Introduction to

New England

The New England states of Massachusetts, Rhode Island, Connecticut, Vermont, New Hampshire, and Maine often regard themselves as the repository of all that is intrinsically American. In this version of history, the tangled streets of old Boston, the farms of Connecticut, and the villages of Vermont are the cradle of the nation. It's a picture which has some truth to it, however, and, although nostalgia plays a big part in the tourist trade here, and innumerable small towns have been dolled up to recapture a past that can occasionally be wishful thinking, the appeal of New England is undeniable. It is indeed the most historic region of the United States; its towns and villages are often rustic and pretty, with white-spired churches sitting beside tidy greens and colonial churchyards; and its landscape can get surprisingly diverse – ranging from some of its stark coastlines to its green rolling hills and mountains further inland. Like most regions that have a well-developed tourist industry, the trick is to find the unspoiled corners, and to distinguish the bogus from the authentic.

Above all, New England packs an enormous amount of variety into what is by American standards a relatively small area. There are the region's **literary connections** – with well-visited shrines to Emily Dickinson, Mark Twain, and Edith Wharton, to name just a few New

New England

this edition researched and updated by

Arabella Bowen, Todd Obolsky, and Ross Velton

www.roughguides.com

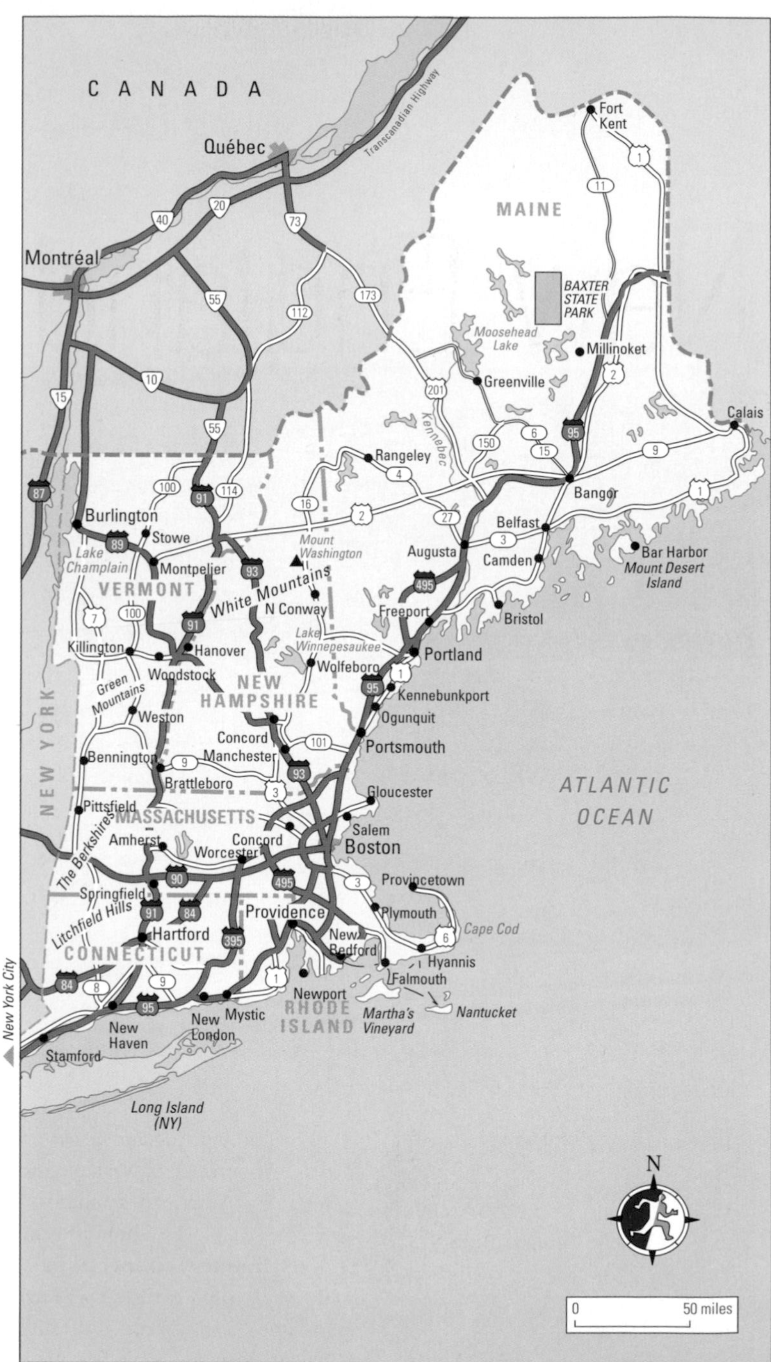
CANADA
Québec
Montréal
Transcanadian Highway
MAINE
BAXTER STATE PARK
Moosehead Lake
Fort Kent
Millinoket
Greenville
Calais
Kennebec
Rangeley
Bangor
Belfast
Augusta
Camden
Bar Harbor
Mount Desert Island
Bristol
Freeport
Portland
Kennebunkport
Ogunquit
Portsmouth
Gloucester
Salem
Boston
ATLANTIC OCEAN
Burlington
Stowe
Lake Champlain
Montpelier
VERMONT
Mount Washington
White Mountains
N Conway
Lake Winnepesaukee
Wolfeboro
Killington
Hanover
Woodstock
Green Mountains
NEW HAMPSHIRE
Weston
Concord
Manchester
Bennington
Brattleboro
NEW YORK
Pittsfield
MASSACHUSETTS
The Berkshires
Amherst
Concord
Worcester
Springfield
Litchfield Hills
Hartford
CONNECTICUT
Providence
Provincetown
Plymouth
Cape Cod
New Bedford
Hyannis
Falmouth
Newport
Martha's Vineyard
Nantucket
RHODE ISLAND
Mystic
New London
New Haven
Stamford
New York City
Long Island (NY)
N
0
50 miles

England writers. There is no shortage of inviting places to **ski**, **hike**, **boat,** or just watch the leaves change color and drop from the trees – which phenomenal numbers of people come to do each fall. And there are the historic sights, which manage to catalog all manner of New England **architecture** and **design**, not to mention Yankee pride and ingenuity. Boston especially is celebrated as the birthplace of American independence – so many of the seminal events of the Revolutionary War took place here, or just outside, in Lexington or Concord; and, although the genteel seaside towns of Massachusetts and Rhode Island can seem a far cry from the first European settlements in New England, plenty of traces of those early years remain. This is, after all, the stretch of the United States where the Pilgrim Fathers and other religious sects put down their stakes, their survival aided by groups of Native

Fact file

- Boston is the only New England city to rank among the top 100 in population in the US.
- The highest point in the region is New Hamphsire's Mount Washington, 6288ft above sea level.
- Cambridge is home to the oldest college in the US, Harvard, founded in 1636.
- The Thanksgiving holiday is often traced back to a harvest celebration that took place in Plymouth back in 1621, though direct correlations are inexact at best.
- Maine has around 3500 miles of shoreline and, at more than 30,000 square miles, is by far the largest state in the region. Rhode Island, at a little more than 1000 square miles, is not only the smallest state in the region, but the entire country.
- Vermont produces around seventy million pounds of cheese a year.

Fall foliage

New England is undoubtedly a year-round destination, with summer resorts dotted along the coast, winter sports destinations in the Green and White mountains, and springtime perhaps the nicest time of all to come, everything considered. But nothing really compares to how towns and tourist bureaus alike make such hay out of the **fall foliage season**. In a way it might seem unbelievable that such a thriving industry can be predicated on watching leaves turn color, but that's how spectacular the display is in some places. If you plan on heading there during the prime times – much of October, though with some variance depending where you are – be sure you make reservations long in advance, and be prepared to pay a bit more than normal. Then take a drive along into the mountains or along some river valley (preferably in the Berkshires, White Mountains, or most anywhere in Vermont), and admire the fiery reds, yellows, and oranges of the maples, birches, and poplars along the way.

Maine has New England's most extreme blend of seaside towns and untamed wilderness

Americans who themselves were eventually displaced, though their legacy remains, too, in place names throughout the region. Later, as the European foothold on the continent became more secure, the coastline became increasingly prime real estate, lined with grand patrician homes, from the Vanderbilt mansions of Newport to the presidential compounds of the Bush and Kennedy families. Inland, the Ivy League colleges of Harvard, Yale, Brown, Dartmouth, and others still embody New England's strong sense of its own superiority, and contribute to accusations of provincialism and snobbishness; in fact, the region's traditional role as home to the WASP elite is due more to the vagaries of history and ideology than to economic realities. Its thin soil and harsh climate made it difficult for the first pioneers to sustain an agricultural way of life, while the industrial prosperity of the nineteenth and early twentieth centuries is now but a distant memory. Indeed, New England has pockets, in Vermont and the other more northerly states, that are as poor as anywhere in the US; and the southern states have all the problems that are normally associated with long-established urban conglomerations.

Despite the apparent gulf between its **interior** and **coast** – and, too, its northern and southern halves – New

England is compact and well defined, and quite easy to get around; only Maine, New England's biggest and most rural state by some way, takes any real time and effort to navigate. Most of its states offer the same mix (to differing degrees) of picturesque small towns and villages, and at times dramatic landscapes, though each has its own distinctive character. When you're working out where to go, plan to include coverage of at least parts of two to three states, in order to pick up on some of that difference. The southern states of Connecticut, Massachusetts, and Rhode Island are more urban and historic and, where nature intervenes, it is usually along the region's spectacular coastline. Here, the tourist facilities are aimed as much at weekenders from the big cities as outsiders – Cape Cod, the Berkshires, Martha's Vineyard, all are convenient (and very popular) targets for moneyed locals. Further north, the lakes and mountains of Vermont, New Hampshire, and particularly Maine, offer wilderness to rival any in the nation.

Maritime history

The region's longtime **connection with the sea** has left its indelible imprint on much of the landscape. The whitewashed houses dotted along the coast make for picture-postcard scenes, complemented by the grand mansions built a bit further from the shore to house the merchants who got rich off the spoils of maritime trade. Both Newport and Marblehead lay claim to the crown of birthplace of the US Navy; Provincetown and Plymouth for where the Pilgrims first alighted from their *Mayflower* voyage (they landed at the former, settled at the latter). As for vintage lighthouses, you can't throw a stone without hitting one – nearly two hundred along the entire coast, and of all shapes and stripes. It's not always a historical legacy either; if the heyday of shipbuilding and whaling, along with much of the canning industry, is long gone, plenty still make their lives hauling in catch up and down the rocky shores. Visit Maine's Mid-Coast (p.540) to see the sea's importance in locals' everyday lives.

Where to go

Boston is the undisputed capital of New England, perhaps America's most historic city, certainly one of its most elegant, full of enough colonial charm and contemporary culture to satisfy most appetites. Together with its energetic student neighbor, **Cambridge**, Boston has plenty to

Food

It is easy to dismiss New England as a non-contributor to any notable culinary innovation – words like "stodgy" and "comfort food" more easily spring to mind when free-associating with Yankee cooking. But pot roast, boiled beef, and Boston baked beans do all have their fans, and they certainly help you make it through the harsh winters. And it's not nearly so grim, really: seafood is prevalent, whether it's lobster every which way (don't miss out on trying a lobster roll – lobster meat mixed with a bit of lemon and mayonnaise, piled high on a hot-dog bun), Ipswich clams, homemade seafood chowders, or broiled scrod. Tomato pies, New Haven's take on pizza, are out of this world. Meanwhile, enough Portuguese and Italian immigrants have made it over to spice up the ethnic offerings in many areas, and Boston and Portsmouth are two of the East Coast's most exciting cities for New American cuisine. For more on food, see p.43; individual recommendations are, of course, listed throughout the guide.

merit a visit of at least a few days, including a fine array of restaurants, bars, and venues for both high- and lowbrow culture. The city also makes a good base for day-trips out to historic Lexington and Concord, the rocky North Shore where the witch sights of Salem probably hold the most interest, and **Cape Cod** – an admittedly somewhat overrated, usually very crowded peninsula, but one which does at least have delightful, quirky Provincetown at its outermost tip.

West of Boston, there's the collegiate **Pioneer Valley**, which gives way to the **Berkshires**, a scenic if hopelessly twee retreat for Boston and New York's cultural elite – much like its Connecticut cousin, Litchfield Hills, just to its south. Southwest of Boston, along the coast, tiny Rhode Island's two main attractions are energetic **Providence** and wealthy **Newport**, beyond which you can take in the better parts of the Connecticut coast

– the seaport of **Mystic**, and, further on, likeable **New Haven**, home to Yale University.

In the opposite direction from Boston, in the three states to the north, New England is more varied: the weekenders are thinner on the ground, there's a greater sense of space, and a simpler way of life rules. In Vermont, outside of the relaxed, pleasant towns of **Brattleboro** and **Burlington**, both worthy of exploration, you're best off just wandering the state's backroads in search of country inns, dairy farms, and some peace and quiet – unless of course you've come to make the pilgrimage to Ben & Jerry's in Waterbury, to see how an ice-cream empire began. Over in New Hampshire, the rugged glory of the **White Mountains** is the most dramatic lure, with the highest peaks in the area and countless outdoor opportunities; indeed, if you're an avid camper or hiker, you won't want to miss this area. Coastal **Portsmouth** is also as nice a town as you'll find most anywhere in the region. Finally, there's Maine, in the far northeast of the country, which has perhaps New England's most extreme blend of seaside towns (Portland, Bar Harbor) and untamed interior wilderness, in which you can spot moose outside of **Rangeley**,

The trick is to find the unspoiled corners and distinguish the bogus from the authentic

Literary heritage

Perhaps fitting for a region dominated by institutions of higher learning, New England has an undeniably strong literary heritage; in fact, Boston was the publishing center of the States before New York copped that mantle. You can do much more than just soak in the highbrow atmosphere at the universities, or linger with a book in one of the many coffeehouses and cafés that inevitably surround those areas; you can go straight to the sources themselves. Visit the homes where Longfellow, Thoreau, Alcott, Frost, Dickinson, Hawthorne, Twain, and many more notables were either born, reared, or spent their time toiling away on the classics so familiar to all. Whether philosophizing by Walden Pond (p.172) or stopping in the snowy woods one evening, near Robert Frost's farm (p.463), you're sure to feel some spirit move you.

whitewater raft near **Moosehead Lake**, and do some remote hiking in **Baxter State Park** along the Appalachian Trail, which actually runs through all three of New England's northern states.

When to go

New England can be a rather pricey place to visit, especially in late September and October, when visitors flock to see the magnificent fall foliage. The region is at its most beautiful during this time, which makes the crowds and prices understandable, if not more bearable. It can get quite cold, unsur-

Average daytime temperatures (°f) and rainfall in New England

	Jan	Feb	March	April	May	June	July	Aug	Sept	Oct	Nov	Dec
Bangor												
max	27	28	37	52	63	73	79	75	68	57	45	30
min	9	10	21	34	43	52	57	55	48	39	30	16
rain	3.0	2.9	3.2	3.3	3.5	3.3	3.3	3.3	3.4	3.4	4.6	3.9
Boston												
max	36	37	45	57	66	77	82	81	72	63	52	39
min	23	25	32	41	50	59	64	64	57	46	39	27
rain	3.6	3.6	3.7	3.6	3.3	3.1	2.8	3.2	3.1	3.3	4.2	4.0
Burlington												
max	25	27	37	54	66	75	81	79	70	57	45	30
min	9	9	21	34	45	54	59	57	48	39	30	16
rain	1.8	1.6	2.2	2.8	3.1	3.5	3.6	4.1	3.3	2.9	3.1	2.4
Hartford												
max	36	37	46	59	70	79	84	82	75	64	52	37
min	18	19	27	37	46	55	63	61	52	41	34	21
rain	3.3	3.0	3.4	3.9	4.0	3.8	3.6	3.5	3.5	3.5	3.7	3.6
Providence												
max	36	37	46	57	68	77	82	81	73	63	52	41
min	19	21	28	37	48	57	63	63	54	43	36	25
rain	3.9	3.6	4.0	4.1	3.8	3.3	3.2	3.6	3.5	3.7	4.5	4.4

prisingly, during winter months, but that's fine if you're thinking of skiing or other winter sports, or a cabin retreat of sorts. Bear in mind, though, that whichever resort you choose, you likely won't be alone. Summers are warm and dry, but this is New England's prime season and it can get extremely crowded, especially in overpopulated getaway towns like those on Cape Cod, Martha's Vineyard, the Rhode Island coast, and in southern Maine – though the upside of coming then is that at least you know everything will be open. On balance, late spring is probably the nicest time to come: the temperature is generally agreeable, if a little unpredictable, the crowds are more dispersed, and prices have yet to go up for the tourist season.

things not to miss

It's not possible to see everything that New England has to offer in one trip – and we don't suggest you try. What follows is a selective taste of the region's highlights: outstanding scenery, picturesque villages, and dramatic wildlife. They're arranged in five color-coded categories, which you can browse through to find the very best things to see and experience. All highlights have a page reference to take you straight into the Guide, where you can find out more.

01 **Burlington, VT** Page **423** • One of New England's most purely enjoyable towns, with an assured sense of vitality, plenty of culture, and a picturesque setting on Lake Champlain.

02 **Canterbury Shaker Village** Page **466** • The only thing missing at this perfectly restored Shaker village near Concord, New Hampshire, are the Shakers themselves.

03 **Tracing colonial history** Pages **91**, **170** & **191**
Very much where the new nation began, New England has all sorts of symbols of its past, from the sights along Boston's Freedom Trail to the battlegrounds at Lexington and Concord to Plymouth Rock itself.

04 **Maine lobsters** Page **556**
Seafood is of course the culinary choice along the coast; lobster pounds and clam shacks provide the setting for many a messy and tantalizing feast.

05 **Harvard Square** Page **131** • The epicenter of Cambridge, Harvard Square buzzes with activity day and night.

07 **The houses of Beacon Hill** Page **108** • Be on the lookout for purple-tinted windowpanes and bow-fronted townhouses as you stroll Boston's most elegant neighborhood.

06 **Mystic Seaport** Page **331** So what if it's a bit of a tourist trap? It's still the easiest way to retreat to port life in the late 1800s.

08 Berkshire's summer festivals Page **272**
Tanglewood is the most celebrated outdoor venue of all, but there are plenty of places to take in music, drama, and much more in the Berkshires.

09 Provincetown's beaches Page **223** • These might be the nicest strips of sand anywhere in the region, and the town itself the most enjoyable on the Cape.

10 Naumkeag Page **275** • One of a handful of magnificent private estates right around Stockbridge, Naumkeag has much less forced opulence than its Newport mansion counterparts, and stunning gardens to boot.

11 Joining the Ivy League Pages **345**, **477** & **131** • Maybe you didn't make it there on academic merit, but the libraries, greens, and stately campuses at Yale, Dartmouth, and Harvard will have you advocating the merits of going back to school.

12 **A day in Nantucket** Page **237** • Or feel free to spend much longer on this lovely island, full of wild beauty, accessible beaches, and a few picture-perfect towns.

13 **Skiing Stowe** Page **421** • Steeps abound in Vermont and New Hampshire, but the oldest resort – and one-time home to the real life Von Trapp family – is still one of the best.

14 **Block Island's inns** Page **321** • Watch the sun set from any of a number of grand Victorian inns perched along the island's Old Harbor.

15 Newport's mansions Page **304** • Such ostentation was called "conspicuous consumption" in Thorstein Veblen's day; in ours, you don't have to be self-conscious at all to gawk at the folly.

16 Mass MoCA Page **285** • The far corner of Western Massachusetts is an unlikely place for a first-class contemporary art museum to be sure, but that only adds a special thrill to seeing such bizarre exhibits.

17 Monhegan Island Page **552** • The kind of splendid, low-tech solitude you just may be looking for, right off the Maine coast.

18 **The hills of Providence** Page **295** & **297** • College Hill and Federal Hill are two of the town's most delightful neighborhoods, the former full of historic houses and the buildings of Brown University, the latter crammed with cafés and Italian groceries.

19 **Worcester Art Museum** Page **250** • Some excellent works by big names on display here, in sculpture, painting, photography, and much more.

20 Eating in Portsmouth Page **456** • There are a raft of surprisingly upscale restaurants in this seafront New Hampshire town, including some enjoyable ones right on the water.

21 Wild blueberries Page **519** They grow all over Maine and crop up in all sorts of delectable dishes, from pancakes to pies to sauce for chicken.

22 Whale watching Page **184** Take advantage of the seasonal migration habits aboard a whale-watching cruise, one of the best wildlife-spotting opportunities around.

23 **Shelburne Museum** Page **428** • Outside of Burlington, this collection of Americana is sometimes beyond description, but never less than enjoyable, as daily life over the past two centuries is recreated in exacting detail.

24 **Cape Cod's north coast** Page **206** • Though there aren't too many spots demanding you to get off the road, a drive along the Cape's north coast should afford you a sense of the surreal quality of light for which the Cape is known.

25 **Montpelier, VT** Page **413** • In an area full of cultivated quaintness, Vermont's tiny state capital exudes plenty of natural charm.

26 **Litchfield Hills, CT** Page **370** • If you're looking for scenic villages and manicured town squares, amidst some surprisingly rural patches, this alternative to the Berkshires should do the trick.

27 **Hiking the Long Trail** Page **397** • The region is perfect for active nature-lovers, who can catch the northern bit of the Appalachian Trail that runs through the mountainous interior.

28 **Revolutionary War Festival** Page **457** • In Exeter, New Hampshire, summer means the chance to elaborately re-create the Revolutionary fervor of a few centuries ago.

29 **Acadia National Park, ME** Page **573** • New England's only national park, and a beauty at that – rugged, varied, and dramatic, even in a relatively small area.

30 **Faneuil Hall** Page **92** • There's lots of history around Boston, and you get a good sense of it at this vaunted longtime meeting place, which also abuts the restaurants and shops of Quincy Market.

31 The Mount Washington Hotel Page **506** • There was once a time when vacationing in the White Mountains was the preserve of the extremely well-to-do; at the grand resort hotel of the *Mount Washington Hotel* you'll understand why.

32 Ben & Jerry's Factory Tour Page **418** • Perhaps the little ice-cream company that could has become a bit co-opted by the mainstream, but that doesn't mean they don't still churn out all manner of irresistible flavors.

Contents

Using the Rough Guide

We've tried to make this Rough Guide a good read and easy to use. The book is divided into five main sections, and you should be able to find whatever you want in one of them.

Color section

The front color section offers a quick tour of New England. The **introduction** aims to give you a feel for the place, with suggestions on where to go. We also tell you what the weather is like and include a basic country fact file. Next, our authors round up their favorite aspects of New England in the **things not to miss** section – whether it's a quaint village, a coastal resort, or an adventurous outdoor activity. Right after this comes a full **contents** list.

Basics

The Basics section covers all the **pre-departure** nitty-gritty to help you plan your trip. This is where to find out which airlines fly to your destination, what paperwork you'll need, what to do about money and insurance, about Internet access, food, security, public transportation, car rental – in fact just about every piece of **general practical information** you might need.

Guide

This is the heart of the Rough Guide, divided into user-friendly chapters, each of which covers a specific region. Every chapter starts with a list of **highlights** and an **introduction** that helps you to decide where to go, depending on your time and budget. Likewise, introductions to the various towns and smaller regions within each chapter should help you plan your itinerary. We start most town accounts with information on arrival and accommodation, followed by a tour of the sights, and finally reviews of places to eat and drink, and details of nightlife. Longer accounts also have a directory of practical listings. Each chapter concludes with **public transportation** details for that region.

Contexts

Read Contexts to get a deeper understanding of what makes New England tick. We include a brief history, coverage of films either shot in or pertaining to the region, and some **literary extracts** that help bring the landscape to life, together with a detailed further reading section that reviews dozens of **books** relating to the country.

Index + small print

Apart from a **full index**, which includes maps as well as places, this section covers publishing information, credits and acknowledgments, and also has our contact details in case you want to send in updates and corrections to the book – or suggestions as to how we might improve it.

Map and chapter list

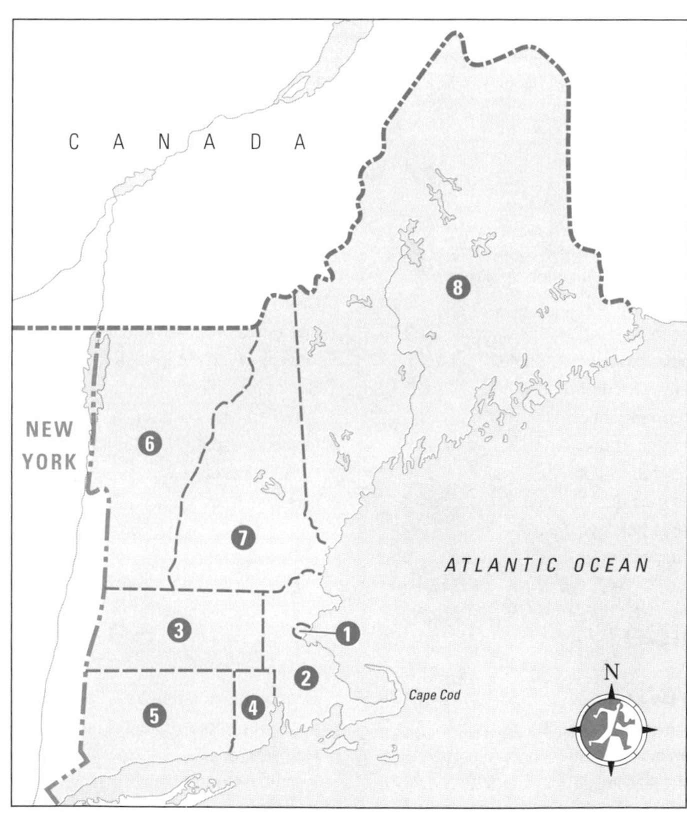

Contents

Color section i–xxiv

Basics 9–68

Guide 69–596

6 Vermont 383–440

7 New Hampshire 441–515

Contexts

Index + small print

Map symbols

maps are listed in the full index using colored text

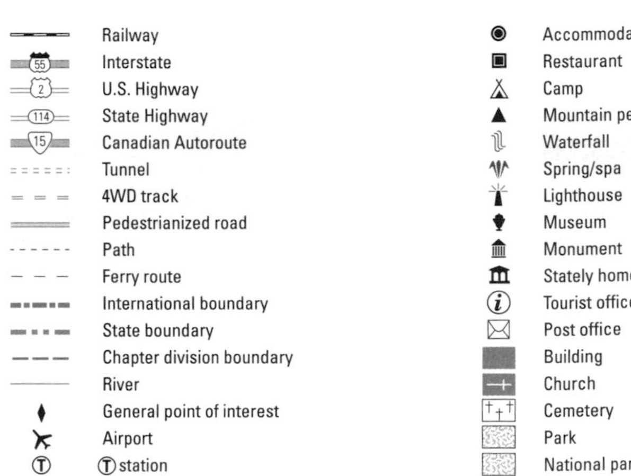

Basics

Basics

Getting there

Getting into New England is easiest from Boston, the region's largest city and busiest airline hub. All the major airlines operate daily scheduled flights to Boston's Logan International Airport from the United States, Canada, and Europe – those coming from further afield typically connect with domestic flights on the West Coast. While air travel may be fastest, New England is also easily accessible by road or rail from points throughout North America.

For visitors coming from outside of North America, air travel – at least to somewhere in the States or Canada – is, of course, a near necessity. Flying can also often be the least expensive option, especially if you land a last-minute deal, which can save you more than half the regular airfare from just about anywhere. Generally, the most expensive time to fly is **high season** which stretches from mid-May to early September; note, though, that inter-regional flights can continue to stay pricey well into November thanks to the popularity of the **fall foliage** season (mid-September to mid-November), when throngs descend upon the region to gape at its glorious arboreal colors. April to May and September to October are considerably less expensive for flights from abroad and the rest of the year – with the exception of Thanksgiving, Christmas, and New Year's, when the prices skyrocket again – is considered low season and is cheaper still.

If you don't want to fly, or have already arrived from abroad somewhere in the US or Canada, the **railroad** is a decent second option for getting to major regional cities – like Boston, Portland, and Providence – and is particularly useful for visitors traveling along the East Coast, where **Amtrak** has a reliable (but not particularly cheap) high-speed route between Washington DC and Boston. From elsewhere in North America, though, the approaches to the region are leisurely at best.

For budget travelers and those without their own car, the **Greyhound** and **Peter Pan bus companies** make good options – and are especially useful for reaching smaller hinterland towns; they tend to have more flexible departure times and destination ranges than either train or plane. Keep in mind, though, that long-haul buses can be uncomfortable, and that, unlike on rail or by plane, you're still at the mercy of the traffic.

Probably the best option if you're planning on covering a lot of New England during your stay is **driving**; that said, car rental in the US is not cheap.

On a final note, **air**, **train**, and **bus passes** are available for **discounted travel** throughout the United States; for foreign visitors, these normally have to be purchased before your trip, and from within your home country.

Shopping for air tickets and passes

Competition on major routes keeps plane fares at a reasonable level, though prices do vary according to numerous factors. Within the US, prices for **domestic flights** to New England are generally determined by the time of departure and seat availability, especially on the busy northeastern commuter routes between Washington, New York, and Boston.

Special seasonal deals or discount fares for students and anyone under 26 can bring the price down, but by far the best deals around are **last-minute fares** for long-weekend travel, usually announced mid-week by airlines that haven't filled their full-fare seats. Of course, there's no guarantee that New England destinations will make the cut on any given week, but if one does, you can count on substantial savings – though ticketing restrictions will affect your departure and return times. You can get first crack at the cheap seats by signing up for email notification at most major airline websites.

It is often possible to cut costs by going through a **specialist flight agent** – either a consolidator, who buys up blocks of tickets from the airlines and sells them at a

One word of **warning**: it's not a good idea to buy a **one-way** ticket to the US. Not only are they rarely good value compared to a round-trip ticket, but US immigration officials usually take them as a sign that you aren't planning to go home and may refuse your entry. With increased airport checks, you are unlikely to be allowed to board your flight to begin with.

discount, or a **discount agent**, who in addition to dealing with discounted flights may also offer special student and youth fares and a range of other travel-related services such as travel insurance, rail passes, car rentals, tours, and the like. Some agents specialize in **charter flights**, which may be cheaper than anything available on a scheduled flight, but departure dates are fixed and withdrawal penalties are high.

For some regional destinations, like Boston or Cape Cod, you may even find it cheaper to pick up a bargain **package deal** from one of the tour operators listed below and then find your own accommodation when you get there. A further possibility is to see if you can arrange a **courier flight**, although you'll need a flexible schedule, and preferably be traveling alone with very little luggage. In return for shepherding a parcel through customs, you can expect to get a deeply discounted ticket. You'll probably also be restricted in the duration of your stay.

If you want a longer stay – or simply the guarantee that you will indeed be going to New England during your predetermined holidays – you'll get the **most savings** by booking a mid-week flight two to three weeks in advance, and staying over a Saturday night. Airlines usually charge $100 to change your departure date once your ticket's been issued, so be sure of your schedule when booking.

Remember also to allow for the extra cost of government **duty fees and airport taxes** whenever, and from wherever, you travel – you'll be quoted an all-inclusive price when you pay for your ticket, but not necessarily when you first make inquiries. On the plus side, none of New England's airports charge a **departure tax** – yet.

Rather than contacting all the separate airlines, you'll save yourself a lot of time, and possibly money, too, by checking out the various **discount travel and flight agents**, which often advertise in the travel sections of the daily and weekend newspapers. Some, such as Council Travel, STA, Travel Cuts, and Usit Campus, specialize in **youth/student fares**, but even if you don't fit into that category, they'll often do their best to find you the cheapest available flight.

Overseas travelers should also keep in mind that many of the main US airlines offer **air passes** for multiple flights within the States. These have to be bought in advance, and are usually sold with the proviso that you reach the US with the same airline. See "Getting around", p.36, for details.

Online booking agents and general travel sites

Many airlines and discount travel websites offer you the opportunity to **book your tickets online**, often at a small discount. Keep in mind, though, that you'll need to be flexible about your departure and return dates to get the best prices from these sites. Make sure you read the small print before buying, too, as it can be difficult, if not impossible, to claim refunds or change your ticket, especially on last-minute deals.

Ⓦ **www.cheapflights.com** Bookings from the UK and Ireland only. Flight deals, travel agents, plus links to other travel sites.

Ⓦ **www.cheaptickets.com** American discount flight specialists.

Ⓦ **www.ebookers.com** and Ⓦ **www.ebookers.com.ie** Low fares on an extensive selection of scheduled flights from the UK and Ireland.

Ⓦ **www.etn.nl/discount.htm** A hub of consolidator and discount agent web links.

Ⓦ **www.expedia.com** Discount airfares, all-airline search engine, and daily deals.

Ⓦ **www.flyaow.com** UK online air travel info and reservations site.

Ⓦ **www.hotwire.com** Bookings from the US only. Last-minute savings of up to forty percent on regular published fares.

Ⓦ **www.lastminute.com** Good last-minute holiday package and flight-only deals; UK bookings only.

Ⓦ **www.orbitz.com** US bookings only for cut-rate international and domestic flights.

Ⓦ **www.priceline.com** and Ⓦ **www.priceline.co.uk** Name-your-own-price website that has deals at around forty percent off standard fares. You cannot specify flight times (although you do specify dates).

Ⓦ **www.skyauction.com** Bookings from the US

only. Auctions tickets and travel packages using a "second bid" scheme. The best strategy is to bid the maximum you're willing to pay, since if you win you'll pay just enough to beat the runner-up regardless of your maximum bid.

ⓦ **www.smilinjack.com/airlines.htm** Lists an up-to-date compilation of airline website addresses.

ⓦ **www.travel.com.au** and ⓦ **www.travel.co.nz** Discount fares and destination advice for Australian/New Zealand travelers.

ⓦ **www.travelocity.com** and ⓦ **www.travelocity.co.uk** Destination guides along with deals for car rental, lodging, and airfares.

ⓦ **www.travelshop.com.au** Australian website offering discounted flights, packages, insurance, and online bookings.

ⓦ **www.travel.yahoo.com** Incorporates a lot of Rough Guide material in its coverage of destination countries and cities across the world, with information about places to eat, sleep, etc.

ⓦ **www.unison.otc-ie.com** Irish site with online flight bookings, car rental, insurance, and more.

From North America

Getting to New England **from anywhere else in North America** is only problematic in the harsh winter months, when roads get icy and airports occasionally close due to inclement weather. All the main airlines operate daily scheduled flights from across the US to Boston's Logan International Airport, and there are daily scheduled flights from Toronto, Montreal, Vancouver, and Ottawa as well. You should be aware that service to airports other than Boston's can be infrequent, and that some local flights to Cape Cod, Hartford, Burlington, Portland, Bangor, and Providence also operate from New York, sometimes with cheaper fares – especially in the fall when Boston-originating flights tend to keep their prices high due to the popularity of the fall foliage season.

While flying remains the best but most expensive way to travel, if you're coming from the mid-Atlantic states, driving may make more sense. Train comes a slow but smooth second, and traveling by bus is the least expensive method, but it's also slow – and much less comfortable.

By plane

Boston's Logan International Airport is by far the biggest and most accessible in New England: direct flights are available from all the major hubs in North America – though you may find yourself connecting through Chicago, New York City, or another large East Coast city. Smaller airports in Manchester (NH), Portland (ME), Bangor (ME), Burlington (VT), and Windsor Locks (near Hartford, CT) are serviced less regularly by smaller aircraft; some have international terminals as well. It's also worth checking flights to New York City, as they are often cheap enough to make taking a bus, train, or rental car the rest of the way to New England worth it. Albany's (NY) international airport is also close by and a good bet for reasonable fares, especially if you're going on to Vermont, western Massachusetts, or Connecticut.

East Coast visitors have the best access to the region, as frequent **shuttles** originate from New York's La Guardia (Delta Airlines; Mon–Fri every 30–60mins 6am–9.30pm, Sat–Sun every 2hrs 8.30am–8.30pm) and Washington DC's Reagan National Airport (US Airways; Mon–Sat hourly 7.30am–8.30pm, Sun every 2–4hrs 8.30am–8.30pm). The following airlines also offer regular daily service to Boston: Air Canada (from Montreal, Ottawa, Toronto, and Vancouver), American Airlines (from Chicago, Dallas, Miami, Philadelphia, and St Louis), Continental (from Houston, Chicago, Miami, Newark, and Seattle), Delta (from Atlanta, Dallas, and Tampa), United (from Chicago, Los Angeles, and San Francisco), Northwest (from Detroit, Memphis, Minneapolis, San Diego, and Vancouver), and US Airways (from Fort Lauderdale, Orlando, and Philadelphia).

Fares are lowest in the heavily trafficked Northeast corridor; a round-trip fare **from New York** can cost as little as $90–100, although $120–170 is the more usual price range; **from Washington DC** and **Miami**, the range is usually $200–250; from **Chicago**, $260–300. The price of flights **from the West Coast** is more likely to fluctuate – round-trip fares from LA, San Francisco, or Seattle typically cost $450 to $550, but can go as low as $300. **From Canada**, be prepared to pay around Can$400–500 from Toronto and Montréal, and closer to Can$700, and as high as Can$1200, from Vancouver.

What makes more difference than your choice of carrier is the conditions governing the ticket – whether it's fully refundable, the time and day, and most importantly the time of year you travel. **Least expensive** of all is a non-high-season midweek flight, booked and paid for at least three weeks in advance. Also keep in mind that **one-way** tickets are sometimes more expensive than round-trip tickets. While it makes sense to call the airlines directly to get a sense of their official fares, it's also worth checking with a reputable **travel agent** to find out about any special deals or student/youth fares that may be available. You can also scout **online** at any of the US-based sites listed on p.12.

In addition to the big-name airlines, a few **lesser-known carriers** run no-frills flights, which can prove to be very good value, especially if you have a flexible schedule and can stand a few delays. Southwest Airlines flies from a host of cities at rock-bottom prices, and although it doesn't fly to Boston's Logan, the airline does service Providence (RI), Manchester (NH), and Hartford's Bradley International Airport.

Airlines in the US and Canada

Air Canada ⓣ1-888/247-2262, ⓦwww.aircanada.ca
Air Tran ⓣ1-800/247-8726, ⓦwww.airtran.com
America West ⓣ1-800/235-9292, ⓦwww.americawest.com
American Airlines and **American Eagle** ⓣ1-800/433-7300, ⓦwww.aa.com
American Trans Air ⓣ1-800/225-2995, ⓦwww.ata.com
Cape Air ⓣ1-800/352-0714, ⓦwww.flycapeair.com
Continental ⓣ1-800/523-3273, ⓦwww.continental.com
Delta Air Lines and **Delta Shuttle** ⓣ1-800/221-1212, ⓦwww.delta.com
Delta Express ⓣ1-866/2-FLYDLX, ⓦwww.flydlx.com
Frontier ⓣ1-800/432-1359, ⓦwww.frontierairlines.com
Midwest Express ⓣ1-800/452-2022, ⓦwww.midwestexpress.com
Northwest ⓣ1-800/225-2525, ⓦwww.nwa.com
Southwest ⓣ 1-800/435-9792, ⓦwww.southwest.com
United ⓣ1-800/241-6522, ⓦwww.ual.com
US Airways, **US Airways Shuttle**, and **US Airways Express** ⓣ1-800/428-4322, ⓦwww.usairways.com

Discount travel and flight agents in the US and Canada

Airtech ⓣ1-877/247-8324 or 212/219-7000, ⓦwww.airtech.com. Standby seat broker; also deals in consolidator fares and courier flights.
Council Travel ⓣ1-800/226-8624, ⓕ617/528-2091, ⓦwww.counciltravel.com. Nationwide organization that mostly specializes in student/budget travel. Flights from the US only. Owned by STA Travel.
Now Voyager ⓣ1-800/255-6951, ⓦwww.nowvoyager.com. San Francisco-based gay- and lesbian-friendly consolidator with Boston-based tours and packages.
Skylink US ⓣ1-800/247-6659 or 212/573-8980, Canada ⓣ1-800/759-5465, ⓦwww.skylinkus.com. Consolidator with multiple offices throughout New England and the US.
STA Travel ⓣ1-800/777-0112 or 1-800/781-4040, ⓦwww.sta-travel.com. Worldwide specialists in independent travel; also student IDs, travel insurance, car rental, etc.

Airports in New England

Connecticut Bradley International Airport, I-91, Exit 40, Windsor Locks, CT (near Hartford) ⓣ860/292-2000 or 1-888/624/1533, ⓦwww.bradleyairport.com

Maine Portland International Jetport, 1001 Westbrook St, Portland, ME ⓣ207/774-7301, ⓦwww.portland jetport.org

Massachusetts Logan International Airport, East Boston, MA ⓣ1-800/235-6426, ⓦwww.massport.com/logan

New Hampshire Manchester Airport, Brown Ave, Manchester, NH ⓣ603/624-6556, ⓦwww.flymanchester.com

Pease International Tradeport, 601 Spaulding Turnpike, Portsmouth, NH (ⓣ603/433-6088, ⓦwww.peasedev.org)

Rhode Island TF Green State Airport, 2000 Post Rd, Warwick, RI ⓣ401/737-8222 or 1-888/268-7222

Vermont Burlington International Airport, 1200 Airport Drive, South Burlington, VT ⓣ802/863-1889, ⓦwww.burlingtonintlairport.com

TFI Tours International ⓣ1-800/745-8000 or 212/736-1140, ⓦwww.lowestairprice.com. Consolidator with flights to Boston from Canadian and US cities.
Travelers Advantage ⓣ1-877/259-2691, ⓦwww.travelersadvantage.com. Discount travel club; annual membership fee required (currently $1 for 3 months' trial).
Travel Cuts Canada ⓣ1-800/667-2887, US ⓣ1-866/246-9762, ⓦwww.travelcuts.com. Canadian student-travel organization.
Worldtek Travel ⓣ1-800/243-1723, ⓦwww.worldtek.com. Discount travel agency.

Package tours

Plenty of travel operators offer **tours** and **camping trips** covering several New England destinations that typically feature a day or two in Boston, followed by visits of Revolutionary War or foliage sites, as part of a seven-day itinerary. Though these are considerably more expensive than a mere weekend getaway (and prices vary wildly as to what's being offered), they can make for a terrific New England vacation.

Tour operators

American Express Vacations ⓣ1-800/241-1700, ⓦwww.americanexpress.com/travel. Flights, hotels, last-minute specials, city-break packages, and specialty tours.
Amtrak Vacations ⓣ1-800/321-8684, ⓦwww.amtrak.com/services/amtrak-vacations/html. Train or Amtrak Air-Rail trips through the Northeast, along with hotel reservations, car rental, and sightseeing tours.
Collette Vacations ⓣ1-800/340-5158, ⓦwww.collettevacations.com. Boston figures in various escorted or independent tour permutations: from the six-night "Discover Boston" option (from $779) to the "New England Foliage" tour, which also covers provincial NE towns like Lexington, Concord, and Killington (from $1369); prices include meals but exclude airfare/travel to the region.
Contiki Holidays ⓣ1-888/CONTIKI, ⓦwww.contiki.com. Trips for the 18–35-year-old crowd; the 12-day "Eastern Canada and the USA" tour (from $1159, airfare not included) takes in Boston and Cape Cod.
Globus and Cosmos ⓦwww.globusandcosmos.com. Deluxe escorted tours. The "Cape Cod Escape" (eight days, from $1599) and "Great Cities of the East" (ten days, from $2299) tours both include significant time in Boston as well as additional outposts like Provincetown; the land-only prices include meals. Request brochures online or via a listed travel agent.
Suntrek Tours ⓣ1-800/SUN-TREK, ⓦwww.suntrek.com. Has 7- to 14-day "Eastern Trails" tours that include a couple of days in the Boston region before heading up the coast ($439–$799), and a three-week "Canadian Pioneer" tour that includes Ontario and Québec in the package, as well ($1252–$1322).
Trek America ⓣ1-800/221-0596, ⓦwww.trekamerica.com. Trekking company geared to 18–38-year-olds with 7–14 day camping tours through the Eastern US, many with a Canadian leg thrown in (from $469).

By train

If you have a bit more money and hanker after a few more creature comforts (all the trains have private cabins and dining cars that can be yours for a premium), or simply have the time and inclination to take in some of the rest of the US on your way to New England, then an **Amtrak train** (ⓣ1-800/USA-RAIL, ⓦwww.amtrak.com) may be just the ticket for you. The most spectacular train journey has to be the **Zephyr** in conjunction with the **Lakeshore Limited**, which runs all the way from San Francisco to Boston (73 hours, including a stopover in Chicago); bus to Emeryville (the nearest *Zephyr* station to San Francisco) departs San Francisco at 8am daily. Alternately, you can get an 8.55am train from Oakland's Jack London Square and connect with the *Zephyr* in Sacramento. After climbing alongside raging rivers through gorgeous mountain scenery east of Salt Lake City, the route drops down the eastern flank of the Rockies and races across the Midwest to Chicago, where you change trains before hitting the rolling greenery of western Pennsylvania and upstate New York. Another major route, the **Crescent**, originates in New Orleans and crosses into Atlanta before making its way north up the East Coast for New York, from where you'll have to board another train bound for Boston.Train travel is much speedier for those heading to New England **from Washington DC and New York** – but likely no less expensive than air travel. The Amtrak trains that service the corridor are the fleet's most reliable, and usually stick to their official schedules. Fares from New York to Boston are $128 round-trip, with the trip taking between four and five hours; double the cost gets you a seat on the cushier Acela Express, which, its name notwithstanding, only shaves about thirty minutes off the trip time. From Washington DC, the regular train runs just shy of eight hours ($162 round-trip) while the express gets you there in 6.5 hours ($341 round-trip).

Although it's possible to haul yourself long-distance **from the West Coast**, the Midwest or the South, the trip is anything but fast – count on three days and up from California – nor is it cost effective, at around $350 round-trip. The same applies to visitors trying to approach the region **from Canada** using Via Rail (ⓣ1-888/842-7245, ⓦwww.viarail.ca); you can only do so by connecting in New York City, and on an indirect itinerary at best. The rail journey can take anywhere from twelve to twenty hours from Toronto and Montréal, and over three days from Vancouver. Fares start around Can$400 round-trip from the closer points – and at those prices, you might as well fly.

Amtrak also offers several **rail passes** for both North American and international travelers that allow unlimited travel within certain time frames in certain areas, which can be good value; see box on p.36 for details.

Although Amtrak's basic fares and passes can be reasonably priced, if you want to travel in a bit more comfort the cost rises quickly. **Sleeping compartments**, which include meals, small toilets, and showers, start at around $160 per night for one or two people for short-haul trips, but can go well over $500 for coast-to-coast travel.

Be sure to check out Amtrak's website for special deals and weekly **rail sales**.

By bus

Considering how expensive rail travel is in the US, getting to New England by **bus** can be an appealing – if less comfortable – option, especially as the buses quite often get there faster than the train does, given the notorious unreliability and tardiness of rail travel outside of the Northeast corridor. Greyhound (ⓣ1-800/231-2222, ⓦwww.greyhound.com) is the sole long-distance operator and has an extensive network of destinations in New England. A good alternative, once you're in the region, is Peter Pan (ⓣ1-800/237-8747, ⓦwww.peterpanbus.com), which runs regular buses up and down the New England coast. Several smaller local bus companies have direct connections with Greyhound's longer routes.

As with air and train routes, Boston is the best-served destination, especially if you're coming from **New York** or **Washington DC**; barring rush-hour traffic and highway accidents, trips typically take four and a half hours from New York and ten and a half hours from Washington; round-trip fares cost $80 and $132, respectively.

Coming from Canada, several daily buses **from Toronto** reach Boston with at least one changeover – usually in Syracuse, New York – contributing to a minimum twelve-hour ride (Can$160 round-trip). Buses **from Montréal** take around seven hours and have the added benefit of direct service (Can$116 round-trip). In both cases, contact Greyhound (ⓣ1-800/229-9424, ⓦwww.greyhound.ca).

The real reason to take the bus is if you're planning on visiting a number of New England destinations; Greyhound's Ameripass is good for unlimited travel within

Green Tortoise

One alternative to Long-Distance Bus Hell is the slightly countercultural Green Tortoise, whose buses, complete with foam cushions, bunks, fridges and rock music, cross the country from California to New York and Boston during the summer. These transcontinental trips amount to mini-tours of the nation, taking 12–14 days at a current cost of $499–539 one-way (plus contributions to the food fund, which amounts to $121–$151 over the course of the trip), and allowing plenty of stops for hiking, river-rafting and hot springs. Other Green Tortoise trips include excursions to the major national parks, south to Mexico and Central America and north to Alaska.

Main Office: 494 Broadway, San Francisco, CA 94133 (ⓣ1-800/867-8647 or 415/956-7500, ⓦwww.greentortoise.com).

a certain time, and costs $199 for seven days, $299 for fifteen days, $389 for thirty days, and $549 for sixty days. Foreign visitors, who are entitled to slightly cheaper rates, can buy the passes before leaving home through Greyhound's website; Canadian and US passengers must purchase them fourteen days ahead of time, while international visitors need at least 21 days' prior reservation; see also p.36. An alternative, in every sense, is the San Francisco-based Green Tortoise bus company (☎415/ 956-7500 or 1-800/867-8647, Ⓦwww.greentortoise.com; $499), which reaches the East Coast after a leisurely (around twelve days) coast-to-coast journey (see box p.16).

By car

Driving your own **car** gives the greatest freedom and flexibility, but if you don't have one (or don't trust the one you do have), one option worth considering is a **driveaway**. Companies operate in most major cities, and are paid to find drivers to take a customer's car from one place to another – most commonly between California and New York, though deliveries terminating in Boston are also available. The company will normally pay for your insurance and your first tank of gas; after that, you'll be expected to drive along the most direct route and to average four hundred miles a day. Many driveaway companies are not keen to use foreign travelers, but if you can convince them you are a safe bet they'll take something like a $250–$500 deposit, which you get back after delivering the car in good condition. Get in touch in advance to spare yourself a week's wait for a car to turn up. Look under "Automobile transporters and driveaway companies" in the *Yellow Pages* and phone around for the latest offers, or try one of the ninety branches of Auto Driveaway, based at 310 S Michigan Ave in Chicago (☎312/939-3600 or 1-800/346-2277, Ⓦwww.autodriveaway.com).

Renting a car involves the usual steps of phoning the local branch, or checking the website, of one of the major companies (see p.33 in "Getting around"), of which Thrifty tends to be the cheapest. Most have offices at destination airports, and addresses and phone numbers are comprehensively documented in the *Yellow Pages*. Also worth considering are fly-drive deals, which give cut-rate (and sometimes free) car rental when buying an air ticket. They usually work out cheaper than renting on the spot and are especially good value if you intend to do a lot of driving. A car rented in Canada can normally be driven across the border into the US, but you will pay a much higher fee if you do not return it to its country of origin. Most of the larger companies have offices in Canada.

Drivers planning on hitting Boston during their New England tour should be prepared for interminable traffic jams and detours caused by ongoing work to put **I-93** underground. If you insist on driving in the city, stay informed of road closures and reroutings by tuning into 1030 AM on the radio. Aside from the Boston headache, the I-93 is useful for visitors heading seaward from New Hampshire, as it connects the state with southern Rhode Island. Several other major highways also transect the region: the **I-95**, which runs along the Atlantic coast south from Canada and circumscribes the Boston area; the **I-90** (the Massachusetts Turnpike or "Masspike"), which approaches Massachusetts from the west and is popular with those arriving from New York State; and the **I-91** which heads south from Québec and rims Vermont and New Hampshire before hitting Amherst, Massachusetts, and Hartford, Connecticut.

Driving to Boston

From Chicago 16 hours, 30 minutes (982 miles)
From Miami 25 hours (1488 miles)
From New York 4 hours (216 miles)
From San Francisco 52 hours (3100 miles)
From Montréal 6 hours (310 miles)
From Toronto 9 hours, 30 minutes (552 miles)

From Britain and Ireland

Flying to New England from Britain is pretty straightforward if you're keen to start your travels in Boston, as most budget options involve non-stop service to the city. That said, visitors to just about any other regional capital will probably have to transfer to a smaller aircraft somewhere en route. The first place the plane lands is your point of entry into the US, which means you'll have to collect your bags and go through customs and immigration formalities there, even if you're continuing on to other regional points on the same plane. This can be a real pain after a seven-hour journey, so it's worth finding out before you book a ticket.

Fares, routes, and agents

Most flights from Britain and Ireland leave early to mid-afternoon and arrive mid-afternoon or evening, though the odd red-eye flight leaves the UK at 8pm and arrives later the same night in Boston. Returning to the UK and Ireland, you're looking at an early morning or early evening departure; the prevailing winds tend to make the trip back modestly shorter than the one over. British Airways, Virgin Atlantic, and American Airlines have the most daily **non-stop flights** from London's Heathrow Airport; travelers from elsewhere in the UK will have to connect in London. Aer Lingus operates the only non-stop service **from Ireland**.

As there's not a lot of price differentiation between the major airlines, you'll have to shop around to get the best deals. Your best bet for finding what cut-rate tickets exist is checking the **travel ads** in the weekend papers, the **holiday pages** of ITV's *Teletext* and, in London, scouring *Time Out* and the *Evening Standard*. Giveaway magazines aimed at young travelers, like *TNT*, are also very helpful. The **internet** is another valuable resource, and you'll often find good deals on any of the travel-based sites shown on p.12.

The standard option, the **Apex** ticket, is a non-refundable round-trip ticket that must be purchased 21 days in advance and requires a minimum seven-night stay, up to a maximum of one month; changing departure dates usually incurs a penalty. With or without an Apex ticket, fares still hover around £250 in low season (Nov to mid-Dec & Jan–March), £350 in spring and fall, and over £400 in high season (May–Sept). Flights from Ireland (Shannon) can ring in over 700 euros. All fares are subject to a tax of approximately £63, and weekend flights incur additional surcharges. A non-restricted economy fare ticket, allowing the greatest flexibility in departure times, can cost you upwards of £1000.

Airlines in the UK and Ireland

The following fares to Boston do not include taxes.

Aer Lingus UK ⓣ0845/973 7747, Republic of Ireland ⓣ01/705 3333 or 01/844 4777, ⓦwww.aerlingus.ie. Daily flights from Dublin and Shannon. Low-season fares start from €325.

American Airlines UK ⓣ0845/778 9789, ⓦwww.aa.com. Two direct flights daily from London Heathrow. Low-season fares start from £186.

British Airways UK ⓣ0845/773 3377, Republic of Ireland ⓣ1800/626 747, ⓦwww.british-airways.com. Three flights daily from London Heathrow. Typical low-season fares start around £176.

Continental UK ⓣ0800/776 464, Republic of Ireland ⓣ1890/925 252, ⓦwww.flycontinental.com. Operates one daily direct flight from London Heathrow with fares as low as £204.

KLM/Northwest UK ⓣ08705/074 074, ⓦwww.klmuk.com. Daily non-direct flights from Heathrow and Gatwick, starting around £176.

United Airlines UK ⓣ0845/844 4777, Republic of Ireland ⓣ1800/535 300, ⓦwww.ual.com. Daily non-direct flights (usually transferring in Washington DC) starting at £188.

US Airways UK 0845/600 3300, Republic of Ireland 1890/925 065, ⓦwww.usairways.com. Daily non-direct flights from Heathrow at £190.

Virgin Atlantic UK ⓣ01293/747 747, Republic of Ireland ⓣ01/873 3388, ⓦwww.virgin-atlantic.com. Daily flight from London Heathrow. A sample low-season fare comes out at £166.

Discount travel and flight agents

In the UK

Bridge the World ⓣ020/7911 0900, ⓦwww.bridgetheworld.com. Specializing in round-the-world tickets, with good deals aimed at the backpacker market.

Destination Group ⓣ020/7400 7000, ⓦwww.destination-group.com. Discount airfares, as well as inclusive packages for US travel.

Dial A Flight ⓣ0870/333 4488, ⓦwww.dialaflight.com. Discounts on airfares, as well as car rental, hotels and insurance.

Flightbookers ⓣ020/7757 2444, ⓦwww.ebookers.com. Low fares on an extensive selection of scheduled flights.

Flight Centre ⓣ08705/666677, ⓦwww.flight centre.co.uk. Large choice of discounted flights.

Flynow ⓣ020/7835 2000, ⓦwww.flynow.com. Wide range of discounted tickets.

London Flight Centre ⓣ020/7244 6411, ⓦwww.topdecktravel.co.uk. Long-established agent dealing in discount flights.
North South Travel ⓣ01245/608 291, ⓦwww.northsouthtravel.co.uk. Discounted fares worldwide; profits are used to support projects in the developing world, especially the promotion of sustainable tourism.
Quest Worldwide ⓣ020/8547 3322, ⓦwww.questtravel.com. Specialists in round-the-world discount fares.
STA Travel ⓣ0870/160 6070, ⓦwww.statravel.co.uk. Worldwide specialists in low-cost flights and tours for students and under-26s (other customers welcome); Amtrak passes also available.
Trailfinders ⓣ020/7628 7628, ⓦwww.trailfinders.com. One of the best-informed and most efficient agents for independent travelers; Amtrak passes also available.
Travel Bag ⓣ0870/900 1350, ⓦwww.travelbag.co.uk. Discount flights to the US.
Travel Cuts ⓣ020/7255 2082, ⓦwww.travelcuts.co.uk. Budget, student, and youth travel, plus round-the-world tickets; Amtrak passes also available.
Usit Campus ⓣ0870/240 1010, ⓦwww.usitcampus.co.uk. Student/youth-travel specialists with an emphasis on North America; offers discount flights and Amtrak passes.

In Ireland

Apex Travel Dublin ⓣ01/671 5933, ⓦwww.apextravel.ie. Specialists in flights to the US.
CIE Tours International Dublin ⓣ01/703 1888, ⓦwww.cietours.ie. General flight and tour agent.
Flightfinders Dublin ⓣ01/676 8326. Discount flight specialists.
Joe Walsh Tours Dublin ⓣ01/872 2555 or 676 3053, Cork ⓣ021/427 7959, ⓦwww.joewalshtours.ie. General budget fares agent.
McCarthy's Travel Cork ⓣ021/427 0127, ⓦwww.mccarthystravel.ie. General flight agent.
Premier Travel Derry ⓣ028/7126 3333, ⓦwww.premiertravel.uk.com. Discount flight specialists.
Rosetta Travel Belfast ⓣ028/9064 4996, ⓦwww.rosettatravel.com. Flight and holiday agent.
Trailfinders Dublin ⓣ01/677 7888, ⓦwww.trailfinders.ie. One of the best-informed and most efficient agents for independent travelers; Amtrak passes also available.
Twohigs Travel Dublin ⓣ01/677 2666. General flight and travel agent.
Usit Now Belfast ⓣ028/9032 7111, Dublin ⓣ01/602 1777 or 677 8117, Cork ⓣ021/4270 900, Derry ⓣ028/7137 1888, ⓦwww.usitnow.ie. Student and youth travel specialists offering flights and Amtrak passes.
World Travel Centre Dublin ⓣ01/671 7155, ⓦwww.worldtravel.ie. Discount flights and other travel services.

Tour operators and fly-drive deals

There are plenty of companies running package deals **from the UK** to New England, and especially to Boston – mostly short city-breaks that span three to five days. For a three-day trip, typical rates will run to around £600 per person in summer, though prices drop to around £450 out of high season, and sometimes less than that. It's usually around £100 more for the five-star or superior-grade hotel package. If you plan to see more of New England, **fly-drive** deals – which include car rental when buying a transatlantic ticket from an airline or tour operator – are always cheaper than renting a car on the spot. Most of the specialist companies offer fly-drive packages, though watch out for hidden extras, such as local taxes, "drop-off" charges, and extra insurance.

American Connections 10 York Way, Lancaster Rd, High Wycombe, Bucks HP12 3PY ⓣ01494/473173, ⓦwww.connectionsworldwide.net. Tailor-made packages, fly-drive, and escorted coach tours; the "New England Delights" package features Boston, Portland, Bar Harbor, Killington, Cape Cod, and Newport, among other attractions.
American Express Vacations ⓣ1-800/241-1700, ⓦwww.americanexpress.com/travel. Flights, hotels, last-minute specials, city-break packages, and specialty tours.
American Holidays Belfast ⓣ028/9023 8762, Dublin ⓣ01/433 1009, ⓦwww.american-holidays.com. Specialists in travel to USA and Canada with independent travel options and escorted tours; a ten-day tour including Boston, Nantucket, and Martha's Vineyard costs £1475.
Amtrak Vacations ⓣ1-800/321-8684, ⓦwww.amtrak.com/services/amtrak-vacations/html. Train or Amtrak Air-Rail trips through the Northeast, along with hotel reservations, car rental, and sightseeing tours.
Bon Voyage 18 Bellevue Rd, Southampton, Hants SO15 2AY ⓣ0800/316 3012, ⓦwww.bon-voyage.co.uk. Flight-plus-accommodation deals and tours covering Stowe, Boston, Plymouth, and Newport.
British Airways Holidays UK ⓣ0870/242 4245, ⓦwww.baholidays.co.uk. Using British Airways and

other international airlines, offers quality package and tailor-made New England holidays by phone; you can book individual amenities like hotel rooms, at a serious discount, online.

Contiki Tours UK ⓣ0208/290 6777, ⓦwww.contiki.com. Trips for the 18–35-year-old crowd; the 12-day "Eastern Canada and the USA" tour (from £749, land only) includes Boston and Cape Cod.

The Destination Group 14 Greville St, London EC1N 8SB ⓣ020/7400 7001, ⓦwww.destinationgroup.co.uk. Tailor-made accommodation, fly-drive deals, and tours in association with Amtrak.

Explore Worldwide 1 Frederick St, Aldershot, Hants GU11 1LQ ⓣ01252/760000, ⓦwww.explore.co.uk. Small-group adventure tours; the 16-day "New England and the Adirondacks" option includes Stowe, Provincetown, Acadia National Park, and Boston starting around £799 for land-only (£1199 including air).

Funway USA UK ⓣ020/8466 0222, ⓦwww.funwayholidays.co.uk. Boston city breaks, flight-only deals, and car rental.

Globus and Cosmos ⓦwww.globusandcosmos.com. Deluxe escorted tours. The "Cape Cod Escape" (eight days, from $1599) and "Great Cities of the East" (ten days, from $2299); the land-only prices include meals. Request brochures online or via a listed travel agent.

Individual Travellers New England Country Homes, Manor Courtyard, Bignor, Pulborough RH20 1QD ⓣ0870/077 4774, ⓦwww.indiv-travellers.com. Complete packages, including select accommodation in traditional New England clapboard cottages, colonial houses, log houses, hunting lodges, and beach houses, usually starting around £1012.

Kuoni 33 Maddox St, London W1S 1PX ⓣ020/7499 8636; 2a Barton Square, Manchester M2 7LW ⓣ0161/832 0667, ⓦwww.kuoni.co.uk. Multi-center flight-plus-accommodation-plus-car deals, as well as organized fly-drive tours; the 12-day "Classic New England" option includes Provincetown, Boston, the Berkshires, Newport, and more.

Media Travel UK ⓣ01784/434 434, ⓦwww.mediatravelco.uk. Tour operator with various eight-day trips through New England with an option of visiting Canada, too (£799–£899).

North America Travel Service 7 Albion St, Leeds LS1 5ER ⓣ0113/246 1466, ⓦwww.americatravelservice.com. Tailor-made holidays. An eight-day fly-drive holiday taking in Boston, Maine, White Mountains, Green Mountains, and Cape Cod costs from £699 per person.

Northwest Flydrive PO Box 45, Bexhill-on-Sea, East Sussex TN40 1PY ⓣ01424/224 400, ⓦwww.holiday-america.net. Flight-plus-accommodation and fly-drive specials. Boston weekend breaks start from £299.

Premier Holidays Westbrook, Milton Road, Cambridge CB4 1YG ⓣ0870/789 3334, ⓦwww.directcollection.co.uk. Flight-plus-accommodation deals starting as low as £295.

Suntrek Tours ⓣ1-800/SUN-TREK, ⓦwww.suntrek.com. Has 7- to 14-day "Eastern Trails" tours that include Providence, Boston, Plymouth, and the Adirondacks ($439–$799), and a two-week "East Coast Adventure" tour that adds Provincetown (and Washington DC) into the package ($1252–$1322).

Thomas Cook UK ⓣ0870/5666 222, ⓦwww.thomascook.co.uk. Long-established one-stop 24-hour travel agency for package holidays, city breaks, and scheduled flights, with bureau de change issuing Thomas Cook travelers' checks, travel insurance, and car rental.

Travelpack Clarendon House, Clarendon Road, Eccles, Manchester M30 9TR ⓣ0870/574 7101, ⓦwww.travelpack.co.uk. Boston city-breaks, escorted New England tours, and tailor-made holidays starting from £526.

TrekAmerica UK ⓣ01295/256 777, ⓦwww.trekamerica.com. Youth-oriented (18–38-year-olds) camping tours including Boston as part of larger tours of the region. The one-week "Eastern Highlights" tour, departing from New York, costs from £308 (flights, meals, and personal expenses extra).

Unijet UK ⓣ0870/600 8009, ⓦwww.unijet.com. City breaks, hotel reservations, and car rental.

United Vacations UK ⓣ0870/606 2222, ⓦwww.unitedvacations.co.uk. One-stop agent for tailor-made holidays, city breaks, fly-drive deals, pre-booked sightseeing tours, etc. Organized tours include a seven-night "Great American Cities" rail tour with Amtrak, from Boston to DC, from £553 (accommodation, transport, and tours included, flights extra).

Virgin Holidays UK ⓣ0870/220 2788, ⓦwww.virginholidays.co.uk. City breaks to Boston; flights are with Virgin Atlantic.

World Travel Centre Dublin ⓣ01/671 7155, ⓦwww.worldtravel.ie. Specialists in flights and packages to the US and Boston.

Courier flights

If you're really penny-pinching, and must go to the region in high season, you might consider flying as a **courier**. In return for cheaper rates, you'd be responsible for checking a package through with your (carry-on only) luggage. Given heightened security following September 11, though, the extra hassle over your relation to the package's contents may not be worth the trouble. To offer your services, call Flight Masters (☎020/7462 0022) or Bridges Worldwide (☎01895/465 065). You can also join the International Association of Air Travel Couriers (☎0800/746 481 or 01305/216 920, Ⓦwww.aircourier.co.uk). Flights leave from either Gatwick or Heathrow, with high season costs reduced to fares nearing spring rates.

From Australia and New Zealand

There are no direct flights to Boston from Australia or New Zealand, and most people reach the eastern United States by way of the West Coast and gateway cities such as Los Angeles and San Francisco. However you do it, it's a pretty long trip, considering that flying time is about fourteen hours to the West Coast and another six to New England.

Fares to LA and San Francisco from eastern **Australian** cities cost the same, while from Perth they're about A$400 more. There are daily non-stop flights from Sydney, to LA and San Francisco on United Airlines and to LA on Qantas, for around A$1800 in low season (Nov to mid-Dec & Jan–March). In addition there are several airlines that fly via Asia, which involves either a transfer or stopover in their home cities. The best deal is on JAL (A$1600–1900), which includes a night's stopover accommodation in Tokyo or Osaka in the fare. If you don't want to spend the night, Cathay Pacific and Singapore Airlines can get you there, via a transfer in the home cities of Hong Kong and Singapore, for around A$1750, and Korean Air (via Seoul) are sometimes a few dollars cheaper. Look out for special deals from agents (see p.22) at slack times, which can see tickets to Los Angeles from Sydney go for as little as A$1279.

From **New Zealand**, most flights are out of **Auckland** (add about NZ$200–250 for Christchurch and Wellington departures). The best deals are on Air New Zealand, to Los Angeles either non-stop or via Honolulu, Fiji, Tonga, or Papeete, or United Airlines, also non-stop to LA or San Francisco (both cost around NZ$2100–2500). Air Pacific via Fiji, and Qantas via Sydney (though direct is cheaper) both start around NZ$1800–2000. Via Asia, Singapore Airlines offers the best connecting service to LA and San Francisco from NZ$2099, while the best value for money (around NZ$1850–2250) is on JAL via either a transfer or stopover in Tokyo.

Once on the West Coast, the most frequent domestic flights to New England gateways are through United Airlines and American Airlines; the most cost-effective way to get to the region might be using an air pass, though you must buy a minimum of three flight coupons (costing between $400 and $800 total) before leaving your home country; see "Getting around," p.36, for details.

If you intend to take in New England as part of a world trip, a **round-the-world** (**RTW**) ticket offers the greatest flexibility. In recent years, many of the major international airlines have aligned themselves with one of two globe-spanning networks: the "Star Alliance," which links Air New Zealand, Ansett Australia, United, Lufthansa, Thai, SAS, Varig, and Air Canada; and "One World," which combines routes run by American, British Airways, Canadian Airlines, Cathay Pacific, LAN Chile, and Qantas. Both offer RTW deals with three stopovers in each continental sector you visit, with the option of adding additional sectors relatively cheaply. Fares depend on the number of sectors required, but a 21-day advance ticket from Australia to Boston, Burlington, Hartford, or Providence usually starts at around A$2500 (low season) for a US–Europe–Asia and home itinerary. If this is more flexibility than you need, you can shave a few hundred dollars off by going with an individual airline (in concert with code-share partners) and accepting fewer stops.

Airlines in Australia and New Zealand

Air New Zealand Australia ☎13 24 76, New Zealand ☎0800/737 000, Ⓦwww.airnz.com
American Airlines Australia ☎1300/650 747, New Zealand ☎0800/887 997, Ⓦwww.aa.com
British Airways Australia ☎02/8904 8800, New Zealand ☎09/356 8690, Ⓦwww.british-airways.com
Continental Airlines Australia ☎02/9244 2242, New Zealand ☎09/308 3350, Ⓦwww.flycontinental.com
Delta Air Lines Australia ☎800/500 992, New Zealand ☎0800/440 876, Ⓦwww.delta-air.com

Japan Airlines (JAL) Australia ⓣ02/9272 1111, New Zealand ⓣ09/379 9906, ⓦwww.japanair.com

KLM Australia ⓣ1300/303 747, New Zealand ⓣ09/309 1782, ⓦwww.klm.com

Northwest Airlines Australia ⓣ1300/303 747, New Zealand ⓣ09/302 1452, ⓦwww.nwa.com

Qantas Australia ⓣ13 13 13, New Zealand ⓣ0800/808 767, ⓦwww.qantas.com.au.

United Airlines Australia ⓣ13 17 77, New Zealand ⓣ09/379 3800, ⓦwww.ual.com

Virgin Atlantic Australia ⓣ02/9244 2747, New Zealand ⓣ09/308 3377, ⓦwww.virgin-atlantic.com

Discount travel and flight agents in Australia and New Zealand

Anywhere Travel Australia ⓣ02/9663 0411 or 018/401 014. General fares agent.

Budget Travel New Zealand ⓣ09/366 0061 or 0800/808 040, ⓦwww.budgettravel.co.nz. Flights, RTW fares, and tours.

Destinations Unlimited New Zealand ⓣ09/373 4033. RTW fares.

Flight Centre Australia ⓣ02/9235 3522 or for nearest branch 13 16 00, New Zealand ⓣ09/358 4310, ⓦwww.flightcentre.com.au. Specialist agent for budget flights, especially RTW.

STA Travel Australia ⓣ13 17 76 or 1300/360 960, ⓦwww.statravel.com.au, New Zealand ⓣ09/309 0458 or 09/366 6673, ⓦwww.statravel.co.nz. Discount flights, travel passes, and other services for youth/student travelers.

Student Uni Travel Australia ⓣ02/9232 8444. Good deals for students.

Thomas Cook Australia ⓣ13 17 71 or ⓣ1800/801 002, ⓦwww.thomascook.com.au, New Zealand ⓣ09/379 3920, ⓦwww.thomascook.co.nz. General flight and holiday agent; Amtrak passes also available.

Trailfinders Australia ⓣ02/9247 7666, ⓦwww.trailfinders.com.au. One of the best-informed and efficient agents for independent travelers; Amtrak passes also available.

Usit Beyond New Zealand ⓣ09/379 4224 or 0800/874 823, ⓦwww.usitbeyond.co.nz. Youth/student travel specialist; also RTW tickets, train passes, and other services.

Walshes World New Zealand ⓣ09/379 3708. Agent for Amtrak rail passes.

Specialist tour operators

Adventure World Australia ⓣ02/9956 7766 or 1300/363 055, ⓦwww.adventureworld.com.au, New Zealand ⓣ09/524 5118, ⓦwww.adventureworld.co.nz. Boston hotel bookings, car rental, and organized tours.

Australian Pacific Tours Australia ⓣ03/9277 8444 or 1800/675 222, New Zealand ⓣ09/279 6077, ⓦwww.aptours.com. Offers eight-day luxury coach tours during September and October of the region's historical sights, architecture, and scenery; from Boston via Cambridge, Lexington, Concord, and Williamstown, then up through Vermont to St Johns, across to the coast of Main to Kennebunkport then back to Boston starting at A$2750/NZ$2999.

Canada and America Travel Specialists Australia ⓣ02/9922 4600, ⓦwww.canada-americatravel.com.au. Can arrange flights and accommodation in North America, plus Greyhound Ameripasses and Amtrak passes.

Contiki Holidays Australia ⓣ02/9511 2200, New Zealand ⓣ09/309 8824, ⓦwww.contiki.com. Frenetic tours for 18- to 35-year-old party animals. Their twelve-day "Eastern Canada and USA" tour includes Boston, Cape Cod, Martha's Vineyard, and Rhode Island before hitting Canadian destinations (from A$2099, NZ$2475).

Creative Holidays Australia ⓣ02/9386 2111, ⓦwww.creativeholidays.com.au. City breaks and other packages.

Sydney International Travel Centre ⓣ02/9299 8000, ⓦwww.sydneytravel.com.au. US flights, accommodation, city stays, and car rental.

United Vacations ⓣ02/9324 1000. Tailor-made city stays or wider American holidays, with departures available from several Australian airports.

Red tape and visas

Under the Visa Waiver Program – designed to speed up lengthy immigration procedures – citizens of Andorra, Australia, Austria, Belgium, Brunei, Denmark, Finland, France, Germany, Iceland, Ireland, Italy, Japan, Liechtenstein, Luxembourg, Monaco, the Netherlands, New Zealand, Norway, Portugal, San Marino, Singapore, Slovenia, Spain, Sweden, Switzerland, the United Kingdom, and Uruguay visiting the United States for a period of less than ninety days only need a passport and a visa waiver form. The latter will be provided either by your travel agency, or by the airline before check-in or on the plane, and must be presented to immigration on arrival. The same form covers entry across the land borders with Canada and Mexico as well as by air. However, those eligible for the scheme must apply for a visa if they intend to work, study, or stay in the country for more than ninety days.

Prospective visitors from parts of the world not mentioned above require a valid passport and a **non-immigrant visitor's visa**. How you'll obtain a visa depends on what country you're in and your status when you apply, so telephone the nearest US embassy or consulate. You'll need a passport valid for at least six months beyond your intended stay, two passport photos, and will be charged the equivalent of $65. Expect it to take up to three weeks, though it could be substantially quicker. More information can be found at Ⓦwww.travel.state.gov/visa_services.

In **Britain**, only British or EU citizens, and those from other countries eligible for the Visa Waiver Program, can apply by post – fill in the application form available at most travel agents and send it with your passport and an SAE to the nearest US embassy or consulate. Expect a wait of ten days to three weeks before your passport is returned. All others must apply in person at the embassy or consulate, making an appointment in advance.

Australian and **New Zealand** passport holders staying less than ninety days do not require a visa, providing they arrive on a commercial flight with an onward or return ticket. You'll need an application form, available from a US embassy or consulate one signed passport photo and your passport, and either post it or personally lodge it at one of the US embassies or consulates. Processing takes about ten working days for postal applications; personal lodgements take two days – but check details with the consulate first.

Whatever your nationality, visas are not issued to convicted felons.

US embassies and consulates abroad

Australia

Canberra Moonah Place, Yarralumla, ACT 2600 Ⓣ02/6214 5600, Ⓕ6214-5970, Ⓦusembassy-australia.state.gov
Melbourne 553 St Kilda Road, PO Box 6722, Vic 3004 Ⓣ03/9526-5900, Ⓕ9510-4646
Sydney MLC Centre, 59th Floor, 19–29 Martin Place, NSW 2000 Ⓣ02/9373-9200, Ⓕ9373-9125
Perth 16 St George's Terrace, 13th floor, WA 6000 Ⓣ08/9202-1224, Ⓕ9231-9444

Canada

Ottawa 490 Sussex Drive, ON K1N 1G8 Ⓣ613/238-5335, Ⓦwww.usembassycanada.gov
Calgary 615 Macleod Trail SE, Room 1000, AB T2G 4T8 Ⓣ403/266-8962, Ⓕ264-6630
Halifax Suite 910, Purdy's Wharf Tower II,1969 Upper Water St, NS B3J 3R7 Ⓣ902/429-2480, Ⓕ423-6861
Montréal 1155 St Alexandre St, Québec H3B 1Z1 Ⓣ514/398-9695, Ⓕ398-0973
Toronto 360 University Ave, ON M5G 1S4 Ⓣ416/595-1700, Ⓕ595-0051
Vancouver 1075 W Pender St, BC V6E 2M6 Ⓣ604/685-4311, Ⓕ685-5285

Denmark

Copenhagen Dag Hammerskjöld Allé 24, 2100 ⓣ3555-3144, ⓕ3543-0223, ⓦwww.usembassy.dk

Ireland

Dublin 42 Elgin Rd, Ballsbridge ⓣ01/668 8777, ⓕ668 9946, ⓦwww.usembassy.ie

Netherlands

Den Hague Lange Voorhout 102, 2514 EJ ⓣ070/310-9209, ⓕ361-4688, ⓦwww.usemb.nl
Amsterdam Museumplein 19, 1071 DJ ⓣ020/575-5309, ⓕ575-5310

New Zealand

Wellington 29 Fitzherbert Terrace, Thorndon ⓣ04/462-6000, ⓕ478-1701, ⓦusembassy.org.nz
Auckland 3rd floor, Citibank Building, 23 Customs St ⓣ09/303-2724, ⓕ366 0870

Norway

Oslo Drammensveien 18, 0244 ⓣ2244-8550, ⓦwww.usa.no

South Africa

Pretoria 877 Pretorius St, Arcadia 0083 ⓣ012/342 1048, ⓕ342 2244, ⓦusembassy.state.gov/pretoria
Cape Town 7th floor, Monte Carlo Building, Heerengracht, Foreshore ⓣ021/421 44351, ⓕ425 3014
Durban 2901 Durban Bay Building, 333 Smith St ⓣ031/304 4737, ⓕ301 0265
Johannesburg 1 River St, Killarney ⓣ011/644 8000, ⓕ646 6913.

UK

London 24 Grosvenor Square, W1A 1AE ⓣ020/749 99000; visa hotline (£1.50 a minute) ⓣ09061/500 590, ⓦwww.usembassy.org.uk
Belfast Queen's House, 14 Queen St BT1 6EQ ⓣ028/9032 8239, ⓕ9024 8482.
Edinburgh 3 Regent Terrace, EH7 5BW ⓣ0131/556 8315, ⓕ557 6023.

Embassies and consulates in New England

All of the following are located in Boston:
Canada 3 Copley Place, Suite 500 ⓣ617/536-4414
Denmark 20 Park Plaza ⓣ617/542-1415
Ireland 535 Boylston St ⓣ617/267-9330
Netherlands 20 Park Plaza, Suite 524 ⓣ617/542-8452
Norway 286 Congress St ⓣ617/423-2515
UK 600 Atlantic Ave ⓣ617/248-9555

Immigration controls

The standard immigration regulations apply to all visitors, whether or not they are using the Visa Waiver Program. During the flight, you'll be handed an **immigration form** (and a customs declaration; see below), which must be given up at immigration control once you land. The form requires you cite your proposed **length of stay** and to list an **address**, at least for your first night. Previously "touring" was satisfactory, but since **September 11**, controls have become more stringent and they require a verifiable address. If you have no accommodation arranged for your first night, pick a plausible-sounding hotel from the appropriate section of the *Guide* and list that.

You probably won't be asked unless you look disreputable in the eyes of the official on duty, but you should be able to prove that you have a return air ticket (if flying in), and enough money to support yourself while in the US; anyone revealing the slightest intention of working while in the country is likely to be refused admission. Around $300–400 a week is usually considered sufficient – waving a credit card or two may do the trick. You may also experience difficulties if you admit to being HIV positive or having AIDS or TB. Part of the immigration form will be attached to your passport, where it must stay until you leave, when an immigration or airline official will detach it.

Customs

Customs officers will relieve you of your customs declaration and check if you're carrying any fresh foods. You'll also be asked if you've visited a farm in the last month – if you have, you may well have your shoes taken away for inspection. The duty-free

Canadian citizens are in a particularly privileged position when it comes to crossing the border into the US. Though it is possible to enter the States without your passport, you should really have it with you on any trip that brings you to New England. Only if you plan to stay for more than ninety days do you need a visa. Bear in mind that if you cross into the US by car, trunks and passenger compartments are subject to spot searches by Customs personnel. Remember too, that without the proper paperwork, Canadians are legally barred from seeking gainful employment in the US.

allowance if you're over 17 is 200 cigarettes and 100 cigars, a litre of spirits (if you're over 21), and $400 worth of gifts, which can include an additional 100 cigars. As well as foods and anything agricultural, it's prohibited to carry into the country any articles from Afghanistan, Cuba, Iran, Libya, North Korea, Serbia, and Sudan, or obscene publications, drug paraphernalia, lottery tickets, chocolate liqueurs, or pre-Columbian artifacts. Anyone caught carrying drugs into the country will not only face prosecution, but be entered in the records as an undesirable and probably denied entry for all time. There are more details on the US Customs website at ⓦwww.customs.treas.gov/travel/travel.

Extensions and leaving

The date stamped on your passport is the latest you're legally allowed to stay. Leaving a few days later may not matter, especially if you're heading home, but more than a week or so can result in a protracted, rather unpleasant interrogation from officials, which may cause you to miss your flight and be denied entry to the US in the future.

To get an **extension** before your time is up, apply as early as possible to the **US Immigration and Naturalization** Service (ⓦwww.ins. usdoj.gov) center which handles the state where you are staying. For New England, all states are handled by the Vermont Service Center, 75 Lower Welden Street, St Albans, VT 05479. Do not go to the local INS office. You must provide evidence of ample finances, and you'll also have to explain why you didn't plan for the extra time initially. The INS must receive your application for extension by the day your authorized stay expires.

Information, websites, and maps

Advance information for a trip to New England can be obtained by calling the appropriate state's information center (see overleaf). A publicly funded firm called Discover New England, PO Box 3809, Stowe, VT 05672 (ⓣ802/253-2500, ⓦwww.discovernewengland.org), also exists to provide advance information on all six states in New England. Anyone can visit their website, while residents of the UK and Germany can get in touch directly with the Discover New England offices in these two countries. In the UK, the office is at Cellet Travel Services, Brook House, 47 High St, Henley in Arden, Warwickshire B95 5AA (ⓣ0906/558 8555; calls charged at £1 per minute to a maximum of £2 to cover the costs of postage and packaging of guides and maps), and in Germany at Roonstr 21, 90429 Nümberg (ⓣ0911/926 9113, ⓔbusscons@aol.com).

Once you've arrived, you'll find most towns have visitors' centers of some kind – often called the **Convention and Visitors Bureau** (CVB) or **Chamber of Commerce**: many are listed within the *Guide*. The essential difference between the two types of visitors' centers is that the former deals exclusively with tourism-related businesses, while the latter represents all types of commerce. Either one will give out detailed information on the local area, and can often help with finding accommodation. Additionally, free **newspapers** in most places carry news of events and entertainment. Of the several **publications** with travel information specific to New England, check out the range of magazines published by Yankee Publishing, PO Box 520, Dublin, NH 03444 (Ⓣ1-800/895-9265 ext 220, Ⓦwww.yankeemagazine.com). *Yankee Magazine* is published ten times a year, and contains travel features and coverage of the latest New England living trends. The annual *Yankee Magazine Travel Guide to New England* ($4.99) also contains travel features, accompanied by plenty of useful practical information. The *New England Navigator* ($8.99) has customized maps and information on six scenic driving tours. The *Yankee Magazine's Bed & Breakfast and Inn Directory* ($4.99) features more than six hundred places to stay in New England. The *Boston Magazine*, 300 Massachusetts Ave, Boston, MA 02115 (Ⓣ617/262-9700, Ⓦwww.bostonmagazine.com), is another publication, published monthly ($3.50), which has feature articles on Boston and the rest of New England.

New England state information centers

Connecticut 505 Hudson St, Hartford, CT 06106 Ⓣ860/270-8080 or 1-800/282-6863, Ⓦwww.ctbound.org
Maine 9 State House Station, Augusta, ME 04333-0059 Ⓣ1-888/624-6345, Ⓦwww.visitmaine.com
Massachusetts 10 Park Plaza, Suite 4510, Boston, MA 02116 Ⓣ617/973-8500 or 1-800/227-MASS, Ⓦwww.mass-vacation.com
New Hampshire 172 Pembroke Rd, Concord, NH 03302 Ⓣ603/271-2665 or 1-800/FUN-IN-NH, Ⓦwww.visitnh.com
Rhode Island One W Exchange St, Providence, RI 02903 Ⓣ401/222-2601 or 1-800/556-2484, Ⓦwww.visitrhodeisland.com
Vermont 6 Baldwin St, Montpelier, VT 05633 Ⓣ802/828-3236 or 1-800/VERMONT, Ⓦwww.1-800-vermont.com

Websites

Though we've listed relevant websites throughout this guide for hotels, organizations, major sights, and so on, the following might help you pursue a few special areas of interest in preparation for your visit.

AlpineZone Ⓦwww.alpinezone.com. Check up on ski and hiking trail reports in the northeast, as well as accommodation on all the mountains.
Boston Online Ⓦwww.boston-online.com. General info on the city, including a dictionary of Bostonian English and a guide to public bathrooms.
Link Pink Ⓦwww.linkpink.com. Comprehensive listings of businesses, hotels, shops, and services catering to New England's gay and lesbian community.
New England History Ⓦwww.newenglandhistory.info. Well-organized site for limited historical background on each state, plus some good old images and notable quotes.
New England Lighthouses Ⓦwww.lighthouse.cc. Organized by state, with photos, history, and pretty much everything you might need to find out about your favorite lighthouse.
New England Rail Photography Archive Ⓦphotos.nerail.org. If you have an unhealthy interest in seeing shots of every imaginable railway and railroad car in New England, check out this archive – and follow the links that lead to sites on the history of railroads in the region.
New England for Visitors Ⓦgonewengland.about.com. Links to all sorts of fairly mainstream info, including tour operators, major ski resorts, and the like.

Maps

Most of the tourist offices we've mentioned here or throughout the *Guide* can supply you with good **maps**, either free or for a small charge, and supplemented with our own, these should be enough for general sightseeing and touring. If you need more specific detail, Rand McNally produces a decent folded map of New England ($3.95), as well as maps focusing on the six individual states of the region, while its *Road Atlas* ($8.99), covering the whole country plus Mexico and Canada, is worthwhile if you're traveling further afield. For driving or cycling through rural areas, Maine-based Delorme (Ⓦwww.delorme.com) publishes their valuable *Atlas & Gazetteer* to each of the New England states ($19.95 each), with detailed city plans, marked campgrounds, and reams of national park and forest information. For travel along the coastline, Delorme's *Street Atlas: Seacoast Region* ($9.95) covers the stretch of coast from Kennebunk, ME, down to Salisbury Beach, MA, and up to 25 miles inland. Several other New England-based publishers also produce good maps, although you may only find them for sale in the region's better bookstores. Arrow Map's *Road Map & Recreation Guide: New England* ($4.95) is colorful and easy to read; while the *Visual Encyclopedia: New England* ($3.50) by Marshall Penn-York Co is a well detailed alternative with a good index, if not as pretty to look at. For detailed hiking maps, check with ranger stations in parks and wilderness areas or with camping stores. The American Automobile Association (ⓣ1-800/922-8228, ⓦwww.aaa.com) has offices in most large cities and provides excellent free maps and travel assistance to its members, as well as to British members of the AA and RAC.

Map and travel book suppliers

In the US and Canada

Adventurous Traveler.com ⓣ1-800/282-3963, ⓦwww.adventuroustraveler.com
The Appalachian Mountain Club 5 Joy St, Boston, MA 02108 ⓣ617/523-0636, ⓦwww.outdoors.org
Distant Lands 56 S Raymond Ave, Pasadena, CA 91105 ⓣ1-800/310-3220, ⓦwww.distantlands.com
Globe Corner Bookstore 28 Church St, Cambridge, MA 02138 ⓣ1-800/358-6013, ⓦwww.globecorner.com
Gulliver's 7 Commercial Alley, Portsmouth, NH 0380 ⓣ603/431-5556, ⓦwww.gulliversbooks.com
Map Link 30 S La Patera Lane, Unit 5, Santa Barbara, CA 93117 ⓣ1-800/962-1394, ⓦwww.maplink.com
Open Air Books and Maps 25 Toronto St, Toronto, ON M5C 2R1 ⓣ416/363-0719
Rand McNally ⓣ1-800/333-0136, ⓦwww.randmcnally.com. Around thirty stores across the US; dial ext 2111 or check the website for the nearest location.
The Savvy Traveller 310 S Michigan Ave, Chicago, IL 60604 ⓣ312/913-9800, ⓦwww.thesavvytraveller.com
Sierra Club Bookstore 85 Second St, San Francisco, CA 94105 ⓣ415/977-5600, ⓦwww.sierraclub.org
The Travel Bug Bookstore 2667 W Broadway, Vancouver V6K 2G2 ⓣ604/737-1122, ⓦwww.swifty.com/tbug
Ulysses Travel Bookshop 4176 rue St-Denis, Montréal, PQ H2W 2M5 ⓣ514/843-9447
World of Maps 1235 Wellington St, Ottawa, ON K1Y 3A3 ⓣ1-800/214-8524; 736A Granville St, Vancouver, BC V6Z 1G3 ⓣ604/687-3320; ⓦwww.worldofmaps.com

In the UK and Ireland

Blackwell's Map and Travel Shop 50 Broad St, Oxford OX1 3BQ ⓣ01865/793 550, ⓦwww.maps.blackwell.co.uk
Daunt Books 83 Marylebone High St, London W1M 3DE ⓣ020/7224 2295; 193 Haverstock Hill, London NW3 4QL ⓣ020/7794 4006
Easons Bookshop 40 O'Connell St, Dublin 1 ⓣ01/858 3881
Heffers Map and Travel 20 Trinity St, Cambridge CB2 1TJ ⓣ01865/333 536, ⓦwww.heffers.co.uk. Mail order available.
Hodges Figgis Bookshop 56–58 Dawson St, Dublin 2 ⓣ01/677 4754, ⓦwww.hodgesfiggis.com.
James Thin Melven's Bookshop 53–62 South Bridge, Edinburgh EH1 1Y3 ⓣ0131/622 8222, ⓦwww.jthin.co.uk. Established 1849; map department with all foreign maps; mail order specialist.
John Smith and Sons 50 Crouper St, Townhead, Glasgow G4 0DL ⓣ0141/552 4394, ⓦwww.johnsmith.co.uk
The Map Shop 30A Belvoir St, Leicester LE1 6QH ⓣ0116/247 1400, ⓦwww.mapshopleicester.co.uk. Mail order available.
National Map Centre 22–24 Caxton St, SW1H 0QU ⓣ020/7222 2466, ⓦwww.mapsnmc.co.uk
Newcastle Map Centre 55 Grey St, Newcastle upon Tyne NE1 6EF ⓣ0191/261 5622, ⓦwww.newtraveller.com
Stanfords 12–14 Long Acre, WC2E 9LP ⓣ020/7836 1321; also a branch within the British Airways offices at 156 Regent St, W1B 5SN ⓣ020/7434 4744; ⓦwww.stanfords.co.uk
The Travel Bookshop 13–15 Blenheim Crescent, W11 2EE ⓣ020/7229 5260, ⓦwww.thetravelbookshop.co.uk

In Australia and New Zealand

The Map Shop 6 Peel St, Adelaide, SA 5000 ⓣ08/8231 2033, ⓦwww.mapshop.net.au
Mapland 372 Little Bourke St, Melbourne, Victoria 3000 ⓣ03/9670 4383, ⓦwww.mapland.com.au
MapWorld 173 Gloucester St, Christchurch ⓣ0800/627 967, ⓦwww.mapworld.co.nz
Perth Map Centre 1/884 Hay St, Perth, WA 6000 ⓣ08/9322 5733, ⓦwww.perthmap.com.au

Specialty Maps 46 Albert St, Auckland 1001 ☎09/307 2217, Ⓦwww.ubdonline.co.nz/maps
Travel Bookshop Shop 3, 175 Liverpool St, Sydney ☎02/9261 8200
Walkers Bookshop 96 Lake St Cairns ☎07/4051 2410
Worldwide Maps and Guides 187 George St, Brisbane ☎07/3221 4330

Insurance

Getting travel insurance is highly recommended, especially if you're coming from abroad and are at all concerned about your health – prices for medical attention in the US can be exorbitant. A secondary benefit is that most policies also cover against theft and loss, which can be useful if you're toting around an expensive camera or any high-tech gear. Before paying for a new policy, check to see if you're already covered: some all-risks home insurance policies may cover your possessions when overseas, and many private medical schemes include cover when abroad. In Canada, provincial health plans usually provide partial cover for medical mishaps outside of the country, while holders of official student/teacher/youth cards are entitled to meager accident coverage and hospital in-patient benefits. Students will often find that their student health coverage extends during the vacations and for one term beyond the date of their last enrollment.

After exhausting the possibilities above, you might want to contact a specialist travel insurance company, or consider the Rough Guides travel insurance deal (see box below). A typical travel insurance policy usually provides cover for the loss of baggage, tickets, and – up to a certain limit – cash or checks, as well as cancellation or curtailment of your journey. Most of them exclude so-called **high-risk activities**, such as skiing, snowboarding, and rockclimbing, unless an extra premium is paid; be sure to check. Many policies can be chopped and changed to exclude coverage you don't need – for example, sickness and accident benefits can often be excluded or included at will. If you

Rough Guides travel insurance

Rough Guides offers its own travel insurance, customized for our readers by a leading UK broker and backed by a Lloyd's underwriter. It's available for anyone, of any nationality and any age, traveling anywhere in the world.

There are two main Rough Guide insurance plans: **Essential**, for basic, no-frills cover; and **Premier**, with more generous and extensive benefits. Alternatively, you can take out **annual multi-trip insurance**, which covers you for any number of trips throughout the year (with a maximum of 60 days for any one trip). Unlike many policies, the Rough Guides schemes are calculated by the day, so if you're traveling for 27 days rather than a month, that's all you pay for. If you intend to be away for the whole year, the Adventurer policy will cover you for 365 days. Each plan can be supplemented with a "Hazardous Activities Premium" if you plan to indulge in sports considered dangerous, such as skiing, scubadiving, or hiking.

For a policy quote, call the Rough Guide Insurance Line on US toll-free ☎1-866/220-5588, UK freefone ☎0800/015 0906, or, if you're calling from elsewhere in the world, dial your international access code, followed by ☎44 1243/621 046. Alternatively, get an online quote or buy online at Ⓦwww.roughguidesinsurance.com.

do take medical coverage, ascertain whether benefits will be paid as treatment proceeds or only after return home, and whether there is a 24-hour medical emergency number. When securing **baggage cover**, make sure that the per-article limit – typically under $500 – will cover your most valuable possession. If you need to make a claim, you should keep receipts for medicines and medical treatment, and in the event you have anything stolen, you must obtain an official statement from the police.

Health

Visitors from Europe, Australia, New Zealand, and Canada don't require any vaccinations to enter the US. All travelers will be comforted to know that if you have a serious accident while you're in New England, emergency services will get to you sooner and charge you later. For emergencies, dial toll-free ⓣ911 from any phone. If you have medical or dental problems that don't require an ambulance, most hospitals will have a walk-in emergency room: for the nearest hospital, check with your hotel or dial information at ⓣ411.

Should you need to see a doctor, lists can be found in the *Yellow Pages* under "Clinics" or "Physicians and Surgeons." Be aware that even consultations are costly, usually around $75–100 each visit, which is payable in advance. Keep receipts for any part of your medical treatment, including prescriptions, so that you can claim against your insurance once you're home. (See "Insurance" above for more).

For minor ailments, stop by a local pharmacy; some are open 24 hours – especially in the larger cities. Foreign visitors should note that many medicines available over the counter at home – codeine-based painkillers, for one – are available by **prescription only** in the US. Bring additional supplies if you're particularly brand loyal.

Costs, money, and banks

To help with planning your vacation in New England, this book contains detailed price information for accommodation, eating, and various activities. Unless otherwise stated, the hotel price codes (explained on p.39) are for the average cost of the least expensive double room typically available, exclusive of any local taxes, while any meal prices quoted include food only and not drinks or tip. For museums and similar attractions, the prices we quote are generally for adults; you can assume that children get in half-price. Naturally, costs will increase slightly overall during the life of this edition, but the relative comparisons should remain valid.

Costs

Accommodation is likely to be your biggest single expense in New England. Few hotel or motel rooms cost under $40; you're likely to pay more than $80 for anything halfway decent in a city, and rates in rural areas are not much cheaper. In Boston, it may well be difficult to find anything at all for less than $75. On the plus side, these prices are almost invariably for a double room, so you will save money if you can split the cost with a travel companion. Hostels offering dorm beds – usually for $15–20 – are available, but they are by no means everywhere, and they save little money for two or more people traveling together. Camping, of course, is cheap (anywhere from free to $25 per night), but rarely practical in the big cities.

As for **food**, $20 a day is enough to get an adequate life-support diet, while for a daily total of around $30 you can dine pretty well. Beyond this, everything hinges on how much sightseeing, taxi-cabbing, and drinking you do. Much of any of these – especially in the cities – and you're likely to be going through upwards of $50 a day (excluding accommodation).

The rates for traveling around, especially on buses, and to a lesser extent on trains and planes, may look inexpensive on paper, but the distances involved mean that costs soon mount up. For a group of two or more, renting a car can be a very good investment (see "Getting around," p.32), not least because it enables you to stay in the ubiquitous budget motels along the interstate highways instead of relying on expensive downtown hotels.

Remember that a **sales tax** of between five and seven percent is added to virtually everything you buy in stores except for groceries, but isn't part of the marked price (there is no sales tax in New Hampshire, however). In addition, many potential accommodations apply a hotel tax; this can add as much as fourteen percent to the total bill.

Cash and travelers' checks

US dollar travelers' checks are the best way to carry money, for both American and foreign visitors; they offer the great security of knowing that lost or stolen checks will be replaced. The usual fee for travelers' check sales is one or two percent, though this fee may be waived if you buy the checks through a bank where you have an account. Don't forget to keep the purchase agreement and a record of serial numbers safe and separate from the checks themselves. In the event that checks are lost or stolen, the issuing company will expect you to report the loss forthwith (see opposite for numbers); most companies claim to replace lost or stolen checks within 24 hours. Throughout New England, you should have no problem using the better-known checks, such as American Express and Visa, in the same way as cash in shops, restaurants, and gas stations (don't be put off by "no checks" signs, which only refer to personal checks). Be sure to have plenty of the $10 and $20 denominations for everyday transactions.

Banks are generally open from 9am until 5pm Monday to Thursday, and 9am to 6pm on Friday. Some have limited hours on Saturdays, and ATMs are usually accessible 24 hours a day. Most major banks change US travelers' checks for their face value (not that there's much point in doing this – and some charge for the privilege, so ask before you do), and change foreign travelers' checks and currency as well. **Exchange bureaux**, found at airports, tend to charge less commission: Thomas Cook and American Express are the biggest names. Rarely, if ever, do hotels change foreign currency. If your checks and/or credit cards are stolen or if you need to find the nearest bank that sells a particular brand of travelers' check, or to buy checks by phone, call the following numbers: American Express (☎1-800/221-7282), Citicorp (☎1-800/645-6556), MasterCard International/Thomas Cook (☎1-800/223-7373) and Visa (☎1-800/227-6811).

Credit and debit cards

Credit cards are a very handy backup source of funds, and can be used either in ATMs or over the counter. MasterCard, Visa, and American Express are accepted just about everywhere, but other cards may not be recognized in the US. Remember that all cash advances are treated as loans, with interest accruing daily from the date of withdrawal; there may be a transaction fee on top of this. However, you may be able to make withdrawals from ATMs using your **debit card**, which is not liable to interest payments, and the flat transaction fee is usually quite small – your bank will able to advise on this. Make sure you have a personal identification number (PIN) that's designed to work overseas.

A compromise between travelers' checks and plastic is Visa TravelMoney, a disposable pre-paid debit card with a PIN which works

Money: a note for foreign travelers

Even when the exchange rate is at its least advantageous, most western European visitors find virtually everything – accommodation, food, gas, cameras, clothes, and more – to be better value in the US than it is at home. However, if you're used to traveling in the less expensive countries of Europe, let alone in the rest of the world, you shouldn't expect to scrape by on the same minuscule budget once you're in the US. Regular upheaval in the world money markets causes the relative value of the US dollar against the currencies of the rest of the world to vary considerably. Generally speaking, one pound sterling will buy between $1.40 and $1.80; one Canadian dollar is worth between $0.60 and $0.80; one Australian dollar is worth between $0.50 and $0.88; and one New Zealand dollar is worth between $0.45 and $0.72.

US currency comes in bills of $1, $5, $10, $20, $50, and $100, plus various larger (and rarer) denominations. All are the same size and color, making it necessary to check each bill carefully. The dollar is made up of 100 cents with coins of 1 cent (known as a penny), 5 cents (a nickel), 10 cents (a dime), and 25 cents (a quarter). New gold dollar coins were recently introduced in the US and are becoming more prevalent. Very occasionally you might find JFK half-dollars (50¢), Susan B. Anthony dollar coins, or a two-dollar bill. Change (quarters are the most useful) is needed for buses, vending machines, parking meters, and telephones, so always have some on hand.

in all ATMs that accept Visa cards. You load up your account with funds before leaving home, and when they run out, you simply throw the card away. You can buy up to nine cards to access the same funds – useful for couples or families traveling together – and it's a good idea to buy at least one extra as a backup in case of loss or theft. There is also a 24-hour toll-free customer assistance number (Ⓣ1-800/847-2911). The card is available in most countries from branches of Thomas Cook and Citicorp. For more information, check the Visa TravelMoney website at Ⓦwww.usa.visa.com/personal/cards/visa_travel_money.html.

ATMs

The two major international cash dispenser networks operate a toll-free line to let customers know the location of their nearest ATM: Plus System is Ⓣ1-800/THE-PLUS and Cirrus is Ⓣ1-800/4CIRRUS.

Wiring money

Having money wired from home using one of the companies listed below is never convenient or cheap, and should be considered a last resort. It's also possible to have money wired directly from a bank in your home country to a bank in the US, although this is somewhat less reliable because it involves two separate institutions. If you go this route, your home bank will need the address of the branch bank where you want to pick up the money and the address and routing number of that bank's state head office, which will act as the clearing house; money wired this way normally takes two working days to arrive, and costs around $40 per transaction.

Money-wiring companies

Thomas Cook US Ⓣ1-800/287-7362, Canada Ⓣ1-888/823-4732, UK Ⓣ01733/318 922, Republic of Ireland Ⓣ01/677 1721, Ⓦwww.us.thomascook.com

Travelers Express Moneygram US Ⓣ1-800/926-3947, Canada Ⓣ1-800/933-3278, Ⓦwww.moneygram.com

Western Union US and Canada Ⓣ1-800/325-6000, Australia Ⓣ1800/501 500, New Zealand Ⓣ09/270 0050, UK Ⓣ0800/833 833, Republic of Ireland Ⓣ1800/395 395, Ⓦwww.westernunion.com

Youth and student discounts

Once obtained, various official and quasi-official **youth/student ID cards** soon pay for themselves in savings. Full-time students are eligible for the International Student ID Card (ISIC, ®www.isiccard.com), which entitles the bearer to special air, rail, and bus fares, as well as discounts at museums, theaters, and other attractions. For Americans there's also a health benefit, providing up to $3000 in emergency medical coverage and $100 a day for 60 days in the hospital, plus a 24-hour hotline to call in the event of a medical, legal, or financial emergency. The card costs $22 for Americans; Can$16 for Canadians; AUS$16.50 for Australians; NZ$21 for New Zealanders; and £6 in the UK.

You only have to be 26 or younger to qualify for the **International Youth Travel Card**, which costs US$22/£7 and carries the same benefits. Teachers qualify for the **International Teacher Card**, offering similar discounts and costing US$22, Can$16, AUS$16.50, and NZ$21. All of these cards are available from student-oriented travel agents in North America, Europe, Australia, and New Zealand. Several other travel organizations and accommodation groups also sell their own cards, good for various discounts. A university photo ID might open some doors, but is not easily recognizable, as are the ISIC cards. However, the latter are often not accepted as valid proof of age, for example in bars or liquor stores.

Getting around

Although rural areas can be nearly impossible to access if you don't have a car, getting from one large city to the next is seldom much of a problem on public transportation in New England. Good bus links and reasonable, though limited, train service are nearly always available. Getting around after you arrive, however, is another story. If you plan to cover any range of different destinations, renting a car is highly recommended, but with adroit forward planning, you can usually get to the main points of interest on local buses and charter services, details of which are in the relevant sections of the *Guide*.

By car

Driving is by far the best way to get around New England. Keep in mind, though, that things get confusing within the larger cities such as Boston, where complicated freeway networks intertwine with narrow one-way city streets that were designed for horse-drawn carriages. Away from the cities, many places are almost impossible to reach without your own transportation; most national and state parks and forests are only served by infrequent public transportation as far as the main visitor's center, if that. What's more, if you are planning on doing a fair amount of camping, renting a car can save you money by allowing access to less expensive out-of-the-way campgrounds, not to mention easing the burden of carting your equipment around.

Drivers wishing to **rent cars** are supposed to have held their licenses for at least one year (though this is rarely checked); people **under 25 years old** may encounter problems, and will probably get lumbered with higher than normal rates. Car rental companies (see opposite) will also expect you to have a credit card; if you don't they may let you leave a hefty deposit (at least $200), but don't count on it. The likeliest tactic for getting a good deal is to phone the major firms' toll-free numbers and ask for their best rate – most will try to beat the offers of their competitors, so it's worth haggling.

In general the **lowest rates** are available at the airport branches – $200 a week for a subcompact is a fairly standard base rate – although many airports now add "Airport Accessibility" fees, calculated in a percentage, which serve to increase your total fairly quickly. Always be sure to get free **unlimited mileage**, and be aware that leaving the car in a different state from the one in which you rented can incur a drop-off charge. However, many companies do not charge drop-off fees to certain cities, so check before you book if you plan a one-way drive. Also, don't automatically go for the cheapest rate, as there's some difference in the quality of cars from company to company; industry leaders like Hertz and Avis tend to have newer, lower-mileage cars, often with stereo cassette or CD as standard equipment.

Alternatively, various local companies rent out new – and not so new (try Rent-a-Heap or Rent-a-Wreck) – vehicles. They are certainly cheaper than the big chains if you just want to spin around a city for a day, but you have to drop them back where you picked them up, and free mileage is seldom included. Addresses and phone numbers are listed in the **Yellow Pages**.

When you rent a car, read the small print carefully for details on **Collision Damage Waiver** (CDW), sometimes called Liability Damage Waiver (LDW), a form of insurance which often isn't included in the initial rental charge but is well worth considering. This specifically covers the car that you are driving yourself, as you are in any case insured for damage to other vehicles. At $9–13 a day, it can add substantially to the total cost, but without it you're liable for every scratch to the car – even those that aren't your fault. Some credit-card companies offer automatic CDW coverage to anyone using their card; read the fine print beforehand in any case.

You should also check your **third-party liability**. The standard policy often only covers you for the first $15,000 of the third party's claim against you, a paltry sum in litigation-conscious America. Companies strongly advise taking out third-party insurance, which costs a further $10–12 a day but indemnifies the driver for up to $2,000,000.

If you **break down** in a rented car, there'll be an emergency number pinned to the dashboard, tucked away in the glove compartment, or printed on your rental contract. You can summon the highway patrol on one of the new emergency phones stationed along freeways (usually at half-mile intervals) and many other remote highways (mostly every two miles) – although as the highway patrol and state police cruise by regularly, you can just sit tight and wait. Raising your car hood is recognized as a call for assistance, although women traveling alone should be wary of doing this.

Another tip, for women especially, is to rent a **mobile telephone** from the car rental agency – you often only have to pay a nominal amount until you actually use it, and in larger cities they increasingly come built into the car. Having a phone can be reassuring at least, and a potential lifesaver should something go terribly wrong.

Major car rental agencies

In North America

Alamo US ⓣ1-800/522-9696, ⓦwww.alamo.com
Avis US ⓣ1-800/331-1084, Canada ⓣ1-800/272-5871, ⓦwww.avis.com
Budget US ⓣ1-800/527-0700, ⓦwww.budgetrentacar.com
Dollar US ⓣ1-800/800-4000, ⓦwww.dollar.com
Enterprise Rent-a-Car US ⓣ1-800/325-8007, ⓦwww.enterprise.com
Hertz US ⓣ1-800/654-3001, Canada ⓣ1-800/263-0600, ⓦwww.hertz.com
National ⓣ1-800/227-7368, ⓦwww.nationalcar.com
Thrifty ⓣ1-800/367-2277, ⓦwww.thrifty.com

In the UK

Avis ⓣ0870/606 0100, ⓦwww.avisworld.com
Budget ⓣ0800/181 181, ⓦwww.budget.co.uk
National ⓣ0870/5365 365, ⓦwww.nationalcar.com
Hertz ⓣ0870/844 8844, ⓦwww.hertz.co.uk
Holiday Autos ⓣ0870/400 00 99, ⓦwww.holidayautos.co.uk
Suncars ⓣ0870/500 5566, ⓦwww.suncars.com
Thrifty ⓣ01494/751 600, ⓦwww.thrifty.co.uk

In Ireland

Argus Republic of Ireland ⓣ01/490 4444, ⓦwww.argus-rentacar.com
Avis Northern Ireland ⓣ028/9024 0404, Republic of Ireland ⓣ01/605 7500, ⓦwww.avis.co.uk
Budget Republic of Ireland ⓣ01/9032 7711, ⓦwww.budgetcarrental.ie
Cosmo Thrifty Northern Ireland ⓣ028/9445 2565, ⓦwww.thrifty.co.uk
Hertz Republic of Ireland ⓣ01/660 2255, ⓦwww.hertz.ie
Holiday Autos Republic of Ireland ⓣ01/872 9366, ⓦwww.holidayautos.ie

In Australia

Avis ⓣ13 63 33, ⓦwww.avis.com.au
Budget ⓣ1300/362 848, ⓦwww.budget.com.au
Dollar ⓣ02/9223 1444, ⓦwww.dollarcar.com.au
Hertz ⓣ13 30 39, ⓦwww.hertz.com.au
National ⓣ13 10 45, ⓦwww.nationalcar.com.au
Thrifty ⓣ1300/367 227, ⓦwww.thrifty.com.au

In New Zealand

Avis ⓣ09/526 2847, ⓦwww.avis.co.nz
Budget ⓣ09/976 2222, ⓦwww.budget.co.nz
Hertz ⓣ0800/654 321, ⓦwww.hertz.co.nz
National ⓣ0800/800 115 or 03/366 5574, ⓦwww.nationalcar.co.nz
Thrifty ⓣ09/309 0111, ⓦwww.thrifty.co.nz

Renting an RV

Besides cars, Recreational Vehicles or **RVs** (camper vans) can be rented from around $450 a week (usually with no or limited free mileage), although outlets are surprisingly rare. The Recreational Vehicle Rental Association, 3930 University Drive, Fairfax, VA 22030 (ⓣ703/591-7130 or 1-800/336-0355, ⓦwww.rvra.org), publishes a directory of rental firms in the US and Canada ($10, $15 outside North America) or you can get details of their many members online. Two of the larger companies offering RV rentals are Cruise America (ⓣ1-800/327-7799, ⓦwww.cruiseamerica.com) and Moturis (ⓣ1-877/668-8747, ⓦwww.moturis.com).

On top of the rental fees, take into account the cost of gas (some RVs do twelve miles to the gallon or less) and any drop-off charges, in case you plan to do a one-way trip across the country. Also, it is rarely legal simply to pull up in an RV and spend the night at the roadside – you are expected to stay in designated parks that cost around $20 or more per night.

Motoring organizations

In North America

American Automobile Association ⓣ1-800/222-4357, ⓦwww.aaa.com. Each state has its own club – check the phone book for local address and phone number.
Canadian Automobile Association ⓣ613/247-0117, ⓦwww.caa.ca. Each region has its own club – check the phone book for local address and phone number.

In the UK and Ireland

RAC UK ⓣ0800/55 00 55, ⓦwww.rac.co.uk
AA UK ⓣ0800/44 45 00, ⓦwww.theaa.co.uk
AA Ireland Dublin ⓣ01/617 9988, ⓦwww.aaireland.ie

In Australia and New Zealand

Australian Automobile Association Australia ⓣ02/6247 7311, ⓦwww.aaa.asn.au
New Zealand Automobile Association New Zealand ⓣ09/377 4660

Roads

There are several types of road in New England. The best for covering long distances quickly are the wide, straight, and fast **interstate highways**, usually at least six-lane motorways and always prefixed by "I" (eg I-95) – marked on maps by a red, white, and blue shield bearing the number. Even-numbered interstates run east–west and those with odd numbers run north–south. Though most roads are free, some of the more traveled highways, known as **turnpikes**, charge anywhere from 50¢ to several dollars to cruise down their broad lanes. You'll be warned in advance that a toll booth is coming. If you're severely strapped for cash, you can usually get to the same destination on smaller – and considerably slower – roads, but the extra effort is usually not worth it.

A grade down, and broadly similar to British dual carriageways and main roads, are the **state highways** (eg Hwy-1) and the **US highways** (eg US-395). Some major roads in cities are technically state highways but are better known by their local names. Hwy-1 in Brunswick, Maine, for instance, is better known as Mill Street. In rural areas, you'll also find much smaller **county roads**, which are known as routes (eg Rte-11).

Rules of the road

Although the law says that drivers must keep up with the flow of traffic, which is often hurtling along at 75mph, the **maximum speed limit** in New England is 65mph, with lower posted limits – usually around 25–35mph – in built-up areas. If given a ticket for speeding, your case will come to court and the size of the fine will be at the discretion of the judge; $100 is a rough minimum.

Foreign drivers

UK, Canadian, Australian, and New Zealand citizens can all drive in the US provided they have a regular driver's license; International Driving Permits are not required. If in any doubt about your driving status in the US, check with your local motoring association (see opposite).

Some foreign travelers have trouble at first adjusting to **driving on the right**. In terms of technical skills, it's actually pretty easy to make the switch; a more common problem is that people simply forget and set out on the left – try taping a reminder to the steering wheel.

Note that rules and regulations aren't always nationally fixed. Some standard rules: no making a U-turn on an interstate or anywhere where a single unbroken line runs along the middle of the road; no parking on a highway; and front-seat passengers must ride with a fastened seat belt. At junctions, one rule is crucially different from the UK: you can **turn right on a red light** if there is no prohibiting sign, and no traffic approaching from the left; otherwise red means stop. Stopping is also compulsory (on both sides of the road) when you come upon a school bus disgorging passengers with its lights flashing. A blinking red light should be treated as a stop sign; for a blinking yellow one, you should cross the intersection with caution, but do not need to come to a complete stop.

If the police do flag you down, don't get out of the car, and don't reach into the glove compartment as the cops may think you have a gun. Simply sit still with your hands on the wheel; when questioned, be polite and don't attempt to make jokes.

As for other possible violations, US law requires that any alcohol be carried unopened in the boot (trunk) of the car, and it can't be stressed enough that **driving while intoxicated** (DWI) or driving under the influence (DUI) is a very serious offense. If a police officer smells alcohol on your breath or has reason to believe that you are under the influence, he/she is entitled to administer a breath, saliva, or urine test. If you fail, you'll be locked up with other inebriates in the drunk tank of the nearest jail until you sober up. Your case will later be heard by a judge, who can fine you as much as $1000, or in extreme (or repeat) cases, imprison you for thirty days.

Hitching

The usual advice given to **hitchhikers** is that they should use their common sense; in fact, of course, common sense should tell anyone that hitchhiking in the US is a **bad idea**. We do not recommend it under any circumstances.

By plane

A plane is obviously the quickest way of getting around New England, and it can be less expensive than you may think. By keeping up with the ever-changing deals being offered by airlines – check with your local travel agent, read the ads in local newspapers, or go on the Web – you may be able to take advantage of heavily discounted fares. Contact details are listed on p.14. At off-peak times, flights between Boston and Portland (ME) cost around $140 round-trip and may require a booking to be made 21 days in advance. See also the box overleaf for information on **air passes**.

By train

Amtrak's four main routes in New England provide decent, though limited, connections between the few major cities in western New England, as well as some of the minor ones. You're assured of a smooth journey with few if any delays and the carriages are clean, comfortable, tidy, and rarely crowded. Probably the prettiest route is the *Vermonter*, which winds from Washington DC up through upstate New York and Vermont all the way up to Montréal; it's particularly popular in the fall, though beautiful vistas whisk by your window at all times of the year. The other major north–south Amtrak routes in and around New England, the *Ethan Allen*

Rail, bus, and air passes

Amtrak rail passes

International travelers can take advantage of two regional **rail passes** that may save money and allow you to see more of the region at the same time: the **Northeast Rail Pass** enables you to jump on and off the train anywhere between Virginia and Montréal ($149–250) in five- to thirty-day increments, while the **Eastern Rail Pass**, between Boston, Florida, Chicago, and New Orleans, allows the same flexibility over 15 or 30 days ($260–320).

Greyhound bus passes

Foreign visitors and US and Canadian nationals can all buy a **Greyhound Ameripass** or **Discovery Pass**, offering unlimited travel within a set time limit: most travel agents can oblige or you can order online at ⓦwww.greyhound.com. They come in several durations and the fare for international visitors is slightly less. A seven-day pass costs $184 for foreign visitors ($199 for North Americans), ten days go for $234 ($249), fifteen days for $274 ($299), thirty days for $364 ($389), forty-five days for $404 ($439), and the longest, a sixty-day pass, is $494 ($549). All kids under 12 go half-price, and there are discounts of around seven percent for North American students and seniors (62+). No daily extensions are available. The first time you use your pass, it will be dated by the ticket clerk (which becomes the commencement date of the ticket), and your destination is written on a page that the driver will tear out and keep as you board the bus. Repeat this procedure for every subsequent journey.

Air passes

Most of the major American airlines (and British Airways, in conjunction with its partners) offer **air passes** for visitors who plan to fly a lot within the US. These must be purchased in advance, and comprise between three and eight **coupons**, each valid for a one-way flight of any duration in the US; in many cases the coupons must be bought in conjunction with a transcontinental flight on the same airline. All the deals are broadly similar, and require that you purchase a minimum of three coupons, costing between $400 and $800 for the first three coupons, and around $60–80 for each additional one.

(Washington, DC to Rutland, VT), the *Twilight Shoreliner* (Boston, MA to Newport News, VA), and the *Acela Regional* (Washington DC to Boston, MA), are almost as scenic, as is the *Downeaster* (Boston, MA to Portland, ME). There's also a route *(Lakeshore Limited)* that travels the length of Massachusetts (from Chicago, IL) and ends up in Boston.

Travelers can cut fares greatly by using one of several Amtrak **rail passes**, which give unlimited travel within certain time periods (see box above).

On production of a passport issued outside the US or Canada, the passes can be bought at travel agents, or at Amtrak stations in the US. In the **UK**, you can buy them from Destination Marketing, 14 Greville St, London EC1 N8SB (ⓣ020/7400 7099); in **Ireland**, contact Usit Now (ⓣ01/602 1600); in **Australia**, Amtrak Rail USA, 4 Davies St, Surry Hills (ⓣ02/9318 1044); and in **New Zealand** passes can be purchased from almost any travel agent.

The 30-day **North America Rail Pass** ($475-674), which can be purchased by travelers from the US, Canada, and abroad, must include travel both in the US and Canada, but allows unlimited rides and stopovers.

Look out also for special deals and weekly **rail sales** for all comers, advertised on ⓦwww.amtrak.com.

There is also the **Visit USA** scheme, only available to non-US residents, which entitles

For all information on Amtrak fares and schedules in the US, use the toll-free number ⓣ1-800/USA-RAIL (1-800/872-7245) or visit the official Amtrak website: ⓦwww.amtrak.com. Do not phone individual stations.

foreign travelers to a thirty percent discount on any full-priced domestic fare, provided you buy the ticket before leaving home. It is certainly worth asking your travel agent, but in many cases there are discount fares available which undercut the Visit USA fare.

By bus

If you're traveling on your own, and making a lot of stops, buses are by far the cheapest way to get around. There are several main bus companies which link the major cities and many smaller towns in New England (see box below). Out in the country, buses are fairly scarce, sometimes appearing only once a day, and here you'll need to plot your route with care. But along the main highways, buses run around the clock to a fairly full timetable, stopping only for meal breaks (almost always fast-food dives) and driver changeovers.

The buses are slightly less uncomfortable than you might expect, too, but it's feasible to save on a night's accommodation by **traveling overnight** and sleeping on the bus – though you may not feel up to much the next day.

To avoid possible hassle, lone female travelers in particular should take care to sit as near to the driver as possible, and to arrive during **daylight hours**, as many bus stations are in fairly unsafe areas. It used to be that any sizeable community would have a bus station; in some places, now, the post office, a convenience store, or a gas station doubles as the bus stop and ticket office, and in many others the bus service has been canceled altogether. Reservations, either in person at the station or on the toll-free number, are not essential but recommended – if a bus is full you may be forced to wait until the next one, sometimes overnight or longer.

Fares average about $0.10 a mile, which can add up quickly; indeed, for long-trip travel, the bus is not that much cheaper than flying. However, it's the best deal if you want to visit a lot of places, and Greyhound's **Ameripasses** are good for unlimited travel nationwide within certain time frames; see box opposite for rates.

The bus companies that specialize in New England each publish comprehensive timetables. Most tourist offices are well supplied with route information and schedules, particularly at Boston's Logan Airport.

Greyhound's nationwide toll-free information service and website can give you routes and times, plus phone numbers and addresses of local terminals. You can also make reservations: ⓣ1-800/231-2222 or ⓦwww.greyhound.com.

New England bus companies

American Eagle ⓣ508/993-5040. Massachusetts only, Boston to New Bedford.

Bonanza One Bonanza Way, Providence, RI ⓣ401/751-8800 or 1-888/751-8800, ⓦwww.bonanzabus.com. Nonstop service between New York and Providence. Also covers Cape Cod, southern Massachusetts (including Boston), Connecticut, eastern New York, and Bennington, VT.

C&J Trailways Sumner Drive, Dover, NH ⓣ1-800/258-7111 or 603/430-1100, ⓦwww.cjtrailways.com. Service from Logan Airport and Boston's South Station through northern MA to southern NH.

Concord Trailways Trailways Transportation Center, 7 Langdon St, Concord, NH (ⓣ1-800/639-3317, ⓦwww.concordtrailways.com. Good coverage of New Hampshire and Maine, with connecting service to Logan Airport.

Peter Pan Trailways 1776 Main St, Springfield, MA ⓣ1-800/237-8747, ⓦwww.peterpanbus.com. Relatively frequent and extensive service between Boston and New York, via Springfield and Hartford.

Plymouth and Brockton Peter Pan Terminal, Boston ⓣ508/746-0378, ⓦwww.p-b.com. Comprehensive service to Cape Cod.

Vermont Transit Lines 345 Pine St, Burlington, VT ⓣ1-800/642-3133 in VT, 1-800/451-3292 out of state, ⓦwww.vermonttransit.com. Service throughout most of New England, plus lines to New York, Toronto, and Montréal. Direct connections with Greyhound.

Cycling

In general, **cycling** is one of the best ways to get around New England. Some of the larger cities have cycle lanes and local buses equipped to carry bikes (strapped to the outside), and even the bustle of Boston can be easily escaped in half an hour by bicycle. Although the terrain is often slightly hilly, there's nothing insurmountable to an experienced cyclist. One is rarely more than an hour's ride from a town or village, and the countryside in between is frequently idyllic, worth taking in at a leisurely pace on two wheels.

Bikes can be rented for less than $25 a day, $90–100 a week, from most bike stores; the local visitors' center will have details (we've listed rental options where applicable throughout the *Guide*). Be sure to carry warm clothing and rain gear on longer rides. Also remember that the further north you go, the lower the temperatures become.

For **long-distance cycling** you'll need a good-quality multispeed bike (but don't immediately splurge on a mountain bike, unless you are planning a lot of off-road use – good road conditions and trail restrictions in national parks make a touring bike an equally good or better choice), maps, spare tires, tools, panniers, and a helmet (not a legal necessity for adults, but a very good idea). A route avoiding the interstates (on which cycling is illegal) is essential, and it's also wise to cycle **north to south**, as the wind blows this way in the summer and can make all the difference between a pleasant trip and acute leg-ache. The main problem you'll encounter is **traffic**: wide, cumbersome recreational vehicles spew unpleasant exhaust in your face and, in northern Maine, and Vermont close to the Canadian border, enormous logging trucks have slipstreams that will pull you towards the middle of the road. Be particularly careful if you're planning to cycle along Hwy-1 on the Maine coast, since besides heavy traffic, it has narrow shoulders; again, you're much better off on the quiet country roads that New England is known for.

When asking for directions, stick to other cyclists or bike shops; others will either look at you in disbelief, or give you directions along the most direct, and therefore the busiest and least scenic route.

A good source for **cycling information** in New England, including trail and bike store locations, is the New England Mountain Bike Association, PO Box 2221, Acton, MA 01720-6221 (ⓣ1-800/576-3622, ⓦwww.nemba.org). If you're **camping** as well as cycling, contact the Adventure Cycling Association, PO Box 8308-W, Missoula, MT 59807 (ⓣ406/721-1776 or 1-800/755-2453, ⓦwww.adv-cycling.org), or try Backroads, 801 Cedar St, Berkeley, CA 94710-1800 (ⓣ510/527-1555 or 1-800/462-2848, ⓦwww.backroads.com).

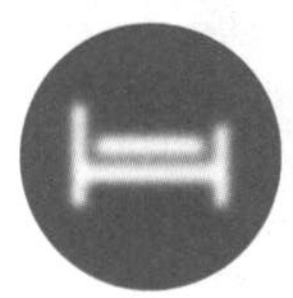

Accommodation

Accommodation standards in New England – as in the rest of the US – are high, and costs inevitably form a significant proportion of the expenses for any trip to the area. It is possible to haggle, however, especially in the chain motels, and if you're on your own, you can possibly pare costs by sleeping in dormitory-style hostels, where a bed will usually cost $15–20. However, groups of two or more will find it only a little more expensive to stay in the far more plentiful budget motels and hotels, where basic rooms away from the major cities typically cost around $40 per night. Many hotels will set up a third single bed for around $5–10 on top of the regular price, reducing costs for three people sharing. By contrast, the lone traveler will have a hard time of it: "singles" are usually double rooms at an only slightly reduced rate. Prices quoted by hotels and motels are almost always for the actual room rather than for each person using it.

Wherever you stay, unless you use a credit card, you'll be expected to **pay in advance**, at least for the first night and perhaps for further nights too, particularly if it's high season and the hotel is expecting to be busy. Payment can be in cash or in US dollar

Accommodation price codes

Throughout this book, accommodation has been price-coded according to the average cost of the least expensive **double room** typically available. Note that there can be a great deal of fluctuation with room rates, especially in areas like the Berkshires during the popular fall foliage season when prices can rise drastically; as well, many establishments charge more on Friday and Saturday nights, while big-city business hotels often slash their prices on weekends. We've listed specific prices for hostels and whole apartments, rather than codes. As the high and low seasons for tourists vary widely across the region, astute planning can save a lot of money. Watch out also for local events, which can raise rates far above normal. Only where we explicitly say so do the price codes include local taxes, which range from seven to thirteen percent.

1 up to $30
2 $30–45
3 $45–60
4 $60–80
5 $80–100
6 $100–130
7 $130–175
8 $175–250
9 $250+

travelers' checks, though it's more common to give your credit card number and sign for everything when you leave. **Reservations** are only held until 5pm or 6pm unless you've told them you'll be arriving late. Most of the larger chains have an advance booking form in their brochures and will make reservations at another of their premises for you.

Since cheap accommodation in the cities and on the popular sections of the coast is snapped up fast, **book ahead** whenever possible, using the suggestions in this book.

Hotels and motels are essentially the same thing, although motels tend to be located beside the main roads away from city centers – and thus are much more accessible to drivers. The budget ones are pretty basic affairs, but in general there's a uniform standard of comfort everywhere – double beds with bathroom, TV, and phone – and you don't get a much better deal by paying, say, $55 instead of $40. Over $55, the room and its fittings simply get bigger and more luxurious, and there may even be a swimming pool which guests can use for free. Paying over $150 or so may allow you to have a suite-type room, or a room which includes a minibar or video games on your television.

A growing number of New England hotels provide a **complimentary breakfast**. Generally, this will be no more than a cup of coffee and a doughnut, but in cities and business hotels it is increasingly a sit-down affair likely to comprise fruit, cereals, muffins, and toast, even made-to-order entrees in the pricier spots. In most places you'll be able to find cheap hotels and motels simply by keeping your eyes open – they're usually advertised by enormous roadside signs. Alternatively, there are a number of budget-priced chains whose rooms start at $40–60, such as *Econolodge*, *Motel 6*, and *Travelodge*. Mid-priced options include *Best Western*, *Howard Johnson*, and *Ramada* – though if you can afford to pay this much ($55–140) there's normally somewhere nicer and more personal to stay. When it's worth splurging on somewhere really atmospheric we've said as much in the *Guide*. Bear in mind the most upscale establishments have all manner of services which may appear to be free but for which you'll be expected to tip in a style commensurate with the hotel's status – ie, big.

Discounts and reservations

During off-peak periods many motels and hotels struggle to fill their rooms and it's worth haggling to get a few dollars off the asking price. Staying in the same place for more than one night may bring further reductions. Read the small print, though: what appears to be an amazingly cheap room rate sometimes turns out to be limited to midweek.

For motels in particular, note also that you might also be able to get a discount by presenting a membership card from a motoring organization like AAA (see p.34). In addition, look out for discount coupon booklets at information centers.

Bed and breakfasts

Bed and breakfasts are everywhere in New England – nearly every town with any tourist

Hotel discount vouchers

For the benefit of overseas travelers, many of the higher-rung hotel chains offer pre-paid discount vouchers, which in theory save you money if you're prepared to pay in advance. To take advantage of such schemes, British travelers must purchase the vouchers in the UK, at a usual cost of £30–60 per night for a minimum of two people sharing. However, it's hard to think of a good reason to buy them; you may save a nominal amount on the fixed rates, but better-value accommodation is not exactly difficult to find in the US, and you may well regret the inflexibility imposed upon your travels. Most UK travel agents will have details of the various voucher schemes.

traffic at all will have one – though some are nothing more than a converted room in the back of someone's home. Typically, the bed-and-breakfast inns, or **"B&Bs"**, as they're usually known, are restored old buildings with fewer than ten rooms and plenty of antique furnishings. Television is refreshingly absent from most, as are in-room phones. Abundant flowers, stuffed cushions, and a contrived homely atmosphere are commonplace. Then, of course, there's the breakfast, often an extravagant feast with French toast or pancakes, eggs, fresh fruit, pastries, coffee, and juice. It's often served around a common dining table (anywhere between 7–9am), which can be fun if you're a "morning person," but a nightmare if you'd rather down your poached pears in peace.

B&B prices vary greatly: anywhere from $60 to $300 depending on location, season, and facilities. Most fall between $80 and $130 per night for a double, a little less for solo travelers. Bear in mind, too, that they are often booked well in advance, and even if they're not full, the cheaper rooms may already be taken.

New England B&B contacts

American Country Collection ⓣ1-800/810-4948 or 518/370-4948, ⓔcarolbnbres@msn.com. Western Massachusetts and Vermont only.

B&B Cape Cod PO Box 1312, Orleans, MA 02653-1312 ⓣ1-800/541-6226; international 1-800/1541-6226; from Republic of Ireland 1-800/220-164, ⓦwww.bedandbreakfastcapecod.com

Boston Area B&B Reservations ⓣ617/964-1606 or 1-800/832-2632, ⓦwww.bbreserve.com. Also includes a couple of choices in Maine, New Hampshire, and Vermont.

New England Innkeepers Association PO Box 1089, 44 Lafayette Rd, N Hampton, NH 03862 ⓣ603/964-6689, ⓦwww.newenglandinns.com

Nutmeg B&B ⓣ1-800/727-7592. Connecticut only.

Yankee Magazine PO Box 520, Dublin, NH 03444 ⓣ603/563-8111. Sells a New England B&B guide for $5.

Hostels and Ys

At an average of $15–20 per night per person, hostels are clearly the cheapest accommodation option in New England other than camping. There are three main kinds of hostel-type accommodation in the US: YMCA/YWCA hostels (known as "Ys") offering accommodation for both sexes or, in a few cases, women-only accommodation; official HI-AYH hostels; and the growing AAIH (American Association of Independent Hostels) organization. There is a fairly good concentration of hostels in New England. HI-AYH are the most prevalent, though there are many unaffiliated hostels as well. For a complete listing of the hostels in the region, check out ⓦwww.hostels.com.

Prices in Ys range from around $15 for a dormitory bed to $35 for a single or double room. Some Ys are basically health clubs and do not offer accommodation. As well, in recent years, many YMCAs have become exclusively long-term residential; indeed, the only Ys currently available lie in Connecticut and Massachusetts. Be sure to call in advance if you intend to stay at a YMCA: some are only open to male travelers. The Ys listed in the *Guide* do offer accommodation to travelers at the present time. Although they are often in older buildings in less than ideal neighborhoods, facilities can include a gymnasium, a swimming pool, and an inexpensive cafeteria.

You'll find HI-AYH hostels (the prefix is usually shortened to HI in listings) in major cities and popular hiking areas, including national and state parks, mostly in Vermont and Massachusetts (there are no HI options in Maine or Rhode Island, and only one each in New Hampshire and Connecticut). Most urban hostels have 24-hour access, while rural ones may have a curfew and limited daytime hours. HI also operates a couple of small "home hostels" in the region, though as with other hostels you need to reserve in advance or there may be no one there to receive you. Rates at HI hostels range from $8 to $24 for HI members; non-members generally pay an additional $3 per night. If you plan on staying in several hostels, it obviously makes sense to join – membership is only $25 a year. Each location will have registration information.

It's advisable to book ahead through one of the specialist travel agents or international youth hostel offices: HI-AYH has a **free booking service** online at ⓦwww.hostel-booking.com. Some HI hostels will allow you to use a sleeping bag, though officially they should (and many do) insist on a sheet sleeping bag, which can usually be rented at the hostel. The maximum stay at each hostel is technically three days, though this is again a rule that is often ignored if there's space. Few hostels provide meals but most have cooking facilities. Alcohol, smoking, and, of course, drugs are banned.

The **independent hostels** in the AAIH group are usually a little less expensive than their HI counterparts, and have fewer rules. The quality is not as consistent; some can be quite poor, while others, which we've included in this book, are absolutely wonderful. There is often no curfew and, at some, a party atmosphere is encouraged at barbecues and keg parties. Their independent status may be due to a failure to come up to the HI's (fairly rigid) criteria, but often it's simply because the owners prefer not to be tied down by HI regulations.

New England **hosteling information services** include Eastern New England Council, 1105 Commonwealth Ave, Boston, MA 02215 (ⓣ617/779-0900, ⓦwww.usahostels.org). *The Hostel Handbook for the USA and Canada*, produced each May, lists over two hundred hostels and is available for $4 from Jim Williams, Sugar Hill House International Hostel, 722 Saint Nicholas Ave, New York, NY 10031 (ⓣ212/926-7030). *USA Hostel Directory*, the HI guide to hostels in the USA and Canada, is available free of charge to any overnight guest at HI-AYH hostels or direct for $3 from the HI National Office, 733 15th St NW, Suite 840, Washington, DC 20005 (ⓣ202/783-6161).

Worldwide youth hostel information

In the US

Hosteling International-American Youth Hostels ⓣ**202/783-6161**, ⓦ**www.hiayh.org.** Annual membership for adults (18–55) is $25, for seniors (55 or over) is $15, and for under-18s and groups of ten or more, is free. Lifetime memberships are $250.

In Canada

Hostelling International Canada ⓣ**1-800/663 5777 or 613/237 7884**, ⓦ**www.hostellingintl.ca.** Rather than sell the traditional one- or two-year memberships, the association now sells one Individual Adult membership with a 28- to 16-month term. The length of the term depends on when the membership is sold, but a member can receive up to 28 months of membership for just $35. Membership is free for under-18s and you can become a lifetime member for $175.

In England and Wales

Youth Hostel Association (YHA) ⓣ**0870/770 8868**, ⓦ**www.yha.org.uk and www.iyhf.org.** Annual membership £13; under-18s £6.50; lifetime £190 (or five annual payments of £40).

In Scotland

Scottish Youth Hostel Association ⓣ**0870/155 3255**, ⓦ**www.syha.org.uk.** Annual membership £6, for under-18s £2.50.

In Ireland

Irish Youth Hostel Association ⓣ**01/830 4555**, ⓦ**www.irelandyha.org.** Annual membership €15; under-18s €7.50; family €31.50; lifetime €75.

Hostelling International Northern Ireland ⓣ**028/9032 4733**, ⓦ**www.hini.org.uk.** Adult membership £10; under-18s £6; family £20; lifetime £75.

In Australia

Australia Youth Hostels Association ⓣ**02/9261 1111**, ⓦ**www.yha.com.au.** Adult membership rate AUS$52 (under-18s AUS$16) for the first twelve months and then AUS$32 each year after.

Reserving a campground

Kampgrounds of America (KOA), PO Box 30558, Billings, MT 59114 (☎406/248-7444, ⓦwww.koakampgrounds.com), privately oversees a multitude of campgrounds all over New England; although these are largely for RVs, there are one-room "Kabins" available in almost all their sites. More tent-friendly (and aesthetically pleasing) sites can be found in the state parks and public lands. These can be booked ahead (for a fee) through a centralized system in each state. To reserve a site at public campgrounds, contact the individual state's division of parks and recreation: CT (☎860/424-3200), MA (☎1-877/422-6762), ME (☎207/287-3821), NH (☎603/271-3556), RI (☎401/884-0088), and VT (☎802/879-6565). The Appalachian Mountain Club also has some very well-maintained camping areas and mountain huts; call their headquarters in Boston for reservation information (☎617/523-0636, ⓦwww.outdoors.org). Additionally, the National Park Service runs a reservation system (☎1-800/365-2267, ⓦwww.nps.gov), through which you can reserve several months in advance but not less than two days before you arrive.

In New Zealand

Youth Hostelling Association New Zealand ☎0800/278 299 or 03/379 9970, ⓦwww.yha.co.nz. Adult membership NZ$40 for one year, NZ$60 for two and NZ$80 for three; under-18s free; lifetime NZ$300.

Camping

New England campgrounds range from the primitive (a flat piece of ground that may or may not have a water tap) to places more like open-air hotels, with shops, pools, game rooms, restaurants, and washing facilities. Naturally enough, prices vary accordingly, from nothing for the most basic plots to $30 a night for something comparatively luxurious. There are plenty of campgrounds but often plenty of people intending to use them as well. Call ahead for reservations at the bigger parks, or anywhere at all during national holidays or the summer, when many grounds will be either full or very crowded. Many save a number of sites for same-day arrivals, but to claim one of these you should plan on arriving early in the day – before 9am to be safe. Vacancies often exist in the grounds outside the parks – where the facilities are usually marginally better – and some of the more basic campgrounds in isolated areas will often be empty whatever time of year you're there. If there's any charge at all you'll need to pay by leaving the money in the bin provided.

Much of the backcountry **forest land** in New England is owned by paper and logging companies, though many cooperate with campers (and hikers) who are hoping to make use of their pristine but soon to be destroyed lands. Contact the local chamber

Camping carnet

If you're planning to do a lot of camping all over the world, an international camping carnet may be a good investment. The carnet gives discounts at member sites and serves as useful identification. Many campsites will take it instead of making you surrender your passport during your stay, and it covers you for third-party insurance when camping. In the **US and Canada**, the carnet is available from home motoring organizations, or from **Family Campers and RVers** (FCRV; ☎1-800/245-9755, ⓦwww.fcrv.org). FCRV annual membership costs $25, and the carnet an additional $10. In the **UK and Ireland**, the carnet costs £4.50, and is available to members of the AA or the RAC (see p.34), or for members only from either of the following: the **Camping and Caravanning Club** (☎024/7669 4995, ⓦwww.campingandcaravanningclub.co.uk), or the foreign touring arm of the same company, the **Carefree Travel Service** (☎024/7642 2024), which provides the carnet free if you take out insurance with them.

of commerce for information on land usage and **wilderness camping**. In other designated public lands you can camp rough pretty much anywhere you want provided you first obtain a wilderness permit (either free or about $5), and usually a campfire permit, from the nearest park rangers' office. You should also take the proper precautions: carry sufficient food and drink to cover emergencies, inform the park ranger of your travel plans, and watch out for bears, and the effect your presence can have on their environment; see "Backcountry camping and wildlife" on p.54. For more information on these undeveloped regions – which are often protected within either "national parks" or "national forests" – contact the **US Forest Service**, Recreation, Heritage & Wilderness Resources, Mail Stop 1125, 1400 Independence Ave SW, Washington, DC 20090-1125 (ⓣ202/205-1706, ⓦwww.fs.fed.us).

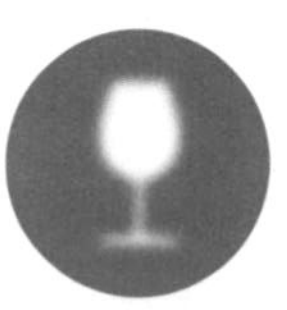

Eating and drinking

Food in New England is difficult to categorize, though there is certainly a tradition of hearty Yankee cooking which permeates the landscape. And as with elsewhere in the US, you'll find a mess of typical all-American family restaurants with lots of basic meat, seafood, and pasta dishes, and little to say in the way of ambience.

New England **seafood** is excellent and loved – lobster almost worshipped – and, especially along the coast, a multitude of "lobster pounds" and low-key seafood joints will try to tempt you with "wicked good" homemade clam-chowder ("chowdah"), oysters, clams, fish, and of course fresh lobsters. Any of these ocean creatures can be part of a traditional New England **clambake** (see box overleaf), a delicious way of enjoying the fruits of the sea. Signature Boston baked beans, a once-popular salty stewed mix of pork, onions, and beans, are still found on more nostalgic New England menus. Good attempts at more refined American and international food are available in touristed areas and the larger urban centers, where New England's version of **California cuisine** – using fresh, locally grown ingredients – has caught on with the well-heeled crowds. Country inns and bed and breakfasts that serve dinner are good bets for high-quality food in a romantic setting; many have professional chefs on staff. And, of course, there's an abundance of pizza, hamburger, and fast-food places that have become the unfortunate (and not always accurate) symbol of American cuisine.

Even though New England is not particularly agriculturally rich, in season, larger grocery stores stock just about every type of **produce** imaginable – from mangos to avocados to chili peppers. The region also produces its own range of highly nutritious goodies: apples, strawberries, blueberries, peaches, plums, and cranberries are all grown locally. **Maple syrup** is a big product in the region, and every New England state produces at least some amount of the sweet sticky liquid. Vermont is known for its quality **dairy** products – cheese, milk, and yogurt – not to mention Ben and Jerry's Ice Cream.

Breakfasts

For the price, on average $5–8, breakfast is the best-value and most filling meal of the day. Diners, cafés, and coffee shops all serve breakfast until at least 11am, with some diners serving it all day.

The breakfasts themselves are pretty much what you'd find all over the country. Eggs are the staple ingredient, often accompanied by some pork product or other: ham, bacon, or sausages.

If you wish, you can add waffles, pancakes, or French toast to the combination, consumed with butter and sweet syrup, flavored to mimic the more delicate and expensive maple syrup – if you're lucky, you'll get the real thing. Typically, fresh fruit such as apple, banana, grapefruit, orange, pineapple, or strawberry is available.

A New England clambake

Clambake is not just the title of a particularly bad Elvis Presley movie, it's a local tradition older than New England itself. Long before the first white settlers arrived, Native Americans had perfected the ritual of cooking plentiful amounts of clams by what now seems a rather unconventional method. A deep pit is dug into a beach's sand, then lined with smooth rocks. Wood is added and ignited; its ashes are eventually swept away, with the rocks left hot enough to cook on. Before the cooking begins, seaweed is piled on these rocks; layers of sweet potatoes, onions, corn, and clams – and/or sometimes lobsters – follow. Then comes another layer of seaweed, and finally a wet canvas covering everything to trap the steam. The result is an unforgettable, and messy, meal, usually eaten with bare hands. Clambakes are usually organized by churches and similar groups that hold fund-raisers; also, a few commercial organizations arrange clambakes in late summer and fall when the fresh corn is at its best. Your best bet if you want to participate in a clambake is to search out local papers for advertisements; towns along the southern coast of Rhode Island are the likeliest sites. In any case, don't think of just staging one on your own unless you want trouble from the authorities.

Bagels are available in larger towns: thick, chewy rolls with a hole in the middle, spread with almost anything you fancy, but generally cream cheese is the standard. They're great for breakfasts-to-go.

Wherever you eat, a dollar or so will entitle you to wash the meal down with as much **coffee** as you can stomach; **tea** is less common, but isn't hard to find.

Lunch and snacks

Between 11am and 3pm look for excellent-value **lunchtime set menus** on offer – Chinese, Indian, and Thai restaurants frequently have help-yourself buffets for $5–8, and many Japanese restaurants give you a chance to eat sushi much more cheaply ($8–12) than usual. Most **diners** are exceptionally well priced all the time: you can get a good-sized lunch for $5–10. Along the coast, many seafood restaurants and shacks sell all manner of **breaded and fried fish**, **clams**, and **various shellfish**, not to mention the prized **lobster roll** – lobster meat mixed with a bit of mayonnaise and lemon, and served on a hot-dog bun. Look, too, for clam chowder, a thick, creamy shellfish soup served almost everywhere for $4–5, sometimes using a hollowed-out sourdough cottage loaf as a bowl.

As you'd expect, there's also **pizza**, available from chains like *Pizza Hut* or local restaurants. Most are dependable and have a similar range of offerings; count on paying around $10 for a basic two-person pizza.

For quick snacks, you'll find many **delis** do a range of sandwiches "to go," which can be meals in themselves: huge French rolls filled with a custom-built combination of meat, cheese, and vegetables. Mexican food is not as prevalent here as on the West Coast, but if you can find it, it will undoubtedly be cheap and goopy – tacos, burritos, quesadillas, and enchiladas are all standard. **Street stands** sell hot dogs, burgers, or a slice of pizza for around $2 and most shopping malls have ethnic fast-food stalls that are usually edible and filling. And of course the burger chains are as ubiquitous here as anywhere in the US: *Wendy's*, *Burger King*, and *McDonald's* are the most familiar. Consider also a favorite healthy fast food: frozen yogurt, which is sold in most places by the tub for $2.

Besides sodas, available everywhere in any number of varieties, a wide stock of

Free food

Some bars are used as much by diners as drinkers, who take advantage of the free hors d'oeuvres often laid out between 5pm and 7pm Monday to Friday – an attempt to nab the commuting classes before they head off to the suburbs. For the price of a drink you can stuff yourself silly on chili, seafood, or pasta, though bear in mind that the food is more often than not downright unappetizing until you've had at least three drinks.

juices is also available at most casual restaurants: Snapple is a favorite, as are locally produced Nantucket Nectars. Each has at least a dozen different flavors, though when you read the fine print you'll be sorry to learn that both have no more than fifteen percent real fruit juice – and plenty of sweeteners. You're better off with a cold jug of **bottled water**, which is also available everywhere, despite the fact that New England tap water is clean and perfectly drinkable.

Restaurants

Traditional American cooking – juicy burgers, steaks, fries, salads (invariably served before the main dish), and baked potatoes – is found in restaurants all over New England. Seafood is particularly abundant along the coast, where it is served in both upscale expensive gourmet restaurants and no-nonsense harborside shacks where you'll sit at an outdoor bench with other hungry tourists. Ethnic cuisines are plentiful too. Chinese food can be found even in the most rural towns. Japanese is more expensive and somewhat fashionable – though sushi is not worshipped here the way it is in, say, New York or California. Italian food is very popular, but can be expensive once you leave the simple pizzas and pastas to explore the specialist Italian regional cooking that's fast catching on. French food, rarely found outside the larger cities, can be quite expensive. Thai, Korean, Vietnamese, Indian, and Indonesian foods are similarly city-based, though usually cheaper.

Drinking

Typical bars and cocktail lounges are prevalent across New England, and in college-dominated Boston the bars are particularly lively with plenty of young, often extremely drunken revelers. Similarly, younger and more tourist-driven towns like Portland, ME, Portsmouth, NH, Burlington, VT, and Providence, RI, hold most of New England's worthwhile pubs and microbreweries.

To **buy and consume alcohol** in New England (or anywhere in the US) you need to be 21, and you could well be asked for ID even if you look much older. Alcohol can be bought and drunk any time between 6am and 2am, seven days a week. Bars and nightclubs are likely to be fully licensed, while restaurants, especially in Boston, may only have half-licenses allowing them to serve beer and wine but no hard liquor. It is sometimes permitted to take your own bottled wine into a restaurant, where the corkage fee will be $5–10. You can buy beer, wine, or spirits more cheaply and easily in supermarkets, delis, and liquor stores. Beware that in some states it's illegal for stores to sell alcohol on Sundays, though you can still buy alcohol in bars and restaurants after noon. Note, too, that many towns and cities have open-container laws, which make it a misdemeanor to carry an open container of alcohol in a public place, including parks and riversides. You'll probably get away with a warning to take it home, but you could get a fine.

American **beers** fall into two diametrically opposite categories: wonderful and tasteless. The latter includes light, fizzy brands such as Budweiser, Miller, and Michelob. The alternative is a fabulous range of "**microbrewed**" beers, the product of a wave of backyard and in-house operations that has matured to the point that many pump out over 150,000 barrels a year and are classed as "regional breweries." Head for one of the brewpubs and you'll find handcrafted beers such as crisp pilsners, wheat beers, and stouts on tap, at prices only marginally above those of the national brews. Bottled microbrews like Boston's Harpoon are found on draft in most New England cities. Sam Adams, the self-proclaimed original microbrewery, is the largest of the regional beers and well known throughout the United States, while Vermont-brewed Long Trail Ale and Otter Creek are both worth seeking out. Portsmouth Ale, found in many parts of northern New England, is also a satisfying choice.

Alternatively, you can always find a selection of **imported beers** from most anywhere. Expect to fork out $3–5 for a glass of draft beer, about the same for a bottle of imported beer. In all but the most pretentious bars, several people can save money by buying a (quart or half-gallon) "pitcher" of beer for $6–10. Six-packs from a supermarket should run $4–5 for domestic, $5–9 for imported brews.

If you're partial to **wine**, you might choose to try lesser-known wines found in the region, for example from Connecticut's Wine

Trail (see p.375). Otherwise, you'll find a wide variety available, hailing from both the US and abroad. Wines are categorized by grape-type rather than place of origin: Cabernet Sauvignon is probably the most popular, a fruity and palatable red. Also widespread are the heavier reds – Burgundy, Merlot, and Pinot Noir. Among the whites, Chardonnay is very dry and flavorful, and generally preferred to Sauvignon Blanc or Fume Blanc, though these have their devotees. The most unusual is the strongly flavored Zinfandel, which comes in white (mocked by wine snobs, but popular nonetheless), red, or rosé. A decent glass of wine in a bar or restaurant costs about $5, a bottle $15–30. Buying from a supermarket is cheaper – a quality bottle can be purchased for as little as $7.

Cocktails are extremely popular, especially during happy hours (usually any time between 5pm and 7pm) when drinks are half-price and there's often a buffet thrown in (see "Free food" box, p.44). Varieties are innumerable, sometimes specific to a single bar or cocktail lounge, and they cost anywhere between $3 and $10.

An alternative to drinking dens, **coffee shops** play a vibrant part in New England's social scene, and are havens of high-quality coffee far removed from the stuff served in diners and convenience stores. In larger towns and cities, cafés will boast of the quality of the roast, and offer specialties such as espresso with lemon peel as well as a full array of cappuccinos, lattes, and the like, served straight, iced, organic, or flavored with syrups. Herbal teas and light snacks are often on the menu.

Communications

Staying in touch with friends and family back home won't be a problem in New England. Virtually every hotel room comes equipped with a phone (though these can be expensive to use), public pay phones are widespread, and many Internet outlets allow you to check your email for free. You can buy stamps at multiple regional post offices, and mailboxes are easy to find.

Mail

Post offices are usually open Monday through Friday from about 9am to 5pm, and in some cases on Saturday from 9am to noon; there are also **blue mailboxes** on many street corners. Ordinary mail within the US costs 37¢ for a letter weighing up to an ounce; addresses must include the zip code (postal code), and a return address should be written on the upper left corner of the envelope; postcards cost 23¢. **Air mail** between New England and Europe generally takes about a week to arrive. Aerograms and international postcards cost 70¢, letters weighing up to one ounce cost 80¢.

Letters can be sent **c/o General Delivery** (what's known elsewhere as poste restante) to any post office in each state, but must include that post office's zip code and will only be held for thirty days before being returned to sender – so make sure there's a return address on the envelope. If you're receiving mail at someone else's address, it should include "c/o" and the regular occupant's name, or it is likely to be returned.

Note that if you want to send any **parcels** out of the country, you'll need a green customs declaration form, available from post offices.

New England state abbreviations

Connecticut: CT
Maine: ME
Massachusetts: MA
New Hampshire: NH
Rhode Island: RI
Vermont: VT

Telephones

New England has several area codes (see below); simply dial 1+area code+seven-digit number to reach a specific town or city from elsewhere in the US or Canada; from abroad, dial your country's international access code, then 1+area code and the seven-digit number.

Local calls range from 20¢ to 50¢ in coin-operated public phones, which accept denominations of 5¢, 10¢, and 25¢; when making a local call in eastern Massachusetts cities, compose all ten digits, including the area code. Operator assistance (☎0) and directory information (☎411) are toll-free from public telephones – not from in-room phones.

Phoning home

With respect to calling abroad from the US, you've got several options, the most convenient of which is using your **credit card** – most pay phones now accept them. A cheaper option is using a **prepaid phone card**, sold at many convenience stores in denominations of $5 and $10. You'll find a phone number and special PIN number on the back – just dial the number, enter the PIN, and compose the number you're trying to reach (see below).

More expensive is using a **telephone charge card** from your phone company back home that will charge the call to your home account. Since most major charge cards are free to obtain, it's certainly worth getting one at least for emergencies, but bear in mind that rates aren't necessarily cheaper than calling from a public phone with a calling card; in fact, they may well be more expensive.

If all else fails, you can call **collect** by dialing ☎0, and then the number you wish to reach; the operator will take it from there. Otherwise, ☎1-800/COLLECT and ☎1-800/CALL-ATT both claim (vehemently) to have the cheapest options.

Mobile phones

If you're from overseas and you want to use your **mobile phone** in New England, you'll need to check with your phone provider whether it will work abroad, and what the call charges are. Unless you have a tri-band phone, it is unlikely that a mobile bought for use outside the US will work inside the States (and vice versa).

In the UK, for all but the very top-of-the-range packages, you'll have to inform your phone provider before going abroad to get international access switched on. You may get charged extra for this, depending on your existing package and where you are traveling. You're also likely to be charged extra for incoming calls when abroad, as the people calling you will be paying the usual rate. If you want to retrieve messages while you're away, you'll have to ask your provider for a new access code, as your home one is unlikely to work abroad.

For further information about using your phone abroad, check out Ⓦwww.telecomsadvice.org.uk/features/using_your_mobile_abroad.htm.

Useful phone numbers and codes

Emergencies and information

Emergencies ☎911; ask for the appropriate emergency service: fire, police, or ambulance.
Directory information ☎411
Directory inquiries for toll-free numbers ☎1-800/555-1212
Long-distance directory information ☎1-(area code)/555-1212
Operator ☎0

New England area codes

Connecticut Northern Connecticut ☎860/959; Southern Connecticut ☎203; Maine ☎207
Massachusetts Boston ☎617/857; Suburban Boston ☎781/339; Cape Cod ☎508/774; Northern MA ☎978/351; Western MA ☎413
New Hampshire ☎603
Rhode Island ☎401
Vermont ☎802

International calling codes

Calling TO New England from abroad
international access code + 1 + area code
For calls **FROM New England**, the codes are as follows: Australia 011 + 61 + city code
Canada 1 + area code
New Zealand 011 + 64 + city code
Republic of Ireland 011 + 353 + city code
UK and Northern Ireland 011 + 44 + city code

Email

Public Internet access in New England is still mostly the reserve of public libraries and universities – what few Internet cafés exist usually charge in the vicinity of $5–$8 for an hour of surfing. While libraries and universities have more limited hours (usually Mon–Fri 9am–5pm, Sat 10am–noon, closed Sun) and time constraints (around 15 minutes per person), their major advantage is that the service is free to everyone.

The media

Despite its legacy as the birthplace of America's first newspaper, *Publick Occurences*, which was published in Boston in 1690, New England hardly ranks among the country's most media-savvy regions today. The better media is intellectual rather than newsy, and you'll certainly be engaged by the *Atlantic Monthly*, one of the US's most venerable monthly magazines, a slew of leftist weeklies, and the two Boston daily newspapers, the *Boston Globe* (ⓦwww.boston.com/globe) and the *Boston Herald*, both of which get wide distribution throughout the region.

Newspapers

Boston's oldest paper, *The Globe* (50¢) remains the region's best general daily; its fat Sunday edition ($2) includes substantial sections on art, culture, and lifestyle. The *Boston Herald* (50¢; ⓦwww.bostonherald.com) is the *Globe*'s tabloid competitor and is best for appeasing your gossip and local sports coverage fix. The two stalwarts are complemented by smaller papers like the *Hartford Courant* (ⓦwww.courant.com), the *Bangor Daily News* (ⓦwww.bangornews.com), and the *Providence Journal* (ⓦwww.projo.com), which tend to excel at local coverage, but typically rely on agencies for foreign and even national news stories.

Every community of any size also has at least a few **free newspapers**, found in distribution bins, cafés, bars, or just lying around in piles. It's a good idea to pick up a full assortment: some simply cover local goings-on, while others provide specialist coverage of interests ranging from long-distance cycling to getting ahead in business – and the classified and personal ads can provide hours of entertainment. Many of them are also excellent sources of **listings information**; we've mentioned the most useful titles where relevant throughout this guide.

Overall, New England's news coverage is parochial at best; you can get your international fix by stopping by a newsstand or library, where you'll find the *New York Times* at the very least, and often the *Observer* and *Independent*, too.

TV and radio

New England TV is pretty much the standard network barrage of sitcoms, newscasts, and talk shows found all over the US, though PBS, the national public television station, broadcasts a steady stream of interesting documentaries, informative (if slightly dry) news programs, and educational children's television. **Cable television** is ubiquitous, and with over seventy channels, there's bound to be something on of at least marginal interest. That said, the major networks will likely carry everything you need or want to see: you'll be able to catch regular **news**, as well as keep abreast of your favorite dramas and sitcoms from the comfort of your hotel room.

Radio stations are also abundant, and run up and down FM and AM dials; the latter is strong on news and chat, while the former carries some of the region's best stations, including National Public Radio (NPR) shows, and college broadcasts of jazz, classical, world music, and hip-hop beats, all found between 88 and 92 FM. Larger cities boast good specialist stations of all stripes, from music to sports. In between, however, you'll have to resort to skipping up and down the frequencies, which will produce everything from Eagles' tracks to fire-and-brimstone Bible thumpers and crazed phone-ins. Driving through rural regions can be especially frustrating, with sometimes only two (dull) stations airing in addition to NPR.

Public holidays, festivals, and opening hours

Someone, somewhere is always celebrating something in New England although, apart from national holidays, few festivities are shared throughout the entire region. Instead, there is a disparate multitude of local events: arts and craft shows, county fairs, ethnic celebrations, music festivals, parades, and many others of every hue and shade. New England tourist offices can provide full lists, or you can just phone ahead to the visitors' center in a particular region to ask what's coming up. The calendar below provides a good overview of unusual or particularly worthwhile area festivals.

Public holidays

The biggest and most all-American of the national holidays is Independence Day on the Fourth of July, when the entire country grinds to a standstill as people get drunk, salute the flag, and take part in fireworks displays, marches, beauty pageants, and more, all in commemoration of the signing of the Declaration of Independence in 1776. Halloween (October 31) lacks any such patriotic overtones, and is not a public holiday despite being one of the most popular yearly flings. Traditionally, costumed kids run around the streets banging on doors demanding "trick or treat," and receiving pieces of candy. These days that sort of activity is mostly confined to rural and suburban areas, while in bigger cities Halloween has grown into a massive drunken celebration of the macabre. More sedate is Thanksgiving Day, on the fourth Thursday in November, essentially a domestic affair, when relatives return to the familial nest to stuff themselves with roast turkey, and (supposedly) fondly recall the first harvest of the Pilgrims in Massachusetts – though in fact Thanksgiving was already a national holiday before anyone thought to make that connection.

On the national, or federal, public holidays listed below, banks and offices (and many shops) are liable to be **closed** all day. Many states also have their own additional holidays, and in some places Good Friday is a half-day holiday. The traditional summer season for tourism runs from Memorial Day to Labor Day, and some tourist attractions are only open during that period.

January 1 New Year's Day
Third Monday in January Martin Luther King Jr's Birthday
Third Monday in February Presidents' Day
Late March/April (varies) Good Friday
Last Monday in May Memorial Day
July 4 Independence Day
First Monday in September Labor Day
Second Monday in October Columbus Day
November 11 Veterans' Day
Fourth Thursday in November Thanksgiving Day
December 25 Christmas Day

Opening hours

Shops and services are generally open Monday to Saturday 8am/9am–5pm/6pm. Many stores are also open on Sundays, and larger towns and cities will invariably have 24-hour supermarkets and pharmacies.

For banking and post office hours, see the relevant sections in this chapter.

Festivals and events

January

Winter Carnival Jackson, NH, first two weeks (☎603/383-9336, ⓦwww.jacksonnh.com). Ice sculptures, sleigh rides, and Nordic skiing.

Stowe Winter Carnival Stowe, VT, last week (☎1-800/247-8693, ⓦwww.stowecarnival.com). Similar to above, with more partying.

February

Railroad Show West Springfield, MA, first weekend (☎413/436-0242). An extravaganza of trains, both model and real.

Winter Festival Newport, RI, second week (☎1-800/976-5122, ⓦwww.newportevents.com). Discounts at area shops and restaurants with the purchase of a festival button ($6), plus hayrides and ice sculpting.

February–March

Mardi Gras Bretton Woods, NH, weekend before Ash Wednesday (☎1-800/258-0330). A masquerade ball held in the historic *Mount Washington Hotel* is the apex of this traditional celebration including beads, bands, and a King Cake.

Saints and Spirits Celebration Rockport/Camden, ME, mid-March (☎207/236-4404). St Patrick's Day parties and Irish singalongs meant to dispel the "mud season blues."

April

Boston Marathon Boston, MA, third Monday (☎617/236-1652, ⓦwww.bostonmarathon.org). Perhaps the premier running event in the US.

Vermont Maple Festival St Albans, VT, last weekend (☎802/524-5800, ⓦwww.vtmaplefestival.org). Maple exhibits/demonstrations, food contests, and, of course, pancake breakfasts.

May

Moose Mainea Greenville, ME, mid-May to mid-June (☎207/695-2702). Moose-watching, boat and bike races, and family activities.

Open Studios VT (statewide), last weekend (☎802/223-3380). Artists open their homes and studios to the public.

June

Ethan Allen Days Sunderland, VT, mid-month (☎802/425-4884). Revolutionary battle enactments along Vermont's Ethan Allen Highway (Rte-7A).

One World, One Heart Festival Warren, VT, late June (☎802/651-9600). Concerts, food, and Ben and Jerry's Ice Cream.

July

Moxie Festival Lisbon Falls, ME, mid-month (☎207/783-2249, ⓦwww.moxiefestival.com). Activities and entertainment in celebration of an odd-tasting soda in a bright orange can.

Revolutionary War Festival Exeter, NH, mid-month (☎603/772-2622). Mock battles (by local militia buffs) are waged, and costumed locals wander the town.

Folk Festival Lowell, MA, last weekend (☎978/970-5000). Traditional music and dance on six outdoor stages, plus food, parades, and crafts.

August

Maine Lobster Festival Rockland, ME, first weekend (☎207/596-0376). Features eight tons of boiled lobster.

Narragansett Powwow Charlestown, RI, second weekend (☎401/364-1100). Native American dancing, music, crafts, and food festival.

Crane Beach Sand Blast Ipswich, MA, late August (☎978/356-4351). Sandcastle-building contest.

Union Fair and Blueberry Festival Union, ME, mid-month (☎207/236-8009, ⓦwww.union-fair.com). One of the oldest traditional fairs in the state.

September

Windjammer Weekend Camden, ME, first weekend (☎207/236-4404, ⓦwww.windjammerweekend.com). Maine's largest windjammer gathering, with boat parade, fireworks, contests, and concerts, set in Camden's beautiful harbor.

Oyster Festival Norwalk, CT, second weekend (☎203/838-9444). Seaport Association extravaganza, featuring tall ships, a juried craft show, and oysters every way.

World's Fair Tunbridge, VT, second weekend (☎802/889-5555). Agricultural fair with butter-churning, cheesemaking, sheepshearing, and the like.

Grand Old Brewers Festival Portsmouth, NH, last weekend (☎603/433-1100). Keg rolling, tug-of-war, and, of course, lots of beer.

October

Rennaisance Faire Woodstock, CT, first two weekends (☎860/928-0600, ⓦwww.ctfair.com). King Arthur comes to Connecticut, with a small realm of archers, merchants, elves, and court entertainers.

Head of the Charles Regatta Cambridge, MA, mid-month (☎617/868-6200, ⓦwww.hocr.org). One of the largest racing shell events in the world, with over 600 teams participating during the weekend.

Haunted Happenings Salem, MA, late October (☎1-877/725-3662). Learn to cast spells and visit haunted houses in the days leading up to Halloween.

November

Antiquarian Book Fair Boston, MA, mid-month (☎617/266-6540). Tons of old books on display and on sale.

Victorian Holiday Portland, ME, weekend after Thanksgiving (☎207/772-6828). Horse-drawn carriages and Victorian garb abound.

December

Christmas Town Festival Bethlehem, CT, first weekend (☎203/266-5557). Caroling, crafts, and the lighting of the town tree by Santa himself.

Christmas in Newport Bethlehem, RI, month-long (☎401/849-6454). *The Breakers Hotel*, decorated in the most festive manner, throws open its doors for holiday music and refreshments on Saturdays, plus make-your-own-gifts workshops, 'The Nutcracker', and the Santa Train throughout the month.

Sports and outdoor pursuits

Boston is the only city in New England with major professional sports teams; excepting football, they have one team in each of the primary sports – baseball, hockey, and basketball. The region's only professional football team is based slightly afield, in Foxboro, MA. Residents in smaller towns often choose instead to root for the teams at their local high school or university, though Boston's professional teams are followed closely in all New England newspapers. College basketball in the region is particularly competitive, and, more locally, minor league baseball teams draw enthusiastic crowds. Locals are also physically active; the most popular outdoor pursuits include fishing, hiking, river-rafting, canoeing, and kayaking.

Football

Football in America attracts the most obsessive and devoted fans of any sport, perhaps because there are fewer games played – only sixteen in a season, which lasts throughout the fall. With many quick skirmishes and military-like movements up and down the field, the game is ideal for television, and nowhere is this more apparent than during the telvised games which are a feature of many bars on Monday nights – though most games are played on Sundays.

The game lasts for four fifteen-minute quarters, with a fifteen-minute break at half-time. But since time is only counted when play is in progress, matches can take up to **three hours** to complete, mainly due to interruptions for TV advertising. Commentators will discuss the game throughout to help your comprehension, though they use such a barrage of statistics to illustrate their remarks that you may feel hopelessly confused. Not that it matters – the spectacle of American football is fun to experience, even if you haven't a clue what's going on. The best players (or the flashiest, most obnoxious ones) become nationally known celebrities, raking in millions of dollars in fees for product endorsements on top of astronomical salaries.

Teams and tickets

All major teams play in the National Football League (NFL), the sport's governing body, which divides the teams into two conferences of equal stature, the National Football Conference (NFC) and the American Football Conference (AFC). In turn, each conference is split into three divisions, East, Central, and West. For the end-of-season playoffs, the best team in each of the six divisions, plus three wildcards from each conference, fight it out for the title.

The NFL season begins in late summer and lasts through the end of January. New England's only team is the **New England Patriots**, who went to (and lost) the Super Bowl in 1985 and 1996, but earned a victory in their return in January 2002 with former backup quarterback Tom Brady against the formidable St Louis Rams. There are no second division equivalents, though the region's college teams serve as a training ground for future NFL stars.

Tickets cost $20–80 for professional games. Ticket sales are handled by Ticketmaster (ⓣ617/931-2000) when they are available (some usually go on sale during the summer), though renewed interest in the team has resulted in over 90 consecutive home sellout games. For **information**, call the New England Patriots (ⓣ508/543-1776, ⓦwww.patriots.com).

Baseball

Baseball, much like cricket in its relaxed, summertime pace and seemingly Byzantine rules, is often called "America's pastime," though its image has been tarnished by numerous bitter strikes by players – one of which shortened the 1994 season and saw the unthinkable canceling of the World Series – and the most recent threatened strike in 2002.

Games are played, 162 each full season, all over the US almost every day from April to September, with the league championships and the World Series, the final best-of-seven playoff, lasting through October. Watching a game, even if you don't understand what's going on, can be at the least a pleasant day out, drinking beer and eating hot dogs; in the unshaded bleachers beyond the outfield, tickets are comparatively cheap ($18–20) and the crowds usually friendly and sociable.

Teams and tickets

All Major League baseball teams play in either the **National League** or the **American League**, each split into three divisions, East, Central, and West. For the end-of-season playoffs and the World Series, the best team in each of the six divisions, plus a second-place wildcard from each league, fight it out for the title.

New England's Major League club is the **Boston Red Sox**. In addition, there are also numerous minor league clubs, known as farm teams because they supply the top clubs with talent. Details are included in relevant chapters of the *Guide*.

Tickets for games cost $18–60 per seat, and are generally available on the day of the game.

League and club contact information

Major League ⓣ212/339-7800, ⓦwww.mlb.com
National League ⓣ212/339-7700
American League ⓣ212/339-7600
Boston Red Sox ⓣ 617/267-9440, ⓦwww.redsox.com

Basketball

Basketball is one of the few professional sports that is also actually played by many ordinary Americans, since all you need is a ball and a hoop. It's a particularly popular sport in low-income inner-city areas, where school playgrounds are packed with young hopefuls.

The professional game is played by athletes of phenomenal agility, seven-foot-tall giants who float through the air over a wall of equally tall defenders, seeming to change direction in mid-flight before slam-dunking the ball to score two points. Games last for an exhausting 48 minutes of playing time, around two hours total.

Teams and tickets

New England's basketball club, the **Boston Celtics** (ⓣ617/523-6050, ⓦwww.nba.com/celtics), have been struggling ever since their domination ended in the late 1980s, when Larry Bird and company parted ways. Call Ticketmaster (ⓣ617/931-2000) for available seating and pricing ($10–85).

The **University of Connecticut**, the **University of Massachusetts**, and **Providence University** all field perpetually competitive college basketball teams. Additionally, in recent years quite a lot of buzz has been generated around the University of Connecticut **women's basketball** team, the 2000 and 2002 NCAA champions. **Tickets** cost $5–25 for college games. Call each school's athletic department (UConn ⓣ1-877/288-2666; UMass ⓣ413/545-0810; Providence ⓣ401/865-4672) for game and ticket info.

Ice hockey

Ice hockey enjoys considerable popularity in New England, not least because the cold winter weather is so conducive to the sport. Many children grow up playing it and go on to compete at the area's highly competitive colleges and universities; a small percentage go on to play in the professional **National Hockey League** (NHL).

Teams and tickets

New England has one NHL team, the **Boston Bruins** (@www.bostonbruins.com), which manages to draw a considerable crowd. **Tickets** start at about $25. Call Ticketmaster (☎617/931-2000) for more information.

Outdoor pursuits

Hunting and fishing are probably the two most popular outdoor pursuits in New England, although the more physically challenging hiking, mountain biking, and kayaking all fall right behind. Duck, deer, and sometimes even the mighty moose are all popular targets, though hunting laws are strict and you'll need a **permit** (ask the local chamber of commerce how you can get one) before you start dropping victims in the forest. Streams, lakes, ponds, and rivers fill up with fishermen (and women) in season, though as with hunting, permits are required and laws are strict. Trout and salmon are found in most bodies of fresh water.

Hiking is huge, especially in the northern areas of New England, although you'll find good places to get out into nature just about anywhere outside of the main cities. Most state and federally operated parks maintain good networks of trails, not least the famous **Appalachian Trail**, which originates in Georgia and winds through the beautiful backcountry of New England before traversing New Hampshire's White Mountains and terminating in desolate northern Maine. We've given plenty more on hiking on p.56, and throughout the *Guide* as well.

Cycling is also extremely popular, particularly longer road rides on New England's many deserted, tree-shaded country roads or hectic trail rides in the mountains. Weekend enthusiasts put their knobby mountain-bike tires to use on the countless trails that weave throughout New England's beautiful wilderness areas. Special mountain- bike parks, most of them operating in summer only, exploit the groomed snow-free runs of northern New Hampshire, Vermont, and Maine. In such places, and throughout New England, you can rent bikes for $20–30 a day; see "Getting around," p.37, for more on general cycling.

Skiing is the biggest mass-market participant sport, with downhill resorts all over northeastern New England – where it snows heavily most winters. In fact, the mountains that cap the northern ends of Maine, New Hampshire, and Vermont offer the best skiing in the eastern US, particularly in **Killington, VT** (see p.405), and **Sugarloaf, ME** (see p.588). You can rent equipment for about $50 a weekend, and lift tickets for the best locations top out at around $50 a day. The Internet is a great source for additional information – for example, @www.skimaine.com has links to Maine's resort-cams, weather information, and most of the ski resorts, and @www.skinh.com has resort reviews and details on New Hampshire snowboarding and snow tubing in addition to skiing. Another good bet is @www.newenglandskiresorts.com, which locates all of the downhill ski resorts in the region on maps and provides extensive descriptions of each. A number of companies run all-inclusive ski trips (including transportation, lift-tickets, equipment, and accommodation) from the larger cities. In addition to convenience, these outfits usually offer good deals; consult the relevant section of the *Guide* or check the **Yellow Pages**.

A cheaper option is **cross-country skiing**, or ski-touring. A number of backcountry ski lodges offer a range of rustic accommodation, equipment rental, and lessons, from as little as $20 a day for skis, boots, and poles, up to about $200 for an all-inclusive weekend tour. For additional information, consult @www.nexcski.com, an exhaustive reference pertaining to the sport in New England, with information on resorts, trail conditions, equipment, and ski shops.

Backcountry camping and wildlife

New England has some fabulous backcountry and wilderness areas, coated by dense forests, splashed with sparkling lakes, and capped by monumental mountains. Unfortunately, while still immensely rewarding – and it's one of the compelling reasons for coming to New England – it isn't all as wild as it once was, thanks to the thousands who tramp through each year. If you're intending to do the same, you can help preserve the special qualities of the environment by observing a few simple rules. For practical information on traveling through the forest, see the box opposite.

The protected backcountry areas in the US fall into a number of potentially confusing categories. Most numerous are **state parks**, owned and operated by the individual states. They include state beaches, state historic parks, and state recreational areas, often around sites of geological or historical importance and not necessarily in rural areas. **Daily fees** are usually less than $5, though a $40–75 annual pass gives free access to most sites for a year.

Acadia National Park in Maine (see p.573), a large, preserved area of great natural beauty is the only national park in New England; entry is $5 for one person on bicycle or motorbike, or $10 for up to four in a car. Excellent free ranger programs – such as guided walks or slide shows – are held throughout the year. The federal government also operates national recreation areas. Campgrounds and equipment-rental outlets are always available, though not always in appropriate numbers.

New England's two **national forests**, the Green Mountain National Forest in Vermont (see p.396) and the White Mountain National Forest in New Hampshire (see p.495), are huge, covering fifty percent of all public land in Vermont and an area larger than the state of Rhode Island in New Hampshire. They are federally administered (by the US Forest Service Ⓦwww.fs.fed.us), but with much less protection than national parks. More roads run through national forests, and often there is some limited logging and other land-based industry operated on a sustainable basis.

All the above forms of protected land can contain **wilderness areas**, which aim to protect natural resources in their most native state. In practice this means there's no commercial activity at all; buildings, motorized vehicles, and bicycles are not permitted, nor are firearms and pets. Overnight camping is allowed, but wilderness permits (free to $5) must be obtained in advance from the land management agency responsible. In New England, the White Mountains and the

Essential equipment

Many campgrounds are on rock with only a thin covering of soil, so driving pegs in can be a problem; freestanding dome-style tents are therefore preferable. Go for one with a large area of mosquito netting and a removable fly sheet: tents designed for harsh European winters can get horribly sweaty once the sun rises, unless, of course, you're camping in the winter.

Most developed campgrounds are equipped with fire rings with some form of grill for cooking, but many people prefer a Coleman stove, powered by white gas, a kind of super-clean gasoline. Both stoves and white gas are widely available in camping stores. Other camping stoves are less common. Equipment using butane and propane – Camping Gaz and, to a lesser extent, EPI gas, Scorpion, and Optimus – is on the rise, though outside of major camping areas you'll be pushed to find supplies, so stock up when you can.

Backcountry dangers and wildlife

You're likely to meet many kinds of wildlife and come upon unexpected hazards if you head into the wilderness, but with due care, many potential difficulties can be avoided.

Hiking in the foothills should not be problematic but you should check your clothes frequently for **ticks** – pesky, blood-sucking, burrowing insects which are known to carry **Lyme disease**, a health hazard especially in southern New England (it's named after a town in Connecticut). If you have been bitten, and especially if you get flu-like symptoms, get advice from a park ranger. Also annoying around water are **mosquitos**; carry candles scented with citronella or insect repellent to keep them at bay. **Black flies** also come out in force in the warm summer months, and, with a tenacious appetite for human heads, ears, and faces, and a perpetual buzz, they can be tremendously annoying; again, carry insect repellent.

You're highly unlikely to encounter a **bear** in New England, though the American black bear is native to the region, and prevalent in the northern wilderness areas. To reduce whatever likelihood, make noise (carrying bells in your pack isn't a bad idea) as you walk. If you do come across one, keep calm, and make sure it is aware of your presence by clapping, talking, or making other sounds. Black bears may **charge** with no intention of attacking when attempting to steal food or if they feel threatened. If you are so unlucky, don't run, just slowly back away.

If a bear visits your camp, it will be after your food, which should be stored in airtight containers. Some campgrounds are equipped with bear-proof lockers, which you are obliged to use to store food when not preparing or eating it. Elsewhere, you should hang both food and garbage from a high branch some distance from your camp. **Never feed a bear**: it will make the bear dependent on humans for food. Bears within state and national parks are protected, but if they spend too much time around people the park rangers are, depressingly, left with no option but to shoot them.

Moose, which live in the lush, unpopulated regions near the Canadian border, seldom attack unless provoked. The largest member of the deer family, they can be up to nine feet tall and weigh as much as 1200 pounds, and look like badly drawn horses. They are mostly active at night, but can also be seen at dusk and dawn, when they may gather to feed near lakes and streams. Though they may seem slow, tame, and passive at first, moose can be unpredictable, especially during the mating season in September and October. If you happen upon one in the forest, move slowly, avoid making any loud noises, and keep your distance. The best place to view a moose is from your automobile, though you should be careful when driving along northern country roads – collisions can be fatal for all involved.

Poison ivy is one thing that isn't going to come and get you, though you may come up against it, especially in the spring. Recognizable by its shiny configuration of variously notched leaves (which secrete an oily juice), greenish flowers, and whitish berries, this twiggy shrub or climbing vine is found in open woods or along stream banks throughout much of New England. It's highly allergenic, so avoid touching it. If you do, washing with strong soap, taking frequent dips in the sea, and applying cortisone cream usually help relieve the symptoms; in extreme cases, see a doctor.

In the mountains, your biggest dangers have nothing to do with the flora or fauna. **Late snows** are common, giving rise to the possibility of **avalanches** and **meltwaters**, which make otherwise simple stream crossings hazardous. Drowning in fast-flowing meltwater rivers is one of the biggest causes of death in New England wilderness areas. The riverbanks are often strewn with large, slippery boulders – keep clear unless you are there for river activities. Sudden changes in the weather are also common in mountainous regions, when temperatures can fluctuate wildly and high winds and storms appear out of nowhere; be sure to have warm clothing with you at all times, and check with park rangers before long backcountry treks.

Green Mountains both have large wilderness areas, with only the regions near roads, visitors' centers and buildings designated as less stringently regulated "front country."

When camping rough, check that fires are permitted before you start one; if they are, use a stove in preference to local materials – in some places firewood is scarce, although you may be allowed to use deadwood. No open fires are allowed in wilderness areas, where you should also try to camp on previously used sites. Where there are no toilets, bury human waste at least four inches into the ground and a hundred feet from the nearest water supply and camp. Burn rubbish, and what you can't burn, carry away.

One potential problem is giardia, a waterborne protozoan causing an intestinal disease, symptoms of which are chronic diarrhea, abdominal cramps, fatigue, and loss of weight, that requires treatment. To avoid catching it, never drink from rivers and streams, however clear and inviting they may look (you never know what unspeakable acts people – or animals – further upstream have performed in them). Water that isn't from taps should be boiled for at least five minutes, or cleansed with an iodine-based purifier (such as Potable Aqua) or a giardia-rated filter, available from camping or sports stores.

Finally, don't use ordinary soaps or detergents in lakes and streams; you can buy special ecological soap for washing needs.

Hiking

Wilderness areas start close to the main areas of national parks. There is normally no problem entering the wilderness for day walks, but overnight trips require wilderness permits (see p.54). In peak periods, a quota system operates for the most popular paths, so if there's a hike you specifically want to do, obtain your permit well ahead of time (at least two weeks, more for popular hikes). When completing the form for your permit, be sure to ask a park ranger for weather conditions and general information about the hike you're undertaking.

In New England, the **Appalachian Mountain Club** (Ⓣ617/523-0636, Ⓦwww.outdoors. org) offers a range of backcountry hikes into otherwise barely accessible parts of the wilderness, with food and guide provided. The hikes happen at all times of the year, cost anywhere from $50 to $800, last from a day to two weeks, and are heavily subscribed, making it essential to book well in advance. Club members pay around $20 less, though you'll also have to pay $40 to join. They also have some very well-maintained camping areas and mountain huts; call their headquarters in Boston for information on making reservations.

Hikes covered in the *Guide* are given with length and estimated walking time for a healthy but not especially fit adult. State parks have many graded trails designed for people who drive to the corner store, so anyone used to walking and with a moderate degree of fitness will find these ratings very conservative.

Crime and personal safety

New England is one of the safest regions in the US, and you're unlikely to incur great risks traveling in any one of its six states. While it pays to be cautious, especially in big cities such as Boston or Hartford, or on lonely country roads, the region is pretty unforeboding. Driving during the harsh winter months in the northern and mountain areas is perhaps the biggest threat to your personal safety, and extreme care should be taken if you'll be making such trips.

Avoiding crime

All over New England, crime has been on the decline since the early 1990s. Even in built-up urban centers where theft and assaults do occur on a somewhat regular basis (namely Boston and the region's other larger cities), tourists are seldom involved or targeted.

In the more risky areas, common sense and a certain degree of caution should be enough to avoid most problems. For instance, seek local advice before exploring unfamiliar and run-down parts of a city, avoid walking along deserted streets at night, leave valuables in hotel safes, don't leave luggage clearly visible in cars (especially rental cars), don't resist violent theft, and beware of various tourist scams. One such scam, by no means restricted to tourists and by no means restricted to New England, is known as "bump and rob." The thief bumps his (usually stolen) car into the back of another, and when the victim gets out to inspect the damage and swap insurance details, the thief drives away in the unoccupied car. Therefore, if you are bumped from behind, indicate to the other driver to follow you to a well-lit, public place before thinking about leaving your vehicle.

The emergency number for police is ⓣ911; numbers for lost or stolen credit cards, travelers' checks, and the like can be found on p.3.

Safe driving

Since driving is by far the best way of getting around New England, many visitors will choose to rent a car to explore the region. If you are unfamiliar with driving in the US, make sure that you learn the traffic laws *before* you set off. Note, also, that speed limits and drunk driving regulations may differ from your own country. For more comprehensive information about getting around by car, see p.32.

In the more northerly states of New England – and particularly in the mountain regions – driving during the winter months, when snow storms, black ice, and generally foul weather are facts of life, is a potentially treacherous undertaking. In the winter, especially during bad weather, you should only make trips which are necessary, and always check road and weather conditions before leaving. It's a good idea to keep your gas tank two-thirds full to prevent the vehicle's fuel line from freezing, and a mobile telephone could be extremely useful in case of emergency. Don't be over-dependent on a phone, however, and consider carrying an **emergency car-care kit** on trips in difficult weather conditions. Such a kit typically contains antifreeze, windshield washer fluid, shovel, ice scraper, jumper cables, flares or reflectors, blankets, non-perishable food, and a first-aid kit.

There are emergency phones stationed along freeways at regular intervals, but you won't find these on quieter roads.

Living and working abroad

Besides students, anyone planning an extended stay in the United States should apply for a special working visa at any American embassy *before* setting off. Different types of visas are issued, depending on your skills and length of stay, but unless you've got relatives (parents or children over 21) or a prospective employer to sponsor you, your chances are slim at best.

Illegal work is not as easy to find as it used to be, especially since the terrorist attacks of September 11, 2001, and with the government's increase in fines (now $10,000) for companies that employ illegal workers. If you do manage to get hired, you're more likely than ever to be hidden out of sight, in lower paid jobs (think dishwasher rather than waiter). The following suggestions for finding work are basic and, if you're not a US citizen, represent the limit of what you can do unless you have a **social security number**, which is technically essential for any kind of legal employment. There are, of course, a number of legal **work and study abroad programs** available, though many of these are for students and recent graduates only.

Useful publications and websites

A good resource for finding work abroad is the *Overseas Jobs Express* (Premier House, Shoreham Airport, Sussex BN43 5FF; ⓣ01273/699 611, ⓦwww.overseasjobs.com), a fortnightly publication with a range of job vacancies, available by subscription only. Vacation Work also publishes books on summer jobs abroad and how to work your way around the world; call ⓣ01865/241 978 or visit ⓦwww.vacationwork.co.uk for their catalogue. Travel magazines like the reliable *Wanderlust* (every two months; £2.80) have a Job Shop section that often advertises job opportunities with tour companies. ⓦwww.studyabroad.com is a useful website with listings and links to study and work programs worldwide.

Au pair work

For young women (in most cases) working as an **au pair** is a viable option. Applicants for au pair visas to the US who will be looking after babies under two will have to prove that they have at least 200 hours' experience with infants, 24 hours' training in child development, and 8 hours' child safety training. Applicants will also have to undergo testing to provide a personality profile. The prospective employers must provide a written description of the job they expect their au pair to perform, so there is protection on both sides. Au Pair in America (see below) can arrange visas and placements.

Study and work programs

From the UK and Ireland

BUNAC (British Universities' North America Club) 16 Bowling Green Lane, London EC1R 0QH ⓣ020/7251 3472, ⓦwww.bunac.org. Organizes working holidays in the US for students, typically at summer camps or training placements with companies.

Camp America/Au Pair in America 37 Queen's Gate, London SW7 5HR. Camp America ⓣ020/7581 7373, ⓦwww.campamerica.co.uk; Au Pair in America ⓣ020/7581 7311, ⓦwww.aupair america.co.uk. The Camp America scheme is similar to that of Camp Counselors USA (see below). The Au Pair scheme is open to both men and women aged 18–26, though women are mostly preferred. There is a placement fee of £40, a £67 contribution towards insurance and a good-faith deposit of £268; the combined amount includes the interviewing and selection process, visa (covering you for 13 months, 12 months working plus optional one month travel at the end), and flight to the US. You receive weekly on-the-job payment, and on completion of the twelve months you get your good-faith deposit back in American dollars (about US$400), which you can then use to fund further US travels.

Camp Counselors USA ⓣ020/8688 9051, ⓦwww.ccusa.co.uk. Volunteer summer work (9 weeks from anytime in June) for over-18s; you need to have experience with children (except for support staff, who must be full-time students) and be a specialist in an area like arts and crafts, drama, or sport. A charge of £215 covers a return flight to New York (and 10 weeks to travel at the end of the camp program), visa, insurance, and travel to the camp. Food and board is provided as well as some pocket money. Also runs a work experience program (see below).

Work Experience USA Green Dragon House, 64–70 High St Croydon CR0 9XN ⓣ020/8688 9051, ⓦwww.ccusa.co.uk. For full-time students only, a chance to live and work in a regular job in the US. £695 covers flights, insurance, guaranteed job offer, orientation, and help with tax forms and other paper work. Minimum 10 weeks, maximum 4 months, plus one month's travel. They also offer a scheme as above but you find your own job in the USA for £595 – check the website for details.

From Australia and New Zealand

Australians Studying Abroad 1/970 High St, Armadale, Melbourne ⓣ1800/645 755 or 03/9509 1955, ⓦwww.asatravinfo.com.au. Study tours focusing on art and culture.

Council on International Educational Exchange 91 York St, Level 3, Sydney ⓣ1300/135 331 or 02/8235 7000, ⓦwww.councilexchanges.org.au. Offers opportunities for work and study abroad, with programs in the US.

Finding a place to live

Apartment-hunting is not the nightmare it is in, say, New York City (with the possible exception of Boston). Accommodation is plentiful and not always expensive, though there is very little really cheap accommodation anywhere except in isolated country areas, and Boston can be downright pricey. Apartments will usually come unfurnished; in Boston, expect to pay at least $900 a month for a studio or one-bedroom apartment and upwards of $1800 (or more) per month for two to three bedrooms. Elsewhere, prices can be half that. Most landlords will expect one month's rent as a deposit, plus one month in advance. There is no area-wide organization for long-term accommodation: near universities or college campuses, where apartment turnover is especially high, the best way to find somewhere is to ask around. Otherwise rooms for rent are often advertised in the windows of houses and local papers have "Apartments For Rent" sections. In Boston, the single best source is the Sunday edition of the *Boston Globe*. The *Yellow Pages* will also sometimes list "apartment-finder" firms under "Apartments," and you might try calling real estate offices for help as well (though rental agents often charge a hefty fee – usually one month's rent – in return). The Internet is another good resource, with numerous sites listing available apartments as well as people looking for roommates.

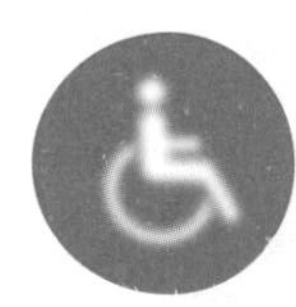

Travelers with disabilities

Travelers with mobility problems or other physical disabilities are likely to find New England – as with the US in general – to be much more in tune with their needs than anywhere else in the world, thanks in part to the 1990 Americans with Disabilities Act (ADA). All public buildings must be wheelchair-accessible and have suitable toilets; most city street corners have dropped curbs; subways have elevators; and most city buses are able to kneel to make access easier and are built with space and handgrips for wheelchair users. Most hotels, restaurants, and theaters (certainly any built in the last ten years or so) have excellent wheelchair access. The golden rule when traveling with a disability is to plan well in advance. Most obstacles can usually be overcome – or avoided altogether – if you call 48 hours or so before your arrival at a bus or train station, airport, hotel, restaurant, park, or other such facility.

Contacts for disabled travelers

In the US and Canada

Access-Able ⓦwww.access-able.com. Online resource for travelers with disabilities.

The Center for Independent Living 2539 Telegraph Ave, Berkeley, CA 94704 ⓣ510/841-4776, ⓦwww.cilberkely.org. Counseling services.

Mobility International USA 451 Broadway, Eugene, OR 97401 ⓣ541/343-1284, ⓦwww.miusa.org. Information and referral services, access guides, tours, and exchange programs. Annual membership $35 (includes quarterly newsletter).

Society for the Accessible Travel and Hospitality (SATH) 347 Fifth Ave, Suite 610, New York, NY 10016 ⓣ212/447-7284, ⓦwww.sath.org. Non-profit educational organization which has actively represented travelers with disabilities since 1976.

Twin Peaks Press PO Box 129, Vancouver, WA 98666 ⓣ1-800/637-2256 or 360/694-2462. Publishes *Travel for the Disabled*, *Wheelchair Vagabond*, and *Directory of Travel Agencies for the Disabled*.

Wheels Up! ⓣ1-888/389-4335, ⓦwww.wheelsup.com. Provides discounted airfare, tour and cruise prices for disabled travelers; also publishes a free monthly newsletter and has a comprehensive website.

In the UK and Ireland

Disability Action Group Portside Business Park, 189 Airport Road West, Belfast BT3 9ED ⓣ028/9029 7880, ⓦwww.disabilityaction.org.

Holiday Care Service 2nd floor, Imperial Building, Victoria Rd, Horley, Surrey RH6 7PZ ⓣ01293/774 535, ⓕ784 647, minicom 776 943, ⓦwww.holidaycare.org.uk. Provides information on all aspects of travel.

Irish Wheelchair Association Blackheath Drive, Clontarf, Dublin 3 ⓣ01/818 6400, ⓕ01/833 3873, ⓦwww.iwa.ie. Useful information provided about traveling abroad with a wheelchair.

Tripscope The Vassall Centre, Gill Avenue, Bristol BS16 2QQ ⓣ08457/585 641, ⓕ0117/939 7736, ⓦwww.tripscope.org.uk. National telephone information service offering free advice on transport and travel (helpline open Mon–Fri 9am–5pm).

Australia and New Zealand

ACROD (Australian Council for Rehabilitation of the Disabled) PO Box 60, Curtin, ACT 2605; Suite 103, 1st floor, 1–5 Commercial Rd, Kings Grove 2208 ⓣ02/6282 4333, ⓦwww.acrod.org. Lists of travel agencies and tour operators.

Disabled Persons Assembly PO Box 27-524, Wellington 6035 ⓣ04/801 9100, ⓦwww.dpa.org.nz. Resource center with lists of travel agencies and tour operators for people with disabilities.

Getting there and around

Most **airlines**, transatlantic and within the US, do whatever they can to ease your journey, and will usually let attendants of people with serious disabilities accompany them at no extra charge. US carriers are not covered by the ADA, although the Air Carriers Access Act does contain a number of requirements pertaining to air travel for handicapped passengers. A free, 28-page booklet available from the Eastern Paralyzed Veterans Association, 75-20 Astoria Blvd, Jackson Heights, NY 11370-1177 (☎718/803-EPVA) will get you up to speed on the Air Carriers Access Act. Another more general publication, *New Horizons: Information for the Air Traveler with a Disability*, is also available from the US Department of Transportation, PVA Distribution Center (☎1-888/860-7244).

Almost every Amtrak **train** includes one or more coaches with accommodation for disabled passengers using wheelchairs. Guide dogs travel free, and Amtrak will provide wheelchair assistance at its train stations, adapted seating on board, and a fifteen percent discount on the regular fare, all provided 24-hours' notice is given. Passengers with hearing impairment can get information at ☎1-800/523-6590.

Traveling by Greyhound or regional **buses** is more difficult for those with disabilities. Only occasionally are Greyhound buses equipped with lifts for wheelchairs, although every effort will be made to assist travelers with disabilities, especially if such assistance is requested 48 hours prior to departure. Contact the Greyhound Customers with Disabilities Travel Assistance Line at ☎1-800/752-4841 to mention specific travel needs; deaf or hearing-impaired passengers should call ☎1-800/345-3109. Under the PCA (Personal Care Attendant) Program, those traveling with disabled passengers in order to help them through their journey may be allowed to travel free of charge.

The major **car rental** firms can, given sufficient notice, provide vehicles with hand controls (though these are usually only available on the more expensive models). The American Automobile Association produces the *Handicapped Driver's Mobility Guide* for drivers with disabilities, available free from the Highway Safety Division Manager, AAA, 815 Farmington Ave, West Hartford, CT 06119 (☎860/236-3261).

As in other parts of the world, the rise of the **self-service gas station** is unwelcome for many disabled drivers. The states of New England have addressed this by changing its laws so that most service stations are required to provide full service to disabled drivers at self-service prices.

Local information

The state information centers (see p.26) all have information on handicapped facilities at places of accommodation and attractions. They should also be able to provide lists of wheelchair-accessible properties – hotels, motels, apartments, B&Bs, hostels, RV parks – in the cities and surrounding countryside, while some of the free tourist guides (notably those produced by the Connecticut, New Hampshire, and Vermont offices) include accessibility ratings for accommodation. Even so, it's always a good idea to call the property in question to confirm details.

Accommodation

The big motel and hotel chains are often the safest bet for **accessible accommodation**; there are plenty of excellent local alternatives, of course, but with a chain at least you'll know what to expect. The ADA obliged all hotels, motels, inns, and other places of lodging designed or constructed after 1993 to be usable by persons with disabilities, be they physical handicaps or other disabilities such as blindness and deafness. This means that, theoretically at least, the newer accommodations should have features such as raised letter signs and cane-detectable warnings of safety hazards, easy-to-use heating, air-conditioning, and faucet controls, as well as ways of moving about the property without having to use steps or stairs. Even if a lodging is described as "accessible" in a brochure, however, always ask about the special facilities on offer before completing a reservation. Where large chains are involved, avoid calling the central reservations number; instead contact the property at which you intend to stay for the most accurate and detailed information about its accessibility.

The great outdoors

Citizens or permanent residents of the US who have been "medically determined to be blind or permanently disabled" can obtain the **Golden Access Passport**, a free lifetime entrance pass to those federally-operated parks, monuments, historic sites, recreation areas, and wildlife refuges which charge entrance fees. The pass must be picked up in person from the areas described, and it also provides a fifty percent discount on fees charged for facilities such as camping, boat launching, and parking. Each state also offers Disabled Discount Passes, which give similar concessions to state-run parks, beaches, and historic sites. Reduced rates are available for permanently disabled people who apply by mail ($3.50 once-only payment) to the relevant state's Department of Parks and Recreation Disabled Discount Pass Program.

Disabled Outdoors Magazine, 5223 South Lorel Ave, Chicago, IL 60608 (☎708/358-4160), is a quarterly magazine covering outdoor activities for disabled sports enthusiasts, with yearly subscriptions costing $10 in the US and $16 in Canada. Also useful, though somewhat outdated, is *Easy Access to National Parks*, a detailed guide to all US national parks for people with disabilities, senior citizens, and families with young children, published in 1992 by the Sierra Club, 85 Second St, San Francisco, CA 94105 (☎415/977-5500), and costing $16. **Acadia National Park**, PO Box 177, Eagle Lake Rd, Bar Harbor, ME 04609-0177 (☎207/288-3338), can also supply general information direct.

Packages

Many US **tour operators** cater to disabled travelers or specialize in organizing disabled group tours. State tourist departments should be able to provide lists of such companies; failing that, ask the National Tour Association, 546 E Main St, PO Box 3071, Lexington, KY 40596 (☎1-800/682-8886, Ⓦwww.ntaonline.com). They can put you in touch with operators whose tours match your needs. **Directions Unlimited**, 123 Green Lane, Bedford Hills, NY 10507 (☎914/241-1700 or 1-800/533-5343), specializes in bookings for people with disabilities; while **The Guided Tour**, 7900 Old York Road, Suite 114-B, Elkins Park, PA 19027-2339 (☎215/782-1317 or 1-800/783-5841, Ⓦwww.guidedtour.com), places the emphasis on travelers with mental or "developmental" disabilities. In the UK, **Accessible America**, Avionics House, Nass Lane, Gloucester GL2 4SN (☎08702/416 127, Ⓦwww.accessibleamerica.co.uk), offers Boston city breaks for wheelchair-users and a category of traveler interestingly described as "slow walkers."

Senior travelers

For many senior citizens, retirement brings the opportunity to explore the world in a style and at a pace that is the envy of younger travelers. As well as the obvious advantages of being free to travel for longer periods during the quieter – and less expensive – seasons, anyone over the age of 62 (with suitable ID) can enjoy a tremendous variety of discounts. Amtrak, Greyhound, local buses, and many US airlines offer (smallish) percentage reductions on fares to older passengers. In addition, museums, art galleries, and even hotels offer small discounts, and since the definition of "senior" can drop to as low as 55, it is always worth asking.

Any US citizen or permanent resident aged 62 or over is entitled to **free admission** to all national parks, monuments, and historic sites using a **Golden Age Passport**, for which a once-only $10 fee is charged; it must be issued in person at any such site, and proof of age is required. This free entry also applies to any accompanying car passengers or, for those hiking or cycling, the passport-holder's spouse and children. It also gives a fifty percent reduction on fees for camping, parking, and boat launching.

The individual states offer senior citizen **discounts** on admission to state-run parks, beaches, and historic sites; these give $1 off parking and $2 off family camping in state-operated parks, except where the fee is less than $2. Several states offer special senior citizen discount passes – contact the relevant state's tourist information center for details (see p.26).

The **American Association of Retired Persons** (AARP), 601 E St NW, Washington DC 20049 (ⓣ202/434-2277 or 1-800/424-3410, ⓦwww.aarp.org), organizes group travel for senior citizens and can provide discounts on accommodation, vehicle rental, airlines, and vacations with selected tour operators. Annual membership (which includes a subscription to their excellent *Modern Maturity* magazine for both North American and international members) is available to anyone over 50, costing $12.50 ($29.50 for three years) for US residents, $17 for Canadians, and $28 for those living in other countries.

There are a number of Boston-based **tour operators** specializing in vacations for seniors. **Elderhostel**, 11 Avenue de Lafayette (ⓣ1/877-426-8056, ⓦwww.elderhostel.org), runs an extensive worldwide network of educational and activity programs for people over 55 (companions may be younger). Trips generally last a week or more, and costs are in line with those of commercial tours. There are numerous programs offered in New England, with themes ranging from brush painting in Massachusetts to sea-kayaking off the Maine coast. **Vantage Deluxe World Travel**, 90 Canal St (ⓣ617/878-6000 or 1-800/322-6677, ⓦwww.vantagetravel.com), specializes in worldwide group travel for seniors, and offers bus tours of New England (essentially Boston and the Maine coastline) and the Atlantic provinces of Canada. The UK-based **Saga Holidays**, The Saga Building, Middelbug Square, Folkestone, Kent CT20 1AZ (ⓣ0130/377 1111 or 0800/096 0078, ⓦwww.holidays.saga.co.uk), is the country's biggest and most established specialist in vacations aimed at older people. New England tours include most of the major sights, and are conducted during the "fall foliage" season. There is also a Boston-based company affiliated to Saga Holidays (ⓣ1-800/343-0273, ⓦwww.sagaholidays.com).

Traveling with children

Traveling with kids in New England is relatively problem-free; children are readily accepted – indeed welcomed – in public places everywhere. Hotels and motels are used to them (although some of the ritzier or smaller bed and breakfasts have a minimum age requirement – ask when making reservations). Most state and national parks organize children's activities, every town or city has clean and safe playgrounds, and there are plenty of commercial attractions that specialize in kids' entertainment – mini-golf, water slides, arcades, and the like. Restaurants make considerable efforts to encourage parents to bring their offspring. All the national chains offer booster chairs and kids' menus, packed with excellent-value (though not necessarily healthy) meals.

Local tourist offices (see p.26) can provide specific information on what their state has to offer children, and various **guidebooks** have been written for parents traveling with children, like the helpful **Trouble Free Travel with Children** ($6.95), available through Publishers Group West. John Muir Publications puts out a series of books for children, called *Kidding Around*, which tell about the history and describe the various sights of major US cities. And **Travel with Your Children** (ⓣ1-888/822-4388 or 212/477-5524) publishes a regular newsletter, *Family Travel Times* (ⓦwww.familytraveltimes.com), as well as a series of books on travel with tykes including **Great Adventure Vacations With Your Kids**.

Getting around

Most families choose to travel by car, and while this is the least problematic way to get around it's worth planning ahead to assure a pleasant trip. Don't set yourself unrealistic targets if you're hoping to enjoy a driving vacation with your kids – long, boring journeys on the interstate can be disastrous. If you're on a fly-drive vacation, note that when renting a car the company is legally obliged to provide free car seats for kids.

Children under two years old **fly free** on domestic routes, and for ten percent of the adult fare on international flights – though that doesn't mean they get a seat, let alone frequent-flier miles. Kids between two and twelve are usually entitled to half-price tickets.

Traveling by **bus** is the most uncomfortable for kids. Under-twos travel (on your lap) for free; ages two to four are charged ten percent of the adult fare, as are any toddlers who take up a seat. Children under twelve years old are charged half the standard fare.

Taking the **train** is by far the best option for long journeys – not only does everyone get to enjoy the scenery, but you can get up and walk around, relieving pent-up energy. Most cross-country trains have **sleeping compartments**, which may be quite expensive but are likely to be seen as a great adventure. On Amtrak, two children aged two to fifteen can travel at half-fare with each adult passenger.

Gay and lesbian New England

Go to the right places, and New England can be a very enjoyable destination for gay and lesbian visitors. The region possesses some firm favorites on the gay North American travel circuit, and gay-friendly accommodations can be found dotted all over the region. However, go to the wrong places – mainly rural areas – and you will find that the narrow-minded attitudes of "small town America" are still alive and well. Be cautious, then, with open displays of affection and the like. As difficult and frustrating as this may be, it's usually the most effective way to keep the bigots at bay.

There are sizeable, predominantly gay areas in almost all of the New England states. The **South End** of Boston is what Greenwich Village is to New York and the Marais is to Paris. Other "gay" cities in Massachusetts include **Provincetown**, one of the world's premier gay beach resorts, and **Northampton**, well known for its large lesbian community. Elsewhere, the Rhode Island city of **Providence**, although some-

Same-sex marriages In Vermont

On July 1, 2000, Vermont, the state with the second largest per capita lesbian population in the US, became the first state in the Union to legally recognize **civil unions** for same sex couples. This groundbreaking move has made Vermont, always one of the country's more gay-friendly states, a prime destination for gay and lesbian couples looking to get married. Hotels, inns, and B&Bs have caught on to the trend, and are now starting to offer their premises for civil wedding ceremonies. Couples interested in marrying, Vermont style, should first get a civil union license ($20) and a Certificate of Civil Union ($7) from a Vermont town clerk. A judge, a justice of the peace, or a member of the clergy must then certify the license within sixty days. Then, within ten days of the certification, the license must be returned by the official who certified it to the town clerk who issued it. Once joined together in civil union, the same-sex couple is given the same benefits, protections, and responsibilities as are granted to spouses in a traditional marriage. For more information, contact The Secretary of State's Office, Redston Building, 26 Terrace St, Drawer 09, Montpelier, VT 05609-1101 (☎1-802/828-2363).

Gay and lesbian publications

Of **national publications** to look out for, most of which are available from any good bookstore, by far the best are the range produced by Damron, PO Box 422458, San Francisco, CA 94142 (Ⓣ415/255-0404 or 1-800/462-6654, Ⓦwww.damron.com). These include the *Men's Travel Guide*, a pocket-sized yearbook full of listings of hotels, bars, clubs, and resources for gay men ($18.95); the *Women's Traveler*, which provides similar listings for lesbians ($15.95); the *Road Atlas*, which shows gay-friendly lodgings and entertainment in major cities ($21.95); and *Damron Accommodations*, which provides detailed listings (with color photos) of over one thousand accommodations for gays and lesbians worldwide ($22.95). Note that all of these titles are offered at a discount on the website. The *Gayellow Pages*, PO Box 533, Village Station, New York, NY 10014 (Ⓣ212/674-0120, Ⓦwww.gayellowpages.com; $16), is a directory of businesses in the US and Canada, with a regional directory for New England. *The Advocate*, PO Box 4371, Los Angeles, CA 90078 (Ⓕ323/467-0173, Ⓦwww.advocate.com; $3.95) is a bimonthly national gay news magazine, with features, general info, and classified ads (not to be confused with *Advocate Men*, which is a soft porn magazine).

There are also a number of **New England publications** covering the gay scene in this part of the US. *Bay Windows*, 631 Tremont St, Boston, MA 02118 (Ⓣ617/266-0393, Ⓦwww.baywindows.com), is New England's largest gay and lesbian weekly, with cultural listings for all of the region's six states. *Out in the Mountains*, PO Box 1078, Richmond, VT 05477 (Ⓣ802/434-6486, Ⓦwww.mountainpridemedia.org), is Vermont's monthly gay newsletter; while the bimonthly *Metroline Magazine*, 495 Farmington Ave, Hartford, CT 06105 (Ⓣ860/231-8845, Ⓦwww.metroline-online.com), has information on the gay scene in Connecticut, Maine, Massachusetts, and Rhode Island. Some tourist information centers stock the free *Pink Pages*, KP Media, 66 Charles St, Boston, MA 02114 (Ⓣ617/423-1515, Ⓦwww.linkpink.com), a complete listing of gay- and lesbian-friendly businesses and community organizations in all six New England states – although about half of the book is devoted to Boston. The text in its entirety is reproduced on the website.

For additional research try one of the Internet's many **online publications**, such as the gay and lesbian travel resources, Ⓦwww.qtmagazine.com and Ⓦwww.gayguide.net, or something more specific to New England, such as Ⓦwww.vermontgaytravel.com and Ⓦwww.gayinmaine.com.

what overshadowed by Boston, has a vibrant gay scene; while **Ogunquit** is the quieter, Maine-version of Provincetown. Indeed in **Maine**, where you would expect there to be a backcountry-fueled opposition to anything different, locals are so obsessed with living life their own way that gays and lesbians are enjoying more public acceptance. In 1998, for example, a Maine antiques dealer walked across the state to encourage opposition to a ballot measure to ban gay rights. **Vermont** is notoriously liberal (see box opposite), while even traditionally conservative **New Hampshire** has recently joined other New England states in passing anti-discrimination laws. The latest show of acceptance was by the venerable *Boston Globe*, which started to include same-sex commitment ceremonies in the "Announcements" section of the paper in the fall of 2002.

Contact the International Gay & Lesbian Travel Association (Ⓣ954/776-2626 or 1-800/448-8550, Ⓦwww.iglta.org), for a list of gay- and lesbian-owned or -friendly **tour operators**. Meanwhile, gaytravel.com (Ⓣ1-800/429-8728, Ⓦwww.gaytravel.com), is a good online travel agency where you can make bookings and get help with travel planning.

Women travelers

Practically speaking, though a woman traveling alone is certainly not the attention-grabbing spectacle in New England that she might be elsewhere in the world, you're likely to come across some sort of minor harassment. More serious than the odd offensive comment, rape statistics in the US are high, and it goes without saying that, even more than anyone else, women should never hitchhike alone – this is widely interpreted as an invitation for trouble, and there's no shortage of weirdos to give it.

Similarly, if you have a car, be careful whom you pick up: just because you're in the driver's seat doesn't mean you're safe. If you can, avoid traveling to or from small towns **at night** by public transportation – deserted bus stations, while not necessarily threatening, will do little to make you feel secure, and where possible you should team up with another woman. On buses, sit as near to the front – and the driver – as possible.

New England cities can feel very safe, but as with anywhere, particular care has to be taken at night, and a modicum of **common sense** can often avert disasters. Walking down unlit, empty streets is never a good idea, and you should take cabs whenever the situation feels remotely sketchy. The advice that women who look confident tend not to encounter trouble is, like all home truths, grounded in fact but not written in stone; those who stand around looking lost and a bit scared are prime targets, but nobody is immune. Provided you listen to advice, though, and stick to the better parts of a town, going into bars and clubs alone should pose no problems, especially in Boston, where there's generally a pretty healthy attitude towards women who choose to do so. If in doubt, gay and lesbian bars are usually a trouble-free alternative.

Small towns in rural areas are not blessed with the same liberal attitudes toward lone women travelers that you'll find in the cities. If your vehicle **breaks down** in a country area, walk to the nearest house or town for help; don't wait by the vehicle in the middle of nowhere hoping for somebody to stop – they will, but it may not be the help you're looking for. Should disaster strike, all major towns have some kind of rape counseling service available; if not, the local sheriff's office will make adequate arrangements for you to get help, counseling, and, if necessary, get you home.

The **National Organization for Women** is a women's issues group whose lobbying has done much to affect positive legislation. NOW branches, listed in local phone books, can provide referrals for specific concerns such as rape crisis centers and counseling services, feminist bookstores, and lesbian bars. Further back-up material can be found in *Women's Travel in Your Pocket* ($15.95; SCB Distributors), a guide for women travelers, last updated in 2000.

Directory

Addresses Though initially confusing for overseas visitors, American addresses are masterpieces of logical thinking. Generally speaking, roads in major cities are laid out to a grid system, creating "blocks" of buildings: addresses of buildings refer to the block, which will be numbered in sequence, from a central point usually downtown; for example, 620 S Cedar will be six blocks south of downtown. In some larger cities, "streets" and "avenues" often run north–south and east–west respectively; streets are usually named (sometimes alphabetically), avenues generally numbered.

Airport tax All airport, customs, and security taxes are included in the price of your ticket.

Cigarettes and smoking Smoking is as much frowned upon in New England as the rest of the US (excepting the fanatic West Coast, perhaps). Cinemas are nonsmoking, and smoking is prohited on public transportation and flights. Restaurants are usually divided into smoking and nonsmoking sections. Cigarettes are sold in almost any food shop, convenience store, drugstore, or bar. A pack of twenty costs upwards of $5.

Drugs Possession of under an ounce of marijuana is a misdemeanor in New England, and the worst you'll get is a $200 fine. Being caught with more than an ounce, however, means facing a criminal charge for dealing, and a possible prison sentence – stiffer if caught anywhere near a school. Other drugs are, of course, completely illegal and it's a much more serious offense if you're caught with any.

Electricity 110V AC. Some foreign travel plug adapters don't fit American sockets.

ID Should be carried at all times. Two pieces will diffuse any suspicion, one of which should have a photo: driving license, passport, and credit card(s) are your best bets. Not having your license with you while driving is an arrestable offense.

Measurements and sizes Measurements are in inches, feet, yards, and miles; weight in ounces, pounds, and tons. American pints and gallons are about four-fifths of Imperial ones. Clothing sizes are always four figures less than what they would be in Britain – a British women's size 12 is a US size 8 – while British shoe sizes are half a size below American ones for women, and one size below for men.

Tax Added on to your bill will invariably be some sort of surcharge, be it a food tax (5–7 percent), hotel tax (7–13 percent), or sales tax (5–7 percent). New Hampshire, however, has no sales tax; Vermont has none for hotels. Car rentals are notorious for loading on taxes for a variety of reasons, which may add up to 30 percent to your final bill.

Temperatures Always given in Fahrenheit.

Time New England runs on Eastern Standard Time (EST), five hours behind GMT in winter and three hours ahead of the US West Coast. British Summer Time runs almost concurrent with US Daylight Saving Time – implemented from the first Sunday in April to the last Sunday in October – causing a four-hour time difference for two weeks of the year.

Tipping You are expected to tip pretty much all service-related help, from waitstaff (15–20 percent) to bartenders (10–15 percent) to cab drivers (15–20 percent).

Guide

Guide

1

Boston

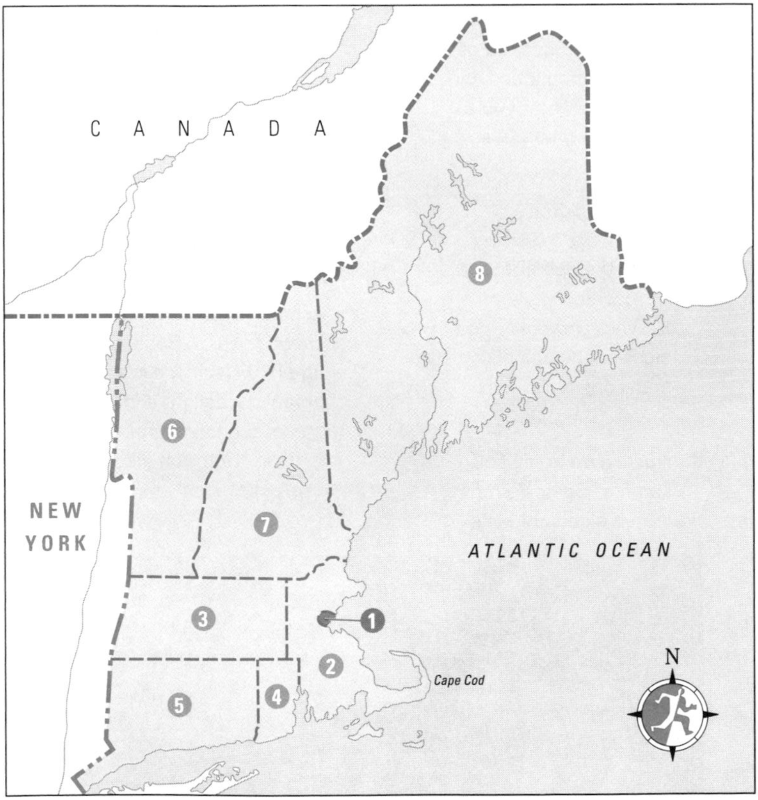
CANADA
NEW YORK
ATLANTIC OCEAN
Cape Cod
N
1
2
3
4
5
6
7
8

CHAPTER 1 Highlights

* **Beacon Hill** Long the neighborhood of choice for the city's elite, with stately red-brick Federalist town houses and gaslights lining the narrow, cobblestoned streets. See p.107

* **Newbury Street** This swanky promenade of designer boutiques and cafés will tempt you to break the bank. See p.116

* **Harvard Square** Cambridge's buzzing heart is steps from the ivy-covered walls of Harvard University and close to the colonial mansions of Brattle Street. See p.000

* **North End** You'll find some of Boston's most famed sights, plus its best *cannoli*, in its most authentic Italian neighborhood. See p.100

* **Isabella Stewart Gardner Museum** Don't miss this delightful museum, with its eclectic collection and sublime central courtyard, styled after a fifteenth-century Venetian palace. See p.125

* **Fenway Park** Watch one of baseball's most storied teams play in one of the country's classic stadiums. See p.123

* **Arnold Arboretum** The crown jewel of Boston's Emerald Necklace is a botanist's delight and one of the finest arboretums in North America. See p.130

1

Boston

Boston might be as close to the Old World as the New World gets, an American city that proudly trades in on its colonial past, having served a crucial role in the country's development from a few wayward pilgrims right through the Revolutionary War. It occasionally takes this a bit too far – what's a faded relic anywhere else becomes a plaque-covered tourist sight here – but none of it detracts from the city's overriding historic charm, nor from its present-day energy. Indeed, there are plenty of tall skyscrapers, thriving business concerns, and cultural outposts that are part and parcel of modern urban America, not to mention excellent mergers of past and present, such as the redeveloped – and bustling – Quincy Market, a paradigm for successful urban renewal. True, nowhere else will you get a better feel for the events and the personas behind the birth of a nation, all played out in Boston's wealth of emblematic and evocative colonial-era sights. But the city's cafés and shops, its attractive public spaces, and the diversity of its neighborhoods – student hives, ethnic enclaves, and stately districts of preserved town houses – are similarly alluring, and go some way to answering the twin accusations of elitism and provincialism to which Boston is perennially subjected.

As the undisputed commercial and cultural center of New England, Boston is the highlight of any trip to the region, truly unmissable because almost every road in the area leads to it (indeed Boston was, until the late 1700s, America's most populous and culturally important city). It's also the center of the American university system – more than sixty colleges call the area their home, including Harvard, in the neighboring city of Cambridge – and it enjoys a youthful buzz that again belies any reputation for stuffiness it might have. This academic connection has also played a key part in the city's left-leaning political tradition, the kind that spawned a line of ethnic mayors and, most famous of all, the Kennedy clan.

Today, Boston's relatively small size – both physically and in terms of population (eighteenth among US cities) – and its provincial feel actually serve the city to great advantage. Though it has expanded since it was first settled in 1630 through landfills and annexation, it has never lost its center, a tangle of streets clustered around Boston Common which can really only be explored on foot. Steeped in Puritan roots, the residents of these areas often display a slightly anachronistic Yankee pride, but it's one that has served to protect the city's identity, while groups of Irish and Italian descent have carved out authentically and

Unless otherwise stated, all phone numbers in this chapter are prefixed by the code ⓣ617.

often equally unchanged communities in areas like the North End, Charlestown, and South Boston. Indeed, the districts around the Common exude almost a small-town atmosphere and, until recently at least, were relatively unmarred by chain stores and fast-food joints. Even as Boston has evolved from busy port to blighted city to the rejuvenated place it is today, it has remained, fundamentally, a city on a human scale.

Some history

Boston's first permanent settlement was started by **William Blackstone**, who split off from the Pilgrims' camp down in Plymouth for more isolated territory. He was soon joined by more Puritan settlers, to whom he sold most of the land he had staked out, then called the Shawmut Peninsula and soon renamed by the Puritans after their hometown in England: Boston.

Early Bostonians enjoyed almost total political autonomy, but with the restoration of the British monarchy in 1660, the crown began appointing governors to oversee the Massachusetts Bay Colony. The colonists clashed frequently with these appointees, their resentment growing with a series of acts over the next one hundred or so years that restricted various civil and commercial liberties. This culminated in such skirmishes as the Boston Massacre and the Boston Tea Party, events that went a long way towards propelling the **Revolutionary War**, which effectively started just outside Boston, in Lexington.

Post-Revolution, Boston emerged as a leading port city, eventually moving on to prominence in textiles and other industries. Its success in these fields brought wave after wave of nineteenth-century immigrants, notably Irish and Italian, ethnicities that still largely populate the city and that have made great inroads into local and regional politics. Despite a strong history of progressive thought in abolitionism, the city has been less successful in integrating African-Americans into the fold, and **racial tensions** flared up frequently in the twentieth century, most recently with the controversial advent of busing in the 1970s. This has been somewhat healed of late, as have any economic doldrums that plagued the city for the latter half of this century, and a new sense of confidence – so emblematic of Boston's storied past – has taken hold.

Arrival, information, and city transit

Boston is the unchallenged travel hub of New England, and if it's not the only place in the region you'll visit, it almost certainly will be the first. Conveniently, all **points of arrival** are located inside the city boundaries, none more than a few miles away from downtown, and all are well connected to public transport.

By air

Busy **Logan International Airport** (Ⓣ1-800/23-LOGAN, Ⓦwww.massport.com/logan), servicing both domestic and international flights, has five terminals lettered A through E that are connected by a series of courtesy buses. You'll find currency exchange in terminals C and E (daily 10am–5pm), plus information booths, car rental, and Automatic Teller Machines (ATMs) in all five.

After arriving at Logan, the most convenient way downtown is by **subway**. The Airport stop is a short ride away on courtesy bus #11, which you can

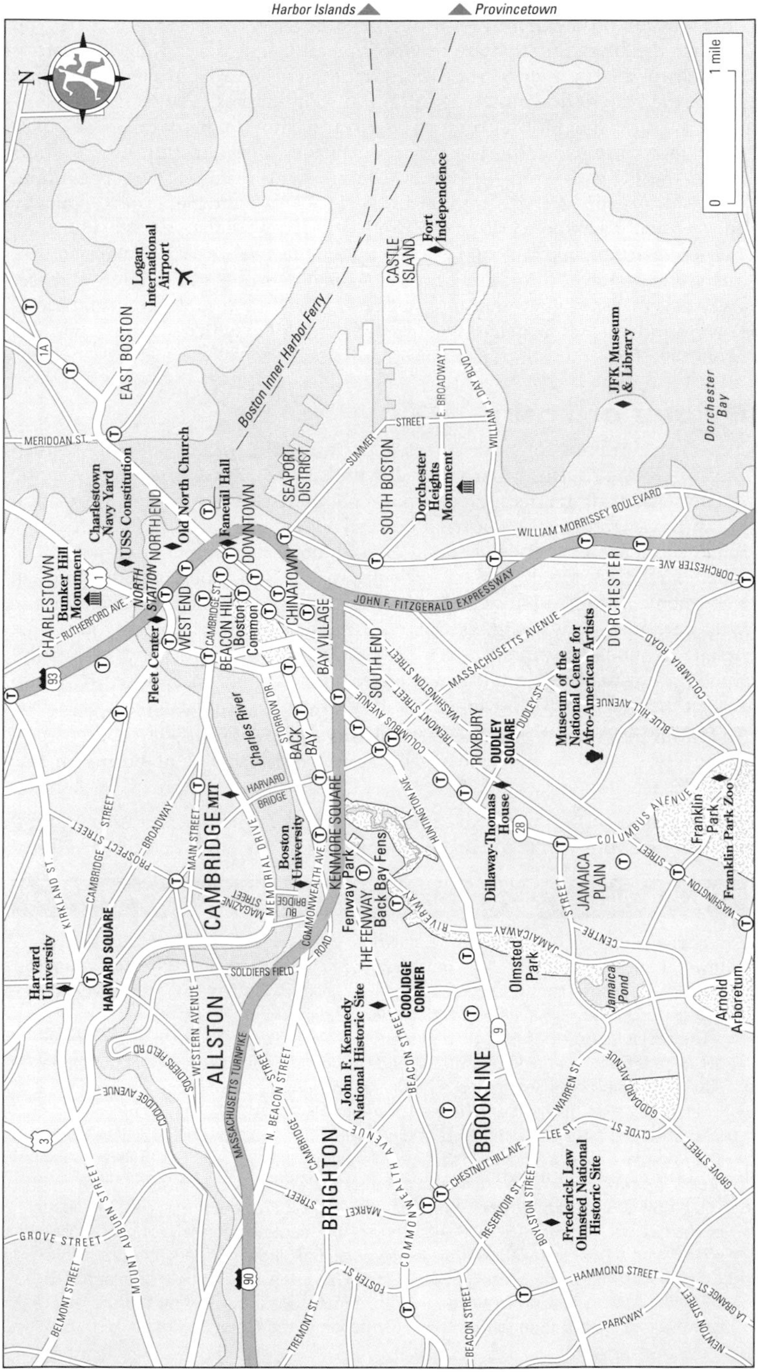
Harbor Islands
Provincetown
N
0
1 mile
CHARLESTOWN
Bunker Hill Monument
Charlestown Navy Yard
USS Constitution
RUTHERFORD AVE.
NORTH STATION
NORTH END
Old North Church
Faneuil Hall
DOWNTOWN
EAST BOSTON
MERIDOAN ST.
Logan International Airport
Boston Inner Harbor Ferry
SEAPORT DISTRICT
CASTLE ISLAND
Fort Independence
SUMMER
STREET
E. BROADWAY
WILLIAM J. DAY BLVD
SOUTH BOSTON
Dorchester Heights Monument
JFK Museum & Library
Dorchester Bay
WILLIAM MORRISSEY BOULEVARD
JOHN F. FITZGERALD EXPRESSWAY
DORCHESTER AVE
DORCHESTER
Fleet Center
WEST END
CAMBRIDGE ST
BEACON HILL
Boston Common
CHINATOWN
BAY VILLAGE
SOUTH END
MASSACHUSETTS AVENUE
WASHINGTON STREET
TREMONT STREET
COLUMBUS AVENUE
Museum of the National Center for Afro-American Artists
COLUMBIA ROAD
BLUE HILL AVENUE
DUDLEY ST.
ROXBURY
DUDLEY SQUARE
Dillaway-Thomas House
COLUMBUS AVENUE
Franklin Park
Franklin Park Zoo
WASHINGTON STREET
JAMAICA PLAIN
CENTRE STREET
Charles River
STORROW DR.
BACK BAY
HARVARD BRIDGE
MIT
CAMBRIDGE
MAIN STREET
BROADWAY
PROSPECT STREET
CAMBRIDGE STREET
KIRKLAND ST.
MEMORIAL DRIVE
MAGAZINE STREET
BU BRIDGE
Boston University
COMMONWEALTH AVE
KENMORE SQUARE
Fenway Park
THE FENWAY
Back Bay Fens
HUNTINGTON AVE
RIVERWAY
JAMAICAWAY
Olmsted Park
Jamaica Pond
Arnold Arboretum
Harvard University
HARVARD SQUARE
SOLDIERS FIELD
ROAD
ALLSTON
WESTERN AVENUE
SOLDIERS FIELD RD
COOLIDGE AVENUE
MASSACHUSETTS TURNPIKE
N. BEACON STREET
CAMBRIDGE STREET
John F. Kennedy National Historic Site
COOLIDGE CORNER
BEACON STREET
BROOKLINE
WARREN ST.
GODDARD AVENUE
CLYDE ST.
LEE ST.
CHESTNUT HILL AVE.
BRIGHTON
MARKET STREET
COMMONWEALTH AVENUE
RESERVOIR ST.
BOYLSTON STREET
Frederick Law Olmsted National Historic Site
GROVE STREET
HAMMOND STREET
LA GRANGE ST.
NEWTON STREET
PARKWAY
BEACON STREET
TREMONT ST.
FOSTER ST.
GROVE STREET
MOUNT AUBURN STREET
BELMONT STREET
93
1
1A
90
3
9
28

catch outside on the arrival level of all five Logan terminals. From there, you can take the Blue Line to State or Government Center stations in the heart of downtown, and transfer to the Red, Orange, and Green lines to reach other points; the ride to downtown lasts about fifteen minutes ($1).

Just as quick, and a lot more fun, is the **water shuttle** that whisks you across the harbor to Rowes Wharf near the Blue Line Aquarium stop (Mon–Thurs every 15min, 6am–8pm; Fri every 30min, 8am–11pm; Sat every 30min, 10am–11pm; Sun every 30min, 10am–8pm; $10). From the airport, courtesy bus #66 will take you to the pier.

By comparison, taking a **taxi** is expensive – the airport to a downtown destination costs $15–20, plus an extra $4.50 or so in tolls – and time-consuming, given Boston's notorious traffic jams. Save yourself the trouble and avoid them. For around the same price, you can ride in style with Boston Town Car (Ⓣ782-4000, Ⓦwww.bostontowncar.com; $20–25).

By bus or train

The main terminus for both **buses** and **trains** to Boston is Boston's **South Station**, in the southeast corner of downtown at Summer Street and Atlantic Avenue. **Amtrak trains** arrive at one end, in a station with an information booth, newsstands, a food court, and several ATMs (but no currency exchange), while **bus carriers** arrive at the clean and modern terminal next door, from where it's a bit of a trek to reach the subway (the Red Line), which is through the Amtrak station and down a level. Those with sizeable baggage will find the walk particularly awkward, as there are no porters or handcarts. Note that despite its modernity, the bus terminal's departure and arrival screens are anything but up-to-date – confirm your gate with an agent to be sure. Trains also make a second stop at Boston's **Back Bay Station**, 145 Dartmouth St, on the Ⓣ's Orange Line – the station has nothing in the way of amenities.

By car

Driving into Boston is the absolute worst way to get there, and is sure to put a damper on your trip if you're a first-time visitor. Two highways provide direct

The Big Dig

Whether you arrive in Boston by air, rail, or highway, you're likely to notice a downtown in seeming disarray. This mess has been created by the **Big Dig**, a grand attempt – and one that has evolved into a political calamity and a logistical nightmare – to bury the city's central traffic artery underground.

The project, approved in 1987 and started in 1991, began as an attempt to alleviate central Boston's heinous traffic – roads are often gridlocked for ten hours a day – by relocating some seven and a half miles of highway underground, a move that would free up an estimated 27 acres of land for use as a downtown park.

The budget, originally estimated at $2.6 billion, is now expected to reach $15 billion since an inquiry discovered that city planners had hidden over $2 billion of their project's cost overruns from the public. While the project is slated for completion in 2004, concerns about the cost overruns have led to talk of auctioning off the space to developers – a move that would change the central artery's proposed "green space" into a conglomeration of high-rise office buildings and parking garages.

If this civic headache interests you, visit the Museum of Science's permanent **Big Dig exhibit**, or go online to Ⓦwww.bigdig.com, to learn that, during the dig, "more earth will be moved than during the construction of the Great Pyramids."

access to the city, **I-90** and **I-93**, though the latter, which cuts north–south through the heart of the city, is the focus of protracted construction with the goal of submerging the highway below ground sometime before 2005 (see box opposite). The result is notorious traffic jams and indecipherable detours that are sure to inspire road rage and get you lost. Consequently, if you're coming along I-90 from **eastern Massachusetts** and **Albany**, you'd do better to get off the highway and head into town before it connects with I-93. Visitors coming from southern points like **New York** or northern states like **New Hampshire** are pretty much stuck, however, as I-93 is the only serviceable road available. A third highway, **I-95**, circumnavigates Boston, and is more useful to drivers trying to avoid the city altogether.

Information

Boston's main public tourist office is the **Boston Visitor Information Pavilion** on Boston Common, near the Park Street subway stop (daily 9am–5pm). You'll find loads of maps and brochures, plus information on historical sights, cultural events, accommodation, restaurants, and bus trips. Across the street from the Old State House, at 15 State St, is a **visitors' center** maintained by the Boston National Historical Park (daily 9am–5pm); it too has plenty of free brochures, plus a bookstore. In Back Bay, there is a visitor **kiosk** in the Prudential Center, 800 Boylston St (daily 9am–5pm). Visitors to **Cambridge** can get all the information they need from the Cambridge Office of Tourism (ⓣ441-2884 or 1-800/862-5678, ⓦwww.cambridge-usa.org), which maintains a well-stocked kiosk in Harvard Square (Mon–Sat 9am–5pm). For advance information, the best source is the Greater Boston Convention and Visitors Bureau's (GBCVB) website, ⓦwww.bostonusa.com.

The city's oldest **newspaper**, *The Globe* (50¢; ⓦwww.boston.com/globe) remains Boston's best general daily; its fat Sunday edition ($2) includes substantial sections on art, culture, and lifestyle. The *Boston Herald* (50¢; ⓦwww.bostonherald.com) is the *Globe*'s tabloid competitor and is best for appeasing your gossip and local sports coverage fix. The rest of the city's print media consists primarily of listings-oriented and **free weeklies**. To know what's on, the *Boston Phoenix* (ⓦwww.bostonphoenix.com), available at sidewalk newspaper stands around town, is essential, offering extensive entertainment **listings** as well as good feature articles. Other freebies like *Improper Bostonian* (ⓦwww.improper.com) and the *Phoenix*'s bi-weekly listings magazine, *Stuff@Night*, both have good listings of new and noteworthy goings-on about town (though the features are primarily ad-driven). *Bay Windows* (ⓦwww.baywindows.com), a small weekly catering to the **gay and lesbian** population, is available free at most South End cafés and bars; the cover price is 50¢ otherwise. The lone monthly publication, *Boston Magazine* ($3.95; ⓦwww.bostonmagazine.com), is a glossy lifestyle **magazine** with good restaurant reviews and a yearly "Best of Boston" roundup.

The **Boston CityPass** (available all over; $30.25; ⓦcitypass.net) is a ticket booklet that covers admission to the Prudential Skywalk Observatory, the Kennedy Museum, the Museum of Fine Arts, the New England Aquarium, the Harvard Museum of Natural History, and the Science Museum.

City transport

Much of the pleasure of visiting Boston comes from being in a city built long before cars were invented. Walking around the narrow, winding streets can be a joy; conversely, driving around them is a nightmare. Be particularly cautious

Guided tours of Boston

Perhaps the best way to orient yourself in Boston, aside from walking, is by taking a trolley tour, on small open-air buslike vehicles painted to look like streetcars. Most of the trolleys let you hop on and off at various locations and they make pick-ups at major hotels; full tours usually last about two hours, and there is little difference from tour to tour in what historical sights you'll actually see.

Narrated trolly tours

Beantown Trolley ⓣ720-6342 or 236-2148, ⓦwww.brushhilltours.com. One of the oldest and most popular history tours, covering the gamut from waterfront wharfs to Beacon Hill Brahmins and Fenway museums, with multiple pick-up and drop-off points around town. $18.

Discover Boston Multilingual Trolley Tours ⓣ742-1440. Tours in English; audio devices available in French, German, Italian, Japanese, and Russian. $24.

Old Town Trolley Tours ⓣ269-7010, ⓦwww.trolleytours.com. Another hop-on, hop-off trolley tour of Boston, this one on ubiquitous orange-and-green trolleys with thematic routes like Sons and Daughters of Liberty and Ghosts and Gravestones. $23.

Other city tours

Boston by Foot ⓣ367-2345, ⓦwww.bostonbyfoot.com. Informative ninety-minute walking tours focusing on the architecture and history of Beacon Hill, Copley Square, the South End, North End, and the Ⓣ, including disused stations. $8–10.

Boston Duck Tours ⓣ723-DUCK, ⓦwww.bostonducktours.com. Excellent tours that take to the streets and the Charles River in restored World War II amphibious landing vehicles; kids get to skipper the bus/boat in the water. Tours depart every half-hour from the Prudential Center at 101 Huntington Ave; reservations advised in summer. $19.

Boston National Historical Park Visitor's Center Freedom Trail Tours ⓣ242-5642. Led by park rangers and taking in a few Freedom Trail sights, these tours run on the hour between 10am and 3pm.

Brush Hill Grayline Tours ⓣ720-6342 or 236-2148, ⓦwww.brushhilltours.com. Day-long coach tours to surrounding towns such as Concord, Lexington, Plymouth, and Salem. Late March to November. $26–45.

L'Arte di Cucinare ⓣ523-6032, ⓦwww.cucinare.com. Award-winning walking and tasting tours of the North End's Italian salumerias, pasticcerias, and enotecas. Often booked up, so reserve well in advance. Wed & Sat 10am & 2pm, Fri 3pm; $39–42.

Literary Trail ⓣ350-0358, ⓦwww.lit-trail.org. A three-hour bus tour that takes in all the local hotshots from Henry Wadsworth Longfellow to Henry David Thoreau. $30.

in traffic circles known as "rotaries": when entering, always yield the right of way. If you have a car, better park it for the duration of your trip (see p.163) and get around either by **foot** or **public transit** – a system of subway lines, buses, and ferries run by the Massachusetts Bay Transportation Authority (MBTA, known as the "T"; ⓣ1-800/392-6100, ⓦwww.mbta.com).

Subway (the Ⓣ)

While not the most modern system, Boston's subway is cheap, efficient, and charmingly antiquated – its Green Line was America's first underground train, built in the late nineteenth century, and riding it today is akin to riding a tram – albeit underground.

Four **subway** lines transect Boston and continue out into some of its more proximate neighbors. Each line is color coded and passes through downtown before continuing on to other districts. The **Red Line**, which serves Harvard, is the most frequent, intersecting South Boston and Dorchester to the south and Cambridge to the north. The **Green Line** hits Back Bay, Kenmore Square, the Fenway, and Brookline. The **Blue Line** heads into East Boston and is most useful for its stop at Logan Airport. The less frequent **Orange Line** traverses the South End and continues down to Roxbury and Jamaica Plain.

All trains travel either **inbound** (towards the quadrant made up of State, Downtown Crossing, Park Street, and Government Center stops) or **outbound** (away from the quadrant). If you're confused about whether you're going in or out, the train's terminus is also designated on the train itself; for instance, trains to Harvard from South Station will be on the "Inbound" platform and heading towards "Alewife."

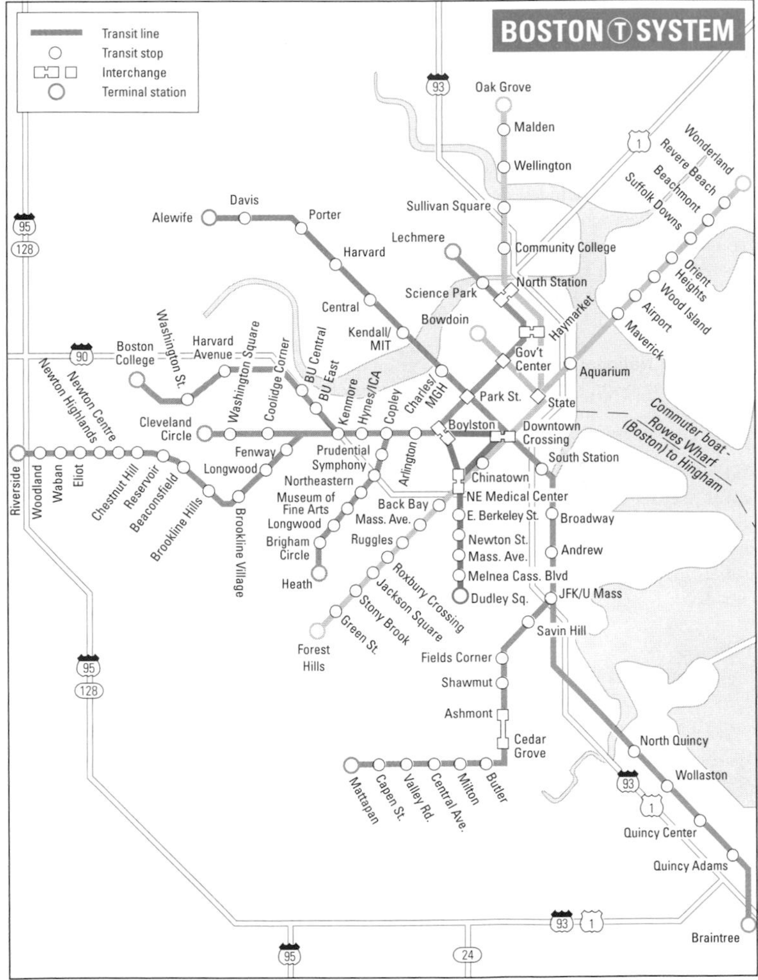

The four lines are supplemented by a bus rapid transit (BRT) route, the Silver Line, which runs above ground along Washington Street from Downtown Crossing Ⓣ. More of a fast bus than a subway, the line cuts through the heart of South End.

The **fare** is $1, payable by tokens purchased at the station or by exact change; when boarding a subway at a station with no token-seller, you can squeeze your dollar bill into the slot at the bottom left of the conductor's till. If you're planning to use public transit a lot, it's a good idea to buy a visitor's pass for one ($6), three ($11), or seven days ($22) of unlimited subway, bus, and harbor ferry use. A cheaper option may be the weekly combo commuter passes ($12.50), which are good from Sunday to Saturday, and are sold from the previous Thursday until the Wednesday of the week they're valid for. Buy them at the Harvard, Kenmore, or Park Street Ⓣ stations.

The biggest drawback to the Ⓣ is its hours (Mon–Sat 5.15am–12.30am, Sun 6am–12.30am); the 12.30am closing time means you'll be stuck taking a taxi home after last-call. Free transit maps are available at any station.

Buses

The MBTA also manages a whopping 170 **bus** routes both in and around Boston. The buses run less frequently than the subway and are harder to navigate, but they bear two main advantages: they're cheaper (75¢, exact change only) and they provide service to many more points. It's a service used primarily by natives who've grown familiar with the byzantine system of routes. If you're transferring from the Ⓣ, you'll have to pay the full fare; transferring between buses is free, however, as long as you have a transfer from your original bus. Note that the Ⓣ's visitor pass (see above) includes unlimited bus access over one, three, or seven days, depending on the package you've purchased. Be sure to arm yourself with the *Official Public Transport Map*, available at all subway stations, before heading out. Most buses run from 5.30am to 1am, but a few "Night Owl" buses run until 2.30am, leaving from Government Center Ⓣ.

Ferries

Of all the MBTA transportation options, the Inner Harbor **ferry** is by far the most scenic: $1.25 gets you a ten-minute boat ride with excellent views of downtown Boston. The boats, covered 100-seaters with exposed upper decks, navigate several waterfront routes by day, though the one most useful to visitors is that connecting Long Wharf with Charlestown (Mon–Fri 6.30am–8pm, Sat & Sun 10am–6pm; every 30min).

Bikes

In and around Boston are some eighty miles of **bike trails**, making it an excellent city to explore on two wheels. The usual precautions – wearing a helmet and carrying a whistle – are advised. You can rent a bike starting at about $25 per day from Community Bicycle Supply, at 496 Tremont St (Ⓣ542-8623, Ⓦwww.communitybicycle.com); Back Bay Bicycles, at 333 Newbury St (Ⓣ247-2336, Ⓦwww.backbaybicycles.com); or Wheelworks Bicycle Workshop, at 259 Massachusetts Ave, Cambridge (Ⓣ876-6555). Wheelworks also does repairs. A copy of *Boston's Bike Map*, available at the Globe Corner Bookstore (see p.158 for store info; $4.25 for map), will help you find all the trails and bike-friendly roads in the area.

Taxis

Given Boston's small scale and the efficiency of its public transport, **taxis** aren't as necessary – or as prevalent – as in bigger cities such as New York or London. You can generally hail one along the streets of downtown or Back Bay, though competition gets pretty stiff after 1am, when the subway has stopped running, and bars and clubs begin to close; in this case, go to a hotel, where cabs cluster, or where a bellhop can arrange one for you. In Cambridge, taxis mostly congregate around Harvard Square.

Boston Cab (Ⓣ262-2227) and Bay State Taxi Service (Ⓣ566-5000) have 24-hour service and accept major credit cards. In Cambridge, call the dispatcher (Ⓣ495-8294) for Yellow Cabs or Ambassador Cabs. As a general rule, the rate starts at $1.50 and goes up by 25¢/mile.

Accommodation

For such a popular travel destination, Boston has a surprisingly limited range of well-priced **accommodation**. Though there are still bargains to be found, prices at many formerly moderate **hotels** have inched into the expense-account range. Your best bet is to come offseason, around November through April, when many hotels not only have more vacancies but offer special discounts too. At any other time of year, be sure to make reservations well in advance. September (start of the school year) and June (graduation) are particularly busy months, due to the large student population. Even if Boston's hotels are not suited to every traveler's budget, they do cater to most tastes, and range from the usual assortment of **chains** to some excellent independently run hotels, the best of which, not to mention the highest concentration, are in Back Bay. Most of the business hotels are located in or around the Financial District.

A surprising number of **bed and breakfasts** are tucked into renovated brownstones in Back Bay, Beacon Hill, and the South End, or outside the city in Cambridge and Brookline. The industry is thriving, largely because it is so difficult to find accommodation here for under $100 a night – and many B&Bs offer just that. You can make reservations directly with the places we've listed; there are also numerous B&B **agencies** that can do the booking for you.

Short-term **furnished apartments**, spread throughout the city, are another option; most have two-week minimums. There are also a handful of decent **hostels** if you're looking for real budget accommodation, though definitely book ahead, especially in summer. Hotels and bed and breakfasts are listed below by neighborhood, with hostels listed separately.

Downtown

Boston Marriott Long Wharf 296 State St Ⓣ227-0800 or 1-888/236-2427, Ⓦwww.marriott.com; Aquarium Ⓣ. All the rooms here boast harbor views, but the stunning, vaulted lobby is what really makes this Marriott stand out. 6–7

Harborside Inn 185 State St Ⓣ723-7500, Ⓦwww.hagopianhotels.com; State Ⓣ. This small hotel is housed in a renovated 1890s mercantile warehouse across from Quincy Market; the rooms – with exposed brick, hardwood floors, and cherry furniture – are a welcome surprise for this part of town. 5

Marriott's Customs House 3 McKinley Square Ⓣ310-6300 or 1-888/236-2427, Ⓦwww.marriott.com; Aquarium Ⓣ. All the rooms at this downtown landmark-turned-hotel are high-end, one-bedroom suites with spectacular Boston Harbor and city views. 7

Le Meridien 250 Franklin St Ⓣ451-1900 or 1-800/543-4300, Ⓦwww.lemeridien.com; State Ⓣ. Located in the heart of the Financial District, this stern granite building is the former Federal Reserve Bank of Boston. The rooms are spacious and modern, but the overall atmosphere is a bit stiff. 5–6

Millenium Bostonian Hotel Faneuil Hall Marketplace ⓣ523-3600 or 1-866/866-8086, ⓦwww.milleniumhotels.com; State Ⓣ. Formerly known as the *Regal Bostonian*, this hotel has splendid quarters, some with fireplaces and en-suite balconies, and is located in the heart of downtown. The rooms and lobby are festooned with portraits of famous Colonials. ❻–❼
Milner 78 Charles St S ⓣ426-6220 or 1-877/MIL-NERS, ⓦwww.milner-hotels.com; Boylston Ⓣ. Uninspiring but affordable digs convenient to Bay Village, the Public Garden, and the Theater District. All room rates include a continental breakfast, served in a European-style nook in the lobby. ❹
Omni Parker House 60 School St ⓣ227-8600 or 1-800/843-6664, ⓦwww.omniparkerhouse.com; Park Ⓣ. No one can compete with the *Omni Parker House* in the history department: It's the oldest continuously operating hotel in the US. Though the present building only dates from 1927, the lobby, decorated in dark oak with carved gilt moldings, recalls the splendor of the original nineteenth-century building that once housed it. The rooms are small, however, and a bit dowdy. ❻
Tremont House 275 Tremont St ⓣ426-1400 or 1-800/331-9998, ⓦwww.wyndham.com; NE Medical Center Ⓣ. The opulent lobby of this 1925 hotel, the former national headquarters of the Elks Lodge, somewhat compensates for its smallish rooms; and, if you want to be in the thick of the Theater District you can't do better. ❹–❺
XV Beacon 15 Beacon St ⓣ670-1500 or 1-877/XVB-EACON, ⓦwww.xvbeacon.com; Park St Ⓣ. Luxurious boutique hotel across from the Boston Athenaeum, with 61 spectacular rooms equipped with marble bathrooms, in-room fax, high-speed Internet connection, Kiehl's toiletries, CD player, decadent upholstery, and working gas fireplaces. Room rates include use of a chauffeured Mercedes. ❾

Charlestown

Bed & Breakfast Afloat 28 Constitution Rd ⓣ241-9640, ⓦwww.bostonharbor.com/bb.html; Community College Ⓣ. Guests at this original B&B hole up on a houseboat, sailboat, or yacht, right in Boston Harbor; the fancier vessels come with DVD players and deck-top Jacuzzis. All come with continental breakfast and access to the marina pool. ❸–❾
Constitution Inn YMCA 150 Second Ave ⓣ241-8400 or 1-800/495-9622, ⓦwww.constitution-inn.com. Despite its billing as a YMCA, this inn, from which downtown is but a ferry ride away, has 150 private rooms equipped with cable TV, a/c, and private baths, in addition to an on-site weight-room, sauna, and pool. Though predominantly servicing military personnel, civilians are more than welcome, though they pay significantly more. ❷

Beacon Hill and the West End

Beacon Hill Bed & Breakfast 27 Brimmer St ⓣ523-7376; Charles Ⓣ. Two spacious rooms with fireplaces in a well-situated brick town house, built in 1869. Sumptuous full breakfasts are served in the morning; two-night minimum stay, three on holiday weekends. ❻
Beacon Hill Hotel 25 Charles St ⓣ723-7575 or 1-888/959-BHHB, ⓦwww.beaconhillhotel.com; Charles Ⓣ. A luxurious boutique hotel set in two mid-1800s brownstones; the twelve sleek chambers come with flat-screen televisions and mahogany fireplaces. ❻
Charles Street Inn 94 Charles St ⓣ314-8900, ⓦwww.charlesstreetinn.com; Charles Ⓣ. Intimate inn with rooms styled after the (presumed) tastes of various Boston luminaries; the Isabella Stewart Gardner room features a rococo chandelier, while Oliver Wendell Holmes' staid chamber boasts a king-sized sleigh bed. All rooms come with working fireplaces. ❽–❾
The John Jeffries House 14 David G Mugar Way ⓣ367-1866, ⓦwww.johnjeffrieshouse.com; Charles Ⓣ. Mid-scale hotel at the foot of Beacon Hill, with a cozy lounge and Victorian-style rooms featuring cable TV and air conditioning; single-occupancy studios include kitchenettes. And, though it's wedged in between a busy highway and the local Ⓣ stop, it's not too noisy. ❷
The Shawmut Inn 280 Friend St ⓣ720-5544 or 1-800/350-7784, ⓦwww.shawmutinn.com; North Station Ⓣ. Located in the old West End near the FleetCenter, the inn has 66 comfortable, modern rooms, all of which have kitchenettes. ❹

Back Bay and the South End

463 Beacon Street Guest House 463 Beacon St ⓣ536-1302, ⓦwww.463beacon.com; Hynes Ⓣ. The good-sized rooms in this renovated brownstone, located in the heart of Back Bay, are available by the night, week, or month, and come equipped with kitchenettes, cable TV, and various hotel amenities (though no maid service); some have a/c, hardwood floors, and ornamental fireplaces. Ask for the top-floor room. ❶–❸
82 Chandler Street 82 Chandler St ⓣ482-0408 or 1-888/482-0408, ⓦwww.channel1.com/82chandler; Back Bay Ⓣ. Basic rooms with mini-

mal service in a restored, 1863 brownstone that sits on an up-and-coming street in the South End. ❸–❹

Boston Park Plaza Hotel & Towers 64 Arlington St ⓣ426-2000 or 1-800/225-2008, ⓦwww.bostonparkplaza.com; Arlington Ⓣ. The *Park Plaza* is practically its own neighborhood, housing the original *Legal Sea Foods* restaurant alongside three other eateries, plus offices for American, United, and Delta airlines. Its old-school elegance and hospitality – plus its central location – make it stand out; the high-ceilinged rooms are quite comfortable, too. ❻

Charlesmark Hotel 655 Boylston St ⓣ247-1212, ⓦwww.thecharlesmark.com; Copley Ⓣ. New, 33-room European-style hotel; while the rooms are on the small side, they compensate with cozy beechwood furnishings and modern accoutrements like in-room CD players, VCRs, and dataports. ❺–❻

The Colonnade 120 Huntington Ave ⓣ424-7000 or 1-800/962-3030, ⓦwww.colonnadehotel.com; Prudential Ⓣ. With its beige poured-concrete shell, the *Colonnade* is barely distinguishable from the Church of Christ buildings directly across the street. Still, there are spacious rooms and, in summer, a rooftop pool – the only one in Boston. ❼

Copley Inn 19 Garrison St ⓣ236-0300 or 1-800/232-0306, ⓦwww.copleyinn.com; Prudential Ⓣ. Comfortable rooms with full kitchens, friendly staff, and a great location make this a fine option in the Back Bay. One night free with a week's stay. ❸

Copley Square Hotel 47 Huntington Ave ⓣ536-9000 or 1-800/225-7062, ⓦwww.copleysquarehotel.com; Copley Ⓣ. Situated on the eastern fringe of Copley Square, this family-run, low-key hotel is popular with a European crowd; the rooms won't win any style awards, but they're spacious enough and equipped with modem hookups, cable TV, coffee makers, and the like. ❻

Eliot 370 Commonwealth Ave ⓣ267-1607 or 1-800/442-5468, ⓦwww.eliothotel.com; Hynes Ⓣ. West Back Bay's answer to the *Ritz*, this calm, plush, nine-floor suite hotel has rooms with kitchenettes and luxurious Italian marble baths. ❻–❾

Fairmont Copley Plaza 138 St James Ave ⓣ267-5300 or 1-800/795-3906, ⓦwww.fairmont.com; Copley Ⓣ. Built in 1912 and it shows – from the somewhat severe facade facing Copley Square to the old-fashioned rooms. It does boast Boston's most elegant lobby, and even if you don't stay here, you should at least have a martini in the fabulous *Oak Bar* (see p.148). ❺–❻

Four Seasons 200 Boylston St ⓣ338-4400 or 1-800/332-3442, ⓦwww.fourseasons.com; Arlington Ⓣ. The tops in city accommodation, with 288 rooms offering quiet, contemporary comfort. ❾

The Lenox 710 Boylston St ⓣ536-5300 or 1-800/225-7676, ⓦwww.lenoxhotel.com; Copley Ⓣ. Billed as Boston's version of the *Waldorf-Astoria* when its doors first opened in 1900, *The Lenox* is a far cry from that now, though it's still one of the most comfortably upscale hotels in the city. ❺–❻

Newbury Guest House 261 Newbury St ⓣ437-7666, ⓦwww.hagopianhotels.com; Copley Ⓣ. Big Victorian brownstone with 32 rooms that run the gamut from cramped chambers with overstuffed chairs to spacious bay-windowed quarters with hardwood floors and sleigh beds. Continental breakfast included. ❸–❺

Ritz-Carlton 15 Arlington St ⓣ536-5700 or 1-800/241-3333, ⓦwww.ritzcarlton.com; Arlington Ⓣ. This is the *Ritz-Carlton* flagship, and even if the rooms are a bit cramped, the hotel retains a certain air of refinement, aided by a view overlooking the Public Garden. ❾

Kenmore Square, The Fenway, and Brookline

Beacon Inn 1087 and 1750 Beacon St ⓣ566-0088 or 1-888/575-0088, ⓦwww.beaconinn.com; Hawes Ⓣ. Fireplaces in the lobbies and original woodwork contribute to the relaxed atmosphere in these two nineteenth-century brownstones, part of the same guest house. ❸–❺

Brookline Manor Inn 32 Centre St ⓣ232-0003 or 1-800/535-5325, ⓦwww.beaconmanorinn.com; Coolidge Corner Ⓣ. This small guesthouse, with private and shared baths, is located on a pleasant stretch off Beacon Street; it's just a short subway ride from Kenmore Square. ❶–❸

The Buckminster 645 Beacon St ⓣ236-7050 or 1-800/727-2825, ⓕ617/262-0068; Kenmore Ⓣ. Though renovated not so long ago, the 1905 *Buckminster* retains the feel of an old Boston hotel with its antique furnishings. ❹

Gryphon House 9 Bay State Rd ⓣ375-9003 or 1-877/375-9003, ⓦgryphonhouseboston.com; Kenmore Ⓣ. This hotel-cum-B&B around the corner from Fenway has eight wonderfully appointed suites equipped with working gas fireplaces, cable TV, VCR, CD player, and high-speed Internet connection. Free parking. ❹–❼

Oasis Guest House 22 Edgerly Rd ⓣ267-2262, ⓦwww.oasisgh.com; Symphony Ⓣ. Sixteen comfortable, very affordable rooms, some with shared baths, in a renovated brownstone near Symphony Hall. ❷–❹

Cambridge

A Cambridge B&B 1657 Cambridge St ⓣ868-7082 or 1-877/994-0844, ⓦwww.cambridgebnb

.com; Harvard Ⓣ. This homely Colonial Revival house has three pleasant rooms outfitted with canopy beds, and a common room furnished with over-stuffed chairs and plenty of lace. Shared bath. ❷

A Friendly Inn 1673 Cambridge St ⓣ547-7851; Harvard Ⓣ. A good deal, and just a few minutes' walk from Harvard Square. The rooms are nothing special and the service doesn't exactly live up to the name, but there are private baths, cable TV, and laundry service. ❸–❹

Charles Hotel 1 Bennett St ⓣ864-1200 or 1-800/882-1818, ⓦwww.charleshotel.com; Harvard Ⓣ. Clean, bright rooms – some overlooking the Charles – that have a good array of amenities: cable TV, three phones, minibar, Shaker furniture, and access to the adjacent WellBridge Health Spa. There's also an excellent jazz club, *Regattabar*, and restaurant, *Henrietta's Table*, on the premises – see p.152 and p.145 for reviews. ❺

Harding House 288 Harvard St ⓣ876-2888, ⓦwww.irvinghouse.com; Harvard Ⓣ. This cozy Victorian home has 14 bright rooms with hardwood floors, throw rugs, TVs, and a/c; includes breakfast. Shared or private bath. ❸–❺

Harvard Square Hotel 110 Mt Auburn St ⓣ864-5200 or 1-800/222-8733, ⓦwww.theinnatharvard.com; Harvard Ⓣ. The rooms here are only adequate, but the Harvard Square location is right. ❺–❻

Hotel @ MIT 20 Sidney St ⓣ577-0200 or 1-800/524-2538, ⓦwww.hotelatmit.com; Kendall Square Ⓣ. Contemporary hotel anchoring an office tower near MIT, with a lobby festooned with AI robots created by the university's tech-savvy students; the modern rooms have nice touches like louvered window shades and muted color schemes, and come with high-speed Internet access. ❹

Inn at Harvard 1201 Massachusetts Ave ⓣ491-2222 or 1-800/222-8733, ⓦwww.theinnatharvard.com; Harvard Ⓣ. This carefully constructed hotel is designed to give the impression of old-school grandeur; plus it's so close to Harvard you can smell the ivy. Pleasant but rather small rooms. ❺–❻

Irving House 24 Irving St ⓣ547-4600, ⓦwww.irvinghouse.com; Harvard Ⓣ. A quaint option near Harvard Square sharing the same management as the *Harding House*, with laundry and kitchen facilities; both shared and private baths. ❸–❺

Mary Prentiss Inn 6 Prentiss St ⓣ661-2929, ⓦwww.maryprentissinn.com; Harvard Ⓣ. Eighteen clean, comfortable rooms in a mid-nineteenth-century Greek Revival building. Full breakfast and snacks are served in the living room, or, weather permitting, on a pleasant outdoor deck. ❹–❻

Hostels

There are fairly limited **hostel** accommodations in Boston, and if you want to get in on them, you should definitely book ahead, especially in the summertime.

Beantown Hostel 222 Friend St ⓣ723-0800; North Station Ⓣ. This former bowling alley, next door to the *Irish Embassy Youth Hostel*, has several co-ed and single-sex dorm rooms, plus a comfy lounge with TV and Internet access. 1:45am curfew. $22/dorm bed.

Berkeley Residence YWCA 40 Berkeley St ⓣ375-2524, ⓦwww.ywcaboston.org/berkeley.html; Back Bay Ⓣ. Clean and simple rooms (for women only) next door to a police station. All rates include breakfast; dinner is an additional $6.50. Singles are $50, doubles $70, and triples $75, plus a $2 membership fee.

Greater Boston YMCA 316 Huntington Ave ⓣ927-8040, ⓦwww.ymcaboston.org; Symphony Ⓣ. Good budget rooms, and access to the Y's health facilities (pool, weight room, etc). Singles are $45–65, but you can get a four-person room for $96. Co-ed facilities are available from late June until early September; the rest of the year it's men only. Ten days maximum stay.

HI–Boston 12 Hemenway St ⓣ536-1027, ⓦwww.bostonhostel.org; Hynes Ⓣ. Around the Back Bay–Fenway border, standard dorm accommodation with 3–4 beds per room. Members $29, nonmembers $32.

Irish Embassy Youth Hostel 232 Friend St ⓣ973-4841, ⓕ720-3998; North Station Ⓣ. Boston's only independent youth hostel is above the *Irish Embassy* pub (see p.147) in the West End, and not far from Faneuil Hall. The place can be noisy, but prices include free admission to pub gigs on most nights, and free barbecues on Tuesday and Sunday. $22/dorm bed.

B&B agencies and short-term accommodation

Bed & Breakfast Agency of Boston 47 Commercial Wharf, Boston, MA 02110 ⓣ720-3540 or 1-800/248-9262, UK ⓣ 0800/895 128, ⓦwww.boston-bnbagency.com. Can book you a room in a brownstone, a waterfront loft, or even on a yacht.

Bed & Breakfast Associates Bay Colony PO Box 57166 Babson Park Branch, Boston, MA 02157 ⓣ781/647-4949 or 1-888/486-6018, ⓦwww.bnbboston.com. Features some real finds in Back Bay and the South End.

Bed & Breakfast Reservations PO Box 590264, Newtown Center, MA 02459 ⓣ964-1606 or 1-800/832-2632, ⓦwww.bbreserve.com. Lists B&Bs in Greater Boston, North Shore, and Cape Cod.

Boston Reservations/Boston Bed & Breakfast ⓣ332-4199, ⓦwww.bostonreservations.com. Competitive rates at B&Bs as well as at leading hotels.

Neighborhoods and orientation

Boston is small for an American city, and its tangle of old streets makes it far easier to get around on foot than by car, especially in the city center. Driving is particularly trying these days due to the ongoing "**Big Dig**" highway reconstruction project, wherein Interstate 93, which cuts through the heart of the city, is being put underground. Boston's **downtown** area is situated on a peninsula that juts into Boston Harbor; most of the other neighborhoods branch out south and west from here mainly along the thoroughfares of Washington, Tremont, and Beacon streets.

Downtown really begins with Boston Common, a large public green that holds either on or near its grounds many of the city's major historical sights, including the State House, Old Granary Burying Ground, and Old South Meeting House. Nothing, however, captures the spirit of the city better than downtown's Faneuil Hall, the so-called "Cradle of Liberty," and the always-animated Quincy Market, adjacent to the hall. On the other side of I-93 from the marketplace is the **North End**, which occupies the northeast corner of the peninsula; aside from being the city's Little Italy, it's home to Old North Church and the Paul Revere House. Just across Boston's Inner Harbor is **Charlestown**, the quiet home of the world's oldest commissioned warship, the *USS Constitution*.

North of the Common are the vintage gaslights and red-brick Federalist town houses that line the streets of **Beacon Hill**, the city's most exclusive residential neighborhood. Charles Street runs south along the base of the hill and separates Boston Common from the Public Garden, which marks the beginning of **Back Bay**. This similarly well-heeled neighborhood holds opulent row houses alongside modern landmarks like the John Hancock Tower, New England's tallest skyscraper; appended south of Back Bay is the gay enclave of the **South End**, known for its hip restaurants. The student domains of **Kenmore Square** and **Fenway** are west of Back Bay: the former has some of the area's best nightlife, while the latter is home to the Museum of Fine Arts, the Isabella Stewart Gardner Museum, and Fenway Park. South of all these neighborhoods are Boston's vast **Southern Districts**, which don't hold too much of interest other than some links in Frederick Law Olmsted's series of parks known as the "Emerald Necklace," such as the dazzling Arnold

Arboretum and Franklin Park, home to the city zoo. Across the Charles River from Boston lies **Cambridge**, a must for its excellent bookstore-and-café scene and, above all, the ivy-covered walls of Harvard University.

Downtown Boston

Boston's compact **downtown** encompasses both the colonial heart and contemporary core of the city, an assemblage of red-brick buildings and modern office towers that, if not rivaling the glamour of other American big-city centers, still holds a number of the best reasons for visiting. Quite lively by day, when commuters and tourists create a constant buzz, the streets thin out come nightfall, with a few exceptions: the touristy **Quincy Market** area, which has a decent, if somewhat downmarket, bar scene; **Chinatown**, with its ever-popular restaurants; and the **Theater District**, particularly animated on weekends.

King's Chapel, on Tremont, and the nearby **Old State House** mark the periphery of Boston's earliest town center, where the first church, market, newspaper, and prison were all clustered. **Spring Lane**, a tiny pedestrian passage off Washington Street, recalls the location of one of the bigger springs that lured the earliest settlers over to the Shawmut Peninsula from Charlestown. The most evocative streets, however, are those whose character has been less diluted over the years – **School Street**, **State Street**, and the eighteenth-century enclave known as **Blackstone Block**, near Faneuil Hall.

You can get the flavor of Boston Harbor, once the world's third busiest, along the **waterfront**, now somewhat isolated on account of the elevated John F. Fitzgerald Expressway, a chunk of I-93 that's to be put underground. The **Freedom Trail**, a self-guided walking tour that connects an assortment of historic sights by a line of red bricks embedded in the pavement, begins in **Boston Common**, a king-sized version of the tidy green space at the core of innumerable New England villages. One of the many historic places it passes is the ever-popular meeting place **Faneuil Hall**, not far from the Common. South is the **Financial District**, its short streets still following the tangled patterns of colonial village lanes; west of it is the small but vibrant Chinatown and adjacent Theater District.

Boston Common and around

Boston's premier piazza is **Boston Common**, a fifty-acre chunk of green, neither meticulously manicured nor especially attractive, which effectively separates downtown from the posher Beacon Hill and Back Bay districts. It's the first thing you'll see emerging from the **Park Street Ⓣ station**, the central transfer point of America's first subway and, unfortunately, a magnet for panhandlers. Established in 1634 as "a trayning field" and "for the feeding of Cattell" – so a slate tablet opposite the station recalls – the Common is still primarily utilitarian, used by both pedestrian commuters on their way to downtown's office towers and tourists seeking the **Boston Visitor Information Pavilion** (see p.77), down Tremont Street from the Park Street Ⓣ and the official starting-point of the Freedom Trail. Along the northern side of the Common, the lovely **Beacon Street** runs from the gold-domed State House to Charles Street, opposite the Public Garden.

Even before John Winthrop and his fellow Puritan colonists earmarked Boston Common for public use, it served as pasture land for the Reverend

William Blackstone, Boston's first white settler. Soon after, it disintegrated into little more than a gallows for pirates, alleged witches, and various religious heretics; a commoner by the name of Rachell Whall was once hanged here for stealing a bonnet worth 75¢. Newly elected president George Washington made a much celebrated appearance on the Common in 1789, as did his aide-de-camp, the Marquis de Lafayette, several years later. Ornate eighteenth-century iron fencing encircled the entire park until World War II, when it was taken down for use as scrap metal: it is now said to grace the bottom of Boston Harbor.

One of the few actual sights here is the **Central Burying Ground**, which has occupied the southeast corner of the Common, near the intersection of Boylston and Tremont streets, since 1756. Artist Gilbert Stuart, best known for his portraits of George Washington – the most famous of which is replicated on the dollar bill – died penniless and was interred in Tomb 61. Among the other notables are members of the largest family to take part in the Boston Tea Party, various soldiers of the Revolutionary Army, and Redcoats killed in the Battle of Bunker Hill. From the Burying Ground it's a short walk to **Flagstaff Hill**, the highest point on the Common, crowned with the granite-pillared Civil War **Soldiers and Sailors Monument**, which is topped by a bronze statue of Lady Liberty and surrounded by two cap-wearing sailors and two bayonet-toting foot soldiers. A former repository of colonial gunpowder, the hill overlooks the **Frog Pond**, once home to legions of unusually large amphibians and site of the first water pumped into the city. These days, it's nothing more than a kidney-shaped pool, used for wading in summer and ice-skating in winter. From here, a path leads to the elegant, two-tiered **Brewer Fountain**, an 1868 bronze replica of one from the Paris Exposition of 1855; the scantily clad gods and goddesses at the base are watched over by cherubs from above.

Park Street Church to the Old Granary Burying Ground

The 1809 **Park Street Church**, on the northeast corner of Park and Tremont streets just across from Boston Common (July–Aug daily 9am–3pm, rest of year by appointment; ☎523-3383; free; Park Street Ⓣ), is an oversized and rather uninteresting mass of bricks and mortar, though its ornate 217-foot-tall white telescoping **steeple** is undeniably impressive. To get an idea of the immensity of the building, including the spire, walk to tiny Hamilton Place, across Tremont Street. Its reputation rests not on size but on events that took place inside: this is where William Lloyd Garrison delivered his first public address calling for the nationwide abolition of slavery (Massachusetts had scrapped it in 1783), and where *America* ("My country 'tis of thee . . .") was first sung, on July 4, 1831.

Park Street itself slopes upward from the church along the edge of Boston Common toward the State House (see p.109). It was once known as **Bulfinch Row**, for its many brick town houses designed by the architect Charles Bulfinch (see p.109), but today only one remains, the imposing bay-windowed **Amory-Ticknor House** at no. 9, built in 1804 for George Ticknor, the first publisher of the *Atlantic Monthly* and, unfortunately, closed to the public.

Adjacent to the church is one of the more peaceful stops on the always busy Freedom Trail, the **Old Granary Burying Ground**, last resting place for numerous leaders of the American Revolution. The entrance, an Egyptian Revival arch, fronts Tremont Street, and it's from the Tremont sidewalk that some of the most famous gravesites can be best appreciated: the boulder and plaque commemorating revolutionary **James Otis**; **Samuel Adams**' tomb;

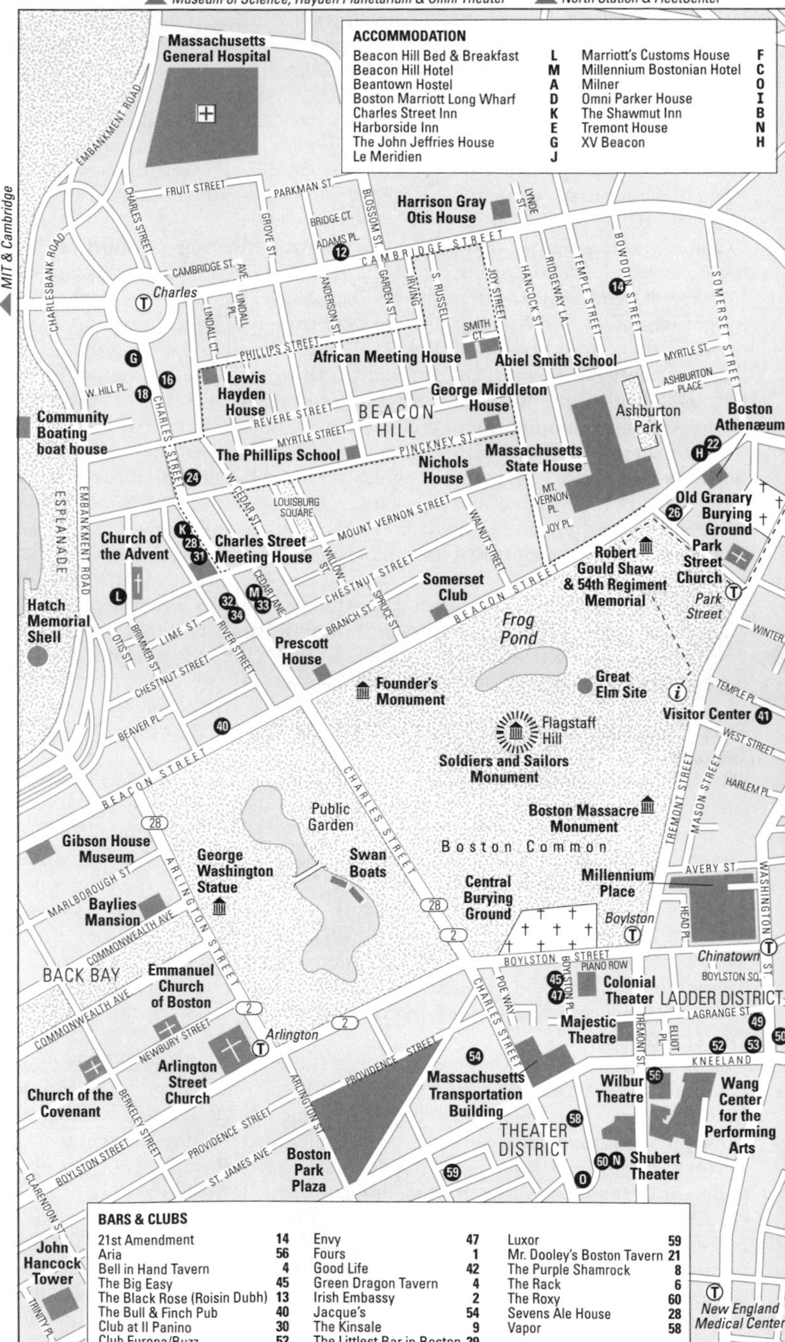
Museum of Science, Hayden Planetarium & Omni Theater
North Station & FleetCenter
MIT & Cambridge
South End
ACCOMMODATION
Beacon Hill Bed & Breakfast L
Beacon Hill Hotel M
Beantown Hostel A
Boston Marriott Long Wharf D
Charles Street Inn K
Harborside Inn E
The John Jeffries House G
Le Meridien J
Marriott's Customs House F
Millennium Bostonian Hotel C
Milner O
Omni Parker House I
The Shawmut Inn B
Tremont House N
XV Beacon H
BARS & CLUBS
21st Amendment 14
Aria 56
Bell in Hand Tavern 4
The Big Easy 45
The Black Rose (Roisin Dubh) 13
The Bull & Finch Pub 40
Club at Il Panino 30
Club Europa/Buzz 52
Envy 47
Fours 1
Good Life 42
Green Dragon Tavern 4
Irish Embassy 2
Jacque's 54
The Kinsale 9
The Littlest Bar in Boston 29
Luxor 59
Mr. Dooley's Boston Tavern 21
The Purple Shamrock 8
The Rack 6
The Roxy 60
Sevens Ale House 28
Vapor 58
Massachusetts General Hospital
Harrison Gray Otis House
Charles
African Meeting House
Abiel Smith School
Lewis Hayden House
George Middleton House
BEACON HILL
Ashburton Park
Boston Athenæum
Community Boating boat house
The Phillips School
Nichols House
Massachusetts State House
Old Granary Burying Ground
Church of the Advent
Charles Street Meeting House
Louisburg Square
Park Street Church
Robert Gould Shaw & 54th Regiment Memorial
Park Street
Hatch Memorial Shell
Somerset Club
Frog Pond
Prescott House
Founder's Monument
Great Elm Site
Visitor Center
Flagstaff Hill
Soldiers and Sailors Monument
ESPLANADE
Public Garden
Boston Massacre Monument
Boston Common
Gibson House Museum
George Washington Statue
Swan Boats
Central Burying Ground
Millennium Place
Boylston
Baylies Mansion
Chinatown
BACK BAY
Emmanuel Church of Boston
Colonial Theater
LADDER DISTRICT
Majestic Theatre
Arlington
Arlington Street Church
Church of the Covenant
Massachusetts Transportation Building
Wilbur Theatre
Wang Center for the Performing Arts
THEATER DISTRICT
Boston Park Plaza
Shubert Theater
John Hancock Tower
New England Medical Center
CAMBRIDGE STREET
BEACON STREET
CHARLES STREET
BOYLSTON STREET
TREMONT STREET
ARLINGTON STREET
COMMONWEALTH AVE.
NEWBURY STREET
PROVIDENCE STREET
ST. JAMES AVE.
MOUNT VERNON STREET
CHESTNUT STREET
PINCKNEY ST.
REVERE STREET
MYRTLE STREET
PHILLIPS STREET
JOY STREET
BOWDOIN STREET
SOMERSET STREET
EMBANKMENT ROAD
CHARLESBANK ROAD
FRUIT STREET
PARKMAN ST.
MARLBOROUGH ST.
BERKELEY STREET
CLARENDON ST.
TRINITY PL.
WASHINGTON ST.
KNEELAND
AVERY ST.
WINTER
TEMPLE PL.
WEST STREET
MASON STREET

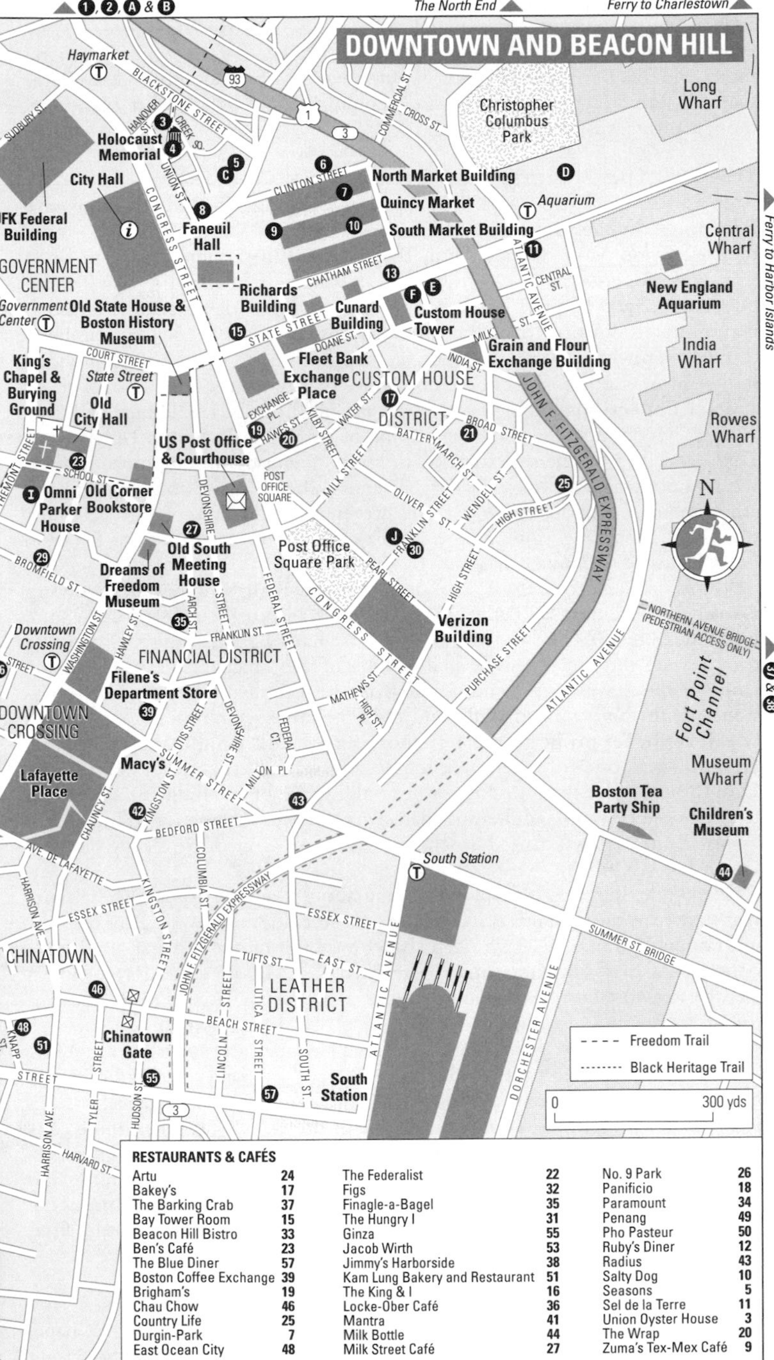

RESTAURANTS & CAFÉS

Artu	24	The Federalist	22	No. 9 Park	26
Bakey's	17	Figs	32	Panificio	18
The Barking Crab	37	Finagle-a-Bagel	35	Paramount	34
Bay Tower Room	15	The Hungry I	31	Penang	49
Beacon Hill Bistro	33	Ginza	55	Pho Pasteur	50
Ben's Café	23	Jacob Wirth	53	Ruby's Diner	12
The Blue Diner	57	Jimmy's Harborside	38	Radius	43
Boston Coffee Exchange	39	Kam Lung Bakery and Restaurant	51	Salty Dog	10
Brigham's	19	The King & I	16	Seasons	5
Chau Chow	46	Locke-Ober Café	36	Sel de la Terre	11
Country Life	25	Mantra	41	Union Oyster House	3
Durgin-Park	7	Milk Bottle	44	The Wrap	20
East Ocean City	48	Milk Street Café	27	Zuma's Tex-Mex Café	9

and the group grave of the five people killed in the **Boston Massacre** of 1770. From any angle inside you can see the stocky **obelisk** at dead center that marks the grave of Benjamin Franklin's parents. Also further inside are **Peter Faneuil**, **Paul Revere**, and, at least according to the pillar, **John Hancock**, though this fact is in some dispute.

The Boston Athenaeum and King's Chapel

Around the block from the Old Granary Burying Ground, the venerable **Boston Athenaeum**, at 10 1/2 Beacon St (Ⓣ227-0270, Ⓦwww.bostonathenaeum.org; Mon 8.30am–8pm, Tue–Fri 8.30am–5.30pm, Sat 9am–4pm; free; Park Street Ⓣ), was established in 1807, and is one of the oldest independent research libraries in the country. In naming their library, the founders demonstrated not only their high-minded classicism but marketing sensibility too, as its growing stature was a potent enough force to endow Boston with a lofty sobriquet – the "Athens of America" – that has stuck. Best known are its **special collections**, including the original holdings of the library of King's Chapel, which included the 1666 edition of Sir Walter Raleigh's *History of the World*, and its prominent **artworks**: an impressive array of sculptures, coupled with paintings by the likes of Sargent and Gilbert Stuart, contribute to the atmosphere of studious refinement. However, unless you're going to go to the trouble of becoming a member, you'll be confined to the first-floor library – not a bad spot to hunker down with a newspaper.

Boston's oldest cemetery, the atmospheric **King's Chapel Burying Ground**, 58 Tremont St (daily: June–Oct 9.30am–4pm; Nov–May 10am–4pm; free; Park Street Ⓣ), not to mention its accompanying church, is well worth a tour despite the din of nearby traffic. One of the chief pleasures of walking amongst the graves is to examine the many beautifully etched ancient tombstones, with their winged skulls and contemplative seraphim, such as that of one **Joseph Tapping**, near the Tremont Street side. King's Chapel Burying Ground was one of the favorite Boston haunts of author **Nathaniel Hawthorne**, who drew inspiration from the grave of a certain Elizabeth Pain to create the famously adulterous character of Hester Prynne for his novel *The Scarlet Letter*. (Hawthorne himself is buried in Concord's Sleepy Hollow Cemetery; see p.171).

Meanwhile, the most conspicuous thing about the gray, foreboding **chapel** that stands on the grounds is its absence of a steeple (there were plans for one, just not enough money). A wooden chapel was built on the site first, amid some controversy. In 1686, King James II revoked the Massachusetts Bay Colony's charter and installed Sir Edmund Andros as governor, giving him orders to found an Anglican parish, a move that for obvious reasons didn't sit too well with Boston's Puritan population. The present chapel was completed in 1749, with the pillar-fronted portico added in 1789, and the belfry boasts the biggest bell ever cast by Paul Revere. Most visitors never go past the entrance, but it is well worth a look inside, ideally during one of the weekly chamber music concerts (Tues 12.15–12.45pm; $2 suggested donation). While hardly ostentatious, the elegant Georgian interior, done up with wooden Corinthian columns and lit by chandeliers, provides a marked contrast to the minimalist adornments of Boston's other old churches. It also features America's oldest pulpit, dating from the late-1600s, and many of its original pews.

Government Center

Most visitors pass through **Government Center**, due north of King's Chapel Burying Ground and west of Faneuil Hall, during their time in Boston, as it's

The Freedom Trail

Boston's history is so visible that the city often stands accused of living in its past, and tourist-friendly contrivances like the **Freedom Trail** only serve to perpetuate the notion. It originated when, like many American cities, Boston experienced an economic slump in the postwar years as people migrated to the suburbs; in response, resident William Schofield came up with the idea of a trail highlighting historic Boston sights to lure visitors – and their money – back into town.

Delineated by a 2.5-mile-long red-brick stripe in the sidewalk, the trail stretches from Boston Common to Charlestown, linking sixteen points "significant in their contribution to this country's struggle for freedom". It's a somewhat vague qualifier that allows for the inclusion of several sights that have little to do with Boston's place in the American Revolution. In the relevant column, there's the Revolutionary-era **Old North Church**, whose lanterns warned of the British arrival (see p.103); **Faneuil Hall**, where opposition to the Brits' proposed tea tax was voiced (see overleaf); the **Old South Meeting House**, wherein word came that said tax would be imposed (see p.97); the **Old State House**, which served as the Boston seat of British government (see p.93); and the site of the **Boston Massacre** (see p.93). Other stops on the trail, however, have nothing whatsoever to do with the struggle for independence, like the **USS Constitution** (see p.105), built fully two decades after the Declaration of Independence (but which failed, notably, to sink under British cannon fire, earning her the nickname "Old Ironsides"); the **Park Street Church** (see p.87), built another fifteen years after that; and the **Old Corner Bookstore** (see p.97), a publishing house for American (and some British) writers. You'll also find two instances of British dominion – the **Bunker Hill Monument** (see p.107), an obelisk commemorating, ironically, a British victory, albeit in the guise of a moral one for America, and **King's Chapel** (see opposite), built to serve the King's men stationed in Boston. Finally, you can check out the digs of the gilt-domed **Massachusetts State House** (see p.109) after visiting the gravesites of the Boston luminaries who fought for it – they lie interred in three separate **cemeteries** (see pp.87, 90 & 103).

Unfortunately, some of the touches intended to accentuate the attractions' appeal move closer to tarnishing it. The people in period costume stationed outside some of the sights can't help but grate a little, and the artificially enhanced atmosphere is exaggerated by the bright-red brick trail and pseudo-old signage that connects the sights. Still, the Freedom Trail remains the easiest way to orient yourself downtown, and is especially useful if you'll only be in Boston for a short time, as it does take in many "must-see" sights. For more info and an interactive timeline of Boston's history, visit Ⓦwww.thefreedomtrail.org. You can also pick up a detailed National Park Service **map** of the trail from the information center in Boston Common.

an essential travel hub located in the midst of the city center – and passing through is just about all there is to do in this sea of towering gray government buildings which stands on the former site of **Scollay Square**, once Boston's most notorious den of porn halls and tattoo parlors. Scollay was razed in the early 1960s, eliminating all traces of its salacious past and its lively character; indeed, the only thing that remains from the Square's steamier days is the Oriental Tea Company's 227-gallon **Steaming Kettle** advertisement. The area is now overlaid with concrete, thanks to an ambitious plan developed by I.M. Pei, and towered over by two monolithic edifices: **Boston City Hall**, at the east side of the plaza, and the **John F. Kennedy Federal Building**, on the north.

Faneuil Hall, Quincy Market, and around

Located between the Financial District and the North End, the **Faneuil Hall Marketplace** is the kind of active, bustling, public gathering ground that's none too common in Boston, popular with locals and tourists alike. Built as a market during colonial times to house the city's growing mercantile industry, it declined during the nineteenth century and, like the area around it, was pretty much defunct until the 1960s, when it was successfully redeveloped as a restaurant and shopping mall.

Much-hyped **Faneuil Hall** (Mon–Sat 10am–9pm, Sun 12–6pm; ⓣ523-1300, ⓦwww.faneuilhallmarketplace.com; State Street Ⓣ) itself doesn't appear particularly majestic from the outside; it's simply a small, four-story brick building topped with a Georgian spire, hardly the grandiose auditorium one might imagine would have housed the Revolutionary War meetings that earned its "Cradle of Liberty" sobriquet. But this was where revolutionary firebrands such as Samuel Adams and James Otis whipped up popular support for independence by protesting British tax legislation on the second-floor meeting space. The first floor now houses a panoply of tourist shops which make for a less than dignified memorial; you'll also find an information desk, a post office, and a BosTix kiosk (see p.154). The second floor is more impressive: the auditorium has been preserved to reflect modifications made by Charles Bulfinch in 1805. Its focal point is a massive – and rather preposterous – canvas depicting an imagined scene in which Daniel Webster speaks in Faneuil Hall to a range of luminaries from Washington to de Tocqueville.

Immediately in front of Faneuil Hall is **Dock Square**, so named for its original location directly on Boston's waterfront; carvings in the pavement indicate the shoreline in 1630. The square's center is dominated by a statue of **Samuel Adams**, interesting mostly for its over-the-top caption: "A Statesman, fearless and incorruptible." A dim, narrow corridor known as Scott's Alley heads north of the market to reach Creek Square, where you enter **Blackstone Street**, the eastern edge of a tiny warren of streets bounded to the west by Union Street. Its uneven cobblestoned streets and low brick buildings have remained largely untouched since the 1650s; many of them, especially those along Union Street, now house restaurants and pubs. The one touch of modernity here is nearby on Union Street, where you'll see six tall hollow glass pillars erected as a **memorial** to victims of the Holocaust. Built to resemble smokestacks, the columns are etched with quotes and facts about the human tragedy – with an unusual degree of attention to its non-Jewish victims. Steam rises from grates beneath each of the pillars to accentuate their symbolism, an effect that's particularly striking at night.

The three oblong markets just behind Faneuil Hall were built in the early eighteenth century to contain the trade that had quickly outgrown its space in the hall. The center building, known as **Quincy Market** (Mon–Sat 10am–9pm, Sun noon–6pm; ⓣ523-1300, ⓦwww.faneuilhallmarketplace.com; State Street Ⓣ), holds a super-extended corridor lined with stands vending a variety of decent though pricey takeout treats – it's the mother of mall food courts. To either side of Quincy Market are **North and South markets**, which hold restaurants and popular chain clothing stores, as well as specialized curiosity shops (one sells only purple objects, another nothing but vests). There's not much to distinguish it from any other shopping complex, save a few good restaurants and some surrounding bars, but sitting on a bench in the carnivalesque heart of it all on a summer day, eating scrod while the mobs of locals and tourists mill about, is a quintessential (if slightly absurd) Boston experience.

Old State House

That the graceful three-tiered window tower of the red-brick **Old State House**, at the corner of Washington and State streets (daily 9am–5pm; $5, children $1; ⓣ720-1713, ⓦwww.bostonhistory.org; State Street Ⓣ), is dwarfed by skyscrapers amplifies, rather than diminishes, its colonial-era dignity. For years this three-story structure was the seat of the Massachusetts Bay Colony, and consequently the center of British authority in New England. Later it served as Boston's city hall, and in 1880 it was nearly demolished so that State Street traffic might flow more freely.

An impassioned speech in the second-floor Council Chamber by James Otis, a Crown appointee who resigned to take up the colonial cause, sparked the quest for independence from Britain fifteen years before it was declared. Legend has it that on certain nights you can still hear Otis hurling his anti-British barbs and the cheers of the crowd he so energized, but the current museum staff has no comment on this. The **balcony** overlooking State Street was the place from which the Declaration of Independence was first read publicly in Boston, on July 18, 1776. Two hundred years later, Queen Elizabeth II – the first British monarch to set foot in Boston – performed the same feat from the balcony as part of the American Bicentennial activities. Inside, a **museum** tracks, through images and artifacts of varying interest, the events that led up to the establishment of the Commonwealth of Massachusetts (though not, curiously, the US), along with Boston's role in the Revolutionary War. Upstairs are rotating exhibits on city history and, somewhat incongruously, a display on old Boston hotels and restaurants.

The waterfront

Stretching from the North End to South Station Ⓣ, Boston's **waterfront** is still a fairly active area, although it's no longer the city's focal point, as it was up until the mid-1800s. Today, the waterfront thrives on tourism, with stands concentrated around **Long Wharf** hawking everything from tacky T-shirts to furry lobsters. Nevertheless, strolling the atmospheric **Harborwalk** that edges the water affords unbeatable views of Boston, and is a pleasant respite from the masses that can clog Faneuil Hall and the Common. You'll also find plenty of diversion, if you've got little ones in tow, as the **Children's Museum** and **Aquarium** are both found here. Otherwise, you can do some waterborne exploring on a number of boat tours, or even escape the city altogether by heading out to the **Harbor Islands**.

The Boston Massacre

Directly in front of the State Street side of the Old State House, a circle of cobblestones embedded in a small traffic island marks the site of the **Boston Massacre**, the tragic outcome of escalating tensions between Bostonians and the British Redcoats that occupied the city. This riot of March 5, 1770, began when a young wigmaker's apprentice began heckling an army officer over a barber's bill. The officer sought refuge in the Custom House, which stood opposite the Old State House at the time, but by this time, a throng of people had gathered, including more soldiers, at whom the mob flung rocks and snowballs. When someone threw a club that knocked a Redcoat onto the ice, he rose and fired. Five Bostonians were killed in the ensuing fracas. Two other patriots, John Adams and Josiah Quincy, actually defended the offending eight soldiers in court; six were acquitted, and the two guilty were branded on their thumbs.

Long Wharf, the New England Aquarium, and around

Long Wharf is the best place to head when hitting the waterfront. Built in 1710, the wharf is still the area's hub of activity. As you might expect, summer is its most active season, when the wharf comes alive with vendors selling kitschy souvenirs and surprisingly good ice cream. This is also the main point of departure for **harbor cruises**, whale-watching trips and ferries to Cape Cod. Walk out to the end of the wharf for an excellent vantage point on **Boston Harbor**. It's perhaps most enjoyable – and still relatively safe – at night, when even the freighters appear graceful against the moonlit water.

Next door to Long Wharf is the waterfront's main draw, the **New England Aquarium**, at Central Wharf (July–Aug Mon, Tues & Fri 9am–6pm, Wed & Thurs 9am–8pm, Sat, Sun & holidays 9am–7pm; Sept–June Mon–Fri 9am–5pm, Sat & Sun 9am–6pm; weekdays $12, kids $6; weekends $13.50, kids $7; CityPass accepted; ⓣ973-5200, ⓦwww.neaq.org; Aquarium Ⓣ). A visit here is most fun for kids, although it's engaging enough for anyone who doesn't set their hopes too high. Currently in the midst of an ambitious expansion, which has already seen the addition of an **IMAX theater** (daily 9.30am–9.30pm; $8, kids $6), the indoor aquarium has plenty of good exhibits, such as the penguins on the bottom floor. Be sure to play with the laser device that maneuvers a red point of light around the bottom of their pool; the guileless waterfowl mistake the light for a fish and follow it around hopefully. In the center of the Aquarium's spiral walkway is an impressive collection of marine life: a three-story, 200,000-gallon cylindrical tank packed with moray eels, sharks, stingrays, and a range of other sea exotica that swim by in unsettling proximity. The Aquarium also runs **whale-watching** trips (April–Oct; 3.5–5hr, call for times; $27, kids $17; ⓣ973-5281).

To the south, moored in the Fort Point Channel alongside the Congress Street bridge, is a replica of the ship raided during the **Boston Tea Party**. The vessel, along with its accompanying museum (ⓣ338-1773, ⓦwww.bostonteapartyship.com), were hit by lightning in August 2001 and have been closed ever since. Spirited re-creations of the Tea Party are still held on occasion here, but don't be taken in: this is not the site of the actual event. It took place on what is today dry land, near the intersection of Atlantic and Congress streets.

The Seaport District and the Children's Museum

It's hard to miss the larger-than-life 1930s-era **Hood Milk Bottle** across the Congress Street bridge in the **Seaport District**, though the only dairy product the 40-foot structure serves is ice cream. In fact, most of its trade is in hot dogs and hamburgers. Behind it, the engaging **Children's Museum**, 300 Congress St (Mon–Thurs, Sat & Sun 10am–5pm, Fri 10am–9pm; $7, kids $6, Fri 5–9pm $1; ⓣ426-8855, ⓦwww.bostonkids.org; South Station Ⓣ), comprises five floors of

The Harborwalk

The **Harborwalk** was conceived as a way to recall Boston's history as a major port, days that seem ever more in the past, especially considering the harbor's notorious recent reputation for pollution. While the sights along the walk don't have the all-star quality of those on the Freedom Trail, it's still a picturesque stroll that provides a historical perspective on the waterfront not otherwise readily evident. Visitor center maps can help steer you on the self-guided walk that starts at the corner of State Street and Merchant's Row, proceeds along the wharves, and ends up on the Congress Street bridge at the Boston Tea Party ship.

△ Boston skyline

educational exhibits, craftily designed to trick kids into learning about a huge array of topics, from kinematics to the history of popular culture. The Seaport District is accessible by a free shuttle from the South Station Ⓣ.

Harbor Islands

Extending across Massachusetts Bay from Salem to Portsmouth, the thirty islands that comprise the bucolic **Harbor Islands** originally served as strategic defense points during the American Revolution and Civil War. It took congressional assent to turn them into a national park, in 1996, with the result that six are now easily accessible by ferry from Long Wharf (see p.94). The most popular and best serviced of the lot, the skipping-stone-shaped **George's Island,** saw heavy use during the Civil War era, as evidenced by the remains of **Fort Warren** (April to mid-Oct, daily dawn–dusk; free), a mid-nineteenth-century battle station covering most of the island. Constructed from hand-hewn granite, and mostly used as a prison for captured Confederate soldiers, its musty barracks and extensive fortress walls have an eerie feel, although the parapets offer some stunning downtown views. You'll get more out of a visit by taking a park ranger tour (free).

The remaining Harbor Islands needn't rank high on your must-see list. The densely wooded and sand-duned **Lovell** is probably your best bet after George's, as it hosts the islands' only life-guarded sand beach. The largest of all, the 134-acre **Peddock**, is laced with hiking trails connecting the remains of Fort Andrews, a harbor defense outpost used from 1904 to 1945, with a freshwater pond and wildlife sanctuary. **Bumpkin**, **Grape**, and **Little Brewster islands** round out the list of accessible stops.

Washington Street shopping district

The **Washington Street shopping district** takes up much of downtown proper, and it holds some of the city's most historic sights – the Old Corner Bookstore, Old South Meeting House, and Old State House – but it tends to shut down after business hours. The stops can be seen in half a day, though you'll need to allow more time if shopping is on your agenda.

Across School Street from King's Chapel is the legendary **Omni Parker House**. It was in this hotel that Boston Creme Pie – really a layered cake with

Island-bound

To visit the Harbor Islands, take the 45-minute ferry ride connecting Long Wharf with central **George's Island** (July–Aug daily on the hour 10am–5pm; May & Sept to mid-Oct daily 10am, noon & 2pm; June daily 10am, noon, 2pm & 4pm; $10, kids $7; Ⓣ227-4321, Ⓦwww.bostonharborcruises.com; Aquarium Ⓣ), the hub from which water taxis (free) shuttle visitors to five of the other thirty islands. You would do well to pack a picnic lunch (best arranged through nearby *Sel de la Terre*, see review p.141), though if you've come without, you can make do on beachfare from George's **snack bar**. If you prefer to forage for your food, you can try berry-picking on Grape and Bumpkin islands. All of the islands lack a freshwater source, so be sure to bring bottled water with you. Note that in the interest of preserving the islands' fragile environment, no bicycles or in-line skates are allowed. You can **camp**, however, for a nominal fee, on four of the islands (May to mid-Oct; Lovell & Peddock Ⓣ727-7676; Bumpkin & Grape Ⓣ1-877/422-6762); you'll need to bring your own supplies. In all cases, good walking shoes are a must, as most of the pathways consist of dirt roads. The Harbor Islands **information** kiosk, at the foot of Long Wharf, keeps a detailed shuttle **schedule** and stocks excellent **maps**.

custard filling and chocolate frosting all around – was concocted in 1855, and the hotel reportedly still bakes 25 of them a day. On a more bizarre note, Ho Chi Minh and Malcolm X each used to wait tables at the hotel's restaurant.

Only one block long, School Street offers up some of the best in Boston charm, beginning with the antique gaslights that flank the severe western wall of King's Chapel. Just beyond is a grand French Second Empire building that served as **Boston City Hall** from 1865 to 1969. A few doors down on the left, the gambrel-roofed, red-brick former **Old Corner Bookstore** anchors the southern end of School Street as it joins Washington. The stretch of Washington from here to Old South Meeting House was nineteenth-century Boston's version of London's Fleet Street, with a convergence of booksellers, publishers, and newspaper headquarters; the bookstore itself – as home to the publishing house of Ticknor & Fields – was the hottest literary salon Boston ever had, with the likes of Emerson, Longfellow, and even Dickens and Thackeray, all of whom Ticknor & Fields published.

Old South Meeting House

Washington Street's big architectural landmark is the **Old South Meeting House**, at 310 Washington St (daily: April–Oct 9.30am–5pm; Nov–March 10am–4pm; $5, kids $1; ⓣ482-6439, ⓦwww.oldsouthmeetinghouse.org; Downtown Crossing Ⓣ), a charming brick church recognizable by its tower, a separate, but attached, structure that tapers into an octagonal spire. An earlier cedarwood structure on the spot burned down in 1711, clearing the way for what is now the second oldest church building in Boston, after Old North Church in the North End. The spacious venue soon saw its share of anti-imperial rhetoric. The day after the Boston Massacre, outraged Bostonians assembled here to demand the removal of the troops that were ostensibly guarding the town. Even more telling was the meeting on December 16, 1773, when nearly seven thousand locals came to await word on whether the Crown would actually impose duty on sixty tons of tea aboard ships in Boston Harbor. When a message was received that it would, Samuel Adams rose and announced, "This meeting can do nothing more to save the country" – the signal that triggered the Boston Tea Party (see p.100).

The Meeting House served as a stable, a British riding-school, and even a bar before becoming the **museum** it is today. One of the things lost in the transition was the famous original high pulpit, which the British tore out during the Revolution and used as firewood; the ornate one standing today is a replica from 1808. There's not much to see other than the building itself – take note of the exterior **clock**, the same one installed in 1770, which you can still set your watch by – but if you take the audio tour, included in the admission price, you will hear campy re-enactments of a Puritan church service and the Boston Tea Party debates, among other more prosaic sound effects.

South of the meeting house, pedestrian-friendly **Downtown Crossing**, centered on the intersection of Washington and Winter streets, brims with department stores and smaller shops that mostly cater to lower-income shoppers. Its nucleus is Filene's Basement, a magnet for bargain hunters of all socioeconomic stripes and the only thing here really worth your time.

Financial District and around

Boston's **Financial District** hardly conjures the same image as those of New York or London, but it continues to wield influence in key areas (such as with mutual funds, invented here in 1925) and is not entirely devoid of historic interest – though this is generally more manifest in plaques rather than actual buildings. Like most of America's business districts, it beats to an office-hours-only schedule, and many of its little eateries and Irish pubs are closed on weekends – though some brave new restaurants are beginning to make inroads. The generally immaculate streets follow the same short, winding paths as they did three hundred years ago, only now, thirty- and forty-story skyscrapers have replaced the wooden houses and churches that used to clutter the area.

The most dramatic approach is east from Washington Street via **Milk Street**. A bust of **Benjamin Franklin** surveys the scene from a recessed Gothic niche above the doorway at 1 Milk St, across from the Old South Meeting House. The site marks Franklin's birthplace, though the building itself only dates from 1874 and now contains the interactive **Dreams of Freedom Museum** (mid-April to Dec daily 10am–6pm; Jan to mid-April Tue–Sat 10am–5pm; $7.50, children $3.50; ⓣ338-6022, ⓦwww.dreamsoffreedom.org; State Street Ⓣ), which extols the virtues of immigration via amusing, and often educational, hands-on displays. Though children are obviously the focus here, adults might enjoy testing their knowledge of American history to see if they, too, could pass the citizenship exam.

A bit farther down Milk Street, at its intersection with Devonshire Street, the somber 22-story **John W. McCormack Federal Courthouse** houses one of Boston's better post offices, with a special section for stamp collectors, though it was an earlier building on this site that gave the adjacent, triangular **Post Office Square** its name. Sneak up to the glass atrium atop the building at **One Post Office Square**; though not really open to the public, it holds jaw-dropping views of Boston Harbor and downtown that make the transgression worth it.

A prime Art Deco specimen is nearby at 185 Franklin St, the head office of telephone company **Verizon**. The step-top building was a 1947 design; more recently the phone booths outside were given a Deco makeover. **Exchange Place**, at 53 State St, is a mirrored-glass tower rising from the facade of the old Boston Stock Exchange; the *Bunch of Grapes* tavern, watering hole of choice for many of Boston's revolutionary rabble-rousers, once stood here. Behind it is tiny **Liberty Square**, once the heart of Tory Boston and now home to an *Aspirations for Liberty* sculpture depicting two rebels upholding each other in honor of the Hungarian anti-Communist uprising of 1956.

The Custom House District

The wedge of downtown between State and Broad streets and the Fitzgerald Expressway is the unfairly overlooked **Custom House District**, dotted with some excellent architectural draws, chief among which is the **Custom House Tower**, surrounded by 32 huge Doric columns. Built in 1847, the thirty-story

Downtown vistas

Whether from in- or out-of-town, people can't seem to get enough of Boston's skyline – its pastiche of brownstone churches and glass-paneled skyscrapers framing Massachusetts Bay ranks among the country's finest. You can check out Boston from every angle by ascending the **Marriot Customs House** (see p.81), **One Post Office Square** (see above), the **Prudential Center** (see p.118), and the **Bunker Hill Monument** (see p.187). The best lay of the land, though, is had from the water – board the **Charlestown ferry** (see p.80) or visit the **Harbor Islands** (see p.96) and watch the city recede.

Greek Revival tower itself was added in 1915. Not surprisingly, it is no longer the tallest skyscraper in New England (a status it held for thirty years), but it still has plenty of character and terrific views – you can check them out from the 360-degree observation deck free of charge (daily 10am–4pm).

Another landmark is the **Grain and Flour Exchange Building**, a block away at 177 Milk St, a fortress-like construction with a turreted, conical roof that recalls the Romanesque Revival style of prominent local architect H.H. Richardson. On **State Street**, which, when it used to extend into Boston Harbor was the focal point of Boston's maritime prosperity, get a look at the elaborate cast-iron facade of the **Richards Building** at no. 114 – a clipper ship company's office in the 1850s – and the **Cunard Building** at no. 126, its ornamental anchors recalling Boston's status as the North American terminus of the first transatlantic steamship mail service.

Chinatown, the Ladder District, and the Leather District

Colorful and authentic, Boston's **Chinatown** lies wedged into just a few square blocks between the Financial and Theater districts, but it makes up in activity what it lacks in size. Lean against a pagoda-topped pay phone on the corner of **Beach and Tyler streets** any time and watch the way life here revolves around the food trade. By day, merchants barter in Mandarin and Cantonese over the going price of produce; by night, Bostonians arrive in droves to nosh in Chinatown's restaurants. Walk down either of those streets – the neighborhood's two liveliest thoroughfares – and you'll pass most of the restaurants, bakeries, and markets, in whose windows you'll see the usual complement of roast ducks hanging from hooks and aquariums filled with future seafood dinners. There's not much else to actually see, though the impressive **Chinatown Gate**, a three-story red-and-gilt monolith guarded by four Fu dogs, overlooks the intersection of Hudson and Beach streets. Chinatown is at its most vibrant during various festivals, none more so than the **Chinese New Year** in late January (sometimes early Feb); at the **Festival of the August Moon**, not surprisingly held in August, there's a bustling street fair. Call the Chinese Merchants Association for more information (Ⓣ482-3972).

The tenor around Washington Street, between Essex and Kneeland, was until recently relatively dodgy. Designated as an "adult entertainment zone" in the 1960s, when it replaced Scollay Square as the city's red light district, and known enigmatically as the Combat Zone, the **Ladder District** was home to a few X-rated theaters and bookshops until trendy restaurants and nightclubs pushed the smut peddlers out. PR hacks successfully renamed the area after its ladderlike layout (Tremont and Washington form the rails, Winter and Avery streets the top and bottom rungs), but failed to alter its daylight character.

Just east of Chinatown are six square blocks, bounded by Kneeland, Atlantic, Essex, and Lincoln streets, that designate the **Leather District**, which takes its name from the days when the shoe industry was a mainstay of the New England economy, and the leather needed to make the shoes was shipped through the warehouses here. Since then, the Financial District – with which it is frequently lumped – has horned in, and the leather industry has pretty much dried up. The distinction between the two areas is actually quite sharp, most evident where High Street transitions into South Street: gleaming modern skyscrapers are replaced by stout brick warehouses, and the place of suited bankers is taken by a melange of merchants and gallery owners, who have taken advantage of the abundance of cheap warehouse space. Some of the edifices

The Boston Tea Party

The first major act of rebellion preceding the Revolutionary War, the **Boston Tea Party** was far greater in significance than it was in duration. On December 20, 1773, a long-standing dispute between the British government and its colonial subjects, involving a tea tax, came to a dramatic head. At nightfall, an angry mob of nearly one thousand, which had been whipped into an anti-British frenzy by Samuel Adams at Old South Meeting House, converged on Griffin's Wharf. Around a hundred of them, some dressed in Indian garb, boarded three brigs and threw their cargo of tea overboard. The partiers disposed of 342 chests of tea each weighing 360 pounds – enough to make 24 million cups, and worth more than one million dollars by today's standards. While it had the semblance of spontaneity, the event was in fact planned beforehand, and the mob was careful not to damage anything but the offending cargo. In any case, the Boston Tea Party transformed protest into revolution; even Governor Hutchinson agreed that afterwards, war was the only recourse. The ensuing British sanctions, colloquially referred to as the "Intolerable Acts," and the colonists' continued resistance, further inflamed the tension between the Crown and its colonies, which eventually exploded at Lexington and Concord several months later.

still have their leather warehouse signs on them, like Boston Hide & Leather Co, 15 East St, and the Fur and Leather Services Outlet, at 717 Atlantic Ave. The nearby **South Street Station** is Boston's main train and bus terminus.

The Theater District

Just south of Boston Common is the slightly seedy **Theater District**, the chief attractions of which are the flamboyant buildings that lend the area its title, such as the Wilbur, Colonial, and Majestic theaters. Not surprisingly, you'll have to purchase tickets in order to inspect their grand old interiors (see p.153), but it's well worth a quick walk along Tremont Street to admire the facades. The **Colonial** – still the grande dame of Boston theater – is just off **Piano Row** – a section of Boylston Street between Charles and Tremont that was the center of American piano manufacturing and music publishing in the nineteenth and early twentieth centuries. There are still a few piano shops around, but the hip restaurants and clubs in the immediate vicinity are of greater interest; many, like *Mistral* (see p.144), are tucked between Charles and Stuart streets around the mammoth **Massachusetts Transportation Building** and cater to the theatergoing crowd.

The North End

The **North End** is a small yet densely populated neighborhood whose narrow streets are chock-a-block with Italian bakeries and restaurants, and also hold some of Boston's most storied sights. Bordered by Boston Harbor and cut off from downtown by the elevated Fitzgerald Expressway (I-93), it may seem an inaccessible district at first, and indeed the protracted dismantling of I-93 can make access a challenge, but you can avoid the hassle – and get a much better sense of the area's attractiveness – by entering from the waterfront Christopher Columbus Park, then taking Richmond Street past quiet North Square to Hanover Street, the North End's main drag, from where you can explore the must-sees fairly quickly.

The North End's detached quality goes back to colonial times, when it was actually an island, later to be joined by short bridges to the main part of town, known then as the South End. Though landfill eventually ended the district's physical isolation, the North End remained very much a place apart. Irish immigrants poured in after the potato famine of 1840, but were just the first of several immigrant groups to settle here, displaced by Eastern European Jews in the 1850s, and southern Italians in the early twentieth century. The latter have for the most part stayed put, and the North End is still Boston's most authentically Italian neighborhood, with its proliferation of bakeries and produce and meat markets. In recent years, however, yuppies have begun to overtake the area's waterfront side and are now making inroads into rehabilitated tenements. You can still see laundry dangling from upper-story windows and grandmothers chattering in Italian in front of their apartment buildings, but it's perhaps only a matter of time before gentrification wins out.

Hanover Street and North Square

Hanover Street has long been the main connection between the North End and the rest of Boston, and it is along here – and its small side streets like Parmenter and Richmond (actually a continuation of each other on either side of Hanover) – that many of the area's trattorias, cafés, and bakeries are located. It's also where you'll find, in its first few blocks, perhaps Boston's most authentically European flavor, though when a CVS drugstore opened here in 1996, it marked the first chain store intruder on the street – and probably not the last.

The little triangular wedge of cobblestones and gaslights known as **North Square**, one block east of Hanover between Prince and Richmond streets, is among the most historic and attractive pockets of Boston, although its actual center is cordoned off by a heavy chain. Here the eateries recede in deference to the **Paul Revere House**, the oldest residential address in the city, at 19 North Square (mid-April to Oct daily 9.30am–5.15pm; Nov to mid-April Tues–Sun 9.30am–4.15pm; $2.50; ⓣ523-2338, ⓦwww.paulreverehouse.org). The small two-story post-and-beam structure, which dates from about 1680, stands on the former site of the considerably grander home of Puritan heavyweight Increase Mather – that one burned down in the Great Fire of 1676. The building, in which Revere lived from 1770 to 1800, was restored in 1908 to reflect its seventeenth-century appearance; prior to that it served variously as a grocery store, tenement, and cigar factory. Though the house is more impressive for its longevity than its appearance, from the outside the second-story overhang and leaded windows providing quite a contrast to the red-brick buildings around it. Examples of Revere's self-made silverware upstairs merit a look, as does a small but evocative exhibit about the mythologizing of Revere's famed horseback ride.

A small courtyard, the focus of which is a glass-encased 900-pound bell that Revere cast, separates the Paul Revere House from the **Pierce/Hichborn House** (tours by appointment only; $2.50; ⓣ523-2338), a simple Georgian-style house built in 1710, making it the oldest surviving **brick house** in Boston. Moses Pierce, a glazier, built the house; it later belonged to Paul Revere's shipbuilding cousin, Nathaniel Hichborn. The interior is typical colonial American – sparsely furnished with some unremarkable period tables, chairs, and a few decorative lamps.

At Hanover's intersection with Clark Street is **St Stephen's Church**, the only still-standing church in Boston built by Charles Bulfinch and one with a striking three-story recessed brick arch entrance. Originally called New North Church, it received its present-day name in 1862, in order to keep up with the

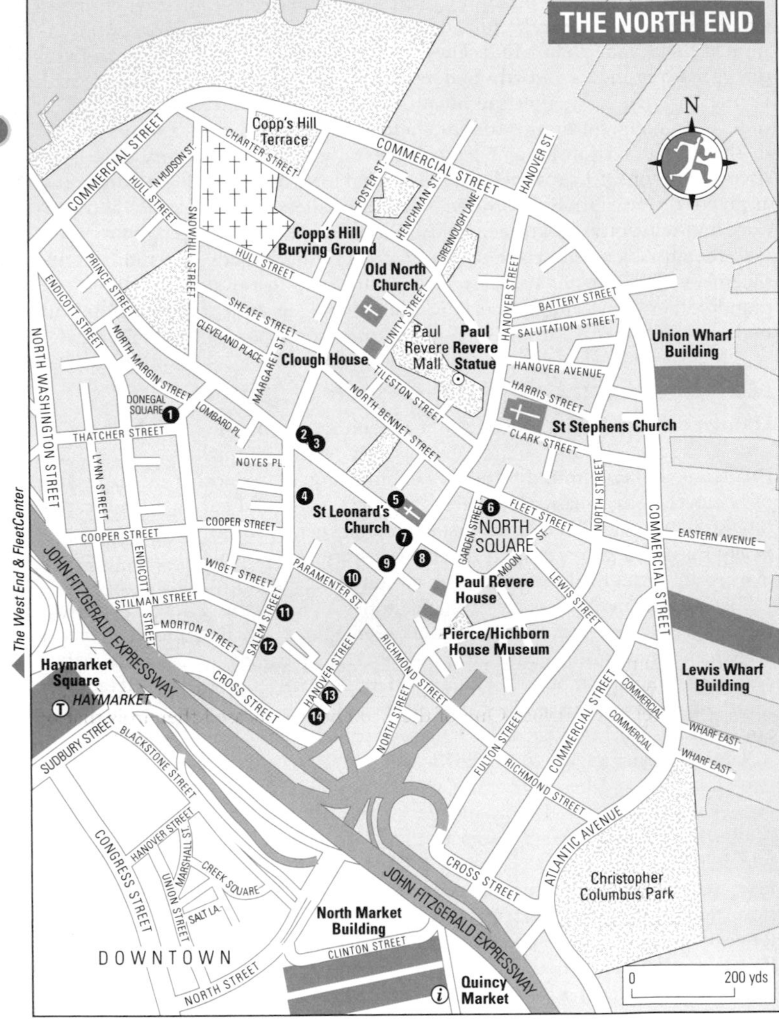

RESTAURANTS & CAFÉS

Assaggio	5	The Daily Catch	8	Marcuccio's	4	Sage	2
Caffé dello Sport	7	Dolce Vita	14	Monica's	3	Trattoria Il Panino	10
Caffé Paradiso	13	Ernesto's	12	Pizzeria Regina	1		
Caffé Vittoria	9	Mama Maria	6	Rabia's	11		

increasingly Catholic population of the North End. Though it seems firmly planted today, the whole building was actually moved back sixteen feet when Hanover Street was widened in 1870.

Just across Hanover, the famous bronze **statue** of Paul Revere astride his borrowed horse marks the edge of the **Paul Revere Mall**, a cobblestoned park space known as the Prado. This much-needed open space was carved out of a chunk of apartment blocks in 1933 and runs back to tiny **Unity Street** – home of the small 1712 red-brick **Clough House**, at no. 21, a private residence built by the mason who helped lay the brick of the nearby Old North Church.

Old North Church

Were it not for **Old North Church**, 93 Salem St (daily: June–Oct 9am–6pm; Nov–May 9am–5pm; free; Ⓦ www.oldnorth.com), as a sign affixed to a collection box just inside its entrance reads, "You Might be Making Donations in Pound Notes." Few places in Boston have as emblematic a quality as the simple yet noble Christ Church (as Old North is officially called), rising unobstructed above the monotonous blocks of red-brick apartments around it. Built in 1723, it's the oldest church in Boston, easily recognized by its gleaming 191-foot **steeple**, which is actually a replica – hurricanes toppled both the original in 1804 and its first replacement in 1954 (the weather vane, however, is the original). What secured its place in history were the two lanterns that church sexton Robert Newman is said to have hung inside it on the night of April 18, 1775, to signal the movement of British forces "by sea" from Boston Common, which then bordered the Charles River. That steeple is clearly visible from Charlestown across the water and even from the other side of I-93, lending a certain credence to its reputation as a watch and signal tower. Still, some historians speculate that the lanterns were actually hung from another church, also called Old North, which occupied the North Square spot where the **Sacred Heart Italian Church** now stands, at no. 12; that irate Tories burned that one for firewood in 1776 adds fuel to the theory. In any case, the spotlessly white interior contains the oldest clock still ticking in an American public building, made in 1726. The timber on which the high box pews rest is supported by 37 basement-level brick crypts. One of the 1100 bodies encased therein is that of John Pitcairn, the British major killed in the Battle of Bunker Hill. His remains were tagged for Westminster Abbey, but didn't quite make it.

On your way out, the quirky **souvenir shop** is worth a stop if only for a look at some of its not-for-sale items, such as a vial of Boston Tea Party tea and the bellringers' contract that Paul Revere signed as a mere lad in 1750. Some of Old North's greatest charms are actually outside the church itself, notably the diminutive Washington Memorial Garden, the brick walls of which are bedecked with commemorative plaques honoring past church members, and the inviting Eighteenth Century Garden.

Copp's Hill Burying Ground

Up Hull Street from Old North Church, atmospheric **Copp's Hill Burying Ground** (daily dawn–dusk), with its eerily tilting slate tombstones and stunning harbor views, holds the highest ground in the North End. Among the ten thousand interred are nearly a thousand men who had lived in the "New Guinea Community," a long-vanished colonial enclave of free blacks at the foot of the hill. The most famous gravesite here is that of the Mather family, just inside the wrought-iron gates on the Charter Street side. Increase Mather and son Cotton – the latter a Salem Witch Trial judge – were big players in Boston's early days of Puritan theocracy, a fact not at all reflected in the rather diminutive, if appropriately plain, brick vault tomb. You'll notice that many gravestones have chunks missing, the consequence of British soldiers using them for target practice during the 1775 Siege of Boston. The grave of one Captain Daniel Malcolm, toward the left end of the third row of gravestones as you enter the grounds, bears particularly strong evidence of this: three musketball marks scar his epitaph, which refers to him as a "true son of liberty" and "enemy of oppression."

The granite **Copp's Hill Terrace**, a plateau separated from the burial ground by Charter Street, was the place from which British cannons bombarded Charlestown during the Battle of Bunker Hill. In 1919, a 2.3-million-gallon tank of molasses exploded nearby, creating a syrupy tidal wave fifteen feet high that engulfed entire buildings and drowned 21 people along with a score of horses. Old North Enders claim you can still catch a whiff of the stuff on an exceptionally hot day.

Across the street from Copp's Hill is Boston's **narrowest house**, at 44 Hull St. It really *is* narrow – 9 1/2 feet wide – and that's about it, as it's a private residence and you can't go in.

Salem and Prince streets

While the Old North Church is **Salem Street**'s star attraction, in the lower blocks between Prince and Cross streets, Salem is arguably the North End's most colorful thoroughfare. The actual street – whose name is a bastardization of "Shalom Street," as it was known to the earlier European Jewish settlers – is so narrow that the red-brick buildings seem to lean into one another, and light traffic makes it a common practice to walk right down the middle of the road. Traveling south, an agreeable onslaught of Italian grocers, aromatic *pasticcerias* and cafés begins at Salem's intersection with Prince; above this point the street is primarily residential. At the southern end, as soon as you traverse Cross Street (which snakes alongside the construction to I-93), the Naples-like bustle ends.

Serpentine **Prince Street** cuts through the heart of the North End on an east–west axis, linking Salem and Hanover streets. Like most in the neighborhood, this appealing artery also has its share of restaurants, but it tends to be more social – locals typically pass the day along the pavement here on folding chairs brought from home. At the corner of Hanover Street, **St Leonard's Church**, 14 N Bennet St (Ⓣ523-2110), was supposedly the first Italian Catholic church in New England. The ornate interior is a marked contrast to Boston's stark Protestant churches, while the so-called "Peace Garden" in front, with its prosaic plantings and tacky statuary, is – in a sense – vintage North End.

Charlestown

Charlestown, across Boston Harbor via Charlestown Bridge from the North End, is a largely Irish working-class neighborhood that's quite isolated from the city, despite its annexation more than a century ago. Its historic core of quiet streets and elegant row houses is now all but surrounded by elevated highways and construction projects, though you won't have to worry much about the inelegant surroundings if you arrive on one of the trolley tours – or even better, by the short $1 ferry trip from Long Wharf to the Charlestown Navy Yard.

The earliest Puritan settlers had high hopes for developing Charlestown when they arrived in 1629, but an unsuitable water supply pushed them over to the Shawmut Peninsula, which they promptly renamed Boston. Charlestown grew slowly after that, and had to be completely rebuilt after the British burned it down in 1775. The mid-1800s witnessed the arrival of the so-called "lace-curtain Irish," somewhat better off than their North End brethren, and the district remains an Irish one at heart. The longtime locals, known as "townies," have acquired a reputation for being standoffish, due to instances such as their resistance to school desegregation in the 1970s. Recent years have seen urban professionals practically take over the Federal- and Colonial-style town homes south of the **Bunker Hill Monument** – Charlestown's other big sight – much to the chagrin of the townies. The rest of the neighborhood is fairly nondescript and even somewhat dodgy in parts.

The USS Constitution ("Old Ironsides")

The sprawling **Charlestown Navy Yard** was one of the first and busiest US naval shipyards – riveting together an astounding 46 destroyer escorts in 1943 alone – though it owes most of its present-day liveliness to being home to the frigate **USS Constitution** (late May to Oct daily 10am–4pm; Nov to late May Thurs–Sun 10am–4pm; free; Ⓦ www.ussconstitution.navy.mil), at Constitution Wharf. In 1974 the Yard became part of the Boston National Historical Park after President Nixon decommissioned it, and since then it has been ambitiously repurposed as marinas, upscale condos, and offices. But its focal point remains the *USS Constitution*, the oldest commissioned warship afloat in the world. Launched two centuries ago to safeguard American merchant vessels from Barbary pirates and the French and British navies, she earned her nickname during the War of 1812, when cannonballs fired from the British *HMS Guerrière* bounced off the hull (the "iron sides" were actually hewn from live oak, a particularly sturdy wood from the southeastern US), leading to the first and most dramatic naval conquest of that war. The ship went on to win more than forty battles before it was retired from service in 1830.

Authentic enough in appearance, the *Constitution* has certainly taken its hits – roughly ninety percent of the ship has been reconstructed. Even after extensive renovations, though, Old Ironsides is still too frail to support sails for extended periods of time, and the only regular voyages it makes are annual Fourth of July turnarounds in Boston Harbor. There's often a line to visit the ship – especially in the summer – but it's worth the wait to get a close-up view of the elaborate rigging that can support some three dozen sails totaling almost an acre in area. After ambling about the main deck, scuttle down to the lower deck, where you'll find an impressive array of cannons. Though most of the ship's 54 cannons are replicas, two functional models face downtown from the bow from where they mark mast-raising and -lowering daily. Were they to fire the 24-pound balls for which they were originally outfitted, they'd topple the Customs House tower across the bay in downtown Boston.

The rest of Charlestown Navy Yard

Housed in a substantial granite building a short walk from Old Ironsides and across from Pier 1, the **USS Constitution Museum** (daily: May to mid-Oct 9am–6pm; mid-Oct to April 10am–5pm; free; Ⓦ www.ussconstitutionmuseum.org), is worth visiting before you board the ship. One especially evocative display consists of curios which sailors acquired during a two-year round-the-world diplomatic mission begun in 1844; these are creatively arranged under a forest of faux palm fronds. Among the souvenirs are wooden carved toys from Zanzibar, a chameleon from Madagascar preserved in a glass jar, and a Malaysian model ship made of cloves. The highlight upstairs is an infectiously fun wooden "deck," replete with sail and spinning helm, that rocks back and forth according to where you throw your weight.

Berthed in between Old Ironsides and the ferry to Long Wharf is the hulking gray mass of the World War II destroyer **USS Cassin Young** (daily: June–Oct

10am–5pm; Nov–May 10am–4pm; free). You're free to stride about the expansive main deck and check out some of the cramped chambers below, but it's mostly of interest to World War Two history buffs. At the northern perimeter of the Navy Yard is the **Ropewalk building**. For years "ropewalkers" made all the cordage for the US Navy in this narrow, quarter-mile-long granite building, the only one of its kind still standing in the country; unfortunately it's not open to the public.

City Square to Bunker Hill Monument

Toward Charlestown's center, there's a wealth of eighteenth- and nineteenth-century town houses, many of which you'll pass on your way from the Navy Yard to the Bunker Hill Monument. John Harvard, the young English minister whose library and funds launched Harvard University after his death, lived in Charlestown and left a legacy of street names here: directly behind **City Square** – a traffic circle anchored by one of Boston's most popular restaurants, *Olives* (see p.142) – Harvard Street curves through the small **Town Hill** district, site of Charlestown's first settled community. You'll also find Harvard Mall and adjacent Harvard Square (not to be confused with the one in Cambridge), both lined with well-preserved homes.

Just up Main Street is the atmospheric **Warren Tavern**, at no. 105, a small three-story wooden structure built soon after the British burned Charlestown in the Battle of Bunker Hill, and named for Dr. Joseph Warren, killed in

The Battle of Bunker Hill

The Revolutionary War was at its bloodiest on the hot June day when British and colonial forces clashed in Charlestown. In the wake of the battles at Lexington and Concord two months before, the British had assumed full control of Boston, while the patriots had the upper hand in the surrounding counties. The British, under the command of generals Thomas Gage and "Gentleman Johnny" Burgoyne, intended to sweep the countryside clean of "rebellious rascals." Americans intercepted the plans and moved to fortify Bunker Hill, the dominant hill in Charlestown. However, when Colonel William Prescott arrived on the scene, he chose to occupy Breed's Hill instead, either due to confusion – the two hills were often confused on colonial-era maps – or tactical foresight, based on the proximity of Breed's Hill to the harbor. Whatever the motivation, more than a thousand citizen-soldiers arrived during the night of June 16, 1775, and fortified the hill with a 160-foot-long earthen redoubt by morning.

Spotting the Yankee fort, the Redcoats, each carrying 125 pounds of food and supplies on their backs, rowed across the harbor to take the rebel-held town. On the patriots' side, Colonel Prescott had issued his celebrated order to his troops that they not fire "'til you see the whites of their eyes," such was their limited store of gunpowder. When the enemy's approach was deemed near enough, the patriots opened fire; though vastly outnumbered, they successfully repelled two full-fledged assaults. Some British units lost more than ninety percent of their men, and what few officers survived had to push their men forward with their swords to make them fight on. By the third British assault, the Redcoats had shed their gear, reinforcements had arrived, and the Americans' supply of gunpowder was dwindling – as were their chances of clinching victory. The rebels continued to fight with stones and musket butts; meanwhile, British cannonfire from Copp's Hill in the North End was turning Charlestown into an inferno. Despite the eventual American loss, the battle did much to persuade the patriots – and the British, who lost nearly half of their men who fought in this battle – that continued armed resistance made independence inevitable.

combat. From the tavern, crooked Devens Street to the south and Cordis Street to the north are packed with historic, private houses; the most imposing is the Greek Revival mansion at **33 Cordis Street**. West on Main Street, the landmark **Five Cents Savings Bank Building**, with its steep mansard roof and Victorian Gothic ornamentation, looms above the street-level convenience stores. Further west is the **Phipps Street Burying Ground**, which dates from 1630. While many Revolutionary soldiers are buried here, it's not part of the Freedom Trail – perhaps even more of a reason to make the detour.

Double back and head up Monument Avenue, toward the Bunker Hill Monument. The red-brick town houses that you'll pass are some of the most eagerly sought residences in town. Nearby is **Winthrop Square**, Charlestown's unofficial common, just south of the monument. The prim rowhouses overlooking it form another upscale enclave.

Bunker Hill Monument

Commemorating the Battle of Bunker Hill is the **Bunker Hill Monument** (daily 9am–4.30pm; free), a gray, dagger-like obelisk that's visible from just about anywhere in Charlestown, thanks to its position atop a butte confusingly known as Breed's Hill (see box). It was here that revolutionary troops positioned themselves on the night of June 16, 1775, to wage what was ultimately a losing battle – despite its recasting by US historians as a great moral victory in the fight for independence. The tower is centrally positioned in **Monument Square** and fronted by a statue of Colonel William Prescott; at its base is a lodge that houses some decent dioramas of the battle. Inside, 294 steps wind up the 221-foot granite shaft to the top; hardy climbers will be rewarded with sweeping views of Boston, the harbor, and surrounding towns – and, to the northwest, the stone spire of the **St Francis de Sales Church**, which stands atop the real Bunker Hill.

Beacon Hill and the West End

No visit to Boston would be complete without an afternoon spent tootling around delightful **Beacon Hill**, a dignified stack of red brick rising over the north side of Boston Common. This is the Boston of wealth and privilege, one-time home to numerous historical and literary figures – including John Hancock, John Quincy Adams, Louisa May Alcott, and Oliver Wendell Holmes – and still the address of choice for the city's elite. Its narrow, hilly byways are lit with gaslights and lined with quaint, nineteenth-century-style town houses, all part of an enforced preservation that prohibits modern buildings, architectural innovations, or anything else to disturb the carefully cultivated atmosphere of urban gentility.

It was not always this way. In colonial times, Beacon Hill was the most prominent of three peaks known as the Trimountain which formed Boston's geological backbone. The sunny south slope was developed into prime real estate and quickly settled by the city's political and economic powers, while the north slope was closer in spirit to the **West End**, a tumbledown port district populated by free blacks and immigrants; indeed, the north slope was home to so much salacious activity that outraged Brahmins termed it "Mount Whoredom." By the end of the twentieth century, this social divide was almost entirely eradicated, though today it can still be seen in the somewhat shabbier homes north of Pinckney Street and in the tendency of members of polite society to refer to the south slope as "the good side." Still, both sides have much to offer, if of very different character: on the south slope, there's the grandiose **Massachusetts State House**, attractive boulevards like **Charles Street** and the **Beacon Street Promenade**, in addition to the residences of past and present luminaries. More down-to-earth are the north slope's **Black Heritage Trail** sights, such as the **African Meeting House**, and some vestiges of the old West End.

Beacon Street

Running along the south slope of Beacon Hill above the Common, **Beacon Street** was described as Boston's "sunny street for the sifted few" by Oliver Wendell Holmes in the late nineteenth century. This lofty character remains today: the row of stately brick town houses, fronted by ornate iron grillwork, presides regally over the area. The story behind the **purple panes** in some of their windows – most visible at nos. 63 and 64 – evinces the street's long association with Boston wealth and privilege. When the panes were installed in some of the first Beacon Street mansions, they turned purple upon exposure to the sun, due to an excess of manganese in the glass. At first, their owners perceived the purple panes as nothing more than an irritating accident, but due to their prevalence in the windows of Boston's most prestigious houses, they eventually came to be perceived as the definitive Beacon Hill status symbol by subsequent generations – in fact, some residents have gone so far as to shade their windows purple in imitation.

While it lacks the purple-tinted panes, the elegant bowfronted 1808 **Prescott House**, at no. 55 (May–Oct Wed, Thurs & Sat 12–4pm, tours every 30mins; $4; ⓣ742-3190, ⓦwww.nscda.org/ma; Park St ⓣ), is nevertheless the only house on Beacon Street with public access to its inner chambers. Designed by an understudy of Charles Bulfinch, the house's most distinguished inhabitant was Spanish historian and Harvard professor William Hickling Prescott, whose family occupied its five floors from 1845 to 1859. Hung above the pastiche of Federalist and Victorian furniture inside are two crossed swords belonging to Colonel William Prescott and British Captain John Linzee – the professor's and his wife's respective grandfathers. The men fought against each other at Bunker Hill (see p.106), and the sight of their munitions here inspired William Thackeray, a frequent house visitor, to write his novel, *The Virginians*.

Across the street, the **Founder's Monument** commemorates Boston's first European settler, William Blackstone, a Cambridge-educated loner who moved from England with his entire library to a piece of wilderness he acquired for next to nothing from the Shawmut Indians – the site of present-day Boston. A stone bas-relief depicts the apocryphal moment in 1630 when Blackstone sold most of his acreage to a group of Puritans from Charlestown.

Back on the north side of Beacon Street, and a few steps past Spruce Court, is the last of a trio of **Charles Bulfinch** (see box opposite) houses commissioned by lawyer and future Boston mayor Harrison Gray Otis over a ten-year period; the four-story Classical house has been home to the American Meteorological Society since 1958. Just east of here, it's hard to miss the twin-swelled granite building at no. 42–43, built for Colonel David Sears' family by Alexander Parris of Quincy market fame (see p.92). Its stern Greek Revival facade has welcomed members of the exclusive **Somerset Club** since 1872, a club so elitist that when a fire broke out in the kitchen, the firemen who arrived were ordered to come in via the cumbersome servants' entrance, a heavy iron-studded portal.

Farther up the street, on the edge of the Commons facing the Massachusetts State House, is the majestic monument honoring **Robert Gould Shaw and the 54th Massachusetts Regiment**. The memorial commemorates America's first all-black company to fight in the Civil War, a group led by Shaw, scion of a moneyed Boston Brahmin clan. Isolated from the rest of the Union army, given the worst of the military's resources, and saddled with menial or terribly dangerous assignments, the regiment performed its service bravely; most of its members, including Shaw, were killed in a failed attempt to take Fort Wagner from the Confederates. Augustus Saint-Gaudens' 1897 high-relief bronze sculpture depicts the regiment's farewell march down Beacon Street, and the names of the soldiers who died in action are listed on its reverse side (though these were belatedly added in 1982). Robert Lowell won a Pulitzer Prize for his poem, *For the Union Dead*, about this monument; the regiment's story was also depicted in the film *Glory*.

Massachusetts State House

Across from the memorial rises the large gilt dome of the Charles Bulfinch-designed **Massachusetts State House** (Mon–Fri 10am–4pm, last tour at 3.15pm; free; Park Street Ⓣ), the scale and grandeur of which recall the heady spirit of the then newly independent America in which it was built. Though only three stories tall, it seems taller sitting at the confluence of the steep grade of Park and Beacon streets. Of the current structure, only the central section was part of Bulfinch's original design; the huge wings jutting out toward the street on either side and the section extending up Bowdoin Street behind the State House were all added much later. An all-star team of Revolution-era luminaries contributed to its construction: built on land donated by John Hancock, its cornerstone was laid by Samuel Adams, and the copper for its dome was rolled in Paul Revere's foundry (though it was covered over with gold leaf in the 1870s).

Once inside the labyrinthine interior, make your way up one flight and proceed to the central hallway, the only section of any real interest to visitors and the easiest to navigate. The best section is the sober and impressive **Hall of Flags**, a circular room surrounded by tall columns of Siena marble, displaying original flags carried by Massachusetts soldiers into battle and lit by a vaulted stained-glass window bearing the state seal. On the third floor, the carved wooden fish known as the **Sacred Cod** hangs above the Senate chambers. The

The architecture of Charles Bulfinch

America's foremost architect of the late eighteenth and early nineteenth centuries, **Charles Bulfinch** developed a distinctive style somewhere between Federal and Classical that remains Boston's most recognizable architectural motif. Mixing Neoclassical training with New England practicality, Bulfinch built residences characterized by their rectilinear brick structure and pillared porticoes – examples remain throughout Beacon Hill, most notably at 87 Mount Vernon St and 45 Beacon St. Although most of his work was residential, Bulfinch, in fact, made his name with the design of various government buildings, such as the 1805 renovation of **Faneuil Hall** and, more significantly, the **Massachusetts State House**, whose dome influenced the design of state capital buildings nationwide. His talents extended to urban planning as well, including the layout of Boston's **South End**, and an area known as Tontine Crescent, a half-ellipse crescent planned around a small park that won Bulfinch praise but ruined him financially; what vestiges remain are found around the Financial District's Franklin and Arch streets.

senators take this symbol of maritime prosperity so seriously that when it was stolen by Harvard pranksters in the 1930s, they shut down the government until it was recovered.

Behind the State House, on Bowdoin Street, lies pleasant, grassy **Ashburton Park**, centered on a pillar that is a replica of a 1789 Bulfinch work. The column indicates the hill's original summit, which was sixty feet higher and topped by a 65ft post with the makeshift warning light – constructed from an iron pot filled with combustibles – that gave Beacon Hill its name.

Nichols House

To the left of the State House, up the slope of Joy Street, and a few steps eastward along Mount Vernon Street, at no. 55, is the only Beacon Hill residence open to the public year-round, the **Nichols House** (May–Oct Tues–Sat 12.15–4.15pm; Nov–Dec & Feb–April Mon & Thurs–Sat noon–4.15pm, tours start fifteen minutes past the hour; $5; ⓣ227-2993; Park Street Ⓣ). It's yet another Bulfinch design, and was most recently the home of eccentric spinster Rose Standish Nichols, who counted among her allegiances Fabian Socialism and the International Society of Pen Pals. She lived in the house until her death in the early 1960s, and left it to the public as a museum rather than bequeathing it to her greedy relatives. Crowded with a patchwork of post-Victorian period pieces, the interior isn't too gripping unless you have an abiding interest in antique furnishings; best go to get some perspective on the interior life of overstuffed leisure led by Beacon Hill's moneyed elite.

Louisburg Square and around

Farther down the street, between Mount Vernon and Pinckney streets, **Louisburg Square** forms the gilded geographic heart of Beacon Hill. The central lawn, surrounded by wrought-iron fencing and flanked by statues of Columbus and Aristides the Just, is owned by local residents, making it the city's only private square. On either side of this oblong green space are rows of stately brick town houses, though the square's distinction is due less to its architectural character than to its long history of illustrious residents and the sense of elite civic parochialism that has made this Boston's most coveted address. Among those to call the area home were novelist Louisa May Alcott and members of the illustrious Vanderbilt family.

Just below Louisburg Square, between Willow and West Cedar streets, narrow **Acorn Street** still has its original early nineteenth-century cobblestones. Barely wide enough for a car to pass through, it was originally built as a minor byway to be lined with servants' residences. Locals have always clung to it as the epitome of Beacon Hill quaint; in the 1960s, residents permitted the city to tear up the street to install sewer pipes only after exacting the promise that every cobblestone would be replaced in its original location. One more block down, **Chestnut Street** features some of the most intricate facades in Boston, particularly Bulfinch's **Swan Houses**, at nos. 13, 15, and 17, with their recessed arches and marble columns, and touches like scrolled door knockers and wrought iron lace balconies.

Smith Court and the African Meeting House

The north side of the slope, across Pinckney Street, is keyed by **Smith Court**, once the center of Boston's substantial pre-Civil War black community when the north slope was still a low-rent district, and now home to a few stops on Boston's Black Heritage Trail (see box opposite). Free blacks, who were not permitted

The Black Heritage Trail

In 1783, Massachusetts became the first state to declare slavery illegal, partly as a result of black participation in the Revolutionary War. Not long after, a large community of free blacks and escaped slaves sprang up in the North End and Beacon Hill. Very few blacks live in either place today, but the **Black Heritage Trail** traces Beacon Hill's key role in local and national black history – and is the most important historical site in America devoted to pre-Civil War African-American history and culture. Starting from the **Robert Gould Shaw Memorial**, the 1.6-mile loop takes in fourteen historical sights, detailed in a useful **guide** available at the African Meeting House and at the information center in Boston Common. Much of what there is to see, however, is quite ho-hum on its own; the best way to experience the trail is by taking a National Park Service **walking tour** (late May to early Sept Mon–Sat 10am, noon & 2pm; Sept–June call to reserve; free; ⓣ742-5415, Ⓦwww.nps.gov/boaf; Park Street Ⓣ.

to participate in Boston's civic and religious life, worshiped and held political meetings in what became known as the **African Meeting House**, at 8 Smith Court (July–Aug daily 10am–4pm; Sept–June Mon–Sat 10am–4pm; donation requested; Ⓦwww.afroammuseum.org; Park Street Ⓣ). Informally called the Black Faneuil Hall, the meeting house grew into a center for abolitionist activism: in 1832, William Lloyd Garrison founded the New England Anti-Slavery Society here. Today, it houses the **Museum of Afro-American History**, which, considering its site, is rather a disappointment. You won't find much in the way of displays, only a rotating exhibit on the first floor – usually contemporary African-American art – and the meeting house on the second, which has been restored to look like the most basic of churches it once was.

At the end of Smith Court, you can walk along part of the old Underground Railroad used to protect escaped slaves, who once ducked into the doors along narrow **Holmes Alley** that were left open by sympathizers to the abolitionist cause. The **Abiel Smith School**, at 46 Joy St (July–Aug daily 10am–4pm; Sept–June Mon–Sat 10am–4pm; donation requested), built in 1834, was the first public educational institution established for black schoolchildren in Boston. It now showcases exhibits for the Museum of Afro-American History; check out "Separate Schools, Unequal Education," which traces, as the name indicates, the history of racial inequality in the American school system.

Charles Street and the Esplanade

Back towards the river, **Charles Street** is the commercial center of Beacon Hill, lined with scores of restaurants, antique shops, and pricey specialty boutiques. A jaunt just off Charles down **Mount Vernon Street** brings you past some of Beacon Hill's most beautiful buildings, none of which you can enter, including the Federal-style **Charles Street Meeting House**, at the corner of the two streets, now repurposed as an office building, and the vegetation-enshrouded Victorian Gothic **Church of the Advent**, at Mount Vernon's intersection with Brimmer Street.

Connected to Charles Street at its north end by a footbridge and spanning nine miles along the Charles River, the **Esplanade** is yet another of Boston's well-manicured public spaces, with the requisite playgrounds, landscaped hills, lakes, and bridges. The stretch alongside Beacon Hill is the nicest, providing a picturesque way to appreciate the Hill from a distance as well as a popular spot for jogging and blading on summer days. Just below the Longfellow Bridge (which connects to Cambridge) is the Community Boating Center, the point of departure for sailing, kayaking, and windsurfing outings on the Charles (daily: April–Oct 9am–5pm; two-day visitor's pass $50; ⓣ523-1038, ⓦwww.community-boating.org). The white half-dome rising from the riverbank along the Esplanade is the **Hatch Shell**, a public performance space best known for its Fourth of July celebration, which features a free concert by the Boston Pops, a pared-down version of the Boston Symphony Orchestra. Free movies and jazz concerts occur almost nightly in summer (ⓣ727-9547 or ⓦwww.state.ma.us/mdc for schedules and events; Charles Ⓣ).

The West End

North of Cambridge Street, the tidy rows of town houses give way to a more urban spread of office buildings and old brick structures, signaling the start of the **West End**. Once Boston's main port of entry for immigrants and transient sailors, this area has seen its lively character pretty much disappear. A vestige of the old West End manages to remain in the small tangle of byways behind the high-rise buildings of **Massachusetts General Hospital**, where you'll see urban warehouses interspersed with Irish bars, some of which swell to a fever pitch after Celtic basketball and Bruin hockey games. Those games take place at the nearby **FleetCenter**, 150 Causeway St (tours daily at 11am, 1pm & 3pm; $5), the slick, corporate-named arena built next to the legendary Boston Garden.

Back along Cambridge Street, at no. 141, the brick **Harrison Gray Otis House** (Wed–Sun 11am–5pm, tours hourly; $5; ⓣ227-3956, ⓦwww.spnea.org; Charles Ⓣ), originally built for the wealthy Otis family in 1796, sits incongruously among mini-malls and office buildings. Its first two floors have been painstakingly restored – from the bright wallpaper right down to the silverware sets – in the often loud hues of the Federal style.

Situated on a bridge over the Charles, Boston's **Museum of Science** (July to early Sept Mon–Thurs, Sat & Sun 9am–7pm, Fri 9am–9pm; Sept–June Mon–Thurs, Sat & Sun 9am–5pm, Fri 9am–9pm; $12, $9 kids; CityPass accepted; ⓣ723-2500, ⓦwww.mos.org; Science Park Ⓣ) consists of several floors of interactive, though often well-worn, exhibits illustrating basic principles of natural and physical science. The best exhibit is the Theater of Electricity in the Blue Wing, a darkened room full of optical illusions and glowing displays on the presence of electricity in everyday life. Containing the world's largest Van de Graaf generator, the theater puts on daily electricity shows in which simulated lightning bolts flash and crackle around the space.

Back Bay and the South End

Back Bay, a meticulously planned neighborhood where elegant, angular, tree-lined streets form a pedestrian-friendly area that looks much as it did in the nineteenth century, right down to the original gaslights and brick sidewalks, is Boston at its most cosmopolitan. A youthful population helps offset stodginess and keeps the district, which begins at the **Public Garden**, buzzing with chic eateries, trendy shops, and the aura of affluence that goes along with both. Its other main draw is its trove of Gilded Age row houses, specifically their exquisite architectural details; there really is no end to the fanciful bay windows and ornamental turrets. On its southern border, the sprawl of the **South End** offers

From swamp to swank: the building of Back Bay

The fashioning of **Back Bay** occurred in response to a shortage of living space in Boston. An increasingly cramped Beacon Hill prompted developers to revisit a failed dam project on the Charles River, which had made a swamp of much of the area. **Arthur Gilman** manned the huge landfill project, which began in 1857. Taking his cue from the grand boulevards of Paris, Gilman decided on an orderly street pattern extending east to west from the Public Garden, itself sculpted from swampland two decades before. By 1890, the cramped peninsula of old Boston was flanked by 450 new acres, on which stood a range of churches, town houses, and schools. You'll notice that, with a few exceptions, the brownstones get fancier the farther from the Garden you go, a result of architects and those who employed them trying to one-up each other. The exteriors of most of the buildings remain unaltered, although visually that's as far as you usually get, unless the place has been converted into a shop, salon, or gourmet eatery; in that case, step inside and hang onto your wallet.

another impressive, if less opulent, collection of Victorian architecture, alongside some of Boston's more inventive restaurants.

Starting with the side closest to the Charles River, the east–west thoroughfares of Back Bay are **Beacon** and **Marlborough** streets, **Commonwealth Avenue**, and **Newbury** and **Boylston** streets. These are transected by eight shorter streets, so fastidiously laid out that not only are their names in alphabetical order, but trisyllables are deliberately intercut by disyllables: Arlington, Berkeley, Clarendon, Dartmouth, Exeter, Fairfield, Gloucester, and Hereford, until you get to Massachusetts Avenue. Generally, the grandest town houses are found on Beacon Street and Commonwealth Avenue, though Marlborough, in between the two, is more atmospheric; Boylston and Newbury are the main commercial drags. In the middle of it all is a small green space, **Copley Square**, surrounded by the area's main sights: **Trinity Church**, the imposing **Boston Public Library**, and the city's classic skyscraper, the **John Hancock Tower**.

The Public Garden

The value of property in Boston typically goes up the closer its proximity to the lovingly maintained **Public Garden**, a 24-acre park first earmarked for public use in 1859. Of the garden's 125 types of trees, many identified by little brass placards, most impressive are the weeping willows which ring the picturesque man-made **lagoon**, around which you can take a fifteen-minute ride in one of six **swan boats** (April to late June daily 10am–4pm; late June to early Sept daily 10am–5pm; early to mid-Sept Mon–Fri noon–4pm, Sat–Sun 10am–4pm; $2; ⓦwww.swanboats.com). There's often a line to hop on board – instead of waiting, you can get just as good a perspective on the park from the tiny **suspension bridge** that crosses the lagoon. The park's other big family draw is the cluster of bronze bird sculptures collectively called **Mrs Mallard and Her Eight Ducklings**, installed to commemorate Robert McClosky's 1941 children's tale *Make Way for Ducklings*, which was set in the Public Garden. Of the many statues and monuments throughout the park, the oldest and oddest is the thirty-foot-tall **Good Samaritan** monument, a granite and red-marble column that is a tribute to, of all things, the anesthetic qualities of ether; controversy as to which of two Boston men invented the wonder drug led Oliver Wendell Holmes to dub it the "Either Monument." Finally, a dignified equestrian statue of **George Washington**, installed in 1869 and his first likeness astride a horse, watches over the Garden's Commonwealth Avenue entrance.

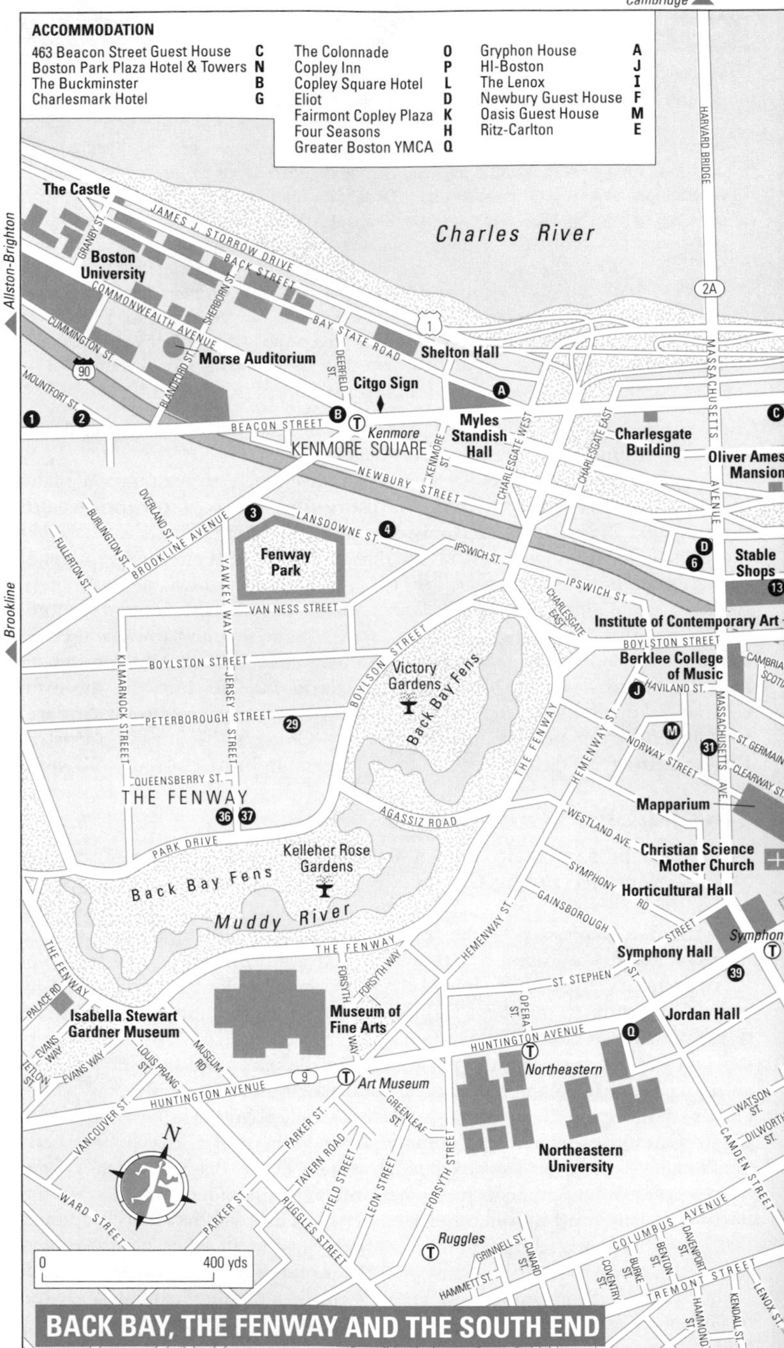
ACCOMMODATION
463 Beacon Street Guest House C
Boston Park Plaza Hotel & Towers N
The Buckminster B
Charlesmark Hotel G
The Colonnade O
Copley Inn P
Copley Square Hotel L
Eliot D
Fairmont Copley Plaza K
Four Seasons H
Greater Boston YMCA Q
Gryphon House A
HI-Boston J
The Lenox I
Newbury Guest House F
Oasis Guest House M
Ritz-Carlton E
Cambridge
Allston-Brighton
Brookline
Charles River
The Castle
Boston University
James J. Storrow Drive
Back Street
Bay State Road
Commonwealth Avenue
Cummington St.
Mountfort St.
Granby St.
Sherborn St.
Blandford St.
Deerfield St.
Morse Auditorium
Shelton Hall
Citgo Sign
Myles Standish Hall
Beacon Street
Kenmore
Kenmore Square
Kenmore St.
Newbury Street
Charlesgate West
Charlesgate East
Charlesgate Building
Oliver Ames Mansion
Harvard Bridge
Massachusetts Avenue
Lansdowne St.
Ipswich St.
Fenway Park
Brookline Avenue
Overland St.
Burlington St.
Fullerton St.
Yawkey Way
Van Ness Street
Stable Shops
Institute of Contemporary Art
Boylston Street
Berklee College of Music
Haviland St.
Cambria
Victory Gardens
Back Bay Fens
Kilmarnock Street
Jersey Street
Peterborough Street
Queensberry St.
The Fenway
Hemenway St.
Norway Street
St. Germain
Clearway St.
Mapparium
Agassiz Road
Park Drive
Westland Ave.
Christian Science Mother Church
Symphony Rd
Horticultural Hall
Gainsborough Street
Kelleher Rose Gardens
Muddy River
Symphony
Symphony Hall
Forsyth Way
St. Stephen St.
Jordan Hall
Opera St.
Huntington Avenue
Northeastern
Palace Rd
Isabella Stewart Gardner Museum
Museum of Fine Arts
Museum Rd
Louis Prang St.
Evans Way
Tetlow St.
Art Museum
Vancouver St.
Parker St.
Greenleaf St.
Forsyth Street
Northeastern University
Watson St.
Dilworth St.
Camden Street
Tavern Road
Field Street
Leon Street
Ruggles Street
Ward Street
Ruggles
Grinnell St.
Cunard St.
Hammett St.
Columbus Avenue
Coventry St.
Burke St.
Benton St.
Davenport St.
Tremont Street
Hammond St.
Kendall St.
Lenox St.
N
0
400 yds
BACK BAY, THE FENWAY AND THE SOUTH END

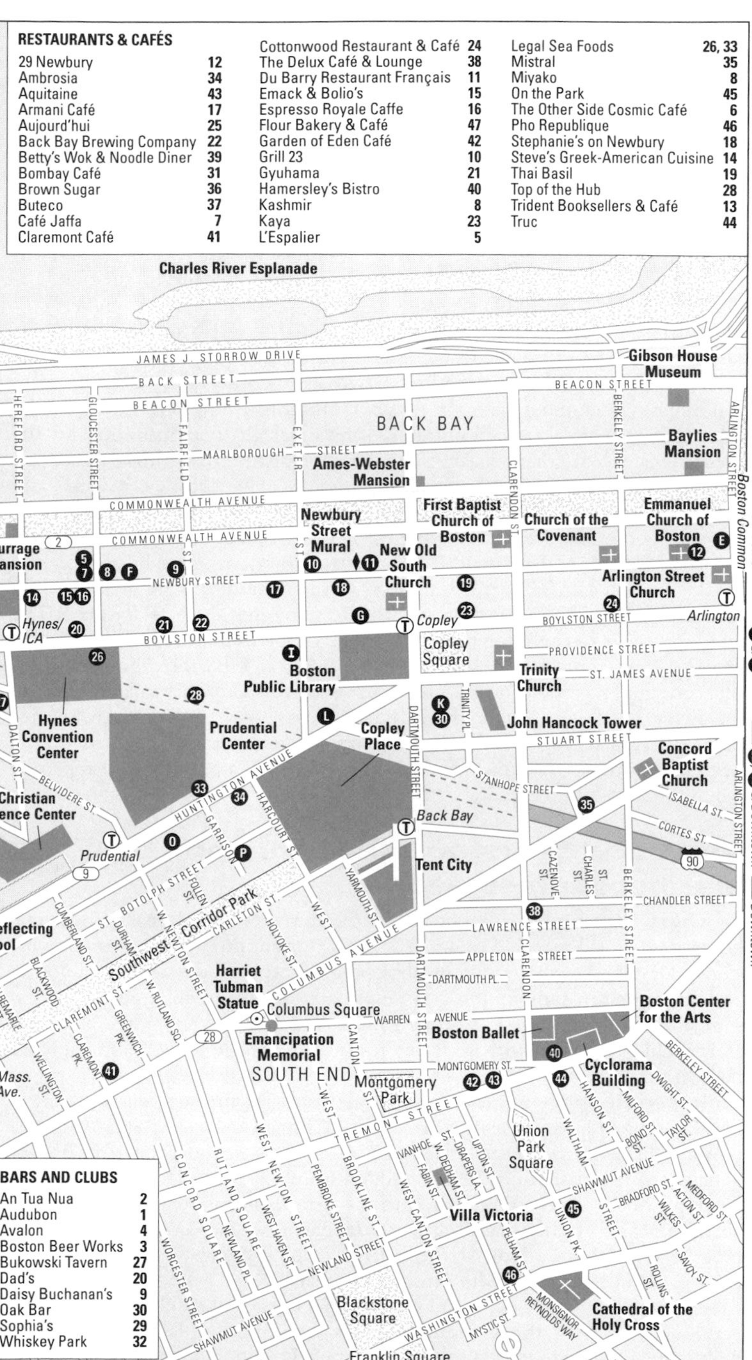
RESTAURANTS & CAFÉS
29 Newbury 12
Ambrosia 34
Aquitaine 43
Armani Café 17
Aujourd'hui 25
Back Bay Brewing Company 22
Betty's Wok & Noodle Diner 39
Bombay Café 31
Brown Sugar 36
Buteco 37
Café Jaffa 7
Claremont Café 41
Cottonwood Restaurant & Café 24
The Delux Café & Lounge 38
Du Barry Restaurant Français 11
Emack & Bolio's 15
Espresso Royale Caffe 16
Flour Bakery & Café 47
Garden of Eden Café 42
Grill 23 10
Gyuhama 21
Hamersley's Bistro 40
Kashmir 8
Kaya 23
L'Espalier 5
Legal Sea Foods 26, 33
Mistral 35
Miyako 8
On the Park 45
The Other Side Cosmic Café 6
Pho Republique 46
Stephanie's on Newbury 18
Steve's Greek-American Cuisine 14
Thai Basil 19
Top of the Hub 28
Trident Booksellers & Café 13
Truc 44
Charles River Esplanade
JAMES J. STORROW DRIVE
BACK STREET
BEACON STREET
BACK BAY
Gibson House Museum
Baylies Mansion
Ames-Webster Mansion
MARLBOROUGH STREET
COMMONWEALTH AVENUE
NEWBURY STREET
BOYLSTON STREET
HEREFORD STREET
GLOUCESTER STREET
FAIRFIELD ST.
EXETER ST.
CLARENDON ST.
BERKELEY STREET
ARLINGTON STREET
Burrage Mansion
Newbury Street Mural
First Baptist Church of Boston
Church of the Covenant
Emmanuel Church of Boston
New Old South Church
Arlington Street Church
Hynes/ICA
Copley
Arlington
Copley Square
Trinity Church
PROVIDENCE STREET
ST. JAMES AVENUE
Boston Public Library
Prudential Center
Hynes Convention Center
Copley Place
John Hancock Tower
STUART STREET
TRINITY PL.
DARTMOUTH STREET
DALTON ST.
BELVIDERE ST.
Christian Science Center
HUNTINGTON AVENUE
Prudential
Back Bay
STANHOPE STREET
Concord Baptist Church
ISABELLA ST.
CORTES ST.
Tent City
GARRISON
HARCOURT ST.
YARMOUTH ST.
CAZENOVE ST.
CHARLES ST.
CHANDLER STREET
LAWRENCE STREET
APPLETON STREET
DARTMOUTH PL.
Reflecting Pool
BOTOLPH STREET
Southwest Corridor Park
CARLETON ST.
HOLYOKE ST.
W. NEWTON STREET
COLUMBUS AVENUE
Harriet Tubman Statue
Columbus Square
WARREN AVENUE
Boston Ballet
Boston Center for the Arts
Emancipation Memorial
SOUTH END
Mass. Ave.
Montgomery Park
MONTGOMERY ST.
Cyclorama Building
TREMONT STREET
Union Park Square
SHAWMUT AVENUE
Villa Victoria
WEST CANTON STREET
BROOKLINE ST.
PEMBROKE STREET
WEST NEWTON STREET
RUTLAND SQUARE
CONCORD SQUARE
WORCESTER STREET
NEWLAND STREET
Blackstone Square
WASHINGTON STREET
Franklin Square
Cathedral of the Holy Cross
MONSIGNOR REYNOLDS WAY
BARS AND CLUBS
An Tua Nua 2
Audubon 1
Avalon 4
Boston Beer Works 3
Bukowski Tavern 27
Dad's 20
Daisy Buchanan's 9
Oak Bar 30
Sophia's 29
Whiskey Park 32
Beacon Hill
Public Garden & Boston Common
25 & H
32, N & Downtown
Downtown
47
Roxbury

Commonwealth Avenue

The garden leads into the tree-lined median of **Commonwealth Avenue**, the 220-foot-wide showcase street of Back Bay. The mall forms the first link in Frederick Law Olmsted's so-called **Emerald Necklace**, which begins at Boston Common and extends all the way to the Arnold Arboretum in Jamaica Plain. "Comm Ave," as locals ignobly call it, is at its prettiest in early May, when the magnolia and dogwood trees are in full bloom.

On the street proper, the **Baylies Mansion**, at no. 5, now houses the Boston Center for Adult Education, so feel free to slip inside for a look at the opulent ballroom Baylies built expressly for his daughter's coming-out (in the old-fashioned sense) party. You'll have to be content to see the **Ames-Webster Mansion**, a few blocks down at the corner of Dartmouth Street, from the outside. Built in 1872 for railroad tycoon, Massachusetts governor, and US congressman Frederick Ames, it features a two-story conservatory, central tower, and imposing chimney. Farther down Commonwealth, at no. 314, is the **Burrage House**, a fanciful synthesis of Vanderbilt-style mansion and the French chateau of Chenonceaux. The exterior of this 1899 urban palace is a riot of gargoyles and carved cherubim; inside it's less riotous – it serves as a retirement home.

Rising above the avenue, at no. 110, is the landmark belfry of the **First Baptist Church of Boston** (Mon–Fri 10am–4pm), designed by architect H. H. Richardson in 1872 for a Unitarian congregation, though at bill-paying time only a Baptist congregation was able to pony up the necessary funds. The puddingstone exterior is topped off by a 176-foot **bell tower**, which is covered by four gorgeous friezes by Frederic-Auguste Bartholdi, of Statue of Liberty fame, a product of his friendship with Richardson that developed at the Ecole des Beaux Arts in Paris. Richardson's lofty plans for the interior never materialized, again for lack of money, but its high ceiling, exposed timbers, and Norman-style rose windows are still worth a peek if you happen by when someone's in the church office.

Newbury, Boylston, Beacon, and Marlborough streets

Newbury Street takes in eight blocks of alternately traditional and eclectic boutiques, art galleries, and designer spas, all tucked into Victorian-era brownstones. Despite the encroachment of big chain stores and the occasional nod to pretentiousness in some of the cafés, especially, it remains an atmospheric and suprisingly inviting place to wander round. And not all is shopping: Newbury and neighboring **Boylston** are home to most of the old schools and churches built in the Back Bay area.

In fact, right on the corner of Boylston and Arlington streets is Back Bay's first building, the squat **Arlington Street Church** (Mon–Fri 10am–5pm), a minor Italianesque masterpiece designed in 1861 by Arthur Gilman; its host of Tiffany stained-glass windows were added from 1895 to 1930. A block down is the prison-like **New England Mutual Life building**, with some national chains on the first floor that do little for its character. However, it's worth nipping inside to have a look at the **murals**, which depict such historic local events as Paul Revere sounding his famous alarm.

Back on the first block of Newbury Street itself, the full-blown Gothic Revival **Church of the Covenant** boasts a soaring steeple and thirty-foot-high stained-glass windows, also from Tiffany's. The church's chapel houses one of Boston's biggest contemporary art spaces in the form of the Gallery NAGA (Tues–Sat 10am–5.30pm; ⓣ267-9060, ⓦwww.gallerynaga.com). Designed as an architect's house, the medieval flight-of-fancy at **109 Newbury St** is arguably more arresting for its two donjon towers than the Cole-Haan footwear inside. A block down at **275 Dartmouth** is the Rodier Paris boutique, but again the burnt sienna-colored building with mock battlements hunkered over it steals the show: originally the *Hotel Victoria* in 1886, it looks like a combination Venetian–Moorish castle, not a bad place to have your in-town condo. A block west, on the exposed side of no. 159, is the **Newbury Street Mural**, a fanciful tribute to a hodgepodge of notables from Sam Adams to Sammy Davis, Jr. A key to who's who is affixed to the parking attendant's booth in the lot next to it. Housed in a Romanesque-style police and fire station built in 1886, half of which Back Bay's firefighters still call home, the **Institute of Contemporary Art**, 955 Boylston St (Wed & Fri–Sun noon–5pm, Thurs noon–9pm; $7, free Thurs 5–9pm; ⓣ266-5152, ⓦwww.icaboston.org), is Boston's main venue for modern art, with no permanent collections.

As a continuation of Beacon Hill's stately main thoroughfare, **Beacon Street** was long the province of blueblood Bostonians. It is the Back Bay street closest to the Charles River, yet its buildings turn their back to it, principally because in the nineteenth century the river was a stinking mess. On the first block of the Back Bay portion of Beacon, at no. 137, is the only house museum in the neighborhood, the **Gibson House Museum** (Wed–Sun 1–3pm, tours hourly; $5; ⓣ267-6338, ⓦwww.thegibsonhouse.org). Built in 1860, this standard-issue Back Bay town house has been more or less preserved as it was, with an almost complete lack of sunlight and a host of Victoriana that includes a still-functioning dumbwaiter, antique globes, and writing paraphernalia (one of the Gibsons was apparently a travel writer), and gilt-framed photos of long-gone relatives of the long-gone Bostonian Catherine Hammond Gibson.

Sandwiched between Beacon Street and Commonwealth Avenue is quiet **Marlborough Street**, which with its brick sidewalks and vintage gaslights is one of the most prized residential locales in Boston, after Louisburg Square in Beacon Hill and the first few blocks of Commonwealth Avenue. Even though the town houses here tend to be smaller than elsewhere in Back Bay, they display a surprising range of stylistic variation, especially on the blocks between Clarendon and Fairfield streets. The final block, which links Massachusetts Avenue to Charlesgate East, is the only street in Back Bay proper that curves.

Copley Square and around

Bounded by Boylston, Clarendon, Dartmouth, and St James streets, **Copley Square** is the busy commercial center of Back Bay. The square itself is a relatively nondescript grassy expanse, but its periphery holds quite a bit of interest.

In his meticulous attention to detail – from the polychromatic masonry on the outside to the rather generic stained-glass windows within – Boston architect H.H. Richardson seemed to overlook the big picture for his 1877 **Trinity Church**, 206 Clarendon St (daily 8am–6pm; $3; ⓦwww.trinityboston.org), which, as one 1923 guidebook averred, "is not beautiful" – despite the reaction of the critics at the time, who dubbed it a masterpiece of Romanesque Revivalism. Skip the rather spartan interior, which feels more empty than awe-inspiring unless, of course, you happen to be there on Friday at 12.15pm, in which case there are often free organ recitals. Indeed, the most interesting aspect of Trinity Church, hulking exterior and all, is probably its juxtaposition to the John Hancock Tower, in whose mirrored panes it's reflected.

A decidedly secular building anchors the end of Copley Square opposite Trinity Church, in the form of the **Boston Public Library** (Mon–Thurs 9am–9pm, Fri & Sat 9am–5pm; ⓣ536-5400, ⓦwww.bpl.org) – the largest public research library in New England, and the first one in America to actually permit the borrowing of books. Architects McKim, Mead & White built the Italian Renaissance Revival structure in 1852; the massive inner bronze doors were designed by Daniel Chester French (sculptor of the Lincoln Memorial in Washington DC). Inside, check out the imposing **Bates Reading Room**, with its barrel-vaulted ceiling and dark oak paneling. The library's most remarkable aspect is tucked away on the top floor, however, where the darkly lit **Sargent Hall** is covered with more than fifteen astonishing murals painted by John Singer Sargent between 1890 and 1916, entitled the *Triumph of Religion*. After viewing, you can take a breather in the library's open-air central **courtyard**, modeled after that of the Palazzo della Chancelleria in Rome.

Just opposite the Boston Public Library, on the corner of Boylston and Dartmouth streets, is one of Boston's most attractive buildings, the **New Old South Church**, 645 Boylston St (Mon–Fri 9am–5pm), a name to which there is actually some logic: the congregation in residence at downtown's Old South Meeting House (and church) outgrew it and decamped here in 1875. You need not be a student of architecture to be won over by the Italian Gothic design, most pronounced in the ornate, 220-foot bell tower – a 1937 addition – and copper-roof lantern, replete with metallic gargoyles in the shape of dragons. Its interior is an alluring assemblage of dark woods set against a forest-green backdrop, coupled with fifteenth-century English-style stained-glass windows.

At 62 stories, the **John Hancock Tower**, at 200 Clarendon St, is the tallest building in America north of New York City, and in a way Boston's signature skyscraper – first loathed, now loved, and taking on startlingly different appearances all depending on your vantage point. In Back Bay, the characteristically angular edifice is often barely perceptible, due to designer I.M. Pei's deft understatement in deference to adjacent Trinity Church and the old brownstones nearby. From Beacon Hill, it appears broad-shouldered and stocky; from the South End, taller than it really is; from across the Charles River, like a crisp metallic wafer. You'd never guess from any angle that soon after its 1976 construction, dozens of windowpanes popped out, showering Copley Square with glass. Though the building serves as an office tower, visitors were, until recently, allowed to ascend to its sixtieth floor **observatory** for some of the most stunning views around – but security concerns have prompted its closure; now, you'll have to head instead to the Prudential Skywalk (see below) for Boston vistas. Next door to the tower is the *old* Hancock Tower, which cuts a distinguished profile in the skyline with its truncated step-top pyramid roof.

Nothing can cloak the ugliness of the **Prudential Tower**, at 800 Boylston St, just west of Copley Square. This 52-story gray intruder to the Back Bay skyline is one of the more unfortunate by-products of the urban renewal craze that gripped Boston and most other American cities in the 1960s – though it did succeed in replacing the Boston & Albany rail yards, a blighted border between Back Bay and the South End. The running joke about the "Pru Tower" is that it offers the best view of Boston – because it's the only view where you don't have to actually look at the Pru Tower. That said, the fiftieth-floor **Skywalk** (daily 10am–10pm; $7; ⓣ859-0648, ⓦwww.prudentialcenter.com) does offer the only 360-degree aerial view of Boston. If you're hungry (or just thirsty) you can avoid the admission charge by ascending two more floors to the *Top of the Hub* restaurant; your bill may well equal the money you just saved, but during most daytime hours it's fairly relaxed, and you can linger over coffee or a drink.

Christian Science buildings

People gazing down from the top of the Prudential Tower are often surprised to see a 224-foot-tall Renaissance Revival basilica vying for attention amidst the urban outcroppings lapping at its base. This rather artificial-looking structure is the central feature of the sprawling world headquarters of the **First Church of Christ, Scientist**, 75 Huntington Ave (Mon–Sat 10am–4pm; free; Ⓦwww.tfccs.com; Symphony Ⓣ), which dwarfs the earlier, prettier Romanesque **Christian Science Mother Church** just behind it, built in 1894. There may be no better place in Boston to contemplate the excesses of religion than around the center's 670-foot-long red granite-trimmed **reflecting pool**.

The highlights of a visit here, though, are on the ground floor of the **Mary Baker Eddy Library**, at 200 Massachusetts Ave (Tues–Fri 10am–9pm, Sat–Sun 10am–5pm, closed Mon; $5; ⓣ1-888/222-3711, Ⓦwww.marybakereddylibrary.org; Symphony Ⓣ), in the Christian Science Publishing building. The entrance foyer alone is worth a peek, as the grand Art Deco lobby recently underwent renovation to accommodate a trippy glass and bronze fountain that appears to cascade with words rather than water; the sayings – mostly to do with peace and humanity – are projected from the ceiling for an effect that verges on holographic. Equally outstanding is the marvelous **Mapparium** tucked behind the lobby, a curious stained-glass globe, whose thirty-foot diameter you can cross on a glass bridge. The technicolor hues of the six hundred-plus glass panels, illuminated from behind, reveal the geopolitical reality of the world in 1935, when the globe was constructed, as evidenced by country names such as Siam, Baluchistan, and Transjordan. Intended to symbolize the worldwide reach of the Christian Science movement, the Mapparium has a more immediate payoff: thanks to the spherical glass surface, which absorbs no sound, you can whisper, say, "What's Tanganyika called today?" at one end of the bridge and someone on the opposite end will hear it clear as a bell – and perhaps proffer the answer (Tanzania).

Bay Village

Back near the Public Garden, one of the oldest sections of Boston, **Bay Village**, bounded by Arlington, Church, Fayette, and Stuart streets, functions now as a small atmospheric satellite of Back Bay. This warren of gaslights and tiny brick houses has managed to escape the trolley tours that can make other parts of the city feel like a theme park; of course, that's in part because there's not all that much to see. The area is, however, popular with Boston's **gay community**, who colonized it over a decade ago, before nearby South End (see overleaf) came into favor.

The area's overall resemblance to Beacon Hill is no accident; many of the artisans who pieced that district together built their own, smaller houses here throughout the 1820s and 1830s. A few decades later, water displaced from the filling in of Back Bay threatened to turn the district back into a swamp, but Yankee practicality resulted in the lifting of hundreds of houses and shops onto wooden pilings fully eighteen feet above the water level. Backyards were raised only twelve feet, and when the water receded many building owners designed sunken gardens. You can still see some of these in the alleys behind slender Melrose and Fayette streets, but a more unusual remnant from the past is the **fortress** at the intersection of Arlington and Stuart streets and Columbus Avenue, complete with drawbridge and fake moat, that was built as an armory for the **First Corps of Cadets**, a private military organization.

Bay Village's proximity to the theater district made it a prime location for **speakeasies** in the 1920s, not to mention a natural spot for actors and impresarios to take up residence; indeed, the building at **48–50 Melrose St** originally housed a movie studio. Around the corner is the site of the **Coconut Grove Fire** of 1942, in which 490 people perished in a nightclub because the exit doors were locked. There's little else to see here by day; Bay Village wakes up after the sun sets, when its clubs get going.

The South End

Trendy **South End**, a predominantly residential neighborhood extending below Back Bay, from Huntington Street to I-93, and loosely cut off from downtown by I-90, is almost always modified by the term "quaint," though for once, the tag fits. The term truly hits home in the heart of the neighborhood, an area loosely shaped like a triangle and bounded by Tremont Street, Dartmouth Street, and Columbus Avenue. The tony enclave, nicknamed the "Golden Triangle" by South End realtors, boasts a spectacular concentration of **Victorian architecture** which, when taken together with the examples found in the rest of the neighborhood, is surely unmatched anywhere in the US. The sheer number of such houses here earned the South End a National Landmark District designation in 1983, making the 500-acre-wide area the largest historical neighborhood of its kind in the country. The South End is also known for its well-preserved **ironwork**; a French botanical motif known as Rinceau adorns many of the houses' stairways and windows. Details like these made the area quite popular in the mid-1990s with upwardly mobile Bostonians, who moved in and gentrified the neighborhood. The result is some of the most upbeat and happening **street life** in town – most clustered on **Tremont Street** and on pockets of **Washington Street**, a few blocks below Back Bay Ⓣ, the neighborhood's only Ⓣ stop.

Dartmouth Street to Columbus Avenue

Dartmouth Street, anchored by Copley Place on the far side of the street, gets tonier the closer it gets to Tremont Street, a few blocks southeast. Immediately below Copley Place, at 130 Tremont St, is the street's most important tenant, **Tent City,** a mixed-income housing co-op that owes its name to the 1968 sit-in protest – tents included – staged on the formerly vacant lot by residents concerned about the neighborhood's dwindling low-income housing. Their activism thwarted plans for a parking garage, and the result is a fine example of environmental architecture planning, built in 1988. The pocket of land separating Tent City from Copley Place marks the start of the five-mile **Southwest Corridor Park**, a grassy promenade that connects Back Bay Ⓣ with the Forest Hill Ⓣ station near the Arnold Arboretum.

The northern edge of the Golden Triangle, **Columbus Avenue**, which runs parallel to the Southwest Corridor Park below Tent City, is itself lined with handsome Victorian houses, though the main interest is a tiny wedge of parkland known as **Columbus Square**, four blocks southwest of Dartmouth, between Pembroke and West Newton streets. The space, which marks the southwestern tip of the Golden Triangle, is the repository of two outstanding bronze relief sculptures commemorating Boston's role as part of the Underground Railroad. The nine-foot-tall **Harriet Tubman "Step on Board" Memorial** depicts the strident abolitionist leading several weary slaves, presumably to safety, while the nearby 1913 **Emancipation Memorial** is a more harrowing portrait of slaves' plight: the foursome here are achingly thin and barely clothed.

Appleton and Chandler streets

Cobblestoned **Appleton Street** and quiet **Chandler Street**, which jut off to the northeast from Dartmouth below Columbus Avenue, are the most sought-after South End addresses. The tree-lined streets are graced with refurbished flat- and bow-fronted row houses that would easily be at home in London's Mayfair. In addition, unlike many of their neighbors, the houses here have an extra, fourth story, and are capped off by mansard roofs. If you're here in October, you can catch the annual South End Historical Society's **house tour** for a better perspective on the area (Ⓦwww.southendhistoricalsociety.org or Ⓣ536-4445 for further information).

Cyclorama Building

The heart of South End is the intersection of Clarendon and **Tremont** streets, where some of the trendiest restaurants operate. The area's only real sight, per se, is the domed **Cyclorama Building**, built in 1884 to house an enormous, 360-degree painting of the Battle of Gettysburg (since moved to Gettysburg itself). Later used as a carousel space, a boxing ring, and even the site of the Boston Floral Exchange in 1923, the repurposing theme continued until 1972, when its current hosts, the **Boston Center for the Arts** (Ⓣ426-7700, Ⓦwww.bcaonline.com), moved in.

Kenmore Square, The Fenway, and Brookline

At the western edge of Back Bay, the decorous brownstones and smart shops fade into the more casual Kenmore Square and Fenway districts, both removed from the tourist circuit but good fun nonetheless, with a studenty vibe and some of the city's more notable cultural institutions. Farther west and more residential is the town of Brookline, which feels like just another sleepy part of the city, though one in which you're unlikely to find yourself spending too much time.

Kenmore Square and Boston University

Kenmore Square, at the junction of Commonwealth Avenue and Beacon Street, is the primary port of entry to Boston University and the unofficial playground for its students. Back Bay's Commonwealth Avenue Mall leads right into this lively stretch of youth-oriented bars, record stores, and casual restaurants that cater to the late-night cravings of local students – as such the Square is considerably more alive when school's in session. Many of the buildings on its north side have been snapped up by BU, such as the bustling six-story Barnes & Noble mall, 660 Beacon St, on top of which is perched the monumental **Citgo Sign**, Kenmore's most noticeable landmark. This sixty-square-foot neon advertisement, a pulsing red triangle that is the oil company's logo, has been a popular symbol of Boston since it was placed here in 1965.

Boston University, one of the country's biggest private schools, has its main campus alongside the Charles River, on the narrow stretch of land between Commonwealth Avenue and Storrow Drive. The school has made inventive reuse of old buildings, such as the dormitory **Myles Standish Hall**, at 610 Beacon St, a scaled-down version of New York's Flatiron Building that was once a hotel where notables like baseball legend Babe Ruth camped out.

Shelton Hall, behind it on Bay State Road, is another hostelry-turned-dorm where playwright Eugene O'Neill undramatically made his long day's journey into night. **Bay State Road** was the westernmost extension of Back Bay, evidenced by its wealth of turn-of-the-century brownstones, most of which now house BU graduate institutes and smaller residence halls. An ornate High Georgian Revival mansion at no. 149 houses the office of the university president. The street ends at **The Castle**, an ivy-covered Tudor mansion now used for university functions. Continuing the theme back on Commonwealth is the domed **Morse Auditorium**, formerly a synagogue. One long block down is the closest thing the BU campus has to a center, **Marsh Plaza**, with its Gothic Revival chapel and memorial to Martin Luther King, Jr., a graduate here.

The Fenway

The Fenway spreads out beneath Kenmore Square like an elongated kite, taking in sights disparate enough to please most any visitor. Just past Landsdowne's clubs, the district starts in earnest with **Fenway Park**, the venerable baseball stadium where the star-crossed Boston Red Sox play, though this is quite removed from the highbrow spaces of Fenway's eastern perimeter, dotted with some of Boston's finest cultural institutions: **Symphony Hall**, the **Museum of Fine Arts**, and the **Isabella Stewart Gardner Museum**. Running down the neighborhood's spine is the **Back Bay Fens**, a huge green space banking the Muddy River and designed by Frederick Law Olmsted, urban landscaper extraordinaire.

The Curse of the Bambino

In 1903, Boston (then nicknamed the "Pilgrims") became the first team to represent the American League in baseball's World Series, upsetting the heavily favored Pittsburgh Pirates to claim the championship; their continued financial success allowed them to build a new stadium, Fenway Park, in 1912. During their first year there, Boston won the Series again, and repeated the feat in 1915, 1916, and 1918, led in the latter years by the young pitcher George Herman "Babe" Ruth, who also demonstrated an eye-opening penchant for hitting home runs.

The team was poised to become a dynasty, when its owner, Harry Frazee, began a fire sale of the team to finance a Broadway play that was to star his ingenue girlfriend. Most of the players sold at bargain prices, including Ruth, who went to the New York Yankees, which of course went on to become the most successful franchise in professional sports history, with the Babe and all his home runs at the forefront. Indeed, Yankee Stadium is often referred to as "The House that Ruth Built." On the other hand, Frazee's play, *No, No, Nanette*, flopped. So did his Red Sox team – the 1918 World Series was the last they won. Their long periods of mediocrity have been punctuated by even more disappointing seasons in which they came agonizingly close to the championship, only to snatch defeat from the jaws of certain victory: in 1978, a late-season collapse was capped off when the Yankees' light-hitting shortstop Bucky Dent slugged a three-run homer to beat the Sox in a one-game playoff; in 1986, the Sox were one strike away from clinching the World Series against the New York Mets when a series of miscues, including the infamous grounder that rolled through the legs of first baseman Bill Buckner, brought about another crushing loss. It's become fodder for the long-suffering fans, who call it "The Curse of the Bambino" (referring back to the Babe); Boston sportswriter Dan Shaughnessy even penned a 1991 book by that same name. Today, fans will no doubt complain that the curse continues, especially with the recent spate of success by their arch rivals, the Yankees.

Fenway Park

Baseball is treated with reverence in Boston, so it's appropriate that it is played here in what may be the country's most storied stadium, unique **Fenway Park**, at 24 Yawkey Way (April–Oct Mon–Fri 10am, 11am, 1pm & 2pm, no 2pm tour on game days; $8 adults, $6 children; Ⓣ236-6666, Ⓦwww.redsox.com; Kenmore or Fenway Ⓣ), whose giant 37-foot-tall left-field wall, aka the **Green Monster**, is an enduring symbol of the quirks of early ballparks. Fenway Park was constructed in 1912 in a tiny, asymmetrical space just off Brookline Avenue, resulting in its famously awkward dimensions – also included in which are an abnormally short right-field line (302ft) and a fence that doesn't at all approximate the smooth arc of most outfields. That the left-field wall was built so high makes up for some of the short distances in the park and also gives Red Sox leftfielders a distinct advantage over their counterparts – it takes some time before one gets accustomed to the whimsical caroms a ball hit off there might take. You can take tours of the stadium, where greats like Ted Williams, Carl Yazstremski, and even Babe Ruth roamed about, but your best bet is to come see a game, really a must for any baseball fan and still a reasonable draw for anyone remotely curious. The season runs from April to October, and tickets are quite reasonable, especially if you sit in the bleachers ($18–30; Ⓣ267-1700, Ⓦwww.redsox.com for ticket info). Sadly, the Red Sox are looking to tear it down and build a huge, more profitable stadium, and foot the bill with tax money and higher ticket prices. Among the many groups opposing the plan, Save Fenway Park (Ⓦwww.savefenwaypark.org) in particular is trying to gain historic landmark status for the beloved stadium.

The Back Bay Fens

The Fenway's defining element is the **Back Bay Fens** (daily 7.30am–dusk; Ⓦwww.emeraldnecklace.org/fenway.htm), a snakelike segment of Frederick Law Olmsted's Emerald Necklace that rather uninspiringly takes over where the prim Commonwealth Avenue Mall leaves off. The Fens were fashioned from marsh and mud in 1879, a fact reflected in the name of the waterway that still runs through them today – the **Muddy River**. In the northern portion of the park, local residents maintain small garden plots in the wonderfully unmanicured **Victory Garden**, the oldest community garden in the US. Nearby, below Agassiz Road, the more formally laid out **Kelleher Rose Garden** boasts colorful hybrid species bearing exotic names like Voodoo, Midas Touch, and Sweet Surrender.

Not far from the Fens' northern tip, the renowned **Berklee College of Music** makes its home on the busy stretch of Massachusetts Avenue south of Boylston Street. A few short blocks south, **Symphony Hall**, home to the Boston Symphony Orchestra, anchors the corner of Massachusetts and Huntington avenues. The inside of the 1900 McKim, Mead & White design resembles an oversized cube, apparently just the right shape to lend it its perfect acoustics. The modern campus of **Northeastern University** spreads out on both sides of Huntington farther south, though it lacks any of the collegiate atmosphere and charm of other Boston schools.

Museum of Fine Arts

Rather inconveniently located in south Fenway – but well worth the trip – the **Museum of Fine Arts**, at 465 Huntington Ave (Mon, Tues, Thurs–Sun 10am–4.45pm, Wed until 9.45pm; West Wing also open Thurs–Fri until 9.45pm; $15; by contribution Wed after 4pm; West Wing only, $13 after 5pm Thurs–Fri; CityPass accepted; Ⓣ267-9300, Ⓦwww.mfa.org; Museum Ⓣ), is

Olmsted and the Emerald Necklace

The string of urban parks that stretches through Boston's southern districts, known as the **Emerald Necklace**, grew out of a project conceived in the 1870s, when landscape architect Frederick Law Olmsted was commissioned to create for Boston a series of urban parks like those he had done in New York and Chicago. A Romantic naturalist in the tradition of Rousseau and Wordsworth, Olmsted conceived of nature as a way to escape the ills wrought by society, and considered his urban parks a means for city-dwellers to escape the clamor of their everyday lives. He converted much of Boston's remaining open space, which was often disease-breeding marshland, into a series of fabulous, manicured parks beginning with the Back Bay Fens, including the Riverway along the Boston–Brookline border, and proceeding through Jamaica Pond and the Arnold Arboretum to Roxbury's Franklin Park (see "Southern Districts," p.128). While Olmsted's original skein of parks was limited to these, further development linked the Fens, via the Commonwealth Avenue Mall, to the Public Garden and Boston Common, all of which now function as part of the Necklace. And which make it all the more impressive in scale, though the Necklace's sense of pristine natural wonder has slipped in the century since their creation – the more southerly links in the chain, starting with the Fens, have grown shaggy and are unsafe at night. The Boston Park Rangers (9am–5pm; ⓣ635-7383) organize free walking tours covering each of the Necklace's segments from Boston Common to Franklin Park.

New England's premier art space. Founded in the 1850s as an adjunct of the Boston Athenaeum when that organization decided to focus more exclusively on local history rather than art, the collection was given public imprimatur and funding by the Massachusetts Legislature in 1870. After moving around at the end of the nineteenth century, it found its permanent home here in 1906.

American collection

On the first floor, a marvelously rich **American collection** features Gilbert Stuart's nationalistic *Washington at Dorchester Heights* and a number of John Singleton Copley portraits of revolutionary figures, plus his gruesome narrative *Watson and the Shark*. Romantic naturalist landscapes from the first half of the nineteenth century – such as Albert Bierstadt's quietly majestic *Buffalo Crossing* – dominate several rooms; and from the latter half of the century there are several seascapes by Winslow Homer, Whistler's morose *Nocturne in Blue and Silver: the Lagoon*, and works from the Boston school, notably Childe Hassan's gauzy *Boston Common at Twilight* and John Singer Sargent's spare *The Daughters of Edward Darley Boit*. Early twentieth-century American work finds Edward Hopper's dour *Drugstore* hanging beside his uncharacteristically upbeat *Room in Brooklyn*, as well as Maurice Prendergast's sentimental renderings of genteel life, *Sunset* and *Eight Bathers*. The standout of early to mid-twentieth century American works, Jackson Pollock's tense, semi-abstracted *Troubled Queen*, pre-dates his famous drip painting style; it hangs near Georgia O'Keeffe's majestically antlered *Deer's Skull with Pedernal* and Charles Sheeler's ironically titled *View of New York* – which you'll have to see for yourself to appreciate the joke. Don't miss the **American Decorative Arts**, either: a gloriously nostalgic assemblage of coffee urns, elaborately styled oak furnishings, and reconstructed living rooms with period furniture.

European collection

The second-floor **European wing** begins with Dutch paintings from the Northern Renaissance, featuring two outstanding Rembrandts, *Artist in his*

Studio and *Old Man in Prayer*, and follows with several rooms of grandiose Rococo and Romantic work from the eighteenth and early nineteenth centuries. The culmination of the wing is the late nineteenth-century collection, which begins with works by the Realist Jean-François Millet, whose *Man Turning over the Soil* and *The Sower* exhibit the stark use of color and interest in common subjects that characterized later French artists. The subsequent **Impressionist** room also contains Monet's heavily abstracted *Grainstack (Snow Effect)* and *Rouen Cathedral (Morning Effect)*, though his tongue-in-cheek *La Japonaise*, a riff on Parisian fashion trends, steals the show. Degas figures prominently here with his agitated *Pagans and Degas' Father* and a bronze cast of the famous *14-Year Old Dancer*, as does Renoir, whose renowned *Dance at Bourgival* looks onto *Psyche*, a delicate Rodin marble. The room's highlight, however, is its selection of Post-Impressionist art, best of which is Picasso's coldly cubist *Portrait of a Woman*, Van Gogh's richly hued *Enclosed Field with Ploughman* and *Houses at Auvers*, and Gauguin's bizarre relief wood sculpture, *Be in Love and you will be Happy*, in which the artist casts himself seizing a woman's outstretched hand and ordering her to do as the title instructs.

Ancient art and other galleries

A series of MFA-sponsored digs at Giza have made its **Egyptian collection** the standout of a fine collection of **ancient art**. Pieces range from prehistoric pots to artifacts from the Roman period. While rather modest by comparison, the Nubian collection is nevertheless the largest of its kind outside Africa. Most of the pieces are funerary and actually quite similar to their Egyptian contemporaries. Not nearly as well-represented, the classical section is worth a glance mostly for its numerous Grecian urns, a fine Cycladic *Female Figure*, and several Etruscan sarcophagi with elaborately wrought narrative bas-reliefs.

Between the second-floor Egyptian and Asian galleries is the outstanding **Shapiro Rotunda**, its dome and en-suite colonnade inset with multiple **murals** and **bas-reliefs** by John Singer Sargent, who undertook the commission following his Boston Public Library work (see p.113). Operating under the belief that mural painting – not portraiture – was the key to "artistic immortality," this installation certainly guaranteed the artist a lasting place in the MFA and some attending controversy to boot: when the ten-year project was completed shortly before Sargent's death in 1925, his Classical theme was falling out of vogue and his efforts were considered the "frivolous works of a failing master." The rotunda leads off to the **Koch Gallery**, which ranks among the museum's more spectacular showings. Designed to resemble a European palace hallway, its wood-inlaid ceilings cap walls hung two-high with dozens of portraits and landscapes of varying sizes, including three religious pieces by El Greco.

For those in the know, the MFA's **Asian Galleries** are a highlight. The Chinese, Indian, Southeast Asian, and Islamic collections are excellent, but the standout is the Museum's **Japanese Collection**, quite simply one of the best in the world. One room is filled with striking displays of intricately decorated samurai swords, lacquer boxes, and kimonos, and another has temple guardian and Buddha statues arranged in a setting designed like the great hall of a temple. There's also an astounding collection of hanging scrolls and *ukiyo-e* (woodblock prints), which, because of their fragility, are exhibited on a rotating basis.

The Isabella Stewart Gardner Museum

Less broad in its collection, but more distinctive and idiosyncratic than the MFA, is its neighbor, the **Isabella Stewart Gardner Museum**, at 280 The

△ Aerial shot of Harvard University, Cambridge

Fenway (Tues–Sun 11am–5pm; $10, $11 on weekends; ⓣ566-1401, ⓦwww.gardnermuseum.org; Museum ⓣ). Eccentric Boston socialite Gardner collected and arranged more than 2500 objects in the four-story Fenway Court building she designed herself, making this the only major museum in the country that is entirely the creation of a single individual. It's a hodgepodge of works from around the globe, presented without much attention to period or style; Gardner's goal was to foster the love of art rather than its study, and she wanted the setting of her pieces to "fire the imagination." Your imagination does get quite a workout – there's art everywhere you look, with many of the objects unlabeled, placed in corners or above doorways, for an effect that is occasionally chaotic, but always striking. To get the most out of a visit, aim to join the hour-long Friday **tours** (free; 2.30pm), but get there early as only twenty people are allowed on a first-come-first-served basis. Alternatively, the **gift shop** sells a worthwhile **guide** ($5) detailing the location and ownership history of every piece on display.

The Gardner is best known for its spectacular central **courtyard**, styled after a fifteenth-century Venetian palace, where flowering plants and trees bloom year-round amid statuary and fountains. However, the museum's greatest success is the **Spanish Cloister**, a long, narrow corridor which perfectly frames John Singer Sargent's ecstatic representation of Spanish dance, *El Jaleo*, and also contains fine seventeenth-century Mexican tiles and Roman statuary and sarcophagi. Gardner had an affinity for **altars**, and the collection contains several, cobbled together from various religious artifacts. Most notable of these is her **chapel**, on the third floor, which incorporates sixteenth-century Italian choir stalls and stained glass from Milan and Soissons cathedrals, as well as assorted unlabeled religious figurines, candlesticks, and crucifixes, all surrounding Paul-Cesar Helleu's moody representation of the *Interior of the Abbey Church of Saint-Denis*.

The **Titian**, **Veronese**, and **Raphael rooms** comprise a strong showing of Italian Renaissance and Baroque work, including Titian's famous *Europa*, Botticelli's *Tragedy of Lucretia*, and Crivelli's mannerist *St George and the Dragon*. What was once a first-rate array of seventeenth-century Northern European works was debilitated by a 1990 art heist in which two Rembrandts and a Vermeer were among ten canvases stolen. But the majority of works in the **Dutch Room** remain, with an early *Self-Portrait* by Rembrandt and Rubens' austere *Thomas Howard, Earl of Arundel*.

Brookline

The leafy, affluent town of **BROOKLINE**, south of Boston University and west of The Fenway, appears as if it's just another well-maintained Boston neighborhood, though in fact it's a distinct municipality. It holds some vaguely diverting attractions, and is centered around bustling **Coolidge Corner**, at the intersection of Beacon and Harvard streets. To reach Brookline, take the Green Line's C branch to Coolidge Corner or D branch to Brookline Village.

Close by Coolidge Corner is the **John F. Kennedy National Historic Site**, at 83 Beals St (Wed–Sun 10am–4.30pm; $2), the outwardly unremarkable house where JFK was born on May 29, 1917. The inside is rather plain, too, though a narrated voiceover by the late President's mother, Rose, adds some spice to the roped-off rooms. Along Brookline's southern fringe is the **Frederick Law Olmsted National Historic Site**, at 99 Warren St (Fri–Sun 10am–4.30pm; free; ⓦwww.nps.gov/frla). Known as Fairsted, the expansive house here doubled as Olmsted's family home and office – almost one million landscape schemes are archived here, ranging from his work on Yosemite Valley to New York's Central Park. It's a dry retrospective that will appeal mostly to Olmsted buffs; that said, the surrounding grounds, unsurprisingly, are quite idyllic.

Boston's Southern Districts

The parts of Boston that most visitors see – downtown, Beacon Hill, Back Bay, the North End – actually only cover a small proportion of the city's geography. To the south lies a vast spread of residential neighborhoods known collectively as the **Southern Districts**, including largely Irish **SOUTH BOSTON**, unlovely **DORCHESTER**, blighted **ROXBURY**, and pleasant, trendy **JAMAICA PLAIN**, which count just a handful of highlights among them, most notably Jamaica Plain's **Arnold Arboretum** and Dorchester's **John F. Kennedy Museum and Library**. These were once rural areas dotted with the swish summer resort homes of Boston's moneyed elite, but population growth in the late nineteenth century pushed middle- and working-class families here from the increasingly crowded downtown area. Three-story rowhouses soon replaced the mansions, and the moniker "streetcar suburbs" was coined as a catch-all for the newly redefined neighborhoods. In the years immediately following World War II, each was hit to varying degrees by economic decline, and the middle class moved farther afield, leaving the districts to the mostly immigrant and blue-collar communities that remain today.

None of these areas, though fairly easily accessible on the Ⓣ from downtown (if not always safe to walk around, especially after dark), will draw your attention for too long, which is one of the reasons we've gone ahead and picked out the best sights for you – as you're likely to target certain attractions rather than wandering around the rather large districts. An exception to this rule is Jamaica Plain (popularly known as "JP"), whose Centre Street has boomed into one of the hippest eating and junk shopping strips in the city – much to the distress of local residents who have seen their rents more than double in the past few years.

Castle Island and Fort Independence

South Boston narrows to an end in Boston Harbor on a strip of land called **Castle Island**, off the end of William J. Day Boulevard, a favorite leisure spot for Southie residents and, in fact, many Bostonians. The island, reachable by bus #9 or #11 from the Broadway Ⓣ, is covered by parks and beaches, though you wouldn't want to swim here, since Boston Harbor's waters, while cleaner than in years past, are far from non-toxic – and they're freezing to boot. At the tip of the island is **Fort Independence** (Sat & Sun noon–3.30pm; free), a stout granite edifice that was one of the earliest redoubts in the Americas, originally established in 1634, though it has been rebuilt several times since. Today, what remains is a skeleton of its 1801 version, and its slate-gray walls aren't much to look at from the outside, though supposedly an incident that happened inside served as inspiration for Edgar Allan Poe's story, "The Cask of Amontillado."

John F. Kennedy Museum and Library

There's not much to see in Dorchester besides the **John F. Kennedy Museum and Library** (daily 9am–5pm; $8; CityPass accepted; Ⓣ929-4500 or 1-877/616-4599, Ⓦwww.cs.umb.edu/jfklibrary; JFK/UMass Ⓣ; free shuttle every twenty minutes), at Columbia Point, spectacularly situated in an I.M. Pei-designed building overlooking Boston Harbor. The museum's presentation opens with a well-done eighteen-minute film covering Kennedy's political career through the 1960 Democratic National Convention. The remaining displays cover the presidential campaign of 1960 and the highlights of the brief Kennedy administration. The campaign exhibits are most interesting for their television and radio ads, which illustrate the squeaky-clean self-image America possessed at that time. The section on the Kennedy administration is more serious, highlighted by a 22-minute film on the Cuban Missile Crisis that well evokes the tension of the event, if exaggerating Kennedy's heroics. The final section of the museum is perhaps its best: a roomy glass-enclosed space overlooking the harbor, with modest inscriptions bearing some of Kennedy's more memorable quotations – affecting enough to move even the most jaded JFK critic. Oddly enough, the museum is also the repository for Ernest Hemingway's original manuscripts. Call for an appointment to see them (Ⓣ929-4523).

Dorchester Heights Monument

Back at the convergence of South Boston and Dorchester rises the incline of **Dorchester Heights**, whose northernmost point, Thomas Park, is crowned by a stone obelisk **monument** commemorating George Washington's bloodless purge of the Brits from Boston. After the Continental Army had held the British under siege in the city for just over a year, Washington wanted to put an end to the whole thing. On March 4, 1776, he amassed all the artillery he could get his hands on and placed it on the towering peak of Dorchester Heights, so the tired Redcoats could get a good look at the patriots' firepower. Intimidated, they swiftly left Boston – for good. The park is generally empty, pristinely kept, and still commands the same sweeping views of Boston and its southern communities that it did during the Revolutionary War. The best vista is from the top of the monument itself, though it's only open sporadically (July–Aug Wed 4–8pm, Sat & Sun 10am–4pm; free) and, anyway, it's quite a bit out of the way from any other major points of interest.

Franklin Park

Roxbury's **Franklin Park Zoo**, 1 Franklin Park Rd in Franklin Park (April–Sept Mon–Fri 10am–5pm, Sat & Sun 10am–6pm; Oct–March daily 10am–4pm; $9.50 adults, $5 kids; Ⓣ442-2002, Ⓦwww.zoonewengland.com; Forest Hills Ⓣ), the southernmost link in the Emerald Necklace, has little besides its backdrop to distinguish it from any other zoo, and is perhaps only an essential stop if you're traveling with kids. It does boast the African Tropical Forest, an impressively re-created savanna that's the largest indoor open-space zoo design in North America, and houses gorillas, monkeys, and pygmy hippos, and Bird's World, a charming relic from the days of Edwardian zoo design: a huge, ornate, wrought-iron cage you can walk through while birds fly overhead.

Franklin Park itself was one of Olmsted's proudest accomplishments when it was completed, due to the sheer size of the place, and its scale is indeed astounding – 527 acres of green space, with countless trails for hikers, bikers, and walkers leading through the hills and thickly forested areas. That's about all that's still particularly impressive, as much of the park is overgrown from years of halfhearted upkeep and it borders some of Boston's more dangerous areas.

Jamaica Plain and the Arnold Arboretum

Diminutive **Jamaica Plain** – "JP" in local parlance – is one of Boston's more successfully integrated neighborhoods, with a good mix of students, immigrants, and working-class families. Located between Roxbury and the section of the Emerald Necklace known as the Muddy River Improvement, the area's activity centers around, appropriately, **Centre Street**, which holds some inexpensive cafés and restaurants.

Jamaica Plain's star attraction – and really the only must-see sight in all the Southern Districts – is the 265-acre **Arnold Arboretum**, at 125 Arborway (daily: March–Oct dawn to dusk; Nov–Feb Mon–Fri dawn to dusk, Sat & Sun 10am–2pm; $1 donation requested; Ⓣ524-1718, Ⓦwww.arboretum.harvard.edu; Forest Hills Ⓣ), the most spectacular link in the Emerald Necklace. Its collection of trees, vines, shrubs, and flowers has benefited from more than one hundred years of both careful grooming and ample funding, and is now one of the finest in North America. The plants are arranged along a series of paths populated by runners and dog-walkers as well as serious botanists, though it certainly doesn't require any expert knowledge to enjoy the grounds. The array of Asian species – the best in the world outside Asia – is highlighted by the **Larz Anderson Bonsai Collection** and is brilliantly concentrated along the Chinese Path, a walkway near the center of the park. Best to visit during spring, when crabapples, lilacs, and magnolias complement the greenery with dazzling chromatic schemes. "**Lilac Sunday**," the third Sunday in May, sees the Arboretum at its most vibrant (and busiest), when its collection of lilacs – the second largest in the US – is in full bloom.

Cambridge

A walk down most any street in **CAMBRIDGE** – just across the Charles River from Boston, but a world apart in atmosphere and attitude – takes you past plaques and monuments honoring literati and revolutionaries who lived and worked in the area as early as the seventeenth century. But along its Colonial-period brick sidewalks and narrow, crooked roads, Cambridge vibrates with a vital present: starched businesspeople bustle past disaffected punks; clean-cut college students coexist right beside a growing homeless population; and busloads of tourists look on as street people purvey goods and perform music. In fact, many residents tend to forget the world beyond the Charles River, and the Puritan parochialism of its founders has turned into a different breed of exclusivity, touched with civic and intellectual elitism. Still, there's plenty here to make this an essential stopover on your trip.

The city is loosely organized around a series of squares – confluences of streets that are the focus of each area's commercial activity. By far the most important of these is **Harvard Square**, center of the eponymous university, and the top draw for Cambridge's visitors. The area around it is home to the city's main sights, particularly the stretch of Colonial mansions in **Old Cambridge**. The squares of **Central** and **East Cambridge** are more down-to-earth. Blue-collar **Central Square** is less touristy but no less urban than its collegiate counterpart: here you can eat at *McDonald's* (a rarity in Cambridge), and enjoy the city's best blues bars and rock music shows. Farther east along the Charles is **Kendall Square**, home to a cluster of technology companies and also the beginning of East Cambridge, a mostly Hispanic working-class district. The only part of this area that really warrants a visit is the

Massachusetts Institute of Technology (MIT), one of the world's premier science and research institutions and home to some peculiar architecture and an excellent museum.

Harvard Square and the University

Harvard Square – a public space in the shadow of Harvard Yard with a buzz generated by outdoor cafés, street performers, and a steady stream of browsers who descend on the square's main tenant, Out of Town News – radiates out from the Ⓣ stop along Massachusetts Avenue, JFK Street, and Brattle Street. A small **tourism kiosk** run by the Cambridge Tourism Office (daily 9am–5pm; Ⓣ441-2884 or 1-800/862-5678, Ⓦwww.cambridge-usa.com) faces the station exit, but more of the action is in the adjacent sunken area known as **The Pit**, a triage center for fashion victims of alternative culture. Moody students spend entire days sitting here admiring each other's green hair and body piercings while homeless locals hustle for change and other handouts. This is also the focal point of the **street music scene**. It's at its most frenetic and fascinating on Friday and Saturday nights and Sunday afternoons, when all the elements converge – crowds mill about; evangelical demonstrators engage in shouting matches with angry youths; and magicians, acrobats, and bands perform on every corner.

A brief history of Cambridge

Cambridge began inauspiciously in 1630, when a group of English immigrants from Charlestown founded **New Towne** village on the narrow, swampy banks of the Charles River. These Puritans hoped New Towne would become an ideal religious community; to that end, they founded a college in 1636 for the purpose of training clergy. Two years later, the college took its name in honor of a local minister, **John Harvard**, who bequeathed his library and half his estate to the nascent institution. New Towne was eventually renamed Cambridge for the English university where many of its figureheads were educated, and became an enormous publishing center after the importation of the printing press in the seventeenth century. Its printing industry and university established Cambridge as a bastion of intellectual activity and political thought. This status became entrenched over the course of the United States' turbulent early history, particularly during the late eighteenth century, when the Cambridge population grew sharply divided between the numerous artisans and farmers who sympathized with the Revolution and the minority of moneyed Tories. When fighting began, the Tories were driven from their mansions on modern-day Brattle Street (then called "Tory Row"), their place taken by Cambridge intelligentsia and prominent Revolutionaries.

In 1846, the Massachusetts Legislature granted a city charter linking Old Cambridge (the Harvard Square area) and industrial East Cambridge as a single municipality. Initially, there was friction between these two very different sections; in 1855, citizens from each area unsuccessfully petitioned for the regions to be granted separate civic status. Though relations improved, the distinctive characters remain. A large immigrant population was drawn to opportunity in the industrial and commercial sectors of East Cambridge, while academics increasingly sought out Harvard, whose reputation had continued to swell, and the Massachusetts Institute of Technology, which moved here from Boston in 1916. The district's political leanings are less liberal today than in the 1960s, when Cambridge earned the name "Moscow on the Charles" due to its unabashedly Red character, but the fact that nearly half of its 90,000-plus residents are university affiliates insures that it will remain one of America's most opinionated cities.

North of Harvard Square along Massachusetts Avenue lies one of Cambridge's first cemeteries, the **Old Burying-Ground**, whose style and grounds have scarcely changed since the seventeenth century. The stone grave markers are adorned in a style somewhere between Puritan austerity and medieval superstition: inscriptions praise the simple piety of the staunchly Christian deceased, but are surrounded by death's-heads carved to ward off evil spirits. You're supposed to apply to the sexton of Christ Church for entry, but if the gate at the path behind the church is open (as it frequently is), you can enter – just be respectful of the grounds.

A triangular wedge of concrete squeezed into the intersection of Massachusetts Avenue and Garden Street, **Dawes Park** is named for the patriot who rode to alert residents that the British were marching on Lexington and Concord on April 19, 1775 – the *other* one that is, William Dawes. While Longfellow opted to commemorate Paul Revere's midnight ride instead, as have all history classes, the citizens of Cambridge and other areas north of Boston must have appreciated poor Dawes' contribution just as much. Bronze hoofmarks in the sidewalk mark the event, and several placards behind the pathway provide information on the history of the Harvard Square/Old Cambridge area.

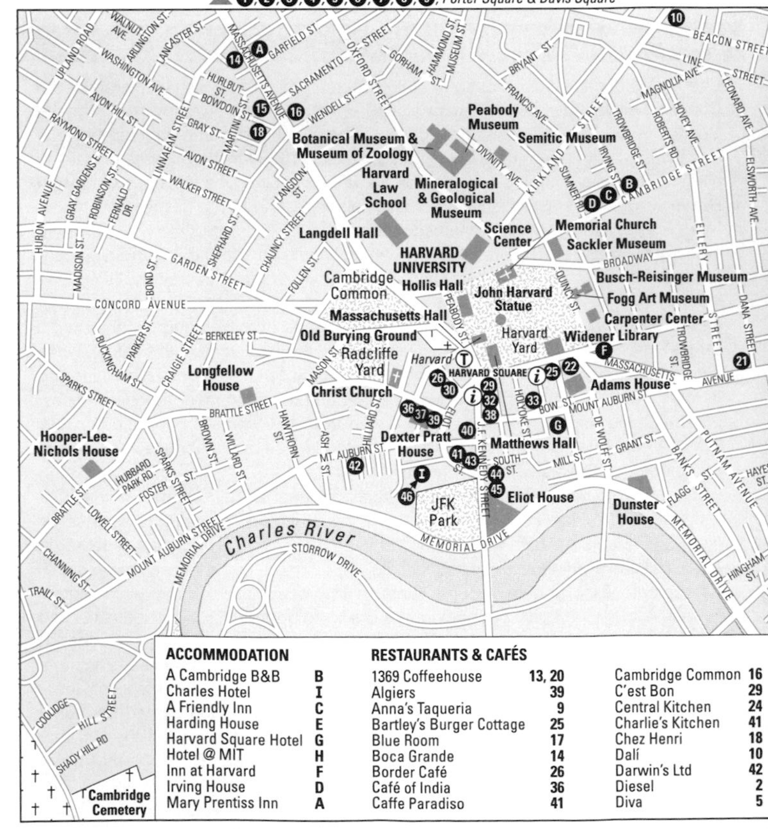

Cambridge Common

In **Cambridge Common**, a roughly square patch of green space between Massachusetts Avenue, Garden Street, and Waterhouse Street, you can retrace the old **Charlestown–Watertown path**, along which Redcoats beat a sheepish retreat during the Revolutionary War, and which still transects the park from east to west. The most prominent feature on the Common is, however, the revered **Washington Elm**, under which it's claimed George Washington took command of the Continental Army. The elm, at the southern side of the park near the intersection of Garden Street and Appian Way, is accompanied by a predictable wealth of commemorative objects: a cannon captured from the British when they evacuated Boston, a statue of Washington, and monuments to two Polish army captains hired to lead Revolutionary forces. What the memorials don't tell you is that the city of Cambridge cut down the original elm in 1946 when it began to obstruct traffic; it stood at the Common's southwest corner, near the intersection of Mason and Garden streets. The present tree is only the offspring of that tree, raised from one of its branches. To further confuse the issue, the Daughters of the American Revolution erected a monument commemorating the south*east* corner of the park as the spot where

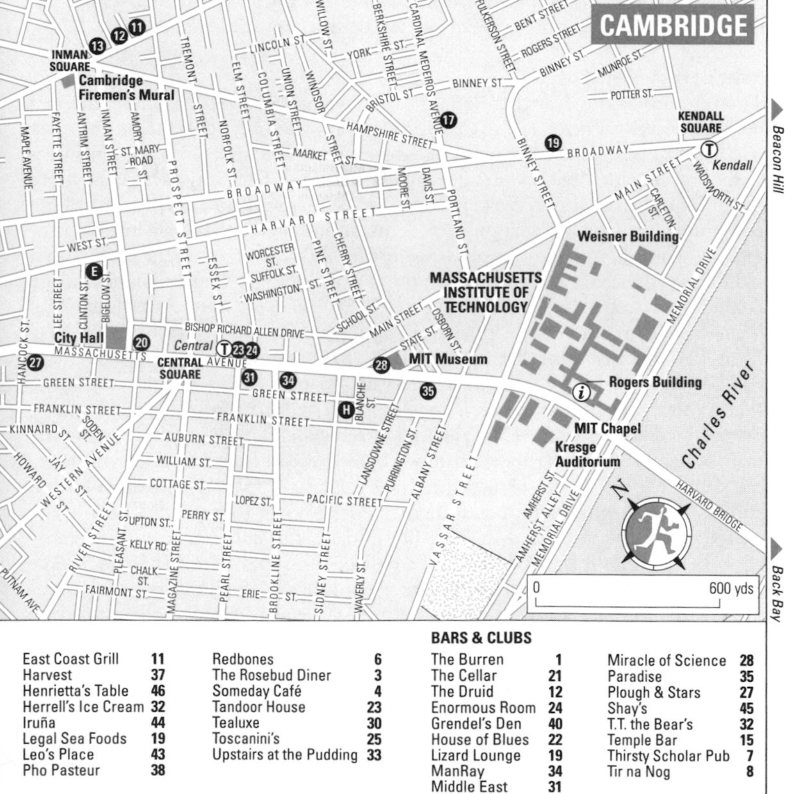

Washington did his historic thing. And recently, historians have suggested that Washington never commissioned the troops on the Common at all, but rather in Wadsworth House at Harvard Yard.

JFK Street and the Harvard Houses

The stretch of JFK Street below Harvard Square holds more of the city's many public spaces, certainly the least of which is **Winthrop Square**, site of the original New Towne marketplace and since converted into a bedraggled park. **John F. Kennedy Park**, where JFK Street meets Memorial Drive, was only finished in the late 1980s, making it an infant among Harvard Square's venerable spaces, though certainly not the first pious shrine to the university's favorite modern son. The unusual **memorial** to Kennedy in its center is worth a look – a low granite pyramid surrounded by a moat, covered constantly but imperceptibly by a thin film of flowing water.

Harvard's fancy upperclassmen's residences, most of which are nested in the area east of JFK Street and south of Harvard Yard, are a visible remnant of the university's elite past. Just south of **Adams House**, once a hotbed of counter-culturalism, juts the graceful, blue-topped bell tower of **Lowell House**, at 2 Holyoke Place, which boasts one of Harvard's most beautiful courtyards. Further west on the banks of the Charles rises the purple spire of **Eliot House**, at 101 Dunster St, a community that remains a bastion of social privilege. To the east, at 945 Memorial Drive, lies **Dunster House**, whose red Georgian top is a favorite subject of Cambridge's tourist brochures.

Harvard Yard

The transition from Harvard Square to **Harvard Yard** – the proper center of the university – is brief and dramatic: in a matter of only several feet, the buzz of car traffic and urban life gives way to grassy lawns and towering oaks pervaded by an aura of Ivy League intellectualism. The atmosphere is more mythological than real, however, as the Yard's narrow, haphazard footpaths are constantly plied by preoccupied students and as many camera-clicking tour groups, who often make the place seem more like an amusement park than a staid university campus. You can join the hullabaloo by taking a free 45-minute guided tour from the Holyoke Center, 1350 Massachusetts Ave (June–Aug Mon–Sat 10am, 11.15am, 2pm & 3.15pm, Sun 1.30pm & 3pm; Sept–May Mon–Fri 10am & 2pm, Sat 2pm; ⓣ495–1573); the Center also stocks maps and brochures detailing everything Harvard-related.

The most common entrance is the one directly across from Harvard Square proper, which leads to the **Old Yard**, a large, rectangular area enclosed by freshman dormitories that has been around since 1636. In front of stark, symmetrical, slate-gray University Hall is the Yard's trademark icon, the **John Harvard statue**, around which chipper student guides inform tour groups of the oft-told story of the statue's three lies (it misdates the college's founding; erroneously identifies John Harvard as the college's founder; and isn't really a likeness of John Harvard at all). While it's a popular spot for visitors to take pictures, male students at the college covet the statue as a site of public urination; it's a badge of honor around here – as a result, there are surveillance cameras trained on the statue.

The architectural contrast between modest **Hollis Hall**, which dates from 1762, and its grandiose southern neighbor, **Matthews Hall**, built around a hundred years later, mirrors Harvard's transition from a quiet training ground for ministers to a wealthy, cosmopolitan university. The **indentations** in Hollis's front steps also hold some historical interest: students used to warm their rooms by heating cannonballs; come time to leave their quarters for the summer, they would dispose of the cannonballs by dropping them from their windows rather than having to carry them down the stairs.

To the east of the Old Yard lie the grander buildings of the **New Yard**, where a vast set of steps leads up to the enormous pillars of **Widener Library**. Named after Harvard grad and *Titanic* victim Harry Elkins Widener, whose mother paid for the project, it's the center of the largest private library collection in the US, which includes a first folio of Shakespeare and a Gutenberg Bible. At the opposite side of the New Yard is **Memorial Church**, whose narrow, white spire strikes a balancing note to the heavy pillared front of Widener.

North lies the main quad of the famed **Harvard Law School**, focusing on the stern gray pillars of **Langdell Hall**, the imposing edifice on its western border. Above Langdell's entrance is a Latin inscription encapsulating the Western ideal of the Rule of Law, tinctured with an unusual degree of religiosity: *"Non sub homine, sed sub deo et lege"* ("Not under man, but under God and law"). Inside is the renovated **Harvard Law Library**, where you can practically smell the stress in the air.

It's hard to miss the conspicuously modern **Carpenter Center** as you walk past down Quincy Street, a slab of slate-gray granite amidst Harvard's ever-present brick motif. Completed in 1963 as a center for the study of visual art at Harvard, the Carpenter Center is the only building in America designed by the French architect Le Corbusier. Be sure to traverse its trademark feature, a **walkway** that leads through the center of the building, meant to reflect the path worn by students on the lot on which the center was constructed. The basement of the building is the place for screenings of the Harvard Film Archives.

Harvard University museums

Harvard's three art **museums** have benefited from years of scholarly attention and donors' financial generosity. Largely underappreciated and underattended by most visitors, not to mention the students themselves, the collections are easily some of the finest in New England. A ticket to one buys you entry to the others (Mon–Sat 10am–5pm, Sun 1–5pm; $6.50, free Sat 10am–noon; ⓣ495-9400, ⓦwww.artmuseums.harvard.edu).

Fogg Art, Busch-Reisinger, and Sackler museums

Housed on two floors which surround a lovely mock sixteenth-century Italian courtyard, the collections of the **William Hayes Fogg Art Museum**, at 32 Quincy St, showcase the highlights of Harvard's substantial collection of Western art. Much of the first floor is devoted to medieval and Renaissance material, mainly religious art with the usual complement of suffering Christs. This part of the collection is best for a series of capitals salvaged from the French cathedral of Moutiers-Saint-Jean, which combine a Romanesque predilection for classical design with medieval didactic narrative. Additional first-floor chambers are devoted to portraiture of the seventeenth and eighteenth centuries, featuring two Rubens, a Rembrandt, and three Poussins, whose startling *Hannibal Crossing the Alps* depicts the great Carthaginian instructing his troops from atop a massive tusked elephant.

The museum's permanent holdings are strongest in Impressionism and modernism, especially the late nineteenth century French contingent of Degas, Monet, Manet, Pissarro, and Cezanne. But it's the focus on American counterparts to European late nineteenth- and early twentieth-century artists that truly distinguishes the collection, from the fine range of John Singer Sargent portraits, his solitary *The Breakfast Table* among them, to an ethereal Whistler *Nocturne* in blue and silver tints. Modernism is represented by, among others, Pollock's narrow beige-and-black *No. 2*, and Sheeler's outstanding *Upper Deck*, a representation of technology that ingeniously combines realism with abstraction.

Secreted away at the rear of the Fogg's second floor is the entrance to Werner Otto Hall, home of the **Busch-Reisinger Museum**, concentrating exclusively on the German Expressionists and the work of the Bauhaus. Despite its small size, it's one of the finest collections of German Expressionists and Bauhaus works in the world. Its six rooms contain *fin de siècle* art, including Klimt's *Pear Tree*, a dappled meditation on the natural environment, and several Bauhaus standouts like Feininger's angular *Bird Cloud* and Moholy-Nagy's *Light-Space Modulator* – a quirky sculpture-machine set in motion for ten minutes just once a week (Wed 1.45pm) due to its fragility. The gallery is strongest in Expressionist portraiture, notably Kirchner's sardonic *Self-Portrait with a Cat* and Beckmann's garish *The Actors*, a narcissistic triptych.

Right out of the Fogg and dead ahead is the five-floor Arthur M. Sackler Building, 485 Broadway, the first, second, and fourth floors of which comprise the **Sackler Museum**, dedicated to the art of classical, Asian, and Islamic cultures. The museum's holdings far outstrip its available space, which is why the first floor is devoted to rotating exhibits. Islamic and Asian art are the themes of the second floor, featuring illustrations from Muslim texts and Chinese landscapes from the past several centuries. The fourth floor is best for its excellent array of sensuous Buddhist sculptures from ancient China, India, and Southeast Asia.

Harvard Museum of Natural History

North past the Sackler Museum, Divinity Avenue holds another series of museums, the bulk of which are grouped together in a consortium called the **Harvard Museum of Natural History** (Ⓦwww.hmnh.harvard.edu), which showcases objects from the natural world in tandem with cultural artifacts discovered on professor-led digs. The result is a pretty specialized collection of academic odds and sods; still, even the most dispassionate observer will find something of interest here.

The most prominent of the group is the **Peabody Museum of Archaeology and Ethnology,** 11 Divinity Ave (Mon–Sat 9am–5pm, Sun 1–5pm; $5, free Sat 9am–noon; Ⓦwww.peabody.harvard.edu), which displays materials culled from Harvard's anthropological and archeological expeditions. The strength of the museum lies in its collection of pieces from Mesoamerica, ranging from digs in the pueblos of the southwestern United States to artifacts from Incan civilizations – though the wax dummies in traditional garb and the miniature dioramas can't help but seem hokey and out of place. Harvard's Mineralogical and Geological Museum is, basically, a bunch of rocks. If you don't know much about geology, this probably won't do too much for you, though most of the gems are aesthetically pleasing. Right next door (you can pass through from one to the other without exiting the building), and similarly narrow in scope, is the **Botanical Museum** at 26 Oxford St. You might think this collection is only of interest to botanists, and much of it may well be, but it's still worth a pass to take in the stunning Ware Collection of Glass Models of Plants. This project began in 1887 and terminated almost fifty years later in 1936, leaving the museum with an absolutely unique and visually awesome collection of flower models constructed to the last detail, entirely from glass. Housed in the same building as the Botanical Museum, but lacking a similar knockout centerpiece, the Museum of Comparative Zoology is really just the tip of the iceberg of the university's collection of zoological materials. Most of the collection is inaccessible to visitors: what is consists of rote displays of stuffed dead animals with some fascinating amber-preserved insects and impressive fossils thrown in.

Harvard Semitic Museum

Facing the Peabody is the **Harvard Semitic Museum**, at 6 Divinity Ave (Mon–Fri 10am–4pm, Sun 1–4pm; free; Ⓦwww.fas.harvard.edu/~semitic), whose informative, if somewhat unfocused, displays chronicle Harvard's century-old excavations in the Near East. Pieces range from Egyptian tombs to Babylonian cuneiform, and include a particularly appealing collection of tiny stone-cut votive figurines. What distinguishes the collection, though, is its focus on the process and methodology of the digs, with concomitant examples of charts, infrared devices, and dusting tools, in addition to their results.

Old Cambridge

After the outbreak of the American Revolution, Cambridge's bourgeois majority ran the Tories out of town, leaving their sumptuous houses to be used as the quarters of the Continental Army. What was then called Tory Row is modern-day **Brattle Street**, the main drag of the **Old Cambridge** district. The area has remained a tree-lined neighborhood of stately mansions, although only two of the houses are open to the public; the rest you'll have to view from across their expansive, impeccably kept lawns.

Just off Harvard Square is the **Brattle House**, at 42 Brattle St, which fails to reflect the unabashedly extravagant lifestyle of its former resident, William Brattle. It doesn't appear nearly as grand as it once did, dwarfed as it is by surrounding office buildings, nor is it open to the public – no great loss since it now only houses offices. A sign on the corner of Brattle and Story streets commemorates the site of a tree which once stood near the **Dexter Pratt House**, home of the village blacksmith celebrated by Longfellow in the popular poem *Under a Spreading Chestnut Tree*. These days the house holds the *Blacksmith House* bakery, producers of some of the finest scones around.

Longfellow House

One house you *can* visit is the recently renovated **Longfellow House** at 105 Brattle St (May–Oct Wed–Sun 10am–4.30pm, tours hourly 10.30–11.30am & 1–4pm; $3; Ⓣ876-4491, Ⓦwww.nps.gov/long; Harvard Ⓣ), the best-known and most popular of the Brattle Street mansions, where the poet Henry Wadsworth Longfellow lived while serving as a professor at Harvard. It was erected for Royalist John Vassal in 1759, who promptly vacated it on the eve of the Revolutionary War. During the war, it was used by George Washington as his headquarters during the siege of Boston, and it wasn't until 1843 that it became home to Longfellow, who moved in as a boarder; when he married the wealthy Fanny Appleton, her father purchased the house for them as a wedding gift. Longfellow lived here until his death in 1882, and the house is preserved in an attempt to portray it as it was during his residence. The halls and walls are festooned with Longfellow's furniture and art collection: most surprising is the wealth of nineteenth-century pieces from the Far East, amassed by Longfellow's renegade son Charlie on his world travels; four of his Japanese screens are included, the best of which, a two-panel example depicting geishas in spring and winter costumes, is in an upstairs bedroom.

Hooper-Lee-Nichols House

The second of the Brattle Street mansions open to the public, half a mile west of the Longfellow House and well worth the trip if you've got the stamina, is the bluewashed **Hooper-Lee-Nichols House**, at no. 159 (Tues & Thurs 2–5pm, tours every hour; $5; Ⓦwww.cambridgehistory.org), one of the oldest residences in Cambridge and the best example of the character of housing design during Cambridge's colonial period. The house began as a stout, post-medieval farmhouse, and underwent various renovations until it became the Georgian mansion it is today. Knowledgeable tour guides open secret panels to reveal centuries-old wallpaper and original foundations; otherwise, you'll see rooms predictably restored with period writing tables, canopy beds, and rag dolls.

At the terminus of Brattle Street is the **Mount Auburn Cemetery**, an unexpected treasure. Laid out in 1831 as America's first "garden cemetery," its 170 acres of stunningly landscaped grounds, with ponds and fountains, provide a gorgeous contrast with the many spare "burying grounds" scattered all over Cambridge and Boston. Resting here are a medley of famous names such as the painter Winslow Homer and Christian Science founder Mary Baker Eddy, among others. Pick up a map at the visitors' center at the entrance to find out who's where and get a sense of its scope by ascending the **tower** that lies smack in its center – from here, you can see not only the entire grounds but all the way to downtown Boston.

Central and East Cambridge

Working-class **Central Cambridge** lacks any semblance of pretension – not to mention any semblance of a reason to visit – unlike its stuffy academic neighbor. **Central Square**, as you might expect, is located roughly in the geographical center of Cambridge, and is appropriately the city's civic center as well, home to its most important government buildings. There's nothing as such to see, but it's a good place to shop and eat, and is home to some of the best nightlife in Cambridge.

Overshadowed by Cambridge's busier districts, **Inman Square** marks a quiet stretch directly north of Central Square, centered around the confluence of Cambridge, Beacon, and Prospect streets. There's little of interest here either, just a pleasant, mostly residential neighborhood where much of Cambridge's Portuguese-speaking population resides. The lone landmark is the charmingly inexpert **Cambridge Firemen's Mural**, at the corner of Cambridge and Antrim streets, a work of public art commissioned to honor local men in red.

Massachusetts Institute of Technology

East Cambridge is mostly taken over by the **Massachusetts Institute of Technology** (MIT), which occupies 153.8 acres alongside the Charles and provides an intellectual counterweight to the otherwise working-class character of the area. Originally established in Allston in 1865, MIT moved to this more auspicious campus across the river in 1916 and has since risen to international prominence as a major center for theoretical and practical research in the sciences.

The campus buildings and geography reflect the quirky, nerdy character of the institute, emphasizing function and peppering it with a peculiar notion of form. Everything is obsessively numbered and coded: you can, for example, go to 1-290 (the Rogers Building) for a lecture in 1.050 (Solid Mechanics), which gets you closer to a minor in 1 (Civil and Environmental Engineering).

Behind the massive pillars that guard the entrance of the **Rogers Building**, at 77 Massachusetts Ave, you'll find a labyrinth of corridors through which students can traverse the entire east campus without ever going outside – known to Techies as the **Infinite Corridor**. Atop the Rogers Building is MIT's best-known architectural icon, a massive gilt hemisphere called the **Great Dome**. Just inside the entrance to Rogers, you'll find the **MIT Information Center** (Mon–Fri 9am–5pm).

MIT has drawn the attention of some of the major architects of the twentieth century, who have used the university's progressiveness as a testing ground for some of their more experimental works. Two of these are located in the courtyard across Massachusetts Avenue from the Rogers Building. The **Kresge Auditorium**, designed by Finnish architect Eero Saarinen, resembles a large tent, though its real claim to fame is that it puzzlingly rests on three, rather than four, corners; the architect allegedly designed it over breakfast by cutting into his grapefruit. In the same courtyard is the red-brick **MIT Chapel**, also the work of Saarinen, and shaped like a stocky cylinder with an abstract sculpture crafted from paper-thin metals serving as a rather unconventional spire; inside, a delicate metal screen scatters light patterns across the floor. The I.M. Pei-designed Weisner Building is home to the **List Visual Art Center** (Tues–Sun noon–6pm; free), which displays student works, often more technologically impressive than visually appealing. Of perhaps more interest, down Massachusetts Avenue at no. 265, the **MIT Museum** (Tues–Fri 10am–5pm, Sat & Sun noon–5pm; $5; ⓣ253-4444, ⓦweb.mit.edu/museum) has two main permanent displays, the Hologram Museum and the Hall of Hacks, the latter of which provides a retrospective on the various pranks ("hacks") pulled by Techies, and details how the madcap funsters wreaked havoc at the annual Harvard–Yale football game, for one, by landing a massive weather balloon in the middle of the gridiron.

Eating

There is no shortage of places to **eat** in Boston. The city is loaded with bars and pubs that double as restaurants, cafés that serve full meals, and plenty of higher-end dinner-only options. There's a new level of dining adventurousness these days, too, partly in response to the traditional New England-type fare that is still the area's hallmark: hearty standbys like broiled scrod, clam chowder, and Yankee pot roast, all of which owe a bit of debt to the cold-winter mentality in Boston. Most of this has shown up in the explosion of restaurants, particularly in Back Bay and the South End, serving modern, eclectic food that unfortunately doesn't always quite hit the mark.

At **lunchtime**, many places offer meals at about half the cost of dinner, a plus if you want to sample some of the food at the city's pricier and more exclusive restaurants. Pubs and taverns are also a good bet, serving sandwiches and old-fashioned grub that won't let you go hungry. **Dinner**, usually from 5pm on, is a much more exciting deal, with a wide array of **restaurants** that range from Boston's own local cuisine to ethnic foods of every stripe. You'll probably want to book ahead if you're planning to show up at a popular place (say, a bistro in the South End or on Newbury) after 6pm; places are generally open until 10 or 11pm, though in Chinatown there are numerous **late-night** spots. Also, many restaurants close on Sundays and/or Mondays, so call ahead for either of those nights, too.

As far as Boston's culinary landscape goes, there are ever-popular **Italian** restaurants, both traditional Southern and more trendy Northern, that cluster in the **North End**, mainly on Hanover and Salem streets. The city's tiny **Chinatown** packs in all types of Asian fare. **Dim sum**, where you choose selections from carts wheeled past your table, is especially big here, and you can find it any time, though mostly at lunch – the best places are always packed on weekends, with lines down the streets. Boston's trendiest restaurants, usually of the **New American** stripe, tend to cluster in **Back Bay** and the **South End**.

Cambridge eating life centers around Harvard, Inman, and Central squares, and is perhaps best distinguished for its **Indian** restaurants, forever competing against each other to offer lower prices – resulting in some of the best food values in the city.

In most places, save certain areas of downtown, you won't have a problem finding somewhere to grab a **quick bite,** whether it's a diner, deli, or some other kind of snack joint. In addition to all the spots listed below, see the bars and cafés starting on p.147, many of which offer food all day long.

Downtown, Chinatown, and the waterfront

Bakey's 45 Broad St ☎426-1710; State Ⓣ. Easily recognized by its decorative sign depicting a man slumped over an ironing board, *Bakey's* was one of the first after-hours Irish pubs to surface in the Financial District.

The Barking Crab 88 Sleeper St (at the Northern Avenue Bridge) ☎426-CRAB; South Station Ⓣ. This endearing seafood shack aims to please with its homely atmosphere, friendly service, and unpretentious, inexpensive menu – centered around anything they can pull from the ocean. On the Boston Harbor with a view of the city skyline.

Bay Tower Room 60 State St ☎723-1666; State Ⓣ. Located on the 33rd floor of a downtown high-rise, the *Bay Tower* is notable mostly for its spectacular views of Boston Harbor. The food is less remarkable, but reliable upscale American cuisine nonetheless.

Ben's Café 45 School St ☎227-3370; Government Center or Park Ⓣ. This relaxed French eatery is situated in a French Second Empire building that for a hundred years served as Boston's City Hall. Ask for a table in "The Vault" and go with the prix fixe menu; otherwise head for its airy, hideaway bar, where the price of a drink includes free hors d'oeuvres. Closed Sundays.

The Blue Diner 150 Kneeland St ☎695-0087; South Station Ⓣ. Campy bar and restaurant with a rare feature among retro diners – genuinely good food. A popular spot for a late-night nosh, open until 4am on weekends.

Chau Chow 52 Beach St ☎426-6266; Chinatown Ⓣ. One of the first Chinatown restaurants to specialize in seafood, and still one of the best. The setting is stripped-down so there's nothing to distract you from delicious salt-and-pepper shrimp or, if you're in a more adventurous mood, sea cucumber. The fancier *Grand Chau Chow*, just across Beach Street, serves basically the same food at somewhat higher prices.

Country Life 200 High St ☎951-2685; Aquarium Ⓣ. An all-vegetarian buffet near the waterfront, whose cheap and quick meal options vary daily; call the menu hotline (☎ 951-2462) to find out what's cooking.

Durgin-Park 340 Faneuil Hall Marketplace ☎227-2038; Government Center Ⓣ. A Boston landmark in operation since 1827, *Durgin-Park* has a no-frills Yankee atmosphere and a somewhat surly waitstaff. That doesn't stop folks from coming for the sizeable, pricey pot roast and roast beef dinners in the upstairs dining room. The downstairs raw bar is considerably livelier.

East Ocean City 25–29 Beach St ☎542-2504; Chinatown Ⓣ. Another seafood specialist full of aquariums where you can greet your dinner before it appears on your plate. They have especially good soft-shell crabs.

Finagle-a-Bagel 70 Frankin St ☎261-1900; Downtown Crossing Ⓣ. A small Boston chain with more than fifteen varieties of bagels that are always served fresh. Additional location in Back Bay at 535 Boylston St (☎ 266-2500; Copley Ⓣ).

Ginza 16 Hudson St ☎338-2261; Chinatown Ⓣ. Open until 4am on weekends, *Ginza* is a popular after-hours spot serving perhaps the best sushi in the city. Additional location in Brookline at 1002 Beacon St (☎ 566-9688; St Marys Ⓣ).

Jacob Wirth 31 Stuart St ☎338-8586; Arlington Ⓣ. A German-themed Boston landmark, around since 1868; even if you don't like bratwurst washed down with a hearty lager, something is sure to please. A Boston must-visit.

Jimmy's Harborside 242 Northern Ave ⓣ423-1000; South Station Ⓣ. Totally tacky, but the harbor views and seafood are beyond reproach. House specialties include the sizeable King Lobsters and the Shore Dinners, a panoply of shellfish harvested along the New England seashore.

Kam Lung Bakery and Restaurant 77 Harrison St ⓣ542-2229; Chinatown Ⓣ. Tiny takeout joint that peddles dim sum, bakery treats (sweet rolls, sugary moon pies), and more exotic delicacies like pork buns and meat pies.

Locke-Ober Café 3 Winter Place ⓣ542-1340; Park Ⓣ. Don't be fooled by the name: *Locke-Ober Café* is very much a restaurant, and one of the most bluebloodеd in Boston. The fare consists of stuff like steak tartare and oysters on the half shell, while the setting is dark, ornate, and stuffy. There's an archaic dress code, too – jacket and tie for men.

Mantra 52 Temple Place ⓣ542-8111; Park St Ⓣ. A snazzy hookah den completes the over-the-top atmosphere at this chi-chi Indian-French restaurant where you can dine on grilled filet mignon and caramelized sweetbreads, or treat yourself to a chocolate "degustation" – four rich, cocoa-infused desserts. All in all, a definite experience.

Milk Bottle 300 Congress St ⓣ482-3343; South Station Ⓣ. This Boston landmark in front of the Children's Museum dishes out bagels and cream cheese, ice cream, and coffee from its tiny kiosk window; patrons content themselves by sitting at nearby picnic tables.

Milk Street Café 50 Milk St ⓣ542-3663; State Ⓣ; Post Office Square Park ⓣ350-7273; Downtown Crossing Ⓣ. Kosher and quick are the key words at these two downtown eateries, popular with suits and vegetarians for the large designer sandwiches and salads.

Mr. Dooley's Boston Tavern 77 Broad St ⓣ338-5656; State Ⓣ. One of the many Irish pubs downtown, though with a quieter and more atmospheric interior than the rest. Also known for its live music acts and Traditional Irish Breakfast Sundays – nice, especially since finding anything open around here on Sunday is a challenge.

No. 9 Park 9 Park St ⓣ742-9991; Park St Ⓣ. Highly recommended restaurant with sedate green walls and plates busy with Southern French and Italian entrées. A seven-course tasting menu ($85; with wine $135) allows you to try almost everything.

Penang 685 Washington St ⓣ451-6373; Chinatown Ⓣ. *Penang* takes its name from an island off the northwest coast of Malaysia. The painfully overdone interior is countered by consistently good food: try the *roti canai* appetizer or the copious yam pot dinner.

Pho Pasteur 682 Washington St and 8 Kneeland St ⓣ482-7467; Chinatown Ⓣ. Two restaurants, both offering a multitude of variations on *pho*, the Vietnamese noodle dish.

Radius 8 High St ⓣ426-1234; South Station Ⓣ. Housed in a former bank, this ultramodern French restaurant tries to inject a dose of minimalist industrial chic to the cautious Financial District with über cool decor and innovative menu. New Yorker Michael Schlow's tasty nouvelle cuisine is complemented by an extensive wine list.

Salty Dog Faneuil Hall Marketplace ⓣ742-2094; Government Center Ⓣ. It's worth braving the long waits here for the fresh seafood, such as the particularly good raw oysters, clams, and generous lobster dinners, all best enjoyed in the outdoor dining area.

Seasons North and Blackstone sts (in the *Bostonian Hotel*) ⓣ523-4119; Government Center or State Ⓣ. With inventive, truly excellent Modern American fare, such as stone crab with smoked corn minestrone, *Seasons* has a knack for attracting up-and-coming chefs before sending them on their way to culinary stardom.

Sel de la Terre 255 State St ⓣ720-1300; Aquarium Ⓣ. The less-expensive sister to upscale *L'Espalier* (see review, p.143) *Sel de la Terre* honors its name (Salt of the Earth) with rustic Provençale fare like hearty bouillabaisse, lamb and eggplant, and perhaps the best french fries in Boston. Conveniently, you can acquire the fixings for a waterfront picnic here, too, by calling ahead to order a hamper ($15, minus the basket), and picking it up on your way to the ferry.

Union Oyster House 41 Union St ⓣ227-2750; Government Center or State Ⓣ. The oldest continuously operating restaurant in America has two big claims to fame: French king Louis-Philippe lived over the tavern during his youth, and, perhaps apocryphally, the toothpick was first used here. The food is good too: fresh, well-prepared seafood, plus one of Boston's best raw bars.

The Wrap 82 Water St ⓣ357-9013; State Ⓣ. Sandwiches rolled in tortillas, fruit smoothies, and other lunchtime treats, all quick, easy, and cheap.

Zuma's Tex-Mex Café 7 N Market St ⓣ367-9114; State Ⓣ. Tex-Mex is a long way from home in Boston, but *Zuma's* comes up with a close approximation. Especially good are the fajitas and the salty, tangy margaritas.

North End and Charlestown

Assaggio 29 Prince St ⓣ227-7380; Haymarket Ⓣ. Reliable, classic Italian fare with contemporary touches and an extensive wine list. The main dining room, with its ceiling mural of the Zodiac and steady stream of opera music, is calm and relaxing.

The Daily Catch 323 Hanover St ⓣ523-8567; Haymarket ⓣ; 261 Northern Ave ⓣ338-3093; South Station ⓣ. Ocean-fresh seafood, notably *calamari* and shellfish – Sicilian-style, with mega-doses of garlic – draws big lines to this tiny storefront restaurant. The downtown location offers a solid alternative to the touristy Yankee scrod-and-chips thing.

Dolce Vita 237 Hanover St ⓣ720-0422; Haymarket ⓣ. Sit in the quiet upstairs dining room in this longstanding North End spot to savor their famous Ravioli Rose, in a tomato cream sauce. Don't come here if you're in a hurry, though – service can be slow.

Ernesto's 69 Salem St ⓣ523-1373; Haymarket ⓣ. The cheap, oversized slices of thin-crust pizza served here can't be beat for a quick lunch.

Mama Maria 3 North Square ⓣ523-0077; Haymarket ⓣ. A favorite special-occasion restaurant, and considered by some to be the best the district has to offer; in any case its location, on historic North Square, is as good a reason as any to come. The Northern Italian fare is of consistently impeccable quality. Dinner only.

Marcuccio's 125 Salem St ⓣ723-1807; Haymarket ⓣ. Contemporary Italian food in a nice setting, with Pop Art updates of Renaissance masterpieces on the walls. The chef has a light, piquant touch that works particularly well with seafood dishes, risottos, and salads. No credit cards; dinner only.

Monica's 67 Prince St ⓣ720-5472; Haymarket ⓣ. Some of the most intensely flavored Italian fare around, prepared and served by Monica's three sons, one of whom drew the cartoons plastered over the walls. They do a brisk takeout (sandwiches and such) at lunch, though the best dishes are reserved for dinner. Monica herself has a gourmet shop around the corner at 130 Salem St (see p.158).

Olives 10 City Square ⓣ242-1999; Community College ⓣ. *Olives* is consistently rated among Boston's best restaurants, and justifiably so. Chef Todd English turns out New Mediterranean food of unforgettable flavor in sizeable portions. No reservations save for parties of six or more; very expensive. Closed Sun and Mon.

Pizzeria Regina 11 1/2 Thacher St ⓣ227-0765; Haymarket ⓣ. Visit *Regina* for tasty, cheap pizza, served in a neighborhood feed station where the wooden booths haven't budged since the 1940s. Vintage North End.

Rabia's 73 Salem St ⓣ227-6637; Haymarket ⓣ. The best thing about this small restaurant is the "Express Lunch" special: a heaped plate of pasta, chicken parmigiana or the like is yours to savor for a mere $5 from noon until 2pm, daily.

Sage 69 Prince St ⓣ248-8814; Haymarket ⓣ. Diminutive Italian restaurant that doesn't scrimp on flavor; the refreshing seasonal menu finds dishes like savory lemon and asparagus risotto and vegetable casseroles; perfect fodder for an intimate tête-à-tête.

Sorelle Bakery and Café 1 Monument Ave ⓣ242-2125. Phenomenal muffins and cookies, plus pasta salads and other lunch fare which you can enjoy on a delightful hidden patio.

Trattoria Il Panino 11 Parmenter St ⓣ720-1336; Aquarium ⓣ. A bona fide Boston best, with incredible pasta specials at lunch; a bit more formal by night.

Beacon Hill

Artu 89 Charles St ⓣ227-9023; Charles ⓣ. Though squeezed into a tiny storefront on Charles Street, *Artu* keeps things fresh, flavorful, and affordable. Authentic Italian country cooking focused on soups, risottos, roast meats, and *panini*.

Beacon Hill Bistro 25 Charles St (in the *Beacon Hill Hotel*) ⓣ723-1133; Charles ⓣ. Sleek New American and French bistro with an upscale neighborhood feel. Short ribs with prunes share counter space with cod with capers and tomatoes; breakfast is traditional American.

The Federalist 15 Beacon St ⓣ670-1500; Park Street ⓣ. The lofty, chandeliered dining room verges on sterile, but the seafood is anything but. The "seafood flight" – a citrus-flavored sea urchin and shrimp concoction – as well as the braised lobster and roasted sea bass with truffles, are out of this world (and so are the prices).

Figs 42 Charles St ⓣ742-3447; Community College ⓣ. This noisy, popular offshoot of *Olives* (see below) has excellent thin-crust pizzas, topped with such savory items as figs and prosciutto or caramelized onions and arugula.

The Hungry I 71 Charles St ⓣ227-3524; Charles ⓣ. Don't sweat the pricey menu and hyped-up, romantic surroundings, because the food here is delectable – classic American fare with creative twists that change nightly; if you're there on a night featuring the signature venison with poivre noir (black pepper), prepare for food heaven.

The King & I 145 Charles St ⓣ227-3320; Charles ⓣ. Excellent, inventive Thai with bold, but not overbearing, flavors. The "Shrimp in Love" is almost worth trying for its name alone.

Paramount 44 Charles St ⓣ720-1152; Charles

Ⓣ. The Hill's neighborhood diner serves Belgian waffles and *frittatas* to the brunch regulars by day, and decent American standards like hamburgers and meatloaf by night.

Ruby's Diner 280 Cambridge St ☎367-3224; Charles Ⓣ. Very basic breakfast chow – eggs and such – done cheaply and well. Open all night Thurs–Sat.

Back Bay

Ambrosia 116 Huntington Ave ☎247-2400; Prudential or Copley Ⓣ. French Provençal meets Asian fusion cuisine. At lunch, most salads, gourmet sandwiches, and other entrées are priced under $12.

Aujourd'hui 200 Boylston St (in the *Four Seasons*) ☎338-4400 or 1-800/332-3442; Arlington Ⓣ. One of Boston's best, this is a good place to splurge. Nibble roasted Maine lobster – accompanied by crabmeat wontons, pineapple compote, and fenugreek broth – from antique china while enjoying the view out over the Public Garden.

Back Bay Brewing Company 755 Boylston St ☎424-8300; Copley Ⓣ. Of all the brewpubs in Boston, this feels the least like a glorified bar: the breakfast fare is every bit as good as the inventive lunch and dinner offerings. If you just want a brew, though, settle into the comfortable second-floor lounge and take your pick.

Betty's Wok & Noodle Diner 250 Huntington Ave ☎424-1950; Symphony Ⓣ. Mix and match from a list of rice, noodles, sauces (from Asian pesto to Cuban chipotle-citrus), vegetables, and meats and, minutes later, you'll be enjoying a piping hot plateful of tasty Chino-Latino food. Open every day until 11pm.

Bombay Café 175 Massachusetts Ave ☎247-0555; Hynes Ⓣ. The chicken tikka and stuffed naan are good bets – as is anything with seafood – at this casual Indian restaurant.

Café Jaffa 48 Gloucester St ☎536-0230; Hynes Ⓣ. Boston's best falafel served in an inviting space.

Cottonwood Restaurant & Café 222 Berkeley St ☎247-2225; Arlington Ⓣ. Creative, tasty Southwestern fare served in a bright setting. Famous for its margaritas, this is also one of Back Bay's best bets for lunch or Sunday brunch with a twist.

Du Barry Restaurant Français 159 Newbury St ☎262-2445; Copley Ⓣ. One of the few classic French restaurants in Boston. Nothing too inventive, just good, hearty staples plus a hidden terrace and a quiet bar popular with locals.

Emack & Bolio's 290 Newbury St ☎247-8772; Copley Ⓣ. Pint-sized ice-cream parlor named for a long-defunct rock band. Try a scoop each of Chocolate Moose and Vanilla Bean Speck in a chocolate-dipped waffle cone to get hooked.

Grill 23 161 Berkeley St ☎542-2225; Arlington Ⓣ. This carnivore-fest is as clubby as Boston gets: the steaks are aged in-house, accompanied by a myriad of wines, and served amidst patrons who are encouraged to smoke ad nauseum – cigars included.

Gyuhama 827 Boylston St ☎437-0188; Hynes Ⓣ. Noisy basement-level sushi bar, favored by students for late-night Japanese snacks.

Kashmir 279 Newbury St ☎536-1695; Hynes Ⓣ. The food and decor are equally inviting at Newbury Street's only Indian restaurant.

Kaya 581 Boylston St ☎236-5858; Copley Ⓣ. This is the place to go when the craving for Japanese–Korean food kicks in.

Legal Sea Foods 27 Park Square (in the *Park Plaza Hotel*) ☎426-4444; Arlington Ⓣ; 100 Huntington Ave, Level Two, Copley Place ☎266-7775; Copley Ⓣ; 800 Boylston St, Prudential Center ☎266-6800; Prudential Ⓣ; 5 Cambridge Center ☎864-3400; Kendall Ⓣ. This local chain is probably the best-known seafood restaurant in America, and for many, it's the best, as well. Go early to avoid long lines, which can be expected no matter the location or day of the week.

L'Espalier 30 Gloucester St ☎262-3023; Hynes Ⓣ. A ravishing French restaurant in a Back Bay brownstone. The food is first-rate, but the lofty prices suggest that ambience is factored into your bill.

Miyako 279 Newbury St ☎236-0222; Copley Ⓣ. Authenticity comes at a price at this Japanese standby, which has a popular terrace on Newbury Street, a sleek sushi bar inside, and a minimalist decor of muted grays and bright floral arrangements.

Stephanie's on Newbury 190 Newbury St ☎236-0990; Copley Ⓣ. Though they pride themselves on their smoked salmon potato pancake, what sets *Stephanie's* apart is their sidewalk dining in the prime people-watching territory of Newbury Street. Open until midnight.

Steve's Greek-American Cuisine 316 Newbury St ☎267-1817; Hynes Ⓣ. Excellent Greek food makes this one of Boston's classic cheap eats.

Thai Basil 132 Newbury St ☎424-8424; Copley Ⓣ. Excellent seafood and vegetarian dishes, plus soothing decor in which to enjoy it.

Top of the Hub 800 Boylston St ☎536-1775; Prudential Ⓣ. Inventive New England fare on the 50th floor of the Prudential Tower.

South End

Aquitaine 569 Tremont St ☎424-8577; Back Bay

Ⓣ. This swanky French brasserie is *the* place to be and be seen; settle into a marvelous leather banquette, gape at the astonishing array of wine, and feast on the best steak frites and foie gras in town.

Claremont Café 535 Columbus Ave ⓣ247-9001; Back Bay Ⓣ. Diverse appetizers (like cornmeal-fried oysters with jicama slaw), imaginatively garnished entrées, and particularly flavorful desserts, including a stellar banana creme pie. Closed Mondays.

The Delux Café & Lounge 100 Chandler St ⓣ338-5258; Back Bay Ⓣ. The South End's cool spot of the moment is this retro hideaway *boîte*; the menu is loosely American fusion – but it doesn't matter, as most go for the buzz more than the food.

Hamersley's Bistro 553 Tremont St ⓣ423-2700; Back Bay Ⓣ. *Hamersley's* is widely regarded as one of the best restaurants in Boston, and with good cause. Every night star chef (and owner) Gordon Hamersley dons a baseball cap and takes to the open kitchen, where he dishes out unusual – and unforgettable – French-American fare that changes with the seasons.

Mike's City Diner 1714 Washington St ⓣ267-9393; Back Bay Ⓣ. Classic diner breakfasts and lunches in an out-of-the way setting in the South End.

Mistral 221 Columbus Ave ⓣ867-9300; Arlington Ⓣ. Still one of *the* places to go in Boston, *Mistral* serves pricey modern Provençal food in a bright, airy space above the Turnpike. Despite the raves, the food doesn't live up to the cost. Dinner only.

On the Park One Union Park ⓣ426-0862; Back Bay Ⓣ. Its secluded setting on the quiet south side of Union Park is as much of a draw as the French bistro fare at this neighborhood restaurant. The vegetarian cassoulet is a winner, and there's an intimate brunch on weekends.

Pho Republique 1415 Washington St ⓣ262-0005; Back Bay Ⓣ. Funky Vietnamese restaurant that attracts a young, stylish clientele who dine on hearty servings of *pho* and sip divine lemongrass martinis; an in-house DJ keeps patrons nodding their heads long after their meal is done.

Truc 560 Tremont St ⓣ338-8070; Back Bay Ⓣ. That Julia Child was a regular (before she left town in 2002) suggests the *hauteur* to which this secluded French bistro aspires. The limited menu doesn't disappoint, with appetizers like warm mushroom salad and entrées like crab-stuffed trout; ask for a table in the romantic greenhouse room at the back, to dine overlooking a charming garden.

Kenmore Square, The Fenway, and Brookline

Anna's Taqueria 1412 Beacon St ⓣ739-7300; Coolidge Corner Ⓣ. Exceptional tacos, burritos, and *quesadillas* are the only things on the menu at this bright and extremely cheap Mexican eatery – but they're so good branches had to be opened around the corner at 446 Harvard St, Coolidge Corner Ⓣ, and in Cambridge at 8222 Sommerville Ave, Porter Ⓣ, to accommodate its legions of devotees.

Brown Sugar 129 Jersey St ⓣ266-2928; Kenmore Ⓣ. Charming neighborhood restaurant near the Museum of Fine Arts, serving Boston's best Thai food. Everything here is wonderfully fresh, and some selections, like the basil chicken, are superbly spicy. There are ample vegetarian options, too.

Buteco 130 Jersey St ⓣ247-9508; Kenmore Ⓣ. The setting's not much, but the downright tasty Brazilian home-cooking served at this no-frills joint more than compensates; the weekend *feijoada* – a sausage, dried beef, and black bean stew – is utterly authentic and is often accompanied by a live Brazilian band.

Matt Murphy's 14 Harvard St, Brookline ⓣ232-0188; Coolidge Corner Ⓣ. Authentic Irish comfort food such as warm potato and leek soup with brown bread and rabbit pie with Irish soda bread crust. The place is tiny, and you may have to wait, but it's well worth it.

Washington Square Tavern 714 Washington St, Brookline ⓣ232-8989; Washington Square Ⓣ. Cozy, off-the-beaten-path restaurant/bar with an eclectic fusion menu that turns out inventive meals like pork tenderloin with fig glaze and sweet potatoes.

Wonder Bar 186 Harvard Ave, Allston-Brighton ⓣ351-2665; Harvard Ave Ⓣ. Popular late twenty-early thirtysomething hangout that scores points with its clay pot concoctions and tapas snacks, though it really comes alive after dark; its strict dress code (no tennis shoes, ripped jeans, or hats) is a bit over-the-top for the neighborhood, however.

Southern districts

Amrheins 80 W Broadway, South Boston ⓣ268-6189; Broadway Ⓣ. A Southie landmark and a favorite of local politicians for generations. The good-ole' American comfort food won't dazzle your palate, but it's reasonably priced and you get a lot of it.

Bella Luna 405 Centre St, Jamaica Plain ⓣ524-6060; Green St Ⓣ. *Nouvelle* pizza with a funky array of fresh toppings (you can order from their list of combinations or design your own) in a festive space. Jazz brunch on Sunday mornings and live entertainment on most weekends.

Bob the Chef 604 Columbus Ave, Roxbury ⓣ536-6204; Mass Ave Ⓣ. The best soul food in New England. Good chitlins, black-eyed peas, and collard greens – and don't miss the "glori-fried chicken," the house specialty. Live jazz on weekends.

Cambridge

Bartley's Burger Cottage 1246 Massachusetts Ave ⓣ354-6559; Harvard Ⓣ. The walls here are decorated with references to political humor and pop culture, while the names of the dishes on the menu poke fun at celebrities of the hour. The food itself is loaded with cholesterol, but a burger and "frappe" (milkshake) here is a definite experience.

Blue Room 1 Kendall Square ⓣ494-9034; Kendall Ⓣ. Unpretentious restaurant with superlative grilled fusion; tuna steak and braised lamb are common, but what accompanies them – cumin and basmati yogurt or tomatillos – isn't.

Boca Grande 1728 Massachusetts Ave ⓣ354-7400; Porter Ⓣ. Somewhere in between a restaurant and a taco stand, crowded *Boca* vends delectable, if not quite authentic, Mexican fare at incredibly low prices – no entrée is above $5.

Border Café 32 Church St ⓣ864-6100; Harvard Ⓣ. Cambridge's most popular Tex-Mex place is pretty good, though not nearly enough to justify the massive crowds that form on weekend nights. The margaritas are salty and strong, and the moderately-priced food is so pungent that you'll carry its aroma with you for hours afterward.

Café of India 52 Brattle St ⓣ661-0683; Harvard Ⓣ. This inexpensive Indian spot stands out primarily because of its uplifting, woody interior; in summer, the facade is removed for semi-alfresco dining. Its best dishes are the tried-and-true Indian standards.

Cambridge Common 1667 Massachusetts Ave ⓣ547-1228; Harvard or Porter Ⓣ. Half bar, half restaurant, *Cambridge Common* is a popular after-work place for young professionals and graduate students. The "Ultimate Nachos" appetizer could stand as a meal on its own. A downstairs music venue, the *Lizard Lounge* (see review p.151), has decent rock and jazz acts almost nightly.

Central Kitchen 567 Massachusetts Ave ⓣ491-5599; Central Ⓣ. Hip Central Square bistro with a delightful chalkboard menu offering French classics (moules frites) and New American twists (grilled octopus with shaved fennel) in an intimate, stylish setting.

C'est Bon 1432 Massachusetts Ave ⓣ661-0610; 110 Mt Auburn St ⓣ492-6465; Harvard Ⓣ (both locations). Small, centrally located shop, in two branches, both of which serve up excellent coffee, fresh baked goods, and the best falafel in the area at inexpensive prices. Open late.

Charlie's Kitchen 10 Eliot St ⓣ492-9646; Harvard Ⓣ. Marvelously atmospheric townie hangout in the heart of Harvard Square, with red vinyl booths, sassy waitresses with beehive hairdos, and greasy diner food. Try the cheap but filling Double Cheeseburger Special.

Chez Henri 1 Shepard St ⓣ354-8980; Harvard or Porter Ⓣ. Does paying more at a fancy restaurant actually mean you'll get a vastly superior meal? At *Chez Henri*, the answer is an emphatic yes. If you can get a table (no reservations, and the weekend wait tops one hour even late at night), you'll enjoy what may well be Cambridge's finest cuisine. Chef Paul O'Connell's experiment in fusion brings Modern French together with Cuban influences, best sampled in the light salads and excellent Cuban crab cake appetizers, and the chicken *asado* that follows.

Darwin's Ltd 148 Mt Auburn St ⓣ354-5233; Harvard Ⓣ. The rough-hewn exterior conceals a delightful deli serving the best sandwiches on Harvard Square – wonderfully inventive combinations, such as roast beef, sprouts, and apple slices, served on freshly baked bread.

East Coast Grill 1271 Cambridge St ⓣ491-6568; Harvard or Central Square Ⓣ. A festive and funky atmosphere – think shades of *Miami Vice* – in which to enjoy fresh seafood (there is a raw bar tucked into one corner) and Southern side dishes such as grilled avocado, pineapple salsa, and fried plantains. The Sunday serve-yourself Bloody Mary bar is reason enough to visit.

Harvest 44 Brattle St ⓣ868-2255; Harvard Ⓣ. Upscale, white-tableclothed Harvard Square institution with an oft-changing menu of rich New American cuisine; the smashing outdoor courtyard is another fine feature.

Henrietta's Table 1 Bennett St (in the *Charles Hotel*) ⓣ661-5005; Harvard Ⓣ. One of the only restaurants in Cambridge that serves classic New England fare. Some might say, however, that a trip to *Henrietta's* is wasted if it's not for their famous brunch, served every Sunday from noon to 3pm; it costs $35 per person but allows unlimited access to a cornucopia of the farm-fresh treats from around New England.

Herrell's Ice Cream 15 Dunster St ⓣ497-2179; Harvard Ⓣ. Both the long lines and the profusion of "Best of Boston" awards that adorn the walls attest to the well-deserved popularity of this local ice-cream parlor. The chocolate pudding flavor is a particular delight, especially combined with "smoosh-ins," such as Junior Mints or crushed Oreo cookies. Open until midnight.

House of Blues 96 Winthrop St ⓣ491-2583; Harvard Ⓣ. The original *House of Blues* serves up mediocre Southern food in a carefully manufactured roadhouse setting. Come here, instead, for the big-name blues and rock acts at the upstairs venue (see p.151).

Iruña 56 JFK St ⓣ868-5633; Harvard Ⓣ. Located in a diminutive, unassuming spot in an alley off JFK Street, this fairly uncrowded spot serves authentic Spanish fare. Lunch specials are incredibly cheap, including *paella* and a rich *arroz con pollo*; dinner is more expensive but equally good.

Leo's Place 35 JFK St ⓣ354-9192; Harvard Ⓣ. Possibly the best-kept secret in Cambridge, *Leo's* red-walled retro diner serves hearty breakfasts until late – and for next to nothing. A real find.

Pho Pasteur 35 Dunster St, in the Garage ⓣ864-4100; Harvard Ⓣ. Upscale Harvard Square incarnation of the successful Chinatown string of Vietnamese joints serving a variety of filling and delicious *pho* noodle soups beginning at $7.

Tandoor House 569 Massachusetts Ave ⓣ661-9001; Central Ⓣ. Consistently at the top of the list of Cambridge's many fine Indian restaurants, *Tandoor* has excellent chicken *saag* and a great mushroom *bhaji*.

Toscanini's 1310 Massachusetts Ave ⓣ354-9350; Harvard Ⓣ. An ever-changing ice-cream list includes original flavors like Khulfee, a concoction of pistachios, almonds, and cardamom.

Upstairs at the Pudding 10 Holyoke St ⓣ864-1933; Harvard Ⓣ. The dining room was converted from what was originally the eating area for Harvard's ultra-elite Hasty Pudding Club – and the attitude lingers on. The food is excellent, though, falling somewhere between New American and Old Colonial. Reservations essential.

Somerville

Dalí 415 Washington St ⓣ661-3254; Harvard Ⓣ. Waitresses dance the flamenco at this upscale tapas restaurant, which features live, energetic Spanish music, excellent sangría, and superlative tapas. Your taste buds will thank you.

Diva 246 Elm St ⓣ629-4963; Davis Ⓣ. This trendy Davis Square spot isn't your typical Indian restaurant: the space is stylishly modern and cushy, the entrées pricey ($12–$16), and the mix of Northern and Southern dishes unusually mild, spice-wise.

Redbones 55 Chester St ⓣ628-2200; Davis Ⓣ. All styles of American barbecue are represented in huge portions here, accompanied by delectable sides such as collard greens and Cajun "dirty rice." After eating, you won't likely have room for dessert – but if you do, the pecan pie is top-notch. Long lines at dinner, so arrive early. No cards.

The Rosebud Diner 381 Summer St ⓣ666-6015; Davis Ⓣ. Authentic diner car, with red vinyl booths, pink neon sign, and chrome detail, that serves the expected burgers, fries, and Boston Creme Pie along with more contemporary favorites like pasta, grilled chicken, and veggie burgers.

Drinking

Despite – or perhaps because of – the lingering Puritan anti-fun ethic that pervades Boston, people here seem to **drink** more than in most other American cities. The most prevalent place to nurse a pint is the **Irish pub**, of which there are high concentrations in the **West End** and downtown around **Quincy Market**. More upscale are the bars and lounges of **Back Bay**, along Newbury and Boylston streets, which offer attitude as much as anything else. The rest of the city's neighborhood bars, pick-up joints, and yuppie hotspots are differentiated by their crowds: **Beacon Hill** tends to be older and a bit stuffy; **downtown**, mainly around Quincy Market and the Theater District, draws a healthy mix of tourists and locals; **Kenmore Square** and **Cambridge** are fairly student-oriented. The **café** scene is not quite as diverse, but still offers a decent range of places to hang out. The toniest spots are again those that line the Back Bay's **Newbury Street**, where you pay as much for the fancy environs as for the quality of the coffee. Value is much better in the **North End**, but the most lively cafés are across the river in **Cambridge**, and cater, unsurprisingly, to the large student population.

Bars

Bars stop serving at 2am (at the latest), and most strictly enforce the drinking-age minimum of 21. Be prepared to show either a driver's license or passport. The one potential for after-hours drinking is **Chinatown**, where some restaurants will bring you a pot of beer if you ask for the "cold tea."

Downtown

Bell in Hand Tavern 45 Union St ⓣ227-2098; State or Government Center Ⓣ. The oldest continuously operating tavern in Boston draws a fairly exuberant mix of tourists and young professionals.
The Black Rose (Roisin Dubh) 160 State St ⓣ742-2286; State Ⓣ. Down-home Irish pub specializing in imported beers from the Emerald Isle.
The Good Life 28 Kingston St ⓣ451-2622; Downtown Crossing Ⓣ. This swanky bar (and restaurant) generates quite a buzz, due as much to its potent martinis as its 1970s decor, which features wicked groovy orange vinyl walls.
Green Dragon Tavern 11 Marshall St ⓣ367-0055; Government Center Ⓣ. Another tavern that dates to the Colonial era. There's a standard selection of tap beers, a raw bar, and a full menu rife with twee historical humor ("One if by land, two if by seafood").
The Kinsale 2 Center Plaza ⓣ742-5577; Government Center Ⓣ. Shipped brick by brick from Ireland to its current location in the shadow of Government Plaza, this outrageously popular Irish pub is as authentic as it gets; the menu even lists beer-battered fish and hot pastrami on a "bulkie" (Boston slang for a sandwich bun).
The Littlest Bar in Boston 47 Province St ⓣ523-9766; Downtown Crossing Ⓣ. The tiny size of this place – it's only allowed 38 people in its cramped quarters at any given time – is part of the charm, as are the quality pints of Guinness.
The Purple Shamrock 1 Union St ⓣ227-2060; State or Government Center Ⓣ. A lively watering hole that draws a broad cross-section of folks, the *Shamrock* has one of Boston's better straight singles scenes. It gets very crowded on weekends.
The Rack 24 Clinton St ⓣ725-1051; Government Center Ⓣ. Well-dressed twenty- and thirtysomethings convene at this pool hall to dine, smoke cigars, drink a bewildering variety of cocktails, and, of course, shoot a rack or two.

Charlestown

Warren Tavern 2 Pleasant St ⓣ241-8142; Community College Ⓣ. An atmospheric place to enjoy a drink, and the oldest standing structure in Charlestown. The *Warren* also has a generous menu of good tavern food.

Beacon Hill and the West End

21st Amendment 148 Bowdoin St ⓣ227-7100; Bowdoin Ⓣ. This dimly lit, down-home watering hole, which gets its name from the amendment that repealed Prohibition, is a favorite haunt of legislators from the adjacent State House and students from nearby Suffolk University.
The Bull & Finch Pub 84 Beacon St ⓣ227-9605; Arlington Ⓣ. If you don't already know, and if the conspicuous banners outside don't tip you off, this is the bar that served as the inspiration for the TV show *Cheers*. If you've gotta go, be warned – it's packed with camera-toting tourists, the inside bears little resemblance to the NBC set, and the food, though cutely named (eNORMous burgers), is pricey and mediocre. Plus, it's almost certain that nobody will know your name.
Fours 166 Canal St ⓣ720-4455; North Station Ⓣ. The classiest of the West End's sports bars, with an army of TVs to broadcast games from around the globe, as well as paraphernalia from the Celtics, Bruins, and other local teams.
Irish Embassy 234 Friend St ⓣ742-6618; North Station Ⓣ. Up in the West End, this is one of the city's most authentic Irish (rather than Irish-American) pubs, with the crowd to match. Live Irish entertainment most nights, plus broadcasts of Irish soccer matches.
Sevens Ale House 77 Charles St ⓣ523-9074; Charles Ⓣ. While the tourists pack into the *Bull & Finch*, you can drop by this cozy wood-paneled joint to watch the game or shoot darts in an authentic Boston neighborhood bar.

Back Bay and the South End

Bukowski Tavern 50 Dalton St ⓣ437-9999; Hynes Ⓣ. Arguably Boston's best dive bar, this parking garage watering hole has views over the Mass Pike and such a vast beer selection that a homemade "wheel of indecision" is spun by waitstaff when patrons can't decide.
Dad's 911 Boylston St ⓣ296-3237; Hynes Ⓣ. Dim lights and scantily clad barmaids make this a fairly un-Back Bay watering hole – all the more so given it's actually set in an old school diner.
Daisy Buchanan's 240A Newbury St

Ⓣ247-8516; Copley Ⓣ. A real-life beer commercial: young guys wearing baseball caps, sports on TV, and a pervasive smell of booze.

Oak Bar 138 St James Ave (in the *Fairmont Copley Plaza*) Ⓣ267-5300; Copley Ⓣ. Rich wood paneling, high ceilings, swirling cigar smoke, and excellent martinis make this one of the more genteel Back Bay spots to drink.

Whiskey Park 64 Arlington St (in the *Park Plaza*) Ⓣ542-1482; Arlington Ⓣ. Owned by Randy Gerber (aka Mr Cindy Crawford), this lounge's chic chocolate-brown leather chair design was conceived by Michael Czysz, the guy behind Lenny Kravitz's swinging Miami pad. The prices match the celebrity name-dropping, but there's hardly a better place in town to grab a cocktail.

Kenmore Square, The Fenway, and Brookline

Audubon 838 Beacon St Ⓣ421-1910; Kenmore Ⓣ. Sleek bar where a well-dressed crowd gathers for cocktails and fancy bar food before and after games at nearby Fenway Park.

Boston Beer Works 61 Brookline Ave Ⓣ536-2337; Kenmore Ⓣ. A brewery located right by Fenway Park, *Boston Beer Works* is a popular place for the Red Sox faithful to warm up before games and drown their sorrows after. Their signature ale is "Boston Red," but the seasonal brews are also worth a taste. Decent food, too.

Southern Districts

Brendan Behan 378 Centre St, Jamaica Plain Ⓣ522-5386; Jackson Square Ⓣ. The godfather of Boston's Irish pubs, this dimly lit institution has the usual friendly staff all week long and live music and free buffets available on most weekends.

James's Gate 5–11 McBride St, Jamaica Plain Ⓣ983-2000; Forest Hills Ⓣ. Beat Boston's harsh winter by sipping Guinness by the blazing fireplace in this cozy pub, or by trying the hearty fare in the restaurant in back.

Cambridge

The Cellar 991 Massachusetts Ave Ⓣ876-2580; Harvard Ⓣ. Two floors, each with a bar, filled with a regular crowd of Harvard faculty members, older students, and other locals imbibing fine beers and killer Long Island iced teas.

The Druid 1357 Cambridge St Ⓣ497-0965; #69 bus. Twee Inman Square bar featuring an old Celtic motif, with murals of druid priests and ever-present pints of Guinness; blessedly free of the college scene.

Enormous Room 577 Massachusetts Ave (no phone); Central Ⓣ. Walking into this comfy lounge tucked above *Central Kitchen* (see p.145) is tantamount to entering an opium den minus the pipe smokers. Sundry good-looking types primp and pose on thick-piled futon mattresses and deep leather sofas, while deep house is piped in over the sound system.

Grendel's Den 89 Winthrop St Ⓣ491-1160; Harvard Ⓣ. A favorite spot of locals and grad students for drinking ale; these dark, conspiratorial environs have a fantastic happy-hour special, with big plates of appetizers for just $1.50 each.

Miracle of Science 321 Massachusetts Ave Ⓣ868-2866; Central Ⓣ or #1 bus. Surprisingly hip despite its status as an MIT hangout. There's noir decor and a trendy crowd of well-dressed professionals; can get quite crowded on weekend nights.

Plough & Stars 912 Massachusetts Ave Ⓣ441-3455; Central or Harvard Ⓣ. Off-the-beaten-path neighborhood hideaway that's very much worth the trek, whether for its animated cribbage games, live UK and European soccer broadcasts, quality pub grub, or its nightly live music.

Shay's 58 JFK St Ⓣ864-9161; Harvard Ⓣ. Relaxed contrast to the crowded and sweaty sports bars of Harvard Square. Unwind with grad students over wine and quality beer.

Temple Bar 1688 Massachusetts Ave Ⓣ547-5055; Harvard or Porter Ⓣ. Cambridge's stand-out scenester bar attracts a chi-chi crowd to its smart digs.

Somerville

The Burren 247 Elm St Ⓣ776-6896; Davis Ⓣ. Busy student bar whose crowds spill out onto its terrace, which is a prime spot for Davis Square people watching.

Thirsty Scholar Pub 70 Beacon St Ⓣ497-2294; Harvard Ⓣ. One of the coziest bars around, *Thirsty*'s warm red-brick and burnished wood interior is matched by a smiling waitstaff and down-home comfort food like shepherd's pie and baked beans.

Tir na Nog 366A Somerville Ave Ⓣ628-4300; Washington Square Ⓣ. Tiny, wonderful pub with a marvelously homely feel, thanks to bookcase-lined walls and friendly bar staff who pour terrific pints behind a gleaming mahogany bar.

Cafés

Although the *Starbuck's* invasion has done some real damage to the eclectic café scene in Boston and Cambridge, there are still any number of independent places to work on your novel and stroke your goatee. At many cafés, you can just as easily get an excellent full meal as you can a cup of coffee. Below are the best choices for casual hanging out; there are also plenty of cafés more suited for meals listed under "Eating" (p.139).

Downtown

Boston Coffee Exchange 101 Arch St ⓣ737-3199; Downtown Crossing ⓣ. Cramped coffee shop with a good selection of pastries and sweets to nosh while imbibing some of the best coffee in town - the decaf is so good, you'll be forgiven for thinking it's made from the real bean.

Brigham's 50 Congress St ⓣ523-9822; State ⓣ. The closest thing downtown has to a coffee shop, with an excellent soda fountain. Stick to basic ice-cream flavors – chocolate chip, vanilla – and you'll be happiest.

North End

Caffe dello Sport 308 Hanover St ⓣ523-5063; Haymarket ⓣ. A continuous stream of Rai Uno soccer matches is broadcast from the ceiling-mounted TV sets, making for an agreeable din amongst a very local crowd. Opens very early.

Caffe Paradiso 255 Hanover St ⓣ742-1768; Haymarket ⓣ. Not much on atmosphere, but the pastries are, hands-down, the best in the North End, and their superb gelato is the only homemade stuff around.

Caffe Vittoria 296 Hanover St ⓣ227-7606; Haymarket ⓣ. A Boston institution, the *Vittoria*'s atmospheric original section, with its dark wood paneling, pressed tin ceilings, murals of the Old Country, and Sinatra-blaring Wurlitzer, is vintage North End. It's only open at night, though a street-level addition next door is open by day for excellent cappuccinos.

Beacon Hill

Panificio 144 Charles St ⓣ227-4340; Charles ⓣ. Fine cups o' Joe, fresh tasty pastries (*biscotti* is the standout), and some of the best home-baked bread in the city.

Back Bay

29 Newbury 29 Newbury St ⓣ536-0290; Arlington ⓣ. A small upscale café/bar and eatery with good, if pricey, salads and the like. Don't miss the 29 Smooch, their signature dessert made with brownies and caramel ice cream. Open until 1.30am.

Armani Café 214 Newbury St ⓣ437-0909; Copley ⓣ. People watching is the *mot du jour* at this fashionista hotspot, though the good contemporary Italian fare shouldn't be overlooked, mind you.

The Other Side Cosmic Café 407 Newbury St ⓣ536-9477; Hynes ⓣ. This ultracasual spot on "the other side" of Massachusetts Avenue offers gourmet sandwiches, "creative green salads," and fresh juices.

Trident Booksellers & Café 338 Newbury St ⓣ267-8688; Copley ⓣ. A window seat at this bookstore café (see p.157), perennially popular with the cool student set, is the ideal vantage point from which to observe the flood of young passersby outside.

The South End

Flour Bakery + Café 1595 Washington St ⓣ267-4300; Back Bay ⓣ. Quite possibly the best café in town, this stylish South End spot has a drool-worthy array of brioche au chocolat, old-fashioned sour cream coffee cake, gooey caramel nut tarts, rich cakes, savory sandwiches, home-made breads, and thirst-quenching drinks. Choosing just one can be torture.

Garden of Eden Café 571 Tremont St ⓣ247-8377; Back Bay ⓣ. The doyen of the South End café scene has a prime streetside terrace, perfect espressos, and delectable morsels like orange-and-pistachio-encrusted paté de canard and chocolate and raspberry mousse cakes.

Kenmore Square and The Fenway

1369 Coffeehouse 757 Massachusetts Ave ⓣ576-4600; Central ⓣ. The *1369* mixes earnest thirty-something leftists with youthful hipsters in a relaxed environment; your best bets are the standard array of caffeinated beverages and particularly exquisite desserts. A second location is at 1369 Cambridge St ⓣ576-1369; #69 bus.

Espresso Royale Caffe 736 Commonwealth Ave ⓣ277-8737; Kenmore ⓣ. Funky little coffee shop serving traditional cups of java alongside original blends like a zesty orange cappuccino; the cheerful decor is enhanced by abstract wall paintings and cozy seats.

Cambridge

Algiers 40 Brattle St ⓣ492-1557; Harvard ⓣ. North African café popular with the artsy set; while the food is so-so and the service slow, there are few more atmospheric spots in which to sip first-rate coffee.

Tealuxe 0 Brattle St ⓣ441-0077; Harvard ⓣ. In a twist on the standard coffeehouse, what was once a curiosity shop called Loulou's Lost and Found has reincarnated itself as the only teahouse in Harvard Square. They manage to stock over 100 varieties of the stuff – loose and by the cup – though the place is smaller than a teacup.

Somerville

Diesel 257 Elm St ⓣ629-8717; Davis ⓣ. They take their caffeine seriously at this trendy, garage-like coffee shop.

Someday Café 51 Davis Square ⓣ623-3323; Davis ⓣ. Ultra-laid-back café as close an approximation to a university common room as you'll find outside of a university dorm.

Nightlife

In recent years the city's **nightlife** has received something of a wake-up call, with stylish new **clubs** springing up in places such as Downtown Crossing that were once ghost towns at night. Though Boston is by no means a 24-hour city, these spots have given a bit of fresh air to a scene that lived in the shadow of the city's so-called high culture. Most of the clubs, however, tend to be geared toward – or at least chiefly attract – either moneyed students, suburbanites, or the secretarial set.

The **live music** scene plays perhaps a bigger part in the city's nightlife. Many of the bars and clubs, especially around Kenmore Square and Harvard Square, are just as likely, if not more, to have a scruffy garage band playing for only a nominal cover as they are to have a slick DJ spinning house tunes. And Boston has spawned its share of enormous **rock** acts, from the ever-enduring Aerosmith, to the Cars, pop ska-sters Mighty Mighty Bosstones, teen heart-throbs Marky Mark and the New Kids on the Block, and, more recently, a deluge of post-punk and indie groups such as the Pixies, Sebadoh, and Folk Implosion. There is a bit less in the way of **jazz** and **blues**, but you can usually find something cheap and to your liking any day of the week.

For **club and music listings**, check Thursday's *Boston Globe* "Calendar" or the *Boston Phoenix*; the two best websites are ⓦwww.boston.com and ⓦwww.stuffatnight.com.

Nightclubs

Boston's **nightclubs** are mostly clustered in downtown's Theater District and around Kenmore Square, with a few prominent ones in Back Bay and the South End. Many of the Back Bay and South End venues are **gay clubs**, often the most happening in town. For a listing of these, see "Gay and lesbian Boston," p.155. Otherwise, a number of the clubs below have special gay nights. **Cover charges** are generally in the \$5–10 range, though sometimes there's no cover at all.

An Tua Nua 835 Beacon St, Kenmore Square ⓣ262-2121; Kenmore ⓣ. Despite its Gaelic name ("the new beginning"), this popular neighborhood hangout is just as much dance bar as it is Irish pub. Thursday's hip-hop nights get especially crowded with BU and Northeastern undergrads.

Aria 246 Tremont, Downtown ⓣ338-7080, ⓦwww.ariaboston.com; Boylston ⓣ. Glamorous lounge-cum-nightclub in the Wilbur Theatre (see p.100) with a rotating cast of hip-hop, top-40, and New York house DJs.

Avalon 15 Lansdowne St, Kenmore Square ⓣ262-2424, ⓦwww.avalonboston.com; Kenmore ⓣ. The biggest dance club in Boston, and any weekend night the place is positively jamming, usually to music spun by top international DJs. Sunday is gay night.

The Big Easy 1 Boylston Place, Back Bay ⓣ351-

7000, Ⓦ www.alleyboston.com; Boylston Ⓣ. Bar and jazz club with a New Orleans theme; for the best people watching go on a weeknight.
Club Europa/Buzz 51 Stuart St, Downtown Ⓣ 482-3939, Ⓦ www.buzzboston.com; Boylston Ⓣ. On the edge of the Theater District, this is one of Boston's better dance clubs. On Saturday night the club becomes "Buzz," the most plugged-in gay disco in Boston.
Club at Il Panino 295 Franklin St, Downtown Ⓣ 338-1000, Ⓦ www.ilpanino.com; State Ⓣ. Downstairs is a classy, reasonably-priced trattoria; upstairs is a three-story disco, one of the hottest in town. Latin house music on Friday and Saturday nights.
Envy 25 Boylston Pl, Downtown Ⓣ 542-3689, Ⓦ www.alleyboston.com; Boylston Ⓣ. What distinguishes this Top-40 club is the plethora of pastel-hued scenic murals that cover the place, painted by Hollywood film artist John P. Moores; the dance floor resembles a goldfish pond.
Milky Way 405 Centre St, Jamaica Plain Ⓣ 524-3740; #39 bus. "Lanes and lounge" – that's right, bowling alley-cum-nightclub, in the heart of Boston's hippest neighborhood.
The Roxy 279 Tremont St, Downtown Ⓣ 338-7699, Ⓦ www.roxyplex.com; Boylston Ⓣ. Cavernous singles' scene nightclub in an old-fashioned dance hall; Thursday Latin nights are particularly steamy.
Sophia's 1270 Boylston St Ⓣ 351-7001, Ⓦ www.sophiasboston.net; Kenmore Ⓣ. This great tapas restaurant is also a great spot for live salsa and Latin jazz, Tues–Sat nights. Dancing Thurs–Sat.

Live music

The strength of Boston's **live music** is its diversity, and the city serves as both a stop on the world tours of superstar performers and a hotbed of small, experimental acts. Two of the biggest venues are out of town: the Great Woods Auditorium, south of the city in Mansfield (Ⓣ 508/339-2333), and the Worcester Centrum, an hour or so west in Worcester (Ⓣ 508/798-8888). There are still, however, plenty of places in town to see either name bands or obscure experimental acts.

Rock

Bill's Bar 5½ Lansdowne St, Kenmore Square Ⓣ 421-9678; Kenmore Ⓣ. Relaxed and homely spot, with lots of beer, lots of TV, and occasional live music – in which case expect a cover charge of $5.
FleetBoston Pavilion Fan Pier, Northern Ave, Downtown Ⓣ 728-1600, Ⓦ www.fleetbostonpavilion.com; South Station Ⓣ. Formerly the Harborlights Pavilion; during the summer, concerts by well-known performers are held here under a huge white tent at Boston Harbor's edge.
FleetCenter 50 Causeway St, West End Ⓣ 624-1750, tickets Ⓣ 931-2000, Ⓦ www.fleetcenter.com; North Station Ⓣ. This arena, in the West End, attracts a decent number of the big-name acts.
Lizard Lounge 1667 Massachusetts Ave, Cambridge Ⓣ 547-0759; Harvard or Porter Ⓣ. Downstairs portion of the restaurant *Cambridge Common*, it has rock and jazz acts pretty much nightly, for a fairly nominal cover charge.
Middle East 472 Massachusetts Ave, Cambridge Ⓣ 354-8238, Ⓦ www.mideastclub.com; Central Ⓣ. Local and regional progressive rock acts regularly stop in at this Cambridge institution. Downstairs hosts bigger acts; smaller acts ply their experimental stuff in a tiny upstairs space.
Orpheum Theater 1 Hamilton Place, Downtown Ⓣ 482-0630; Park or Downtown Crossing Ⓣ. Once an old-school movie house, it's now a venue for big-name music acts. The small space means you're closer to the action, but it sells out quickly and cramped seating discourages dancing.
T.T. the Bear's 10 Brookline St, Cambridge Ⓣ 492-2327, Ⓦ www.ttthebears.com; Central Ⓣ. A downmarket version of the *Middle East*: lower-quality acts, but in a space with a grittiness and intimacy its neighbor lacks. Mostly punk, rock, and electronica acts.

Jazz, blues, and folk

Cantab Lounge 738 Massachusetts Ave, Cambridge Ⓣ 354-2685; Central Ⓣ. Although from the outside, it looks like the kind of sleazy place your mother wouldn't want you to set foot in, it's actually one of the few truly bohemian spots in town, with hopping live jazz and blues, and poetry slams every Wednesday night.
The House of Blues 96 Winthrop St, Cambridge Ⓣ 491-2583, Ⓦ www.hob.com; Harvard Ⓣ. The first in the corporate monolith spawned by the same evil geniuses who started the Hard Rock Café conglomerate. The faux-roadhouse decor and stiff,

middle-class patrons are painfully inauthentic, but the house still features top national blues acts.

Johnny D's Uptown 17 Holland St, Somerville ☎776-2004, ⓦwww.johnnyds.com; Davis Ⓣ. A mixed bag: acts include garage bands, progressive jazz sextets, traditional blues artists, and some beyond categorization.

Passim 47 Palmer St, Cambridge ☎492-7679, ⓦwww.clubpassim.org; Harvard Ⓣ. Folkie hang-out where Joan Baez and Suzanne Vega got their starts. There's also world music and spoken word performances.

Regattabar 1 Bennett St, Cambridge ☎876-7777, ⓦwww.regattabar.com; Harvard Ⓣ. The *Regattabar* draws top national jazz acts, although, as its location in the swish *Charles Hotel* might suggest, the atmosphere – and clientele – is decidedly sedate. Dress nicely and prepare to pay at least $10 cover.

Scullers Jazz Bar 400 Soldier's Field Rd in *Doubletree Guest Suites Hotel*, Brighton ☎562-4111, ⓦwww.scullersjazz.com; Harvard Ⓣ. The fact that *Scullers* is in a hotel lounge does little to dampen the enthusiasm of the first-rate jazz performers and the devoted listeners who trudge out here to see them.

Wally's Cafe 427 Massachusetts Ave, Roxbury ☎424-1408, ⓦwww.wallyscafe.com; Massachusetts Avenue Ⓣ. This refreshingly unhewn bar hosts lively jazz and blues shows that draw a vibrant crowd. No cover.

Western Front 343 Western Ave, Cambridge ☎492-7772; Central Ⓣ. The *Front* puts on rollicking jazz, blues, and reggae shows for a dance-crazy audience. Drinks are cheap, and the Jamaican food served on weekends is delectably authentic.

Performing arts and film

Boston's **cultural scene** is famously vibrant, and many of the city's artistic institutions are second to none. Foremost among them is the **Boston Symphony Orchestra**, which gave its first concert on October 22, 1881; in fact, Boston is arguably at its best in the **classical music** department, and there are many smaller but internationally-known chamber and choral music groups, from the Boston Symphony Chamber Players to the Handel & Haydn Society, to shore up that reputation. The **Boston Ballet** is also considered world-class, though it's probably best known in Boston itself for its annual holiday production of *The Nutcracker*.

The **theater** here is quite active too, even if it is, in a way, a shadow of its 1920s heyday. Boston remains a try-out city for Broadway productions, and smaller companies have increasingly high visibility. Still, it's a real treat to see a play or musical at one of the opulent old theaters such as the **Colonial** or **Emerson Majestic**. For current productions, check the listings in the *Boston Globe*'s Thursday "Calendar" section or the *Boston Phoenix*.

The **film** scene is dominated by the Sony conglomerate, which runs several multiplexes featuring major first-run movies. For foreign, independent, classic, or cult cinema, you'll have to look to other municipalities – Cambridge is best, though Brookline and Somerville have art-movie houses, too.

Classical music

Boston prides itself on being a sophisticated city of high culture, and nowhere does that show up more than in its proliferation of **orchestras** and **choral groups** – and the venues to house them. This is helped in no small part by the presence of three of the foremost music academies in the nation: Peabody Conservatory, New England Conservatory, and Berklee College of Music.

Chamber music ensembles

Alea III ⓣ353-3340 and **Boston Musica Viva** ⓣ354-6910, ⓦwww.bmv.org. Two regulars at BU's Tsai Performance Center.

Boston Baroque ⓣ484-9200, ⓦwww.boston-baroque.org. One of the country's oldest baroque orchestras is now a resident ensemble at BU.

Boston Camerata ⓣ262-2092, ⓦwww.bostoncamerata.com. Regular performances of choral and chamber concerts, from medieval to early American, at various locations in and around Boston.

Boston Chamber Music Society ⓣ349-0086, ⓦwww.bostonchambermusic.org. This society has soloists of international renown who perform in Jordan Hall (Fridays) and the Sanders Theater at Harvard (Sundays).

Boston Symphony Chamber Players ⓣ638-9289 or 1-888/266-1200, ⓦwww.bso.org. The only permanent chamber group sponsored by a major symphony orchestra and made up of its members; they perform at Jordan Hall.

The Cantata Singers & Ensemble ⓣ267-6502, ⓦwww.cantatasingers.org. Boston's premier choral group, which also performs at Jordan Hall.

Handel & Haydn Society ⓣ266-3605, ⓦwww.handelandhaydn.org. Performing chamber and choral music since 1815, these distinguished artists can be heard at Symphony Hall.

Pro Arte Chamber Orchestra ⓣ661-7067, ⓦwww.proarte.org. Cooperatively run chamber orchestra in which musicians have full control. Sunday afternoon concerts in Harvard's Sanders Theater.

Dance

The city's longest-running **dance** company is the **Boston Ballet** (ⓣ695-6950 or 1-800/447-7400, ⓦwww.bostonballet.org), with an unparalleled reputation in America and beyond; their biggest blockbuster, the yearly performance of *The Nutcracker*, has an audience attendance of more than 140,000. The troupe performs at the Wang Center (see overleaf).

Venues

Berklee Performance Center 136 Massachusetts Ave ⓣ747-2261 for scheduling information or 931-2000 for tickets, ⓦwww.berkleebpc.com; Symphony Ⓣ. Berklee College of Music's main performance center, known for its quality contemporary repertoire.

Isabella Stewart Gardner Museum 280 The Fenway ⓣ278-5150, ⓦwww.gardnermuseum.org; Museum Ⓣ. Chamber and classical concerts, including many debuts, are held regularly at 1.30pm on weekends (Sept–May) in the museum's decadent Tapestry Room. The $18 ticket price includes museum admission.

Jordan Hall 30 Gainsborough St ⓣ536-2412, ⓦwww.newenglandconservatory.edu; Symphony Ⓣ. The impressive concert hall of the New England Conservatory, just one block west from Symphony Hall, is the venue for many chamber music performances as well as those by the Boston Philharmonic (ⓣ868-6696).

Museum of Fine Arts 465 Huntington Ave ⓣ369-3770 or 369-3306, ⓦwww.mfa.org; Museum Ⓣ. During the summer, the MFA's jazz, folk, and world music "Concerts in the Courtyard," take place each Wednesday at 7.30pm; a variety of indoor performances are also scheduled for the rest of the year.

Symphony Hall 301 Massachusetts Ave ⓣ266-1492 for concert information, 638-9289 or 1-888/266-1200 for tickets, ⓦwww.bso.org; Symphony Ⓣ. This is the regal, acoustically perfect venue for the Boston Symphony Orchestra; the famous Boston Pops concerts happen in May and June; in July and August, the BSO retreats to Tanglewood, in the Berkshires (see p.272).

Tsai Performance Center 685 Commonwealth Ave ⓣ353-TSAI for event information or ⓣ353-8725 for box office, ⓦwww.bu.edu/tsai; Boston University Ⓣ. Improbably tucked into Boston University's School of Management, this mid-sized hall is a frequent venue for chamber music performances, prominent lecturers, and plays; events are often affiliated with BU and either free or very inexpensive.

Theater

It's quite possible to pay dearly for a night at the **theater**. Tickets to the bigger shows range from $25 to $75 depending on the seat, and there is, of course, the potential of a pre- or post-theater meal (see p.140 for restaurants in the Theater District). Your best option is to pay a visit to **BosTix** (ⓣ482-BTIX) – a half-price, day-of-show ticket booth with two outlets; in Copley Square, at the corner of Dartmouth and Boylston streets, and Faneuil Hall, by Abercrombie & Fitch (ⓣ482-2849; Mon–Sat 10am–6pm, Sun 11am–4pm) – tickets go on sale at 11am, and only cash is accepted. Full-price tickets can be had by phoning **Ticketmaster** (ⓣ931-2000, ⓦwww.ticketmaster.com) or contacting the individual theater directly in advance of the performance. The **smaller venues** tend to showcase more offbeat and affordable productions; shows can be under $10 – though you shouldn't bank on that.

Major venues

American Repertory Theater at the Loeb Drama Center, 64 Brattle St ⓣ547-8300, ⓦwww.amrep.org; Harvard Ⓣ. Excellent theater near Harvard Square known for staging plays by the likes of Shaw, Wilde, Ionesco, and Stoppard.

Charles Playhouse 74 Warrenton St ⓣ426-6912, ⓦwww.broadwayinboston.com; Boylston Ⓣ. The Charles has two stages, one of which is more or less the permanent home of *Shear Madness*, a participatory, comic murder mystery that's now the longest-running non-musical in American theater (ⓦwww.shearmadness.com; $34). The other stage hosts somewhat edgier material.

Colonial Theatre 106 Boylston St ⓣ426-9366, ⓦwww.broadwayinboston.com; Boylston Ⓣ. Built in 1900 and since refurbished, this is the glittering grande dame of Boston theaters, known primarily for its Broadway-scale productions.

Emerson Majestic Theatre 219 Tremont St ⓣ824-8725, ⓦwww.maj.org; Boylston Ⓣ. Emerson College, a communications and arts school, took stewardship of this 1903 Beaux Arts beauty in 1983. The lavish venue, with soaring Rococo ceiling and Neoclassical friezes, is set to reopen in 2003 following renovations, and resume hosting productions of the Emerson Stage company and the Boston Lyric Opera.

Huntington Theatre Company 264 Huntington Ave ⓣ266-8488, ⓦwww.bu.edu/huntington; Symphony Ⓣ. Productions here range from the classic to the contemporary, but they are consistently well staged at this small playhouse, the official theater of Boston University.

Shubert Theatre 265 Tremont St ⓣ482-9393 or 1-800/447-7400, ⓦwww.wangcenter.org; Boylston Ⓣ. Stars from Sir Laurence Olivier to Kathleen Turner have played the city's "Little Princess" at some point in their careers. Recent renovations have restored the 1680-seat theater to its prettier early-1900s appearance to boot, with white walls and gold leaf accents replacing the previous gaudy brown tones.

Wang Center for the Performing Arts 270 Tremont St ⓣ482-9393 or 1-800/447-7400, ⓦwww.wangcenter.org; Boylston Ⓣ. The biggest performance center in Boston opened in 1925 as the Metropolitan Theater, a movie house of palatial proportions – its original Italian marble, gold leaf ornamentation, crystal chandeliers, and 3800 seats all remain. The Boston Ballet (see p.153) is headquartered here; when their season ends, Broadway musicals often take center stage.

Wilbur Theatre 246 Tremont St ⓣ423-4008, ⓦwww.broadwayinboston.com; Boylston Ⓣ. *A Streetcar Named Desire*, starring Marlon Brando and Jessica Tandy, debuted in this small Colonial Revival theater before going to Broadway, and the Wilbur has been trying to live up to that production ever since. In winter, avoid the seats toward the back, where the loud, old heating system may leave you straining to hear.

Small venues

Boston Center for the Arts 539 Tremont St ⓣ426-2787, ⓦwww.bcaonline.org; Back Bay Ⓣ. Several theater troupes, many experimental, stage productions at the BCA, which incorporates a series of small venues on a single South End property. One of these is the Cyclorama Building (see p.121).

Hasty Pudding Theatre 12 Holyoke St ⓣ495-5205, ⓦwww.hastypudding.org; Harvard Ⓣ. Harvard University's Hasty Pudding Theatricals troupe, one of the country's oldest, mounts one show per year (usually a musical comedy; Feb & March) at this theater, then hits the road, after which the Cambridge Theatre Company moves in.

Institute of Contemporary Art Theatre 955 Boylston St ⓣ927-6620, ⓦwww.icaboston.org; Hynes Ⓣ. Boston's leading venue for all things cutting-edge.

Lyric Stage 140 Clarendon St ⓣ437-7172, ⓦwww.lyricstage.com; Copley Ⓣ. Both premieres and modern adaptations of classic and lesser-known American plays take place at this small theater within the big YWCA building.

Cinemas

In Boston, as in any other large American metropolis, it's easy enough to catch general release **films** – the usual listings sources carry all the details you'll need. If you're looking for out-of-the-ordinary film fare, however, you'll have to venture out a bit from the center. Whatever you're going to see, admission will cost you between $7 and $9, though matinees before 6pm can be cheaper. You can call ⓣ333-FILM for automated film listings.

Brattle Theater 40 Brattle St ⓣ876-6837, ⓦwww.brattlefilm.org; Harvard Ⓣ. A historic basement indie cinema that pleasantly looks its age. They have thematic film series plus occasional author appearances and readings.

Coolidge Corner Moviehouse 290 Harvard St, Brookline ⓣ734-2500, ⓦwww.coolidge.org; Coolidge Corner Ⓣ. Film buffs flock to this classic theater for foreign and independent movies. The interior has balconies and is adorned with Art Deco murals.

Harvard Film Archive Carpenter Center, 24 Quincy St ⓣ495-4700, ⓦwww.harvardfilmarchive.org; Harvard Ⓣ. A mixed bag of artsy, foreign, and experimental films.

Kendall Square Cinema One Kendall Square, Cambridge ⓣ494-9800, ⓦwww.landmarktheatres.com/Market/Boston; Kendall Ⓣ. All the neon decoration, cramped seating, and small screens of your average multiplex, but this one has the area's widest selection of first-rate foreign and independent films. It's actually located on Binney Street near Cardinal Medieros Avenue.

Museum of Fine Arts Theater 465 Huntington Ave ⓣ267-9300, ⓦww.mfa.org/film; Museum Ⓣ. Offbeat art films and documentaries, mostly by locals, and often accompanied by lectures from the filmmaker, in addition to hosting several showcases like the Boston Jewish Film and the Boston French Film festivals.

Somerville Theatre 55 Davis Square, Somerville ⓣ625-5700, ⓦwww.somervilletheatreonline.com; Davis Ⓣ. Wacky home for camp, classic, cult, independent, foreign, and first-run pictures. Also doubles as a venue for live music. It's way out there – in more ways than one – past Cambridge, but well worth the trip.

Sony Nickelodeon 606 Commonwealth Ave ⓣ424-1500; Kenmore Ⓣ. Originally an art-flick place, now taken over by the Sony group, but it features the better of the first-run features.

Gay and lesbian Boston

Boston is a fairly gay-friendly city and has a decent number of establishments that cater to a gay crowd. The center of the **gay scene** is the South End, a largely residential neighborhood whose businesses, mostly restaurants and cafés, are concentrated on a short stretch of Tremont Street above Union Park. Adjacent to the South End, on the other side of Arlington Street, is tiny **Bay Village**, which has several gay bars and clubs. The **lesbian scene** is pretty well mixed-in with the gay scene, and there are very few exclusively lesbian bars or clubs.

Boston's two free **gay newspapers** are *in newsweekly* (ⓦwww.innewsweekly.com) and *Bay Windows* (ⓦwww.baywindows.com). The latter is one of two good sources of **club information**, the other being the gay-friendly alternative paper, *The Boston Phoenix*. All can be found in various venues and bookstores, notably We Think the World of You, 540 Tremont St, Glad Day Bookstore, 673 Boylston St, and New Words, 186 Hampshire St. The latter two's vestibules have gay and lesbian community bulletin boards, with postings for apartment rentals, club happenings, and so forth. If you need to hit the **gym** whilst on vacation, head to gay-friendly Metropolitan Health Club, 209 Columbus Ave (ⓣ536-3006; $30).

Accommodation

All of Boston's **accommodations** are gay-friendly but none endorse a strict gay-only clientele policy. That said, you're likely to find more gay visitors than straight ones crashing at the city's few **gay-run** hotels, which usually attract a good mix of gay, lesbian, and gay-positive guests. Most of these are situated in the Back Bay and South End; a quieter option is Jamaica Plain. You can either book them yourself, or save some money by going through City Wide Reservations (ⓣ267-7424 or 1-800/468-3593, ⓦwww.cityres.com), a **discount reservation agency** with a Boston-area hotel category devoted to "celebrating diversity."

463 Beacon Street Guest House 463 Beacon St ⓣ536-1302, ⓦwww.463beacon.com; Hynes Ⓣ. The good-sized rooms in this renovated brownstone, in the heart of Back Bay, are available by the night, week, and month, and come equipped with kitchenettes, cable TV, and various hotel amenities (though no maid service); some have a/c, hardwood floors, and ornamental fireplaces. Ask for the top-floor room. ❹–❻

Chandler Inn 26 Chandler St ⓣ482-3450 or 1-800/842-3450, ⓦwww.chandlerinn.com; Back Bay Ⓣ. Small, comfortable 56-room European-style hotel above the popular *Fritz* bar (seebelow); perks like satellite TV, in-room Internet hook-up, and continental breakfasts are included in the rates. ❻

Oasis Guest House 22 Edgerly Rd ⓣ267-2262, ⓦwww.oasisgh.com; Symphony Ⓣ. Sixteen comfortable, affordable rooms, some with shared baths, in a renovated brownstone near Symphony Hall with continental breakfast and nightly cocktail at 8pm – they supply the hors d'oeuvres, you bring the booze. ❺–❼

Taylor House 50 Burroughs St, Jamaica Plain ⓣ1-888/228-2956, ⓦwww.taylorhouse.com; Green Street Ⓣ. This delightful B&B is a bit out of the way, but its three charming rooms, tucked away on the second floor of an 1855 Italianate house, include queen-sized beds, TV with VCR, Internet access, continental breakfast, and two friendly golden retrievers. ❻–❼

Bars, clubs, and cafés

Only one **club** in Boston maintains its gay banner seven days a week, the long-standing *Vapor* (formerly *Chaps*); to pick up the slack, some of Boston's more popular clubs designate one or two nights a week as gay nights. The best ones, Campus at *ManRay* (Thurs), *Buzz* (Sat), and *Avalon* (Sun) draw a good mix; see "Nightlife," p.150, for further details on nightclub venues. Friday night's Circuit Girl party at *Club Europa* is the hottest lesbian night around. For those night owls who haven't gotten their fill of dancing after the clubs close, ask around for an invite to Boston's hush-hush after-hours private party, "Rise," at 306 Stuart St; the member's-only stomping ground for gays and straights only gets going at 2am.

Buzz 51 Stuart St ⓣ267-8669, ⓦwww.buzz-boston.com; New England Medical Ⓣ. Resident DJs Michael Sheehan and MaryAlice lay down dance and house tracks at this two-floor dance club where the drinks are poured by pumped and shirtless bartenders. $10 cover charge.

Club Café 209 Columbus Ave ⓣ536-0966, ⓦwww.clubcafe.com; Back Bay Ⓣ. This combination restaurant/video bar popular among South End guppies has two back lounges, *Moonshine* and *Satellite*, showing the latest videos and making a wide selection of martinis with fey names like Pouty Princess and Dirty Birdie ($8).

Fritz 26 Chandler St ⓣ482-4428; Back Bay Ⓣ. South End sports bar below *Chandler Inn* (see above), often likened to the gay version of *Cheers* thanks to its mix of casually attired locals and visitors, and friendly staff.

Jacque's 79 Broadway ⓣ338-7472; Boylston Ⓣ. *Priscilla, Queen of the Desert* invades New England at this drag dream where past-it divas lip-synch *I Love the Nightlife* while youngsters explore gender issues and transvestite/transsexual prostitutes peddle their wares. Showtime is 10.30pm Tues–Sun.

Luxor 69 Church St ⓣ423-6969; Arlington Ⓣ. Not as popular as it once was, but still a good place to drink and cruise, either in the upstairs gay video bar or downstairs at the sports bar.

Machine 1254 Boylston St ⓣ266-2986; Kenmore

Ⓣ. A favorite with the gay crowd on Fridays and Saturdays when the club's large dance floor and top-notch music has the place pumping. The pool tables and bar near the dance floor let you take a breather and soak up the scene. Sundays attract a lesbian crowd as Mix Mistress gets on the decks for *Trix*.

ManRay 21 Brookline St, Cambridge ⓣ864-0400, ⓦwww.manrayclub.com; Central Ⓣ. Five bars, two dance floors, and four very different theme nights. Campus (Thurs) is relatively wholesome, with J Crew types and plenty of straights. The scene is altogether different on Fridays, when a fetish-and-bondage fest, replete with leather and dominatrixes galore, takes over.

Midway Café 3496 Washington St, Jamaica Plain ⓦwww.dykenight.com; Green Street Ⓣ. Neighborhood hangout with a popular Thursday dyke night; there's free pool 8–10pm, $2 drink specials from 9–10.30pm, and dancing til 2am. Cover $2.

Ryle's 212 Hampshire St, Cambridge ⓣ628-0288, ⓦwww.nestofvipers.org; Central Ⓣ. The last Sunday of the month brings The Amazon Slam, a poetry-slam and dance hosted by the crew from *Nest of Vipers*, an on-line lesbian magazine; words start flying at 8pm, music at 10pm. Cover $8.

Vapor 100 Warrenton St ⓣ695-9500; Arlington Ⓣ. Returning visitors will recognize this hot spot for the 19+ set as the former home of *Chaps*. Little has changed in the weekly repertoire which starts off chill with Piano Bar (Mon) and Oldies (Tues), and heats it up from Wed–Sat with Latino (Wed), Mocha (Thurs), and House (Fri & Sat). The usual Tea Dance still prevails Sun at 6pm. Cover from $3–8.

Shopping

Boston is an extremely pleasant place to shop, with attractive stores clustered on atmospheric streets like **Charles Street** in Beacon Hill, and **Newbury Street** in Back Bay. **Harvard Square** is another excellent place for such a wander, with especially good **bookstores** in the vicinity. Otherwise, most of the action takes place in various downtown quarters, first and foremost at the **Faneuil Hall Marketplace**. This area has become more commercialized over the years, but there's still enough homespun boutiques, plus the many food stalls of **Quincy Market**, to make a trip here worthwhile. There's also the somewhat downmarket **Downtown Crossing**, at Washington and Summer streets, centered on Filene's Basement, a bargain-hunter's delight.

Books

Boston has a history as a literary city, enhanced by its numerous universities and the authors and publishing houses that once called it home. This is well reflected in the quality and diversity of **bookstores** to be found both in Boston and neighboring Cambridge.

New books

Barnes & Noble Downtown Crossing ⓣ426-5502; Downtown Crossing Ⓣ; 660 Beacon St ⓣ267-8484; Kenmore Ⓣ. Two large outposts of the national bookstore chain. The one on Beacon Street is capped by the neon Citgo sign (p.121).

Brookline Booksmith 279 Harvard St ⓣ566-6660, ⓦwww.brooklinebooksmith.com; Coolidge Corner Ⓣ. This cozy shop doesn't seem to have a particular specialty, but its friendly staff makes it perfect for browsing.

Harvard Book Store 1256 Massachusetts Ave ⓣ661-1515, ⓦwww.harvard.com; Harvard Ⓣ. Three huge rooms of new books upstairs, a basement for used volumes and remainders downstairs. Academic and critical work in the humanities and social sciences dominate, with a healthy dose of fiction thrown in.

Trident Booksellers & Café 338 Newbury St ⓣ267-8688; Copley Ⓣ. A preferred lair of Back Bay's New-Agers. If the aroma of one too many essential oils doesn't deter you, buy an obscure magazine and pretend to read it over coffee in the café (see p.149).

WordsWorth Books 30 Brattle St ⓣ354-5201, ⓦwww.wordsworth.com; Harvard Ⓣ. Discount bookstore with regular readings by well-known authors.

Secondhand books

Brattle Book Shop 9 West St ⓣ542-0210, ⓦwww.brattlebookshop.com; Downtown Crossing Ⓣ. One of the oldest antiquarian bookstores in the country. Three levels, with a good selection of yellowing travel guides on the second.
Bryn Mawr Book 373 Huron Ave ⓣ661-1770; Porter Ⓣ. This neighborhood bookstore vends used titles in a relaxed Cambridge setting. Weather permitting, there are sidewalk displays for pedestrian browsers.
House of Sarah 1309 Cambridge St ⓣ547-3447; Central Ⓣ. A wacky Inman Square spot in which to peruse used fiction and scholarly work – sit in an overstuffed red couch and look up at various stuffed creatures hanging from the ceiling. You may find a 25¢ copy of a Danielle Steele novel or some remaindered Foucault, and there are often coffee and snacks, compliments of the proprietors.

Specialist

Boston Globe Store 1 School St ⓣ367-4000; Park Street Ⓣ. Small shop in the historic Old Corner Bookstore (see p.97) building with New England travel guidebooks, Internet access, and lots of stuff emblazoned with the *Boston Globe* logo.
Glad Day Bookshop 673 Boylston St ⓣ267-3010; Copley Ⓣ. This second-floor gay bookstore is easily recognized from the sidewalk by the big rainbow flag in the window. A good selection of reasonably priced books, cards, and pornography, and a vast community bulletin board at the entrance.
Globe Corner Bookstore 28 Church St ⓣ497-6277, ⓦwww.globecorner.com; Harvard Ⓣ. These travel specialists are well stocked with maps, travel literature and guidebooks, with an especially strong New England section.
Grolier Poetry Bookstore 6 Plympton St ⓣ547-4648; Harvard Ⓣ. With 14,000 volumes of verse, this tiny shop has gained an international following among poets and their fans. Frequent readings.
Kate's Mystery Bookstore 2211 Massachusetts Ave ⓣ491-2660, ⓦwww.katesmysterybooks.com; Davis Ⓣ. Mystery-only bookstore selling both old and new titles; you'll know the place from the faux gravestones in the front.
Schoenhof's 76A Mt Auburn St ⓣ547-8855, ⓦwww.schoenhofs.com; Harvard Ⓣ. Well-stocked foreign language bookstore that's sure to have that volume of Proust you're looking for, as well as any children's books you might want.
We Think the World of You 540 Tremont St ⓣ423-1965, ⓦwww.wethinktheworldofyou.com; Back Bay Ⓣ. With its cool music and good selection of international magazines, this bright, upscale South End gay bookstore invites lingering.
Willowbee & Kent 519 Boylston St ⓣ437-6700; Copley Ⓣ. The first floor of this roomy store has a good range of travel guidebooks and gear; the second is given over to a travel agency.

Food and drink

Eating out in Boston may prevail, but should you choose to cook your own **food**, or get provisions for a picnic, you won't do so badly either. There are also some excellent spots to pick up pastries, pies, and other dessert-oriented items.

Gourmet food

Barsamian's 1030 Massachusetts Ave ⓣ661-9300; Harvard or Central Ⓣ. Gourmet meats, cheeses, coffee, and bread, plus a great range of desserts – including the best tart in Cambridge.
Formaggio Kitchen 244 Huron Ave ⓣ354-4750, ⓦwww.fromaggiokitchen.com; Harvard Square Ⓣ; 268 Shawmut Ave, ⓣ350-6996; Back Bay Ⓣ. Although regarded as one of the best cheese shops in Boston, the gourmet meats, salads, sandwiches, and baked goods here are also worth sampling.
Monica's Salumeria 130 Salem St ⓣ742-4101; Haymarket Ⓣ. Lots of imported Italian cheeses, cooked meats, cookies, and pastas.
Salumeria Italiana 151 Richmond St ⓣ523-8743 or 1-800/400-5916, ⓦwww.salumeriaitaliana.com; North Station Ⓣ. Arguably the best Italian grocer this side of Roma, this shop stocks only the finest cheeses, meats, and more.
Savenor's 160 Charles St ⓣ723-6328; Charles Ⓣ. Known for its meats, this small gourmet food shop in Beacon Hill also has a produce selection, in addition to prepared foods – ideal for taking to the nearby Charles River Esplanade for an impromptu picnic.
See Sun Co 19 Harrison St ⓣ426-0954; Chinatown Ⓣ. The most accessible of Chinatown's markets has all the basics plus a few exotic delicacies.

Health food

Bread & Circus 15 Westland Ave ⓣ375-1010; Symphony Ⓣ. The Boston branch of this New

England Whole Foods chain, near Symphony Hall, has all the alternative foodstuffs you'd expect, plus one of Boston's best salad bars.

Nature Food Centers GNC 545 Boylston St ⓣ536-1226; Copley Ⓣ. If you're looking for vitamin-enriched fruit juices, organic produce, and other healthful items, this small store in Copley Square is bound to have it.

Pastries and cakes

Bova's Bakery 76 Prince St ⓣ523-5601; Haymarket Ⓣ. The North End's all-night bakery, vending delights like plain and chocolate cannolis, oven-fresh cakes, and whoopie pies, is famously cheap, with most items around $5.

LMNOP Bakery 79 Park Plaza ⓣ338-4220; Arlington Ⓣ. Purveyor of bread to neighboring restaurants, this hideaway is the best gourmet bakery in Boston. They also have great sandwiches and pasta specials at lunchtime.

Maria's Pastry Shop 46 Cross St ⓣ523-1196 or 1-888/688-2889; North Station Ⓣ. The place doesn't look like much but *Maria's* has the best Neapolitan treats in town.

Mike's Pastry 300 Hanover St ⓣ742-3050; Haymarket Ⓣ. The famed North End bakery is one part Italian and two parts American, meaning in addition to cannoli and tiramisu, you'll find counters full of brownies and cookies. The homemade ice cream is not to be missed, but expect to wait in line for it.

Rosie's Bakery 243 Hampshire St ⓣ491-9488, ⓦwww.rosiesbakery.com; #69 bus. This bakery features the richest, most decadent desserts in Cambridge. Their specialty is a fudge brownie called the "chocolate orgasm," though the less provocatively named lemon squares are just as good.

Malls and department stores

Boston's **malls** are well scattered about, good places if you need to pick up a number of diverse items on the same shopping trip. They often contain the city's biggest **department stores**, though a few unattached ones stand out, mostly around Downtown Crossing.

The malls

CambridgeSide Galleria 100 Cambridgeside Place ⓣ621-8666, ⓦwww.cambridgesidegalleria.com; Kendall Ⓣ. Not too different from any other large American shopping mall. The haze of neon and packs of hairsprayed teens can be exhausting, but there's no similarly dense and convenient conglomeration of shops in Cambridge.

Copley Place 100 Huntington Ave ⓣ375-4400, ⓦwww.shopcopleyplace.com; Copley Ⓣ. This ambitious, upscale office-retail-residential complex features more than 100 stores and an 11-screen multiplex. The best of the shops are a Rizzoli bookshop, a Neiman Marcus department store, the gift shop for the Museum of Fine Arts, and the Artful Hand Gallery, representing solely American artists; the rest is pretty generic.

Faneuil Hall Marketplace Faneuil Hall ⓣ523-1300, ⓦwww.faneuilhallmarketplace.com; Government Center Ⓣ. The city's most famous market, with a hundred or so shops, plus next door's Quincy Market. It's a bit tourist-oriented, but still worth a trip (see p.92).

The Heritage on the Garden 300 Boylston St ⓣ423-0002; Arlington Ⓣ. Not so much a mall as a very upscale mixed-use complex across from the Public Garden that consists of condos, restaurants, and boutiques.

The Shops at Prudential Center 800 Boylston St ⓣ267-1002; Prudential Ⓣ. This is a fairly new conglomeration of a hundred or so mid-market shops, heavily patronized by local residents and conventioneers from the adjacent Hynes Convention Center who seem to genuinely enjoy buying commemorative T-shirts and ties from the center-atrium pushcarts.

Department stores

Filene's 426 Washington St ⓣ357-2100, ⓦwww.filenes.com; Downtown Crossing Ⓣ. The merchandise inside downtown Boston's oldest department store is standard issue; the stunning 1912 Beaux Arts facade is not.

Filene's Basement 426 Washington St ⓣ542-2011, ⓦwww.filenesbasement.com; Downtown Crossing Ⓣ. Discounted merchandise from Filene's upstairs and other big-name department stores, plus a few Boston boutiques.

The Harvard Coop 1400 Massachusetts Ave ⓣ499-2000, ⓦwww.thecoop.com; Harvard Ⓣ. Harvard's local department store, with a wide selection of fairly expensive insignia clothing and the like.

Neiman Marcus 5 Copley Place ⓣ536-3660, ⓦwww.neimanmarcus.com; Copley Ⓣ. Boston's most luxurious department store, with prices to match.

Boston festivals

It's always good to know ahead of time what festivals are scheduled to coincide with your trip to Boston, though even if you don't plan it, there's likely to be some sort of celebration or seasonal event going on. Summer is usually best for these, as the warmer weather allows for more outdoor festivals to take place. For written information, call the Boston Convention and Visitors Bureau (ⓣ1-888/SEE-BOSTON); the City of Boston Special Events Line (ⓣ822-0038) has recorded information on the month's festivals.

January

Late Chinese New Year. Dragon parades and firecrackers punctuate these festivities throughout Chinatown. It can occasionally fall in February, depending on the Chinese lunar calendar (ⓣ542-2574).

February

First two Mondays The Beanpot. At the FleetCenter, Boston's four major college hockey teams (Boston University, Boston College, Northeastern, and Harvard) compete for bragging rights (ⓣ624-1000).

March

17 St Patrick's Day Parade and Festival. Boston's substantial Irish-American community, along with much of the rest of the city, parade through South Boston, which culminates in Irish folk music, dance, and food at Faneuil Hall (ⓣ536-4100).

April

Third Monday Patriot's Day. A celebration and re-creation of Paul Revere's (and William Dawes') famous ride, from the North End to Lexington, that alerted locals that the British army had been deployed against the rebel threat (ⓣ236-4100).
Third Monday Boston Marathon. One of America's premier running events with a world-class field (ⓣ236-1652).

May

Early Blacksmith House Dulcimer Festival. In Cambridge, workshops and performances by experts of both mountain and hammer dulcimers (ⓣ547-6789).
Mid Greater Boston Kite Festival. Franklin Park is taken over by kite-lovers during this celebration, which also has kite-makers, flying clinics, and music (ⓣ635-4505).

June

First week Boston Dairy Festival. Cows and other animals are brought back to Boston Common to graze. For a modest donation, you can indulge in unlimited samples of Boston's best ice creams.
Early to mid Boston Early Music Festival. This Renaissance fair only happens every other year, the next one scheduled for 2003. Concerts, costume shows, and exhibitions take place throughout town (ⓣ661-1812, ⓦwww.bemf.org).
Mid to late Boston Globe Jazz Festival. The city's leading newspaper sponsors a weeklong series of jazz events at various venues, usually in mid -to late June. Some are free, though shows by big names can be pricey (ⓣ929-2000).

Music

The best places for new and used **music** in Boston are on Newbury Street in Back Bay, around Massachusetts Avenue near Kenmore Square, and up in Harvard Square, basically all the places students can be found hanging about.

July

Week leading up to 4 Harborfest hosts a series of jazz, blues, and rock concerts on the waterfront. On the weekend of July 4, there's the annual turnaround cruise of the *USS Constitution*, the highly competitive "Chowderfest," and tons of fireworks (Ⓣ227-1528).

4 Boston Pops Concert and Fireworks. A wildly popular yearly event at the Hatch Shell, for which people sometimes line up at dawn to get good seats for the evening concert by the scaled-down version of the Boston Symphony Orchestra (Ⓣ266-1492).

Throughout July and August Commonwealth Shakespeare Company on the Boston Common. First-rate, free Shakespeare productions, performed in the evening outside on the Tremont side of the Common (Ⓣ423-7600).

August

End of month August Moon Festival. Chinatown's merchants and restaurateurs hawk their wares on the street amid dragon parades and firecrackers (Ⓣ542-2574).

Last two weekends Italian Festas. Music, dancing, and games throughout the North End. In weekend parades, statues of the Virgin Mary are borne through the streets as locals pin dollar bills to the floats.

September

Early to mid Boston Film Festival. Area theaters screen independent films, with discussions by directors and screenwriters.

Mid Cambridge River Festival. Memorial Drive is closed off from JFK Street to Western Avenue for music shows, dancing, and eclectic food offerings, all along the Charles River (Ⓣ349-4380).

October

Second Monday Columbus Day Parade. Kicked off by a ceremony at City Hall at 1pm, the raucous, Italian-flavored parade continues into the heart of the North End.

Second to last weekend Head of the Charles Regatta. Hordes of well-off prepsters and the like descend on the Harvard Square area, ostensibly to watch the crew races, but really more to pal around with their cronies and get loaded (Ⓣ864-8415).

December

Sunday nearest 16 Boston Tea Party Re-enactment. A lusty re-enactment of the march from Old South Meeting House to the harbor, and the subsequent tea-dumping that helped spark the American Revolution, hosted by the Boston Tea Party Museum (Ⓣ338-1773).

31 First Night. Big, though not at all wild, New Year's Eve celebration, with open galleries, performances by mimes and musicians, and other artsy happenings citywide (Ⓣ542-1399).

New

Boston Beat 279 Newbury St Ⓣ247-2428, Ⓦwww.bostonbeat.com; Hynes Ⓣ. A first-floor store stocking lots of independent dance and techno labels.

Newbury Comics 332 Newbury St Ⓣ236-4930, Ⓦwww.newbury.com; Hynes Ⓣ. Boston's biggest alternative record store carries lots of independent labels you won't find at the national chains along with a substantial array of vinyl, posters, 'zines,

and kitschy T-shirts. It's also a good place to pick up flyers on local club happenings.
Nuggets 486 Commonwealth Ave ⓣ536-0679, ⓦwww.nuggetsrecords.com; Kenmore Ⓣ. American jazz, rock, and R&B are the strong suits at this venerable new and used record store.
Satellite 49 Massachusetts Ave ⓣ536-5482, ⓦwww.satelliterecords.com; Hynes Ⓣ. This storefront hideaway has a great selection of imported techno and trance, in both CD and vinyl format.

Used and vintage

Disc Diggers 401 Highland Ave, Somerville ⓣ776-7560; Davis Ⓣ. The largest selection of used CDs in New England, though higher in quantity than quality. Forgotten albums by one-hit wonders abound.
Pipeline 257 Washington St ⓣ591-0590; #63 bus. This alluringly bizarre store defies categorization. Mainly used CDs and vinyl, particularly deep on indie and imports. Also new music, kitsch Americana, and videos of the Russ Meyer film ilk.
Skippy White's 538 Massachusetts Ave ⓣ491-3345; Central Ⓣ. Excellent collection of jazz, blues, R&B, gospel, funk, P-funk, funkadelic, and hip-hop. Hum a few bars and the salesfolk will guide you to the right section.
Smash City Records 304 Newbury St ⓣ536-0216, ⓦwww.velvetcityrecords.com; Arlington Ⓣ. Aside from its velvet Elvis collection, what distinguishes this record store from the others is its massive stock of vinyl for $1; there's even a free bin.
Stereo Jack's 1686 Massachusetts Ave ⓣ497-9447, ⓦwww.stereojacks.com; Porter Ⓣ. Jazz and blues specialists, mostly used, but with some new stuff, too.
Twisted Village 12 Eliot St ⓣ354-6898, ⓦwww.twistedvillage.com; Harvard Ⓣ. A strange mix of fringe styles, among them beat, spoken word, and psychedelic rock.

Specialty shops

Black Ink 101 Charles St ⓣ723-3883; Charles Ⓣ; 5 Brattle St ⓣ497-1221; Harvard Ⓣ. Eclectic assortment of things you don't really need but are cool anyway: rubber stamps, a smattering of clothes, and a wide assortment of vintage postcards.
Fresh 121 Newbury St ⓣ421-1212; Arlington Ⓣ. More than three hundred varieties of French milled soaps, lotions, oils, and makeup, packaged so exquisitely you won't want to open them.
Justin Tyme Emporium 91 River St ⓣ491-1088; Central Ⓣ. Justin's is all about pop culture artifacts, featuring boffo American detritus like lava lamps, Donny and Marie Osmond pin-ups, and campy T-shirts with iron-ons.
Leavitt and Pierce 1316 Massachusetts Ave ⓣ547-0576; Harvard Ⓣ. Old-school tobacconists with an outstanding selection of cigars, imported cigarettes, and smoking paraphernalia, plus an upstairs smoking loft right out of the carefree past.
The London Harness Company 60 Franklin St ⓣ542-9234, ⓦwww.londonharness.com; Downtown Crossing Ⓣ. Chiefly known for its high-quality luggage goods, this atmospheric shop reeks of traditional Boston – indeed, Ben Franklin used to shop here. They also vend a wide array of items like chess sets, clocks, candlesticks, and inlaid decorative boxes.
Loulou's Lost & Found 121 Newbury St ⓣ859-8593; Arlington Ⓣ. They say Loulou scours the globe in search of such essentials as tableware embossed with French cruise ship logos and silverware from long-gone five-star restaurants.
Marquis 73 Berkeley St ⓣ426-2120; Back Bay Ⓣ. Proffering a wide range of leather items and hardcore sexual paraphernalia, this South End shop leaves little to the imagination.
Million-Year Picnic 99 Mt Auburn St ⓣ492-6763; Harvard Ⓣ. For the comic obsessive. Japanese anime and Superman, Tank Girl, and Dilbert. Stronger on current stuff than old material. The staff has encyclopedic knowledge, and is tolerant of browsers.

Listings

Airlines American Airlines (ⓣ1-800/433-7300, ⓦwww.aa.com); British Airways (ⓣ1-800/247-9297, ⓦwww.ba.com); United Airlines (ⓣ1-800/241-6522, ⓦwww.ual.com); US Airways (ⓣ1-800/428-4322, ⓦwww.usairways.com); Virgin Atlantic ⓣ1-800/862-8621, ⓦwww.virgin-atlantic.com). American and United have offices in the *Park Plaza Hotel* (in addition to one at Logan

Airport); British Airways' office is across from the Government Center Ⓣ station.

Banks and currency exchange Fleet Bank is the biggest bank, with branches and ATMs throughout the city. Bureaux de change are not very prevalent. You can find locations at Logan Airport Terminal E (International); Thomas Cook, 399 Boylston St; and many Fleet Bank branches.

Bowling Boston's variation on tenpin bowling is "candlepin" bowling, in which the ball is smaller, the pins narrower and lighter, and you have three rather than two chances to knock the pins down. Try the Ryan Family Amusement Center, 82 Landsdowne St (Sun, Mon, Wed & Thurs noon–11pm, Tues 9am–11pm, Fri & Sat noon–midnight; Ⓣ267-8495, Ⓦwww.ryanfamily.com).

Consulates Canada, 3 Copley Place, suite 400 (Ⓣ262-3760, Ⓦwww.dfait-maeci.gc.ca); France, 31 St James Ave, suite 750 (Ⓣ542-7374, Ⓦwww.consulfrance-boston.org); UK, One Memorial Dr, Cambridge (Ⓣ245-4500, Ⓦwww.britainusa.com/boston).

Hospitals Massachusetts General Hospital, 55 Fruit St (Ⓣ726-2000, Ⓦwww.mgh.harvard.edu; Charles/MGH Ⓣ); Beth Israel Deaconess Medical Center, 330 Brookline Ave (Ⓣ667-7000, Ⓦwww.bidmc.harvard.edu; Longwood Ⓣ); New England Medical Center, 800 Washington St (Ⓣ636-5000, Ⓦwww.nemc.org; NE Medical Ⓣ); the Women's Hospital, 75 Francis St (Ⓣ732-5500 or 1-800/BWH-9999, Ⓦwww.bwh.partners.org; Longwood or Brigham Circle Ⓣ); Children's Hospital, 300 Longwood Ave (Ⓣ355-6000, Ⓦwww.tch.harvard.edu; Longwood Ⓣ).

Internet Pop into a local university and use one of their free public computers. Harvard's Holyoke Center, at 1350 Massachusetts Ave in Cambridge, has a couple of stations with 10-minute access maximum. The same goes for MIT's Rogers Building, at 77 Massachusetts Ave (also in Cambridge). Boston's main public library, at 700 Boylston St, has free 15-minute Internet access on the ground floor of the Johnson building. Cybercafés are limited to *Designs For Living*, at 52 Queensberry St (Mon–Fri 7am–6.30pm, Sat 8am–6.30pm, Sun 9am–6.30pm; Ⓣ536-6150, Ⓦwww.bosnet.com; $8/hr; Kenmore Ⓣ) and *Adrenaline Zone*, at 40 Brattle St, lower level (Mon–Thurs & Sun 11am–11pm, Fri–Sat 11am–12am; $5/hr; Ⓣ876-1314, Ⓦwww.adrenzone.com; Harvard Ⓣ).

Laundries Back Bay Laundry Emporium, 409A Marlborough St (daily 7.30am–11pm, last wash at 9pm), is a good, clean bet; drop-off service is 90¢ per pound of clothing.

Parking A nightmare. The cheapest parking lots downtown are Center Plaza Garage, at the corner of Cambridge and New Sudbury streets ($9/hr up to $25 max; Ⓣ742-7807) and Garage at Post Office Square ($3.50/30min up to $29 max; Ⓣ423-1430). The parking limit at nonmetered spots is two hours, whether posted or not.

Pharmacies The CVS drugstore chain has locations all over the city, though not all have pharmacies. For those, try the branches at 155–157 Charles St, in Beacon Hill (open 24 hours; Ⓣ227-0437, pharmacy Ⓣ523-1028), and 35 White St, in Cambridge's Porter Square (Ⓣ876-4037, pharmacy Ⓣ876-5519).

Police In case of emergency, get to a phone and dial Ⓣ911. For non-emergency situations, contact the Boston Police, headquartered at 154 Berkeley St, in Back Bay (Ⓣ343-4200).

Post office The biggest post office downtown is J. W. McCormack Station in Post Office Square, at 90 Devonshire St (Mon–Fri 7.30am–5pm; Ⓣ720-4754); Cambridge's central branch is at 770 Massachusetts Ave, in Central Square (Mon–Fri 7.30am–6pm, Sat 7.30am–3pm; Ⓣ876-0620). The General Post Office, 25 Dorchester Ave, behind South Station, is open 24 hours a day (Ⓣ654-5326).

Sports Baseball: Boston Red Sox (Ⓣ267-1700, Ⓦwww.redsox.com) play at Fenway Park, seats $10–70; Basketball: Boston Celtics (Ⓣ523-3030, Ⓦwww.nba.com/celtics) play at the FleetCenter, 150 Causeway St, in the West End, seats $10–$550; Hockey: Boston Bruins (Ⓣ931-2222, Ⓦwww.bostonbruins.com), also at the FleetCenter, seats $25–85.

Travel agents Council Travel, 12 Eliot St, 2nd Floor, Harvard Square, Cambridge (Ⓣ497-1497), specializes in student and youth travel; American Express Travel, 170 Federal St (Ⓣ439-4400), provides general services.

Eastern Massachusetts

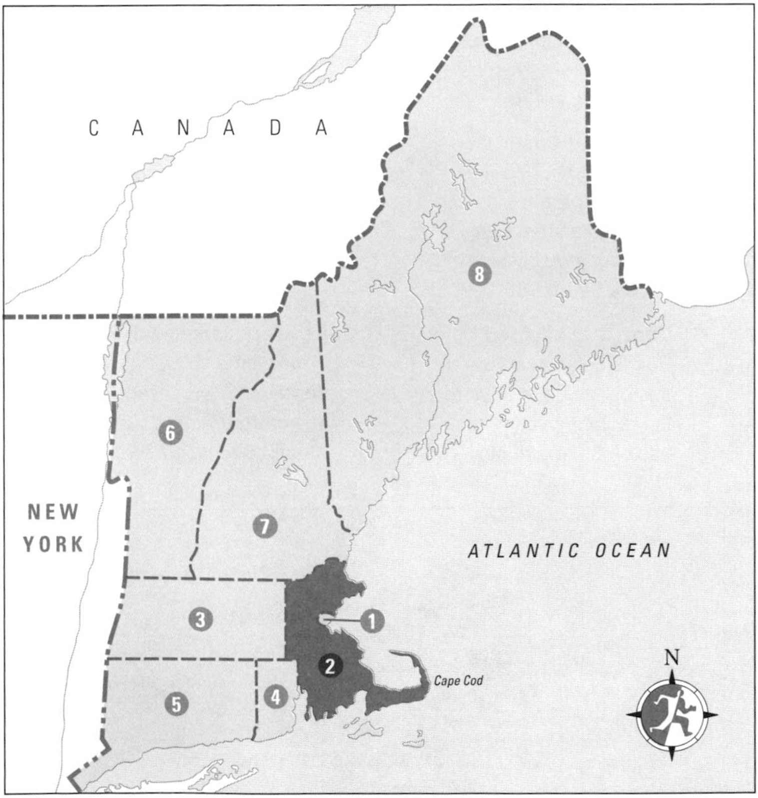

CANADA

NEW YORK

ATLANTIC OCEAN

Cape Cod

N

8

6

7

3

1

2

5

4

CHAPTER 2 Highlights

* **Colonial battlefields** Think revolutionary thoughts while walking Lexington's Battle Green, the site of the first armed confrontation that led to the birth of America. See p.170
* **Salem** The witch-related spots get all the hype, but the maritime legacy here impresses just as much. See p.175
* **Hammond Castle Museum, Gloucester** See how bizarrely some New Englanders lived, at this eccentric cliffside house. See p.185
* **Cape Cod seafood** Roadside seafood stands are ubiquitous to the region; dive into fresh lobster and scallops at places like *Captain Frosty's Fish and Chips* and the *Lobster Pot*. See pp.211 & 224
* **Provincetown** Perhaps the lone must-see on the Cape, a lively town with great beaches, tasty seafood, and an anything-goes mentality. See p.218
* **Hit the beach** The region's bountiful beaches make a fine excuse to laze about. See pp.216, 234 & 242.
* **House hunting in Nantucket** Leaf through Melville's *Moby Dick* while admiring the digs of one-time whaleboat captains in Nantucket Town, the *Pequod's* port of call. See p.237

2

Eastern Massachusetts

The vast majority of Massachusetts' six million residents live within a few miles of its eastern coast, many of them direct descendants of successive waves of Europeans, going all the way back to the Mayflower Pilgrims, who arrived here, miles off course, in 1620. They were heading, in fact, for Jamestown, Virginia, though after the initial disappointment wore off they must have been impressed by what they had found: natural harbors to facilitate trade and commerce, waters teeming with fish for food, virgin forests providing endless supplies of wood for fuel and for building, even creeks and salt marshes that reminded them of their native England. Heartened by their initially friendly contact with indigenous Native Americans who were willing to share their agricultural knowledge of the terrain, the Pilgrims stayed put. The rest, as they say, is history.

That's apt, considering that **Eastern Massachusetts** has quite a bit to offer in the way of history, cradle as it is of much early American development. The coast itself can hardly be said to be spectacular, like that of California, or even nearby Maine (though for stupendous geological formations, you can't get much more impressive than Cape Cod); rather, the shoreline draws its charm from the diversity it offers – surf-lashed promontories, windswept offshore islands, pristine beaches, and the laid-back towns that surround them along the way. Wherever you happen to take a short stay – there's no overwhelming need to spend more than a few days, if that, in any one area – you likely won't be more than a stone's throw away from a vast number of historical sights, even at the very end of Cape Cod, where you probably thought you could escape from it all.

Just inland from Boston, and easily done as a day-trip, are the towns of **Lexington** and **Concord**, major players during the Revolutionary War. Otherwise, Massachusetts' long coast can be divided into four sections, all linked by the major highways which radiate from Boston: the **North Shore**, which stretches from Boston's bland northern suburbs to the New Hampshire border, including the famous Witch Trial town of **Salem** and the rocky **Cape Ann** peninsula with the old fishing ports of **Gloucester** and **Rockport**; the **South Shore**, extending from the southern outskirts of Boston towards **Plymouth**, with its Pilgrim-related sights, all the way to the Rhode Island border, passing the partially restored whaling port of **New Bedford**, among

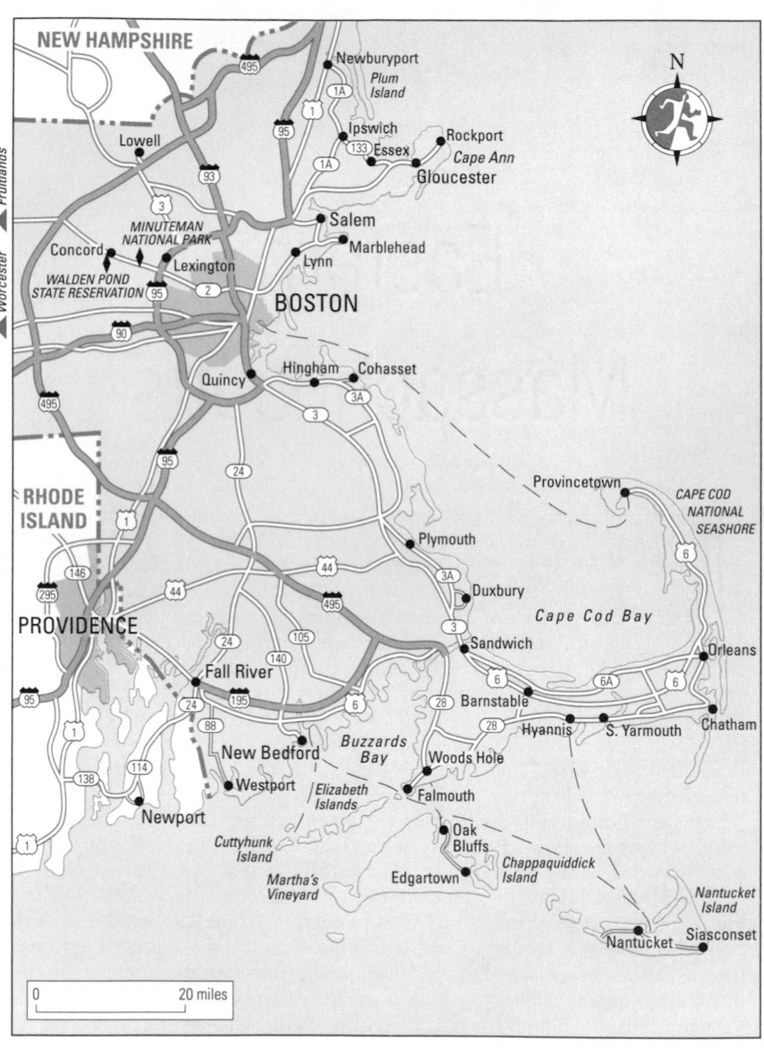

more dreary outposts, in its course; the outstretched arm of **Cape Cod**, a vast glacial deposit reaching more than seventy miles into the Atlantic, and splattered with a range of popular resorts, none better than bohemian **Provincetown**; and the relaxed, upmarket holiday islands of **Martha's Vineyard** and **Nantucket**, playgrounds of the rich and famous.

Lexington and Concord

The sedate towns of **Lexington** and **Concord**, almost always mentioned in the same breath, cash in on their fame as the locations of the Americans' first armed confrontation with the British. Lexington is mostly suburban today, while Concord, five miles east, still has the flavor of a genteel country town. Most of the area's historical sights have been incorporated into the **Minute Man National Park**, which takes in the Lexington Battle Green, the North Bridge area in Concord, and much of Battle Road, the route the British followed on their retreat from Concord to Boston. The battles of Lexington and Concord are evoked in a piecemeal but relentless fashion throughout, with visitors' centers full of scale models and remnant musketry, and old colonial houses boasting the odd preserved bullet hole, though only a few of these spots are worth any more than a quick look. The whole affair tends to be overly structured – in many instances you must take hour-long tours of tiny houses you could walk through in two minutes. The Park also includes the **Old Manse** and **The Wayside**, two rambling old Concord houses with bookish pasts, though some other "literary" sites, such as **Walden Pond** in Concord, are just beyond its boundaries.

Some history

What finally precipitated the celebrated battle of April 19, 1775, was the march of British troops to Concord to seize the munitions that the Americans had squirreled away there. Such plans were hardly a secret; the "Minute Men" were so called because they knew they might have to fight at a moment's notice. When the British troops disembarked from Boston Common, Paul Revere and William Dawes set out on separate routes to sound the alarm. Within minutes, church bells were clanging and cannons roaring throughout the countryside, signaling the rebels to head for Lexington Green; hundreds more converged around the North Bridge area of Concord. Revere, who was questioned at gunpoint en route to Lexington but managed to escape, gave the final alarm to John Hancock and Samuel Adams (who were in town to attend a provincial congress) at the Hancock-Clarke House.

John Parker, the colonial captain, was down the street at the Buckman Tavern, when he received word that the British were closing in on the Green. "Don't fire unless fired upon," he ordered the men, "but if they mean to have a war, let it begin here." With only 77 Americans pitted against 700 British regulars, it was more a show of resolve than a hope for victory. Who fired the first shot remains a mystery, but in the fracas that followed, eight Americans were killed, including Parker. The British suffered no casualties, and marched three miles west to Concord.

By the time they arrived, it was already after sunrise on April 19, and hundreds more Minute Men had amassed on a farm behind North Bridge near where the lion's share of munitions were stored. When a British officer accidentally set fire to a building the Americans believed that the town was going up in smoke. They fired on the British guarding the other side of the bridge: the "shots heard round the world," as history books have it. The British were now outnumbered four to one, and suffered heavily in the ensuing battle, which continued all the way back to Boston.

Getting to Lexington and Concord

Despite their rural setting, Concord and Lexington are only about a dozen miles from downtown Boston, and therefore readily accessible from the city. The MBTA (ⓣ617/222-3200, ⓦwww.mbta.com) operates trains to Concord from North Station ($4 one-way) and also runs buses to Lexington from Cambridge's Alewife Station. Journey time ranges from 40 minutes to one hour. If you are coming from Boston by car, take Rte-2 (Mass Ave) out of the city to Arlington Center, then follow the signs to Lexington. If you're in shape and the weather permits, the Minuteman bike path goes from Cambridge to Lexington Green. The easiest places to pick up the bike path are behind Davis or Alewife Ⓣ stations on the red line.

Lexington

The main attraction in **LEXINGTON** itself is the grassy, meticulously manicured **Battle Green**, where, appropriately enough, the American flag is flown 24 hours a day. The land serves as Lexington's town common and is fronted by Henry Kitson's diminutive but dignified statue of *The Minute Man*. Though this musket-bearing figure of **Captain John Parker** was not dedicated until 1900, it stands on boulders dislodged from the stone walls behind which the colonial militia fired at British troops on April 19, 1775. The **Lexington Visitor Center**, 1875 Massachusetts Ave, on the eastern periphery of the Green (daily: April–Oct 9am–5pm; Nov–March 9am–4pm; free; ⓣ781/862-7753, ⓦwww.nps.gov/mima), has a diorama that shows the detail of the battle, while in the **Buckman Tavern** (mid-March to Nov Mon–Sat 10am–5pm, Sun 1–5pm; 30–45min guided tour; $5; ⓣ781/862-5598), facing the Green at 1 Bedford St, a bullet hole from a British gun has been preserved in an inner door near the restored first-floor tap room. A couple of blocks north, at 36 Hancock St, a plaque affixed to the brown, two-story **Hancock-Clarke House** (mid-March to late-Oct Mon–Sat 9am–5pm, Sun 1–5pm; 30–45min guided tour; $5; ⓣ781/862-1703) solemnly reminds us that this is where "Samuel Adams and John Hancock were sleeping when aroused by Paul Revere"; the latter was the grandson of Reverend John Hancock, the man for whom the house was built in 1698, and enlarged in 1738. Exhibits on the free-admission first floor include the drum on which William Diamond beat the signal for the Minute Men to converge and the pistols that British Major John Pitcairn lost on the retreat from Concord. Less interesting is the small wooden **Munroe Tavern**, somewhat removed from the town center, at 1332 Massachusetts Ave (mid-March to late Oct Mon–Sat 9am–5pm, Sun 1–5pm; 30–45min guided tour; $5; ⓣ781/862-2016), which served as a field hospital for British soldiers, though only for a mere hour and a half. If you intend to visit all three sights, you'll save a bit by getting a combination ticket ($10), available at each site. Just outside of Lexington town, a contemporary brick-and-glass building houses the **National Heritage Museum**, 33 Marrett Rd (Mon–Sat 10am–5pm, Sun noon–5pm; free; ⓦwww.monh.org), which tries to be just that, with rotating displays on all facets of American history, daily life, and culture, plus a permanent exhibit on the battle events of Lexington.

Practicalities

Accommodation in Lexington includes the *Battle Green Motor Inn*, 1720 Massachusetts Ave (ⓣ781/862-6100 or 1-800/537-8483; ❹), with 96 comfortable, basic rooms; the *Desiderata Bed & Breakfast*, 189 Wood St

(Ⓣ781/862-2824; $85), is cozier, a Victorian farmhouse with three basic guestrooms, all non-smoking, with private baths; *Fireside Bed & Breakfast*, 24 Eldred St (Ⓣ781/862-2053, Ⓦwww.firesidebb.com; ❺), is another small family-run establishment with three flouncy rooms, private baths, and a pool. If you're looking to have a **meal**, you might want to try *Via Lago*, at 1845 Massachusetts Ave (Ⓣ781/861-6174), a casual counter-service spot serving fresh, tasty pastas, sandwiches, and salads, or head to *Vinny Testa's*, 20 Waltham St (Ⓣ781/860-5200), for heaping portions of reliable Italian fare like fennel sausage lasagna and spaghetti bolognese.

Concord

CONCORD was one of the few sizeable inland towns of New England at the time of the Revolution, but it hasn't grown much since, and you can see the major sights in a matter of minutes. It's a good spot to explore by bike; the countryside around town is some of the most pristine in this part of the state, filled with bucolic fields and historic colonial houses. The business district hugs **Main Street**, which intersects Monument Street right by the historic **Colonial Inn**, where many of the wounded from the battles of Lexington and Concord were tended; today it is an atmospheric place to stay or just to eat a tavern lunch of fish cakes and chips. Main Street crosses Lexington Road at the **Hill Burying Ground**, from the top of which you can survey much of Concord. A few blocks behind the grounds, off Rte-62, lies **Sleepy Hollow Cemetery**, where Concord literati Ralph Waldo Emerson, Nathaniel Hawthorne, Henry David Thoreau, and Louisa May Alcott are interred atop "Authors' Ridge," a centrally located crest.

The most vaunted spot in Concord is the **North Bridge Area**, slightly removed from the town center and site of the first effective armed resistance to British rule in America. If you approach from Monument Street, as most tourists do, you'll be following the route the British took, as a plaque on a group grave of some British regulars reminds: "They came 3000 miles and died to keep the past upon its throne." The focal point, of course, is the bridge, which, though photogenic enough, looks a bit too groomed to provoke much patriotic sentiment – indeed, it's a 1954 replica of an earlier replacement. On the far side of the bridge is another Minute Man statue, this one sculpted by Daniel Chester French, of Lincoln Memorial fame. A short walk takes you to a **visitors' center**, 2 Heywood St (May–Oct daily 9.30am–4.30pm), where a diorama of the battle is displayed along with assorted military regalia.

Literally a stone's throw from North Bridge is the **Old Manse** (mid-April to Oct Mon–Sat 10am–5pm, Sun noon–5pm; $7; Ⓣ978/369-3909), a gray clapboard house built for Ralph Waldo Emerson's grandfather, the Reverend William Emerson, who was able to witness the nearby hostilities from his window. Of the numerous rooms in the house, all with period furnishings intact, the most interesting is the small upstairs study, which is where Nathaniel Hawthorne, who rented the house in the early 1840s, wrote *Mosses from an Old Manse*, a rather obscure book that endowed the place with its name; it's also here that his wife used her diamond wedding ring to etch the words "Man's accidents are God's purposes" into a window, following a miscarriage. On the first floor, a framed swath of original English wallpaper features the British "paper" stamp-tax mark on the reverse side.

Another Concord literary landmark is the seventeenth-century **Wayside**, 455 Lexington Rd (April–Oct Tues–Sun 10am–5.30pm; $4; ⓣ978/369-6975), a 300-year-old yellow wooden house once home to both the Alcotts and Hawthorne, albeit at different times. Louisa May Alcott's girlhood experiences in the house are said to have inspired *Little Women*, by far her best-known novel. Amongst the many antique furnishings, including an original Franklin stove in the kitchen, the most evocative is in the fourth-floor "tower" that Hawthorne had added on: the slanted writing desk at which the author toiled, standing up. If you don't feel like taking a guided tour, you can stop in at the small but very well-done **museum** at the admissions area to get a flavor of the personalities behind the famous bylines.

Alcott actually penned *Little Women* right next door at the gloomy, brown-clapboard **Orchard House**, 399 Lexington Rd (April–Oct Mon–Sat 10am–4.30pm, Sun 1–4.30pm; Nov–March Mon–Fri 11am–3pm, Sat 10am–4.30pm, Sun 1–4.30pm; closed Jan 1–15; $7; ⓦwww.louisamayalcott.org), where the family lived from 1858 to 1877. Next door to the Wayside is the **Concord Grape Cottage**, where in 1849 Ephraim Bull developed the Concord grape, one of only three fruits native to North America (the others are the cranberry and blueberry). You can see the vines that stemmed from the first successful fruit, but that's about it – it's a private home and not open to the public.

Just past the Orchard House, at the intersection of the Cambridge Turnpike and Lexington Road, is what has become known as the **Ralph Waldo Emerson House**, 28 Cambridge Turnpike (mid-April to Oct Thurs–Sat 10am–4.30pm, Sun 2–4.30pm; $6; ⓣ978/369-2236), where the essayist and poet lived from 1835 until his death in 1882. Emerson's study has been reconstructed across the street at the excellent **Concord Museum**, 200 Lexington Rd (Jan–March Mon–Sat 11am–4pm, Sun 1–4pm; April–Dec Mon–Sat 9am–5pm, Sun noon–5pm; $7; ⓦwww.concordmuseum.org), where his apple orchard once stood. The museum has more than a dozen galleries which display period furnishings from eighteenth- and nineteenth-century Concord, including a sizeable collection of Thoreau's personal effects, such as the simple bed from his Walden Pond hut. More interesting, however, are the Revolutionary War artifacts, including one of the signal lanterns hung from the Old North Church in Boston.

Practicalities

For somewhere to **stay**, the *Amerscot House B&B,* 61 West Acton Rd, Stow (ⓣ978/897-0666, ⓦwww.amerscot.com; ❺), offers attentive hospitality in a restored 1734 farmhouse, while the inexpensive *Concordian Motel*, a few miles west of downtown Concord on Rte-2 at Hosmer Street, Acton (ⓣ978/263-7765; ❹), has 52 comfortable air-conditioned rooms. If you're looking for a bite to **eat**, try the *Cheese Shop*, at 29 Walden St (ⓣ978/369-5778), a great place to stop for deluxe picnic fixings from paté and jellies to, of course, all manner of cheeses. For a sit-down meal, head to *Walden Grille*, 24 Walden St (ⓣ978/371-2233), for baby shrimp quesadillas, lamb salad, or crabcake sandwiches in a refurbished nineteenth-century firehouse.

Walden Pond State Reservation

The tranquility which Thoreau sought and savored at **Walden Pond**, just south of Concord proper off Rte-126 (daily 7am–4.30pm, until sundown in summer; $5 parking fee), is for the most part gone, thanks mainly to the masses of tourists

Concord and Transcendentalism

A half-century after the social tumult that precipitated independence, Concord became the center of a revolution in American thinking known as **transcendentalism**, a cerebral mix of religion, philosophy, mysticism, and ethics. Heavily influenced by Unitarianism and the teachings of **Reverend Ellery Channing**, the transcendentalists, many of them Harvard-educated Unitarian ministers unhappy with their church's conservatism, denied the existence of miracles, and stressed the conviction that insight and intuitive knowledge were the ways to enhance the relationship between man, nature, and the "over-soul." These beliefs, originating in the Platonic belief of a higher reality not validated by sense, experience, or pure reason, were borne of a passion for rural life, liberty, and intellectual freedom. Indeed, the free thinking that transcendentalism unleashed put area writers at the vanguard of American literary expression.

In 1834, **Ralph Waldo Emerson** moved into the Old Manse (see p.171), the house his grandfather had built near the North Bridge; there, in 1836, he wrote the book that would signal the birth of the movement, *Nature*, in which he argued for the organicism of all life, and the function of nature as a visible manifestation of invisible spiritual truths. His stature as an intensely pensive, learned scribe drew other intellectuals to Concord, notably Thoreau, Hawthorne, and the Alcotts, and in 1840 he co-founded *The Dial*, the literary magazine which became the movement's semi-official journal, with Margaret Fuller. The Concord authors formed a close-knit group. Nathaniel Hawthorne, a native of Salem, rented out the Old Manse for three happy years, returned to his hometown, then moved back to Concord permanently in 1852. Meanwhile, Emerson financed Thoreau's Walden Pond sojourn and the Alcotts lived in Orchard House, on Lexington Road. It was a largely wholesome literary movement and the short-lived utopian farming communities it spawned – Hawthorne's Brook Farm and Bronson Alcott's Fruitlands (see overleaf) – seem almost quaint in retrospect. Its effect was longer lasting than these communities, however, as its proponents were to play an important role in supporting educational innovation, abolitionism, and the feminist movement.

who pour in to retrace his footsteps. The place itself, however, unremarkable but for its literary connection, has remained much the same since the author's famed exercise in independence from 1845 to 1847. Thoreau described his experiment in solitude and self-sufficiency in his 1854 book *Walden*, where he concluded, "A man is rich in proportion to the number of things which he can afford to let alone." Of his life in the simple log cabin, he wrote, "I did not feel crowded or confined in the least." A reconstructed single-room hut, replete with a journal open on its rustic desk, is situated near the parking lot (you'll have to be content with peering through the windows), while the site of the original cabin, closer to the shores of the pond, is marked out with stones. The pond, popular with swimmers, was spared from development by a band of celebrities led by ex-Eagle Don Henley. It looks best at dawn, when the pond still "throws off its nightly clothing mist"; late risers should plan an offseason visit to maximize their transcendental experience of it all.

DeCordova Museum, Codman House, and Fruitlands

Though technically a part of the town of Lincoln, the **DeCordova Museum and Sculpture Park**, 51 Sandy Pond Rd (Tues–Sun 11am–5pm; museum $6; Ⓦ www.decordova.org), is only a few miles south of downtown Concord and very much worth a visit. All manner of contemporary sculpture peppers the museum's expansive 35-acre grounds, but most fascinating are the bigger works, like John Buck's *Dream World* and Paul Matisse's *Musical Fence*, which look like they busted the walls of a museum and tumbled into their present positions; Matisse's piece is interactive – tap it with a wooden stick like you would a xylophone. Most of the sculptures are by American (and in particular New England) artists, and are sufficiently impressive to make the garden overshadow the small on-site museum, whose rotating special exhibits are often just as eye-catching, with an emphasis on contemporary multimedia art.

Also in Lincoln, the three-story, gray-shingled **Codman House**, Codman Road (June to mid-Oct Wed–Sun 11am–5pm; tours on the hour; $5), which dates from 1735, and was home to five generations of the Codman family, contains eclectic architectural features from every period, from Georgian paneling through to a Victorian dining room. The grounds resemble those of an English country estate and include a hidden Italianate garden with its own reflecting pool.

Twenty miles west of Lincoln, the small town of **HARVARD** is home to the collection of museums known as **Fruitlands**, 102 Prospect Hill Rd (mid-May to Oct Mon–Fri 11am–3pm, Sat & Sun 10am–5pm; $10; Ⓦwww.fruitlands.org), which tell the story of the daily life, art, and beliefs of a high-minded group, headed by **Bronson Alcott**, that aimed to create a "New Eden." Alcott started the idealistic but short-lived commune here with his English friend Charles Lane in 1843, espousing vegetarianism, freedom of

Lowell

Perhaps more properly part of New Hampshire's Merrimack River Valley than Massachusetts proper, **LOWELL**, sixteen miles north of Lexington, is filled with grim and derelict factories that make it appear more like a midwestern Rust Belt town than a New England village. The one portion that remains intact and attracts visitors is the **Lowell National Historic Park**, in the center of downtown, a preserved factory city founded in the 1820s by Boston industrialist and anthropologist Francis Cabot Lowell. The modern housing was considered a humane alternative to the smog-choked slums of England's industrial cities and for a while it was; workers were not only well paid but also encouraged to attend literacy classes in their spare time. Charles Dickens was one of many British visitors favorably impressed by the place. With the advent of cheap Indian cotton, however, the textile mill fell on hard times, and never recovered. Of the many factories and buildings that have been preserved, the mill at 246 Market St, also the site of the **visitors' center**, functions as a gloomy but interesting open-air **museum** (daily 9.30am–5pm; Ⓦwww.nps.gov/lowe), its web of streets and industrial canals still intact; you can also poke around the Boott Cotton Mills Museum (same hours; $4), where early twentieth-century looms are still put in motion by electric generators.

The city grew up around the manufacturing site, attracting immigrant workers from all over the world; French-Canadians at first, through to the Cambodian immigrants of today – but driving around its depressing streets, it's no wonder that Lowell native **Jack Kerouac** hit the road at the earliest opportunity. A guide to the sights associated with Kerouac, including the University of Massachusetts' **Patrick J. Mogan Cultural Center**, 40 French St (Mon–Fri 9am–5pm, Sat 10am–3pm; free), where you can see his Underwood typewriter and copies of some of his better-known works, can be picked up at the park's visitors' center. Kerouac is buried in the **Edson Cemetery**, at the corner of Gorham Street and the Lowell Connector, which links Lowell to I-95. If hunger strikes along the way, head to the *Southeast Asian Restaurant*, 343 Market St (Ⓣ978/452-3182), which offers an excellent $5 lunch buffet incorporating dishes from all over Southeast Asia.

expression, and celibacy (the latter after siring four daughters, including Louisa May), but talk of living off the "fruits of the land" proved much easier than actually doing it. True to Alcott's pastoral proclivities, today there are two hundred acres of woodlands and meadows on the site, which you can explore on four well-marked nature trails. The original farmhouse now houses a **museum** with exhibits on the transcendentalist movement, including letters and memorabilia of Alcott, Emerson, and Thoreau. The **Shaker Museum** has displays of furniture, crafts, and artifacts retrieved from a Shaker community that once existed here; the **Picture Gallery** features a collection of American art, including New England landscape paintings by Hudson River School artists Thomas Cole and Frederick Edwin Church; and an **Indian Museum** highlights Native American handicrafts and design, including richly decorated clothing, headdresses, pottery, dolls, and carved wood.

The North Shore

The mainly rocky **North Shore**, which extends north of Boston to the New Hampshire border, takes in some of Massachusetts' most disparate geography and culture. Outside Boston a series of glum working-class suburbs – Revere, Saugus, and Lynn – gradually yield to such bedroom communities as Swampscott and Beverly Farms, then to the charming waterfront towns of **Marblehead** and **Salem**, the first real places of any interest, and the latter synonymous with the infamous Witch Trials which took place there in 1692. Just north juts the promontory of scenic **Cape Ann**, the so-called "other Cape"; with its lighthouses, seafood shanties, and rocky shores pummeled by the cold Atlantic, it's a scaled-down version of the Maine coast. Highlights include the fishing port of **Gloucester** and the laid-back oceanfront village of **Rockport**. Further up the coast, the land becomes flatter, with acres of salt marshes and white sands, some of the finest in New England, particularly on **Plum Island**. If the beach is not your thing, here, too, are sleepy villages like **Essex** and **Ipswich**. Closer to the New Hampshire border, the elegant old fishing burg **Newburyport** is of some historical interest, with scores of Federal mansions and a red-brick commercial district built in the early 1800s. Any of these North Shore towns can be reached in an easy day-trip from Boston, and none should take more than a day to explore, with the possible exception of Salem.

The quickest route north from Boston is **Rte-1**, but the more scenic (and closer to the coast) is **Rte-1A**, which also traverses the bucolic horse country of Hamilton and Ipswich between Salem and Newburyport. From Rte-1, **Rte-127** branches off to loop around Cape Ann.

Salem

The Witch Trials of 1692 put **SALEM** on the map for all the wrong reasons, but this unpretentious coastal town sixteen miles north of Boston has done little since to distance itself from such macabre associations; indeed, a number of its attractions focus on the witch-related activity. It's all a bit misleading, considering Salem was the site where the Massachusetts Colony was first established – with the most elevated of intentions – and also for years an immensely prosperous port, the history of which has been largely forgotten. A walk around downtown, however, does much to demonstrate this other legacy: the stately sea captains' houses in the square-mile **McIntire District**; the **Essex Street Mall**, a pedestrian area with shops, cafés, and the **Peabody Essex Museum** – a treasure-trove of merchandise brought home by sea captains on their travels round the world; and the **harbor** area, which includes the famed **House of the Seven Gables** and the **Salem Maritime National Historic Site**, recalling the period of prosperity immediately after the Revolution when Salem boasted no fewer than 185 vessels in its merchant fleet.

Indeed, Salem had such a maritime empire that at one time many Asian merchants were under the impression that the town was the capital of the United States. A deep, well-protected harbor lured a handful of English settlers from Cape Ann to the spot they first called **Naumkeag**, and the Massachusetts Bay Colony was born. By 1683, Salem was one of the few lawful ports of entry for foreign cargos in British America, and by the time the Revolutionary War broke out, good fortune on the high seas had turned Salem into an unrivaled commercial dynamo. **Elias Derby**, said to be America's first millionaire, built his fortune by running privateers from Salem during the war; afterwards, when British ports barred American vessels, he simply had his ships sail farther afield, most gainfully to China and the East Indies.

Of the many goods on the outbound ships of Salem traders, the most lucrative by far was **cod**, which found a huge market in Catholic Europe. Salem's "merchant princes" brought back everything from spices to olive oil to fine china, for a while fairly monopolizing the luxury goods trade in America. At a time when most of the federal government's income came from customs duties, millions of dollars poured in by way of Salem's **Federal Customs House**. But the California Gold Rush, the Civil War, and silting up of the harbor all conspired to rob Salem of its generations of prosperity. Today the harbor is still home to hundreds of boats, though mostly pleasure craft.

Arrival, information, and city transit

MBTA (ⓣ617/222-3200, ⓦwww.mbta.com) commuter **trains** run hourly (every two hours on weekends; $3 one-way) between Salem and Boston's **North Station**, and there's a regular **bus service**, also operated by MBTA, from Haymarket Square in Boston. If you are traveling by **car** from Boston, you can choose between the slow but more interesting Rte-1A, which reaches Salem via the Dalton Parkway, or the much faster Rte-128, which heads to town from exit 25A. Once you've arrived, downtown Salem is so compact you're unlikely to need anything more than a pair of feet to get around; the **Salem Heritage Trail**, a painted red line on Salem's sidewalks, links some of the key sights, similar to Boston's more well-known Freedom Trail. The **Salem Trolley** (April–Oct daily 10am–5pm; March & Nov Sat–Sun 10am–4pm; $10; ⓣ978/744-5469, ⓦwww.salemtrolley.com), also links the main sights; the tickets are valid for a whole day, so you can jump on and off as you please. The town's **information center**, at 2 New Liberty St (daily 9am–5pm; ⓣ978/740-1650 or 1-877/SALEM-MA, ⓦwww.salem.org), serves as the Salem Heritage Trail's unofficial starting point.

The Salem Witch Trials

By their quantity alone, Salem's witch memorials and "attractions" speak of the magnitude of the hysteria that gripped the town for much of 1692 and 1693. Bostonians had overthrown the Massachusetts Bay Colony's first royally-appointed governor, Sir Edmund Andros, in 1689, plunging the region, already under constant threat of French and Indian attack, into political instability. That same year, Boston minister and eventual Witch Trial judge **Cotton Mather** published his popular book *The Wonders of the Invisible World*, a sort of Rough Guide to the supernatural that would help feed the imagination of the town's gullible inhabitants later on. Salem itself was experiencing identity trouble: Salem Village, slightly inland, was a struggling community of farmers mired in property disputes and personality clashes, while Salem Town was an increasingly affluent port. Those caught up in the intrigue lived in Salem Village (which separated to form the town of Danvers in 1752), while the actual trials took place in Salem Town, which is known today simply as Salem.

The first casualties of the villagers' Calvinist lifestyle were their young and supremely bored teenage daughters, who reported as truth fireside tales of the occult as told by **Tituba**, a West Indian slave woman. The children ate up the stories and washed them down with hard cider and various potions, also proffered by Tituba. The fun and games took a sinister turn when the daughter of a new clergyman, Samuel Parris, and his niece experienced convulsive fits and started barking. Whether it was epilepsy or the adverse effects of eating mold-contaminated bread – or witchcraft – other girls started to copy them, and when the village doctor failed to diagnose the problem, the girls' accusations of witchcraft began to be taken seriously.

The trials that ensued pitted neighbor against neighbor, even husband against wife. Confessing to witchcraft spared you the gallows but meant castigation and the confiscation of your land. Mary Lacy of Andover, for instance, "confessed" that "me and Martha Carrier did both ride on a stick when we went to a witch meeting in Salem Village." Another accused, Giles Cory, first testified that his wife was a witch, then refused to agree that the court had the right to try him. To coerce him into acknowledging the court's authority, he was staked on ground under planks while heavy stones were pressed on top of him. He lasted two days, and died without confessing.

The trials were also marked by the girls' crazed ravings: in a scene re-enacted at the Witch Dungeon Museum, Ann Putnam claimed that Sarah Good, a pipe-smoking beggar woman, was biting her, right in front of the judge. Such "**spectral evidence**" was accepted as fact, and the trials soon degenerated into the definitive case study of guilt by association. More than 150 villagers were accused and imprisoned (this in a village of 500), nineteen were hanged and four died in jail. Tituba, who readily confessed to sorcery, was not among them. Two dogs were even hanged after some girls claimed they had given them "the evil eye."

The most grisly day in Salem's history came on **September 22, 1692**, when, on the final day of execution, eight villagers were hanged on **Gallow's Hill**, the precise location of which is not known. Though the hysteria continued for a while unabated, with another 21 people tried in January 1693, the court's legitimacy, shaky from the start (it was formed in direct response to the accusations), was starting to wear thin. One of the judges, Jonathan Corwin, and his family, stood to gain heavily from the proceedings; indeed, much purloined land fell into the hands of his son George. The new royal governor, **William Phipps**, appalled by the sordid state of affairs, finally intervened after his wife was accused. He responded by forbidding the use of spectral evidence as proof, and all of the accused were acquitted that May, with families of the victims eventually awarded damages.

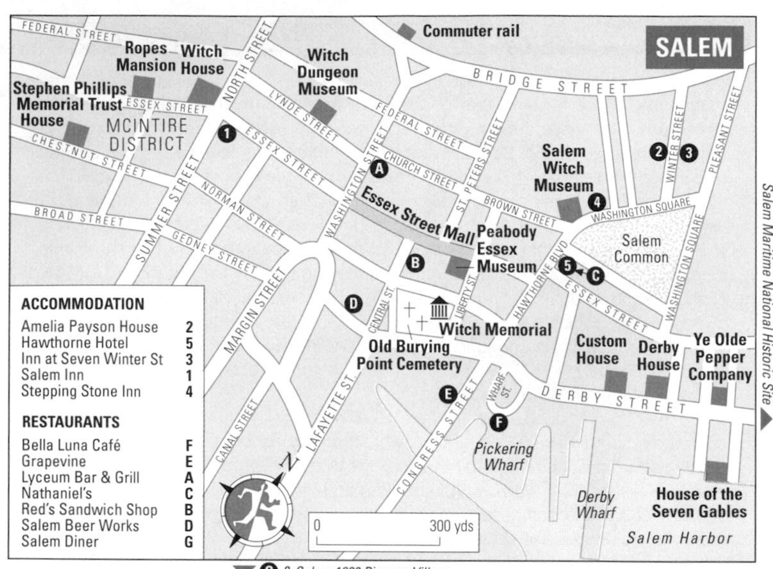

Accommodation

Salem is perhaps the only town in America where **hotels** are booked for Halloween months in advance; if you plan on coming any time in late October, beware of high prices and full houses. Otherwise, apart from the peak summer period when the town is crammed with tourists, you should have no difficulty in finding a room, although none are cheap.

Amelia Payson House 16 Winter St ⓣ978/744-8304, ⓦwww.ameliapaysonhouse.com. Small, friendly, historic B&B in a restored 1845 Greek Revival home, where each room is furnished with period antiques. ❺

Hawthorne Hotel 18 Washington Square W ⓣ978/744-4080 or 1-800/SAY-STAY, ⓦwww.hawthornehotel.com. Salem's only full-service hotel is right in the heart of things and home to two of the town's better restaurants. ❺

The Inn at Seven Winter Street 7 Winter St ⓣ978/745-9520 or 1-800/932-5547, ⓦwww.inn7winter.com. Ten elegant air-conditioned rooms, some with fireplace and antique bed, in an 1871 Victorian house. ❻

The Salem Inn 7 Summer St ⓣ978/741-0680 or 1-800/446-2995, ⓦwww.saleminnma.com. Located on the south side of the McIntire District, this historic inn comprises 38 well-maintained rooms in the Captain West House, the main central building, and the Curwen and Peabody houses, smaller ones on either side of the Captain West, with all non-smoking rooms. Many rooms have working fireplaces. ❻

The Stepping Stone Inn 19 Washington Square N ⓣ978/741-8900 or 1-800/338-3022, ⓦwww.thesteppingstoneinn.com. An unassuming B&B in an 1846 building across from Salem Common and next to the Witch Museum. ❻

The Town

You're never very far from the Puritans' woeful legacy in Salem, with its plethora of witch-related museums, exhibits, and memorials – most child-oriented and some frighteningly tacky, but others unexpectedly enlightening. There's no shortage of witches, either, as a sizeable and highly visible contingent of latter-day sorceresses has staked Salem out as their turf. Many of the so-called witches keep storefronts, and are more than willing to read your palm or otherwise prognosticate your future for a modest fee. Indulge if you must, but bear in mind they're as much a part of the tourist industry as everything else in Salem. Ironically, Salem's witch heritage has proved to be its ultimate salvation, because were it not for the spruced-up center that capitalizes on it, all of the once-proud port might look as industrial and unsightly as some neighboring North Shore towns.

Essex Street Mall

The **Essex Street Mall** is the closest thing Salem has to a main drag, a car-free, boutique-filled stretch of Essex Street that is convenient to many of the city's best sights. At its northern end, the hokey **Salem Witch Museum**, at 191/2 Washington Square (July–Aug daily 10am–7pm; Sept–June daily 10am–5pm; $6; ⓣ978/744-1692 or 1-800/544-1692, ⓦwww.salemwitchmuseum.com), provides some entertaining, if kitschy, orientation on the Witch Trials. It's really just a sound-and-light show that makes ample use of wax figures to depict the events of 1692, housed in a suitably spooky Romanesque building that once served as a church. In front of it is the imposing statue of **Roger Conant**, founder of Salem's first Puritan settlement. Cheesier, but actually far more evocative of Salem's darker hours, is the **Witch Dungeon Museum**, on the west side of town at 16 Lynde St (April–Nov daily 10am–5pm; $6; ⓣ978/741-3570, ⓦwww.witchdungeon.com), occupying a 19th-century clapboard church situated on the site of the prison where the accused witches were locked up, uncovered during preliminary construction by the local phone company. Inside you're again treated to reconstructions of key events, this time by real people: upstairs are surprisingly well-done re-enactments – based on actual transcripts – of the farcical trial of Sarah Good, a beggar falsely accused of witchcraft. Afterwards the actors escort you to a re-created "dungeon," where you see that some of the prison cells were no bigger than a telephone booth. Dank and supremely eerie, it's not hard to believe claims that the place is haunted. If it's all a bit too theatrical, head to the simple and moving **Witch Trials Memorial**, at Charter and Liberty streets, a series of stone blocks etched with the names of the hanged. It's wedged into a corner of the **Old Burying Point Cemetery**, where one of the witch judges, **John Hathorne**, forebear of Salem's most famous son, Nathaniel Hawthorne, is buried. The author of *The Scarlet Letter* added a "w" to his name in an attempt to exorcise the shame.

Peabody Essex Museum

The best thing going in Salem, and a good primer before heading down to the harbor area, is the medley of red-brick and glass buildings that comprise the **Peabody Essex Museum**, at East India Square (April–Oct Mon–Sat 10am–5pm, Sun noon–5pm; Nov–March Tues–Sat 10am–5pm, Sun noon–5pm; $10; ⓣ978/745-9500 or 1-800/745-4054, ⓦwww.pem.org), the oldest continuously operating museum in the US. Currently undergoing a major facelift and expansion at the hands of Canadian architect Moishe Safdie, whose trademark use of atrium entranceways will be in evidence once the structure is complete in June 2003, the museum's vast space incorporates more than thirty galleries displaying art and artifacts from around the world that illustrate Salem's past importance as a major point of interaction and trade between the East and West. Founded by ship captains in 1799 to exhibit their exotic items obtained while overseas, the museum also boasts the biggest collection of nautical paintings in the world. Other galleries hold Chinese and

Japanese export art, Asian, Oceanic, and African ethnological artifacts, American decorative arts, and, in a preserved house that the museum administers, court documents from the Salem Witch Trials.

Currently, the first floor is home to the core museum displays, with creatively curated whaling exhibits that feature not only the requisite scrimshaw but Ambrose Garneray's famous 1835 painting, *Attacking the Right Whale*, and the gaping lower jaw of a sperm whale. Upstairs highlights include a cavernous central gallery with the fanciful figureheads from now-demolished Salem ships hung from the walls and the reconstructed salon from America's first yacht, *Cleopatra's Barge*, which took to the seas in 1816. The collections are likely to be considerably reorganized during a three-month closure in early 2003, so be sure to pick up a new floor plan at the admissions desk.

Salem Harbor

Little of Salem's original waterfront remains, although the 2000ft-long **Derby Wharf** is still standing, fronted by the imposing Federalist-style **Custom House** at its head. These two, and ten other mainly residential buildings once belonging to sea captains and craftsmen, help comprise the **Salem Maritime National Historic Site**, which maintains a **visitors' center** at 174 Derby St (daily 9am–5pm; ⓣ978/740-1650, ⓦwww.nps.gov/sama). The Custom House is where Nathaniel Hawthorne worked as chief executive officer for three years, a stint which he later described as "slavery." The office-like interior is rather bland, as is the warehouse in the rear, with displays of tea chests and such. Rangers also give free tours of the adjacent **Derby House** (daily 9am–5pm), whose millionaire owner, Elias Derby, received it as a wedding gift from his father; it overlooked the harbor to better allow him to monitor his shipping empire. Next door, the **West India Goods Store** emulates a nineteenth-century supply shop by stocking its shelves with nautical accoutrements like fish-hooks and ropes, as well as supplies like molasses candy and "gunpowder tea" – a tightly-rolled high-grade Chinese green tea.

The most famous sight in the waterfront area is undoubtedly the **House of the Seven Gables**, at 54 Turner St (daily: July–Oct 10am–7pm; Nov–June 10am–5pm; closed Jan; $10; ⓣ978/744-0991, ⓦwww.7gables.org), a rambling old mansion by the sea that served as inspiration for Hawthorne's eponymous novel. Forever the "rusty wooden house with seven acutely peaked gables" that Hawthorne described, this 1688 three-story house has some other notable features, such as the bricked-off "Secret Stairway" that leads to a small room. The house was inhabited in the 1840s by Susan Ingersoll, a cousin of Hawthorne whom he often visited. The author's birthplace, a small undistinguished house built before 1750, has been moved to the grounds, which also feature a wishing well amidst lovely surrounding gardens; the grounds are a great place to nibble candies from **Ye Olde Pepper Company** nearby at 122 Derby St (ⓣ978/745-2744), which claims (with some justification) to be the country's oldest candy store.

The McIntire District

The witch attractions pick up again at the so-called **Witch House**, 310 Essex St, west of the Essex Mall (daily: mid-March–June 10am–4.30pm; July–Aug 10am–6pm; Sept–Nov 10am–4.30pm; $6; ⓣ978/744-0180), the well-preserved former home of Judge Jonathan Corwin where the preliminary examinations of those accused of witchcraft took place. It's a good point of departure for exploring the **McIntire District**, a square mile of sea captains' homes west of downtown between Federal and Broad streets, named after a prominent local architect of the late eighteenth century, Samuel McIntire. The most picturesque stretch of these mansions, built after the Revolutionary War for sea captains who wanted to escape the congested waterfront, is along **Chestnut Street**. Of these, the **Stephen Phillips Memorial Trust House**, at no. 34 (mid-May to Oct Mon–Sat 10am–4.30pm; last tour at 4pm; free; Ⓦwww.phillipsmuseum.org), is the one to tour, for its trove of bric-a-brac from around the world, including Chinese porcelain, Oriental rugs, and Fijian throwing clubs. The **Ropes Mansion**, at 318 Essex St, is run by the Peabody Essex Museum (you'll have to request entrance permission there at Ⓣ1-800/745-4054, ext 3011), but you can skip the interior anyway – there's little to distinguish it from similar ones – and instead check out the delightful formal gardens surrounding the residence, admission to which is free.

Salem 1630 Pioneer Village

A bit outside of town (too far to walk, but feasible by bike or car), off of Rte-1A South, is the **Salem 1630 Pioneer Village** (July–Aug Mon–Sat 10am–5pm, Sun noon–5pm; May–June & Sept–Oct tours by appointment only; $7.50; Ⓦwww.7gables.org), run by the House of the Seven Gables (see p.176) and yet another of New England's colonial villages staffed with period-costumed interpreters. It was, in its defense, one of the first of its kind, built in 1930 to celebrate the 300th anniversary of the Naumkeag settlement (and perhaps in a vain attempt to give colonial Salem a reputation as something other than "that place where they hanged all those witches"). The twelve buildings, primarily thatch-roofed cottages, represent a seventeenth-century fishing village, and, while it's no old Sturbridge Village (see p.252), it is a pleasant enough place to spend an hour or two. The most notable building is the Governor's Faire House, a rare example of a grand early Colonial mansion. Should you intend to visit both The Gables and the Village, you'll shave a dollar or so off the price by buying a combo-ticket ($16) at either locale.

Eating and drinking

It's inevitable that a town as geared to the tourist as Salem will have a range of places to **eat and drink**, though there's nothing too out of the ordinary here. Most of the top seafood spots are situated near the harbor.

Bella Luna Café 62 Wharf St Ⓣ978/744-5555. A bistro-style restaurant where you will find blackened seafood, pastas with sun-dried tomatoes, and other trendy fare at reasonable prices (lunch usually under $10).

Grapevine 26 Congress St Ⓣ978/745-9335. Top-notch, expensive bistro with exotic dishes like Cambodian mussels, roasted red snapper with Thai sauce, and good vegetarian options. Dinner entrées range from about $10 to $24.50.

Lyceum Bar and Grill 43 Church St Ⓣ978/745-7665. Affordable Yankee cooking with modern updates at this popular eatery. Try their grilled pork tenderloin with garlic mashed potatoes.

Nathaniel's at the *Hawthorne Hotel*, 18 Washington Square W Ⓣ978/744-4080. One of two restaurants in the hotel, and the fancier by far, creating moderately-priced concoctions like rope-grown mussels steamed in ale with roasted shallots.

Red's Sandwich Shop 15 Central St Ⓣ978/745-3527. Downright cheap and hearty breakfast and lunch fare served in a stone house built in 1700; a hamburger special costs a mere $2.50.

Salem Beer Works 278 Derby St Ⓣ978/745-2337. The microbrew phenomenon hits Salem, with all the requisite and slightly pricey nouveau pub grub to wash down with your beer.

Salem Diner 70 Loring Ave Ⓣ978/741-7918. Your basic diner fare in an original 1941 Sterling Streamliner diner car, one of only four remaining in the US.

Marblehead

Just a few miles on from Salem, **MARBLEHEAD** sits on a peninsula thrusting out into Massachusetts Bay, its rocky shoreline cliffs overlooking a wide natural harbor – which has helped to make it one of the East Coast's biggest yachting centers. Thanks to its occupants' affluence, though, and, strangely, a severe shortage of parking, Marblehead has managed to escape the ravages of rampant commercialism typical of such playpens.

Founded by hardy fishermen from Devon and the English West Country in 1629, Marblehead prides itself on being the birthplace of the US Navy. Originally part of Salem, whose harbor it sits opposite, Marblehead gained its **independence** in 1648 and was incorporated as a town the following year. It became a thriving **fishing and trading port**, especially in the years leading up to the Revolution, and by 1760 was the sixth largest town in the colonies, with a population in excess of five thousand. Any aspirations of becoming one of the nation's great cities were soon dashed, however, after Marblehead sent a regiment to fight in the Revolution that successfully repelled 4000 British in Pelham, New York. Their prowess was recognized by George Washington, who commissioned the local schooner *Hannah*, and four subsequent made-in-Marblehead vessels for use in what became the US Navy. Ironically, his nod to their efforts effectively wiped out the town's prospering commercial fishing trade. Though fishing made a brief comeback, followed by shoemaking, it's boating that the town has become known for. In fact, Marblehead is at its most animated during the annual **Race Week** (the last week of July).

Winding streets lined with old clapboard houses trail down to the waterfront in testimony to the thriving early colonial community, most of them quite modest, their tiny gardens witness to the fact that only fishermen, not farmers, lived downtown. A bit further back from the oceanfront, along **Washington Street**, are the much larger and more sumptuous homes of the wealthy merchants who prospered during the pre-Revolutionary period. Among them is the 1768 **Jeremiah Lee Mansion** (mid-May through mid-Oct Mon–Sat 10am–4pm, Sun 1–4pm; $5; ⓣ781/631-1069), the Georgian home of former shipping magnate Jeremiah Lee, who imported the decorative materials, including English wallpaper and South American mahogany, for his magnificent home. In fact, Lee's wallpaper is the only eighteenth-century hand-painted paper in existence today. Nearby, at the early eighteenth-century **King Hooper Mansion**, 8 Hooper St (Tues–Sat 10am–4pm, Sun 1–5pm; free; ⓣ781/631-2608, ⓦwww.marbleheadarts.org), you can contrast the slave quarters with a lavish third-floor ballroom, and check out local art as well. While you're in the area, stop by **Abbot Hall**, Washington Square (Mon–Tues & Thurs–Fri 8am–5pm, Wed 7.30am–7pm, Sat 9am–6pm, Sun 11am–6pm), Marblehead's uninspiring red-brick town hall, which houses Archibald Willard's famous patriotic painting *The Spirit of '76*.

Abbot Hall can actually be seen from far out at sea, but to get a sweeping view of the port, head to **Fort Sewall**, at the end of Front Street, the remnants of fortifications the British built in 1644, then enlarged in 1742 to protect the harbor from French cruisers (and that later protected the frigate *USS Constitution* in the War of 1812). Closer to the center of town, but with similar panoramic views, is **Old Burial Hill**, Orne Street, which holds the graves of more than six hundred Revolutionary War soldiers.

Practicalities

The Marblehead Chamber of Commerce maintains an **information booth** at the corner of Pleasant and Essex streets (late May to early Sept Mon–Fri 2–6pm, Sat 11am–6pm, Sun 11am–5pm; ⓣ781/639-8469) and an **office** at 62 Pleasant St (Mon–Fri 9am–5pm; ⓣ781/631-2868, ⓦwww.marbleheadchamber.org).

Of the posh places to **stay** in Marblehead, most of which are **B&Bs**, best is *Spray Cliff on the Ocean*, 25 Spray Ave (ⓣ781/631-6789 or 1-800/626-1530, ⓦwww.spraycliff.com; ⑧), a restored 1919 mock-Tudor mansion with large rooms that afford sweeping ocean vistas. Given Marblehead's waterfront location, seafood headlines the town's **dining** options. If you're looking for a snack, try *Flynnie's at the Beach*, on Devereaux Beach (summers only), for inexpensive fish and chips. Alternatively, *The Landing*, 81 Front St, serves pricier fresh seafood in a room overlooking the harbor. You can also tuck into a reasonably-priced steak at *The Barnacle*, 141 Front St, while sitting on an outdoor waterfront terrace.

Cape Ann

Gloucester and **Rockport** are the two principal, but quite different, towns on low-key **Cape Ann**, which reaches into the Atlantic some forty miles north of Boston. The area draws plenty of visitors mainly on account of its salty air and seafood restaurants, but there aren't many sights per se, and in fact the best thing about the place is its unspoiled scenery, the kind of setting that inspired T.S. Eliot, who came here for his family holidays – "The Dry Salvages" in the third of his *Four Quartets* refers to a group of offshore rocks. Rocky headlands, lighthouses, and sea spray define Cape Ann more than the little towns and villages do, and it's quite easy to feel very far from civilization here, if only for an afternoon. From I-95, Rte-128 East will take you all the way to Gloucester, then it's either Rte-127 or scenic Rte-127A to Rockport.

Gloucester

Founded in 1623, gritty **GLOUCESTER** is the oldest fishing port in Massachusetts, though years of over-fishing the once cod-rich waters have robbed the town of any aura of affluence it may have had in the past, and federal regulations threaten to reduce the current fleet of fishing boats still further. The town has long had an artistic identity as well, initially established by the painter **Winslow Homer**, who summered out in the harbor on Ten Pound Island in 1880. Homer was followed by a bevy of other artists who set up a colony on **Rocky Neck**, just east of downtown, where they converted fishermen's shacks into studios. The now run-down district whose modern galleries are salt-box shacks selling the kinds of tacky nautical prints that end up in motel bathrooms, was also once the temporary home of Rudyard Kipling, whose 1897 novel *Captains Courageous* involved a Gloucester ship. Recently Gloucester has seen a bit of a tourist boom, triggered by the popular film version of Sebastian Junger's 1997 book *The Perfect Storm* (see p.627 for an excerpt); the **Crows Nest**, a bar and lodge depicted in the film, is the object of most visitors' affections (see review under "Practicalities" below). The friendly folk in the **visitors' center**, located down by the harbor at Stage Fort Park, Rte-127 (June to mid-Oct daily 9am–5pm; ⓣ978/281-8865), can give you a map of locations used in the film, and it seems nearly everyone has a story about how nice George Clooney was during his stay.

Whale watching and sailing on Cape Ann

One of the most popular and exhilarating activities along this stretch of coast is whale-watching; trips depart from Gloucester, Salem, and Newburyport to the important whale feeding grounds of Stellwagen Bank and Jeffreys Ledge, where an abundance of plankton and small fish provide sufficient calories (around one million a day) to keep a 50ft, 25-ton humpback happy. Ongoing narration throughout the trips from a marine scientist interprets the sightings and behavior of all whales and marine life encountered, and researchers are available to answer questions on the return journey. Several of the companies rely on reports from deep-sea fishing boats which radio back the location of the feeding whales, so the whale-watch boats know where to go before they even leave the docks. Most claim a 99 percent or higher sighting record, though this does not necessarily mean that you're going to see a whale performing a photogenic pirouette just a few feet away – sometimes you may catch no more than a glimpse of a tail. Even on a hot day, it can be quite cool twenty miles offshore, so bring a jacket or sweater, sunglasses, rubber-soled shoes, and a hat to protect you from the powerful sun; though there's little likelihood of spray, you might also bring a rain jacket. Two of the leading companies operate out of Gloucester Harbor. The Yankee Fleet is at 75 Essex Ave (ⓣ978/283-0313 or 1-800/WHALING, ⓦwww.yankeefleet.com), and Captain Bill's (ⓣ978/283-6995 or 1-800/33WHALE, ⓦwww.captainbillswhalewatch.com) is next to *Captain Carlo's* restaurant on the Harbor Loop. Both offer two daily four-hour trips during the summer season, probably the best time to see the whales, for around $28.

From Gloucester, a worthwhile alternative to whale watching is a schooner trip aboard the *Thomas E. Lannon*. Built in 1997, but modeled after a 1903 sword-fishing schooner, the 65-foot vessel takes up to 49 passengers on two-hour sailing tours of the Gloucester coast. The *Lannon* makes up to four sails daily from Seven Seas Wharf at the *Gloucester House Restaurant*, 10am to 8pm in July and August; once daily on weekends early September to October 15; at a cost of $30 per adult. Call ⓣ978/281-6634 or check ⓦwww.schooner.org for booking information.

The Town

Coming into town, which you can do either via Rte-128 or 127, both of which feed into Main Street, you'll likely be drawn toward one of Gloucester's sources of pride, the 1923 bronze *Man at the Wheel*, right on the waterfront near the drawbridge, an overhyped statue of an angler at the wheel of a ship. To learn a bit more about the port's fishing past, head to the excellent **Cape Ann Historical Association**, 27 Pleasant St, near the docks (Tues–Sat 10am–5pm; $5; ⓦwww.cape-ann.com/historical-museum), where the history of Gloucester and Cape Ann is well documented through old photographs, fishing implements, and paintings of mostly local scenes by a variety of artists including Winslow Homer, Milton Avery, Augustus Buhler, and Gloucester-born marine artist Fitz Hugh Lane. Over in East Gloucester, at Eastern Point off Rte-127A, **Beauport** (tours hourly, mid-May to mid-Sept Mon–Fri 10am–4pm; mid-Sept to mid-Oct Mon–Fri 10am–4pm, Sat & Sun 1–4pm; $5; ⓣ978/283-0800) is a 45-room mansion perched on the rocks overlooking Gloucester Harbor. Started in 1907 as a simple summer retreat for the collector and interior designer Henry Davis Sleeper, the house evolved over the following 27 years into a gabled, turreted villa filled with vast collections of European, American, and Asian objects. Sleeper wasn't interested in the historical integrity of his aggregation so much as the aesthetic balance, and the house is an intriguing mixture of styles and themes, each room strikingly different from the next, with cozy, dark Colonial rooms leading directly into bright, open Mediterranean-style rooms with jaw-dropping ocean views. The tour, which meanders through the structure, provides a fascinating view of the lifestyles of the rich and famous in the early part of the twentieth century.

On the southwestern corner of Gloucester's harbor is the imposing **Hammond Castle Museum**, 80 Hesperus Ave (June–Aug daily 10am–5pm; Sept–May weekends only 10am–3pm; $8; ⓣ978/283-7673, ⓦwww.hammondcastle.org), once the home of the eccentric financier and amateur inventor John Hays Hammond, Jr. (he made some advances in guided missile and radio communications technology), who wanted to bring medieval European relics back to the US. By all accounts, he succeeded: the austere fortress, which overlooks the ocean and site of the spot that inspired Longfellow's poem *The Wreck of the Hesperus*, is brimming with them, from armor and tapestries to the elaborately carved wooden facade of a fifteenth-century French bakery. Also among the artifacts is the partially crushed skull of one of Columbus's shipmates. A murky 30,000-gallon pool inside the castle can, at the switch of a lever, change from fresh to sea water; it's said that Hammond himself liked to swan dive into it from his balcony.

Practicalities

Gloucester is just over an hour by **commuter rail** from Boston's North Station (ⓣ617/222-3200, ⓦwww.mbta.com; $4.50 one-way) and trains arrive about half a mile from the harbor. That said, to get the most out of the town's spread-out sights and the area in general, you should probably count on some other means of transportation – either a car or a bike. **Accommodation** options range from fairly inexpensive bed and breakfasts like *Julietta House*, 84 Prospect St (ⓣ978/281-2300, ⓦwww.juliettahouse.com; ❻), and *The Harborview Inn*, 71 Western Ave (ⓣ978/283-2277 or 1-800/299-6696, ⓦwww.harborviewinn.com; ❺), both quiet, friendly establishments minutes from all of Gloucester's attractions, to five or six motels, several with impressive water views, like the *Cape Ann Motor Inn*, 33 Rockport Rd (ⓣ978/281-2900 or 1-800/464-VIEW, ⓦwww.capeannmotorinn.com; ❻), a three-story establishment right on Long Beach, with airy rooms equipped with kitchenettes and balconies.

As is to be expected, many of the city's **restaurants** specialize in fresh seafood, like *Captain Carlo's* at Harbor Loop (ⓣ978/283-6342), which has the added bonus of being right where the professional fishing action is; *The Studio*, 51 Rocky Neck Ave (ⓣ978/283-4123), also serves steak; and *Madfish Bar & Grill*, 77 Rocky Neck Ave (ⓣ978/281-4554; closed winters), has an airy, waterfront setting perfect for downing creatures of the sea – don't miss the tuna carpaccio with wasabi. More upscale is the *Franklin Café*, 118 Main St (ⓣ978/283-7888), a New American bistro. If you're looking for action at night, the likeliest places to start are **bars** like *The Crows Nest*, 334 Main St (ⓣ978/281-2965), long a fisherman's hangout (and with great clam chowder), though it has lost some of its rough-and-tumble feel in the wake of its *The Perfect Storm* success, and the *Blackburn Tavern*, 2 Main St (ⓣ978/282-1919), a cozy neighborhood pub with live music.

Rockport

ROCKPORT, about five miles north of Gloucester, is the more scenically situated of the two towns, and also the more self-consciously quaint, though only oppressively so on crowded summer weekends. It, too, started life as a fishing village, then became an important granite-quarrying center, a business that fizzled out here during the 1920s and 1930s and hasn't found much of a replacement since.

From early on, Rockport attracted summer vacationers and artists, drawn by the picturesque harbor and the surrounding shingled shacks, and has some renown as a one-time artists' colony: a red lobster shed near the harbor's edge has been christened "Motif #1" because it's been painted so many times. Works by contemporary local artists, some of them terribly kitsch, can be seen at the **Rockport Art Association**, 12 Main St (mid-May to mid-Oct Mon–Sat 10am–5pm, Sun noon–5pm; Oct–Dec & March to mid-May Tues–Fri 10am–4pm, Sat 10am–5pm, Sun noon–5pm; free; ⓣ978/546-6604, ⓦwww.rockportusa.com/RAA), and at a number of small shops and galleries throughout town. The main drag is a thin peninsula called **Bearskin Neck**, lined with old saltbox fishermen's cottages transformed into art galleries and restaurants. The neck rises as it reaches the sea, and there's a nice view of the rocky harbor from the end of it. Otherwise, aside from shopping and strolling, there isn't much doing here. Inside the aptly named **Paper House**, just outside Rockport in Pigeon Cove, Pigeon Hill Street (daily April–Oct 10am–5pm), everything is made of paper, from chairs and a piano (keys excepted) to a desk fashioned from copies of the *Christian Science Monitor*. It's the end result of a twenty-year project undertaken in 1922 by a local mechanical engineer who "always resented the daily waste of newspaper." He hasn't really helped the cause.

Practicalities

Rockport is the last stop on the Rockport Line from Boston's North Station (ⓣ617/222-3200, ⓦwww.mbta.com; $5 one-way). The town has plenty of **accommodation**, mostly in inns and B&Bs situated near the center; among these, the *Pleasant Street Inn*, 17 Pleasant St (ⓣ978/546-3916 or 1-800/541-3915, ⓦwww.pleasantstreetinn.net; ❺), is a gracious eight-room Victorian inn perched on a knoll overlooking the village; a separate carriage house contains a two-bedroom apartment. There's also the delightful *Addison Choate Inn*, 49 Broadway (ⓣ978/546-7543 or 1-800/245-7543, ⓦwww.addisonchoateinn.com; ❻), a Greek Revival house with a lovely shaded porch, pool, and complimentary breakfast buffet. Like Gloucester, Rockport's **restaurants** mainly focus on moderately-priced fresh seafood dishes; the added incentive of a waterfront view is often the only distinction between restaurants. The *Greenery Restaurant*, at 15 Dock Square (ⓣ978/546-9593), has a pleasant atmosphere, with a light seafood and vegetarian menu, but no seaside view. More upscale is *My Place by the Sea*, on Bearskin Neck (ⓣ978/546-9667), which has a stupendous waterfront setting to match its delicious lobster. If you want wine with your meal, you'll have to bring your own, however, as there's none sold here; Rockport is a "dry town."

Ipswich and Essex

Though it was founded in 1633, little **IPSWICH**, a few miles northwest of Gloucester along Rte-133, isn't much of a town, its dubious claim to fame

Route 127's Coastal Trail

Rte-127A ends shortly after Rockport, after which you can catch 127 South back inland, or continue along scenic 127 North to **Halibut Point State Park**, a beautiful stretch of rocky, wooded coast with **hiking trails** to the northernmost tip of Cape Ann. From there, 127 turns back in toward Gloucester and Essex, but stays close to the coast all the way, yielding majestic vistas of ocean and coves. It's one of the most **scenic drives** you'll find along the Massachusetts coast.

being that it has more houses built before 1725 than any other community in the country. One of these, the double-gabled **John Whipple House**, 53 S Main St (May to mid-Oct Wed–Sat 10am–4pm, Sun 1–4pm; $7), built in 1640 and one of the nation's first homes to be restored – in 1898 – is filled with a variety of antiques and Arthur Wesley Dow paintings, and an outside herb garden contains some fifty varieties of medicinal plants. The price of admission includes entry to the nearby **John Heard House**, 40 S Main St (same hours as Whipple House), a 1795 sea captain's home built in the Federal style, with Chinese and early American furnishings and a collection of carriages. Most people come to Ipswich, however, to visit **Crane's Beach**, part of the Crane Memorial Reservations, Argilla Road (daily 8am–sunset), four miles of beautiful sand lining Ipswich Bay. There's a large parking lot that fills up on summer weekends, despite a $20-per-car parking fee; weekday visitors get charged $10. You can get a better vantage on the oceanside by ascending to **Castle Hill**, 290 Argilla Rd (May–Oct 10am–4pm, $8; tours: mid-May to Sept Wed & Thurs 11am–4pm; grounds open year-round, free; ⓣ978/356-4351), a reproduction 59-room English-style mansion built by plumbing tycoon Richard Crane in the 1920s; you might recognize it as the setting for the movie *The Witches of Eastwick*. Unfortunately it's often rented out for private events, so call ahead.

To best soak up the pristine tidal flats, take a boat out to the **Crane Wildlife Refuge** (late May to late Oct 9am–3.30pm; $5; ⓣ978/356-4351), a spectacular, 650-acre expanse of dunes, woodlands, and five islands, all maintained by the Trustees of Reservations, a historical conservation group that runs seasonal twice-a-day (10am and 2pm) tours of the refuge aboard the *Osprey*, a 22-seater pontoon. The trip includes a stop at **Hog Island**, where the film of *The Crucible* was filmed; you can hike up to the top of the island for great tri-state views.

The former shipbuilding town of **ESSEX**, off Rte-1A, though somewhat of a noted antiques center, should be visited primarily for the splendid **Essex Shipbuilding Museum**, 29 Main St (May–Sept Wed–Mon 10am–5pm; Oct–April Wed–Sun noon–4pm; $4; ⓣ978/768-7541, ⓦwww.essexshipbuildingmuseum.org), right in the center of the village, where more than four thousand ships have been constructed over the years, including schooners, steamers, and yachts. The museum traces their fascinating history through models of ships, tools, and old photographs. At the **Shipyard**, 66 Main St, also part of the museum, you can see the *Evelina M. Goulart*, one of five surviving Essex-built schooners, drydocked near the spot where she was first launched in 1927.

Practicalities

Among the few places to **stay** in these parts is the *Essex River House Motel*, Rte-133 (ⓣ978/768-6800; April–Oct; ❺), right on the river, with comfortable, air-conditioned rooms and efficiencies; and the *George Fuller House*, 148 Main St, also in Essex (ⓣ978/768-7766 or 1-800/477-0148, ⓦwww.cape-ann.com/fuller-house; ❼), a rambling old Federal home with Victorian additions with attractive, air-conditioned rooms, some featuring views over the marshes, and a full breakfast. Cheaper is the *Whittier Motel*, 120 County Rd, Ipswich (ⓣ978/356-5205 or 1-877/418-0622, ⓦwww.whittiermotel.com; June–Oct; ❺), fairly standard but close to the local attractions.

Most of the best **restaurants** in the area are in Essex. *Jerry Pelonzi's Hearthside*, Rte-133 (ⓣ978/768-6002), is a lovely old farmhouse with views over the marshes where you can tuck into marine delights like finnan haddock, done the traditional Scottish way with eggs, as well as steaks and a range of sandwiches. *Woodman's*, 121 Main St (ⓣ978/768-6057), lays claim to being the first restaurant to serve fried clams; less famous, but certainly no less good, is *J. T. Farnham's Seafood and Grill*, Rte-133 (ⓣ978/768-6643). Over in Ipswich, try the *Choate Bridge Pub*, on South Main Street (ⓣ978/356-2931) for standard pub fare like steak sandwiches, burgers, and pizza, or head to the *White Cap Restaurant and Tavern*, 141 High St (ⓣ978/356-5276), which also specializes in fried clams, shucked daily on the premises.

Newburyport and around

Further up I-95, just south of the New Hampshire border, **NEWBURYPORT** is Massachusetts' smallest city and one of its most appealing, a pleasant and unsullied mix of upscale boutiques and historic homes that still functions as a fishing port. Its location at the mouth of the Merrimack River proved convenient to the English fishermen who settled here as early as 1635, and to shipbuilders in the two centuries that followed, resulting in the accumulation of an enormous amount of shipbuilding wealth, attested to by the imposing mansions on **High Street**, on the northern rim of town. Today Newburyport exudes a real flavor of the past, but the **Market Square Historic District**, with its bricked sidewalks, old lampposts, and upscale shops and eateries, is not quite as historic as you'd think – a fire destroyed the area in 1811, and everything had to be rebuilt.

Your best bet is to simply stroll the streets of the city center, especially **State Street**, sample some incredibly fresh seafood, and watch the boats from the two-acre Waterfront Park and Promenade, which faces the Merrimack River as it spills into the ocean. Near the waterfront, the **Custom House Maritime Museum**, 25 Water St (April–Dec Mon–Sat 10am–4pm, Sun 1–4pm; $4), is a one-time custom house that seems to have far more empty space than exhibits. What little there is consists of old model ships and a rather dreary re-created tidepool. On the other side of downtown, the handsome 22-room Federal-style **Cushing House**, 98 High St (May–Oct Tues–Fri 10am–4pm, Sat 11am–2pm; guided tours only, $4; ⓦwww.newburyhist.com/collections), once home to Caleb Cushing, the nation's first ambassador to China, has among its rather musty antique furnishings a lovely hand-painted Dutch baby cradle in the canopy bedroom. You're better off milling about the eerie **Old Hill Burying Ground**, adjacent to the beautiful Bartlett Mall on High Street, where many Revolutionary War veterans and prominent sea captains are interred.

If you don't have your own transport, Newburyport is also accessible by commuter rail (ⓣ617/222-3200, ⓦwww.mbta.com) from Boston's North Station. When you get to the train station, it's less than a mile walk to the center of town.

Plum Island

Plum Island, a nine-mile barrier beach just south of Newburyport on Rte-1A, is mostly occupied by the remote **Parker River National Wildlife Refuge** (daily dawn–dusk; $5 per car, $2 walk-in; ⓦwww.plum-island.com), a bird-watching sanctuary located on the migratory route of a vast number of different species. As such it is populated in summer by great blue herons, glossy ibises, and snowy egrets, though a less impressive array year-round. The beach itself here gets better, and less developed, the further south you go. Outside of the refuge, the beach is free save for a small fee for parking ($3–5).

Practicalities

Newburyport is an ideal place to spend an afternoon or stop over for **dinner**. Some of the more reliable spots in town that won't break the bank are *Glenn's*, 44 Merrimac St (Ⓣ978/465-3811), where you can savor big portions of grilled seafood; and *The Bayou*, 50 State St (Ⓣ978/499-0428), an excellent Cajun restaurant. For **accommodation**, try *The Windsor House,* 38 Federal St (Ⓣ978/462-3778, Ⓦwww.bbhost.com/windsorhouse; ❻), an eighteenth-century Federal mansion with four comfortable rooms, delicious English breakfasts, and enjoyable afternoon tea. Just slightly more modern, *The Clark Currier Inn*, 45 Green St (Ⓣ978/465-8363 or 1-800/360-6582, Ⓦwww.clarkcurrierinn.com; ❺), dates from 1803, and has plenty of common areas in which to relax, including an outdoor garden with gazebo and pond. *The Essex Street Inn*, 7 Essex St (Ⓣ978/465-3148; Ⓦwww.essexstreetinn.com; ❺), is an attractive Colonial-style house right off the main drag, State Street, with beautiful large rooms and private baths.

The South Shore

The **South Shore** makes a clean sweep of the Massachusetts coast from suburban Quincy, just south of Boston, to the former whaling port of New Bedford, west of Cape Cod. **Plymouth** is the only really tourist-driven place along this stretch, on account of the **pilgrim** associations; if you're not interested in reliving the coming of the *Mayflower*, the town, while pleasant enough, will probably not merit more than a few hours' exploration. **New Bedford** has fewer sights, one of which is a well-conceived whaling museum, but its historic associations feel a bit more authentic than those of Plymouth. Still, the South Shore's biggest draw may be its unclogged seaside villages and miles of coastal scenery that in other parts of the country would doubtless have already succumbed to strip-mall mania; likely the only reason this hasn't happened is because everybody is too geared up for Cape Cod and the islands beyond to stop off. You won't be able to stop yourself, however, without your own wheels: while Plymouth and Quincy are easily accessible by commuter rail from Boston, the rest of the towns aren't.

Route 3A: Quincy to Duxbury

Although Rte-3 is the most direct route from Boston to Cape Cod, you'll hardly catch a glimpse of the coast from it. A better alternative is to take **Rte-3A**, which splits off from I-93 just south of Boston. Although not by any means a "scenic drive," the road does go through some pretty residential neighborhoods and affords occasional harbor and beach views. The first town you hit on this route is **QUINCY**, not much more than part of the urban sprawl of metropolitan Boston, but which bills itself rather imperiously as the "City of Presidents" – it was the birthplace of John Adams and his son John Quincy Adams, the second and sixth presidents of the United States. This grasp at heritage is preserved at the **Adams National Historic Site**, 1250 Hancock St (mid-April–Nov daily 9am–5pm; grounds open year-round; trolley tours $2; ⓣ617/770-1175, ⓦwww.nps.gov/adam), highlighted by the Adams Mansion, residence of the family for four generations and boasting, out in the garden, the magnificent cathedral-ceilinged **Stone Library**, which houses presidential books and manuscripts. Just a short walk away on the grounds stands the modest 1681 saltbox where the elder Adams entered the world, and adjacent to that, the 1663 house where his son was born.

If for some reason you find yourself **staying** here, there are a few large, insipid chain hotels and motels which straddle the expressway to Boston and the surrounding roads. There are, however, some decent places for a bite to **eat**: *Tullio's*, 150 Hancock St (ⓣ617/471-3400), does admirable pastas, while lighter fare, including good wraps and burritos, is available at *Blackboard Café*, at 1515 Hancock St (ⓣ617/847-1605). You can reach Quincy by commuter rail from Boston (ⓣ617/222-3200, ⓦwww.mbta.com).

Hingham

After a few twists and turns through heavy industrial areas, Rte-3A opens up to picturesque **HINGHAM**. Founded in 1635, it's the kind of affluent place you would more expect to find on Cape Cod, though considerably quieter and less visited, of course. **Main Street** is lined with small, black-shuttered eighteenth- and nineteenth-century houses, none of which are open to the public; in fact, the only house in Hingham you can visit is the **Old Ordinary**, 21 Lincoln St (mid-June to early Sept Tues–Sat 1.30–4.30pm; $3; ⓦwww.hinghamhistorical.org), its name a reference to "ordinary" meals at fixed prices that used to be served at this former stagecoach stop between Boston and Plymouth. Today it's the house museum of the Hingham Historical Society, with a tap room set up as it would have been when the house was a tavern, and a dining room with various Hepplewhite and Chippendale furnishings. Back on Main Street, at no. 107, the **Old Ship Church**, whose roof resembles an inverted ship's hull (it was built by ship carpenters), claims to be the oldest building in continuous ecclesiastical service in the United States – since 1681. Behind the church an attractive garden-style cemetery offers good views of the harbor. If you want to get a bit closer to the water, head to the peninsula of parkland known as **World's End** (daily 9am–5pm; parking $4.50); the five-mile spit isn't quite the end of the world, but it's a sufficiently nice place for a walk or picnic, with impressive views of the distant Boston skyline.

Cohasset and Duxbury

Further south is the quiet, moneyed town of **COHASSET**, where according to maritime historian Samuel Eliot, "the granite skeleton of Massachusetts protrudes for the last time." Captain John Smith, who in 1607 had helped establish the first permanent English colony in North America at Jamestown, Virginia, disembarked briefly here in 1614 in his initial exploration of New England. Make your detour at the enclave of **Cohasset Village**, slightly east of Rte-3A, a pristine blink-and-miss-it town featuring a wide town green perhaps recognizable from the movie *The Witches of Eastwick*. From here, a drive along **Jerusalem Road** reveals stunning views of the coast and rambling (private) mansions.

Another fifteen miles down 3A is affluent **DUXBURY**, settled in 1627 by Myles Standish and other Plymouth Pilgrims who needed more land for their cows. It has a beautiful five-mile barrier **beach** on Rte-139, access to which is nearly impossible due to residents-only parking. You can, however, get to isolated smaller beaches by parking along the residential streets. The only real sight of note is the **John Alden House**, 105 Alden St (mid-May to mid-Oct Mon–Sat noon–4pm; $4; Ⓦwww.alden.org), originally built in 1653 for John and Priscilla Alden, passengers on the *Mayflower*, and just having undergone minimal structural change since. Check out the East Chamber, or master bedroom, with its post-and-beam construction clearly visible and canopy bed with trundle bed underneath, and the Great Room (living room), centered on an eighteenth-century gate-leg table. South of town, the **Myles Standish State Forest**, 14,000 hilly acres of mostly pine woodlands and meadows, is a good place to stretch, traversed by hiking trails and bicycle paths, and dotted with fifteen ponds. A 116-foot granite shaft at its center, the **Myles Standish Memorial**, is capped by a statue of the strident Plymouth colony captain; if it's open, head up the 125 inside steps for stunning South Shore views.

You probably won't have much need to linger in Duxbury, especially with Plymouth just down the road, but if you're looking for a place to **eat** *and* **stay**, the *Windsor House Inn*, 390 Washington St (Ⓣ781/934-0991; ❼), is an 1803 inn with two guestrooms and two suites done out with reproduction antique furniture. The elegant main dining room is open weekends only, though there's a carriage room restaurant open daily; both specialize in moderately-priced seafood (especially lobster) and meat dishes.

Plymouth

PLYMOUTH, dubbed "America's hometown," is one of the largest towns in area in the United States, about the same size as Boston, though its population is largely clustered round the waterfront area where the Pilgrims landed in December 1620 (they had landed prior to this near Provincetown, on Cape Cod). Much of the town is given over to commemorating, in various degrees of taste and tact, this event: apart from the expected crop of Pilgrim-related monuments and museums, there would be little to distinguish Plymouth's concentration of fast-food restaurants, gas stations, and mini-malls from any of America's other hometowns.

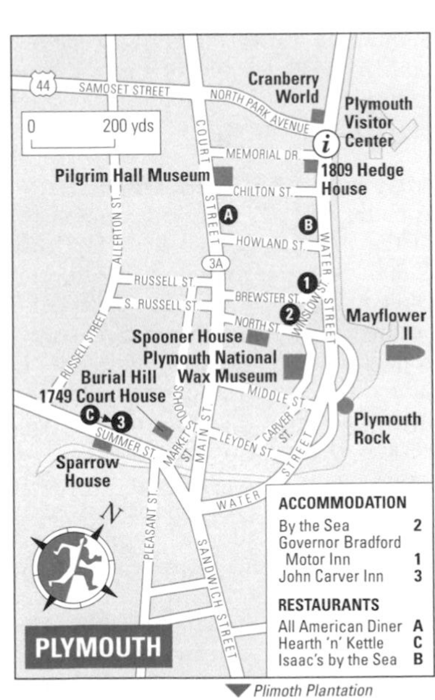

The Town

The proceedings start off with a solemn pseudo-Greek temple by the sea that encloses the otherwise nondescript **Plymouth Rock**, where the Pilgrims are said to have touched land. As is typical with most sites of this ilk, it is of symbolic importance only – they had already spent several weeks on

Cape Cod before landing here. On the hill behind the venerable stone, the **Plymouth National Wax Museum**, at 15 Carver St (daily: March–May & Oct–Nov 9am–7pm; June–Sept 9am–9pm; closed Dec–Feb; $5; ⓣ508/746-6468), charges admission to its inadvertently kitsch sound-and-light tableaux of the early days of settlement. Down the street is the similarly unconvincing **Pilgrim Hall Museum**, at 75 Court St (Feb–Dec daily 9.30am–4.30pm; $5; ⓣ508/746-1620, ⓦwww.pilgrimhall.org), where you enter a room filled with furniture which may or may not have come over on the *Mayflower*, along with numerous pairs of shoes which the Pilgrims may or may not have worn.

Close to the waterfront are a couple of historic homes which were indeed inhabited by early settlers of the area. The **1809 Hedge House**, 126 Water St (tours hourly, early June through early Oct Thurs–Sat 10am–4pm; $5; ⓣ508/747-1240), is an impressive Federal-style mansion built by a wealthy shipping family filled with stylish period furnishings that include a remarkable collection of imported Chinese porcelain. The older **Spooner House** at 27 North St (tours hourly, June 1–Oct 7 Thurs–Sat 10am–4pm; $5; ⓣ508/747-1240) was home to five generations of Spooners, a noted mercantile family, and is decorated with their family heirlooms. However, the most interesting feature is the secret garden out back, though the tours are pretty tight affairs and you can't simply stroll the gardens at your own leisure.

Since "how old is it?" is a question that seems to thread itself throughout a tour of Plymouth, it is worth heading over to two of the oldest structures in the town. The **1749 Court House and Museum**, 12 Market St (daily, late May Day to early Sept; free; ⓣ508/830-4075), is distinguishable as America's oldest wooden courthouse. The courthouse almost went the way of every other wooden courthouse in the country in the early 1950s when it was slated for demolition, but was saved as a historical site and still stands as it always has for the past two hundred years. The museum attached is little more than a collection of tools, housewares, and the usual assorted artifacts, but it's fun anyway. Just a little further south on Market Street is the **Sparrow House**, 42 Summer St (daily 9am–5pm except Wed; $5.50), the oldest house in Plymouth, built in 1640 by one of the *Mayflower's* brave passengers; the ground-floor gallery contains local pottery and crafts while the upper rooms are decorated in the threadbare style of early settlers.

Mayflower II and Plimoth Plantation

A better way to spend your time in Plymouth is at the newly restored replica of the *Mayflower*, called the **Mayflower II** (April–Nov daily 9am–5pm; $8; ⓣ508/746-1622, ⓦwww.plimoth.org), on the State Pier in Plymouth Harbor. Built in Britain by English craftsmen following the detailed and historically accurate plans of an American naval architect at MIT, the *Mayflower II* was ceremoniously docked in Plymouth in 1957 and given to America as a gesture of goodwill. This version meticulously reproduces the buff brown hull and red strapwork ornamentation that are typical of a seventeenth-century merchant vessel – which is what the original *Mayflower* was, before being outfitted for passengers prior to its horrendous 66-day journey across the Atlantic. Notice the hawthorn, or English mayflower, carved into the stern; whether the original ship was so adorned is unclear. On board, role-playing "interpreters" in period garb, meant to be representatives of the 102 Pilgrim passengers, field visitors' questions. Below the main deck, you can have a look at the "tween decks" area, where the Pilgrims' cramped cabins would have been.

Similar in approach and authenticity is the **Plimoth Plantation**, three miles south of town off Rte-3 (April–Nov daily 9am–5pm; $20; ⓣ508/746-1622,

The world's cranberry capital

If you're fortunate enough to visit Plymouth during the first half of October, you'll coincide with cranberry country's **annual wet harvest**. Nearly half the country's crop of cranberries come from Plymouth County, its boggy terrain and acidic soil just perfect for this creeping evergreen of the heath family, as the Native Americans discovered centuries before the first colonists arrived. Cultivation involves planting cuttings in about three or four inches of sand laid over the soil. The planting area is then flooded for a day or two to secure the cuttings in the ground, a ploy that is also used in the winter to protect the plants from frost. After four or five years, they are ready to be harvested. The farmers flood the bogs, which are surrounded by forest, with about a half-meter of water and the berries float to the surface in an explosion of glittering crimson. Most of the bogs are situated around **Carver** and **South Carver**, in particular the stretch of Rte-58 between routes 44 and 28. Every Columbus Day weekend, South Carver plays host to the **Cranberry Harvest Festival**, at the Edaville Cranberry Bogs off Rte-58. There are parades, baked goods, and helicopter rides over the bogs. Contact the festival organizers (Ⓣ508/759-1041 ext 13, Ⓦwww.cranberries.org) for details.

If you miss it, you can head ten miles north of Plymouth Rock to **Cranberry World**, 158 Water St (May–Nov daily 9.30am–5pm; free; Ⓣ508/747-2350), a slick little museum sponsored by juice giant Ocean Spray. Tours display the harvesting processes above (and then the juicing), and they conclude with free juice samples.

Ⓦwww.plimoth.org), also staffed by costumed interpreters, each of whom acts out the part of a specific Pilgrim or Indian. The charade that visitors are expected to perform – pretending to have stepped back into the seventeenth century – can be a little tiresome, but the sheer depth of detail ultimately wins you over, so long as you are not too critical of the villagers' taste in decor. Everything you see in the plantation, such as the Pilgrim Village of 1627 and the Wampanoag Indian Settlement, has been created using traditional techniques; even the farm animals were "backbred" to resemble their seventeenth-century counterparts. Again, actors dressed in period garb try to bring you back in time – ask one of the pseudo-farmers what crop he's planting, or his wife what she's cooking, and you'll get an answer in an English dialect appropriate to the era and the individual's place of origin. The only part of Plimoth Plantation that makes concessions to the modern age is the crafts center, where interpreters not only weave baskets, which is historically accurate, but make pottery and ceramics, which is not (the Pilgrims had to import that stuff from England). Even the name, "Plimoth," is spelled thusly in deference to an antique map and to distinguish the Plantation from modern-day Plymouth. Depending on your level of resistance, the whole affair can be quite enjoyable. If you intend to see both the Plantation and the *Mayflower*, you'd do better to buy a combo ticket ($22) from either admissions counter.

Practicalities

Plymouth's **visitors' center** is in a park on North Park Avenue (Mon–Sat 9am–5pm, Sun noon–5pm; Ⓣ508/747-7525, Ⓦwww.visit-plymouth.com) and stocks information on local attractions, dining, and accommodations. Plymouth & Brockton **buses** (Ⓣ508/746-0378, Ⓦwww.p-b.com) run back and forth to Boston, stopping at various points in downtown Plymouth. The best **accommodation** in Plymouth is the *John Carver Inn*, 25 Summer St (Ⓣ508/746-7100 or 1-800/274-1620, Ⓦwww.johncarverinn.com; ❻), a modern, 79-room inn close to the waterfront and all the downtown attractions. Less expensive options include *By the Sea*, 22 Winslow St (Ⓣ508/830-9643 or 1-800/593-9688, Ⓦwww.bytheseabedandbreakfast.com; ❺), a harborview B&B with two spacious suites with private bath; and the *Governor Bradford*, 98 Water St (Ⓣ508/746-6200, Ⓦwww.governorbradford.com; ❺), another modern hotel overlooking the water, though its oceanfront rooms cost more. America's hometown isn't much of a **restaurant** center, but the casual *Hearth 'n' Kettle*, in the *John Carver Inn*, is a safe bet for well-priced New England specialties, as is *Isaac's on the Waterfront*, 114 Water St (Ⓣ508/830-0001), a favorite with locals who also come for the ocean views. For standard breakfast fare, drop by *All American Diner*, 60 Court St (Ⓣ508/747-4763), before 2pm any day of the week.

New Bedford and around

Don't be put off by **NEW BEDFORD**'s grimy appearance. This once-prosperous whaling port, 45 miles south of Boston, is still home to one of the nation's largest fishing fleets and although new development and a waterfront highway have hardly contributed to the aesthetic appeal of the place, the old mercantile buildings, nineteenth-century houses and cobblestoned streets in the city center still manage to conjure up the atmosphere that inspired Herman Melville to set the beginning of *Moby Dick* here. These four square blocks are assembled as the recently christened New Bedford Whaling National Historic Park, whose centerpiece is the uncluttered **New Bedford Whaling Museum** at 18 Johnny Cake Hill (daily: 9am–5pm, second Thurs of the month to 9pm; $8; Ⓦwww.whalingmuseum.org). Scrimshaw and whale jaws abound, but more stimulating is the half-scale model of the whaling vessel *Lagoda*, housed in a necessarily immense building – formerly a church – that also contains harpoons, artifacts whalemen retrieved from the Arctic and Pacific, and fascinating black-and-white photos of whaling journeys from the 1880s. A smaller section of the museum has the roster of the whaling ship *Acushnet*, which shows Melville as one of its crew. Here you'll also see "tally pages" from the whalemen's logbooks, with rubber stamps depicting sperm whales to indicate the ones killed (a vertical stamp meant the whale was harpooned but lost to the sea). A recent addition is a modern building housing the 66-foot skeleton of a blue whale named Kobo, King of the Blue Ocean, that had the bad fortune to be washed up on the South Shore in 1998. Immediately opposite the museum stands the **Seamen's Bethel**, the famous "Whaleman's Chapel" built in 1832 and described in *Moby Dick* (May–Oct daily 10am–5pm; mid-Oct to April Mon–Fri 11am–1pm, Sat 10am–5pm, Sun 1–5pm; donation requested). It features a rather disappointingly small replica of the ship-shaped pulpit described in Melville's book. More evocative are the memorials to those who died at sea that line the walls of the chapel.

There are a few other remnants of New Bedford's whale-derived wealth, chief among which are the old Federalist and Victorian mansions around **County Street**, of which Melville commented:

> **Had it not been for us whalemen, that tract of land would this day perhaps have been in as howling condition as the coast of Labrador . . . all these brave houses and flowery gardens came up from the Atlantic, Pacific and Indian oceans. One and all, they were harpooned and dragged hither from the bottom of the sea.**

Generally speaking, the mansions did not belong to working ship captains, but rather to those who had turned to international trade and investment in the whaling industry. The Greek Revival **Rotch-Jones-Duff House & Garden Museum,** 396 County St (Mon–Sat 10am–4pm, Sun noon–4pm; $4; Ⓦwww.rjdmuseum.org), built by a Quaker whaling captain in 1834, retains many of its original decorations and furnishings and is festooned with decadent marble fireplace mantles and oriental rugs. The formal gardens, laid out in their original style, with boxwood hedges, roses, and wildflowers, occupy an entire city block. Neighboring **Madison**, **Maple**, and **Orchard streets** also contain a number of fanciful, brightly repainted mansions. It's worth driving by – about all you can do, as they're all private – before heading out of town.

Practicalities

If you want to **stay** in New Bedford, the town's **visitors' center** at Pier 3 (Ⓣ508/991-6200 or 1-800/508-5353) can pre-book accommodation, but in reality a couple of hours of wandering about the town should be enough before moving on. Still, the *Orchard Street Manor* is an atmospheric B&B at 139 Orchard St (Ⓣ508/984-3475, Ⓦwww.the-orchard-street-manor.com; ❻). *Spearfield's*, 1 Johnny Cake Hill (Ⓣ508/993-4848), is as good as any place for a quick bite to **eat**, serving omelettes and salads in a cottage across from the whaling museum. For a more substantial meal, try the authentic Portuguese dishes at *Antonio's*, 267 Coggeshall St (Ⓣ508/990-3636).

Westport

On either side of New Bedford, fronting Buzzards Bay and Rhode Island Sound, run a series of coastal villages usually consisting of little more than a post office and a general store. By far the most attractive is **WESTPORT**, on the Rhode Island state line, where the Westport River spills into the ocean, forming a natural harbor. Positioned here is **Horseneck Beach**, a two-mile-long stretch of sand that is a favorite with students from the nearby University of Massachusetts at Dartmouth, but never overcrowded because of its vast size. There's ample parking, which costs $10 per car on summer weekends ($8 during the week). For a much starker seascape, head east along Rte-88 to **East Beach**, a half-mile of pebbly shoreline once the site of dozens of homes until the hurricane of 1938 (and the subsequent hurricane of 1954) swept them all away. What's left are dozens of telephone and power poles and lines, but no homes to attach themselves to.

In an area that was just far enough away from the ocean to survive the devastation is **Westport Point**, just off Rte-88, a village built on a neck of land leading down to a quay, its main street lined with the white-clapboard eighteenth- and nineteenth-century homes of sea captains. At the foot of the street, nearest the water, the charming *Paquachuck Inn* (Ⓣ508/636-4398, Ⓦwww.paquachuck.com; ❻) occupies an 1827 building with lovely views over the harbor. Nearby is a stellar seafood **restaurant** right on the water, *The Back Eddy*, 1 Bridge Rd (Ⓣ508/8636-6500); it's not cheap, but the chef's fresh clam and roasted corn chowder alone is worth the visit.

Fall River

The fate of **FALL RIVER**, a glum-looking town about fifteen miles west of New Bedford, will forever be linked to the sensational trial of **Lizzie Borden**, a spinster Sunday school teacher accused of the axe murders of her wealthy father and stepmother in August 1892; in many ways, the town plays up the associations. Borden was at home when the murders took place, but the prevailing notion that such brutal crimes were beyond a woman's capability bolstered her case. Her lawyer even made her wear antiquated Victorian dresses to the thirteen-day trial to help conceal her sizeable wrists. It must have worked – she was acquitted, though perhaps not in the public's opinion: as the popular rhyme goes, "Lizzie Borden took an axe and gave her mother forty whacks/When she saw what she had done, she gave her father forty-one." The **Fall River Historical Society**, 451 Rock St (April to mid-Nov Tues–Fri 9am–4.30pm, summer weekends also 1–5pm; tours on the hour; $5; Ⓦwww.lizzieborden.org), contains the inevitable exhibits of the affair, including some vintage photographs of Lizzie and her family, as well as more general information about the city, particularly its industrial heritage. There's also a **museum** at the **Lizzie Borden B&B**, 92 Second St (July–Aug daily 11am–2.30pm; mid-May to July & Sept–mid-Oct Sat & Sun 11am–2.30pm; tours on the hour; $7.50; Ⓣ508/675-7333, Ⓦwww.lizzie-borden.com), where the awful deeds were done; see also "Practicalities" below for lodging details.

Aside from Lizzie-mania, Fall River is better known as a mill town. Though its prosperity from wool manufacture unraveled ages ago, dozens of huge old mills remain, many of which have been transformed into **factory outlets**, the greatest concentration of them at the confluence of I-195 and Rte-24. Though the stores are far from original, you can still find some decent bargains in shoes, designer clothing, jewelry, and household goods, all tax-free. The town's other attraction, as it were, is **Battleship Cove**, I-195 to exit 5 at the Braga Bridge (April–June 9am–5pm; July–Aug 9am–5.30pm; Sept–March 9am–4.30pm; $10; Ⓦwww.battleshipcove.org), site of an impressive assemblage of World War II naval craft), most intriguing of which are the enormous *USS Massachusetts* and the submarine *USS Lionfish*.

Practicalities

Fall River's Chamber of Commerce provides **tourist information** at its office at 200 Pocasset St (Mon–Fri 10am–4pm; Ⓣ508/676-8226, Ⓦwww.fallriverchamber.com), but a safer bet (if you're driving) might be the **Bristol County Visitors' Bureau** (daily 9am–5pm; Ⓣ1-800/268-6263, Ⓦwww.bristol-county.org) located between exits 1 and 2 on I-195 eastbound in neighboring Swansea. One of the few places to **stay** in Fall River is the suitably gloomy *Lizzie Borden B&B*, 92 Second St (Ⓣ508/675-7333; ❻). You can stay in the rooms where Lizzie's parents were found, savor the same kind of breakfast enjoyed by the family on the day of the murders and load up on Lizzie memorabilia in the gift shop. More mundane is the *Best Western*, 360 Airport Rd (Ⓣ508/672-0011; ❺), just up the hill from Battleship Cove, the only hotel within the city boundaries. New Bedford supports a large Portuguese population, a fact reflected in its proliferation of Portuguese **restaurants**. Two of the better spots are *Sagres*, 181 Columbia St (Ⓣ508/675-7018), a casual, well-priced restaurant with a good wine list and music on weekend nights, and *Giorgio's*, 30 Third St (Ⓣ508/672-8252; closed Sun & Mon), a rare South Shore spot serving upscale steak and pan-seared duck breast with raspberry demi-glace – as opposed to seafood.

Cuttyhunk Island

If you're really desperate to get away from the crowds, take a one-hour boat trip from Pier 3 in New Bedford out to minuscule **CUTTYHUNK ISLAND**, an entirely uncommercialized chunk of land, with unpaved roads and beaches lined with glorious wildflowers throughout the summer months such as **Channel Beach**, just a short walk from the ferry dock, and **Church's Beach** on the other side of the island, ideal for swimming or a peaceful stroll. The outermost of the **Elizabeth Islands**, which stretch for sixteen miles from Buzzards Bay, and one of the few not privately owned, Cuttyhunk was the site of the first English settlement in the Bay State: a short, 22-day sojourn which resulted in the building of a stockade and the planting of a medicinal garden. A small stone tower on an island in **Gosnold Pond**, at Cuttyhunk's western end, honors the event.

A **ferry**, run by Cuttyhunk Boat Lines (July–Aug: Mon–Thurs 10am, returning at 3pm; Fri 10am & 6pm, returning 3pm and 7pm; Sat 9am & 12pm, returning 10.30am & 4pm; Sun 9am & 3.30pm, returning 2pm & 5.30pm; mid-to end June & early to mid-Sept: Mon–Fri 10am and Sat & Sun 9am, returning 3pm; late May to mid-June & mid-Sept to mid-Oct: Tues & Fri 10am, returning 2pm, Sat & Sun 9am, returning 3pm; mid-Oct to late May: Fri 10am, returning 2pm; Ⓣ508/992-1432, Ⓦwww.cuttyhunk.com) charges $20 round-trip for same-day travel ($13 each way otherwise), plus $1 per unit baggage charge. The ride can be an experience in its own right: it's the only means of transporting goods back and forth, meaning you may find yourself squeezed into a corner surrounded by towers of six-packs – or blocked in by a car.

The tiny island has a year-round population of around 26 and **bicycles** are really the best way to get around; rent one in New Bedford and take it over with you on the ferry. There are only a couple of **restaurants** on the island, too, so you're best off bringing your own lunch; again, the main reason you're here is to get away from it all. A few commercial establishments are located at **Four Corners**, the island's hub, such as gift shops and markets. Also nearby is the tiny **Historical Society Museum** (July–Aug Tues, Fri–Sat 10.30am–12.30pm & 2–4pm, Thurs 10.30am–12.30pm, Sun 10am–4pm; free; Ⓣ508/984-4611), which traces the history of the island through an assortment of artifacts.

If you want to **stay**, the *Cuttyhunk Fishing Club* close to the ferry has an inn which offers clean and comfortable rooms in an idyllic setting (Ⓣ508/992-5585, Ⓦwww.cuttyhunkfishingclub.com; ❻); you can also rent cottages by the week or month through the island website (Ⓦwww.cuttyhunk.com).

Cape Cod

CAPE COD, one of the most celebrated slices of real estate in America, boasts a consistently stunning quality of light that mostly compensates for its flat, lackluster landscape and sometimes suffocating quaintness. The slender, crooked Cape gives Massachusetts an extra three hundred miles of coastline, access to much of which is hampered by shore-hugging upper-middle-class homes. Those parts of the Cape that haven't fallen prey to suburban overdevelopment have been preserved as the snug, rather humorless villages they were a hundred or more years ago, replete with town green, white steeple church, and the odd lighthouse. Only **Provincetown**, at the very tip, manages to successfully mesh the past with the present; its unique art galleries, shops, and restaurants make it far and away the destination of choice here. It's also perched on the best stretch of the extensive **Cape Cod National Seashore**, so there's no overwhelming need to go elsewhere, though tiny upscale towns like **Sandwich**, **Brewster**, and **Chatham** make for scenic stops along the way. In recent years local chambers of commerce have been trying to lure tourists in the offseason by touting the region's "historical attractions" – the museums, the Kennedy associations, and so on – in lieu of its more typical shore-oriented ones, but the reality is that for most visitors the beach reigns supreme. It's also worth noting that sights and beaches are heavily geared toward families, not independent travelers.

Some history

In all the hype about Plymouth and its associations with the Pilgrims, it's often forgotten that they first set foot on North American soil at Provincetown – despite the presence of an enormous monument there to commemorate the event. Immigration to the Cape up to 1700 was almost exclusively made up of homesick Englishmen who crossed the Atlantic to take advantage of the bur-

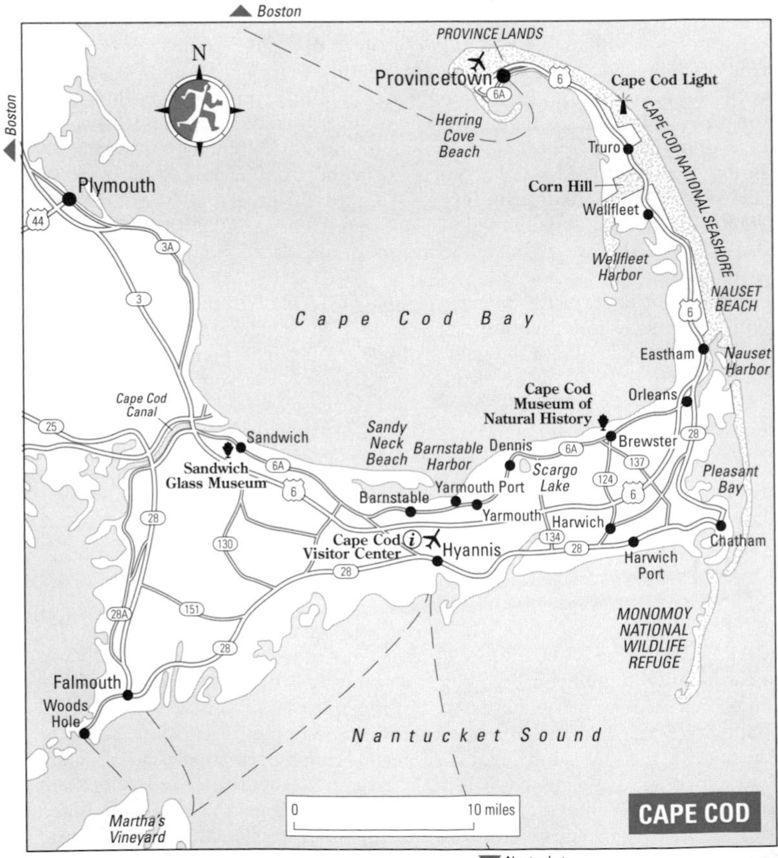

geoning markets of the New World, and who named the places after towns back home, such as Sandwich, Falmouth, and Barnstable. Indeed, during the Revolutionary War many Cape Codders sided with the Crown; how much of this was genuine affection for British rule and how much was prompted by their vulnerability to British naval strength is debatable. By the early 1800s, whaling had become the Cape's primary industry, the ports of Provincetown, Barnstable, Wellfleet, and Truro doing particularly well, while other Cape Codders were employed in the fishing and agricultural industries, including the harvesting of cranberries. By the time of the Civil War, with the whaling industry in serious decline, Cape Cod inhabitants began to look to the burgeoning railways for salvation.

Cape Cod's rise as a tourist destination is mainly attributable to the development of the motor car and the railway. Wealthy Bostonians and New Yorkers were, for the first time, able to get to the Cape with relative ease, many purchasing land to build summer homes and returning to live on the Cape permanently on retirement, so much so that parts of the Cape resemble leafy Boston suburbs. Today, the year-round population more than doubles in the summer, when more than 80,000 cars a day cross the Cape Cod Canal.

But nature is the real arbiter of the Cape's fate. During the last Ice Age, glaciers moved down across Canada and New England. The vast sheet of ice deposited huge amounts of debris as it began to melt and retreat, forming Cape Cod, the islands of Martha's Vineyard and Nantucket, and Long Island. Because it lacks the solidity of other sections of the New England coast, and due to rising sea levels, Cape Cod is particularly vulnerable to erosion. Between Wellfleet and Provincetown the land is scarcely one mile wide, and narrowing all the time. The one benefit of the adverse environmental situation is that it keeps development in check, especially in the vicinity of the protected National Seashore. Even highly developed areas are interspersed with pockets of untrammeled meadowland and seagrass, lending the Cape at least the illusion of wide-open spaces.

The shape of the Cape

The Cape is shaped like a **flexed arm**, with Sandwich at the shoulder, Chatham at the elbow, and Provincetown the clenched fist at the very end. According to local parlance, the "Upper Cape" is the area you come to after crossing the Sagamore or Bourne bridges from the mainland, the "Lower Cape" is the forearm that stretches approximately from Orleans to Provincetown, and the "Mid-Cape" is everything in between, including the main commercial center of Hyannis. From a traveler's perspective, however, things make more sense in terms of the **north coast** of the Cape from Sandwich to Brewster, the **south coast** from Falmouth to Chatham, and the **outer Cape**. The best plan of attack is Rte-6A, the Old King's Highway, from Sandwich to Brewster. At Orleans, just past Brewster, Rte-6A joins Rte-6, the Mid-Cape Highway, an exceedingly dull road that does little else than get you to Provincetown in a hurry. With a very few exceptions, Rte-28, the main thoroughfare on the south coast, wends past baleful outcroppings of suburbia – even Cape Codders will tell you that it's a byway best avoided in favor of its scenic northern cousin.

Arrival, information, and getting around

The main way of reaching the Cape is by **car**, though if you're heading there on a summer weekend, you may well regret this choice. On a fairly quiet day it takes about two hours to get from downtown Boston to the Sagamore Bridge, but expect this to double on summer weekends and holidays. Bonanza Buses (Ⓣ1-800/556-3815, Ⓦwww.bonanzabus.com) operate a **bus** service in

The Cape Cod Canal

Between 1909 and 1914 a **canal** was dug across the westernmost portion of Cape Cod, effectively making the Cape an island. It was an old idea – the Pilgrims who landed on the Cape some three hundred years earlier had talked about building a canal as a means of avoiding the shipwreck-prone 135-mile trip around the Cape, thus facilitating trade between the Plymouth colony and the Dutch colony of New Amsterdam (New York), but they lacked the manpower to get the work done. Later on, George Washington, contemplating the advantages a canal would have in protecting naval ships and commercial vessels during war, resurrected the idea, but it was not until 1880 that work finally started on building a canal. The Cape Cod Canal Company employed more than five hundred immigrant workers to begin the laborious process – hand shovels were used, and the debris carted away in wheelbarrows. In 1899 wealthy New York businessman Augustus Belmont took over the project; ten years later, state-of-the-art earthmoving equipment was introduced, and the canal was completed in 1914, though at the time it was too shallow and narrow to allow anything but one-way traffic. In 1928 the canal was bought by the federal government, which subsidized the modifications necessary to permit larger vessels to trawl the waters. Hundreds of boats now use the canal every day, many of them leisure craft that have to contend with dramatic shifts in water currents and tides. You can join them on a **boat trip** with Hy-Line Cruises ($10–14; ⓣ508/295-3883, ⓦwww.hy-linecruises.com), which runs a variety of trips ranging from straightforward tours to three-hour jazz outings from Onset Bay Town Pier off routes 6 and 28. Still, you don't have to be on the canal to enjoy it; the view of the canal and its verdant shores from the Sagamore and Bourne bridges is one of the most dramatic on the East Coast. There is also a **bike trail** on either side of the canal.

summer from Boston to Woods Hole and Falmouth, while the Plymouth & Brockton buses (ⓣ508/746-0378, ⓦwww.p-b.com) ply the route from various points in Boston to Hyannis. You can also take a **ferry** from Boston to Provincetown. Bay State Cruise Company (ⓣ617/748-1428, ⓦwww.baystatecruisecompany.com) runs two boats daily throughout the summer months from Boston's Commonwealth Pier; the 90-minute express costs $60 round-trip; the three-hour equivalent costs $39. Boston Harbor Cruises (ⓣ617/227-4371, ⓦwww.bostonboats.com) also runs an express service, leaving Long Wharf twice a day and reaching Provincetown ninety minutes later for $49. A Plymouth to Provincetown ferry service is run by Captain John's Boats (ⓣ508/746-2400 or 1-800/242-2469, ⓦwww.provincetownferry.com) and costs $28 round-trip for the ninety-minute journey (bicycles are an extra $3). Finally, a number of **airlines** fly direct to Cape Cod – perhaps the best way to dodge traffic – including US Airways (ⓣ1-800/428-4322, ⓦwww.usairways.com), which goes to Hyannis from Boston, and Cape Air (ⓣ1-800/352-0714, ⓦwww.capeair.com), which heads to Hyannis and Provincetown from Boston several times a day, even in winter.

Once on the Cape, you can **get around** how most island visitors do – by **car** – though doing so will add to the notorious congestion; rentals are available through *Thrifty*, in Orleans (ⓣ508/255-2234, ⓦwww.thrifty.com), or *Enterprise*, 332 Iyannough Rd, Hyannis (ⓣ508/771-1792 or 1-800/736-8222, ⓦwww.enterprise.com). Alternatively, the *Cape Cod Regional Transit Authority* (ⓣ1-800/352-7155, ⓦwww.thebreeze.com) runs frequent public buses (6.30am–7pm) along routes 28 and 132 connecting the Cape's outlying towns; simply flag them down on the side of the road and cough up $1.50–3. The Cape also has plentiful and scenic **bike** paths; you can rent two-wheels at *Bike*

Zone (ⓣ508/775-3299, ⓦwww.bikezoneinc.com), which has a location in Hyannis, at 323 Barnstable Rd, and Falmouth, 273 Teaticket Hwy; bikes rent for $15/day. A more touristy option, from Hyannis anyway, is the **Cape Cod Scenic Railroad** (late May to Oct; $15; ⓣ508/771-3800, ⓦwww.capetrain.com) which runs from Center Street along a meandering two-hour circuit west through cranberry bogs to the Cape Cod Canal and Sandwich.

The main Cape Cod **visitors' center**, situated at the junction of routes 6 and 132 in Hyannis, has information about all the towns on the Cape (Mon–Fri 8.30am–5pm; summer weekends also 10am–4pm). You can also research the area and make reservations online before you go, at the Cape Cod Chamber of Commerce's website, ⓦwww.capecodchamber.org.

Cape Cod's south coast

Route 28, which hugs the Nantucket Sound coast of the Cape until it merges with routes 6 and 6A at Orleans, is certainly not the most attractive or scenic route on the Cape; much of it is lined with motels and commercial buildings, and it can get seriously clogged up with traffic during the summer. Nonetheless, it runs through a number of important hubs along the south coast, notably **Falmouth** and **Hyannis**, that many find themselves visiting for one reason or other. At its culmination are the two best reasons for hitting this path, the quiet town of **Chatham** and the even quieter **Monomoy National Wildlife Refuge**, reachable only by ferry.

Falmouth and Woods Hole

FALMOUTH boasts more coastline than any other Cape Cod town and no fewer than fourteen harbors among its eight villages, at the center of which is **Falmouth Village**, with its prim, picket-fence-encircled central green surrounded by Colonial, Federal, and Greek Revival homes. Typical of New England, a number of these old sea captains' houses now serve as B&Bs, and are complemented by a touristy mixture of clothing shops, ice-cream parlors, and real estate agents. The **First Congregational Church**, right on the green at 68 Main St, is also picture-perfect New England, a white-steepled church with a bell commissioned from Paul Revere. Nearby, at 55–65 Palmer Ave, the 1794 **Conant House** (mid-June to mid-Sept Mon–Fri 10am–4pm; mid-Sept to late Oct Sat & Sun 1–4pm; $4; ⓣ508/548-4957, ⓦwww.falmouthhistoricalsociety.org), run by the Falmouth Historical Society, contains scrimshaw, rare glass and china, and sailors' memorabilia. There's also a room dedicated to local girl **Katherine Lee Bates**, who composed **America the Beautiful**; she was born in 1859 down the road at 16 Main St, where a plaque commemorates the event. The Historical Society also maintains the **Julia Wood House**, next door to the Conant House (same hours and price), an early nineteenth-century doctor's home, one room of which is set up as a clinic, with a horrifying display of primitive dental utensils – doctors doubled up as dentists in those days. To get the most out of a visit, you might consider hopping aboard one of the society's narrated **trolley tours** (mid-July to late Sept every other Wed 10am–noon; $12) available at the Conant House.

The salty drop of a town that is **WOODS HOLE** owes its name to the water passage, or "hole" between Penzance Point and Nonamesset Island, linking Vineyard Sound and Buzzards Bay. It's little more than a clump of casual restaurants and convenience stores clustered around the harbor and the **Woods Hole Oceanographic Institute**, 15 School St (late May to early Sept Mon–Sat 10am–4.30pm, Sun noon–4.30pm; early Sept to Oct Tues–Sat 10am–4.30pm, Sun noon–4.30pm; Nov–Dec Tues–Fri 10am–4.30pm; April Fri & Sat 10am–4.30pm, Sun noon–4.30pm; closed Jan–March; $2; Ⓦwww.whoi.edu), which houses an exhibit on the rediscovery of the *Titanic* in 1986, a project the institute spearheaded, and some neat submarine capsules that children will enjoy, but little else besides. More worthwhile are the ocean forays that depart from the harbor, where **OceanQuest** runs informative and hands-on cruises – lobster and scallop traps are pulled up for inspection and those on board are encouraged to handle the sealife (July–Aug Mon–Fri 10am, noon, 2pm & 4pm; Ⓣ1-800-37-OCEAN, Ⓦwww.oceanquestonline.org; $19). Back on land, much of the sealife that lurks off the Cape's shores is kept behind glass at the National Marine Fisheries Service, which maintains America's oldest **aquarium** at the corner of Albatross and Water streets (mid-June to early Sept daily 10am–4pm; early Sept to mid-June Mon–Fri 10am–4pm; free; Ⓣ508/495-2000, Ⓦwww.nefsc.noaa.gov). With a mission to preserve local marine life, its displays are mostly limited to the likes of codfish, lobster, and other piscine creatures that are more appealing on a plate; the exception, the institute's pet seals, Coco and Sandy, give visitors a thrill at feeding time (daily 11am & 4pm).

Accommodation

Despite having little in the way of in-town diversions, Falmouth has some lovely **accommodation** options that make a good base for exploring the Cape and catching the **ferry** from Woods Hole to Martha's Vineyard.

Mostly Hall 27 Main St, Falmouth Ⓣ508/548-3786 or 1-800/682-0565, Ⓦwww.bbonline.com/ma/mostlyhall. An amiably run 1849 mansion with queen-sized canopy beds in each of the six rooms. Closed Jan. ❼

Scallop Shell Inn 16 Massachusetts Ave, Falmouth Ⓣ508/495-4900 or 1-800/249-4587, Ⓦwww.scallopshellinn.com. The best in-town spot: a deluxe seven-room inn with views of Nantucket and Martha's Vineyard, and several rooms outfitted with fireplaces and whirlpool tubs. ❽

Wildflower Inn 167 Palmer Ave, Falmouth Ⓣ508/548-9524 or 1-800/294-5459, Ⓦwww.wildflower-inn.com. Well situated, with expansive, well-lit rooms furnished with country quilts and wicker chairs; the top-floor quarters have skylights and whirlpool tubs. ❻

Woods Hole Passage 186 Woods Hole Rd Ⓣ508/548-9575, Ⓦwww.woodsholepassage.com. Brightly painted chambers in a refurbished red-shingled carriage house set on spacious grounds, and the place to go to save some money in the area. ❻

Eating and drinking

Betsy's Diner 457 Main St, Falmouth Ⓣ508/540-0060. Worth stopping for – an authentic 1950s diner serving no-nonsense fare and beckoning you to "Eat Heavy."

The Clam Shack 227 Clinton Ave, Falmouth Ⓣ508/540-7758. A local institution which serves up heaping plates of fried seafood (and obviously clams) on outside picnic tables and a smashing rooftop deck with prime waterfront views.

Chapaquoit Grill 410 Rte-28A, West Falmouth Ⓣ508/540-7794. Popular roadside restaurant serving wood-oven-fired pizzas and grilled fish.

Fishmonger's Cafe 56 Water St, Woods Hole Ⓣ508/548-9148. Laid-back natural-foods eatery with a surprising number of vegetarian dishes in addition to seafood standards; try the fine fisherman's stew loaded with shrimp, scallops, and mussels ($16.95).

Hyannis

The largest town on the Cape, and its main commercial hive, **HYANNIS** somewhat desperately clings to its JFK heritage; the so-called **Kennedy Compound**, the family's best-known summer home, is located in **Hyannis**

Port, an upscale residential section a couple of miles southwest of the town's business district. This connection is by far the most glamorous bit in Hyannis's long history. Settled by Eastern Algonquan Indians over one thousand years ago, the first documented exploration by a European came from Captain **Bartholomew Gosnold** in 1602. Shortly after that, settlers persuaded the local Native American chief **Ianno** to sell them what is now Hyannis and Centerville for about $30 and two pairs of trousers; it's from the name Ianno that Hyannis derives. When the first railway trains reached the place in 1854, the economy skyrocketed, further boosted by the development of transportation links to Martha's Vineyard and Nantucket. Today, Hyannis is, not surprisingly, clogged up with traffic in summertime, which at least means there's some semblance of shopping and nightlife, though most is directed towards a more upscale clientele.

If it's Kennedy memorabilia you've come to see, probably the best place to start is the **John F. Kennedy Hyannis Museum**, 397 Main St (mid-May to Oct Mon–Sat 10am–5pm, Sun noon–5pm; Nov to mid-Dec Wed–Sat 9am–5pm; $5; ⓣ508/790-3077), which displays the expected Kennedy nostalgia, mainly in the form of old black-and-white photographs. More Kennedy fare is found ten minutes south, along Ocean Street; here, a pebbly **Kennedy Memorial** made of island stone and adorned with a bronze likeness of the country's 35th president anchors Veteran's Park.

Visitors who come to Hyannis expecting to take a guided tour round the **Kennedy Compound** will be disappointed: this group of houses is concealed by tall fences, and it's best glimpsed, if you must, out on the water – Hy-Line Cruises, Ocean Street Docks (mid-April to late Oct; $12; ⓣ508/778-2600, ⓦwww.hy-linecruises.com), runs hour-long cruises that peek in on the compound. Joe and Rose Kennedy bought their house here in 1929, and immediately set about remodeling it to accommodate their burgeoning family; Jack and Bobby Kennedy bought neighboring houses in the 1950s.

For a welcome non-Kennedy diversion, you might take a free tour round the **Cape Cod Potato Chip Factory**, on Breed's Hill Road near the Cape Cod Mall (Mon–Fri 9am–5pm; free; ⓣ508/775-7253, ⓦwww.capecodchips.com). The tasty chips, once a local phenomenon but now to be found almost everywhere, are made with natural ingredients hand-cooked in kettles; it's hard to resist the free samples, in any case.

Practicalities

The local Chamber of Commerce maintains an **information center** at 1481 Rte-132 (Mon–Sat 9am–5pm; summer also Sun 9am–5pm; ⓣ1-877-HYANNIS, ⓦwww.hyannis.com), not to be confused with the Cape Cod Visitor Center just up the road (see p.201). If you have a boat to catch and need to **stay** in Hyannis, options include the *Inn on Sea Street*, 358–363 Sea St (ⓣ508/777-8030, ⓦwww.innonseastreet.com; ❺), with nine expansive rooms tucked into two Victorian homes complete with antique furnishings and candelabra; the wood-shingled *Sea Breeze Inn*, 270 Ocean Ave (ⓣ508/771-7213, ⓦwww.seabreezeinn.com; ❹), with ten frilly queen-bedded rooms with shared bath; and the *Simmons Homestead Inn*, 288 Scudder Ave (ⓣ508/778-4999 or 1-800/637-1649, ⓦwww.simmonshomesteadinn.com; ❽), the only B&B in Hyannis Port, thirteen rooms with private baths in an 1820 sea captain's home. To access many of the **restaurants**, it's helpful to have a car, since they are quite spread out and public transport stops at 7pm. Reasonably-priced options are *Alberto's*, 360 Main St (ⓣ508/778-1770), for Northern Italian dishes; *Cooke's Seafood*, 1120 Iyanough Rd/Rte-132 (ⓣ508/775-0450), where it's hard to go wrong with the fresh broiled and fried seafood – especially the clams; *The Egg & I*, 521 Main St (ⓣ508/771-1596), a great spot for big breakfasts; *Sam Diego's*, 950 Rte-132 (ⓣ508/771-8816), a dependable, casual restaurant serving Mexican, Southwestern, and barbecue fare; and *Harry's*, 700 Main St (ⓣ508/778-4188), a Cajun spot with spicy jambalaya and ribs on the menu.

Harwich

Sleepy **HARWICH**, about ten miles east of Hyannis on Rte-28, is not a bad place to get close to the ocean, boasting three scenic harbors – including man-made **Wychmere Harbor**, once a landlocked salt pond, and the naturally formed **Saquatucket Harbor**, the largest municipal marina on the Cape – and some excellent beaches. At the latter, parking tends to be restricted to residents and visitors with stickers, but a free bus service can drop you off at **Red River Beach**, Uncle Venies Road, off Rte-28, which offers a full range of facilities.

Harwich Port, the central village in Harwich, has a fairly active main street that boasts some well-preserved nineteenth-century architecture, including the **Brooks Academy Museum**, 80 Parallel St (mid-May to mid-Oct Thurs–Sun 1–4pm; free), an 1844 Greek Revival school building which housed one of the nation's first schools of navigation; inside are exhibits on local history. The town springs to life for ten days every September during the **Harwich Cranberry Festival**, a small-town extravaganza marked by crafts fairs, a parade, and fireworks.

Practicalities

You likely won't be **staying** here, though there are a couple of good budget options: *Harbor Walk*, 6 Freeman St (ⓣ508/432-1675; ❸), a pleasant B&B close to scenic Wychmere Harbor, where two of the six guestrooms have shared baths; and *Cape Winds by the Sea*, 28 Shore Rd (ⓣ508/432-1418, ⓦwww.capewinds.com; ❺), which has four bright, cottage-like rooms with quilts and hardwood floors; some have sea-views. If you're looking to **eat**, sample the French take on local seafood at the upscale *L'Alouette*, 787 Main St/Rte-28 (ⓣ508/430-0405), or tuck into inexpensive broiled and fried seafood fare at *Seafood Sam's*, 302 Rte-28 (ⓣ508/432-1422), which also serves burgers.

Chatham

Few of the pocket-sized towns on the southern flank of the Cape are as genteel as **CHATHAM**, six miles east of Harwich Port and one of the few Cape destinations worth an overnight **stay.** The quiet and posh small-town atmosphere is largely attributable to some strictly enforced zoning laws, which have prevented the kind of indiscriminate attract-tourists-at-all-costs mentality evident in so many other Cape communities. The focal point is **Chatham Village**, whose **Main Street** is home to a variety of upscale boutiques, provisions stores, and some sophisticated restaurants and charming inns. Just off Main Street is one of the town's best historical attractions, the gambrel-roofed **Atwood House and Museum**, 347 Stage Harbor Rd (early June to Sept Tues–Fri 1–4pm, Sat 9.30am–12.30pm; $3; ⓦwww.atwoodhouse.org), built in 1752 as a sea captain's home, with a variety of seafaring artifacts, antique dolls, seashells, toys, and a herb garden. The adjacent Mural Barn houses the rather gaudy *Stallknecht Murals*, a triptych painted in 1931 by Alice Stallknecht Wight that depicts recognizable Chatham townsfolk listening in awe to a contemporarily-dressed Christ. Further north along Stage Harbor Road finds the Gothic **Railroad Museum**, on Depot Road (mid-June to mid-Sept Tues–Sat 10am–4pm; free; no phone), topped by a tapered turret; the highlight of the railway-related gear inside is a 75-year-old walk-in refurbished caboose complete with bells and whistles. Back on Main Street, at no. 540, is the adorable 1818 **Mayo House** (mid-June to mid-Sept Tues–Thurs 11am–4pm; free), its upstairs dormer bedrooms furnished with kitschy needlepoint renditions of Cape Cod scenery. Tour maps of Chatham are available from the **information booth** at 533 Main St (May–Oct Mon–Fri 9am–5pm; ⓣ508/945-5199 or 1-800/715-5567, ⓦwww.chathamcapecod.org).

A few minutes' drive outside the village, the 1877 **Chatham Light** stands guard over a windswept bluff beyond which many a ship had met its doom on the "Chatham bars," a series of sandbars that served to protect the town from the worst of the Atlantic storms – until in January 1987, when a fierce nor'easter broke through the barrier beach to form the **Chatham Break**, leaving Chatham exposed to the vagaries of the ocean. Right below the lighthouse is a nice beach, but with parking limited to half an hour, you're better off biking there from town if you want to do anything other than take a brief walk along the shore. A mile north on Rte-28, the **Fish Pier** on Shore Road provides a spot to wait for the fleet to come in mid-afternoon. From here you can also take a $10 water taxi to Monomoy Island, a 2700-acre wildlife refuge (see box below).

Accommodation

Chatham is well endowed with tasteful **accommodation**, mostly the kind of romantic **B&Bs** found throughout the Cape. Despite the ample selection, reservations are strongly advised, even outside of high season.

Monomoy National Wildlife Reserve

Stretching out to sea for nine miles south of Chatham, desolate **Monomoy National Wildlife Refuge** is a fragile barrier beach that was attached to the mainland until breached by a storm in 1958. A subsequent storm in 1978 divided the island in half, and today the islands are accessible by boat only – when weather conditions permit. The refuge spreads across 2750 acres of sand and dunes, tidal flats and marshes, with no roads, no electricity, and, best of all, no human residents, though a small fishing community once existed here. Indeed, the only man-made buildings on the islands are the South Monomoy Lighthouse and lightkeeper's house.

It's a perfect stopover point along the North Atlantic Flyway for almost three hundred species of shorebirds and migratory waterfowl, including many varieties of gull and the endangered piping plovers, for whose protection several sections of the refuge have been fenced off. In addition, the islands are home to white-tailed deer, and harbor and gray seals are frequent visitors in winter. Several organizations conduct island tours, among them the Cape Cod Museum of Natural History (ⓣ508/349-2615, ⓦwww.ccmnh.org) and the Wellfleet Bay Wildlife Sanctuary (ⓣ508/349-2615, ⓦwww.wellfleetbay.org); prices vary, depending, among other things, on the number of people in your group. In any case, if there are six or more of you, you'll need to get a special permit from the headquarters of the Wildlife Refuge, located on Morris Island (ⓣ508/945-0594), which also has a visitors' center offering leaflets on Monomoy. Morris Island is accessible from Morris Island Road, south of the Chatham Light.

The Captain's House Inn 369–371 Old Harbor Rd ⓣ508/945-0127 or 1-800/315-0728, ⓦwww.captainshouseinn.com. Easy elegance prevails at this sumptuously renovated 1839 Greek Revival whaling captain's home; most rooms have fireplaces, and prices include gourmet breakfasts and afternoon tea with freshly baked scones. ❽.

Chatham Bars Inn 297 Shore Rd ⓣ508/945-0096 or 1-800/527-4884, ⓦwww.chatham-barsinn.com. The grande dame of Cape Cod's seaside resorts, the 205 rooms and cottages spread out over a 22-acre oceanfront property are decorated in country-chic, with luxurious linens, hand-painted wood furniture, and bay windows; some have decks and fireplaces. ❾

Chatham Tides Waterfront Motel 394 Pleasant St, South Chatham ⓣ508/432-0379, ⓦwww.chathamtides.com. Choose between standard hotel rooms or self-catering town-house suites at this relative bargain directly on Nantucket Sound. Closed Oct–May. ❼

Chatham Wayside Inn 512 Main St ⓣ508/945-5550 or 1-800/391-5734, ⓦwww.waysideinn.com. This 56-room refurbished 1860 sea captain's home is one of the finer inns in the area, though at a price. ❼

Cyrus Kent House 63 Cross St ⓣ508/945-9104 or 1-800/338-5368, ⓦwww.cyruskent.com. Ten graciously appointed guestrooms, all with private baths, in a stately 1877 home one block from the center of town. ❼

Eating

Not surprisingly, given its status as one of the more sophisticated destinations on Cape Cod, Chatham abounds in upmarket **restaurants**, as well as the more casual eateries typical in these parts.

Carmine's Pizza 595 Main St ⓣ508/945-5300. Casual checked-tablecloth joint serving inexpensive and tasty pizzas with an accent on spice – the Pizza from Hell combines garlic, red pepper, jalapeños, and pineapple slices.

Chatham Bars Inn 297 Shore Rd ⓣ508/945-0096 or 1-800/527-4884. The hostelry's formal dining room offers expensive New England cuisine with wonderful ocean views.

Chatham Squire 487 Main St ⓣ508/945-0945. This informal and affordable spot has a raw bar, an eclectic menu incorporating elements of Mexican and Asian cuisine, and often live acoustic bands at night.

Christian's 443 Main St ⓣ508/945-3362. The movie posters upstairs are fitting, considering that the menu items are named after films; hard to go wrong with the well-priced Roman Holiday (Caesar salad) followed by A Fish Called Wanda (salmon sautéed with mushrooms).

The Impudent Oyster 15 Chatham Bars Ave ⓣ508/945-3545. Popular upscale bistro with generous portions of inventively prepared fresh seafood.

Vining's Bistro 595 Main St ⓣ508/945-5033. Imaginative offerings at this appealing low-cost dinner spot range from Thai Street Vendor's Beef Salad to a warm lobster taco.

Cape Cod's north coast

The meandering stretch of highway that parallels the Cape Cod Bay shoreline between Sandwich and Orleans is among the most scenic in New England, affording glimpses of the Cape Cod of popular imagination: salt marshes, crystal-clear ponds, ocean views, and tiny villages. What began as a Native American pathway from Plymouth to Provincetown became the Cape's main road in the seventeenth and eighteenth centuries. There are hundreds of historic buildings along the 34-mile stretch, a frightening number of which have been turned into antiques shops or bed and breakfasts, and the towns that hold them are pleasant enough, though **Sandwich** and **Brewster** have the highest concentration of well-preserved historical homes. Even if you're traveling by car, it's worth it to temporarily ditch the wheels in favor of a bike to take the **Cape Cod Rail Trail**, a totally flat but popular bike path on the site of the former Old Colony Railroad track, running from **Dennis**, about fifteen miles past Sandwich, through Brewster to **Wellfleet**, a distance of twenty miles up the Cape.

Sandwich

Overlooked **SANDWICH** kicks off Rte-6A with little of the crass commercialization common to so many Cape towns, thanks in part to its position so close to the mainland. The first permanent settlement on Cape Cod, Sandwich traces its roots to Pilgrim traders in the late 1620s who appreciated its proximity to the **Manomet Trading Post**, where they could barter goods and knowledge with the local Native Americans. The salt marshes in the area also provided an abundant supply of hay for their animals. Unsurprisingly, agriculture was Sandwich's main industry until the 1820s, when Bostonian Deming Jarves established a glassmaking factory here. Though the dense woodlands provided plenty of fuel for the furnaces, by the 1880s the Sandwich factory was no longer able to compete with the coal-fired glassworks of the Midwest. Today, tourism plays a role in the local economy, but, unlike so many other Cape communities, Sandwich is not totally dependent on it.

A stroll around Sandwich's old **village center** gives you a good taste of things to come along Rte-6A: a little village green, white steepled church, a smattering of bed and breakfasts, antiques shops, and a general store. Near Main and River streets, the **Shawme Duck Pond** and adjacent **Dexter Grist Mill**, a replica of one built in 1654, make for a pleasant, peaceful stop, especially if you want to hear about the milling process (mid-June to mid-Sept daily 10am–4pm; $1.50; ⓣ508/888-4910). On Water Street, overlooking the pond, and well worth a visit, the **Hoxie House** (mid-June to mid-Oct Mon–Sat 10am–5pm, Sun 1–5pm; $1.50, combination ticket with Dexter Grist Mill $2.50; ⓣ508/888-1173) is a seventeenth-century shingled saltbox house claimed by some to be the oldest on the Cape. It showcases authentic Colonial furniture on loan from the Museum of Fine Arts in Boston, rare diamond-shaped lead-glass windows and antique textile machines. Close to the shore, at 129 Main St, the **Sandwich Glass Museum** (April–Dec daily 9.30am–5pm; Feb–March Wed–Sun 9.30am–4pm; closed Jan; $3.50; ⓦwww.sandwichglassmuseum.org) contains fourteen galleries that house artifacts from the Boston & Sandwich Glass Company, which set up shop here in 1825. Besides thousands of functional and decorative pieces, a diorama re-creates the factory interior, a video describes the demise of the industry, and demonstrations of glassmaking are routinely held.

The other museums dotted around town are only really recommended for those with an abiding passion for Americana, primarily the **Heritage Plantation of Sandwich** at Grove and Pine streets (mid-May to late Oct Sat–Wed 9am–6pm, Thurs–Fri 9am–8pm; Nov–April Tues–Sun 10am–4pm; $12; ⓦwww.heritageplantation.org), which features a mega-attic of Currier and Ives prints, old American firearms, a working 1912 carousel, replicas of American flags, and, inexplicably, a collection of polished old cars housed in a reproduction of the Shaker round barn in Pittsfield, a western Massachusetts town. The seventy-plus-acre gardens on the grounds are beautiful in season, especially July when the rhododendrons typically bloom. A couple of miles to the east, on Rte-6A in East Sandwich, the **Green Briar Nature Center & Jam Kitchen**, 6 Discovery Hill Rd (April–Dec Mon–Sat 10am–4pm, Sun 1–4pm; Jan–March Tues–Sat 10am–4pm; free; ⓦwww.thorntonburgess.org), run by the Thornton W. Burgess (of *Peter Rabbit* fame) Society, seems mainly geared for toddlers, housing such wonders as a stuffed beaver, a live garden snake, a box turtle, and assorted snapshots of the turtle.

Sandwich's attractions also include several miles of **beach** on Cape Cod Bay, but, like all the Cape's bayside beaches, the water is several degrees cooler than over on the Nantucket Sound side (cut off from the warming influence of the Gulf Stream). It will cost you $5 to park at **Town Neck Beach**, Town Neck Road, off Rte-6A.

Practicalities

The place to **stay** in Sandwich is the *Dan'l Webster Inn* at 149 Main St (Ⓣ508/888-3622 or 1-800/444-3566, Ⓦwww.danlwebsterinn.com; ❼), a rambling Colonial-style hostelry, modeled on an earlier building that was a haunt of Revolutionary patriots, with first-rate rooms and charming courtyards. Nearby, the *Captain Ezra Nye House*, 152 Main St (Ⓣ508/888-6142 or 1-800/388-2278, Ⓦwww.captainezranyehouse.com; ❻), has six handsome rooms with private baths in an 1829 sea captain's home. The best **meals** are also served at the *Dan'l Webster Inn:* top-notch, classic American dishes are served, for a price, every evening, but it's worth it for the compelling opportunity to nibble edible flowers (among other things) from the inn's aquafarm; they also serve breakfast and lunch in a sunlit conservatory.

Barnstable

BARNSTABLE, ten miles east of Sandwich on Rte-6A, was, after Sandwich, the second town to be founded on Cape Cod, in 1639. Early prosperity was attained thanks to its trade in whale products, and Barnstable's harbor was the busiest port on the Cape until it silted up earlier this century. Wayward cetaceans would frequently wash ashore at **Sandy Neck**, a beautiful eight-mile barrier beach, the best on Cape Cod Bay that protects Barnstable's harbor. No longer used as a site for burning blubber, the beach is probably your main reason for checking out the town, though parking will set you back $8. Follow Sandy Neck Road, just over the Sandwich line.

Evidence of Barnstable's earlier prosperity can be seen in several imposing domestic and civic buildings in the leafy village center, among them the impressive granite mass of the **Barnstable County Superior Courthouse** at 3195 Rte-6A, a reminder that Barnstable is also the county seat for the whole of the Cape. Nearby, the dignified red-brick **Donald G. Trayser Memorial Museum**, 3353 Rte-6A (July & Aug Tues–Sat 1.30–4.30pm; free), was built in 1855 as the town's Customs House. Nowadays, it contains an eclectic array of Americana, from vintage clothes to Sandwich glass and, on the grounds, an eighteenth-century jail cell which, according to Henry David Thoreau, was often shut up during the 1850s as, "when the court [came] together at Barnstable, they [had] not a single criminal to try."

Many former residences of Barnstable's hundreds of sea captains survive to this day, including that which belonged to **William Sturgis**, who set out to sea at the age of fifteen after the death of his father and returned four years later as a captain. Sturgis, uneducated, but an avid reader, bequeathed his house to the town for use as a library; the resultant **Sturgis Library**, 3090 Rte-6A (Mon, Wed, Fri 10am–5pm, Tues & Thurs 1–8pm, Sat 10am–4pm, Sun 1–5pm; free), contains genealogical records dating back to the area's first European settlers, an original 1605 Lothrop Bible, and an extensive collection of maritime maps, charts, and archival material. A few miles away, in West Barnstable, the majestic Neoclassical **West Parish Meetinghouse**, Rte-149 at Meetinghouse Way, is the oldest surviving Congregationalist building in the US, constructed in 1717. The bell tower contains a bell cast by Paul Revere in 1806.

Practicalities

For something to **eat** in Barnstable, try the *Barnstable Tavern* at 3176 Main St (Ⓣ508/362-2355), offering casual American food with an unusual Lebanese touch and a good list of wines by the glass. Waterfront views and classic American seafood can be had at the more expensive *Mattakeese Wharf*, 271 Mill Way (Ⓣ508/362-4511; May–Oct). If you want to **stay** overnight, *Beechwood*, 2839 Rte-6A (Ⓣ508/362-6618 or 1-800/609-6618, Ⓦwww.beechwood-inn.com; ❻), an 1853 Queen Anne-style house, has six romantic rooms decorated Victorian style. Another lovely option is the *Honeysuckle Hill B & B*, 591 Old King's Hwy/Rte-6A (Ⓣ508/362-8418 or 1-866/444-5522, Ⓦwww.honeysucklehill.com; ❻), four rooms and one suite in a quintessential Cape Cod 1810 National Register home. In addition to the full breakfast, you can enjoy sitting by the fireplace in the living room, perhaps accompanied by the owners' friendly black Labrador.

Yarmouth Port

The only part of Yarmouth, the closest thing the Cape has to an urban sprawl, that's worth visiting is **YARMOUTH PORT**, a delightful hamlet eastward on Rte-6A, marked by a series of old sea captains' houses that have been converted into bed and breakfasts. Indeed, along one two-mile stretch, no building was constructed later than the turn of this century, creating somewhat of a time-warp effect, augmented all the more by a visit to **Hallet's**, at 139 Rte-6A, a general store that started out as a pharmacy in 1889 – later serving as a post office and town meeting hall – and still has an original oak counter and old-fashioned soda fountain. Upstairs, a memorabilia-filled museum traces local history. Nearby, on the town green off Rte-6A at 11 Strawberry Lane, the **Captain Bangs Hallet House** (tours hourly, June to mid-Oct Wed–Sun 1–3pm; $3; Ⓦwww.hsoy.org) is a Greek Revival mansion built in 1740 by one of the town's founders, though its name comes from the successful sea captain who lived here in the late 1800s. The original kitchen comes complete with beehive oven, and a glorious weeping beech tree enhances the view from the back of the house. The recently refurbished 1780 **Winslow Crocker House**, 250 Rte-6A, (call for new hours; Ⓣ508/362-438, Ⓦwww.hsoy.org; $4), is a two-story Georgian home moved from West Barnstable to its present site in 1936 by Mary Thacher, a descendant of one of the original town founders, Thomas Thacher. The dwelling holds a range of seventeenth- to nineteenth-century furniture, rugs, and ceramics collected by Mrs. Thacher.

In decent weather, you might walk amongst the 53 acres of the **Botanic Trails of Yarmouth**, entered right behind the post office, on Rte-6A (trails open year-round during daylight hours; suggested donation $1). This peaceful park contains oak and pine woods, and a wealth of flora, including rhododendrons, blueberries, hollies, and lady's slippers. An extension of the trail leads to **Kelley's Chapel**, a seaman's bethel built in 1873 by a father for his daughter who was grieving the death of her son; Kelley is not a surname but the first name of the daughter.

Practicalities

Though there's absolutely no good reason to **stay** here, except to get a dose of good old-fashioned seafaring days, the *Wedgewood Inn*, 83 Main St, Yarmouth Port (Ⓣ508/362-5157, Ⓦwww.wedgewood-inn.com; ❻), does offer quintessential country inn ambience in six rooms with canopy beds and fireplaces. You can **eat** Italian fare year-round at *abbicci*, 43 Main St/Rte-6A (Ⓣ508/362-

3501), which serves excellent and pricey seafood as well as more traditional meat and pasta dishes; another option, *Jack's Outback*, 161 Rte-6A (Ⓣ508/362-6690), a local institution with the motto "Good food, lousy service," is not for the fainthearted, but the down-home American grub *is* good and cheap. If you simply fancy an old-fashioned milkshake, head straight for *Hallet's*, 139 Rte-6A (Ⓣ508/362-3362; closed Dec–March), an 1889 drugstore with an original marble soda fountain.

Dennis

In **DENNIS**, just down the road from Yarmouth, detour onto Old Bass River Road to pristine **Scargo Lake** for sweeping views from a thirty-foot **stone observation tower** built on a bluff overlooking it. The town itself, named after its founder, the Rev. Josiah Dennis, retains much of its colonial feel, notably in places like the clergyman's home, the **Josiah Dennis Manse** at 77 Nobscusset Rd (July–Aug Tues & Thurs 2–4pm; small donation requested), a saltbox built in 1736 and set up to reflect life in the Reverend's day, filled with antique toys and furniture, china and pewter, plus the inevitable portraits of sea captains. There's also an attic containing spinning and weaving equipment, and, on the grounds, a one-room schoolhouse dating from 1770. One of the most famous summer theaters in the US, the **Cape Playhouse**, Rte-6A between Nobscusset and Corporation roads (late June to early Sept daily except Sun; Ⓣ508/385-3838, Ⓦwww.capeplayhouse.com for ticket info), was a Unitarian Meeting House until its purchase in 1927 by Raymond Moore, a Californian who had intended to start a theater company in Provincetown but found it too remote. Famous names who have trod the boards here include Basil Rathbone (who starred in the first performance, *The Guardsman*), Lana Turner, Gregory Peck, Humphrey Bogart, and Bette Davis, who also worked here as an usherette. The complex also contains an art cinema, 35 Hope Lane (Ⓣ508/385-2503, Ⓦwww.capecinema.com; $7.50), open year-round, modeled after a Congregational church. On the ceiling is a 6400-square-foot romantic astrological mural designed by Rockwell Kent and Jo Mielziner; look for entwined couples making their way through the Milky Way. Also on-site, the **Cape Museum of Fine Arts** (mid-May to mid-Oct Mon–Sat 10am–5pm, Sun 1–5pm; mid-Oct to April Tues–Sat 10am–5pm, Sun 1–5pm; $7; Ⓦwww.cmfa.org) showcases more than one thousand works of local artists with a penchant for seascapes and sealife portraits that's to be expected. For cycling enthusiasts, the **Cape Cod Rail Trail**, a tarred bicycle path that was formerly the Old Colony Railroad, extends 26 miles from Dennis to Wellfleet (beginning in South Dennis, on Rte-134 south of Rte-6); Barbara's Bike & Sports, 430 Rte-134 (Ⓣ508/760-4723), rents bikes for about $10 a day and stocks copies of the free *Cape Cod Bike Guide* (Ⓦwww.capecodbikeguide), which details this, and a few other island trails as well.

Practicalities

If you're looking to **stay** in Dennis, the *Four Chimneys Inn*, 946 Main St/Rte-6A (Ⓣ508/385-6317 or 1-800/874-5502, Ⓦwww.fourchimneysinn.com; ❺), is an appealing B&B with high ceilings and marble fireplaces in most rooms; while the *Isaiah Hall B&B Inn*, 152 Whig St (Ⓣ508/385-9928 or 1-800/736-0160, Ⓦwww.isaiahhallinn.com; ❻; closed Nov–May), is an 1857 Greek Revival farmhouse with nine attractive rooms equipped with VCRs, all within walking distance of village and beach. For more resort-like accommodations, check into the *Lighthouse Inn*, 1 Lighthouse Inn Rd (Ⓣ508/398-2244,

Ⓦwww.lighthouseinn.com; ❽), an expansive compound with private beach, minigolf, tennis, and shuffleboard on-site. You can **eat** generous portions of tried-and-true New England staples at the inexpensive *Captain Frosty's Fish & Chips*, 219 Rte-6A, Dennis (Ⓣ508/385-8548), or go Italian at *Gina's by the Sea*, 134 Taunton Ave (Ⓣ508/385-3213; closed Dec–March), and dive into moderately-priced fare like mouthwatering shrimp scampi and ravioli stuffed with smoked mozzarella. Off Rte-28 south of Dennis proper, you can also load a hotdog with all the fixings for next-to-nothing at the *Dog House*, 189 Lower Country Rd (Ⓣ505/398-7774), before heading to the *Sundae School Ice Cream Parlor*, 387 Lower County Rd, Dennisport (Ⓣ508/394-9122) for home made ice cream, topped with real whipped cream, from an antique marble soda fountain.

Brewster

BREWSTER is yet another agreeable, if anodyne, Cape Cod town, known as a leading antiques center and popular with young couples who choose to tie the knot here, usually in one of the many bed and breakfasts that line Rte-6A. The town, as ever, traces its affluence to the sea captains who settled here – even though Brewster doesn't have a harbor. The **cemetery** in which many of these seamen are buried is adjacent to the 1834 **First Parish Church**, at 1969 Rte-6A; it has one of New England's more fascinating legends attached to (or buried in) it. One of the gravestones bears the names of two men lost at sea: Captain David Nickerson and his adopted son, Captain René Rousseau. Nickerson was in Paris during the French Revolution when a veiled woman handed him the infant René; longtime locals maintain he was the son of Louis XVI and Marie Antoinette. More picturesque is the town's last remaining windmill, the 1795 **Higgins Farm Windmill**, 785 Rte-6A (July–Aug Tues–Fri 1–4pm; June & Sept Sat–Sun 1-4pm; free; Ⓣ508/896-9521), with its roof resembling a capsized dory, and the still-functioning water wheel at the **Stony Brook Mill and Museum**, 830 Stony Brook Rd, just off Rte-6A (May & June Thurs–Sat 2–5pm, July & Aug Fri 2–5pm; $1), built in 1873 on the site of an earlier mill that churned out cloth, boots, and ironwork for over a century; the second-story museum today displays local bric-a-brac including some recently recovered arrowheads.

Brewster also boasts the **New England Fire & History Museum**, 1439 Rte-6A (late May to early Sept Mon–Fri 10am–4pm, Sat & Sun noon–4pm; early Sept to mid-Oct Sat & Sun noon–4pm; $5; Ⓦwww.nefiremuseum.org), which lures visitors with the tantalizing invitation to "see the fire fighting apparatus of yesteryear." That includes more than thirty buffed and polished fire engines, one of which is a one-and-only 1929 Mercedes-Benz Nurburg 460. There is also an extensive collection of fire helmets and a sizeable diorama of the Chicago Fire of 1871. Further down the road, at 869 Rte-6A, the **Cape Cod Museum of Natural History** (Mon–Sat 9.30am–4.30pm, Sun 11am–4.30pm; $5; Ⓦwww.ccmnh.org) makes for a somewhat more enlightening alternative – especially for kids – with its exhibits on the fragile Cape environment, whales, other sealife, and short nature trails that straddle cranberry bogs and salt marshes. The museum also organizes several nature tours, the most popular of these, a two-hour seal cruise, observes gray seals flopping around on the shores of Monomoy National Wildlife Refuge (see box, p.205); the institution also arranges overnight stays at the Refuge.

Accommodation

Bramble Inn 2019 Main St ⓣ508/896-7644, ⓦwww.brambleinn.com; closed Nov–April. This lovely old inn takes in two rustic homes, with country-style fittings and a posh restaurant to boot (see below). ❼

Brewster Farmhouse Inn 716 Main St/Rte-6A ⓣ508/896-3910 or 1-800/892-3910, ⓦwww.brewsterfarmhouseinn.com. Typical Cape B&B where you're likely to get a personalized experience (there are only eight rooms) and a delicious breakfast. ❼

The Captain Freeman Inn 15 Breakwater Rd ⓣ508/896-7481 or 1-800/843-4664, ⓦwww.captainfreemaninn.com. An 1866 post-and-beam structure, with high-ceilinged rooms outfitted with fireplaces, whirlpool tubs, and VCRs, as well as a delightful wraparound porch with rocking chairs. ❼

Eating and drinking

Bramble Inn see details above. One of the Cape's finest gourmet restaurants, offering pricey seafood in a romantic setting; look for dishes like lobster in an open shell, filled with scallops, shrimp, and cod covered in toasted almonds and coconut. Prix-fixe menu available.

Brewster Coffee Shop 2149 Main St ⓣ508/896-8224. Laid-back place serving cheap American chow – from turkey sandwiches to scrambled eggs.

Brewster Fish House 2208 Rte-6A ⓣ508/896-7867. A good spot to get a moderately priced meal of creatively prepared seafood, but be sure to arrive early to avoid a wait.

Café Alfresco 1097 Main St ⓣ508/896-1741. Informal café where you'll find tasty pastries and sandwiches.

Chillingsworth 2449 Rte-6A ⓣ508/896-3640 or 1-800/430-3640. For contemporary French cuisine, this is one of the Cape's more celebrated restaurants, with a sumptuous setting and superb food; if you're going to splurge, you may as well go for its seven-course *table d'hôte* menu (about $50).

Cobie's 3260 Main St ⓣ508/896-7021. This white clapboard clam shack serves excellent fried seafood and lobster rolls, as well as ice cream, at inexpensive prices.

High Brewster 964 Satucket Rd ⓣ508/896-3636 or 1-800/203-2634. Like *Chillingsworth* and the *Bramble Inn*, another romantic and expensive place, serving the kind of food Americans think English aristocrats still eat (pheasant, rabbit sausage pie, tea-smoked salmon, etc).

Outer Cape: Orleans to Wellfleet

ORLEANS, at the southernmost portion of the Outer Cape, was named after Louis-Philippe de Bourbon, duc d'Orleans, who is said to have visited the area at the time of his exile from France in the 1790s. Such grasps at royalty are long forgotten, as modern Orleans is basically a series of strip malls on either side of Rte-6A, a place to stock up on snacks for a trip to the beach or to fuel up for the ride onward to Provincetown. In the "town," which is a generous designation, the **Bird Watcher's General Store**, 36 Rte-6A (ⓣ508/255-6974), is worth a stop, just to partake of the store tradition of telling the cashier a joke. If he likes it, he'll ring a little bell and reward you with a gift. On Rte-6A at Town Cove Park, the well-traveled **Jonathan Young Windmill** (July & Aug daily 11am–4pm; free) started life in the 1720s in East Orleans, was subsequently moved to the center of town, then to Hyannisport, and finally, in 1983, moved back to Orleans. Although no longer in operation, this gristmill does have its machinery intact, and there's a resident miller who will explain how it all works. A much better diversion is a visit to atmospheric **Rock Harbor**, at the end of Rock Harbor Road off Main Street, a former landing place for packet ships until it silted up, and now a small fishing port and a departure point for charter fishing trips; you can book one with Captain Cook Sport Fishing (ⓣ508/255-2065 or 1-888/772-9695). Over in East Orleans is one of the Cape's better beaches, the nine-mile-long oceanside **Nauset Beach**, off

Beach Road ($10 parking fee).You can also hook up with the **Cape Cod Rail Trail** here; find it just past the Mid-Cape Home Center. Rent bikes in town at Orleans Cycle, 26 Main St (Ⓣ508/255-9115).

Orleans has a few surprisingly good **restaurants**, in all price ranges. Among the high-end choices, *Captain Linnell House*, 137 Skaket Beach Rd (Ⓣ508/255-3400), serves expensive New England fare in a candelit 1840 clipper captain's mansion; budget-minded travelers can hit *Land Ho!*, 38 Main St (Ⓣ508/255-5165), for generous portions of burgers and fried seafood; and mid-range prices are the norm at *Mahoney's Atlantic Bar & Grill*, 28 Main St (Ⓣ508/255-5505), a great place for pasta and seafood. **Accommodation** in Orleans is plentiful, with a combination of modestly priced motels along Rte-28 and close to Nauset Beach, and several comfortable bed and breakfasts. *The Cove*, 13 S Orleans Rd (Ⓣ508/255-1203 or 1-800/343-2233, Ⓦwww.thecoveorleans.com; ⑤), is a 47-room motor inn on Town Cove with an outdoor pool, while *Parsonage Inn*, 202 Main St, East Orleans (Ⓣ508/255-8217 or 1-888/422-8217, Ⓦwww.parsonageinn.com; ⑥), is an eighteenth-century house with eight antique-furnished rooms. *Nauset Knoll Motor Lodge*, Nauset Beach, East Orleans (Ⓣ508/255-2364, Ⓦwww.capecodtravel.com/nausetknoll; ⑦), stands just steps from the ocean, and has the requisite accompanying views.

Eastham

Largely undiscovered **EASTHAM**, up Rte-6 past Orleans as the Cape begins to curve up toward Provincetown, is home to fewer than five thousand residents, most of whom are quite content to sit and watch the summer traffic pass by on its way to Provincetown. Though the sum of Eastham's commercial facilities is little more than a small strip of shopping malls and gas stations along Rte-6, if you veer off the highway in either direction you will capture some authentic Cape flavor.

The first detour is the **Fort Hill area**, part of the Cape Cod National Seashore, with a scenic overlook for sweeping views of **Nauset Marsh**,

Cape Cod National Seashore

The protected **Cape Cod National Seashore**, which President Kennedy saved from development because of his fondness for it, extends along much of the Cape's Atlantic side, stretching forty miles from Chatham north to Provincetown. It's a fragile environment: three feet of the lower Cape is washed away each year, and much of it ends up as extra sand on the beach before the sea takes that away, too. Environmentalists are hoping that an extensive program of grass-planting will help prevent further erosion.

It was on these shifting sands of the outer Cape that the **Pilgrims** made their first home in the New World. They obtained their water from Pilgrim Spring near Truro; at Corn Hill Beach they uncovered a cache of corn buried by the Wampanoag Indians who had been living on the Cape for centuries – a discovery which kept them alive their first winter, before moving on to Plymouth.

Displays and films at the **Salt Pond Visitor Center**, on Rte-6 just north of Eastham (closed until 2004; call for hours and exact reopening dates, Ⓣ508/255-3421), trace the geology and history of the Cape. A pretty road and hiking/cycling trail head east to the sands of **Coast Guard Beach** and **Nauset Light Beach**, both of which offer excellent swimming. You can also catch a free shuttle ride there from the visitors' center in summer. Another fine beach is **Head of the Meadow**, halfway between Truro and Provincetown. In several areas parking is restricted to residents only, but you can often park by the road and strike off across the dunes to the shore.

a bay, but which became a marsh when **Coast Guard Beach** was formed. Along the way, you'll pass the **Captain Edward Penniman House**, Fort Hill Road (Ⓣ508/255-3421), a partly restored Second Empire-style house with an octagonal roof that looks straight out of the movie *Psycho*. Unfortunately, it's only open to the public sporadically – but worth it if you can get in. North of Coast Guard Beach, at the corner of Ocean View Drive and Cable Road, is the red and white **Nauset Light**, originally located in Chatham, but installed here in 1923 and moved back 350 feet in 1996 when it was in danger of crumbling into the sea. In 1838, this spot was home to no fewer than three brick lighthouses, known as the "Three Sisters," and built 150 feet apart to protect ships from dangerous shoals off the coast. In 1892, serious erosion necessitated their replacement by three wooden towers; two were eventually moved away in 1918 and the third in 1923. Having been acquired by the National Park service, they now stand in the woods well away from today's coastline. **First Encounter Beach**, off Samoset Road on the town's bayside, refers to the first meeting of Pilgrims and Native Americans in 1620. It was hardly a cordial rendezvous; with the *Mayflower* anchored in Provincetown, an exploration party led by Myles Standish came ashore only to meet a barrage of arrows. Things settled down after a few gunshots were returned, and since then the beach has been utterly tranquil. A plaque set back in the dunes describes the encounter in detail.

Practicalities

The place to **stay** in Eastham is the *Whalewalk Inn*, 220 Bridge Rd (Ⓣ508/255-0617 or 1-800/440-1281, Ⓦwww.whalewalkinn.com; ❼), where immaculate guest rooms and tasty breakfasts are the big draws; the cottages are more spacious than the rooms in the main inn building. There's also a **hostel**, *Mid-Cape American Youth Hostel*, 75 Goody Hallet Dr (mid-May to mid-Sept; Ⓣ508/255-2785, Ⓦwww.usahostels.org/about_eastham.shtml; $21 non-members, $19 members), with dorm-style accommodation in a collection of woodsy cabins. For something to **eat**, *Arnold's Lobster & Clam Bar*, 3580 Rte-6 (Ⓣ508/255-2575), provides generous portions of fried New England seafood, while *Box Lunch*, 4205 Rte-6 (Ⓣ508/255-0799), as its name suggests, is the place to go for packed pita sandwiches to take to the beach.

Wellfleet

WELLFLEET, with a year-round population of just 2500, is, like Eastham eight miles to the south, one of the least developed towns on Cape Cod. Once the focus of a thriving oyster fishing industry, today it is a favorite haunt of writers and artists who come here to seek inspiration from the unsullied landscapes and the constantly heaving ocean. Despite the fact that a number of art galleries have surfaced – most of them along **Main Street** or **Commercial Street** – the town remains a remarkably unpretentious place, with many of the galleries themselves resembling fishing shacks and selling highly distinctive original work aimed at the serious collector, alongside mass-market souvenirs. The **Art Gallery Association** produces a guide to the galleries which can be picked up at the **information booth** at the corner of Rte-6 and LeCount Hollow Road (Ⓣ508/349-2510).

The **Wellfleet Historical Society Museum**, 266 Main St (late June to early-Sept Tues & Fri 10am–4pm; Wed, Thurs & Sat 1–4pm; $1; Ⓦwww.wellfleethistoricalsociety.com), has an interesting collection of furniture, items salvaged from shipwrecks, nautical artifacts, and photographs as well as exhibits on the local oyster industry. Close by at no. 200, the **First Congregational Church** is worth a peek inside for its curved pews and restored Hook and Hastings organ.

The most scenic part of town is actually outside the center, at the bluff-lined **Marconi Beach**, east off Rte-6 in South Wellfleet, where Guglielmo Marconi issued the first transatlantic radio signal on January 18, 1903, and announced greetings from President Roosevelt to King Edward VII. Nothing remains of the tall radio towers built for that purpose, but there are some scale models beneath a gazebo-type structure overlooking the ocean. A short trail up the cliffsides leads to a vantage point from which you can see horizontally across the entire Cape – just a mile wide at this point.

Practicalities

If you want to **stay** the night in Wellfleet, try the laid-back *Holden Inn*, 140 Commercial St (Ⓣ508/349-3450, Ⓦwww.theholdeninn.com; closed Oct–May; ❹), a farmhouse-style structure with 27 rooms, some with shared baths, or the charming *Inn at Duck Creeke*, 70 Main St (Ⓣ508/349-9333, Ⓦwww.innatduckcreeke.com; May–Oct; ❹), a cozy country inn with shared and private baths situated on five woodland acres. Tiny though Wellfleet is, there are a number of casual seafood **restaurants** worth checking out, such as the *Bayside Lobster Hutt*, 91 Commercial St (Ⓣ508/349-6333), an old oyster shack, and *Moby Dick's*, Rte-6, across from Gull Pond Road (Ⓣ508/349-9795), which offers family seafood dining. More upscale is *Painter's Restaurant & Studio Bar*, 50 Main St (Ⓣ508/349-3003), a former tavern that doesn't look like much from the outside, but has funky and moderately-priced American fusion fare and a festive atmosphere, and *Finely JP's*, 554 Rte-6 (Ⓣ508/349-7500), a deceptively plain roadside shack that actually serves downright tasty oysters and other delicious dishes at a good price; try the oysters Bienville, a baked extravaganza of mushrooms, parmesan, cream, and white wine. The finest (and most expensive) restaurant around is *Aesop's Tables*, 316 Main St (Ⓣ508/349-6450), which, in addition to serving divine fresh-caught seafood, boasts terrific home-baked desserts to boot.

Truro

Most of **TRURO**, a sprawling town that continues on Rte-6 right up to Provincetown, falls within the boundaries of the Cape Cod National Seashore, allowing it to keep preserved the kind of natural beauty that has attracted the likes of artists, writers, even politicians – Edward Hopper built a summer house here which he used from 1930 to 1967 and Vice President Al Gore and his

Oyster shucking

No visit to Wellfleet would be complete without a taste of the town's famous oysters. In fact, the little molluscs are so abundant here that the French explorer Samuel de Champlain named the town "Port aux Huitres" (or oyster port) when he disembarked in 1606. The current name of Wellfleet, granted by the English in 1763, also has an oyster heritage – it's a nod to England's own Wellfleet oyster beds. One of the best places to dive into a plate of the raw variety is the rowdy *Beachcomber*, on Cahoon Hollow Beach (Ⓣ508/349-6055): a fun beach shack with awesome waterfront views. You can also attend the Wellfleet Oyster Weekend (annually mid/late October; Ⓦwww.wellfleetshellfishdepartment.org), a jamboree complete with raw oyster bars and shucking contests.

Cape Cod beaches

With over 300 miles of coastline, Cape Cod certainly doesn't lack sand. What it does lack is facilities at its beachfront locations; what few have the full gamut of services (restrooms, lifeguards, and snackbars) are, not surprisingly, usually busiest. The island's southern stretches, facing Nantucket Sound, tend to be calmer and warmer than its northern options, making this coast more family-oriented than its Atlantic side, where the water tends to be chillier and rougher, but also good for surfers. Parking across the Cape is a bit of a crapshoot: some counties allow daily non-permit beach parking (usually $10/day), whereas others limit beach parking to residents, or visitors with temporary parking stickers. Your best bet, if you're planning on hitting the beach a good deal during your stay, is to visit the local town hall and inquire about non-resident parking permits (which can range from $20 for the length of your stay to $50 per week).

The following list is a selection of some of the Cape's best beaches:

Around Hyannis

Craigville Beach off Craigville Beach Road in Centerville. Well-oiled and toned sun-worshippers flock to this broad expanse of sand nicknamed "Muscle Beach."

Kalmus Beach off Gosnold Street in Hyannisport. A big windsurfing destination at the mouth of the busy harbor, with full facilities.

Brewster

Breakwater Beach off Breakwater Road. Close to town, this shallow-water beach has restrooms.

Pains Creek Beach off Paines Creek Road. 1.5-mile bay beach with great body surfing when the tide comes in.

Dennis

Corporation Beach off Rte-6A. One of the best-maintained beaches on the Cape, it has wheelchair-accessible boardwalks, a children's play area, lifeguards, and full facilities.

Mayflower Beach off Rte-6A. Popular family spot thanks to naturally formed tidal pools.

West Dennis Beach off Rte-28, West Dennis. Well-equipped and narrow 1.5-mile beach with a kite-flying area to boot.

Eastham

Coast Guard Beach off Ocean View Drive. Pristine and picturesque Cape Cod National Seashore beach with views for miles, as well as lifeguards and restrooms; Atlantic setting can mean chilly swimming, however.

Nauset Light off Ocean View Dive. Scenic Atlantic-facing beach connected to Coast Guard Beach by shuttle bus and also part of the Cape Cod National Seashore; serviced by lifeguards and has restrooms.

Falmouth

Old-Silver Beach off Rte 28-A in North Falmouth. Popular, calm beach with great sunsets; college kids and young families gather here, the latter drawn to its natural wading pool.

Surf Drive Beach off Shore Street. Another family favorite; a shallow tidal pool between jetties is known as "the kiddie pool."

family vacationed here in 1997. Although at over 43 square miles it's one of the largest towns on the Cape in area, it's the smallest in population – no surprise, then, that downtown is little more than a strip mall with just a few shops, a post

Harwich

Bank Street Beach off Bank Street. Pretty stretch within walking distance of town; the swimming conditions here are good, and the beach attracts a mix of families and college-aged crowds.

Orleans

Nauset Beach East Orleans. Arguably the Cape's biggest beach scene, this 10-mile-long barrier beach has terrific facilities (and regular sunset concerts), and prime windsurfing and boogie-boarding conditions.

Skaket Beach off Skaket Beach Road. Calm bay beach ideal for families; when the tide goes out, kids take to the pools left behind.

Provincetown

Long Point Beach. A blissfully quiet beach at the end of a trail lined with scented wild roses and beach plums; you can get there on foot or by frequent shuttle from MacMillan Wharf (see p.222).

Herring Cove Beach off Rte-6. Easily reached by bike or through the dunes, and famous for sunset watching, this beach is actually more crowded than those nearer town, though never unbearably so.

Province Lands off Race Point Road. Beautiful, vast, sweeping moors and bushy dunes are buffeted by a crashing surf; the site has seen some three thousand known shipwrecks.

Race Point Beach off Race Point Road. Abutting Province Lands (see above), this wide swath of white sand is backed by beautiful, tall dunes – the archetypal Cape Cod beach.

Sandwich

Sandy Neck Beach off Sandy Neck Road, East Sandwich. Six-mile-long barrier beach loaded with low dunes favored by off-roaders; the paths are shut down in summer to encourage the local bird population's hatching season.

Town Neck Beach off Town Neck Road. Narrow and rocky beach 1.5 miles out of town with pretty views of passing ships and decent facilities.

Wakeby Pond Ryder Conservation Area, John Ewer Road. The Cape's largest fresh-water pond has a life-guarded beach and full facilities.

Truro

Head of the Meadow off Head of the Meadow Road. Remote National Seashore beach with great surfing conditions and restrooms; easily accessed by boardwalk from the parking lot.

Wellfleet

Cahoon Hollow Beach off Ocean View Drive. Good surfing and full facilities make this town-run beach popular with the 30-something set. Don't miss the famous *Beachcomber* shack for delicious oysters (see p.215).

Marconi Beach off Marconi Beach Road. Dramatic cliff-framed beach best hit in the morning before the sun falls behind the bluffs.

White Crest off Ocean View Drive. The main distinction between White Crest and neighboring Cahoon is the clientele – here, it's a predominantly young college crowd.

office, town hall, and police station.

It was in windswept Truro that Pilgrim leader Myles Standish and his companions from the *Mayflower* found the cache of Indian corn that helped them survive their first New England winter in 1620; a plaque at **Corn Hill** marks the exact spot. It wasn't until 1697, however, that the first permanent settlement was established. Originally called Pamet, after the Native American tribe that once lived here, it was changed in 1705 to Dangerfield due to the particularly treacherous offshore currents, and finally to Truro, after the town in Cornwall, England. In its early days, Truro depended on the sea for its economic well-being, even becoming the site of Cape Cod's first lighthouse in 1797, powered by whale oil. Today a golf course unappealingly sidles up to the lighthouse's 1857 replacement, the **Cape Cod Light** on Lighthouse Road. Also known as the Highland Light, it was automated as recently as 1986, and even more recently moved back 450 feet from the eroding shoreline where it was in danger of collapsing into the ocean. Thoreau stayed at the old lighthouse during his travels around the Outer Cape, a place where he said he could "put all America behind him." You can visit it, and the nearby **Highland House Museum**, Lighthouse Road (June–Sept daily 10am–4.30pm; $3, $5 with lighthouse; ⓣ508/487-3397, ⓦwww.trurohistorical.org), a 1907 hotel that's now home to some rather prosaic remnants of yesteryear like fishing and whaling equipment, old photographs, and seventeenth-century firearms; better are the objects obtained from the many shipwrecks that have occurred offshore, as well as the second-floor rooms done up in Victorian style – they emulate the chambers this former hotel's guests occupied in the early 1900s, for a price of $8/week.

Practicalities

Other than privately owned summer homes, which can be rented by the week from Duarte/Downey Real Estate, 12 Truro Center Rd (ⓣ508/349-7588, ⓦwww.ddre.com), places to **stay** in Truro are mainly confined to a strip of sandy terrain which hugs the bay shoreline west of Shore Road (Rte-6A) in North Truro. Here *Kalmar Village* (ⓣ508/487-0585, ⓦwww.kalmarvillage.com; ❻) consists of 45 spacious and well-kept one- and two-bedroom cottages in an oceanfront community. In July and August, these can only be rented by the week; at other times, nightly rentals are possible. The *Top Mast Motel*, 209 Shore Rd (Rte-6A), North Truro (ⓣ508/487-1189, ⓦwww.capecodtours.com/topmast; ❺; closed Oct–May), has beachfront rooms rented on a weekly basis, and non-beachfront rooms rented by the night. There's a pool and a restaurant on the premises. For something to **eat**, *Adrian's*, 535 Rte-6, North Truro (ⓣ508/487-4360), serves affordable breakfasts and dinners with an Italian touch, while the *Blacksmith Shop*, Truro Center Road off Rte-6A (ⓣ508/349-6554), is a local institution, mainly for its hefty portions of moderately-priced prime rib and shrimp.

Provincetown

"Far from being out of the way, Provincetown is directly in the way of the navigator...
It is situated on one of the highways of commerce, and men from all parts of the globe touch there in the course of a year."

from *Cape Cod* by Henry David Thoreau

The brash fishing burgh of **PROVINCETOWN**, at the very tip of Cape Cod, is a popular summer destination for bohemians, artists, and fun-seekers lured by the excellent beaches, art galleries, and welcoming atmosphere. While it's become a major **gay** resort destination, complete with frequent festivals and theme weekends to match, P-town – as this coastal community of five thousand year-round inhabitants is commonly known – also has a drop of **Portuguese** culture to embellish it, after a smallish population of fishermen began settling here starting in the mid-1800s; their legacy is now celebrated in an annual June festival complete with music and Portuguese soup-tasting competitions. Throughout the summer, P-town's population swells into the tens of thousands, and there's often a carnival atmosphere in the bustling streets. The appealing hamlet should not be missed by anyone, especially as it's just a few hours' ferry ride from Boston.

Some history

Provincetown has a number of Pilgrim-related monuments – after all, they landed here before heading to Plymouth – but the Pilgrims were not the first European visitors to arrive at Provincetown. Way back in 1004, Leif Erikson's brother, **Thorvald**, disembarked here to repair the broken keel of his ship and named the place "Cape of the Keel," and in 1602 the area was visited by explorer **Bartholomew Gosnold**, the first European to visit southeastern New England, who dubbed it "Cape Cod" on account of the profusion of cod in the local waters. The Pilgrims came ashore here and stayed for five weeks in 1620, signing the **Mayflower Compact**, one long and rather vaguely worded sentence espousing a democratic form of self-government, before sailing across Cape Cod Bay.

The town was incorporated in 1727, and soon became a thriving fishing, salt-processing, and whaling port; indeed, by 1880, the town was the richest per capita in Massachusetts. Fishing retains its importance here, and many of the fishermen working today are direct descendants of the Portuguese from the Azores who settled here in the 1800s. Its destiny to become one of the East Coast's leading **art colonies** was assured in 1899, when painter Charles W. Hawthorne founded the **Cape Cod School of Art**, which encouraged artists to explore the outdoors and exploit the Mediterranean-like quality of the light. So many of his friends came to investigate the place that it became known as the "Greenwich Village of the North." By the early 1900s, many painters had begun to ply their highbrow trades in abandoned "dune shacks" by the sea, and by 1916 there were no fewer than six art schools here. The natural beauty and laid-back atmosphere also began to seduce rebellious young writers like Mary Heaton Vorse, who established the **Provincetown Players** theater group in 1915. **Eugene O'Neill** joined the company in 1916, premiering his *Bound East for Cardiff* in a waterfront fish house done up as a theater, and **Tennessee Williams** was another frequent visitor.

As much of an impact as its colorful residents have had, equally important in Provincetown's history has been its **geography**. The entire Cape is a glacial deposit on a crooked sliver of bedrock, but due to its position at the very tip, Provincetown is particularly susceptible to the vagaries of wind and water, the fragile environment lending a certain legitimacy to the strict **zoning laws** that have kept major development at bay and, consequently, continue to preserve the flavor of the old town. There's also evidence that the shifting dunes of this part of the Cape Cod National Seashore, including the barren but beautiful **Province Lands**, were once covered with topsoil and trees that were cut for fuel, thus hastening the process of erosion – a further example of the need for conservation.

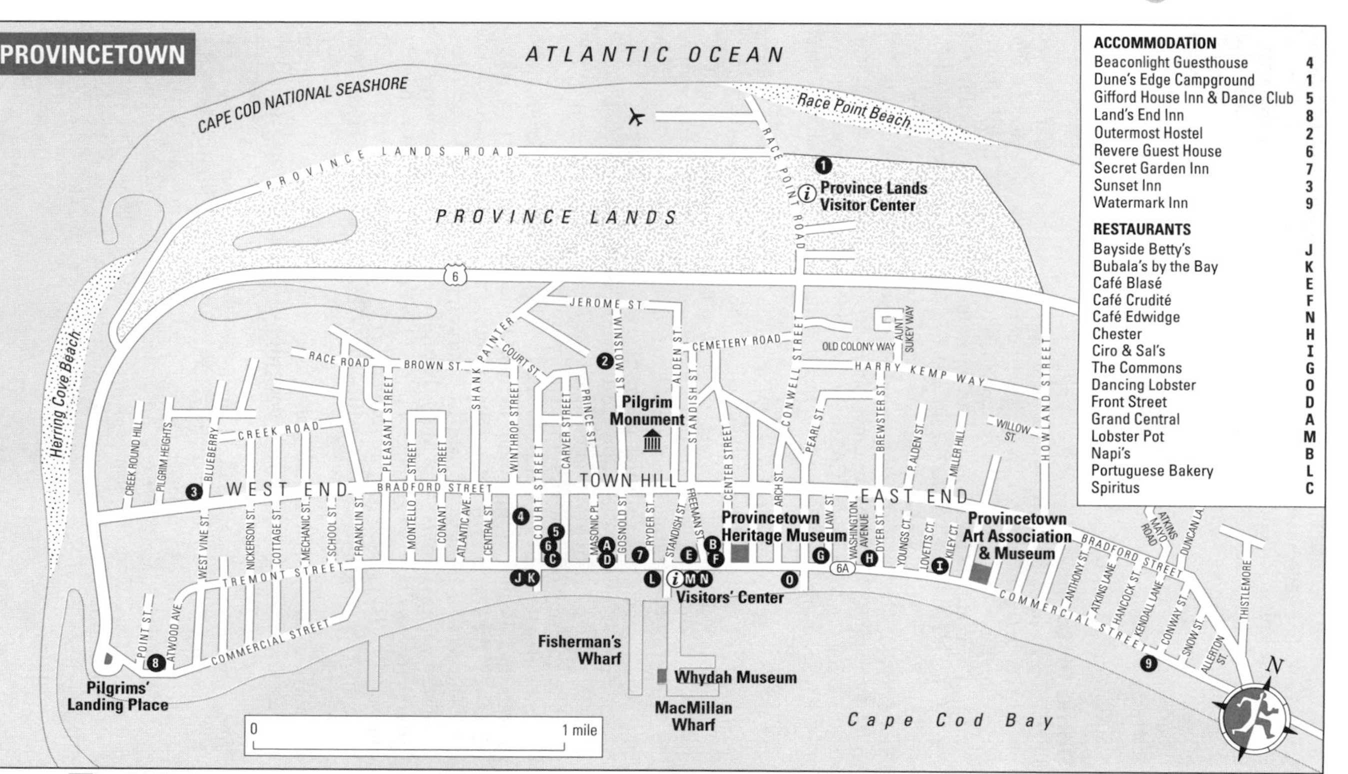
PROVINCETOWN
ACCOMMODATION
Beaconlight Guesthouse 4
Dune's Edge Campground 1
Gifford House Inn & Dance Club 5
Land's End Inn 8
Outermost Hostel 2
Revere Guest House 6
Secret Garden Inn 7
Sunset Inn 3
Watermark Inn 9
RESTAURANTS
Bayside Betty's J
Bubala's by the Bay K
Café Blasé E
Café Crudité F
Café Edwidge N
Chester H
Ciro & Sal's I
The Commons G
Dancing Lobster O
Front Street D
Grand Central A
Lobster Pot M
Napi's B
Portuguese Bakery L
Spiritus C
ATLANTIC OCEAN
CAPE COD NATIONAL SEASHORE
PROVINCE LANDS
Race Point Beach
Herring Cove Beach
Province Lands Visitor Center
Pilgrim Monument
Provincetown Heritage Museum
Provincetown Art Association & Museum
Visitors' Center
Whydah Museum
MacMillan Wharf
Fisherman's Wharf
Pilgrims' Landing Place
Cape Cod Bay
Long Point Beach
TOWN HILL
WEST END
EAST END
0
1 mile
N

Arrival, information, and getting around

Two companies make the ninety-minute trip across Massachusetts Bay to Provincetown: **Boston Harbor Cruises** departs from **Long Wharf** (daily late May to mid-June leaving 9am, returning 4pm; late June to early Oct Mon–Wed leaving 9am, returning 4pm, Thurs leaving 9am & 6.30pm, returning 4pm & 8.30pm, Fri–Sun leaving 9am, 2pm & 6.30pm, returning 11am, 4pm & 8.30pm; $49 round-trip; ⓣ617/227-4321, ⓦwww.bostonharborcruises.com), while **Bay State Cruises** leaves, somewhat inconveniently, from the **Commonwealth Pier** by the World Trade Center (daily late May to early Oct leaving 8am & 5.30pm, returning 10am & 7.30pm; daily late June to early Oct leaving 8am, 1pm & 5.30pm, returning 10am, 3pm & 7.30pm; $60 round-trip; ⓣ617/748-1428, ⓦwww.boston-ptown.com). The latter has an excellent **excursion fare** for weekend day-tripping, too: $15 round-trip will get you to P-town and back with a three-hour window to tool around in – but keep in mind the boats also take three hours each way (late May to early Sept Fri–Sun leaving 9.30am, returning 3.30pm). Provincetown is at the end of **Rte-6**, the Cape's main, though unscenic, highway, and **buses** regularly trawl this stretch from Boston and all the major Cape towns; Bonanza Bus Lines (ⓣ401/751-8800 or 1-888/751-8800, ⓦwww.bonanzabus.com) and Plymouth & Brockton buses (ⓣ508/746-0378, ⓦwww.p-b.com) are the ones to call. Buses stop right in the middle of town near MacMillan Wharf. There is a **visitors' center** right by the bus stop, 307 Commercial St (ⓣ508/487-3424), where you can pick up all sorts of information. You can get online information before you go at ⓦwww.provincetown.com; gays and lesbians may also want to check ⓦwww.gayprovincetown.com.

Transit and tours

However you've gotten here, you'll find Provincetown a very **walkable** kind of place; **bicycles** can come in handy, though, especially if you want to venture a bit further afield. For rentals, Arnold's, 329 Commercial St (ⓣ508/487-0844), right in the center of town, is open from mid-April to mid-October, as is Nelson's Bike Shop, 43 Race Point Rd (ⓣ508/487-8849), located close to the **bike trails** that meander through the Province Lands. Bikes go for about $17 per day. Provincetown also claims the title of first **whale-watching** spot on the East Coast; the most renowned company is the Dolphin Fleet (ⓣ508/349-1900 or 1-800/826-9300, ⓦwww.whalewatch.com; $20), with cruises leaving frequently from MacMillan Wharf between June and October.

If you want to take a **boat ride**, Provincetown Harbor Cruises, MacMillan Wharf (ⓣ508/487-4330), run forty-minute trips round the bay hourly from 11am to 7pm in season ($7), while Flyer's Boat Rentals, 131A Commercial St (ⓣ508/487-0898 or 1-800/750-0898, ⓦwww.flyersrentals.com), provides a range of rental boats, from sloops to powerboats. Alternatively, take their **shuttle** across Cape Cod Bay to Long Point Beach (mid-June to mid-Sept; $8 one-way, $12 round-trip). You can also opt to ramble about the dunes in a four-wheel-drive vehicle with **Art's Dune Tours**, at Commercial and Standish (April–Oct 10am–dusk; $12; ⓣ508/487-1950, ⓦwww.artsdune-tours.com), or fly over them in a replica 1938 biplane (ⓣ1-888/BIPLANE or 508/428-8732; $60; advance reservations required). Twenty-minute flights take off from the Cape Cod Airport, near the intersection of Race Lane and Rte-149; or, if you wish, you and two friends can also opt to board a Cessna (same phone; $69) instead.

Accommodation

Many of the most picturesque cottages in town are **guesthouses**, some with spectacular views over Cape Cod Bay. The best place to be is the quiet West End, though anything on Bradford Street will also be removed from the summertime racket. Prices are generally very reasonable until mid-June, and off-season you can find real bargains. In addition, there are a few **motels**, mostly confined to the outskirts of town, towards the Truro line.

Provincetown Reservations (ⓣ508/487-2400 or 1-800/648-0364) and the gay-oriented Intown Reservations (ⓣ508/487-1883 or 1-800/67P-TOWN) can usually rustle up lodgings at busy times. The welcoming **Dune's Edge Campground**, on Rte-6 just east of the central stoplights (ⓣ508/487-9815), charges $22 for use of one of its wooded sites.

Beaconlight Guesthouse 12 Winthrop St ⓣ1-800/696 9603, ⓦwww.beaconlightguesthouse.com. Stylish ten-room guesthouse with individually appointed rooms, equipped with air conditioning, TV, and VCR. ❻

Gifford House Inn & Dance Club 9–11 Carver St ⓣ1-800/434-0130, ⓦwww.giffordhouse.com. Popular gay resort with lobby piano bar, restaurant, and dance floor; continental breakfast included in rates. ❺

Land's End Inn 22 Commercial St ⓣ1-800/276-7088, ⓦwww.landsendinn.com. Meticulously decorated rooms and suites, many with sweeping ocean views, in a fanciful turreted house; continental breakfast included. ❼

Outermost Hostel 28 Winslow St ⓣ508/487-4378. Hostel with thirty $15 beds in five cramped dorm cabins; includes kitchen access and parking.

Revere Guest House 14 Court St ⓣ508/487-2292 or 1-800/487-2292, ⓦwww.reverehouse.com. This pleasant B&B has a garden patio and antiques-accented rooms, some with shared bath. ❻

Secret Garden Inn 300a Commercial St ⓣ866/786-9646, ⓦwww.provincetown.com/secretgardeninn. Four quaint rooms in a house with a verandah, done up in country furnishings, and with modern touches like TVs and air conditioning; country breakfast included. ❹

Sunset Inn 142 Bradford St ⓣ508/487-9810, ⓦwww.sunsetinnptown.com. Clean, quiet rooms in an 1850 captain's house with double or queen beds and private or shared bath. ❹

Watermark Inn 603 Commercial St ⓣ508/487-0165, ⓦwww.watermark-inn.com. Ten immaculate and contemporary suites, several of which come with private decks and ocean views, are rented by the week in summer ($1050–$2175), and by night the rest of the year. ❺

The Town and around

The town center is essentially two three-mile-long streets, **Commercial** and **Bradford**, connected by about forty tiny lanes of no more than two short blocks each. Though much diluted by tourism, the beatnik spirit is still in evidence, most pronounced in regular Friday-night expositions in the many art galleries along Commercial Street. On summer evenings the narrow street fills with hordes of sightseers, locals, and, amazingly, cars, even though they can do little more than crawl along. **Fisherman's Wharf**, and the more touristy **MacMillan Wharf**, busy with whale-watching boats, yachts, and colorful old Portuguese fishing vessels, split the town in half. MacMillan Wharf also houses the **Whydah Museum**, 16 Macmillan Wharf (June–Aug daily 10am–7pm; May & Sept–Oct daily 10am–5pm; Nov–Dec Sat & Sun 10am–5pm; $8; ⓣ508/487-8899, ⓦwww.whydah.com), which displays some of the bounty from a famous pirate shipwreck off the coast of Wellfleet in 1717. The lifelong quest of native Cape Codder Barry Clifford to recover the treasure from the one-time slave ship *Whydah* – repository of loot from more than fifty ships when it sank – paid off royally with his discovery of the ship in summer 1983. Thousands of coins, gold bars, pieces of jewelry, and weapons were retrieved, ranging from odds and sods like silver shoe buckles and flintlock pistols to rare African gold jewelry attributed to West Africa's Akan people that was likely en-route to England, where it would have been melted to make guineas. The most evocative display in the museum, glimmering gold coins notwithstanding, is the ship's **bell**, a little rusty but not so corroded that you can't read "The Whydah Galley – 1716" clear as day.

Two blocks north of the piers, atop aptly named Town Hill, is the 252-foot granite tower of the **Pilgrim Monument** (daily: July–Aug 9am–7pm; May–June & Sept–Nov 9am–4.15pm; $6; ⓣ508/487-1310, ⓦwww.pilgrim-monument.org), modeled on a bell tower in Siena, Italy. It commemorates the Pilgrims' landing and their signing of the Mayflower Compact. From the observation deck, the whole Cape (and, on a clear day, Boston) can be discerned. At the bottom of the hill on **Bradford Street**, the second of the two main roadways, is a bas-relief monument to the Pilgrims' **Mayflower Compact**. Not far away in the lively East End, the **Provincetown Heritage Museum**, 356 Commercial St (daily 10am–6pm; $3), is housed in an 1860 Methodist church. This comprehensive collection of Provincetown memorabilia includes a 68-inch striped bass, a Portuguese altar, and a reconstruction of the "dune shack" of Harry Kemp, beach-bum poet and crony of Eugene O'Neill. The second floor houses an impressive half-scale model of the *Rose Dorothea*, a much-loved old Provincetown fishing schooner. Further out, the delightful **Provincetown Art Association and Museum**, 460 Commercial St (July–Aug daily noon–5pm & 8–10pm; mid-May to June & Sept daily noon–5pm, Sat & Sun noon–5pm & 8–10pm; Oct–April Sat & Sun noon–4pm, April to mid-May Sat & Sun noon–5pm; $5; ⓦwww.paam.org), rotates works from its collection of nearly two thousand, with equal prominence given to local artists as well as established figures. Do your best to come on a Friday night, when openings by new artists frequently take place.

On the other side of the wharves is the quieter and slightly less cramped **West End**, where many of the weathered clapboard houses are cheerfully decorated with colored blinds, white picket fences, and wildflowers spilling out of every possible orifice. At Commercial Street's western end, the actual Pilgrim **landing place** is marked by a modest bronze plaque on a boulder.

A little ways beyond the town's narrow strip of sand, a string of **undeveloped beaches** is marked only by dunes and a few shabby beach huts

. The **visitors' center** (late May to early Sept daily 9am–5pm; early Sept to late Oct & April to late May daily 9am–4.30pm; ⓣ508/487-1256), in the middle of the dunes off Race Point Road, has an observation deck from which you might spot a whale – or even, when the tide is right, the ruins of the **HMS Somerset**, a sunken British battleship from the Revolutionary War.

Eating

Food in Provincetown can be expensive: the snack bars around MacMillan Wharf are generally extortionate, and the eclectic cuisine in the sometimes precious restaurants can hit $10 for a salad and a coffee. Still, there are some real discoveries to be made, and they need not break your budget – look out in particular for the Portuguese restaurants that can be found throughout the town. Whenever possible, especially in the few restaurants where it's possible to eat al fresco (mosquitos can be a big problem), arrive early or call ahead to make a reservation; many restaurants are packed in season, and just as many close for the winter.

Cafés and bakeries

Café Blasé 328 Commercial St ⓣ508/487-9465. Touristy pastel café, one of the few places with outdoor seating for great people watching. Pricey for pasta and steak dinners (and only average at that), but delicious $6 fresh fruit and waffle breakfasts, and pre-dinner cocktails.

Café Crudité 336 Commercial St ⓣ508/487-6237. Casual upstairs eatery serving exclusively vegetarian fare, like delicious tofu salad.

Café Edwidge 333 Commercial St ⓣ508/487-2008. Breakfast's the thing at this popular second-floor spot; try the homemade Danish pastries and fresh fruit pancakes. Creative bistro fare at dinner time.

Portuguese Bakery 299 Commercial St ⓣ508/487-1803. This old standby is the place to come for cheap baked goods, particularly the tasty fried *rabanada*, akin to portable French toast.

Restaurants

Bayside Betty's 177 Commercial St ⓣ508/487-6566. Funky waterfront eatery with hearty breakfasts and seafood dinners that's also a popular martini bar.

Bubala's by the Bay 183 Commercial St ⓣ508/487-0773. Snappy seafood with international influences is the signature of the brightly painted West End eatery, where the service is not quite so snappy; additional seating on a big outdoor deck.

Chester 404 Commercial St ⓣ508/487-8200. Preciously chic spot with an award-winning wine list. Menu changes weekly, emphasizing fresh ingredients, unusual combinations like sea scallops with apples and sage, and high prices.

Ciro & Sal's 4 Kiley Court ⓣ508/487-0049. Traditional Northern Italian cooking with plenty of veal and seafood choices; a bit on the pricey side, but worth it.

The Commons 386 Commercial St ⓣ508/487-7800. French bistro food and tasty pizzas from a wood-fired oven make this a popular spot.

Dancing Lobster 373 Commercial St ⓣ508/487-0900. The Tuscan-prepared seafood and sunset views pack them in here, so arrive early to avoid a wait.

Front Street 230 Commercial St ⓣ508/487-9715. Popular Italian and Continental restaurant located in a Victorian house; menu changes weekly, but you might find dishes like potato-crusted salmon with raspberry butter, and chick-pea and artichoke flan.

Grand Central 5 Masonic Place ⓣ508/487-7599. Romantic and expensive bistro directly across from the *Atlantic House* bar.

Lobster Pot 321 Commercial St ⓣ508/487-0842. Its landmark neon sign is like a welcome mat for those who come from far and wide for the ultra-fresh crustaceans. Affordable and family-oriented.

Napi's 7 Freeman St ⓣ508/487-1145. Popular dishes at this art-strewn spot include pastas and seafood items, notably a thick Portuguese fish stew.

Spiritus 190 Commercial St ⓣ508/487-2808. Combination pizza place and coffee bar with an especially lively after-hours scene.

Nightlife and entertainment

Each in-season weekend, boatloads of revelers seek out P-town's notoriously wild **nightlife**. Heavily geared towards a gay clientele, resulting in ubiquitous tea dances, drag shows, and video bars, some establishments have terrific waterfront locations and terraces to match, making them ideal spots to sit out with a drink at sunset. Any cover charge you may come across will fall somewhere in the $5–10 range. You'll also find that many of Provincetown's restaurants have a lively bar scene, too.

Atlantic House 6 Masonic Place, behind Commercial Street ⓣ508/487-3821. The "A-House" – a dark drinking hole that was a favorite of Tennessee Williams and Eugene O'Neill – is now a trendy (and still dark) gay dance club and bar.

Boatslip 161 Commercial St ⓣ800/451-SLIP, ⓦwww.boatslipresort.com. The Sunday tea dances at this resort are legendary; you can either dance away on a long wooden deck overlooking the water, or cruise inside under a disco ball and flashing lights.

Chaser's 293 Commercial St ⓣ508/487-7200. Subterranean disco for women, with occasional live music, right in the heart of the action.

Club Euro 258 Commercial St ⓣ508/487-2505. Music videos, world-beat sounds, and a good buzz in an 1843 former Congregational church with 3-D mermaid emerging from the wall.

Crown and Anchor 247 Commercial St ⓣ508/487-1430, ⓦwww.onlyatthecrown.com. A massive complex housing several bars, including *The Vault*, P-town's only leather bar, *Wave*, a video-karaoke bar, and *Paramount*, a cabaret with nightly acts.

Pied Piper 193 Commercial St ⓣ508/487-1527, ⓦwww.thepied.com. Though largely a lesbian club (it's the oldest one in the country), the outdoor deck and inside dance floor at this trendy waterfront space attract a good dose of men, too, for their longstanding After Tea T-Dance (Sun 6.30–9pm). Thursday is Classic Disco night; Friday and Saturday are house nights.

Steve's Alibi 291 Commercial St ⓣ508/487-2890, ⓦwww.stevesalibi.com. Campy bar with four daily drag shows (4pm, 7pm, 9pm & 11pm).

Martha's Vineyard and Nantucket

Just five miles south of Cape Cod, the sedate, forested island of **Martha's Vineyard** has long been one of the most popular and prestigious vacation destinations in the US, a status that has only grown in recent years, as a gaggle of celebrities from Carly Simon to President Clinton have come for its mannerly New England towns, untouched beaches, and, above all, peace and quiet. Like its slightly further afield cousin, **Nantucket**, it mingles an easygoing cosmopolitan atmosphere, assured by some of the best restaurants and bed and breakfasts on the East Coast, with a taste of remoteness, even though Boston and New York are just short flights away. Neither island boasts much in the way of traditional sights, and almost all locals are more than happy to keep it that way.

Martha's Vineyard

The largest offshore island in New England, 20-mile-long **MARTHA'S VINEYARD** encompasses more physical variety than Nantucket, with hills and pasturelands providing scenic counterpoints to the beaches and wild, windswept moors on the separate island of **Chappaquiddick**. Roads throughout the Vineyard are framed by knotty oak trees, which lend a romantic aura to an already pretty landscape. The most genteel town on the island is **Edgartown**, all prim and proper with its freshly painted, white-clapboard Colonial homes and manicured gardens. The other main town, **Vineyard Haven**, has a more commercial atmosphere, not surprising considering that it is one of the main places where the ferries come in. **Oak Bluffs**, in between the two (and the other docking point for ferries), has an array of wooden gingerbread cottages and inviting eateries. Regardless of where you visit, watch out for the terminology: heading "Up-Island" takes you, improbably, southwest to the wondrous cliffs at **Gay Head**; conversely, "Down-Island" refers to the easterly towns of Vineyard Haven, Oak Bluffs, and Edgartown.

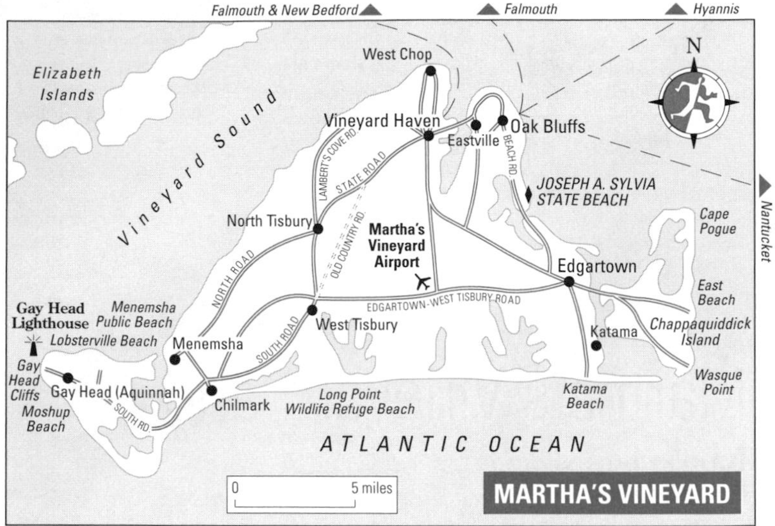

Some history

Martha's Vineyard was reputedly named by the British explorer who discovered it in 1602, **Bartholomew Gosnold**, for his daughter, **Martha**. The "Vineyard" part was for its fertile store of vines – back then the triangular-shaped island was virtually covered with wild grapes, none of which remain. While Gosnold spent only three days on the island, **Wampanoag Indians** had been calling it home for at least ten thousand years, and a small community of around three hundred remains at **Aquinnah**, near the multicolored limestone cliffs of Gay Head. They claimed that in order to separate his tribe from enemies on the mainland, the Indian chief **Moshup** placed his cape on the ground and created Vineyard Sound, though geological records put that event as happening about 50,000 years ago.

For a few decades after Gosnold's departure the island was once again the exclusive province of the natives, but in 1642 one **Thomas Mayhew** bought it from the earl of Stirling for forty pounds and a beaver hat, paving the way for other English Puritan farmers to settle here. They learned tricks of the whaling industry from the natives, and the economy flourished: while Martha's Vineyard never ousted Nantucket or New Bedford as whaling capital of the East, many of its captains did very nicely out of the industry, evidenced by the gracious sea captains' houses that remain in Edgartown and Vineyard Haven. By the time of the Civil War in the 1860s, however, whaling was in serious decline, and had it not been for the **Methodist camp meetings** that started here in 1835, the island's tourist industry might never have taken root. Dozens of Methodist families from churches all over the nation started gathering in tents at sparsely populated Oak Bluffs for two weeks of vigorous preaching and recreation; they were looking for an isolated location far away from the temptations of the flesh. As the movement grew, so did the desire of many families to return, some building permanent platforms, arranged around the preachers' tent, and later constructing small cottages with extraordinarily fancy facades, now familiar as "gingerbread" style – more than half of which remain clustered round the village green. In 1867, recognizing the island's potential as a resort, developers constructed a separate secular community next to the original campground, and large hotels were soon constructed around the harbor.

Though the tourism has never abated, today strictly enforced **zoning** laws insure that major development is kept to a minimum; billboards, neon signs, even parking meters, are outlawed. Concerned residents come out in force at the slightest whiff of change; a car sticker campaign a few years ago urged "Mac to Keep Off Martha," in response to an application by *McDonald's* to open a franchise here – the campaign was successful.

Arrival, information, and getting around

Most people come to Martha's Vineyard by **ferry**, arriving at either Oak Bluffs or Vineyard Haven (see box p.228 for schedules and fares). You can also **fly** via Cape Air (Ⓣ508/771-6944 or 1-800/352-0714, Ⓦwww.flycapeair.com) from Boston (from which there's an hourly shuttle in the summer), Hyannis, Nantucket, or New Bedford. The Vineyard's **airport** (Ⓣ508/693-7022) is in West Tisbury. **Taxis** greet all arriving ferries and flights; reputable companies include Martha's Vineyard Taxi (Ⓣ508/693-8660 or 693-9611), All Island Taxi (Ⓣ508/693-3705), and Accurate Taxi (Ⓣ508/627-9798), which has the only late-night service.

A white public **bus** operated by the Martha's Vineyard Transit Authority connects the main towns on the island year-round, from around 7am to 12.45am daily (Ⓣ508/627-7448, Ⓦwww.vineyardtransit.com); tickets cost $1 in between towns and an unlimited pass is $5 per day. You can also join a three-hour pithily narrated **trolley tour** run by Island Transport (Ⓣ508/693-4681, Ⓦwww.mvtour.com; $15), which is a good way of getting oriented; the trolleys operate from spring to autumn from all ferry arrival points. Still, it's best to explore the island for yourself. Bringing a **car** over is expensive and rather pointless, but as soon as you get off the ferry you encounter rows of **bike** rental places; other rental options are Anderson Bike Rentals on Circuit Avenue in Oak Bluffs (Ⓣ508/693-9346), or R.W. Cutler Bikes at 1 Main St, Edgartown (Ⓣ508/627-4052, Ⓦwww.edgartownbikerentals.com). Wherever you get it from, a basic mountain bike generally starts at $20 a day. If you just can't do without a car, you can rent one from Budget, in both Vineyard Haven and Edgartown (Ⓣ508/693-1911 or 1-800/527-0700, Ⓦwww.budget.com), go upscale with Vineyard Classic Cars, Lake Avenue, Oak Bluffs (Ⓣ508/693-5551), or arrange wheels through Adventure (Ⓣ508/696-0909, Ⓦwww.adventurerentalsmv.com), which has a

Name confusion on the Vineyard

There's no way around the **name confusion** of Martha's Vineyard towns other than acquainting yourself with a bit of island history. Most muddled of all are Vineyard Haven and West Tisbury. Where, you might wonder, is Tisbury? The answer is, nowhere. Well, officially, but not really. Vineyard Haven, north of West Tisbury, is incorporated as Tisbury, but no one ever calls it that. Back in 1642, the settlement of Nunnepog was renamed Great Harbor, but in 1673, Governor Thomas Mayhew opted for another name, Edgar Towne, a nod to the son of the Duke of York and heir presumptive of Charles II, the reigning monarch at the time. The habit has proven hard to break. Oak Bluffs was called Cottage City until 1907. Gay Head, home of the famous cliffs, recently reverted, officially, to its Wampanoag Indian name of Aquinnah, though people still refer to it as Gay Head. Then there is the matter of Chilmark, which, though endowed with a town hall, is not endowed with a town. It's all very fitting for a place that, after all, neither belongs to "Martha" nor is a vineyard.

convenient airport kiosk and also rents mopeds, even though they are frowned on by many residents because of the resultant noise and accidents.

You can get **tourist information** at the Martha Vineyard Chamber of Commerce in Vineyard Haven (see opposite), which stocks the requisite pamphlets and island maps.

Accommodation

There's a tremendous variety of **accommodation** on the island, ranging from resort hotels with every conceivable creature comfort, to old sea captains' homes oozing with charm and personality, and rental cottages, usually booked on a weekly basis. Keep in mind that, whatever type of lodging you decide on, summer accommodation in Martha's Vineyard gets booked up very early, so reserve well in advance. If you do get stuck with nowhere to stay, the main Chamber of Commerce office will always do their best to help. Remember too, that in-season and off-season prices can vary dramatically, hence the big range in some of the prices listed below. If you want (or need) to save money, check out the **campground** in Edgartown, 569 Edgartown Rd (ⓣ508/693-3722, ⓦwww.campmvfc.com; $36 for two).

Oak Bluffs

Admiral Benbow Inn 520 New York Ave ⓣ508/693-6825, ⓦwww.admiral-benbow-inn.com. Seven pleasant, non-smoking rooms in a newly restored landmark inn close to the harbor. ❻

Ferries to Martha's Vineyard

Unless otherwise specified, the ferries listed below run several times daily in the peak mid-June to mid-September holiday periods. Most have fewer services from mid-May to mid-June, and between mid-September and October. There is at least a skeleton service to each island, though not on all routes, year-round. Round-trip passenger fares from **Woods Hole** cost $11; **Falmouth** $20–26, depending on whether you're arriving in Oak Bluffs or Edgartown; **Hyannis**, $27; and **New Bedford**, $20. The ferry from **Montauk**, Long Island, which operates only in summer, costs $40. Round-trip costs for cars (mid-May to mid-Sept) are around $104 ($48–60 off-season), not including passengers. You *must* have a reservation for cars; book early if possible. Large parking lots are provided for day-trippers and for those who want to stay overnight, costing $10–12 per car per day. Most ferries also charge extra for bikes (up to $6).

From Cape Cod

Falmouth to Oak Bluffs (about 35min). Passengers only. The *Island Queen* (ⓣ508/548-4800, ⓦwww.islandqueen.com).

Falmouth to Edgartown (1 hour). Passengers only. Falmouth Ferry Service (ⓣ508/548-9400, ⓦwww.falmouthferry.com).

Woods Hole to both Vineyard Haven and Oak Bluffs (about 45min). Car ferry. Steamship Authority (ⓣ508/447-8600, ⓦwww.islandferry.com).

Hyannis to Oak Bluffs (about 1hr40min). Passengers only. Hy-Line (ⓣ508/778-2600 in Hyannis; ⓣ508/693-0112 on Martha's Vineyard, ⓦwww.hy-linecruises.com).

From elsewhere in Massachusetts and New York

New Bedford to Vineyard Haven (90min). Passengers only. The *Schamonchi* (ⓣ508/997-1688, ⓦwww.mvferry.com).

Montauk, Long Island, NY to Oak Bluffs (about 6 hours). Passengers only, summer Thursdays only. Viking Ferry (ⓣ631/668-5700, ⓦwww.vikingfleet.com).

Attleboro House 11 Lake Ave ⓣ508/693-0085. Charming, old-fashioned guesthouse with a distinguished harbor-view terrace ; no private bathrooms. Open May–Sept. ❹

Nashua House B&B 30 Kennebec Ave ⓣ508/693-0043, ⓦwww.nashuahouse.com. Small rooms, shared baths, but one of the less expensive choices in these parts. ❹

Wesley Hotel 1 Lake Ave ⓣ508/693-6611 or 1-800/638-9027, ⓦwww.wesleyhotel.com. The last of Oak Bluff's grand hotels, with plenty of character intact. Prices rise significantly in the summer months. ❻

Edgartown

Colonial Inn 38 N Water St ⓣ508/627-4711 or 1-800/627-4701, ⓦwww.colonialinnmvy.com. Extremely central white-clapboard inn with well-appointed airy rooms, some off-season bargains, and high midsummer rates. ❼

Edgartown Commons Pease's Point Way ⓣ508/627-4671 or 1-800/439-4671, ⓦwww.edgartowncommons.com. Adequate and inexpensive one- and two-bedroom efficiencies in Edgartown's historic district. ❻

Harborside Inn 3 S Water St ⓣ508/627-4321 or 1-800/627-4009, ⓦwww.theharborsideinn.com. Comfortable rooms on the waterfront with heated pool and sauna. ❼

Shiretown Inn 21 N Water St ⓣ508/627-3353 or 1-800/541-0090, ⓦwww.shiretowninn.com. Variety of different-styled B&B rooms, including some very costly ones, slap bang in the center of town. ❼

Tuscany Inn 22 N Water St ⓣ508/627-5999, ⓦwww.tuscanyinn.com. Savor an unexpected slice of Italy in the center of (somewhat stuffy) Edgartown, reflected mainly in the food and decor. ❼

Elsewhere on the island

HI-Martha's Vineyard Edgartown–West Tisbury Road ⓣ508/693-2665, ⓦwww.usahostels.org. A nice setting, but a bit off the beaten track, with 78 beds in dormitory accommodation, with shared bath and a full kitchen. April to mid-Nov only; $19 members, $22 nonmembers.

Lambert's Cove Country Inn Lambert's Cove Road, West Tisbury ⓣ508/693-2298 or 1-888/LAMBINN, ⓦwww.lambertscoveinn.com. Quiet, secluded country inn on idyllic grounds that include access to a private beach. ❼

Menemsha Inn & Cottages North Road, Menemsha ⓣ508/645-2521, ⓦwww.menemshainn.com. Lovely pine-furnished carriage house suites, main building rooms, and 12 cottages, all with private decks. Open May–Nov; book early. ❽

The island

The Vineyard is basically divided in two sections, the far busier of which is "**Down-Island**," which includes the ferry terminals of **Vineyard Haven** and **Oak Bluffs**, and smart **Edgartown**. The largely undeveloped western half of the island, known as "**Up-Island**," comprises woods, agricultural land, ponds, and nature reserves, with a smattering of tiny villages thrown in between, including **West Tisbury**, **Chilmark**, and **Gay Head**. Although there are plenty of trails to explore, much of the land belongs to strictly private estates and as such is out of bounds to the public.

Vineyard Haven

Most visitors by boat arrive at **VINEYARD HAVEN** (officially named Tisbury), at the northern tip of the island. Founded by islanders from Edgartown disillusioned with the iron-fist Puritan rule of the Mayhew family, Vineyard Haven supplanted Edgartown as the island's main commercial center in the mid-1800s, because ferries preferred the shorter run to the mainland; today, the town, which may well be the least attractive on the island, retains its distinctively business-like ambience, its late-Victorian main street lined with a mix of shops, banks, law and real estate offices, and ice-cream parlors.

The brand-new **bus terminal**, visible as you get off the ferry, is also home to a small **visitors' kiosk**, but for more detailed information and help in finding accommodation, walk up Beach Road to the **Martha's Vineyard Chamber of Commerce**, 24 Beach Rd (late May to early Sept daily 9am–5pm; early Sept to late May Mon–Fri 9am–5pm; ⓣ508/693-0085,

Ⓦwww.mvy.com). Along the way, you'll pass the legendary **Black Dog Tavern**, as famous for its souvenirs as for its food and drink; see also p.236. More sanctimonious is the nearby **Seamen's Bethel Museum**, at 15 Beach Rd (hours vary; free; Ⓣ508/693-9317), set in a wayfarer's synagogue and chock-full of maritime tidbits given in thanks by homecoming mariners; in addition to the expected carved whale teeth and model schooners, there's a lifebelt from the *Titanic* among the motley collection. From here, it's just a few yards up to **Main Street**, many of whose original buildings were destroyed in the Great Fire of 1883, though it's rebuilt and thriving now. One that escaped the blaze is the 1829 **Mayhew Schoolhouse**, at no. 110, the town's first school (and now a private business); the **liberty pole** out front honors three young island girls who crept out of their homes and risked their lives one night in 1776 to blow up the town's captured liberty pole, rather than allow the British sea captain who had seized it to keep it. Close by, **William Street** also escaped the ravages of fire and is now a historical district brimming with elegant Greek Revival sea captains' houses from the prosperous whaling days. Just round the corner, at 51 Spring St, the 1844 Association Hall houses both the **Tisbury Town Hall** and the **Katharine Cornell Theatre**, the latter partly created with funds donated by the famous actress, a long-time summer resident, in her will. Miss Cornell is buried close by in the pine-shaded **Center Street Cemetery**, which dates back to 1817, with simple gray slate slabs marking the resting places of early nineteenth-century islanders.

Oak Bluffs

OAK BLUFFS, just across Lagoon Pond from Vineyard Haven, is the newest of the island's six towns, a quiet farming community until the Methodists established their campground, known as "Wesleyan Grove," here in the 1850s. This section of Oak Bluffs remains a relatively tranquil haven filled with the brightly colored "carpenter Gothic" or "gingerbread" cottages they built. Family-oriented events and Sunday morning services are still held in the iron and wood-constructed **tabernacle** during summer. At one end of the circle, the sweet 1867 **Cottage Museum** at 1 Trinity Park (mid-June to Sept Mon–Sat 10am–4pm; $1.50 donation) offers a charming collection of photographs, old Bibles, and other artifacts from the campground's history. In a frenzy of post-Civil War construction, speculators built up the area near the waterfront with dance halls, a skating rink, a railway linking "Cottage City" to Edgartown, and resort hotels, of which only the 1879 **Wesley Hotel**, on Lake Avenue, survives. Most of the current action focuses on **Circuit Avenue**, where the shops and bars attract a predominantly young crowd. The recently restored **Flying Horses Carousel**, at Circuit and Lake avenues (mid-April to mid-Oct daily 10am–10pm; $1 a ride), is reputedly the oldest operating carousel in the country; hand-carved in 1876, the 22 horses on parade here have bona fide horsehair manes.

Oak Bluffs also has a few beaches worth checking out, though the **town beach**, on Sea View Avenue, can get very noisy and crowded in season. Further south, the **Joseph A. Sylvia State Beach**, a sandy six-mile stretch of shore, is more appealing, and it parallels an undemanding pedestrian/cycle path that leads all the way to Edgartown, with pleasant views to accompany you.

Edgartown

Six miles southeast of Oak Bluffs, **EDGARTOWN**, originally known as Great Harbor, is the oldest and swankiest settlement on the island, and has been extravagantly dolled up for visitors, its elegant Colonial residences glistening

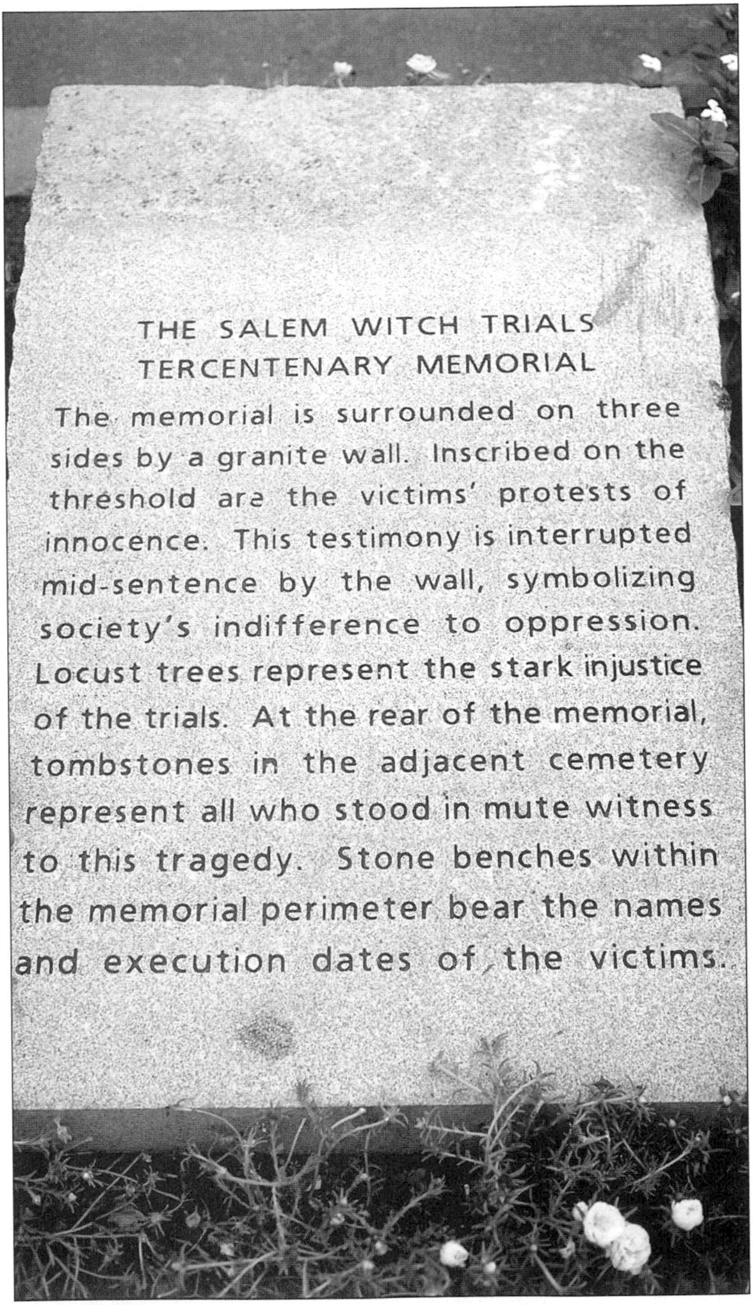

THE SALEM WITCH TRIALS
TERCENTENARY MEMORIAL

The memorial is surrounded on three sides by a granite wall. Inscribed on the threshold are the victims' protests of innocence. This testimony is interrupted mid-sentence by the wall, symbolizing society's indifference to oppression. Locust trees represent the stark injustice of the trials. At the rear of the memorial, tombstones in the adjacent cemetery represent all who stood in mute witness to this tragedy. Stone benches within the memorial perimeter bear the names and execution dates of the victims.

△ Witch Trials Memorial, Salem

white and surrounded by exquisitely maintained gardens and trimmed hedges. It doesn't end there, of course: downtown brims with upmarket boutiques, smart restaurants, and artsy galleries. You may recognize the place as the location for the *Jaws* films – rumor has it that filming for Steven Spielberg's blockbuster movie was delayed when the Californian-built monster shark began to disintegrate in the salty New England brine.

Once you've got your bearings at the seasonal **Edgartown Visitors' Center**, Church Street (late May to early Sept daily 9am–5pm), which has a full range of facilities, but no phone, it's a short walk to the **Vineyard Museum**, Cooke Street at School Street (mid-June to mid-October Tues–Sat 10am–5pm; rest of year Wed–Fri 1–4pm, Sat 10am–4pm; $7; Ⓦwww.marthasvineyardhistory.org), a complex of buildings maintained by the Martha's Vineyard Historical Society. One of them, the 1845 **Captain Frances Pease House** is full of whaling relics and native arrowheads and, best of all, an Oral History Center, which traces the history of the island through more than 250 recorded narratives of older locals; another, the pre-Revolution **Thomas Cooke House**, is decorated in the Colonial style befitting the means of the island's one-time Customs Officer; while the **Carriage Shed** serves as a hodgepodge storeroom for, among other things, a peddler's cart and a whaleboat.

A couple of blocks to the east, on Main Street, the massive **Old Whaling Church**, whose 92ft-high clock tower is visible for miles around, started life in 1843 as a Methodist church and is now used as a performing arts center, among other things. Its impressive six-column portico leads into a simple, elegant interior, where the original box pews are still in place. Just behind the church, the 1672 **Vincent House Museum** (May to mid-Oct daily 10.30am–3pm; $5, $8 combo admission includes tours of Fisher House and Whaling Church) is the oldest house on the island, and has the furniture to prove it. Also on Main Street, the Federal-style **Dr. Daniel Fisher House** was built in 1840 for the entrepreneurial Fisher (who, besides serving as a doctor, owned a whale-oil factory, and founded the Martha's Vineyard National Bank); exquisitely preserved features include an enclosed cupola, and roof and porch balustrades. A short walk along North Water Street leads past more charming sea captains' houses to the white cast-iron **Edgartown Lighthouse** – it's a replacement of the 1828 original, destroyed in the hurricane of 1938. There's a pleasant **public beach** here, though if you want to swim, you'll have to deal with an abundance of smelly seaweed.

Chappaquiddick

Though in truth inordinately peaceful, **Chappaquiddick Island** instantly conjures up the political strife of Senator Edward J. Kennedy, in whose car 28-year-old Mary Jo Kopechne drowned in the summer of 1969 at **Dike Bridge**, circumstances that conspiracy theorists still debate. The island is an easy five-minute jaunt from Edgartown via the *On Time* ferry (so called because it has no regular schedule and is thus always "on time"; $1, $2.50 with bicycle), which departs frequently from a ramp at the corner of Dock and Daggett streets, or by walking along the long sandy spit from South Beach in **Katama**. This latter entrance leads to the **Wasque Reservation**, largely a continuation of the beach on the Vineyard's "mainland." Indeed, most of Chappaquiddick's space is given over to beautiful beaches and wildlife reservations, such as the **Cape Pogue Wildlife Refuge**, on the island's eastern side, five hundred acres of dunes, salt marshes, ponds, scrubland, and barrier beach, and an important habitat and migration stopover for thousands of birds. Half the state's scallops

ings," like beer cans and condoms. Off South Road, a dirt track leads to **Lucy Vincent Beach**, named after the town's prim and proper librarian, who saw it as her mission to protect Chilmark residents from corruption by cutting out from her library books all pictures she deemed to be immoral. Rather ironically, the beach, which is open only to residents and their guests in the summer, today doubles as a **nudists'** spot. Off North Road, pick up a map at the trailhead of **Waskosim's Rock Reservation** for a fascinating three-mile hike through a variety of habitats including wetlands and black gum and oak woods. The rock itself was dumped here by retreating glaciers ten thousand years ago.

In the northern part of Chilmark, another tiny village, **Menemsha**, is a picturesque but hodgepodge collection of gray-shingled fishing shacks with a man-made harbor used for location shots in the making of *Jaws*. The harbor also serves as an important commercial and sports-fishing port, much of the catch ending up at restaurants all over the island. Stroll past the fish markets of **Dutcher's Dock** for a real sense of the island's maritime heritage, or bring an early-evening picnic to pebbly **Menemsha Beach** to enjoy the spectacular sunsets. The **Menemsha Hills Reservation**, just north of the beach, is also well worth a visit, its mile-long rocky shoreline and sand bluffs along Vineyard Sound peaking at **Prospect Hill**, the highest point on the Vineyard, with wonderful views of the Elizabeth Islands.

Gay Head (Aquinnah)

In 1997, the people of **GAY HEAD** voted to revert the town's name back to its original Wampanoag Indian name of **Aquinnah**, the culmination of a ten-year-plus court battle in which the Wampanoags won guardianship of 420 acres of land, to be held in perpetuity by the Federal Government and known as the **Gay Head Native American Reservation**. Gay Head is also the location of the estate of the late **Jacqueline Onassis**, though it's strictly private and hidden by trees.Most people come to this part of the island (its westernmost point), to see the multicolored clay **Gay Head Cliffs**, whose brilliant hues are the result of millions of years of geological work. When the oceans were high, and the Vineyard was underwater, small creatures died and left their shells behind to form the white layers. At other times, the area was a rainforest and vegetation compressed to form the darker colors. The weight of the glaciers thrust the many layers of stone up at an angle to create the cliffs, dubbed "Gay Head" by passing English sailors in the seventeenth century, on account of their bright colors. The clay was once the main source of paint for the island's houses, but now anyone removing any (unless you're a Wampanoag Indian) faces a substantial fine; in any case, the cliffs are eroding so fast that it's not safe to approach them too closely anyway. A short steep path lined with seafood shacks and craft stalls leads the way from the parking lot to the **overlook**, which affords stunning views to the Elizabeth Islands, and, on a clear day, as far as the entrance to Rhode Island's Narragansett Bay. The imposing red-brick **Gay Head Lighthouse** (mid-June to mid-Sept Fri, Sat & Sun evenings only; $3), built in 1854 to replace a wooden structure that dated from 1799, is well situated for sunset views, on the edge of the cliffs. Below the lighthouse, though not accessible from it, a **public beach** provides an equally impressive view of the cliffs from a different angle. To reach it, take the wooden boardwalk from the **Moshup Beach** parking lot to the shore, then walk round towards the lighthouse.

Martha's Vineyard eating and drinking

It's easy enough to find something to **eat** on Martha's Vineyard. The ports in particular have rows of places to tempt tourists who've just disembarked the ferries. With four of the island's six towns dry, only in Edgartown and Oak Bluffs can you order booze with meals, but you can bring your own bottle(s) elsewhere. Many pubs, too, serve inexpensive food, though the people partaking of it often look as if they've just stepped out of a Ralph Lauren catalog.

Vineyard Haven

The Black Dog Bakery Water Street ☎508/693-4786. You'll see these T-shirts all over the island and the mainland but it's best to skip the touristy and overrated *Black Dog Tavern* next door (☎508/693-9223), which serves full (and somewhat expensive) dinner, and stock up on delicious muffins or bagels here for the return ferry ride. Either way, both spots feel like pretty unavoidable places, especially located as they are right near the terminal.

Café Moxie 70 Main St ☎508/693-4480. A trendy neighborhood seafood and pasta joint with surprisingly fair prices.

Oak Bluffs

Giordano's 107 Circuit Ave ☎508/693-0184. Popular and reasonably priced Italian family restaurant. Their chicken cacciatore is particularly good.

Jimmy Seas Pan Pasta 32 Kennebec Ave ☎508/696-8550. Huge portions of tasty pasta in this small, casual eatery favored by locals. Not especially inexpensive, but on the whole worth the price, especially considering where you are.

Zapotec 10 Kennebec Ave ☎508/693-6800. Exciting seafood variations on Mexican cuisine, like swordfish fajitas, at slightly elevated prices.

Edgartown

Main Street Diner 65 Main St, Old Post Office Square ☎508/627-9337. Down-to-earth 1950s-style diner offering good-value traditional home cooking. Open for breakfast, lunch, and dinner.

The Newes from America 23 Kelley St ☎508/627-7000. Swill five hundred beers in this atmospheric pub (not necessarily all the same night) and they'll name a stool after you. Decent and filling pub food, on the relatively affordable side, to help prevent the alcohol from going to your head.

The Wharf Lower Main Street ☎508/627-9966. One of the better-priced seafood joints on the island, on the east side of town.

Elsewhere on the island

Homeport North Road, Menemsha ☎508/645-2679. Unpretentious place serving affordable lobster, swordfish, and steaks, with lovely views of Menemsha Creek.

Lambert's Cove Inn Lambert's Cove Road, West Tisbury ☎508/693-2298. The reasonably-priced restaurant at this hideaway inn – surrounded by forest and apple orchards – is a gem; try the delectable soups.

Nightlife and entertainment

Much of the Vineyard's evening entertainment comes in the form of private dinner parties, but that doesn't mean there's nothing to do if you're not invited to one. First-run **movies** can be seen at Capawok, an Art Deco theater on Main St, Vineyard Haven (☎508/696-9200), or in Edgartown at Entertainment Cinemas, 65 Main St (☎508/627-8008). Also in Edgartown, the **Old Whaling Church**, 85 Main St (☎508/627-4442), hosts regular arts performances, readings, lectures, and other intellectual pursuits. Weekend **cabaret** and **musical productions** are staged at the **Vineyard Playhouse**, 24 Church St, Vineyard Haven (☎508/696-6300, Ⓦwww.vineyardplayhouse.org), housed in a former Masonic lodge dating from 1833. In Chilmark, **The Yard**, off Middle Road near Beetlebung Corner in Chilmark (☎508/645-9662, Ⓦhome.tiac.net/~theyard), hosts **modern dance** performances by a resident choreographer troupe. Oak Bluffs has some of the most happening **nightlife** around, with a fun bar scene, regular live acts, and boisterous streetlife. Charges for venues listed below range from free to $15.

For current listings information, check the *Vineyard Gazette* (Ⓦwww.mvgazette.com) and the weekly *Martha's Vineyard Times* (Ⓦwww.mvtimes.com).

Oak Bluffs

Atlantic Connection 124 Circuit Ave ☎508/693-7129. A catch-all space that always has something going on, whether it be live music, comedy, or karaoke; everyone from button-down college-aged kids to stars like Spike Lee tend to descend on it

at least once during their stay.
Lola's *Island Inn*, Beach Road ⓣ508/693-5007, ⓦwww.lolasonline.com. Trendy 30-something disco with a Top-40 dance floor and nightly live acts during the summer; weekends only rest of the year.
Offshore Ale Company 30 Kennebec Ave ⓣ508/693-2626. Friendly local brewpub with wooden booths, toss-on-the-floor peanuts, and live shows almost nightly in season.
Ritz Café 1 Circuit Ave ⓣ508/693-9851. This cupboard-sized bar is anything but ritzy, but its pool tables and live music acts (nightly in summer; weekends only rest of the year) make a nice escape from the scene.

Elsewhere on the island

David Ryans 11 N Water St, Edgartown ⓣ508/627-4100. Loud two-story bar with a chichi martini lounge upstairs and raucous dancing to rock 'n' roll downstairs – usually on the tables.
Hot Tin Roof Airport, West Tisbury ⓣ508/693-1137, ⓦwww.mvhottinroof.com. The biggest nightclub and live music venue on the Vineyard, this Carly Simon – owned venture blends Top-40 and reggae hits on the dance floor with almost nightly live entertainment during the summer; several murals by local artist Margot Datz bring Vineyard vistas indoors.

Nantucket

The thirty-mile, two-hour sea crossing to **NANTUCKET** from Cape Cod may not be an oceangoing odyssey, but it does set the "Little Gray Lady" apart from her larger, shore-hugging sister, Martha. Just halfway out from Hyannis, neither mainland nor island is in sight, and you realize why the Native Americans dubbed it "distant land." Once you've landed, you can avert your eyes from the smart-money double-deck cruisers with names like *Pier Pressure* and *Loan Star* and let the place remind you that it hasn't always been a rich folks' playground. Indeed, despite the formidable prowess of its seamen, survival for settlers on the island's barren soil was always a struggle. The tiny, cobbled carriageways of **Nantucket Town** itself, once one of the largest cities in Massachusetts, were frozen in time by economic decline 150 years ago. Today, this area of delightful old restored houses is very much the center of activity, while, seven flat, easily cyclable miles to the east, the pretty, rose-covered cottages of **Siasconset** (always abbreviated to 'Sconset) give another glimpse of days gone by. But however appealing the island's man-made attractions are, it's Nantucket's gentle natural beauty that's the real draw, with heaths and moorlands, mile after mile of fabulous beaches, and a network of bicycle paths that connect the many spots maintained by conservation trusts.

Some history

European settlement on Nantucket dates from 1659, when **Thomas Mayhew**, who had originally purchased the island sight unseen, sold it on the cheap to a group of nine shareholders from Massachusetts who were anxious to escape the repressive policies of the Massachusetts Bay Colony. Those nine then sold half-shares to people whose skills they thought would be needed to expand the new settlement. Even this wasn't enough; the settlers, who landed at **Madaket**, were only able to survive their first winter thanks to assistance from the Wampanoag natives living on the island at the time. In time the number of settlers began to rival that of the natives, who were decimated by disease, and they maintained themselves by developing the business of **whaling**. Though they had learned to spear whales from the shore, where they basically waited at home for the whales to pass by, they began to sail the neighboring ocean to pursue their prey. It paid off in 1712, when one of the ships was blown far out to sea and managed to harpoon a sperm whale, whose highly sought-after oil would fetch very high prices. For the next 150 years,

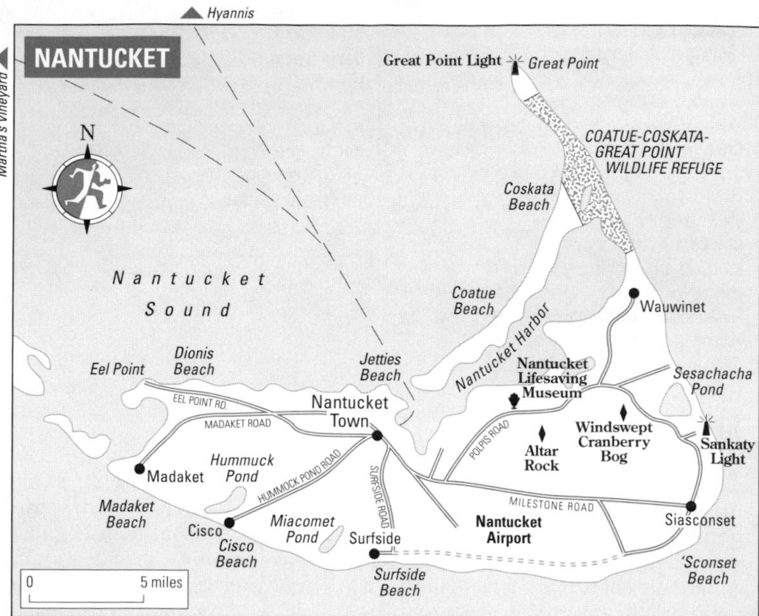

the trade flourished, as did the island; the population grew to more than 10,000, and Nantucket became synonymous with whaling – at its peak, the harbor was base to some one hundred whaling boats plying their trade. The beginning of the end came when larger ships were needed to cater for the longer (up to five-year) periods at sea. These ships were unable to cross the shallows, and much of Nantucket's whaling activity transferred to the deep-water harbors at New Bedford and Edgartown. Then, a major **fire** in 1846, which started in a hat shop on Main Street, spread to the harbor, where it set light to barrels of whale oil. The harbor was virtually destroyed, along with up to a third of Nantucket Town. The final blow was whale oil's replacement as the fuel of choice by the much cheaper kerosene. Nantucket declined for the next century, until a local entrepreneur revamped the waterfront in the 1950s; suddenly people began work to preserve the old buildings and salt-encrusted cottages that still stood. There's little doubt that visitors from all over have taken notice once again.

Arrival, information, and getting around

Most likely you'll arrive in Nantucket by **ferry**. Both the Steamship Authority (Ⓣ508/447-8600, Ⓦwww.islandferry.com) and Hy-Line (Ⓣ508/778-2600, Ⓦwww.hy-linecruises.com) run year-round passenger services to the island from Hyannis, but only the Steamship Authority's service takes cars. Both have fast ferries that charge from $24 to $33 each way for passengers; the Steamship Authority's car ferry ($165 per vehicle, mid-May to mid-Oct) allows passengers-only at $13. Passenger ferries from Harwich Port to Nantucket are run by Freedom Cruise Line (Ⓣ508/432-8999, Ⓦwww.nantucketislandferry.com), but only from June to October. Fares are around $29 each way. A much quicker way to get to the island is by **air**: Island Airlines (Ⓣ1-800/248-7779, Ⓦwww.nantucket.net/trans/islandair) and Cape Air (Ⓣ1-800/352-0714,

Ⓦwww.capeair.com) run year-round daily services from Hyannis to Nantucket; Cape Air also offers daily services to and from Boston, Providence, and Martha's Vineyard. The **airport** (Ⓣ508/325-5300, Ⓦwww.nantucketairport.com) is about three miles southeast of Nantucket Town.

Once you've arrived, **getting around** should pose no problem. From the moment you get off the ferry you're besieged by **bike** rental places and tour companies. Try Young's Bicycle Shop (Ⓣ508/228-1151, Ⓦwww.youngsbicycleshop.com), conveniently located on Steamboat Wharf; it should cost $25 per day for a standard mountain bike. Driving a **car** makes little sense, especially in peak season, when island arteries can easily get clogged, and it won't endear you to the locals. If you didn't bring one with you on the ferry, there is a limited on-island supply available from Windmill (Ⓣ508/228-1227 or 1-800/228-1227, Ⓦwww.nantucketautorental.com) and two airport Budget (Ⓣ508/228-5666, Ⓦwww.budget.com) and Hertz (Ⓣ508/228-9421, Ⓦwww.hertz.com) outlets; none will come cheap, mind you. A better way to get around is by **bus**: five shuttle routes round the island are operated between June and September by the Nantucket Regional Transit Authority (7.30am–11.30pm; Ⓣ508/228-7025), with fares starting at just 50¢ per journey for in-town travel; you can get unlimited travel for three days ($10), a week ($15), or a month ($30). There are also shuttle buses to the beaches from Nantucket Town with Barrett's Tours (Ⓣ508/228-0174 or 1-800/773-0174); the ninety-minute narrated bus rides cost $12. You probably won't need the aid of **taxis** while here, but they are usually available at the airport or by the ferry terminal; A-1 Taxi (Ⓣ508/228-3330) and All Points Taxi (Ⓣ508/228-5779) are both reliable.

Visitor information is available from the Nantucket **Chamber of Commerce**, 48 Main St (Mon–Fri 9am–5pm; Ⓣ508/228-1700, Ⓦwww.nantucketchamber.org), or from the helpful **Nantucket Information Bureau**, 25 Federal St (June to early Sept 9am–9pm; rest of year Mon–Sat 9am–6pm; Ⓣ508/228-0925, Ⓦwww.nantucket.net). The **Nantucket Historical Association**, 15 Broad St (Mon–Fri 9am–5pm; Ⓣ508/228-1894, Ⓦwww.nha.org), which maintains fourteen historical properties on the island, offers a

The whalers of Nantucket

The whalers of Nantucket commanded the attention of many with their whaling skill and resultant domination of such a treacherous trade. The early chronicler Crèvecoeur provided an extensive account of Nantucket as it was in 1782 in his *Letters from an American Farmer*. Although perturbed by the islanders' universal habit of taking a dose of opium every morning, he held them up as a model of diligence and good self-government. Whaling was a disciplined profession, unmarred by the stereotyped debauchery of sailors elsewhere, and to feed themselves and equip their ships the islanders kept up a shrewd and extensive trade with the mainland. At that time there were already more than a hundred ships. The whalemen were not paid; instead each had a share (a *lay*) of the final proceeds of the voyage. Crèvecoeur was impressed by the Nantucketers' ambition: "Would you believe that they have already gone to the Falkland Islands and I have heard several of them talk of going to the South Sea." They did indeed reach the Pacific, though Nantucket will always be the locale most closely associated with the whaling industry. Read about the whalers in Herman Melville's *Moby Dick*, a valediction of sorts; by the time it was published in 1851, Nantucket's fortunes had gone into an abrupt decline. As a magazine article of 1873 reported, "Let no traveler visit Nantucket with the expectation of witnessing the marks of a flourishing trade . . . of the great fleet of ships which dotted every sea, scarcely a vestige remains."

worthwhile $15 **combination ticket** for entrance to all its buildings (which cost $5 individually). The sights are generally open daily from late May to mid-October, 10am until 5pm; from mid-October to early November, daily from 11am to 4pm; and closed the rest of the year.

Accommodation

There's a wide range of accommodation in Nantucket Town, from resorts with pools, health clubs, and sophisticated restaurants to cozy inns and B&Bs; further afield, you can rent private homes by the week. Be sure to book well in advance, especially for stays during the hectic summer season, when the island fills up. For hassle-free booking contact **Martha's Vineyard and Nantucket Reservations**, Box 1322, Lagoon Pond Road, Vineyard Haven, MA 02568 (ⓣ508/693-7200 or 1-800/649-5671). If you're stuck at the last minute with nowhere to stay, try the **Nantucket Visitors Service and Information Bureau**, 25 Federal St, Nantucket Town (ⓣ508/228-0925), which maintains a list of vacancies during the season. All of the places listed below are in **Nantucket Town**, unless otherwise indicated in the address.

Anchor Inn 66 Center St ⓣ508/228-0072, ⓦwww.anchor-inn.net. Rooms with period-style furnishings and queen-sized canopy beds in the heart of the historic residential district. ❼

Century House 10 Cliff Rd ⓣ508/228-0530, ⓦwww.centuryhouse.com. Elegant rooms with private baths and country-house ambience in this 1833 late-Federal home. ❻

Cliff Lodge 9 Cliff Rd ⓣ508/228-9480, ⓦwww.clifflodgenantucket.com. Quiet B&B in a residential area with some low-priced singles in the off season. ❼

Hawthorn House 2 Chestnut St ⓣ508/228-1468, ⓦwww.hawthornhouse.com. Central, well-appointed guesthouse with handsome rooms outfitted with tapestries, quilts, and antique furnishings. ❼

HI-Nantucket Surfside Beach ⓣ508/228-0433, ⓦwww.usahostels.org. Dorm beds at Surfside Beach, just over three miles south of Nantucket Town. $19 members, $22 nonmembers. Lockout 10am–5pm, curfew 11pm. April–mid Oct only.

Jared Coffin House 29 Broad St ⓣ508/228-2400 or 1-800/248-2405, ⓦwww.jaredcoffinhouse.com. Sixty rooms, all with period furniture in four adjacent buildings in the town center. Superb restaurant and pleasant bar. ❻

Martin House Inn 61 Center St ⓣ508/228-0678. Thirteen lovely rooms offer good value in this 1803 seaman's house. ❺

The Nesbitt Inn 21 Broad St ⓣ508/228-0156. The central location and affordable rooms, most with original furniture, compensate for the shared baths in this Victorian inn, built in 1872. ❹

Ship's Inn 13 Fair St ⓣ508/228-0040 or 1-800/564-2760, ⓦwww.theshipsinn.com. Three-story whaling captain's home with ten biggish rooms, all with private bath. ❹

The Wauwinet Wauwinet Road, Wauwinet ⓣ508/228-0145 or 1-800/426-8718, ⓦwww.wauwinet.com. For many, *the* place to stay on the island, and out a bit from the main town. Luxury historic resort hotel restored in 1986, offering full range of leisure facilities, beautifully appointed rooms, excellent dining, and great views. ❾

Nantucket Town

Very much the center of activity on the island, the cobbled walkways of **NANTUCKET TOWN** boast a delightful array of eighteenth- and nineteenth-century homes, most of them concentrated around **Main Street**. Before you hit there, though, you can get the salty feel of the half-dozen **wharves** around Nantucket's harbor when arriving on the ferry, which docks at **Steamboat Wharf**. A number of private summer homes are perched on Old North Wharf just south of that, while lively **Straight Wharf**, which dates to 1723, contains souvenir shops, restaurants, and the restored red-brick building of the **Museum of Nantucket History** (hours vary; free; ⓣ508/228-3899), originally a warehouse for whaling supplies. Exhibits include early firefighting apparatus, old photographs, and a diorama depicting the waterfront's busy goings-on before the fire. Straight Wharf leads directly onto Main Street, where, at its junction with South Water Street, the **Pacific Club**, a three-story Georgian edifice built as a country house for William Rotch, owner of two of the three ships involved in the Boston Tea Party, once served as a US customs house, but has been used since 1861 as an elite private club (meaning you can't go in) for retired whaling captains. A short walk north along Federal Street leads to the **Athenaeum**, 1 Lower India St (hours vary; ⓣ508/228-1110), the town library and repository for various antiques, scrimshaw, and old island newspapers.

Continue up Federal Street to Broad Street, where the **Nantucket Whaling Museum** (late May to mid-Oct Mon–Sat 10am–5pm, Sun noon–5pm; $10) is housed in an old candlemaking factory built just before the big fire. Among its intriguing collection of exhibits, look out especially for such scrimshaw artifacts as a set of 21 whale types carved from whales' teeth, the astonishing harpoon corkscrewed in the "flurry" or last struggle of a dying whale, and the original 16ft-high prism from the Sankaty Lighthouse. Just steps away, the **Peter Foulger Museum**, 15 Broad St (daily: late May to mid-Oct 10am–5pm; mid-Oct to early Nov 11am–4pm; closed rest of year; $5), dedicated to one of the island's first settlers, displays an extensive collection of portraits, textiles, and furniture, plus the fascinating "Away from the Shore" exhibit, which traces the island's geological origins. More history can be found in the Nantucket Historical Association's Research Center, in the same building, though the ships' logs and genealogical records there are only available for those doing research.

Back on Main Street, at nos. 75 and 78, the **Henry Coffin House** and the **Charles Coffin House** belonged to two brothers who inherited a fortune from their father's candlemaking business. Their houses were built opposite each other, employing the same carpenters and masons, but in completely different styles: Charles's house a simple yet dignified Greek Revival, Henry's a late Federal-style home with ornate marble tower and cupola. Though you can't visit their interiors, you can stop by another grand house nearby, the Greek Revival **Hadwen House**, 96 Main St (daily: late May to mid-Oct 10am–5pm; mid-Oct to early Nov 11am–4pm; closed the rest of the year; $5; ⓣ508/228-1894, ⓦwww.nha.org), which contains gas chandeliers, a circular staircase, and silver doorknobs, with a lovely period garden out back.

Built in 1834, the **First Congregational Church**, 62 Center St (mid-June to Sept Mon–Sat 10am–4pm; $1.50 donation to climb tower), is famous for its 120ft steeple, from which you can get a spectacular bird's-eye view of the island. The inside is worth a peek, too, for its restored *trompe l'oeil* ceiling, 600-pound brass chandelier, and rows of old box pews. Follow Center Street and West Chester Street past Lily Pond Park to the aptly named **Oldest House** (the Jethro Coffin House), on Sunset Hill Road (daily: late May to mid-Oct 10am–5pm; mid-Oct to early Nov 11am–4pm; closed the rest of the year; $5; ⓣ508/228-1894, ⓦwww.nha.org), though there's not much to see other than the central brick chimney; the house is sparsely decorated, with an antique loom serving as the most prominent feature inside.

Polpis Road

Polpis Road, an indirect and arcing track from Nantucket Town to 'Sconset, holds a number of natural attractions both on and off its main course, though your first stop off should be the less wild **Nantucket Life Saving Museum**, off the northern side of the road at no. 158 (mid-June to mid-Oct daily 9.30am–4pm; $5; ⓦwww.nantucketlifesavingmuseum.com), filled with two lifesaving surfboats, buoys, rescue equipment, photographs, artifacts from the *Andrea Doria*, which sunk off Nantucket forty years ago, and a horse-drawn

Nantucket beaches

With fifty miles of beaches, most of which are open to the public, Nantucket is more accessible than Martha's Vineyard for water enthusiasts. The island's southern and eastern flanks, where the water tends to have rougher surf, is ideal for surfers, while the more sheltered northern beaches are good for swimming. With extremely limited, albeit free, parking, it makes sense to walk or cycle to all but the most far-flung of the strands. You can rent **watersports equipment** (kayaks, windsurfers, and the like) from Nantucket Community Sailing, on Jetties Beach (ⓣ508/228-5358, ⓦwww.nantucketsailing.com; $15–30).

Nantucket Town

Brant Point off Easton Street. Strong currents at the harbor entrance mean this beach is better equipped for tanning and watching the comings and goings of boats in the harbor.

Children's Beach off South Beach Street. Just minutes from Steamboat Wharf, this calm harbor beach is perfect for children, and has a full range of facilities.

Dionis Beach Eel Point Road. A quiet beach with high dunes and calm waters.

Jetties Beach off Bathing Beach Road. Catch the shuttle bus or leg it to this popular beach whose facilities include lifeguards, changing rooms, and a snack bar.

East of Town

'Sconset Beach (known also as Codfish Park). Sandy beach with moderate surf and a full range of facilities. Just a short walk to several eating places.

South Shore

Cisco Beach Hummock Point Road. Long, sandy beach with lifeguards and restrooms; again, ideal for surfing.

Madaket Beach at the end of the Madaket Bike Path. Another long beach with strong surf and gorgeous sunsets. Portable restrooms (not for the squeamish), lifeguards, and shuttle bus.

Surfside Beach off Surfside Road. Wide sands attract a youthful crowd of surfers; there's a large parking lot, but you'd do better to take the shuttle bus from town.

carriage from the Henry Ford Museum. Further on, an unmarked track leads south to **Altar Rock**, where you'll want to walk around for views of the surrounding bogs. One of these, the 200-acre **Windswept Cranberry Bog**, east on Polpis Road, is a feast of color at most times of the year, especially so in mid-October, when the ripened berries, loosened from the plants by machines, float to the top of the water.

Siasconset, Great Point, and Coatue

Seven flat miles east of Nantucket Town, the village of **SIASCONSET**, or 'Sconset as it's known, is filled with venerable cottages literally encrusted with salt and covered over with roses. Once solely a fishing village, it began to attract visitors eager to get away from the foul smells of Nantucket Town's whale-oil refineries, and in the late 1800s, enough writers and actors came from big cities to give 'Sconset some modicum of artistic renown.

There's not too much to see, other than the houses themselves along Broadway and Center streets – certainly picturesque enough – and the year-round population of 150 only supports a few commercial establishments, all close to one another in the center of town. A few miles north, the red-and-white striped **Sankaty Light**, an 1849 lighthouse, stands on a 90ft bluff,

△ Lighthouse, Nantucket

though it seems only a matter of time until it falls victim to the crashing waves below. North of here, and also accessible heading east on Polpis Road from Nantucket Town, **Wauwinet** is largely notable for holding the inn of choice on the island, simply titled *The Wauwinet* (see p.240 for review and opposite for details on its restaurant, *Toppers*).

Further north still, **Coatue-Coskata-Great Point**, a five-mile-long, razor-thin slice of sand, takes in three separate wildlife refuges, and is accessible only by four-wheel-drive (for which you'll need a special $20 permit; call ⓣ508/228-0006) or on foot. If you don't feel like walking (the sand is very soft and taxing on the feet), you could take one of the tours offered by Ara's Tours, 25 Federal St (90min; $12; ⓣ508/221-6852, ⓦwww.arastours.com). In the Coskata section, the somewhat wider beaches are backed by salt marshes, and some trees: with binoculars, you may catch sight of plovers, egrets, oyster-catchers, terns, and even osprey. The beach narrows again as you approach the 70ft **Great Point Light**, at the end of the spit, put up in 1986 after an earlier light was destroyed during a 1984 storm; the new one is said to be able to with-stand 240mph winds and 20ft waves. Unsurprisingly, this is not the safest place to swim, even on a calm day. Coatue, the last leg of the journey, is the narrow stretch that separates Nantucket harbor from the ocean; so narrow, in fact, that stormy seas frequently crash over it, turning Great Point into an island.

Madaket and the South Shore

At the western tip of Nantucket, rural **MADAKET** is the small settlement located on the spot where Thomas Macy landed in 1659. There's little in the way of visitor attractions, but the area's peacefulness and natural beauty makes up for that. Unspoiled **Eel Point**, a couple of miles north, sits on a spit of sand covered with all manner of wild plants and flowers, including wild roses and bayberries, which attract an array of birds, including the graceful egrets which can be seen in late spring and summer stalking the shallow offshore sandbars. **Maps** and **self-guided tours** are available for $4 from the Nantucket Conservation Foundation, 118 Cliff Rd (ⓣ508/228-2884, ⓦwww.nantucketconservation.com), and for $4.50 from the Maria Mitchell Association, 2 Vestal St (ⓣ508/228-9198, ⓦwww.mmo.org). East of Madaket, and only about three miles from Nantucket Town, **Cisco**'s windswept beach faces water popular with surfers, and erosion due to windy blasts here has resulted in several houses being lost. Two miles east of Cisco, freshwater **Miacomet Pond**, surrounded by reeds and grasses, and a favorite haunt of swans and ducks, is a prime spot for a picnic.

Nantucket eating and drinking

The early chronicler Crèvecoeur, in an extensive account on Nantucket published in 1782, stated that on Nantucket "music, singing and dancing are holden in equal detestation." Thankfully, **eating** is not: the island abounds in first-rate restaurants, most of them located in Nantucket Town and specializing in seafood. Be prepared, however, for the shock of the bill: it's often Manhattan prices, and then some. As far as **drinking** goes, many of the restaurants have bars attached to them, though there are also a few pubby places to get boozed up. All of the establishments below, unless otherwise indicated, are in **Nantucket Town**.

Cafés and bakeries

Espresso Cafe 40 Main St ⓣ508/228-6930. Inexpensive, mostly healthy sandwich and salad lunches, including some vegetarian dishes, and the finest coffee on the island.

Nantucket Bake Shop 79 Orange St

ⓣ508/228-2797. Terrific bakery and coffee shop with a delectable array of warm scones, gruyere cheese puffs, and Portuguese bread.

Restaurants

Arno's 41 Main St ⓣ508/228-7001. Good-value breakfasts, lunches, and dinners in this atmospheric and kid-friendly eatery with nightly steak and pasta specials.

Bluefin 15 S Beach St ⓣ508/228-2033. Japanese-influenced restaurant with innovative dishes like sake-marinated halibut and shrimp tempura martini, as well as sushi and steak, served in a casual space.

Boarding House 12 Federal St ⓣ508/228-9622. Romantic downstairs dining room with contemporary pan-Asian and Mediterranean cuisine; lively bar upstairs with lighter (and cheaper) bistro fare. Definitely order the double lobster soup with fresh corn and truffle mousseline.

Brandt Point Grill at the *White Elephant Hotel*, Easton Street ⓣ508/228-2500 or 1-800/475-2637. Enjoy spectacular harbor views while dining on local Nantucket specialties with a Tuscan influence – like Tuscan Oricchioni with crab, artichokes, olive oil, and lemon thyme.

Centre Street Bistro 29 Centre St ⓣ508/228-8470. Intimate (seven tables) café specializing in light seafood fare – the seared salmon with lemon aioli is gorgeously fresh – with wonderful homemade desserts to top it off. Serves a mean weekend brunch, too.

Cioppino's 20 Broad St ⓣ508/228-4622. Stylish Mediterranean and New American cuisine in the center of town. Try their grilled lobster tails and fresh shrimp on a bed of pesto pasta.

Nantucket Lobster Trap 23 Washington St ⓣ508/228-404. Dinner-only establishment specializing, as its name indicates, in lobster.

Nantucket Tapas 5 S Beach St ⓣ508/228-2033. Globally inclined menu takes the Spanish idea of tapas, throws in things like "spicy fried Thai calamari" and "Sechwan (*sic*) style grilled filet of beef," and takes advantage of the location to throw in a very fresh sushi bar.

Pearl 12 Federal St ⓣ508/228-9701. Very chic restaurant upstairs from the *Boarding House* (see above), with a stand-out menu featuring the likes of oyster shooters, scallop ceviche, and tempura of Maryland soft-shell crabs with lemongrass risotto.

Rose & Crown 23 S Water St ⓣ508/228-2595. Traditional pub-style saloon that offers sand wiches, chicken wings, and the like. Music and comedy in the evenings.

SeaGrille 45 Sparks Ave ⓣ508/325-5700. One of the best places for seafood, whether grilled, blackened, steamed, or fried, and not badly priced at that; award-winning wine list too.

Ships Inn 13 Fair St ⓣ508/228-0040. Choose from California-French style dishes, such as pan-roasted striped bass, served in a bright and airy space.

Topper's 120 Wauwinet Rd, Wauwinet ⓣ508/228-8768. Pricey but outstanding New American cuisine in this quiet, upscale restaurant at the *Wauwinet* hotel and resort a few miles outside Nantucket Town.

Vincent's 21 S Water St ⓣ508/228-0189. Moderately priced Italian dishes in a casual, relaxed atmosphere.

Nightlife and entertainment

There are two **movie theaters** on Nantucket; the Dreamland Theater, 19 S Water St (ⓣ508/228-5356), which shows first-run movies from June to September, and the Gaslight Theater, 1 N Union St (ⓣ508/228-4435), for more arty flicks year-round. Also in Nantucket Town, the Theater Workshop of Nantucket puts on **plays** and musicals at Bennett Hall, next to the First Congressional Church, at 62 Centre St (ⓣ508/228-4305, ⓦwww.theatreworkshop.com), while Actors Theater of Nantucket (ⓣ508/228-6325, ⓦwww.nantuckettheatre.com) produces Broadway-type plays, comedy nights, and children's matinees at the Methodist Church, 2 Centre St. Additionally, the Nantucket Musical Arts Society stages **classical concerts** with renowned musicians through July and August, in the First Congregational Church, 62 Centre St (ⓣ508/228-1287).

In terms of tried-and-true **nightlife**, Nantucket is quieter than the Vineyard, but Nantucket Town still has some good options to keep you out 'til after midnight (though not much later). There's certainly no shortage of live music, especially jazz and folk, to help you kick up your heels, but if you're after a big city nightclub, you won't find it here. Current **listings** can be found in the weekly *Yesterday's Island* (Ⓦ www.yesterdaysisland.com), and the daily *Inquirer and Mirror* (Ⓦ www.ack.net).

Brotherhood of Thieves 23 Broad St (no phone). This basement bar is a Nantucket institution and the place to go for live folk music, year-round.

Club Car 1 Main St Ⓣ 508/228-1101. Piano bar doubling as a big singles scene.

The Muse 44 Surfside Rd Ⓣ 508/228-6873. A mix of rock, reggae, and just about anything else you can dance to, as well as a few pool tables, keep this venue popular.

Tap Room 29 Broad St Ⓣ 508/228-2400. This rollicking pub has live jazz Wednesday through Saturday in the basement of the Jared Coffin House – but only during the season.

Central and Western Massachusetts

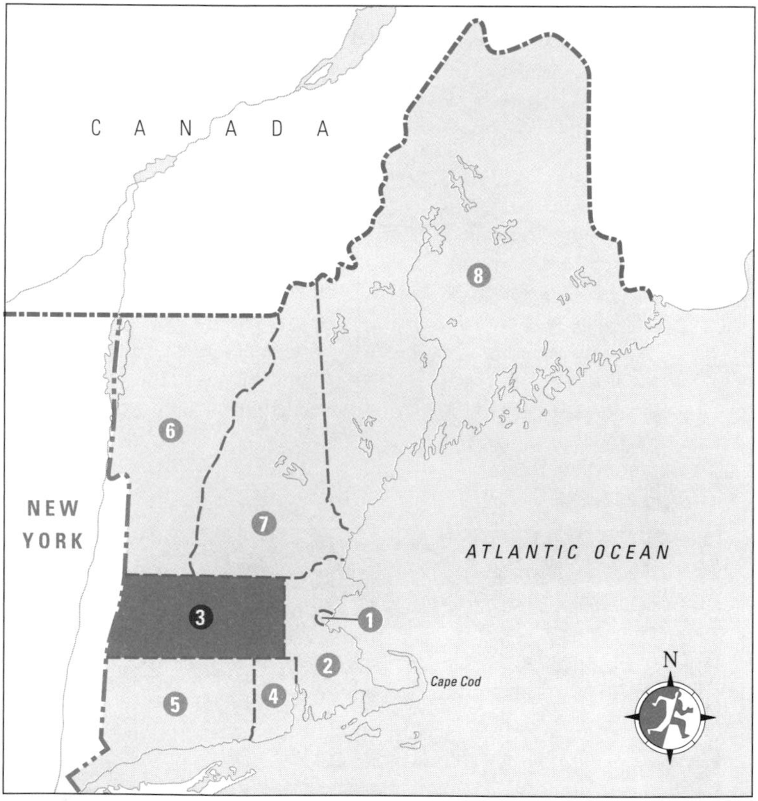

CANADA
NEW YORK
ATLANTIC OCEAN
Cape Cod
N
1 2 3 4 5 6 7 8

CHAPTER 3

Highlights

* **Worcester Art Museum** One of the largest art collections in New England, featuring an impressive photography collection and dazzling mosaics from Antioch. See p.250

* **Basketball Hall of Fame** A real treat for hoops fans, the recently renovated Hall resides in Springfield, the birthplace of the sport. See p.254

* **Five College Consortium** The college towns of Northampton, Amherst, and South Hadley are less crowded – and less precious – than the Berkshires, but still offer plenty in the way of arts, culture, and entertainment. See pp.257–264

* **Berkshires festivals** The Berkshires in summer is a one-stop-shop for music, dance, and drama junkies, with many performances taking place at open-air venues in the countryside for which the area is renowned. See p.272

* **Naumkeag** Best of the Newport-style summer "cottages" to be found in the Berkshires. See p.275

* **North Adams** A fine contemporary art museum is the centerpiece of a town that has transformed from a post-industrial eyesore to the hippest place in the Berkshires. See p.285

3

Central and Western Massachusetts

Moving west from the coast, Massachusetts' well-preserved and cultivated charm quickly dissolves amid the strip malls, franchises, and faded storefronts of the area loosely known as Central Massachusetts. Comprised mostly of semi-industrial towns still struggling to redefine their identities in the shadow of labor migrations, recessions, and Boston's thriving tourist industry, this area is not going to be the focal point of your itinerary, and it will likely not detain you for too long. But it does have one or two things worth checking out. Worcester, the first town you reach traveling west from Boston, has one of the state's best collections of art, and Springfield, a bit further west, is home to the Basketball Hall of Fame, and where the game was invented. Springfield is also the most sensible jumping-off point for the **Pioneer Valley**, which stretches north from here, where small-town charisma and New England gentility begin to reassert themselves. Home to four separate colleges and a major university, the "Valley" supports a year-round population of down-to-earth academics, artists, and community activists who, in turn, patronize a bevy of restaurants, cafés, and bookstores – giving the area a continuous, if low-key, buzz. You can base yourself in any one of three or four locations to explore this region, but **Northampton** is probably the liveliest, with a good range of places to stay and most of the area's nightlife.

From the Pioneer Valley, most roads lead west to the **Berkshires** – as the smattering of tiny towns nestled in among the Berkshire Mountains, dividing Massachusetts from New York State, are collectively known. This area holds some of the Northeast's most desirable vacation spots for local city-dwellers, and is the adopted summer stage of many Boston and New York dance companies, orchestras, and theater troupes. With its spas, pricey inns, and sophisticated cultural happenings, it's a lovely spot – if you can afford it. And even if you can't, the region's simpler pleasures – such as camping, hiking, and biking – are all available in abundance. You can either base yourself in the slightly precious small towns of **Lenox** or **Stockbridge** in the southern Berkshires, or **Williamstown** in the north, which has a good selection of museums and galleries to explore. There's also the outstanding Massachusetts Museum of Contemporary Art (MASS MoCA) in nearby **North Adams**. Williamstown and North Adams are the first two towns of any note along the 63-mile **Mohawk Trail**, which stretches from the Massachusetts–New York border to the town of Millers Falls on the Connecticut River, and offers perhaps the best scenic driving opportunities in this part of the state.

Central Massachusetts

Central Massachusetts is hardly the highlight of the state, and many will experience it from a car or bus window as they travel to the Berkshires or Pioneer Valley. This said, the towns of Central Massachusetts are close enough to Boston to be visited in a day-trip, and the region does have one or two spots worth exploring, most notably Worcester's Art Museum and Springfield's Basketball Hall of Fame.

Worcester

Forty miles west of Boston on I-90, **WORCESTER** is Massachusetts' second largest city (the third largest in New England behind Providence, Rhode Island), and the only major industrial city in the US beside neither sea, lake, nor river. Incorporated in 1722, Worcester enjoyed a century and a half of unbridled prosperity and was a thriving multi-ethnic town of Greek, Yiddish, and Italian bakeries, textile mills, and close-knit immigrant communities before lapsing into recession during the Seventies and Eighties. Famous as the birthplace of such American icons as the Valentine's Day card (the card's creator made and marketed them here), the yellow Smiley Face which became synonymous with the phrase "Have a nice day," the birth control pill, and Abbie Hoffman – the spiritual father of the rabble-rousing Yippies of the Sixties – it's only now beginning to pick itself up – which means that for the moment its downtown area doesn't have much to lure you beyond an excellent museum, good shopping opportunities, and a reasonable selection of restaurants.

The Town

Worcester's solution to its defunct business district has been to park the enormous **Worcester Common Fashion Outlet Mall**, just off I-290 (exit 14 or 16), smack in the center of town. With almost a hundred designer and designer-like stores under one roof, the outlet mall has brought a bit of vitality and a much-needed influx of cash back into the city.

What charm Worcester does possess rests not on its attempts at rejuvenation, but in its preservation of the past. The **Worcester Art Museum**, 55 Salisbury St (Wed, Fri & Sun 11am–5pm, Thurs 11am–8pm, Sat 10am–5pm; $8; free Sat 10am–noon; ⓣ 508/799-4406, ⓦ www.worcesterart.org), located in a leafy part of town dominated by brick terraces about two miles north of downtown, is the city's major attraction – and is an absolute gem. Its vast holdings include a Romanesque chapter house from the twelfth century, shipped from Europe and reassembled in Worcester, a permanent gallery of American portrait miniatures, and an impressive collection of mosaics from Antioch. In addition, there are lesser-known paintings by Braque, Cezanne, Gainsborough, Gauguin, Goya, Kandinsky, Matisse, Turner, and Renoir, and the museum is blessed with an expansive photography collection, with works from the Civil War to the present day, including recognizable images from Cartier-Bresson, Stieglitz, and Weston. The museum also stages frequent exhibitions that draw from its holdings of over two thousand prints.

Just outside the downtown area is the **American Antiquarian Society**, 185 Salisbury St (Mon–Fri 9am–5pm, tours Wed 2pm; free; ⓣ508/755-5221, ⓦwww.americanantiquarian.org), which holds copies of two-thirds of all the material published in America before 1821, more even than the Library of Congress in Washington DC. Among the highlights are impressions of nearly all the prints of Paul Revere and an excellent collection of the works and private papers of James Fenimore Cooper. Further down the road, off of Rte-122A, the remarkable castle-like **Higgins Armory Museum**, 100 Barber Ave (Tues–Sat 10am–4pm, Sun noon–4pm; $6.75; ⓣ508/853-6015, ⓦwww.higgins.org), is also worth a visit, representing years of careful collecting in post-World War I Europe by John Woodman Higgins, the founder of the Worcester Pressed Steel Company. It's chock-full of armor, swords, knives, chain mail, and helmets from ancient Greece and Rome, medieval and Renaissance Europe, and feudal Japan.

Practicalities

There are two **train stations**, Amtrak and MBTA; if you're coming from Boston, the latter is less than a third of the Amtrak fare, but either way, you'll have to navigate across four lanes of traffic, with nary a crossing signal or sidewalk in sight to get into town. It's not deadly, just annoying. The Peter Pan Trailways Terminal, 75 Madison St (ⓣ508/753-1515), is a short walk from downtown, and is served by regular **buses** to Boston and Springfield, from where there are connections to the Pioneer Valley. The well-equipped **Central Massachusetts Convention and Visitors Bureau**, downtown at 30 Worcester Center Blvd (Mon–Fri 8.30am–5pm; ⓣ508/755-7400 or 1-800/231-7557, ⓦwww.worcester.org), has information on Worcester and the rest of Central Massachusetts. A comprehensive **local bus** service is provided by the RTA (ⓣ508/791-9782).

Worcester works best as a day-trip from Boston or Northampton. However, if you need a **place to stay**, you'll find plenty of reliable hotel chains in and around the city. The *Crowne Plaza*, 10 Lincoln Square (ⓣ508/791-1600; ❻), *Regency Suites*, 70 Southbridge St (ⓣ508/753-3512, ❺), and the *Hampton Inn*, 110 Summer St (ⓣ508/757-0400 or 1-800/426-7866; ❺), are all centrally located hotels with comfortable rooms. Another good choice, albeit about three miles north of the center, is the *Holiday Inn*, 500 Lincoln St (ⓣ508/852-4000 or 1-800/782-7306, ⓦwww.holiday-inn.com/worcesterma; ❻).

For **food**, the *Sole Proprietor*, 118 Highland St (ⓣ508/798-3474), is a reliable seafood restaurant, not especially cheap but well worth the price. The *Living Earth Garden Café*, 232 Chandler St, at Park Avenue (ⓣ508/753-1896), is a friendly health-food store with an attached café where you can munch on bison and ostrich burgers – a welcome oasis in an otherwise impersonal area of gas stations and convenience stores. For good Italian, head to *Anthony's*, 172 Shrewsbury St (ⓣ508/757-6864), where the appetizer of choice is the "172 ravioli," a single gargantuan pasta shell enfolding a center of artichoke and roasted garlic. One of the more atmospheric places to eat a steak or some seafood is *Maxwell Silverman's Toolhouse*, just off Worcester Center Boulevard at

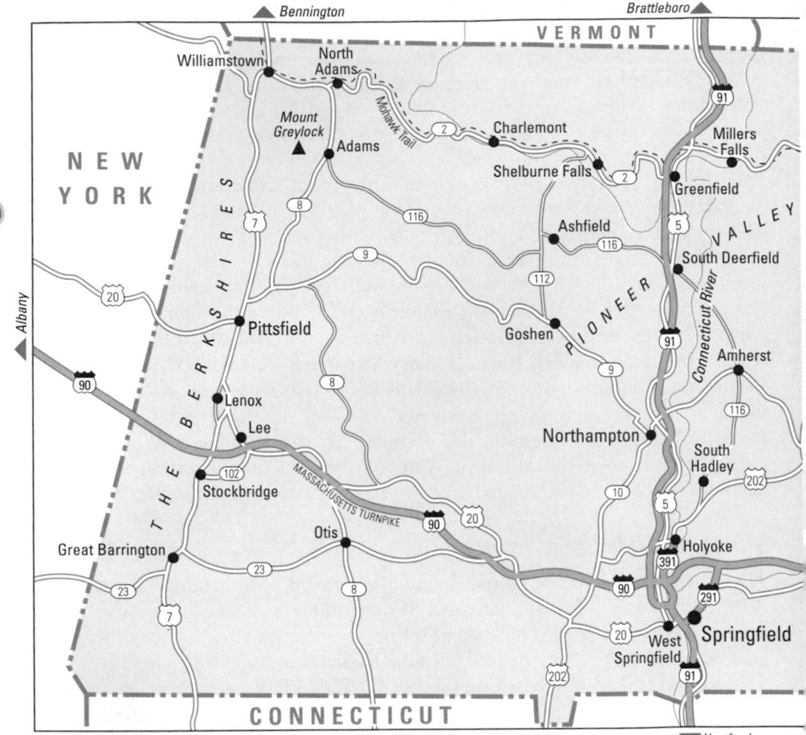

25 Union St (☎508/755-1200), which has a cavernous dining room in a restored old factory building. *El-Basha*, 424 Belmont St (☎508/797-0884), is a popular Lebanese spot near the UMass Medical Center, where nothing on the menu will set you back more than around $10. About twenty miles west of Worcester, but worth the detour, is the *Salem Cross Inn*, on Rte-9 in West Brookfield (☎508/867-2345), a rambling restaurant in a restored 1705 farmhouse which serves consistently high-quality Yankee cooking.

On from Worcester: Sturbridge

Around fifteen miles southwest of Worcester, on US-20 near the junction of I-90 and I-84, the small town of **STURBRIDGE** holds but one spot of interest, the restored and reconstructed **Old Sturbridge Village** (daily: winter 9.30am–4pm; rest of year 9am–5pm; $20; ☎508/347-3362 or 1-800/SEE-1830, Ⓦwww.osv.org), a little way west of the town center, made up of preserved buildings brought from all over the region to present a somewhat idealized but engaging portrait of a small New England town of the 1830s. It's the usual heritage hokum, with lots of costumed interpreters acting out roles – working in blacksmiths' shops, planting and harvesting vegetables, tending cows, and the like – but they pull it off with some style. And the 200-acre site, with mature trees, ponds, and dirt footpaths, is very pretty, making for a pleasant place to while away half a day or so. There is an **information center**

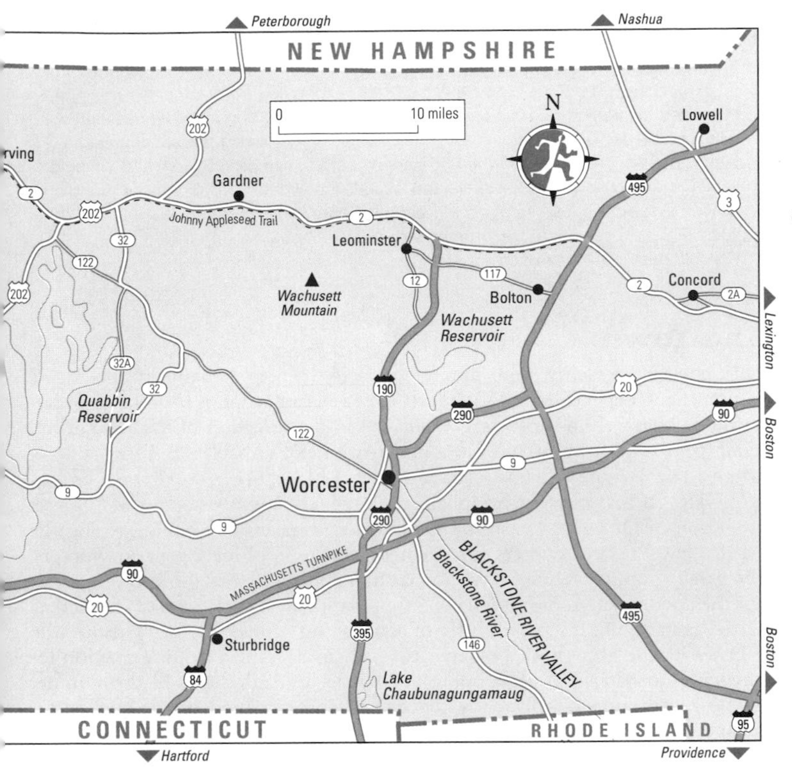

just opposite the entrance to Old Sturbridge Village at 380 Main St (ⓣ508/347-7594 or 1-800/628-8379, ⓦwww.sturbridge.org), should you need brochures and more detailed information. The nearby *Old Sturbridge Village Lodges*, 371 Main St (ⓣ508/347-3327; ❺–❻), owned by the Old Sturbridge Village, is a reasonable **place to stay**; the *American Motor Lodge*, 350 Main St (ⓣ508/347-9121 or 1-800/528-1234; ❹), costs a bit less and has an indoor heated swimming pool and sauna as well as a playground and game room for the kids.

Springfield

SPRINGFIELD, situated at the point where I-90 crosses I-91, ninety miles from Boston at the southern end of the Pioneer Valley (see p.257), sprang up along the banks of the Connecticut River, and was once the industrial hub of Central Massachusetts. America's first frozen foods were made in Springfield; it was the home of the Springfield rifle, and the late children's author **Dr Seuss**, née Theodore Geisel. But, like so many places in this part of the state, the city was hit by recession and became rapidly depopulated. Today, blessed with a central location and the optimistic nickname "The Comeback City of America," it's slowly restoring its fortunes. Most importantly, Springfield is the town where the sport of **basketball** was invented, and therein lies the main reason for any visit.

The Nashoba Valley Winery

The Nashoba Valley Winery, on Wattaquadoc Hill Road (daily 11am–5pm with tours weekends 11.30am–4pm; $3; ⓣ978/779-5521, ⓦwww.nashobawinery.com), is located on a pastoral hillside in the town of **BOLTON**, approximately seventeen miles northeast of Worcester. Activities range from picking seasonal peaches, plums, apples, and berries in their 55-acre orchard to sampling their award-winning wines and microbrews. Complete the experience with lunch, dinner, or Sunday brunch at their in-house café, *J's at Nashoba Valley* (closed Mon, dinner not served Tues & Sun, reservations recommended; ⓣ978/779-9816). From Worcester, take Rte-290 east to I-495, exit 27 to Rte-117.

The Town

Springfield's unwieldy and unattractive city center is split by the wide Connecticut River. There's not much to see here beyond a handful of museums (see below), and most signs point you in the direction of the **Basketball Hall of Fame** at 1150 W Columbus Ave, next to the river just south of Memorial Bridge (daily 10am–5pm; $14; ⓣ413/781-6500 or 1-877/4HOOPLA; ⓦwww.hoophall.com), which commemorates the 1890s invention of Dr James Naismith. Designed as a means of exercise during the harsh New England winters for athletes at the School for Christian Workers, the game's popularity spread with amazing rapidity. After Naismith took a trip to the Berlin Olympics in 1936, the National Association of Basketball Coaches started to discuss the idea of establishing a museum, finally realized in 1959. With the growth of the game, the hall has become a major attraction for anyone who's dreamed of stepping in Michael Jordan's shoes. In the summer of 2002, a revamped hall nearly twice the size of its predecessor opened for business. The renovated hall includes movies, videos, memorabilia, statistical databases, and some high-tech interactive gadgets such as the "Electronic Coach Telestrator," "You Call the Play," and "You Are the Sports Anchor," where you can test your skills as a coach, referee, and basketball commentator respectively. The centerpiece, visible from all three floors, is a full-sized basketball court complete with suspended arena scoreboard.

Back in the center of town, Springfield's other museums are located at **The Quadrangle**, a tree-lined square at the corner of State and Chestnut streets (all museums Wed–Fri noon–4pm, weekends 11am–4pm, call for additional summer opening hours; $7; ⓣ413/263-6800, ⓦwww.quadrangle.org). They're not all that interesting individually, but taken together can make for a decent afternoon diversion. The **Smith Art Museum**, housed in an airy Italian palazzo-styled building blessed with Tiffany stained-glass windows, displays the eclectic collection of George Walter Vincent and Belle Smith (local art collectors), which focuses on Asian decorative arts, including the largest collection of Chinese cloisonné pottery outside of Asia, but also takes in nineteenth-century American painting and rugs from the Middle East. **The Museum of Fine Arts** is slightly more coherent, proudly displaying Winslow Homer's *The New Novel* and Frederic Church's *New England Scenery* alongside lesser-known pieces by Monet, Calder, and Georgia O'Keeffe. Also of local interest, the **Connecticut Valley Historical Museum** has an interactive exhibit on "The World of Doctor Seuss" to keep the kids busy while you check out their collection of furniture, toys, paintings, games, and artifacts that were once the possessions of settlers in the region. This museum also houses a **Genealogy and Local History Library** with its database, Project Shamrock, which allows the descendants of Irish immi-

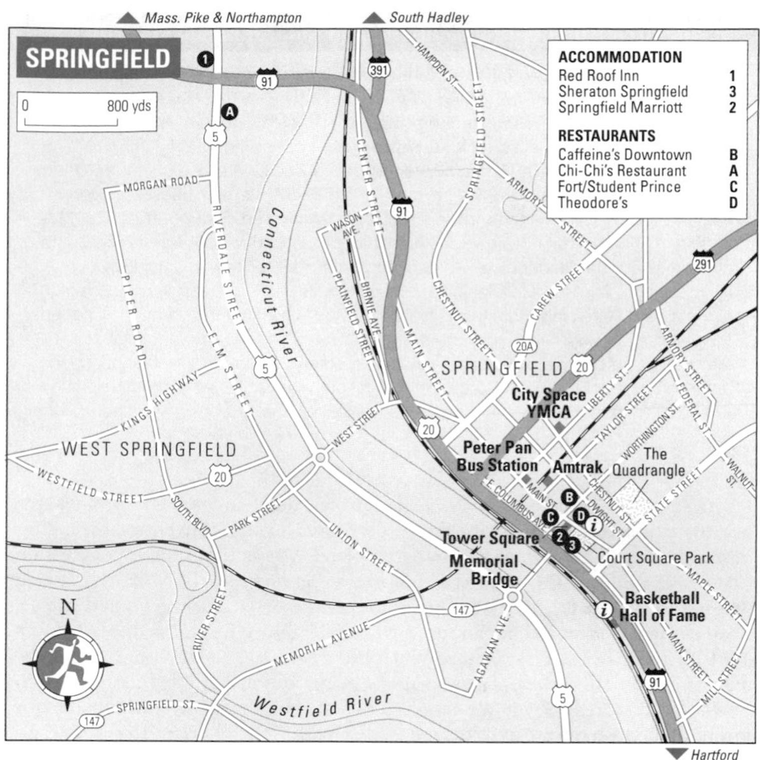

grants to search for relatives who may have been living in the greater Springfield area between 1840 and 1900. Finally, the **Springfield Science Museum** has a crowd-pleasing life-sized replica of Tyrannosaurus Rex, an exhibit on life under the Connecticut River, lots of hands-on displays, and a **planetarium** with daily shows – though these cost extra. In the middle of The Quadrangle, the **Dr Seuss National Memorial Sculpture Garden** (daily 7am–8pm) contains metallic sculptures of various characters and scenes created and inspired by the Springfield-born children's writer and illustrator, Theodore Geisel.

Practicalities

Amtrak **trains** regularly stop at Springfield's downtown station at 66 Lyman St, about a mile from The Quadrangle. Peter Pan Trailways, which provides daily **bus** services to and from Boston and New York, the Pioneer Valley, and the Berkshires, operates out of the nearby bus station at 1776 Main St (Ⓣ413/781-3320). The **Greater Springfield Convention & Visitors Bureau** (Ⓦwww.valleyvisitor.com) has two information centers: one opposite Tower Square at 1441 Main St (Mon–Fri 9am–5pm; Ⓣ413/787-1548 or 1-800/723-1548), the other by the river next to the Basketball Hall of Fame at 1200 W Columbus Ave (daily 8am–8pm; late May to mid-Oct weekends 8am–10pm; Ⓣ413/750-2980). **Local transportation** is provided by the PVTA (Ⓣ413/781-PVTA), and includes a trolley service (route 26) which does a loop of the downtown area.

Scenic drives and outdoor activities in Central Massachusetts

The northern strip of Central Massachusetts is good **scenic driving** country, with the **Johnny Appleseed Trail** taking over from the Mohawk Trail (see p.284) as Rte-2 passes the Quabbin Reservoir and heads east towards Concord, Massachusetts. Named after the so-called Johnny Appleseed (real name: John Chapman), a nurseryman born in 1774 in Leominster, Massachusetts, who dedicated his life to planting apple trees and spreading the word of God, the trail passes 25 towns, numerous orchards, wineries, rolling hills, and **Wachusett Mountain** (Ⓣ978/464-2300 or 1-800/SKI-1234, Ⓦwww.wachusett.com), a popular spot for **skiing**. South of Worcester, the **Blackstone River Valley** stretches all the way to Providence, Rhode Island. The 46-mile Blackstone River brought great prosperity to the region at the time of America's Industrial Revolution in the late eighteenth century, although today the waterway sees more **canoeing** and **kayaking** than commercial activity. There is also a **bicycle path** that follows the course of the river and the long-since defunct Blackstone Canal. Contact the Blackstone River Valley National Heritage Corridor (Ⓣ401/762-0250) for more information on the activities available in the area.

You shouldn't need to stay, but if you do, there are several options for **accommodation** in Springfield, mostly geared to the convention-attending businessperson. The *Springfield Marriott*, Boland Way at East Columbus Avenue (Ⓣ413/781-7111; ❻), and the *Sheraton Springfield*, 1 Monarch Place (Ⓣ413/781-1010; ❻), are both smack in the middle of downtown and pricey. Also enjoying a central location, but considerably cheaper, is the *Cityspace YMCA*, 275 Chestnut St (Ⓣ413/739-6951 ext 130; ❸), which has rooms for men and women. Other places to stay can be found sprinkled along Rte-5, otherwise known as Riverdale Street, across the river in West Springfield, with most hotels clustered around its intersection with I-91. The *Red Roof Inn*, 1254 Riverdale St (Ⓣ413/731-1010; ❸), and the *Super 8 Motel*, 1500 Riverdale St (Ⓣ413/736-8080; ❹), are good, clean, standard choices.

For **food**, *Chi-Chi's Restaurante*, 955 Riverdale St in West Springfield (Ⓣ413/781-0442), is a local institution, a massive pseudo-adobe Mexican restaurant on Hwy-5, just south of the I-91 bridge. *Caffeine's*, 1338 Memorial Ave in West Springfield (Ⓣ413/731-5282), serves a range of entrées, from barbecued chicken pizza to soy burgers and focaccia, and has a counterpart in the center of Springfield, at 254 Worthington St (closed Sun; Ⓣ413/788-6646). Across the street from that outlet, at 201 Worthington St, *Theodore's Booze, Blues and Barbecue* (Ⓣ413/736-600) pulls no punches with its offering of barbecued ribs and chicken (even salmon), a solid beer selection, and live blues most nights. Tiny Fort Street has been home to the *Fort/Student Prince* (Ⓣ413/734-7475) for over sixty years, a local favorite for German Wiener schnitzel, goulash, and sauerbraten. *Gus & Paul's* has two Springfield locations with distinctly different attitudes. The 1500 Main St branch, at Tower Square (closed Sun; Ⓣ413/781-2253), has an urban bistro feel, while the 1209 Sumner Ave option (Ⓣ413/782-5710) leans towards Old World-style deli. Either way, the food is fresh and tasty.

The Pioneer Valley

The Pioneer Valley, a verdant corridor shaped by the Connecticut River and centuries of glacial activity, is the epicenter of recreational and cultural activity in Central Massachusetts. The towns of **Northampton**, **South Hadley**, and **Amherst** share between them no less than five colleges: Smith College (in Northampton), Mount Holyoke College (in South Hadley), Amherst College, the University of Massachusetts, and Hampshire College (all in Amherst) – schools that have formalized their relationship through the creation of the co-operative "Five College Consortium," which links the communities academically, economically, and culturally. One and a half hours from Boston and just three hours from New York City, the Valley is a good, less expensive and much less popular alternative to the Cape or the Berkshires – an excellent choice for those who like to hike, bike, hang out in cafés, browse bookstores, and pretend, if only for a weekend, that they actually live in this idyllic little spot.

Northampton

In 1654, the Puritans purchased some of the most fertile farmland in the densely-wooded hills of Central Massachusetts from the Nonotuck Indians for ten coats, several trinkets, and 100 fathom of wampum and christened it **NORTHAMPTON**. These vast land holdings became a liability after the Revolutionary War, however, when depressed and indebted farmers were in danger of losing their property to creditors looking to recover the war debt. Rising to meet this injustice in 1786 was farmer Daniel Shays, who rustled up hundreds of his compatriots and marched to the county courthouse in Northampton, and soon after attacked the federal arsenal in Springfield in what would later come to be known as **Shays' Rebellion**.

Northampton's canal connection to New Haven, Connecticut, and the Atlantic was completed in 1835, only to be overshadowed by the 1845 arrival of the railroad. Transportation, in turn, encouraged the development of industry, which by the early to mid-twentieth century was undermined by the rush to use cheaper southern and international labor. In retrospect, Northampton's saving grace has been its investment in education and the intellectual environment it has fostered. Smith College, founded in 1871 by Sophia Smith and financed with her personal inheritance, survives as a prestigious women's college.

Today, liberal, progressive, and content to march to a different drummer, Northampton (population 30,000 or so), fondly nicknamed "NoHo," has settled into its role as a tolerant town of artists, writers, students, teachers, and activists. Oddly enough, it was cited in *Parents' Magazine* as one of the best small towns in America to raise a family and in *Newsweek* as the "lesbian capital of the Northeast" – both distinctions it accepted with pride.

Accommodation

You shouldn't have a terrible time finding somewhere reasonable to stay in town, though, that said, many of the places tend to be of the stylish inn variety, similar to the way things are over in Amherst (see p.261).

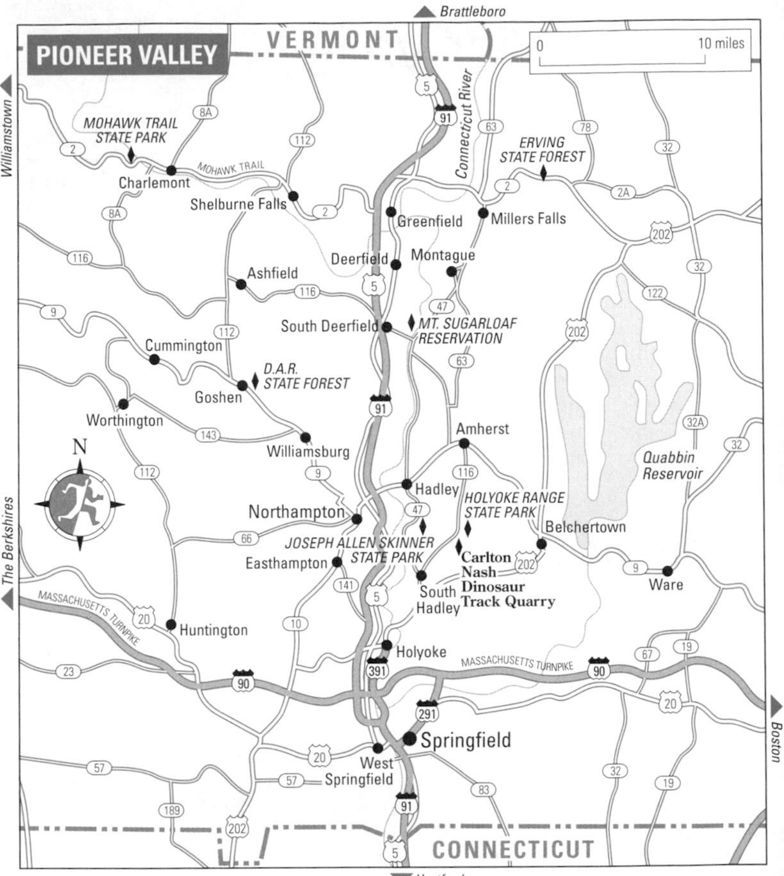

Autumn Inn 259 Elm St ⓣ413/584-7660, ⓦwww.hampshirehospitality.com. A Colonial-style inn boasting an attractive outdoor swimming pool and barbecue area surrounded by trees. Clean, comfortable, and close to the action. Reservations required. ❺

Clarion Hotel and Conference Center 1 Atwood Drive ⓣ413/586-1211, ⓦwww.hampshirehospitality.com. Formerly the *Inn at Northampton*, this place is now part of a local chain of hotels. Wood paneling and a roaring fireplace in the lobby set the tone, an indoor pool topped with a glass dome completes the scene. The smallest bed is a queen-size. Friendly staff. ❺

Hotel Northampton 36 King St ⓣ413/584-3100, 1-800/547-3529, ⓦwww.hotelnorthhampton.com. Copious flower arrangements in the entryway of this over-sized historic 1927 hotel give an immediate sense of its inflated – though entirely deserved – self-importance. The attention to detail and charm makes up for the smallish rooms. ❼

Lupine House 185 N Main St, Florence ⓣ413/586-9766 or 1-800/890-9766. Three antique-furnished rooms with private bath in a lovely Colonial house three miles from downtown Northampton. Continental breakfast included. ❹

North King Motel 504 N King St ⓣ413/584-8847. Fifteen clean and basic rooms in a well-worn Fifties-style roadside motel. The chatty owners give this otherwise slightly dreary place a comfortable, lived-in feel. ❸

The Saltbox 153 Elm St ⓣ413/584-1790. A lovely 1780s house near Smith College, with three cozy sunlit suites, complete with kitchen and overstuffed armchairs, for monthly rental (from $1175). Weeklong stays possible (from $750) depending on availability.

Pioneer Valley practicalities

Arrival and information

By **car**, Northampton is off of I-91 approximately fifteen miles north of the Massachusetts Turnpike (I-90). All exits marked "Northampton" lead to the center of town. During the foliage season, those coming from Boston should consider taking the less traveled and more scenic Rte-2 from Concord west to Rte-202 through the woods skirting the Quabbin Reservoir and picking up Rte-9 into Amherst. The closest commercial airport is **Bradley International Airport** (℡203/627-3000) in Windsor Locks, Connecticut, roughly 45 minutes south of Northampton on I-91. Amtrak's *Vermonter* **train** service between Montréal, New York, and Washington DC pulls in to Amherst at 13 Railroad St. The region is also served by Peter Pan Trailways **buses**, with direct services to Boston, Hartford, and New York. Purchase tickets and catch the bus at 1 Roundhouse Plaza in Northampton (℡413/586-1030), 79 S Pleasant St in Amherst (℡413/256-0431), and Redfern Travel Connection, 29 College St in South Hadley (℡413/534-1190).

The **Greater Northampton Chamber of Commerce**, 99 Pleasant St (Mon–Fri 9am–5pm; May–Oct weekends 10am–2pm; ℡413/584-1900, Ⓦwww.northamptonuncommon.com), and the **Amherst Area Chamber of Commerce**, 409 Main St (Mon–Fri 8am–5pm; ℡413/253-0770, Ⓦwww.amherstarea.com), both offer the usual array of maps and recommendations; the Northampton chamber also stocks copies of the *Pink Pages* for gay and lesbian travelers (see p.65). **Bookstores** in both towns are a significant source of local maps and advice. *The Valley Advocate*, a free weekly newspaper available in any café, prints a complete listing of area happenings, movie listings, and restaurant reviews. Look out for their "Best of the Valley" Readers Poll, which gives restaurants, bars, and cafés awards for excellence in a variety of categories. Contact the **Northampton Conservation Commission** (℡413/586-6950) or the **Amherst Conservation Commission** (℡413/256-4045), which between them oversee the maintenance of 37 distinctly different nature preserves, for suggestions and listings of nature hikes and recreation areas.

Public transportation

Shuttling between Northampton, Amherst, and South Hadley, and stopping at points in between, is the **Pioneer Valley Transit Authority (PVTA)** (℡413/586-5806 or 1-877/779-PVTA). Financed and operated by the area colleges and driven by UMass students, the PVTA is a free service available to anyone who wants to use it. Generally, buses begin circulating at 6am and head home at around midnight (later on Thurs, Fri & Sat), passing each stop every thirty minutes or so. Schedules are available on each bus and posted at the sidewalk stops. The paved **Norwottuck Trail Bike Path** weaves its way for around eight miles between Northampton and Amherst in the footprint of a former railroad bed. Used for biking, walking, and rollerblading, the path, though crowded in nice weather, offers an attractive alternative to driving the very developed Rte-9.

The Town

Although Northampton doesn't have much in the way of tourist attractions per se, the town itself has a well-earned reputation as one of the most liveable places in the US. Judging by the wealth of shops, restaurants, cafés, and the diversity of the population along Main Street, you could be in a major city, rather than a small college town. The traffic, however, remains relatively light (except for the snail's pace rush-hour commutes to and from Amherst), and the streets clean and safe.

The main thing to see in Northampton is on the grounds of the institution that most defines the town, Smith, whose **Smith College Museum of Art**

(☎413/585-2760) is superb for an institution of its size. The recently-renovated museum focuses on nineteenth- and twentieth-century art, with works by Monet (*Field of Poppies*), Georgia O'Keeffe (the nearly translucent *Squash Flowers, #1*), Jean Arp (a languid *Torso*), and Frank Stella, who is represented by the enormous *Damascus Gate (Variation III)*. In addition, it boasts an 8000-strong print collection which contains a startling number of prints and engravings by Daumier, Delacroix, Dürer, Munch, Picasso, and Toulouse-Lautrec. There are also more than a few off-beat items sprinkled throughout the museum, such as an exquisite Luba ceremonial axe from Zaire.

You may want to call in at other areas on the attractive campus, such as the **botanic garden**; tours can be made from the admissions office, pretty much on the hour during weekday mornings and early afternoons. Besides exploring Smith and taking in the laid-back vibe of Northampton's student community, the biggest attraction is the city's nightlife and coffee culture. It's worth slowing down the pace of your travels here and taking in some music at the legendary *Iron Horse* or a couple of pints at the *Brewery* (see reviews below).

Eating and drinking

Northampton is the top place in the Pioneer Valley for eating, and establishments are typically a lot less precious here than they are over in the Berkshires.

Bart's Homemade 235 Main St ☎413/584-0721. From cow to cone, *Bart's* reputation for using quality local ingredients to create melt-in-your-mouth indulgences is well deserved. A great place to nurse a novel and a latte. Also one in Amherst at 103 N Pleasant St (see p.263).

Del Raye 1 Bridge St ☎413/586-2664. A sophisticated urban-style bistro serving French-inspired steaks and seafood. Chic and rather pricey (entrées around $30).

Eastside Grill 19 Strong Ave ☎413/586-3347. A well-established steakhouse serving steaks, chicken, and seafood with a Cajun bite. Extensive menu, attentive service, but often crowded.

Haymarket Café & Juice Joint 185 Main St ☎413/586-9969. Popular hangout for people looking for a cheap fix of the healthy variety. Soups, salads, and sandwiches for around $5. Drinks served in the street-level café, food in the dimly-lit basement.

Java Net Café 241 Main St ☎413/587-3401. A comfortable cybercafé serving up just what you'd expect – coffee, tea, croissants, and muffins – all at reasonable prices. Internet access at fancy computers costs $6 per hour.

La Veracruzana 31 Main St ☎413/586-7181. Bright, cheerful, and informal, the folks at *La Veracruzana* are credited with bringing the take-out burrito to the Valley. There's another branch in Amherst (see p.263).

Paul and Elizabeth's 150 Main St, in Thorne's Marketplace ☎413/584-4832. Vegetarian and seafood entrées, homemade breads, and desserts served in a serenely airy dining room.

Pizzeria Paradiso 12 Crafts Ave ☎413/586-1468. A cozy pizza place kept warm with wood-fired ovens imported from Italy. The extensive choice of toppings, drinks, and desserts make this much more than just another pizza joint.

Spoleto 50 Main St ☎413/586-6313. Fabulous pasta creations, an extensive wine list, and wonderful desserts. Always busy – and deservedly so. Takeout available at 255 King St ☎413/586-TOGO.

Sylvester's 111 Pleasant St ☎413/586-1418. Housed in the former home of Sylvester Graham, the inventor of the Graham Cracker, *Sylvester's* serves up tasty fare, including delightful breakfast treats such as banana-bread French toast. Very child-friendly staff.

Nightlife and entertainment

The Pioneer Valley's most active **nightlife** is in Northampton, though most cafés are open late in Amherst, which gives the town a bit of a nocturnal buzz. Thanks to its relatively close proximity to New York and Boston, and energetic local promoters such as "The Iron Horse Entertainment Group," Northampton attracts some of the biggest names in most branches of the performing arts. This being college-student country, expect your ID to be checked if you look a day under 60. You can reserve tickets for many shows playing in Northampton at the **Northampton Box Office**, 150 Main St, on the second floor of Thorne's Marketplace (☎413/586-8686 or 1-800/THE-TICK).

The Calvin Theater and Performing Arts Center 19 King St ☎413/584-1444. The folks responsible for *The Iron Horse* (see below) have lovingly transformed this 75-year-old movie house into a beacon of the performing arts. Live theater, music, and dance performance for all ages and tastes.

Fire & Water 5 Old South St ☎413/586-8336. If your idea of comedy is a hairy hippie dressed in a sack talking gibberish, then this is the place for you. Equally off-the-wall poetry evenings and live folk music. Mandatory monetary contribution for all performances.

FitzWilly's 23 Main St ☎413/584-8666. Smack in the middle of it all, this established local bar is a relaxing place to knock a few back and soak up the atmosphere.

The Iron Horse 20 Center St ☎413/585-0479. An institution in the world of folk music, this small, coffeehouse-style venue has been cheering on emerging artists for twenty years and still has a knack for booking the big names of folk, bluegrass, jazz, and blues. Call ☎413/586-8686 or 1-800/THE-TICK for information and reservations.

Northampton Brewery 11 Brewster Court, behind Thorne's Marketplace ☎413/584-9903. With a solid selection of high-quality microbrews on tap, an extensive munchies menu, and a relaxing outdoor patio, this is a great place to while away a summertime happy hour or a snowy winter night.

Packards's 14 Masonic St ☎413/584-5957. The plush billiards tables on the third floor give the place a rather gentleman's club-type atmosphere, in stark contrast to the video games and televised football downstairs. Featuring the usual selection of beers and bar food.

Pearl Street Night Club 10 Pearl St ☎413/586-8686 or 1-800/THE-TICK. Two-story live music and dance club. Reggae, alternative, hip-hop, and Grateful Dead tribute acts abound.

Pleasant Street Theater 27 Pleasant St ☎413/586-0935. Independent, classic, and foreign films are screened in this intimate movie theater – a worthy leftover from the pre-multiplex era. Check out the "Forgotten Film at Five" for 5pm screenings of films which, especially in the case of non-English-language productions, never got the chance to be remembered in the first place.

Amherst

Settled in 1727, incorporated in 1759, and named for General Jeffrey Amherst, **AMHERST** developed for the most part like its neighbor, Northampton, as a college town. In 1821, the citizens of Amherst financed and opened the Collegiate Charitable Institution to educate the town's young men, and by 1825 this had become Amherst College. In 1866, the Massachusetts Agricultural College opened in Amherst to teach military, agricultural, and technical skills, and today, as the renamed University of Massachusetts at Amherst, it is the main cog in the Massachusetts public university system. Hampshire College, just outside town on the road to South Hadley, was founded in the Seventies by the presidents of four local colleges as an experiment in true liberal arts study, one that emphasized the individual and interdisciplinary nature of education.

Today, Hampshire has only recently begun to outgrow its reputation as a flaky hippie haven, but the town as a whole maintains the feel of a small, bookish community, a bit larger but in fact less hurried than Northampton, with a healthy mix of college students, hippies, young families, and professionals – all in all a good place to kick back for a day or two and explore the surrounding countryside.

Accommodation

Amherst's **accommodation** options range from expensive inns and intimate bed and breakfasts with an ecological bent to predictable branches of the national chains. The best bet for inexpensive lodging is to drive the length of Rte-9 and check out some of the smaller, slightly rumpled-looking motels along the way. Many of them are safe and clean, if visually unappealing. Remember, wherever you stay, you can expect to pay more during foliage season.

Allen House Victorian Inn 599 Main St ⓣ413/253-5000, ⓦwww.allenhouse.com. A charming, award-winning Victorian B&B just past the Emily Dickinson Homestead. The *Amherst Inn*, directly opposite the Dickinson Homestead on a quiet, leafy part of Main Street, is the *Allen House's* sister inn. ④

Delta Organic Farm 352 E Hadley Rd ⓣ413/253-1893, ⓦwww.deltaorganicfarm.com. An organic Nirvana for health-conscious travelers. Special needs and requests are welcomed by the concerned and accommodating owners. Organic breakfast. ⑤

Howard Johnson 401 Russell St (Rte-9), Hadley ⓣ413/586-0114, ⓦwww.hampshirehospitality.com. Despite looking like little more than a cement block airlifted into place along the highway between Amherst and Northampton, this motor lodge is clean, comfortable, and everything you have come to expect from "HoJo." Managed by a local hotel chain. ④

Lord Jeffrey Inn 30 Boltwood Ave ⓣ413/253-2576 or 1-800/742-0358, ⓦwww.lordjeffreyinn.com. Situated on Amherst Common, this is a quintessential rambling and richly decorated New England inn – so much so that it is often used for weddings. The rooms are a luxurious treat. ⑤

The Town

Just about everybody who comes to Amherst visits the **Emily Dickinson Homestead**, 280 Main St (guided tours March & Nov to mid-Dec, Wed & Sat 1–5pm on the hour; April–May & Sept–Oct Wed–Sat 1–5pm hourly; June–Aug Wed–Sat 10am–5pm, Sun 1–5pm every half-hour; $5, reservations advised; ⓣ413/542-8161), where the celebrated American poet Emily Dickinson lived all her life. Born in Amherst in 1830, Emily Dickinson attended nearby Mount Holyoke College, but loneliness drove her back home without finishing her studies, and she shortly afterwards began a life of self-imposed exile in the family home here on Main Street. Emily Dickinson read voraciously, wrote incessantly, corresponded with friends, and over the course of her life penned some 1800 poems, most of which mirrored her lifelong struggle between isolation and an intense search for inspiration. Despite this literary hyperactivity, she published less than a dozen poems during her life, and was a completely unknown woman, much less poet, when she died in 1886. Her work was collected and published four years later by her sister, and she has since been recognized as influential in giving American poetry its own resounding voice.

The world Dickinson wrote of from her house no longer exists, but her room here is frozen in time, with an array of personal effects, such as the desk where Dickinson's poems were found after her death. It's a pretty low-key display on the whole, but for most visitors – especially those who also visit **Dickinson's grave** in the nearby West Cemetery, off Pleasant Street – this seems to be just enough. Also of notable literary interest, the original copy of *Stopping by Woods on a Snowy Evening* written by the American poet Robert Frost, who was a professor at Amherst College for thirty years, sits under glass in the **Jones Library** on Amity Street.

There's further cultural interest in the **Mead Art Museum**, on the lovely campus of **Amherst College** (academic year Tues–Sun 10am–4.30pm, Thurs 10am–9pm; summer Tues–Sun 1–4pm; free), where works by Frederic Church, Thomas Cole, John Singleton Copley, Thomas Eakins, and Winslow Homer dominate a collection strong on early twentieth-century American art. There's also a sprinkling of Renaissance European works, notably a seductive *Salome* by Robert Henri and a gory *Still Life with Dead Game* by Frans Synders.

There's a small **Museum of Natural History** in the Amherst precincts (academic year Mon–Fri 9am–3.30pm, Sat 10am–4pm & Sun noon–5pm; summer Sat 10am–4pm & Sun noon–5pm), but you might be better off heading on to Hampshire College, where the campus is home to the **National Yiddish Book Center** (Sun–Fri 10am–3.30pm; closed on Jewish holidays; free), which houses one of the world's largest collections of Yiddish books – many culled from New York City dumpsters – in a sprawling building designed to emulate an Eastern European *shtetl*.

Eating and drinking

Though Amherst doesn't have as many **restaurants** as Northampton, you surely won't go hungry. The high student population has led to a large percentage of sandwich places, pizza joints, chain coffee shops, and casual eateries. A stroll along either Main Street or North Pleasant Street pretty much sums up the choices.

Amber Waves 63 Main St ⓣ413/253-9200. Southeast Asian noodle soups and stir fries designed to please carnivores, vegetarians, and vegans alike.

Amherst Brewing Company 24–36 N Pleasant St ⓣ413/253-4400. The brass bar and exposed brick add a touch of upscale yearning to this prime drinking spot. Live music – mostly jazz – and a street terrace are added attractions.

Amherst Chinese Food 62 Main St ⓣ413/253-7835. Believe it or not, the owners of this restaurant grow the organic vegetables they use in their dishes and add nothing artificial as they pick, steam, sauté, fry, and deliver them piping hot to your table. Unsurprisingly popular with a health-conscious crowd.

Antonio's 31 N Pleasant St ⓣ413/253-0808. Just a few benches and stools to eat at, but this is *the* pizza place in town, where the slices are always just out of the oven and good.

Bart's Homemade 103 N Pleasant St ⓣ413/253-9371. Amherst branch of a Northampton favorite (see p.260). The street terrace is as welcome as the sundaes, smoothies, and ice creams on warm days.

The Black Sheep 79 Main St ⓣ413/253-3442. Stacked sandwiches, pastries, coffee, and desserts served in a down-to-earth café. Open late for coffee and occasional music, including open-mike nights. Highly recommended.

Boltwood Tavern 30 Boltwood Ave ⓣ413/253-2576. Part of the *Lord Jeffrey Inn*, this is a popular spot for good beers and pub grub. Upstairs is the *Windowed Hearth*, a more expensive and upscale counterpart where you're likely to find professors rather than students.

Bub's BBQ Rte-116, Sunderland ⓣ413/548-9630. Despite the address, this is only minutes by car from Amherst. From Rte-9, take Rte-116 N, look for the fluorescent pink porker on the right inviting you to "Pig out in style." Smokin' barbecue and homestyle sides.

Judie's 51 N Pleasant St ⓣ413/253-3491. Famous for meal-sized salads, huge homemade popovers served with apple butter, and award-winning deserts. Closed Mon.

La Veracruzana 63 S Pleasant St ⓣ413/253-6900. Burrito joint that's the sister restaurant of the Northampton place of the same name (see p.260).

South Hadley

Located at the intersection of routes 116 and 47, **SOUTH HADLEY**, the home of bucolic Mount Holyoke College, completes the circle of towns in the Five College Consortium. Founded in 1836 by education pioneer Mary Lyon, Mount Holyoke is the oldest college for women in America and, like its neighbor Smith, is considered to be one of the most prestigious of the "Seven Sisters" group.

The Town

Though the smallest of the area's towns, South Hadley is a worthwhile destination in its own right, mainly due to the presence of the **Mount Holyoke**

The forgettable legacy of Jeffrey Amherst

The town of Amherst takes pride in its scholars as well as its famous poet-in-one-time residence, Emily Dickinson. Less attention is given to the achievements of **General Jeffrey Amherst** – perhaps for good reason.

Amherst was a popular British general when the town was named after him in 1759, best known for his many victories during the French and Indian War. After the French surrendered, Amherst was fairly charitable to the defeated French troops; however, continuing a well-established practice in Colonial times, he was allegedly brutal and cruel to the Native Americans.

Although it is uncertain with whom the idea originated, a series of correspondences between Amherst and Colonel Henry Bouquet in the summer of 1763 refer to "innoculat[ing] the Native Americans by means of blankets," some historians believing that the idea was to spread the disease of smallpox by distributing infected blankets to the natives. Smallpox is not specifically mentioned, although other documents do confirm its presence among the British in the area. General Jeffrey's intentions are made clearer by his urging of Colonel Bouquet to "try Every other method that can serve to Extirpate this Execrable race." Although no follow-up to this plan has been discovered in the correspondences, and debate rages on over Amherst's burden of responsibility, smallpox did appear among the native peoples at about this time – perhaps one of the earliest instances of biological warfare.

College Art Museum, Rte-116 (Tues–Fri 11am–5pm, Sat–Sun 1–5pm; free), which has an impressive permanent collection of Asian, Egyptian, and Mediterranean paintings, drawings, and sculpture, and regularly mounts high-quality special exhibitions. The museum has acquired a *Head of Faustina the Elder*, a marble Roman sculpture, of the second-century Empress Faustina, whose likeness was reproduced on coins and statues of the period, and whose elaborate braided hairstyle is a feat of both the art of sculpting and hairdressing.

There's also the **Joseph Allen Skinner Museum**, 35 Woodbridge St/Rte-116 (May–Oct Wed & Sun afternoons; free), which has fantastic exhibits of period glassware, musical instruments, housewares, antique furniture, and weaponry. The museum, a Congregational church built in 1846 and moved to this site from its original resting place – now under the placid waters of the nearby Quabbin Reservoir – houses the eclectic collection of Mr. Skinner, a wealthy mill-owner and world traveler. There's very little organization to speak of, and those who have tried to trace and label the various bows and arrows, pistols, knick-knacks, harpoons, and farm implements were obviously defeated by the Sisyphean futility of their task.

Just outside town, the **Carlton Nash Dinosaur Track Quarry**, Amherst Rd/Rte-116, is one of the more surreal local sights (late May to early Sept Mon–Sat 10am–4pm, Sun noon–4pm; $2 adults, $1 children; ⓣ413/467-9566), a roadside collection of locally excavated dinosaur bones and footprints. In its previous incarnation as Nash Dinosaur Land, it was something of a roadside legend, as its elderly proprietor would not only show you the dinosaur bones but also spin animated tales about the property to all that would listen. Carlton has since passed away, and the place is a bit more low-key.

For **something to eat**, your only sure bet for several miles is *Tailgate*, in the shopping area across the street from Mount Holyoke (ⓣ413/532-7597), which has a large selection of bagels, pasta salads, and gourmet treats. If you need a snack before heading to one of the nearby parks, be sure to stop here first, as you won't pass any other options en route.

Around South Hadley

Farther along Rte-116 between South Hadley and Amherst, **The Notch**, an impasse between Bare Mountain and Mount Norwottuck, is the location of the entrance and visitors' center of the **Holyoke Range State Park** (for information, call the Joseph Allen Skinner State Park – see below), which consists of 2936 acres spread out over nine miles and rising to heights of over a thousand feet, with marked hiking trails throughout. On Rte-47, about halfway between South Hadley and Northampton, is the entrance to the **Joseph Allen Skinner State Park** (Ⓣ413/586-0350), which sits proudly perched atop Mount Holyoke. Head up to the aptly named **Summit House** (late May to mid-Oct weekends), where the park's visitors' center has wide and stunning views of the river valley, particularly the bend referred to as the "Ox Bow" – immortalized in Thomas Cole's painting of the same name.

The Upper Pioneer Valley

If you have a car and the desire to hit the back roads, exploring the area known as the **Upper Pioneer Valley** can offer many pleasant surprises. In sharp contrast to the relative economic and cultural stability of the college towns of Northampton and Amherst, the smaller rural towns surrounding them embrace an entirely different lifestyle. With the harsh weather, instability of the family farm, and the loss of industrial dollars, life in these hills can be grueling – and the picturesque scenery sometimes masks a rural poverty uncharacteristic of this part of New England. Yet the hills in these parts yield simple pleasures: the odd roadside vegetable stand, good local diners, disarming vistas, eclectic yard sales, maple syrup farms, and, especially in the summer, numerous festivals ranging from the Riverfest in Shelburne Falls (June) to the Turn of the Century Ice Cream Social in Deerfield (July).

The only two towns in the Upper Pioneer Valley accessible by **bus** are Greenfield and Deerfield, with Peter Pan Trailways stopping in front of the Town Hall in Greenfield and at Savage Market, 470 Greenfield Rd in Deerfield.

Quabbin Reservoir, Mount Sugarloaf, and beyond

Leaving the Five College area, the Pioneer Valley becomes quite rural quite quickly. The beauty of **Quabbin Reservoir** (entrance on Rte-9 between Ware and Belchertown) belies its origins: in 1939, in a bureaucratic decision designed to benefit the eastern part of the state, the Swift River was dammed and the towns of Dana, Greenwich, Enfield, and Prescott were evacuated and flooded with some 39 square miles of water, since which time the metropolitan Boston area has had to give little thought to the source and availability of its water. And while you cannot swim, camp, or barbecue at Quabbin, its 81,000 acres of protected wildlife reservation land provide a fair degree of serenity.

Just outside South Deerfield (see overleaf), the **Mount Sugarloaf Reservation** (Rte-116) consists of North and South Sugarloaf mountains, the latter of which has a paved road allowing cars to climb to the summit. Scenic views and good picnicking make this a popular spot, and there are opportunities for camping, too – though reservations are advised. On the other side of

Maple syrup

Though the raw, muddy, unpredictable, and seemingly endless weeks of March in New England have few virtues, one is the proximity of spring and the other is **maple syrup**. The sugar shacks of the Upper Pioneer Valley are responsible for producing most of the maple syrup made in Massachusetts. Surrounded by ancient maples and using time-honored methods, these tiny, often family-owned and -run, sugar houses welcome visitors, give tours, and even offer weekend brunches where the maple syrup flows generously. The season usually begins the first weekend of March and continues for six weekends afterward. Calling ahead is wise and arriving early is even wiser, as the farms are quite popular. Try **South Face Farm**, Watson-Spruce Corner Rd, off Rte-116 in Ashfield (March to mid-April Sat–Sun 8.30am–3.30pm; ⓣ413/628-3268), where they make pancakes, waffles, and fried corn fritters and dare you to top them with both syrup and ice cream.

Deerfield, the **Daughters of the American Revolution (D.A.R.) State Forest**, Rte-112, Goshen (ⓣ413/268-7098), is also a good place for camping, with tent and RV sites available (late May to early Sept; $12). The **Mohawk Trail State Forest**, Rte-2, Charlemont (ⓣ413/339-5504), offers 56 campsites and six cabins (tent sites available mid-April to mid-Oct, cabins year-round). **Erving State Forest**, Wendell Depot Road, off Rte-2A at Erving Center (late May to early Sept; ⓣ413/544-7745), is a bit more rough-and-ready, with no showers or flush toilets, but makes up for it by allowing almost every outdoor activity you could think of, from snowshoeing to fishing.

South Deerfield

Despite the sedate appearance of present-day **SOUTH DEERFIELD**, its history is punctuated by violent episodes of unusual intensity, even for America. The town was first settled in 1669 as a frontier outpost of British North America. Its position in the woods far away from established colonial centers on the coast left it vulnerable to attack, which local Indians did on September 18, 1675. One of the bloodiest clashes of King Philip's War (see p.602), this culminated in the death of 64 men at "Bloody Brook" in South Deerfield. But it was in February 1704, in a colonial extension of Queen Anne's War, that Deerfield earned its notoriety. In a raid that began at dawn and lasted five hours, some 350 Indians – led by the French – killed 49 settlers and set fire to the town. More than a hundred prisoners were promptly marched 300 miles to Canada; one-fifth of this number perished en route. Deerfield was abandoned afterward, but it eventually became a prosperous farming town. Today South Deerfield, along routes 5 and 10 (exit 24 off I-91), is home to both Historic Deerfield and the Yankee Candle Company.

Accommodation

Charlemont Inn Rte-2, Charlemont ⓣ413/339-5796, ⓦwww.charlemontinn.com. Travelers from Benedict Arnold to Mark Twain have homed in on this Mohawk Trail inn since 1787. Full of character and comfort, it drips with New England charm. The cheapest rooms come with shared bath. ❸

Deerfield Inn 81 Old Main St (The Street) ⓣ413/774-5587 or 1-800/926-3865, ⓦwww.deerfieldinn.com. The one and only place to stay in Historic Deerfield itself, this commodious and expensive country inn has good dining, too. ❽

Motel 6 Rte-5, South Deerfield ⓣ413/665-7161. Completely lacking in rustic charm, but offering clean rooms, friendly service, and reasonable rates. Located in a conifer grove off of I-91 at exit 24. ❸

The Town

Historic Deerfield, with dutifully preserved old houses girdled by a thousand acres of lush meadows and farmland, is a destination frozen in time. It considers itself the home of the preservation movement in New England, and also one of the first to milk the appeal of Olde New England. Restoration began here as early as the 1890s, when Alice Baker purchased the Frary House, restored it and opened the doors to the public. This was something of a first back then, and today, of the 65 or so eighteenth- and nineteenth-century structures on either side of **The Street** (the main drag), fourteen house museums are open for guided tours. These small-scale studies in simple elegance are filled with over 20,000 objects, from furniture and fabrics to silver and glass, either made or used in America between 1650 and 1850. About the only thing that infuses the strip with a touch of modernity (other than the tourists) is the presence of the 1797 **Deerfield Academy**, an American answer to Eton. If you don't have the patience for guided tours – and unless you have an overriding interest in antique home decor you probably need not go on more than one or two – the best thing is to peruse the new Flynt Center for Early American Life and take in the excellent Memorial Hall Museum, both of which are self-guiding.

Housed around the corner from The Street in the original building of the Deerfield Academy, the three-story **Memorial Hall Museum**, 8 Memorial St (daily: May–Oct 9.30am–4.30pm; $5), houses a superb collection of New England antiquities, and, on the second floor, a door destroyed during a 1704 raid by Native Americans. Judging by the hole in the center left by a battering axe, the wielder of the weapon didn't quite make it inside, but to get a sense of that moment of terror all you have to do is walk behind the door, preserved in a glass case. The door was pried off the 1698 John Sheldon House, itself demolished in the 1840s. Other exhibits include Native American artifacts, New England quilts, and well-curated period rooms with ceramics, glassware, paintings, and similar accoutrements of a generally placid past.

The best way to orient yourself is to check in at the **Hall Tavern Information Center**, across from the *Deerfield Inn*, and where you have to purchase house tickets anyway (daily 9.30am–4.30pm; $6 single house admission, $12 unlimited admission ticket good for two consecutive days; ⓣ413/774-5581, ⓦwww.historic-deerfield.org). There's a small museum inside, but the main thing is to check to see which of the fourteen historic houses are open for touring on the day you happen to be there. Next to Hall Tavern is the 1799 **Stebbins House**, one of the most interesting of the houses for its spiral staircase, stately New England furniture, and ornate French wallpaper. Tackling The Street from north to south, the 1825 brick **Wright House** is noted for Federal-style furniture and clocks, and Chinese export porcelain. A few doors down, The **Henry N. Flynt Silver & Metalware Collection** has on display both English and American silver and pewterware, some crafted by Paul Revere. Across the way is the **Ashley House**, with the upscale furnishings of the eighteenth-century Connecticut River Valley elite. Four doors down from the latter is the **Indian House Memorial**, a reconstruction of the Sheldon House, the earliest-known Deerfield house. From here you can take the short but enchanting **Channing Blake Meadow Walk** down to the Deerfield River. The **Wells-Thorn House**, at the corner of The Street and Memorial Street, has period rooms that depict the lifestyle of Deerfield residents from 1725 to 1850. One short block south is the **Dwight House**, a circa-1725 merchant's home that was moved here from Springfield. Behind the Dwight House is the modern **Flynt Center for Early American Life**, which houses some 10,000 objects of interest, and is the only place in

Historic Deerfield with rotating exhibits. Allow an hour or more to take it all in, including the Helen G. Flynt Textile Collection.

There's not much to the rest of Deerfield, although if you have the energy, the **Yankee Candle Company** on routes 5 and 10 (daily 9.30am–6pm), and the shopping complex it shares with the tourist-targeted Bavarian Christmas Village and Kringle Market, is worth a brief stop off for its regular demonstrations of traditional candlemaking techniques using 200-year-old equipment. If you tire of the candles, the adjacent Yankee Candle Car Museum ($5 admission) has a display of eighty antique and exotic cars.

Eating and drinking

As you exit I-91 and turn north onto routes 5 and 10 (which are, at this point, one road), you will pass the Sugarloaf Shoppes and *Motel 6* and arrive at a stop light. Take a right at the light on to Elm Street, cross the railroad tracks, and the small business district you see represents the extent of the South Deerfield area's offerings. Neighboring Greenfield, ten minutes to the north on Rte-5, has a bit more going on.

The Deli and Bakery The Sugarloaf Shoppes. Bagels, sandwiches, and coffee for hungry picnickers heading up Mount Sugarloaf (see p.265).

The People's Pint 24 Federal St, Greenfield ⓣ413/773-0333. Local brewpub even makes its own sodas, as well as serving well-prepared dishes using local and organic ingredients.

Sienna 6 Elm St (closed Mon & Tues) ⓣ413/665-0215. It may be the fact that it is only open for dinner or possibly that its storefront, when not lit, has the look of an abandoned dime store, but it is easy to miss *Sienna*. Whatever the reason, its unassuming nature undoubtedly contributes to its status as one of the area's best-kept secrets. A warm terracotta-colored interior, candles, and dishes ranging from Chilean swordfish with goat cheese ravioli to jumbo scallops and crabmeat mashed potato, this is a dining experience you will not quickly forget. Entrées in the $21–26 range, desserts and appetizers $7–11.

Shelburne Falls

Nestled in the Berkshire foothills and straddling the Deerfield River approximately two miles from Rte-2 is the tiny town of **SHELBURNE FALLS**, a community whose buzz of artistic activity and scenic surroundings give a taste of modern New England small-town life. You wouldn't make a special trip to Shelburne Falls, but the scenic drive you have to make to get here and its eminently strollable Main Street, dotted with antique shops and glass-blowing galleries, make it a pleasant enough, if low-key, spot. Be warned, though, that what one would logically consider Shelburne Falls is actually the two towns of Shelburne Falls and Buckland, each on its respective side of the river – this is momentarily confusing when you drive into what you expect to be Shelburne Falls and are greeted by the Buckland Town Hall.

The Town

The most prominent thing to see in Shelburne Falls is the **Bridge of Flowers**, an old trolley bridge which is festooned with flowering foliage each spring by the Shelburne Falls Women's Club. Although the event is celebrated by the local authorities as "internationally known," it's basically a well-executed show of civic pride rather than a botanical wonder. That said, all the hype doesn't detract from the bridge's appeal. The town's other attraction is a naturally occurring one, a series of geologically bizarre **glacial potholes**, east of Bridge Street at Salmon Falls, formed by several hundred million years of erosion and pitted by the splashing from the waterfalls upstream. Worth a quick look, they resemble an enormous solid mass of once-molten stone that has now been whittled into a svelte sculpture along the riverbed.

The Book Mill

Lovers of books will feel right at home at the **Book Mill**, 440 Greenfield Rd, off Rte-63 in Montague (daily 10am–6pm; ⓣ413/367-9206, ⓦwww.montaguebookmill.com), which accurately bills itself as offering "books you don't need in a place you can't find." With 40,000 used and discount books, well-seasoned armchairs, and large windows overlooking the river, the Book Mill is a pleasant place to spend a couple of lazy hours. There is also an on-site **café** with reasonable coffee and tables with reading lights. For something more substantial, consider having a meal (Sunday brunch is particularly good) next door at the *Blue Heron Restaurant* (closed Mon & Tues; ⓣ413/367-0222).

Practicalities

Shelburne Falls is located approximately two miles south of Rte-2 and 10 miles west of the intersection of Rte-2 and I-91 at Greenfield. If you are coming from Northampton, consider taking the more scenic Rte-9 N to Goshen and climbing Rte-112 north to Shelburne Falls. If you are coming from Amherst or South Deerfield, you can take the equally scenic Rte-116 north to Rte-112 N (Ashfield is a worthwhile stop, but mostly closed on Sundays). Antique shops, two grocery stores, and restaurants line State Street in Buckland and Bridge Street in Shelburne Falls. In the latter town, you'll also find the **Village Information Center**, 75 Bridge St (daily: May–Oct 10am–4pm; ⓣ413/625-2544).

Accommodation options are spread out, but the *Bear Haven Bed & Breakfast*, 22 Mechanic St (ⓣ413/625-9281, ⓦwww.bearhaven.com; ❹), is centrally located, home to the large collection of teddy bears of its owners and a nice resting-place for humans as well. You can't miss its rambling blue and lavender exterior. It is hard to go wrong stopping for a **bite to eat** in Shelburne Falls; the town's culinary offerings are packed into the little commercial center and the quality is surprisingly good for a town this small.

Margo's Bistro (ⓣ413/625-0200) offers innovative fare with trendy ingredients such as gorgonzola and Thai peanut sauce, wooing clients with their terrific brunch served with a complimentary tea tray of fruit and homemade biscuits. Another option, *Mother's* (ⓣ413/625-6300), offers sandwiches galore plus hearty breakfasts, in a welcoming environment. Finally the *Copper Angel*, 2 State St (ⓣ413/625-2727), offers resourceful vegetarian and non-red-meat dishes such as honey-coriander grilled chicken on its summertime outdoor terrace above the Bridge of Flowers.

The Berkshires

A rich cultural history, world-class summer arts festivals, and a bucolic landscape of forests and verdant hills – reminiscent of the English Lake District – make **the Berkshires**, at the extreme western edge of Massachusetts, an unusually civilized region. Since the mid-nineteenth century, the beauty and

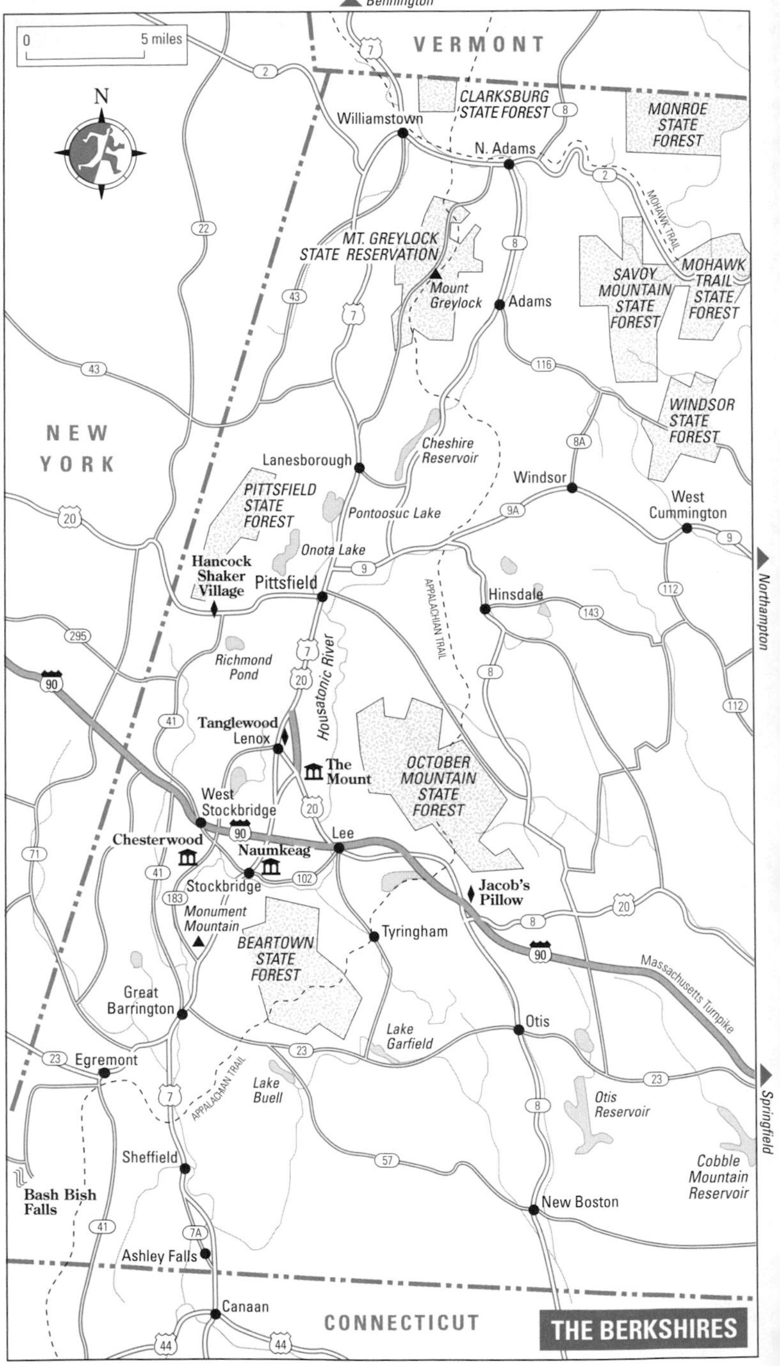
Bennington
0
5 miles
VERMONT
CLARKSBURG STATE FOREST
MONROE STATE FOREST
Williamstown
N. Adams
MOHAWK TRAIL
MT. GREYLOCK STATE RESERVATION
Mount Greylock
Adams
SAVOY MOUNTAIN STATE FOREST
MOHAWK TRAIL STATE FOREST
WINDSOR STATE FOREST
NEW YORK
Cheshire Reservoir
Lanesborough
PITTSFIELD STATE FOREST
Pontoosuc Lake
Windsor
West Cummington
Onota Lake
Hancock Shaker Village
Pittsfield
APPALACHIAN TRAIL
Hinsdale
Northampton
Richmond Pond
Housatonic River
Tanglewood
Lenox
The Mount
OCTOBER MOUNTAIN STATE FOREST
West Stockbridge
Lee
Chesterwood
Naumkeag
Stockbridge
Jacob's Pillow
Monument Mountain
BEARTOWN STATE FOREST
Tyringham
Massachusetts Turnpike
Great Barrington
Lake Garfield
Otis
Egremont
Lake Buell
Otis Reservoir
Springfield
APPALACHIAN TRAIL
Sheffield
Cobble Mountain Reservoir
Bash Bish Falls
New Boston
Ashley Falls
Canaan
CONNECTICUT
THE BERKSHIRES

tranquility of this region have attracted a moneyed crowd, the most visible manifestations of which are sumptuous Newport-style summer "cottages" nestled in the woods around the sedate villages of **Stockbridge** and **Lenox**. The latter is also home to **Tanglewood**, summer quarters of the Boston Symphony Orchestra and symbol of putative East Coast cultural superiority. But venture beyond these bastions of gentility and the more typical aspects of New England quickly re-emerge, from the economically battered old mill town of **Pittsfield** to dignified **Williamstown** and time-warp hill towns as remote as any in Vermont or New Hampshire.

More so than other parts of New England, tourism in the Berkshires is **seasonal**. Traveling in the off season has its rewards, but you'll miss out on virtually all of the big cultural festivals and find most of the museums either closed or on skeleton winter schedules. On the other hand, in the summer you're competing with East Coasters who have been coming here for years, which makes planning far in advance to secure accommodations and/or tickets less a good idea than a requirement. Perhaps the best times to visit are late May – spring is delightful in the Berkshires – or September, when the leaves are changing but before the October "leaf peepers" arrive in force. Note that when booking accommodation during the summer season, there is often a three-night minimum stay.

Getting around the Berkshires is not difficult, as long as you have a car and a good map – road signage is decidedly geared to residents, not visitors. The main highway, **Rte-7**, runs the length of the region (and the state) from north to south, following the cleft between the Taconic Mountains on the New York border and Hoosic ranges to the east. Because the Berkshires are at the end of the end of the state, the biggest decision you have to make in terms of driving – assuming you are coming from points east – may well be how you want to arrive. The **Massachusetts Turnpike** takes you from Boston to West Stockbridge in a stupendously dull three hours; a more appealing option might be to pick up I-91 south from Rte-2, sampling the Pioneer Valley (see p.257) before striking off west on pristine Rte-9, which takes you past tourist-free villages such as Williamsburg and Cummington and into Pittsfield, which is very close to Lenox. In the fall, you might opt to take scenic secondary routes that branch west off Rte-9 itself, notably routes 112 and 143. Alternatively, you may want to take Rte-2 all the way to Williamstown – the stretch from Miller's Falls (just east of I-91) to the New York border follows the very picturesque **Mohawk Trail** (see p.284); in fact, if you don't take this route into the Berkshires, you'd be remiss not to take it on the way out.

Your options by **public transport** are predictably limited. Peter Pan Trailways and Bonanza **buses** stop in Lee (at H.A. Johansson's, 50 Main St), Lenox (at the Village Pharmacy, 5 Walker St), Pittsfield (at the Pittsfield Bus Terminal, 57 S Church St), and Williamstown, on their way to and from Boston and Albany, New York. Hopping from one Berkshire town to another, however, is simplest using the local buses run by the **Berkshire Regional Transit Authority** (☎413/499-2782 or 1-800/292-BRTA), which cover a surprisingly large number of towns and villages between Great Barrington in the south and Williamstown in the north of the region. The maximum fare is $3.

Stockbridge

Strolling the spotless main street of **STOCKBRIDGE** either entices or unsettles, depending on whether you see it as the picture-postcard New England village it touts itself as or the essence of prefabricated quaint. Accordingly, you can either credit or curse Norman Rockwell, who lived and painted here for 25 years, for your reaction to the place. His Stockbridge paintings, like all the rest, capture a small-town American charm that may have only ever existed on the surface; regardless, his illustrations pass for great art in these parts (especially at his eponymous museum), and buying into the illusion of all-pervasive gaiety – the legacy of his work – for the length of your visit will at least increase your enjoyment. The social reality of Stockbridge is not quite Rockwell: the majority of the residences in town are summer homes for wealthy New Yorkers. Ironically, Stockbridge's other, uncelebrated, claim to fame is at quite the other end of the socio-cultural spectrum: the town is the setting for Arlo Guthrie's classic anti-draft song/monologue "Alice's Restaurant." White-clapboard schmaltz aside, there's actually quite a bit to see and do in and around

Culture in the Berkshires

There are several **summer cultural festivals** in the Berkshires, but none so prominent as the big three of Tanglewood, Jacob's Pillow, and the Williamstown Theatre Festival. Virtually every concert and performance at the more established festivals is well attended, and tickets for the more popular events sell out far in advance, so plan accordingly. For a current calendar that includes all of the festivals, contact the

Berkshire Visitors' Bureau, Berkshire Common, Pittsfield, MA 01201 (①413/443-9186 or 1-800/237-5747, ⓦwww.berkshires.org).

Aston Magna Festival St James Church, Rte-7 and Taconic Avenue, Great Barrington (July to early Aug Sat; ①413/528-3595 or 1-800/875-7156). The country's oldest annual summer festival, devoted to performances of Baroque music played on period instruments.

Berkshire Theatre Festival Main Street, Stockbridge (late June to Aug Mon–Sat; ①413/298-5576). Best known for its four summer productions at the Berkshire Playhouse Mainstage, but also noteworthy for Unicorn Theatre readings of plays in progress.

Jacob's Pillow Rte-20 between Becket and Lee (late June to Aug Tues–Sat; ①413/243-0745). Perhaps the most famous contemporary dance festival in the country, improbably located in the middle of (an admittedly lovely) nowhere. Artists-in-residence give free performances of works in progress before the main programs.

Shakespeare & Company The Mount, 70 Kemble St, Lenox (May–Nov; ①413/637-3353). One of the country's biggest Shakespeare festivals uses The Mount, former summer estate of Edith Wharton, as its venue. Productions are not limited to Shakespeare, and include new plays, dance, and dramatizations of stories by Wharton, Henry James, and the like.

Tanglewood West Street/Rte-183, Lenox. From July to late August the Boston Symphony Orchestra gives concerts at this, perhaps the most celebrated outdoor cultural venue in the country. Full orchestral concerts take place weekends at the Shed; the newer Ozawa Hall is used on other days, mainly for chamber-music concerts. The musical options include open rehearsals for the BSO on Saturday mornings, and jazz and pop performances. Though tickets are sold for the Shed and Ozawa Hall, it is cheaper and arguably more enjoyable to sit on the grass – but if you do, bring a towel or lawn chair. When ordering tickets in advance, call ①617/266-1492 September through May; otherwise ①413/637-1600.

Williamstown Theatre Festival 84 Spring St, Williamstown (mid-June to late Aug Tues–Sun; ①413/597-3400). Every summer some of the most accomplished actors from American stage and screen converge on this stately college town for a series of nearly a dozen productions, both time-tested and experimental.

Stockbridge, from the sprawling Newport-style estates of Naumkeag and Chesterwood outside town to other historical houses and relics within easy reach of the town.

Stockbridge has the bulk of weighty historical associations in a region that has relatively few, especially compared to Eastern Massachusetts. When in 1722 pioneers wrested a chunk of land along the Housatonic River from local Indians, they set aside a bit as "Indian Town," where they attempted to "English" them – with limited success. Indian Town was soon renamed Stockbridge, and, in the days before it attracted a wealthy summer population, owed its sustained existence to farming and its location on the stagecoach route between Boston and Albany, New York. On February 26, 1787, disenfranchised Revolutionary War veterans plundered Stockbridge houses and holed up for the night in the *Red Lion Inn*; the ill-fated Shay's Rebellion ended the next day with a shoot-out in Great Barrington, the next town south on Rte-7. Incidentally, the *Red Lion Inn*, depicted in Norman Rockwell's *Main Street Stockbridge at Christmastime*, was built on the site of the original, which burned in 1896.

Accommodation

The Stockbridge Chamber of Commerce (Ⓣ413/298-5200, lodging hotline Ⓣ413/298-4321, Ⓦwww.stockbridgechamber.org) can help you with accommodation and other information.

Berkshire Thistle Bed and Breakfast 19 East St/Rte-7 Ⓣ413/298-3188, Ⓦwww.berkshirethistle.com. This oversized residence resting confidently on five forested acres has five beautifully furnished rooms waiting to comfort tired travelers. Full breakfast on weekends, generous continental breakfast buffet during the week. ❺

Meadowlark Chesterwood Ⓣ413/298-5545. The second, smaller studio built by Daniel Chester French on his large estate is rented out in season; staying in this unusual spot grants you free admission to the rest of Chesterwood. Make reservations through the *Red Lion Inn* ❾

One Main Street Bed and Breakfast 1 Main Street Ⓣ413/298-5299, Ⓦwww.onemainbnb.com. Although not on the stretch of Main Street immortalized by Norman Rockwell, still a central – and quiet – location. Three comfortable rooms with private bath and mountain views in an 1825 Colonial-style home. Hearty breakfast included.

Red Lion Inn 30 Main St Ⓣ413/298-1690, Ⓦwww.redlioninn.com. Brimming with the kind of bric-a-brac you wish your grandmother would toss, what for many is the quintessential New England hostelry – and therefore popular with tour groups – is for others a case study in quaintness run amok. The gift shop is called The Pink Kitty. Draw your own conclusions. ❹

Stockbridge Country Inn 26 Glendale Rd/Rte-183 Ⓣ413/298-4015, Ⓦwww.stockbridgecountryinn.com. Set in an 1856 Federal country house on four acres of private land, this seven-room B&B is close to the Rockwell Museum and offers queen-sized four-poster canopy beds, a heated pool, attractive gardens, and porches from which to view them. Full country breakfast included. ❽

The Town and around

The actual town of Stockbridge is tiny, basically consisting of a few nineteenth-century buildings on Main Street and those around the corner on Elm Street. Unless they're staying at the grandmotherly **Red Lion Inn**, most people tend to park their car near it and wander from there, either having iced tea on the inn's venerable front porch, or else stocking up on provisions at one of the numerous good country markets such as Williams and Sons.

There are few specific sights in the town center. The Historical Room of the **Stockbridge Library**, at the corner of Main and Elm streets (Mon–Fri 9am–5pm, Sat 9am–4pm), contains artifacts from the Mahican Indians, who first lived in the area. The small **Mission House**, at the corner of Main and

Sergeant streets (daily: late May to mid-Oct 10am–5pm; $5), is where the Reverend John Sergeant planned his missionary work, under the auspices of the London Society for the Propagation of the Gospel in Foreign Lands. Though built in 1739, it was relocated here from a nearby site in 1928. The exterior has a pretty, arched Connecticut River Valley–style doorway, while the inside is noteworthy mainly for the eighteenth-century chairs on which Sergeant is said to have sat. Opposite the Mission House, the **Merwin House** is another period residence (tours temporarily suspended at the time of writing), normally open to public viewing by way of regular guided tours. The elegant Federal-style building exemplifies gracious Stockbridge living in the early part of the nineteenth century, and is stocked with an interesting selection of paintings and antiques.

Most people skip all this, however, in favor of the **Norman Rockwell Museum** (May–Oct daily 10am–5pm; Nov–April Mon–Fri 10am–4pm, Sat–Sun 10am–5pm; $12), just outside the town center off Rte-183. Given the steep admission, the selection is more limited than one might expect, but the two floors of Rockwell originals and reproductions are well displayed in a $10 million facility, built in part with a donation from Steven Spielberg. Even the biggest fan of his work may have the limits of their admiration tested by the gallery of Rockwell's advertising endorsements, for everything from cereal to cars, which make it seem like he would have given his name to just about anything. The facility itself is rather sterile, looking like nothing so much as a nursing home from the outside, but the grounds include the little red building that was Rockwell's own studio.

Beyond the Rockwell Museum, the **Berkshire Botanical Garden**, at the junction of routes 102 and 183 (daily: May–Oct 10am–5pm; $7), is home to around fifteen acres of landscaped gardens, with wildflowers on display in spring and roses during summer. You can also make a fragrant loop through the woods.

Norman Rockwell

Love him or hate him, if you spend any time in western New England, it's hard to avoid the work of **Norman Rockwell**. The man dubbed "America's best-loved artist" lived and painted in Arlington, Vermont, and, more famously, in Stockbridge, Massachusetts, and there are no fewer than three museums in his honor. For more than half a century, Rockwell was a fixture on the landscape of American popular culture, known as much for his product endorsements as for his *Saturday Evening Post* covers. Of American artists, perhaps only Warhol, in many ways his spiritual opposite, is so easily recognizable.

Born in 1894 in New York City, Rockwell dropped out of high school to attend classes at the National Academy of Design, and at the age of 22 sold his first painting to the *Saturday Evening Post*; in the forty years that followed, he contributed more than 300 paintings to that publication alone. His work presented, in the artist's own words, "life as it should be": children playing, adults relaxing, doctors examining healthy patients, family struggles that seemed certain to have a happy ending. His work stands in dramatic contrast to the "serious artists" of the twentieth century, the surrealists, dadaists, cubists, and abstract expressionists, much as his idyllic images stand in contrast to the often turbulent times in which he lived.

Many have questioned the veracity of these images, yet it seems doubtful that Rockwell saw much in the way of war, riots, or lynchings during his placid suburban life. However, later in his career, working for *Look* magazine, Rockwell did take on such issues as integration of schools and neighborhoods, and did so with the same gentle dignity that he had devoted to more insular concerns.

There's another, rather overrated, attraction just down the road in the form of **Chesterwood**, at 4 Williamsville Rd (daily: May–Oct 10am–5pm; $10, grounds only $5), the former summer home of sculptor Daniel Chester French, best known for his oversized rendition of President Lincoln that sits in his eponymous memorial in Washington DC. The humdrum plaster models in the artist's studio perhaps betray the fact that he had no formal training. His 130-acre estate is idyllic, though, as he averred, "I live here six months of the year – in heaven. The other six months I live, well – in New York."

With its spectacular views of the Stockbridge hills, distinctive gardens and aesthetically balanced interiors, the Gilded Age estate of **Naumkeag**, on Prospect Hill Road (daily: late May to mid-Oct 10am–5pm; $9, gardens only $7), nestled amongst several other sumptuous private estates (including the nearby Oronoque, a stylized royal hunting lodge built the same year as Naumkeag), is like a Newport mansion without the forced opulence. It was built by Stanford White in 1886 as a family home for the prosperous attorney Joseph Hodges Choate, later made ambassador to the Court of St James (the estate's name, pronounced "Nómkeg," derives from the Native American word for Salem, Choate's birthplace). The touches of a master architect are evident everywhere, from the synthesis of American elements such as a shingle roof with European-style brick and stone towers to understated flourishes throughout the 26 rooms of the house, including a combination of cherry, oak, and mahogany paneling and a three-story handcarved oak staircase. Original furnishings and domestic accoutrements, from European tapestries to Asian ceramics, give the impression that the Choates have just slipped out for a ride in the country; indeed, there are even coats left hanging in the closet. Although only guided tours of the inside are available, this is one of the few country "cottages" in the Berkshires where taking one is truly worthwhile.

As impressive as the house is, the real attraction here is the eight acres of meticulously planned and tended **gardens**, subtly studded with contemporary sculpture. The first green space of note, more like an adjunct to the house, is the Afternoon Garden, a 1928 addition remarkable for its vividly painted Venetian-style oak posts. The Perugino View, named for a sixteenth-century landscape painter, adjoins the Top Lawn and affords intoxicating views over the grounds and across to Monument Mountain. From here it's a short walk to the Blue Steps, named for a succession of blue-colored fountains flanked by stairs that lead to yet more gardens. The atmospheric Linden Walk ends with a statue of the Roman goddess Diana.

Eating and drinking

Boiler Room Café 405 Stockbridge Rd/Rte-7 ⓣ413/528-4280. It comes as a pleasant surprise to find such toothsome Mediterranean cooking, with an emphasis on Provençal and Catalan dishes, just outside of Stockbridge.

Glendale River Grille Rte-183 ⓣ413/298-4711. Elegant, spacious grill and tavern, about five miles south of the Norman Rockwell Museum. Some adventurous entrées – such as roast duckling Cantonese with hoisin sauce – in addition to standard grill treats like steaks and swordfish.

The Red Lion Inn Main Street ⓣ413/298-5545. Repair to the old inn's atmospheric tavern room for big portions of reliable Yankee fare, from prime rib to *sole meunière*.

Lenox

From Stockbridge, a slight detour off Rte-7 takes you to Rte-7A and the genteel village of **LENOX**, the cultural nucleus of the Berkshires by virtue of its proximity to Tanglewood, the summer home of the Boston Symphony Orchestra. It's a quiet place for most of the year, but on summer weekends during its music festival, traffic jams are not uncommon. Summering in Lenox has been a New York (rather than Boston) tradition since the mid-nineteenth century, and, not surprisingly, although the number of shops and restaurants is necessarily limited by the town's small size, in terms of both price and attitude their atmosphere is more Manhattan than New England.

Accommodation

The **Lenox Chamber of Commerce**, 5 Walker St (⊕413/637-3646, ⊛www.lenox.org), will help you to find a place to stay, although don't expect to stroll into town and find a room while Tanglewood is in session.

Blantyre Blantyre Road ⊕413/637-3556, ⊛www.blantyre.com. A roomy Scottish Tudor mansion with Gothic flourishes – a former summer "cottage" – that has been purposed as one of the country's most luxurious resorts, and as such is almost a destination in itself. Closed for winter. 9

Brook Farm Inn 15 Hawthorne St ⊕413/637-3013 or 1-800/285-POET, ⊛www.brookfarm.com. The innkeepers at this twelve-room 1870 Victorian B&B are poetry aficionados, so in summer you can borrow a tape recorder and listen to the bard of your choice, on the porch or by the pool, and in winter curl up with a book of verse in front of a fireplace, either in the common area or in your room. 6

Gateways Inn 51 Walker St ⊕413/637-2532, ⊛www.gatewaysinn.com. Choose from four-poster, canopy, or sleigh beds at this centrally located inn with attractive wooden interiors and well-kept gardens. 6

The Village Inn 16 Church St ⊕413/637-0020 or 1-800/253-0917, ⊛www.villageinn-lenox.com. A country inn-style hotel – with 32 rooms with antiques, bountiful breakfasts, and afternoon English tea – in the center of Lenox. Good-value rooms if you visit during spring. 4

Walker House 64 Walker St ⊕413/637-1271, ⊛www.walkerhouse.com. This informal eight-room B&B is pet-friendly – the innkeepers have five cats which roam the jungle-like gardens surrounding the house. 6

Wheatleigh Hawthorne Rd ⊕413/637-0610, ⊛www.wheatleigh.com. Built by a New York financier in 1893 as a wedding present for his daughter, who married a Spanish count, today this Florentine palazzo-style estate-cum-resort combines antique and contemporary decor to sumptuous, successful effect. The lush grounds were landscaped by Frederick Law Olmsted, designer of New York's Central Park, and to stay any closer to Tanglewood you'd have to camp on its lawn. 9

The Town and around

Even if you're visiting after late August, it's well worth making a stop off West Street (Rte-183), about a mile outside town, to walk around **Tanglewood**. Though its lush grounds were formerly part of the estate of a wealthy Boston banker, it was Nathaniel Hawthorne who coined the name – today musicians practice in a reconstruction of the little red farmhouse where he lived with his wife Sophia in 1850 and 1851, penning *The House of the Seven Gables* on the premises. On summer weekends, concerts are given in the aptly named "Shed," a barebones, indoor/outdoor hall, as well as the newer Ozawa Hall (see p.272). From the edge of the sprawling lawn there is a good view of the Stockbridge Bowl, a mile-wide pond – a view which is even better from the more elevated Kripalu Center for Yoga and Health, across the street from Tanglewood's main entrance (just drive through the parking lot and pretend to be in meditation if questioned). Another way to appreciate the countryside around here is on horseback; **Undermountain Farm** (⊕413/637-3365) offers guided trail rides.

While most of the expansive "cottages" that transformed Lenox and vicinity into "the inland Newport" at the turn of last century remain in private hands (as homes, hotels, and even medical facilities), **The Mount**, at the southern junction of routes 7 and 7A, at the corner of Plunkett Street and Rte-7 (early June to early Nov house 9am–5pm, grounds 9am–6pm; $16; ⓣ413/637-1899), the summer home of novelist Edith Wharton from 1902 until 1911, is open to the public. Its order, scale, and harmony are a reflection of the principles Wharton promoted in her first successful book, *The Decoration of Houses*, published a few years before she moved in. One of her precepts was to ease the transition from outdoors to inside – an example of which is the indoor wrought-iron stair rails, a material typically associated with exterior ornamentation. Though Wharton's years at The Mount were productive – among other things, she wrote *Ethan Frome* here – they were not entirely happy; boredom with her husband and unapologetic disgust for the turpitude of American culture sent her packing for France, where she lived out her final years. These days the Mount is another performance space, with four stages, the main one of which is open-air; adaptations of stories by Wharton and her soul mate, Henry James, also take place in season in the drawing room.

Eating and drinking

Bistro Zinc 56 Church St ⓣ413/637-8800. Power-lunch spot filled with diners on cell phones gobbling up flavorful French fare at reasonable prices – dinner is considerably more expensive.
Café Lucia 90 Church St ⓣ413/637-2640. It may not be on the menu, but you're likely to get a serving of attitude along with your pricey, if tasty, Italian entrées at this popular, bustling spot where a Manhattan ambience prevails. Closed Mon.
Church Street Café 69 Church St ⓣ413/637-2745. Updated New England fare, from sautéed Maine crab cakes to maple- and cider-glazed pork chops, wins accolades for this eatery – more restaurant than café – in the center of Lenox.
Wheatleigh Hawthorne Road ⓣ413/637-0610. Very highly priced, but you get what you pay for – outstanding flavors of contemporary continental cuisine, including low-fat and vegetarian menus, artfully prepared desserts, and impeccable service. The decor, from crystal chandeliers to Italianate paintings, is undeniably soothing.

Lee and Tyringham

During the busy summer cultural season, many last-minute travelers who think they'll find a room in Lenox end up staying in nearby **LEE**, which is just as well, for there is a genuine aspect to the place altogether lacking in its ritzier neighbor. Plus, there are many small inns and B&Bs, all of which have the advantage of being near the thick of things yet removed from the commotion. Like other Berkshire towns, Lee was once a papermaking center, but it was better known for its unusually strong marble – which found its way to the US Capitol, the Empire State Building, St Patrick's Cathedral, and other East Coast landmarks. It's also in evidence in Lee itself, for example in certain buildings along the archetypal **Main Street**. McClelland's Drug Store, here at no. 43, replete with vintage soda fountain – which unfortunately uses Ben & Jerry's instead of homemade ice cream – is a big draw, as is the perennially busy *Joe's Diner* at Main and Center streets (see overleaf), where quality eats from omelets to club sandwiches come at ridiculously low prices.

One of the better-kept secrets in Massachusetts is the incredibly scenic Tyringham Valley (see overleaf), practically hidden between routes 102 and 23. **TYRINGHAM** itself, which basically consists of a post office and a church, was settled as a hinterland community in the eighteenth century and hasn't perceivably changed since. The only tangible sight is an unusual museum called **Santarella** at 75 Main Rd (daily: late May–Oct 10am–5pm; $4), designed and built by Englishman Sir Henry Hudson Kitson – the sculptor of the *Minute Man* in Lexington – as his sculpture studio in the Thirties. Its signature feature is the eighty-ton roof, a sculpted simulation of thatching that succeeds in conveying the image of the undulating Berkshire Hills in autumn. Despite a few noteworthy works, Kitson was a minor figure on the American artistic landscape, and the "museum" in his honor isn't all that impressive. What makes Santarella worth a stop, however (other than getting a look at its fantastic roof), is the contemporary art gallery inside, which spills onto the serene gardens and around a lily pond behind the house.

Just south of Santarella, Tyringham Road opens onto the **Tyringham Valley**, which is more reminiscent of an unsullied Irish glade than any part of New England proper. The highest spot, on the right, is the **Tyringham Cobble**, a forest-covered outcropping of limestone and quartzite that rises 400 feet over the valley: to hike it, make a right on Jerusalem Road, after the village, and proceed for a quarter of a mile. The reward for your two-mile endeavor will be views that are breathtaking, and on a clear spring or fall day, positively immobilizing. A right turn on Art School Road, the next street down, takes you to the highly-regarded Joyous Spring Pottery (daily during summer 10am–5pm; ⓣ413/528-4115), where you can view pottery made using Japanese techniques and fired in a *nobori gama* (a kiln that can hold up to fifteen hundred pieces). A couple of miles farther south, the road intersects Rte-23, heading west on which takes you through equally tiny Monterey and back to Rte-7.

Practicalities

The **Lee Chamber of Commerce**, 3 Park Place (ⓣ413/243-0852, ⓦwww.leechamber.org), operates an information booth on weekends (10am–5pm). There is a good range of **accommodation**, especially in Lee, and this may be a good alternative base if nearby Lenox is either too full or too expensive. *Applegate*, 279 W Park St (ⓣ413/243-4451 or 1-800/691-9012, ⓦwww.applegateinn.com; ❺), is a calm, ship-shape B&B, in a Southern-style Georgian colonial home, whose six guestrooms have old-fashioned character but a contemporary feel; fresh baked goods contribute to great breakfasts. The *Chambéry Inn*, 199 Main St (ⓣ413/243-2221 or 1-800/537-4321; ❺), has seven meticulously refurbished suites with high ceilings, big windows, and modern touches such as in-room phones and cable TV (there are also two standard double rooms) in an 1885 French country house, built as the country's first parochial school. Just south of town between Stockbridge and Lee, the atmospheric old nine-room *Historic Merrell Inn*, 1565 Pleasant St/Rte-102, South Lee (ⓣ413/243-1794 or 1-800/243-1794, ⓦwww.merrell-inn.com; ❺), has some interesting relics from its days as a stagecoach stop, such as a vintage birdcage bar in the Tavern Room, where breakfast is served. Ask for a room overlooking the meandering Housatonic River. Meanwhile, old New England lives on in Tyringham at the *Sunset Farm Bed & Breakfast*, 74 Tyringham Rd (ⓣ413/243-3229, ⓦwww.sunsetfarminn.com; ❺), a blissfully isolated farmhouse on a hillock in the gorgeous Tyringham Valley. Four rooms, of which three have private baths, are a bit frayed at the edges, but the feel is very authentic without being twee. The owners are warm, the food good, and there's a nice place to hike out back.

The best **place to eat** in Lee, whether you want a weighty corned beef sandwich, tuna salad on rye, or scrambled eggs and waffles, is *Joe's Diner*, 85 Center St, South Lee (ⓣ413/243-9756), a very popular spot with extremely low prices and attendant lines at peak grazing times. Also with reasonable

△ Pontoosuc Lake, near Pittsfield

prices, and an informal atmosphere in which to eat a variety of seafood and pasta dishes, is the *Salmon Run Fish House*, 78 Main St (Ⓣ413/243-3900).

Great Barrington

South of Stockbridge, the landscape takes on a more rusticated flavor, one that colors the only town of any size, **GREAT BARRINGTON**. It was the site of the last attempt of the British to hold court in America: Shay's Rebellion ended with five casualties here on February 27, 1787, when the Sheffield militia confronted one hundred anti-government insurgents and the hostages they had taken from Stockbridge. Another claim to fame is **Monument Mountain**, on US-7, five miles north of the town center, a picturesque peak known in literary lore as the place where Nathaniel Hawthorne and Herman Melville met during an afternoon hike in August 1850. In a thunderstorm-induced interlude, they and some other climbers drank champagne and recited poetry; the two authors became fast friends. Yet Great Barrington is perhaps most notable as the unlikely birthplace of one of the greatest civil rights leaders in US history, Dr. **W.E.B. Dubois**, a well-regarded writer and one of the founders of the National Association for the Advancement of Colored People (NAACP).

Today **Great Barrington** is still a modest country town, though one with alternately hip and hippie touches. What buzz there is centers on **Main Street** near Railroad and Castle streets, where up-market home decor shops bestride a number of good eateries, such as *20 Railroad Street* (Ⓣ413/528-9345) for casual American food and *Bev's* (Ⓣ413/528-6645) for even more casual American dining, including homemade ice cream. The old-fashioned **Mahaiwe Theater** on Castle Street has recently been bought by the Berkshire Opera Company (Ⓣ413/644-9988), and is the place to go for classical music concerts. If it's the season (mid-Aug to mid-Oct), you may want to pick apples at **Windy Hill Farm**, 686 Stockbridge Rd (Ⓣ413/298-3217), or pumpkins at **Taft Farms**, Rte-183 (Ⓣ413/528-1515 or 1-800/528-1015). Just south of town on Rte-7, Guido's (Ⓣ413/528-9255) is a popular gourmet food market.

Practicalities

The Great Barrington **Chamber of Commerce** can arrange for accommodation via their lodging hotline (Ⓣ413/528-4006 or 1-800/269-4825). If you're looking for a **place to stay**, the *Wainwright Inn*, 518 S Main St (Ⓣ413/528-2062, Ⓦwww.wainwrightinn.com; ❻), occupies a huge 1766 mansion right outside the center of town, while the *Windflower Inn*, 684 South Egremont Rd/Rte-23 (Ⓣ413/528-2720 or 1-800/992-1993; Ⓦwww.windflowerinn.com; ❻), is a relaxed country inn with thirteen guest rooms, most with fireplaces – the biggest of which is in Room 12. Sitting quietly five minutes outside of town, the *Manor Lane B&B*, 145 Hurlburt Rd (Ⓣ413/528-8222; ❻), offers all the amenities you could ask for. Make sure to reserve one of the three large rooms ahead of time, and be sure to take advantage of the outside pool, tennis courts, and walking trails.

In addition to *20 Railroad Street* and *Bev's* (see above), there are several other decent **places to eat** in Great Barrington. For excellent wood-fired sourdough pizzas made with local organic produce, head to *Babalouie's*, 289 Main St (Ⓣ413/528-8100); if it's sushi you crave, go to *Bizen*, 17 Railroad St (Ⓣ413/528-4343), which has Japanese chefs and an energetic atmosphere; or wolf down "Le Burger" and other good French bistro food at *La Tomate*, 293

Main St/Rte-7 (ⓣ413/528-3003). Just north of Great Barrington along Rte-183, in the small village of Housatonic, *Jack's Grill* (ⓣ413/274-1000) is worth the detour more for the lavish romper-room decor – which features a model train that chugs around a track suspended from the ceiling, lunch boxes and tube radios from the 1950s, and very funky bathrooms – than for the rather mediocre American comfort food.

South of Great Barrington

Rte-23 southwest from Great Barrington takes you to tiny **SOUTH EGREMONT**, near which are the **Bash Bish Falls**, named for the Indian girl whose amorous woes prompted her to plunge fifty feet to her demise in a rock-bottomed pool. Water tumbling through a series of gorges and finally dropping 80 feet into a sparkling pool make this one of the more dramatic waterfalls in the state. Heading east on Rte-23 from Great Barrington, meanwhile, takes you on a more serene trajectory to Monterey, from where you can head back to Tyringham and Lee.

There's little need to proceed much farther south on Rte-7 unless you want to go antique shopping or hiking. **SHEFFIELD**, the next town down from Great Barrington, is the antique capital of the region. There's not much of a town center, however; if you see an antiques store that grabs your fancy, just pull over by the side of the road and check out the merchandise. **ASHLEY FALLS**, practically straddling the Connecticut border, is the site of **Bartholomew's Cobble**, a mineral outcropping that rises above the placid Housatonic River. A contiguous **nature reserve**, known for its abundant ferns, has a series of easy walking trails that are heavily trodden in summer and fall. Very nearby, on Cooper Hill Road, is the white-clapboard **Ashley House**, a rather unremarkable colonial abode. Built in 1735, this is said to be the oldest house in Berkshire County, but is more interesting for its historical associations than anything inside. In 1773, townsmen here drafted the "Sheffield Declaration," a statement of grievances against English rule; in 1781 Ashley's slave, Mum Bet, sued for freedom – which she won two years later.

One of the more quirky **places to stay** in the Berkshires, largely by virtue of its chintz-free feel, is the *Race Brook Lodge*, 864 S Undermountain Rd (Rte-41), Sheffield (ⓣ413/229-2916 or 1-888/RB-LODGE, ⓦwww.rblodge.com; ④), which has thirty rooms in a cluster of restored nineteenth-century farm buildings, with cheaper, quite basic cabins also available. For **eating**, *John Andrew's*, Rte-23, South Egremont (ⓣ413/528-3469), has been roundly praised for its contemporary American fare, excellent wine list, and tasteful decor – a triple surprise for what appears from the outside to be just another building at the edge of a forest. Less upscale, *The Old Mill*, Rte-23, South Egremont (ⓣ413/528-1421), serves reliably good-tasting New England fare, and sizeable portions of it, in a cozy riverside building that – you guessed it – used to be an old mill.

Pittsfield and around

PITTSFIELD, once a prosperous center for paper milling and the home of GE's plastics division, is now the grim epitome of a town that has failed to reinvent itself. Perhaps Pittsfield suffers in comparison to its northerly neighbor,

North Adams (see p.285), an ugly old industrial town which *has* undergone a renaissance in recent years, or perhaps arriving at a gritty mill town after several carefree days spent in the refined Berkshire villages to the south is just too much of a culture shock. Either way, Pittsfield is not a highlight of the region, and the interminable talk of historic buildings being bought and restored by various philanthropic groups remains just that – talk. The town is home, however, to the excellent **Berkshire Visitors Bureau**, at the Berkshire Common Plaza, next to the *Crowne Plaza* (Mon–Fri 8.30am–5pm; ⓣ413/443-9186 or 1-800/237-5747, ⓦwww.berkshires.org), which has information and a seasonal hotel reservation service (July–Aug Thurs–Fri 8.30am–7pm, Sat 8.30am–5pm) covering the entire Berkshires region.

Crane and Company, one of the few paper manufacturers still operating in the vicinity and, since 1879, the sole producer of paper used to make US dollar bills, maintains the **Crane Museum** off routes 8 and 9 (June to mid-Oct Mon–Fri 2–5pm; free), housed in an old stone mill in nearby Dalton, where the exhibits focus on American paper manufacture since the Revolutionary years. The only other sight that might keep you in Pittsfield is **Arrowhead**, just south of the town center on Holmes Road (daily: late May–Oct 9.30am–5pm; $6), the eighteenth-century farmhouse where Herman Melville lived for thirteen years and wrote *Moby Dick*. In Pittsfield itself, the generic art-and-science **Berkshire Museum**, 39 South St (Mon–Sat 10am–5pm, Sun noon–5pm; $7.50), has little that can't be found at similar, smaller collections around the country – you're better off heading out to the Hancock Shaker Village (see below).

The most obvious **place to stay** in Pittsfield is the *Crowne Plaza*, 1 West St (ⓣ413/499-2000, ⓦwww.berkshirecrowne.com; ❻), which dominates downtown and has comfortable rooms. If you're looking for a much more personal experience, however, head about three miles out of town along Barker Road to *Hollyhock House* (ⓣ413/443-6901, ⓔhollyhockhouse@worldnet.att.net; ❸), a friendly, intimate, and spotlessly clean bed and breakfast with three recently renovated rooms which are good value for money. For something to **eat**, *Dakota*, 1035 South St/Rte-7 (ⓣ413/499-7900), is a capacious place with updated hunting lodge decor, a bit of a relief from the faux hipness of so many Berkshire restaurants. Big portions of American staples such as Maine lobster and mesquite-grilled chicken are the draws, as is the large salad bar. Meanwhile, the *Court Square Breakfast & Deli*, 95 East St (ⓣ413/442-9896), across from the courthouse, is one of the brighter, more pleasant places in town to eat straightforward breakfasts and lunches.

Hancock Shaker Village

Our tools are kind and gentle words, our shop is in the heart, And here we manufacture peace, that we may such impart.

from a Shaker song

From 1790 until 1960, the **Hancock Shaker Village**, at the junction of routes 20 and 41, five miles west of Pittsfield (daily: late May to late Oct 9.30am–5pm; rest of year 10am–3pm; summer and fall $15, rest of year $12; ⓣ413/443-0188 or 1-800/817-1137, ⓦwww.hancockshakervillage.org), was an active community of the famous offshoot of Quakers from Manchester, England, so named for their convulsive fits of glee experienced when worshipping. The pacifist cult, which was renowned for its vegetable seeds and simply but elegantly crafted furniture, all but disappeared, partly due to its members' vows of celibacy, although one community shakes on at Sabbathday

Lake in Maine. Hancock was the third Shaker village established, and retains one of the biggest collections of Shaker furniture and objects. Its twenty preserved buildings, located in fairly close proximity amid 1200 acres, are well worth poking about. The most interesting, and most photographed, is the **Round Stone Barn**, built in 1826 and the only one of its kind. Its circular shape allowed a single man to feed 54 cows at the same time from the center. In another unsung instance of Shaker ingenuity, manure was dropped through trap doors to the barn's cellar, where it was stored until needed as fertilizer. Other structures include a schoolhouse, meeting house, privies, and a two-car garage added in 1914.

Much of the fun to be had at the Hancock Shaker Village is of the pastoral variety. In the Barn Complex you can try your hand at a spinning wheel or quill pen, or try on a range of Shaker fashions. You can also milk a plastic cow – if the teats seem spent, ask a guide to turn the heifer on – or chat with a guide tending one of the gardens, where heirloom vegetables are raised. Other activities and demonstrations vary from day to day, but could include anything from a plowing match to sheep shearing. The highlight of a visit, however, may well be lunch or a snack in the on-site *Village Café*, which serves inexpensive and surprisingly tasty Shaker-inspired dishes, such as ham baked in cider, and devilishly savory baked goods. During fall and winter, Shaker dinners are held on certain dates only.

Mount Greylock

To Americans from the western states it will never be more than a sizeable hill, but those from Massachusetts take no small amount of pride in **Mount Greylock**, the tallest peak in the state. Though somewhat short of spectacular, it does make for a scenic hike or drive, especially in the fall. From the peak, at 3491 feet, you can sometimes see five states, though admittedly they all look pretty much the same from here. The ninety-foot-tall **War Memorial Tower**, erected to honor the Massachusetts casualties of all wars, stands near the top. Access to Mount Greylock is easy enough: from Rte-7 one mile north of Lanesborough, turn right (east) on to Rockwell Road, where in two miles there's a **visitors' center** (☎413/499-4262) with trail maps and such like; the summit is eight miles further. Note that the summit is accessible by vehicle from May through October. If you want to **eat** a cheap, bountiful coffee shop-style breakfast or lunch before or after your hike up Mount Greylock, *Bob's Country Kitchen* (closed Wed; ☎413/442-1075) in not unlovely Lanesborough is a good place to stop.

Williamstown

Pretty **WILLIAMSTOWN**, at the northwesternmost corner of the state, may seem a bit remote to be one of the region's premier art destinations, but the presence of the **Clark Institute**, with its excellent Impressionist collections, and the **Williams College Museum of Art** has put it on the map. These two, plus the beautiful campus of Williams College and the town's prime location at the terminus of the Mohawk Trail, make Williamstown a choice spot to spend a few days. Most of the action, of which there is actually little save for during the summertime **Williamstown Theatre Festival** (see box, p.272), centers on block-long **Spring Street**, with the requisite range of shops and restaurants, most infused with an unmistakable upscale collegiate atmosphere.

The Mohawk Trail

The best-known scenic route in the Berkshires is the **Mohawk Trail**, otherwise known as Rte-2, from the Massachusetts–New York border to the town of Millers Falls on the Connecticut River. Originally, the 63-mile Mohawk Trail was used by Native Americans of the Five Nations to travel between the Hudson and Connecticut river valleys. During the French and Indian War, they put it to use as an invasion route. Today, the main appeal of the trail – especially during fall foliage – is simply taking in the bucolic vistas it affords. Tourist facilities in the form of country inns, bed and breakfasts, gift shops, and private and public campgrounds are in plentiful supply along the way, and the attractions are many and varied. Working from west to east, there are the culturally-rich towns of **Williamstown** (see p.283) and **North Adams** (see opposite), with their museums and festivals, as well as Massachusetts' highest peak, **Mount Greylock**, which lies just south of the road, roughly halfway between the two towns. In North Adams, New England's only **natural bridge**, a white marble arch formed by melting glaciers, is worth a visit. Just before Charlemont, you'll pass the **"Hail to the Sunrise" monument**, a huge statue of a Native American with outstretched arms, the trail's symbol. Here, you can access the **Mohawk Trail State Forest** (Ⓣ413-339-5504), a scenic woodland with many tall pine trees, hiking trails, and a 56-place campsite (mid-April to mid-Oct; $12 per site). Straddling the Deerfield River, the **Bridge of Flowers** is another highlight, especially if you happen to be passing through in spring when it's adorned with colorful foliage. Just downstream, check out the bizarre glacial potholes on the riverbed at **Salmon Falls**. Turn south at the town of Greenfield and travel a short way down Rte-10 to **Historic Deerfield** (see p.267), a profusion of well-preserved historic homes which are the main thing to see in the Upper Pioneer Valley.

For more information on the Mohawk Trail, contact the **Mohawk Trail Association**, North Adams (Ⓣ413/743-8127 or 1-866/743-8127, Ⓦwww.mohawktrail.com).

Accommodation

The 1896 House Cold Spring Road/Rte-7 Ⓣ413/458-1896 or 1-888/999-1896, Ⓦwww.1896house.com. Close to the center of Williamstown, this easily found hostelry proffers spotless "brookside," "pondside," and "barnside" accommodations and a good restaurant. ❸

Bed & Breakfast at Field Farm Guest House 554 Sloan Rd Ⓣ413/458-3135. Five bedrooms, each with private bath, in a 1948 country estate surrounded by nearly 300 acres of meadows and woodlands. ❻

Maple Terrace Motel 555 Main St/Rte-2 Ⓣ413/458-9677, Ⓦwww.mapleterrace.com. Reliable motel set off from the street, within easy walking distance of the Williamstown Theatre Festival. ❸

The Orchards 222 Adams Rd t413/458-9611 or 1-800/225-1517, wwww.orchardshotel.com. Modern hotel with a country-inn theme, with English antiques, afternoon tea, and several rooms with fireplaces. The spacious rooms also have TVs and VCRs. ❼–❽

Steep Acres Farm B&B 520 White Oaks Rd Ⓣ413/458-3774. Four rooms with shared baths in a 1900 cottage on fifty very scenic acres with an orchard and spring-fed pond; the breakfast is as filling as the environs are relaxing. ❹

The Town

What makes Williamstown an essential ingredient of any Berkshires tour is not the college itself – attractive as it is – but rather two superb museums, one of which, the **Sterling and Francine Clark Art Institute**, 225 South St (Tues–Sun 10am–5pm; $10 June–Oct, free Nov–May), is known for its extensive collection of French Impressionist paintings, including thirty by Renoir. There are also paintings by Fragonard, Géricault, Rembrandt, and

Alma-Tadema, as well as a sizeable collection of American works by Homer, Sargent, and Remington. Allow two hours or so to take it all in, longer if you have a snack or light lunch at the excellent museum café.

Located on the Williams campus, the **Williams College Museum of Art**, 15 Lawrence Hall Drive (Tues–Sat 10am–5pm, Sun 1–5pm; free) is ravishing on two counts: its facility and its collections. Part of it is housed in an 1846 two-story brick octagon, capped by a Neoclassical rotunda; a three-story entrance atrium connects it to a contemporary addition, and from the polished floors to lighting and crisply painted walls, the place could not be more immaculately maintained. The thrust of the exceedingly well-curated collection is American visual art from the late eighteenth century to the present day, and some of the best exhibits are those by contemporary artists. The non-Western collections include Asian art and a small but stunning selection of Mesopotamian and ancient Greek antiquities.

Music junkies will want to stop at the **Toonerville Trolley**, 131 Water St (Ⓣ413/458-5229), one of the best record stores in the region. There's a cheap selection of used vinyl in the back, an excellent selection of jazz, rock, blues, and world music, as well as a staggering, if pricey, selection of concert recordings. A must for serious collectors.

Eating and drinking

Chopsticks Chinese Restaurant 412 Main St Ⓣ413/458-5750. This minimal Chinese probably won't win any awards, but can be a welcome find in an area with very few non-American restaurants.

Clarksburg Bread Company 37 Spring St Ⓣ413/458-2251. Sure, they have bread galore, but the coffee, cakes, and cookies – especially the peanut butter chocolate chip – are what you'll want to fill up on.

Cobble Café 27 Spring St Ⓣ413/458-5930. Whether the menu is infused with attitude or innovation is up to you, but stick to the quesadillas, salads, and such and you'll be fine.

North Adams

Settled in the 1730s and, during the nineteenth century, a fairly prosperous mill town, **NORTH ADAMS**, five miles east of Williamstown on the Mohawk Trail, might have been just another post-industrial eyesore if it weren't for the **Massachusetts Museum of Contemporary Art** (MASS MoCA), 87 Marshall St (June–Oct daily 10am–6pm; Nov–May Mon, Wed–Sun 11am–5pm; $9 June–Oct, $7 Nov–May, free tours Sat–Sun noon & 3pm; Ⓣ413/662-2111; Ⓦwww.massmoca.org), a huge arts center housed in a resurrected old mill site. MASS MoCA mounts an extensive range of exhibits in its 27 refurbished red-brick buildings, linked by a web of bridges, passageways, viaducts, and courtyards. Most of the work inside is installation-oriented, and although much of the content may provoke even the most open-minded to wonder aloud, "Can you really call this *art*?," there's an undeniable neo-funhouse pleasure in wandering through the configurations of materials, collages, video monitors, found objects, oversized photographs, and flashing lights. The space also hosts modern dance performances, concerts, and a film series.

Practicalities

The opening of MASS MoCA in 1999 spawned a renaissance in North Adams, with trendy restaurants, boutiques, lounges, and cafés now inhabiting many of the town's previously empty factory buildings – and most forsaking the quaintness quotient so prevalent in other Berkshire towns. Just across the street from MASS MoCA, for example, *The Porches Inn*, 231 River St (☎413/664-0400, ⓦwww.porches.com; ❻–❼), is an ultra-modern **hotel** with DVD players, high-speed Internet connections, and not an antique in sight, occupying a row of houses formerly lived in by mill workers' families. At *Eleven*, in Building 11 at MASS MoCA (☎413/662-2004), you can **eat** spring pea risotto or seared *ahi* with *wasabi* cream sauce, and sip urban-chic cocktails on Martini-shaped bar stools. A similar vibe can be found at the *Joga Café*, 23 Eagle St (☎413/664-7122), the town's late-night **drinking** spot, where there's **live music** and bartenders wearing cowboy hats. If you'd prefer something more down-to-earth, head a few miles south on Rte-8 to the town of **ADAMS**, where the *Miss Adams Diner*, 53 Park St (☎413/743-5300), has been serving homemade cream pies and classic diner fare long before North Adams had even heard of spring peas.

Rhode Island

CANADA
8
6
NEW YORK
7
ATLANTIC OCEAN
3
1
2
Cape Cod
N
4
5

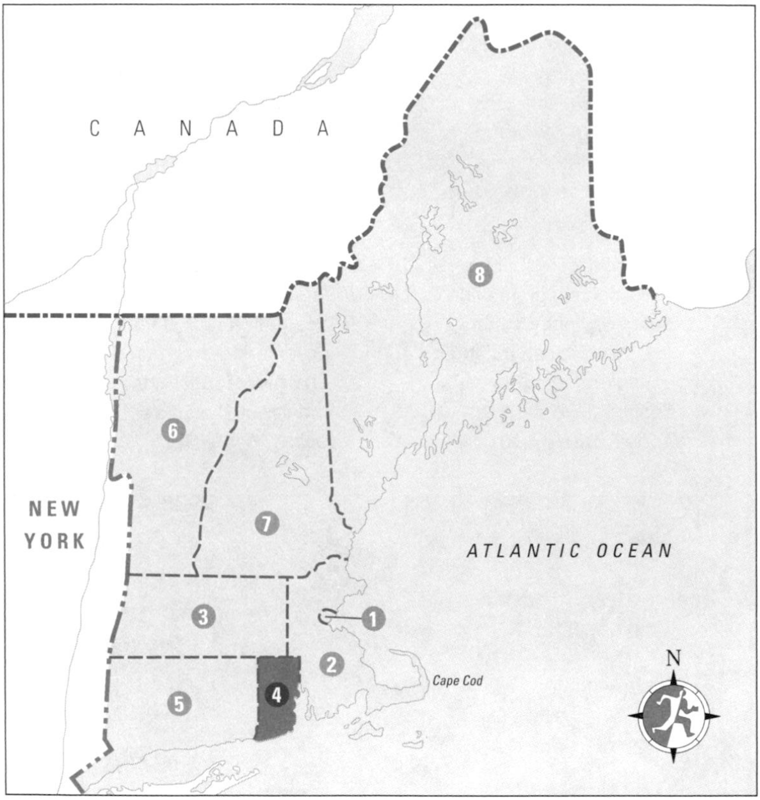

CHAPTER 4

Highlights

* **Federal Hill, Providence** This firmly established Italian community west of the Providence River has (almost) as much charm as Naples itself. See p.297

* **Blithewold Mansion and Gardens** In Bristol's otherwise drab surroundings, Blithewold is an oasis of blooming gardens, exotic trees, and giant sequoias. See p.300

* **Newport** With its phenomenal mansions, fine beaches, fancy yachts, and world-class summer music concerts, this coastal town has real appeal. See p.300

* **Blackstone Riverboat Tour** Get off the road and experience Rhode Island as the early settlers did: slowly, along the Blackstone River. See p.301

* **South County** Native American tribal gatherings, green parks, historical sites, and attractive beaches jockey for your attention in this overlooked corner of the state. See p.312

* **Mohegan Bluffs, Block Island** Experience pure desolation at 200 feet up, peering down on the charming tourist community of Block Island below. See p.323

4

Rhode Island

Just 48 miles long by 37 miles wide, tiny **Rhode Island** is easily the smallest state in the Union, barely even noticeable on a map of the country. For that reason alone, it often tends to be overlooked as a tourist destination, even if it is home to more than twenty percent of the nation's historical landmarks. Indeed, locals take great satisfaction in pointing out the state's disproportionately large influence on national life: it enacted the first law against slavery in North America on May 18, 1652, and was one of the first of the thirteen original colonies to declare independence from Great Britain. Rhode Island also claims the city of Newport as the birthplace of the US Navy (though Marblehead, Massachusetts, has a rival claim), and the Blackstone River Valley, which runs northwest from Providence, as the cradle of the Industrial Revolution, an event that followed the 1793 construction of America's first water-powered cotton mill in Pawtucket.

Despite its size, Rhode Island has more than four hundred miles of impressive, sometimes spectacular, coastline with more than one hundred public and private beaches, not to mention thousands of acres of pristine woodlands within a surprisingly diverse geography. Most of this coastline is hacked out of the state's most conspicuous feature, **Narragansett Bay**, a vast expanse of water that has long been a determining factor in Rhode Island's economic development and strategic military importance. In fact, more than thirty tiny islands make up the state, including Hope, Despair, and the bay's largest island, Rhode Island, which gives the state its name – though it's more often referred to by its Native American name, "Aquidneck."

Rhode Island's size and compactness is, ultimately, one of its most endearing features, and means that you are rarely more than an hour's drive or bus ride away from any other point in the state. The prime destinations are the colonial college town of **Providence**, right on I-95, the main highway that runs through the state (and indeed, the East Coast), and well-heeled **Newport**, yachting capital of the world, with good beaches and outrageously extravagant mansions. More scenic than I-95, US-1 hugs the coast of Narragansett Bay – which presents endless opportunities for swimming, boating, and other water-related leisure activities – and parallels the Atlantic Coast through **South County** into Connecticut. Along the coast are plenty of sleepy small towns and ports worth a look, most notably **Watch Hill** and **Galilee**. The latter also happens to be the main point of departure for ferries to **Block Island**, a popular excursion for visitors seeking a pleasant stretch of sand.

While in a state this small, traveling by **car** is really your best bet, getting to and around Rhode Island using public transport is also an option. **T.F. Green Airport** near Providence has **bus** links to Boston and most of the rest of New England, while RIPTA, or the Rhode Island Public Transit Authority,

(☎1-401/781-9400) is the means for traveling within state borders, whatever your point of origin. Stops at Westerly, Kingston, and Providence are your scant options via Amtrak's **train** service (☎1-800/USA-RAIL), though the trains are clean, reliable, and make for easy connections if you're traveling between here and Massachusetts or Connecticut.

Some history

The first European to explore the shores of Rhode Island may have been Portuguese navigator **Miguel de Cortereal** who sailed along the coast in

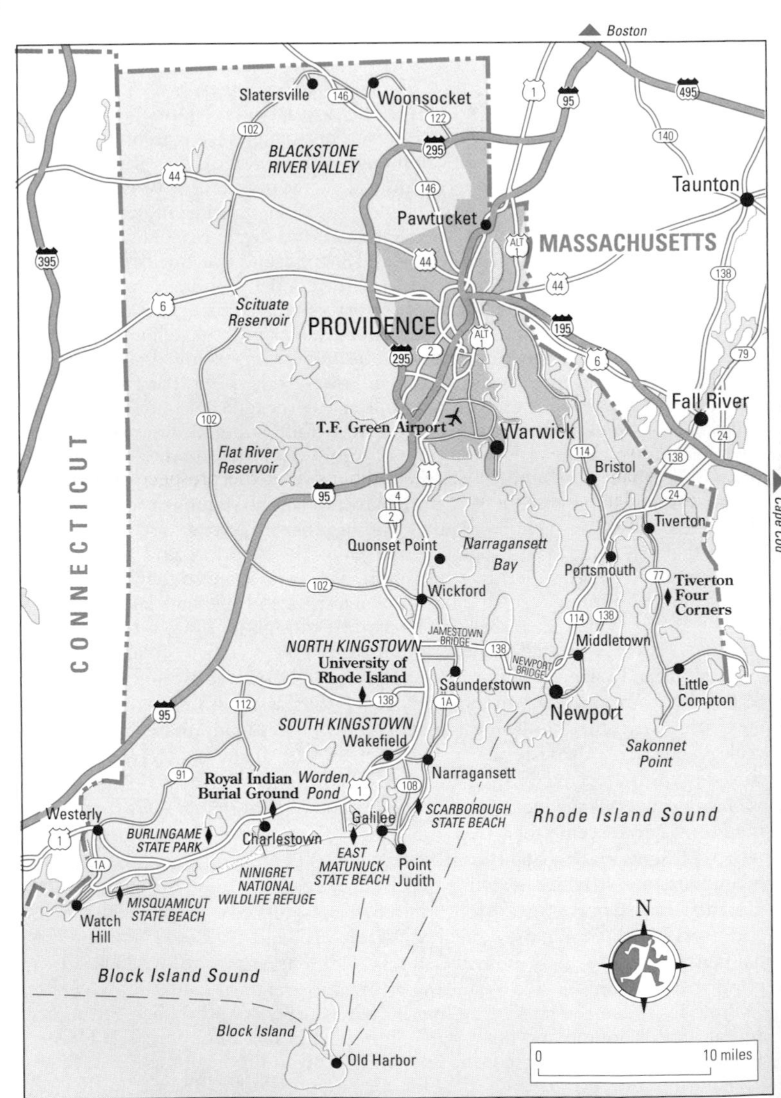

1511, but it was **Giovanni da Verrezano**, an Italian explorer working for France, who arrived in 1524 and remarked on its striking resemblance to the Greek island of Rhodes. One can only surmise either that the weather was foggy, or that the summer heat (and a bottle or two of rum) had gone to his head. Others claim that the name is associated with Dutch explorer **Adrian Block**, who in 1614 named an island in Narragansett Bay *Roodt Eylandt* (Red Island) because of its prominent red clay and rocks.

In 1636, dissent among the ranks of the colonists in Plymouth prompted the **Reverend Roger Williams** to establish a new colony as a "lively experiment" in religious freedom. Williams did not leave fully of his own accord, though – his revolutionary ideas (including the notions of Indians' rights, and total separation of church and state) had incurred the wrath of the Puritan zealots, and they covertly arranged to ship the radical cleric back to England. He got word of the plan and managed to escape to present-day Providence, safely out of the jurisdiction of the Massachusetts authorities, where he declared the place a refuge for the oppressed and sent word to his freethinking colleagues in Massachusetts to join him. Relations with local Native Americans – longtime settlers in the region – which had been good up to this point, soured in 1675, when Wampanoag chief King Philip (Metacomet) attacked New England colonists to protect tribal lands in Massachusetts, resulting in what became known as **King Philip's War**. A series of battles culminated in the **Great Swamp Fight** in what is now South Kingstown, where the Wampanoags were virtually wiped out.

By 1680 the first wharf was built, encouraging maritime trade and commerce, especially whaling; a good deal of smuggling occurred, too, helping earn the state the unflattering nickname of "Rogues' Island." Bolstered by economic power and prosperity, self-assured Rhode Islanders were at the forefront of Revolutionary feeling, resenting the stringent economic pressures placed on them from England and declaring independence from the Old Country prior to the other twelve states. However, no Revolutionary battles were ever fought on Rhode Island soil, and the state, apprehensive at the prospect of yielding power to a federal government, was the last to ratify the Constitution.

Between the Revolution and the Civil War, the economic focus shifted from maritime trade to manufacturing, and Rhode Island became the birthplace of the American **Industrial Revolution**, when, in 1790, Pawtucket became the site of the nation's first water-powered **textile mill**, the brainchild of local entrepreneur Samuel Slater. The textile industry lured thousands of immigrant workers, including Russians, French-Canadians, and British, into Rhode Island, resulting in the ethnic mix that exists today. Manufacturing still plays an important role in the life of the state, though not in the places that people come to see: Providence and Newport both originated as port cities.

In recent years, Rhode Island's economic fortunes have fluctuated, but confidence took a major nosedive in 1990, in a disastrous **banking crisis** which closed many of the state's credit unions and resulted in the loss of millions of dollars from the savings accounts of thousands of ordinary Rhode Islanders. A tightening of regulations has helped put the state on a more secure financial footing, prompting improvements to the state's infrastructure – including repairs to its crumbling roads – along with some decent urban renewal programs and modernization of the state's main airport, T.F. Green, at Warwick. Meanwhile the vastly improved east coast rail link to Boston and New York has made the state more easily accessible; perhaps as a result, travel and tourism sales for the year 2000 topped $3.25 billion, a massive increase of about 16 percent over the previous year.

Providence

Until the past half-decade or so, the millions who whizzed towards New York or Boston in either direction on I-95 had little incentive, or so they thought, to stop in **PROVIDENCE**, which had always languished in the shadow of its larger and more self-assured neighbors. Put off by the towering chimneys of the elephantine Narragansett Power Station, drab office buildings, and ugly oil tanks and empty shop-fronts along once-prosperous Westminster Street, few took the time to notice that the city center holds more intact Colonial and early Federal buildings than any other community in the nation. After an aggressive urban renewal program throughout the late 1990s – during which the move was on to open up entire sections of the Providence River and create the new Waterplace Park, a four-acre green space south of the State Capitol – the city has emerged with a new sense of pride and vigor.

Stretching across seven hills on the Providence and Seekonk rivers, Providence was Rhode Island's first settlement, established "in commemoration of God's Providence" on land given to **Roger Williams** by the Narragansett Indians, in exchange for Williams' continued assistance and future gifts from the trading post established there. The city flourished as one of the most important ports of call in the notorious "**triangle trade**," where New England rum was exchanged for African slaves to be exchanged in turn for West Indian molasses. Many lavish homes were constructed during this period, some of which can still be seen in the Benefit Street district. Among those who prospered was **James Brown**, who opened a lucrative distillery and slaughterhouse, while also entering the shipping trade. His four sons found success, too: Joseph, an architect responsible for many of the city's most elegant buildings; John, a somewhat ruthless merchant; Nicholas, who donated land for the university that bears his name; and Moses, who helped Samuel Slater introduce the nation's first water-powered cotton mill in nearby Pawtucket, insuring that the textile industry was to become a mainstay of the local economy.

Rhode Island's **capital** since 1901, the city proper, with a population of 160,000, is the third largest city in New England (after Boston and Worcester) – and the second largest conurbation, with a population of around 1.1 million. The compactness of its **downtown** area, bounded on the south by I-195, to the west by I-95, to the east by College Hill and to the north by Constitution Hill – bursting with energy and full of cafés, restaurants, shops, and nightclubs – allows you to see most of the main attractions on foot. The city's **ethnic diversity**, one of its greatest strengths, is reflected in the large Italian community on **Federal Hill**, west of the river and I-95, and by fairly voluble Greek and Portuguese – especially Cape Verdean – communities elsewhere in the city.

The oldest and most interesting section of Providence, where founder Roger Williams and his followers first settled, lies on the eastern side of the riverfront area along North and South Main streets and Benefit Street. Known as the **East Side**, it's crowned by **College Hill**, a showcase of architectural preservation, and home to Ivy League **Brown University** and the **Rhode Island School of Design** (RISD or "Rizdee"), both of which give the place a certain cultural verve, at least in their immediate vicinities.

Arrival, information, and getting around

T.F. Green Airport is on Post Road, just off I-95 in **Warwick** (ⓣ401/737-4000), nine miles south of downtown Providence. It's not an international airport (unless flights to Canada count), but there are connections to all main US cities. The Amtrak **train station**, 100 Gaspee St (ⓣ1-800/USA-RAIL), is housed in a domed building a short walk southeast of the capitol building. Greyhound and Bonanza **buses** stop downtown at Kennedy Plaza; Bonanza's main terminus is considerably further out at 1 Bonanza Way, off I-95 (Ⓣ401/751-8800). Local bus transportation is provided by RIPTA (Rhode Island Passenger Transport Association; Mon–Sat 7am–7pm; Ⓣ401/781-9400), with most city and statewide services operating from Kennedy Plaza. Particularly useful for getting around downtown are RIPTA's Gold Line – which runs from north to south across the central area – and its Green Line, running from east to west. Services run every eleven minutes, and cost $1.25, however many stops you're traveling. There's a transport **information booth** near Kennedy Plaza (129 Washington St; Mon–Fri 8am–5pm, Sat 8am–4pm), and bus schedules are available. You don't really need a **car** to get around – Providence is a very walkable city and sightseeing best done on foot – but just

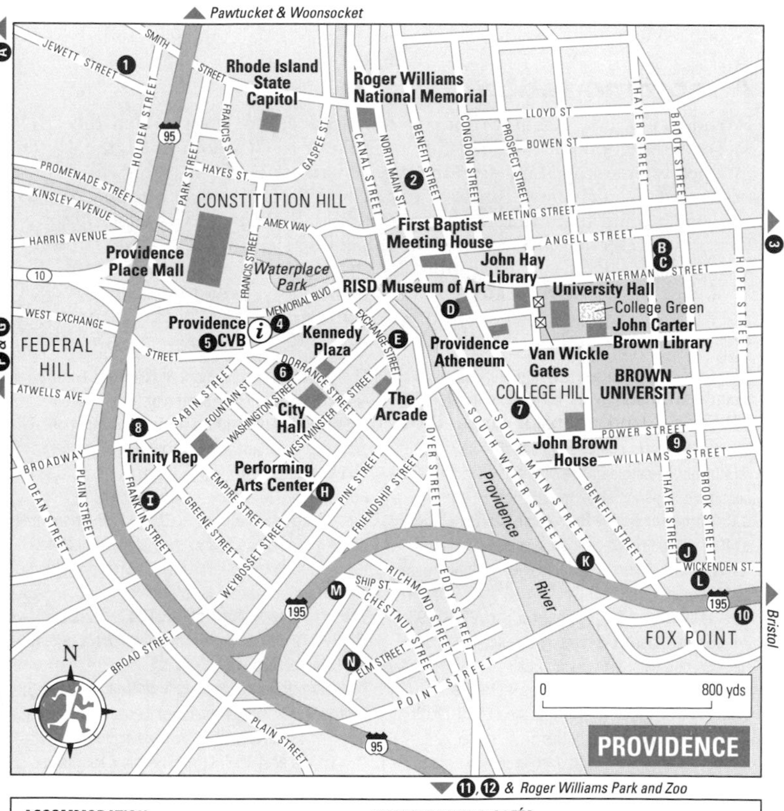

ACCOMMODATION

Annie Brownell House B&B	3
C.C. Ledbetter Bed & Breakfast	7
The Cady House	9
Comfort Inn	12
Fairfield Inn	11
Holiday Inn Downtown	8
The Old Court	2
The Providence Biltmore	6
The Providence Marriott	4
Radisson Hotel at Providence Harbor	10
State House Inn	1
The Westin	5

RESTAURANTS & CAFÉS

Al Forno	K
Angelo's	F
Anthony's	A
Atomic Grill	M
Caffe Dolce Vita	G
CAV	N
Coffee Exchange	J
Hemenways	D
Intermezzo	H
Kabob 'n' Curry	B
New Japan	I
Pot au Feu	E
Tealuxe	C
Z Bar and Grille	L

in case, **taxis**, which aren't always readily available on the street, can be arranged by calling Providence Taxis (ⓣ401/521-4200) or Yellow Cab (ⓣ401/941-1122). All the major **car rental** outfits are represented at the airport, including National (ⓣ401/737-4800) and Budget (ⓣ401/739-8986), and there's a downtown location for Enterprise at 90 Weybosset St (ⓣ401/861-4408).

The **CVB**, 1 W Exchange St (Mon–Fri 10am–5pm; ⓣ401/751-1177 or 1-800/233-1636), provides maps and brochures, as does the **Providence Preservation Society** located in the 1772 Shakespeare's Head, 21 Meeting St (Mon–Fri 9am–5pm; ⓣ401/831-7440), a pre-Revolutionary wood-frame dwelling which once housed the family and printing press of John Carter, a prominent local worthy and publisher of the *Providence Gazette*. Information on self-guided historic tours is available here, including ones on the area's churches, and the innovative **Banner Trail**, which takes in the city's main cultural, historic, and architectural sights. There's yet another **information center** in the Roger Williams National Memorial Park, 282 N Main St (daily 9am–4.30pm; ⓣ401/521-7266).

Accommodation

Providence is not exactly brimming with **places to stay**, though the city's recent redevelopment included the building of a 350-room hotel, the *Westin* (see below); the hopes are – among city officials at least – that this will be the first of many such new constructions. There are fairly few **budget rooms** available around town, and no **hostels**, although **B&Bs** are a viable option – Citywide Reservation Services (ⓣ1-888/248-9121) will almost certainly be able to help you if you have difficulty securing a room. Motorists can take advantage of the swath of mid-priced **motels** along I-95 towards Pawtucket, north of the city, and to the south near the airport in Warwick. **Camping** is not much of an option, with the closest sites fifteen miles away in Coventry.

Annie Brownell House B&B 400 Angell St ⓣ401/454-2934. Nice and spacious Colonial Revival house built in 1899, within walking distance of the city's main attractions. The newly refurbished guestrooms are bright and airy and are decorated in period style; friendly owner, too. ❺

C.C. Ledbetter Bed & Breakfast 326 Benefit St ⓣ401/351-4699. Clean rooms, some with harbor views, in a 200-year-old house filled with hand-stitched quilts and Delft tile. ❻

The Cady House 127 Power St ⓣ401/273-5398. An elegant, Classical Revival house set on College Hill, adorned with antiques and folk art. A good location for Brown, RISD, and downtown. ❺

Comfort Inn 1940 Post Rd, Warwick ⓣ401/732-0470. Adequate lodging in this chain motel, located right by the airport. Also a branch at 2 George St, in nearby Pawtucket (see p.299; ⓣ401/723-6700). ❺

Fairfield Inn 36 Jefferson Blvd, Warwick ⓣ401/941-6600, ⓦwww.marriott.com. Comfortable rooms in Marriott's less expensive chain. Outside the city, but still close to I-95 for easy access. ❻

Holiday Inn Downtown 21 Atwells Ave ⓣ401/831-3900. Standard chain hotel next to the Civic Center and close to the restaurants of Little Italy. ❻

The Old Court 144 Benefit St ⓣ401/751-2002, ⓦwww.oldcourt.com. Charming B&B in an old red-brick rectory near RISD, featuring ten rooms done the Victorian way. ❼

The Providence Biltmore Kennedy Plaza ⓣ1-800/294-7709, ⓦwww.providencebiltmore.com. A Providence landmark since 1922, the *Biltmore* may be the prime place to stay here, if you can afford it: elegant, newly restored city-view rooms in a convenient downtown location. ❽

The Providence Marriott Charles & Orms streets ⓣ401/272-2400, ⓦwww.marriott.com. Large luxury hotel located downtown. ❽

Radisson Hotel at Providence Harbor 220 India St ⓣ401/272-5577. Reasonably priced accommodation with all the amenities, overlooking India Point Park on the east side of town, next to I-195. ❼

State House Inn 43 Jewitt St ⓣ401/351-6111, ⓦwww.providence-inn.com. Pleasant, central B&B in a restored former tenement near the state capitol; rooms are outfitted with antique furnishings. If full, ask the friendly proprietors about their other inns nearby. ❻

The Westin 1 W Exchange St ⓣ401/598-8000 or 1-800/937-8461, ⓦwww.westin.com. Deluxe modern accommodation, which shows in the prices, in this multistory hotel close to all the city sights. ❽

The City

Providence's main attractions focus around three of its seven hills. Downtown, which centers on **Kennedy Plaza**, is sited just below **Constitution Hill**. **City Hall**, at the western end of the Plaza, is mostly notable for a star-spangled midnight-blue ceiling in the Alderman's Chamber; though designed in the style of the Louvre and the Tuileries palaces in Paris, you'll find nothing to compare with the *Mona Lisa* here. The nearby Beaux Arts **Union Station**, built in 1898 but no longer in use as a train terminal, is a fine example of the kind of historic restoration at which the city excels. To the south of the Plaza, in Westminster Mall, is the 1828 **Arcade**, the sole survivor of many such "temples of trade" built in America during the Greek Revival period and America's oldest indoor shopping mall. It's still a marketplace, though a fairly subdued one, with plenty of places to eat, drink, and explore small specialty shops.

The state's only National Park Service property, the **Roger Williams National Memorial**, at the corner of North Main and Smith streets, was the site of the original settlement of Providence in 1636, and is now a small four-acre green space; its small visitors' center includes replicas of Williams' compass, an Indian bible, and papers documenting Williams' efforts. At the top of Constitution Hill the white marble **State Capitol** (Mon–Fri 8.30am–4.30pm; guided tours by appointment only; ⓣ401/222-2357) sports a vast dome, supposedly the fourth largest self-supported dome in the world, that dominates the city skyline. Inside, you can view the original Rhode Island Charter of 1663 and, in the Reception Room, a portrait of George Washington by Rhode Island artist Gilbert Stuart.

Benefit Street and around

Most of Providence's historic legacy can be found in the **College Hill** area, across the river from downtown – an attractive tree-lined district of Colonial buildings, museums, and **Brown University** facilities. Part of Roger Williams' religious experiment was the establishment of a Baptist church, the first in America, in 1638: the white-clapboard **First Baptist Meeting House**, at 75 N Main St, is the third such church building on the site, built in 1775 and topped by a tall steeple inspired by St Martin-in-the-Fields in London. North Main logically leads into **South Main Street**, once bustling with waterfront activity and now home to a number of new upmarket restaurants, though the real action is a block up the hill, on **Benefit Street**. This is Providence's "mile of history" – the most impressive collection of original Colonial homes in America. Lined with the beautifully restored white-clapboard residences of Providence's merchants and sea captains, it was just a dirt track leading to graveyards until it was improved in the eighteenth century "for the benefit of the people of Providence," hence its name.

The elegant **John Brown House**, 52 Power St at Benefit Street (March–Dec Tues–Sat 10am–5pm, Sun noon–4pm; Jan & Feb closed Tues–Thurs; $7), a three-story residence constructed in 1786, was home to one of the city's most aggressive merchants, who made his money trading in slaves and building commercial links with China. Designed by his brother Joseph, the house has a lovely central hall flanked by large formal rooms used by Brown to entertain his illustrious guests; it also retains much original furnishing, silverware, and china, and holds displays on the formidable Brown family and Rhode Island history in general. The plain but dignified **Old State House**, 150 Benefit St (Mon–Fri 8.30am–4.30pm; free), built in 1762, is where the Rhode Island General Assembly renounced allegiance to King George III on May 4, 1776, two months before the Declaration of Independence.

Buddy, can you spare a dime?

The year 2002 was seen as the end of an era in Providence, as the city's wildly popular **Vincent "Buddy" Cianci**, was convicted on a racketeering conspiracy charge. A doctor's son who got his start in the public eye as a child singer on the radio, Cianci was elected to office in 1974, Providence's first Republican mayor in over thirty years and the city's first Italian-American to hold this position. After three terms, he resigned from his post after pleading "no contest" to beating his estranged wife's lover (and getting five years' probation). In his downtime, he returned to the radio, offering the city his views on a variety of topics. In 1990 he campaigned again, winning the mayoral seat by a narrow margin of 317 votes; four years later, he won again by 5000 votes. Cianci's popularity was due in large part to the virtue of his concern and consideration for all different factions of the community, sometimes reaching approval levels over eighty percent. (His likeness can even be found on the "Mayor's Own" brand of pasta sauce.) However, following a four-year FBI investigation (labeled Plunder Dome) of bribes in exchange for favors, tax breaks, and jobs, Cianci and his co-defendants were indicted in 2001 with thirty counts of corruption charges, and the charismatic ex-mayor was sentenced in September 2002 to more than five years in prison.

Further up the street, the small but excellent collection of the **RISD Museum of Art**, 224 Benefit St (Tues–Sun 10am–5pm; $6, free last Sat of the month; ⓣ401/454-6500), Rhode Island's leading museum of fine and decorative arts, is worthy of its association with one of the foremost art schools in the country. The antiquities section contains a Ptolemaic Egyptian mummy, Roman frescoes, and a fabulous array of Greek coins, while the Asian art collection includes more than six hundred Japanese bird-and-flower woodblock prints and a Heian Buddha – the largest historic Japanese wooden sculpture in the US. Other wings are devoted to textiles and costumes, paintings and prints, and multimedia contemporary art. Across the road, the Greek Revival **Providence Atheneum**, 251 Benefit St (Mon–Thurs 9am–7pm, Fri & Sat 9am–5pm, Sun 1–5pm; closed Sat afternoon & Sun in summer; free), is where Edgar Allan Poe and Sarah Whitman carried on their courtship among the stacks. The library, one of America's oldest, holds original Audubon prints and rare books, and the piano and hand-painted chairs in the cozy reading rooms give it the feel of someone's living room.

Brown University

The extensive campus of Ivy League **Brown University**, a short walk up Waterman Street from RISD, occupies 133 acres of College Hill, giving the whole neighborhood a relaxed, intellectual feel. The third oldest college in New England, and seventh oldest in the nation, it was founded in 1764 in Warren as Rhode Island College before it moved forty years later to Providence, where it was renamed after Nicholas Brown II, who donated substantial funds and extensive land. The wrought-iron **Van Wickle Gates**, on Prospect Street, lead on to the historic core of the university, pleasant **College Green**, skirted by a collection of mostly Colonial and Greek Revival buildings. Among them stands the 1904 Beaux Arts **John Carter Brown Library** (Mon–Fri 8.30am–5pm, Sat 9am–noon; free), with an extensive collection of Americana, including the first printed accounts of Columbus's arrival in the New World. Nearby, the school's oldest building – dating from 1770 – **University Hall**, which stood alone on College Hill for its first fifty years, was used as a barracks for the Revolutionary troops and their French allies.

Of the other 150 or so buildings that constitute the university, don't miss the **John Hay Library**, just down the road from University Hall, home to Brown University's special collections, where you can see hundreds of Abe Lincoln manuscripts and a vast display of miniature soldiers (Mon–Fri 9am–5pm; free). For **free tours** of the Brown University campus, contact the admissions office, 45 Prospect St (Mon–Fri 8am–4pm; tours 5 times daily, except during Christmas and Spring Break; mid-Sept to mid-Nov Sat am tours only).

Behind College Hill, happening **Thayer Street** and neighboring streets are home to the half dozen or so best bookstores in the area, while at the eastern end of the hill, **Wickenden Street** buzzes with an assortment of thrift stores, cafés, galleries, and restaurants. Further towards Gano Street lies the increasingly gentrified **Fox Point** district, once Providence's main Portuguese neighborhood, with many pastel-shaded dwellings, and bakeries selling Portuguese delicacies.

The rest of the city

Back west of downtown, **Federal Hill** – also known as Providence's **Little Italy** – can be entered through a large arch topped with a bronze pinecone at Atwells Avenue. Long a powerful Mafia stronghold, this area is one of the safest and friendliest in the city, where you can savor the nuances of Italian culture and cuisine in dozens of restaurants, bakeries, and grocery stores. If it's just a drink you want, head to the bars and cafés around the **Piazza DePasquale**, where there's even a large Italianate fountain, reminiscent of the kind found in Naples. South of Federal Hill, at 100 South St, accessed by bus #1 or #3 from Kennedy Plaza, or from I-95 exit 20, is the excellent **Providence Children's Museum** (April–Aug daily 9.30am–5pm, Fri until 8pm; Sept–March Tues–Sun 9.30am–5pm; $4.75; ⓣ401/273-KIDS), where the range of interactive displays includes a fun look at teeth in a giant mouth, a walk-in kaleidoscope, a time-traveling adventure through Rhode Island's history, and a chance to climb down a manhole and explore the world below street level.

A wealth of food history, including ancient utensils, recipes, and menus, can be found at the **Culinary Archives & Museum**, 315 Harborside Blvd (Tues–Sat 10am–4pm; $5; ⓣ401/598-2805, ⓦwww.culinary.org), a satellite of nearby **Johnson & Wales University** (ⓦwww.jwu.edu), one of the country's premier culinary colleges, located three miles south of the Children's Museum. The exhibits, which could keep one occupied through several meals, rotate seasonally, and range from restaurant development, to mini kitchen replicas, to historical biographies of significant "food people" like Earle MacAusland (founder of *Gourmet Magazine*), culinary writer Clementine Paddleford, and Julia Child.

Several miles west of the museum, off exit 17 of I-95 S, the 430-acre **Roger Williams Park** spills with serpentine paths, rolling hills, and peaceful ponds. Aside from a **carousel** and a **Museum of Natural History**, there's the **Roger Williams Zoo**, with nearly a thousand animals, including giraffes, cheetahs, and zebra in a "Plains of Africa" area, a tropical rainforest, an exhibit of endangered Madagascar lemurs, and an Australasian section with an open-air aviary and clouded leopard exhibit. Even if zoos aren't normally your thing, you can't help but admire the imaginative way this one has been laid out, with its close attention to culture and history alongside zoology (daily: end of May–Aug 9am–5pm; rest of year 9am–4pm; $7, children $4.50; ⓣ401/785-3510).

Eating

Providence's ethnic diversity means that it's never difficult to find good food here. **Thayer Street** is lined with inexpensive eateries, almost all of which stay open until late. Nearby **Wickenden Street** is more alternative, and more expensive, while the family-run Italian restaurants on **Federal Hill** offer superb value; **downtown** is home to a burgeoning bevy of up-and-coming establishments.

Al Forno and **Provincia at Al Forno** 577 S Main St ⓣ401/273-9760. Upstairs, at *Al Forno*, you can try the wood-grilled pizzas, pasta, and interesting twists on steak and seafood at what has been called one of the five best restaurants in America; downstairs, the newer *Provincia* features a mix of Italian and Provençal dishes. Whichever spot – or cuisine – you choose, expect to pay upwards of $20 a dish.

Angelo's 141 Atwells Ave ⓣ401/621-8171. Affordable Italian standards in a family-style restaurant, with half and full portions available.

Anthony's 1065 Chalkstone Ave ⓣ401/331-6401. Established over sixty years in the same location, this moderately priced restaurant is one of Providence's best Italian joints.

Atomic Grill 99 Chestnut St ⓣ401/621-8888. Full dinners served Fri and Sat only (lounge menu the rest of the week) at this lively, off-beat restaurant, with a wide range of moderately priced choices from steaks to quesadillas. Live jazz on Mondays.

Caffe Dolce Vita 59 DePasquale Square ⓣ401/331-8240. Sandwiches, salads, and desserts made with fresh and imported Italian ingredients.

CAV Restaurant, Antiques and Gifts 14 Imperial Place ⓣ401/751-9164. Trendy Mediterranean mid-priced meals in an atmospheric historic loft; live jazz after 9.30pm from Thurs to Mon. Stop by next door at 18 Imperial Place to check out the working studio and glass gallery featuring art and jewelry by local stand-out David Van Noppen and other glass artists.

Coffee Exchange 207 Wickenden St ⓣ401/273-1198. This happening coffee bar is a popular meeting place for would-be intellectuals; deck chairs and barrels act as pavement seating and tables.

Hemenways 1 Old Stone Square, South Main St ⓣ401/351-8570. Classic international seafood like Norwegian salmon and Alaskan king crab, to be eaten in an attractive glass atrium setting. Entrées $15–30.

Intermezzo 220 Weybosset St ⓣ401/331-5100. Conveniently located next to the Providence Performing Arts Center, this cozy New York-style bistro restaurant with Rhode Island prices is a great place for a pre- or post-theater meal, and it's got an excellent reputation for fine service.

Kabob 'n' Curry 261 Thayer St ⓣ401/273-8844. Above-average Indian meals (at above-average value for $6–15) on lively Thayer Street.

New Japan 145 Washington St ⓣ401/351-0300. Reasonably priced Japanese place, with excellent tempura and teriyaki; sushi only served on Sundays.

Pot au Feu 44 Custom House St ⓣ401/273-8953. Expensive salon dining upstairs, moderately priced bistro downstairs, and a cozy, romantic atmosphere in both. Try the bouillabaisse, or the namesake dish resembling a soupier beef stew, with the meat and vegetables hugging the sides of the pot and the broth pooled in the center.

Tealuxe 231 Thayer St ⓣ401/453-4832. Bordering the Brown campus, this tranquil spot has almost 90 teas available to drink here or steep at home. Simple sandwiches like grilled cheese or peanut butter and honey are also served to enhance the tea experience.

Z Bar and Grille 244 Wickenden St ⓣ401/831-1566. Boxing matches once took place in this spot, the former *Ringside Café*. Today it retains that boisterous environment while serving up decent salads, burgers, steaks, and the like.

Nightlife and entertainment

Providence's **nightlife**, concentrated mainly in the city's commercial core off Kennedy Plaza, is largely student-generated, which means things can get a bit quiet during the vacations, though **Thayer Street** is always throbbing.

For those less inclined towards drink, the Cable Car Cinema, 204 S Main St (ⓣ401/272-3970), and the Avon Rep Cinema, 260 Thayer St (ⓣ401/421-3315), show good independent and art **films**, while the Tony Award-winning Trinity Rep, 201 Washington St (ⓣ401/351-4242, ⓦwww.trinityrep.com), one of America's foremost regional theaters, puts on innovative productions of contemporary and classic **plays** in two different theater spaces year-round. The Providence Performing Arts Center, 220 Weybosset St (☎401/421-2787), hosts **musicals** and other lavish productions in a grand old (recently restored) Art Deco movie house. On Gallery Night, the third Thursday of each month (except Dec), the free ArTrolley stops at most of the city's museums and galleries, where admission is free for the evening. And in the warmer months, **WaterFire** (several times a month May–Oct) enthralls visitors and locals alike with over 80 small bonfires set in the center of the Providence River starting at Waterplace Park, tended by gondoliers and accompanied by rousing music. Complete entertainment listings can be found in the free weekly *Providence Phoenix* and the *Providence Journal*'s Thursday edition.

Bars

AS220 115 Empire St ☎401/831-9327. Unabashedly artsy café/bar hangout for locals and students. Also a music venue featuring everything from mellow jazz to performance art; there's a gallery on the second floor. Cover $2–5.

Finnegan's Wake 397 Westminster St ☎401/751-0290. Authentic Irish pub, right down to the corned beef and cabbage.

Snooker's Café 145 Clifford St ☎401/351-7665. Lively pool hall with a variety of table games. Its green room features alternative DJs and is one of the city's most sociable spots. No cover.

Trinity Brewhouse 186 Fountain St ☎401/453-2337. Everything on tap is brewed in-house. Hang out here after a Providence Bruins (minor league hockey) or Friars (college basketball) game to quaff in either celebration or despair.

Union Street Station 69 Union St ☎401/331-2291. Lively gay bar attracting a fairly mixed crowd for nightly carousing.

Clubs and live music

Lupo's Heartbreak Hotel 239 Westminster St ☎401/272-5876. This is *the* spot in town to see nationally recognized bands rock Providence. Tickets generally $15 in advance, $20 day of show.

Metropolis 172 Pine St (☎401/454-5483). Downtown hotspot, offering international DJs and a spectacular light show. Free for ages 21 and over, $10 for 19+.

Strand Theater 79 Washington St ☎401/751-2700. The place to go for heavy metal and rock music, with a large space for dancing. Thurs–Sun cover charge $5–10.

Around Providence: Pawtucket, Woonsocket, and Bristol

Northwest of Providence, the **Blackstone River Valley** has been given special status by the Department of the Interior for its role in America's development as the world's leading industrial power. It's a gritty strip, really, with not much of a future, but clearly plenty of past, beginning with **PAWTUCKET**, just a few short miles up I-95 from downtown Providence. Here you can start your explorations back through time at the **Slater Mill Historic Site**, where the **Old Slater Mill** was built to house the innovative machinery Samuel Slater developed (see box p.301). Today, the mill contains a copy of an original carding engine, a spinning frame and mule, and some very rare textile machines that date from 1838 up to the 1960s, all conspiring to illustrate the process of transforming raw cotton to yarn. Also included is the 1810 **Wilkinson Mill**, where a nineteenth-century machine shop, complete with belt-driven machine tools, still operates, and the 1758 **Sylvanus Brown House**, 67 Roosevelt Ave, an early skilled worker's home furnished as it was in the early 1800s. (Historic site open May–Nov Mon–Sat 10am–5pm, Sun noon–5pm; Dec–April Sat 10am–5pm, Sun noon–5pm; $6; ☎401/725-8638).

Slater and a group of business partners, including his brother John, pioneered the building of **Slatersville**, nineteen miles away off Rte-146 in North Smithfield, a model village constructed in 1808 to accommodate the workers who labored in the two mills they had built nearby. The village remains intact, restored earlier this century, its small, white-clapboard homes, churches, schools, and meeting house still visible round a pretty village green.

A few miles east in **WOONSOCKET**, another major manufacturing center, the fascinating **Museum of Work and Culture**, at 42 S Main St (Mon–Fri 9.30am–4pm, Sat 10am–5pm, Sun 1–5pm; $5; ⓣ401/769-WORK), opened in 1997, traces the story of mill workers who came from the farms of Quebec in the last third of the eighteenth century to work in the shoe and textile factories of New England. A self-guided journey through the workaday world of Woonsocket's residents and immigrant arrivals takes you from the shop floor of a textile mill to the porch of a three-story tenement house and lets you out on today's city streets.

Bristol

Fifteen miles southeast of Providence on Ferry Road (Rte-114), the town of **BRISTOL** holds, unexpectedly, the oldest and largest **Fourth of July** celebration in the nation, a parade and fireworks spectacular that attracts hundreds of thousands of spectators. Otherwise, the only thing to bring you here is the **Blithewold Mansion and Gardens** at 101 Ferry Road (ⓣ401/253-2707, ⓦwww.blithewold.org, grounds open year-round daily 10am–5pm; mansion open mid-April to mid-Oct Wed–Sun 10am–4pm; $10; $5 gardens only when house is closed). This is the one-time summer residence of Pennsylvania coal magnate Augustus Van Wickle and his wife Bessie, who filled the 45-room manor house with knick-knacks from her globetrotting adventures. The arboretum merits a wander too; seek out the 100-foot-tall giant sequoia, an anomaly in these parts, for a good photo opportunity.

Newport

NEWPORT, named "America's First Resort," is probably best known for its summer "cottages" – more like huge palaces – which were built by nineteenth-century industrial magnates and business tycoons each trying to outdo one another. These monuments to opulence and greed, like **Rosecliff** and **Beechwood** on **Bellevue Avenue**, give a glimpse into the ostentatious lives behind such names as the **Astors** and **Vanderbilts**, but even before those families arrived on the scene, Newport had established itself as a major port, rivaling New York and Boston in size and importance.

First settled in 1639 by refugees from neighboring Massachusetts seeking **religious freedom**, the area was soon recognized for its excellent **trade location** and quickly developed into a bustling seaport. Although the city became renowned for its liberal approach in matters of religion, which brought an influx of Jews, Quakers, and Baptists, such charity did not extend to the slave trade; in the eighteenth century, the local fleet was heavily involved in trading African **slaves** for West Indian sugar and molasses, and the city was a haven for privateers, often barely distinguishable from pirates.

The prosperity that international trade had brought suffered a severe setback when British and Hessian troops occupied Newport in 1776, blockading the harbor and forcing residents to use the city's timber wharves as firewood during the brutally cold winter. During the next three years, many locals fled, buildings were either destroyed or left to decay, and the city floundered. By the end of the war, so poor was the city that townsfolk wanting to expand their properties could not even afford to tear down their own homes, let alone rebuild. This is largely the reason for the wealth of fine **Colonial buildings** still seen today.

In the 1850s, the town became fashionable again as a resort for wealthy Southern merchants, and very soon nouveau riche industrialists such as the Astors, Belmonts, and Vanderbilts were building the mansions along the coast-

The birthplace of the Industrial Revolution

The Blackstone River cuts through the northeastern portion of Rhode Island, not much of a landmark in and of itself – but it was largely along these riverbanks that the seeds of the Industrial Revolution began to grow in America. Dubbed the **Blackstone River National Heritage Corridor** and stretching from Providence to Worcester, Massachusetts, it encompasses two dozen of the original manufacturing communities where thousands of Americans and immigrants came to work and live, at least until the valley's demise.

The area was a desolate wilderness when its first white settler, **Reverend William Blackstone**, arrived here in 1635 after fleeing the intolerant Puritan regime in Boston. More settlers came, of whom one Joseph Jencks, Jr, a blacksmith by trade, realized that the vast forests of **Pawtucket** would provide a virtually inexhaustible supply of timber to fire a forge. His new smithy boomed, and soon other blacksmiths began to settle here, setting the stage for future development.

The industrial expansion received a huge boost in 1793, when **Samuel Slater**, a manufacturer's apprentice originally hailing from Derbyshire, England – with the help of entrepreneur Moses Brown, of the wealthy Providence family – used new technology surreptitiously imported from his native land to produce cotton yarn. The resultant success fueled another century of high prosperity, but as you'll find touring the preserved mills, much of the machinery has not been spinning for some time, most of the companies having relocated to the South, where overhead and labor were much cheaper.

For an unusual perspective of the Blackstone River Valley's history and environment, a narrated **riverboat tour** departs from various locations, run by Blackstone Valley Explorer (May–Oct Sat–Sun; ⓣ401/724-1500 or 1-800/454-BVTC, ⓦwww.tourblackstone.com).

line for which the city has become known. Despite an end to the decadence, the city remained a major naval town, home to the **United States Naval War College**, and is a prime playpen for the yachting set: in 1980 and 1983 the **America's Cup Race** was held off Newport, and every summer the harbor is lined with majestic sailboats, pleasure boats, and touring vessels. There's no question that today's Newport is unashamedly geared to the tourist, as a stroll around the tacky harbor area will testify. Somehow, though, the rough old port still manages to linger, with beer and R&B clubs as evident as cocktails and cruises, making this an essential urban stop, especially during the summer **festival season**. Additionally, Newport is a good base for exploring the more peaceful neighboring towns of **Portsmouth** and **Middletown**, and, across the bay, the appealing villages of **Tiverton Four Corners** and **Little Compton**, full of stone-walled country lanes, rocky shorelines, and idyllic beaches.

Arrival, information, and getting around

Newport, Middletown, and Portsmouth are all located on **Aquidneck**, also known formally as Rhode Island. The island is connected to the mainland from I-95 and the west by Rte-138, which crosses the impressive **Newport Bridge** ($2 toll). The nearest Amtrak (ⓣ1-800/USA-RAIL) **station** is on Rte-138 at Kingston, some nineteen miles away. The RIPTA buses (ⓣ401/781-9400) available here can take you the rest of the way.

Newport itself, spanning only ten miles, is eminently walkable. **Thames** (pronounced *Thaymz*) **Street** is the main drag; it's separated from the shops and restaurants of the harbor district by **America's Cup Avenue**, a wide, ugly road that doesn't even succeed in speeding up traffic through the town, at its worst in the summer. It's here, at no. 23, that you will find Newport's main **visitors' center**, a vast, glitzy operation with plenty of maps, brochures, and advice to keep you busy (daily 9am–5pm; ⓣ401/849-8048 or 1-800/976-5122, ⓦwww.gonewport.com). Parking in the adjacent Gateway Center's parking lot is free for the first hour.

The **Gateway Center** is the terminal for Bonanza Buses (ⓣ401/846-1820) and RIPTA buses, which run through town and out to the beaches and Providence ($1–3). The Center is also the terminus for the summer **trolleys** which run daily 10am to 7pm and connect downtown, the mansions, and shopping areas – for $5 a person (or $10 for a family pass) an all-day ticket allows you to hop on and off at will. Also located here are Viking Tours, whose bus and harbor excursions include admission to one or more mansions ($18–29; ⓣ401/847-6921) and Newport Trolley Tours ($18; ⓣ401/849-8005), offering a 90-minute city tour. Rental **bikes** are good for getting around, especially if you're heading to one of the beaches; it's $5 per hour ($25 per day, $70 per week) from Ten Speed Spokes, 18 Elm St (ⓣ401/847-5609).

The Newport Historical Society, 82 Touro St (Tues–Fri 9.30am–4.30pm, Sat 9.30am–noon; ⓣ401/846-0813, ⓦwww.newporthistorical.org), next door to the Touro Synagogue, organizes **walking tours** through Colonial Newport on summer Thursdays, Fridays, and Saturdays at 10am, with a $7 fee. Other walking tours are provided on a daily basis between April and October by **Newport On Foot** (ⓣ401/846-5391; $8). If you must rent a **car**, International Car Rental, 6 Valley Rd, Middletown (ⓣ401/847-4600), will deliver the vehicle to your hotel, but be warned: parking is a major problem on the city's narrow streets. Easily the best and most relaxing way of getting a good overview of the mansions and town is on a **boat tour**: you can take the beautiful 72-foot schooner *Madeleine*, which departs four times a day from Bannister's Wharf for a ninety-minute tour ($25), or the motor yacht *Rum Runner* for $17 (75min narrated), both of which are organized by Classic Cruises of Newport (ⓣ401/847-0298).

Accommodation

Newport has plenty of reasonably priced **guesthouses**, but it's always a good idea to **book ahead**, especially on summer weekends when prices can sky-rocket. The visitors' center (see above) has free phone links to inns and motels in all price ranges. Due in part to the abundance of Victorian mansions, the most common form of accommodation here is the **B&B**. Large rooms – often with fireplaces and ocean views – can be expected, and prices can get a little steep. To find something a bit more stripped down and for a better price, there are a couple of established agencies: Bed and Breakfast of Rhode Island (ⓣ401/849-1298 or 1-800/828-0000), which can find rooms from around $125 in season ($75 in winter), and Bed & Breakfast of Newport, 33 Russell Ave (ⓣ401/846-5408 or 1-800/800-8765), which specializes in smaller B&Bs you might otherwise find difficult to locate. One problem you might run into throughout Newport: limited accommodation options for travelers with children under twelve. Make sure to call ahead and confirm individual policies.

1855 Marshall Slocum Guest House 29 Kay St ⓣ401/841-5120 or 1-800/372-5120, ⓦwww.marshallslocuminn.com) Close to Bellevue Ave, this unpretentious inn is located in a former parsonage. Each room is unique, and yours might feature a mahogany sleigh bed, an antique four-poster, a maple Colonial frame, or a queen-sized brass bed. ❼

Admiral Fitzroy Inn 398 Thames St ⓣ401/848-8000 or 1-800/343-2863, ⓦwww.admiralfitzroy.com. Cheerfully decorated B&B in the heart of the action, with a roof deck overlooking the harbor and excellent breakfasts. ❼

Chase Farm B&B 308 Chases Lane, Middletown ⓣ401/845-9338. Romantic Victorian farmhouse with wonderful waterview sunsets and just a few minutes to Newport's main attractions. ❻

The Clarkeston 28 Clarke St ⓣ401/849-7397 or 1-800/524-1386, ⓦwww.innsofnewport.com.

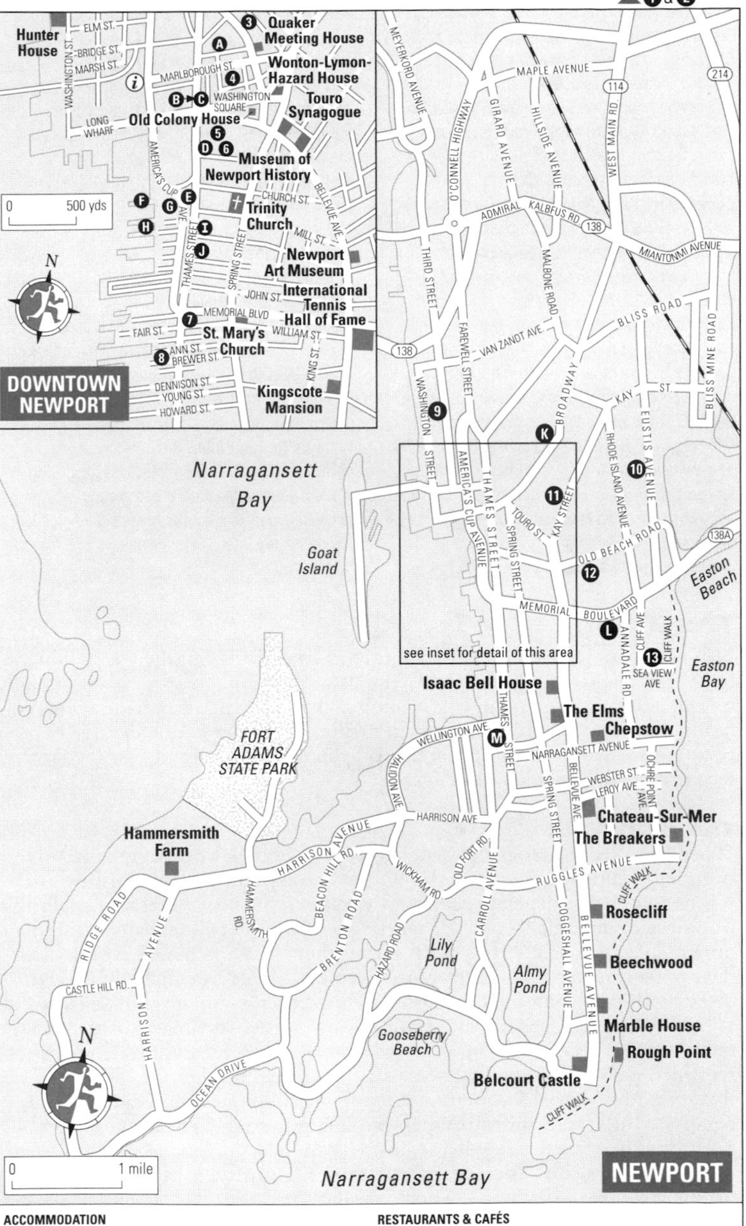

ACCOMMODATION

1855 Marshall Slocum Guest House	11
Admiral Fitzroy Inn	8
Chase Farm B&B	2
The Clarkeston	6
Cliffside Inn	13
Commodore Perry Inn	7
Elm Tree Cottage	10
Howard Johnson Lodge	1
Jailhouse Inn	4
Las Palmas Inn	3
Melville House	5
The Old Beach Inn	12
Willows Romantic Inn	9

RESTAURANTS & CAFÉS

Aloha Café	G
Asterix & Obelix	M
The Black Pearl	F
Brick Alley Pub and Restaurant	D
Café Zelda	J
Christie's	E
Mudville Pub	B
Ocean Coffee Roasters	C
Puerini's	L
Salvation Café	K
Scales and Shells	J
Smokehouse Café	H
Via Via	I
White Horse Tavern	A

Sumptuous circa-1705 colonial inn with working fireplaces, Jacuzzi tubs, canopy and feather beds. ❼
Cliffside Inn 2 Seaview Ave ⓣ401/847-1811, ⓦwww.cliffsideinn.com. Gorgeous 1876 Victorian manor house, one minute from the Cliff Walk and First Beach. All rooms have fireplaces, private baths, telephones, a/c, and cable TV plus full breakfast and afternoon tea. ❾
Commodore Perry Inn 8 Equality Park West ⓣ401/846-5603. Clean and comfortable rooms in a quiet area a half mile from downtown. ❺
Elm Tree Cottage 336 Gibbs Ave ⓣ401/849-1610 or 1-888/ELM-TREE, ⓦwww.elmtreebnb.com. This former summer house with frilly and lushly decorated antique-filled rooms, is tucked away on an acre of land in a peaceful neighborhood overlooking Easton Pond and First Beach. ❽
Howard Johnson Lodge 351 W Main Rd, Middletown ⓣ401/849-2000 or 1-800/446-4656, ⓦwww.hojo.com. Two miles north of downtown Newport, this represents the best hotel value in the area. Much-reduced rates outside of July/August peak season. ❸
Jailhouse Inn 13 Marlborough St ⓣ401/847-4638 or 1-800/427-9444. Spacious modern rooms with jailhouse trimmings in this restored 1772 clink, right in the center of town. ❻
Las Palmas Inn 12 Collins St ⓣ401/848-0708, ⓦwww.newportlaspalmas.com. Unusual inn done out in "Key West Victorian" style and close to all the main attractions. ❼
Melville House 39 Clarke St ⓣ401/847-0640, ⓦwww.melvillehouse.com. Colonial B&B in a tranquil location two blocks from the harbor; the rooms are small, but pleasant. ❼
The Old Beach Inn 19 Old Beach Rd ⓣ401/849-3479 or 1-888/303-5033, ⓦwww.oldbeachinn.com. A romantic and handsome B&B boasting seven rooms, each decorated in a different floral theme; all with private bath, some with fireplaces and a/c. Generous continental breakfasts and private parking. ❻
Willows Romantic Inn 8–10 Willow St ⓣ401/846-5486, ⓦwww.thewillowsofnewport.com. If you like the Astor's Beechwood (see opposite) you'll feel right at home with the daily "living history lesson" that comes with your breakfast in bed. ❽

The Town

Newport's main attractions are obviously its **mansions**, but there is nothing to be gained by attempting to tour them all, and although it is pleasant enough to stroll around the predominantly colonial **downtown**, the ever-growing profusion of souvenir shops is somewhat off-putting. Otherwise, if you don't fancy beautiful-people-spotting on the harbor, you'll do better following the crowds to one of Newport's fine **beaches**.

The mansions

When horrified sociologist Thorstein Veblen visited Newport at the turn of the twentieth century and coined the phrase "**conspicuous consumption**," he was criticising the desperate need felt by some of the new entrepreneurial **millionaires** of the time to define their fragile identities and perhaps establish an instant American aristocracy by flaunting their newly acquired wealth. More than just a summer resort, Newport became an arena in which families competed, with increasing mania, to outdo each other – though the "**season**" of wild and decadent parties lasted only a few weeks and many of the multi-million-dollar homes, described as "white elephants" by author Henry James, remained empty for months, even years, at a time. It's difficult to take in the sheer wealth involved by merely gawking at the impressive facades, but after being herded in and rushed through more than a couple of Newport's famous mansions, the opulence rapidly begins to pall.

The **Preservation Society of Newport County**, at 424 Bellevue Ave (ⓣ401/847-1000, ⓦwww.newportmansions.org), manages the bulk of the mansions open for public view – though not Beechwood or Belcourt Castle. Their properties are open April–Oct daily from 10am (Breakers at 9am) through 5pm (last admission), and during the rest of the year the schedule varies. Entrance to the Breakers is $15, all others $10, and a combination ticket to any five Society properties is $31.

You can peek at the Bellevue Avenue mansions on the cheap by taking the invigorating **Cliff Walk**, which begins on Memorial Boulevard where it meets First (Easton) Beach. This three-and-a-half-mile oceanside path alternates from pretty sections meandering among jasmine and wild roses to ugly concrete underpasses and dangerous stretches across perilous rocks.

Beechwood

The Astors' **Beechwood**, 580 Bellevue Ave (June–Oct daily 10am–5pm, may close early for special events; Nov–May hours vary; ⓣ401/846-3772, ⓦwww.astors-beechwood.com; $15), is an entertaining antidote to the drier historical drills given on other tours. Inside the stucco house, costumed actors welcome visitors as houseguests who have arrived for a party to be given by Mrs Caroline Astor, the self-proclaimed queen of American society, known for her attempts to stave off the advances of "new money" families into society's inner circles. Anecdotes, bitchy asides, and a constant stream of activity – as well as strawberry tea in the servants' kitchen – make it all a great deal of fun.

Marble House, Rosecliff, Kingscote, and the Breakers

Just to the south of the Preservation Society's headquarters is **Marble House**, the most over-the-top example of Gilded Age excess, with a golden ballroom and a Chinese teahouse on the grounds; both this and **Rosecliff** (on the other side of Beechwood), with its colorful rose garden and heart-shaped staircase, were used as sets during the filming of *The Great Gatsby*. **Kingscote**, further up the avenue, is a quirky Gothic Revival cottage, built in 1839, and expanded in 1876 by the firm of McKim, Mead & White; its lovely interior features mahogany paneling and a Tiffany glass wall in the dining room.

The biggest and best of the lot, however, is Cornelius Vanderbilt's four-story **The Breakers**, on Ochre Point Avenue, an extravagant Italian Renaissance palace built for president and chairman of the New York Central Railroad Cornelius Vanderbilt II by renowned architect Richard Morris Hunt. Located on a 13-acre oceanfront estate, the imposing "cottage," completed in 1895, includes a 45-foot-high central Great Hall and seventy additional rooms, many of which were constructed overseas by European craftsmen then shipped to Newport. The waves crashing on the rocks below give the house its name. The Society has five other homes, most along Bellevue Avenue, open for public viewing, from **Chateau-Sur-Mer** (the first Newport mansion) and the Italian country house **Chepstow** (on Narragansett Avenue), to the ornate French *maison* **The Elms**, and the simpler **Hunter House** (see overleaf) and **Isaac Bell House**. All of these homes can be seen with combination tickets (see opposite), which help to beat the hefty admission prices to individual properties.

Belcourt Castle

Standing slightly apart from this parade, but a competitor nonetheless, **Belcourt Castle**, 657 Bellevue Ave at Lakeview (weekdays 10am–4pm, most Sundays 12–5pm; $10; ⓣ401/846-0669;), was built to echo owner Oliver Belmont's love for equines and armor, and guides are decked out in medieval costume when you enter. As yet another Newport example of excess, Belmont's horses slept in white linen sheets in a specially designed stable.

Hammersmith Farm

For those with a car, Ocean Drive continues from Bellevue Avenue where the Cliff Walk ends, following the coast eastwards and passing the shingle-sided **Hammersmith Farm**, John and Jackie Kennedy's 28-room summer home, originally owned by Jackie's mother. The Kennedys' wedding reception was held here in 1953, and the couple were such frequent visitors that it became known as the "**summer White House**." The selling of the estate some years ago means that the farm is no longer open to the public.

Rough Point

Near the southern end of Bellevue Avenue stands **Rough Point** (June–Oct Tues–Sat 10am–4pm; $25; ⓣ401/845-9130, ⓦwww.newportrestoration.org), which showcases the home of Doris Duke, the only child of James B. Duke, tobacco magnate and benefactor of Duke University. Of particular note are the mansion's textiles (including Flemish tapestries dating to 1510), ornate eighteenth-century French furniture, and a fine collection of brilliant blue Ming vases. Like the Breakers, it's just steps away from the sea cliff, leading to a rock-strewn beach and an empty horizon. In an effort to preserve the property (just opened to the public in 2000), there is no parking available; visitors must reserve and take a shuttle van from the Visitors' Center (see p.302).

Downtown Newport

Colonial Newport's political and commercial center, **Washington Square**, starts just south of the Gateway Center, where Thames Street meets the **Brick Market**. The 1762 market, off **Long Wharf** (the most important of Newport's colonial wharves), has been reconstructed to include a mixture of galleries and pricey souvenir shops. Also inside, the **Museum of Newport History** (Mon & Wed–Sat 10am–5pm, Sun 1–5pm; $5) gives a good overview of Newport's past through interactive exhibits, photographs, and pithy oral histories. Across the square stands the **Old Colony House**, one of Rhode Island's few pre-Revolutionary brick buildings and seat of government from 1739 to 1900 – the second oldest capitol building in the United States. It was here that in May 1776, Rhode Island became the first state to declare its independence from Britain – two months before the official proclamation. Just up from Washington Square, at 17 Broadway, the **Wanton-Lyman-Hazard House** (mid-June to early Sept Thurs–Sun 1–5pm; $3) appears uncomfortably hemmed in among surrounding commercial buildings for good reason: it is one of the oldest dwellings in Newport, built sometime between 1650 and 1700. The central chimney and pitched roof are typical of the early settlers' homes; inside, the surviving original plasterwork is made from ground shells and molasses. To the north, the **Easton's Point** district, between Washington Square and Spring Street, is lined with the eighteenth-century homes of ship captains. Of these, the 1748 **Hunter House**, 54 Washington St (March–Oct daily 10am–5pm; $9), the only one open to the public, has been carefully restored to reflect its original state.

The oldest religious building in town is the 1699 **Quaker Meeting House**, at the corner of Farewell and Marlborough streets (free tours by appointment; ⓣ401/846-0813), restored to its nineteenth-century state and completely free of adornment. The Quakers, like other religious sects, received a warm welcome in Rhode Island; indeed, the state's penchant for religious tolerance is echoed by the presence of the elegant **Touro Synagogue**, at 85 Touro St, the oldest house of Jewish worship in America. Built in 1763 and modeled on Sephardic Jewish temples in Portugal and Holland, the synagogue displays a letter to the Jewish community written by George Washington himself, advocating religious freedom (tours given July through early Sept Sun–Fri 10am–5pm; mid-Sept to Oct & May–June Mon–Fri 1–3pm, Sun 11am–3pm; rest of year Fri 1pm only, Sun 11am–3pm; free). Rhode Island's tolerance even extended to the much-despised Anglicans, who were the main reason for the Puritan exodus from England. Their 1726 **Trinity Church** on Queen Anne Square (mid-June to July 4 Mon–Fri 10am–4pm, July 4 to early Sept daily

10am–4pm; rest of year 10am–1pm; free) was based on the Old North Church in Boston and the designs of Sir Christopher Wren, with a bleach-white 150-foot tower which acts as a beacon for ships as well as worshippers. Inside, the only triple-decked, freestanding pulpit left in America stands in its original position in front of the altar, evidence of the emphasis at the time on preaching rather than communion. The Roman Catholic **St Mary's Church**, Spring Street and Memorial Boulevard (Mon–Fri 7–11.30am; free), completed in 1848, witnessed the union of Jacqueline Bouvier and John Kennedy on September 12, 1953.

Bellevue Avenue, the street of Newport's mansions and green-awninged shops, is also home to two noteworthy museums not far from downtown. The **Newport Art Museum**, at no. 76 (June to mid-Oct Mon–Sat 10am–5pm, Sun noon–5pm; rest of year Mon–Sat 10am–4pm, Sun noon–4pm; $6), exhibits New England art from the last two centuries in the 1864 mock-medieval Griswold House; the grand **Newport Casino**, no. 194, was an early country club which held the nation's first tennis championships in 1881. It now houses the **International Tennis Hall of Fame** (daily 9.30am–5pm; $5; ⓣ401/849-3990 or 1-800/457-1144), and still keeps its grass courts open to the public for play (mid-May to Sept; individual $35 for 90min, group $55–75 per hour; indoor and hard outdoor courts also available). Exhibits include the original patent for the game granted by Queen Victoria in 1874, displays on tennis fashion, a portrait of Chris Evert by Andy Warhol, and a video theater where you can watch classic matches.

The beaches

The indubitable attraction of Newport's shoreline, with its rocky coves and gently sloping sandy beaches, is slightly marred by the fact that several stretches are strictly private; still, some of the best strands remain within the public domain. The calm waters of **Gooseberry Beach**, nestled among the rocks in an attractive inlet off Ocean Avenue, appeals to families and charges a $1 admission for parking. The town beach, also known as **First** or **Easton Beach**, is a wide stretch at the east end of Memorial Boulevard that gets very busy despite the relatively high $8 parking fee ($10 on weekends). There's also an aquarium with a tide pool and tanks of local sea life. The most attractive of all the Aquidneck Island beaches is further east in neighboring Middletown, pleasant **Second (Sachuest) Beach**, with acres of soft gray sand and good surf ($10 weekdays; $15 weekends). You can combine a few hours on the beach with a visit to the nearby **Norman Bird Sanctuary**, 583 Third Beach Rd (daily 9am–5pm; $4), home to more than ten miles of trails, a nature museum, and education building. Peaceful **Third Beach**, further on, is not technically an ocean beach as it's on the inner side of Narragansett Bay; parking is $10 weekdays, $15 at weekends.

Eating

Many of Newport's **restaurants** are smug and overpriced, with the result that visitors on strict budgets have to make do with snacks. However, there are some notable exceptions and the seafood here is worth the blowout if you can handle it.

Aloha Cafe 18 Market Square ⓣ401/846-7038. Inexpensive sandwiches and salads in a small café inside the Seamen's Institute.

Asterix & Obelix 599 Thames St ⓣ401/841-8833. Happening eatery in a former garage, with abstract paintings on the walls and Oriental rugs covering an orange cement floor. Entrées ($18–32) are eclectic, with Asian flourishes.

The Black Pearl Bannister's Wharf ⓣ401/846-5264. This Newport institution is famed for its chunky clam chowder; repair to the Commodore Room for more formal (and more expensive) dining.

Brick Alley Pub & Restaurant 140 Thames St ⓣ401/849-6334. Attracts a good mix of locals and tourists for lunch, dinner, and cocktails; Sunday brunch is especially popular. The cheap to moderately priced offerings are fairly straightforward: burgers, some seafood options, and the like.

Café Zelda 528 Thames St ⓣ401/849-4002. This attractive corner restaurant with a friendly face features dressed-up standards like nori-wrapped tuna and Long Island duck with ginger glaze. Entrées $16–23.

Christie's 351 Thames St ⓣ401/847-5400. Very popular – and expensive – waterfront seafood restaurant, established in 1945. Try their scrumptious house specialty, Narragansett fish pie, or one of the awesome lobsters. Wed, Thurs, and Sun dinner specials offseason.

Mudville Pub 8 W Marlborough St, adjacent to the Cardine's Field Baseball Stadium ⓣ401/849-1408. Lively sports bar serving sandwiches and burgers, and packed out especially after a home game.

Ocean Coffee Roasters 22 Washington Square ⓣ401/846-6060. Hip, upbeat café serving aspiring artists and poets rather than yacht club types. Crepes from $4, lunch specials with an international twist from $5.50, flavored coffees and teas. Occasional poetry readings and exhibitions.

Puerini's 24 Memorial Blvd W ⓣ401/847-5506. Classic Italian fare make this a firm favorite with locals and visitors alike.

Salvation Café 140 Broadway ⓣ401/847-2620. Healthy, largely vegetarian food with an Asian focus (vegetable pakora, little necks with udon noodles) at reasonable prices.

Scales and Shells 527 Thames St ⓣ401/846-FISH. Casual "only fish" restaurant with high-quality seafare and a sense of humor.

Smokehouse Café America's Cup Avenue ⓣ401/848-9800. It's an oddity in Newport's world of seafood, but the *Smokehouse* has great barbeque for under $20 and a lively crowd.

Via Via 372 Thames St ⓣ401/848-0880. Specialty oven-fired pizza like shrimp pesto or chicken and goat cheese; can also be delivered until 2am.

White Horse Tavern Marlborough and Farewell streets ⓣ401/849-3600. Intensely atmospheric restaurant (the building dates from 1687) serving hearty American fare such as New York sirloin, sautéed lobster, and baked Atlantic salmon. Expensive, but more affordable at lunchtime.

Nightlife and entertainment

Newport has a reputation for being a lively party town, with fairly unrefined **nightlife**, which irks many of its residents – to the point that the town council has tried to tone things down through various regulations and restrictions. Most, but by no means all, of the noisiest **bars** and **clubs** are found in the waterfront area.

The Boom-Boom Room downstairs at the *Clarke Cooke House*, Bannister's Wharf ⓣ401/849-2900. One of the most popular discos in town, the *Boom-Boom Room* attracts a fairly mixed crowd with standards, oldies, and Top-40.

Newport Blues Café 286 Thames St ⓣ401/841-5510. Live blues and jazz from 9.30pm nightly in an old bank building overlooking the harbor. Elegant dining through 10pm.

One Pelham East Corner of Thames and Pelham sts ⓣ401/847-9640. Long-established and still popular venue that has been hosting live bands for over twenty years.

The Red Parrot 348 Thames St ⓣ401/847-3140. This small, dark, and cramped storefront is the place for live jazz and world music nightly.

The Rhino Bar & Grille 337 Thames St ⓣ401/846-0707. Original live bands (in the bar) and the best area DJs (playing dance, hip-hop, and techno in the Mamba Room) keep this safari-themed place hoppin'. Food options range from conventional bar appetizers to shrimp scampi and pasta dinners.

Sports Ticket 15 Aquidneck Ave, Middletown ⓣ401/847-7678. Sports bar with 32 TV screens and an outdoor deck overlooking First Beach.

The Wharf Deli & Pub 37 Bowen's Wharf ⓣ401/846-9233. Somewhat touristy microbrewery in the heart of it all that puts on R&B and jazz.

Around Newport

Newport has plenty to keep you occupied, no matter what your proclivities, but if you are interested in getting out of town for a while, there are some worthwhile detours nearby, the best of which are on the **Sakonnet**

Peninsula, a remote area that was once part of Massachusetts, and bears little of the development characteristic of other coastal sections of the state. Sakonnet is basically an island, with virtually no public transport; **cars** and **bicycles** can be rented in Fall River, a couple of miles across the border in Massachusetts. If you are driving from Newport, just take Rte-77 south off I-24 and follow it down the length of the land.

Portsmouth

Founded in 1638 by Anne Hutchinson, another refugee from Massachusetts, **PORTSMOUTH**, about ten miles north of Newport on Rte-138, was until recently a small rural community; now it's little more than a bedroom suburb of Newport.

The **Portsmouth Historical Society** (June–Aug Sat & Sun 1–4pm; free), based in the Old Union Church, 870 East Main Rd at Union Street, comprises several interesting buildings, including what may be the oldest one-room schoolhouse in the country, completed in 1723, as well as the original Portsmouth Town Hall and the church itself, once home to a nineteenth-century religious sect with connections to the abolitionist movement. Displays feature local artifacts like coal fossils from the town's now-derelict coal mines and various Native American tools. For something a little different, the Preservation Society of Newport also administers the **Green Animals Topiary Gardens** (Cory's Lane, off Rte-114), which has more than eighty sculpted trees and animal-shaped shrubs set on an idyllic lawn that slopes down to Narragansett Bay. There are espaliered fruit trees, a rose arbor, formal flower beds, and a small Victorian **toy museum** (May–Oct daily 10am–5pm; $10; see the Newport section for details on combination tickets with Newport's mansions).

Those that choose to **stay** – not a bad option, as it is little more than a twenty-minute drive from downtown Newport – typically do so at the *Founder's Brook Motel*, 318 Boyd's Lane, at the junction of routes 138 and 24 (Ⓣ401/683-1244; ⑤). **Eating** revolves around Portsmouth's star contender: the **Seafare Inn**, 3352 East Main Rd, Portsmouth (Ⓣ401/683-0577). It would be a shame to miss this excellent fish venue, which has been voted one of the top ten seafood restaurants in the US year after year.

The Sakonnet Peninsula: Tiverton and Little Compton

The rather nondescript and tatty northern section of **TIVERTON** that you immediately encounter after traveling five miles and crossing Rte-24 is

Newport's music festivals

Newport is nearly world famous for the plethora of prominent annual music festivals that take place here in the summer months, the two most popular of which are the **Apple & Eve Folk Festival**, in late July or early August, followed by the **JVC Jazz Festival**, in the middle of **August**. Both feature big-name performers in their respective fields; call Ⓣ401/847-3700 for details. Labor Day weekend in early September, the **Waterfront Irish Festival** held at the Newport Yachting Center (Ⓣ401/846-1600, Ⓦwww.newportfestivals.com), includes several music performance stages and exhibits of Irish and Celtic literature, art, and stepdancing. The lesser-known two-week **Newport Music Festival** (Ⓣ401/846-1133) emphasizes classical music and takes place during July in a number of Newport's mansions. The program features world-class artists performing everything from chamber and orchestral music to sea shanties.

redeemed only by some delightful views of the **Sakonnet River**, which parallels Rte-77 the length of Sakonnet Peninsula. Heading south, the first spot of interest is **Fort Barton**, on Highland Street, an original redoubt built during the American Revolution and named after Colonel William Barton, who captured Newport's British commander during the war. A climb of the observation tower affords a spectacular view of neighboring Aquidneck Island. Two miles south, Seapowet Avenue leads to the **Ruecker Wildlife Refuge**, forty acres of shallow marshes and upland woodlots donated to the Rhode Island Audubon Society in 1965. Trails are well marked, and all kinds of birdlife can be seen, including herons and egrets, catbirds and cardinals (daily dawn to dusk; free; ⓣ401/624-2759).

Further south on Rte-77, **Tiverton Four Corners** is a motley collection of specialty stores and art galleries, as well as historic homes, several of which date from the eighteenth century, among them the 1730 gambrel-roofed **Chase Cory House**, 3980 Main Rd (June–Sept Sun 2–4.30pm; free; ⓣ401/625-5174), now the base for the Tiverton Historical Society. The home retains many features indigenous to colonial village farms, such as an eight-foot-tall kitchen fireplace with beaded chimney. **Pond Bridge Road**, a mile south of Four Corners, a pretty country lane bordered by lush hedges and rugged stone walls, traverses gentle farmland to reach **Fogland Beach** (parking $5), Tiverton's shingly but safe town beach that skirts the southern edge of a comma-shaped peninsula jutting out into the Sakonnet River. There are splendid views down the river, with the Sakonnet Lighthouse and the various elephantine rocks that surround it looming in the distance.

Little Compton

The 4500 year-round residents of tiny but wealthy **LITTLE COMPTON**, ten miles from Tiverton, owe their place on the map to a bird – the Rhode Island Red chicken was developed here, and even has a small granite monument honoring it in the Adamsville section of town. Fowl history notwithstanding, residents are ultra-protective of their environment, as evidenced by car stickers that bluntly demand "Keep Little Compton Little," and the conspicuous absence of places to stay. Rumor has it that its classic village center, **Little Compton Commons**, was the favored location for the film *The Witches of Eastwick* (eventually filmed in Cohasset, Massachusetts; see p.190), but that the residents turned down the opportunity for fear that it would put the town rather too firmly on the tourist trail. Though its population does increase during the summer, it manages to retain its composed self – thanks to a planning code that prohibits the construction of fast-food joints and unnecessary malls.

You can check out the town square on Meetinghouse Lane, where the commons is dominated by the lofty, brilliant-white spire of its 1832 **Congregational Church**, with an adjacent burial ground that predates the building by 150 years. It contains the grave of one **Benjamin Church**, an Indian-fighter who took part in the execution of King Philip back in the 1600s. Opposite the church, the meandering maze of rooms that is **Wilbur's Store**, established more than two hundred years ago, is Little Compton's own Lilliputian department store, selling everything from food to hardware.

At 548 W Main Rd, the **Wilbor House** (late June to Aug Thurs–Sun 1–5pm; Sept to mid-Oct Sat–Sun 1–5pm; $5) is a restored 1690 structure with low ceilings and exposed wooden beams that contains numerous examples of eighteenth- and nineteenth-century domestic furniture. Far more interesting than the house is the accompanying barn, where old farm implements and vehicles are on display, along with photographs and items celebrating Little Compton's Portuguese heritage and a replica of a one-room schoolhouse.

Nearby, evocatively named Swamp Road leads to the town-owned **Wilbour Woods**, which contain, among all the maples, hollies, and ferns, a monument to **Queen Ashawonk**, a Native American woman who chose to side with the new settlers rather than the Wampanoag tribe during King Philip's War. In case you're wondering, the many variations on the Wilbur name derive from one **Samuel Wilbore**, an early settler of the Little Compton area. It was he who built the Wilbor House and so established the legacy of Little Compton's would-be first family, which, as it branched out geographically, began to utilize different spellings.

Main Road struggles south toward the Atlantic to **Sakonnet Point**, where a broad, sweeping vista of an often angry seascape is framed on one side by a newly restored **lighthouse** and on the other by the rocky crags and promontories of Newport and Middletown. In between, the graceful mock English Gothic tower of St George's School punctuates the horizon. With all the watercraft around, it's far too dangerous to swim at the nearby harbor; instead, park at the **Little Compton Town Beach**, at the end of South Shore Road ($7 weekdays, $12 weekends), and walk on to pretty **Goosewing Beach**, sandier and quieter than the town beach, at least for the moment – the question of better access – meaning in turn, more visitors – is perennially up in the air.

Four and a half miles on, the **Sakonnet Vineyard**, 162 W Main Rd/Rte-177 (daily: June–Sept 10am–6pm; Oct–May 11am–5pm; free; ⓣ1-800/91-WINES), is New England's largest winery, at which you can take a guided or unguided tour that includes free samples. Nearby, local shrine **Walker's Farm Stand**, 251 W Main Rd (ⓣ401/635-4719), is a veritable kaleidoscope of colorful produce, especially in the late summer and autumn when bright orange pumpkins bask seductively in the golden autumnal glow, and you can snack on juicy fresh-picked apples.

Tiverton and Little Compton practicalities

While most visitors spend only an hour or two in these towns (or just pass through), should you desire a break on your way to or from Newport, it is possible to spend the night with a little advance planning (you won't stumble on lodging by accident here). One of the few places to stay if you're visiting Little Compton or Tiverton (save a few small B&Bs) is the *Stone House Club*, 122 Sakonnet Point Rd, Little Compton (ⓣ401/635-2222; ❺), housed in a rugged three-story granite building overlooking the Atlantic. This local gathering spot is technically a private club, but you can book a room as long as you pay the $25 membership fee; there's also a decent restaurant open to the public with basic American entrées ($11–25) like crispy roast duck, and a cellar bar on the premises. If you really want to relax and don't mind splurging a bit, your best bet is to rent a cottage way down in the town of Sakonnet, a pricey option (starting at $850 per week – try local agents T.L. Holland at ⓣ401/624-8469) – or try the lovely bed and breakfast *The Roost*, at the Sakonnet Winery, (ⓣ401/635-8486; ❻), which occupies the former property's farmhouse, right on the vineyard.

Places to eat are few and far between as well. The Provender, 3883 Main Rd, Tiverton (ⓣ401/624-8096), is a delightful gourmet food store where you can choose from an exotic array of designer sandwiches and freshly baked desserts, while Gray's Ice Cream, at the intersection of routes 77 and 177, also in Tiverton (ⓣ401/624-4500), vends numerous homemade flavors of the sweet stuff. Local no-frills institution the *Commons Lunch*, East Side, Little Compton Commons (ⓣ401/635-4388), serves luscious lobster rolls, stuffed quahogs, and johnnycakes.

South County: Rhode Island's Southern Coast

SOUTH COUNTY is the unofficial name given to Rhode Island's southernmost towns along a coastal stretch that begins with North Kingstown, twenty miles south of Providence, and runs past gently rolling hills, quaint villages, and gray sandy beaches to Westerly, just this side of the Connecticut border. Further inland the geography is a bit more diverse, full of dense woodlands, wildlife reserves, and oversize ponds, but somewhat lacking in must-see sights that would make you stray very far off the coastal highway of **US-1**, actually once the main connecting route between New York and New England. In any case, the construction of I-95 some miles north has insured that this chunk of Rhode Island remains relatively unscathed by the kind of overdevelopment seen in other parts of the state. Indeed, many visitors bypass this area entirely while wending their way over to Cape Cod or up into northern New England – which makes it all the more appealing.

The place is alive with reflections of its Colonial and Native American heritage, the latter attested to by such place names as Misquamicut and Quoquonset. Historic points of interest include **Smith's Castle**, America's oldest plantation house, and, in North Kingstown, the **birthplace of Gilbert Stuart**, the portraitist, whose painting of George Washington is seen on all US dollar bills. **Watch Hill** and **Narragansett**, on the coast, are – like Newport – known for their massive summer "cottages" and resort facilities, while **Galilee** is the point of departure for ferries to unspoilt Block Island, as well as being one of the busiest fishing ports in New England, a great place to enjoy a seafood meal while watching the boats come in.

North Kingstown

NORTH KINGSTOWN, known as "plantation country" for its many long-standing farms, is less a town than a collection of rural communities straddling Rte-1A on the eastern shore of Narragansett Bay. The best-known of these is the harborside village of **Wickford**, full of shady tree-lined lanes and handsomely preserved eighteenth- and nineteenth-century homes. Wickford is also home to the oldest Episcopal (Anglican) church north of Virginia, **Old Narragansett Church**, at 55 Main St (July–Aug Thurs–Sun 11am–4pm, other times by appointment; free; ⓣ401/294-4357), built in 1707 in the square "preaching box" style which makes it look more like a congregational meetinghouse from the outside. Among its treasures are a Queen Anne communion set and reputedly the oldest organ in America, dating back to 1680. Box pews and a slave gallery are reminders of a grim and turbulent past. The **Wickford Town Dock**, at the end of Main Street, was a bustling waterfront for years, especially when it was trading with the West Indies; today it's a peaceful, relaxing place where local quahog skiffs rub shoulders with posh yachts and the only bustle of any kind comes when the annual Arts Festival is held here in July.

Just north of town off Rte-1 is **Smith's Castle**, 55 Richard Smith Drive (May & Sept–Oct Fri–Sun noon–4pm; June–Aug Thurs–Mon noon–4pm; other times by appointment; free for gardens, $5 for house tour; ⓣ401/294-3521). A red-clapboard plantation house that dates back to 1678, it was the site of much of Roger Williams' preaching activity. It replaced an earlier trading post that was destroyed by Native Americans in 1676, having been used to plan the attack against King Philip of the Wampanoags. The castle was recently restored to resemble how it appeared in 1740. Also north of town (3.5 miles east of the castle), the only brick hangar on the East Coast houses the **Quonset**

Getting around South County

Southern Rhode Island has much to offer in terms of attractions, but woefully little as far as public transportation goes. **Amtrak**'s (T 1-800/USA-RAIL) sole South County stop is in Westerly, and RIPTA **buses** connect North and South Kingstown with Providence (bus #66) and Newport (#64). Most people travel between the sights and beaches by **car**. US-1 is the main thoroughfare spanning the county; offshoot Rte-1A is best for getting to Narragansett or the Watch Hill area.

Local **information** can be found at the South Kingstown Chamber of Commerce, 328 Main St, in Wakefield (T 401/783-2801, W www.skchamber.com); you might also try W www.narragansettri.com or W www.charlestownri.com, though both sites are somewhat limited.

Air Museum, 488 Eccleston Ave, Quonset Naval Air Base, North Kingstown (Fri–Sun 10am–3pm; $4; T 401/294-9540), which displays vintage aircraft, both military and commercial, such as a Russian MIG-17 and an A-4 Skyhawk.

Most of North Kingstown's other points of interest are further south, in and around **Saunderstown**, including the three-hundred-acre **Casey Farm**, 2325 Boston Neck Rd, also known as Rte-1A (June–mid-Oct Tues, Thurs & Sat 1–5pm; $4) and, in business since 1702, one of the oldest working farms in the United States. It was originally the center of a plantation that produced food for local and foreign markets, and today, resident farmers raise organically grown vegetables, herbs, and flowers for subscribing households in a Community Supported Agriculture Program. The farmhouse contains original furniture and family memorabilia; in the parlor door, a musket hole bears witness to a British attack on the property when it was used as a garrison by American military during the Revolutionary War. The **Gilbert Stuart Birthplace and Museum**, 815 Gilbert Stuart Rd (April–Oct Thurs–Mon 11am–4pm; $3; T 401/294-3001), childhood home of the celebrated eighteenth-century portraitist, disappoints in that it only contains one reproduction of the 111 portraits of George Washington that Stuart painted during his lifetime.

Few people choose to **stay** or **eat** in North Kingstown, electing to find such practicalities in more tourist-friendly **Narragansett** and **Galilee**, described below.

Narragansett

Eleven miles along Rte-1A, **NARRAGANSETT** (meaning "little spit of land") occupies a narrow patch snaking out into the Atlantic, its long coastline of rocks interspersed by broad expanses of sand – a major attraction for swimmers, watersports enthusiasts, bird watchers, and fishermen. The town center, known as **Narragansett Pier** (though it's only a seawall and sidewalk along the ocean), had its heyday during the Victorian era, when the town competed with Newport as a major resort destination. It succeeded to some extent, luring visitors particularly with the **Narragansett Casino Resort**, designed by the architectural firm of McKim, Mead & White in 1884. Hopes of lasting fame and prosperity came to an abrupt end in 1900, however, when fire swept through the casino complex, destroying all but its turreted towers, which today remain the most striking feature of the town center, and which house the Narragansett Historical Society and the **visitor information center**, 35 Ocean Rd (Mon–Fri 9am–4pm; T 401/783-7121). For additional explication of Narragansett's role over the years, visit the **South County Museum**, Rte-1A at Canonchet Farm, opposite Narragansett Beach Pavilion (May & Sept–Oct Fri–Sun 10am–4pm, June–Aug Wed–Sun 10am–4pm; $4;

☎401/783-5400), which contains thousands of local artifacts, a replicated print shop, smithy, general store, and one-room schoolhouse.

Narragansett's long coastline boasts several outstanding **beaches** (see box opposite) and the charmingly chaotic fishing port of **Galilee**, four miles south of the town center. The port's potholed main drag, where the fishy whiff can at times be overwhelming, is home to a large commercial fishing fleet, half a dozen fish markets, two or three fish-processing works, beach accessory stores, and the **Block Island Ferry** (see p.319 for details). If you want to go on a guided **whale-watch**, the boats of Francis Fleet (July & Aug daily 1pm; $32 adults, $20 children under 12; ☎401/783-4988 or 1-800/662-2824) depart from a point just behind *Finback's* restaurant. A mile east, the **Point Judith Lighthouse**, at the end of Ocean Road, has been warning ships off the rocky coast since the early 1800s. The present lighthouse, built in 1857, is closed to the public, but the view from the parking lot is breathtaking, especially on a stormy day.

Practicalities

Accommodation is never hard to come by in Narragansett, except at the height of the season, when it's advisable to book well in advance. In Galilee, opposite the Block Island ferry at Great Island Road, is the *Lighthouse Inn* (☎401/789-9341 or 1-800/336-6662; 4), a comfortable 100-room hotel near all the beach and boating activities. More atmospheric digs are available in the Narragansett Pier area, where, at 59 Kingstown Rd, the *1900 House* (☎401/789-7971; 5) is a remnant of Narragansett's glory days. If you prefer to rent a cottage, Durkin Cottage Realty (☎401/789-6659) has the largest selection in the area, starting at around $800 a week.

The Narragansett Pier area boasts several upmarket **restaurants**, including the *Coast Guard House*, 40 Ocean Rd (☎401/789-0700), where the view, if not the food, is spectacular; *Basil's*, at 22 Kingstown Rd, on the pier (☎401/789-3743), has established a strong local following for its fine French cuisine. Galilee is home to a number of excellent seafood spots, the most popular of which are *George's*, 250 Sand Hill Cove Rd (☎401/783-2306), and *Champlin's*, 256 Great Island Rd (☎401/783-3152), which has nice views of the fishing boats from an upstairs covered deck. Not far away, *Aunt Carrie's*, 1240 Ocean Rd (summer only; ☎401/783-7930), is a Rhode Island institution, the place for traditional shore dinners in an unpretentious, relaxed atmosphere, while *Spain*, 1144 Ocean Rd (☎401/783-9770), serves a variety of Spanish, American, and seafood dishes in a contemporary setting.

South Kingstown

SOUTH KINGSTOWN's 62 square miles – in area, Rhode Island's largest town – takes in fourteen separate villages covering both sides of Rte-1, quite different in nature depending on whether you're traveling on the inland or coastal side of the highway. Inland, dense woods hide well-preserved colonial villages, potato farms, and wildlife refuges; the most logical first stop here is **Kingston**, founded in 1674, and a seat of Rhode Island government until it was centralized in Providence. Many well-preserved examples of Federal-style architecture can still be seen, including the 1775 **Kingston Free Library**, 2605 Kingstown Rd, originally the Washington County Courthouse, where the state's General Assembly, Supreme Court, and local town council all shared their sessions. Nearby, in the **Old Washington County Jail**, at 2036 Kingstown Rd (April–Oct Tues, Thurs & Sat 1–4pm; $3 donation), you can see old jail cells which have been around since 1792, along with a decent museum containing changing exhibits on South County life over the past three hundred years. Rural Kingston is also the unlikely location of the **University of**

South County beaches

Many of Rhode Island's best **saltwater beaches** can be found in South County, and are generally open to the public, although access to some of them is virtually impossible without a car, and there is usually a hefty parking fee in summer, especially on weekends. Outside of season, parking is often free and the beaches, on weekdays at least, are deserted. Ocean temperatures peak at a refreshing 70–75 degrees during the dog days of August. Amounts listed below are per car.

Charlestown Town Beach Charlestown Beach Road, Charlestown. This beach looks like it belongs in California: lots of volleyball players, surfers, and bronzed bodies. $5 weekdays, $10 weekends.
East Beach Ninigret Conservation Area off East Beach Road, Charlestown. An almost Caribbean-like beach, with sugar-fine sand and aquamarine waters in a protected area. $12 weekdays, $14 weekends.
East Matunuck State Beach Succotash Road, South Kingstown. A beach with a gradual dropoff that is good for sand-fishing and popular with teens. $8 weekdays, $10 weekends.
Misquamicut State Beach Misquamicut. Only half a mile long, but incredibly crowded. Amusements and fast food are close at hand. $12 weekdays, $14 weekends.
Napatree Point Watch Hill. A complete contrast to Misquamicut; limited access only to this pretty, ecologically fragile beach. No parking.
Narragansett Town Beach Rte-1A, Narragansett. A half-mile-long beach popular with families. $6 per car parking, plus $5 per person.
Roger Wheeler Beach Cove Wood Drive, Narragansett. A mile of gray sand with excellent facilities and expansive parking. $12 weekdays, $14 weekends.
Scarborough State Beach, Ocean Drive, Narragansett. Popular with students from nearby University of Rhode Island. $12 weekdays, $14 weekends.
South Kingstown Town Beach South Kingstown. Beautiful beach backed by dunes. $10 daily.

Rhode Island (URI), on North Road, whose leafy 1200-acre campus once centered on a small farmhouse – fitting, as this was started as an agricultural school. On Rte-2, a mile south of the junction with Rte-138, a dilapidated sign points the way to the **Great Swamp Fight Monument**, which commemorates the bloody 1675 battle in which King Philip's Wampanoag tribe was decimated by colonial forces. Rte-108 leads south from here to the village of **Wakefield**, whose Main Street holds a pleasant mix of antique shops, restaurants, and historic buildings, though nothing of particular interest.

Meanwhile, to the south of Rte-1, a succession of laid-back coastal communities are separated by a series of saltwater ponds protected by fragile barrier beaches. Seaside villages worth stopping by include **Jerusalem** and **Snug Harbor**, with their clutch of summer cottages and stately homes. Otherwise, the main reason for coming down here is to join the crowds at the beaches, namely **Green Hill** and **East Matunuck**, a favorite with URI students. Summer crowds are entertained at the barn-like **Theatre-by-the-Sea**, 364 Cards Pond Rd (shows nightly June–Sept, except Mon; matinees Thurs; tickets $25–35; ⓣ401/782-8587) – an absolute must if you enjoy jolly musicals of the *South Pacific* variety.

Practicalities

The sheer size of South Kingstown means a wide variety of accommodation and dining choices are available; you can find simple motels and cozy B&Bs,

plain diners, and elegantly prepared meals. **Places to stay** in the area include the *Admiral Dewey Inn*, 668 Matunuck Beach Rd, Matanuck (☎401/783-2090 or 1-800/457-2090; ❻), a traditional beach lodging house where you can relax and unwind on the wraparound porch. In Wakefield, the 160-year-old family-run *Larchwood Inn*, 521 Main St (☎401/783-5454; ❻), offers twelve cozy rooms, a nice complement to the elegant **restaurant** on the premises, which serves well-priced classic American fare with a Scottish twist. For generous portions of seafood, head to *Cap'n Jack's* in Jerusalem, 584 Succotash Rd (☎401/789-4556; closed Mon).

Charlestown

Laid-back **CHARLESTOWN**, South Kingstown's western neighbor along Rte-1, is one of the fastest-growing communities in the state, its recent arrivals having been seduced by an attractive coastline – miles of barrier beach backed by pristine salt ponds. First settled by the Narragansett Indians, Charlestown received its charter from King Charles II in 1663, and was thus named for him. The Narragansetts, however, still own plenty of land in town, and maintain a significant cultural impact, best observed during their **Annual Pow-Wow**, held the second weekend of August on tribal lands just off Rte-2 and featuring Native American dancing, crafts, food, and storytelling (☎401/364-1100 for details). Also located on these lands are the **Royal Indian Burial Grounds**, used for centuries as the resting place for tribal chiefs, and the **Narragansett Indian Church**, a reconstruction of an 1859 granite Greek Revival building reopened in 1998 after a disastrous fire. The church is not generally accessible to the public, though you can try to check it out during Sunday services.

The **Ninigret National Wildlife Refuge**, 3769 Old Post Rd (☎401/364-9124), highlights Charlestown's protected coastline and consists of four hundred acres of diverse upland and wetland habitats. Nine miles of trails yield many opportunities for bird watching or a bit of exercise. It's merely one of a number of recreational areas that surround **Ninigret Pond**.

Inland, off Rte-1, the **Burlingame State Park** (☎401/322-7337) is crossed by trails through a variety of habitats, where foxes, deer, wild turkeys, coyotes, and ruffed grouse might be seen from mid-October through May; outside of those months, you can only enter if you're camping. Further in, a number of tiny communities provide a glimpse into rural Rhode Island life, especially **Shannock**, on Rte-112, a disarmingly pretty New England mill village of white-clapboard houses near the Pawcatuck River. Once virtually abandoned, the whole place was purchased and restored by a local developer, with the express intention of turning upwardly mobile young couples on to the charms of country living, to date only a partly successful venture.

Practicalities

Much of Charlestown's accommodations, a mix of motor courts and intimate inns, lines the main US-1 road, including the *General Stanton Inn*, 4115 Old Post Rd (☎401/364-8888; ❻), which has been a resting place for travelers on the Providence–New London run since Revolutionary days. An adjacent flea market keeps guests busy at weekends. *One Willow By the Sea*, 1 Willow Rd (☎401/364-0802; ❺), is a peaceful hostelry near the wildlife refuges. The bulk of the town's restaurants specialize in moderately priced seafood, like the casual *Charlestown Lobster Pot* on Old Post Road (☎401/322-7686).

Westerly and Watch Hill

WESTERLY, as its name implies, occupies the most westerly point of Rhode Island, eleven miles on from Charlestown, sharing the Pawcatuck River with

△ Canoeing on the Blackstone River

the town of Pawcatuck, Connecticut. Once a prosperous manufacturer of textiles and fine-grained granite, its downtown area holds few reminders of those days. The most impressive specimen left is the **Babcock-Smith House**, 124 Granite St (May–June & Sept–Oct Sun 2–5pm; July–Aug Sun & Wed 2–5pm; $3), built in 1734 for Dr Joshua Babcock, Westerly's first physician, who moonlighted as the town's postmaster, the chief justice for Rhode Island, and major-general in the Revolutionary army. The handsome two-story gambrel-roofed building contains much of its original trimmings, including the wooden paneling, the open fireplace in the kitchen, a Queen Anne daybed, and, above the mantelpiece in the dining room, an engraving that depicts Babcock engaged in an act of diplomacy at the French court.

Most visitors, however, forsake Westerly's downtown in lieu of the **Watch Hill** area a few miles south, which, after Newport, is Rhode Island's most select resort, with salty seaside shops and 1900s-era **cottages** overlooking the Atlantic. One holdover from its birth as a resort is the **Flying Horse Carousel** at the end of Bay Street, which, like several others in New England, is claimed to be the nation's oldest (1879). The twenty horses are not attached to the floor but instead suspended from a central frame, swinging out or "flying" when in motion. The other highlight in town, the granite **lighthouse** on Lighthouse Road, built in 1856 to replace an earlier wooden edifice, houses a small **museum** containing the usual bits on lighthouse history (July & Aug Tues & Thurs 1–3pm; free). To the west, accessible from Watch Hill Beach, the two-mile-long barrier beach of **Napatree Point** once supported a number of homes before they were destroyed by the devastating hurricane of 1938. Today it is a peaceful conservation area filled with myriad bird species and affording stunning ocean views.

Practicalities

Perhaps the most tourist-friendly of South County towns, Westerly has upwards of thirty hotels, motels, and B&Bs; some of these have more of a resort feel than most any Rhode Island town except for Newport. For a good **lodging** option, try the *Shelter Harbor Inn*, 10 Wagner Rd (Ⓣ401/322-8883; ❺), a 24-room country inn done out in early American fittings, with an excellent restaurant to boot. Alternately the *Winnepaug Inn*, 169 Shore Rd (Ⓣ401/348-8350 or 1-800/288-9906; ❻), is a well-appointed three-story motor hotel set on beautifully manicured grounds overlooking a golf course.

Of the best places to **eat**, the spacious *Mary's Italian Restaurant*, 336 Post Road (Ⓣ401/322-0444), doles out relatively inexpensive Italian home-cooking in unpretentious surroundings; closer to downtown, *W.B. Cody's*, 265 Post Rd (Ⓣ401/322-4070), is also a good alternative to the local fish fare, serving authentic Western BBQ and steaks at respectable prices. Just outside of town, the *Weekapaug Inn*, 25 Spray Rock Rd, Weekapaug (Ⓣ401/322-0301), offers creative American dishes in a bright and airy dining room. Down in Watch Hill, *St Clair Annex*, 141 Bay St (May–Oct; Ⓣ401/348-8211), run by the same family for over 100 years, serves wonderful breakfasts and home-made ice cream in thirty flavors. For something more substantial, the *Olympia Tea Room*, 74 Bay St (May–Oct; Ⓣ401/348-8211), has a variety of seafood dishes and mouth-watering desserts.

Entertainment in Westerly centers on theater: the Granite Theater, 1 Granite St (March–Dec Thurs–Sat, Sun matinees; $17; Ⓣ401/596-2341), in a former church building, presents drama, comedy, and, every summer, a classic American musical. There's also the Colonial Theatre's free professional Shakespeare-in-the-Park productions in July in Wilcox Park, which have been a highlight of the summer since 1991 (Ⓦwww.colonialtheatrerict.org). Wilcox Park is also the venue for the renowned **Westerly Chorus**'s Summer Pops concert, which draws up to 25,000 people. Throughout the rest of the year

(Nov to June) the ensemble puts on classical concerts at the **Westerly Performance Hall**, 119 High St (☎401/596-8663). A former Immaculate Conception Church blessed with excellent acoustics, this is one of the best small concert halls in the the Northeast.

Block Island

It may not be the "Bermuda of the North," or "one of the last great places on earth," as it is also sometimes described, but **BLOCK ISLAND**, twelve miles off the coast of southern Rhode Island, has managed to preserve its melancholy, seductive charm even in the face of growing hordes of visitors and the rampant construction of summer homes in the 1970s and 1980s, which threatened to disfigure the landscape's simple beauty as well as destroy its unique natural environment. Inhabited by 800 year-round residents, who scatter themselves around the gently rolling hills and broad expanses of moorland, Block Island still exudes an air of desolation, a mood exacerbated offseason when the island ferries are incapacitated due to bad weather. There's not much to see once you get over, just lovely coves and sandy beaches, but, like its Massachusetts cousins Martha's Vineyard and Nantucket, the island gets chock-a-block between July 4th and early September, when tourists, part-time residents, and day-trippers all seem to take to the small island's scant network of roads at once.

Some history

Native Americans, who called it "Manisses" or "Island of the Little God," had inhabited Block Island for centuries before Giovanni de Verrezano spotted it in 1524. With the prospect of a substantial bonus in sight, he cannily named it **Claudia**, after the mother of the French King, Francis I, who had commissioned him. Later on, in 1614, the intrepid Dutch explorer, Adrian Block, stopped for a time on the island and gave it the name "**Adrian's Eyelandt**" which eventually became **Block Island**.

A group of English settlers seeking religious freedom arrived here in 1661 and established a small farming and fishing community that still exists today. A relatively quiet couple of hundred years followed until 1842, when the island's first hotel was built and visitors began to recognize Block Island's many charms; thirty years later a new breakwater was built, meaning that larger ships could dock – bringing even more travelers. Things took a turn for the worse with the 1938 hurricane that devastated much of the New England coast: it destroyed nearly all of Block Island's fishing fleet and caused considerable structural damage to the hotels and other buildings around Old Harbor, the island's commercial center.

There's little remnant of hard times today: Block Island has only become increasingly fashionable, a highly sought-after real estate destination with many properties surpassing the million-dollar mark. In recent years, residents of **New Shoreham** (the island's official title) passed a number of measures designed to preserve the relative tranquility and natural environment they had so expensively become privy to: camping and tenting were banned, the operation of mopeds and motorcycles between midnight and 6am prohibited, and shellfishing without a license no longer tolerated.

Arrival, information, and getting around

Most people arrive on Block Island by **ferry**. From the Galilee State Pier in Narragansett (also known as Point Judith), the Interstate Navigation Co. (☎401/783-4613, Ⓦwww.blockislandferry.com) runs at least six ferries a day during the summer months (sometimes as many as ten) and one to three a day

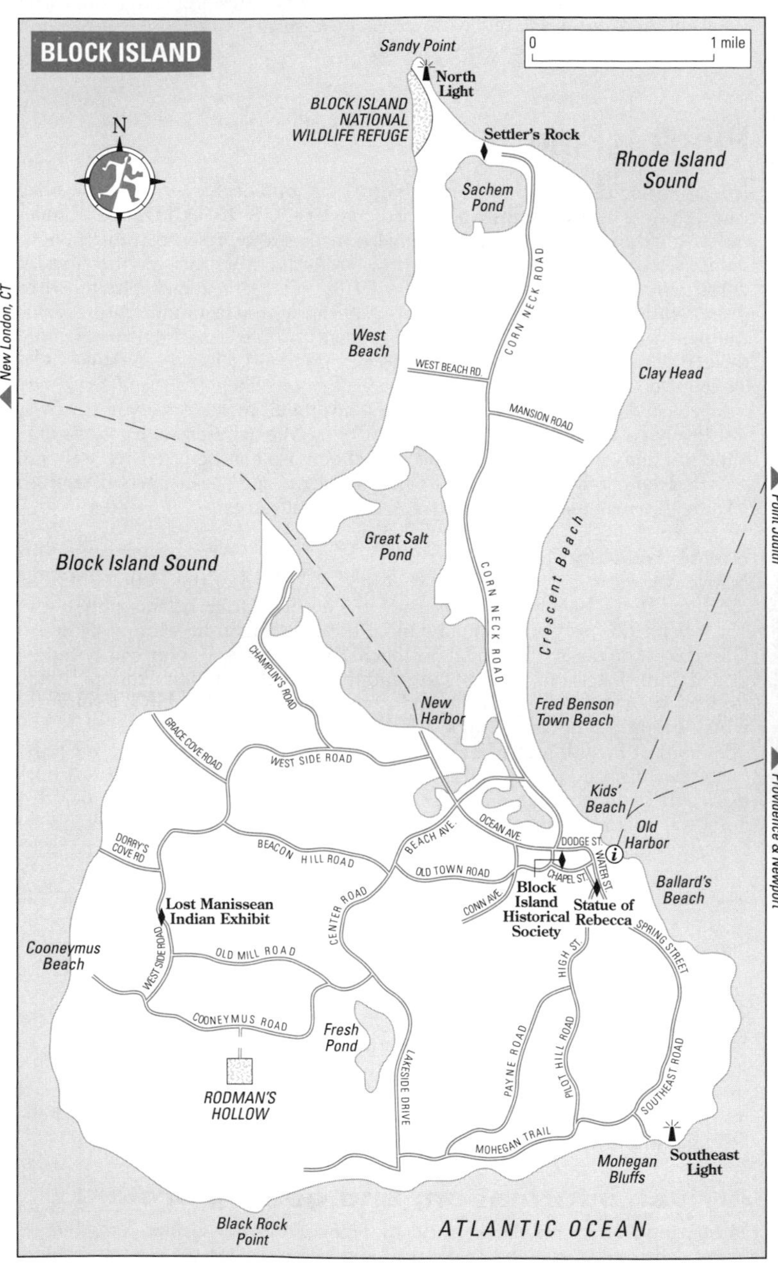
BLOCK ISLAND
Sandy Point
0 1 mile
North Light
BLOCK ISLAND NATIONAL WILDLIFE REFUGE
N
Settler's Rock
Rhode Island Sound
Sachem Pond
CORN NECK ROAD
West Beach
WEST BEACH RD.
Clay Head
New London, CT
MANSION ROAD
Point Judith
Great Salt Pond
Block Island Sound
Crescent Beach
CORN NECK ROAD
CHAMPLIN'S ROAD
New Harbor
Fred Benson Town Beach
GRACE COVE ROAD
WEST SIDE ROAD
Providence & Newport
Kids' Beach
Old Harbor
OCEAN AVE.
BEACH AVE.
DODGE ST.
DORRY'S COVE RD
BEACON HILL ROAD
WATER ST.
CHAPEL ST.
OLD TOWN ROAD
Ballard's Beach
CENTER ROAD
CONN AVE.
Lost Manissean Indian Exhibit
Block Island Historical Society
Statue of Rebecca
SPRING STREET
HIGH ST.
Cooneymus Beach
OLD MILL ROAD
WEST SIDE ROAD
COONEYMUS ROAD
Fresh Pond
PAYNE ROAD
PILOT HILL ROAD
SOUTHEAST ROAD
LAKESIDE DRIVE
RODMAN'S HOLLOW
MOHEGAN TRAIL
Mohegan Bluffs
Southeast Light
Black Rock Point
ATLANTIC OCEAN

during the winter. The seventy-minute trip costs $8.30 one-way, $13.65 for same-day return. Passengers taking cars ($26 each way) need to make reservations in advance; foot passengers just need to arrive 45 minutes early. The same company runs daily ferries (no cars) from Newport's Fort Adams State Park from late June to early September at 9.15am ($8.25 one-way, $11.85 for same-day return), as well as from New London, Connecticut, leaving at 9am daily (and 7.15pm on Fridays) from early June to early September ($15 one-way, $19 for same-day return, cars $28 each way). From Point Judith, it is also possible to catch the Island Hi-Speed Ferry, which takes approximately 30 minutes; for information, contact them at ⓣ(877/733-9425 or ⓦwww.blockislandhighspeedferry.com. If you'd rather fly, **New England Airlines** (ⓣ1-800/243-2460) provides hourly flights from Westerly all year for $45 one-way, $76 round-trip.

The Block Island Chamber of Commerce (ⓣ401/466-2982, ⓦwww.blockislandchamber.com) operates an **information center** right where you come off the ferry, set to open and shut with ferry times, or you can check the Block Island Tourism Council at 23 Water St (ⓣ1-800/383-BIRI). The other thing you'll see as you disembark is a bewildering array of **bike**, **moped**, and **car rental** agencies, with still more lurking behind the shops. Prices vary, so you might want to shop around. Two good options are the Old Harbor Bike Shop (ⓣ401/466-2029), a dockside shack just left as you disembark the ferry, and Block Island Bike and Car Rental, Ocean Avenue (ⓣ401/466-2297). There are plenty of **taxis** lined up too, at least on summer days, useful if you're weighed down with luggage or if your accommodation is located at some far-flung corner of the island. Most of the cabs provide narrated (and fairly pithy) **island tours**, at $35 for two people and a further $5 for each additional person; in the absence of tour buses, this can be a good way to get oriented. Uncle Lou's Taxi (ⓣ401/466-2124) is one of the best for these.

Still, you'll mostly want to get around **on foot**. There are some 25 miles of walking trails, a system known as **The Greenway** and maintained by the Nature Conservancy (ⓣ401/466-2129), which gives guided nature walks during the summer. If your wanderings take you through grassy terrain, be especially wary of ticks, which delight in attaching themselves to your socks before they proceed to other parts of your anatomy.

Accommodation

If you want to **stay** in Block Island during the summer, it's advisable to book well in advance; even with more than seventy hotels, inns, B&Bs, and studio rentals, accommodation fills up rapidly, especially at weekends. Expect to pay anything from $80 to $350 per night for a room, and $750 a week up to an incredible $4000 for a cottage rental. Because the island is so small, numbers are rarely, if ever, used in addresses; fortunately, it's virtually impossible to get lost. Most hotels are located in any case on **Old Harbor**; the only one listed below that's not is the *Hygeia House* on Beach Avenue. **Block Island Reservations** on Water Street (ⓣ1-800/825-6254), across from the ferry landing, will help you to choose rooms and supply other general information. You can also check out ⓦwww.blockislandchamber.com.

1661 Inn & Guest House Spring Street, Old Harbor ⓣ401/466-2421. Nine quietly luxurious rooms opposite the *Manisses*, set on a hill overlooking the sea. ❻

Atlantic Inn High Street, Old Harbor ⓣ401/466-5883, ⓦwww.atlanticinn.com. Laden with mainly Victorian antiques and set on six acres, *The Atlantic* has superior rooms, many with superb views. Guests who feel so inclined can enjoy a game of tennis at the *Inn's* two courts, or a game of croquet on the lawn. Good restaurant, too – see p.323. ❼

Blue Dory Inn Dodge Street, Old Harbor ⓣ401/466-5891 or 1-800/992-7290. A guest-house since it was constructed in 1898, several of the rooms in this romantic Victorian home have ocean or harbor views. ❼

The Gothic Inn Dodge Street, Old Harbor ⓣ401/466-2918 or 1-800/944-8991. Perched high above Crescent Beach, this Victorian, family-run inn has oodles of character; unusually steep gables complete with gingerbread trimmings and a wide, relaxing porch above Dodge Street. It's just three minutes from the ferry. ❻

Hotel Manisses Spring Street, Old Harbor ⓣ401/466-2421 or 1-800/MANISSES. Seventeen comfortable antique-filled rooms, some affording views of the ocean, each named after local shipwrecks. ❺

Hygeia House Beach Avenue, New Harbor ⓣ401/466-9616, ⓦwww.hygeiahouse.com. This creamy yellow homestead, purchased in 1999 and restored by the great grandson of Dr. John C. Champlain (the original 1883 owner and the island's only doctor at the time) offers ten attractive rooms and suites and overlooks both harbors. ❽

National Hotel Water Street, Old Harbor ⓣ1-800/225-2449. This vast Victorian pile dominates everything else on Water Street. There's a delightful wraparound porch and all mod cons, none at the expense of its charm. Fills up fast, so book early. ❻

Spring House Hotel High Street, Old Harbor ⓣ401/466-5844 or 1-800/234-9263, ⓦwww.springhousehotel.com. Built in 1854, the distinctive *Spring House* has hosted notables such as Ulysses S. Grant, Mark Twain, and a Kennedy or two. Rooms, studios, and suites available, with a fancy and expensive well-regarded dining room for lovers of chops, steaks, and seafood on the premises. ❼

The island

Most visitors' first – and last – picture of Block Island is **Old Harbor**, the island's only village, which developed after 1870 when the federal government built the two breakwaters. Huge Victorian hotels were built along **Water Street** to encourage the fledgling tourist industry, many boasting cupolas, porches, and flamboyant gingerbread architecture redolent of Oak Bluffs on Martha's Vineyard. Some of these grand structures still stand, albeit amidst a touristy mix of shops, boutiques, restaurants, and smaller, less atmospheric B&Bs. At the western end of Water Street, smack in the middle of the road, stands the **Statue of Rebecca**, an 1896 recasting of a biblical allegory, 'Rebecca at the Well', erected by the Women's Christian Temperance Movement to remind folks of the dangers of alcohol.

Close by, the **Block Island Historical Society**, Old Town Road at Ocean Avenue (July & Aug daily 10am–5pm; offseason by appt; $3; ⓣ401/466-2481), has a number of exhibits describing the island's farming and maritime past. This 1850 structure, once an inn, is furnished with antiques, though it's mostly useful as a place to get your bearings. Further west, at Rustic Rides Farm, 1173 West Side Road, **The Lost Manissean Indian Exhibit** features arrowheads, axe heads, knives, and ancient mortars and pestles made by the Manissean Indians dating back 450 years (June–Aug daily 9am–5pm; ⓣ1-401/466-5060; $1). You can also rent horses for trail riding at the Farm.

New Harbor, perhaps a mile northwest of Old Harbor along Ocean Avenue, boasts the only other would-be commercial area on the island: a handful of waterfront restaurants and shacks, some facilities for sailing enthusiasts, and, perched on the hill overlooking the Great Salt Pond, the *Hygeia House*, one of several here. The pond was totally enclosed by land until a channel from the ocean was dredged to allow boats entry into the newly fashioned harbor; indeed, this is where ferries from Long Island dock. There's not much to see, but the place comes to life on summer weekends with myriad sailboat races, fishing tournaments, and watersports activities.

Continuing north, accessible via Corn Neck Road, **Settler's Rock** is not much more than a quick stopping-off point – fitting for a place that commemorates where the settlers first landed in 1661 – before the walk up to **North Light**, at Block Island's isolated northern tip. The current incarnation is the fourth go-round for this lighthouse, a grim reminder of the power of nature, since the previous three were destroyed by the elements. A museum traces the island's maritime history and displays old life-saving equipment (July & Aug daily 10am–4pm; $2).

Block Island's beaches

Block Island has some fine **beaches** (all of which are blessedly free of charge), and even in the peak of the summer season it's possible to get far from the madding crowd and find the bliss of solitude. The main "family" beach is the **Fred Benson Town Beach**, a two-mile-long swath of sand with showers, lockers, and chairs, umbrellas and kayaks to rent, and lifeguards to keep an eye on things. There's ample free parking and extensive bicycle racks. At its sheltered southern tip, known as **Kids' Beach**, children can play in relatively shallow water, and look for small crabs, mussels, and the like. **Ballard's Beach**, just south of Old Harbor, is the island's only other lifeguard-staffed beach. Quiet **West Beach**, on the northwestern coast, is backed by dunes that you must keep off: they are part of a bird sanctuary. **Cooneymus Beach**, at the southwest corner of the island, may look like a lovely sandy stretch, but the water is somewhat dangerous due to strong currents. Last, a venture to beautiful **Black Rock Point**, on the island's southern shore, rewards not with swimming opportunities but with a dramatic seascape at which many ships have met their untimely end.

Back from Old Harbor, Spring Street trails to the southernmost tip of the island, where **Mohegan Bluffs**, the spectacular 150-foot cliffs named for an Indian battle that occurred at their base, tower over the Atlantic. Positioned atop is the red-brick **Southeast Light**, built in 1873 but not moved to its present position until 1993 after erosion threatened its survival. It, too, hosts a small museum (July–Sept daily 10am–4pm; $5 donation); better yet are the stunning **ocean views** to be glimpsed from here.

Further west, a dirt track (Black Rock Road) leads from Cooneymus Road to the preserved sanctuary of **Rodman's Hollow**, a deep glacial depression offering more panoramic views of the Atlantic.

Eating

For such a small island, there is a remarkable variety of good **places to eat**, a result of the high number of visitors. Not surprisingly, **fresh seafood** tops the bill at many of the establishments, with lobster a firm favorite. Remember that all of these places reduce their hours drastically for the spring and autumn and all but one or two close for the entire winter. Summer weekends in particular can be very crowded, and not all restaurants take reservations.

Atlantic Inn High Street, Old Harbor ⓣ401/466-5883. This restaurant's main claim to fame is that President Clinton dined here in the summer of 1997 – though no one can tell you what he chose from the excellent $42 four-course prix-fixe menu. Contemporary American cuisine like delicious grilled shark on a bed of spinach is complemented by fantastic ocean views, best enjoyed accompanied by a cocktail or two on the verandah.

Ballard's Restaurant Water Street, Old Harbor ⓣ401/466-2231. Overlooking the beach, this casual standby offers seafood classics like fish and chips, clam cakes, and fried clams. July and August only.

Bethany's Airport Diner State Airport, Center Road ⓣ401/466-3100. Sunup to sundown meals in an informal atmosphere, plus daily homecooked specials like meatloaf and London broil.

Finn's Seafood Restaurant Water Street, Old Harbor ⓣ401/466-2473. Fresh-caught fish and shellfish, with hamburgers and other options.

Hotel Manisses Spring Street, Old Harbor ⓣ401/466-2421. Elegant dining in a Victorian inn (see opposite) featuring an innovative menu with tasty twists on local seafood.

The Oar West Side Road, New Harbor ⓣ401/466-8820. Island landmark famous for the scores of painted oars that hang from the ceiling. The seafood bar's got cheap chowder, peel-and-eat shrimp, fried scallops, and the like; you can take your food outside and enjoy superb views of the Great Salt Pond from the porch.

Rebecca's Water Street, Old Harbor ⓣ401/466-5411. Affordable breakfasts, tasty and inventive sandwich wraps, clam cakes, and chowder at this island favorite, conveniently open 7am to 2am in season.

Nightlife and entertainment

Although Block Island is so quiet for most of the year you can hear the grass grow, on summer nights the **nightlife** picks up, mostly centering on the ample selection of **bars**. Some of these are staid and courtly; others are renowned for their boisterous weekend parties. In recent years, the **Spring House Music Festivals** (several per summer) have even brought full-blown rock concerts to the island (call the *Spring House Hotel* for details; see p.322). More "wholesome" entertainment is provided by two **cinemas**: the Empire Theater, Water Street (Ⓣ401/466-2555), shows first-run movies and midnight cult films, while the Oceanwest Theater, Champlin's Marina, New Harbor (Ⓣ401/466-2971), offers more first-runs and childrens' matinees. Pick up one of the local papers, the *Block Island Times* or the *Cable*, for current listings and special events.

Albion Pub Ocean Avenue, Old Harbor Ⓣ401/466-9900. Comfortable, dark, and smoky pub on the main strip.

Captain Nick's Rock & Roll Bar Ocean Avenue, Old Harbor Ⓣ401/466-5113. The island's biggest nightclub, featuring live music at weekends that ranges from national headliners to locals eager to strut their stuff.

Club Soda Connecticut Avenue, Old Harbor Ⓣ401/466-5397. Drinks and music amidst strange, sort of kitsch, decor.

McGovern's Yellow Kittens Tavern Corn Neck Road, Old Harbor Ⓣ401/466-5855. This 126-year-old institution has no shortage of activities in which to engage – pool, ping-pong, darts, pinball – while imbibing. Live classic rock throughout the summer, too.

Mohegan Café & Brewery Water Street, across from the ferry on Old Harbor Ⓣ401/466-2145. Microbrews direct from an in-house brewery, plus nightly entertainment in season.

Mohogany Shoals Payne's Dock, New Harbor Ⓣ401/466-5572. Dockside bar featuring an Irish folk guitarist on Wednesdays and weekends during the summer.

5

Connecticut

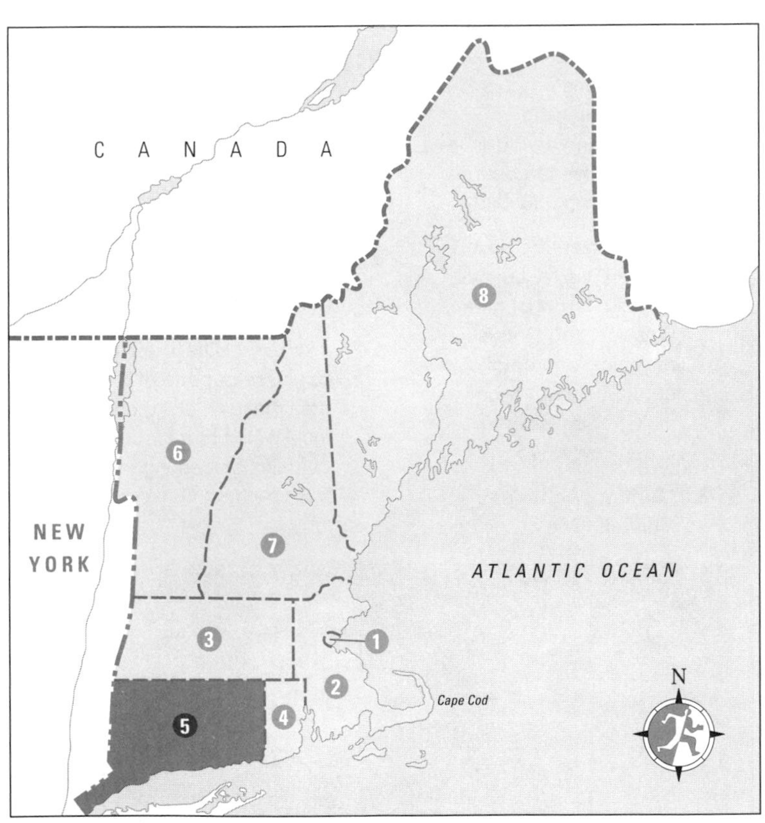

CHAPTER 5

Highlights

* **Mystic** Though the seaport can verge on tacky, you'll still be able to trace the authentic maritime history here. See p.331
* **Guilford–Madison–Clinton** This trinity of Connecticut's prettiest small towns offers pristine lawns, historic homes, and an old-fashioned sense of community. See pp.338–340
* **Yale University, New Haven** This Ivy League school's lawns of green, Classical and Gothic buildings, and erudite but non-snobby vibe make for a welcome oasis. See p.345
* **Maritime Aquarium, Norwalk** One of the best maritime collections to be found anywhere. See p.353
* **Bruce Museum, Greenwich** A broad collection of fine art pieces, anthropological artifacts, and natural science exhibits makes this one of the state's top draws. See p.355
* **Mark Twain House, Hartford** The esteemed Samuel Clemens' eccentric hideaway, befitting the imaginative author. See p.363
* **Litchfield Hills** The stark ruralness of parts of this area makes looking for local wines or antique bargains something of a treasure hunt. See p.370

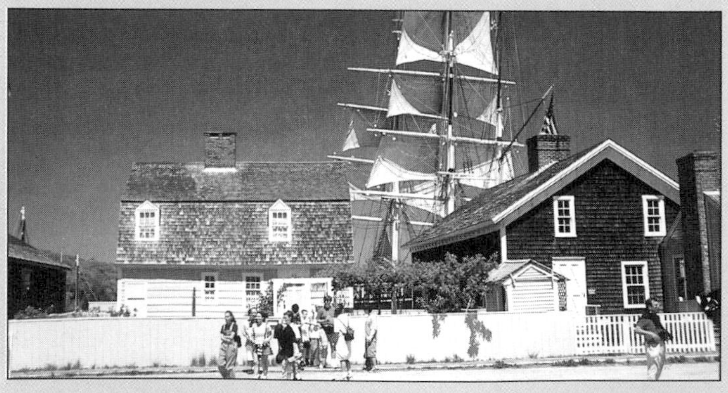

Connecticut

New England's southernmost state, **CONNECTICUT**, a rectangle about 90 miles long by 55 miles wide, was named *Quinnehtukqut* ("great tidal river") by the Native Americans after the river that bisects it and spills into Long Island Sound. It's a small and densely populated state, despite being predominantly rural: the vast majority of residents live in the large coastal cities, in and around the state capital **Hartford**, or in the southwestern corner of the state, which is little more than a conservative, high-rent suburb of New York City where commuters can earn Big Apple salaries while avoiding its high taxes.

Connecticut's first white settlers came in the 1630s when **English** refugees from Massachusetts seeking political and religious freedom arrived at the town of Windsor. Settlements followed in Wethersfield and Hartford, and in 1636 the three united to form the **Connecticut Colony**, adopting the "**Fundamental Orders**," a charter which was later used as a model for the American Constitution; indeed, Connecticut is still sometimes referred to as the "**Constitution State**." After the Pequot War of 1637, which effectively displaced the Native Americans from their home of several thousand years, more communities were established, and a **second colony**, composed of the coastal towns surrounding New Haven, was formed in 1643, only to unite with the first around twenty years later.

Connecticut soon became a center for "**Yankee ingenuity**," principally the invention and marketing (often by notorious and not always honorable Yankee peddlers) of many a useful household object. Meanwhile, on the coast, locals were turning to the sea for their livelihood; shipbuilding and whaling were both big business. The Puritan infatuation with education resulted in the establishment of **Yale University**, founded in 1701 as the Collegiate School in Killingsworth before moving to Saybrook, and eventually New Haven in 1716. Among its earliest students was **Noah Webster**, whose *American Dictionary of the English Language*, published in 1828, became the definitive dictionary for American English and helped standardize spelling and pronunciation.

Although the colony was hit very badly by English raids during the Revolutionary War, its role in providing the war effort with crucial supplies earned it the nickname of the "**Provisions State**." This period also produced one of Connecticut's great folk heroes, **Nathan Hale**, hanged by the British for spying.

Connecticut continued to prosper during the late eighteenth and nineteenth centuries, with steady industrialization helped along by **Eli Whitney**, developer of efficient machine tools, and entrepreneurs like Hartford's **Samuel Colt**, inventor of the repeating pistol. While it was producing some of the nation's great businessmen, the state was also having a cultural impact – during a long

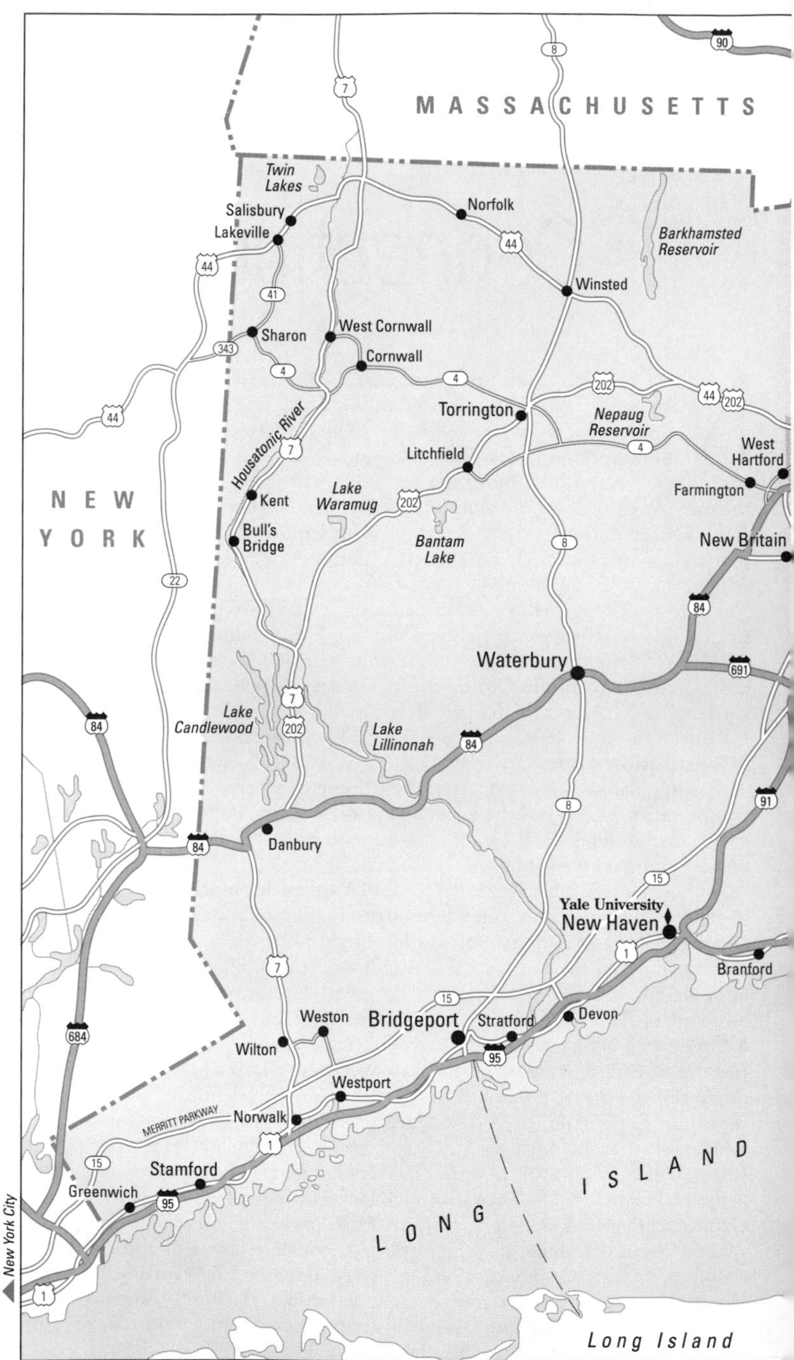
MASSACHUSETTS
NEW YORK
LONG ISLAND
Long Island
Twin Lakes
Salisbury
Lakeville
Norfolk
Barkhamsted Reservoir
Winsted
Sharon
West Cornwall
Cornwall
Torrington
Nepaug Reservoir
Housatonic River
Litchfield
West Hartford
Farmington
Kent
Lake Waramug
Bull's Bridge
Bantam Lake
New Britain
Waterbury
Lake Candlewood
Lake Lillinonah
Danbury
Yale University
New Haven
Branford
Weston
Bridgeport
Stratford
Devon
Wilton
Westport
MERRITT PARKWAY
Norwalk
Stamford
Greenwich
New York City

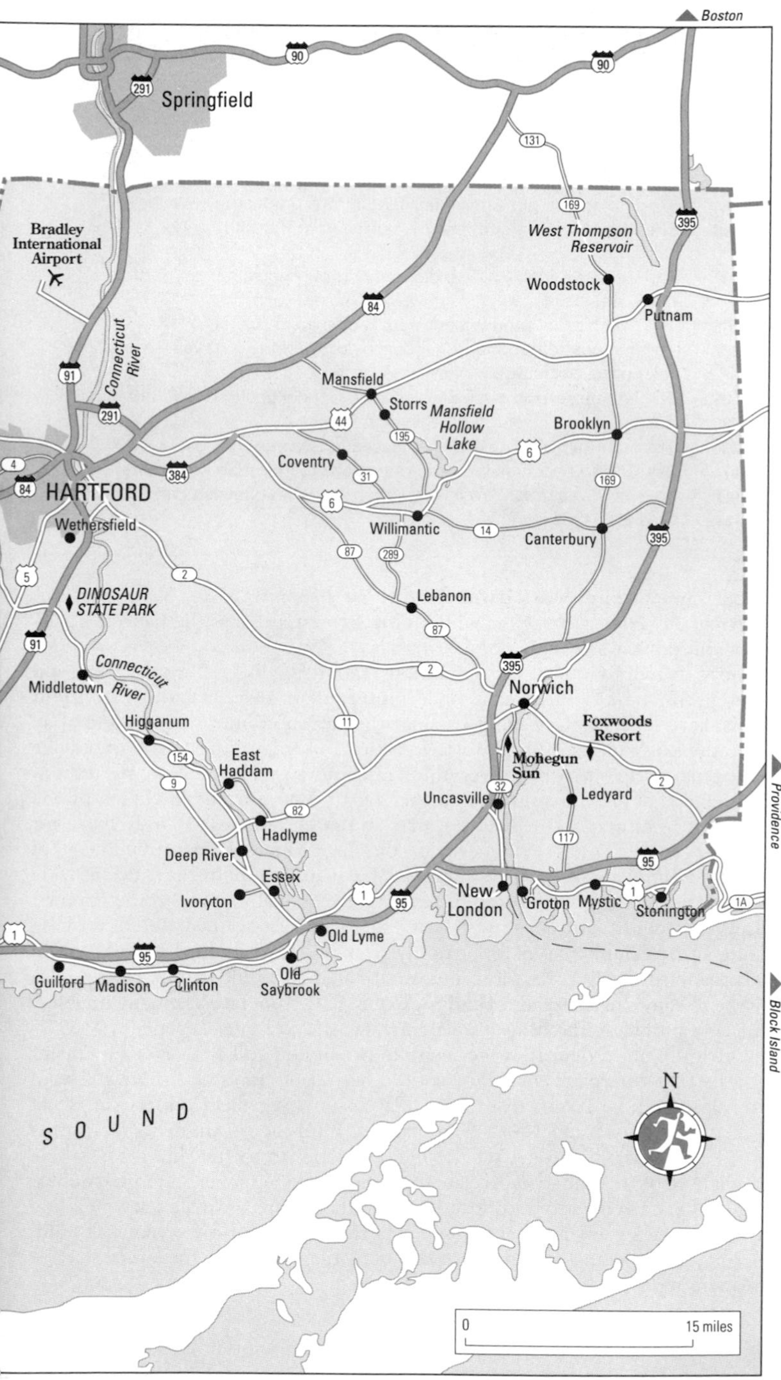
Boston
Springfield
Bradley International Airport
Connecticut River
West Thompson Reservoir
Woodstock
Putnam
Mansfield
Storrs
Mansfield Hollow Lake
Brooklyn
Coventry
HARTFORD
Wethersfield
Willimantic
Canterbury
Lebanon
DINOSAUR STATE PARK
Connecticut River
Middletown
Norwich
Foxwoods Resort
Higganum
Mohegun Sun
East Haddam
Uncasville
Ledyard
Hadlyme
Deep River
Essex
Ivoryton
New London
Groton
Mystic
Stonington
Old Lyme
Guilford
Madison
Clinton
Old Saybrook
Providence
Block Island
SOUND
N
0
15 miles

Some Connecticut firsts

1639	Connecticut produces the first **written constitution** in the colonies, *The Fundamental Orders*.
1656	The nation's first **public library** is opened in New Haven.
1775	The world's first **submarine** is launched by David Bushnell of Saybrook.
1784	The nation's first **law school** is established in Litchfield by Tapping Reeve.
1794	The first **cotton gin** is manufactured by Yale graduate Eli Whitney.
1796	The first **American cookbook** is published in Hartford, written by Amelia Simmons.
1806	The first **American English dictionary** is published in West Hartford by Noah Webster.
1846	The nation's first **amusement park** is opened in Bristol.
1877	The first **pay telephone** is introduced, followed the next year by the first **telephone exchange** in New Haven with 21 subscribers.
1881	The first **three-ring circus** is staged by Connecticut native P.T. Barnum.
1920	The **Frisbee** is invented in Bridgeport.
1934	The first **Polaroid camera** is produced in Bridgeport.
1975	Ella Grasso becomes the nation's first **elected woman governor**.
2000	Joseph I. Lieberman, from New Haven, is the first **Jewish candidate** on a presidential ticket.

sojourn in Hartford, **Mark Twain** wrote *The Adventures of Tom Sawyer* and *The Adventures of Huckleberry Finn*, while **John Brown**, perhaps the nation's greatest abolitionist, was a native of Torrington.

Today, many of Connecticut's traditional industries, like the iron, copper, and brass production facilities that once prospered in areas like the **Litchfield Hills**, have faded away, leaving large areas of green countryside a world away from the noisy interstate highways, vast tracts of verdant forests, and the idyllic archetypal villages that have everything in common with their counterparts in Vermont and New Hampshire further north. The current linchpins of the economy – insurance, medical research, and military bases – hardly make for pleasing aesthetics, as evidenced in the high-rise corporate buildings of Hartford and the submarine fleet in **Groton**, though they do provide Connecticut's citizens with the highest average annual income in the country. **Southeastern Connecticut**, a series of rocky surf-washed outcrops along Long Island Sound, makes for a mostly scenic trek, while further west on the coast towards New York, more industrial-based cities like **New Haven**, also home to Yale University, and **Bridgeport**, in particular, face distinctly un-New England problems like drug wars, homelessness, and violent crime.

Though Connecticut is easy enough to get around and well served by major roads – I-95 runs parallel to the coast of Long Island Sound from New York to Rhode Island; I-91 runs from New Haven up along the Connecticut River Valley to Vermont; and I-84 cuts a diagonal from the southeast to the northwest – it's more fun to get off the highways and on to the side roads, where you'll have more time to appreciate the attractive rural scenery and pretty colonial villages. Even getting lost can be fun; distances are so small that you'll find your way back sooner rather than later. Public transportation, on Amtrak trains or any of the major bus lines, covers both the coast and the more sizeable inland towns.

Southeastern Connecticut

The much-visited **southeastern coast** of Connecticut stretches fifty miles from Stonington in the east to Branford in the west, bisected by the Thames (pronounced *Thaymz*) River. A succession of picturesque colonial communities, old whaling towns, and unattractive industrial cities characterize this section of Long Island Sound. No longer are they the iniquitous and rumbustious ports that so inspired Melville, but they're still keen to preserve – with varying degrees of success – a sense of their history. Among the highlights is **Mystic Seaport**, a reconstructed nineteenth-century maritime village with a fine collection of restored ships; the salty old whaling city of **New London** is dealing with the consequences of economic decline brought about by defense cutbacks at neighboring **Groton**, but it has a cluster of halfway decent galleries and museums as well as some fine old sea captains' houses; further west, the prosperous towns of **Old Lyme** and **Old Saybrook** are home to a number of beguiling art galleries and museums; while **Guilford** has one of the largest collections of seventeenth- and eighteenth-century homes in the Northeast, several of which are open to the public. A bit inland, the massive casinos opened by local Native Americans at **Foxwoods** and **Mohegan Sun** attract millions of visitors annually; if you're looking to get well away from such bustle, there's no better place than off the coast of **Branford**, where you'll encounter a series of rocky outcrops (some inhabited, some not) known as the **Thimble Islands**.

Mystic

As purists will tell you, the town of **MYSTIC**, right on I-95, does not really exist; it's an area governed partly by Groton and partly by Stonington. Nonetheless, the old whaling port and shipbuilding center does have a small, well-kept, and rather touristy **downtown**, lined with typical New England-quaint clapboard galleries and antique shops. Before going on to see Mystic's main attractions in and around the seaport, you might first want to take a look at the **Mystic Art Association Gallery**, 9 Water St (daily 11am–5pm; $2 donation; ⓣ860/536-7601), with changing exhibits and a section devoted to the works of modern impressionist William North, many of which depict local landscapes. Not far away, the **Portersville Academy**, 74 High St (June–Oct Tues, Thurs & Sat hours vary; ⓣ860/536-4779), contains a restored classroom where you can enjoy the thrill of sitting at a school desk more than a hundred years old. The old drawbridge across the **Mystic River**, which divides the town down the middle, is still raised hourly. Along the western bank of the river is River Road, a four-mile stretch ideal for walking or cycling, which passes **Downes Marsh**, a sanctuary where you may catch a glimpse of osprey and cranes.

Mystic Seaport and around

What tourists come to Mystic to see is on the other side of the bridge, the meticulously constructed waterfront village of **Mystic Seaport**, at the mouth of the river (daily: April–Oct 9am–5pm; rest of year 10am–4pm; $17, children

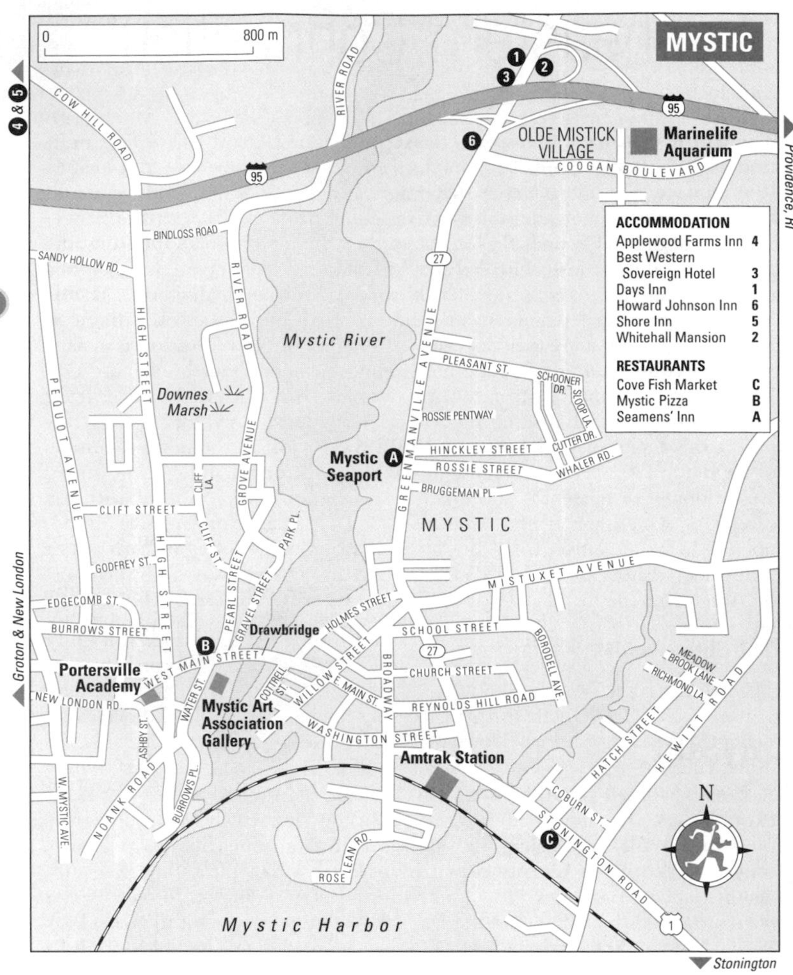

$9; ⓣ860/572-0711, ⓦwww.mysticseaport.org), where more than sixty weathered buildings house old-style workshops and stores, including an apothecary and a printing press. The **Stillman Building** contains beautifully carved scrimshaw, ornate figureheads, and vast numbers of objects made from whales' wax-like spermaceti, as well as disturbing video footage of a bloody whale hunt. Demonstrations of sea-shanty singing, fish-splitting, sail-setting, and knot-tying vie with storytelling and theater, and state-of-the-art interactive computers enable visitors to track hurricanes and encourage children to become sailors. In the **Henry Dupont Preservation Shipyard**, you can watch the building, restoration, and maintenance of a vast collection of wooden ships, among them the *Joseph Conrad*, an 1882 training ship, the *L.A. Dunton*, a 1921 fishing schooner, and the restored *Charles W. Morgan*, a three-masted wooden Yankee **whaling ship** built in 1841, and the last of its kind. Done up as if ready to embark on a two-year voyage, the ship is filled with whaling memorabilia;

below deck, accessed by perilously narrow stairs, the blubber room is crowded with huge iron try-pots for melting down the stinking stuff. The Seaport also boasts the nation's largest maritime bookstore and the **Mystic Maritime Gallery**, a center for contemporary marine art with a display of model ships.

About a mile north of the Seaport, adjacent to I-95, the **Marinelife Aquarium** is Mystic's other major draw (daily: March–Nov 9am–6pm, rest of year Mon–Fri 10am–5pm, Sat–Sun 9am–6pm; $16, children $11; ⓣ860/572-5955, ⓦwww.mysticaquarium.org), where more than four thousand weird and wonderful marine specimens glug about. Beyond the striking glass entrance, visitors are confronted with a recreated bayou, with Spanish moss and baby alligators, and a thirty-thousand-gallon reef display. Also good are the sea lion theater, and a captivating collection set of frogs from around the world. Nearby, not-so-quaint factory outlets occupy the overdone **Olde Mistick Village**, at the intersection of I-97 and Rte-27, an outdoor mall with more than sixty upmarket shops in mock-Colonial buildings.

Practicalities

There's a **train station** in Mystic where Amtrak calls in on its Boston-to-Washington route (for schedule information call ⓣ1-800/872-7245), and South East Area Transit provides a regular **bus** service to Mistick Village (ⓣ860/886-2631). Mystic's **information office** is in the Olde Mistick Village Shopping Mall (Mon–Sat 9am–6pm, Sun 10am–5pm; ⓣ860/536-1641); accommodation information is available there. It may be useful to take advantage of their help, as it's very difficult to find a place to stay in the town in the peak summer months; definitely reserve your room well in advance if it's July or August. You can also seek out the local Convention and Visitors' Bureau, called Connecticut's Mystic and More! (ⓣ1-800/TOENJOY or ⓦwww.mysticmore.com). Convenient **lodging** options include chains like the *Howard Johnson Inn*, 253 Greenmanville Ave (ⓣ860/536-2654; ❻), the *Days Inn*, 55 Whitehall Ave (ⓣ860/572-0574 or 1-800/572-3993; ❻), and the *Best Western Sovereign Hotel*, 9 Whitehall Ave (ⓣ860/536-4281 or 1-800/363-1622; ❻), all of which are close to the Seaport, though not high on character. Also on Whitehall Avenue, the *Whitehall Mansion*, no. 42 (ⓣ860/572-7280 or 1-800/572-3993; ❼), is a painstakingly restored 1771 mansion with five guestrooms, each furnished with antiques and queen-sized canopy beds. For options in a quieter area, try either the *Shore Inn*, 54 East Shore Ave (ⓣ860/536-1180; April–Oct only; ❻), about five miles west of Mystic Village on Groton Long Point, a turn-of-the-twentieth-century residence, with private beach and fishing opportunities, or the *Applewood Farms Inn*, 528 Ledyard Hwy, Ledyard (ⓣ860/536-2022; ❻), a delightful antique-filled Colonial farmhouse just five minutes north of downtown; if you call ahead, the owners will collect you from the train station. The Seaport **campground** is on Rte-184 in Old Mystic, three miles from the Seaport (ⓣ860/536-4044).

Much the best-known **restaurant** in town, *Mystic Pizza*, 56 W Main St (ⓣ860/536-3700), is a small, family-run place that for $10–15 serves huge pies; it remains relatively unruffled by its status as pilgrimage site for movie fanatics (see "Films," p.613). Also worth a try, the *Seamen's Inn*, 105 Greenmanville Rd (ⓣ860/572-5303), serves excellent prime rib and other entrées for $14–22, or you can grab some fried seafood and an outdoor picnic table at *Cove Fish Market*, 20 Old Stonington Rd (ⓣ860/536-0061).

Around Mystic

Not far away from Mystic are a few hard-working towns, especially charming **Stonington**, which may lack obvious attractions, but certainly make for a more complete picture of the area, and are worth a poke around if you've got more than a short afternoon to devote here. If you're interested in a bit of glitz, just inland are Connecticut's gambling facilities, on Native American land.

Stonington

STONINGTON, just south of I-95 near the state's eastern border, is a disarmingly pretty old fishing village, originally settled by Portuguese, but now very much New England with its attractive whitewashed cottages, white picket fences, colorful gardens, and peaceful waterfront. Its main street, **Water Street**, is brimming with antique shops and upmarket thrift stores, packed with well-to-do bargain hunters on weekends. At no. 7, the **Old Lighthouse Museum** (July–Aug daily 10am–5pm; May–June & Sept–Oct Tues–Sun 10am–5pm; $4), moved back a bit from its original position due to the dangers of erosion, dates from 1823 and is full of local memorabilia, maps, drawings, and whaling and fishing gear. You can climb the stone steps and iron staircase for views over Long Island Sound. Close to Lambert's Cove Bridge, the Italianate **Captain Nathaniel B. Palmer House**, 40 Palmer St (May–Oct Tues–Sun 10am–4pm, last tour 3pm; $4), celebrates the life of Palmer, whose main claim to fame was the discovery of the Antarctic landmass in 1820. The mansion, topped by an octagonal cupola from which Palmer and his family could identify ships arriving from far-off ports, contains exhibits about his work.

A few miles out of the village center, at exit 91 off I-95, follow the "Wine Trail" signs to the **Stonington Vineyards**, 523 Taugwonk Rd (daily 11am–5pm; tour at 2pm), for a look around a local wine producer, and some free tastings of their concoctions like Seaport White and Seaport Blush. (For more on Connecticut's Wine Trail, see box p.375).

Practicalities

If you'd like to **stay** in Stonington, *Lasbury's Guest House*, 24 Orchard St (☎860/535-2681; ④), offers three pleasant rooms decorated with a nautical theme in a secluded cottage at the rear of a much larger house. Alternatively, try the *Cove Ledge Motel*, Whewell Circle (☎860/599-4130; ⑤), where you'll find simple, uncluttered rooms close to the water. Authentic clam chowder, as well as full **meals**, can be had at *Noah's*, 115 Water St (☎860/535-3925), an old Portuguese restaurant with a friendly atmosphere. Two seafood restaurants, *Water St Café* and *Skipper's Dock*, are within a hop and a skip of one other, the former, at 142 Water St (☎860/535-2122), is for elegant dining, the latter, at no. 66 (☎860/535-0111), is less expensive and rowdier, with a deck offering fantastic ocean views.

Groton

Seven miles west of Mystic Seaport, **GROTON** is a suitably unpleasant name for the home town of the hideous **US Naval Submarine Base**, Crystal Lake Road, off Rte-12 (mid-May to Oct Wed–Mon 10am–5pm, Tues 1–5pm; Nov to mid-May Wed–Mon 9am–4pm; free; ☎860/343-0079). Headquarters for the North Atlantic Fleet, it's also the place where the **USS Nautilus**, America's first nuclear-powered submarine, was built. You can tour the submarine, winding your way through narrow, claustrophobic passages past the wardroom and officers' berthing area and the attack center, down a short, steep staircase to the control room, the radio room, and the crew's quarters, with bunks stacked three and four high, complete with pin-ups of Marilyn Monroe. The **Submarine Force Museum** next door traces the history of submersibles from Bushnell's *American Turtle*, used in the Revolutionary War, to the powerful *Trident*. The main hall features a re-created World War II attack center, where you can look through one of three periscopes and take aim on cars in the parking lot. For a different perspective, the tour boat *Enviro-Lab* makes summer excursions up and down the Thames, gathering plankton, water, sand, and oceanographic information with the help of paying customers ($17, children $12; ☎860/445-9007). They also do tours of the Ledge Lighthouse, stuck out in the middle of the river in New London, a mansard-roofed, square red-brick structure with a rich history, and – for those who believe – a resident ghostly presence.

New London

On the opposite bank of the Thames from Groton, **NEW LONDON**, with 26,000 residents, is the largest city along this stretch of the coast, though it's hardly a metropolis and spreads over but six square miles. It was a wealthy whaling port in the nineteenth century, and by the 1850s was second only to New Bedford, Massachusetts, for the size of its whaling fleet. Today, the city is struggling to come to terms with the economic realities brought about by cuts in military spending, though it is trying very hard to liven up the downtown area, still shabby in parts, but with enough historical interest to warrant perhaps a half-day detour.

Its most popular attraction, the **US Coast Guard Academy**, Mohegan Avenue off I-95, spreads out on an attractive sloping campus overlooking the Thames. Visitors can tour the *USS Eagle*, the only tall ship on active duty, and now used as a training ship. The **US Coast Guard Museum** explores two centuries of coast guard history and includes ships' portraits and the figurehead from the *Eagle* (Mon–Fri 9am–5pm, Sat 10am–5pm, Sun noon–5pm; free; ☎1-800/343-0079). Just opposite the Academy entrance, the **Lyman Allyn Art Museum**, 625 Williams St (Tues–Sat 10am–5pm, Sun 1–5pm; $5), contains all varieties of American fine arts and crafts, including a silver tankard made by Paul Revere and a superior collection of dolls, dollhouses, and toys from the eighteenth and nineteenth centuries.

The **Southeastern Connecticut CVB**, 470 Bank St (☎860/444-2206), provides maps for a self-guided walking tour of New London's downtown, which takes you past **Whale Oil Row**, a short line of 1832 Greek Revival houses once owned by leaders in the whale-oil business (though none is open to the public). Just round the corner, **Captain's Walk** is New London's main street, lined with a variety of shops and restaurants. Nearby, on Eugene O'Neill Drive, the **Nathan Hale Schoolhouse**, first called Union Schoolhouse, is where Nathan Hale, the Revolutionary War hero famed for his last words, "I only regret that I have one life to lose for my country," taught for sixteen months before starting his military service. A bit west, the **Shaw-Perkins Mansion**, 11 Blinman St (Wed–Fri & Sun 1–4pm, Sat 10am–4pm; $5), a stone house built in 1756 for wealthy shipowner and trader Nathaniel Shaw, has unusual paneled-cement fireplace walls and some period furnishings and portraits. Meanwhile, New London's oldest house, the 1678 **Joshua Hempstead House**, 11 Hempstead St at Jay Street (mid-May to mid-Oct

Gambling on Connecticut's Native American reservations

Until the late 1980s, the $400 billion-a-year gambling business was confined to just two states, Nevada and New Jersey, but a lobbying push from Native American tribes, eager for greater self-determination to manage their own affairs, moved Congress to pass the Indian Gambling Regulatory Act. This reform recognized the rights of Native American tribes in the US to establish gambling and gaming facilities on their reservations, so long as the states in which they are located have some form of legalized gambling, and, indeed, today gambling is only not legal in the two states of Hawaii and Utah.

Connecticut has since become home to two major Native Indian casinos, over objections from environmentalists, anti-gambling agencies, and residents. The massive **Foxwoods Casino and Resort**, Rte-2, Ledyard (Ⓣ1-800/752-9244, Ⓦwww.foxwoods.com), rises dramatically above the virgin pine forests north of New London and draws millions of visitors annually. Built by the Mashantucket-Pequot Indians, the casino's visitors have three huge hotels to accommodate them, as well as all manner of slots, gaming tables, and bingo to entertain. Just a few miles away, the **Mohegan Sun Casino**, Rte-2A, Uncasville (Ⓣ1-888/226-7771, Ⓦwww.mohegansun.com), opened its doors in 1996, as Foxwood's much smaller and quieter competitor. But after a $1 billion expansion effort which concluded in 2002 with the introduction of a new 1200-room hotel and the largest ballroom in the Northeast, the Sun has become more of a commercial draw, while managing to retain some of the traditional Indian reverence for nature – readily apparent in the planetarium ceiling and the crystal mountain installed on one of the casino walls.

Thurs–Sat noon–4pm; $5), was said to have been used as a safe haven on the Underground Railroad, though you'll find nothing too special here to mark it as such. Admission also gets you into the **Nathaniel Hempstead House** – Nathaniel was Joshua's grandson – across the lawn, which stands out for its two-foot-thick stone walls and outdoor stone beehive oven.

New London is also renowned as the birthplace of boozy playwright **Eugene O'Neill**, whose childhood home, the **Monte Cristo Cottage**, 325 Pequout Ave (June to mid-Sept Tues–Sat 10am–5pm, Sun 1–5pm; $5), can be toured complete with juicy details of his trauma-ridden early life – though they may already be familiar to you from his *Long Day's Journey into Night*. The author's influence is felt further at the O'Neill Memorial Theater Center at 305 Great Neck Rd in nearby **Waterford** (I-95 exit 82), an acclaimed testing-ground for playwrights and actors, where audiences can watch new, often experimental shows in rehearsal (performances held sporadically May–Aug; Ⓣ860/443-5378). Just beyond the Monte Cristo Cottage, **Ocean Beach Park**, 1225 Ocean Ave (summer daily 9am-11pm; $8–12 parking includes admission for all occupants, or $4 walk-in), holds a "sugar sand" beach with a wooden boardwalk and arcade, mini-golf, waterslide, and a massive pool.

Groton and New London practicalities

You could be forgiven for thinking that, thanks to New London's proximity to I-95, everyone arrives by road. Not so. There's a **car ferry** from Orient Point on Long Island (Cross Sound Ferry; Ⓣ860/443-5281), and even an **airport**, with a limited service to the rest of New England (and several car rental outfits). Amtrak runs a regular **train** service to New London from New York, Boston, and other points along the main East Coast line. Greyhound and Bonanza **buses** both serve the city, and there's a **local bus** network, too (SEAT: Southeast Area Transit Ⓣ860/886-2631); the #2 and #3 lines can take you around Groton and New London, but they don't run on Sundays. New London is generally a less expensive place to **stay** than touristy Mystic, ten miles away, with several reasonably priced motels along I-95, including the *Holiday Inn*, I-95 and Frontage Road (☎860/442-0631; ❹), and the *Red Roof Inn*, 707 Colman St (☎860/444-0001 or 1-800/843-7663; ❸), while Groton also boasts plenty of budget motels off I-95 exit 86, including a *Super 8* (☎860/448-2818 or 1-800/800-8000; ❸).

New London has a few good **restaurants** worth stopping into, including *Timothy's*, 181 Bank St (☎860/437-0526), where, from your vantage point on the Long Island Sound, you can sample Long Island duckling. On the cheaper side is the *Recovery Room*, 445 Ocean Ave (☎860/443-2619), an award-winning pizzeria. Over the water in Groton, *G. Williker's*, 156 King's Hwy (☎860/445-8043), with an enormous menu, is a good place for steaks, seafood, and sandwiches, while the *Abbot's Lobster in the Rough*, 117 Pearl St (☎860/536-7719), serves the delicious creatures in the summer, and on weekends only in the fall. For more eating and accommodation information, try Connecticut's Mystic and More! Visitors Bureau (☎1-800/TOENJOY or Ⓦwww.mysticmore.com), or you can check out the Eastern Connecticut Chamber of Commerce at 1 Whale Oil Row (☎860/443-8332 or 1-800/222-6783).

West to New Haven

Fifteen miles west of New London, at the mouth of the Connecticut River, sits **OLD LYME**, the site of an Impressionist art colony dating from the end of the nineteenth century. It was started when three sisters and their mother began to attract a regular clientele of artists to their boarding house each summer. The **Florence Griswold Museum**, 96 Lyme St (Jan–March Wed–Sun 1–5pm; Apr–Dec Tues–Sat 10am–5pm, Sun 1–5pm; $7), named after the sister – "Miss Florence" – most involved in developing the colony, is located in the very boarding house the family managed. Guided tours of the 1817 house cover its history, Griswold's life, and the work of the various artists who stayed there, including Willard Metcalfe, Childe Hassam, and William Chadwick, whose studio is set up just as it was during his lifetime. A few doors away, the **Lyme Academy of Fine Arts**, at 84 Lyme St (Tues–Sat 10am–4pm, Sun 1–4pm; donation), founded in 1976, features drawing, painting, and sculpture by contemporary artists housed in a Federal-style house also dating from 1817.

There are no trains that stop in Old Lyme, though local **bus** services through Old Lyme and the surrounding communities are provided by the Estuary Transit District (☎860/388-1919).

Old Saybrook

The former shipbuilding center of **OLD SAYBROOK**, opposite Old Lyme on the western bank of the Connecticut River, claims a few historic houses along its main road. Though there's little else to draw your attention, it's a good, centrally-located base for a more complete exploration of Connecticut's south-eastern coast. Puritan settlers arrived in 1635 and soon erected a fort to guard the river entrance to the town, an act remembered in **Fort Saybrook Monument Park**, at the stronghold's former site, though nothing of the fort remains today. In 1701 the town became the venue for the **Collegiate School**, later to move to New Haven and rename itself **Yale University**.

Commercial activity centers on Boston Post Road, while the unusually wide **Main Street** becomes progressively more interesting the further south you get toward Saybrook Point, showcasing architectural styles from seventeenth-century saltboxes to nineteenth-century Federal buildings. Of these, the 1767 **General William Hart House**, 350 Main St (late mid-June to mid-Sept Fri–Sun 12.30–4pm; suggested donation $2), once the residence of a prosperous merchant who owned a fleet of sailing ships and served in the Revolutionary War, has been restored to its original elegance. It contains eight corner fireplaces, one decorated with Sadler and Green transfer print tiles illustrating scenes from Aesop's fables, as well as local history exhibits and a reference library. The **James Gallery**, 2 Pennywise Lane at Main Street (summer daily noon–10pm; ⓣ860/395-1229), is an unusual art gallery and soda fountain, housed in a former general store and pharmacy.

Practicalities

Local **bus** services are provided by the Estuary Transit District (ⓣ860/388-1919), and some Amtrak **trains** stop at Old Saybrook (ⓣ1-800/872-7245), with a local commuter service between New Haven and New London provided by Shore Line East (ⓣ1-800/255-7433). The **Old Saybrook Chamber of Commerce** maintains an office at 146 Main St (Mon–Fri 9am–5pm; ⓣ860/388-3266). They'll have info about the wide variety of **accommodation** in the area, ranging from historic **B&Bs** like the 1746 *Deacon Timothy Pratt House B&B*, 325 Main St, Old Saybrook (ⓣ860/395-1229; ❻), with rooms furnished in period (ie 1746) style, with working fireplaces and four-poster beds, and the luxurious *Saybrook Point Inn*, 2 Bridge St, Old Saybrook (ⓣ860/395-2000 or 1-800/243-0212, ⓦwww.saybrook.com; ❾), where most rooms have water views and balconies, to a number of motels and inns all located along Boston Post Road (Rte-1). These include the friendly, 45-room *Sandpiper Motor Inn*, no. 1750 (ⓣ860/399-7973 or 1-800/323-7973, ⓦwww.thesandpiper.com; ❹), the smaller but equally comfortable *Heritage Motor Inn*, no. 1500 (ⓣ860/388-3743; ❺), and the *Water's Edge Inn & Resort*, no. 1525 (ⓣ860/399-5901; ❻), on a lovely setting overlooking the Sound. Many of Old Saybrook's **restaurants** are also to be found on Boston Post Road: the moderately priced *Old Saybrook Diner*, at no. 809 (ⓣ860/395-1079), a town fixture, serves great spinach pie, while *Cuckoo's Nest*, at no. 1712 (ⓣ860/399-9060), offers tasty and plentiful Mexican, southwestern, and Cajun dishes for $11–20. Away from Boston Post Road, *Dock & Dine*, College Street, Saybrook Point (ⓣ860/388-4665 or 1-800/362-3625), has lovely views over the Connecticut River to go with classic American steak and seafood dishes – though you'll pay for it.

Clinton

CLINTON, eight miles west of Old Saybrook, pushes itself as one of the most visited leisure ports on Long Island Sound, thanks to an abundance of well-equipped marinas. Its historic district includes the **John Stanton House**, 63 East Main St (June–Sept Sat–Sun 2–5pm; donation requested), built around 1790 and where the Marquis de Lafayette stayed in 1824; the bed in which he slept is still displayed in its original surroundings. The house served as a general store for many years, supplying goods and services to the sailors whose boats docked nearby; on display are items that were sold back in those days, together with a collection of antique American and Staffordshire dinnerware. Today Clinton is better known for its **Clinton Crossing Premium Outlets**, just off

I-95 (Mon–Sat 10am–9pm, Sun 10am–8pm), with more than seventy upmarket stores that offer savings on designer goods. You're unlikely to **stay** in town, though it is pleasant enough; if you do, for something a bit different, consider *A Victorian Village – Marina Cottages*, 345 East Main St (ⓣ860/669-3009) – a cluster of comfortable, antique-filled cottages around a landscaped garden, available by the week only, starting at $300.

Madison

Just a few miles west on Rte-1, posh **MADISON** sits on the waterfront with an attractive shady green overlooked by a white-spired church and a broad main street lined with upmarket boutiques and trendy cafés. There's not much to distinguish it from nearby Clinton, though it does contain two historic buildings of note. The **Deacon John Grave House**, 581 Boston Post Rd (mid-June to early Sept Wed–Sat 1–4pm; early Sept to mid-Oct Sat & Sun 10am–4pm; $2), Madison's oldest residence, built in 1685 and used over the years as a school, a wartime infirmary and weapons depot, an inn, a tavern, and a courtroom, has nevertheless remained all this time under the auspices of the Grave family. Indeed, there's even a surviving ledger of their household expenditures from 1678 to 1895. Further down the road, the white-clapboard saltbox **Allis-Bushnell House**, at no. 853 (Wed, Fri & Sat 1–4pm; donation), dates from about the same period, and contains original paneling and unusual corner fireplaces. One room has been restored as a turn-of-the-twentieth-century doctor's office in memory of **Dr Milo Rindye**, a popular physician who lived and worked in the house. There's also an interesting collection of artifacts and the like, from costumes and kitchenware to a Victorian hearing aid and working looms. About two miles east of downtown Madison, off Rte-1, **Hammonasset Beach State Park** (daily 8am–sunset; in summer, parking $8 weekdays, $12 weekends) maintains two miles of prime sandy beach, backed by dunes and a salt marsh. If you don't fancy a swim, there's a **nature center** in the park that contains exhibits about the wildlife and history of the area.

Practicalities

Good **accommodation** choices are *The Inn at Café Lafayette*, 725 Boston Post Rd (ⓣ203/245-7773 or 1-866/623-7498; ❻), a smart downtown establishment with antique furnishings, the *Dolly Madison Inn*, 73 West Wharf Rd (ⓣ203/245-7377; ❺), just two minutes from the water, with cozy rooms and access to one of the town beaches, and the *Tidewater Inn B&B*, 949 Boston Post Rd, a pleasant retreat in a woodsy area (ⓣ203/245-8457; ❻). Places to **eat** include the casual *Perfect Parties*, 885 Boston Post Rd (ⓣ203/245-0250), with offerings ranging from good inexpensive salads, soups, and sandwiches to gourmet dinners for eat-in or take-out, and *The Wharf*, 94 West Wharf Rd at the *Madison Beach Hotel* (ⓣ203/245-0005), where mid-priced, good-value seafood – baked, grilled, fried, or stuffed – is their thing.

Guilford

First settled by English vicar Reverend Henry Whitfield in 1639, **GUILFORD** has one of the largest collections of seventeenth- and eighteenth-century homes in New England; only three, unfortunately, are open to the public. Among them, Whitfield's own home at 248 Old Whitfield St, the oldest surviving stone house in New England, has been transformed into the **Henry Whitfield State Museum** (Wed–Sun 10am–4.30pm; closed Dec

15–Jan 31; $2). The fortress-like dwelling also served as a church and meeting hall for the village community, and currently contains a collection of antique furniture, weaving and textile equipment, and the first tower clock made in the colonies, dating from 1726; today it's also the home of the **Guilford Tourism Office** (Mon–Fri 9am–3pm; Ⓣ203/453-2457, Ⓦwww.guilfordct.com). Nearby, at 84 Boston St, the **Hyland House** (June–Aug Tues–Sun 10am–4.30pm; Sept to mid-Oct Sat & Sun 10am–4.30pm; $2), a saltbox built in the 1660s, belonged to esteemed clockmaker Ebenezer Parmelee. Little refurbishment has gone on since; the house is held together by the same old nails and bolts, and has its original casement window and hand-hewn floorboards. The last of the three houses open to the public is a short walk away at 171 Boston St, the **Thomas Griswold House** (June to Sept Tues–Sun 11am–4pm; Oct Sat & Sun 11am–4pm; $2.50), another saltbox, built in 1774, and full of period furniture and clothing, photographs, and changing local history exhibits. Outside, there's a working blacksmith's shop and Colonial-style garden. Guilford's large **village green** is the attractive location for summer concerts and recitals, lined on two sides with boutiques and restaurants.

Practicalities

For pleasant **accommodation** in Guilford, try the Georgian-style *Guilford Corners Bed & Breakfast*, 133 State St (Ⓣ203/453-4129; ❻), which has private gardens; slightly less charm can be had at the *Guilford Suites Hotel*, 2300 Boston Post Rd (Ⓣ203/453-0123 or 1-800/626-8604; ❺), though their suites do contain small refrigerators and microwaves. There's no shortage of excellent **restaurants** along this stretch of the coast. A good stop is *Guilford Mooring*, 505 Old Whitfield St (Ⓣ203/458-2921), where not surprisingly, the focus is on moderate to expensive seafood. For a more casual, and somewhat less costly, dining experience, *The Place*, Boston Post Road (Ⓣ203/453-9276), does grilled seafood outdoors, where diners sit on logs and toss their shells onto the gravel.

Branford and the Thimble Islands

You'll have little reason to stop in **BRANFORD**, despite its surprisingly good collection of restaurants, other than perhaps its proximity to the **Thimble Islands**. If you do find yourself with an extra couple of hours to kill in town, however, stop by the **Harrison House**, 124 Main St (June–Sept Thurs–Fri 2–5pm; donation requested), built in 1724 but altered many times since, and containing an interesting display of farm implements in its barn.

Branford's main attraction is unquestionably the **THIMBLE ISLANDS**, a group of 365 tiny islands off the nearby village of **Stony Creek**, best accessed by exit 56 off I-95. The so-called chain of islands is in reality a cluster of granite rocks within a three-mile radius of shore, ranging in size from one large enough to support a small community of 24 homes, to some that actually disappear at high tide. Years ago, they provided a perfect hiding place for pirate ships waiting to attack passing boats in Long Island Sound; one of the individuals who purportedly used these waters to this end was **Captain Kidd**, who is said to have hidden treasure here (he could hardly have buried it) when being chased by the British. You can hear the colorful narratives spun about the islands by taking a tour on either the *Islander* ($8; Ⓣ203/397-3921) or the *Volsunga IV* ($8; Ⓣ203/481-3345), two boats that offer 45-minute daily trips from mid-May until mid-October, departing from the Town Dock at the end of Thimble Island Road.

Practicalities

Branford's many fine **restaurants** are primarily located around the Branford Green, like the *Café Bella Vita*, 2 East Main St (☎203/483-5639), with Northern Italian specialities, and *Le Petit Café*, Branford Green, opposite Trinity Church (☎203/483-9791), one of the best restaurants around for French bistro cuisine. Much more casual is *Lenny's*, Rte-146 (☎203/488-1500), a seafood shack teeming with noisy kids and their parents; dinner specials start at $9.95. Near the dock in Stony Creek, the *Stony Creek Market*, 178 Thimble Islands Rd (☎203/488-0145), sports a combined restaurant, bakery, deli, and (in the evenings) pizzeria, with stunning views of the Thimbles from its deck. Branford's absence of inns and B&Bs is compensated for by the abundance of inexpensive and generally basic **hotels** and **motels**, most of which are located on East Main Street, such as the *Motel 6*, no. 320 (☎203/483-5828; ❸), and the *Branford Motel*, no. 470 (☎203/488-5442; ❸).

New Haven and southwestern Connecticut

An essential stop on any tour of Connecticut, **New Haven** is one of the state's more bearable bigger cities, given life by its intriguing mix of downbeat industrial center and college town. It practically divides the shoreline in half, and can really be visited in conjunction with the coastal stretch on either side, or even Hartford, its urban rival just over thirty miles away. Still, it's most similar in character to the built-up coast in the **southwestern** portion of the state, which leads all the way to the outskirts of New York City. Indeed, the southwest is by far the most developed part of Connecticut, and the former hub of its manufacturing base. It's an unattractive region on the whole, a result of the decline in industry, alleviated only in parts by the odd historic building and the grassy sights on **Merritt Parkway**, also known as **Rte-15**, a good alternative to the parallel – and much busier – I-95, which runs directly along the coast throughout the region. The state's largest city, **Bridgeport**, despite valiant attempts to reverse its urban decline, is still a depressing place to visit, while **Stamford**, marginally less ugly, has been quite successful in managing to entice leading business corporations away from New York City. **Norwalk** is another city which had fallen on bad times and is now working hard to improve things, while, inland, predominantly residential **Danbury**, the city once known as the nation's "hat capital," sits in the **Housatonic Valley**, a pleasant, hilly landscape dotted with rivers and lakes.

New Haven

Don't be put off by the grubby initial impression you get when you arrive in **NEW HAVEN** on I-95 or by train: the grimy factories, the tall chimneys, and architecturally nondescript office blocks. Tucked away, in fact, are some of the best restaurants, most exciting nightspots, and diverting cultural activities in all of New England – not to mention, of course, the idyllic, leafy Ivy League campus of **Yale University**. The resultant tensions between these two very different facets once made New Haven a somewhat uneasy place. However, town-versus-gown conflicts have been minimized since the early 1990s when Richard C. Levin became president of the university, with a goal of fostering cooperation. Now there's an active symbiosis, as residents are encouraged to take advantage of Yale's cultural and public offerings, and over half of the student body, eager to contribute to their 'home' community, volunteers in some sort of local outreach program. New Haven is certainly less WASPish and smug than many other Ivy League towns, and aside from the usual city problems like drugs and homelessness, ethnic and racial groups coexist ambivalently in a way unseen in the rest of New England. Even the students themselves seem to be a less snooty, less smug breed than their counterparts at Princeton or Harvard.

Some history

Founded in 1638 by a group of wealthy Puritans on a large natural harbor at the mouth of the Quinnipiac River, New Haven started life as an independent colony, the early settlers living in relative harmony with the native Quinnipiac Indians. Very early on, the town was laid out in nine "**squares**" that can still be seen today in the downtown area's grid pattern. The efforts of the community's leaders to create a prosperous economy foundered, however, and in 1662 New Haven became part of the Connecticut Colony, based in Hartford. In 1701 Connecticut's first university, the Collegiate School, was founded, and classes met in a variety of towns, until, in 1716, the school established a permanent home in New Haven, eventually becoming Yale University as a sign of respect to **Elihu Yale**, a wealthy Anglican who made generous donations. Meanwhile, New Haven's shipping industry was finally beginning to flourish, the result of a fine deepwater harbor.

Still, it was manufacturing that would lead the city forward. During the Revolutionary War, the city produced gunpowder and cannonballs, and towards the end of the eighteenth century, Yale-educated **Eli Whitney** started manufacturing mass-produced firearms, the result of using standardized parts as the basis of the assembly line in his factory outside of town, dubbed Whitneyville. New Haven also churned out Winchester rifles, musical instruments, tools, carriages, and corsets. Local entrepreneurs, realizing that the city could do better still if it had access to interior New England, decided to build an eighty-mile canal which would extend as far as Northampton, Massachusetts. The canal, however, was a financial flop. Nevertheless, New Haven continued to progress until the middle of the twentieth century, when the problems of unplanned urban growth and increasing economic competition from the suburbs began to take their toll. Millions of dollars in federal funds were then pumped into the city to begin the process of urban renewal, but unemployment continued to grow and, today, there is little manufacturing activity left in New Haven.

Arrival, information, and city transit

New Haven lies at the fork of I-91 and I-95. Parking downtown is atrocious: parking lots are few and far between (though several of the major hotels have their own lots), and meters often allow a maximum stay of only half an hour. New Haven is on the main **train** line between Washington, New York, and Boston; services also run to Canada. Amtrak's main terminal is in the colossal and newly renovated **Union Station**, on Union Avenue six blocks southeast of the Yale campus downtown. You can also get here from New York on the Metro North Commuter Railroad (ⓣ1-800/METRO-INFO), which runs from Union Station or the station at State Street. The terminal for Greyhound, Bonanza, and Peter Pan **buses** is at 45 George St; whether you're arriving by train or bus, it makes sense to grab a **cab** to your hotel, as the bus and train stations are in potentially unsafe areas. Metro Taxi (ⓣ203/777-7777) has a good reputation.

Local public transit within New Haven and its outlying areas is provided by Connecticut Transit, 470 James St (ⓣ203/624-0151), but the service deteriorates rapidly after 6pm. An **information booth** (Mon–Fri 9am–5pm) at 200 Orange St, two blocks east of the Green, has schedules and the **Greater New Haven CVB**, at 59 Elm St, on the Green (Mon–Fri 8.30am–5pm; ⓣ800/332-7829, ⓦwww.newhavencvb.org) has a helpful staff and publishes a comprehensive visitors guide. Yale University runs its own **information center** at 149 Elm St, on the north side of the Green (Mon–Fri 9am–4.45pm, weekends 10am–4pm; ⓣ203/432-2300), whose staff gives tours of the university and can tell you about campus events.

Accommodation

New Haven has surprisingly few **hotels** for a city of its size; not even expensive ones for parents visiting their Yalie offspring. **B&Bs** from around $80 can be arranged in advance through Nutmeg Bed & Breakfast in West Hartford (ⓣ1-800/727-7592). The downtown hotels, though somewhat overpriced, are worth it for their proximity to the main sights and for the comparative safety of the location. Because of the shortage of rooms, make sure to book well in advance if you're intending to visit during graduation in early June, or Parents' Weekend in October, always the busiest times of the year here.

Best Western Executive Hotel – West Haven 490 Sawmill Rd, West Haven ⓣ203/933-0344, ⓦwww.bestwestern.com. Standard rooms not far from downtown at I-95 exit 42. Hotel features swimming pool and fitness center, and a free hot breakfast buffet. ❺

Colony Inn 1157 Chapel St ⓣ203/776-1234 or 1-800/458-8810, ⓦwww.colonyatyale.com. Intimate full-service hotel with colonial trimmings. ❻

Days Inn New Haven North 270 Foxon Blvd ⓣ203/469-0343. Inexpensive but comfortable motel located just off I-91 north of town. ❹

Fairfield Inn 400 Sargent Drive ⓣ203/562-1111. Good-value *Marriott* relation with 152 rooms overlooking the harbor. ❺

Holiday Inn 30 Whalley Ave ⓣ203/777-6221. Generic rooms in a good central location. ❻

Hotel Duncan 1151 Chapel St ⓣ203/787-1273. Comfortable rooms in an old-fashioned hotel, on one of New Haven's main thoroughfares. ❸

New Haven Hotel 229 George St ⓣ203/498-3100 or 1-800/NH-HOTEL, ⓦwww.newhavenhotel.com. Small, quiet hotel with better-than-adequate rooms, a health club, and indoor pool. ❻

Omni New Haven Hotel at Yale 155 Temple St ⓣ203/772-6664 or 1-800/THEOMNI, ⓦwww.omnihotels.com. Recently refurbished, New Haven's plushest hotel has 306 luxury rooms, health club, and a superb (though expensive) restaurant with spectacular city views. ❼

Oyster Point Inn 104 Howard Ave ⓣ203/773-3334 or 1-866/978-3778, ⓦwww.oysterpointinn.com. Six beautifully decorated theme rooms, in an extremely comfortable gay-friendly establishment near the harbor. ❼

Quality Inn 100 Pond Lily Ave (exit 59 off Rte-15) ⓣ203/387-6651, ⓦwww.schafferhotels.com. Good-value standard rooms, all with queen-sized beds; there's also an indoor pool and Jacuzzi. ❺

Residence Inn 3 Long Wharf Drive ⓣ203/777-5337 or 1-800/331-3131, ⓦwww.residenceinn.com. Luxurious, all-suites waterfront hotel that's part of the *Marriott* empire. ❼

Swan Cove B&B 115 Sea St, exit 44N off I-95 ⓣ203/776-3240, ⓦwww.swancove.com. Pleasant 1890s historic district house with views over Long Island Sound. ❻

Three Chimneys Inn 1201 Chapel St ⓣ203/789-1201, ⓦwww.threechimneysinn.com. This elegant Victorian B&B is central to Yale, and local theaters and museums. Formal parlor with complimentary port, sherry, teas, and fruit, and a porch overlooking a landscaped courtyard. ❽

The City

A succession of remarkably ugly buildings put up during the 1950s rather blighted New Haven, but its **downtown**, centered on the **Green**, remains both attractive and walkable, thanks in part to some sensitive restoration. The Green, laid out in 1638 and originally called "**The Marketplace**," was the site of the city's original settlement, and also functioned as a meeting area and a burial ground. Around it are three churches, a grand library, and a number of stately government buildings, and it borders the student-filled College and Chapel Street district.

The Green

Standing in the middle of the Green, and flanked by two other churches, the **Center Church on the Green**, built in 1812, is the successor to New Haven's first religious building, the First Church of Christ. Though it once held nearly a dozen Tiffany windows, all but one were given away during a renovation in the 1960s (some of which can be viewed at the Southern Connecticut State

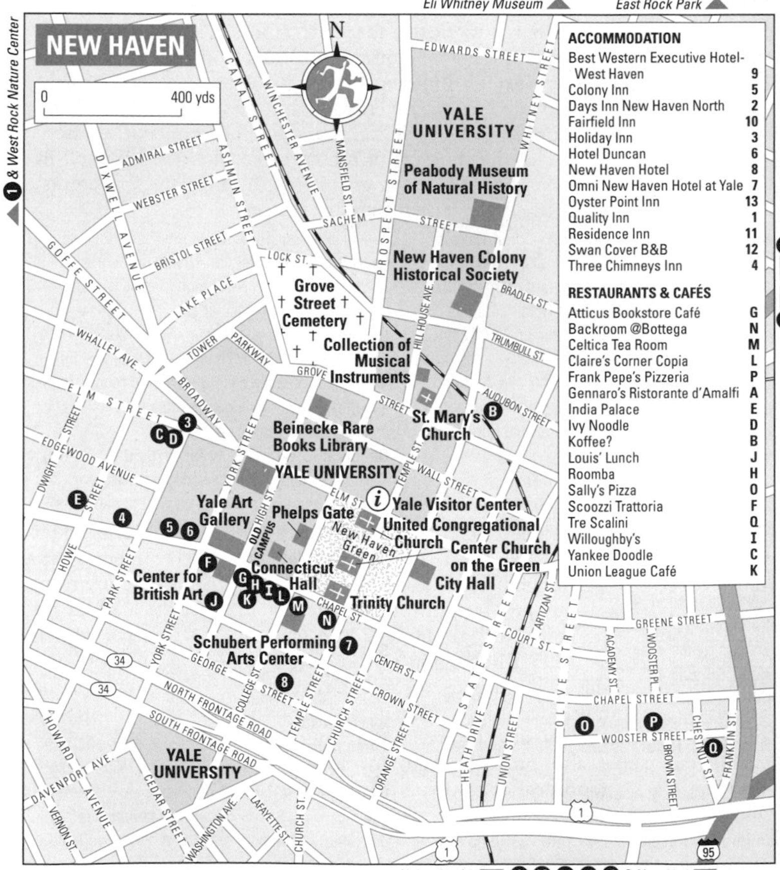

The Amistad

In the spring of 1839, more than 500 Mendi tribesmen were illegally kidnapped from their Sierra Leone homes and brought to Havana, Cuba. Fifty-three of them were placed on a smaller ship, the *Amistad*, for delivery to another Cuban port. Three days after setting sail, the Africans, led by Joseph Cinque, revolted and took control of the ship with the intent to return home, killing several crew members in the process. After 63 days the ship arrived off Long Island, where it was intercepted by the US Navy. The Africans were taken into custody and charged as pirates and murderers, despite the protests of abolitionists. A series of trials in both Hartford and New Haven followed; after two years of legal wrangling, the case went all the way to the US Supreme Court. Having received the powerful backing by that time of none other than the president himself, John Quincy Adams, the tribesmen were eventually acquitted and released. In 1842, the 35 survivors were able to return home, though slavery was not to be abolished for another twenty years. Steven Spielberg dramatized the incident in the 1997 film *Amistad*.

University, 501 Crescent St); the remaining window sits in a place of honor over the pulpit, and depicts John Davenport, the first minister, preaching the first service in New Haven colony. Below the church, a fascinating **crypt** holds tombs from as far back as 1687. (Tours of church and crypt Tues, Thurs & Sat 11am–1pm & Sun after 11am service; donation.) Close by, fronting Temple Street, the Gothic Revival **Trinity Episcopal Church**, built in 1816, holds even more Tiffany windows; the **United Church**, originally known as the **North Church** when it was built in 1813, is based on a design copied from a French book on English architecture. At the southern end of the Green is the recently restored High-Victorian **City Hall**, built in 1861. Behind the unusual, wrought-iron staircase in the building's graceful, spacious lobby you can see a scale model of the city. City Hall overlooks the 1992 **Amistad Memorial** (see box, above), a three-sided bronze-relief monument on the site of the former New Haven Jail.

Following Court Street east, you'll hit New Haven's close-knit **Italian District**, featuring the well-kept brownstones and colorful window boxes of **Wooster Street** and Wooster Square, where the city's original Italian immigrants settled when they came to work on the railway. There's little to see here in the way of attractions, but there are some incredibly popular restaurants, and it's well worth stopping by when there's a festival on; see "Eating" on p.348).

Yale University and around

At the opposite end of the Green, Yale University's **Connecticut Hall**, built in 1750 and based on Harvard's Massachusetts Hall, is notable for being the oldest surviving building in New Haven and the only remaining structure from Yale's Old Brick Row. Just outside of Connecticut Hall stands a statue of Revolutionary War hero **Nathan Hale**, a Yale graduate. A short way down College Street, the 1895 **Phelps Gate** is known as "Yale's front door" and allows access to the Old Campus of **Yale University**, New Haven's prime attraction. You can wander at will, though free hour-long student-led **tours** set off daily from the Yale Visitor Information Center at 149 Elm St (Ⓣ203/432-2300); the center also provides maps for self-guided tours. Whatever you decide, expect a good deal of trooping to and fro, as the University's buildings are strewn out over several blocks.

It makes sense to start with the cobbled courtyards of the Old Campus (mostly built in the 1930s but constructed in Gothic Revival style, and painstakingly manicured to look suitably ancient) and ending up at the remarkable **Sterling Memorial Library**, 120 High St (Mon–Fri 8.30am–5pm, Sat 10am–5pm, Sun 1–5pm, closed Sun in summer; free). Designed by alum James Gamble in modern Gothic style, and with fifteen butresses, it has the symbolic appearance – inside and out – of a cathedral, albeit one to the power of knowledge and the written word. Inside, leaded glass windows illustrate the history of the Library, Yale, New Haven, and the history of books and printing, and at the would-be altar (the Circulation Desk), the Alma Mater receives gifts from Light, Truth, Science, Labor, Music, Fine Arts, Divinity, and Literature in a fifteenth-century-Italian-style mural that's highly expressive. Directly in front of the Library is the **Women's Table**, an ovate granite fountain commemorating the enrollment of women at Yale. It was designed by alum Maya Lin, who also designed the Vietnam Veterans' Memorial in Washington DC.

Also nearby is the **Beinecke Rare Books Library**, 121 Wall St (Mon–Fri 8.30am–5pm, Sat 10am–5pm; free), where priceless ancient manuscripts and hand-printed books are viewed with the aid of natural light seeping through the translucent Vermont marble walls. The marble also blocks out the harmful solar radiation that would otherwise cause them to deteriorate, while providing stunning interior artwork as the sun rises and falls. There's a 1300-page Gutenberg Bible (the first major book to be printed using moveable type, in 1455), along with some original Audubon prints in the collection. Other buildings of interest include the modernist, Louis Kahn-designed **Yale Center for British Art**, 1080 Chapel St (Tues–Sat 10am–5pm, Sun noon–5pm; free), which prides itself on having the most comprehensive collection of British art outside the UK. The collection traces the development of British art, beginning with paintings from the sixteenth and seventeenth centuries, highlighting the period from William Hogarth in the early eighteenth century to J.M.W. Turner in the mid-nineteenth, and moving through to the twentieth century boasting works by Walter Sickert and the Bloomsbury Group, with a special emphasis on Alfred Munnings and Ben Nicholson – favorites of the center's founder, Paul Mellon. The Center's large collection of portraits contains full-lengths by Van Dyck, Gainsborough, and Reynolds and some fine landscapes including Turner's *Dort and Staffa* and John Constable's *Hadleigh Castle*. The modern building opposite houses the **Yale University Art Gallery**, 1111 Chapel St (Tues–Sat 10am–5pm, Sun 1–6pm; free), the nation's most venerable university art collection. Founded in 1832 with John Trumbull's original donation of 100 paintings to Yale, the collection now boasts more than 100,000 objects from around the world, dating from ancient Egyptian times to the present, and features American decorative arts, Etruscan vases, regional design and furniture, and African and pre-Columbian works. Among the highlights are Vincent Van Gogh's famous 1888 composition *Night Café*, which the artist complained was "one of the ugliest pictures I have done," and works by Manet, Monet, Picasso, and Homer. The surrounding five blocks are a genuinely lively area in which to hang out, filled with bookstores, cafés, clubs, and hip clothes shops; the **Neon Garage**, an art exhibit in a real parking lot on Crown Street, is particularly notable. There are some rough pockets, but generally speaking, New Haven is reasonably safe to wander around, especially during term-time, when the streets are brimming with students.

A short walk two blocks east of the Green, **Hillhouse Avenue**, designed by James Hillhouse in the 1790s and completed by his son in 1837, is one of New Haven's most attractive thoroughfares – so attractive that when Charles Dickens visited he proclaimed it to be the most beautiful street in America. Once the domain of New Haven's rich and famous, much of it is now taken up with Yale University's administrative offices. A quirky, 800-strong **Collection of Musical Instruments**, some dating back as far as the sixteenth century, can be seen at no. 15 (Tues–Thurs 1–4pm; closed summer), while at the street's lower end, Gothic **St Mary's Roman Catholic Church**, the first Roman Catholic parish in New Haven, is the place where Friar Michael McGivney founded the Knights of Columbus charitable order in 1882.

Whitney Avenue

Whitney Avenue leads north from the Green, with several worthy stops along the way. The **Peabody Museum of Natural History**, 170 Whitney Ave (Mon–Sat 10am–5pm, Sun noon–5pm; $5), one of the largest museums in New England, hosts exhibits of dinosaur skeletons, including a 67ft brontosaurus, a 75-million-year-old turtle and a vast section on America's ancient civilizations, in particular the Native Americans of Connecticut. On the same street, the **New Haven Colony Historical Society**, at no. 114 (Tues–Fri 10am–5pm, Sat & Sun 2–5pm; $2; ⓣ203/562-4183), housed in a handsome 1930s Georgian Revival building, traces New Haven's history through a series of fine art displays, industrial artifacts, maps, and genealogical records. One of the galleries is dedicated to the maritime history of the city and the much-reproduced Nathaniel Jocelyn portrait of the leader of the *Amistad* slaves, Cinque; you can also see Eli Whitney's original cotton gin and Charles Goodyear's rubber inkwell. More Whitney-related exhibits can be seen at the **Eli Whitney Museum**, two miles further out at 915 Whitney Ave (Wed–Fri & Sun noon–5pm, Sat 10am–3pm; $2), housed in the original gun factory where mass production originated. The museum includes an 1816 barn that was part of Whitney's factory town and a glut of hands-on experiments, mostly designed for children.

The city outskirts

When you've had enough traipsing around museums and galleries, head for **East Rock Park**, East Rock Road (daily sunrise–sunset, summit open April–Nov), named for the huge outcrop of reddish rock that dominates the skyline for miles around, and from which there are spectacular views of New Haven, Long Island Sound, and beyond. On the other side of town, at the **West Rock Ridge State Park**, Wintergreen Avenue at Baldwin Drive (Mon–Fri 10am–4pm; $1 for cars), the Regicides Trail leads to Judges' Cave, where two of the men who signed Charles I of England's death warrant fled after the restoration of the monarchy.

At the extreme southeastern tip of the city, follow Lighthouse Road off I-95 to the **Pardee-Morris House**, 325 Lighthouse Rd (late May to end of Aug Sat & Sun 11am–4pm; $2), a small but worthwhile museum housed in a 1750s Georgian farmhouse rebuilt after an earlier one was burnt to the ground by the British. It's furnished with period antiques, some of them original to the house, and there are demonstrations of butter- and ice cream-making. At the end of Lighthouse Road, **Lighthouse Point Park** (daily 7.30am to sunset; parking fee late May to end of Aug), an eighty-acre park with a sandy public beach, nature trails, and a restored antique carousel, is a stopover point for hawks, eagles, and falcons on their winter migration. Nearby, on Woodward Avenue, are **Black Rock Fort** and **Fort Nathan Hale** (late May to end of Aug daily 10am–4pm), the remains of two forts from the Revolutionary and Civil wars, both offering spectacular views of New Haven Harbor, though there's not enough left of either to warrant anything more than a quick poke round.

Eating

Don't leave New Haven without trying the local **pizza** (known by the cognoscenti as tomato pies), available at all the family Italian restaurants in Wooster Square. There are plenty of other ethnic cuisines to savor in New Haven as well, with many of the best places to eat located around the Green and on Chapel and College streets.

Cafés

Atticus Bookstore Café 1082 Chapel St, next to the Yale Center for British Art ☎203/776-4040. Salads, soups, sandwiches, brioches, and great coffee in a relaxed bookstore open until midnight.

Celtica Tea Room 260 College St ☎203/777-7893. A comforting tea room set back in a gift shop also offering all things Irish.

Koffee? 104 Audubon St ☎203/562-5454. Casual, whimsical all-day hang out. There's also **Koffee Two** at 276 York St ☎203/787-9929.

Willoughby's 1006 Chapel St ☎203/789-8400. Self-consciously trendy gourmet coffee bar frequented by hip intellectuals and fashionable townies. Superb coffee and sticky cakes.

Yankee Doodle 260 Elm St ☎203/865-1074. Yalies' favorite low-cost café, with original 1950s fittings. Open 6am–8pm, Mon–Sat; during the summer, 6am–2pm.

Restaurants

Backroom @ Bottega 956 Chapel St rear, Temple St Courtyard ☎203/562-5566. Homestyle (think Grandma) rustic Italian dining, in a funky flower-strewn loft, with live music weekends and some Thursdays. Cost is moderate. Closed Mon.

Claire's Corner Copia 1000 Chapel St ☎203/562-3888. Corny name, but excellent Mexican and Middle Eastern food at moderate prices. The local vegetarian for 26 years.

Frank Pepe's Pizzeria 157 Wooster St ☎203/865-5762. Most popular of the Wooster Street establishments; plain, functional, and friendly, with huge and delicious "combination pies", like white clam for $19. The secret, allegedly, is in the coal-fired ovens and genuine Italian tomatoes. Closed Tues.

Gennaro's Ristorante d'Amalfi 937 State St ☎203/777-5490. Excellent Italian restaurant serving specialties including traditional Amalfian dishes. For around $25, sample their *linguini in cartoccio* – clams, anchovies, olives, white wine, and tomatoes served in a brown bag. Closed Sun.

India Palace 65 Howe St ☎203/776-9010. Serviceable North Indian restaurant, most noteworthy for its $6 buffet lunch.

Ivy Noodle 316 Elm St ☎203/562-8800. Quick, decent, and cheap Chinese noodles, almost everything under $6.

Louis' Lunch 261–263 Crown St ☎203/562-5507. Small, dark, and ancient burger institution which claims to have served the first hamburger sandwich in the US in 1900. The meat, cooked in an upright broiler which reduces the fat, is presented between two slices of toast, and it's perfect in every way. It's also very cheap and popular, so expect lines, and don't ask for ketchup, either – it's only accompanied by onions, tomato, and/or cheese. Closed Sun and Mon.

Roomba 1044 Chapel St, Sherman's Alley ☎203/562-7666. Innovative Nuevo Latino cuisine in a stylish room. Trendy and loud.

Sally's Pizza 237 Wooster St ☎203/624-5271. Another top-notch Wooster Street pizzeria, and a good alternative to *Pepe's* (above). Closed Mon.

Scoozzi Trattoria 1104 Chapel St ☎203/776-8268. Northern Italian restaurant (with a summer outdoor courtyard) specializing in pasta – eighteen varieties for $16–24 – and fish.

Tre Scalini 100 Wooster St ☎203/777-3373. Upmarket Italian restaurant in an elegant setting, with entrées like chicken breast with olives, sun-dried tomatoes, wild mushrooms, and fresh sage.

Union League Café 1032 Chapel St ☎203/562-4299. Fairly expensive, very French bistro known as one of the finest restaurants in the city.

Nightlife and entertainment

New Haven has an undeniably rich **cultural scene**, especially strong on **theater**. The Yale Rep Company, 1120 Chapel St (☎203/432-1234, ⓦwww.yalerep.org), which boasts among its eminent past members Jodie Foster and Meryl Streep, turns out consistently good shows during term-time. The Long Wharf Theater (☎203/787-4282), 222 Sargent Drive, just off I-95, has a nationwide reputation for quality performances, as does the refurbished Shubert Performing Arts Center, 247 College St (☎203/562-5666).

As you'd expect with such a large student population, there are plenty of excellent **bars** and **clubs**, mostly concentrated around Chapel and College streets. The *New Haven Advocate*, a free weekly news and arts paper, has detailed listings of what's on in and around the city, while a free biweekly, *Hip*, available from the clothes shops along Chapel Street, lists trendy goings-on.

168 York Street Café 168 York St ⓣ203/789-1915. New Haven's oldest gay joint has two downstairs bars, and a quieter upstairs bar with lots of TV screens. Busy, especially at weekends.
Anchor Bar 272 College St ⓣ203/865-1512. Authentic 1950s bar, one of the best spots in town (and Jodi Foster's favorite while an undergrad). Snug plastic booths, dim orange lighting, frosted windows, and a formidable matronly hostess.
Bar 254 Crown St ⓣ203/495-8924. Simple name, outrageous place – this is where the New Haven gay community lets its collective hair down on Tuesday nights.
Cafe Nine 250 State St ⓣ203/789-8281. Intimate club with live jazz and blues on the weekends.
Gotham Citi 130 Crown St ⓣ203/498-2484. Large, steamy club where those "in-the-know" head for a late night of drinking, dancing, and simply looking good. Gay night on Mon and Sat.
GYPSCY Bar 204 York St ⓣ203/432-2638. On-campus bar at Yale, open to the general public; live music at weekends.
New Haven Athletic Club 806 State St ⓣ203/777-6670. Open to the public Sunday nights for live blues or jazz.
The Playwright 144 Temple St ⓣ203/752-0450. Five bars, ranging from rowdy pub to dance club, inside a church bought in Ireland, dismantled, and reassembled here. An unusual must-stop.
Toad's 300 York St ⓣ203/624-8623, ⓦwww.toadsplace.com. Mid-sized nationally renowned live-music venue, where Bruce Springsteen and the Stones used to "pop in" occasionally to play impromptu gigs. Tickets $15–25.

Bridgeport and around

Long the state's leading industrial center, **BRIDGEPORT**, not quite twenty miles southwest from New Haven, suffered greatly during the economic decline of the 1960s and 1970s, when dozens of factories and businesses closed down, giving rise to some serious social and environmental problems. Now littered with abandoned factories, boarded-up stores, and run-down neighborhoods, the city is gloomy at best, though it does contain some diverting attractions, especially if you're traveling with kids. The **Beardsley Zoo**, the largest in the state, is still small enough to appear intimate by big-city standards, while the entertaining, hands-on **Discovery Museum** is one of the better children's museums on the East Coast. On top of that, the city has close ties to showman **P.T. Barnum**, a one-time mayor of Bridgeport; there's a downtown museum in his honor.

The City

The **Barnum Museum**, 820 Main St (Tues–Sat 10am–4.30pm, Sun noon–4.30pm; $5; ⓦwww.barnum-museum.org), Bridgeport's most endearing visitor attraction, gets off to an uninspiring start on its first two floors, which are devoted to the city's industrial history. The third level, however, is entirely dedicated to Barnum, with exhibits on General Tom Thumb and Jenny Lind, the "Swedish Nightingale," various props and memorabilia, and, most impressive of all, the "Three Ring Circus," a complete scale model of nearly 4,000 pieces. A block away, the **Housatonic Museum of Art**, 900 Lafayette Blvd (Sept–May Mon–Fri 8.30am–5.30pm, Sat 9am–3pm, Sun noon–4pm; free; ⓣ203/332-5000), holds works by Picasso, Matisse, and Warhol, plus African and Asian ethnographic collections, contemporary Latin American art, and decent local pieces. Located at Black Rock Harbor, at the end of Bostwick

Southwestern Connecticut practicalities

In addition to the straightforward road system, and train and bus services (see Basics, "Getting around") linking the various cities in the region, you might consider commuter trains run by Metro-North (ⓣ1-800/METRO-INFO) and the limited services of the Greater Bridgeport Transit Authority (ⓣ203/333-3031) and Milford Transit District (ⓣ203/874-4507). A year-round **ferry** service operated by the Bridgeport & Port Jefferson Steamboat Co (ⓣ203/355-2040) links Bridgeport with Port Jefferson, on Long Island. For tourist information, there are year-round **visitors' centers** at 5 Broad St, Milford (Mon–Fri 8.30am–4.30pm; ⓣ203/878-0681), and 297 West Ave, Norwalk (daily 10am–5pm; ⓣ1-800/866-7925).

Avenue, **Captain's Cove Seaport** consists of a boardwalk, craft shops, a restaurant, and a large Victorian home which contains an exhibit on local history and Connecticut's oyster industry. The *Chief*, a 40-foot Navy launch, will take you on a harbor tour past the Black Rock lighthouse (May–Sept weekends; ⓣ203/335-1433).

A little way out of the city center, the **Discovery Museum**, 4450 Park Ave (Tues–Sat 10am–5pm, Sun noon–5pm; adults $7, children $5.50; ⓣ203/372-3521, ⓦwww.discoverymuseum.org), is an interactive art and science museum with a planetarium and more than a hundred engaging exhibits on topics like electricity, nuclear energy, and the science of color. Best of all, perhaps, is the Challenger Learning Center, honoring the memory of the ill-fated *Challenger* crew. Another top-drawer destination for kids, the fifty-two-acre **Beardsley Zoological Gardens**, 1875 Noble Ave (daily 9am–4pm; $7, children 3–11 $5; ⓦwww.beardsleyzoo.org), has exhibits ranging from North American mammals like the Canadian lynx and bison to exotic animals from South American rainforests. There's also a farmyard-like children's zoo and a splendid working carousel on the grounds.

Around Bridgeport: Stratford and Putney

Adjacent to Bridgeport, **STRATFORD**, named after its English counterpart Stratford-upon-Avon, shares a connection with that city's most famous son as the longtime home to the prestigious **American Shakespeare Theatre**, located near the Housatonic Boat Club. While it closed down in 1982, the Chamber of Commerce hopes to have a plan in place by 2004 to renovate the existing theater. Also in town are the **Catharine B. Mitchell Museum**, 967 Academy Hill (mid-May to Oct Wed, Sat & Sun 11am–4pm; $2), with displays on local American Indian and African-American history, and the **Stratford Antique Center**, a group of over 200 dealers of collectible furniture, copper, glassware, and artwork set up in a huge blue building at 400 Honeyspot Rd (daily 10am–5pm; ⓣ203/378-7754).

One of New England's most bizarre museums can be found nearby in **PUTNEY**. The **Boothe Memorial Park & Museum**, Main Street (park open daily June–Sept 9am–5pm; museum Tues–Fri 11am–1pm, Sun 1–4pm; free), for almost three hundred years the estate of the wealthy Boothe family, comprises an assortment of some fifteen buildings bequeathed to the community by the last surviving members of the family – two eccentric, globetrotting brothers. Among the highlights are a 44-sided blacksmith's shop, a redwood "cathedral" with an antique organ, an Americana Museum focusing on nineteenth-century farming techniques and domestic life, and a collection of odds and ends collected by the brothers on their travels.

P.T. Barnum

Phineas Taylor Barnum, world's greatest showman (and huckster), was born in Bethel, Connecticut, in July 1810, and worked as a lottery ticket salesman before he ventured into the world of show business – and forever altered history – in 1835. With an eye for the bizarre, he purchased a frail hymn-warbling old black woman, and exhibited her as George Washington's 161-year-old nurse. Further "success" followed with the "Feejee mermaid," in reality the upper half of a monkey sewn to the body of a fish. Barnum made his fortune out of the midget Tom Thumb – actually a native of Bridgeport – and the Swedish singer Jenny Lind, both of whom drew massive crowds thanks to Barnum's publicity efforts. Barnum plowed much of the profits from these efforts into the American Museum in New York City, which he acquired in 1841 and where dozens of curiosities, both of the human and animal variety, were put on show. Part of the complex, a large, well-equipped theater known as the "lecture room," became the venue for a variety of popular dramatic productions and one of New York's most popular places of entertainment. Buoyed by this venture, in 1871 Barnum fulfilled a personal dream by launching a huge traveling circus and museum. Attracting vast crowds wherever it performed, it eventually merged with James A. Bailey's London Circus and became known as the Barnum & Bailey Show, until it was bought out by the Ringling Brothers. Throughout his life, Barnum maintained strong links with his home city and state, serving in the Connecticut state legislature, and as one of Bridgeport's most popular mayors. Today, a statue commemorating Barnum's contribution to the city stares out to Long Island Sound from a plinth in Bridgeport's Seaside Park, which he himself gave to the city; three showpiece homes Barnum owned in the city, including Iranistan, an eccentric model of a Persian mosque, no longer exist.

Bridgeport area practicalities

With very few B&Bs in the area, most of the **accommodation** on offer is in larger chain hotels and motels. Since most of their clientele are business travelers, rates will be substantially lower at weekends. The exception to the B&B rule is the *Nathan Booth House*, 6080 Main St, Putney (☎203/378-6489; ❼), a restored Greek Revival farmhouse near the Booth Museum. There's a conveniently located *HoJo Inn* at 360 Honeyspot Rd, off I-95, Stratford (☎203/375-5666; ❹), while the *Holiday Inn*, 1070 Main St (☎203/334-1234; ❻), is the only major hotel in downtown Bridgeport. If you're stuck, the Coastal Fairfield County Tourism District (☎203/840-0770 or 1-800/473-4868) can provide extensive listings.

There's no shortage of **places to eat** in the area: *Scribner's*, 31 Village Rd, Milford (☎1-800/828-7019), is the place for seafood; in downtown Bridgeport, *Ralph & Rich's*, 121 Wall St (☎203/366-3597), has excellent pasta, and the *King & I*, 545 Broadbridge Rd (☎203/374-2081), serves good-value Thai dishes. Over in Stratford, try the prime rib at the expensive *Blue Goose*, 326 Ferry Blvd (☎203/375-9130), or, slightly more exotic, French tavern fare at the equally steep *Plouf Bistro de la Mer*, 14 Beach Drive (☎203/386-1477), in a pleasant setting overlooking the Long Island Sound.

Westport and around

Artsy **WESTPORT**, another fifteen miles down the road from Stratford, has spent this century shedding its industrial image, and in place of its mills and tannery now sit the designer boutiques and upmarket galleries of a chic downtown. Lending to the proceedings is the prestigious **Westport Country Playhouse**, 25 Powers Court (ⓣ203/227-4177), one of the oldest repertory theaters in the country, housed in a rustic rural barn, where stars like Henry Fonda, Gene Kelly and Liza Minnelli, first strutted their stuff. One of the few sights, the 1795 **Wheeler House**, 25 Avery Place (Mon–Fri 10am–4pm, Sat–Sun 11am–3pm; donation requested), sports beautifully restored Victorian rooms and a Victorian costume and textile collection. The adjacent Bradley-Wheeler Barn, the only documented octagonal cobblestone barn in the state, contains local historical archives and genealogical information. The lone public beach in southwestern Connecticut, the **Sherwood Island State Park**, Sherwood Connector Road, exit 18 off I-95 (8am–sunset; May–Sept $5 weekdays for Connecticut-registered vehicles, $8 out-of-state; weekends $7 CT vehicles, $12 out-of-state; rest of year free), also happens to be one of the best in the state, with miles of sandy shoreline and a small nature center with hiking trails.

Practicalities

If you fancy a splurge, there's nowhere better in the area to **stay** than *The Inn at National Hall*, 2 Post Rd (ⓣ203/221-1351 or 1-800/NAT-HALL, ⓦwww.innatnationalhall.com; ❾), a lavish hotel with eighteen-foot-high ceilings, and individually decorated rooms and suites, some with sweeping river views. By contrast, the simple *Westport Inn*, 1595 Post Rd E (ⓣ203/259-5236; ❼), offers 116 reasonably priced units, with a smart lounge and fitness center. There are some fine **restaurants** in downtown Westport, too, among them *Sakura*, 680 Post Road E (ⓣ203/222-0802), for relatively inexpensive traditional Japanese dishes, sushi, and hibachi dinners, and the luxuriously expensive *Miramar* at *The Inn at National Hall* (ⓣ203/221-7572), where you can dine on celebrity chef Todd English's sirloin with Tuscan *bruschetta* while you gaze out past tasseled drapes across the Saugatuck River.

Around Westport: Weston and Wilton

A few miles inland from Westport, in the town of **WESTON**, the 1746-acre **Devil's Den Preserve** (dawn to dusk; free; ⓣ203/226-4991), 33 Pent Rd, is so named for the strange hoof-like rock formations which charcoal makers who once worked here believed were the footprints of the devil. Several rare species of plant can be found in this nature conservancy, including the hog peanut and Indian cucumber root. In nearby **WILTON**, don't miss the **Weir Farm National Historic Site**, 735 Nod Hill Rd (grounds open daily, dawn–dusk; visitors' center open Wed–Sun 8.30am–5pm; free; ⓣ203/834-1896), Connecticut's only national park, which once served as the summer home and studio of prominent Impressionist **J. Alden Weir**, who acquired the 150-acre site in 1882 in exchange for a painting (not one of his own) and a measly $6. Its proximity to New York City enticed a group of artists including John Twachtman, Albert Pinkham Ryder, and Childe Hassam to visit and subsequently form an informal art colony that became known as the "School of Ten." The Weir House remains a private artists' residence, and is not generally open to the public, but a visitors' center in the **Burlingham House** contains historical background – though don't expect to see any of the original canvases. You can combine a visit to Weir Farm with a look around the enchanting **Wilton Heritage Museum**, 224 Danbury Rd (Mon–Thurs 9.30am–4.30pm; $2), a 1756 center-chimney farmhouse with a heavy concentration of dolls and dollhouses.

Norwalk

It was in 1651 that **NORWALK** was first settled by Europeans, soon becoming the largest population along this stretch of the coast, thanks to the economic prosperity brought about by a thriving oyster-fishing industry, and, later, by the prolific output of the Silvermine River mills, which produced among other things, shoes and boots, hats, earthenware, candles, and ships. The arrival of the railway in 1840 provided another major boost to the city, but many of the factories closed down in the 1960s and 1970s. Today the area is thriving, thanks to numerous large companies that are headquartered here, and to the vision of city officials and private individuals who initiated a massive renovation of **South Norwalk**, affectionately known as "SoNo," full of restaurants, clubs, and galleries.

The Town

South Norwalk is anchored by the fabulous **Maritime Aquarium**, 10 N Water St (July–Aug 10am–6pm; Sept–June 10am–5pm; $9.25, children $7.50; Ⓦwww.maritimeaquarium.org), which presents a methodical look at the marine life and culture of Long Island Sound, taking you from the creatures at the surface level of salt marshes down through to those of the deep – culminating in a 110,000-gallon tank filled with sharks. Seals, jellyfish, river otters, and 125 other species of marine life are also on display, and you can even take a boat study cruise out into the Sound and get a firsthand look at the catch of the day and see how lobsters are tagged. A boat ride of a different sort is available from adjacent Hope Dock out to the 1868 **Sheffield Island Lighthouse**, whose function was to prevent boats from running aground on the Norwalk Islands, a chain of thirteen islets across the mouth of the Norwalk River. Visitors can take a brief tour of the ten-room lighthouse, abandoned since 1902, and then spend a bit of time on the island, depending on ferry times (June to early Sept; $15, children $12; call Ⓣ203/838-9444 for schedule information). Back on the mainland, head to the Second Empire–style **Lockwood-Mathews Mansion Museum**, 295 West Ave (mid-March to Dec Wed–Sun 12–5pm; $8; Ⓣ203/838-9799), built in 1864 as the summer home of Norwalk resident LeGrand Lockwood, who made his immense fortune in the insurance and railway industries. Nicknamed "America's first chateau," it would seem more at home with Newport's grand palaces (see p.300). Of the mansion's 62 rooms, best is the drawing room, in the rear, where above all the stenciling and grand inlaid woodwork, the ceiling boasts a spectacular gilt chandelier and an oil painting, *Venus at Play with her Cupids*, by Pierre-Victor Galland. It's a short walk to the **Norwalk Museum**, 41 N Main St (Wed–Sun 1–5pm; free; Ⓣ203/866-0202), where the history of the city (and its people) is told with historical documents, maps, and such exhibits as a collection of hats manufactured in the area. Just to the rear, the handsome **Pelissier Gallery**, at 10 Marshall St, presents American iron and glass works that are intriguing as well as functional (and also for sale). **Norwalk City Hall**, 125 East Ave (Mon–Fri 8.30am–4.30pm; information for self-guided tour of building available in Room 236), contains part of a rare collection of WPA murals commissioned during the Great Depression in the mid-1930s, notably *Steamboat Days on the Mississippi*, from the Mark Twain series, and the bright colors and sharp detail of the Marco Polo series. Other rescued murals can be seen at the public library, the Norwalk Transit District, and the aquarium.

Practicalities

Pleasant Norwalk **accommodation**, in a refined Yankee kind of way, is available at the *Silvermine Tavern*, 194 Perry Ave (ⓣ203/847-4558; ❺), which boasts ten delightful rooms in a 1758 Colonial next to a waterfall. Budget options abound on Westport Avenue, where the *Round Tree Inn*, no. 469 (ⓣ203/847-5827 or 1-800/275-2290; ❹), the *Garden Park Motel*, no. 351 (ⓣ203/847-7303; ❹), and the *Norwalk-Westport Motel*, no. 344 (ⓣ203/847-0665; ❹), all provide perfectly adequate accommodation.

Norwalk's best **restaurants** are found in South Norwalk around Washington Street, where *Siam Rialto*, 128 Washington St (ⓣ203/852-7000), is good for Thai curries, *The Brewhouse*, 13 Marshall St (ⓣ203/853-9110), offers standard American fare alongside microbrewed beer, the *Rattlesnake Bar and Grill*, 15 N Main St (ⓣ203/852-1716), tastes like the Southwest, and *Habana*, 70 N Main St (ⓣ203/852-9790), offers its uniquely Caribbean dishes with decor and laid-back attitude to match.

For **nightlife**, again explore the SoNo district, full of lively bars and clubs, some of which, like *Shenanigans*, 80 Washington St (ⓣ203/853-0142), offer live music. For more options, you can always check the listings in the free *Fairfield County Weekly*.

Stamford

While for many years **STAMFORD** had benefited from its proximity to New York, it's only in the last twenty or thirty years that businesses have moved to make it their home, attracted by the lower taxes. The results have not been entirely welcome for the city: the upswing in the local economy has been accompanied by the kinds of modern corporate office buildings and chain hotels that taint its downtown area.

Still, Stamford does have a few spots worth a visitor's time: check out the 1958 **First Presbyterian Church**, 1101 Bedford St (July & Aug Mon–Fri 9am–5pm; Sept–June Mon–Fri 9am–5pm; free), a unique fish-shaped building, designed by architect Wallace K. Harrison, that contains the largest mechanical pipe organ in Connecticut. North of downtown, off Rte-15, the **Stamford Historical Society Museum**, 1508 High Ridge Rd (Tues–Sat noon–4pm; $2), gives a good insight into local history and is worth a quick visit, mostly for the admission it provides to the **Hoyt-Barnum House**, a restored blacksmith's home at 713 Bedford St. Nearby, the **Stamford Museum & Nature Center**, 39 Schofield Rd (Mon–Sat 9am–5pm, Sun 1–5pm; $5), a nineteenth-century working farm and country store, was once the home of prosperous New York clothier Henri Bendel. Its seven galleries display an array of farm tools, Americana, and fine art. Another good place for nature-lovers, **Bartlett Arboretum** at 151 Brookdale Rd (daily 8.30am to sunset; free; ⓣ203/322-6971, ⓦwww.bartlettarboretum.org), contains 63 acres of forest and gardens, with a greenhouse, nature trails, and a special collection of large trees among its assets.

Practicalities

Many of Stamford's often huge chain **hotels** are located downtown and are geared primarily to corporate travelers; the *Stamford Marriott*, 2 Stamford Forum (ⓣ203/357-9555; ❼), and the *Sheraton Stamford*, 1 First Stamford Place

(Ⓣ203/967-2222; ❻), are particularly good places to take advantage of weekend deals; they also offer nicer than average rooms.

There's no shortage of **restaurants** in Stamford, one of the few benefits of its development as a business center. For generous portions of mid-priced steaks and seafood try *Giovanni's Steakhouse*, 1297 Long Ridge Rd (Ⓣ203/322-8870); surprisingly affordable Italian standards can be had at the classy *Il Falco*, 59 Broad St (Ⓣ203/327-0002). Tasty lamb cutlets and "Celtic Supreme of Chicken" are the good-value standouts at the *Druid Restaurant*, 120 Bedford St (Ⓣ203/708-9000); if it's cheaper pub fare (and a nice Guinness) you want, the *Temple Bar* downstairs will suit you fine. *The Sandwich Maestro*, 90 Atlantic St (daily 7am–4pm; Ⓣ203/325-0802), offers gourmet sandwiches (with musical names like "Mostly Mozartrella") for about $6.

After dark, check what's on at the two **theaters** maintained by the Stamford Center for the Arts (Ⓣ203/325-4466): the Rich Forum, 307 Atlantic St, has mainly plays, and The Palace, 61 Atlantic St, is a wonderfully restored music hall primarily hosting musical events.

Greenwich

GREENWICH, nearly as populated as Stamford, has a much more casual feel, with a main thoroughfare, Greenwich Avenue, that's eminently walkable and lined with fine shops, boutiques, and restaurants. Originally a sleepy farming community, the arrival of the railroad in the 1840s benefited the town by facilitating its development as both an industrial power and choice resort for New Yorkers. Indeed, Greenwich remains home to a host of media celebrities as well as the CEOs of several multinational corporations – its private beaches are backed by luxurious homes and fronted by marinas stocked with lavish yachts.

The Town

No visitor should miss the **Bruce Museum**, 1 Museum Drive (Tues–Sat 10am–5pm, Sun 1–5pm; $4, Tues free; Ⓣ203/869-0376, Ⓦwww.brucemuseum.org), which originated in a private home that looks like something out of a Hitchcock movie, and has now developed into a major museum with collections on American cultural history and the environmental sciences. Exhibits include a small collection of nineteenth- and early twentieth-century paintings by the noted Cos Cob School of American Impressionism, and a new science and environment wing features a mine shaft, woodland habitat, minerals, fossils, and a marine touch-tank.

Greenwich's other star attraction is the **Bush-Holley Historic Site & Visitor Center**, 39 Strickland Rd (Jan–March Sat 11am–4pm, Sun 1–4pm; April–Dec Wed–Sun 1–4pm; $6; Ⓣ203/869-6899), a two-story white-clapboard building turned into a boarding house by the Holley family in the late 1800s. Like the Griswold home in Old Lyme (see p.340), the Holley residence began to attract artists eager to escape the summer heat and humidity of the big city – among them, Childe Hassam, John Henry Twachtman and J. Alden Weir, some of whose original works hang today in the house. In addition, there is the fine late-eighteenth-century Connecticut furniture and the ornate woodwork of the house itself, not to mention the studio of Elmer Livingston McRae, the husband of a subsequent owner and himself an artist, which has been left virtually intact. Look out, too, for pottery by Leon Volkmar.

The scalloped, shingle-sided **Putnam Cottage**, 243 E Putnam Ave (Fri & Sun 1–4pm; $2), built in 1690 and licensed as the *Knapp Tavern* from 1732, has a bit of romantic history to it: legend has it that one day in 1779, local patriot General Israel Putnam, a regular here, was busy shaving when he noticed advancing British troops in his mirror. Forced to flee, he jumped on a horse and managed to escape down a steep cliff, returning later with reinforcements to rout the enemy. The cottage contains original fieldstone fireplaces, antique furniture, and Putnam's uniform.

Practicalities

Accommodation in Greenwich tends to be of the B&B variety. Of these, the 1799 *Homestead Inn*, 420 Fieldstone Point Rd (ⓣ203/869-7500; ❾), is perched on a hill in a peaceful residential area, while the *Harbor House Inn*, 165 Shore Rd (ⓣ203/637-0145; ❼), is close to the water in Old Greenwich, as is the *Cos Cob Inn*, 50 River Rd (ⓣ203/661-5845; ❼), an 1870s Federal-style mansion with oodles of "olde worlde" charm in its 14 guestrooms.

You're spoiled for choice in Greenwich as far as **eating** is concerned – though, not surprisingly, in such an affluent place, restaurants can be pricey. If you're up for a splurge, try *La Maison Indochine*, 107 Greenwich Ave (ⓣ203/869-2689), for excellent Vietnamese cuisine, or *Thomas Henkelmann* at the *Homestead Inn*, 420 Field Point Rd (ⓣ203/869-7500), for top-notch French food; at *L'Escale*, 500 Steamboat Rd, in the brand new, luxury hotel *Delamar Greenwich Harbor* (ⓣ203/661-9800), you can dine in style while gazing at the posh yachts in Greenwich Harbor. Less expensive options include the *Stationhouse*, 99 Railroad Ave (ⓣ203/661-1374), with its pubby atmosphere and *Viscardi's Colonial Inn*, 220 Sound Beach Ave (ⓣ203/637-0367), a local institution known for its traditional American, Italian, and Greek dishes.

Danbury and the Housatonic Valley

The company town of **DANBURY**, 25 miles north of Norwalk on Rte-7, became famous as the "hat capital" of America; the ten-gallon Stetson was first fashioned here, and at one point, there were more than three dozen factories engaged in the hatmaking industry. When that industry declined in the 1960s and 1970s, Danbury's savior became **Union Carbide**, whose headquarters are still located here.

There's little of interest in the drab downtown area, where Danbury Green is the focus of an ambitious series of festivals and concerts. Nearby, the **Scott-Fanton Museum and Danbury Historical Society**, 43 Main St (Wed–Fri 1–4pm; donation; ⓣ203/743-5200), housed in the 1785 John and Mary Rider House, is mostly of note for its nostalgic exhibits relating to the city's hat industry. The hatmaking industry developed in Danbury during the Colonial period, thanks to an abundant supply of natural resources, especially water. The museum's hatting exhibit is displayed in a replica of an eighteenth-century shop, and interprets the impact of the industry on Danbury and surrounds. The Society also maintains, at 5 Mountainville Ave, the birthplace of Charles Ives, the local boy who went on to win a Pulitzer in 1947 for his *Third Symphony*, forty years after it was written. The house, built in 1780 by New York silversmith Thomas Tucker, is open by appointment only; call the museum for details. The **Military Museum of Southern New England**, 125 Park Ave, I-84 exit 3 (Tues–Sat 10am–5pm, Sun noon–5pm; $4; ⓣ203/790-9277), con-

△ The American Clock and Watch Museum, Bristol

tains enough life-size dioramas of World War II scenes to sate most any military buff. There's also a 1917 Renault, the first tank ever made in the US, and one of the original self-propelled Howitzers. Danbury's other main visitor attraction is the **Danbury Railway Museum**, 120 White St (April–Dec Tues–Sat 10am–5pm, Sun noon–5pm; Jan–March Wed–Sat 10am–4pm, Sun noon–4pm; $4), with a station and accompanying railroad yard.

About ten miles south of Danbury, picturesque **RIDGEFIELD** nearly seems an extension of the Litchfield Hills, its early buildings having escaped the rampant development so typical in Connecticut. If you make it here, check out the **Keeler Tavern Museum**, 132 Main St (Feb–Dec Wed, Sat & Sun 1–4pm; $5; ⓣ203/438-5485), which was a popular drinking place even before the Revolutionary War, but a hotbed of patriotic fervor during, especially after it was hit by British artillery. The offending cannonball is still embedded in the building. Down the street, the **Aldrich Museum of Contemporary Art**, 258 Main St (Tues–Sun 1–5pm; $5), was the first museum in America devoted solely to contemporary art. Its nine galleries hold a series of rotating exhibitions, and there's a lovely two-acre sculpture garden out back.

Apart from Danbury and Ridgefield, the Housatonic Valley offers a few natural attractions, with much of its landscape set aside as nature reserves and sanctuaries. **Candlewood Lake**, just north of Danbury, is Connecticut's largest freshwater lake, with opportunities for swimming, boating, and fishing. Further south, **Saugatuck Reservoir**, near Redding, is so peaceful and undeveloped you'd swear you were in northern Maine, while **Huntingdon State Park** is a great place for mountain biking. For avid hikers, east of Danbury, in Newtown, you can walk along the banks of the Housatonic River in the **Paugussett State Forest**.

Practicalities

A detailed brochure and map, available from the **Housatonic Valley Tourism Commission**, 30 Main St, Danbury (ⓣ203/743-0546 or 1-800/841-4488), outlines the architectural or historic interest of many of the structures along Ridgefield's Main Street, and the side streets off of it. If you're interested in **staying** in the area, Danbury's *Ethan Allen Inn*, exit 4 off I-84 (ⓣ203/744-1776 or 1-800/742-1776; ❻), is a large, modern hotel, though rooms are stocked with authentic Ethan Allen furniture. Quieter Ridgefield's *Stonehenge Inn*, Rte-7, Stonehenge Road (ⓣ203/438-6511; ❺), is an 1827 Colonial inn in an idyllic garden setting next to a duck pond. Also in Ridgefield, the peaceful *West Lane Inn*, 22 West Lane (ⓣ203/438-7323; ❻), contains twenty antique-stuffed rooms. For something to **eat**, try *Ondine*, 69 Pembroke Rd, Danbury (ⓣ203/746-4900), for contemporary French cuisine, though it's a bit pricey; by contrast, *Rosy Tomorrows*, 15 Old Mill Plain Rd (ⓣ203/743-5845), also in Danbury, is the place for American staples – barbecued ribs, huge sandwiches, burgers, onion rings, and so on, at moderate prices – with boisterous character. In Ridgefield, the *Stonehenge Inn* (see above) serves classic French cuisine, though at more than $40 for a Saturday night prix-fixe meal, it's not exactly cheap.

Hartford and the Connecticut River Valley

The Connecticut River, New England's largest, rises in the mountains of New Hampshire close to the Canadian border and runs all the way down to Long Island Sound. Growing up along either side of it, at least in Connecticut, has been a stretch of relatively peaceful towns, unable to make much industrial use of the river due to its shallowness. The one exception to the slow-paced communities is Hartford, the state capital, an unattractive and largely dull city of some importance as a stronghold of the Connecticut economy. A mile west of the city, Nook Farm was home in the late nineteenth century to some of the greatest literary figures of the age, including such as Mark Twain and Harriet Beecher Stowe, while **West Hartford** is where Noah Webster published his *American Dictionary* in 1828. Further west, gentle countryside leads to the pleasant town of **Farmington**, and the less attractive, but stimulating industrial city of **New Britain**, one of the nation's main producers of hardware. South of Hartford, the Connecticut River wends its way past **Wethersfield**, where Washington planned the final stages of the Revolutionary War; **Rocky Hill**, whose 185-million-year-old dinosaur tracks can be seen in Dinosaur State Park; **East Haddam**, site of the Goodspeed Opera House and the unusual hilltop Gillette Castle, one of the state's leading peculiarities. **Ivoryton**, famed for its summer theater, and **Essex**, with the excellent Connecticut River Museum, complete the picture, as the river widens and nears the sea.

Hartford

The town that Mark Twain once described as "the best built and handsomest town I have ever seen" is today hardly recognizable as such – a hodgepodge of ugly office buildings, multistory parking garages, factories, and sprawling suburbs. Indeed, the modern capital of Connecticut, **HARTFORD**, on the Connecticut River, is actually best known as the insurance center of the United States, and will probably not take more than a day or so of your time to explore – though the longer you stay, the more unexpected charms you are likely to find. Highlights include the 1878 **State House** with its golden dome and verdant grounds, the superb **Wadsworth Atheneum**, the nation's oldest continuously operating public museum, and the whimsical mansion **Mark Twain** built.

Some history

Originally known by the Indian name of *Suckiaug* ("black earth"), Hartford was dubbed "House of Good Hope" by Dutch merchants who established a trading post here in 1633. When a group of Puritans from Massachusetts arrived in 1635, they named the place "Newtown" after their Massachusetts home, then renamed it Hartford after the town of Hertford, England. From its earliest days, it was an important center for government: Connecticut's governor John Winthrop, Jr, set out from here in 1661 on a mission to seek from

King Charles II a charter guaranteeing the colony certain rights. Charles' more authoritarian successor, James II, attempted to rescind those rights and establish his own authority over the colony by dispatching his emissary to the city in 1687. The charter was whisked away by stealth and hidden in the hollow bark of an oak tree on land belonging to Samuel Wyllys. The "Charter Oak" was destroyed during a violent storm in 1856, but the legend lives on in the names Charter Oak Avenue and Charter Oak Place, at which corner it stood.

Leading the manufacturing charge, the Hartford Woollen Company became the first in the country to devote itself to producing woollen cloth; other goods manufactured locally included Colt revolvers, Sharps rifles, and the Pope motor car, and the pioneering city was the first in the nation to be lit by electricity. Hartford's greatest claim to fame, though, has been its position as the nation's insurance capital, a status begun with a policy issued in 1794 by the Hartford Fire Insurance Company. By the middle of the twentieth century, there were up to fifty insurance companies based in the city, providing twenty percent of the nation's coverage on certain types of policies; today the downtown Travelers Tower (which, until the 1980s, was the third tallest building in New England behind Boston's John Hancock Tower and Prudential Tower) still

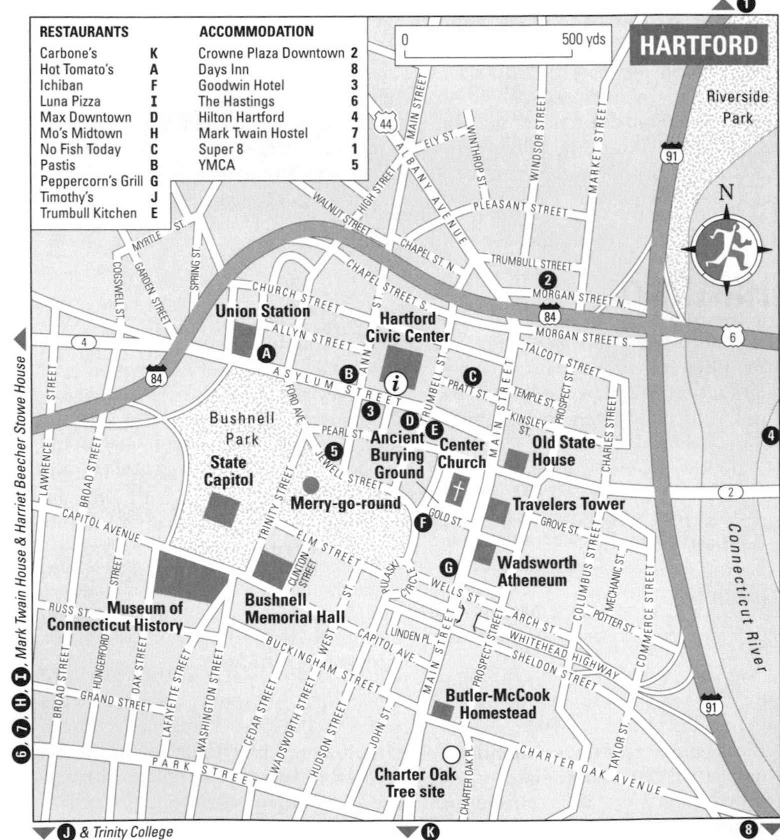

dominates for miles around, while Phoenix Home Life, Aetna, and a host of other insurers maintain headquarters here. However, the turn of the twenty-first century saw a downturn in the insurance industry, especially after 2001, and Hartford has, by most accounts, failed to revitalize itself as Providence (see p.292) and Portland (see p.529) have.

Arrival, information, and city transit

Hartford lies at the junction of the north–south highway I-91 and I-84 (east–west) so the city is easily accessible by **car**. It's also well served by long-distance **buses**, which all pull in to the Union Station terminal. The **local bus** system is operated by Connecticut Transit (ⓣ860/247-5329), which maintains an information bureau at State House Square and Market Street (weekdays 10am–6pm). If you're coming by **train**, the main Amtrak (ⓣ1-800/872-7245) services also pull in to Union Station. If you're traveling to Hartford by **air**, Bradley International Airport, just twelve miles north of town, is Connecticut's main airport. Several reliable **taxi** companies serve the city, among them Yellow Cabs (ⓣ860/666-6666) and Valley Cab Service (ⓣ860/673-4250). Hartford's downtown is also "patrolled" by the **Hartford Guides** (ⓣ860/522-0855), who can help with directions and information. The **Greater Hartford CVB**, Civic Center Plaza (ⓣ860/728-6789 or 1-800/446-7811), can help you find accommodation and provide information on attractions and current events.

Accommodation

Hartford has a limited range of **accommodation** possibilities, from a few budget motels and a couple of hostels, to three or four large (and usually pricey) downtown hotels which cater mainly to business visitors and where, consequently, big reductions can be had at weekends. For something a little quieter, check out the accommodation options in nearby Farmington (p.366), a charming and convenient spot just southwest of the city center.

Crowne Plaza Downtown 50 Morgan St ⓣ860/549-2400, ⓦwww.sixcontinentshotels.com. Large 350-room hotel with well-lit, oversized rooms in the center of town, close to all the main attractions. 7

Days Inn 207 Brainard Rd ⓣ860/247-3297 or 1-800/325-2525. Comfortable, good-value motel that's three miles from downtown. 4

Goodwin Hotel Goodwin Square, 1 Haynes St ⓣ860/246-7500 or 1-800/922-5006, ⓦwww.goodwinhotel.com. Elaborately restored luxury hotel opposite the Civic Center downtown, with a full range of facilities, including an excellent restaurant. 6

The Hastings 85 Sigourney St ⓣ860/727-4200. Originally a conference center, a recent $6 million renovation has made this a comfortable 270-room hotel with fairly plain rooms. 5

Mark Twain Hostel 131 Tremont St ⓣ860/523-7255. Twenty-five beds are available for $21 a night in communal rooms; some private rooms also available. Reservations are advisable, as the place gets full.

Hilton Hartford 315 Trumbull St ⓣ860/728-5151. Large, conveniently located downtown hotel with health club and indoor pool. 7

Super 8 I-91 exit 33 ⓣ860/246-8888 or 1-800/800-8000, ⓦwww.super8.com. Another budget motel offering basic, inexpensive accommodation, close to the Meadows Music Theatre. 3

YMCA 160 Jewell St ⓣ860/246-9622. Economy rooms with shared bath start at around $20; with private bath, from $25.

The City

Bleak insurance towers dominate the skyline of downtown Hartford, but despite that it's a surprisingly open city, with wide streets and plenty of greenery to break up the concrete and steel. The broad lawns and plantings of **Bushnell Park**, designed by eminent landscape architect Frederick Law

Olmsted, surround the golden-domed **State Capitol** (free tours given Sept–June Mon–Fri 9.15am–1.15pm, July–Aug additional tour at 2.15pm; also April–Oct Sat 9.15am–2.15pm), an 1878 mixture of Gothic, Classical, and Second Empire styles. Its ornate exterior, with niches containing statues of Connecticut political worthies, looks more like a church; inside, massive granite columns, stained-glass windows, and lofty ceilings continue the ecclesiastical ambience. The Hall of Flags contains some fascinating relics of Connecticut's history, including bullet-ridden flags and the camp bed Lafayette slept on when he visited the city. After you have traipsed round the Capitol you can take a ride on the antique **merry-go-round** in the park, which gives jangling rides for a mere fifty cents. The **Museum of Connecticut History**, across the road at 231 Capitol Ave (Mon–Fri 9am–4pm, Sat 10am–4pm; free), holds an impressive collection of Colt rifles and revolvers, the desk at which Abraham Lincoln signed the paper that emancipated all slaves during the Civil War, and the original Connecticut Royal Charter.

Main Street

Many of Hartford's most important buildings are located on **Main Street**, starting (from south to north) with the white-clapboard **Butler-McCook Homestead**, no. 396 (Wed–Sun 10am–4pm; $3), one of the few surviving historic homes in Hartford. Owned by the same family for more than two hundred years, it contains a collection of armor from Japan and some antique toys and furniture; behind the house, an 1860s formal garden designed by Jacob Weidenmann is reputed to be the oldest domestic garden in the US. Hartford's pride and joy is the Greek Revival **Wadsworth Atheneum**, 600 Main St (Tues–Fri 11am–5pm, Sat–Sun 10am–5pm; $9, free before noon Sat; ⓣ860/278-2670), founded by Daniel Wadsworth in 1842 and the nation's oldest continuously operating public art museum. The Atheneum collection, spanning over 5000 years, includes ancient Egyptian, Greek, and Roman bronzes; Renaissance and Baroque paintings; seventeenth- and eighteenth-century American furniture and decorative arts; and a host of Old Masters, including Rubens' *The Return of the Holy Family from Egypt* and, in the French Impressionists collection, Pierre-Auguste Renoir's *Monet Painting in His Garden at Argenteuil*. Of particular note are the Wallace Nutting collection of "Pilgrim-century" American furniture and decorative arts; the largest of its kind, and the "*Amistad*" collection, documenting the development of African-American culture from the slave period to the present. Lectures and films are put on at the Atheneum Theater, and there's an excellent café, too, that's open for lunch Tuesday to Saturday, and for Sunday brunch. In a bid to increase its display size (currently the museum can only show two thousand of its 45,000 items), the Atheneum will close for a two-year, $120 million renovation starting in 2004, and much of its collection will travel around the country, vacationing in other museums.

A few hundred yards north, on the corner of Main and Gold streets, the lofty 527-foot-high **Travelers Tower**, corporate headquarters of Traveler's Assurance, though no longer the tallest building in Hartford, can be ascended for spectacular views of the city and beyond from an open-air **observation deck**. You'll have to be fit: after the 24-floor climb or ride up, you'll need to climb a further 72 steps up a spiral staircase. The half-hourly tours are free, though you'll need to make a reservation (ⓣ860/277-4208). The elegant **Center Church** across the street at no. 675 was established by Thomas Hooker, the leader of the band of dissenters from Newtown, Massachusetts. Modeled, like so many others, on London's St Martin-in-the-Fields, the church holds no fewer than five Tiffany windows and a barrel-vaulted ceiling. It overlooks the tranquil **Ancient Burying Ground**, established in 1640, and the final resting-place for many of the city's first settlers, including Hooker, who died in 1647 (daily 10am–4pm; ⓣ860/561-2585; free).

At 800 Main St, the red-brick **Old State House** (Mon–Fri 10am–4pm, Sat 11am–4pm; free), a 1796 Federal-style building designed by Boston architect Charles Bulfinch – his first public commission – provides a dignified contrast to the drab modern office buildings that surround it, especially since its renovation in 1996, when the early-nineteenth-century ornamental iron fencing and gaslights were restored. Inside, the Court Room, which witnessed, among others, the *Amistad* and Prudence Hill trials, has been restored to its initial appearance; downstairs, a new, imaginative museum traces the state's history through various interactive displays and hands-on exhibits. The Connecticut Historical Society, which maintains the museum in the Old State House, is also obviously the force behind the **Connecticut Historical Society Museum**, 1 Elizabeth St (Tues–Sun noon–5pm; $6), with its large collection of eighteenth- and nineteenth-century Connecticut furniture, and Connecticut landscape paintings.

Trinity College

South of downtown, at 300 Summit St, the beautiful and compact campus of **Trinity College** is located at the highest point in the city and is a pleasant place to spend an hour or two. Founded in 1823, it hosts an array of stunning architecture, particularly on the main square, known as the Long Walk, notable for its three very impressive brownstone Victorian Gothic buildings. Also notable is the college chapel, purported by some to be the best example of Victorian Gothic in the nation. Organ and chamber concerts are held here regularly while across the green the college's CineStudio hosts independent and classic movies nightly, and is open to the public. The campus is also home to the excellent Gallows Bookstore, which presents weekly readings with visiting authors. For details on current events at the College, call ⓣ860/297-2001.

Mark Twain House and Harriet Beecher Stowe House

About a mile west of downtown Hartford on Rte-4, a hilltop community known as Nook Farm was home in the 1880s to next-door neighbors **Mark Twain** and **Harriet Beecher Stowe**. Today their Victorian homes, furnished much as they were then, are open for tours. The bizarre **Mark Twain House**, 351 Farmington Ave (May–Oct & Dec Mon–Sat 9.30am–4pm, Sun noon–4pm; rest of year closed Tues; $9; ⓣ860/297-0998), which the author built in 1874 and lived in with his family until 1891, saw him write many of his classic works, such as *The Adventures of Huckleberry Finn*. Looking at the newly restored house, it's easy to see where the author spent the publishing royalties from those books: designed by Edward Tuckerman Potter, the place is outrageously ornate, with black-and-orange brickwork, decorative work by the Associated Artists, an important collection of fine and decorative arts, and the only remaining domestic interior by Louis Comfort Tiffany. Note especially the elaborate woodwork and furnishing in the library, where guests were regaled with readings of Twain's own works-in-progress, and the dining room, where Twain and his wife Livy entertained such luminaries as William Dean Howells and General Sherman.

The much less flamboyant **Harriet Beecher Stowe House**, 77 Forest St (summer Mon–Sat 9.30am–4.30pm, Sun noon–4.30pm; rest of year closed

Mon; $6.50; ☎860/522-9258), celebrates the life of the author of *Uncle Tom's Cabin*, one of the most important American literary works of the nineteenth century. Stowe, who lived here from 1873 until her death in 1896, was an ardent abolitionist, but also found time to write about housekeeping ideals in the book she penned with her sister, Catherine Beecher, *The American Woman's Home*. The house, built in 1871, is a fine example of a nineteenth-century "cottage" with a hint of the romantic villas made popular by Andrew Jackson Downing and Calvert Vaux. Inside you can see Stowe's writing table and some of her paintings.

West Hartford

Farmington Avenue, a long strip with a mix of cheap diners, fast-food joints, and a few quaint gourmet shops and bookstores, continues out of the capital to **WEST HARTFORD**, home to a few scattered highlights, namely the **Noah Webster House**, 227 S Main St (Sept–June Mon & Thurs–Sun 1–4pm; July–Aug Mon, Thurs & Fri 11am–4pm, Sat & Sun 1–4pm; $5), an eighteenth-century farmhouse that was home to Webster, compiler of the pioneering *American Dictionary*, first published in 1828 (see box below). Also in town is the **Museum of American Political Life**, University of Hartford, 200 Bloomfield Ave (Sept–May Tues–Fri 11am–4pm, Sat & Sun noon–4pm; rest of year closed Sun; donation), which holds all sorts of political memorabilia and thematic exhibits on political movements. Particularly topical to these days, "The Presidency and the Press" surveys the use of newspapers in political campaigns and examines the relationship between television and presidential politics.

Back closer to town, north of Farmington Avenue, at Prospect and Asylum avenues, **Elizabeth Park** was the first municipal rose garden in the nation. In addition to the more than 800 varieties of roses, including rarities such as Earth Song and Grenada, there are rock gardens, greenhouses (Mon–Fri 8am–3pm; free), and miles of tranquil walking paths.

Eating

To take advantage of the surprisingly good **eating** options Hartford has to offer, you'll probably end up touring a few different neighborhoods. For home-cooking, head to Farmington Avenue, which offers the city's top diners and cafés. Many of downtown Hartford's choice Italian eateries can be found along Franklin Avenue, the heart of the city's Italian district, while more sophisticated and expensive French and American restaurants operate along the

Hartford's defining resident

Noah Webster was born in West Hartford on October 16, 1758. A lexicographer and author, he wrote educational textbooks before eventually compiling the **first dictionary** to distinguish American usage of the English language from British usage. His spelling book – *The Blue-backed Speller* (1783) – helped standardize American spelling and greatly contributed to the country's growing national identity. Encouraged by the enormous success of the first book, he compiled and edited a series of dictionaries culminating in the extensive, two-volume *American Dictionary of the English Language* (1828), which went on to become the nation's most trusted and well-known dictionary. Webster later co-founded Amherst College in Massachusetts (see p.262) and *Webster's Dictionary* keeps his name synonymous with the development of the English language in America.

axis of downtown's Main and Asylum streets. While you should not have a problem during the week getting a table, reservations are always a good idea at the upscale eateries – and a must on weekends.

Carbone's 588 Franklin Ave ⓣ860/296-9646. Excellent and expensive Italian restaurant – probably the best in town – opened in 1938. Lots of veal and poultry, good pastas, and a winning lobster *fra diavolo*.

Hot Tomato's 1 Union Place ⓣ860/249-5100. A relaxed, energetic Italian spot, popular for its huge garlicky portions and fair bill.

Ichiban 1 Gold St ⓣ860/560-1414. *The* place for sushi in downtown Hartford, but check out the Korean menu, too, where fish broths, stews, and fried meat dishes offer a welcome alternative for those who can't cope with raw fish.

Luna Pizza 999 Farmington Ave, West Hartford ⓣ860/233-1625. Brick-oven thin-crust pizza with a somewhat unusual variety of tasty toppings, such as salmon and capers.

Max Downtown 185 Asylum St ⓣ860/522-2530. Considered Hartford's best restaurant, this dynamic spot, brimming with creative flair, prepares impeccable American-nouveau dishes at a considerable (but worthwhile) cost.

Mo's Midtown 25 Whitney St ⓣ860/236-7741. You get the greatest breakfast to cure all hangovers at this friendly and hugely popular diner right off Farmington Ave. Recommended is the "Papa Mo" breakfast – a classic "fry-up" – and for those with smaller stomachs, the "Momma Mo" and "Baby Mo" still get the job done. Beware of daunting lines on weekends; however they move along fairly fast.

No Fish Today 80 Pratt St ⓣ860/244-2100. Despite its name, seafood – Italian-style – is the thing in this relaxed, moderately-priced downtown restaurant.

Pastis 201 Ann St ⓣ860/278-8852. The closest to a Paris bistro you'll find in the city, with the likes of braised sea bass and steak frites for under $20.

Peppercorn's Grill 357 Main St ⓣ860/547-1714. One of the better eateries in Hartford, rivalling *Max Downtown*, is this minimalist American-nouveau standout. The menu is sophisticated and creative and the staff attentive without being overbearing. The bill can get pricey, however, with an appetizer and entrée running to about $30 – worth it nonetheless.

Timothy's 243 Zion St ⓣ860/728-9822. Super little inexpensive restaurant serving an eclectic menu (Thai chicken, Indian-spiced shrimp) using local and organic produce. Burgers and some vegetarian dishes available as well.

Trumbull Kitchen 150 Trumbull St ⓣ860/493-7417. Popular, trendy eatery with an eclectic menu featuring a bit of everything, from dim sum and tapas and fondue, to pizza (prosciutto, figs, and gorgonzola) and grilled lamb sirloin, with a kaffir lime crème brulée for dessert. Not very pricey, either, for a hot spot – you can do very well for $20–25 a head.

Nightlife and entertainment

There's no shortage of **nightlife** in Hartford, whether you want to see a play, listen to a symphony concert, or bop till the wee hours in a nightclub. Among the main music venues are the **Bushnell Memorial Hall**, 166 Capitol Ave (ⓣ860/987-8900), home to the Hartford Symphony Orchestra, the Hartford Ballet, and the Connecticut Opera; the **Meadows Music Theatre**, 92 Weston St (ⓣ860/548-7370), venue for rock, pop, country, blues, and jazz; and the **Hartford Civic Center Coliseum**, Trumbull and Asylum streets (ⓣ860/727-8010), home of the American Hockey League (minor league NHL) Wolfpack hockey team and host to a variety of sports competitions and rock and pop concerts. Meanwhile, the award-winning **Hartford Stage Company**, 50 Church St (ⓣ860/527-5151), holds classic plays and bold experimental productions, while **Theaterworks**, 233 Pearl St (ⓣ860/527-7838), is a local professional company presenting contemporary pieces.

Hartford's **bars** and **nightclubs** are mainly confined to the downtown area. For current listings, check out the free arts and entertainment weekly the *Hartford Advocate* or the city's daily newspaper, the *Courant*.

Black-eyed Sally's 350 Asylum St ⓣ860/278-7427. Live blues music Thurs to Sun ($5–10 cover) and hearty Cajun cooking in this atmospheric restaurant/club.

The Brickyard 113 Allyn St ⓣ860/249-2112. Multi-level hangout with a casual sports bar (with pool tables), a lounge, and dance floor.

Coach's 187 Allyn St ⓣ860/522-6224. As the name implies, this bar/restaurant has a sports theme, with the typical memorabilia to show for it. $5 on band nights.

Hartford Brewery 35 Pearl St ⓣ860/246-BEER. Beer is brewed on the premises at this friendly, unpretentious spot.

Roo Bar 482 Farmington Ave ⓣ860/232-2260. Live music Fri and Sat, and live reggae shows in the summer, for the twenty-somethings.

Standing Stone 111 Allyn St ⓣ860/246-4400. Irish whiskey and beer line the walls of this pub which features acoustic sets Thurs through Sat ($3 after 9.30pm).

Around Hartford

A cluster of towns within ten miles to the **south and west of Hartford** have managed to retain much of their traditional New England atmosphere, even in the face of Hartford's growing suburban sprawl. None exactly overwhelm with things to do, but they make a decent alternative if you tire of spending time in the city. While they're best accessed by car, Connecticut Transit (ⓣ860/247-5329) has extensive routes in the Greater Hartford area.

Farmington

Lush **FARMINGTON**, about ten miles southwest of Hartford, had its heyday in the 1830s and 1840s, when the Farmington Canal operated between New Haven and Northampton, Massachusetts. Though today a more mundane suburb, it still merits a visit in order to see the **Hill-Stead Museum**, 35 Mountain Rd (May–Oct Tues–Sun 10am–5pm; rest of year Tues–Sun 11am–4pm; $9), an impressive turn-of-the-century Colonial Revival house that belonged to industrial magnate Alfred A. Pope. Designed by his daughter, Theodate – one of the nation's first female architects, whose illustrious career nearly ended while aboard the ill-fated *Lusitania* (she escaped by hanging on to an oar) – it now holds an outstanding assortment of American and European furniture and a collection of Impressionist paintings, including works by Monet, Manet, Degas, and Whistler. Also in Farmington, the **Stanley-Whitman House**, 37 High St (May–Oct Wed–Sun noon–4pm; Nov–April Sun noon–4pm: $5), is a Colonial homestead dating from 1720, with some interesting architectural features, such as its narrow casement windows with small diamond panes.

Practicalities

If you prefer to **stay** here rather than in downtown Hartford, options include the *Farmington Inn*, 827 Farmington Ave (ⓣ860/677-2821 or 1-800/648-9804, ⓦwww.farmingtoninn.com; ⑥), a large, luxury facility whose comfortable rooms and suites contain paintings by local artists, while the *Hartford Marriott*, 15 Farm Springs Rd (ⓣ860/678-1000; ⑥), has just what you expect from a large chain – and with big weekend bargains. For something to **eat**, *Apricots*, 1593 Farmington Ave (ⓣ860/673-5405), is a true gem with an English-style pub downstairs (typical entrées $10–14), and two formal (and expensive) dining rooms offering Continental cuisine upstairs. The *Connecticut Culinary Institute*, 230 Farmington Ave (ⓣ860/677-7869), is a training school for future chefs, with a varied, good-value menu.

New Britain

Industrial **NEW BRITAIN**, ten miles southeast of Farmington, once one of the country's leading producers of locks, tools, ball bearings, and other hardware items, is the unlikely location for one of the Northeast's best collections of American art, with galleries housing more than 5,000 exhibits including oils, watercolors, drawings, and sculpture spanning 250 years. The **New Britain Museum of American Art**, 56 Lexington St (Tues, Thurs, Fri & Sun noon–5pm, Wed noon–7pm, Sat 10am–5pm; $5, free Sat 10am–noon), boasts representative works by Whistler, Copley, Sargent, and Church, and murals by Thomas Hart Benton, all housed in an attractive nineteenth-century mansion. The town's manufacturing past and present is the focus of the **New Britain Industrial Museum**, 185 Main St (Mon–Fri 2–5pm; free), with exhibits devoted to the large manufacturing companies, such as Stanley Tools and Fafnir Bearings, that brought the city prosperity (and employment). Items on display include everything from tools to Art Deco kitchenware.

Wethersfield

Just six miles south of downtown Hartford, **WETHERSFIELD** had its own harbor on the Connecticut River until a major flood in 1692 rerouted the water and so stripped much of the town's wealth; indeed, by the late 1700s, farming had overtaken trade as the main economic activity. Today, a few well-preserved homes lend the place a certain picturesqueness. Much of the historical interest focuses on the **Webb-Deane-Stevens Museum**, 211 Main St (May–Oct Wed–Mon 10am–4pm; Nov–April Sat & Sun 10am–4pm; $8), made up of three eighteenth-century houses. The **Webb House**, built in 1752 by a prosperous merchant, Joseph Webb, Sr, and notable for its wide, central hall and well-proportioned rooms, contains period furnishings and decorative arts in its rooms, one of which was a bedroom especially designed for the arrival of George Washington, who came here to plan the Yorktown campaign with Jean-Baptiste Rochambeau. The 1766 **Silas Deane House** was home to a lawyer-diplomat who played an important role in the First Continental Congress and traveled to Paris to seek French assistance for the forces of the Revolution. In an all-too-familiar story, Deane became involved in some dubious business deals while abroad that led him to be accused of treason, and he spent much of the rest of his life in an unsuccessful attempt to clear his name. The more modest **Stevens House** was built in 1788 by a local leatherworker for his bride, its simple decor and lack of embellishments proving that not everyone here was a member of the aristocracy. Down the road, at 150 Main St, **The Old Academy** (Tues–Fri 10am–4pm, Sat 1–4pm; $2) is a handsome brick building which has served as a town hall, library, women's seminary, and now as the unexciting headquarters of the Wethersfield Historical Society. Just behind it, at 249 Broad St, the charming **Buttolph-Williams House** (mid-May to mid-Oct Wed–Mon 10am–4pm; $5), built in 1700, is one of the oldest surviving homes in the town, with the dark clapboards and small windows that were characteristic of the earliest homes. A massive fireplace dominates the main living room, and the whole place is filled with period furniture. Not far away, the 1764 **First Church of Christ, Congregational**, at 250 Main St, boasts a cupola that's an exact replica of the one at Old North Church in Boston. Main Street ends at the Wethersfield Cove, where the lone survivor of the flood stands – the **Cove Warehouse** (opening times vary; call the Historical Society ⓣ860/529-7656; $1).

Dinosaur State Park

In 1966, the discovery of hundreds of dinosaur tracks in Rocky Hill, south of Wethersfield, led to the foundation of the **Dinosaur State Park**, a mile east of exit 23 off I-91 (park open daily, parking free; exhibition center open Tues–Sun 9am–4.30pm; $2, Ⓦwww.dinosaurstatepark.org), where you can see hundreds of dinosaur prints and explore the park's nature trails. The trails take you through a variety of natural environments, including a prehistoric swamp. You can even make your own dinosaur print; you just need ten pounds of plaster of Paris, one cup of cooking oil, and a five-gallon plastic bucket. If you don't happen to have these upon your person at the time, the museum will point you in the direction of local stores that can provide them.

Practicalities

There isn't too much to choose from regarding **restaurants** in Wethersfield, mainly chain standards for seafood and fast food. An exception from the rule, *Amici's*, 672 Silas Deane Hwy (Ⓣ860/529-8825), serves a wide-ranging menu of Italian favorites at around $15, with some surprises like chicken ravioli in cognac cream sauce. In the event that you want to **stay** in Wethersfield, the *Chester Bulkley House*, 184 Main St (Ⓣ860/563-1651; ❺), has elegant and fairly inexpensive rooms in an 1830 Greek Revival home right in the center of things.

The Connecticut River Valley

The suburbs end and the valley starts in earnest again with **MIDDLETOWN**, once the busiest port on the Connecticut River, which retains a number of gracious nineteenth-century merchants' homes, to be found on the attractive campus of prestigious **Wesleyan University**. Of these, the most prominent is the brick Federal-style **General Mansfield House**, 151 Main St (Sun 2–4.30pm, Mon 1–4pm; $2), constructed in 1810. Also on campus, the **Zilkha Gallery**, Washington Terrace/Wyllys Avenue (Tues–Fri noon–4pm, Sat & Sun 2–5pm; free; Ⓣ860/685-2695), showcases a rotating display of modern works in various media. Middletown's **Harbor Park** is the departure point for a gorgeous four-hour waterway **foliage cruise** on October weekends ($25); contact Deep River Navigation (Ⓣ860/526-4954, Ⓦwww.deeprivernavigation.com) for details on this and its other launches from Hartford and Old Saybrook.

South on Rte-154, **HIGGANUM** contains little save the yellow-clapboard **Thankful Arnold House**, corner of Hayden Hill and Walkley Hill roads (open year-round by appointment; Ⓣ860/345-2400), a three-story gambrel built between 1794 and 1810, with entrances on two levels and tours given by a resident "ghost." The magnificent **herb and vegetable garden** has been carefully researched to reflect the plantings of the period. Another horticultural treat nearby, the **Sundial Herb Garden**, Brault Hill Road (gardens: mid-May to mid-Sept and first two weeks Oct Sat & Sun 10am–5pm; $2; shop: Jan to mid-Sept and first two weeks Oct Sat & Sun 10am–5pm; tea: Feb–Sept one Sat afternoon a month, reservations required; Ⓣ860/345-4290), contains a series of interrelated formal gardens based on seventeenth- and eighteenth-century principles, with topiary, avenues, knots, statuary, and sundials. Even more enticing are the **afternoon teas** put on by the husband-and-wife proprietors.

East Haddam

About seven miles south, on the opposite side of the river, the village of **EAST HADDAM** is the unlikely location for the amazing **Goodspeed Opera House**, Goodspeed Landing, off Rte-82 (tours June–Oct Sat 11am–1.30pm, Mon 1–3pm; $2; performances April–Dec; ⓣ860/873-8668), which rises above the water like a giant wedding cake. Built in 1876 by shipping and banking magnate William Goodspeed to provide a venue for his love of theater, the Opera House later served as a military base and as a storage depot for the Connecticut Highway Department, until, in the late 1950s, restoration work on the run-down structure was initiated by a group of local preservationists. East Haddam's other notable feature is the **Nathan Hale Schoolhouse**, Main Street behind St Stephen's Church (May–Sept weekends & holidays 2–4pm; donation requested), where Hale taught from 1773 to 1774. The one-room schoolhouse contains a small collection of his possessions as well as items of local historical interest.

A further five miles south, on the east bank of the river, is the **Gillette Castle** (daily: end of May to mid-Oct 10am–5pm; mid-Oct to late Dec Sat–Sun 10am–5pm; $4; ⓣ860/526-2336), the centerpiece of **Gillette Castle State Park**, a prime hiking and picnicking venue. This 24-room granite castle-at-the-top-of-a-hill was built between 1914 and 1919 by actor/playwright William Hooker Gillette, known for his portrayal of cool, unruffled men of action in plays like *Held by the Enemy* and *Secret Service*, and, more famously, in the title role of *Sherlock Holmes*, first produced in New York in 1899. Gillette's performances must have been good; not only did he play the part until five years before his death in 1937, but the result of his fortune was this mansion, into which he built incredible features: a dining table on tracks; a grand hall with balconies on three sides and a mirror which allowed Mr Gillette to seize the correct moment for his grand entrance; and a replica of the sitting room at 221B Baker St, complete with violin, chemistry set, scattered copies of the *London Times* and *Illustrated London News*, and pipe.

Practicalities

Among the **places to stay** in East Haddam are *Gelston House*, 8 Main St (ⓣ860/873-1411; ❻), providing luxurious and spacious accommodation adjacent to the Goodspeed Opera House, and the *Bishopsgate Inn*, Rte-82 (ⓣ860/873-1677; ❼), a charming Colonial house built in 1818 with six cozy rooms, each sporting a wood-burning stove. *Gelston House* has an elegant **restaurant** serving American and French dishes, or you could opt for *Hale 'n' Hearty*, 381 Town St (ⓣ860/873-2640), for casual mid-priced American dining of the broiled seafood, steak, and pot roast variety.

Ivoryton and Essex

Back across the river on Rte-9 is the village of **IVORYTON**, formerly known as Centerbrook until it became a hub – along with the nearby towns of Chester, Deep River, and Essex – for the production of ivory. Beginning in 1789, when Phineas Pratt first manufactured ivory combs here, the industry grew to include piano keys, crochet needles, brushes, and organ stops. It is estimated that more than three-quarters of all the ivory exported from Zanzibar in 1884 found its way to Ivoryton and Deep River. However, these days the hamlet is best known for its summer theater, the **Ivoryton Playhouse**, 103 Main St (ⓣ860/767-7318). Many a showbiz career has been launched from this fairly insignificant-looking dark-brown wooden structure, including that of local girl Katharine Hepburn. For more pomp and circumstance, head to the **Museum of Fife and Drum**, 62 N Main St (June–Sept Sat & Sun 1–5pm; $2; ⓣ860/767-2237), where the history of military music is traced through costumes, photographs, sheet music, and instruments from early Colonial days through the Revolutionary period to the present. The museum sponsors occasional concerts in the summer.

The river begins widening noticeably as you head further south towards tiny **ESSEX**, everyone's idea of how a quaint New England town should look, with some lovely Colonial homes, a main street brimming with inviting stores and boutiques, and a riverfront marina lined with posh boats. At the end of Main Street, in an 1878 waterfront dockhouse, the **Connecticut River Museum** (Tues–Sun 10am–5pm; $4) traces local history through paintings, photographs, models, and artifacts. The chief item of interest is a full-sized reproduction of the *American Turtle*, the world's first submarine, powered by foot pedals. The **waterfront park** outside is a great place to watch the boats coming and going. Just south of downtown, the 1701 **Pratt House**, at 19 West Ave (June to mid-Sept Sat & Sun 2–4pm, other times by appt; $3; ⓣ860/767-1191), is the oldest house in the area, and belonged to the town founders. Besides the usual period furnishings, there's ironwork created by the former Pratt smithy, and a reproduction post-and-beam barn at the back, containing exhibits on Essex's agricultural and domestic history. For something completely different, the restored steam trains of the **Valley Railroad**, Railroad Avenue (May–Dec; ⓣ860/767-0103; $10.50, $5.50 ages 3–11), can take you an hour upriver; you can return either by boat or train.

Practicalities

Accommodation options in Ivoryton and Essex include the *Griswold Inn*, 36 Main St, Essex (ⓣ860/767-1776; ❺), open since 1776, with some luxurious suites complete with four-poster beds and wood-burning stoves, and the *Copper Beech Inn*, 46 Main St, Ivoryton (ⓣ860/767-0330; ❻), a restored carriage house with spacious, well-appointed guestrooms and a fine French **restaurant** spread out over three elegant rooms. If it's just a snack you want, try *Crow's Nest*, 35 Pratt St, Essex (ⓣ860/767-3288), for fresh-baked breakfast treats, excellent coffee, and lunchtime soups and sandwiches.

The Litchfield Hills

The rolling, tree-clad **LITCHFIELD HILLS**, tucked away in Connecticut's tranquil northwestern corner, provide a vivid contrast to the hustle and bustle of the coastal stretch, not to mention the industrial centers of New Haven and Hartford. Lakes, rivers, clear rushing brooks, and dense pine-scented forests permeate the area, interrupted by picturesque villages. Right at the center, the small town of **Litchfield** is prototypical New England: a wide, maple-dotted village green surrounded by elegant clapboard homes, all overlooked by a dazzling white church steeple. North of Litchfield are equally attractive but much smaller locales, like the peaceful rural community of **Winsted**, and pretty

Norfolk, home of the Yale Summer School of Music. In the far northwestern corner, **Salisbury** and **Lakeville** are close to Connecticut's tallest peaks, **Bear Mountain** and **Bald Peak**, while further south are **West Cornwall**, with its famous covered bridge, **Cornwall**, and **Kent**, virtually unheard of until it was "discovered" by artists, craftspeople, and designers from New York City in the 1980s. All these places abound with traditional country inns, some surprisingly inexpensive. The area's commercial center, **Torrington**, about seven miles northeast of Litchfield, is insignificant save for being the birthplace of abolitionist John Brown.

Arrival and information

The nearest **train** station to Kent, the southernmost of the Litchfield Hills towns, is some thirty miles away in Danbury (see p.356). Metro North (☎1-800/METRO-INFO) runs daily train service to Danbury from Grand Central Station in New York City; connecting bus service along Rte-7 in the Litchfield Hills area to Kent and West Cornwall (but not to Litchfield itself) is provided by Bonanza Buses (☎1-888/751-8800). But by far the best way to get to the region, and to explore it fully, is by **car**. From New York City, take the Henry Hudson Parkway North to the Saw Mill River Parkway to I-684 West to I-84, which heads northeast past Danbury, then passes along the southern fringe of the region on its way to Hartford. From I-84, take Rte-7 north for Kent, Rte-202 for Litchfield. From Boston, take the Massachusetts Turnpike (I-90) west to Sturbridge, then join I-84 west past Hartford to Rte-8 north, as far as

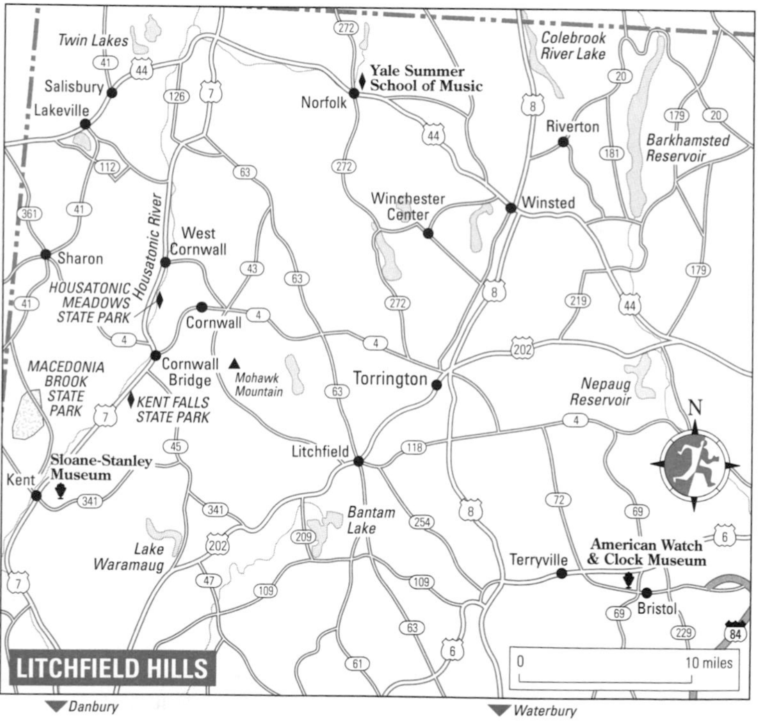

Rte-202 west to Litchfield. Although Litchfield, the center of the region, is only thirty miles west of Hartford, even with such short distances, journeys can often take well over an hour, since the mostly four-lane roads have their share of traffic lights and are well-traveled by locals.

A good source of **information** for the area is the Litchfield Hills Visitors Bureau (Ⓣ860/567-4506, Ⓦwww.litchfieldhills.com).

Litchfield and around

LITCHFIELD, first settled in 1720 by families from Hartford, Windsor, and Farmington, spreads out around an exceptionally long and pretty village green from which radiate quaint streets lined with centuries-old churches and private homes. During and immediately after the Revolutionary War, the town was a hive of activity: thanks to the abundance of iron ore in the hills, Litchfield became a major center for the manufacture of supplies for George Washington's war effort, even producing one of the Revolution's great heroes, Ethan Allen, born here in 1738. After the war, the town achieved fame as the home of **Tapping Reeve's Litchfield Law School**, the first in the nation, and the highly esteemed finishing school which later became the **Litchfield Female Academy** and the Litchfield Female Seminary, one of whose students was Harriet Beecher Stowe. Since then, a new kind of notoriety has developed from its popularity with day-trippers and short-break visitors from New York.

The Town

Much of Litchfield's interest focuses on **North Street**, with its stately white-clapboard mansions, many dating from the eighteenth century and designed by the popular architect William Spratt. The best way to explore is by picking up a walking map from the **visitor's kiosk**, right on **the Green** (June to mid-Sept daily 10am–4pm and weekends in Oct 10am–4pm; Ⓣ860/567-4506), but unless you strike lucky and arrive here on the one day in July each year when these private homes open to raise money for a local children's charity, you'll have to be content simply to view them from the outside. Look out anyway for the 1760 **Sheldon Tavern**, North Street, a graceful mansion with entrance portico and Palladian window that were added some time after the building had ceased to function as a public house. The most striking feature of the Green is the graceful 1829 **Congregational Church**, restored a century later after being used as an armory, hall, and theater. One of the early pastors here was Reverend Lyman Beecher, father of locals Henry Ward Beecher and Harriet Beecher Stowe. The **Litchfield Historical Society Museum**, also on the Green, at the corner of East and South streets (mid-April to Nov Tues–Sat 11am–5pm, Sun 1–5pm; $5), traces the development of northwestern Connecticut with special emphasis on the so-called "golden age" of the late 1700s and early 1800s, when the area was expanding rapidly.

The Historical Society also maintains the **Tapping Reeve House & Litchfield Law School** (same hours as Historical Society Museum; $5 entry also good for museum), former home of the College of New Jersey (now Princeton) graduate who started practicing law in Litchfield in 1772 and opened the law school in 1774, the first such school in the United States. Among many of his notable achievements was his instigation of the movement to allow married women to control their own property. Under his guidance, later students of the school were Aaron Burr, John C. Calhoun, and Horace

Mann. As the size of the student body grew, Reeve required more room and eventually built the adjacent one-room schoolhouse, which now contains exhibits on the life and work of Reeve, his influence on legal education in America, and the achievements of some of his students after graduation.

About two miles south of the Green, on Rte-202 West, the **White Memorial Foundation** (daily dawn–dusk; free), at four thousand acres the largest wildlife sanctuary in the state, has miles of trails for hiking and horse-back riding; there are also plenty of bird watching, fishing, and picnicking opportunities. For a complete contrast, the **Lourdes of Litchfield Shrine**, east of Litchfield Green on Rte-118, liberally re-creates the famous shrine of Our Lady of Lourdes, France, by means of a grotto built into the natural rock, where services are held regularly. Even if you don't subscribe to the faith, it's a fine place for a bit of quiet reflection.

Practicalities

There are plenty of charming **places to stay** in Litchfield, starting with the *Abel Darling B&B*, 102 West St (☎860/567-0384; ❻), a 1782 Colonial building close to Litchfield's main attractions. South of the Green, *The Litchfield Inn*, Rte-202 (☎860/567-4503; ❼), is a modern hotel built in the Colonial style, with spacious, elegant rooms and many extras, and the *Tollgate Hill Inn*, Rte-202 and Tollgate Road (☎860/567-4545; ❻), is an eighteenth-century inn with twenty gracious rooms containing antique reproduction furniture.

Many of Litchfield's **restaurants** line the Green along West Street. Casual *Aspen Garden*, 51 West St (☎860/567-9477), has a large outdoor patio and Mediterranean-influenced dishes. Close by, you can hobnob with the rich and famous and dine on pork chops or steak at the excellent but expensive *West Street Grill*, West Street (☎860/567-3885). For a cheaper alternative, *The Village*, 25 West St (☎860/567-8307), offers inexpensive, homestyle cooking, while *Litchfield Gourmet*, 33 West St (☎860/567-4882; closed Mon), is an upmarket café, bakery, and gourmet food store serving homemade soups, sandwiches, pastries, and desserts. Slightly further afield, *The Bistro East*, Rte-202, inside the *Litchfield Inn* (☎860/567-9040), does contemporary American cuisine (entrées $14–21) in a relaxed, torch-lit bistro setting.

This is a great area for hiking and cycling, with miles of trails, including a stretch of the Appalachian Trail. For **information**, go to the visitors' kiosk on the Green (see opposite). For **bike rental**, try the Wilderness Shop, 85 West St (☎860/567-5905), which also rents out skis and snowshoes.

Around Litchfield: Terryville and Bristol

An unusual opportunity avails itself in the village of **TERRYVILLE**, once an important lock and key manufacturing town, about twelve miles south of Litchfield on Rte-6: the **Lock Museum of America**, 230 Main St (May–Oct Tues–Sun 1.30–4.30pm; $3; ☎860/589-6359), standing on the site of the old Eagle Lock company factory, holds the largest collection of locks and keys and ornate Victorian hardware in the US. Key items, so to speak, include a combination padlock dating back to 1846, a 4000-year-old Egyptian-made pin tumbler lock, and the original patent model of the mortise cylinder pin lock designed by Linus Yale, Jr, in 1865.

In neighboring **BRISTOL**, once the largest clock manufacturing center in the world, make time for the **American Clock & Watch Museum**, 100 Maple St (April–Nov daily 10am–5pm; $5; ☎860/583-6070), reputed to be the finest collection of American clocks in existence – more than three thousand of them, including "Dewey," one of a series of six clocks introduced in 1899 to commemorate the Spanish–American War, with a likeness of Admiral Dewey at the top. Be prepared to cover your ears at the top of the hour, when hundreds of chimes resonate around the museum house. For the rabid fan of all things athletic, Bristol is also home to the sports cable television and radio networks **ESPN** and **ESPN2**, which provide game coverage/commentary, sporting news, documentaries, and even the occasional topical movie. Unfortunately, tours of the facility were not being conducted at time of publication, but sports fans especially might want to call ⓣ860/766-2000 for information in case they are reinstated.

Torrington and around

It's no coincidence that **TORRINGTON**, the largest and least attractive town in northwest Connecticut, is also the area's business center. Even its main claim to fame – being the birthplace, in 1800, of abolitionist **John Brown** – fails to provide a reason for visiting, as the house in which he was born no longer stands. One house that does, the **Hotchkiss Fyler House**, 192 Main St (mid-April to Oct Tues–Fri 10am–4pm, Sat & Sun noon–4pm; $3), a grand Victorian mansion constructed in 1900 by one of the town's industrial magnates, holds some interest in its original family furnishings and rare paintings by artists Winfield S. Clime and Ammi Philips. Nearby, the **Warner Theatre**, 68 Main St (ⓣ860/489-7180), is a huge restored Art Deco movie palace that hosts musicals, concerts, comedy, and ballet.

At the very least, Torrington does budget **accommodation**, like that at the *Super 8 Motel*, 492 E Main St (ⓣ860/496-0811 or 1-800/800-8000; ❹). More expensive, but full of character, is the *Yankee Pedlar Inn*, 93 Main St (ⓣ860/489-9226 or 1-800/777-1891; ❻), opposite the Warner Theatre. Its sixty rooms come complete with Hitchcock furnishings (see below). For something to **eat**, *Marino's*, 12 Pinewoods Rd (ⓣ860/482-6864), serves Italian-American cuisine in a casual, laid-back atmosphere, while *The Venetian Restaurant*, 52 E Main St (ⓣ860/489-8592), is one of the best Italian restaurants around, and not overly expensive; try the *osso buco*.

North from Torrington

From Torrington, Rte-8 leads north to the tranquil rural village of **WINSTED**, which hosts an annual summer festival in honor of the mountain laurel, Connecticut's state flower, which grows in profusion around here. On the corner of Lake and Prospect streets, the **Solomon Rockwell House** (June–Sept Thurs–Sun 2–4pm; free), a Greek Revival mansion built in 1813 by a prosperous iron manufacturer, displays period furnishings, rare nineteenth-century portraits, clocks, toys, war memorabilia, and a collection of wedding gowns.

Four miles west, **WINCHESTER CENTER** maintains a post-colonial charm, its village green an intersection of narrow roads and open fields populated by maples, and a cluster of pristine early nineteenth-century buildings, including several traditional farmhouses and a classic New England church, complete with Doric portico. Near the church is an early nineteenth-century post office, where you can glimpse a remarkable private collection of more than five hundred antique kerosene lamps in the **Kerosene Lamp Museum**, 100 Waterbury Turnpike (daily 9.30am–4pm; free). North of Winsted on Rte-20, **RIVERTON** was once known as Hitchcocksville thanks to its **Hitchcock**

Connecticut's Wine Trail

Contrary to popular belief, it *is* possible to create quality wines away from the West Coast's ideal climes. In Connecticut, wineries flanking the state borders and a few others scattered around the state comprise what is known as Connecticut's **Wine Trail**. The Farm Winery Act, passed in 1978 by the State House, opened up the soil to such establishments, and **Haight Vineyard** was soon growing Chardonnay and Riesling grapes behind their handsome English Tudor building in Litchfield. **Hopkins Vineyard**, on land in New Preston settled by the original Hopkins family in 1787, conducts tastings in a huge, renovated, bright red 1800s barn; furthermore, it's the only Connecticut grape farm to benefit from a microclimate (yielding a longer season) due to its location on Lake Waramaug. Some interesting choices are produced by the folks at **DiGrazia Vineyards** in Brookfield, who add honey (eliminating the need for sulfites), brandy, or pears to their formula. Across the state, picturesque Rte-169 (see p.379) leads to **Heritage Trail Vineyard** in Lisbon, established in 1996 by a transplanted Californian on the site of an eighteenth-century farmstead.

Tastings are available at these and other Wine Trail vineyards; opening times, driving directions and other information can be found at Ⓦwww.ctwine.com, or by calling Ⓣ860/868-7954.

Chair Factory, where Lambert Hitchcock began manufacturing the elaborately stenciled chairs and cabinets that became famous throughout America. The factory is still in operation, but to see the work on display, head for the **Hitchcock Museum**, housed in the sturdy 1826 **Old Union Church** (by appointment through Hitchcock Fine Home Furnishings at School Street and Rte-20; free; Ⓣ860/379-4826), which contains an extensive and rare collection of original hand-painted and-decorated antique furnishings.

Norfolk

Rte-44 leads west from Winsted through dairy farming country to **NORFOLK**, a relatively undeveloped spot whose tall church steeple stands sentinel over a lush **village green**. Note the elaborate **Eldridge Fountain**, designed by Stanford White, that has been quenching people's thirst for years; also on the green, the so-called White House was once part of the **Ellen Battell Stoeckel Estate**, after a music-loving local resident who here entertained such luminaries of the music world as Fritz Kreisler, Rachmaninov, and Sibelius. The estate was left to the **Yale Music School**, which organizes the Norfolk Chamber Music Festival each July and August. Concerts take place in the 950-seat "Music Shed" at the estate, at the intersection of routes 44 and 272 (Ⓣ860/542-3000, Ⓦwww.yale.edu/norfolk). Also in town, the **Norfolk Historical Society Museum**, 13 The Green (June to mid-Oct Sat & Sun 1–4pm; free), housed in the former Norfolk Academy, has on permanent display a traditional Norfolk country store and post office.

If you want to **stay** in Norfolk, the *Blackberry River Inn*, 536 Greenwoods Rd, Rte-44 West (Ⓣ860/542-5100 or 1-800/414-3636; ❺), offers peace and quiet (and a pool) in an eighteenth-century Colonial, and the romantic *Manor House*, 69 Maple Ave (Ⓣ860/542-5690; ❻), was built by the architect of the London Underground system, and features Tiffany windows, with extensive gardens just outside them. Another accommodation option is the *Mountain View Inn*, 67 Litchfield Rd (Ⓣ860/542-6991; ❹), a beautifully restored 1875 house overlooking Norfolk that's particularly noted for its excellent breakfasts. For something to **eat**, the *Pub & Restaurant*, Rte-44 (Ⓣ860/542-5716), with English pub decor (if not atmosphere) offers good-value American fare. If you're really hungry, you can even order a roast suckling pig – just give them six days' advance notice.

The northwest corner: routes 41 and 7

Further west, **LAKEVILLE** and neighboring **SALISBURY** are situated amid some of the state's most attractive scenery and an abundance of quaint guesthouses and inns. Lakeville's chief attraction, the **Holley Willams House**, routes 41 and 44 (mid-June to Aug Sat & Sun noon–5pm; $3), was built in 1808 by a local "iron baron" and is now a museum containing items collected by the Holley family during the 170 years they lived here. The **Salisbury Cannon Museum**, housed in the adjacent Carriage House (mid-June to Aug Sat & Sun 10am–5pm; free), tells the story of the Revolutionary War cannon factory that provided ammunition for Washington's army. There's also a scale model of an iron furnace and a display of tools.

South of Lakeville on Rte-41, **SHARON** is yet another quintessential New England village with a long, narrow green, some pristine nineteenth-century homes, and a white-steepled church. At the **Sharon Audubon Center** on Rte-4, you can explore 1200 acres and eleven miles of nature trails where you may see beavers, muskrats, and even otters, and visit the interpretive center (trails open daily dawn–dusk; interpretive center Tues–Sat 9am–5pm, Sun 1–5pm; $3; ⓣ860/364-0520).

West Cornwall, Cornwall, and Mohawk Mountain

Due east of Sharon, on Rte-7, the minuscule village of **WEST CORNWALL** has a number of craft shops and restaurants, but is mainly known for its bright-red, much-photographed **covered bridge**, built in 1837 of native oak and restored a few years ago. **CORNWALL**, a quite separate village three miles east on Rte-4, is where the **Cornwall Foreign Mission School** was located from 1817 to 1827. Henry Obookiah, a young Hawaiian who managed to stow away on a New Haven – bound ship after his family was killed in a tribal war, converted to the Christian faith and spent several years preaching in and around the Litchfield Hills until dying of typhoid at the age of 26. His enthusiasm for the faith inspired the American Missionary Board to send a group of missionaries to Hawaii, a story fictionalized in James Michener's *Hawaii*. Close by, the **Mohawk Mountain Ski Area**, Great Hollow Road (ⓣ860/672-6100 or 1-800/895-5222, ⓦwww.mohawkmtn.com), is the largest in the state with 23 trails good for all levels; a full day-pass costs only $37.

There's very little in the way of **lodgings** around here, but you could try *The Hitching Post Country Motel*, Rte-7, Cornwall Bridge (ⓣ860/672-6219, ❹), a small motel with slightly better than average rooms. Better still is the *Housatonic Meadows Inn*, 13 Rte-7, Cornwall Bridge (ⓣ860/672-6064, ❺), where wood floors and country quilts adorn five rooms in an attractive red lodge. For **food**, there's hearty American fare at the *Cornwall Inn*, Rte-7, Cornwall Bridge (ⓣ860/672-6884), where the juicy sirloin ($24) is the most expensive of the dinners.

Kent

Locals wax lyrical about **KENT**, nestled on a flat alluvial plain among the hills which border the Housatonic Valley, though in truth it's hard to understand why. This relatively nondescript town was virtually unknown, other than to members of the famous Kent School, until the 1980s, when it became a choice spot for country homes of various New York artists, designers, and craftspeople. As a result, **Main Street**, which straddles busy Rte-7, is lined with a slightly incongruous mixture of art galleries, trendy boutiques, coffee shops, and bookstores – perhaps a pleasant enough place for a swig of *caffè latte* or a quick shopping spree, but little else.

The Town and around

Chief among the town's sights is the **Sloane-Stanley Museum**, Rte-7, one mile north of downtown (mid-May to Oct Wed–Sun 10am–4pm; $3.50), which houses a unique assortment of hand tools and implements made by early settlers and collected by noted Connecticut writer and artist Eric Sloane. One of the items on display, a leather-bound 1805 diary of one Noah Blake, was discovered by Sloane in a nearby house; Blake describes his austere house in great detail, parameters Sloane used to build a replica small wooden cabin next to the museum. The museum stands on the site of the once-thriving **Kent Iron Furnace**, which began production of pig iron in 1826 – ceasing seventy years later – and whose ruins can be seen adjacent to the museum.

Kent combines opportunities to browse local galleries and bookstores with a chance to explore the countryside, namely in the three state parks that lie within the town's 49-square-mile administrative district. About seven miles north of downtown, the **Kent Falls State Park** has a cascading 200-foot waterfall with trails on either side that allow you to climb to the top, where you are rewarded with a spectacular view (daily 8am–dusk; free parking weekdays; on summer weekends $5 parking fee for CT residents, $8 for non-residents). A couple of miles further north on Rte-7, the **Housatonic Meadows State Park**, a densely forested area which stretches for two miles along the Housatonic River, is popular with hikers and picnickers. Four miles northwest of downtown Kent, on Macedonia Brook Road, beautiful **Macedonia Brook State Park** holds deep gorges, falls, and the 1350-foot summit of Cobble Mountain, which commands views as far as the Catskills in New York State. At the southern end of town, five miles south of downtown, a right turn at Bulls Bridge Road leads to **Bulls Bridge**, one of only two original covered bridges in the state which is open to vehicular traffic. Restored a few years back, it's certainly in better condition today than when George Washington crossed it on horseback. The horse stumbled on a broken plank, so the story goes, forcing its illustrious rider into an overnight stay.

Practicalities

There are several nice **places to stay** in Kent. Located at the top end of Kent's shopping district, *Fife 'n' Drum*, 42 N Main St (ⓣ860/927-3509; ❻), is an above-average small motel that also contains a rustic restaurant; also within walking distance of the center, *Chaucer House*, 88 N Main St (ⓣ860/927-4858; ❻), is a small, pleasant B&B. The *Bulls Bridge Inn*, 333 Kent Rd (ⓣ860/927-1000), is an inexpensive dinner and Sunday brunch-only **restaurant** serving classic American fare. Good for soups, sandwiches, and American and European desserts is the *Stroble Baking Company*, Main Street (ⓣ860/927-4073), but it's only open until 6pm.

Waterbury

At the very southern edge of Litchfield Hills, and certainly no part of them in spirit, **WATERBURY** – known to the Indians as "the place where no trees will grow" because of persistent flooding – valiantly celebrates its glorious past of brass-and coppermaking. That's not necessarily a reason to come, though if you do, you'll find the requisite history in the **Mattatuck Museum**, 144 W Main St (Tues–Sat 10am–5pm, Sun noon–5pm; closed Sun July–Aug; $4), which also includes a permanent collection of nineteenth- and twentieth-century art such as *Adirondack Landscape: Mount McIntire* by John Frederick Kennsett and Frederic Edwin Church's *Icebergs*. The rest of downtown is pleasing enough, with red-brick and white marble municipal buildings, including the **Chase Building** and the **Waterbury National Bank**, designed by Cass Gilbert, architect of the Woolworth Building and the George Washington Bridge in New York. Look, too, at 389 Meadow St, for the current home of the *Waterbury Republican-American* newspaper. The building is the town's **former main railroad station**, and is modeled on City Hall in Siena, Italy, with a tall campanile-style tower that is the city's most notable landmark. If you want to **stay** in Waterbury, *The House on the Hill*, 92 Woodlawn Terrace (☎203/757-9901; ❻), is a large 1888 home containing guestrooms and suites filled with antiques, and boasting fireplaces and an attractive wraparound porch, while *Seventy Hillside*, 70 Hillside Ave (☎203/596-7070; ❼), an elegant mansion with cozy rooms, fireplaces, and a sweeping staircase, is situated in a glorious park setting. *Dreschler's*, 25 Leavenworth St (☎203/573-1743), a **restaurant** open since 1868, offers a variety of German and American dishes (most under $15) in a delightful antique-filled dining room.

Northeastern Connecticut

Once a prosperous textile-manufacturing region which spewed out cotton and silk, the predominantly rural **northeastern corner** of Connecticut, bordering the Rhode Island and Massachusetts state lines, has remained almost entirely devoid of major development and large-scale tourism. Its rolling hills and blossoming orchards are best viewed by driving (or if you're game, biking) along the 32-mile stretch of scenic **Route 169**, from Canterbury to Woodstock – along the way, you'll also spot some of the redundant old mills and warehouses, many of which have been carefully restored or converted into businesses. The best detours are in **Coventry**, home of Revolutionary War hero Nathan Hale; **Lebanon**, whose historic village green stretches a mile along Rte-87; and **Putnam**, named after the famous Revolutionary General Israel Putnam, alleged to have made the famous "whites of their eyes" command at the Battle of Bunker Hill (see p.106). Bonanza **buses** (☎401/331-7500), originating in Providence, RI, run through the region, with stops at Willimantic and Danielson; **local transportation** is virtually non-existent. **The Northeast Connecticut Visitors' District**, 13 Canterbury Road, PO Box 145, Brooklyn, CT 06234 (limited hours; ☎860/779-6383 or 1-888/628-1228,

Ⓦwww.ctquietcorner.org), publishes several useful guides for visitors, including an accommodation list, a bicycle guide, and a "Waters Guide" of the lakes and ponds that dot the area, good for fishing and canoeing enthusiasts.

Scenic Route 169: Woodstock to Canterbury

PUTNAM, just off I-395 in the northeast corner of the region, has a bit of history to it, having been named for Revolutionary War general Israel Putnam, and having been an important stop on the Underground Railroad prior to the Civil War. After years in economic doldrums, it's now one of the hottest antique-shopping areas in the Northeast. Most of the shops are on or around Main Street, where the highlight is a former Victorian department store that has been renovated to form the **Antiques Marketplace**, with more than 300 dealers plying their trade. Apart from browsing the shops, there's little else of interest in Putnam. North of the town, on East Putnam Road, the 120-acre **Quaddick State Park** is a good place to relax, with a vast, 466-acre reservoir and a separate swimming pond, with ample opportunities for hiking, boating, and fishing.

Just north on Rte-169, peaceful **WOODSTOCK** is notable as the site of the 1846 **Roseland Cottage** (June to mid-Oct Wed–Sun 11am–5pm; $4), the former summer retreat of Henry C. Bowen, publisher of abolitionist weekly paper the *Independent*. The striking salmon-colored Gothic Revival residence, designed by English architect Joseph Wells, is particularly interesting for its steep gables, profuse Gothic tracery, stained-glass windows, and opulent interior – a suitable setting for Bowen to entertain four US presidents (Grant, Hayes, Harrison, and McKinley) at his lavish Fourth of July parties. The house, which contains its original furnishings, also includes an antique bowling alley.

Canterbury

A small community at the junction of routes 14 and 169, **CANTERBURY** is home to the **Prudence Crandall Museum** (April to mid-Dec Wed–Sun 10am–4.30pm; $2.50; Ⓣ860/546-9916), housed in an attractive 1805 home that became New England's first academy to admit black women. From 1834 to 1844 the academy was run by Baptist schoolmistress Crandall, who gained notoriety when she accepted a young African-American girl in her school. The residents' violent response – the building was stoned – led to the school's closure, and Crandall was taken to court, though later exonerated. There is a permanent display devoted to Crandall's life and work, and others on black history, abolitionism, and women's rights.

Practicalities

Places to stay in the area include the *King's Inn*, 5 Heritage Rd, Putnam (Ⓣ860/928-7961 or 1-800/541-7304; ❸), a friendly hotel with well-appointed rooms plus its own steakhouse, and the *Inn at Woodstock Hill*, 94 Plaine Hill Rd, Woodstock (Ⓣ860/928-0528; ❻), with spacious, yet cozy rooms. The *Inn* also boasts an excellent **restaurant**, which features a sumptuous and pricey French-influenced American menu, with entrées like poached salmon tarragon. Back in Putnam, *Mrs. Bridge's Pantry*, 136 Main St (Ⓣ860/963-70040; 11am–5pm, closed

Tues), is a British-style tearoom, serving Lapsang Soochong, Oolong, and everything in between. South towards Canterbury, in **Brooklyn**, the *Golden Lamb Buttery*, 499 Wolf Den Rd (ⓣ860/774-4423), offers an unusual (and expensive) dining experience, where diners meet at a set time in the barn, then are invited to take a hayride to view the pastoral setting. Dinner, accompanied by a singing guitarist, includes entrées like roast pork with apricots, garlic, and mushrooms.

Storrs, Mansfield, and Coventry

West on Rte-44, **STORRS** is home to the campus of the **University of Connecticut**, site of a few decent museums. The **Connecticut State Museum of Natural History**, 2019 Hillside Rd, next to the Gampel Pavilion (Mon–Fri 9am–4pm; free; ⓣ860/486-4460), with only somewhat interesting exhibits of mounted hawks and owls, insects, minerals, and mammals, and the occasional archeological display. Also on campus is the **William Benton Museum of Art** (Tues–Fri 10am–4.30pm, weekends 1–4.30pm; free; ⓣ860/486-4520), with a program of changing exhibits, and a permanent collection of over 4,000 items, which includes European and American paintings, among them works by Henry Ward Ranger, Ernest Lawson, Gustav Klimt, and Edward Burne-Jones; drawings, prints, and sculptures from the sixteenth century to the present day, and a large collection of theater drawings by Reginald Marsh. If you're green-thumbed, be sure not to miss the **University of Connecticut Greenhouses,** 75 N Eagleville Rd, Storrs (Mon–Thurs 9am–4pm, Fri 9am–3pm), a complex by the university's department of ecology and evolutionary biology, containing more than 3000 species of plants, including orchids, cacti, palm trees, a redwood, and even carnivorous aquatic plants. On Stone Mill Road, the **Gurleyville Grist Mill** (mid-May to mid-Oct Sun 1–5pm; free), by the Fenton River, built in 1830 to replace an earlier construction, contains a miller's house that was once the home of Governor Wilbur Cross, and now houses a small museum.

Just north, **MANSFIELD** has some of the area's better spots for **eating** and **accommodation**. The *Fitch House B&B*, 563 Storrs Rd (ⓣ860/456-0922; ❺), an elegant Greek Revival mansion, has three large, tastefully decorated rooms. Down the road, you can enjoy Continental cuisine at the moderate to steep *Altnaveigh Inn,* 957 Storrs Rd (ⓣ860/429-4490), an atmospheric country farmhouse, or dine more casually at *The Depot*, 57 Middle Turnpike/Rte-44 (ⓣ860/429-3663), in an original train depot setting popular with students from UConn.

Coventry

COVENTRY, west of Storrs, is another quiet former mill community, though with a decent selection of restaurants and shops, plus the **Nathan Hale Homestead**, 2299 South St (mid-May to mid-Oct Wed–Sun 1–4pm; $4), a three-story farmhouse rebuilt in 1776 by his father, Deacon Richard Hale, just after Hale was hanged by the British as an American spy. More Hale memorabilia can be viewed close by at the **Strong-Porter House**, 2382 South St (mid-May to mid-Oct Sat & Sun 1–5pm; $1), one-time home to Hale's maternal ancestors.

Coventry makes for a nice place to **stay**, with inns like the *Bird-in-Hand*, 2011 Main St (ⓣ860/742-0032; ❹), an attractive antique-filled Colonial house. Its **restaurants**, too, are good, including the *Bidwell Tavern*, 1260 Main St, South Coventry (☎860/742-6978), with all-American food in a historic tavern that dates back to 1822.

Willimantic and Lebanon

South of Coventry, on the Willimantic River, lies **WILLIMANTIC** (in Native American language, "land of the swift running waters"), yet another mill village, once home to the Willimantic Thread Company. The company's former complex contains the **Windham Textile and History Museum**, 157 Union St (June to mid-Oct Wed–Sun 1–4.30pm; rest of year Fri–Sun 1–4pm; $4), which preserves the thread-making machinery and workers' quarters typical of the time.

Straddling a village green that stretches more than a mile along Rte-87, **LEBANON** was home to one **Jonathan Trumbull**, ardent patriot and the only Crown-appointed governor to side with the Revolutionaries. It was his presence that encouraged a battalion of hussars under the leadership of the duc de Lauzun to camp here in 1780, awaiting Rochambeau and his men for the final push of the Revolutionary War. Two Trumbull homes are open to the public: the **Jonathan Trumbull House**, 169 W Town St (mid-May to mid-Oct Tues–Sat 1–5pm; $2), built in 1735 and furnished with period pieces; and the Georgian **Jonathan Trumbull Jr House** (mid-May to mid-Oct Sat & Sun 1–5pm; donation $2), built in 1769 by his son – a noted artist in his own right – and which contains intricate woodwork and a beautifully carved cherrywood banister in the main hall. Close by on West Town Street, you can see Trumbull Sr's **Revolutionary War Office** (June–Sept Sat & Sun 1.30–4.30pm; free), a two-room office and store which became the headquarters of the Council of Safety, which plotted strategy and coordinated supplies during the war.

6

Vermont

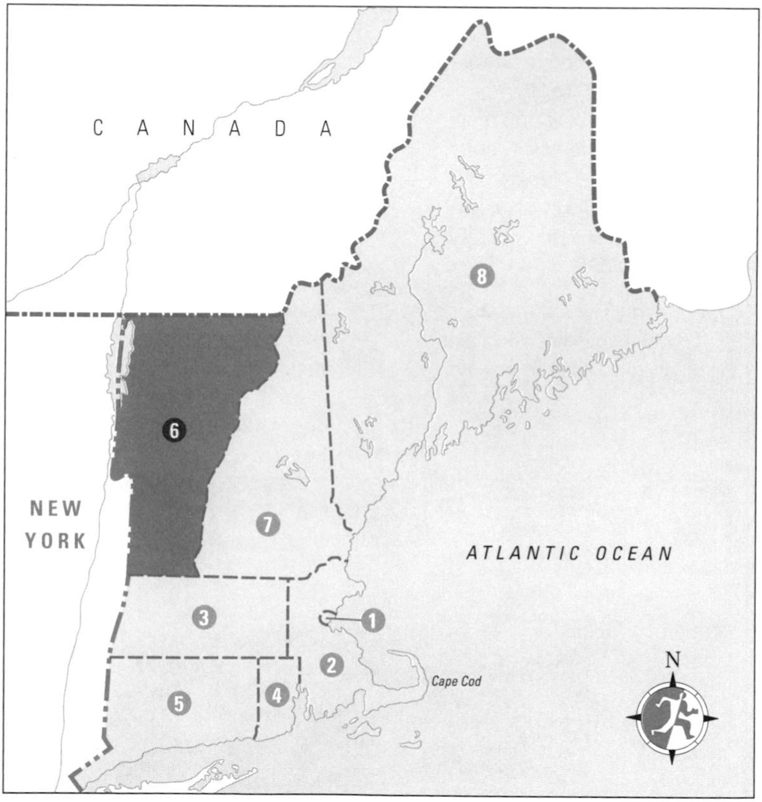
CANADA
NEW YORK
ATLANTIC OCEAN
Cape Cod
N
1
2
3
4
5
6
7
8

CHAPTER 6

Highlights

* **Long Trail** Walking across the entire state wins serious bragging rights for competitive hikers; for others, the magnificent vistas from Vermont's highest peaks will more than justify the effort. See p.397

* **Calvin Coolidge State Historic Site** He may not have been the most famous president, but Coolidge's presidential historic site is arguably the finest in the country. See p.398

* **Skiing** The state abounds with excellent mountains and facilities. See p.405

* **Montpelier** Relaxed, friendly, genuine, relatively tourist-free, bounded by rivers and a forest of tall trees – and the only state capital without a McDonalds. See p.413

* **Burlington** The perfect antidote for those charmed-out by Vermont's profusion of perfect villages: a real city, with a waterfront, a vibrant downtown, and the state's best restaurants and nightlife. See p.423

* **Shelburne Museum** Two centuries of American life stuffed into fifty acres of northern Vermont. See p.428

6

Vermont

In many ways, **Vermont** comes closer than any other New England state to fulfilling the quintessential image of small-town Yankee America, with its white churches and red barns, covered bridges and clapboard houses, snowy woods and maple syrup. No city manages a population of forty thousand (only Burlington even comes close) and the chief tourist attraction is none other than Ben and Jerry's ice-cream factory in Waterbury. Though rural, the landscape is not all that agricultural, and much is covered by verdant, mountainous forests (the state's name supposedly comes from the French *vert mont*, or green mountain). True, in certain areas, the bucolic image proffered can seem a bit packaged, but you probably won't tire of trawling the state's many scenic byways and village greens.

The people who choose to live here represent a number of seemingly disparate groups – hippies, diehard conservatives, taciturn codgers who have never left the state – who tend to band together to preserve their environment and lament the advent of yet another ski resort. However, their political philosophies remain fiercely in contrast, which became all too clear when Governor Howard Dean signed Vermont's **civil union** bill into law in 1999, making Vermont the first state in the US to sanction same-sex marriage. While the governor and the action were widely praised, giving proof to those who proudly proclaimed Vermont "the most progressive state in the nation," another, more conservative, contingent condemned Dean as a "coward" giving in to pressure from "flatlanders" – a derogatory term for Vermont residents transplanted from other parts. Although Dean narrowly won re-election in 2000, the debate rages on, and in front of many a dilapidated farmhouse it's possible to see signs reading "take back Vermont."

Its liberal voice could be traced to it being the youngest of New England's states, settled last, early in the eighteenth century. As French explorers worked their way down from Canada, American colonists began to spread north; but even as that rivalry died down, a further antipathy developed between settlers from New Hampshire and those from New York. The wealthy New York merchants who built fine homes along the Connecticut River Valley thought of themselves as "River Gods," but the hardy settlers of the lakes and mountains to the west had little time for their patrician ways. Their leader was the now-legendary Ethan Allen, who formed his Green Mountain Boys in 1770, proclaiming that "the gods of the hills are not the gods of the valley." When the Revolutionary War superseded such conflicts, this all-but-autonomous force captured Fort Ticonderoga from the British and helped to win the decisive Battle of Bennington. For fourteen years, Vermont was an independent republic (it was not one of the original thirteen states), with the first constitution in

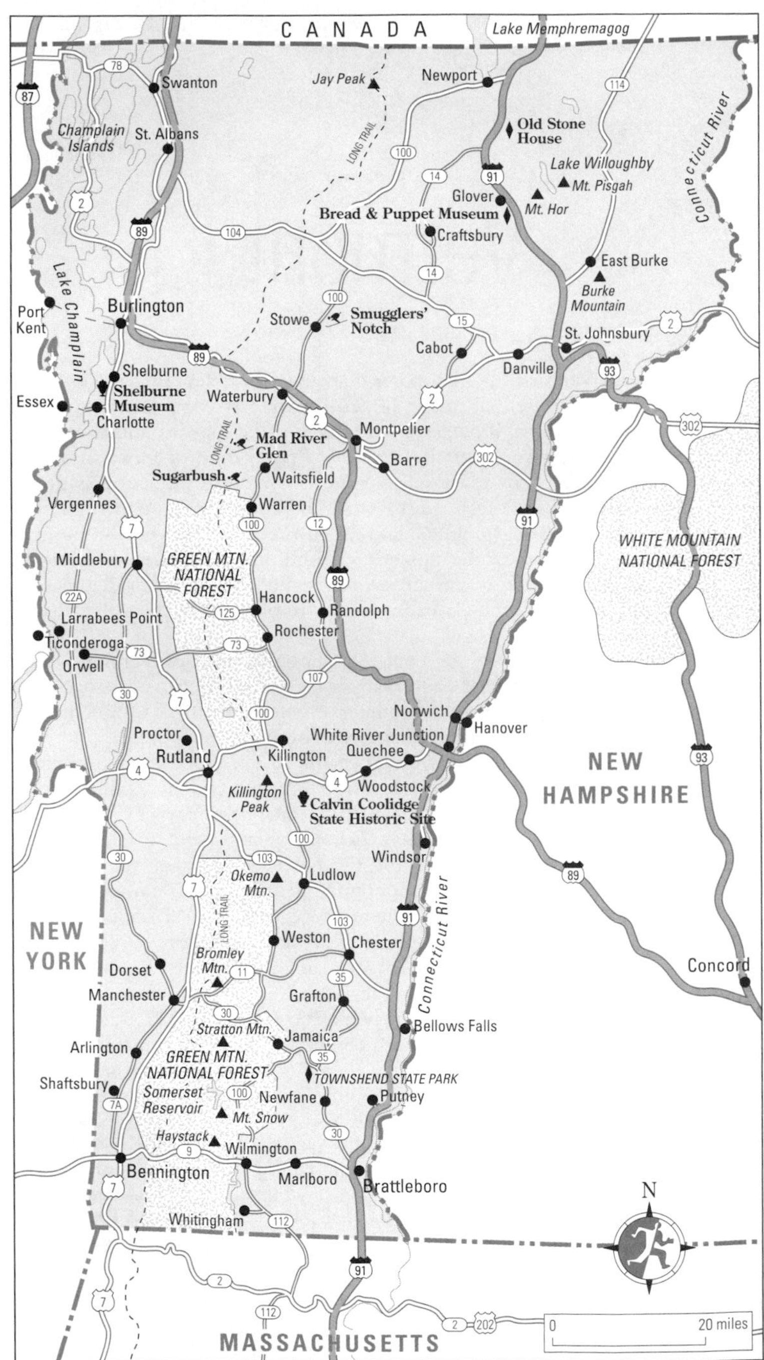
CANADA
Lake Memphremagog
Swanton
Jay Peak
Newport
Champlain Islands
St. Albans
LONG TRAIL
Old Stone House
Lake Willoughby
Mt. Pisgah
Glover
Mt. Hor
Bread & Puppet Museum
Craftsbury
Connecticut River
East Burke
Burke Mountain
Lake Champlain
Port Kent
Burlington
Stowe
Smugglers' Notch
Cabot
St. Johnsbury
Danville
Shelburne
Shelburne Museum
Essex
Charlotte
Waterbury
Montpelier
Mad River Glen
Barre
Sugarbush
Waitsfield
Vergennes
Warren
WHITE MOUNTAIN NATIONAL FOREST
Middlebury
GREEN MTN. NATIONAL FOREST
Hancock
Randolph
Larrabees Point
Rochester
Ticonderoga
Orwell
Norwich
Hanover
Proctor
White River Junction
Rutland
Killington
Quechee
NEW HAMPSHIRE
Woodstock
Killington Peak
Calvin Coolidge State Historic Site
Windsor
Okemo Mtn.
Ludlow
NEW YORK
Weston
Chester
Bromley Mtn.
Dorset
Concord
Manchester
Grafton
Bellows Falls
Stratton Mtn.
Jamaica
Arlington
GREEN MTN. NATIONAL FOREST
TOWNSHEND STATE PARK
Shaftsbury
Somerset Reservoir
Newfane
Putney
Mt. Snow
Haystack
Wilmington
Bennington
Marlboro
Brattleboro
N
Whitingham
MASSACHUSETTS
0
20 miles

the world to explicitly forbid slavery and grant universal (male) suffrage, but once its boundaries with New York were agreed, it joined the Union in 1791. Incidentally, the two seminal figures of the Mormon religion were born in Vermont shortly thereafter – Joseph Smith in 1805 and his lieutenant and successor Brigham Young in 1801.

With the occasional exception, such as the extraordinary assortment of Americana at the **Shelburne Museum** near Burlington (a lively city worth visiting in any case), there are few specific sights as such to seek out; indeed, tourism here is more activity-oriented, with most visitors coming during two well-defined seasons: to see the **fall foliage** in the first two weeks of October, and to **ski** in the depths of winter, when resorts such as **Killington** and **Stowe** (home of The Sound of Music's Von Trapp family) spring to life. For the rest of the year, you might just as well explore any of the state's minor roads that strike your fancy, confident that some impressive village will be around the corner, doubtless surrounded by lakes and mountains, and punctuated by lovely country inns in which to lodge overnight.

Southern Vermont

Of the two towns located at either end of Vermont's southern corridor – a mere forty miles from east to west linked by Hwy-9 – **Brattleboro**, probably your best bet around these parts, has the atmosphere of a college town, but not the college, while **Bennington** has the college but not the atmosphere. In between, the Green Mountain National Forest is dotted with traditional resort villages such as **Newfane** and **Mount Snow**, worth investigating though not for any extended period of time. Nearer to Bennington, hikers can pick up the **Long Trail** close to its southern terminus.

Brattleboro

If **BRATTLEBORO**, in the southeastern corner of the state, just off I-91, is your first taste of Vermont, it may come as a surprise. Not the quaint, 1950s-throwback village you might expect, its style owes more to the central and northern Massachusetts college towns, with numerous little stores and coffeehouses, not to mention the liveliest nightlife scene in the state outside of Burlington, all catering to the youthful and vaguely "alternative" population that has moved into the surrounding hills during the past few decades. Sitting beside the Connecticut River, the city lies near the site of **Fort Dummer**, the first English settlement in the state, which was built to protect neighboring Massachusetts from Indian raids. Gradually businesses and farms sprang up alongside the river and the fort, and in the 1800s Brattleboro enjoyed a modest reputation as a railroad town and a mill town, even briefly as a health care center, after pure springs were discovered along the Whetstone Brook. Rudyard Kipling penned his two *Jungle Books* here, giving the town its lone claim to fame, though one you can't really experience – the only site related to him is his former home **Naulakha**, used only for private parties.

Arrival, information, and city transit

If you're flying in, the closest major **airport** is in Hartford, Connecticut, approximately ninety minutes south of the Vermont border. Brattleboro is more easily reached by **train**; two Amtrak lines pass through daily, and the station is centrally located on Vernon Street. Meanwhile, Vermont Transit interlines with Greyhound **bus service** in these parts, and their terminal is located a couple of miles from downtown at the junction of US-5 (Putney Road) and I-91 (ⓣ802/254-6066). There are services from Brattleboro to Rutland, White River Junction, and destinations in Massachusetts such as Boston and Northampton. Brattleboro's **town bus**, The Brattleboro BeeLine (ⓣ1-888/869-6287), can get you to the bus terminal, as well as various other points in and around town. The single fare is 75¢.

The **Chamber of Commerce**, 180 Main St (Mon–Fri 9am–5pm, Sat 10am–2pm; ⓣ802/254-4565, ⓦwww.brattleboro.com), has a standard selection of brochures on area attractions, and operates an information **kiosk** on the Brattleboro Town Common, just north of town on Putney Road. The **Southeast Vermont Welcome Center**, on I-91 south of Brattleboro in Guilford (daily 7am–10pm; ⓣ802/254-4593, ⓦwww.southernvermont.com), can lay claim to being the most elaborate visitors' center in the whole state, and has plenty of information about the various attractions in the Brattleboro area.

6 VERMONT | Brattleboro

If you're interested in seeing the town from the **water** nearby, Connecticut River Safaris, north of town on Putney Road (Ⓣ802/257-5008), rents motorboats, canoes, and kayaks. The *Belle of Brattleboro*, also on Putney Road (June–Oct, plus special foliage cruises; $8; Ⓣ802/254-1263), seats about fifty people and runs cruises on the Connecticut with a narrative outlining its history, folklore, and wildlife. Sunset cruises are a bit lower key, with cruise guides letting the view speak for itself.

Accommodation

A number of chain and independently owned **motels** line Putney Road (US-5) north of town, though the independent ones are cheaper and have a bit more character. The best **camping** in the area is at *Hidden Acres Campground*, 792 Rte-5 (Ⓣ802/254-2098), two miles north along Putney Road after its intersection with Rte-9, where you'll pay $20 for one of its forty spacious sites.

Artist's Loft B&B and Gallery 103 Main St Ⓣ802/257-5181, Ⓦwww.theartistsloft.com. Tiny B&B above art gallery offers only one suite, but it's a luxurious two-room overlooking the Connecticut River. Private entrance, video and book libraries available. ❻

Colonial Motel & Spa Putney Road, US-5 and Rte-9 Ⓣ802/257-7733 or 1-800/239-0032, Ⓦwww.colonialmotelspa.com. This family-owned and -operated lodge has quality rooms with indoor pool, sauna, health club, and Redwood hot tub. Their in-house restaurant serves fine breakfasts (available at a discount for guests). ❸

Crosby House 1868 175 Western Ave Ⓣ802/257-4914 or Ⓣ1-800/528-1868, Ⓦwww.crosbyhouse.com. Restored Italianate Victorian home with luxurious accommodations: queen-sized beds, fireplaces, Jacuzzi, book and video library, and elegant breakfast settings. Geared more toward couples than families. ❻

Forty Putney Road 192 Putney Rd Ⓣ802/254-6268 or Ⓣ1-800/941-2413, Ⓦwww.putney.net/40putneyrd. Bed and breakfast in a French Baronial house decorated with antique furnishings. A lengthy, but manageable, walk to the town center. ❻

Lamplighter Motel 1336 Putney Rd Ⓣ802/254-8025. The basic rooms look like they haven't been redecorated since the 1960s, but they're clean and very cheap. One step up from a hostel. ❷

Latchis Hotel 50 Main St Ⓣ802/254-6300, Ⓦwww.brattleboro.com/latchis. Small, well-placed thirty-room Art Deco hotel which, depending on your mood, has either been elegantly restored or is in need of a lick of paint. Either way, the centrally controlled air conditioning means that the rooms are invariably either too hot or too cold. The four-person suites are good value, though. The hotel shares a roof with a good restaurant, *Lucca's Bistro* (see overleaf). ❹

The Town

Main Street spans the length of Brattleboro's diminutive downtown, lined with hip coffeehouses, art galleries, holistic apothecaries, and used-CD shops. You could spend time browsing in any of them, including the funky **Windham Art Gallery**, 69 Main St, an artists' co-operative, exhibiting an eclectic array of fine arts; the featured artists can occasionally be seen prowling the halls.

Just west off the southern end of Main Street is the center of Brattleboro's concentration of **bookstores**. Brattleboro Books, 36 Elliot St, purveys a staggering array of used volumes at incredibly cheap prices. Across the street, at 25 Elliot, Everyone's Books is part leftist bookstore, with special sections for indie zines and anarchic political tracts, and part community center for the local counterculture (it's located right downstairs from the *Common Ground* restaurant; see overleaf).

At the foot of Main Street, just before it intersects with Bridge Street, the 1930s Art Deco **Latchis Hotel** is worth a look for its old sign, a sleek chrome example of high Deco style, and interior trimmings, including a series of faux-Greek friezes, even if you have no intention of staying the night. Across the bridge, the **Brattleboro Museum and Art Center** (Tues–Sun noon–6pm; $3) occupies the old railroad station building. It features changing – and usually rather nondescript – exhibits on contemporary art and regional history, as well as several locally-made Estey organs, which the town produced and shipped to churches throughout the world during the early part of the twentieth century.

A couple of miles north of town, off I-91 in the village of Dummerston, is **Naulakha** (call the Landmark Trust for information ⓣ802/254-6868), the home of Rudyard Kipling. Kipling designed it and lived there from 1891 to 1896, writing some of his most celebrated works during the time, including *Captains Courageous* and *The First and Second Jungle Books*. Named after a temple in Janakpur, Nepal, the two-and-a-half-story shingle-clad house sits atop a hill, with views of the Connecticut River Valley and Mount Monadnock, across the border in New Hampshire. It's not regularly open for tours, but you may be able to call ahead and arrange one – or if you're a Kipling diehard, rent the place out and stay there (around $2000 a week; $250 a night in winter).

Eating, drinking, and entertainment

Brattleboro's **restaurants** cater to the youthful counterculture with a variety of styles, ranging from cosmopolitan and sophisticated to low-budget and health-conscious, rarely duplicated in Vermont. Most of the best options are located on or just off Main Street, and the same goes for **bars** in the town. A good place to stock up for a camping trip is the Brattleboro Food Co-op, 2 Main St (ⓣ802/257-0236), in the Brookside Plaza at the intersection of Canal and Main streets, which stocks a wide selection of organically produced foods. The local **music scene** bops with pretty good local acts on a nearly nightly basis; pick up a Thursday edition of the *Brattleboro Reformer* for an exhaustive listing of the week's events. The Latchis Theatre, next to the hotel of the same name, is a meticulously restored **cinema** that shows both studio and indie flicks.

Back Side Café 24 High St ⓣ802/257-5056. One of the town's older cafés, where most items on the menu are homemade. Good omelets, burgers, soups, and desserts at bargain prices.

The Café Beyond at Collected Works Bookstore 29 High St ⓣ802/254-2920. Above-average Euro-style sandwiches, espresso drinks, soups, and desserts served in a bright, industrial-chic setting surrounded by windows, books, and art. Takeout available. Closed Sun.

Carol's Main Street Café 71 Main St ⓣ802/254-8380. Chow on soups and fresh bagels while jawing with crusty locals at the old-fashioned lunch counter. Closed Sun.

Common Ground 25 Elliot St ⓣ802/257-0855. A variety of inventive daily specials, like Jamaican tofu jerk-adilla, are served at this long-established vegetarian restaurant, organic wherever possible, a gathering ground for the crunchiest of the crunchy. Live music provided by groups with names like Timeship Earth and Incognito Sofa Love complement the hippy-friendly atmosphere perfectly. Free food on Tuesdays.

Letamaya 51 Main St ⓣ802/254-2352. Small, relatively up-market restaurant using organic, natural, and locally produced ingredients in dishes with a distinctly Japanese flavor. Closed Sun & Mon "for meditation."

Lucca's Bistro 6 Flat St ⓣ802/254-4747. Good quality Tuscan-inspired cuisine, well presented, quite copious, and not overly expensive. Quality beer and tapas available at the *Cerveceria Lucca* upstairs. Salsa dancing (with no cover charge) on Friday nights.

McNeill's Brewery 90 Elliot St ⓣ802/254-2553. Rough-hewn bar where you can sample eleven different varieties of local microbrews, including Apocalypse Now and Old Ringworm. Closed Sun.

Mocha Joe's 82 Main St ⓣ802/257-7794. Good caffeine-filled beverages in a stylish basement below Main Street. A dark and dingy alternative to the comfy chairs and soothing music found at *Starbucks* and the like.

Mole's Eye Café 4 High St ⓣ802/257-0071. Brattleboro's most happening nightspot, bar, and dance floor, with a wide range of live music most nights – blues, Latin, R&B, jazz, calypso – for about a $4 cover. Talented locals enjoy the open-mike night every Thursday. Closed Sun.

Riverview Restaurant 3 Bridge St ⓣ802/254-9841. The tasty, cheap seafood makes for an ample meal, but the real treat is the outdoor dining available on the deck, accompanied by great views of the Connecticut River.

North from Brattleboro: Newfane and Grafton

Slightly inland and north from Brattleboro, **NEWFANE** and **GRAFTON** are two beautifully restored villages offering the best of small-town Vermont with their white churches and romantic inns. There's nothing of real note to see in the former, but it boasts a town green flanked by no less than three white-steepled buildings: the union hall, the Congregational church, and the county courthouse – pretty enough if you're stopping through. Just a few miles north of Newfane, **Townshend State Park** (ⓣ802/365-7500) provides excellent opportunities for both casual and serious hikers. Its trails, open May through mid-October, include the steep, rocky, 1680-foot climb to the summit of Bald Mountain; other trails are not quite as challenging. There's swimming, tubing, and canoeing at the nearby Townshend Dam. Jamaica State Park (ⓣ802/874-4600), situated on a bend in the West River half a mile from the town of Jamaica, has a trail along the river which follows the old track of the Brattleboro Railroad and leads to the Ball Mountain Dam. On two weekends a year (in late April and late September) the dam is opened and water released on to the river, an event which attracts numerous adrenaline-seeking canoeists and kayakers. The park is open from the end of April to mid-October.

If you're looking for a **place to stay** in Newfane, try the *West River Lodge & Stables*, 117 Hill Rd (ⓣ802/365-7745, ⓦwww.westriverlodge.com; ❺), a nineteenth-century farmhouse where you can eat hearty breakfasts around an open fireplace before hitting the nearby hiking trails. In Newfane itself, smack on the green, the *Four Columns Inn*, 230 West St (ⓣ1-800/787-6633, ⓦwww.fourcolumnsinn.com; ❻), has comfortable rooms, many with Jacuzzis, as well as a gourmet **restaurant** where the likes of Mick Jagger, Henry Kissinger, and Tom Cruise have sampled carefully prepared New American, Asian, and French cuisine. Also on the green, the *Old Newfane Inn* (ⓣ802/365-4427) – an old stagecoach stop – continues to serve up tasty capon and venison dinners to hungry travelers.

There's marginally more to do in Grafton than there is in Newfane, though still, the biggest draw here is a cheese shop, the **Grafton Village Cheese Company**, on Townshend Road, a half-mile south of the village (Mon–Fri 8am–4pm, Sat–Sun 10am–4pm; ⓣ802/843-2221 or 1-800/472-3866). Take some of their excellent cheddar with you on a picnic to nearby Townshend State Park. A little closer to town, the **Nature Museum**, 186 Townshend Rd (Sat–Sun 10am–4pm, also open Mon–Fri during fall foliage; $3; ⓣ802/843-2111), is a somewhat haphazard taxidermic and geological collection crammed into a former hall. If you've got time to kill and an abiding interest in local history, the Grafton Historical Society runs the **History Museum** at 147 Main St (late May to mid-Oct Sat–Sun 10am–noon & 2–4pm, daily during fall foliage; $3 donation), a collection of relics from Grafton homesteads, such as soapstones from the local quarries, textiles, and photos. They can also provide you with a helpful **walking tour** map. The *Old Tavern*, 92 Main St (ⓣ1-800/843-1801, ⓦwww.old-tavern.com; ❽), is an up-market **inn** and **restaurant** which sits in the heart of the tiny village and has been around since 1801, having accommodated such luminaries as Ulysses S. Grant, Nathaniel Hawthorne, and Henry David Thoreau. Continuing a few miles north on Rte-35, you will come to a junction and the pretty village of Chester (see p.399).

West to Bennington

Route 9 heads west from Brattleboro not forty miles to Bennington; the first town of any size along the way is uninspiring **MARLBORO**, just a few miles along. In midsummer, the town is besieged by chamber music fanatics, as it plays host to the **Marlboro Music Fest** (Ⓣ802/254-2394, www.marlboro-music.org). South along Hwy-100, the birthplace of Mormon prophet Brigham Young is marked by a granite monument at **WHITINGHAM**'s town common.

Further on, **MOUNT SNOW** and **HAYSTACK MOUNTAIN** provide perfectly fine places to ski, both officially part of the **Green Mountain National Forest**, though not getting quite as much press as the mountains' other major snowbound havens such as Killington and Stowe. Still, that may be reason enough to opt for it, if you're looking to avoid the crowds while having your choice of types of run. Mount Snow is the larger, and more popular, of the two, offering some 130 trails; Haystack, by contrast, has less than fifty. You'll also find plenty of outdoorsy stuff to occupy you here in the summer. For more information, contact the **Mount Snow Valley Chamber of Commerce**, West Main Street, Wilmington (Ⓣ802/464-8092 or 1-877/VTSOUTH, Ⓦwww.visitvermont.com).

Bennington

Little has happened in **BENNINGTON** in the past two hundred years to match the excitement of the days when Ethan Allen's Green Mountain Boys were based here and known as the "Bennington Mob." Today, despite the presence of the exclusive, arts-oriented **Bennington College** – which has seen the likes of hot young authors Bret Easton Ellis and Donna Tartt pass through its halls – the city is a sleepy town most notable for its rich Revolutionary history and one fine museum of American folk art.

Settled in 1761 on a rise by the Walloomsac River, overlooking the valley between the Green and Taconic mountains, the town became a leading nineteenth-century industrial outpost for paper mills, potteries, gristmills, and the largest cotton-batting mill in the US. That heritage is preserved today in **Old Bennington**, just up the hill from the center of town, and the one obvious spot to explore.

Arrival and information

Bennington is centered on the intersection of US-7 and Hwy-9, an intersection known locally as the "Four Corners." In town, Hwy-9 is referred to as Main Street, while the local stretches of US-7 above and below the Corners are called North and South streets. The nearest commercial **airport** is forty miles away in Albany, New York. The Vermont Transit **bus** terminal (Ⓣ802/442-4808) is in the center of town, one block from Main Street. There are services to New York (via Albany), Boston (via Rutland), and Burlington. A more convenient (and free) alternative if you're heading along Historic Route 7A is the Green Mountain Express (Ⓣ802/442-9458), which runs

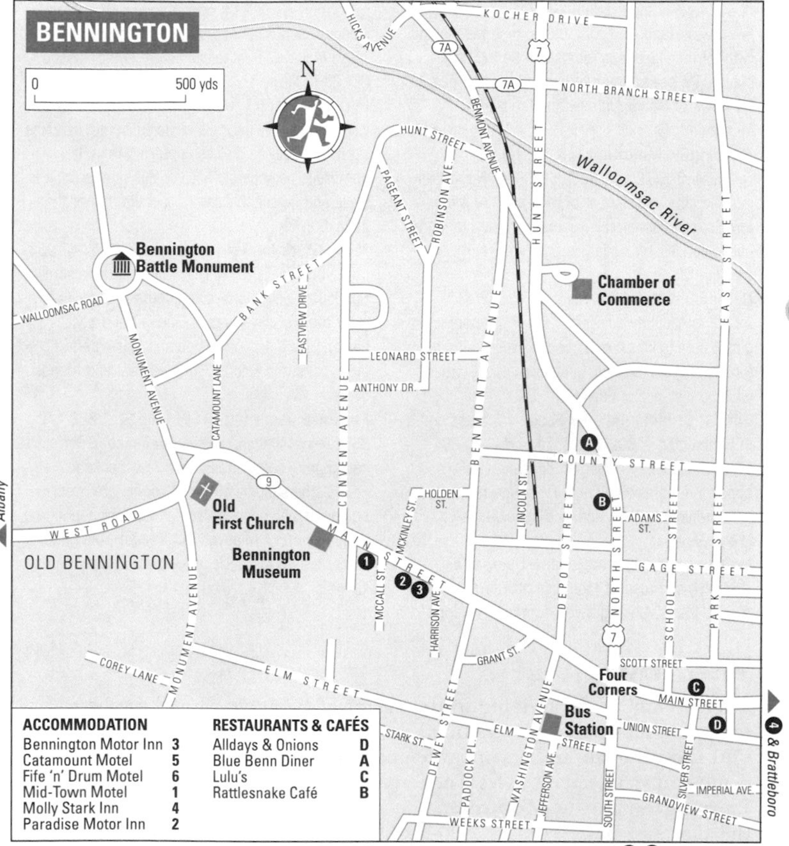

between Bennington, Manchester, and Rutland. The Bennington stop is at the Bank North parking lot.

The **Bennington Area Chamber of Commerce**, 100 Veterans Memorial Drive (Mon–Fri 9am–5pm; ⓣ802/447-3311, ⓦwww.bennington.com), should be your first stop for information on nearby and surrounding attractions; it has clean public restrooms to boot. There's also a **kiosk** with basic practical information at the Four Corners.

Accommodation

Cookie-cutter **budget motels** line South Street and West Main Street, and there are a few other options scattered about. Those who might prefer "name brand" chain motels will be disappointed in what the Bennington area has to offer (namely just a *Best Western* on Northside Drive), but its independent motels and hotels are generally clean and far less expensive than those found in other Vermont cities and towns.

Alexandra Inn Rte-7A and Orchard Road ⓣ802/442-5619 or 1-888/207-9386, ⓦwww.alexandrainn.com. Clean, restored Colonial with thirteen luxurious rooms and baths, fireplaces, TV, hearty gourmet breakfasts, and beautiful views of Mount Anthony and the Battle Monument. ❻

Bennington Motor Inn 143 W Main St ⓣ802/442-5479 or 1-800/359-9900. Family-run inn, the smaller neighbor of the *Paradise Motor Inn*. Sixteen comfortable rooms with the standard conveniences, plus complimentary in-room movies. ❹

Catamount Motel 500 South St ⓣ802/442-5977. Immaculate quarters, featuring a pool and a picnic area in which to barbecue. Rural setting (plenty of green spaces, in any case), yet within walking distance of downtown. ❸

Fife 'n' Drum Motel US-7 South, 1.5 miles south of Bennington ⓣ802/442-4074 or 442-4730, ⓦwww.sover.net/~toberua. Pleasant, well-appointed rooms with cable TV, coffee makers, and air conditioning. Pool, spa, and spacious lawn with grills. ❷

Greenwood Lodge Hostel and Campsites (HI/AYH) on Prospect Mountain off Rte-9 ⓣ802/442-2547, ⓔgrnwd@compuserve.com. Clean dorm beds with access to kitchen and recreation areas. $14, non-members $17. Twenty wooded campsites nearby do not include access to lodge facilities. Best to call before going. Closed Oct 23 to May.

Mid-Town Motel 107 W Main St ⓣ802/447-0189. Extremely basic efficiencies, somewhat less expensive and much less appealing than its numerous neighbors. Consider this one for its low rates and reasonably central location rather than its luxury. ❷

Molly Stark Inn 1067 E Main St ⓣ802/442-9631 or 1-800/356-3076, ⓦwww.mollystarkinn.com. Six double-occupancy guestrooms with quilts and claw-footed tubs in a cozy Queen Anne-style house, plus a self-contained and self-catering cottage facing the woods. Full breakfast and friendly owners. ❹

Paradise Motor Inn 141 W Main St ⓣ802/442-8351, ⓦwww.theparadisemotorinn.com. Perfectly satisfactory accommodation a few blocks from the Four Corners (some of the 76 rooms are even equipped with saunas). Heated outdoor pool and tennis courts. A relatively large hotel, so a good place to try if there are no vacancies elsewhere. ❹

The Town

There's nothing much doing in the center of Bennington, and the best place to begin your wanderings is around the western end of Main Street, in historic **Old Bennington**, an assortment of public and residential buildings done in all manner of architectural styles. The town's most prominent icon is nearby at the **Bennington Battle Monument**, 15 Monument Circle (daily: mid-April to late Oct 9am–5pm; $1.50), a 306-foot hilltop obelisk that commemorates the August 1777 Battle of Bennington. This pivotal conflict pitted the Continental Army against the superior forces of General Burgoyne, who had made it an objective to seize the arsenal depot at Bennington. The unexpected victory of the Revolutionaries bolstered their morale and debilitated Burgoyne's troops, contributing to their ultimate defeat at the subsequent Battle of Saratoga, the major turning point of the war. The monument is located on the hilltop that was the site of Burgoyne's objective (though the battle actually took place just over the Walloomsac River, in New York State). Just down Monument Avenue, **Old First Church**, Monument Circle, erected in 1805, abuts a well-preserved cemetery holding the grave of poet and adoptive Vermonter Robert Frost. His tombstone, well marked by directional signs, reads simply, "I had a lover's quarrel with the world," an epitaph that never ceases to amuse the church's many visitors.

East of here, the **Bennington Museum and Grandma Moses Gallery**, West Main Street (daily: June–Oct 9am–6pm; rest of year 9am–5pm; $6), contains a fine array of Americana, including several Tiffany lamps, what may be the oldest American flag in existence, and *The Wasp*, a 1925 luxury touring car, built in Bennington and the only surviving example of its kind. The highlight of the collection, however, is its exhibit on American folk artist Anna Mary

Robertson Moses, known popularly as **Grandma Moses**. Moses, who first exhibited her simple, pleasing representations of rural life at the age of 80, experienced a meteoric rise to fame in the worlds of high art and popular culture, and eventually lived to enjoy national adulation upon reaching her 100th birthday. In addition to the largest public collection of her work, the museum has a reconstruction of the schoolhouse she attended as a youngster, which displays many of her personal belongings, photographs, painting equipment, and awards.

Rte-7A splits off from US-7 and continues on to North Bennington, where three **covered bridges** – the Silk Road, Paper Mill Village, and the Burt Henry – span the Walloomsac River. This area is marked by reminders of late eighteenth-century industrial activity, notably the mill housing along Sage Street. Also here is the elaborate Greek Revival **Park-McCullough House**, Park and West streets (daily: late May to late Oct 10am–4pm, tours hourly; $8), a sumptuous 1864 mansion filled with most of its original period furnishings, including horse-drawn carriages and children's toys.

In the nearby village of Shaftsbury, the **Robert Frost Stone House Museum**, 121 Rte-7A (Tues–Sun 10am–5pm; $5), is yet another memorial to one of New England's favorite poets. The house should appeal to Frost-enthusiasts who are dying to see the rooms in which poems like *Stopping by Woods on a Snowy Evening* were crafted, and the surrounding scenery which no doubt provided valuable inspiration. For others, it will be just another pretty countryside dwelling in a part of the world where they're certainly not in short supply.

Eating, drinking, and entertainment

There's not an overwhelming variety when it comes to **restaurants** in Bennington, most seeming to serve the simple omelets-and-burgers-type fare found in most diners. Nights are fairly quiet, too, as the college population rarely gets too rowdy.

Alldays and Onions 519 Main St ☎802/447-0043. Creative meat and fish dishes at reasonable prices, served with bread from the in-house bakery. Essentially a breakfast and lunch place, although it's also open for dinner Thurs–Sat.

Blue Benn Diner 102 Hunt St ☎802/442-5140. Authentic, 1940s-era diner draws a diverse crowd of hard-boiled locals and artsy students. In a break with the unwritten code of diners, vegetarian dishes feature on the menu. Open from 6am daily.

Lulu's 520 Main St ☎802/442-9833. "Unusual meals from around the world," which basically translates to meatloaf with mashed potatoes and shepherd's pie. You can't complain about the prices, though.

Madison Brewing Co 428 Main St ☎1-800/44BREWS. Fun, stylish brewpub with hearty burgers and six varieties of in-house beer. Live blues most nights of the week. Open daily until 2am.

McMorland's 782 Harwood Hill, near the intersection of US-7 and Historic Rte-7A ☎802/442-7500. Remodeled barn turned gourmet restaurant, located on a hill with excellent views of New York, New Hampshire, and Massachusetts. Excellent – though expensive – steaks and seafood.

Rattlesnake Café 230 North St ☎802/447-7018. A popular Mexican joint – about the closest you'll come to exotic cuisine in Bennington.

The Green Mountains

The **Green Mountains** that form the backbone ofVermont are not as harsh as New Hampshire's White Mountains, though the forests for which they are named are invariably buried in snow for most of the winter, and the higher roads are liable to be blocked for long periods. For the most part, the sides and the summits are covered with evergreens such as spruces, hemlocks, and firs, the inspiration to the French colonialists for the state's name (and, more obviously, the name of the range). Here and there, denuded patches mark where trees have been shaved away to create ski runs, but otherwise the usually peaceful Rte-100 and US-7, which run along the base of the mountains to the east and west respectively, offer unspoiled mountain views as well as a few charming towns along the way. When accessible (mostly in summer), the mountains are excellent opportunities for hiking, camping, fishing, canoeing, and swimming.

The Green Mountain National Forest runs from the southern border of Vermont nearly up to the state capital, Montpelier, interrupted only around the city of **Rutland**, notable for a nearby museum devoted to the work of **Norman Rockwell**. West of Rutland lies **Killington**, the state's most popular ski resort and one of the access points to the **Long Trail**, a hiking trail which cuts across the Green Mountains on its way from Massachusetts to the Canadian border. In the first stretch of the mountains, outside of the expected quaint towns, there's not much to divert you other than **Manchester**, the outlet shopping center ofVermont, fairly tacky but with an authentic enough historic core. The second stretch, however, has probably the most interesting, and certainly the most cosmopolitan, village in the area, **Middlebury**, home to a noted university of the same name.

Scenic Hwy-100

North of Mount Snow, Hwy-100 snakes along the east of the Green Mountains and continues up to Killington (see p.405) and beyond. Along the way, the road passes through its share of predictably charming villages, of which **Weston** stands out as being one of the more attractive. A little farther north, the town of **Ludlow** is at the base of **Okemo Mountain**, another of the state's fine ski resorts. A slight detour south along Rte-103 brings you to **Chester**, a pretty enough village in its own right and the departure point for scenic train rides on the **Green Mountain Flyer**. Back on Hwy-100, between Ludlow and Killington, **Plymouth Notch** is the home of one of the finest presidential historic sites in the country, the **Calvin Coolidge State Historic Site**. Past Killington, Hwy-100 continues to hug the eastern edge of the Green Mountains, passing through the pleasant town of **Rochester**, where there are some good places to stay.

Weston

One of the prettier villages along Hwy-100, **WESTON** spreads beside a little river and is centered on an idyllic green, where a stone slab commemorates the seventeen local soldiers who were killed on the same day during the Civil War,

store (where Coolidge's father was storekeeper) give the impression that there was an actual town here, too.

Practicalities

The **Okemo Valley Regional Chamber of Commerce**, on Rte-103 in the Okemo Market Place (ⓣ802/228-5830, ⓦwww.okemovalleyvt.com), is an excellent source of information and advice, particularly if you've arrived in the area without pre-booked accommodation; they'll do their best to find something suitable, even during the busiest times of the year. A **local bus** called The Town and Village Bus (ⓣ1-888/869-6287) connects Ludlow to Okemo Mountain.

Ludlow has no shortage of **places to stay**, although you should obviously plan ahead if you intend to arrive during the ski season or fall foliage. Luxurious lodgings within a mile of the lifts include the *Andrie Rose Inn*, 13 Pleasant St (ⓣ802/228-4846 or 1-800/223-4846, ⓦwww.andrieroseinn.com; ❻), and the *Governor's Inn*, 86 Main St (ⓣ802/228-8830 or 1-800/468-3766, ⓦwww.thegovernorsinn.com; ❻). Also close to the slopes, the *Best Western Ludlow Colonial Motel*, 93 Main St (ⓣ802/228-8188, ⓦwww.bestwesternludlow.com; ❹), has 48 comfortable rooms. The *Happy Trails Motel*, one mile south of town on Rte-103 (ⓣ802/228-8888 or 1-800/228-9984; ❹), has rooms with balconies and views of Okemo Mountain, as well as three self-catering suites and two cottages. Ludlow is one of the relatively few Vermont towns to have a **youth hostel**, the *HI-Trojan Horse Hostel*, 44 Andover St (open all year; ⓣ802/228-5244 or 1-800/547-7475; $17 for dorm beds).

Finding a reasonable place to **eat** after an exhausting day on the slopes should not be too difficult. *Wicked Good Pizza*, 117 Main St (ⓣ802/228-4131), sells New York-style pizza, calzone, sandwiches, and other stomach-fillers, which can be delivered free of charge if you can't be bothered to budge from your hotel room. Slightly more effort is required to eat at *Sam's Steakhouse*, Rte-103 (ⓣ802/228-2087), but the steaks and prime rib are worth it. For coffee, hot chocolate, soups, and the like, head for *A State of Bean*, in the Okemo Market Place (ⓣ802/228-2326), where the cozy atmosphere and comfy couches are welcome during the winter months.

Chester

It's easy enough to miss tiny **CHESTER**, at the junction of routes 103, 11, and 35, twelve miles south of Ludlow, though its prototypical Vermont charm may well draw you in. If so, drop by to see the chatty folks at the **Historical Society** on Main Street and Chester Green who can give you a walking-tour brochure to the historic houses scattered about town. Besides wandering through, you can jump aboard the **Green Mountain Flyer** (June–Aug Tues–Sun, mid-Sept to mid-Oct daily; 1 departure at 12.10pm; $12; ⓦwww.rails-vt.com), a sightseeing train that runs two-hour round-trips down to Bellows Falls, right at the New Hampshire border. The engine chugs along slowly, crossing rivers and passing covered bridges at a leisurely pace, leaving lots of time to take in the scenery, which is spectacular in the fall.

There is a good range of predictably quaint **accommodation** in Chester, much of it around the village green. The *Inn Victoria*, Main Street (ⓣ802/875-4288 or 1-800/732-4288, ⓦwww.innvictoria.com; ❻), goes to town on the Victorian theme with its ornate and comfortable rooms, although the friendly New Jersey owners are about as un-Victorian as they come. You could also try the *Chester House Inn*, 166 Main St (ⓣ1-888/875-2205,

Chester's gentleman robber

In 1886 began a dark, sixteen-year period of Chester's otherwise unremarkable history during which almost every store on Main Street was burgled at least once – the unfortunate Pollard's General Store being hit no less than six times. In the absence of an official police force in those days, the Board of Selectmen was charged with the responsibility of catching the thief, and First Selectman **Clarence Adams**, who was also a state legislator, library deacon, bank incorporator, and farm owner, took a particular interest in solving the mystery. He collaborated on precautionary measures with local businessmen, but all to no avail, as the rash of burglaries continued. Finally, one local proprietor devised an elaborate trap which involved rigging a shotgun to a window favored by the thief so that it would fire the gun when opened, a plan he was sure that Adams would approve of had the Selectman not been out of town when he thought of it. On July 29, 1902, news broke that Chester's most respected citizen, Clarence Adams, had been shot and wounded in the leg by highwaymen. It did not take long for the real truth to surface: Adams was Chester's notorious burglar. "What I have done I attribute to a spirit of adventure that was born in me," explained Adams in his confession. Sentenced to ten years in state prison for his multiple crimes, Adams died of pneumonia after two.

Ⓦwww.chesterhouseinn.com; ❺), which has seven rooms with private baths, each decorated in a different style and color. Just off the green, *Rose Arbour* (Ⓣ802/875-4766; ❺) is a pretty B&B with an attached tearoom; the top floor is a five-room suite, complete with kitchen. About one mile west of town along Rte-11, the *Motel-in-the-Meadow*, 936 Rte-11 (Ⓣ802/875-2626, Ⓦwww.motelinthemeadow.com; ❹), is a friendly "mom and pop" motel with perfectly comfortable, well-kept rooms and a small crafts shop featuring rag dolls made by Pat, the gregarious owner. The best place to **eat** in town is *Raspberries and Tyme*, on the green (Ⓣ802/875-4486), serving large portions of creative salads, soups, and sandwiches.

Rochester

Smack on Rte-100, some twenty miles north of Killington, lies pleasant **ROCHESTER**, a good base for exploring the Green Mountains, thanks to its absence of tourist traffic and a few nice places to stay. Of these, most central is the *Cooper-Webber House* (Ⓣ802/767-4742; ❹), right on the village green, an eighteenth-century home decorated in high-Yankee style, with white walls, sturdy wooden furniture, and traditional open kitchen. South of town, the unpretentious *New Homestead* (Ⓣ802/767-4751; ❷) has a lived-in appearance, five comfortable, simply decorated rooms, and good breakfasts. Finally, there's the *Apple Hill Farm* (Ⓣ802/767-6088; ❹), the most secluded option, on Rte-73 just off Rte-100 about three miles out of town. It is an 1850s farmhouse, with wooded hiking paths, grazing sheep, and a three-story barn in the back.

Arlington and Historic 7A

US-7 and **Historic Route 7A** parallel each other as they run from Bennington north to Manchester, though the latter is the preferable path to take, not only a more picturesque drive but with a few notable stopoffs along the way. The great spine of the Green Mountains rises up to the east, with the

Taconics somewhat more irregularly splayed out along the west, putting it smack in the so-called "Valley of Vermont."

About halfway up Rte-7A, the small town of **ARLINGTON** is the former home of illustrator Norman Rockwell, who created some of his most memorable *Saturday Evening Post* covers while living here between 1939 and 1954. Though there is an **exhibit** in his honor here (daily: May–Oct 9am–5pm; $2; Ⓣ802/375-6423), it only contains models of what he painted rather than actual paintings, and is easily missed. Four miles north, the **Equinox Sky Line Drive** (May–Oct; $8 toll per car and driver, $2 per additional passenger; Ⓣ802/362-1114) branches off the highway, a six-mile stretch that winds and elbows its way around Mount Equinox, eventually reaching the 3816-foot summit, which offers views clear across to New Hampshire and Maine. Although the view is impressive, it's worth pointing out that in a region so rich in scenery, it arguably doesn't justify the cost.

Running alongside Rte-7A are the tracks of the old **Rutland Railway**, built in the 1850s and setting Vermont on its way toward prominence as a crossroads for north–south New York–Montréal and east–west Boston–Chicago rail traffic. "The Rutland" still traverses Bennington County, but its track bed is in need of such extensive repairs that a 10mph speed limit restricts the line to local freight use. Passenger traffic was mostly phased out by 1950.

Practicalities

There is a **visitors' center** in Arlington on Rte-7A next to Stewarts convenience store, with all of the usual maps and brochures. The Green Mountain Express, a free **bus service** which runs between Bennington and Manchester four times daily, also leaves from Stewarts, while Vermont Transit buses leave from in front of the town hall.

There is **accommodation** both in Arlington and along Rte-7A. The lovely landscaped grounds and two pet llamas at the *West Mountain Inn*, about half a mile west of Arlington on Rte-313 (Ⓣ802/375-6516, Ⓦwww.westmountaininn.com; ❼) will, for some, excuse the telephone- and TV-free rooms and hefty price tag. The *Arlington Inn*, Rte-7A (Ⓣ802/375-6532 or 1-800/443-9442; ❺), is another very comfortable place to stay, this time in the middle of town. Cheaper lodgings can be found north of Arlington on Rte-7A at *Cut Leaf Maples Motel* (Ⓣ802/375-2757, Ⓔcutleafsandy@webtv.net; ❷) and the *Governor's Rock Motel* (closed Dec–May; Ⓣ802/442-4737, Ⓦwww.rockmotel.com; ❹). You can **camp** at *Camping on the Battenkill*, less than one mile west of Arlington (Ⓣ802/375-6663 or 1-800/830-6663), which has 111 sites starting at $19. The **restaurant** at the *West Mountain Inn* serves gastronomic six-course dinners for $38. Otherwise, grab a soggy sandwich at Stewarts.

Manchester and around

The last town on Rte-7A before it merges with US-7 is **MANCHESTER**, which has served as a summer resort hot spot for more than two hundred years, a fact evidenced by the town's ritzy accommodation and numerous shopping opportunities. Manchester and the surrounding area is also well situated for outdoor pursuits, especially skiing on nearby **Bromley** and **Stratton** mountains, and **fly-fishing** in its many trout streams, particularly the Batten Kill River. It's no small coincidence that **Charles Orvis**, founder of fly-rod manufacturer Orvis Company, is a Manchester native. A visit to the company's recently opened flagship store is also a worthwhile excursion, even if you have no intention of making a purchase.

The Town

Route 7A heads right through the town center, known as **Manchester Village**; the first spot of interest here is **Historic Hildene** (daily: mid-May to Oct 9.30am–5.30pm; $5 for grounds, $10 for tour; ⓦwww.hildene.org), the 24-room Georgian Revival mansion belonging to longtime Manchester resident Robert Todd Lincoln, son of Abraham Lincoln and a prominent diplomat and businessman in his own right. It's a magnificent estate, set on more than four hundred acres, and many of the Lincoln family's personal effects – hairbrushes, mirrors, and such – are on display inside, along with a working antique pipe organ. More Vermont residents are celebrated at the **Gallery North Star**, Rte-7A a block north of the Equinox (daily 10am–5pm; ⓣ802/362-4541), which shows paintings, sculptures, and limited-edition prints of local artists, as does the somewhat larger and less Vermont artist-centric **Southern Vermont Art Center**, Rte-7A (Tues–Sat 10am–5pm, Sun noon–5pm; ⓣ802/362-1405).

Farther up Rte-7A is **Manchester Center**, where **Northshire Bookstore** ranks as one of the finest independent bookstores in New England. The flagship **Orvis Store**, a little farther north on Rte-7A (ⓣ802/362-3750), was opened in 2002, and doubles as a shrine to the company's locally born founder. As well as the extravagantly expensive fly-fishing rods, there's a trout-filled pond for casting demonstrations and beautiful handcrafted hunting rifles, yours for $10,000 and up. Go half a mile back down Rte-7A to the **Orvis Factory Outlet**, opposite the Equinox at 74 Union St (ⓣ802/362-6455), to pick up last year's models for around fifty percent less.

On a less commercialized note, the **Vermont Institute of Natural Science**, 109 Union St (ⓣ802/362-4374), offers natural history walks around the region. The **Bushee Battenkill Valley Farm**, 2545 Richville Rd (hours and days vary; ⓣ802/362-4088), is more entertaining, with its demonstrations of wool processing and milking, and its petting corrals. **Riley Rink at Hunter Park**, on Rte-7A (ⓣ802/362-0150), functions as an Olympic-sized ice rink during winter and a performing arts center in summer; throughout July and August, the Vermont Symphony Orchestra (ⓣ802/864-5741 or 1-800/VSO-9293) also plays here.

Skiing: Bromley and Stratton

The two **ski resorts** within striking distance of Manchester, both a short drive into the Green Mountains, offer quite different winter vacation experiences. The **Bromley Mountain Resort**, six miles east of Manchester on Rte-11 (one-day lift tickets $46 midweek, $52 weekend; ⓣ802/824-5522, ⓦwww.bromley.com), is the archetypal family resort – though whatever your level or age, you may want to avoid Bromley on Thursday afternoons, when Manchester's schoolchildren have time off to learn how to ski on many of the resort's 43 trails. Larger and slightly higher than Bromley, the **Stratton Mountain Resort** (one-day lift tickets $59 midweek, $72 Sat, $69 Sun; ⓣ802/297-2200 or 1-800/STRATTON, ⓦwww.stratton.com) ranks right up there with Killington and Stowe as one of Vermont's premier ski destinations. Although it's certainly a better choice for serious skiers than Bromley, you should also be aware that this far south you may be sliding on artificial snow the majority of the time.. There is also good **cross-country skiing** on the twenty-plus miles of trails at the Stratton Nordic Center, some of the routes weaving through secluded forests and others cutting across open countryside.

Practicalities

Vermont Transit **buses** (ⓣ802/362-1226) pass through several times a day, either on their way north to Rutland and Burlington or south to Bennington and Albany, stopping at the Village Valet launderette in Manchester Center. Meanwhile, the **Green Mountain Express** (ⓣ802/442-9458) provides a local service to Bennington, Rutland, and the ski resorts at Bromley and Stratton during the winter season (Dec 1 to April 15). You'll find plenty of information at the **Manchester and the Mountains Chamber of Commerce**, 5046 Main St, Suite 1, Manchester Center (ⓣ802/362-2100, ⓦwww.manchestervermont.net), or the Visitors Information Center on the green nearby.

Manchester's resort status weighs heavily on the rates at the area's **inns and motels**. One of the swankiest digs in town – which just got swankier with the recent addition of a new spa – is the rambling, colonnaded *Equinox*, Rte-7A (ⓣ802/362-4700 or 1-800/362-4747, ⓦwww.equinoxresort.com; ⑨), full of restored Victorian-style rooms and upscale amenities. Of course, the truly discriminating visitor will stay next door at the *Charles Orvis Inn*, which is part of the same resort. A measly $600-plus a night gets you access to a billiards room, a self-serve honor bar (with cigars), complimentary copies of *Millionaire* magazine, and numerous other luxuries, all in the former home of Charles Orvis himself. More moderately priced lodgings, though still not exactly cheap, include the *Reluctant Panther Inn*, West Road (ⓣ802/362-2568 or 1-800/822-2331, ⓦwww.reluctantpanther.com; ⑧), which has splendid rooms with modern furnishings and optional fireplaces and Jacuzzis, and the *1811 House*, right across the street (ⓣ802/362-1811 or 1-800/432-1811, ⓦwww.1811house.com; ⑥), with fourteen immaculate rooms, each with private bath and shower, plus friendly owners and home-baked cookies. Relatively inexpensive accommodation can be found along routes 7, 11, and 30, including the *Four Winds Country Motel*, Rte-7A (ⓣ802/362-0905 or 1-877/456-7654, ⓦwww.fourwindscountrymotel.com; ④), which boasts large rooms and better-than-expected service. The *Stamford Motel*, Rte-7A, Manchester Center (ⓣ802/362-2342, ⓦwww.stamfordmotel.com; ④), is a tastefully decorated budget motel, including a heated pool, and great mountain views from most rooms. The longstanding, family-run *Aspen Motel*, north on Rte-7A

Route 7: north to Rutland

Shortly after the end of Rte-7A, US-7 opens up into the "Valley of Vermont," between the Green and Taconic mountain ranges, making for a lovely drive, though there are few convenient stopping places, and the presence of a four-lane highway doesn't encourage a leisurely pace.

If you're looking to stop longer, **camping** can be done at the **Emerald Lake State Park**, about nine miles north of Manchester on US-7 (mid-May to mid-Oct; ⓣ802/362-1655), which offers 105 campsites, 36 lean-tos, and easy access to the Long Trail, all on 430 acres that sit alongside Dorset Mountain. Unfortunately, the traffic noise from US-7 imposes upon the tranquility. The 84-acre **Lake Shaftsbury State Park**, two miles south of Arlington on Rte-7A (mid-May to early Sept; ⓣ802/375-9978), is farther from the highway, and it has a developed beach, too.

(☎802/362-2450; ❹), has comfortable rooms, a pool, and a two-bedroom cottage with kitchen and fireplace for family or group stays.

As with the town's accommodation, the **places to eat** in Manchester tend to be upscale and pricey – albeit rather good. On Rte-7A, try the *Little Rooster Café* (☎802/362-3496) for European cuisine, *Ye Olde Tavern* (☎802/362-0611) for authentic Yankee cooking, and the *Panther Bar*, in the *Reluctant Panther Inn*, for good bar fare along the meat-and-potatoes line. And for all-day breakfasts, or at least until closing time at 1pm, *Up for Breakfast & Beyond*, 4935 Main St (☎802/362-4204), is the obvious choice.

Rutland

When Vermonters describe **RUTLAND**, halfway between Bennington and Burlington along US-7, as "a little bit of New Hampshire in Vermont," it is not meant as a compliment. Rather, the indictment is of a bland town dominated by a steady, though modest, industrial base and afflicted by a burgeoning strip-mall aesthetic. It is, in fact, the state's second largest city after Burlington, with a population of about thirty thousand, most of whom are local laborers. Rutland's history as a marble-manufacturing center is still evident in its extensive use in the construction or embellishment of its downtown buildings. You may very well pass through, as Rutland is a key travel hub, but passing through is about all you'd need – or want – to do here.

Rutland's few attractions lie outside of town, most notably the **Norman Rockwell Museum**, east along US-4 (daily 9am–5pm; $3; ☎802/773-6095), which displays more than two thousand reproductions of Rockwell paintings, including early material and all of his *Saturday Evening Post* covers. It's a well-contextualized retrospective of his work, which is at times irritatingly wholesome but nevertheless an important contribution to American graphic art. The **Vermont Marble Exhibit**, 62 Main St (daily: mid-May to late Oct 9am–5.30pm; $6; ☎802/459-2300 or 1-800/427-1396), in the town of **PROCTOR**, northeast of Rutland, has two stories of displays on the state's favorite rock. The displays are a treasure trove of kitsch, particularly the "Hall of Presidents," featuring inexpertly carved marble busts of the 41 chief execs; a vast warehouse filled with marble kitchen and bathroom fixtures; and a hilariously self-serious 1950s-documentary-style film on the history of Vermont marble. A short drive southwest from Proctor, the **Wilson Castle** (daily: late May to mid-Oct 9am–6pm; $7) is an intriguing relic of an aristocrat's past glory. The castle was built in 1867 by Dr. John Johnson, who had married into English nobility and decided to take advantage of his wife's fortune by constructing a castle in a "blend of European styles." He spared no expense, recruiting the best craftsmen and materials from across Europe. The Wilson family owns it today, having added to the already oversized manor complete with Italian woodwork and stained-glass ceilings. One of the strangest rooms that the Wilsons completed is the "art gallery," constructed before they realized that they had no *art*. Now it contains a small collection of works by local artists and designers. Upstairs in the bedrooms, the paint is peeling a bit, adding strangely to the air of faded grandeur.

Practicalities

Trains call in at the station in the Rutland Plaza, Merchants Row; the bus terminal is in the center of town at 122 Merchants Row (☎802/773-2774). A

local bus company called The Bus (☎802/773-3244) can get you to Killington, if you want to base yourself here for ski season. The **Rutland Region Chamber of Commerce**, 256 N Main St (☎802/773-2747 or 1-800/756-8880, Ⓦwww.rutlandvermont.com), open year-round, is your best bet for information.

Aside from the standard hotel and motel chains, most of Rutland's **places to stay** are nondescript, independent motels, but they're generally cheap, clean, and located close to major highways. Among the almost indistinguishable accommodation that lines US-7 are the *Cold River Motel* (☎802/747-6922; ❷), the *Sun-Set Motel* (☎1-800/231-1709 or 802/773-2784; ❸), and the *Green-Mont Motel* (☎802/775-2575; ❷). *Iröquois Land* (May to mid-Oct; $20; ☎802/773-2832), three miles south of Rutland in Clarendon, is an adequate **campground**, though it tends to be dominated by the RV crowd.

Should you be waiting for a bus or train, there are, surprisingly, a few quite good **places to eat** interspersed among the fast-food joints. *Sweet Tomatoes Trattoria*, 88 Merchant's Row (☎802/747-7747), has light, modern Italian dishes in a sleek setting. The selection of vino at *Bistro Cafe's* wine bar, 103 Merchant's Row (☎802/747-7199), is excellent, as is its continental menu, though both are on the expensive side. The *Coffee Exchange*, Merchant's Row at Center Street (☎802/775-3337), is good for a light snack and a caffeinated beverage, with the added advantage of being near enough to the bus station to be able to see your bus arriving. *Pony's*, on Center Street (☎802/773-6171), is an occasionally raucous bar and dance venue, featuring **live music**.

Killington

Twelve miles east of Rutland off US-4, **Killington Resort** (☎802/422-6200 or 1-800/621-6867, Ⓦwww.killington.com), has grown out of nothing since 1958 to become the most popular ski resort in the state. Indeed, Killington is often considered to be the eastern equivalent of Vail in the west, and the resort does provide the longest ski and snowboarding season in the eastern US (especially since the expansion of its snowmaking facilities by thirty percent in 2001). Killington's permanent population is still tiny (around fifty), but it's estimated that in season there are enough beds within twenty miles to accommodate some ten thousand people each night. Sometimes called the "Beast of the East," on account of its size – its 200 trails sprawl over seven mountains – and its notoriously rowdy nightlife, Killington sports a freewheeling and wild attitude that can be fun, if a bit dangerous in the early season. Lift tickets cost $49 per day or $1199 per season. A less boisterous option is nearby **Pico Mountain**, along US-4 (☎1-800/621-6867), which is officially a part of Killington but in style and scale much tamer and smaller. Its 48 trails are best for skiers of mid-range ability, and there's not as much hotdogging as you'll

Vermont skiing

Killington is probably the best known – and certainly the largest – of all Vermont ski resorts, but in a mountainous state that gets plenty of snow, certainly not the only one. The variety of resorts on offer is very diverse, and you should have no problem finding one to suit your needs. Consider other options such as Stowe (see p.419), Stratton and Bromley (see p.402), Okemo (see p.398), Sugarbush and Mad River Glen (see p.422), Burke Mountain (see p.438), and Jay Peak (see p.439).

find on the other peaks. Lift tickets cost $39 per day or $549 per season. (Killington lift tickets are also valid here.) **Hiking** is one of the few things that goes on in the area during the summer. The Long and Appalachian trails meet just north of here. Hikers can take the K-1 Gondola ($9 one-way, $13 round-trip) to the summit of Killington and hike down. If you must, there is also an **Alpine Slide** ($7) at the base of Pico.

Accommodation

You're spoiled for choice in terms of **accommodation** around these parts, though you may wind up paying a pretty penny, especially during prime skiing season. Wise Vacations, 405 Killington Access Rd (Ⓣ802/773-4202 or 1-800/642-1147, Ⓦwww.wisevacations.com), rents private homes in and about Killington; prices vary, but they are only a bit higher than the average inn or B&B.

Cedarbrook Motor Inn US-4, near junction with Hwy-100 Ⓣ802/422-9666 or 1-800/446-1088. Good-value option outside the main ski area. ❸

Cortina Inn 103 US-4 Ⓣ802/773-3333 or 1-800/451-6108, Ⓦwww.cortinainn.com. An excellent luxury inn, if not as close to the ski area as some. ❺

Inn at Long Trail Sherburne Pass Ⓣ802/775-7181 or 1-800/325-2540, Ⓦwww.innatlongtrail.com. Hikers on the Long Trail will appreciate the comfort of this after several nights spent in primitive shelters with no electricity and running water. ❹

Inn of the Six Mountains 2617 Killington Access Rd Ⓣ802/422-4304 or 1-800/228-4676, Ⓦwww.sixmountains.com. The *Inn* offers well-appointed quarters and proximity to skiing and Killington village. ❻

Mountain Meadows Lodge 285 Thundering Brook Rd Ⓣ802/775-1010, Ⓦwww.mtmeadowslodge.com. To the side of Killington Access Road off US-4, about five minutes from Killington, you'll find a relatively unspoiled lakeside farm setting on the Appalachian Trail; it also has an above-average restaurant. ❺

Val Roc Motel US-4, near junction with Hwy-100 Ⓣ802/422-3881 or 1-800/238-8762. Cheap spot, and quiet too. ❸

Eating and drinking

Hemingway's US-4 Ⓣ802/422-3886. One of Vermont's finest restaurants, with a formal waitstaff, impeccable surroundings and presentation, and excellent, vegetarian-friendly though expensive nouvelle cuisine.

Moguls Saloon Killington Road. Bar with cheap draft specials during happy hour.

Mother Shapiro's Killington Road Ⓣ802/422-9933. American comfort food is served all day long at this spot, quite popular with locals.

Panache at the *Woods Resort*, Killington Road Ⓣ802/422-8622. Grill fare with a spicy, modern twist. Adventurous offerings on the meaty menu include emu, wild boar, and yak.

Pickle Barrel Killington Road Ⓣ802/422-3035. A rowdy bar and a dance scene that gets crazy on winter weekends.

Middlebury

In 1800, a small group of local citizens banded together to form a "town's college," primarily to train young men for the ministry. Two centuries later, Middlebury College, in the center of the town of **MIDDLEBURY**, is one of the most endowed (and expensive) colleges in the US, while the village numbers among the prettiest and most diverse in Vermont. Located at the intersection of routes 125, 30, and 7, about equidistant from Rutland and Burlington, the town was actually named for its central location between Salisbury and New Haven, two Vermont towns whose prominence has receded in the past two centuries. All roads converge at the **Middlebury Town Green**, an idyllic place with a pretty and ornate white **Congregational church** at its northern end, not to be confused with the more somber gray church on the green itself. Middlebury's small downtown has a fairly hip collection of shops, with a few bookstores, a record shop, and the **Vermont Craft Center at Frog Hollow**, 1 Mill St (Ⓣ802/388-3177, Ⓦwww.froghollow.com), a bright space showcasing high-quality crafts from all over the state. The **Henry Sheldon Museum of Vermont History**, 1 Park St (Mon–Sat 10am–5pm; $3), is an endearingly quirky collection of tools, household objects, and "one-of-a-kind oddities," such as the alleged remains of the "Petrified Indian Boy," actually a mid-nineteenth-century hoax bought into by, among others, the collector who established this museum.

Catch Rte-125 west to the **Middlebury College Museum of Art**, off Rte-30 (Tues–Fri 10am–5pm, Sat–Sun noon–5pm; free), for a look at the small permanent collection of nineteenth-century European and American sculpture and modern prints on display; the campus spreads out around it, with no other individually compelling sights, though it makes for a nice wander.

Farther down Rte-125, turn north on Rte-23 for the **UVM Morgan Horse Farm** (daily: May–Oct 9am–4pm) where you can tour the stables and admire the beautiful world-famous descendants of Justin Morgan's stallion, the first native breed in North America.

Practicalities

The village green boasts two lovely **inns**. Open since 1827, the *Middlebury Inn* (Ⓣ802/388-4961 or 1-800/842-4666, Ⓦwww.middleburyinn.com; ❺), with 75 rooms, a porch with rocking chairs, an operational 1926 elevator, and a good restaurant, is possibly the pick of the two, while the aptly named *Inn on the Green* (Ⓣ802/388-7512 or 1-888/244-7512, Ⓦwww.innonthegreen.com; ❺) has eleven rooms in a graceful landmark building, with continental breakfast in bed included. Television junkies will want to make sure they check out the *Waybury Inn* (Ⓣ802/388-4015 or 1-800/348-1810, Ⓦwww.wayburyinn.com; ❺), whose exterior was used on the TV show *Newhart*. The relationship with the show ends there, but it has fourteen comfortable, well-kept rooms inside. There are a couple of **motels** two or three miles south of town along Rte-7. Of these, the *Greystone Motel* (Ⓣ802/388-4935, Ⓔgreystone@yahoo.com; ❹) and the *Blue Spruce Motel* (Ⓣ802/388-4091 or 1-800/640-7671; ❸) are clean and comfortable places to spend the night. A small, eight-bed **youth hostel**, the *Covered Bridge Home Hostel* (open all year; Ⓣ802/388-0401; $14 for dorm beds) can also be found in Middlebury; reservations are required.

The **restaurant** scene in Middlebury is pretty good for a town of this size. If you're in the mood for meat – and lots of it – check out the carvery at the *Middlebury Inn,* where $16.95 buys you as much as you can eat from a selection of three types of meat and a fish of the day. The ostentatious *Fire and Ice*, 26 Seymour St (Ⓣ802/388-7166), is a cavernous steak-and-seafood place, with a massive salad bar and enough memorabilia to fill a museum, the centerpiece of which is a 22-foot motorboat from the Twenties. *Tully and Marie's* (Ⓣ802/388-4182), 5 Bakery Lane, is more of a chic urban bistro, with sleek interior and views of Otter Creek. Also with views of the creek, *The Taste of India*, 1 Bakery Lane (Ⓣ802/388-4856), has plenty of curry-and-rice dishes for a very reasonable $10 or so. Another ethnic eatery worth considering, if only for the slightly surreal experience of eating tacos in an icily air-conditioned dining room covered with frescoes of marlins and idyllic beaches whilst looking out on a Vermont village green, is the *Amigos Cantina*, 22 Merchant's Row (ⓣ802/388-3624). *The Dog Team Tavern*, Dog Team Road, off Rte-7 two miles north of town in New Haven (ⓣ802/388-7651), lets you have a proper Vermont feast, with local produce and specialties like maple oatmeal pie. Less expensive are *Rosie's*, south on Rte-7 (ⓣ802/388-7052), for hearty diner-style fare; *Green Peppers* at Grand Union Plaza (ⓣ802/388-3164), for the best pizza in town; and *Baba's Market and Deli*, 54 College St (ⓣ802/388-6408), with Middle Eastern specialties such as falafel, as well as wood-fired pizzas, sandwiches, and the like.

West on Hwy-125: Robert Frost country

Robert Frost spent 23 summers in Vermont on land that has been overrun by Hwy-125 (also called the Robert Frost Memorial Highway), which cuts right across the Green Mountains from East Middlebury to Hancock. The small cabin where he stayed, now a National Historic Landmark and owned by Middlebury College, still stands a few miles down a dirt road from the **Robert Frost Wayside**, a small, peaceful picnic area right by the highway (a quiet two-lane road). Across the street from the Wayside is the **Robert Frost Interpretative Trail**, a mile-long loop trail punctuated by placards displaying poems and excerpts of his work. Although it may not sound like much, it is actually quite evocative – an affecting environment in which to read his deceptively simple, old-fashioned works.

A few miles west along Hwy-125 is the small campus of **Bread Loaf**, the highly-regarded summer writers' conference initiated at Frost's suggestion while he was a professor at Middlebury College. Though there's nothing much to see, just a few sturdily constructed beige wooden buildings, budding writers may want to stroll here and commune with the spirits of the notables, such as Frost, Willa Cather, and John Gardner, who have taught or studied here.

Central and eastern Vermont

Interstate 89 crosses the Connecticut River and enters Vermont at the town of **White River Junction** – a major hub for north–south, Montréal–Boston traffic – before continuing up the eastern side of the state for about fifty miles roughly parallel to the Green Mountain National Forest. It veers west at Vermont's lovely state capital, **Montpelier**, turning towards Burlington and the Canadian border and passing the **Ben and Jerry's Ice Cream Factory** in Waterbury, perhaps the purest embodiment of Vermont activism-cum-tourist attraction. Other firm favorites on the tourist circuit include genteel **Woodstock**, a few miles west of White River Junction, and the ever-popular ski resort of **Stowe**, ten miles north of Waterbury.

Woodstock and around

Since its settlement in the 1760s, **WOODSTOCK**, a few miles west of the Connecticut River on US-4, has considered itself a bit more refined than its rural neighbors, making much, for instance, of its status as the home of a few minor artists, such as sculptor Hiram Powers and novelist Sinclair Lewis. The town has only submitted to the most cultured elements of the tourist industry, hence the distinguished houses that surround its oval green, most of which have been taken over by antiques stores and tearooms, and its tiny downtown area, which is populated by art galleries and upscale eateries. In any case, it should most certainly not be confused with the Woodstock of festival fame, which is in New York. This Woodstock draws well-heeled WASPs looking for a civilized getaway, and the closest it came to radical action during the Sixties was to build a new covered bridge.

Arrival and information

Vermont Transit **buses** plying US-4 between Rutland and White River Junction stop at the village green in Woodstock four times daily. The **Woodstock Area Chamber of Commerce**, 18 Central St (ⓣ802/457-3555 or 1-888/4WOODSTOCK, ⓦwww.woodstockvt.com), has tons of visitors information, and also operates an information booth on the oval town green (June–Oct 9am–5pm; ⓣ802/457-1042), from where you can take **walking tours** of the village (Fri–Sun 11.30am).

Accommodation

Places to stay in Woodstock's center are plentiful and luxurious, but expensive. Sites farther from town get less expensive; there are relatively cheap cookie-cutter motor lodges along US-4 east of town. The information booth on the green can organize accommodation in private homes ("overflow homes") during very busy periods such as fall foliage.

1830 Shiretown Inn 31 South St, Rte-106 ⓣ802/457-1830, ⓦwww.1830shiretowninn.com. In downtown Woodstock, this tiny (three distinct rooms), restored 1830 farmhouse offers mammoth beds, clawfoot tubs, and good breakfasts, across the street from Vail Field. ⑤

Applebutter Inn US-4 in Taftsville ⓣ802/457-4158, ⓦwww.bbonline.com/vt/applebutterinn. Cozy B&B with comfortable beds, personable proprietors, and breakfasts featuring homemade granola. Four miles east out of town. ⑤

Braeside Motel US-4 ⓣ802/457-1366, ⓦwww.braesidemotel.com. Not quite a mile east of the village, you'll find clean and basic family-owned motel digs with very few extra amenities, save for a swimming pool. ③

Shire Motel 46 Pleasant St ⓣ802/457-2211, ⓦwww.shiremotel.com. A recent facelift has done this place absolutely no harm at all. A good mid-range option on the eastern edge of town. Some rooms overlook the Ottauquechee River. ④

Three Church Street 3 Church St ⓣ802/457-1925, ⓦwww.scenesofvermont.com/3church. Impressive, pet-friendly Georgian mansion with eleven bedrooms, a music room, and a library. Its lawns and gardens adjoin the Ottauquechee River which runs through the heart of Woodstock. Breakfasts are Herculean and made to order. There's a clay tennis court and a large swimming pool. ⑤

Village Inn of Woodstock 41 Pleasant St ⓣ802/457-1255 or 1-800/722-4571, ⓦwww.villageinnofwoodstock.com. Quaint B&B with an inviting front porch and attractive gardens. Dinner served as well, for which you don't have to be a guest. ⑤

Woodstock Inn and Resort 14 The Green ⓣ802/457-1100 or 1-800/448-7900, ⓦwww.woodstockinn.com. The largest, fanciest, and best around, with sumptuous rooms, beautiful grounds, an eighteen-hole golf course, and gourmet restaurant. ⑧

The Town

Woodstock's center is an oval green at the convergence of Elm, Central, and Church streets, which are lined with architecturally diverse houses – New England clapboard is not nearly as prevalent here – that provide a genteel foreground to the landscape of rolling hills. The **Woodstock Historical Society**, 26 Elm St (May–Oct Mon–Sat 10am–5pm, Sun 2–5pm; $2; ⓣ802/457-1822), is one of the best museums of its kind, with well-organized multimedia displays including tape recordings of older residents' reminiscences and an admirably complete town archive. Next door to the multimedia center, and included in the admission, is a slightly musty old house with a varied collection of artifacts. Don't miss the assemblage of children's toys and dolls, and the elegant drawing room with an antique harpsichord and gilt mirror from the 1790s. Also in this area are the town's many galleries, the most notable of which are **Woodstock Folk Art Prints and Antiquities**, 6 Elm St (ⓣ802/457-2012), which displays provocative local folk-art prints, and the **Steven Huneck Gallery**, 49 Central St (ⓣ1-800/449-2580), full of idiosyncratic sculpture and furnishings employing animal forms.

Three of the town's attractions located further afield, but still within walking distance, are devoted to the inimitable pleasure of seeing animals close up. The museum section of **Billings Farm and Museum**, off Rte-12 north of town (May–Oct daily 10am–5pm; Dec weekends 10am–4pm; $9; ⓣ802/457-2355), puts on demonstrations of antiquated skills, while the grounds are run as a modern dairy farm where you can pet cows and churn a bit of butter, if you're so inclined. Be sure not to miss the Academy Award-nominated film, *A Place in the Land*, which introduces the major players in the farm's – and the surrounding countryside's – history. Across the street from the Billings Farm, the **Marsh-Billings-Rockefeller National Historic Park** (house and garden tours daily: late May–Oct 10am–4pm; $6) was originally the home of George Perkins Marsh, whose 1864 book *Man and Nature*, inspired by his distress at the deforestation of his native Vermont, is a seminal work of ecological thought. The house was later purchased in 1869 by Frederick Billings, who, greatly influenced by Marsh's image of responsible farming and sustainable forestry, decided to put those principles into action on the property. The 553 acres of forest, replanted by Billings in the late nineteenth century, contain a network of **hiking trails**, some leading to splendid vistas with Mount Tom in the distance. The **Vermont Raptor Center** – on Church Hill Road south of town, but due to move to a new site on US-4 in Quechee (see opposite) by the fall of 2003 (May–Oct Mon–Sat 10am–4pm; $7; ⓣ802/457-2779) – treats injured birds of prey and offers tours of their grounds, where you can see the process by which rescues are made and view a few recovering falcons in the flesh. Most popular is **Sugarbush Farm**, 591 Sugarbush Farm Rd (Mon–Fri 7.30am–5pm, Sat–Sun 9am–5pm; ⓣ802/457-1757 or 1-800/281-1757), which claims to produce a more authentic cheddar and maple syrup than other Vermont farms.

Eating and drinking

Woodstock's **restaurants** cater to an upscale crowd, but although they're expensive, they're undeniably good. In any case, it's a good bet to make reservations ahead of time. Restaurants attached to inns and B&Bs tend to be just a bit cheaper.

Bentley's 3 Elm St ⓣ802/457-3232. Upmarket versions of traditional bistro food (buffalo wings, nachos, and the like) and a good range of microbrews.

Jackson House Inn and Restaurant US-4, 1.5 miles west of the village green ⓣ802/457-2065. Very upscale New American cuisine. Try to get a table offering a view of the lovely four-acre garden. Extensive wine list and knowledgeable sommelier.

Mountain Creamery 33 Central St ☎802/457-1715. Filling country breakfasts and lunch fare served daily, as well as some fine homemade ice cream.

Pane Salute 61 Central St ☎802/457-4882. Italian bakery where the fresh pastries don't quite match the quality of the cappuccino, which is the best available in Woodstock.

The Prince and the Pauper 24 Elm St ☎802/457-1818. Expensive continental cuisine – braised veal, filet mignon, and the like – in an incongruously casual dining room.

Wild Grass US-4, a mile east of the village green ☎802/457-1917. Nouvelle cuisine, American style, with organic game meats featured regularly, though still fairly vegetarian-friendly. Expensive – but worth it.

East of Woodstock: Quechee

Six miles east of Woodstock, **QUECHEE** is a peculiar mixed bag: the **town** proper is a combination of quaint Vermont village and expensive tract housing development, where you'll find several upmarket restaurants and B&Bs; just down US-4 is **Quechee Gorge**, Vermont's greatest natural wonder, and a great place to camp; and adjacent Quechee Gorge Village is a mire of cheap tourist kitsch, hard not to notice but very easy to skip.

Even if you're just passing through the area, be sure to stop and ogle Quechee Gorge, so-called "Grand Canyon" of Vermont. A delicate bridge spans the 165ft chasm of the Ottauquechee River, and hiking trails lead down through forests to the base of the gorge, where its scale seems even more impressive. If you have more time, hit the town of Quechee, where a waterfall on the river turns the turbines of **Simon Pearce Glass** on Main Street (daily 9am–9pm; ☎802/295-2711). Housed in a former wool mill, this is an unusual combination of glass-blowing center and restaurant, where you can watch bowls and pots being made and then eat off them. The hills behind Quechee Town have challenging trails for **hiking** and **cross-country skiing** in season. There is also a good path for **biking**, known locally as the River Road, which starts in Main Street, Quechee Town, and leads west into Woodstock, following the Ottauquechee River and running parallel to US-4. Wilderness Trails, on Dewey's Mills Road next to the *Quechee Inn at Marshland Farm* (☎802/295-7620), dispenses information and rents bikes ($17/day) and cross-country skis ($13/day).

Practicalities

If you're equipped to **camp**, the best place to stay is in the **Quechee Gorge State Park**, on Dewey Mills Road off US-4 (☎802/295-2990; $13), which has 47 well-maintained sites (no hookups) ensconced in a forest of fir trees, and offers foot-trail access to the gorge. The *Quality Inn*, on US-4 between the gorge and the village (☎802/295-7600 or 1-800/732-4376, Ⓦwww.qualityinnquechee.com; ④), offers the least expensive accommodation in the area. But if you're willing to shell out more, the town of Quechee has a few sumptuous **inns**. The *Quechee Inn at Marshland Farm* is located just outside the town, on Quechee Main Street (☎802/295-3133 or 1-800/235-3133, Ⓦwww.quecheeinn.com; ⑤). In addition to the inn's comfy 24 rooms with period furnishings and fabulous country setting, visitors can take advantage of its association with Wilderness Trails and the Vermont Fly-fishing School (☎802/295-7620). The *Parker House Inn*, located in a beautiful red-brick Victorian building at 16 Main St (☎802/295-6077, Ⓦwww.theparkerhouseinn.com; ⑤) is another good choice.

Most **restaurants** in the area are either painfully chichi affairs or dreary "family" establishments. The most notable exceptions are *Firestone's*, at

Waterman Place along US-4 (Ⓣ802/295-1600), serving creative pasta dishes, flatbread pizzas, and traditional Vermont fare, such as game and fish and chips, which you can enjoy on their pleasant rooftop patio, and the *Quechee Village Deli*, 91 The Village Green (Ⓣ802/295-2786), which has tasty soups and sandwiches. Also, the restaurant at *Simon Pearce Glass* (Ⓣ802/295-1470) serves inventive New American-type entrées starting at around $15, as well as no-nonsense Irish dishes such as beef and Guinness stew and shepherd's pie. If there's anything authentic at Quechee Gorge Village, it's probably the 1946 Worcester diner car which houses the *Farina Family Diner and Restaurant*, US-4 (Ⓣ802/295-8955), where the food is filling and inexpensive.

White River Junction and around

Perhaps the most exciting thing ever to happen in **WHITE RIVER JUNCTION** was the first use of nitrous oxide (laughing gas) as an anesthetic, in 1844. Still, it's an important travel hub – as far back as the mid-1860s five different railroads had terminal points in White River, and the community grew steadily until the rail transport industry went bust in the early 1900s. The town hosts an annual downtown street party celebrating its railroading history each September, and the train station even has a small, well-organized **Transportation Museum** (Tues–Sat 9.30am–3pm; free).

The pride of White River Junction these days is the **Northern Stage**, at Briggs Opera House across from the train station (Ⓣ802/296-7000), an ambitious year-round stage company which performs, with the help of some top local and imported talent, a varied program of contemporary and classical pieces, musicals, and straight drama.

Fifteen miles north of White River Junction along I-91, in the town of **NORWICH**, is the **Montshire Museum of Science**, 1 Montshire Rd, exit 13 off I-91 (daily 10am–5pm; $5.50, children $3; Ⓣ802/649-2200), intended for kids but well worth the detour even for adults. You'll see several aquariums with peculiar species of fish as well as machines illustrating the weirder side of physics, but the most engaging displays are the interactive brain-teasing puzzles. Admission includes access to its several easy hiking trails and picnic areas.

Practicalities

Amtrak *Vermonter* **trains** stop right by North Main Street, and buses come and go from the Vermont Transit Terminal right off I-91 exit 11 (Ⓣ802/295-3011). There is a very good **Welcome Center** at the train station (daily 8am–8pm; Ⓣ802/281-5050), where you can read numerous brochures over free cups of coffee. If you're going to be here overnight, the best **place to stay** is the *Hotel Coolidge*, 39 Main St (Ⓣ802/295-3118 or 1-800/622-1124, Ⓦwww.hotel-coolidge.com; ❹), right in the town center, an old-fashioned railroad hotel with reasonable prices. The HI-affiliated **hostel** wing has clean dorm beds and kitchen access from $19 per night. On the outskirts of town, at I-91 exit 11, a number of hotel and motel chains offer similar accommodation at similar prices.

In the same building as the *Coolidge*, the *Gandy Dancer Café* (Ⓣ802/280-2233) serves light **lunch** fare – mostly cheap soups and sandwiches – with Americana on the walls and books to peruse. The *Polka Dot Restaurant*, 1 N Main St (Ⓣ802/295-9722), is a shrine to camp, looking as if it were decorated largely by kids, but fixing up good milkshakes and patty melts. Unusually for a restaurant in a bus station, the recently opened *China Moon Buffet*, at the Vermont Transit Terminal (☎802/291-9088), has been getting rave reviews for its fresh and cheap buffet food. Far and away the most interesting culinary option in town is *Karibu Tulé*, 2 N Main St (☎802/296-3756). Translated from the Swahili as "Welcome, let's dine," the pan-African cuisine includes *mafé* (chicken in peanut sauce) from Mali, *kofta* (beef curry) from Egypt, *dangue* (slow-cooked mug beans) from Kenya, and the various delicious side dishes which constitute an Ethiopian meal.

Windsor

WINDSOR, tucked into a bend in the Connecticut River just this side of the New Hampshire border, about fifteen miles south of White River Junction, is where the original constitution of the Republic of Vermont was drawn up, in 1777, an event which led it to be termed the "birthplace of Vermont." Today, the distinction is preserved in one of its two excellent museums, the **Old Constitution House**, Main Street (late May to mid–Oct Wed–Sun 11am–5pm; $2.50). Housed in the original tavern where the delegates met and constitutional debates took place, it contains a well-preserved re-creation of the tavern's interior plus a fascinating series of history-related displays, featuring rare artifacts such as coins and, more interestingly, newspapers from the brief republican period. Farther south on Main Street along the banks of a Connecticut River tributary, the **American Precision Museum** (daily: late May to Oct 10am–5pm; $4) is oriented around the idea of mechanization – the construction, function, and historical significance of machinery, with a particular focus on the Industrial Revolution. The small but impressive displays of items (many still in working condition) such as "Mississippi" rifles and sewing machines incorporate original antique machine tools and creative interactivity to illustrate not only the importance of technology but also the peculiar beauty of its precision. Halfway between the two museums, Bridge Street branches off to the east from Main Street; at its terminus, you'll find the **Cornish/Windsor covered bridge**, the longest such bridge in the US, which is open to traffic crossing over to New Hampshire.

For affordable **accommodation**, it's best to backtrack to White River Junction, or farther afield in Woodstock or Quechee. However, the *Juniper Hill Inn*, off US-5 on Pembroke Road (☎802/674-5273 or 1-800/359-2541, Ⓦwww.juniperhillinn.com; ❻), has thirty fastidiously kept rooms in a mansion overlooking the town. They also serve excellent, if rather formally presented, continental-style **food**. **Mount Ascutney State Park**, off Rte-44A, nine miles west of Windsor (May–Oct; ☎802/674-2060), maintains several **campsites** in a secluded setting, along with hiking trails and excellent views of the Green Mountains.

Montpelier

With fewer than ten thousand residents, **MONTPELIER** (mont-PEEL-ier), situated in a beautiful valley on the Winooski and North Branch rivers, is the smallest state capital in the country. Its residents have cultivated a vital downtown area around the **capitol** building, urban in style but not in scale, lined exclusively with nineteenth-century buildings – some with a slightly Southern antebellum flavor – and boasting a number of fine restaurants, museums, and theaters. Despite its considerable charms, the city still bears a low tourist profile, and it is this lack of commercialism that makes Montpelier a refreshing counterpoint to the cultivated rural quaintness that pervades the rest of the state.

Arrival, information, and city transit

Knapp Airport, a postage stamp-sized airport about four miles from I-89 exit 7, serves Montpelier and surrounding communities. Montpelier shares a stop on Amtrak's *Vermonter* line with its neighbor Barre, the station lying two miles west of downtown near I-89. The **bus** terminal is next to the river a block from State Street (Ⓣ802/223-7112), one of the town's main thoroughfares.

In town, the **Vermont Division of Travel and Tourism**, 134 State St (daily 8am–8pm; Ⓣ802/828-5981), offers plenty of information on local and statewide attractions. The nearby **kiosk**, just down State Street across from the capitol, crams a large assortment of brochures and guides to area attractions into a small but well-kept space. Check out the daily *Times-Argus* for arts and entertainment schedules and listings. Students and locals take advantage of the town's free **shuttle bus**, Wheels (Ⓣ802/223-2882), hopping on at any downtown Montpelier stop. The same company also makes runs to nearby Berlin and Barre.

Accommodation

There's a decent range of affordable **places to stay** in Montpelier, with some of the better options being, not surprisingly, bed and breakfasts. The town has a very small, three-bed **hostel**, *The Capitol Home Hostel* (Ⓣ802/223-2104), open all year and charging $10–15 per night; while the riverside *Green Valley Campground*, northeast of town at the intersection of Rte-2 and Rte-302, four miles from exit 7 or 8 off I-89 (May–Nov; Ⓣ802/223-6217), offers 35 campsites from $24, with swimming, showers, convenience store, and a laundry room.

Betsy's Bed & Breakfast 74 E State St Ⓣ802/229-0466, Ⓦwww.betsysbnb.com. Relatively large, twelve-room B&B on a quiet, leafy street a few minutes' walk from downtown which retains a personal touch without being claustrophobic. Bathrooms in all rooms are a definite plus – and a rarity for this type of accommodation. ❹

Capitol Plaza Hotel and Conference Center 100 State St Ⓣ802/274-5252 or 1-800/274-5252, Ⓦwww.capitolplaza.com. Luxurious digs across from the gorgeous Art Deco Capitol Theater. Friendly, family-run, and aimed at the business traveler. ❻

Gamble's Bed and Breakfast 16 Vine St Ⓣ802/229-4810. Three large and colorful rooms with shared baths show a little wear and tear, but you can't beat the price. No in-room phones or TV. ❸

Inn at Montpelier 147 Main St Ⓣ802/223-2727, Ⓦwww.innatmontpelier.com. Spacious, well-appointed rooms in a pair of Federal-style buildings. The continental breakfast is a bit skimpy, but access to common areas and a pleasant wrap-around porch are both welcome. ❻

Montpelier Guest Home 138 North St Ⓣ802/229-0878, Ⓦwww.guesthome.com. Three comfortable rooms with handmade quilts, hand-stenciled walls and shared bath. Pleasant deck and gardens, central location. No smoking, no pets. ❸

Twin City Motel 478 Barre–Montpelier Rd, on US-302 just off I-89 exit 7 Ⓣ802/476-8541 or 1-877/476-3104, Ⓦwww.twincitymotel.com. Probably the pick of the several motels located a few miles southeast of town on the Barre–Montpelier Road. Rooms have usual motel amenities, like cable TV, fridge, and telephone. ❸

The Town

Diminutive **downtown Montpelier** is home to four college campuses – New England Culinary Institute, Woodbury College, Vermont College of Norwich

University, and Community College of Vermont – though it feels nothing like a college town. Its most visible landmark, the gilt-domed **State Capitol** rises high above the town center on State Street. While most visitors just stroll around the impeccably kept exterior gardens, particularly brilliant during fall, and photograph the statue of **Ethan Allen** guarding the front doors – although the statue of Vermont's first governor **Thomas Chittenden**, to the left of the main entrance, is more attractive – you should feel free to take a pass through the capitol's refurbished vaulted marble hallways to see the vast painting representing the Battle of Cedar Creek, a Civil War skirmish in which Vermonters played a pivotal role, and the permanent exhibit of Vermont artists. Informative and enthusiastically-given free **guided tours** are available on the half-hour (Mon–Fri 10am–3.30pm; July to mid-Oct also Sat 11am–2.30pm; ⓣ802/828-2228).

East of the Capitol district, in College Hall on the campus of Norwich, lies the small but distinguished **T.W. Wood Gallery**, College Street (Tues–Sun noon–4pm; $2, free on Sun; ⓣ802/828-8743), highlighted by a fascinating array of Vermont painter T.W. Wood's oil paintings of Civil War residents and experimental WPA American folk art and photos.

Montpelier's best spot for outdoor recreation is **Hubbard Park**, north of town on Hubbard Park Drive, 180 acres of grassy space, picnic areas, ponds, and trails. Ascend the fifty-foot stone **observation tower** in the park's center for spectacular views of the Montpelier area. Several hiking and mountain-biking trails wind through the hills, and in winter the trails are used for cross-country skiing and the ponds freeze over for ice-skating. Onion River Sports, 20 Langdon St (ⓣ802/229-9409), rents bikes in summer, snowshoes and skis in winter.

Eating, drinking, and entertainment

Students from the New England Culinary Institute (NECI) have lent their influence to Montpelier's cuisine, resulting in a number of less expensive, experimental **restaurants**. The area is blissfully resistant to fast-food and chain joints – it's the only US state capital without a *McDonald's*, though a *Subway* has found its way on to Main Street. Montpelier's **Farmers Market** (May–Oct Sat 9am–1pm) sells the produce, herbs, flowers, and baked goods of numerous organic gardeners and farmers.

The town's main drama venue is the **Lost Nation Theater**, in the City Hall Arts Center on Main Street, where the local Lost Nation Theater Company performs everything from Shakespeare epics to experimental contemporary plays (ⓣ802/229-0492). Across the street, the **Savoy Theater** (ⓣ802/229-0598) shows first-rate foreign, classic, and independent films. During the summer, the city band holds well-attended evening concerts on the State House lawn and the Vermont Philharmonic stops by in July.

South of Montpelier: Route 12

If you're in no hurry on your way from Montpelier to points south, a worthwhile alternative to I-89 is little-traveled **Rte-12**, which passes through the towns of Riverton, Northfield, Randolph, and Bethel. You'll find very few B&Bs or country stores along this road; just thirty miles of rolling hills, farmland, and lakes. This is the real Vermont, and its lush beauty and traditional charm are as genuine as you'll find anywhere in the state. Be advised, though, that this is also a road with a fairly high concentration of "Take back Vermont" signs (see p.385).

Coffee Corner Main Street, at State ⓣ802/229-9060. A Montpelier standard for over sixty years. Scarf cheap diner food at Formica tables or rub elbows with Vermont's political potentates at the lunch counter. Serves breakfast all day.
Julio's 44 State St ⓣ802/229-9348. Pretty good Tex-Mex for this area of New England. Cheap, filling burrito and enchilada dishes washed down with zippy margaritas. Don't blink or you'll miss the unobtrusive green door entrance.
La Brioche Bakery & Cafe 89 Main St ⓣ802/229-0443. Cheerful, well-designed bakery run by NECI. Good bread, espresso drinks, and the smell of the on-site bakery (but only so-so pastries) lure townies of all stripes. The outside terrace on Main Street, at State, is perfect for people watching.
Main Street Grill and Bar 118 Main St ⓣ802/223-3188. Delectable, inventive specialties from NECI alums, sort of pricey but worth it. American grill fare and shellfish are standouts. Also serves breakfast. The next-door *Chef's Table* (ⓣ802/229-9202), run by the same folks, doesn't serve breakfast and is a bit pricier, but also very good.
McGillicuddy's Irish Pub 14 Langdon St ⓣ802/223-2721. Standard bar fare, most notable for its really hot hotwings. Wide selection of microbrews, and a ripping Long Island Iced Tea. Draws a lively, younger crowd and gets loud and busy on weekends.
Mountain Café 7 Langdon St ⓣ802/223-0888. Continuing the wholesome and organic traditions of the now closed *Horn of the Moon Café*, with huge, tofu- and tempeh-stuffed burritos, brought to life by zesty sauces. Certain "healthy" meats such as chicken and turkey also available. Closed Mon.
Rhapsody 28 Main St ⓣ802/229-6112. Hippy-friendly restaurant where you can wolf down curried tofu and vegan chocolate cake from the organic buffet. No meat here.
Sarducci's 3 Main St ⓣ802/223-0229. Long-established, Tuscan-inspired trattoria next to the river. Pasta dishes will set you back around $10, or you could opt for a house specialty such as wood-roasted salmon in a white-wine sauce.
Wayside Restaurant and Bakery 1873 Barre–Montpelier Rd/Rte-302 ⓣ802/223-6611. Classic Yankee cooking, with New England standards such as baked haddock and pot roast at moderate prices.

Barre

BARRE (pronounced "berry") is Vermont's immigrant center, having attracted Scots, Italians, and other ethnic groups almost a hundred years ago to work for the city's booming granite industry. Even today, a visitor to Barre may hear several languages spoken freely on the streets and in the stores – not that people come here to note its diversity. Indeed, the main draw these days is the same thing that lured immigrants a century ago: granite, the rock on which this city was literally built.

Barre's main sight, while awaiting the opening of a new Granite Museum (ⓣ802/476-4605), is the **Rock of Ages Quarry**, I-89 exit 6 (May–Oct Mon–Sat 8.30am–5pm, Sun noon–5pm; tours June to mid-Oct Mon–Fri 9.15am–3pm; $4; ⓣ802/476-3119, ⓦwww.rockofages.com), which is actually southeast of town on Hwy-63 in the municipality of **Graniteville**. This is the world's biggest granite quarry, as you'll almost certainly be told by the fleet of helpful guides who will rush to greet you as soon as you enter the visitors' center. You can check out one of the smaller but still connected quarries, grab a piece of granite, and watch the campy *You'll dig the Rock of Ages!* informational film all for free – ask for the map of the self-guided tour. If you've come all this way, though, it's just as well to shell out a few bucks for the narrated shuttlebus tour that takes you to the far more impressive fifty-acre working quarries and through the manufacturing centers where artisans busy themselves making fleets of tombstones.

Meanwhile, the **Vermont Historical Society Museum**, 60 Washington Rd (US-302) (ⓣ802/479-8500, ⓦwww.state.vt.us/vhs), has relocated here from Montpelier, to provide an engaging view of the state's past – much more than just the dusty muskets and documents.

More history, specifically the city's turbulent early times – its laborers have long been famed for their militancy – is outlined in the **Barre Museum and Archives**, on the second floor of the Aldrich Public Library, near the intersection of Main and River streets. Newspaper articles, photos, and transcribed oral histories detail various immigrant fracases; even the naming of the town in 1793 spurred a fist-fight (won by Jonathan Sherman of Barre, Massachusetts). This free collection also contains cultural paraphernalia and radical socialist political tracts from the early twentieth century.

Barre's cultural heritage is also painfully evident in a pair of ostentatious granite monuments downtown. The 23-foot-tall **Italian-American Stonecutters' Monument**, at the intersection of North Main and Maple streets, captures a stoneworker in action and pays homage to the town's immigrant past. Similarly, the **Robert Burns Monument**, at Academy and Washington streets, celebrates the great Scottish poet. More interesting than either are the elaborate gravestones of **Hope Cemetery**, just north of town on Hwy-14. While the city's stonecutters lived modestly, they knew how to die in grand style, commemorating themselves and their families with massive, elaborately wrought granite tombstones ranging to ten feet in height, and bearing impressively detailed artwork.

On a more contemporary cultural note, dance and musical performances take place at Main Street's **Barre City Hall and Opera House** (Ⓣ802/476-8188), a fanciful building that has seen the likes of John Philip Sousa and Helen Keller on its stage.

Practicalities

The **local bus** company, Wheels, plies US-302, stopping in downtown Barre. For **visitor information**, stop in at the kiosk in the Price Chopper parking lot along Main Street at the intersection with Hwy-14.

Low demand makes for cheap **accommodation** in Barre. The *Hollow Inn and Motel*, 278 S Main St (Ⓣ802/479-9313 or 1-800/998-9444, Ⓦwww.hollowinn.com; ❹), is on the fancy side, with a fitness center and complimentary continental breakfast. *Reynold's House B&B*, 102 S Main St (Ⓣ802/476-8313; ❻), offers three well-lit, spacious guestrooms with detailed wood molding, bird's-eye maple, and well-chosen antiques. The *Days Inn*, 173–175 S Main St (Ⓣ802/476-6678 or 1-800/325-2525; ❸), has clean and reasonably priced rooms, along with an indoor pool.

Barre's Italian-American population may be deeply entrenched in the granite industry, but it hasn't created the profusion of authentic ethnic **restaurants** you might expect. The exception is *Del's*, 248 N Main St (Ⓣ802/476-6684), which serves up cheap, tasty pasta dinners and pizza on classic red-and-white checked tablecloths. For a quick, light lunch, *Simply Delicious*, 160 N Main St (Ⓣ802/479-1498 or 1-888/479-1498), vends a complement of homey soups and sandwiches, which you can enjoy while reading volumes donated by its next-door neighbor, Barre Books, an independent bookstore.

Waterbury

Few people gave much notice to **WATERBURY** before 1978; even then, no one could have expected the opening of a homemade ice-cream stand at the front of a Burlington gas station to excite any interest. But since aging hippies Ben Cohen and Jerry Greenfield started their mini-empire (and chose Waterbury as its headquarters), **Ben and Jerry's Ice Cream Factory**, one mile north of I-89 in the village of Waterbury Center, on the way up to Stowe, has grown so huge, so fast, that it is now the number-one tourist destination in Vermont. Half-hour tours run by friendly, almost evangelical youths (daily: July to late Aug 9am–8pm; late Aug to Oct 9am–6pm; Nov–May 10am–5pm; June 9am–5pm; $2; ⓣ1-866/BJ-TOURS; ⓦwww.benjerry.com), feature a short film on the boys' early days, then head into the production factory where machines turn cream, sugar, and other natural ingredients into over fifty flavors. Afterwards, you get a free mini-scoop of the stuff that made it all possible – you can buy more at the top-price gift shop and ice-cream stall outside.

There's not really much else to see in Waterbury; even the **culinary outlet shops** clustered together along Hwy-100, each of which offer free samples of their wares in an attempt to seduce travelers into purchasing them, fail to raise much excitement. The pick of the bunch is probably the **Cabot Annex Store** (ⓣ802/244-6334), where you can taste several varieties of the well-known Vermont cheddar cheese (see p.437 for more). However, if you're really looking for something to do, stop by the Waterbury Public Library at 28 N Main St and ask the librarians to let you into the **Waterbury Historical Society and Museum** (Mon–Wed 1–8pm, Fri 10am–5pm, Sat 10am–3pm; ⓣ802/244-7036) upstairs, where they'll have to turn on the lights to let you into the small collection of musty Civil War and medical memorabilia. There are plenty of **craft** outlets, too, on the road, if you're so inclined. Otherwise, you might opt for the surprisingly thrilling goings-on at the **Thunder Road Speedbowl** ($6; ⓣ802/244-6963), which regularly offers stock-car racing on a short-track, high-banked motor speedway. It's loud, cheap, pulsating entertainment.

Practicalities

Amtrak's *Vermonter* **trains** pull into downtown Waterbury, either in the morning heading south or the evening heading north. There is also a Vermont Transit stop in Waterbury at Depot Beverage, 1 River St (ⓣ1-800/552-8737), although **buses** are only scheduled to stop there a couple of times a day. For general tourist information, contact the **Waterbury Tourism Council** (ⓣ802/244-1209) on Rte-100 near its intersection with Stowe Street.

There are several top-notch **accommodation** options in and around town. The Cape Cod-clapboard *Inn at Blush Hill*, 784 Blush Hill Rd just off Rte-100 (ⓣ802/244-7529 or 1-800/736-7522, ⓦwww.blushhill.com; ❺), sits atop a hill with fantastic views, and has Colonial antiques and canopy beds in each room. The Teutonic-themed *Grunberg Haus* (ⓣ802/244-7726 or 1-800/800-7760, ⓦwww.grunberghaus.com; ❹), on Rte-100, is a woodsy A-frame with great breakfasts and reasonable rates. Other quality establishments along Rte-100 near Waterbury Center include the *Black Locust Inn* (ⓣ802/244-7490 or 1-800/366-5592, ⓦwww.blacklocustinn.com; ❻) and the *Old Stagecoach Inn* (ⓣ802/244-5056 or 1-800/262-2206, ⓦwww.oldstagecoach.com; ❸).

One of the better **restaurants** around is *Arvad's*, 3 S Main St (ⓣ802/244-8973), which serves up fresh grill fare with tasty pints of ale. For a light lunch, the deli sandwiches and soups at *Park Row Cafe*, Park Row (ⓣ802/244-5111), are cheap and satisfying. *K.C.'s Bagel Cafe*, Stowe Street (ⓣ802/244-1740), has fresh bagels and other light breakfast foods baked daily.

Stowe

Unlike most of Vermont's other ski towns, there is still a beautiful nineteenth-century village at the heart of **STOWE**, with a white-spired meeting house and a green to stroll around. Though Stowe was actually a popular summer destination even before the Civil War, what really put the town on the map as a ski resort was the arrival of the **Von Trapp family**, of *The Sound of Music* fame. After fleeing Austria during World War II, they settled here and established a lodge – since burned down – where Maria Von Trapp held her singing camps.

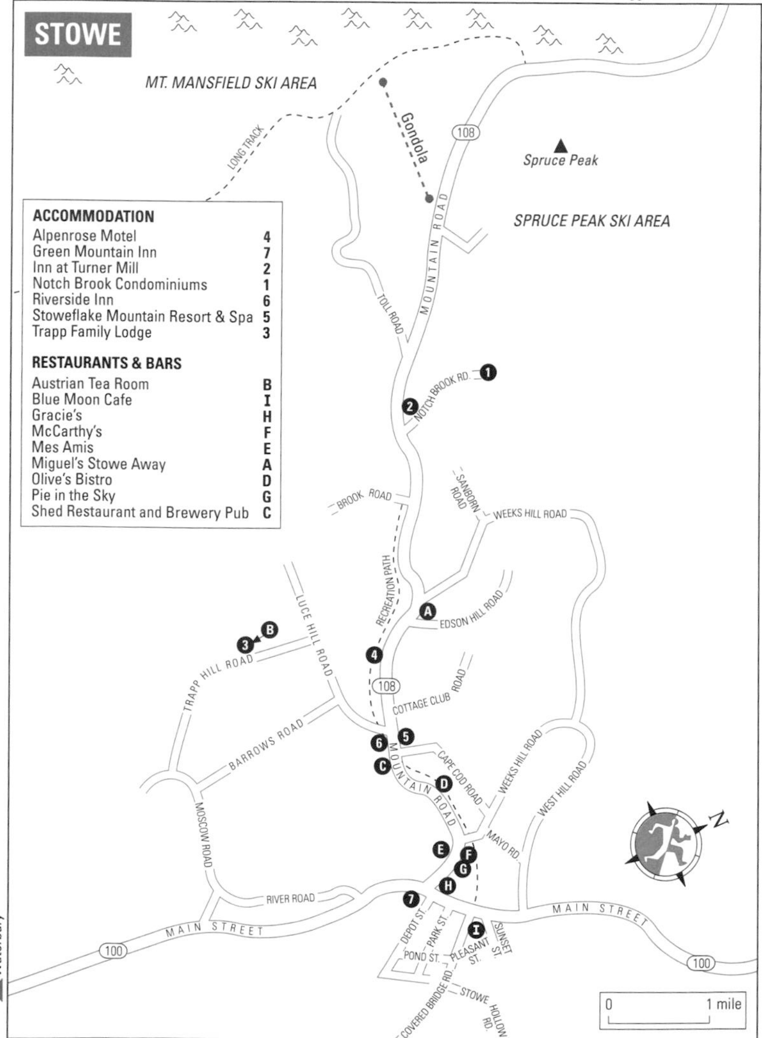

A complex composed of a newly rebuilt lodge, restaurant, and mini-theme park devoted to the celebration of Alpine culture has taken its place. Interfamily squabbling over the direction the lodge and its offshoots will take in the future doesn't seem to have interfered with its popularity. Regardless, a century's worth of experience catering to increasingly large crowds of skiers has rather swamped the approach road to the main ski area with malls, equipment stores, and sprawling condominium complexes – extremely at odds with the village below. Nonetheless, the setting remains spectacular, at the foot of Vermont's highest mountain, the 4393-foot **Mount Mansfield**.

Arrival and information

To get to Stowe by public transport, catch the bus or train to Waterbury, then, as there is no bus service between Waterbury and Stowe, take a taxi the ten miles up Hwy-100. **Taxi** companies in the area include C&L in Waterbury (Ⓣ802/244-6311) and Stowe Taxi in Stowe (Ⓣ802/253-9433). If you are staying at the one of the more expensive hotels in Stowe, they will usually be happy to collect you in Waterbury. **Mountain Road** (Rte-108) is Stowe's primary thoroughfare, stretching from the main village up through the mountain gap known as "Smugglers' Notch," so named because forbidden trade with Canada passed through here during the War of 1812 at the time of Jefferson's Embargo Act. It has also lived up to its nickname via its popularity with fugitive slaves on their way to Canada and, in the early part of last century, Prohibition-era bootleggers. It's generally closed during winter. The Mountain Road Shuttle runs up and down Mountain Road, stopping at the Town Hall in Stowe Village and the base of Mount Mansfield ($1). The Stowe Trolley (Ⓣ802/253-7585) is a winter shuttle service connecting the resort properties with the village. The staff at the **visitors' center**, Main Street, at Mountain Road (Mon–Fri 9am–5pm, Sat–Sun 10am–5pm; Ⓣ802/253-7321 or 1-800/GOSTOWE, Ⓦwww.gostowe.com), are very helpful should you require further information or help finding accommodation.

Accommodation

Multiple **accommodation** options line Mountain Road, and range from luxury resorts to modest B&Bs. During winter, reserve as far ahead as possible; otherwise, you'll probably be shut out. In summertime, many places close, but those that stay open can usually find a room for you – you might even be able to wrangle a discount if you're bold enough to ask the innkeeper. The closest **campground** is *Gold Brook Campground* (Ⓣ802/253-7683), two miles south on Rte-100, with the usual amenities and sites from $18.

Alpenrose Motel 2619 Mountain Rd Ⓣ802/253-7277 or 1-800/962-7002. Affordable, small hotel located halfway between the ski slopes and Stowe Village, just off the Stowe Recreation Path. Rooms and efficiencies with private baths, cable TV, and refrigerators. German spoken. ❸

Green Mountain Inn 1 Main St Ⓣ802/253-7301 or 1-800/253-7302, Ⓦwww.greenmountaininn.com. Stately hotel built in 1833, centrally located (at a busy intersection) and amply accoutered. Offers not one but two good restaurants, complimentary health club, and afternoon tea and cookies. ❺

Inn at Turner Mill 56 Turner Mill Lane Ⓣ802/253-2062 or 1-800/992-0016, Ⓦwww.turnermill.com. Quaint streamside quarters in log-cabin buildings at the foot of Mount Mansfield. Swimming pool and excellent home-made breakfasts. ❹

Notch Brook Condominiums 1229 Notch Brook Rd Ⓣ802/253-4882 or 1-800/253-4882, Ⓦwww.notchbrook.com. A secluded complex of fully-equipped studio apartments with fireplaces and patios, good for large groups. Well-behaved pets welcome. ❺–❽

The Pines Motel 1203 Waterbury Rd ⓣ802/253-4828. Cheap, fairly clean, basic motel rooms, one step above your average hostel. ❷

Riverside Inn 1965 Mountain Rd ⓣ802/253-4217 or 1-800/966-4217, ⓦwww.rivinn.com. Modest, basic hostelry with all the essentials including bed, bath, and phones, though not much more. ❸

Stoweflake Mountain Resort & Spa 1746 Mountain Rd ⓣ802/253-7355 or 1-800/253-2232, ⓦwww.stoweflake.com. Sumptuous rooms filled with tasteful antiques and homemade quilts, coffee and snacks throughout the day, well-informed and courteous staff, all set on sweeping grounds with pool, sauna, spa, and sports club. Definitely the best place to stay if you can afford it. ❼

Trapp Family Lodge 42 Trapp Hill Rd ⓣ802/253-8511 or 1-800/826-7000, ⓦwww.trappfamily.com. On the site of the original Trapp family house, also the first cross-country ski center in America. Now a Teutonically-themed ski resort with nightly entertainment, as fancy as it is expensive, occasionally graced by some of the original Trapp kids, who are now in their eighties. Concerts in the Trapp Meadow. ❼

Skiing and other outdoor recreation

Alpine experts hotly debate whether the **Stowe Mountain Resort** (ⓣ802/253-3500, ⓦwww.stowe.com) is still the "ski capital of the east," a distinction it clearly held until Killington and other eastern ski centers began to challenge its supremacy a decade or so ago. Regardless, it's an excellent mountain, refurbished to the tune of $20 million a few years back, and its popularity remains intact, as traffic through Stowe Village on winter weekends makes all too painfully clear. There are 48 well-kept trails spread over two ski areas, Mount Mansfield and Spruce Peak, with excellent options for skiers of every level (lift ticket $58 per day). A less crowded option is the family-oriented **Smugglers' Notch** (ⓣ802/664-8851 or 1-800/451-8752, ⓦwww.smuggs.com), on the other side of the mountain, a dramatic narrow pass with high cliffs on either side that actually has more trails than Stowe (72), and is cheaper ($54 per day). In vindication of its suitability for parents and kids alike, the respected *Ski* magazine has consistently rated Smuggler's Notch as having the top ski-school program for families.

Stowe offers almost as much to do in the **summer**, when the crowds thin out considerably. Ascending to the peak of **Mount Mansfield** is a challenge no matter how you do it, and rewards with spectacular views all the way to Canada and the shores of Lake Champlain. Weather permitting, the easiest approach is the **Toll Road**, a winding ascent that starts seven miles up from the village (daily: late May to mid-Oct 9am–4pm; $15 per car), or by **gondola** (daily: mid-June to mid-Oct 10am–5pm; $11; ⓣ802/253-7311), which affords great views and drops off at Cliff House, a brief hike from the summit. If you've got the stamina, the most rewarding approach is to **hike** the full way to the Mansfield summit, a steep, steady, 4.7-mile climb up a section of the Long Trail with a trailhead on Rte-108 halfway through Smugglers' Notch. The notch is laced with miles of **hiking trails**; some of the best start out from Smugglers' Notch State Park, 7248 Mountain Rd (mid-May to mid–Oct; ⓣ802/253-4014).

Stowe's cross-country skiing trails double as **mountain-bike routes** during summer. AJ's Ski & Sports, Mountain Road (ⓣ1-800/226-6257 or 802/253-4593, ⓦwww.ajssports.com), offers rentals and organized tours for which advance reservations (possible online) are highly recommended (mid-May to Oct; rentals $24 per day, tours $30). Nearby streams and small rivers offer ample opportunity for **canoeing** and **kayaking**: Umiak Outdoor Outfitters, 849 S Main St (ⓣ802/253-2317), rents full sets of equipment, including watercraft, paddles, and life jackets, for $30–38 per day. There's also a rollerblading park ($15 a day) which offers lessons and rentals, plus an Alpine slide ($9 a ride).

People who would rather keep to lower elevations would do well to use the **Stowe Recreation Path**, a 5.5-mile paved trail for bikers, runners, walkers, and rollerbladers which starts in the village behind the Community Church. Despite its heavy usage, it never feels too crowded; better still, it offers scenic views of the West Branch River and Mount Mansfield along the way. Be warned that the path does not make a full circuit, so plan ahead if you're going the entire length.

Eating and drinking

There is a big choice of places to **eat** in and around Stowe, ranging from low-budget delis, bakeries, and pizza joints to rather pricey restaurants, frequently run by a nearby inn or resort. Its **drinking** and **entertainment** scene draws together lounging après-skiers, hard-boiled locals, and well-heeled yuppies in its various watering holes.

Austrian Tea Room 42 Trapp Hill Rd ⓣ802/253-5705. The high prices are more for the kitschy, Germanic atmosphere than the food, but the cuisine's still authentic enough and the setting fun (in season, try to get seated on the flower-lined balcony).

Blue Moon Cafe 35 School St ⓣ802/253-7006. Inventive, surprisingly inexpensive New American fare featuring local game (braised venison and the like) and seafood; probably Stowe's best all-round dining choice. Good wine list.

Gracie's in the Carlson Building, 2 Main St ⓣ802/253-8741. Good for lunchtime salads and sandwiches, many of them Mexican-style; also open well into the night for fuller dinners.

McCarthy's Mountain Road ⓣ802/253-8626. Irish-themed joint with great heaping breakfasts.

Mes Amis 311 Mountain Rd ⓣ802/253-8669. A local favorite serving rich French cuisine (homemade truffle pâté and the like) for dinner. Excellent service and affordable prices. Live jazz and blues Thurs and Sun. Closed Mon.

Miguel's Stowe Away 3148 Mountain Rd ⓣ802/253-7574. Spicy, tangy Mexican and Tex-Mex treats, excellent by New England standards. Its lively margarita bar can get rowdy on weekends.

Olive's Bistro 1036 Mountain Rd ⓣ802/253-2033. Top-notch tapas bar in addition to other French-inspired Mediterranean specialties. Great selection of martinis, single malt scotches, and assorted cocktails.

Pie in the Sky 492 Mountain Rd ⓣ802/253-5100. Casual café offering wood-fired specialty pizzas you can design yourself, plus vegetarian entrées.

Shed Restaurant and Brewery Pub 1859 Mountain Rd ⓣ802/253-4364. Hearty American fare, specializing in the ample "Mighty Shed Burger." The attached bar has great daily specials on pints and bar chow. Stowe's only brewpub. Open late.

Sugarbush and the Mad River Valley

Instead of taking Hwy-100 north to Stowe, you could turn south just before arriving at Waterbury Center and travel twelve miles down Hwy-100 to the town of **WAITSFIELD** in the Mad River Valley. The river runs through the town, while two of Vermont's most popular ski resorts lie to the west. The **Sugarbush Resort** (ⓣ802/583-6160 or 1-800/53-SUGAR, ⓦwww.sugarbush.com), which is actually closer to the town of **WARREN**, about five miles south of Waitsfield on Hwy-100, is the larger and more commercialized of the two, with its 115 trails (midweek lift tickets $48) and year-round activities. Meanwhile, the cooperatively-owned **Mad River Glen** (ⓣ802/496-3551, ⓦwww.madriverglen.com), a short drive west of Waitsfield along Rte-17, is one of the most unadulterated resorts in North America, with narrow, unforgiving trails which look pretty much as they did when they were cut fifty years ago. In keeping with tradition, no snowboards are allowed here, although

Telemark skiing is promoted aggressively. There are 44 trails (lift tickets $42), of which nearly half are considered to be suitable for the expert skier.

You'll really need a car to get to the Mad River Valley. A taxi from Waterbury to Waitsfield is a possibility, albeit an expensive one. Once at Waitsfield, however, Mad River Valley Transit (Ⓣ802/496-7433) has a **shuttle** service during ski season to Warren and the ski resorts. Information on the plentiful lodging possibilities in the area can be obtained at the **Sugarbush Chamber of Commerce** (Ⓣ802/496-3409 or 1-800/828-4748, Ⓦwww.madrivervalley.com).

Lake Champlain

The 150-mile-long **Lake Champlain** forms the boundary between Vermont and New York, and just nudges its way into Canada in the north, never exceeding twelve miles across at its widest point – in all, an area of about 490 square miles, making it the sixth largest body of freshwater in the US. Across the water from the flatlands of the Champlain Valley, the impassive Adirondack Mountains are always visible, looming up in the west. The first non-native to see the lake was French explorer **Samuel de Champlain** in 1609, who named it in his own honor. The life and soul of the valley is the French Canadian-influenced city of **Burlington**, whose longstanding trade links with Montréal have filled it with elegant nineteenth-century architecture. Within just a few miles of the center, US-2 leads north onto the supremely rural **Champlain Islands**, covered in meadows and farmlands.

Burlington

The closest Vermont gets to a city, with a population of just around forty thousand, lakeside **BURLINGTON** is one of New England's most purely enjoyable destinations, a hip, relaxed fusion of Montréal, eighty miles to the north, and Boston, over two hundred miles southeast. In fact, from its earliest days, Burlington looked as much to Canada as to the south. Shipping connections with the St Lawrence River were far easier than the land routes across the mountains, and the harbor became a major supply center. The city's founders included Ethan Allen and family – far from being some impoverished Robin Hood figure, Ethan was a wealthy landowner, having purchased large tracts of Vermont land from New Hampshire royal governor Benning Wentworth, and his brother Ira set up the University of Vermont.

Burlington today is the definitive youthful university town. From its waterfront walkways to its lively brewpubs, the city is at once cosmopolitan and pleasantly manageable in scale. It's one of the few American cities to offer something approaching a café society, with a downtown – especially around the Church Street Marketplace – you can stroll around on foot, and plenty of open-air terraces. Politically, too, it's unusual: Bernard Sanders, the former

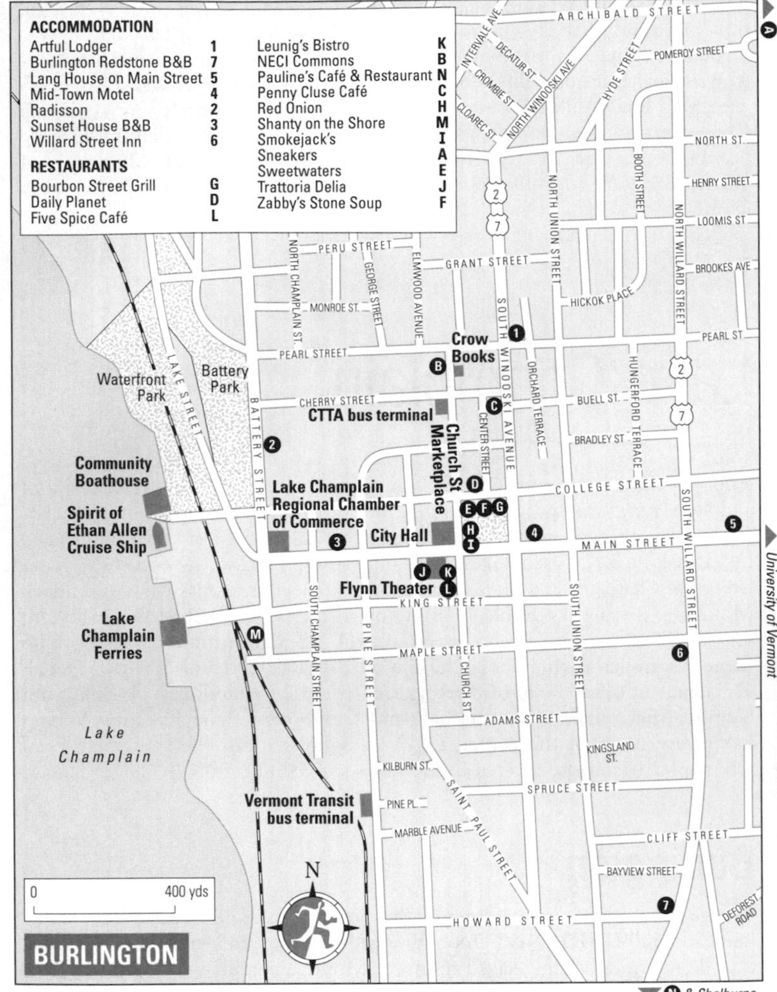

"socialist" mayor of Burlington, was in 1990 elected to the House of Representatives from Vermont, the first political independent to go to Congress in forty years.

Arrival, information, and city transit

Burlington sits at the confluence of several major highways, US-7, US-2, and I-89. Amtrak *Vermonter* **trains** haul into the town of Essex Junction, an inconvenient five miles northeast of town (connecting buses run every half-hour 6.30am–9.30pm; $1). Note that the booking office is closed on weekends, at which time no tickets are sold. Vermont Transit **buses**, on the other hand, stop in downtown Burlington at 345 Pine St, four blocks south of Main Street

(☎802/864-6811). Vermont's only sizeable commercial **airport**, the Burlington International Airport (☎802/863-1889), is a few miles east of town along US-2 (buses to downtown run every half-hour 6.30am–10pm; $1); Continental Airlines and US Airways have services to and from Boston and New York City.

Practical information is available from the **Lake Champlain Regional Chamber of Commerce**, 60 Main St (July–Sept Mon–Fri 8.30am–5pm, Sat–Sun 11am–3pm; Oct–June Mon–Fri 8.30am–5pm; ☎802/863-3489 or 1-877/686-5253, Ⓦwww.vermont.org). There is also an **information booth** (☎802/658-6673) in the middle of Church Street between Cherry and College streets, which has a range of maps and brochures, as well as a courtesy phone for booking accommodation.

The local **CCTA** bus company (☎802/864-2282) connects points all over the downtown area, and travels to the nearby cities of Winooksi, Essex, and Shelburne ($1). You can get a route map and details of schedules at the main downtown terminal on the corner of Cherry and Church streets. CCTA also operates a very convenient – and free – shuttle, which runs along College Street between the University of Vermont and the waterfront with stops at the Fleming Museum and the Church Street Marketplace (every 15–30min; Mon–Fri 6.30am–9pm, Sat–Sun 9am–9pm). The **Champlain Flyer** (☎802/951-4010) is a commuter rail service which travels along the shoreline of Lake Champlain from Union Station at the end of Main Street to South Burlington, Shelburne, and Charlotte ($1).

Lake Champlain Ferries (☎802/864-9804, Ⓦwww.ferries.com) cross the lake to New York from **Burlington** (to Port Kent; hourly; $13.25), **Charlotte** (to Essex; every half-hour; $7.50), and **Grand Isle** (to Plattburgh; every 20min; $7.50). All of these rates are one-way for a car and driver; for additional passengers as well as for cyclists and walk-ons the rate ranges from $2.50 to $3.50. You can rent **bikes** at North Star Sports, 100 Main St (☎802/863-3832), and Skirack, 85 Main St (☎802/658-3313), which also rents skis, snowboards, kayaks, and in-line skates.

Accommodation

The Burlington area has no shortage of moderately priced **accommodation**, though much of it is removed from the downtown area, along Williston Road (just west along US-2, off I-89 exit 14) and Shelburne Road (south of town along US-7). Downtown, there are several good places to stay within striking distance of the town's major attractions.

Hostels and camping

Lone Pines Campsite 52 Sunset View Rd, Colchester ☎802/878-5447, Ⓦwww.lonepinecampsites.com. About eight miles north of town, with 200 sites starting at $26 a night. No beach here, though two swimming pools should be adequate compensation. In any case, Lake Champlain is not too far away.

Mrs Farrell's Home Hostel (HI-AYH) 27 Arlington Court ☎802/865-3730. Only six dorm beds at $15 for HI members and $18 non-members, so reservations are essential. Three miles out from the town center. 10pm curfew. Closed Nov–April.

North Beach Campground 60 Institute Rd ☎802/862-0942 or 1-800/571-1198. Less than two miles north of town on the shores of Lake Champlain. A total of 137 sites ranging from $20 to $30, various other facilities (including plenty for the kids), and access to a sandy beach.

Downtown hotels, motels, and B&Bs

Artful Lodger 15 Lafayette Place ☎802/658-2046, Ⓦwww.theartfullodger.com. Only two rooms at this renovated carriage house. Goes out of its way to welcome artists, although evidently not penniless ones. ❺

Burlington Redstone B&B 497 S Willard St ☎802/862-0508, Ⓦwww.burlingtonredstone.com. Red-brick home, a little cluttered with antiques and work by local artists, convenient to downtown. Nice lake and mountain views from patios and porches. Reservations recommended. ❺

Lang House on Main Street 360 Main St ⓣ802/652-2500 or 1-877/919-9799, ⓦwww.langhouse.com. Handsome Victorian conveniently located between UVM campus and downtown, offers eleven rooms, many with views of Lake Champlain. ❻

Mid-Town Motel 230 Main St ⓣ802/862-9686, ⓔmid-town@juno.com. A classic roadside motel – and an ugly one at that – transplanted right into the center of downtown Burlington. Clean, basic, and affordable rooms, which probably haven't changed much since this place opened for business in the Fifties. ❸

Radisson Hotel 60 Battery St ⓣ802/658-6500 or 1-800/333-3333, ⓦwww.radisson.com/burlingtonvt. Extravagant – and extravagantly expensive – hotel centrally located on a hillside right on the Lake Champlain shore. The lounge hosts surprisingly popular comedy nights on some weekends. ❽

Sunset House B&B 78 Main St ⓣ802/864-3790, ⓦwww.sunsethousebb.com. Good choice if you enjoy staying in family-run places with homely decor, "lived-in" rooms, and shared bathrooms. Prime location right in the center of downtown. ❺

Willard Street Inn 349 S Willard St ⓣ802/651-8710 or 1-800/577-8712, ⓦwww.willard-streetinn.com. Bills itself as "Burlington's first historic inn." If you choose the more luxurious rooms with lakeside views, which are very good from this hilly part of town, it's also Burlington's most expensive. ❻

Out-of-town hotels and motels

Colonial Motor Inn 462 Shelburne Rd, South Burlington ⓣ802/862-5754. The 1960s-era decor lends a campy touch to this meticulously clean motel featuring pool and cable TV. ❹

Comfort Inn 1285 Williston Rd ⓣ802/865-3400. Chain motel with clean, basic, recently redecorated rooms, pool and spa, coffee round the clock, and free continental breakfast and local calls. Most rooms are non-smoking. ❹

Heart of the Village Inn 5347 Shelburne Rd, Shelburne ⓣ802/985-2800 or 1-877/808-1834, ⓦwww.heartofthevillage.com. Nine beautifully decorated rooms in a pair of Victorian houses with period antiques and delectable breakfast. Cable TV available on request. ❺

Ho-Hum Motel 1660 Williston Rd ⓣ802/863-4551. This simple and reasonably priced motel, three miles east of downtown, almost lives up to its name. Four adjacent restaurants and a bike path nearby help liven it up. There is another motel of the same ilk south of the center at 1200 Shelburne Rd ⓣ802/658-1314. ❸

Inn at Essex 70 Essex Way, Essex Junction ⓣ802/878-1100 or 1-800/727-4295, ⓦwww.innaressex.com. Country inn meets business hotel at this classy establishment about eight miles from Burlington, which has a complimentary shuttle to the nearby Amtrak station, IBM offices, and airport, a newly opened golf course, a pool, comfortable rooms, and two excellent restaurants run by the New England Culinary Institute (see p.430). ❽

Inn at Shelburne Farms 1611 Harbor Rd, Shelburne ⓣ802/985-8498, ⓦwww.shelburne-farms.org/comevisitus/inn. Posh digs, perhaps the nicest around, in a mansion on the lovely Shelburne Farms (see p.429). May–Oct. ❺

The City

Your natural inclination on setting out to explore Burlington might be to head for the **waterfront**, one of the city's top destinations; indeed, kayaks seem to be strapped to the roof of every third car in Burlington. The aptly named **Waterfront Park** stretches a couple of miles along Lake Champlain, with ample green spaces, gorgeous swing benches that people tactfully fight to get to, and a popular dog run. At its northern end, **Battery Park** makes a particularly good place to watch the sun go down over the Adirondacks – especially when there's a band playing, as there usually is on weekends. Winding on and about the shoreline, the 6.5-mile **bike path** follows a scruffy former railroad bed from the south end of the city to the north, a good way to see the waterfront and some of the city beaches if you've got wheels. If you're looking to actually get on the water, rather than just admire it from the path, convivial cruises set out from the Community Boathouse at the end of College Street on the

Ethan Allen and his Green Mountain Boys

"I am as resolutely determined to defend the independence of Vermont as Congress are that of the United States ..."

Flamboyant and controversial, folk hero **Ethan Allen** (1738–1789) represents to many the independent ethos Vermont has long been known for, ironic considering his humble beginnings as a Connecticut farmer. An early convert to the concept of republicanism, Allen gained renown as a statesman who united Vermonters in their cause for independence and their right to own land. He also helped establish the image of the rugged individualist, contemptuous of federal authority (be it the Crown or Congress), that is carried on by second-amendment fanatics and militiamen to this day.

In the 1760s, Benning Wentworth, the royal governor of New Hampshire, under the assumption that his authority would naturally extend to the unclaimed territory to the north and west, began issuing New Hampshire Grants for the area now known as Vermont. After Wentworth had been distributing these grants for more than a decade, the King decided that New York's governor actually wielded the rightful authority over the territory, and the original settlers and their townships were subjected to burdensome New York fees or, worse, had their lands confiscated.

The settlers responded by forming a citizens' militia, the **Green Mountain Boys**, to protect their rights, electing Ethan Allen as their colonel. Shortly thereafter, Allen and other family members formed the Onion River Land Company to speculate on the contested Wentworth land grants. This appears to have been a brilliant double strategy: as the Allens sold off the cheap grants to would-be settlers in Massachusetts and Connecticut, they increased the strength of their numbers opposing the Yorkers. And as the numbers increased to back up their claim to the land, the previously worthless grants increased in value accordingly. Eventually, the Allens were selling grants purchased at ten cents an acre for five dollars an acre, a pretty profit indeed. In the meantime, Allen and his fellow settlers were developing the area, building roads and establishing a population center on Burlington Bay.

Allen and (future traitor) Colonel Benedict Arnold were behind the assault on Fort Ticonderoga, the first British property taken by America. Allen eventually became commander of the armed forces of the Commonwealth of Vermont. While defending America's northern border from a renewed British assault from Canada, Allen and other Vermont representatives petitioned Congress to recognize Vermont and to admit her into the American Confederacy. When New York succeeded in blocking Vermont's attempts, the Allens began secret negotiations with the British to guarantee their sovereignty. These negotiations became considerably less attractive after the defeat of Cornwallis (1781) and the Treaty of Paris (1783).

With the coming of peace, Ethan Allen had begun to put together an impressive farm on the Winooski (Onion) River at Burlington, now known as the Ethan Allen Homestead (see overleaf), where he settled down to become a philosopher and writer. Allen died in 1789, only six years after peace with England, with Vermont still yet to join the Union.

Spirit of Ethan Allen III (Ⓣ802/862-8300; $9.95), or you can rent motorboats and jet skis at Winds of Ireland (Ⓣ802/863-5090), also in the Community Boathouse. Nearby is the **Lake Champlain Basin Science Center** which affords the opportunity to handle all sorts of slimy lake-dwelling fauna and peek in on intriguing exhibits on area marine life; more for the kids than their parents, perhaps.

The **Church Street Marketplace**, a pedestrian mall just a few blocks from the waterfront, holds Burlington's finest old buildings – including an attractive

City Hall – and most of its modern cafés and boutiques. Although locals will complain that the marketplace has become inundated with chain stores in recent years, it still supports a number of unique businesses. Avoid the huge Borders and head instead to the Crow Bookshop, 14 Church St (☎802/862-0848), or North Country Books, 2 Church St (☎802/862-6413), two of the better **independent bookstores** that pepper downtown. Another spot with local flavor is **Lake Champlain Chocolates**, 65 Church St (☎802/862-5185), a gourmet chocolate shop and café which offers hot chocolate and espresso, homemade ice cream, fudge, and, of course, chocolate. The market's busiest on nights and weekend days, both good people-watching times.

Up College Street from the marketplace is the sleepy campus of the University of Vermont (better known as UVM, for Universitas Viridis Montis, a Latin rendering of the state's alleged, and grammatically dubious, French nomenclature), a comprehensive research university which houses Vermont's largest collection of art and anthropological pieces. The **Robert Hull Fleming Museum** (May–Sept Tues–Fri noon–4pm, Sat–Sun 1–5pm; Sept–April Tues–Fri 9am–4pm, Sat–Sun 1–5pm; $3) houses some good examples of European Baroque paintings and pre-Columbian artifacts. To catch more art, arrive on the first Friday of each month, when Burlington City Arts sponsors the free First Friday Artwalk, which traverses over fifteen downtown galleries (April–Oct; ☎802/865-7166).

North of Burlington along Rte-127, in the town of **WINOOSKI**, lies the **Ethan Allen Homestead** (daily: mid-May to mid-June 1–5pm; mid-June to mid-Oct Mon–Sat 10am–5pm, Sun 1–5pm; rest of year call ☎802/865-4556 for hours; $5), the 1787 farmhouse and 1400-acre farmland on which the Revolutionary War hero spent the last years of his life. The attached museum is housed in a re-created eighteenth-century tavern, where you can quaff an ale while viewing a fairly intriguing video and slide show as you sit on uncomfortable, but true to period, furniture.

More raucous fun can be had at the **Magic Hat Brewing Company**, five minutes south of downtown at 5 Bartlett Bay Rd, South Burlington (store open Mon–Thurs & Sat 10am–6pm, Fri 10am–9pm; mid-May to Dec also Sun noon–5pm; tours every half-hour Wed–Fri 3.30–5pm, Sat 1–2.30pm; ☎802/658-BREW), which offers free tours which make the science of beer-making look fun, and free samples that enhance the experience even further.

The Shelburne Museum

It takes a whole day, if not more, to fully appreciate the fabulous fifty-acre collection of unalloyed Americana gathered at the **Shelburne Museum**, three miles south of Burlington on US-7 in Shelburne (daily: late May to mid-Oct 10am–5pm, guided tours at 1pm; $17.70; April to late May & mid-Oct to early Dec 1-4pm, only select buildings open; $10). The brainchild of heiress Electra Havemeyer Webb, who aimed to create a distinctly American "collection of collections," the museum centers on her parents' nineteenth-century French Impressionist paintings, housed in a reconstruction of their New York apartment. However, Electra's own interests ran far wider, and she put together what is probably the nation's finest celebration of its own inventive past.

More than thirty buildings, some original and some newly constructed, dot the grounds. Besides seven fully furnished historic houses, moved intact from other locations in the region, there's a blacksmith, a jail, and a general store, all of which aim to re-create aspects of everyday life over the past two centuries. Of the several buildings devoted to American high art, the most notable is the

Webb Gallery, which focuses on nineteenth-century pieces. Much of this collection consists of naturalist work, such as a fine range of James Audubon's bird prints; and there is also an intriguing portrait of Seneca Indian leader Sagayewatha and one of twentieth-century painter Anna Mary Robertson Moses' (known also as Grandma Moses) few cityscapes, *Cambridge, ca. 1944*. However, the collection is most notable for its assemblage of folk art, including decoys, weather vanes, tools, quilts, carriages, and circus memorabilia. The carnivalesque theme continues over at the **Circus Museum**, a homage to spectacle, American-style, featuring Barnum and Bailey ads with harrowing representations of clowns and wild animals, as well as Roy Arnold's woodcarving, *Circus Parade*, a cortege in miniature. Don't miss, too, the **Stagecoach Inn**, which holds a wonderfully nostalgic assemblage of trade and tavern signs, most notably "cigar store Indians," and the hilariously grotesque burled woodcarvings of Gustav Hertzberg.

The collections go beyond Americana – one of the best buildings is a meticulous reconstruction of Electra Webb's New York apartment, the Greek Revival **Electra Havemeyer Webb Memorial Building**, constructed between 1960 and 1967. Despite the towering Ionic columns that front the place, it's the interior that makes a visit worthwhile: each of the six rooms duplicates the arrangements of furniture and decorative arts – including works by Rembrandt, Manet, and Degas – from Webb's extravagant Manhattan home.

The museum grounds themselves are a joy to browse; a stroll around will bring you past lilac gardens in spring and stunning foliage in fall, over covered bridges, and to a working blacksmith shop. The village includes a **Shaker barn**, a **schoolhouse**, a railroad station, even an enormous, fully reconstructed steam **paddlewheeler**, the *SS Ticonderoga*, with its own rock-surrounded lighthouse.

Shelburne Farms

Next to the Shelburne Museum, **Shelburne Farms**, 1611 Harbor Rd (late May to mid-Oct 9am–5pm; $10 walking trails plus tour, $6 for just trails; ⓣ802/985-8686), a working farm reborn as a non-profit environmental education center on Lake Champlain. A guided tour of railroad mogul Dr Seward Webb's estate reveals his descendants' commitment to sustainable farming – though on an incongruously large and impressive scale. The undulating landscape is punctuated by three massive buildings: the main house, which overlooks Lake Champlain and the Adirondacks, a coach barn, and a horseshoe-shaped farm barn. The farm's mansion is the *Inn at Shelburne*, open mid-May to mid-October, with 26 deluxe guestrooms and a dining room which serves breakfast, dinner, and Sunday brunch.

Eating

Burlington's best **restaurants** are located along Main and Church streets and feature a few ethnic eateries as alternatives to the American cuisine which often seems to dominate the town. The presence of ten thousand students ensures that there are plenty of inexpensive places to eat, while the academic tone brings a certain sophistication to the café culture. Keep in mind that this is one of the most vehement anti-smoking towns in the state, and smoking is banned in most eateries.

Bourbon Street Grill 211 College St ⓣ802/865-2800. Dimly lit restaurant – indeed, at first glance it seems to be closed – serving spicy Cajun specials such as fried catfish, gumbo, and jambalaya.

Daily Planet 15 Center St, behind the Church Street Marketplace ⓣ802/862-9647. This brightly colored spot offers a creative menu melding Asian and Mediterranean cooking with old-fashioned American comfort food, à la *satay* burgers and *saag paneer* with mashed potatoes. Highly recommended.

Five Spice Café 175 Church St ☎802/864-4045. Excellent Southeast Asian fare, with vegetarian options, and elaborate, delightfully named dishes such as Evil Jungle Prince (chicken and veggies in a sort of coconut milk curry). Inventive desserts (ginger tangerine cheesecake, for instance) and a popular dim sum brunch (for which reservations are essential) on Sundays.

Leunig's Bistro 115 Church St ☎802/863-3759 or 1-800/491-1281. Sleek, modern bistro serving contemporary continental cuisine at surprisingly reasonable prices. Outdoor dining when weather permits and live jazz Tues–Thurs.

NECI Commons 25 Church St ☎802/862-6324. One of the seven Vermont restaurants operated by the New England Culinary Institute. You can sit at tables inside or on the street terrace, but it's more fun to take one of the high stools facing the open kitchen and watch the students churn out halibut in plum wine broth, vegan risotto, and "uncommon meatloaf," all under the watchful eye of the teacher chef. Very popular, so reservations are recommended. The on-site *Deli* also features student creations, and many of the cakes and sandwiches are half price after 6pm.

Pauline's Café and Restaurant 1834 Shelburne Rd, South Burlington ☎802/862-1081. Inventive American cuisine with a continental flavor, using local produce. Light meals in a casual setting downstairs, more formality and higher prices upstairs.

Penny Cluse Café 169 Cherry St ☎802/651-8834. Omelets made to order, pancakes, sandwiches, salads, and good vegetarian lunches for under $10. Only open for breakfast and lunch.

Red Onion 140 Church St ☎802/865-2563. The best sandwiches in town are made to order here in this small shop with a mouth-watering menu, which includes some good vegetarian options. The "red onion" sandwich is a standout, and can easily fill two people for the price of one.

Shanty on the Shore 181 Battery St ☎802/864-0238. Absolutely fresh seafood in a laid-back setting with views of Lake Champlain. Burlington's best – if not only – raw bar.

Smokejack's 156 Church St ☎802/658-1119. Innovative American cuisine as well as standard steak and seafood, all smoked over an oak-wood grill. Liquid refreshment comes in the form of punchy Bloody Marys, six different types of martinis, and comforting hot chocolate and homemade marshmallows for the winter.

Sneakers 36 Main St, Winooski ☎802/655-908. This is the place for breakfast, and you ought to arrive early for it on weekends. Delicious waffles, homemade granola, eggs Benedict (try the smoked turkey eggs Benedict) and fresh squeezed juices served in a diner-like decor with Art Deco mirrors lining the walls. Good weekday lunches too.

Sweetwaters 120 Church St ☎802/864-9800. American grill standards in a converted bank with sidewalk dining, most notable for its bison burgers and extensive Sunday brunch. Attractive raised street terrace – open in good weather, with windows in bad.

Trattoria Delia 152 St Paul St ☎802/864-5253. Modern Italian fare that goes beyond the usual pasta dishes – try the wild boar served over soft polenta – and a great wine list, at reasonable prices.

Zabby's Stone Soup 211 College St ☎802/862-7616. Excellent "mostly vegetarian" café, featuring a wide variety of sandwiches, homemade soups, cakes, and the like.

Nightlife and entertainment

The **drinking** scene here is at its most active when school is in session, but Burlington's cafés and bars come to life during the summer as well. Though there are a handful of dance clubs, the **nightlife** in Burlington revolves mostly around live music. Pick up a copy of the free newspaper, *Seven Days*, which has listings of music and stage shows. Several of its concert venues are big enough to draw indie bands from New York and around New England, but the local band scene is a formidable presence in its own right. Downtown's Art Deco-style **Flynn Theater**, 153 Main St, across from City Hall and the Church Street Marketplace (☎802/863-5966), plays host to a wide array of talent, from concerts by local hippie heroes Phish to works by Broadway touring companies. The Comedy Slam, inside the *Radisson Hotel*, 60 Battery St (☎802/658-6500), hosts nationally acclaimed comics about once a month. Beware that bars and clubs are quite strict about checking IDs, as this is a college town. Make sure to have proper proof of age with you when venturing out for the evening or you are guaranteed to be disappointed.

Club Metronome 188 Main St ☎802/865-4563. This very hip club above *Nectar's* (see below) hosts some live acts, but is mainly a funked-out dance scene featuring house and techno music. Saturday nights is "Retronome" when Seventies and Eighties music dominates the dance floor. Over-21 only.

Liquid Energy 57 Church St ☎802/860-7666. The "energy" in the title refers more to the stimulating effects derived from invigorating and imaginative fruit juices and smoothies than from the small selection of coffees. Serves equally creative alcoholic cocktails in the evenings.

Millennium 165 Church St ☎802/660-2088. The fancy Art Deco interior here (formerly *Club Toast*) serves as the backdrop for dancing, usually to hip-hop and techno, with the occasional theme night thrown in for variety.

Muddy Waters 184 Main St ☎802/658-0466. Crazy interior lined with used furniture and thrift store rejects. Colorful, crunchy clientele adorn this popular coffeehouse. Extremely potent caffeine beverages.

Nectar's 188 Main St ☎802/658-4771. Follow the rotating neon sign to this retro lounge lined with vinyl booths and Formica tables. Sip a stylish cocktail, smoke a Lucky Strike, and tap your feet to lounge acts. This was the inspiration for Phish's 1995 album title *In the Face of Nectar*, as the club hosted many of their earliest shows.

Rasputin's Church Street ☎802/864-9324. Popular UVM hangout with a rowdy drinking scene that carries on until late in the evening. Good DJs pump up the energy level to new heights on weekends.

Red Square 136 Church St ☎802/859-8909. For those in the mood for a cosmopolitan experience in the depths of the Green Mountains, *Red Square* is the place to sip cocktails amidst a highbrow clientele. The food menu is also quite inviting and worth investigating further. Live music, often jazz, played outside when the weather permits.

Ruben James 153 Main St ☎802/864-0744. This joint brings in a slightly older crowd for delectable microbrews, loud live bar music, pool tournaments, and the viewing of football games.

Three Needs 207 College St ☎802/658-0889. This bar does a fine job of taking care of its customers' three most important needs: great beer, cheap pool, and Sunday night *Simpsons* parties with excellent drink specials.

Vermont Pub and Brewery 144 College St ☎802/865-0500. Roomy and convivial brewpub, offering free tastes of its various beers – Dogbite Bitter is the best – plus a good menu with live music on some weekends.

South of Burlington: underwater preserves

Vermont is one of the few states with designated **Underwater Historic Preserves** (details on ☎802/828-3226), where divers can see wrecks on the lake floor. There are several of these underwater "state parks" close to Burlington, and the best place to find out about them is at the **Lake Champlain Maritime Museum** in Basin Harbor, six miles east of **VERGENNES** (daily: May–Oct 10am–5pm; $5; ☎802/475-2022). The museum boasts a life-sized replica of the 1776 gunboat *Philadelphia II*, displays on Lake Champlain shipwrecks and the technology used to research them, and details of the horse-powered ferry that plied the lake a century ago. The museum is on the grounds of the Basin Harbor Club, where the *Red Mill Restaurant* serves three meals a day in summer, breakfast-only at other times.

Mount Independence

Outside of the town of Orwell, 25 miles south of Vergennes at the very south-eastern tip of Lake Champlain, is **Mount Independence**, site of a major American defeat in the Revolutionary War. Mount Independence was built as a fort in 1776, along with the more famous Fort Ticonderoga on the opposite shore, to repel a British attack from Canada. The two forts initially provided such an intimidating sight that British general Guy Carleton aborted his invasion in October 1776. However, the following winter was brutal, and most of the troops deserted, leaving 2500 American soldiers behind to fall ill or freeze to death. Springtime brought reinforcements insufficient to withstand an attack from General Burgoyne, and the fort was abandoned on July 5, 1777. The British occupied the Mount until November of the same year, when they burned the fort in response to General Burgoyne's surrender across the water at Saratoga. Today, the **Mount Independence State Historic Site** (daily: late May to mid-Oct 8.30am–5pm) is a pleasingly low-key affair, just a small museum with a few artifacts and some documentation of that dreadful winter, plus four hiking trails around the Mount, with a few spots marking relics of the fort (mostly piles of rocks that had been foundation). It's a relaxing place, with relatively few visitors and nice views of the lake by which to enjoy the solitude.

Champlain Islands

The sparsely populated **Champlain Islands** curl southward into Lake Champlain from Canada, comprising four narrow, oblong land masses – **NORTH HERO**, **GRAND ISLE**, **ALBURG**, and **ISLE LA MOTTE** – that never really caught on development-wise, despite being the site of the first settlement in Vermont, way back in 1666. After the Revolutionary War, Vermonters Ira and Ethan Allen staked claims to much of the islands' area, modestly naming them North and South Hero (the latter was later changed to Grand Isle). Today, though, the islands' only real industry is farming, evidenced by the silo-dotted hayfields and ubiquitous bovine odor.

French explorer Pierre de St-Paul's short-lived encampment is now occupied by **St Anne's Shrine**, West Shore Road, Isle La Motte, a statue of a prayerful St Anne that during the season is surrounded by visiting groups of devoted Catholics and amateur miracle purveyors; the shrine is right near a popular beach. Also on the island is a massive granite statue of **Samuel de Champlain**, who first landed here in 1609. Grand Isle's claim to historical fame is the **Hyde Log Cabin**, US-2 (late May to mid-Oct Thurs–Mon 11am–5pm; free), built in 1783 and housing a modest museum, notable for its collection of household artifacts like churns, rusty bedpans, and makeshift ovens from Vermont's earliest frontier days.

There is surprisingly little outdoor activity in these parts save for hunting and fishing, though some good opportunities exist for swimming during summertime. The area's best beach is the nearly half-mile strand at **Sand Bar State Park** (☎802/893-2825), actually on the mainland just below the US-2 bridge to Grand Isle. If that one's too crowded (as it often is in summer), head to **Knight Point State Park**, North Hero (☎802/372-8389), a placid, sandy shoreline enclosed by a bay.

Practicalities

The Champlain Islands are accessible by road along US-2, which is linked to Grand Isle, North Hero, and Alburg by a network of bridges. Isle La Motte lies at the end of Rte-129. The best way of getting to the Champlain Islands if you don't have your own motorized transport is by **bicycle** (for more on renting bikes in Burlington, see p.425), via the **Island Line Rail Trail**, which follows the dramatic path of a railroad causeway built by the Rutland Railroad in 1900 to connect the Great Lakes with the New England seacoast. Much of the old rail bed is now a trail for walkers and non-motorized traffic, starting a couple of miles south of Burlington and continuing up across Lake Champlain and its islands.

△ Tractor, Vermont farm

Should you desire to find a **place to stay** on the islands, the *Thomas Mott Homestead*, along Rte-78, Alburg (Ⓣ802/796-3736 or 1-800/348-0843, Ⓦwww.thomas-mott-bb.com; ❺), is the superior B&B choice, with large rooms, comfortable beds, modern furniture, and fantastic cooking in its accompanying restaurants. Less expensive is *Charlie's Northland Lodge*, along US-2 in North Hero (Ⓣ802/372-8822, Ⓔdorclrk@aol.com; ❹), a cozy hostelry with shared baths. The Champlain Islands do offer some of Vermont's best **camping**. Knight Island State Park (Ⓣ802/524-6353) is enormously secluded, with a multitude of unspoiled nature trails, though you should reserve early to get one of the seven primitive campsites ($13). Grand Isle State Park, 36 E Shore Rd S, Grand Isle (Ⓣ802/372-4300), provides a suitable alternative, with 156 highly developed campsites ($15), replete with restrooms, hot showers, and RVs galore.

The islands offer nothing special in the way of **eating**, though carnivores will enjoy the *Sand Bar Inn*, US-2, Grand Isle (Ⓣ802/372-6911), an all-American steakhouse with sweeping lake views. The *Ruthcliffe Lodge and Restaurant*, Old Quarry Road, Isle La Motte (Ⓣ802/928-3200 or 1-800/769-8162), serves decent steak-and-potatoes type fare for daily dinner, though lodgers get breakfast too.

For information on attractions and accommodation, contact the **Lake Champlain Islands Chamber of Commerce**, US-2, North Hero (Ⓣ802/372-8400 or 1-800/262-5226, Ⓦwww.champlainislands.com).

St Albans and around

Sleepy **ST ALBANS**, about halfway between Burlington and the Canadian border along I-89, is a town only by Vermont's standards, able to be seen by foot in less than an hour. Although there's some ugly mall sprawl to the north, St Albans' center has a large town green, landscaped on the slope of a hill, lined with churches at the top and small, mostly local, shops at the bottom. It's most notable for its curious distinction as the site of the northernmost engagement of the Civil War. The "St Albans Raid" took place on October 22, 1864, when disguised Confederate soldiers entered the town from Canada, robbed its three banks of over $200,000, took some hostages, killed one citizen, and decamped to Québec, where they were arrested and tried but never extradited back to the US. The town makes much of this event, particularly during the Civil War Days festival in late October, when history buffs descend here to re-create the event. Meanwhile, the **St Albans Historical Museum**, Church Street, at Bishop (mid-June to Sept Mon–Fri 1–4pm; $3; Ⓣ802/527-7933), also has displays on the raid, as well as a range of exhibits that vary greatly in quality. The best of these are the collections of artifacts from the town's earliest days, including military memorabilia, a re-created railroad station, and arcane remedies and antique medical devices recovered from local physicians and apothecaries. St Albans is also, as seat of the largest maple-producing county in the US, home to Vermont's Annual Maple Festival, held in April, locally known as the "Sugarin' Off" party.

Practicalities

The **St Albans Area Chamber of Commerce**, 2 N Main St (Ⓣ802/524-2444 or 1-800/262-5226, Ⓦwww.stalbanschamber.com), is probably your best bet for tourist information. **Accommodation** in and around the town is

The legacy of Chester A. Arthur

One of the least celebrated famous figures in Vermont history, President **Chester A. Arthur**, hailed from the small community of Fairfield, about seven miles east of St Albans along Rte-36. Or did he? His rather undistinguished presidency came under fire over a dispute about his upbringing.

Arthur, widely regarded as an ineffectual man with a few powerful connections, ascended from the vice-presidency to commander-in-chief when the twentieth president of the United States, James A. Garfield, was shot in 1881. He was not made more popular by the fact that the assassin's last words were, "I am a Stalwart and Arthur will be President," implying that Garfield was killed not for anything he had done, but to make way for an Arthur presidency. This controversy was followed by the publication of a political tract entitled "How a British Subject Became President of the United States," by feisty journalist A.P. Hinman, who claimed that Arthur had actually been born over the Canadian border, rendering him ineligible for the presidency. No hard evidence was ever produced, just a lot of debate and argument. Regardless, the president failed to win re-election (or even his party's nomination); indeed, he was dogged by kidney disease that would fell him not two years after the end of his term.

Today, you can visit the **Chester A. Arthur Historic Site** (daily: late May to mid-Oct 10am–4pm) in Fairfield, which celebrates his humble origins and otherwise unremarkable presidency while painting a pleasant picture of the murkiness surrounding the actual site of his birth.

reasonable compared to the rest of the state. Least expensive is the *Cadillac Motel*, 213 S Main St (Ⓣ802/524-2191, Ⓦwww.motel-cadillac.com; ❸), which is low on amenities, but very clean and surrounded by pleasant grounds replete with waterfall. The area's best B&B is the *Old Mill River Place*, 6206 Georgia Shore Rd (Ⓣ802/524-6953; ❹), featuring antique-filled rooms in a restored 1799 farmhouse with views of Lake Champlain.

Eating options won't dazzle or disappoint. Hearty meat-and-potatoes fare can be had at *Diamond Jim's Grille*, north of town along US-7 (N Main Street), in the Highgate Mall Shopping Center (Ⓣ802/524-9280). *Simple Pleasures Café*, 84 N Main St (Ⓣ802/527-0669), serves tasty light lunches, while the ethnically confused bar/restaurant *McGuel's Irish Burro Café*, 18 Lake St (Ⓣ802/527-1276; closed Sun), has south-of-the-border fare and a dizzying array of beers. There's also *The Brew Lab*, 201 Main St (Ⓣ802/524-2772), home of Franklin County Brewery, for quality microbrews.

Around St Albans

The coast of Lake Champlain beckons a mere three miles west of town along Rte-36, where the **Kill Kare State Park** (Ⓣ802/524-6021; summer only) has some decent swimming and boating facilities, though it tends to be crowded. Better to take the $3 ferry to the state park on nearby **Burton Island** (Ⓣ802/524-6353; summer only), much more secluded, with three miles of shoreline, hiking trails, and boat and canoe rentals, as well as 42 **campsites**. North of St Albans along I-89, just below the Canadian border, Rte-78 veers west to the **Missisquoi National Wildlife Refuge** in **SWANTON** (Ⓣ802/868-4781; free), a remote lakeside nature preserve where you can meet Vermont's native beasts face-to-face. The fauna range from the mundane (ducks, deer, and turtles) to the borderline scary (vampire bats). Best to bring along bug repellent, especially during summer.

Northeast Kingdom

Remote and relentlessly rural, Vermont's **Northeast Kingdom** takes its name from a remark made by Vermont Senator George Aiken in 1949, referring to the several counties that bulge out eastward to form the state's uppermost corner. The only locales approaching town status are **St Johnsbury** and **Newport**, at the region's southern and northern boundaries, each of which has less than nine thousand inhabitants. I-91 slices through the kingdom, but you can't really appreciate the area's intense quiet and natural beauty without traveling along its innumerable back roads. Here you can drive for hours, passing through vast expanses of green, punctuated by cows, barns, and other bucolic accessories. Aside from its idyllic character, the region offers little in the way of formal sights, with a few notable exceptions such as Glover's **Bread and Puppet Museum**, though opportunities for recreation abound; indeed two of the state's least crowded and most challenging ski areas, **Jay Peak** and **Burke Mountain**, are in this region.

St Johnsbury and around

The town of **ST JOHNSBURY** imagines itself a thriving metropolis in the midst of Vermont's sparsely populated northeast corner; however, its abundance of elaborate architecture, all turrets and marble and stained glass, seems terribly out of proportion to its size. Still, it's the biggest municipality around (the nearest town is Barre, 35 miles away on US-2), and an important travel hub if you happen to be heading this far up.

St J, as it's referred to by locals, grew from a frontier outpost to its current size thanks to the ingenuity of resident **Thaddeus Fairbanks**, the "scale king," who earned his fortune and a minor place in history by inventing the platform scale in the 1830s. Much of his riches were showered on the city in the form of funding for new municipal buildings and elaborate churches. One place that celebrates his legacy, the Romanesque **Fairbanks Museum and Planetarium**, 1302 Main St, at Prospect (Mon–Sat 9am–5pm, Sun 1–5pm, planetarium shows Sat & Sun 1.30pm; museum $5, planetarium $3; ⓣ802/748-2372, ⓦwww.fairbanksmuseum.org), has the predictable range of platform scales, plus a varied collection of historical and scientific artifacts, from Civil War pieces to Zulu war shields to various Japanese handicrafts, including an excellent collection of tiny *netsuke* figurines. It also serves as an official US **weather station**, though some of this is out of sight of the viewing public. Just down Main Street, the **St Johnsbury Athenaeum** (Mon & Wed 10am–8pm, Tues, Thurs & Fri 10am–5.30pm, Sat 9.30am–4pm, closed Sun; free; ⓣ802/748-8291) houses a number of excellent paintings from the Hudson River school, including Andrew Bierstadt's gargantuan *Domes of the Yosemite*.

If you're caught in this part of the world with a yearning for something to *do*, you may find your needs fulfilled by the surprisingly eclectic offerings at the **Catamount Arts Center**, 139 East Ave (ⓣ802/748-2600 or 1-888/757-5559). The small brick building houses a movie theater showing foreign and art films, a concert hall where the offerings focus on jazz, New Age, and world music, a café, and an excellent video store, specializing in foreign films.

Practicalities

Vermont Transit **buses** arrive in St Johnsbury twice a day at Champlain Farms, 125 Railroad St (Ⓣ802/748-4000). The **Northeast Kingdom Chamber of Commerce**, 357 Western Ave (Mon–Sat 10am–5pm; Ⓣ802/748-3678 or 1-800/639-6379, Ⓦwww.nekchamber.com), dispenses information on the whole region, and has a **booth** at the intersection of Main and Eastern streets during summer and fall.

Accommodation is limited mostly to relatively cheap, independent motels packed with travelers taking respite from their sojourns along I-91. One of the more well-accoutered is the *Fairbanks Inn*, 401 Western Ave (Ⓣ802/748-5666; ⑤), which has a heated pool, putting green, and cable TV. There's also the *Yankee Traveler Motel*, 342 Portland St (Ⓣ802/748-3156; ③), a 42-room hotel with a pool, cable TV, and cheerful staff. Cheaper and closer to the town center, the *Maple Center Motel*, 20 Hastings St (Ⓣ802/748-2393; ③), and the *Holiday Motel*, 25 Hastings St (Ⓣ802/742-8192; ③), have comfortable rooms with all the basics.

There is not as much choice as far as **eating** goes. Try *Gerardo's*, 215 Railroad St (Ⓣ802/748-6772; closed Mon), which serves light, inexpensive modern Italian dishes. For a quick pastry or sandwich and some strong coffee, there is the *Northern Lights Book Shop and Cafe*, 79 Railroad St (Ⓣ802/748-4463), which also offers a quirky collection of books.

West of St Johnsbury

DANVILLE, a nondescript town that lies about ten miles west of St Johnsbury at the intersection of US-2 and Rte-15, stakes its limited claim to notoriety as the headquarters of the American Society of Dowsers, based in

Vermont's cheeses

An economic lightweight at a national – and even a regional – level, Vermont does have a habit of doing a few things very well: ice cream, maple syrup, and, perhaps most notably, cheese. Of course, nostalgic cheese historians will look back to the heady days at the turn of last century when eighty percent of Vermont's milk was being made into butter and cheese, and lament that things aren't what they once were. Still, the state produces a very respectable seventy million pounds of cheese a year, with a significant amount coming from family farms using traditional methods: the type of product good enough to scoop twelve awards at the eighteenth American Cheese Society Annual Conference & Judging in 2001. Predictably, the tourist industry has cashed in on the reputation of Vermont cheese, and refrigerators containing the most sought after brands hum and rattle in gift shops statewide. If it's cheddar you're after, the best known is probably Cabot Cheddar, which comes in a variety of sharp flavors. Crowley Cheddar is less acidic and moister than the English-style cheeses made elsewhere in Vermont; Grafton Village Cheese is known for its older cheddars with an earthy, creamy taste; and Neighborly Farms for its organic cheddar. Cheeses made with sheep's milk, such as feta, camembert, and brie, are produced by Peaked Mountain Farm and Vermont Shepherd, among others; while Lazy Lady Farm and Vermont Butter and Cheese Company are the top names in goat's-milk cheese. Such is the pull of cheese in this state, that several of the above-mentioned producers – and others not featured here – have formed the **Vermont Cheese Trail**, opening their doors to the paying public to reveal cheese-making methods and give away pounds and pounds of free samples. For more information, contact the Vermont Cheese Council (Ⓣ1-888/523-7484).

Dowser's Hall, on Danville Green (Ⓣ802/684-3417), where you'll find displays and literature on the practice of intuitively identifying underground water sources using a forked branch or pendulum.

Vermont is justifiably proud of its cheese (see box, p.437), and the small town of **CABOT**, a few miles further west from Danville, is the epicenter of the state's cheese production. The **Cabot Creamery** (visitors' center daily: late May to Oct 9am–5pm; winter closed Sun) churns out around fifteen million pounds of cheese a year, or approximately twenty percent of the total state production. Tours leave every thirty minutes ($1), starting with a twelve-minute video explaining how Cabot got to where it is today, a walk through the plant itself, and ending with an opportunity to gorge yourself on the several different varieties of cheddar for which the company has become known.

CRAFTSBURY, farther north on slow, bumpy Rte-14, is just about in the middle of nowhere – which is exactly its appeal. This is as perfectly lovely a tiny Vermont town as you're likely to see, with a history that stretches back to the mid-eighteenth century and includes one native son who served as Vermont's governor. It has seen virtually no growth in the 200-plus years since its inception; the town center, **Craftsbury Common**, consists of little more than a post office and some lovely inns, best of which are the very upmarket *Inn on the Common* (Ⓣ802/586-9619 or 1-800/521-2233, Ⓦwww.innonthecommon.com; ⑨), whose dining room serves excellent traditional American fare, and the homey *Whetstone Brook B&B*, 1037 S Craftsbury Rd (Ⓣ802/586-6916; ④). While the main recreation here is getting away from activity, the surrounding hills are crisscrossed with a web of **trails** popular for mountain biking and skiing. The Craftsbury Outdoor Center (Ⓣ802/729-7751 or 1-800/729-7751) provides service for all your needs in these activities.

North to Canada

From St Johnsbury, I-91 runs north up to Canada; everything east of the highway is fairly mountainous, and there are a few good diversions not too far off the main road – though if you wander too far off you could easily get lost, as much of the region is undeveloped. This part of the Kingdom is home to a number of pristine lakes and abundant wildlife, including some ten thousand moose.

Burke Mountain and Lake Willoughby

The cream of the United States' crop of young downhill skiers train at the **Burke Mountain Resort**, Mountain Road, East Burke (Ⓣ802/626-3322, Ⓦwww.skiburke.com), best approached from I-91 exit 23 onto US-5, then north on Rte-114. Because of the mountain's isolation, Burke's 43 trails are virtually deserted compared to places such as Killington and Stowe, but they're all tough; indeed, intermediate range is as easy as it gets (lift tickets $29 Mon–Fri, $39 Sat–Sun). East Burke is also one of the access points to the **Kingdom Trails** (Ⓣ802/626-0737, Ⓦwww.kingdomtrails.org), a hundred miles of publicly and privately owned land where you can go **mountain biking**, **hiking**, or **cross-country skiing**. Purchase trail passes ($5 a day) and get information on trail routes and access points at East Burke Sports, Rte-114, East Burke Village (Ⓣ802/626-3215, Ⓦwww.eastburkesports.com). Venture up US-5 to its intersection with Rte-5A and continue north for several miles to be rewarded with views of spectacular **Lake Willoughby**, which is flanked on either side by **mounts Hor** and **Pisgah**. Recreational opportunities abound, from jet-skiing to swimming (there are sand beaches at the lake's north and south ends). Be sure to take note of the waterfalls that line the mountainsides along Rte-5A. Few people **stay** in areas this remote, but the *Willough Vale Inn* (ⓣ802/525-4123 or 1-800/594-9102, ⓦwww.willoughvale.com; ❺), just off Rte-5A, offers both rooms and lakefront cottages in a wonderfully secluded setting; there's also a first-rate restaurant.

Glover and Newport

The only reason to hit **GLOVER**, fifteen miles north of St Johnsbury on Rte-122, is to stop by the **Bread and Puppet Museum** (daily 10am–5pm; free; ⓣ802/525-3031), which got its start in the 1960s from a traveling dramatic troupe that performed anti-Vietnam War puppet shows. The remarkably over-sized puppets – they can be as big as five feet and require up to four people to operate – can now be viewed in this peaceful barn setting, a far cry from the group's more volatile protest days. There are free performances every Sunday.

The obscurely located **Old Stone House**, about ten miles south of Newport, just off Rte-58 in Brownington (daily: July–Aug 11am–5pm; mid-May to June & Sept to mid-Oct Fri–Tues 11am–5pm; $5; ⓣ802/754-2022), is tricky to find but worth the trouble. Originally a schoolhouse built by the **Reverend Alexander Twilight**, said to be the country's first African-American college graduate and legislator (a point contested by some historians, due to Twilight's mixed-race background), today the building is home to an array of Vermont artifacts, including, most interestingly, schoolroom supplies from the period.

The final stop on I-91 before the Québec border, unassuming **NEWPORT** seems more French-Canadian than New England in character. Its main draw is **Lake Memphremagog**, which spans the international border and was once a choice resort area surrounded by grand homes. The lake area is no longer quite so upscale, but still popular enough with vacationing Québecers, who flock here to boat, jet-ski, and swim. The town's drag, Main Street, is lined with quaint brick buildings, many of which are restored relics from the Victorian era and house twee **cafés** with bilingual menus. The best of these are *Miss Newport Diner*, 429 E Main St (ⓣ802/334-7742), one of Vermont's more celebrated diners, serving breakfast all day, and *Brown Cow*, 350 E Main St (ⓣ802/334-7887), for fresh salads and excellent soup. Should you need to **stay** in Newport, the *Newport City Motel*, 974 E Main St (ⓣ802/334-6558 or 1-800/338-6558; ❸), is a decent, if bland, option.

Jay Peak

The 4000-foot summit of the **Jay Peak Resort**, on Rte-242 (ⓣ802/988-2611 or 1-800/451-4449, ⓦwww.jaypeakresort.com), looms just south of the Canadian border, about fifteen miles west of I-91. Jay's 75 trails are some of New England's toughest, and typically only serious skiers venture this far out – unless coming down from Québec. Indeed, those visitors who can prove Canadian residency are allowed to buy the $53 lift tickets with the same amount of Canadian dollars, a concession which results in a considerable saving. Jay Peak consistently receives more snow than any other New England resort, an average of 351 inches a year, something which makes deep-powder skiing a distinct possibility through late April. It has also given the resort a name as the most exciting glade (or tree) skiing in North America. The most popular **accommodation** is *Hotel Jay* (make reservations through the resort at ⓣ1-800/451-4449; ❹), a snazzy ski lodge at the base of the peak; the hotel has deals on lift tickets, a hot tub, and the *Golden Eagle Lounge*, which hosts the area's best après-ski scene. The nearby *Jay Village Inn*, Jay Village (ⓣ802/988-2306 or 1-800/227-7452; ❹), offers fifteen snug rooms, a busy recreation room, and a quaint French-Canadian restaurant. For a good meal, venture a few miles from Jay, where *The Belfry*, on Rte-242 in Montgomery Center (ⓣ802/326-4400), has a relaxed pub atmosphere and meaty specials.

7

New Hampshire

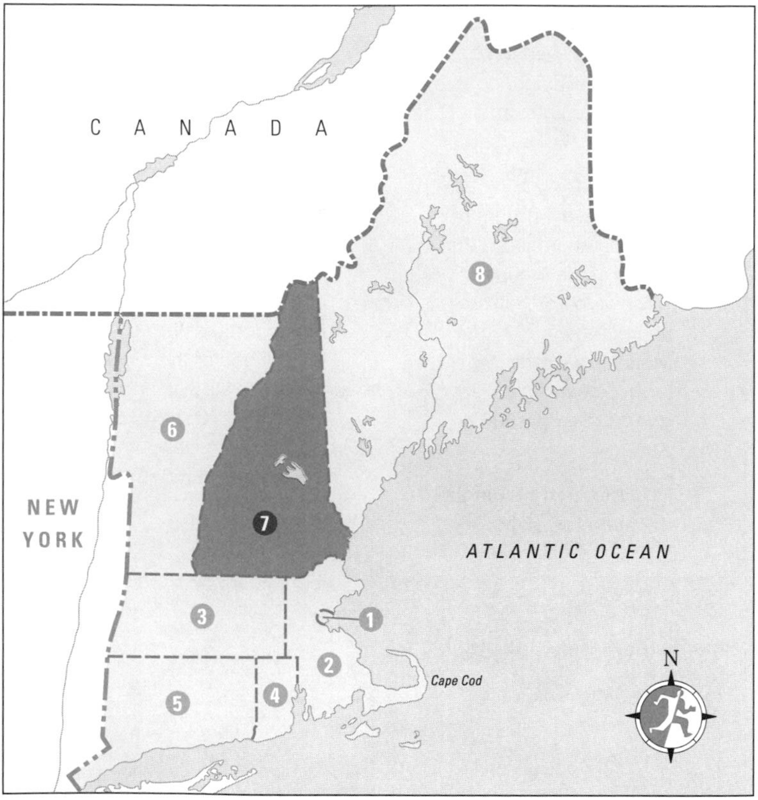
CANADA
NEW YORK
ATLANTIC OCEAN
Cape Cod
N
1
2
3
4
5
6
7
8

CHAPTER 7 Highlights

* **Canterbury Shaker Village** A bit of a living museum near Concord, where you can see traditional Shaker values put to work. See p.466
* **Portsmouth** That rare commodity: a seaside town with culture and class, displayed in its historic buildings, gourmet restaurants, and highbrow shows. See p.448
* **Grand resort hotels** If you can afford it, hit the luxury of the *Mount Washington* or *Balsams* up in the White Mountains – a far cry from a local campground. See pp.506 & 515
* **Cross-country skiing, Jackson** For all its mountainous terrain, New Hampshire still has some excellent places for cross-country skiing, none finer than the pristine and varied trails at Jackson. See p.510
* **Story Land, Glen** With so many attractions geared to adults, the region's answer to Disneyland will keep the kids amused for hours. See p.511
* **Mount Washington** So what if there's a road leading up to the summit of the highest mountain in the northeastern US – it's still one of the most remote, awe-inspiring, and unpredictably exciting places in New England. See p.513

7

New Hampshire

Similar to Rhode Island, **New Hampshire** is a relatively small state (the 44th largest in the US), with surprisingly diverse terrain. The short coastline is strewn with mellow, sun-drenched beaches and capped by **Portsmouth**, a well-preserved colonial town with a crop of excellent restaurants and stylish inns. Further inland, there are over 1300 lakes to explore, the largest, **Lake Winnipesaukee**, ringed with both developed tourist resorts and quiet villages. To the north, the splendor of the **White Mountains** spreads right across the state, culminating in the highest peak in New England, the formidable **Mount Washington**. Apart from these obvious attractions, quaint and relaxing communities scatter in particular abundance across the southern part of the state, connected by shaded, winding country roads and the enduring small-town pride of their residents.

These days most visitors come to New Hampshire for its outdoor activities. In the warm summer months you can kayak, canoe, swim, fish, hike, climb, or bike, while during winter you can cross-country and downhill ski at one of over a dozen ski areas – the **Franconia Notch** area has a high concentration of downhill resorts, while tiny **Jackson** is famous for cross-country skiing. As with much of the rest of New England, fall is a popular time to come, when the trees turn vibrant shades of red, orange, and yellow, and the air temperature drops refreshingly.

All of which makes New Hampshire a busy place, even by New England standards. Much of the state is blanketed with bucolic rural scenery – around **Canterbury Shaker Village** near Concord, for example – but the current tourist authority's motto, "The Road Less Traveled," is not entirely accurate. Some of the major destinations, such as **Weirs Beach**, **North Conway**, and **Hampton Beach**, are extremely well traveled. But if you steer clear of these main draws, the lakes, islands, and snowcapped peaks that define New Hampshire remain both resoundingly spectacular and remote.

Some history

The people of New Hampshire have been an independent and individualistic lot ever since the first settlers of the region survived out of sheer persistence. Though originally explored by Martin Pring in 1603, the first European settlement was not established until 1623, when Englishman David Thomson brought a small group to **Odiorne Point**, at the mouth of the Piscataqua River.

Soon after, the Royal Council of New England issued land grants to two of its most prominent members, Sir Ferdinando Gorges and John Mason, who founded the Laconia Company with the intention of turning a profit in the

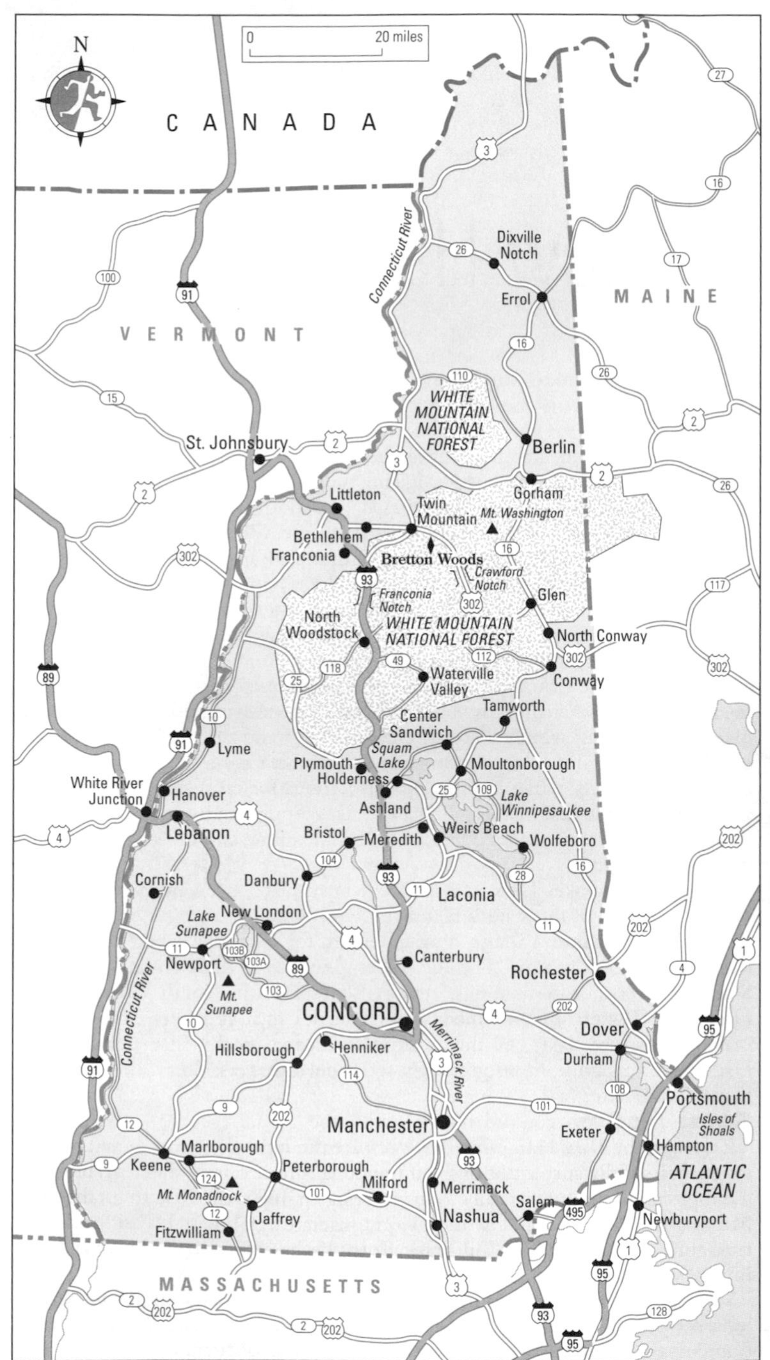
N
0
20 miles
CANADA
VERMONT
MAINE
MASSACHUSETTS
ATLANTIC OCEAN
WHITE MOUNTAIN NATIONAL FOREST
WHITE MOUNTAIN NATIONAL FOREST
Connecticut River
Connecticut River
Merrimack River
Dixville Notch
Errol
Berlin
Gorham
St. Johnsbury
Littleton
Twin Mountain
Mt. Washington
Bethlehem
Franconia
Bretton Woods
Crawford Notch
Franconia Notch
Glen
North Conway
Conway
North Woodstock
Waterville Valley
Tamworth
Center Sandwich
Squam Lake
Moultonborough
Plymouth
Holderness
Ashland
Lake Winnipesaukee
Lyme
White River Junction
Hanover
Lebanon
Bristol
Meredith
Weirs Beach
Wolfeboro
Cornish
Danbury
Laconia
Lake Sunapee
New London
Newport
Mt. Sunapee
Canterbury
Rochester
CONCORD
Dover
Durham
Hillsborough
Henniker
Portsmouth
Isles of Shoals
Manchester
Exeter
Hampton
Keene
Marlborough
Peterborough
Milford
Merrimack
Mt. Monadnock
Jaffrey
Fitzwilliam
Nashua
Salem
Newburyport

fur trade between the Merrimack and Sagadahock rivers. Without ever having laid eyes on the land, Mason named the region New Hampshire, after his home county in England. Their colony struggled, and after Mason died in 1635, the company was dissolved. A small group of settlers, however, endured at **Strawbery Banke**, now Portsmouth, ignoring land ownership laws and taking large plots for themselves.

While only the few miles of seashore held sizeable seventeenth-century communities of European settlers, the harsh, glacier-scarred interior of New Hampshire, with its dense forests and forbidding mountains, remained the exclusive preserve of the Abenaki and Pennacook tribes of the **Algonquin Indians**. Relations with the Indians, though initially amiable, turned sour as settlers became more ambitious, damming rivers, logging the forests, introducing livestock, and scaring away game. Fearing they would lose their natural resources to the new settlers forever, the Indians attacked European settlements throughout New Hampshire in 1675. The conflict, known as King Philip's War, continued for several decades, but by the turn of the century the Indian population had been reduced from tens of thousands to less than a thousand – and more or less vanished from the state by 1730.

By this time, **Portsmouth** was a thriving port, and the financial backbone of the colony. Timber companies and shipbuilding businesses flourished as loggers pushed further inland from Portsmouth and up the Connecticut River from the south. By the mid-eighteenth century, an extremely profitable mast trade had been established, fueled by the region's dense supply of pine trees and the expansion of England's merchant marine fleet, and a wealthy upper class had developed in the thriving colony. Portsmouth resident Benning Wentworth was appointed the colony's governor in 1741, and under his leadership settlement continued to spread west. Just before the Revolutionary War, upon hearing that the king had issued an edict forbidding shipment of gunpowder to the colonies, some four hundred New Hampshire residents invaded **Fort William and Mary**, one of the first overt acts in defiance of England. In January 1776, New Hampshire became the first American state to declare its independence.

Life remained a struggle for many of the settlers of the rugged interior. When it became clear that farmers could make little agricultural impact on the rocky terrain of the "granite state," many laborers departed for more fertile lands to the west. With the coming of the Industrial Revolution, however, towns in the Merrimack Valley, such as Nashua, Concord, and Manchester, became major manufacturing centers. Water-powered textile mills were set up along the Merrimack River, and at one point the enormous brick **Amoskeag Mills** in Manchester produced more cloth than any other textile facility in the world.

For a while, the ruthless timber companies looked set to strip all northern New Hampshire bare, but the pristine landscape of the White Mountains turned out to be the state's greatest asset. Indeed, large-scale summer tourism began in the latter half of the nineteenth century, when city folk checked in to one of several dozen grand resort hotels (the *Mount Washington* in Bretton Woods and the *Balsams* in Dixville Notch are the only two that remain), which stood majestically at the foot of the mountains. At one stage, fifty trains brought travelers to the mountains daily to see such increasingly famous sites as the **Old Man of the Mountain**, now the ubiquitous state symbol. Many also rode the rickety **Cog Railway** (still operational) to the harsh and unpredictable summit of Mount Washington.

Tourism has now surpassed industry as the state's top money earner, but many long-time New Hampshire residents remain suspicious and unaccepting of outsiders, opting for a less intrusive government with fewer laws and

New Hampshire transport

Several major airlines fly in and out of the state's main **airport**, Manchester International (☎603/624-6539), which is conveniently located just off I-93. That's about all that is convenient as far as public transport in New Hampshire is concerned. **Train** services are limited to the tourist trains which run in the mountain areas and Amtrak's new *Downeaster*, which only stops in at the sleepy towns of Exeter, Durham, and Dover. You can get to a few more places by **bus**, but don't bank on seeing much of the northern part of the state if you don't have your own car. Companies which serve New Hampshire include Concord Trailways (☎1-800/639-3317), C&J Trailways (☎603/430-1100 or 1-800/258-7111), and Vermont Transit Lines (☎1-800/552-8737).

regulations. There is no sales or even personal income tax here – in fulfillment of the state motto, "Live Free or Die." Alternative sources of revenue include restaurant, hotel, and hefty property taxes, in addition to state-owned liquor stores – set up after prohibition and enthusiastically promoted: they even have them in freeway rest areas.

New Hampshire has also gained inordinate political clout as the venue of the **first primary election of each presidential campaign**, with its villages well used to playing host to would-be presidents on the stump. The New Hampshire presidential primary is viewed by many as a make-or-break event, and since the first one in 1952 the state has picked the candidates eventually nominated by both the Democrats and the Republicans eleven out of thirteen times. When perpetual rival Vermont suggested that it might have its primary first, New Hampshire quickly passed a law stating that its primaries would be held "on the Tuesday preceding the date on which any other New England state shall hold a similar election."

The seacoast region

New Hampshire's **coastline** stretches for just eighteen miles, the shortest of any US state with ocean access. Its sandy length, filling up the area between Hampton Beach on the south end and Portsmouth on the north, is well developed, but it's not difficult to find sparsely populated beaches.

Though separated by such a short distance, the two main coastal towns couldn't be less similar. **Portsmouth**, New Hampshire's resurgent cultural center, is bursting with well-preserved Colonial architecture, gourmet restaurants, and historic attractions; **Hampton Beach** is a sprawling arc of sand packed in summer with giggling teenagers and lined with a corresponding collection of video arcades, ice-cream parlors, and waterslides. In between, sleepy towns – small collections of a few elegant white-clapboard buildings and some ill-placed strip malls, really – blend into each other, spilling into laid-back beaches, such as **Jenness State Beach**, **Wallis Sands State Beach**, and **Rye Beach**.

West of busy I-95 – situated three miles inland and the main thoroughfare up from Massachusetts – the density of attractions (and people) drops off sharply.

The handsome and historically significant town of **Exeter**, with its shady streets lined with stately mansions, is home to the country's premier college preparatory school, Phillips Exeter Academy; to the north, **Durham** is centered around the University of New Hampshire's flagship campus.

Hampton Beach and around

It's difficult to understand why **HAMPTON BEACH** is so popular. The favorite vacation spot of many thousands of East Coasters – who gorge happily in the town's bad restaurants and pack themselves onto the crowded band of white sandy beach that stretches along the tacky strip – the town's ugly sprawl of cheaply constructed condominiums spreads across the flat, narrow peninsula that juts into the mouth of the Hampton River. It's a decidedly family-friendly resort, with enough arcades and waterparks to keep youngsters happy for days, but that aside there aren't many good reasons to stop here, unless you enjoy watching sunburned vacationers waddle from hot-dog stand to ice-cream shop to the beach and back again. One bright spot is the well-known *Hampton Beach Casino Ballroom*, a large performance venue right along the strip at 169 Ocean Blvd (call ⓣ603/929-4100 for information; tickets $15–30). This is the top choice for touring performers in the state, hosting nationally known rock bands and comedians. If you absolutely must **stay** here, the **Hampton Beach Chamber of Commerce** (ⓣ1-800/GET-A-TAN, ⓦwww.hamptonbeach.org) will help with room reservations. If you're **hungry**, you could stop at *Jack's Seafood*, 539 Ocean Blvd (ⓣ603/926-8053), for lobster "in the rough" and other seacoast specialties, but keep your expectations moderate.

The beach is more pleasant a few miles north along Rte-1A at **NORTH HAMPTON BEACH**, a more peaceful stretch of sand with abundant metered parking – though it still catches a bit of the slough from Hampton Beach. If you're in the area, you might also stop by the colorful **Fuller Gardens** (daily mid-May to mid-Oct 10am–5.30pm; $6), at the junction of Rte-1A and Rte-111. Designed in 1939 for Massachusetts governor Alvin Fuller, the gardens include over two thousand rose bushes and a Japanese section complete with bonsai trees.

Continuing north, Rte-1A winds along a picturesque strip of rocky coastline that includes "millionaires' row," where a collection of stately homes greets the ocean from enormous bay windows. There's a paved **walking path** along the water if you decide you'd like to take in the finely restored private oceanfront mansions at a more leisurely pace. In **RYE HARBOR**, at the State Marina, you can go **whale watching** with Atlantic Fleet (late May to mid-Oct; $25 ⓣ603/964-5220 or 1-800/WHALE-NH). Popular with surfers and families alike, **Jenness State Beach**, a little further north along Rte-1A, is even more serene, with few buildings and a protected stretch of white sand. Nearby **Wallis Sands State Beach** is also a good bet for swimming and sunning.

North towards Portsmouth

The mouth of the Piscataqua River along Rte-1A, **Odiorne Point State Park** ($3; ⓣ603/436-7406) marks the site of New Hampshire's first settlement, established in 1623 but vacated shortly after in favor of what is now Portsmouth. The park consists of some three hundred acres of protected coast

Seabrook Nuclear Power Station

Talk of a New England nuclear power plant began as early as the 1950s, but it wasn't until the energy crisis of the mid-1970s that legislators got serious. Construction of the **Seabrook Nuclear Power Station**, located about five miles south of Hampton on Rte-1, with funding from First National Bank, began in 1976, and vocal **protest** followed soon after. What started as a grassroots campaign, however, exploded into a national debate about the safety and feasibility of nuclear power. The construction spawned an outburst of vocal environmental groups, most notably the so-called **Clamshell Alliance**, which by the early 1980s had thousands of members. New Hampshire residents and politicians – including then-governor John Sununu – generally supported the construction, seeing it as a long-term energy saver, while residents of neighboring Massachusetts and their governor, Michael Dukakis, fearing negative environmental impacts, remained staunchly opposed. Even ice-cream maker **Ben and Jerry's** out in Vermont got involved in the fray, erecting a billboard in Boston that read "Stop Seabrook. Keep our customers alive and licking." Nevertheless, construction continued, and in 1990, after four years of testing and safety inspections, the nuclear plant began producing power. In the process, as expenses ballooned a staggering $4 billion over budget, New Hampshire's largest utility, the Public Service Company of New Hampshire, went bankrupt. The station is now owned jointly by eleven utility companies – although it was officially put up for auction in December 2001 – providing power for about one million New England homes, and spewing out more than eight million megawatt hours of electricity per year. New Hampshire residents currently pay the highest electric rates in the country, roughly twice the national average.

One small consolation that accompanied Seabrook's construction was the opening of the **Science and Nature Center at Seabrook Station**, on US-1 in Seabrook (by appointment only, call for reservations ⓣ603/773-7219 or 1-800/338-7482), where you can explore various exhibits about nuclear energy, electricity, and the environment, including displays of flora and fauna that populate the salt marshes nearby.

line with a well-maintained network of trails that includes a beautiful seaside bike path and picnic benches (see p.451 for information on bike rental). The park is also home to the **Seacoast Science Center**, 570 Ocean Blvd (daily 10am–5pm; $3), which presents a vaguely diverting array of science and natural history exhibits and has an indoor tide pool touch-tank and a small aquarium.

Along the eastern shore on the island of **New Castle**, a wealthy suburb of Portsmouth, there are a couple of historically relevant forts. **Fort Constitution** (formerly Fort William and Mary), along Rte-1B at the mouth of Portsmouth Harbor, was the site of one of the first overt acts of rebellion against the British, when, at the urging of Paul Revere, angry colonists attacked, pilfering gunpowder and cannons from unsuspecting British soldiers. Only the base of the walls remains, however. Just south stands **Fort Stark,** active in every war from the Revolutionary War through World War II. You can make a self-guided tour of the ten-acre site, including parts of the remodeled fort, but the ocean views are more eye-catching.

Portsmouth

Surprisingly attractive **PORTSMOUTH**, off of I-95 at the mouth of the Piscataqua River, blends small-town accessibility with the enthusiasm of a rejuvenated city. Having endured the many cycles of prosperity and hardship typical of many New England Colonial towns – including, most devastatingly, several major fires and the inevitable loss of its prominence as a port – Portsmouth has found its most recent triumphs in the cultural arena. Artists, musicians, writers, tourists, and, notably, gourmet chefs, attracted by Portsmouth's affordability, authentic Colonial flavor, and youthful exuberance, have converged on the quaint seaside town in recent years, paving the way for the yuppies who now populate the town's streets with their BMWs and modern brewpubs. This has made the town exceptionally young (the average age is 24), if a bit racially homogenous; still, with an attractive town center, a wealth of good restaurants, clean, uncongested streets, an inviting riverside park, and an unusual abundance of well-preserved Colonial buildings, it certainly makes for pleasant exploration.

Some history

Founded in the 1620s by English merchants hoping to turn a quick profit in the fur and fish trade, Portsmouth was, after Jamestown, the second New World commercial settlement of any size. Though initial efforts faltered with the death of leader John Mason in 1635, the immigrants soon established Portsmouth as a premier **seaport**, with thriving **shipbuilding** and commercial **fishing** industries. Demand for manual labor at the busy port was high, and religious

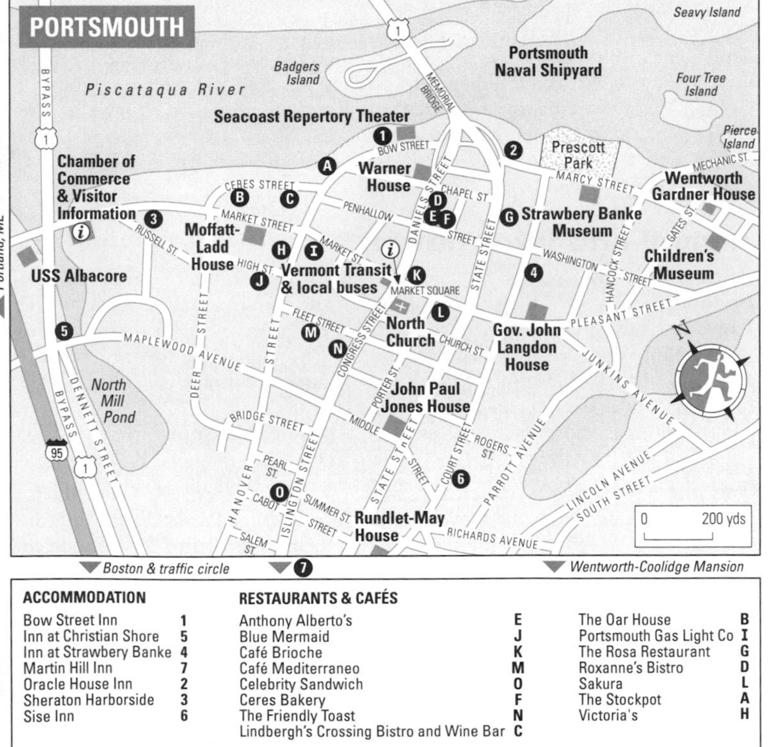

dissenters and common criminals from Puritan Massachusetts fled to Portsmouth during its early years, prompting complaints that the settlement attracted, and even welcomed, "desperately wicked" characters. With an abundance of timber in the surrounding regions, which was easily transported along the fast-flowing Piscataqua River, the prosperous shipyards produced enormous masts, entire trading vessels, and warships more cheaply than their British counterparts, and Portsmouth's boats were soon carrying goods – and fighting wars – all over the world.

As industry flourished, so did a well-heeled aristocratic class of merchants and ship captains, who constructed many of the fine eighteenth-century mansions and commercial buildings that remain prominent in the town today. However, the city's golden age peaked in 1800, after which the combination of the 1807 Embargo Act, the War of 1812, and three devastating **fires** plunged the city into decline.

Portsmouth went on to become a major center for **beer and ale** production after the Civil War, when the brick buildings along Market Street all housed breweries – though this industry, too, was to practically disappear half a century later with the onset of Prohibition. By the turn of the twentieth century, the **Portsmouth Naval Shipyard**, founded in 1800 by John Paul Jones as the US government's first shipyard (and still active, just across the Piscataqua River), had become the area's largest employer. As a result, Portsmouth became notorious as a seedy port of call, complete with a busy **red-light district**, a skyrocketing crime rate, and a raucous assortment of grungy taverns.

After angry citizens drove the revelers and prostitutes from their city in the early 1900s, Portsmouth settled into a long period of stagnation, still heavily dependent on the government-sponsored shipyard for its well-being. It wasn't until the 1950s that the city began to actively preserve and restore its colorful Colonial past, as citizens organized to save the area now known as the "Strawbery Banke Museum" from demolition. Their efforts were largely successful, and today Portsmouth remains one of the best-preserved Colonial towns in New England.

Arrival and information

Portsmouth's city center is huddled along the southern bank of the **Piscataqua River**, at the mouth of one of the finest natural harbors on the East Coast, just across from Kittery, Maine. Surrounded by water on three sides (South Mill Pond, North Mill Pond, and the Piscataqua), the town is compact and easily manageable on foot. At its heart, **Market Square** is flanked by the towering North Church, an easily located landmark.

Portsmouth is most easily accessible via **public transport** from Boston, either on C&J Trailways (Ⓣ1-800/258-7111), with frequent daily services from Boston, Newburyport (MA), and Durham (NH), or Vermont Transit Lines (Ⓣ603/436-0163), which runs buses five times daily along the coast between Boston and Portsmouth, stopping in Market Square opposite North Church. COAST (Cooperative Alliance for Seacoast Transportation; Ⓣ603/862-2328) connects Portsmouth with smaller cities in the Seacoast Region, such as Exeter, Dover, Hampton, and Seabrook. By **car**, the easiest way to reach downtown Portsmouth is via exit 7 (Market Street) off of **I-95**. **Rte-1A**, which becomes Miller Avenue, and **US-1**, which becomes Middle Street, both pass directly through the city center and continue into Kittery, Maine (see p.523), across the Memorial Bridge. **Parking** near the waterfront is scarce in the summer; there's a public garage at the intersection of Hanover and High streets. You can usually find non-metered parking next to South Mill Pond, along Parrot Avenue, a short walk from Market Square.

The **Greater Portsmouth Chamber of Commerce**, 500 Market St (late May to mid-Oct Mon–Fri 8.30am–5pm, plus Sat & Sun 10am–5pm in summer; ⓣ603/436-1118, ⓦwww.portsmouthchamber.org), a fifteen-minute walk from Market Square, houses an extensive collection of brochures and can help you find a room, although your choices will be limited to chamber members. They also operate an information **kiosk** in Market Square during the summer (daily 9am–5pm). For travel books, guides, and maps, you can't do much better than Gulliver's, downstairs at 7 Commercial Alley near Market Square (ⓣ603/431-5556, ⓦwww.gulliversbooks.com).

City transit

The **Coast Trolley** (Mon–Sat 8.45am–8.45pm, Sun 11.45am–8.45pm; ⓣ603/743-5777; $1) runs in a small loop around the city, stopping at most attractions to pick up and drop off visitors. It makes for a good way to get an overview of what sights the city has to offer. The **Seacoast Trolley** ($1 per ride or $5 for five-day pass; ⓣ603/431-6975) links historic Portsmouth with several beaches, shopping malls, and local sights, and stops at Market Square hourly. You can rent **bikes** from Portsmouth Rent & Ride, 37 Hanover St (ⓣ603/433-6777) for $29 a day, $19 for a half-day, which also rents kayaks ($49), cross-country skis ($19), and snowshoes ($15).

Several companies run **cruises** of varying lengths in Portsmouth Harbor and beyond. Portsmouth Harbor Cruises, at the Ceres Street Dock, features several trips, and has a full bar aboard every boat (90min harbor cruise $13; 150min Isles of Shoals $17; 60min evening cruise $10; call ⓣ603/436-8084 or 1-800/776-0915 for departure times). The Isles of Shoals Steamship Company, nearby at 315 Market St (ⓣ603/431-5500 or 1-800/441-4620, ⓦwww.islesofshoals.com), offers similar trips, including a $24 journey to the Isles of Shoals, ten miles off the coast, with three hours on Star Island, which, since 1897, has hosted summer religious and educational conferences for those interested in a bit of spiritual reflection and inspiration. With both companies, you need to call to make reservations, or to buy your tickets well in advance, to guarantee a spot. If you'd rather see the coastline up close, daily kayaking tours are offered by Portsmouth Kayak Adventures, 185 Wentworth St (ⓣ603/559-1000; $55), which originate at their store in Witch Cove Marina, south of the town center.

Accommodation

As might be expected, **accommodation** in and around Portsmouth's historic district can be expensive – in high season on weekends you'll likely pay $100 or more for a good room in a bed and breakfast. A collection of slightly cheaper – and less pleasant – **motels** can be found at the traffic circle where I-95, the Rte-1 bypass, and routes 4 and 16 intersect. If you can afford it, staying in a restored old inn is well worth the extra cash. Call ahead to reserve a room on summer weekends or holidays and be aware that prices can go up by as much as forty percent during high season; midweek accommodations can also be considerably less expensive. **Camping** in the area is limited to crowded RV-type parks, such as the *Shel-Al Campground*, US-1, North Hampton (ⓣ603/964-5730, ⓦwww.shel-al.com; $18), and the *Wakeda Campground*, Rte-88, Hampton Falls (ⓣ603/772-5274, ⓦwww.wakedacampground.com; $21.50).

In town

Bow Street Inn 121 Bow St ⓣ603/431-7760, ⓦwww.bowstreetinn.com. Portsmouth's only waterfront inn is centrally located and comfortable. The ten cozy rooms occupy a remodeled brick brewery; two rooms offer full harbor views. Continental breakfast included. ❻

Inn at Christian Shore 335 Maplewood Ave ⓣ603/431-6770. Early nineteenth-century Federal-style house with six rooms full of tasteful antique furnishings, and big, tasty gourmet breakfasts. ❺

Inn at Strawbery Banke 314 Court St ⓣ603/436-7242 or 1-800/428-3933, ⓦwww.innatstrawberybanke.com. One of the most central of Portsmouth's bed and breakfasts, in a sumptuous old Colonial home near the waterfront. Reservations strongly recommended. ❻

Martin Hill Inn 404 Islington St ⓣ603/436-2287. Meticulously furnished house with seven guest-rooms and a shaded garden within walking distance of the city center. Excellent full breakfast and helpful innkeepers. ❺

Oracle House Inn 38 Marcy St ⓣ603/433-8827. Painstakingly restored 1702 home located just outside Strawbery Banke with period furniture and views of Prescott Park. Each room has its original working fireplace. Breakfast included. ❻

Sheraton Harbourside 250 Market St ⓣ603/431-2300 or 1-877/248-3794, ⓦwww.sheratonportsmouth.com. Large hotel with conference facilities and a predominantly business clientele. Predictably comfortable and expensive, but enjoys a central location on Market Street. ❼

Sise Inn 40 Court St ⓣ603/433-1200, ⓔsiseinn@cybertours.com. One of the larger inns in Portsmouth, with phones and TVs in 34 elegantly appointed, luxurious rooms, and a Queen Anne-style exterior. The breakfast is a delicious self-serve buffet. ❻

Near the traffic circle

Anchorage Inn 417 Woodbury Ave ⓣ603/431-8111 or 1-800/370-8111, ⓦwww.anchorageinns.com. A large and comfortable modern hotel with 93 rooms, an indoor pool, sauna, and whirlpool. ❹

Fairfield Inn 650 Borthwick Ave ⓣ603/436-6363. Formerly independent hotel, now operated by the *Marriott* chain. Standard – yet comfortable – rooms, outdoor pool, and free continental breakfast. ❹

Port Inn Rte-1 Bypass South ⓣ603/436-4378 or 1-800/282-PORT, ⓦwww.theportinn.com. These good-value, comfortable rooms, some with microwaves and refrigerators, are (depending on the season and day) among the cheapest in Portsmouth. ❹

The Town

Market Square, where Daniel, Pleasant, Congress, and Market streets all converge, has been Portsmouth's commercial center since the mid-eighteenth century. Once a military training site, the brick-dominated square is now surrounded by a bustling assortment of cafés and gift shops. Despite the upscale shopping, the square maintains an unpretentious, lived-in feel – almost everywhere you turn, evidence of the town's history reveals itself in the architecture of old brick buildings such as the **Athenaeum**, 9 Market Square (open to the public Tues & Thurs 1–4pm, Sat 10am–4pm; ⓣ603/431-2538), one of the oldest private libraries in the country. The 1854 **North Church**, also constructed with bricks, flanks the southwest side of the square, and its towering spire makes it the tallest building you'll see in town. It's the best spot to get oriented and begin your wanderings; in fact, this is where you pick up the informative **Portsmouth Harbor Trail** walking-tour guide and map (32-page color guide and map $2; guided tours $8; ⓣ603/436-3988), detailing a series of three walks tracing the city's history that originate in the square.

If you are around on the second Saturday of June, you'll catch **Market Square Day** (ⓣ603/431-5388), when the streets are closed to traffic so that craft booths, musical entertainment, good food, and over thirty thousand pedestrians can fill them up. For a scaled-down version, check out the **Portsmouth Marketplace** (ⓣ603/431-4333), where artisans sell their works and local restaurants showcase their food every summer weekend in the parking lot adjacent to Eagle Photo.

Market Street

Scanning the chic boutiques and fashionable restaurants that line **Market Street**, it's hard to believe the brick buildings that house them were once occupied by breweries. In the late nineteenth century, when Portsmouth's **beer and ale industry** was booming, Frank Jones, its most famous brewer and founder of the Portsmouth Brewery Company, created and brewed what was once considered to be the best beer in the nation here – aptly named "Frank Jones Ale." Jones and his competitors were shut down during Prohibition and never recovered. The company's old brick warehouse, at 125 Bow St, was transformed in 1979 into a theater (see p.457), presenting mostly mainstream plays and musicals. You can learn more about Jones and Portsmouth's brewing history and get drunk on modern microbrews from all over New England during the **Grand Old Portsmouth Brewers Festival**, held the last weekend in September at the Strawbery Banke Museum (see overleaf; admission to the festival is $5).

Of the striking selection of grand old timber mansions in Portsmouth, the **Moffatt-Ladd House**, 154 Market St (mid-June to mid-Oct Mon–Sat 10am–4pm, Sun 2–5pm; $5), is one of the most impressive. Completed in 1763, after no less than 467 days of construction, the house is particularly notable for its Great Hall, which occupies more than a quarter of the first floor. Using inventories left by Captain John Moffatt, who designed the home and later monitored his lucrative shipping business from an office on the second floor, historians have transformed the Yellow Chamber (also on the second floor) into one of the best-documented eighteenth-century American rooms. Portraits of past occupants by artists such as Gilbert Stuart hang throughout the home and include a painting of William Whipple, who signed the Declaration of Independence and lived here in the late eighteenth century. For information on other historic homes which are open to the public, see box on p.455.

Further up Market Street, next to the salt piles along the river, is the departure point for harbor cruises and for boats that take you to the Isles of Shoals, a summer meeting place for many well-known writers of the nineteenth century, including Nathaniel Hawthorne and Annie Fields, ten miles off the coast.

Still further along Market Street, at no. 600, you'll find the **USS Albacore Park and Port of Portsmouth Maritime Museum** (daily: late May to mid-Oct 9.30am–5pm; rest of year 9.30am–3.30pm, closed Tues & Wed; $5), a worthwhile diversion highlighted by a 205-foot, 1200-ton **submarine**. Built in 1952, it was then the fastest electric/diesel submarine in the world. Tours of the underwater vessel offer glimpses of the cockpit, cramped living quarters, and the engine room.

Prescott Park and the Children's Museum

At the other end of the historic district, along the river and adjacent to the Strawbery Banke Museum, is beautiful **Prescott Park**, Marcy Street (☎603/431-8748), a welcoming expanse of grass and shrubbery that slopes gently toward the water's edge. Featuring free music and entertainment throughout the summer, the park is immaculately maintained – especially the colorful All-American Show Garden – and is a great spot for a picnic or afternoon nap. You could also check out the **Sheafe Warehouse Museum,** in Prescott Park on the waterfront (summer only; ☎603/431-8748), which houses a mildly engaging free collection of mostly nautical paraphernalia. The **Point of Graves cemetery**, a creepy plot of crumbling headstones across from Prescott Park on the southeast corner of Mechanic Street near the bridge to Pierce Island, is the oldest in the city – the oldest headstone dates from 1682.

Though you'd never suspect it now, **Marcy Street**, which borders Prescott Park on its west side, was once home to a strip of notorious brothels, patronized by sailors from across the river. A source of town shame, and with an international reputation, the street's name was changed from Water to Marcy in the early twentieth century, after prostitution had subsided. Few reminders of those days are left, but the otherwise undistinguished home of one of Portsmouth's most prominent madames, **Alta Roberts**, who greeted her customers with a mouthful of gold teeth, still stands at 57 Marcy St. Somewhat ironically, the **Children's Museum of Portsmouth**, with hands-on exhibits that investigate a range of diverse topics, such as anatomy, lobstering, sound, and earthquakes, is close by at 280 Marcy St (summer Mon–Sat 10am–5pm, Sun 1–5pm; closed Mon rest of year; $5).

The Strawberrry Banke Museum

Although historic buildings can be found all over Portsmouth, for a more concentrated look at American architecture over the last three centuries, pay a visit to the **Strawbery Banke Museum**, 64 Marcy St (May–Oct Mon–Sat 10am–5pm, Sun noon–5pm; $12; tickets good for two consecutive days; Ⓣ603/433-1100, Ⓦwww.strawberybanke.org), a fenced-off ten-acre neighborhood that takes in a collection of meticulously restored and maintained old wooden buildings. This area began life as the home of wealthy shipbuilders and was successively the lair of privateers and a red-light district before turning into a respectable – and, in the 1950s, decaying – suburbia. It was decided to re-create its former appearance, mainly by clearing away the newer buildings (only two of the houses on display had to be moved here). A few people still live here, tucked away on the upper floors, but the complex really serves as a living museum that you can explore either on a guided tour or at your own whim; in either case, several of the houses have well-informed attendants.

Each building is shown in its most interesting former incarnation, whether that be 1695 or 1955; in the **Drisco House**, the first you come to, each individual room dates from a different era. The 1766 **Pitt Tavern** holds the most historic significance, having acted as a meeting place during the Revolution for patriots and loyalists (it still functions as a Masonic lodge – one of the four oldest in the US – which explains why you can't go upstairs). Tiny glasses remind you that its clientele drank gin rather than beer. The museum also contains the boyhood home of novelist **Thomas Bailey Aldrich** (1836–1907), which he depicted in his most famous novel, *The Story of a Bad Boy*.

Although you may have to struggle to keep ahead of school groups, Strawbery Banke continues to host serious academic research. Traditional crafts are studied and practiced here; in the **Dinsmore Shop**, an infinitely patient cooper manufactures barrels with the tools and methods of 1800. The **Mils Zoldak pottery shop**, open year-round, produces attractive low-priced ceramics. After 5pm, the museum opens its gates, and you can wander around for free and observe the building's exteriors in the waning hours of the day (though it's hardly the same experience).

If you've had your fill of historic houses and are looking for something a bit less serious, try vampire hunting with **Ghostly Tours** (Ⓣ603/433-8888), which offers walking candlelit tours through town, while the guides share various maudlin lore from these parts. One shouldn't take this tour expecting to come across hard historical information, but it can be fun; reservations are recommended.

Portsmouth's historic homes

Beyond the walls of Strawbery Banke, Portsmouth is home to an uncharacteristically large offering of painstakingly restored **Colonial homes**, which, during the summer, are open to the public. Almost as impressive as the buildings themselves is the unrelenting resolve of the people who devote their lives to the structures' impossibly finicky restoration, with attention given even down to the exact pattern and dye-type used in eighteenth-century wallpapers. The hourly tours, led by scholars full of arcane knowledge and stories, can be fascinating, although after one or two, you will have probably had your fill. Most cost $5 and last about an hour. The presence of a blue flag outside a building indicates its status as a historic home which welcomes visitors.

Governor John Langdon House 143 Pleasant St (June to mid-Oct Wed–Sun 11am–5pm; $5; ⓣ603/436-3205). Three-term governor, New Hampshire Senate president, and delegate to the 1787 Constitutional Convention, John Langdon and his wife, Elizabeth, hosted many big-name visitors here, including George Washington. The home, constructed in 1784 with particular attention to interior detailing and woodwork, is in every way a tribute to his affluence and influence.

John Paul Jones House 43 Middle St (June to mid-Oct Mon–Sat 10am–4pm, Sun noon–4pm; $5; ⓣ603/436-8420). Home to the Portsmouth Historical Society's museum, this 1761 Georgian structure was where John Paul Jones, the US's first great naval commander, stayed while his ships, the *Ranger* and the *America,* were being outfitted in the Langdon shipyards. Inside the boxy yellow structure – featured in Sears paint commercials – you can view some of his naval memorabilia and period-furnished rooms.

Rundlet-May House 364 Middle St (July–Aug Wed–Sun 11am–5pm; $5; ⓣ603/433-2494). Wealthy merchant-importer James Rundlet had this symmetrical Neoclassical mansion built in 1807, when he was 35 years old. The walls are adorned with imported English wallpaper and the rooms filled with a fine collection of Federal period furniture – most built by local craftsmen. Notable features include an indoor well and an early coal-fired heating system.

Warner House 150 Daniel St (early June to late Oct Mon–Sat 10am–4pm, Sun 1–4pm; $5; ⓣ603/436-5909). Built for local merchant and shipowner Captain Archibald MacPhaedris in 1716, the Warner House was one of the first buildings in America to be designated a national historic landmark – and examining its laundry list of other "firsts," it's not hard to see why: it was the first brick house constructed in the state; it contains New Hampshire's oldest murals, painted on the staircase wall; and the murals contain some of the earliest known images of Native Americans. Additionally, Benjamin Franklin is said to have installed the lightning rod on the west wall.

Wentworth-Coolidge Mansion 375 Little Harbor Rd, off of Rte-1A (daily: mid-May to early Sept 10am–3pm; $3; ⓣ603/436-6607). Home to Royal Governor Benning Wentworth, who was in office from 1741 to 1766, this massive 42-room, mustard-yellow mansion hosted the Royal Council meetings of the earliest New Hampshire state government. The rambling building, which is beautifully situated on an isolated plot overlooking Little Harbor, now hosts occasional concerts and classes during the summer. It is not furnished, but the wallpaper in several of the rooms is original (though faded), and there are several original Wentworth items on display – among them some fancy imported Chinese porcelain.

Wentworth-Gardner House 50 Mechanic St (mid-June to mid-Oct Tues–Sun 1–4pm; $5; ⓣ603/436-4406). Painstakingly restored, and complete with a gray blocked facade, this house is considered one of the finest examples of Georgian architecture in America. The 1760 home was given by Madam Mark Hunking to her son Thomas Wentworth, nephew of Benning. Her other son, John, was the last royal governor of the province of New Hampshire.

Eating

Portsmouth likes to bill itself as the "food capital of New England," and while this may be an exaggeration, there are undoubtedly plenty of good spots in town to grab an excellent – even gourmet – meal. Portsmouth's **restaurants** include both expensive highbrow **bistros** and cheap, down-to-earth **cafés**. You can still stretch your culinary dollar quite a long way in this town, although the recent surge in tourism is already effecting menu prices at the most well-known spots. There is a particularly high concentration of places to eat along Ceres Street and Bow Street, and you should treat yourself to at least one waterfront meal at one of the outdoor patios or decks that line the Piscataqua River.

Cafés and bakeries

Café Brioche 14 Market Square ☎603/430-9225. A good selection of pastries, sandwiches, and gourmet coffees, with outdoor seating right in the center of town. Perfect for a relaxing afternoon tea.

Ceres Bakery 51 Penhallow St ☎603/436-6518. Excellent fresh breads, good soups, and an assortment of fine pastries in this down-to-earth café with a bright blue exterior.

Restaurants

Anthony Alberto's 59 Penhallow St ☎603/436-4000. Excellent, cozy Italian restaurant, frequent recipient of *Yankee Travel* and *Wine Spectator* awards. Try the homemade ravioli of the day.

Blue Mermaid 409 The Hill, Hanover and High streets ☎603/427-2583. A carefully selected, though not particularly large, selection of mid- to high-priced grill food with Caribbean and Pacific Rim influences. Meals come with homemade fire-roasted salsa.

Café Mediterraneo 152 Fleet St ☎603/427-5563. Reasonably priced (entrées are $10–20), authentic, fresh, and delicious southern Italian meals near Market Square.

Celebrity Sandwich 171 Islington St ☎603/433-2277. Great, enormous deli sandwiches (all named after celebrities, though only a few, such as the "David Letterman ham sandwich," make much sense) with cheap daily specials and a handful of tables.

The Friendly Toast 121 Congress St ☎603/430-2154. Kitschy thrift-store decor with an interesting selection of inexpensive sandwiches and omelets, a huge drink menu that includes mixed drinks, shakes, and coffees, and an equally eclectic crowd. The portions are enormous – try Matt's Sandwich, with black beans, avocado, and cheese. Open 24hr on weekends, 7am–11pm during the week.

Lindbergh's Crossing Bistro and Wine Bar 29 Ceres St ☎603/431-0887. One of Portsmouth's newer eateries is fast becoming one of its most popular. The creative French cuisine, which ranges from seared tuna to crispy duck, is expensive (around $19 per entrée) but worth it.

The Oar House 55 Ceres St ☎603/436-4025. One of Portsmouth's several slightly old-fashioned gourmet standbys, serving standard seafood and grilled meat entrées for $20 and up. There's a great deck outside.

Portsmouth Gas Light Co 64 Market St ☎603/430-8582. Portsmouth's favorite pizza joint, with a wide selection of brick-oven pizzas, which includes the "Strawbery Banke," a bizarre but tasty combination of tomato, teriyaki chicken, crushed pineapple, sliced almonds, and mozzarella cheese. All-you-can-eat pizza special for $6.50, weekdays 11.30am–2pm.

The Rosa Restaurant 80 State St ☎603/436-9715. Longstanding straightforward Italian dining in an intimate, friendly setting. Most dishes, including the delicious Chicken Rosa, a lightly breaded chicken breast sautéed in garlic over fresh pasta, go for $8–16.

Roxanne's Bistro 105 Daniel St ☎603/431-1948. A cute and unpretentious tiny restaurant, serving heaping home-cooked portions of creative American *nouvelle cuisine*. Try "Roxanne's bouillabaisse" (fish, shrimp, mussels, and bacon in a white-wine sauce). Breakfast and lunch daily, dinner Fri–Sat 5.30–9pm.

Sakura 40 Pleasant St ☎603/431-2721. The best Japanese restaurant in the area, with fresh sushi, sashimi, tempura, and teriyaki. The combination sushi platter ($21) is enough for four or five; the raw lobster is arguably too much, even for one. You can eat at the bar or at a table.

The Stockpot 53 Bow St ☎603/431-1851. Reasonably priced hearty American food, including bulging sandwiches, salads, burgers, and lobster, with a superb view of the Piscataqua and a popular outdoor seating area.

Victoria's 51 Hanover St ☎603/431-0693. The healthiest hole-in-the-wall in Portsmouth – if not the state. Order something fruity from the organic juice bar, or try one of several vegan wraps. Take-out only.

Nightlife and entertainment

Despite its size, Portsmouth's **social scene** can be pretty stimulating. Although the place tends to shut down well before midnight, on summer weekends the streets – particularly around **Market Square** and along **Bow Street** and **Ceres Street** – are full of well-dressed couples, noisy high-school kids, tattooed slackers, and fun-seeking tourists. The city is home to several vibrant **cafés**, a host of well-attended **bars**, and its several **live music** venues present a diverse range of bands – from punk to folk to jazz. If theater is your thing, the **Seacoast Repertory Theatre**, 125 Bow St (☎603/433-4472 or 1-800/639-7650), housed in a converted brewery, is Portsmouth's major performing arts theater, presenting mainstream professional stage productions. For complete up-to-date listings, the *Portsmouth Herald* prints an exhaustive **entertainment** supplement every Thursday, while *Spotlight* also has arts and entertainment listings for the Seacoast Region.

Breaking New Grounds 16 Market St ☎603/436-9555. This friendly coffee shop is more low-key than its neighbor across the street, *Café Brioche* (see above). Grab an excellent cup of freshly ground coffee and relax with a book or a friend at one of several indoor tables.

The Music Hall 28 Chestnut St ☎603/436-2400. Boasting some 900 seats, Portsmouth's largest performance space hosts well-known nationally touring folk, rock, jazz, and blues bands, classical concerts, plus dance, theater, and other performances throughout the year.

Poco's Bow Street Cantina 37 Bow St ☎603/430-9122. The passable food is typical Mexican fare, but the real reason to come here is for great margaritas (and perhaps a plate of nachos) on the riverfront patio.

Portsmouth Brewery 56 Market St ☎603/431-1115. A typical microbrew pub, with attractive wood paneling, extensive pizza and burger menu, visible beer tanks, towering ceilings, and a rowdy young crowd. The beer here is exceptional; don't miss the Old Brown Dog. Open until 1am nightly with occasional live music.

Press Room 77 Daniel St ☎603/431-5186. Popular for its nightly live jazz, blues, folk, and bluegrass performances, which feature local and national talents. Also serves inexpensive salads, sandwiches, and soups in a casual pub-style setting.

Around Portsmouth

Inland from Portsmouth, the area between I-95 and Rte-125 has a few historically notable cities, namely **Exeter**, **Durham**, and **Dover**, although aside from Exeter's colonial charm and historic architecture, there's really not much in the way of sightseeing. With most of the tourists heading the opposite way toward Hampton Beach and Portsmouth, however, the region's small towns and deserted backcountry roads can be refreshing. Perhaps the simplest way of **getting to this area** if you haven't got your own transport is by hopping on Amtrak's *Downeaster* service between Boston and Portland, Maine, which stops three times a day in either direction at Exeter, Durham, and Dover.

Exeter

Situated just eight miles west of the Atlantic down Rte-101 from Portsmouth, along the banks of the Squamscott River, friendly **EXETER** was settled in 1638 by a rebellious Bostonian preacher, the Reverend John Wheelwright. With an abundance of timber, Exeter, like other coastal New Hampshire towns, thrived in the eighteenth century, selling masts and lumber to both local and English shipbuilders. It became the state capital in 1775 (the Revolution was fast approaching, and Portsmouth, the previous capital, was too Loyalist), and by early 1776, the provincial congress had signed a state constitution, making New Hampshire the first state to formally declare its independence from England. Exeter's tree-shaded avenues and stately old neighborhood architecture make the charming town worth a stop, if only for a couple of hours. If you choose to stay, there are a few excellent old inns near the town center, making it a good base from which to explore the coast.

The Town

Phillips Exeter Academy, one of the top college preparatory schools in the United States, occupies a large portion of the attractive town center, its heavy-set regal brick buildings sprawling over several acres of well-manicured lawns. Founded in 1781 by Dr John Phillips, the school counts among its long list of prominent alumni the great orator Daniel Webster (see p.478). Along Front Street (Rte-111), near Elm Street south of the center of town, the school's boxy brick **library**, featured in many architecture textbooks, was designed by architect Louis Kahn in 1971. Though the building's exterior is rather plain, inside the space is both practical and inviting – each symmetrical floor looks out through a huge circular window into a naturally lit central atrium. Begin your self-guided walking tour of the campus at the admissions office (Ⓣ603/777-3433) on Front Street across from the Phillips Church.

The well-preserved Art Deco **Ioka Theater**, right in the center of town at 55 Water St, has been in continuous operation since it opened with a screening of *The Birth of a Nation* in 1915. It now shows middle-of-the-road Hollywood blockbusters (call Ⓣ603/772-2222 for listings), though you can usually take a peek inside during off-hours. A hundred yards down the street, in the center of the traffic circle, the **Swasey Pavilion**, a prominent circular bandstand, was designed by Henry Bacon, the architect of the Lincoln Memorial. The Exeter Brass Band, founded in 1847, still plays concerts in the bandstand during the summer. Exeter native Daniel Chester French, who sculpted the sternly seated Abe Lincoln inside the Lincoln Memorial, also created **Exeter's WWI Memorial**, in Gale Park on Front Street.

The **American Independence Museum**, in the Ladd-Gilman House at 1 Governors Lane, just north on Water Street (tours hourly May–Oct Wed–Sat 10am–4pm, Sun 11am–4pm; $5), houses an important, if slightly dull, collection of documents and artifacts investigating New Hampshire's role in the American Revolution, including the copy of the Declaration of Independence that was read to the Exeter townspeople by a fiery John Taylor Gilman, only 22 years old at the time. Gilman was a resident of the Ladd-Gilman House and later served fourteen years as governor of the state. The museum also has annotated draft copies of the US Constitution and a few oddities, including a ring containing a piece of George Washington's hair in a tiny glass case. Exeter stages the elaborate **Revolutionary War Festival** (Ⓣ603/772-2622 for details) every year during the third weekend in July, when the grounds of the museum are transformed into a militia encampment. During the event, some ten thousand people descend upon the town, many in full colonial militia garb; the vigor with which the battles and costumes are re-created is both frightening and fascinating – if you're in the area, don't miss it.

The **Gilman Garrison House**, 2 Water St (June to mid-Oct weekends 11am–5pm; $4), a massive seventeenth-century log cabin (clapboards have covered the logs), offers tours that reflect three hundred years of Exeter's history through furniture, decorations, and narrative. The **Moses-Kent House Museum**, 1 Pine St (summer Thurs & Sat 1–4pm; $5; Ⓣ603/772-2044), built in 1868 for Henry Moses, a local wool merchant, and later occupied by George

Kent, who owned the Exeter Cotton Mill, retains its original furnishings and is open to the public. Its grounds were laid out by Frederick Law Olmsted, best known for designing New York City's Central Park.

Practicalities

For local information, contact the **Exeter Area Chamber of Commerce**, 120 Water St (Ⓣ603/772-2411, Ⓦwww.exeterarea.org). There are several upscale **places to stay** in Exeter's town center, although the affluence of parents visiting their Exeter children keeps the rates relatively expensive. The *Inn by the Bandstand*, in the center of town at 4 Front St (Ⓣ603/772-6352, Ⓦwww.innbythebandstand.com; ❻), is a lovingly restored Federal-style inn, constructed in 1809; many rooms have brick fireplaces. Down the road, the *Inn of Exeter*, 90 Front St (Ⓣ603/772-5901 or 1-800/782-8444; ❻), offers easygoing elegance and superior service in a three-story brick Georgian-style building. There's also a decent gourmet, yet casual, restaurant here serving particularly good Sunday brunches, as well as various meat and fish dishes for lunch and dinner. The *Governor Jeremiah Smith House Inn*, 41 Front St (Ⓣ603/778-7770; ❺), is a friendly bed and breakfast across from the Exeter campus with eight antique-furnished rooms; a full breakfast is included. You can **camp** at the wooded *Exeter Elms Family Campground*, 188 Court St, two miles south on Rte-108 (Ⓣ603/778-7631 or 1-866/778-7631, Ⓦwww.exeterelms.com), for $22 per site.

While Exeter does not have any great wealth of good **places to eat**, there are a few affordable options worth noting. The *Green Bean on Water*, 33 Water St (closed Sun; Ⓣ603/778-7585), serves cheap, fresh sandwiches on homemade bread and creatively prepared salads in a casual café with a walk-up counter and outdoor seating. The *Tavern at River's Edge*, 163 Water St (Ⓣ603/772-7393; closed Sun), has a good range of international cuisine in a cozy, more formal Victorian dining room along the river. As its name suggests, *Penang and Tokyo*, 97 Water St (Ⓣ603/778-8388), offers well-prepared Malaysian and Japanese cuisine, something of a rarity in these parts. For pastries, fresh breads, light salads, coffee, and espresso, head to the *Baker's Peel*, at 231 Water St (Ⓣ603/778-0910). Well worth the ride, *Memories Ice Cream*, Rte-111, four miles outside of town in **Kingston** (Ⓣ603/642-3737), has a peaceful farm setting and delicious homemade ice cream.

Durham and Dover

Along US-4 northwest of Portsmouth, the University of New Hampshire's flagship campus dominates **DURHAM**, which was originally settled in 1635, and the university maintains the youthful exuberance of a typical college town during the school year. Between 1675 and the early eighteenth century, the town was the site of some of the worst Indian massacres in America. Commanded by the French, the natives attacked repeatedly and often, destroying homes and killing British settlers; a painting that hung in the Durham Post Office (at 2 Madbury Rd) for many years depicted a Native American poised to set fire to a local garrison. There's little reminder of this past today: Durham's **Main Street** is a collection of used bookstores, such as the Durham Book Exchange, 36 Main St (Ⓣ603/868-1297), and cafés like the *Licker Store*, 44 Main St (Ⓣ603/868-1863), which serves coffee, ice cream, sandwiches, and baked goods. The campus's main **theater**, in the Paul Creative Arts Center (Ⓣ603/862-2290), puts on several respectable productions each year.

DOVER, a former mill town just off the Spaulding Turnpike (Rte-16) near the Maine border, was one of the first four cities to be established in the state.

You might stop off for a meal at one of the several affordable **eateries** along its pleasant downtown strip – try *Firehouse One*, 1 Orchard St (Ⓣ603/749-2220), which serves an interesting mix of seafood with an Asian emphasis. Otherwise, there's nothing to see here.

The Merrimack Valley

The financial and political heartland of New Hampshire is the **Merrimack Valley**, which – first by water along the Merrimack River and now by road via I-93 – has always been the main thoroughfare north to the lakes, the White Mountains, and Québec. First settled by the Penacook Indians, early pioneers had established a trading post near Concord by 1660, and by the 1720s large groups of Protestant Anglo-Saxons were calling the area home. In the nineteenth century, the valley was booming with industrialization and Nashua, Manchester, and Concord were all major manufacturing centers. **Concord** became the state's capital in 1784 and it remains the center of New Hampshire's political life – particularly evident during the quadrennial presidential primaries – while **Manchester** is the most populous city in the state, with ample evidence of its gritty industrial past.

Manchester

Although **MANCHESTER** is New Hampshire's largest city (population 106,000) and a major business hub, it does not hold much interest for visitors, aside from an excellent art museum. Indeed, the Chamber of Commerce's tourist guide lists the city's proximity to everywhere else in the state as its major attraction. The place is rather rough around the edges and unmistakably urban, and, although town officials are constantly dreaming up new ways to revitalize the downtown and riverfront areas, most of these efforts reek more of desperation than genuine civic improvement.

Once a prosperous mill-town, Manchester has been in a perpetual state of recovery ever since the **Amoskeag Manufacturing Company** went belly-up here in 1935. From 1838 to 1920, the company was the world's largest textile manufacturer, employing 17,000 people at its peak – many of them women, dubbed "mill girls" – and spewing out over four million yards of cloth per week. The textile company – and the entire town of Manchester, for that matter – was the brainchild of a group of Boston entrepreneurs, who purchased 15,000 acres of land around the Amoskeag Falls, acquired the rights to water power along the entire length of the Merrimack River, built a dam, and constructed the enormous brick Amoskeag Mills in the early 1830s. Once cutting-edge examples of manufacturing efficiency, the mills, which stretch for over a mile along the eastern side of the river, are now run down and largely deserted – depressing reminders of the prosperity the city once enjoyed.

That isn't to say that the entire grouping of buildings remains dormant; a group of local businessmen bought the crumbling structures for $5 million and the slow process of converting the mills into apartments, offices, classrooms, and retail space is well under way. Optimistic residents claim Manchester is going through a "renaissance" of sorts, and it's hard not to admire their gumption, but they're still a long way from restoring the booming prosperity of the early part of last century.

Arrival, information, and city transit

Manchester is one of New Hampshire's few transportation hubs, and getting to the city is not particularly difficult. **Manchester International Airport** (Ⓣ603/624-6556), off of Rte-3A, is served by several major carriers. From downtown's **Manchester Transportation Center**, 119 Canal St, at Granite (Ⓣ603/668-6133), you can get to just about anywhere that buses run to in the state, and beyond. The **Greater Manchester Chamber of Commerce**, 889 Elm St (Ⓣ603/666-6600, Ⓦwww.manchester-chamber.org), has brochures and the like, and there is also an **information kiosk** in the city center on Elm Street next to Veteran's Park and at the airport. The **Manchester Transit Authority** (Ⓣ603/623-8801) runs an extensive network of buses all over town (90¢), although apart from the service to the airport (6.30am, 7am, 3pm & 3.30pm from the Manchester Transportation Center), tourists will not have much cause to use it, since most of the city's limited attractions are concentrated in the downtown area and easily accessible by foot.

Accommodation

With little tourism to speak of, the city's few **hotels** count the infrequent presidential primary as their major source of business. Most of the politicos stay at the *Center of NH Holiday Inn*, 700 Elm St (Ⓣ603/625-1000 or 1-800/465-4329; ❻), which becomes a media circus during the primary. At other times it's as comfortable a hotel as you'll find in these parts, with a downtown location second to none. Elsewhere, you might try the *Rice Hamilton*, 123 Pleasant St (Ⓣ603/627-7281; ❹), which has surprisingly well kept, spacious rooms with kitchens in a run-down brick boarding house, or the *Fairfield Inn*, 860 S Porter St (Ⓣ603/625-2020 or 1-800/258-1980; ❹), a fairly standard but quite clean and adequate place for a night's sleep. The *Derryfield Bed and Breakfast*, 1081 Bridge St (Ⓣ603/627-2082; ❹), has three quiet, affordable rooms and great breakfasts. You can **camp** at the family-oriented *Calef Lake Camping*, 593 Chester Rd, thirteen minutes outside of town off of Rte-121 in Auburn (Ⓣ603/483-8282).

The City

Manchester's main commercial drag, **Elm Street**, runs north to south along the Merrimack River and doubles as US-3. The **Amoskeag Mills** are several blocks west along the banks of the river between Bridge and Granite streets. You can get a good look at the mills, the **Amoskeag Dam**, and the city skyline from the **Amoskeag Falls Scenic Overlook** (daily: mid-April–Oct 8am–6.30pm; free), along the river north of Bridge Street. Alternatively, take a stroll along the **Riverwalk**, a pedestrian path on the river's east bank, or visit the Manchester Historic Association's recently opened **Millyard Museum**, Commercial Street, at Pleasant (daily Tues–Sat 10am–4pm, Sun noon–4pm; $5), which has exhibits chronicling the town's history, including looms from the mills and a re-creation of what Elm Street looked like back in the days when Manchester was an economic player to be reckoned with.

Horace Greeley

Northwest of Nashua, the tiny, unassuming town of **AMHERST** is the birthplace of **Horace Greeley**, prominent entrepreneur, orator, politician, and the most celebrated newspaperman of his time. Born in 1811, Greeley founded the *New York Tribune* in 1841 and turned it into one of the major public opinion vehicles of the mid-nineteenth century. At its height in the late nineteenth century, the *Tribune* counted among its contributors Henry Wadsworth Longfellow, Charles Dickens, Mark Twain, Bret Harte, and Karl Marx. Self-educated, Greeley had no problems matching wits with such intellectual luminaries, impressing them with his astute editing. He was also always amazingly adept at placing himself at the center of attention. He challenged slavery (his political maneuverings helped Abraham Lincoln win the presidency in 1860) as morally wrong, contested exploitative corporations, and opposed capital punishment. But he also opposed women's suffrage and dismissed Native Americans as "slaves of appetite and sloth." Perhaps best known for popularizing the phrase, "Go West, young man, and grow up with the country," Greeley's robust personality was well known throughout the country. A politician at heart, Greeley served for a brief time in Congress, but his New York gubernatorial and senatorial aspirations were repeatedly denied by voters and colleagues, apparently wary of his somewhat unpredictable behavior, which included a strong fondness for the bottle. He even made a bid for the presidency in 1872, which failed miserably, and when he returned to the *New York Tribune* offices expecting to resume his former position, his old associates refused to relinquish control. He died several months later, after suffering a nervous breakdown, at the age of 61, on November 29, 1872. His small one-story **boyhood home**, just off of Rte-101 on Horace Greeley Road, is privately owned, but there is a historical marker nearby that is inscribed with a list of his greatest accomplishments.

As New Hampshire's best fine arts museum, the **Currier Gallery of Art**, just north of Bridge Street between Union and Beech streets at 201 Myrtle Way (Mon, Wed, Thur & Sun 11am–5pm, Fri 11am–8pm, Sat 10am–5pm; $5, free Sat 10am–1pm), featuring works by such well-known European and American painters as Monet, O'Keeffe, Hopper, Matisse, and Wyeth, is well worth the stop. Notable paintings include Picasso's colorful *Spanish Woman Seated in a Chair*, from 1941, and Winslow Homer's straightforward watercolor *American in the Woods*. There's also a fair number of local paintings, such as Jasper Francis Cropsey's glowing *American Indian Summer Morning in the White Mountains*, from 1857. The museum also maintains the nearby **Zimmerman House** (Thurs–Mon; tours $9; ⓣ603/626-4158), designed in 1950 by Frank Lloyd Wright. Tours of the house, a one-story wooden structure epitomizing Wright's vision of form in harmony with landscape, depart from the Currier Gallery. For more lively entertainment, ice hockey fans might want to see who's playing at the brand new **Verizon Wireless Arena**, 555 Elm St (ⓣ603/644-5000), which also presents rock concerts and other spectacles.

West of the river, **West Manchester** is best known for its ethnic neighborhoods, most notably a large French Canadian contingent, whose ancestors came in droves to work in the textile mills. Making up nearly forty percent of the population, there are still pockets of French speakers and the **Franco American Centre**, on the east side of the river at 52 Concord St (Mon–Fri 9am–5pm; free; ⓣ603/669-4045), is a leading source of information about French culture, heritage, and history in North America, with a small art gallery. The town also features considerable Greek, Polish, Italian, and Turkish populations.

Eating and drinking

Manchester does not boast any great wealth of **restaurants** either, although there are a few of note. Local institution *Red Arrow Diner*, 61 Lowell St (ⓣ603/626-1118), is a greasy diner open 24hrs and usually filled with talkative patrons, while the newer and considerably pricier *Richard's Bistro*, across the street at 36 Lowell St (ⓣ603/644-1180), serves up creative California cuisine in a modern dining room. For good Italian food, head to the elegant *Café Pavone*, 75 Arms Park Drive (ⓣ603/622-5488), or the bustling *Fratello's*, 155 Dow St (ⓣ603/624-2022). The *Bean-n-Bagel*, 25 Stark St (closed weekends; ⓣ603/623-2328), is good for gourmet **coffee** and snacks. The city's younger crowd **drinks** beer and listens to live music at *Jillian's*, right along the river at 50 Phillippe Cote (ⓣ603/626-7636).

South of Manchester

South of Manchester along US-3 near the Massachusetts border, **NASHUA**, New Hampshire's second largest city (population 84,000), does not hold much interest for tourists either, its suburban sprawl dominated by strip malls and car dealerships. Plenty of its citizens still choose to work in Boston, though Massachusetts no longer allows employees to escape state taxes by living across the border in New Hampshire. The **downtown** area, along Main Street, is pleasant enough, with a short strip of shops and *Michael Timothy's*, 212 Main St (ⓣ603/595-9334), one of the state's top restaurants, which serves creative wood-grilled fare, such as sea bass, duck, and pizza alongside an excellent wine list.

Alongside the Daniel Webster Highway (Rte-3) in **MERRIMACK**, the massive **Anheuser Busch Brewery** (daily: May & Sept–Dec 10am–4pm; June & Aug 9.30am–5pm; Jan–April Thurs–Mon 10am–4pm; ⓣ603/595-1202, ⓦwww.budweisertours.com), the largest beer brewer in the world, offers free tours of its beer-making facility – one of thirteen it operates nationwide. Afterwards, you're treated to complimentary tastings of several of its well-known (and lesser-known) products. Outside, you can wander over to see the **Clydesdale stables**, where the enormous horses associated with the brewery are groomed, trained, and usually on display.

The **Robert Frost Farm** (daily: late June to early Sept 10am–5pm; late May to late June & early Sept to mid-Oct weekends 10am–5pm; $2.50), just off of Rte-28 (take exit 4 from I-93), north of Salem and south of Derry, is slightly difficult to find, but worth visiting for its small exhibit of Frost's handwritten poems and photos, a short house tour, and an annotated nature trail. Frost lived here between 1900 and 1911, and composed or drew inspiration for many of his most famous poems here, including *Stopping by Woods on a Snowy Evening* and *Mending Wall*. He gave such a moving reading of his poem *Tuft of Flowers* to the local Derry Village Men's Club that the teachers in the group convinced him to take up a position teaching English at the nearby Pinkerton Academy, where he worked for two years before deciding to turn to writing full time. Another of the poet's homes can be found in Franconia (see p.502).

A rather unusual attraction, **America's Stonehenge**, is off of Rte-111 in North Salem (daily: Feb–late June & early Sept to late Oct 9am–5pm; late June to early Sept 9am–7pm; Nov–Jan 9am–4pm; $8.50; ⓣ603/893-8300, ⓦwww.stonehengeusa.com). This grouping of stone slabs and tunnels purports to be a site of ancient and mysterious origins – perhaps some sort of sacrificial altar. There is undoubtedly an atmosphere to the place, but note that it has been private property for the last 250 years, and that all the experts featured in the portentous documentary that visitors are shown are employed by the site.

If you're looking for a **place to stay** in the Merrimack area, the best choice is the *Radisson*, on the Daniel Webster Highway close to the Anheuser Busch Brewery (ⓣ603/424-8000; ❺), a business hotel (like many this close to Manchester Airport) with pool, fitness center, and comfortable rooms. They also have a free shuttle to and from the airport and Manchester's downtown bus terminal.

Concord and around

Just twenty minutes north by car from Manchester along I-93, New Hampshire's state capital, **CONCORD** (pronounced "conquered"), like its larger neighbor, does not hold much fascination for travelers. Much of its population lies in the rather spread-out suburbia that surrounds the town. Downtown, the highlights are the State House and the Museum of New Hampshire History, both close to one another and easily seen in a morning or an afternoon. The Christa McAuliffe Planetarium is a good option for the other half of the day, while the nearby Canterbury Shaker Village, the area's outstanding attraction and the best reason for coming to Concord, has enough to keep you busy for at least a day or two.

Arrival and information

Concord is readily accessible via **public transport** and easily reached by **car** from I-93, which passes through the eastern side of the town. Concord Trailways and Vermont Transit Lines stop at the **Concord Trailways Terminal**, 30 Stickney Ave, and provide service to other parts of New Hampshire and New England. Concord Area Transit (CAT) provides a decent **local transportation** service (ⓣ603/225-1989); note, however, that it does not go to the nearby Canterbury Shaker Village.

The **Greater Concord Chamber of Commerce** (Mon–Sat 9am–5pm, Sun 9am–3pm; ⓣ603/224-2508, ⓦwww.concordnhchamber.com) has recently taken up residence in plush new offices about a mile north of the town center at 40 Commercial St, next to the *Courtyard Marriott*. It also maintains an **information kiosk** in front of the State House (Fri–Sun 9am–5pm), which distributes historical walking-tour brochures. The local newspaper, the *Concord Monitor*, is widely available and offers **entertainment listings**.

Accommodation

Concord is short on remarkable **accommodation**, although a minimum of basic, cheap lodging is available on the outskirts of town near the interstate. Smaller towns in the surrounding countryside, such as Henniker (see p.467), feature some first-rate bed and breakfasts.

Brick Tower Motor Inn 414 S Main St ⓣ603/224-9565. Basic, comfortable rooms, two miles from downtown. A decent alternative to the chain motels. ❸

Centennial Inn 96 Pleasant St ⓣ603/225-7102. Probably the most upscale choice of Concord's lodging options, with spacious rooms, grand Victorian touches, and amenities such as in-room phones and cable TV. Also has live music on Sunday evenings. ❼

Holiday Inn 172 N Main St ⓣ603/224-9534, ⓦwww.holiday-inn.com/concordnh. Popular with visiting politicians and business people due to its proximity to the State House and other public buildings. Predictably comfortable rooms and good facilities, including pool, sauna, and fitness center. Also holds comedy evenings about once a month. 6

A Touch of Europe 85 Centre St ⓣ603/226-3771, ⓦwww.members.aol.com/euro1943/home.htm. Choose from Bavarian-, Parisian-, or Scottish-themed guestrooms in this tiny but friendly bed and breakfast offering a German morning meal. 4

The Town

Government is the main focus in Concord, employing almost a third of its residents, and the town consequently seems to revolve, both physically and spiritually, around the gold-domed **State House** on Main Street (Mon–Fri 8am–4.30pm; ⓣ603/271-2154). The building's handsome stone facade was quarried from local granite (once a major local export) using convict labor. Designed by Stuart J. Park, the original structure was completed in 1819, to be expanded and twice remodeled later. The state legislature – the largest in the country, with some 400 members – has met continuously in the same chambers since June 2, 1819, the longest such tenure in the US. Inside, haunting portraits of over 150 legislators hang on all three floors. Both self-guided and guided tours are available from the visitors' center on the first floor (Room 119). Outside, bronze statues of New Hampshire political notables, including Daniel Webster and President Franklin Pierce, strike dignified poses.

The small **Museum of New Hampshire History** (Tues, Wed, Fri & Sat 9.30am–5pm, Thurs 9.30am–8.30pm, Sun noon–5pm; July–Oct 15 & Dec also open Mon 9:30am–5pm; $5; ⓣ603/228-6688, ⓦwww.nhhistory.org) is tucked behind the brick buildings on Main Street across from the State House, in **Eagle Square**, a large open space between buildings back from the road. In the gallery on the first floor, you can browse the well-presented collection of paintings, photographs, maps, and artifacts, including a restored Concord coach (see box below) and a Native American canoe, which chronologically trace the state's history. Upstairs is devoted to rotating displays and various hands-on exhibits for the kids. The museum gift shop has a very extensive selection of **books** on New Hampshire and the rest of New England.

At the north end of Main Street, at 14 Penacook St, is the **Pierce Manse** (mid-June to early Sept Mon–Fri 11am–3pm; $3), where Franklin Pierce lived

Concord coaches

Carriage manufacturing became one of Concord's best-known industries in the mid-nineteenth century, when Abbot, Downing & Co became the major supplier for Ben Holladay's Overland Trail Stage Route. Locals Lewis Downing and Stephen Abbot had constructed the first Concord coach in 1827, and their beautifully painted stagecoaches were soon known throughout the developing West as the best mode of transportation available. In addition to durable construction and dependable quality, Concord coaches earned a good reputation for their wheels, which were made with seasoned white oak and fitted with handmade spokes, making them more likely to maintain a round shape. The coaches used three-inch-thick leather bands rather than springs to support the passenger compartment, prompting Mark Twain to describe a Concord coach as a "cradle on wheels" in his novel *Roughing It*. Weighing over a ton and costing roughly $1000 at the time, Concord coaches carried up to twelve passengers, and, with four to six horses out front, could travel fifteen miles an hour. Used by Wells Fargo Bank, they soon became familiar sights in such far-off places as South America and Australia. You can see a real one at the Museum of New Hampshire History (see above).

with his family between 1842 and 1848. Notable mainly as one of the United States' least successful presidents (see box, p.471), Pierce set up a successful private law practice while in residence here. The restored white two-story 1838 home is now a museum filled with the former president's personal effects, such as his top hat and some period furniture, including the family's writing table. It's open for tours during the summer. Pierce is buried in the **Old North Cemetery**, near the intersection of North State Street and Keane Avenue, in the northern end of the downtown area.

Across the river, the **Christa McAuliffe Planetarium**, 3 Institute Drive (Mon–Wed 10am–2pm, Thurs–Sat 10am–5pm, Sun noon–5pm; $8; Ⓣ603/271-7827, Ⓦwww.starhop.com), named for the Concord High School teacher who perished in the Space Shuttle *Challenger* disaster in 1986, stages impressive public astronomy shows in its 92-seat theater and hosts various sky-watch events. The planetarium also has interactive exhibits, such as the Pathfinder, where you rescue a team of three astronauts lost in space in the year 2058. McAuliffe was selected from a pool of 11,500 applicants to participate in the tragic space trip that ended her life just 73 seconds after lift-off.

Canterbury Shaker Village

About twenty minutes north of Concord, in Canterbury Center, **Canterbury Shaker Village**, exit 18 off I-93, 288 Shaker Rd (daily: May–Oct 10am–5pm; Nov, Dec & April weekends 10am–5pm; $12; Ⓣ603/783-9511, Ⓦwww.shakers.org), is New England's premier museum of Shaker life (for another good one, see "Central and Western Massachusetts" on p.282), and perhaps the most fascinating tourist destination in New Hampshire. The tranquil village, a collection of simple, box-like buildings, is beautifully spread out over a set of rolling hills, overlooking the greenery of the countryside, and the site's quiet isolation is soothing. Founded by Mother Ann Lee in 1774, the Shakers, after breaking off from the Quakers, were one of the religious sects that sought refuge in the New World. In 1792, Canterbury became the sixth of nineteen Shaker communities, and, at its zenith in the mid-nineteenth century, there were some 300 people living on the grounds. Sister Ethel Hudson, the last Shaker living in Canterbury, died in 1992 at age 96; today, only a handful of Shakers remain in the world – all live in New Gloucester, Maine (see p.538).

So named because of their tendency to dance in church (thereby shaking off sins and evil), the Shakers lived apart from the world in communities devoted to efficiency, equality, pacifism, a strong work ethic, co-operative living, and celibacy. Shakers relied upon conversion and adoption to expand their influence; orphans were readily accepted into the community, and at one point the state of New Hampshire opened a foster home in Canterbury Village. However, in the face of industrialization and the opening of the West, the Shakers' decline in the early twentieth century was ultimately exacerbated by their self-imposed sexual chastity.

Believing that technology would create more time for worship, the Shakers were creative and industrious inventors. Several of these inventions, such as a seed spreader used in agriculture, as well as some fine examples of Shaker furniture craftsmanship, are presented during three different thirty-minute **tours** of the village. Led by Shaker experts, the engrossing tours also introduce the ideals, day-to-day life, and architecture (there are 25 perfectly restored buildings on the site) of these people as you wander from building to building – including the church, the schoolhouse, and the laundry room. There is also an acclaimed restaurant on the property, the *Creamery*, serving Shaker specialties (see review opposite).

Eating, drinking, and entertainment

Concord's **restaurants** can seem uninspired when compared with those of Portsmouth. However, you can find some good-value lunches around the State House, and Loudon Road, east of the Merrimack River, is lined with fast-food and national chain restaurants. Note that many of the town's eateries are closed on Sundays, if not the whole weekend. Other than a couple of basic, typical bars, some with **live music**, there is really no nightlife to speak of here. About once a month, the *Holiday Inn* hosts **North Shore Comedy Shows** ($10; ⓣ1-800/923-0879), featuring stand-up comedy acts by performers of regional and occasionally national renown.

Barley House 132 N Main St ⓣ603/228-6363. Watering hole for state legislators on lunch breaks from the State House opposite. Pub-style food and live music, especially jazz, Thurs, Fri & Sat. Closed Sun.

Capitol Grille 1 Eagle Square ⓣ603/228-6608. The restaurant serves sandwiches, steaks, pasta, and seafood dishes, but patrons come as much for the karaoke on Tues, Wed & Thurs, and the disco on Fri & Sat.

Creamery 288 Shaker Rd, Canterbury ⓣ603/783-9511. Imaginative Shaker-inspired specialties such as iced strawberry soup, seared salmon with mint sweet pea cream, herbal tartar sauce, and chocolate cheesecake with fresh berry syrup. Lunches and four-course candlelight dinners are served.

Eagle Square Deli 5 Eagle Square ⓣ603/228-4795. Excellent deli sandwiches-to-go across from the History Museum. You can eat outside on the patio. Closed weekends.

Hermanos Cocina Mexicana 11 Hills Ave ⓣ603/224-5669. Slightly more expensive than the other Mexican restaurant in town (see below), but the food is more authentic and the scene less noisy. The *quesadillas* are particularly good. Live jazz Sun–Wed.

Margaritas 1 Bicentennial Square ⓣ603/224-2821. Housed in a former police station, this popular chain serves some of the biggest Mexican dishes around. You can sit in a former jail cell downstairs while you sip your margarita and carouse with local singles – very atmospheric.

Tea Garden Restaurant 184 N Main St ⓣ603/228-4420. Despite its dirty yellow sign and grim-looking exterior, this place serves some of the most authentic Chinese food in the state. Try the sesame sparkling beef or the Mandarin crispy shrimp.

West of Concord: Henniker

The pleasant, relatively tourist-free residential town of **HENNIKER** ("The only Henniker on Earth!"), west of Concord on Rte-114 along the border of the Merrimack Valley, was settled by families from the *Mayflower*, many of whose descendants still live in the area. Residents enjoy the peaceful seclusion, so much that they raised $100,000 in a successful campaign to keep retail giant Rite Aid Pharmacy from building a store in the quaint downtown area.

In Henniker's center, along the Contoocook River ("Tooky"), **Main Street** is home to an agreeable group of shops, including the nostalgic Henniker Pharmacy, where you can order ice cream and sandwiches at an old-fashioned soda counter in back. The Old Number Six Book Depot, 26 Depot Hill Rd (up the hill from the Town Hall), with an enormous stock of new and used **books** on all subjects, is worth a browse. Just across the double-arched Edna Dean Proctor Bridge, along Bridge Street, **New England College**, with some one thousand students, lends a youthful feel to the area during the school year. There are also a couple of good **hikes** in the area: try the Mount Liberty Extension trail, which winds up a gentle slope to the top of Mount Liberty, one mile west of the center of town off of Western Avenue at the end of Liberty Hill Road. Baseball great Ted Williams regularly went **fly-fishing** along the Contoocook River between Henniker and Hillsborough (see p.470), and it's still a popular spot between May and October. During the winter, you can **ski** at the family-oriented **Pats Peak Ski Area** (Ⓣ603/428-3245, Ⓦwww.patspeak.com), although with only 700 vertical feet of trails the terrain is rather limited.

Practicalities

Henniker has several excellent **accommodation** options, none better than the *Colby Hill Inn*, half a mile from the center of town off of Western Avenue(Ⓣ603/428-3281 or 1-800/531-0330, Ⓦwww.colbyhillinn.com; ❻), a romantic 1795 country farmhouse with friendly owners, delicious breakfasts, and a gourmet restaurant. The *Meeting House Inn*, 35 Flanders Rd (Ⓣ603/428-3228, Ⓦwww.meetinghouseinn.com; ❹), is a similarly cozy and romantic bed and breakfast. Closer to town, the *Henniker House*, 2 Ramsdell Rd (Ⓣ603/428-3198, Ⓦwww.hennikerhouse.com; ❹), offers unpretentious lodging along the river in a converted hospital. You can **camp** at the family-oriented *Keyser Pond Campground*, 47 Old Concord Rd (mid-May to mid-Oct; Ⓣ603/428-7741 or 1-800/272-5221, Ⓦwww.keyserpond.com; $25 per site with water and electricity), or *Mile-Away Campground*, 41 Old West Hopkinton Rd (Ⓣ603/428-7616; $26 per tent site).

There are also a few good **places to eat** in Henniker. The *Colby Hill Inn* (see above) features expertly prepared upscale food (entrées are $19–31), including honey-glazed salmon and lobster-stuffed chicken breast, in a relaxed but elegant setting overlooking a garden. The *Meeting House Restaurant*, also part of an inn (see above), is another pricey gourmet spot, serving American fare in a converted old barn. Along the river, *Daniel's Restaurant and Pub*, Main Street (Ⓣ603/428-7621), serves reasonably priced soups and salads, pastas, and meat entrées on a riverside dock. The *Coffee Grind*, 9 Bridge St (Ⓣ603/428-6397), is a cute little spot for lunch, with sandwiches, bagels, salads, and good coffee.

The Monadnock region

Known as the "quiet corner," the **Monadnock region**, which occupies the southwestern portion of New Hampshire, traverses deserted country roads and typically quaint church spire-filled New England towns that center around the lonely 3165-foot peak of **Mount Monadnock**. Aside from the gentle slopes of the mountain itself, which attract plenty of outdoor enthusiasts, the region boasts no real stand-out tourist attractions, and, although the slow pace and rolling hills can be infectious, you may very well find yourself restless with the desire to move on after a day or so of exploring.

Although you can get a good feel for small-town New England living at any of the region's many picturesque villages, several are worth highlighting. **Keene**, an amiable place with a provincial disposition and a range of services and stores, is the area's most populous community; **Peterborough**, along US-202, is the region's – perhaps the state's – artistic center; **Hillsborough** was the birthplace of New Hampshire's only US president, Franklin Pierce; **Jaffrey** rests quietly at the base of Mount Monadnock next to the state park; and **Fitzwilliam**, a classic New England community incorporated in 1773, has some nice accommodations. Other attractive places to stay, mainly of the bed-and-breakfast and country inn variety, can also be found in Peterborough and Jaffrey, as well as in Keene, which, as the region's main commercial center, also has a spattering of chain hotels. Those who have come to climb Mount Monadnock, will find reasonable places to camp near the mountain.

Arrival, information, and getting around

Vermont Transit **buses** going to Boston, Montréal, and various points in Vermont stop at a terminal in downtown Keene (ⓣ603/352-1331), where you can also catch various local buses. Along with Keene, Peterborough is the only town in the Monadnock region which is easily accessible by public transport. The Vermont Transit bus between Rutland and Boston stops at Carr's Store (ⓣ603/563-8478) in Peterborough, but only once a day in either direction.

By far the best way to get around is by **car**, which will allow easy access to the region's many quiet backcountry roads. You can **rent** a vehicle in Keene from National (ⓣ603/357-4045) or Enterprise (ⓣ603/358-3345), or in Peterborough from Enterprise (ⓣ603/924-9058). **Biking** is also a good way to explore the pleasant countryside of the Monadnock region, although the terrain can at times be a bit hilly. To rent bikes, head to Eclectic Bicycle, 76 Grove St, Peterborough (ⓣ603/924-9797); they'll also give you plenty of advice on potential routes.

For tourist **information** and accommodation bookings, try the Greater Keene Chamber of Commerce, 48 Central Square in Keene (ⓣ603/3521303, ⓦwww.keenechamber.com), the Peterborough Chamber of Commerce, at the junction of Rte-101 and US-202 (ⓣ603/924-7234, ⓦwww.peterboroughchamber.com), or the Jaffrey Chamber of Commerce, Main Street, Jaffrey (ⓣ603/532-4549, ⓦwww.jaffreycoc.org), for more information on the town of Jaffrey and the Monadnock State Park. Meanwhile, the *Monadnock Magazine*, published in Peterborough and distributed throughout the region, has entertainment listings and local-interest stories.

Keene

KEENE, with 23,250 residents, is the most populous of the cities in the Monadnock region, though in truth it has little competition, and you would hardly call it cosmopolitan. The architecture here is noticeably more modern, and, although the town manages to maintain a friendly, if somewhat dull charm, there's not much to do other than shop and eat in the downtown area, along the unusually wide **Main Street**, allegedly the "widest Main Street in the US," which culminates in the lovely **Keene Common**. For what it's worth, the town was a well-known crafts center in the early nineteenth century, when **glass** and **pottery** production was at its peak; a marker along Main Street denotes the site of the **Hampshire Pottery Works**, the most successful of the local manufacturers. Still standing at 399 Main St, the **Wyman Tavern** (June to early Sept Thurs–Sat 11am–4pm; $2; ⓣ603/352-1895) was built in 1762 by Isaac Wyman, a staunch patriot who later led a group of Minute Men from the tavern south to fight in the Revolutionary War. The tavern was also the sight of the first official meeting of the trustees of Dartmouth College (see p.477), which was founded in 1769. The restored taproom, living quarters, and ballroom are open to the public. While you're down in that part of town, it's worth stopping in at the **Thorne-Sagendorph Art Gallery**

Burdick Chocolates

Northwest of Keene, off of Rte-12, in the tiny white-clapboard town of **Walpole**, where Louisa May Alcott summered, and where documentary filmmaker Ken Burns currently lives, you can find one of New Hampshire's most delectable stores, **Burdick Chocolates** (ⓣ603/756-3701 or 1-800/229-2419, ⓦwww.burdickchocolate.com). Situated in an unassuming storefront along Main Street, the chocolate here has been rated the best in the country by *Consumer Reports* magazine – and deservedly so. Swiss-trained Larry Burdick makes his homemade treats from French Valrhona chocolate before shipping them to the nation's finest restaurants and shops, such as *Bouley* in New York City. If the chocolate isn't enough, you can get coffee and pastries in the adjoining café.

(daily noon–4pm, except Fri noon–7pm; free) on the attractive campus of Keene State College. It's pretty tiny (one room for the permanent collection and one for temporary exhibits), but the eclectic permanent collection ranges from African statues to Robert Mapplethorpe photographs to a Goya print. Take some time to peruse Peter Milton's print, *20th Century Limited*, which depicts last century's cultural achievements as a train wreck, from which only a few things have been rescued.

Practicalities

Apart from a few chain hotels on the outskirts of town, Keene plays host to a couple of slightly more intimate **places to stay**. The *Carriage Barn Bed and Breakfast*, 358 Main St (ⓣ603/357-3812, ⓦwww.carriagebarn.com; ❹), has four guestrooms with private bath in a cozy house just a few minutes' walk from the shops, restaurants, and entertainment of downtown Keene. A little further from the town center, next to the pond which shares its name, the *Goose Pond Guest House*, East Surrey Road (ⓣ603/357-4787, ⓦwww.goosepondguesthouse.com; ❺), enjoys an idyllic location among orchards and berry patches, with cozy rooms packed with antique furnishings.

If you're looking for a bite to **eat**, there are a few of places worth noting. The popular *176 Main*, 176 Main St (ⓣ603/357-3100), has a huge varied menu of excellent-value salads, soups, sandwiches, and main meals, served in a rustic and intimate dining room, as well as a large selection of tap and bottled beers. For authentic Italian food in a warm, plant-decorated setting, head to *Nicola's Trattoria*, 39 Central Square (ⓣ603/355-5242), which serves traditional pasta and meat entrées. *Brewbakers*, 97 Main St (ⓣ603/355-4844), is a hip coffee joint with comfy couches that also serves cheap soups, sandwiches, and salads. One of the top spots for **shopping** is the Colony Mill Marketplace, 222 West St, a converted brick woolen mill with an interesting grouping of relatively upscale shops. The Marketplace also houses the best **place to drink** in town, the *Elm City Brewery and Pub* (ⓣ603/355-3335), which serves hearty American meals in addition to its own microbrewed beers.

Hillsborough

About twenty-five miles northeast of Keene on Rte-9, the tiny town of **HILLSBOROUGH** – actually a grouping of four small villages (Hillsborough Bridge Village, Center Village, Lower Village, and Upper Village) – is the birthplace of Franklin Pierce (see box opposite), fourteenth president of the United

States and the only New Hampshire native to have attained the position. You can tour his painstakingly restored boyhood home, the **Franklin Pierce Homestead**, at the intersection of Rte-9 and Rte-31 (daily: July & Aug 10am–4pm; late May to mid-Oct Sat 10am–4pm, Sun 1–4pm; $3), where the docents downplay Pierce's shortcomings – alcoholism, ineffective leadership – to portray him as a misunderstood hero. The building is a fine (if slightly larger) example of the Federal-style homes that were common in the region, and Franklin lived here on and off until he was thirty. The rooms inside are relatively bare, though there are a few nicely painted wallpapers, including one that depicts the harbor at Naples.

The house was built by Franklin's father, **Benjamin Pierce**, who first came to Hillsborough in 1786, after having served as a general in the Revolutionary War under George Washington. He was elected a representative to the legislature for the towns of Hillsborough and Henniker in 1789 and went on to a 57-year career in public office, including two terms as governor of New Hampshire.

On the outskirts of Hillsborough there is some stunningly ugly development, courtesy of Rite Aid and *McDonald's*, but if you follow the roads off Rte-9 to **Hillsboro Center,** ironically not the center of anything any more, you'll pass through some rolling countryside crisscrossed by stone fences.

Franklin Pierce

Not highly rated in history's annals, **Franklin Pierce** was born in Hillsborough, New Hampshire, on November 23, 1804. Though Ralph Waldo Emerson wrote that Pierce was "either the worst, or one of the weakest of all our Presidents," modern New Hampshire residents overlook his shortcomings in the White House and have in fact transformed him into something of a local hero. The biographical brochure published by the New Hampshire Historical Society, for example, dramatically proclaims Pierce's presidency as "one of the great tragedies of our history," although the Friends of Franklin Pierce maintain their mission is to "rescue him from the obscurity he so richly deserves."

Handsome, charming, and amiable in his younger years, Pierce studied law at Bowdoin College in Maine before returning to New Hampshire to win his first election to public office. Only 25 years old at the time, he served in the state legislature under his father, Benjamin, and became speaker of the New Hampshire House at age 28. Pierce served five terms in the House of Representatives before being elected to the United States Senate. But his love of the law ultimately led him to return to Concord, where he set up a successful private law practice. After serving in the Mexican War, he unexpectedly received the nomination for president at the Democratic National Convention in 1852, when his party could not make a decision on any of the other four candidates. Even more surprisingly perhaps, Pierce edged out Whig candidate Whitfield Scott in the general election.

Pierce's presidency began on a particularly black note, when his only remaining son, Bennie, was killed in a train accident just before the inauguration. Pierce's wife, Jane, was rarely seen in public afterwards, and it was said that Pierce himself never recovered. At a time when the nation was severely divided over slavery, Pierce remained staunchly opposed to antislavery legislation, wrongly believing that his status as a Northerner with Southern values would strike an acceptable compromise with the nation. With his signing of the 1854 Kansas–Nebraska Act, which allowed settlers to choose whether to allow slavery, conflict erupted in Kansas, and Pierce effectively lost his authority over the American people. By then he'd become a problem alcoholic, and it is said that Pierce's parting words from the White House were, "Well, I guess there's nothing left to do but go get drunk." To this day, Pierce is the only US president not to have been nominated by his party for a second term.

One of Hillsborough's four municipalities, **Hillsborough Bridge Village**, at the intersection of Rte-9 and Rte-149, is home to the area's one-street downtown area. You can still see the structural remnants of the nineteenth-century **Contoocook Mills**, abandoned in the early 1900s, along the banks of the river, reminders of the town's once successful textile manufacturing industry. Also worth a quick look, the **Kemps Truck Museum**, along the river on River Street off of Rte-149, is really more like a parking lot full of rusting old trucks, though it supposedly holds the biggest collection of Mack trucks in the world.

Once you've tired of the **antique shops** in the center of town, head for the **Fox State Forest**, a state-maintained nature preserve south of town, which has over twenty miles of good hiking and cross-country skiing trails, as well as some interesting wetland areas. You can get a trail map and advice at the Fox Forest Headquarters (ⓣ603/464-3453), along Center Road south of town.

The quiet country roads of Hillsborough span some well-constructed old **stone arch bridges**. Built by skilled Scotch-Irish stonemasons in the mid-nineteenth century, the bridges, some built without mortar, are still in use. The finest bridge can be seen near the Pierce House, at the junction of Rte-9 and US-202, where there is also a small park with picnic benches.

While Hillsborough has a number of things to keep you busy, you're better of heading to either Keene or Peterborough for places to stay or eat.

Peterborough

The proud riverfront town of **PETERBOROUGH**, south of Hillsborough along Rte-202, has a youthful artistic focus these days. Immortalized by Thornton Wilder in the play *Our Town* and now boldly claiming to be "an entire community devoted to the arts," Peterborough is home to a wide range of cultural activities, but really centers on the **MacDowell Colony**, 100 High St (ⓣ603/924-3886, ⓦwww.macdowellcolony.org), which hosts over 200 artists – including musicians, painters, filmmakers, and photographers – in its 32 private studios each year. Dedicated to providing an environment free of distraction since its founding in 1907, the privately funded colony has hosted such notables as Alice Walker, Studs Terkel, Milton Avery, Thornton Wilder, Oscar Hijuelos, and Willa Cather. Artists open their studios to the public only once a year on Medal Day, usually in mid-August (call the Colony for exact date), when the Edward MacDowell Medal is awarded to "an American creative artist whose body of work has made an outstanding contribution to the national culture." Other than the artists' studios, the main building, **Colony Hall**, is open to visitors most afternoons, but there's nothing particularly of interest inside.

The tiny brick-dominated **downtown**, centered around **Grove Street**, was largely the inspiration of architect Benjamin Russell, who designed the **Town House**, where the city still holds town meetings, as well as the Historical Society and the Guernsey Building office complex. Inside the **Historical Society** building, 19 Grove St (Mon–Fri 1–4pm; ⓣ603/924-3275), a dusty hodgepodge of old artifacts, including photographs and farming tools, describes the "story of a typical New Hampshire town."

Three miles east of Peterborough along Rte-101, **Miller State Park** (ⓣ603/924-3672; $3) has a few excellent hikes. Try the **Wapack Trail**, which takes you to the 2290-foot summit of **Pack Monadnock** (2.8 miles round-

Summer arts in Peterborough

Each year in mid-July, Peterborough hosts the **Monadnock Festival for the Arts** (☎603/924-7234), a weekend of dance, art, theater, and music. From late June through mid-September, the **Peterborough Players** (☎603/924-7585, Ⓦwww.peterboroughplayers.com) stage acclaimed traditional and experimental theater performances in a renovated eighteenth-century barn on Hadley Road off of Hancock Middle Road, a few miles outside of town.

trip), from which you can sometimes see the Boston skyline to the southeast and Mount Washington to the north.

Practicalities

The most convenient **place to stay** is the *Peterborough Manor Bed and Breakfast*, 50 Summer St (☎603/924-9832, Ⓦwww.peterboroughmanor.com; ❹), which has six sunny rooms with private bath in an 1890s Victorian mansion. Otherwise, the *Apple Gate Bed and Breakfast*, 199 Upland Farm Rd, two miles from downtown (☎603/924-6543; ❹), offers pretty much the same level of comfort at similar prices.

Of several **places to eat** in Peterborough, *Latacarta at the Boilerhouse*, US-202 south of town in an old mill building (closed Mon; ☎603/924-6878), is the most interesting, serving delicious and creative fusion fare made with fresh ingredients and presented thoughtfully. *Harlow's Deli and Café*, 3 School St (☎603/924-6365), serves up good sandwiches and pizza as well as a healthy dose of town gossip in a friendly, relaxed pub where the bartender knows the customers by name. For upscale gourmet sandwiches, head to *Twelve Pine*, Depot Square (☎603/924-6140), which also serves espresso and fresh juice and has café seating. One of the finest **bookstores** in the state, the Toadstool Bookshop, 12 Depot Square (☎603/924-3543), has a huge selection of fiction, nonfiction, and travel books.

Jaffrey and the Monadnock State Park

The area commonly referred to as **JAFFREY** actually takes in the towns of Jaffrey and Jaffrey Center. Not much goes on in the former, and you're better off concentrating on picturesque Jaffrey Center, long the domain of novelist Willa Cather, who came to Jaffrey Center every fall during the early twentieth century to work and enjoy the quiet countryside. In a studio in the woods, Cather wrote parts of the novels *My Ántonia* (1918) and *One of Ours* (1922). Cather is buried beside her lover, Edith Lewis, in the **Old Town Burial Ground**, along Rte-124 in Jaffrey Center.

Beyond that, you really visit Jaffrey for **Mount Monadnock**, reputedly the second most-climbed mountain in North America and the centerpiece of **MONADNOCK STATE PARK** (open year-round; ☎603/532-8862; $3), just outside town heading west on Rte-124. The park is the most striking natural feature of the Monadnock region, a rolling countryside carpeted with dense stands of birch and pine trees. Although the mountain is only 3165 feet high, its gently sloping peak seems dominant because it is so isolated. The peak was a popular spot with nineteenth-century writers and artists; indeed, by 1900 it was so renowned that *Webster's Dictionary* recognized its name as a noun meaning "a hill or mass of rock rising above a peneplain." Henry David

Thoreau hiked and camped around the top of the mountain many times, writing of the experience, "It is a very unique walk . . . it often reminded me of my walks on the beach, and suggested how much both depend for their sublimity on solitude and dreariness. In both cases we feel the presence of some vast, titanic power." You can read more from Thoreau's journals and learn about the history of the park at the **visitors' center**, near the parking lot. They also have information about the park's forty miles of scenic hiking trails; the White Dot Trail is the most popular and direct route to the summit, taking about three-and-a-half hours round-trip. If you reach the peak (which will likely be crowded) on a clear day, you'll be able to see all six New England states.

Practicalities

You can **camp** in the park at the base of Mount Monadnock all year round, with the 21 basic tent sites costing $12 (Ⓣ603/271-3628 for reservations). Closer to Jaffrey, the *Emerald Acres Campground*, 39 Ridgecrest Rd (open May to mid-Oct; Ⓣ603/532-8838), has 52 pleasant sites in a pine forest bordering a small pond for $15.

The Inn at Jaffrey Center, 379 Main St (Ⓣ603/532-7800, Ⓦwww.theinnatjaffreycenter.com; ④), enjoys, as its name suggests, a central location in Jaffrey Center, with eleven individually decorated rooms in a house nicely situated in a shady garden. Meanwhile, *The Currier's House*, 5 Harkness Rd (Ⓣ603-532-7670, Ⓦwww.thecurriershouse.com; ④), also in town, has views of Mount Monadnock and a back porch from which to enjoy them. Just outside of town, the antique-filled *Benjamin Prescott Inn*, 433 Turnpike Rd, off of Rte-124E (Ⓣ603/532-6637 or 1-888/950-6637, Ⓦwww.benjaminprescottinn.com; ④), offers ten quiet rooms and gourmet New England breakfasts which, on Saturdays at least, include sweet strada (a sort of soufflé) with raspberry syrup and toffee-pecan coffee cake.

Fitzwilliam

Apart from being one of the more eye-pleasing towns in an undeniably picturesque region, the main reason for visiting **FITZWILLIAM**, south of Keene on Rte-12, is for its concentration of good accommodation. Otherwise, once you have absorbed the village's simple charms, consider making a trip to the nearby **Rhododendron State Park**, on Rte-119 five miles west of town (year-round; Ⓣ603/239-8153), particularly in mid-July when the park's sixteen acres of wild rhododendron are in full bloom.

Despite the temporary absence of the longstanding *Fitzwilliam Inn*, Rte-119 (Ⓣ603/585-9000), closed for renovation at the time of writing, there are **places to stay** worth seeking out. The *Amos A. Parker House*, 149 Rte-119 (Ⓣ603/585-6540, Ⓦwww.amosparkerhouse.com; ⑤), is a small, homely bed and breakfast surrounded by beautifully manicured gardens; the *Hannah Davis House*, 106 Rte-119 (Ⓣ603/585-3344; ④), another fine B&B occupying an elegantly restored and furnished 1820s Federal-style home; and the five suites and two cottages at *The Unique Yankee Water View Lodge*, 27 Main St (Ⓣ603/242-6706; ⑥), all with romantic open fireplaces and good views of nearby Mount Monadnock.

Dartmouth – Lake Sunapee Region

The **Connecticut River** forms the entire western border of New Hampshire. Along its banks, a smattering of typically quaint New England villages, connected by empty, winding country roads, are spread between serene stretches of misty, rolling, green farmland. At the region's heart, **Hanover** is New Hampshire's intellectual center, the home of arch-conservative **Dartmouth College**, which draws some of the country's best students and maintains an active arts scene. Nearby, **West Lebanon** and **Lebanon** are more laid-back but less interesting, with ample shopping malls in their quiet suburban sprawl. To the south, tiny **Cornish** was once a popular artists' colony, while **Lyme**, north of Hanover, is centered around a particularly attractive town green. As I-89 runs south from Hanover towards Concord, it grazes the northern tip of Lake Sunapee, a quieter alternative to more developed lake areas further east.

Hanover

Almost everyone in **HANOVER** has some connection to **Dartmouth College**. Indeed, the city and college are pretty much one and the same thing. Hanover received its official charter in 1761, just eight years before Dartmouth was founded. The college's reputation as one of the more conservative Ivy League schools is not unfounded; in fact, as you walk around, you'll notice that many of the students look strikingly alike: clean-cut preppy-types, most of them white. Stereotypes aside, though, it's an active place, with all the cultural and other benefits you expect from a college town: a good museum; regular performances by international musicians, dancers, and actors; good bookstores; and a smattering of decent places to eat and drink.

Arrival, information, and city transit

Amtrak's *Vermonter* **train** stops across the river in White River Junction, less than five miles from Hanover, once a day; local buses (see below) will get you into town from there. Vermont Transit **buses** between Boston and Montréal stop in Hanover at the *Hanover Inn*. There is a major terminal in White River Junction (Ⓣ802/295-3011), with buses south to Boston via Manchester (NH), and as far north as Montréal, via Burlington (VT). The Concord Trailways-affiliated Dartmouth Coach also has services to and from Boston and its airport, although fares are steeper than on Vermont Transit. Like the rest of New Hampshire, the upper Connecticut River Valley is most easily accessible by **car**. From the south, **I-91** blasts up the western side of the Connecticut River in Vermont, while **Rte-12A** and **Rte-10**, the slower, more scenic choices, trace the riverbank on the New Hampshire side. From Concord, I-89 passes through Lebanon and West Lebanon before crossing into Vermont; to get to Hanover, take Rte-120 north from Lebanon or Rte-10 north from West Lebanon.

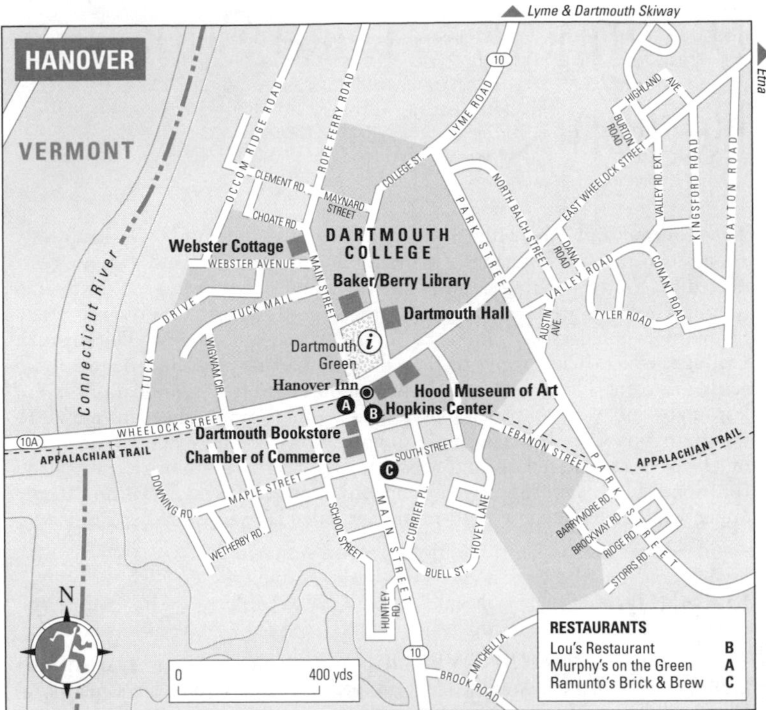

The **Hanover Chamber of Commerce**, 216 Nugget Building, Main Street (Mon–Fri 9am–4pm; ⓣ603/643-3115, ⓦwww.hanoverchamber.org), has only a moderate selection of brochures and tourist information. Probably your best bet during summer is the **information booth** on the green, jointly maintained by Hanover and Dartmouth College, and usually attended by enthusiastic alumni eager to spread the word about their old stomping grounds.

In and around Hanover, Advance Transit (ⓣ802/295-1824, ⓦwww.advance-transit.com; $1.25 one-way) provides a comprehensive **local bus** service, stopping in front of the *Hanover Inn* and at the Dartmouth Bookstore (as well as other places throughout town) and connecting Hanover with Lebanon and West Lebanon, as well the nearby Vermont towns of Norwich, Wilder, Hartford Village, and White River Junction. Trips within Hanover or between Hanover and Lebanon are free. You can get a schedule and route map at the Chamber of Commerce.

Accommodation

Accommodation in Hanover tends to be tidy, expensive, and luxurious – just the sort visiting parents, scholars, and performers appreciate. Things are mellower (though usually just as expensive) in the surrounding countryside.

Chieftain Motor Inn 84 Lyme Rd ⓣ603/643-2550, ⓦwww.chieftaininn.com. About two-and-a-half miles south of Hanover center, the best of the few budget accommodations in the area has access to a guest kitchen, and complimentary canoes for use in the nearby river. ⑤

Hanover Inn corner of Main and Wheelock streets ⓣ603/643-4300 or 1-800/443-7024,

Ⓦwww.hanoverinn.com. The top end of Hanover's accommodation options, with dozens of spacious, elegantly furnished rooms, overlooking Dartmouth Green. See below. ⑨

Moose Mountain Lodge end of Moose Mountain Road, Etna Ⓣ603/643-3529, Ⓦwww.moose-mountainlodge.com. Just east of Hanover, in Etna, the *Lodge* is a marvelously remote option year-round, but is best as a base in winter for cross-country skiing. Closed mid-Oct to late Dec. ⑦

Trumbull House Bed and Breakfast 40 Etna Rd Ⓣ603/643-2370 or 1-800/651-5141, Ⓦwww.trumbullhouse.com. Four miles east of Dartmouth Green, *Trumbull House* offers luxury accommodation in a quiet country setting. ⑥

The Town

Fittingly, the town's focal point remains the grassy **Dartmouth Green**, bounded by Main, Wheelock, Wentworth, and College streets. The Dartmouth-owned **Hood Museum of Art**, on Wheelock Street on the green, is Hanover's main draw off the central campus (Tues & Thurs–Sat 10am–5pm, Wed 10am–9pm, Sun noon–5pm; free; Ⓣ603/646-2808, Ⓦwww.dartmouth.edu/~hood), with paintings by Picasso and Monet as well as outstanding works by several American artists – Gilbert Stuart, Thomas Eakins, and John Sloan. The standouts include Frederick Remington's hauntingly realistic painting of three Native Americans and a settler, *Shotgun Hospitality*; a fine collection of portraits, including Joseph Steward's *Portrait of Eleazar Wheelock*, the founder of Dartmouth College; and a selection of detailed etchings by Rembrandt. In addition to a collection of Greek, Assyrian, and African objects, the museum also stages special exhibits of works from around the world. The adjacent cultural complex, the **Hopkins Center for the Creative and Performing Arts** (Ⓣ603/646-2422, Ⓦwww.dartmouth.edu/~hop), screens international art and classic movies year-round (tickets $6). They also present internationally acclaimed musicians, acting companies, and dance troupes, as well as student performances.

Next door, the venerable **Hanover Inn**, founded by General Ebenezer Brewster in 1780, is a longstanding local landmark, standing five stories high with a classic-looking brick facade. Although devastating fires and extensive renovations have obscured the inn's colonial charm, its lobby is still bustling with visiting parents, scholars, and performers. Recent guests at the inn, owned and operated by the college, include then-President Clinton, dancer Mikhail Baryshnikov, and the rock band Kiss. **South Main Street**, which runs along the west side of the inn, holds most of the town's eateries, bars, and shops, and is pleasant enough to wander around.

Dartmouth College

Majestic **Dartmouth College** (Ⓦwww.dartmouth.edu), founded by Reverend Eleazar Wheelock in 1769, is the ninth oldest college in the United States. The school was initially an outgrowth of a school for Native Americans that Wheelock had established in Connecticut, but in reality few Native Americans ever studied here. Named for its financial backer, the Earl of Dartmouth, the Ivy League institution attracts some of the top students in the world today, with particularly strong programs in medicine, engineering, and business.

The stately 200-acre campus is spread out around **Dartmouth Green**, and this is a good starting point for a look at the grounds. Flanking the north end of the green, along Wentworth Street, the looming **Baker/Berry Library**, with its 207-foot bell tower, is an imposing landmark. Inside, it holds the most arresting attraction on the campus, José Clemente Orozco's series of enormous **frescoes**, on the lower level. The Mexican artist painted these politically

Birthplace of Daniel Webster

New Hampshire's best known statesman, orator, and public figure, **Daniel Webster**, was born in 1782 in the tiny two-room farmhouse on Flaghold Road off of Rte-127 in **FRANKLIN**, twelve miles west of Laconia (see p.487). Now known simply as the **Daniel Webster Birthplace** (mid-May to mid-Oct weekends 10am–5pm; $3; ⓣ603/934-5057 or 924-5976), the restored home contains period furniture, antiques, and some Webster memorabilia, including books he read as a child. Webster attended Phillips Exeter Academy, graduated from Dartmouth College in 1801, and went on to build a successful law practice before serving in Congress from 1813 to 1817 and in the US Senate from 1827 to 1841. He loomed large on the political scene in his day, delivering persuasive speeches on topics as far-ranging as states' rights, slavery, the Union, the US–Canadian border, and Dartmouth College. As Secretary of State under presidents William Henry Harrison, Tyler, and Fillmore, Webster remained a staunch defender of the Union. During a particularly heated discussion in 1850, in which Webster debunked the idea of states' rights, he coined the memorable phrase "Liberty and Union, now and forever, one and inseparable." In perhaps his most famous debate, the Dartmouth College Case of 1817, Webster defended his alma mater before the Supreme Court, which decided that states could not interfere with royal charters.

rousing murals, commissioned by the trustees of the college, between 1932 and 1934, while he was an artist-in-residence and visiting professor at Dartmouth. It's easy to see why conservative college officials and alumni viewed the violent depiction of the artist's stated theme, *An Epic of American Civilization*, as a direct insult. On one of the detailed, realistic panels, for example, a skeleton gives birth while lying upon a bed of dusty books, as a group of arrogant, robed scholars look on. In another panel, a large Jesus-like figure stands angrily next to a felled cross with an axe in his hand. Though college officials initially threatened to paint over the murals, they soon backed down, careful to avoid living up to Orozco's vision. Upstairs on the ground floor, check out the library's map room, which holds 150,000 sheet maps and 7000 atlases.

On the east side of the green stands **Dartmouth Row**, a collection of four impressive old buildings that look out over the grass from a slightly raised position. **Dartmouth Hall**, an imposing white building with a large "1784" on its hulking pediment, was the college's first permanent structure and remains a symbol of Dartmouth's academic prowess. Although it burned to the ground in 1904, the restored structure, which today houses Dartmouth's language and literature departments, remains on its original foundation. The other three halls in the row, **Reed**, **Thornton**, and **Wentworth**, house Dartmouth's history and philosophy departments, and the Dean's office, respectively.

Further north along Main Street, the memory of the school's most celebrated graduate, Daniel Webster, the brilliant lawyer, senator, and orator, is preserved in **Webster Cottage**, 32 N Main St (late May to mid-Oct Wed, Sat & Sun 2.30–4.30pm; free; ⓣ603/646-3371), where he lived as an undergraduate. Webster later succeeded in defending the college before the Supreme Court in the landmark Dartmouth College Case of 1817, which determined that the power to make an institution public rests with those who control it, rather than with those who have funded it.

Eating and drinking

Daniel Webster Room inside the *Hanover Inn*, corner of Main and Wheelock streets ⓣ603/643-4300. The most elegant (and most expensive) restaurant in town, boasting a traditional menu of finely grilled meats at $17–27 per entrée.

Dirty Cowboy Café 7 S Main St ☎603/643-1323. Next door to *Murphy's* (see below), the *Dirty Cowboy* serves the usual coffee drinks, as well as smoothies and fresh-squeezed juices.

Lou's Restaurant 30 S Main St ☎603/643-3321. Filling breakfasts of tasty hashbrowns, eggs, and sausage for under $10. Serves lunch also, but it's not as good. Closes at 5pm.

Murphy's on the Green 11 S Main St ☎603/643-4075. *Murphy's* is the best spot in town for a drink, and it also has a popular restaurant, which serves an eclectic array of healthy American cuisine.

Ramunto's Brick and Brew 68 S Main St ☎603/643-9500. Serves delicious and affordable pizzas and has several beers on tap; open every night until at least midnight.

Sweet Tomatoes Trattoria 1 Court St, Lebanon ☎603/448-1711. Excellent fresh Italian specialties, such as wood-fired pizzas and tortellini with four cheeses; located in nearby Lebanon.

Shopping

Dartmouth Bookstore 33 S Main St ☎1-800/624-8800, Ⓦwww.dartbook.com. This sprawling bookstore, owned and operated by the same family since 1883, is so big it publishes its own four-page map and guide, available at the door.

Powerhouse Mall Rte-10, West Lebanon. A gathering of the usual stores, selling shoes, clothing, electronics, and the like at tax-free prices, atmospherically housed in an old brick electric powerhouse.

Around Hanover: Lyme and Cornish

Time stands still in tiny **LYME**, only ten miles north of Hanover along Rte-10. The grassy town center is perfect for an evening stroll, which will take you past the attractive 1811 white-clapboard **Lyme Congregational Church**, featuring a bell supposedly cast by Paul Revere. After checking out the church's beautiful interior woodwork, have a look at the creepy old cemetery in back. Of the few places to stay in Lyme, which could be a good – although not

Outdoor activities in the Dartmouth area

Quick to take advantage of their rather isolated location, Dartmouth students and Hanover residents alike take their **outdoor** time seriously. Hiking, biking, rowing, and swimming are all popular during the warmer months, while skiing (both cross-country and downhill) and skating are the activities of choice during the winter. The town's residents include best-selling travel author Bill Bryson, one of whose books, *A Walk in the Woods*, chronicled his adventures along the 3000-mile Appalachian Trail, which runs right through Hanover along Rte-10A – during the summer, grizzled hikers trudge into town with some regularity. The Dartmouth Outing Club, in Robinson Hall (☎603/646-2428), maintains hundreds of additional miles of **hiking trails** in the area and also leads group **bike rides**.

You can **rent bikes** (and snowshoes in the winter) for $20 per day from Omer and Bob's Sportshop, 7 Allen St (☎603/643-3525). **Rowing** on the Connecticut River remains an extremely popular way to take in the scenery while getting some exercise; Dartmouth Recreation Rowing (☎603/646-3434) and the Ledyard Canoe Club (☎603/643-6709) rent **canoes** and **kayaks** and can suggest routes. In the winter, Dartmouth's very own **alpine ski** area, the Dartmouth Skiway, ten miles north in Lyme (☎603/795-2143; $22 weekdays, $34 weekends), rents skis and snowboards. The Silver Fox Ski Touring Center in Hanover (☎603/643-6534) maintains 35km of **cross-country skiing** trails and rents skiing and **ice-skating** equipment.

If you're in the mood for an Ivy League-flavored **workout**, Dartmouth's enormous athletic facility (☎603/646-2109, Ⓦwww.dartmouth.edu/~athfac), centered around the **Alumni Gymnasium**, along East Wheelock Street, has a modern fitness center, two pools, tennis courts, racquetball and squash courts, and a basketball court. Non-students can buy an all-day guest pass for $10.

△ Sap bucket

necessarily cheaper – alternative to the Hanover accommodation options, the *Alden Country Inn*, 1 Market St, off Rte-10, on the common in the center of town (Ⓣ603/795-2222 or 1-800/794-2296, Ⓦwww.aldencountryinn.com; ❻), is the best, offering fourteen sizeable upstairs rooms and a full breakfast. On the first floor, the candle-lit *Tavern and Grille* is a good place to **eat**, serving hearty portions of New England chow.

Other than a collection of scenic pastures and a few covered bridges, there's not much left in the town of **CORNISH**, south of Hanover along Rte-120, which was a well-known artistic center in the late nineteenth century. The thing to see here is the **Saint-Gaudens National Historic Site**, off Rte-12A (daily: late May to late Oct 9am–4.30pm; $5; Ⓣ603/675-2175, Ⓦwww.sgnhs.org), where sculptor Augustus Saint-Gaudens lived and worked between 1885 and 1907, when he died. Saint-Gaudens was best known for his lifelike heroic bronze sculptures, including the Shaw Memorial in Boston and the General William T. Sherman Monument in New York City. Many well-known artists, writers, poets, and musicians, including Maxfield Parrish, Kenyon Cox, and Charles Platt, followed Saint-Gaudens to Cornish, establishing the **Cornish Colony**, an informal and supportive group. Saint-Gaudens' house, his studio, and several galleries displaying his sculptures, are open to the public. Take the time to wander around the beautiful grounds, which feature well-cared-for gardens, two wooded nature trails, and a relaxing expanse of green grass. You can also check out works in progress by the artist-in-residence at the **Ravine Studio**, in the woods along the northern edge of the property. Just north along Rte-12A, works by many of the area's famed artists are on display at the small **Cornish Colony Gallery and Museum** (late May–Oct 9am–5pm; $5; Ⓣ603/675-6000), whose gardens were designed by Rose Standish Nichols, the first female landscape architect in America.

A few minutes south of town off of Rte-12A, the **Cornish-Windsor covered bridge**, connecting New Hampshire with Vermont, is the longest covered bridge in the US, though unless you're an enthusiast, it may not be worth seeking out. It was constructed in 1866 and restored in 1989. A little further south, on Springfield Road just off of Rte-11 in **Charleston**, the **Fort at No. 4** (daily: late May to late Oct 10am–4pm; $10) hokily re-enacts colonial life in the 1740s and 1750s. Costumed interpreters roam the grounds, acting out the chores and activities of the day in various re-created living quarters and work areas, including old blacksmith and candlemaking shops.

If you're looking for a comfortable **place to stay**, the best is the luxurious *Chase House Bed and Breakfast*, on Rte-12A (Ⓣ603/675-5391, Ⓦwww.chasehouse.com; ❻). The well-decorated nineteenth-century mansion is also the birthplace and one-time residence of Salmon Portland Chase, Chief Justice of the US Supreme Court in the 1860s, in whose honor the former Chase Manhattan Bank was posthumously named. Today the inn features seven exquisitely furnished rooms and delicious breakfasts (included).

Lake Sunapee

LAKE SUNAPEE, the northern tip of which just brushes I-89, lies about twenty-five miles south of Hanover in the southerly portion of the region. The lake had been popular as a summer escape since the beginning of the nineteenth century, but with the arrival of train connections to Newbury Harbor at the lake's southern tip, the area exploded with a booming tourist trade.

Steamboats full of vacationing Bostonians and New Yorkers plied the waters, while mansions and luxury hotels began appearing on the coast. Among the notables who made their homes here were the Colgates (of Colgate-Palmolive fame) and Secretary of State John Milton Hay, whose mansion The Fells still stands. The advent of the automobile effectively ended Sunapee's boom time and saved it from development on the atrocious scale of its huge northeastern neighbor, Lake Winnipesaukee. Today, the Sunapee region is a very low-key place, although recent heavy investment, especially in Mount Sunapee (see below), while no doubt providing a new boom, may also sound the death knell for its secluded charm. Enjoy it while it lasts, and know that you're still in rockin' good company – Aerosmith's Steven Tyler has a house on the lake.

Sunapee Harbor and around

The action, such as it is, is all on **Sunapee Harbor**. A far cry from the lake's heyday, the only boats on the clear, clean waters (Sunapee is a spring-fed lake) now are the occasional mail boat and regular **boat tours**, such as those run by Sunapee Cruises (daily: July to early Sept 2pm; late May–June & early Sept to mid-Oct weekends 2pm; $14; ⓣ603/763-4030, ⓦwww.sunapeecruises.com). The knowledgeable captain will share Sunapee lore and point out the sights, such as the former Colgate estate and the lake's three lighthouses. True boat aficionados won't want to miss the annual **Classic Boat Parade** in August (contact the Lake Sunapee Protective Association in Sunapee Harbor for details; ⓣ603/763-2210).

On the opposite shore stands the Hay family estate, **The Fells**, off Rte-103A (grounds open year-round, dawn to dusk; $4; house tours, late May to mid-Oct weekends and holidays 10am–4pm; $5, including grounds admission). John Milton Hay was an advisor and friend of Abraham Lincoln, who later became Secretary of State under Teddy Roosevelt. He built his mansion here in the 1870s, and it was passed on to his son, Cecil, who just happened to be a talented landscape artist and designed the grounds of the mansion in a pleasing mix of Asian and European styles. Cecil was also a concerned preservationist, and his distress at the rapid deforestation of the area led him to donate 675 acres of **forest** to the Society for the Protection of New Hampshire Forests. These days, the mansion itself is empty, and the guided tours, while enjoyable, tend to make visitors feel as if they are being shown the house for prospective purchase. Far more interesting are the **gardens** that surround the house, with the borrowed scenery of the lake and forests adding to their charm. There are also **nature trails** through those 675 acres, which provide good opportunities for bird-watching.

Winter activities in the area take place at **Mount Sunapee** (ⓣ603/763-2356, ⓦwww.mountsunapee.com; lift passes from $48), a family-oriented resort at the northern end of the lake. Thirteen million dollars' worth of investment over the past four seasons has led to improvements to lifts, snowmaking facilities, and transportation to the mountain, as well as the opening of two new teaching trails. Indeed, the gentle slopes of Mount Sunapee will suit learners and the mildly proficient more than expert skiers.

Practicalities

About four miles west of Lake Sunapee, the biggest town in the area, Newport, is nothing like its opulent namesake in Rhode Island, and won't prompt more than a glance, but its **Chamber of Commerce** (ⓣ603/863-1510, ⓦwww.newportnh.org), in a small booth right on the town green, should be able to help you orient yourself to the area. The friendly folks at the **Lake Sunapee Business Association** (Ⓣ603/763-2495 or 1-800/258-3530) will happily help you find **accommodation**. Overlooking the lake, with a view as well of nearby Mount Sunapee, the *Inn at Sunapee*, 125 Burkehaven Hill Rd (Ⓣ603/763-4444 or 1-800/327-2466, Ⓦwww.innatsunapee.com; ❺), is a converted 1875 farmhouse with sixteen rooms decorated with a mixture of period items and Asian antiques. There's also an attached **restaurant**, specializing in creative, fresh American food with an Asian flair. The *Best Western Sunapee Lake Lodge*, 1403 Rte-103 (Ⓣ603/763-2010 or 1-800/606-5253, Ⓦwww.sunapeelakelodge.com; ❻), is within walking distance of the ski resort, and while the rooms are much like any other hotel of this genre (comfortable and impersonal), there are plenty of them. Even so, reservations are essential during busy times.

The Lakes Region

The vacation-oriented **LAKES REGION**, occupying the state's central corridor, east of I-93, almost doubles its population between May and September, when throngs of visitors crowd the area's restaurants, hotels, lakefront cottages, beaches, and crystal-clear waters. The lakes themselves – **Winnipesaukee** and **Squam** being the two largest – are the obvious attractions here, and on warm summer weekends they can seem overrun with pleasure craft, all of which are available for rent at the many town marinas. Fishing, swimming, camping, and relaxing on the beach are also popular, and you can enjoy a view of the lakes from afar after hiking to the top of one of several peaks that wrinkle the countryside.

There are literally hundreds of lakes here, created by the snowmelt flowing south from the White Mountains, and the biggest by far is **Lake Winnipesaukee**, which forms the definitive center of the region. Long segments of the enormous lake's shoreline, especially in the east, are carpeted with thick forests that sweep down from surrounding hills to the water's edge. Covering some 72 square miles, the lake is dotted with 274 islands – most of which are privately owned – and its irregular shape, a seemingly endless continuum of inlets and peninsulas, resembles that of a giant paint splatter. The eastern and western shores of Lake Winnipesaukee are quite distinct: sophisticated **Wolfeboro** is the center of the sparsely populated and more upscale region to the east of the lake, while **Weirs Beach** is the most developed stretch of the crowded western shore. Further north, the down-to-earth nineteenth-century towns around beautiful **Squam Lake** are some of the most inviting in the region.

The western Winnipesaukee shore

The western Winnipesaukee shore, the most visited part of the Lakes Region, can be a relaxing or lively spot to spend a day or two depending on where you

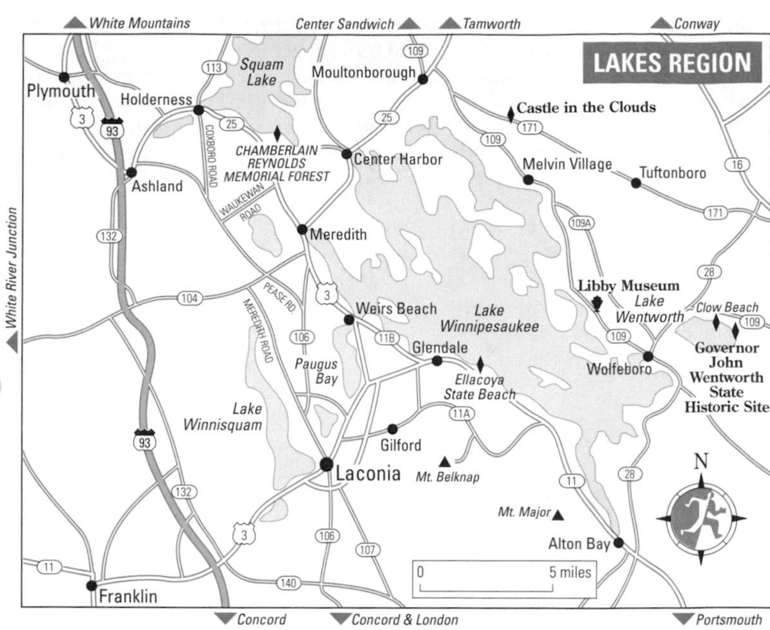

chose to go. Once inhabited by the Abenaki Indians, its position on the major north–south stagecoach route in the early nineteenth century, and, later, the railroad route north to the increasingly popular White Mountains, made it a major stopover. Nowadays, gas stations, cheap hotels, and convenience stores line the major roadways, such as US-3 and Rte-11, although nearly every town in the area boasts sweeping views of some body of water. Downtown **Meredith**, squeezed between Lake Waukewan and Lake Winnipesaukee, is an appealing collection of shops, restaurants, and sumptuous lodgings, while **Weirs Beach**, south along US-3, is the epitome of summertime overkill, with enough arcades, ice-cream parlors, and roadside fun-parks to keep the kids happy for weeks. Undistinguished **Laconia** is the biggest town in the area, while the resort town of **Gilford** maintains a more relaxed disposition.

Arrival, information, and getting around

Public transport is somewhat limited around Lake Winnipesaukee, although Concord Trailways calls in at Laconia (at the train station), in Meredith (at Mobil Mart, close to the center on Rte-25), in Center Harbor (at Fred Fuller's Oil on Rte-25), and in Moultonborough (at the Moultonborough Emporium on Rte-25). The best source of **information** on the western shore is the **Meredith Area Chamber of Commerce** (Ⓣ603/279-6121 or 1-877/279-6121, Ⓦwww.meredithcc.org), on US-3 just south of downtown Meredith. They distribute loads of brochures about local attractions and restaurants, and can provide details on lodging availability and help with reservations. The **Greater Laconia Transit Agency** (Ⓣ603/528-2496 or 1-800/294-2496) operates the Gilford and Meredith **trolleys** from late June through early September, which connect Gilford and Meredith with Weirs Beach, stopping at major restaurants and shopping spots along the way; all-day tickets go for $2. You can **rent a car** from Meredith Ford (Ⓣ603/279-4521), at the intersection

> **The New Hampshire International Speedway**
>
> Twenty miles south of Laconia in **LOUDON**, and just one mile from the serenely peaceful Canterbury Shaker Village (see p.466), the **New Hampshire International Speedway** (ⓣ603/783-4931, ⓦwww.nhis.com) holds car and motorcycle races from May through October, sometimes attracting more than 90,000 beer-swilling motorsports enthusiasts. The NASCAR Winston Cup, held in mid-July, is the most popular event here, and during this time many of the hotels and inns in the Lakes Region fill up well in advance. Tickets for the races cost $15–50. If watching fast cars whirl around a track in a deafening frenzy while shielding your eyes from the burning sun is your idea of a good time, this may be just the event for you.

of US-3 and Rte-25 in Meredith, or a **bicycle** at the Greasy Wheel, 40 S Main St, Plymouth (ⓣ603/536-3655), where you can also get advice on local trails and routes.

Weirs Beach

The short boardwalk at **WEIRS BEACH**, the very essence of seaside tackiness – despite being fifty miles inland – is in summer the social center of the Lakes Region. Its wooden jetty overflows with vacationers from all over New England, and its amusement arcades jingle with cash; there's even a little crescent of sandy beach, suitable for family swimming. The roads are lined with neon signs, mini-golf courses, waterslide playland extravaganzas, and motels clogged with family-filled minivans in summer, when the crowds can be almost overwhelming.

You'd best head elsewhere if you're looking for a relaxing lakeside afternoon. If you're up for a few hours of slippery diversion in the sun, however, you might try the better of the two competing **water parks**, Surf Coaster (daily: late June to early Sept 10am–6pm; $25), which offers dramatic rides and a wave machine on Rte-11B just south of town. Failing that, a great way to take in Winnipesaukee's beautiful expanse of inlets and peninsulas while getting away from the ugliness of Weirs Beach is a cruise aboard the landmark **MS Mount Washington** (mid-May to mid-Oct; ⓣ603/366-5531 or 1-888/843-6686, ⓦwww.cruisenh.com; $19, 150min), a 230-foot monster of a boat which departs from the dock in the center of town several times a day to sail to Wolfeboro on the western side of the lake. The ship also sets sail for dinner and dance cruises several times per week (around $30). Other day cruises are available on the smaller *MV Doris E* ($10, one hour) and the US mail boat, *MV Sophie C* ($16, two hours), which gives you a better opportunity to see some of the lake's many islands close up as *Sophie C* delivers the mail.

Practicalities

If you want to find a **place to stay** within earshot of the amusement arcades and close enough to smell the hot dogs, there are plenty of choices on Tower Street, up the hill behind the jetty. There is a real army barracks feel to the *Half Moon Motel & Cottages* (ⓣ603/366-4494, ⓔhalfmoonmotel@weirsbeach.com; ❸), where a block of motel rooms and individual cottages (some with kitchens) are laid out around the austere pool with military precision. Slightly cozier and compact is the *Lakeview Hotel*, a little further up the hill at 58 Tower St (ⓣ603/366-4621, ⓦwww.stayatlakeview.com; ❶), which also has a pool and cottages, and where offseason room rates are among the cheapest you'll find anywhere in New Hampshire. For something to eat, you're better off heading to nearby Meredith. If, however, you simply need to line your stomach with something to see you through the night, the hot-dog stands and burger bars by the jetty will do the trick.

Meredith

MEREDITH, four miles north of Weirs Beach, is more upscale than its neighbor. The friendly town center, up the hill behind the Mill Falls Shopping Center development, spills into the pleasant **Meredith Marina**, 2 Bayshore Drive (ⓣ603/279-7921), where you can rent a motor boat for a mere $215 per day, $165 per half-day. The **Winnipesaukee Scenic Railroad** (late May to early June & early Sept to mid-Oct weekends; daily: mid-June to early Sept; $9.50 for 1hr, $10.50 for 2hr; ⓣ603/745-2135) operates scenic trips along the lakeshore between Meredith and Weirs Beach. The sandy town **beach**, with mountain views, is located on Waukewan Street along the shores of tiny **Lake Waukewan**. Right outside the center of town, a pretty little **lakeside park** makes for a pleasant stroll; while you're there, you can ponder who decided to mount the anti-aircraft gun from a WWII battle cruiser there on the grass.

Just outside Meredith, off of US-3, the only thing to admire is **Annalee's Doll Museum** (museum late spring to early fall only; shop daily 9am–5pm; ⓣ603/279-6542 or 1-800/433-6557), in reality a hard-sell toy shop, specializing in painted-felt dolls. Those items onto which they've managed to stitch the heads backwards are offered at a 25-percent reduction.

Accommodation

Chieftain Motor Inn 95 Pleasant St ⓣ603/279-8584. Basic rooms here at the sister location of Hanover's *Chieftain Motor Inn* (see p.476) – the lakeside setting is nice, though. ❺

Clearwater Campground Rte-104, 3 miles east of I-93 ⓣ603/279-7761, ⓦwww.clearwatercampground.com. Located out on Permigewassat Lake, with 150 shaded sites and hot showers. $34/site.

Harbor Hill Camping Area 189 Rte-25 E ⓣ603/279-6910, ⓦwww.hhcamp.com. This family-oriented campground has 33 tent sites, 82 full-hookup RV sites, a pool, and a children's playground. Open mid-May to mid-October; $24/tent site, $50/RV site.

The Inns at Mill Falls 312 Daniel Webster Hwy ⓣ603/279-7006 or 1-800/622-6455, ⓦwww.millfalls.com. This group of three hotels is unquestionably the best choice for accommodation in the area. Choose from the *Inn at Mill Falls* or the *Chase House at Mill Falls*, both on the hill overlooking the lake, or the *Inn at Bay Point*, directly on the lake with some balconied rooms offering unrivalled lake views. ❼

Meredith Inn corner of Main and Waukewan streets ⓣ603/279-0000, ⓦwww.meredithinn.com. A quaint Victorian B&B with eight rooms, and a good choice near the center of town. ❻

Tuckernuck Inn 25 Red Gate Lane ⓣ603/279-5521 or 1-888/858-5521, ⓦwww.thetuckernuck-inn.com. A good-value B&B near the center of town; some rooms have shared bath. ❺

Eating and drinking

Boathouse Grille 1 Bay Point, at intersection of Rte-3 and Rte-25 ⓣ603/279-2253. This relaxed dining room on the water is a nice place for good steak and seafood.

Mame's 8 Plymouth St ⓣ603/279-4631. Besides an excellent selection of creative and affordable sandwiches for lunch, and gargantuan seafood, chicken, and steak dinners, *Mame's* also has a cozy pub, which can get crowded on weekend nights. Definitely the best place to eat in Meredith.

Phu Jee 55 Main St ⓣ603/279-1129. Offers a dizzying array of authentic Chinese food, with house specialties for under $15.

Laconia, Gilford, and Glendale

LACONIA, southwest from Lake Winnipesaukee on the shores of **Winnisquam Lake**, has long been the most populated town in the Lakes Region, established as a trading and manufacturing center after the railroad reached the city in 1848. Some of the factories in use back then – when they produced such things as nails and hosiery – continue as office space. Today Laconia is mostly just convenient as a place to pick up supplies. If you do venture past the commercial strip of malls, car dealerships, and fast-food joints to Laconia's downtown, the payoff will be a short and fairly depressed stretch of empty storefronts.

The pleasant villages of **GILFORD** (east of Laconia along Rte-11A) and **GLENDALE** (beside the lake on Rte-11) are worth a quick detour, though there is not a whole lot to actually see or do in either of them. When in Glendale, be sure to check out the huge marina filled with the boats of wealthy visitors. For excellent vistas of the lake and surrounding region, head for the top of **Mount Belknap**, which at 2384 feet is the highest peak in the Belknap Range, along the west side of the lake, east of Laconia. The easiest and shortest route up the mountain begins along Belknap Mountain Carriage Road; turn off Rte-11A at the lights in the center of Gilford, drive through the village on Cherry Valley Road and follow the signs for the Fire Tower on Belknap. If you're feeling more sedentary, **Ellacoya State Beach**, along Rte-11 east of Glendale (late May to mid-Oct; ⓣ603/293-7821), is one of the finer sandy beaches – and the only one that's state maintained – on Lake Winnipesaukee, with 600 feet of sand, and a **campground** that affords some great views of the lake from many of its 38 sites ($35).

Practicalities

If you prefer the more laid-back atmosphere here than at Meredith and certainly Weirs Beach, you will find some reasonable **places to stay** in Guilford. The *Belknap Point Motel*, 107 Belknap Point Rd (ⓣ603/293-7511 or 1-888/454-2537, ⓦwww.bpmotel.com; ⑤), offers somewhat modern lakeside accommodations in a boxy, white building with a good view of the lake and surrounding mountains. Some rooms have full kitchens and can be rented by the week. Slightly more upscale, *B Mae's Inn & Suites*, 17 Harris Shore Rd (ⓣ603/293-7526 or 1-800/458-3877, ⓦwww.bmaesresort.com; ⑤), has two pools, a Jacuzzi, and an exercise room – all within walking distance of the beach. Just past Gilford on Rte-11A, *Gunstock* (ⓣ603/293-4341 or 1-800/486-7862, ⓦwww.gunstock.com) doubles as an alpine ski area during the winter and a recreation area during the summer, as well as offering lodging. Summer activities include mountain-bike riding (you can rent bikes for $30 per day at the camp store), horseback riding ($40 for a one-hour trail ride), and hiking (visit the store for trail maps and advice). **Campsites** are available for $25 per night, while camping cabins, with electricity and water, can be had for $60 per night or $360 per week.

For a **drink** or hearty snack in Gilford, try *Patrick's Pub*, at the intersection of Rte-11 and Rte-11B (ⓣ603/293-0841). If you're looking for **entertainment**, the Meadowbrook Farm Musical Arts Center, also in Gilford (ⓣ603/293-4700, ⓦwww.meadowbrookfarm.net), is the largest musical venue in the Lakes Region.

The eastern Winnipesaukee shore

The eastern shore of Lake Winnipesaukee is a lot less developed than the western shore, with a more polished and elegant air about it, and the refined quality of the food, lodging, and atmosphere is reflected in steeper prices. First established as a popular summer destination in the late eighteenth century by Governor John Wentworth, tourism is still the major industry here, but in a much more relaxed fashion: there are no mini-golf courses and waterslides, and fewer children. Wealthy families vacation year after year at the many stately privately owned homes along Lake Winnipesaukee's shore, and couples flock to the many secluded country B&Bs of the region. This side of the lake is also better for walking and outdoor activities, although most visitors in search of rugged adventure head further north for the popular peaks of the White Mountains. Water-based activities are the rule here, and there are several good public beaches around **Wolfeboro**, the most populated and interesting town in the area. North of Lake Winnipesaukee is the quiet town of **Moultonborough**, home to one of the oldest country stores in the US. Nearby, architecturally-eclectic **Castle in the Clouds** makes for an interesting diversion, as does the **Loon Center**. **Melvin Village** and **Tuftonboro** are unobtrusive and sparsely populated, with winding tree-shaded country roads, the occasional antique shop, and some alluring nineteenth-century architecture.

Many **hotels, inns, and B&Bs** are only available seasonally, so call to be sure, especially in winter months. If you find the prices too steep, or prefer to sleep under the stars, camping in the quiet birch forests that crowd the lake's shore is also a pleasant summer option, although insect repellent is an absolute must. There are plenty of upscale and expensive **places to eat** on this side of the lake, with seafood and panoramic lake views being the norm. Hidden along the area's quiet rambling country roads, there are several out-of-the way eateries that are worth hunting down. The generally quiet **nightlife** centers around a few low-key local pubs.

Arrival, information, and getting around

If you're going to the eastern side of the lake from the western side by **car**, the drive along Rte-25 and Rte-109 is the easiest and most scenic route; using Rte-11 and Rte-28 through Alton Bay around the south end of the lake is slightly faster. Miller Rent-a-car has an office in Wolfeboro along Rte-28 (Ⓣ603/569-1068 or 1-800/287-1068), where you can **rent a car**. You can also cross the lake from west to east by **boat**. The *MS Mount Washington* (see opposite) runs at least two round-trips a day from Weirs Beach to Wolfeboro, so you'll get a minimum of about three hours on the eastern shore if you go out on the first departure and return on the last. Alternatively, if you want to stay in Wolfeboro, you can skip the return portion of the cruise. The best source for **information** on the eastern shore is the **Wolfeboro Chamber of Commerce**, in the old red railroad building on Railroad Street in the center of town (Ⓣ603/569-2200 or 1-800/516-5324, Ⓦwww.wolfeborochamber.com). They stock a dizzying array of brochures and will give the lowdown on local attractions and lodging. **Local transportation** is scarce, although the Wolfeboro Trolley Company (Ⓣ603/569-5257; $3) operates a short narrated loop around Wolfeboro and tickets are good for an entire day.

Wolfeboro

Because Governor John Wentworth built his summer home nearby in 1768, upscale **WOLFEBORO** claims to be "the oldest summer resort in America."

Sandwiched between lakes Winnipesaukee and Wentworth, at the intersection of Rte-109 and Rte-28, it has little to show for that history, but it's a relaxing place to spend a bit of time. The short, bustling Main Street (Rte-109) can be fun if you want to while away a few hours strolling from boutique to boutique, with fine views of the lake never too far away, although the town's attractions as such are actually a short distance from the center. The 4300-square-foot summer mansion of Governor John Wentworth, known as the Wentworth House Plantation, with its own saw mill, orchards, workers' village, and 600-acre deer park, was, at the time, a sort of Hearst Castle of New Hampshire. It burned to the ground in 1820 and was never rebuilt, but the area once occupied by the plantation, on Rte-109 three miles southeast of Rte-28, is now the **Governor John Wentworth State Historic Site** (summer only; $3), an undeveloped park and archeological site.

Another worthwhile stopoff, a few miles north of downtown Wolfeboro on Rte-109, is the eclectic **Libby Museum** (June to mid-Sept Tues–Sat 10am–4pm, Sun noon–4pm; $2), where early twentieth-century dentist Henry Forset Libby's obsession with evolution is manifested by various ineptly stuffed animals (one can only hope he was a better dentist than taxidermist) and the skeletons of bears, orangutans, and humans. There's also a mastodon's tooth, a "Niddy-Noddy" spinning device, a random collection of fossils and insects, Native American artifacts, and a fingernail supposedly pulled out by its Chinese owner to demonstrate his newfound Christian faith. The setting of the museum, in a 1912 Historic Landmark house with a superb view of the lake from the front steps and a grassy lakefront park, makes the detour even more rewarding.

A great way to take in Lake Winnipesaukee's grandeur is aboard the famous **MS Mount Washington** (see p.485), a 230-foot cruiser that departs from the dock in the center of town and connects with Weirs Beach across the lake. You could also hop aboard the smaller *Winnipesaukee Belle* (summer only; ⓣ603/569-3016 or 1-800/451-2389; 90min; $12), a 65-foot replica of an early twentieth-century paddle steamer which departs from the *Wolfeboro Inn* and tours the eastern end of the lake.

Accommodation

Lake Motel 280 S Main St ⓣ603/569-1100 or 1-888/569-1100. Modern accommodation, with tennis courts and private sandy beach; some rooms with kitchen. ❹

Lakeview Inn and Motorlodge 120 N Main St ⓣ603/569-1335, ⓦwww.lakeviewinn.net. Nicely decorated rooms with modern amenities, in a restored inn and two-story hotel overlooking Wolfeboro. ❹

Tuc' Me Inn B&B 118 N Main St (Rte-109N) ⓣ603/569-5702, ⓦwww.tucmeinn.com. Homely 1850 Federal/Colonial inn with tastefully furnished rooms and full breakfast close to the lake and town. ❺

Willey Brook Campground Rte-28 ⓣ603/569-9493, ⓦwww.willeybrookcampground.com. Located three miles north of Wolfeboro and only one mile from Wentworth State Beach. Open mid-May to mid-Oct; sites $16–25.

Wolfeboro Campground 61 Haines Hill Rd ⓣ603/569-9881. Fifty wooded family campsites ($16) with hot showers located close to downtown Wolfeboro. Open mid-May to mid-Oct; sites $16.

Wolfeboro Inn 90 N Main St ⓣ603/569-3016 or 1-800/451-2389, ⓦwww.wolfeboroinn.com. Built in 1812 with 44 well-appointed rooms, this stately inn is situated along the waterfront just a few yards from the town proper. ❺

Eating and drinking

The Cider Press Middleton Road, South Wolfeboro ⓣ603/569-2028. Hearty American food – ribs, steak, grilled salmon – in a rustic, candlelit dining room.

East of Suez Rte-28, just south of Wolfeboro ⓣ603/569-1648. Huge portions of pan-Asian food, from Thai to Chinese to Korean, authentically prepared and served in a high-ceilinged dining room. The pad thai is especially good. Summers only.

Lydia's Café Main Street ⓣ603/569-3991. Fruit smoothies, espresso drinks, bagels, and excellent sandwiches are served in this cute little café in the center of town.
The Strawberry Patch 33 Pine St ⓣ603/569-5523. Excellent, freshly prepared breakfasts and lunches in a homely and unpretentious dining room just off Main Street.
Wolfeboro House of Pizza Main Street ⓣ603/569-8408. Good Greek-owned place, serving tasty pizzas, pastas, and submarine sandwiches – though not a *souvlaki* or *baklava* in sight.
The Wolfeboro Inn 90 N Main St ⓣ603/569-3016. Of the inn's restaurants, the fancy *1812 Room* serves good, expensive, New England-style cuisine, but *Wolfe's Tavern*, a dark pub-like eatery with a huge selection of burgers, sandwiches, pasta, soups, and salads, is the better value of the two. The tavern also has 72 beers on tap; if you want to get your own iron mug (check the ceiling for the 1300 or so that have already been claimed) you have to drink one of each type and then kiss the stuffed moose head (only two beers count per day).
Wolfetrap Grill and Rawbar 19 Bay St ⓣ603/569-1047. Unpretentious and basic restaurant just outside of town with a range of seafood plates including lobster, clams, and softshell crab dinners. Open Thurs–Sat.

Moultonborough and around

Other than some remote B&Bs and quiet country roads, there's not much to the sprawling town of **MOULTONBOROUGH**, north of Lake Winnipesaukee on Rte-25. If you're passing through, however, you might stop off in the **Old Country Store**, at the intersection of routes 25 and 109. One of the oldest of its kind, it sells everything from homemade dill pickles to penny candy to brass door knockers and carved wooden ducks. The bizarre "museum" upstairs houses a dusty collection of artifacts, including axes, saws, and carved Indian sculptures. If, on the other hand, you'd like to spend some time in the sun, off of Rte-25, near the end of Moultonborough Neck Road on Long Island, the **town beach** is a particularly good spot for picnicking and swimming. There's also a popular beach at the intersection of routes 25 and 25B.

A little way east of town on Rte-171, **Castle in the Clouds** (May 11–June 1 weekends only; daily: June 3–Sept 1 9am–4.30pm; daily: Sept 2–Oct 20 9am–4pm; $12 for tours, $6 for access to grounds; ⓣ1-800/729-2468), the 5200-acre mountain estate of eccentric millionaire Thomas Plant, stops just short of being a complete tourist trap. It's saved by the uniqueness of the house itself, an interesting amalgamation of various architectural styles from around the world, betraying Spanish, Japanese, and Swiss influences. The roof, for example, is covered with red tiles, while the facade recalls a ski chalet. Built in 1913 and designed by Plant, the massive hilltop mansion was somewhat advanced for its time, with a centralized vacuum system, intercom, and a self-cleaning oven. These days, they've also added a brewery (whose Lucknow Beer can be found at local stores) and spring mountain water bottling plant, also included in the tour.

The Loon Preservation Committee maintains the small **Loon Center**, along quiet Lee's Mills Road off of Blake Road (Mon–Fri 9am–5pm; July to mid-Oct also weekends 9am–5pm; free; ⓣ603/476-5666), which houses a collection of exhibits about the endangered and much-loved birds, focusing on environmental awareness and the negative impact of pollution. You can view Lake Winnipesaukee from several vantage points along the the **Loon Nest Trail**, which begins at the Loon Center and winds through upland forests and marshes near the lakeshore, and maybe even catch a glimpse (or at least hear the distinguished sounds) of one of the speckled birds.

A good place to **stay** is the *Olde Orchard Inn*, Lee Road (ⓣ603/476-5004 or 1-800/598-5845; ❹), a relaxing bed and breakfast in the middle of an apple

Eastern shore outdoor activities

The eastern shore has enough **outdoor activities** to keep even the most avid enthusiast busy. Hiking, boating, sailing, fishing, swimming, mountain-biking, and kayaking are all big in summer, while cross-country skiing and snowmobiling should sate any outdoor urges during the winter.

The best public **beach** for swimming and picnicking in the Wolfeboro area is **Clow Beach** (mid-June to mid-Oct; ⓣ603/569-3699) in Wentworth State Park on Lake Wentworth. **Brewster Beach** (mid-June to mid-Oct; ⓣ603/569-1532) on Lake Winnipesaukee at the end of Clark Road south of town is also good for sunbathing and swimming. Once you've done sunning yourself, there are a couple of decent, if gentle, local **hiking routes**. The **Mount Major Trail**, north of Alton on Rte-11, offers excellent lake views and takes about an hour and a half to cover the 1.75 miles. The scenic trail to the top of **Bald Peak**, at the Moultonborough–Tuftonboro town line on Rte-171, is a mile long. The Mount Flag Trail in Tuftonboro is a strenuous seven-mile loop. For a shorter jaunt (half a mile), with rewarding panoramic views of the lake and surrounding forests, try the **Abenaki Tower Trail**, off of Rte-109 in Tuftonboro across from Wawbeek Road, featuring an eighty-foot tower overlooking Lake Winnipesaukee and the Ossipee Mountains. **Snowmobiles** and **cross-country skiers** fill the trails during winter months. Call the Cross Country Ski Association (ⓣ603/569-3151) or the New Hampshire Snowmobile Club (ⓣ603/271-3254) for information and guidance.

As for **watersports**, Goodhue Hawkins Navy Yard, at 244 Sewall Rd in Wolfeboro (ⓣ603/569-2371), rents several types of **boats,** ranging from $85 to $275 per day. Wet Wolfe Rentals, 19 Bay St, Wolfeboro (ⓣ603/569-3200), rents boats for a minimum of two hours ($100) and gives tours of the lake in its antique wooden boat. You can take an all-inclusive light tackle guided **fishing** trip with Gadabout Golder, 79 Middleton Rd, Wolfeboro (ⓣ603/569-6426), for $225 per person. The Winnipesaukee Kayak Company, 17 Bay St in Wolfeboro (ⓣ603/569-9926), rents **kayaks** for $40 per day and canoes for $50 per day and also leads various tours and multi-day excursions. For a truly unique lake experience, try a **seaplane** ride, which departs from Wolfeboro and costs $20 per person per flight, with a two-person minimum (ⓣ603/569-1310 for information).

orchard with nine rooms, some featuring fireplaces and Jacuzzis. Meanwhile, the best place to **eat** in town (dinner only) is *The Woodshed*, Lee Road (closed Mon; ⓣ603/476-2311), an old barn-turned-restaurant where prime rib is the specialty, and moderately-priced lamb chops, lobster, and grilled fish are also on the menu. Ask for a table in the screened-in patio on warm summer evenings.

Squam Lake

Much smaller than its sprawling neighbor, but still the second largest body of water in the state, beautiful **Squam Lake** can actually hold more appeal than Lake Winnipesaukee. The pace here is slower, the roads less crowded, and, thanks to a conscientious group of old-money landowners, the land has been less developed.

Most of the activities here revolve around the **outdoors**; hiking, boating, swimming, or simply relaxing on the beach are all popular during the summer months. It's easy to see why producers chose this lake as the setting for the 1981 film *On Golden Pond*, starring Jane and Henry Fonda – the lake is pristine and glassy, and the setting sun brings a quiet calm over the water and surrounding forests. With a population of 1700, **Holderness** is the largest town on the lake, although it's really nothing more than a gas station, a few stately old inns, a couple of restaurants, and a dock. **Center Sandwich**, to the north of Squam Lake, and **Center Harbor**, to the south of Squam Lake on the Lake Winnipesaukee shore, also maintain their nineteenth-century quaintness, while **Ashland**, closer to I-93, near Little Squam Lake, has several good restaurants and a slightly more cosmopolitan feel.

Holderness

Named for the Earl of Holderness, a friend of Governor Wentworth's, **HOLDERNESS**, at the intersection of US-3 and Rte-113, was granted its original town charter in 1751. The popular statesman, Samuel Livermore, had acquired half of the town's land by the late eighteenth century through grants and purchases, building a church and housing, and although nothing of much historical significance ever happened here, the Holderness School has remained a prestigious college preparatory school since its founding in 1879. The unpretentious village brings together a loosely defined grouping of buildings along the lakeshore next to a well-used public dock. The general store in town is the place to come for supplies and provisions before you head out for a day on the lake.

The beach, the forest, and the science center

The best local **beach** is accessible along a short trail through the **Chamberlain-Reynolds Memorial Forest**, off of College Road. To get there from Holderness, follow US-3 south, take a left on Rte-25B, and a left on College Road. The forest is on your right; park in the small lot and follow the Ant Hill Trail for about twenty minutes – be sure to bring some insect repellent. The most popular **hike** in the area begins at the Rattlesnake Trailhead along Rte-113 and follows the **Old Bridle Path** to the top of **Rattlesnake Mountain**, providing spectacular views of Squam Lake and the surrounding hills, with only half an hour of effort. Other trails to the top of Rattlesnake Mountain, such as the **Ramsey Trail**, begin along Pinehurst Road, off of Rte-113. The **Mount Morgan Trail**, which begins at the trailhead along Rte-113, 5.4 miles northeast of US-3, and ascends 1400 feet along a 2.1-mile trail, is also a rewarding hike. Additional hiking suggestions are available at the SLA headquarters (see opposite).

A delicate glimpse of the area's natural habitat and inhabitants is afforded by the **Squam Lake Natural Science Center**, near the intersection of Rte-113 and Rte-25 in the center of town (daily: May–Nov 9.30am–4.30pm; $9 July & Aug, $7 rest of year; ⓣ603/968-7194, ⓦwww.nhnature.org), which features live animals – including bears, bobcats, owls, and otters – housed in settings that resemble their natural habitats along a quarter-mile nature walk. Compared to a typical zoo, it's refreshingly spacious, though numerous hands-on exhibits and educational presentations tend to attract large groups of schoolchildren.

Watersports and activities

Squam Lakes Tours (ⓣ603/968-7577) is one of several companies offering **boat rides** in and out of the picturesque lake's many coves and inlets. Its two-hour jaunts ($14), which depart from the dock a half-mile south of town at 10am, 2pm, and 4pm, include a look at the **Thayer Cottage**, where the bulk of *On Golden Pond* was filmed. The ninety-minute trips offered by Golden Pond Tours (ⓣ603/968-7194; $14) at 11am, 1pm, and 3pm are more focused

The Barnstormers

Founded in 1931 by Francis Cleveland (son of 22nd US president Grover Cleveland), his wife, Alice, and Edward Goodnow, the **Barnstormers** (Ⓣ603/323-8500, Ⓦwww.barnstormerstheatre.com) is the oldest professional summer theater group in the state. It is also one of the few theater companies in the country in which the same actors perform a different play each week, rehearsing the following week's play during the day while acting in the current production at night. Presenting a wide range of productions – from classics such as Arthur Miller's *Death of a Salesman* to comedies like a *Lady from Maxim's*, by Georges Feydeau – the theater company plays to consistently large crowds. Housed in a refurbished old store in the center of **Tamworth Village** since 1935, the company typically produces eight plays per summer. Call Ⓣ603/323-8500 from late May until the end of the season for schedule and ticket information.

Just across the street from the theater, the *Tamworth Inn* (Ⓣ603/323-7721 or 1-800/642-7352, Ⓦwww.tamworth.com; ❻) is a pleasant 1833 inn with comfortable **accommodation** and an elegant **restaurant** serving gourmet homemade American cuisine (Tues–Sat).

on observing the endangered loons which inhabit the lake; and the final cruise of the day is led by a qualified naturalist. If you'd rather steer your own boat, rent a five-person motorboat for $119 per day or a three-person canoe for $49 per day from Squam Lakeside Farm, on US-3 (Ⓣ603/968-7227). The **Squam Lakes Association** (SLA), with a helpful office on US-3 (Ⓣ603/968-7336, Ⓦwww.squamlakes.org), rents **canoes** ($45/day), **kayaks** ($40/day), and **sailboats** ($50/day), and sells trail guides to the region ($6). They also run half-day kayak tours for $50 and give three-and-a-half-hour kayak lessons for $50.

Practicalities

By far the ritziest and most expensive **place to stay** in Holderness is the *Manor on Golden Pond*, on US-3 overlooking the lake (Ⓣ603/968-3348 or 1-800/545-2141, Ⓦwww.manorongoldenpond.com; ❼), an elegant mansion complete with crystal chandeliers, sweeping vistas, and roaring stone fireplaces. Their *Wine Spectator* Award-winning dining room offers gourmet New American cuisine. Less expensive and more down-to-earth, the welcoming *Inn on Golden Pond*, on US-3 along Little Squam (Ⓣ603/968-7269, Ⓦwww.innongoldenpond.com; ❻), has eight large rooms, friendly hosts, full breakfasts, and table tennis in the game room. Though its rooms are nothing special, the well-situated *White Oak Motel*, at the intersection of Rte-25 and US-3 (Ⓣ603/968-3673 or 1-888/965-1850, Ⓦwww.whiteoakmotel.com; ❹), is the cheapest place around. They also rent cottages for $595–899 per week. The Squam Lakes Association maintains primitive **camping sites** on Moon Island, Bowman Island, and in the Chamberlain Reynolds Forest, costing $40 per site (up to six people) on weekends, $32 per site weekdays (reservations required; call Ⓣ603/968-7336; May–Oct).

The only waterfront **restaurant** in town, *Walter's Basin*, on US-3 (Ⓣ603/968-4412), serves decent rainbow trout and other seafood dishes in a pleasant setting. The Golden Pond Country Store (daily 6am–10pm; Ⓣ603/968-3434), at the intersection of US-3 and Rte-113, sells pizza, deli sandwiches, fishing supplies, groceries, beer, newspapers, gas, and just about anything else you might need while traveling in the area.

Center Harbor and Center Sandwich

The relaxing village of **CENTER HARBOR**, nicely situated close to Squam's eastern shore, is a good base from which to explore the Lakes Region, especially if you have a car. There isn't much here except for the usual lake-based diversions of canoeing, kayaking, and boat cruises (the *MS Mount Washington* stops here on Mondays – see p.485 for more details), but it's close to the larger settlements of Lake Winnipesaukee if you're looking for some action. You can also get to Center Harbor by **bus**, with Concord Trailways stopping at Fred Fuller's Oil on Rte-25 four times a day. If you're looking for a **place to stay**, the *Kona Mansion Inn* (ⓣ603/253-4900, ⓦwww.konamansioninn.com; ❻) has tennis, golf, and swimming in a tranquil lakeside setting with a country club atmosphere. For a more rugged experience, at the south end of town on the shore of Lake Winnipesaukee, the enormous (151-site) family-oriented *Arcadia Campground* (ⓣ603/253-6759) offers such amenities as a grocery store and video room.

Nine miles northeast along Rte-113, at the base of the Sandwich Range, **CENTER SANDWICH** groups a string of white-clapboard buildings, including a general store and typically-steepled church, in a quaint version of a New England town. Though it's right next to Squam Lake, you'd never know it; the dense forest along the shoreline, which is largely privately owned, obscures the view. The best **place to stay** in town is the *Corner House Inn* (ⓣ603/284-6219; ❺), an inviting, informal, and popular bed and breakfast that's been around for over 150 years. You could also try the *Overlook Farm B&B*, 14 Mountain Rd (ⓣ603/284-6485; ❹), with four cozy rooms (some with shared bath) in a quiet setting.

Ashland

Though tiny **ASHLAND** was a thriving manufacturing town in the nineteenth century, producing lumber, wool, gloves, and paper, it's now little more than a sleepy village. There's not much to stop for, unless you need a quick bite to eat or a place to sleep without straying too far from I-93. If you decide to **stay the night**, the *Glynn House Inn*, 59 Highland St (ⓣ603/968-3775 or 1-800/637-9599, ⓦwww.glynnhouse.com; ❻), with ornate woodwork, a wrap-around porch, fireplaces in most rooms, hearty breakfasts, and afternoon tea and sherry is one of the better-looking and more comfortable B&Bs in the state. Slightly cheaper, the well-situated *Black Horse Motor Court*, on US-3 (ⓣ603/968-7116 or 1-877/968-7116, ⓦwww.blackhorsemotorcourt.com; ❸), has motel suites and cottages nightly or weekly. For a bite to **eat**, hit the *Common Man*, in a rustic brick building in the center of town along Main Street (ⓣ603/968-7030); they serve great lunches and gourmet dinners, specializing in lobster bisque and roast prime rib. Less formal is the *Ashland House of Pizza*, also on Main Street (ⓣ603/968-3686), which has good pizzas and sandwiches.

North to the White Mountains

US-3 west from Ashland intersects with I-93, which heads north to Lincoln and North Woodstock in the White Mountains. At the foot of the mountains, in **Plymouth**, you can either continue north along the interstate or head another five miles west to the **Polar Caves** (daily: early May to late Oct 9am–5pm; $9.50) – though these are not so much caves as a cascade of clammy granite boulders tumbled against a hillside, between which visitors find pleasure in squeezing themselves – while paying handsomely for the privilege.

A large gift shop sells some supremely irrelevant "souvenirs." For inexpensive food in town, try *Jigger Johnson's* (ⓣ603/536-4386), where you can gorge on big sandwiches, hamburgers, pizzas, and salads as well as more expensive steak and seafood entrées.

The White Mountains

Thanks to their accessibility to both Montréal and Boston, the **WHITE MOUNTAINS** have become a year-round tourist destination, popular with summer hikers and winter skiers alike, and attracting over six million annual visitors. It's a commercialized region, with quite a lot of tourist development flanking the main highways, but the great granite massifs retain much of their majesty and power. **Mount Washington**, the highest peak not only in the range, but in the entire Northeast, can claim some of the severest weather in the world – conditions harsh enough to produce a timberline at four thousand feet, as compared to around ten thousand feet in the Rockies.

Vacationing in these mountains is not a new thing, and this area has long been appreciated for its exquisite beauty. After railroads were built through here during the mid-nineteenth century, lumber companies bought up much of the land and began to log the forest. However, quick to recognize the value of the mountains' beauty, local residents formed influential conservationist groups, such as the **Appalachian Mountain Club**, and eventually ensured the passage of the Weeks Act in 1911, which allowed the federal government to purchase the land to preserve it. The national forest area here now encompasses almost 800,000 acres, covering much of the northern part of the state and even spilling over into Maine.

Only a few high passes – here called "**notches**" – discovered by early pioneers through arduous crossings pierce the range, and the roads through these gaps, such as the **Kancamagus Highway** between **Lincoln** and **Conway**, make for predictably scenic routes. However, you won't really have made the most of the White Mountains unless you also set off, on foot, bike, or skis, across the long expanses of thick evergreen forest that separate them, with mountain peaks poking out in all directions. Some of the best hiking trails are in the state parks of **Franconia Notch**, straddling I-93, **Crawford Notch**,

White Mountains parking fee

You will need a **parking pass** for your vehicle when you park and leave it unattended in the White Mountains National Forest, though not if you're just stopping briefly to take pictures or use restrooms, nor if you're staying in a National Forest campground. Passes cost $5 for seven consecutive days, or $20 for an annual pass. You can buy them from many local stores and at all Forest Service offices. If you have not had time to buy a seven-day or annual pass, or you decide on the spur of the moment to hike to the top of a mountain or spend the afternoon at a swimming hole, you can purchase a day-pass for $3 at self-service machines at sixty selected sites across the forest.

straddling US-302, and **Pinkham Notch**, along the eastern base of Mount Washington. Downhill skiing is popular at resorts such as **Waterville Valley** and **Loon Mountain**, both a few miles east of I-93, while cross-country skiing is particularly good at **Jackson** in the eastern part of the White Mountains, which, along with **North Conway** and **Glen**, make up the region's most built-up area, the **Mount Washington Valley**. Also, even if you don't intend to stay, check out the grand resort hotels in **Bretton Woods** and **Dixville Notch** (the first town in New Hampshire – and therefore the nation – to announce the results of its primary elections).

It's best to have your own transport, as ever, but somewhat regular **bus services** to the White Mountains from the southern part of the state are provided

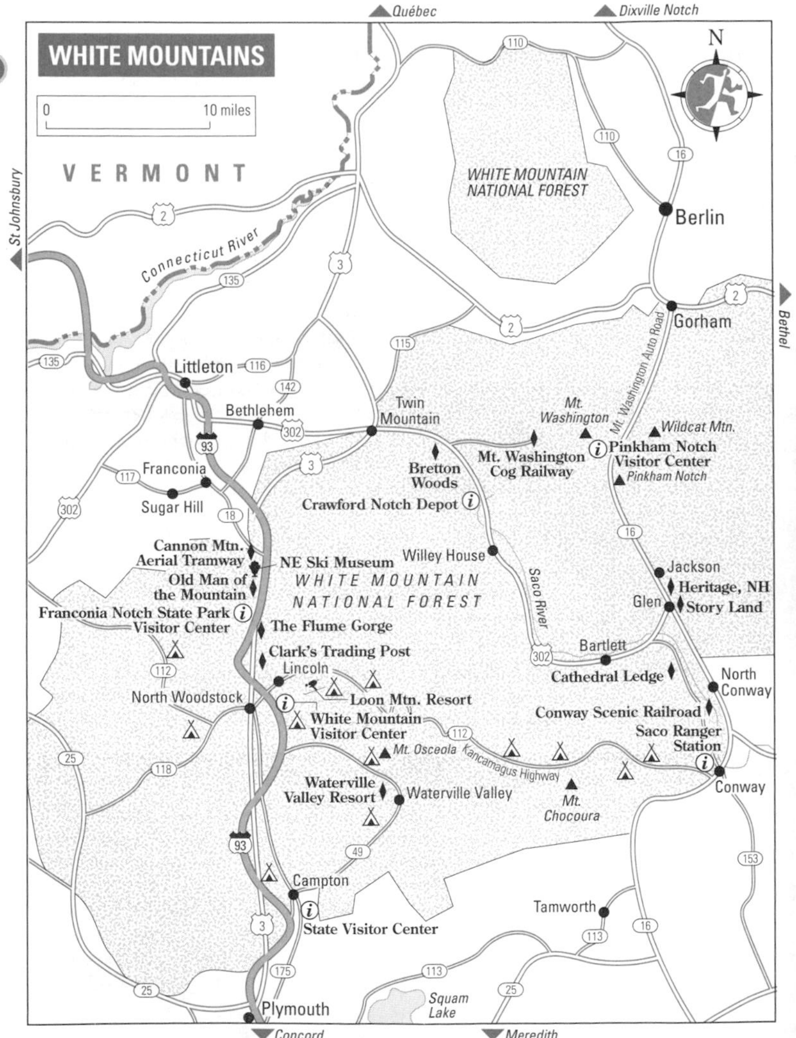

by Concord Trailways, stopping at Berlin, Conway, Franconia, Gorham, Jackson, Lincoln, Littleton, and at the Pinkham Notch AMC Camp.

Waterville Valley

East of I-93 along Rte-49, the sparkling **Waterville Valley Resort** (ⓣ603/236-8311 or 1-800/468-2553, ⓦwww.waterville.com) was the brainchild of shrewd developer Tom Corcoran, who bought the *Waterville Valley Inn* and its surrounding land in 1965 with the intent of creating a happy family-oriented outdoor center. The many resort-goers enjoying rollerblading, mountain-biking, boating, tennis, hiking, and golf during the summer, and skiing, snowmobiling, and ice skating in the winter, are evidence enough that he succeeded – not altogether surprising considering the stunning tree-covered setting.

At the center of the resort is the creatively named **Town Square**, a contrived development of shops and restaurants alongside the smallish **Corcoran's Pond**, where you can lounge on a short strip of sand or rent a kayak ($9/hr), canoe ($11/hr), or paddleboat ($13/hr). Nearby, the Adventure Center (ⓣ603/236-4666) rents **bikes** for $30 per day and sells trail maps for $2.50. You can also rent bikes and ride the lift to the top of the hill at **Snow's Mountain** ($20 per day). In **Campton**, back where Rte-49 first veers off I-93, Ski Fanatics, Rte-49 (ⓣ603/726-4327), rents kayaks for $25 a day and also runs a shuttle to suitable places for kayaking.

Though relatively active in summer, Waterville Valley really comes to life in the winter months, and the intermediate slopes of the **ski** area (lift tickets $39, equipment rental $30), a network of chairlifts covering 2020 vertical feet on Mount Tecumseh and Snow's Mountain, is usually packed. The Nordic Center at Waterville Valley has over forty miles of **cross-country trails** (ⓣ603/236-4666; $13 trail fee, $18 equipment rental).

The rugged area surrounding Waterville Valley makes for excellent **hiking** and **camping**. Of several notable hikes that originate along Tripoli Road, a partially unpaved alternate route between I-93 and Waterville Valley, the **Mount Osceola Trail**, originating four miles from town and winding five miles to a ridge at 4300 feet, is the best. If you plan to park your car at the trailhead, or anywhere in the National Forest for that matter, you'll need a **pass** (see box, p.495), available locally at the Waterville Valley Recreation Department, Noon Peak Road (ⓣ603/236-4695; $5), and at the Tripoli Road Fee Station, just past the Russell Pond Road.

Practicalities

The **Waterville Valley Region Chamber of Commerce** (daily 9am–5pm; ⓣ603/726-3804 or 1-800/237-2307, ⓦwww.watervillevalleyregion.com) is your best bet for information on hiking, camping, and lodging in the area; they stock the usual range of brochures and have helpful attendants and good maps. The **Pemigewasset Ranger District** office on Rte-175 in Plymouth (ⓣ603/536-1310) is also a good source of information on hiking and camping in the region. The **Waterville Valley Recreation Department** (ⓣ603/236-4695) sells trail maps, passports to the White Mountains National Forest, and fishing licenses.

Accommodation options in the immediate Waterville Valley area are geared to families and all-inclusive vacationers, though, in nearby Campton, you'll find a selection of more intimate bed and breakfasts and inns. During the summer, prices are surprisingly reasonable, and rates at all nine of the resort's lodges, inns, and condos include use of the athletic club, mountain bike rental, golf, tennis courts, and kayak rental. The *Best Western Silver Fox Inn* (ⓣ1-888/236-3699, ⓦwww.silverfoxinn.com; ❺) is one of the cheaper places in the resort, and at the *Black Bear Lodge*, 3 Village Rd (ⓣ603/236-4501 or 1-800/349-2327, ⓦwww.black-bear-lodge.com; ❺), you can get a room that sleeps four for under $100 outside of tourist season. The *Snowy Owl Inn*, 4 Village Rd (ⓣ603/236-8383 or 1-800/766-9969, ⓦwww.snowyowlinn.com; ❺), has 85 rooms with cozy fireplaces and homely furnishings, and feels least like a huge lodging complex. Be aware, though, that prices go up by as much as fifty percent in winter. In Campton, the *Osgood Inn*, 14 Osgood Rd (ⓣ603/726-3543; ❹), is one of the better B&Bs, housed in a stately old home; some rooms come with a shared bath.

You can **camp** at the *Waterville Campground*, with 25 wooded sites off of Tripoli Road, ten miles east of I-93 (open all year; ⓣ603/536-1310; $14), or the privately owned *Branch Brook Campground*, Rte-49, Campton (ⓣ603/726-7001; $15). There are thirteen tent sites at the *Osceola Vista Campground* (ⓣ603/536-1310; $15), just outside of Waterville Valley on Tripoli Road, and undeveloped wilderness sites with no facilities along Tripoli Road between Waterville Valley and I-93; obtain a parking/camping permit at the Tripoli Road Fee Station, I-93 exit 31.

Most of the **places to eat** in the Waterville Valley are just the sort you'd expect in a heavily marketed resort community: slightly monotonous and not great value for money. There's a no-nonsense pizza joint, the *Waterville Pizza Company* (ⓣ603/236-FOOD), in the lower level of the Town Square, and a more upscale restaurant serving creative American cuisine with a seasonally changing menu, the *Wild Coyote Grill*, above the White Mountain Athletic Club (ⓣ603/236-4919). For better value, you're better off in Campton, where you can stuff your face with large portions of well-prepared pasta, seafood, chicken, steak, or, on Wednesday evenings, Mexican food at the *Mad River Tavern*, Rte-49 just off of I-93 exit 28 (closed Tues; ⓣ603/726-4290). The *William Tell*, Rte-49 (ⓣ603/726-3618), is a bit more expensive and less relaxed, but nonetheless serves good Swiss and German specialties. The *Jugtown Country Store*, in Town Square (ⓣ603/236-3669), with a full-service deli and wide selection of cheeses, meats, and breads, is a good place to buy picnic supplies.

Lincoln and North Woodstock

Straddling opposite sides of I-93 at the entrance to the Kancamagus Highway (see p.501), the twin towns of Lincoln and North Woodstock maintain relatively distinctive personalities while catering to both skiers and hikers. **NORTH WOODSTOCK**, a small-town mountain retreat at the intersection of Rte-3 and Rte-112, is the nicer and more low-key of the two, with a short, attractive row of restaurants and shops and a couple of good places to stay. On the other hand, **LINCOLN**, a continuous strand of strip malls and condominium-style lodgings, is less appealing, though it makes a good base from which to explore the western White Mountains. Neither town offers much in the way of things to see, and the real attraction lies in getting out of town and into the forest or onto the slopes.

The area was sparsely peopled until 1892, when lumber baron James Henry transformed the town into a bustling logging center, complete with a school, hospital, and housing for his hundreds of workers. By the mid-twentieth century, after Henry's relatives had sold his operation, logging faded and tourism became the town's livelihood. Today, it's difficult to recognize that the **Millfront Market Place**, surrounded by enormous parking lots along Main Street in Lincoln, was once a timber mill, although logging trucks from points further north still occasionally rumble past town along I-93.

Information and accommodation

The enormous **White Mountains Visitor Center** in Lincoln near I-93 (daily 9am–5pm; ⓣ603/745-8720 or 1-800/FIND-MTS, ⓦwww.visitwhitemountains.com) gives lodging advice and sells maps of the region, including the excellent *Trail Map & Guide to the White Mountain National Forest* ($4.95), which lists 250 trail descriptions and is essential if you plan on embarking on any extended hiking expeditions. The **Lincoln-Woodstock Chamber of Commerce**, in the Depot Mall on the east side of town along Main Street (daily 9am–5pm, winter until 7pm; ⓣ603/745-6621, ⓦwww.lincolnwoodstock.com), has more brochures and serves as a room reservation center for the region.

Hotels and inns

Drummer Boy Motor Inn just off I-93 exit 33, Lincoln ⓣ603/745-3661 or 1-800/762-7275, ⓦwww.drummerboymotorinn.com. Slightly more luxurious than the *Franconia Notch*, the *Drummer Boy* is better value, too, with a pool, sauna, Jacuzzi, and exercise room. ❹

Franconia Notch Motel US-3, 1 mile from I-93 exit 33, Lincoln ⓣ603/745-2229 or 1-800/323-7829, ⓦwww.franconianotch.com. Standard, clean lodging along an alarmingly tacky strip of US-3; rooms have cable TV and a/c. ❹

Indian Head Resort Rte-3, Lincoln ⓣ1-800/343-8000, ⓦwww.indianheadresort.com. An unpretentious resort motel with plenty of facilities and outdoor activities, as well as a restaurant which serves decent food. ❹

Wilderness Inn intersection of US-3 and Courtney Street, just south of Rte-112, North Woodstock ⓣ603/745-3890 or 1-800/200-9453, ⓦwww.thewildernessinn.com. Features seven antique-furnished guestrooms and sumptuous breakfasts. ❹

Woodstock Inn Rte-3, Main Street, North Woodstock ⓣ603/745-3951 or 1-800/321-3985, ⓦwww.woodstockinnnh.com. In the center of town, comfortable carpeted rooms, an outdoor Jacuzzi, and reasonable ski/lodging packages. ❹

Campgrounds

Lost River Valley Campground 951 Lost River Rd (Rte-112) ⓣ603/745-8321 or 1-800/370-5678, ⓦwww.lostriver.com. Just over four miles west of North Woodstock, Lost River has swimming and a kids' playground near its 125 wooded sites. Open May–Oct 11; $22–30/site.

Russell Pond Campground south of Lincoln, off I-93 exit 31 ⓣ603/726-7737 or 1-888/CAMPSNH. 86 well-maintained camping spots, plus coin-operated hot showers – all in a scenic setting next to Russell Pond, where you can swim and boat. Open May to mid-Oct; $16/site.

Wildwood Campground 9 miles west of Lincoln along Rte-112 ⓣ603/726-7737 or 1-888/CAMP-SNH. 26 campsites with opportunities for fishing, hiking, and picnicking; well-maintained by the USDA Forest Service. Open May 15–Dec 1; $14/site.

Loon Mountain Resort

Though Lincoln and North Woodstock are relatively busy in summer months, they really come to life in the winter with enthusiastic skiers and snowboarders who hit the slopes at the nearby **Loon Mountain Resort** (ⓣ603/745-8111, ⓦwww.loonmtn.com), two miles east of I-93 on the Kancamagus Highway. Lift tickets for adults cost $49 at Loon ($54 on weekends), and equipment rental is available at the base of the mountain. The trails, while interesting for intermediate skiers, might not be challenging enough for the expert. During the summer, Loon offers many of the activities you'd expect from a large full-service mountain resort – swimming, tennis, aerobics, horseback riding, mountain-biking – and if you'd like a nice view of the surrounding terrain without going through the trouble of hiking or biking up the mountain, you can ride the **gondola** to the top for $9.50 (Ⓣ603/745-6281). You can rent a **mountain bike** for $33 per day at the base of the mountain ($59 with unlimited gondola service) or rent rollerblades for $9 per hour. There's also a stable offering **horseback** trail rides from $39 per hour. In Lincoln, you can rent bikes at White Mountain Cyclists, Main Street (Ⓣ603/745-6466).

Clark's Trading Post

A mile north of town along Rte-3, local landmark **Clark's Trading Post** (daily June 22–Sept 2 10am–5pm; closed weekdays May 25–June 16 & Sept 7–Oct 14; $10; Ⓣ603/745-8913, Ⓦwww.clarkstradingpost.com) is a much-touted, family-friendly collection of tourist attractions, including a haunted house, an 1890s fire station, bumper boats, a functional wood-burning steam locomotive, and a thirty-minute black bear show, in which a group of bears do tricks for their longtime trainer – just the ticket if you're in the mood for some hokey tourist fodder, or have kids in tow.

Eating, drinking, and entertainment

There's ample selection in both Lincoln and North Woodstock for food and drink; the **Papermill Theatre Company** in the Mill at Loon Mountain on Main Street, Lincoln (Ⓣ603/745-2141), presents "Broadway blockbusters" and children's plays during the summer.

Chieng Gardens Main Street, Lincoln Ⓣ603/745-8612. Featuring a typically enormous menu of traditional Chinese dishes for around $10.

Clement Room Grille in the *Woodstock Inn*, Rte-3, Main Street, North Woodstock Ⓣ603/745-3951. Here you can feast on duck, veal, seafood, or steak; definitely North Woodstock's most elegant dining experience.

GH Pizza Main Street, Lincoln Ⓣ603/745-6885. *GH* has the best pizza in town – though the dining room's not particularly pleasant.

Gordi's Main Street, Lincoln Ⓣ603/745-6635. Catering to the jovial after-ski crowd, *Gordi's* is more upscale than other Lincoln restaurants, specializing in seafood and straightforward meat dishes.

Govoni's Lost River Road, North Woodstock Ⓣ603/745-8042. The best place to eat in North Woodstock, the atmospheric, homely *Govoni's* serves delicious Italian specialties such as veal parmigiana and baked penne casserole in an inviting old building perched above the river. The most expensive entrées are just under $20. Summer only, Wed–Sat 4.30–9pm.

Kimber Lee's Deli in the Lincoln Depot, east edge of town Ⓣ603/745-3354. Good sandwiches and deli salads.

Olde Timbermill Restaurant and Pub in the Millfront Market Place on Main Street, Lincoln Ⓣ603/745-3603. Has one of the largest draft beer selections in the area; live music, too.

Truant's Taverne 98 Main St, North Woodstock Ⓣ603/745-2239. A cozy, affordable restaurant serving well-cooked standard American grill fare.

Woodstock Station in the *Woodstock Inn*, Rte-3, Main Street, North Woodstock. Just down the hall from the *Clement Room Grille*, here you can get a great range of hearty food including pizza, burgers, pasta, steak, seafood, and burritos. Good place to go for drinks, too – the beer is brewed on the premises, and there's live entertainment nearly every night.

The Kancamagus Highway

Affording plenty of panoramic glimpses of the tree-coated peaks and valleys that fade into a sunny horizon to the south, the **KANCAMAGUS HIGHWAY**, running 34 miles between Lincoln and Conway, is one of only two National Scenic Byways in northern New England (see box, below). You can easily pass a pleasant afternoon driving the length of the road and parking briefly at a couple of the designated lookouts, but you'll gain a better appreciation for the area if you get out of the car and take a hike or have a swim in the Swift River, which runs parallel to the highway for twenty miles. Better still, plan to camp at one of the many well-maintained campgrounds along the road (see overleaf).

The road is named for **Chief Kancamagus** ("Fearless One"), whose grandfather united seventeen Indian tribes into the Panacook Confederacy in 1627. Though Chief Kancamagus struggled to maintain peace between the Indians and pioneering whites, bloodshed eventually forced the tribes to scatter to the north. The region was finally re-settled in the late eighteenth century, though the **Russell Colbath House**, roughly thirteen miles west of Conway – built in 1800 and now a historic site, with a small display of antique furniture and old cooking gear – is the only remaining evidence. There are convenient car pullouts all along the road, and many have picnic tables, though no motorist services are available; don't forget to pick up your supplies and gas in Lincoln or Conway.

Hiking along the Kancamagus

The **Saco Ranger Station**, 33 Kancamagus Hwy near Rte-16 in Conway (☎603/447-5448), is staffed with friendly rangers who can give advice on hiking and camping along the road. They sell trail maps, which you are well advised to pick up. You can also get information about hiking and camping at the **Pemigewasset Wilderness Center**, just past the *Hancock Campground* on the highway (☎603/536-1310). Among the particularly good **hikes** along the Kancamagus are the **Lincoln Woods Trail** (five miles east of I-93), an easy 2.8-mile walk to the Franconia Falls, which are good for swimming and sunbathing; the **Greeley Ponds Trail** (nine miles east of I-93), a five-mile jaunt to a dark aqua body of water; the **Mount Potash Hike** (thirteen miles west of the Saco Ranger Station), a more difficult four-mile trip to the summit of Mount Potash (2660 feet); and the **Sabbaday Falls Hike**

White Mountains Trail

The Kancamagus Highway, as well as being an official National Scenic Byway in its own right, also forms part of the only other National Scenic Byway in northern New England, which also happens to be in the heart of the White Mountains. The **White Mountains Trail** is a hundred-mile loop which starts and finishes at the White Mountains Visitor Center in Lincoln (see p.498). From the visitor center, go north along I-93/US-3 through the Franconia Notch State Park (see p.503). Turn east along US-3 when it diverges from I-93, and continue in the same direction along US-302 as it passes Bretton Woods (see p.506) before veering south through the Crawford Notch State Park (see p.508). Passing the town of Bartlett, US-302 joins Rte-16 and the White Mountains Trail heads south past North Conway (see p.509). At Conway, the eastern terminus of the Kancamagus Highway, turn west and follow Rte-12 back to the visitor center.

(fifteen miles west of the Saco Station), a half-mile walk to the waterfalls, which, although stunning, are not suitable for swimming.

Camping along the Kancamagus

The **campgrounds** along the well-traveled Kancamagus Highway are usually populated with vacationing families, and most crowded in July and August. They will often be rather primitive affairs (many have vault toilets, for instance), and reservations are not normally accepted; sites are allocated on a first-come-first-served basis. Working from Lincoln to Conway, the first campground along the highway is *Big Rock*, six miles east of Lincoln (mid-May to mid-Oct; ⓣ603/536-1310; $14), which has 28 secluded wooded sites. Fifteen miles west of Conway, the *Passaconway Campground* (mid-May to mid-Oct; ⓣ603/447-5448; $14), is more primitive than the *Jigger Johnson Campground*, twelve-and-a-half miles west of Conway (late May to mid-Oct; ⓣ603/447-5448; $16), which is situated near the Russell Colbath House, and has hot showers and flush toilets. Also twelve-and-a-half miles west of Conway, the *Hancock Campground* (all year; ⓣ603/536-1310; $14) has 56 campsites and a swimming hole. You might also camp at the *Blackberry Crossing Campground* (all year; ⓣ603/447-5448; $14) or the *Covered Bridge Campground* (mid-May to mid-Oct; ⓣ603/447-5448; $12), both six miles west of Conway. Note that reservations are accepted at the *Covered Bridge*.

Franconia and around

North on I-93, past Lincoln and North Woodstock, the White Mountains continue to rise dramatically above either side of the freeway, boldly announcing their presence with enormous tree-covered peaks. **Franconia Notch State Park** is the highlight of the area, with miles of hiking trails and several natural wonders, including the well-known **Old Man of the Mountain**. Past the White Mountains, further north along I-93, the landscape flattens into an inviting valley dotted with former resort towns turned quiet mountainside retreats, such as pleasant **Franconia**, secluded **Sugar Hill**, sleepy **Bethlehem**, and the largest town in the area, **Littleton**.

Franconia

FRANCONIA, a friendly village along I-93 in the rolling grassy hills just north of Franconia Notch State Park and the White Mountains, began attracting summer vacationers, such as the literary notables Nathaniel Hawthorne and Henry Wadsworth Longfellow, soon after railroad tracks made the town accessible in the mid-nineteenth century; today, skiers and leaf-peepers come in droves to check out the area's fall foliage and snow-covered slopes. The town is best known as the one-time home of poet **Robert Frost**. After owning a small farm in Derry (see p.463), and living for a stint in England, Frost settled here in 1915 at the age of forty. You can visit his old home, now known as the **Frost Place**, Ridge Road off of Bickford Hill Road one mile south on Rte-116 (July to mid-Oct Wed–Mon 1–5pm; June weekends only; $3), where he lived with his wife and children for five years and wrote many of his best-known poems, including *The Road Not Taken*. Memorable largely for the inspiring panorama of mountains in its backdrop, the poet's former home is now a Center for Poetry and the Arts, with a poet-in-residence, readings, workshops, and a small display of Frost memorabilia, such as signed first editions and photographs. There's a short **nature trail** complete with placards displaying Frost's poetry and signs that supposedly mark the exact spot certain poems were composed. A longer and more rewarding hike begins 3.4 miles south of Franconia on Coppermine Road off of Rte-116, following the **Coppermine Trail** to the beautifully cascading **Bridalveil Falls**. The wooden Coppermine Shelter, near the end of the 2.5-mile excursion, is a good spot to camp, although there are no facilities. For advice on **bike routes** in the area and to rent bikes ($19 per day), stop in at the Franconia Sport Shop, Main Street, Franconia (Ⓣ603/823-5241).

Accommodation

Bungay Jar 15 Easton Valley Rd, Franconia Ⓣ603/823-7775 or 1-800/421-0701, Ⓦwww.bungayjar.com. Good mountain views, and a popular place with skiers in winter. ❻

Foxglove, A Country Inn Rte-117, Sugar Hill Ⓣ603/823-8840 or 1-888/343-2200, Ⓦwww.foxgloveinn.com. This secluded inn is ideal for romantic getaways, with private porches, fountains, and fireplaces. ❺

Fransted Campground Rte-18, Franconia Ⓣ603/823-5675, Ⓦwww.fransteadcampground.com. This family-oriented campground is a developed site with private streamside tent sites. Open mid-May to mid-Oct; $20/site.

Franconia Inn Easton Valley Road/Rte-116 Ⓣ603/823-5542 or 1-800/473-5299, Ⓦwww.franconiainn.com. 31-bed inn two miles south of Franconia, with great views, a relaxing porch, and an excellent restaurant; it's a good cross-country ski base, too. ❻

Gale River Motel 1 Main St, Franconia Ⓣ603/823-5655 or 1-800/255-7989, Ⓦwww.galerivermotel.com. Slightly cheaper lodgings than the rest nearby at the *Gale*, a sweet little ten-room motel, with heated outdoor pool, hot tub, and two cottages sleeping four to six people. ❹

Hilltop Inn Main Street/Rte-117, Sugar Hill Ⓣ603/823-5695 or 1-800/770-5695, Ⓦwww.hilltopinn.com. A country inn with a quiet atmosphere. ❺

Lovett's Inn Rte-18, Sugar Hill Ⓣ603/823-7761 or 1-800/356-3802, Ⓦwww.lovettsinn.com. *Lovett's*, peacefully set at the foot of Cannon Mountain (see overleaf), is a 1794 Cape Cod-style home complete with swimming pool, a comfortable common area, cozy rooms, an excellent restaurant, and charming staff. ❻

Eating

The Franconia region is not known for fine **dining**, although many of the inns and B&Bs in the area serve excellent (if expensive) food in dining rooms that welcome non-guests.

Franconia Inn Easton Valley Road/Rte-116 Ⓣ603/823-5542. The inn Offers elegant first-class service in its candlelit dining room, and features well-prepared steak and seafood dishes. See also accommodation review above.

Grateful Bread Main Street, Franconia Ⓣ603/823-5228. Purveyors of nutritious home-made organic breads, muffins, and croissants.

Lovett's Inn Rte-18, Sugar Hill Ⓣ603/823-7761. Some of the best gourmet food in the area, including well-prepared classics such as grilled salmon and stuffed chicken breast. Entrées go for $16–22, and reservations are required. See also accommodation review above.

Polly's Pancake Parlor I-93 exit 38, Rte-117, Sugar Hill Ⓣ603/823-5575. *Polly's* might be in the middle of nowhere, but it's well worth the trip if you love pancakes. The original menu – around since the opening 65 years ago – has since been supplemented by healthier options.

Franconia Notch State Park

I-93, speeding up towards Canada, and the more leisurely US-3 merge briefly as they pass through **Franconia Notch State Park** (Ⓣ603/823-8800). Though it's dwarfed by the surrounding national forest, and split in two by the noisy interstate, the park, which features excellent hiking and camping, has several sights that are well worth a visit, including the somewhat overblown Old Man of the Mountain – for which the area is famous.

From the **Flume Gorge Visitor Center**, I-93 exit 33 (daily: May to late Oct 9am–5pm; ⓣ603/745-8391), where there is a helpful information desk, a cafeteria, and a gift shop, you can walk or ride the shuttle bus to the short trail that leads through the narrow riverbed gorge, otherwise known as the **Flume** (entry $8). Formed nearly 200 million years ago, but discovered in 1808 by 93-year-old "Aunt" Jess Guernsey, the 800-foot gorge has been fitted with a wooden walkway that weaves back and forth across cascading falls and between towering sheer granite walls. With the sound of rumbling water echoing through the damp and misty crevice, it's more impressive than you might expect, though during high season the tourist crush can be overwhelming. From the visitor center parking lot, the 1.4-mile **Mount Pemigewasset Trail** leads up a moderate incline to the 2557-foot summit of Mount Pemigewasset, affording views of the Franconia Range.

The Old Man of the Mountain and Cannon Mountain

A mile or so north, you can admire the **Basin**, a curious 25,000-year-old 20-foot-wide granite pothole that catches the surging waters of a cascading waterfall. From the Basin, a marked trail links with the **Cascade Brook Trail**, traversing three miles to **Lonesome Pond**. Back on I-93, follow the signs to a roadside pullout, from where you can look upwards at the diminutive **Old Man of the Mountain**. This natural rock formation, resembling an old man's profile, will no doubt already be familiar from scores of powerfully magnified photographs – and New Hampshire's license plates. Much less impressive from a thousand feet below, it nevertheless inspired Daniel Webster to pen the following lines:

> **Men hang out their signs indicative of their respective trades.**
> **Shoemakers hang out a gigantic shoe;**
> **Jewelers, a monster watch;**
> **Even the dentist hangs out a gold tooth;**
> **But in the Franconia Mountains, God Almighty has**
> **Hung out a sign to show that in New England He makes men.**

These days, it all has to be held together with wires, and one particular family has the annual responsibility of climbing up to plug the cracks made by the winter's ice.

Just north of the lookout, state-owned **Cannon Mountain** offers rides to the top of its 4180-foot peak in an aerial tramway (daily: mid-May to mid-Oct 9am–5pm; $10 round-trip, $8 one-way; ⓣ603/823-8800), displaying panoramic views of the surrounding mountains that are especially impressive – and popular – during the early fall foliage season. During the winter, Cannon Mountain (ⓣ603/823-5563, ⓦwww.cannonmt.com; adult full-day lift ticket $34) offers some of the more challenging **alpine skiing** terrain in the state. You can browse through a collection of old ski equipment and photos or watch a vintage ski flick at the **New England Ski Museum**, next to the tramway (late May to mid-Oct & Dec–March noon–5pm; free; ⓣ603/823-7177). If you'd rather hike to the top of the mountain, take the slightly difficult, roughly two-mile **Kinsman Ridge Trail** from the southwest corner of the tramway parking lot. An equally rewarding, but shorter and less strenuous half-mile hike leads to **Artists Bluff** overlooking Echo Lake; the trail begins in the parking area on the north side of Rte-18, across from the Peabody Base Lodge. At **Echo Lake**, overlooked by Artist's Bluff, you can swim, rent a canoe ($10 per hr), or just enjoy the short stretch of sand (daily: mid-June to mid-Oct 10am–5.30pm; $3).

Practicalities

As well as the Flume Gorge Visitor Center (see opposite), advice about the outdoor activities available in the park is given at the **Franconia Notch State Park Visitor Center** (ⓣ603/271-3628) located at the *Lafayette Place Campground* off of I-93 (mid-May to mid-Oct; ⓣ603/823-9513; $16), which, despite being a bit close to the interstate, is a good place to **camp**. The quieter sites are to be had along the western edge of the grounds where car noise is minimal.

Bethlehem and Littleton

Northeast of Franconia along US-302, **BETHLEHEM**, an attractive community composed mostly of old resorts and counting among its regular summer visitors a large sect of Hasidic Jews, boasts one of the more remarkable sights in the area at the **Crossroads of America**, corner of US-302 and Trudeau Road (June to mid-Oct Tues–Sun 9am–5pm; $3.50; ⓣ603/869-3919), where an obsessively detailed model railroad set – one of the largest in the world – is on display. Lights are controlled to reflect the passage of day and night, and the display is punctuated by some amusing attention to detail, such as a wandering cow scared off the tracks by an oncoming train.

A few miles northwest along US-302, **LITTLETON**, straddling the Ammonoosuc River, has a compact Main Street that's lined with attractive old brick buildings and the largest population in the area at 6000. Though there's really not much to see, the town is a good place to find reasonably priced accommodations. Main Street, with a number of good shops, such as the Village Book Store, 81 Main St (ⓣ603/444-5263 or 1-800/640-9673), is good for an hour or so of browsing.

Information and accommodation

The **Bethlehem Visitors Center** is at 2182 Main St (Thurs–Sat noon–5pm in summer & fall, 10am–2pm in winter & spring; ⓣ1-888/845-1957, ⓦwww.bethlehemwhitemtns.com), while the **Littleton Area Chamber of Commerce** (June–Oct; ⓣ603/444-6561 or 1-888/822-2687 for room reservations, ⓦwww.littletonareachamber.com) has an information booth downtown across from *Thayer's Inn*, and is a good bet for information on lodging and area activities. The **Ammonoosuc Ranger Station**, Trudeau Road, Bethlehem (ⓣ603/869-2626), is particularly good for backcountry wilderness help.

As a general rule, Bethlehem is the place to go for superior **accommodations**, while Littleton has a number of reasonably priced places to stay.

Adair Country Inn 80 Guider Lane, Bethlehem ⓣ603/444-4823 or 1-888/444-2600, ⓦwww.adairinn.com. Offers deluxe antique-furnished rooms, sweeping views of the landscaped grounds, and an impeccable staff – all of which are reflected in the steep prices. ❼

Beal House Inn 2 W Main St, Littleton ⓣ603/444-2661 or 1-888/616-2325, ⓦwww.bealhouseinn.com. A charming, friendly inn, housed in an 1833 farmhouse. ❻

Continental 93 Traveler's Inn I-93 exit 42, Littleton ⓣ603/444-5366, ⓦwww.continental93.com. Fairly standard rooms at cheap rates, some with kitchenettes. There's an indoor pool and sauna, too. ❸

Eastgate Motor Inn US-302, I-93 exit 41, Littleton ⓣ603/444-3971, ⓦwww.eastgatemotorinn.com. Ordinary motel rooms, but at cheaper rates than other accommodations around here. ❸

Mulburn Inn 2370 Main St, Bethlehem ⓣ603/869-3389 or 1-800/457-9440, ⓦwww.mulburninn.com. A good choice near the center of Bethlehem, the *Mulburn* has spacious rooms and a relaxing atmosphere. ❹

Thayer's Inn 111 Main St, Littleton ⓣ603/444-6469 or 1-800/634-8179, ⓦwww.thayersinn.com. Somewhat creaky, but comfortable and even classy old inn right in the center of Littleton, *Thayer's* has hosted such notables as Ulysses S. Grant and Richard Nixon. ❸

Wayside Inn US-302 at Pierce Bridge, Bethlehem ⓣ603/869-3364 or 1-800/448-9557, ⓦwww.thewaysideinn.com. This 170-year-old inn – originally a homestead for Franklin Pierce's nephew – has fourteen recently renovated rooms; there's also a twelve-room motel overlooking the Ammonoosuc River. ❺

Eating and drinking

Flying Moose Café 2 W Main St, Littleton ⓣ603/444-2661. This outstanding restaurant is an intimate bistro serving a mix of classic cuisines with contemporary flair, such as braised lamb shank over polenta. There's also a less-expensive tavern menu featuring well-prepared steak and seafood dishes.

Littleton Diner 145 Main St, Littleton ⓣ603/444-3994. Large, greasy portions of typical diner food, plus extra-thick shakes are served up at the counter here, or in one of seven booths.

Lloyd Hills 2061 Main St, Bethlehem ⓣ603/869-2141. A comfortable, popular spot to have a sandwich or nurse a beer, with a huge five-page menu that includes burgers, pasta, and steak.

Rosa Flamingoes Main Street, Bethlehem ⓣ603/869-3111. Basic Italian dishes served here – also doubles as one of the area's more popular and lively places to drink.

Bretton Woods and around

The ease with which US-302 now crosses the middle of the mountains belies the effort that went into cutting a road through **Crawford Notch**, a twisty and beautiful pass halfway between the Franconia area and Conway. Just north, the magnificent **Mount Washington Hotel** stands in splendid isolation in the wide mountain valley of **Bretton Woods**. West of Bretton Woods lies **Twin Mountain**, a good place for cheap accommodation, while a few miles east the **Mount Washington Cog Railway** is probably the most romantic way of getting to the summit of Mount Washington.

The Mount Washington Hotel

In **BRETTON WOODS**, at the grand opening of the **Mount Washington Hotel** (ⓣ603/278-1000 or 1-800/258-0330, ⓦwww.mtwashington.com; ❽) in the summer of 1902, developer Joseph Stickney reputedly exclaimed, "Look at me gentlemen . . . for I am the poor fool who built all this!" Its glistening white facade, capped by red cupolas and framed by the western slopes of Mount Washington rising behind it, has barely changed since then. In its heyday, a stream of horse-drawn carriages brought families (and servants) up from the train station, deliberately located at a distance to increase the sense of grandeur. Displays in the lobby commemorate the **Bretton Woods Conference** of 1944, which laid the groundwork for the postwar financial structure of the capitalist world, by setting the gold standard at $35 an ounce (it's now about $310), and creating the International Monetary Fund and the World Bank.

Restoration by a group of investors who purchased the decaying building and surrounding property in 1991 for a mere $3.1 million has insured that the cruise ship-sized hotel remains marvelously – if somewhat eerily – evocative of past splendor, with its quarter-mile terrace, white wicker furniture, cool verandahs, and 24-carat views. The hotel is not the one featured in the movie *The Shining*, but it's said to have inspired the story and is worth checking out even if you're not staying. None other than Babe Ruth reputedly got sauced in the former speakeasy downstairs – fittingly known as the "Cave" because of its faux-rocky walls – before sauntering to the indoor pool down the hall and taking a fully clothed dip; these days, the bar hosts more mellow live entertainment nightly, though the rock walls are still there. Weekend golfing and tennis packages are available, and in the 1990s the resort opened its doors to the winter ski crowd. On the property, the 33-room *Bretton Arms Country Inn* (Ⓣ603/278-1000; ❻), has more affordable rooms, while the *Lodge at Bretton Woods*, across US-302 from the *Mount Washington* (same phone; ❹), has modern rooms even cheaper.

Mount Washington Cog Railway

It took a hundred men three years to build the **Mount Washington Cog Railway**, off of Mount Clinton Road at the base of Mount Washington. Completed in 1869, its rickety trains lumber up gradients as steep as 38 per cent – the second steepest railway in the world – while consuming a ton of coal and a thousand gallons of water and spewing out thick gray clouds of heavy smoke. It's a truly momentous experience, inching up the steep wooden trestles while avoiding descending showers of coal smut – although anyone who's not a bona fide antique train aficionado might find it not really worth the money. The three-hour round-trip (with twenty minutes at the summit) costs $49, and trains leave hourly (late May to late Oct; call for other dates and times; Ⓣ603/278-5404 or 1-800/922-8825).

If you'd rather **hike** up Mount Washington, the **Ammonoosuc Ravine Trail** starts in the Cog parking lot, hooking up with the Crawford Path at the AMC's *Lakes of the Clouds* hut (see p.512). If you're in good physical shape (this hike is not for the faint of heart), the four-mile trip takes roughly four and a half hours one-way. Take warm clothing (temperatures above the tree line can be fifty degrees colder than at the base), plenty of water and food, and do not hesitate to turn back if the weather turns foul; several hikers die of exposure to the harsh weather atop the mountain every year. Another option, the **Jewell Trail**, also originating in the parking lot, zigzags up the north shoulder to the summit in 4.6 miles (roughly four hours).

Twin Mountain

Five miles west of Bretton Woods, **TWIN MOUNTAIN**, a blue-collar town that spreads out around the intersection of US-302 and US-3, is mostly notable for its grouping of cheap, no-frills **motels**. If you're not bothered by run-down surroundings and are cash-conscious, this is a good place from which to explore the area. In July, the town hosts a **Native American Cultural Weekend** (Ⓣ603/869-3326 for schedule and additional information, including precise dates), a lively celebration of song and dance. The Abenaki claim they are native to New Hampshire, though they have never been recognized by the state or federal government, which are content to perpetuate the idea that the tribe immigrated from Canada in post-Colonial times. The best bets for **places to stay** include the *Four Seasons Motor Inn*, US-3 (Ⓣ603/846-5708 or 1-800/228-5708, Ⓦwww.4seasonsmotorinn.com; ❸), the *Northern Zermatt Inn*, US-3 (Ⓣ603/846-5533 or 1-800/535-3214, Ⓦwww.zermattinn.com; ❸), and *Carlson's Lodge*, US-302 (Ⓣ603/846-5501 or 1-800/348-5502,

Ⓦwww.carlsonslodge.com; ④). Alternatively, you can **camp** at the *Sugarloaf II Campground*, three miles east of US-302 on Zealand Road (mid-May to mid-Dec; ⓣ603/869-2626; $14), which is maintained by the US Forest Service.

Crawford Notch State Park

Crawford Notch State Park is split in two by US-302, which winds through the dramatic gap formed by the steep slopes of Mount Field to the west and Mount Jackson to the east. Discovered in 1771 by hunter Timothy Nash, who was tracking a moose through the woods, the notch was soon recognized as a viable route through the White Mountains to points further north. A railroad was completed at great expense in 1857, and the old **Crawford Notch Depot** along US-302 south of Bretton Woods across from tiny Saco Lake is now a helpful AMC-maintained **information center** and retail store selling back-country necessities (May–Oct Mon–Sat 9am–5pm; ⓣ603/466-2727). Recommended **hikes** in the area include the **Mount Willard Trail**, a 1.4-mile (one hour) jaunt up to amazing views of Crawford Notch starting at the Crawford Notch Depot, and the **Zealand Trail**, which begins at the end of Zealand Road and ends, 2.7 miles and ninety minutes later, at the Zealand Pond, Zealand Falls, and the AMC *Zealand Falls* hut (see p.512). In the shadow of Mount Crawford, the **Willey House**, named for a family who lived on the site and died in a terrible landslide in 1826, now serves as the **park headquarters** (ⓣ603/374-2272), selling maps and trail guides and offering advice on camping; they also maintain a small café. Behind the headquarters, the **Ethan Pond Trail** leads to the *Ethan Pond* shelter, a somewhat remote **camping** spot with no facilities. Half a mile south, the **Arethusa Falls Trail** is a short but steep walk to the highest falls in the state. Just across US-302, the *Dry River Campground* (May to mid-Dec; ⓣ603/374-2272; $14) has 31 wooded sites, thirty of which are by reservation only. Also note that there is no water after mid-October. Operations at the AMC's *Crawford Notch Hostel*, US-302 just north of the park, have been suspended as construction proceeds on the *Highland Center at Crawford Notch* (call ⓣ603/466-2721 ext 195 for more information), an environmental education center which plans to also offer accommodation in dorms and private rooms when it opens in September 2003.

The Mount Washington Valley

There are no clear boundaries to the **Mount Washington Valley**, though it is generally thought to center around the crowded town of **North Conway**, a once-beautiful mountainside hamlet now overwhelmed by outlet malls and other modern encroachments. In general, the region is more congested than the western White Mountains, but if you can avoid the crowds that cram their cars onto the mile-long strip of Rte-16/US-302 south of downtown North Conway, you'll find there's plenty to do around here. In the winter, there are numerous trails for **cross-country skiers**, while in the summer **rock climbers** test their skills on the highly popular **Cathedral Ledge**. North of North Conway, the pace slows and opportunities for solitary hiking and camping are more accessible. The low-key town of **Glen** is home to **Story Land,** a children's fantasy park, while peaceful **Jackson** has excellent cross-country skiing trails and an unusual concentration of first-class lodging and eating, presenting a good opportunity to spoil yourself amid the quiet splendor of the greenery.

The hiker shuttle service

The AMC runs a hiker **shuttle service** daily from June through mid-October with vans which make stops at many of the trailheads and AMC lodges throughout the Mount Washington Valley region (call ⓣ603/466-2727 for information and reservations), including the Crawford Notch Depot (see opposite) and the Pinkham Notch Visitor Center (see p.513). Drivers will stop anywhere along the route if requested, and the trips cost $10, no matter how long you ride.

North Conway

Whichever way you approach **NORTH CONWAY**, you're in for a depressing time. From the north, the joining of Rte-16 and US-302 eventually becomes a veritable turmoil of shopping malls and theme parks, while from the south, the strip between Conway and North Conway is an orgy of factory outlets, fast-food places, and the over-eager shoppers who have sought them out. Fortunately, there is some relief in the town itself, a touristed village that manages to maintain a hint of rustic backcountry appeal. The centerpiece of downtown is the **North Conway Railroad Station**, a hulking brown and yellow 1874 Victorian structure that you won't miss along Main Street. From here, the **Conway Scenic Railroad** (mid-April to late Dec, call for reservations and schedule; ⓣ603/356-5251 or 1-800/232-5251, ⓦwww.conwayscenic.com) runs antique steam trains to Bartlett ($17 round-trip, 105min), Conway ($10 round-trip, 55min), the Crawford Notch Depot ($35 round-trip, 5hr), and the Fabyan Station in Bretton Woods ($39 round-trip, 5.5hr). The trains are especially worth the money in early fall, when the trees are at their brightest – reservations are a must.

West of town along River Road, you can go for a swim at refreshing **Echo Lake** (not to be confused with the Echo Lake in Franconia Notch State Park) beneath the towering granite face of the White Horse Ledge. Just north off of West Side Road, scores of rock climbers test their skills on the wall of the steep, sheer faces of towering **Cathedral Ledge**, the most popular spot for the sport in the state. Chauvin Guides in North Conway (ⓣ603/356-8919, ⓦwww.chauvinguides.com) offer various **guided climbs** and lessons starting at $105. You might also check with Eastern Mountain Sports in North Conway for guidance (ⓣ603/356-5433). If you'd rather not spend agonizing hours (and lots of money) tethered to the cliff's sheer face, you can simply drive to the top, where you're presented with views of the entire area. You can also hike to the ledge, along the **Bryce Path**, a steep trail that originates at the base of the auto road and takes about an hour each way. North of the entry to **Cathedral Ledge State Park** on North River Road, you can hike to **Diana's Bath**, an easy half-mile walk to a cool running mountain stream along the Moat Mountain Trail. For a longer trek, head to the top of **Mount Kearsarge** from the north side of Hurricane Mountain Road, one and a half miles west of Rte-16; it's a three-hour trip that is rewarded with panoramic vistas.

Just outside of Conway lies **Mount Chocoura**. Although only 3475 feet high, the little curved granite notch on the top, looking like a perched cap, makes it one of the most distinctive mountains visible from this area. It's an easy climb, and it should take about two hours to reach the summit if you're in good shape via the Champney Falls Trail (parking lot ten miles west of Rte-16 on the Kancamagus Highway). The top – that notch you can see – is particularly beautiful, as you emerge from the forest to a stretch of pure rock. The views, including the "Presidential Range," are, of course, stunning.

Practicalities

The **Mount Washington Valley Chamber of Commerce** in North Conway (Ⓣ603/356-3171 or 1-800/367-3364, Ⓦwww.mtwashingtonvalley.com) has a reservation service and information on local attractions, while the **Conway Village Chamber of Commerce**, south of town along Rte-16 (Ⓣ603/447-2639, Ⓦwww.conwaychamber.com), will also help with places to stay and has hiking maps.

There is an HI/AYH **hostel** in Conway called the *Albert B. Lester Memorial Hostel*, 36 Washington St (closed Nov during midweek; Ⓣ603/447-1001 or 1-800/886-4284), which has particularly clean dorm lodging for $19 per night and private rooms for around $35. **Camping** in the area is available at the *Saco River Camping Area*, in North Conway off of Rte-16 (early May to mid-Oct; Ⓣ603/356-3360; $20), whose wooded and open sites are nicely located along the Saco River, well enough away from the highway, and the US Forest Service's *White Ledge Campground*, Rte-16 five miles south of Conway in Albany (mid-May to mid-Oct; Ⓣ603/447-5448; $14). Otherwise, there are plenty of **places to stay** in North Conway. Though it's right on the busy main road, the spacious rooms, gracious hosts, delicious food, and mountain view at the *1785 Inn*, Rte-16 (Ⓣ603/356-9025 or 1-800/421-1785, Ⓦwww.the1785inn.com; ❹), make this a good base from which to explore the area (or to shop). Another good base, this time for rock climbers and other outdoors types, is the *Sunny Side Inn*, Seavey Street (Ⓣ603/356-6239 or 1-800/600-6239, Ⓦwww.sunnyside-inn.com; ❹), which occupies a quiet spot well off the main drag, and has nine homely rooms and five cottages. The *Nereledge Inn*, River Road (Ⓣ603/356-2831 or 1-888/356-2831, Ⓦwww.nereledgeinn.com; ❹), is a reasonably priced, friendly, and informal Colonial inn near skiing, the Saco River, and rock climbing, while the *School House Motel*, on Rte-16 near the shopping outlets (Ⓣ603/356-6829 or 1-800/638-6050, Ⓦwww.schoolhousemotel.com; ❷), is probably the cheapest option in town.

Probably the best **place to eat** in North Conway is the *1785 Inn*, Rte-16 (Ⓣ603/356-9025 or 1-800/421-1785), with its highly praised, expensive gourmet food, such as boned rabbit in a cream sherry sauce ($18), served in a dark, romantic dining room. You can get big portions of freshly prepared Italian dishes at *Bellini's*, 33 Seavey St (closed Mon & Tues; Ⓣ603/356-7000), all served in an attractively decorated dining room. If you're after something a little spicier, *Shalimar*, 27 Seavey St (Ⓣ603/356-0123), has a huge menu of reasonably priced authentic Indian dishes, with a good selection of vegetarian specialties. For **enterntainment**, *Horsefeather's*, Main Street (Rte-16) at Kearsarge (Ⓣ603/356-6862), has live music at weekends, in addition to what many consider to be the best burgers in town.

Jackson and Glen

With a high concentration of first-class lodgings and restaurants, a close-knit local population, and hundreds of miles of trails within easy reach, **JACKSON** is one of the premier **cross-country ski** centers in the country. Indeed, the **Jackson Ski Touring Foundation** (Ⓣ603/383-9355, Ⓦwww.jacksonxc.org), with 154km of trails over 60 square miles, has frequently been rated the number one cross-country ski area in the East by various big-name industry magazines. The trails run over rolling countryside, woodland terrain, mountain descents, and race course areas, and are all perfectly maintained. In order to use them, you have to be a member of the Ski Touring Foundation. Day memberships cost $14, and you can rent equipment for $16 a day. On hot summer days, a great place to cool off is at **Jackson Falls**, which tumble down a stretch of boulders and rocks in the riverbed along Rte-16B.

If you're traveling with children, don't miss New Hampshire landmark **Story Land**, on Rte-16 in **GLEN** (daily: mid-June to early Sept 9am–6pm; late May to mid June & early Sept to mid-Oct weekends only 10am–5pm; $19), a colorful children's theme park, akin to a miniature Disneyland, with immaculately maintained grounds, rides such as the "Turtle Twirl" and "Bamboo Chutes," and lots of places for climbing and exploring – including the "Oceans of Fun Sprayground" and "Professor Bigglestep's Loopy Labs." Next door, **Heritage New Hampshire** (daily: May to mid-Oct 9am–6pm; $10; ⓣ603/383-9776) takes a somewhat hokey and outdated Anglocentric look at New Hampshire history through interactive exhibits and badly animated mannequins. You start with a simulated ride aboard a creaky ship bound for the New World and end with a rickety "train ride" through the White Mountains.

The Red Jersey Cyclery on US-302 in Glen (ⓣ603/374-2700) is the place to go for **mountain-bike** trail advice, with a knowledgeable staff and lots of **rental** bikes. Next door, Northern Extremes (ⓣ603/383-8117 or 1-877/722-6748) rents **canoes** and **kayaks** and offers organized kayaking trips to the Saco River and Conway Lake, both south of Glen around the town of Conway. For any general or specific information, contact the **Jackson Area Chamber of Commerce** (ⓣ603/383-9356 or 1-800/866-3334, ⓦwww.jacksonnh.com).

Accommodation

Bernerhof Inn US-302, Glen ⓣ603/383-9132 or 1-800/548-8007, ⓦwww.bernerhofinn.com. Nine comfortable and elegant guestrooms, with conscientious service. There's also a pub and a gourmet restaurant on the first floor. ⑤

Christmas Farm Inn Rte-16B, Jackson ⓣ603/383-4313 or 1-800/443-5837, ⓦwww.christmasfarminn.com. Another of the town's classier and more expensive digs; rates include dinner and breakfast. ⑧

Covered Bridge House US-302, Glen ⓣ603/383-9109 or 1-800/232-9109, ⓦwww.coveredbridgehouse.com. The homely *Covered Bridge House* is a good, moderately priced option. ④

Covered Bridge Motor Lodge Rte-16, Jackson ⓣ603/383-9151 or 1-800/634-2911, ⓦwww.jacksoncoveredbridge.com. Fairly standard resort motel with clean rooms, a pool, tennis courts, and a games room. ④

Inn at Thorn Hill Thorn Hill Road, Jackson ⓣ603/383-4242 or 1-800/289-8990, ⓦwww.innatthornhill.com. A luxurious hillside inn designed by renowned architect Stanford White, complete with designer furnishings, whirlpool tubs, and private cottages in back. Though the main building was recently badly damaged by fire. Rates include a three-course dinner at the inn's gourmet restaurant. ⑧

Village House Rte-16A, Jackson ⓣ603/383-6666 or 1-800/972-8343. A pleasant B&B just beyond the covered bridge, with private baths and a great big porch. ④

Wildcat Inn & Tavern Rte-16A, Jackson ⓣ603/383-4245 or 1-800/228-4245, ⓦwww.wildcattavern.com. Cozy and unpretentious, the *Wildcat* is right in the center of town and has a comfortable ski-cabin feel. Especially popular in winter (as is the tavern), so call for reservations. ⑥, except between Oct 22 and Dec 20, when rooms are $79/night.

Will's Inn US-302, Glen ⓣ603/383-6757 or 1-800/233-6780, ⓦwww.willsinn.com. Family-friendly, cheap, and perfectly satisfactory. Plus, there's a heated pool. ③

Eating, drinking, and nightlife

As You Like It Jackson Falls Marketplace, Jackson ⓣ603/383-6425. Great homemade coffee cake, cookies, pies, brownies, and bread.

Inn at Thorn Hill Thorn Hill Road, Jackson ⓣ603/383-4242. A romantic spot good for special occasions, serving "New England fusion" dishes such as sake-marinated halibut with a jasmine rice cake and sisho broth, using seasonally grown organic produce, and featuring an extensive wine list.

Red Parka Pub US-302, Glen ⓣ603/383-4344. A favorite place in Glen for a few drinks, especially during ski season and at weekends, when there's live music; Mondays is open-mike night.

Shannon Door Rte-16, Jackson ⓣ603/383-4211. The town's longstanding Irish pub, with a suitably dark bar, plenty of Guinness, and live entertainment. Thurs–Sun.

Thompson House Eatery (T.H.E.) Rte-16 and Rte-16A, Jackson ⓣ603/383-9341. Well known for its homemade root beer and ice cream.

Wildcat Inn & Tavern Rte-16A, Jackson ⓣ603/383-4245. Gourmet country cuisine in the dining room and garden, while cheaper sandwiches and appetizers are served in the less-formal couch-filled tavern, which is often lively in winter with skiers in from a day on the slopes.

Yesterday's Rte-16A, Jackson ⓣ603/383-4457. Big, cheap American breakfasts are the order of the day here.

Pinkham Notch and Mount Washington

Roughly ten miles north of Jackson along Rte-16, **PINKHAM NOTCH**, along the eastern base of towering **MOUNT WASHINGTON**, is as beautiful a mountain pass as there is in the National Forest, with a reputation for serious outdoor activity. The Appalachian Trail and a number of other remote wilderness trails converge here, making the Notch overrun with adventurers

AMC mountain huts

The Appalachian Mountain Club (AMC) operates eight delightfully remote mountain huts in New Hampshire along a 56-mile stretch of the famed Appalachian Trail, each about a day's hike apart. Generally open from June through mid-October, these spots offer full-service lodging in season, and two hot meals per day, for $69 per night, making them a fairly popular choice – reservations are required (ⓣ603/466-2727). At some of the huts, self-service lodging is available (without sheets, heat, or food) for $21. For additional information, contact the Appalachian Mountain Club, 5 Joy St, Boston, MA 02108 (ⓣ617/523-0636, ⓦwww.outdoors.org).

Carter Notch (self-service all year). Accessible via the Nineteen Mile Brook Trail and the Wildcat Ridge Trail, both originating along Rte-16 north of Jackson.

Galehead (full service in season: June to mid-Oct). On the Garfield Range, this is the most remote hut in the chain. Accessible via the Gale River Trail and the Garfield Ridge Trail, both originating off of US-3 south of Bethlehem.

Greenleaf (full service in season: June to mid-Oct). Accessible via the Greenleaf Trail and the Old Bridle Path Trail, off of I-93 in Franconia Notch State Park (see p.503).

Lakes of the Clouds (full service in season: June to mid-Sept). On the southern shoulder of Mount Washington, this is the highest and most popular of the huts. Accessible via the Ammonoosuc Ravine Trail and Crawford Path, off of Mount Clinton Road, just south of Bretton Woods.

Lonesome Lake (full service in season: June to mid-Oct). Good family destination, with daily hikes and activities. Accessible via the Cascade Brook Trail, Dodge Cutoff Trail, Fishin' Jimmy Trail, Lonesome Lake Trail, and the Whitehouse Trail, west of I-93 in Franconia Notch State Park.

Madison Spring (full service in season: June to mid-Sept). Great sunsets from a perch above the Madison Gulf. Accessible via the Crawford Path, Gulfside Trail, Westside Trail, and the Valley Way Trail, southwest of Gorham off of US-2.

Mizpah Spring (full service in season: June to mid-Oct). On Mount Clinton above Crawford Notch. Accessible via the Mount Clinton Trail and the Webster Cliff Trail near Crawford Notch State Park along US-302.

Zealand Falls (full service in season: June to mid-Oct). Open all year, near waterfalls and good backcountry skiing. Accessible via the Zealand Trail, off of Zealand Road south of Twin Mountain.

during the summer. Luckily, the crowds don't detract too much, and they're easy to forget once you've made your way into the forest.

The best place to get information on hiking, camping, and a whole range of other outdoor activities is at the AMC's **Pinkham Notch Visitor Center**, Rte-16 (daily 6.30am–10pm; ⓣ603/466-2727), where you can buy the indispensable and exhaustive *AMC White Mountain Guide* ($21.95), good hiking maps, supplies, and basic camping/mountaineering equipment. The center organizes workshops, guided trips, and programs that cost anywhere from a couple of dollars to a couple hundred dollars. They serve three hearty family-style **meals** per day at long picnic tables in a huge, noisy dining room at the visitor center; the fixed-price dinner ($15) includes salad, soup, vegetables, homemade breads and dessert, an entrée, and plenty of conversation about the day's hike. As if that weren't enough, the club maintains the *Joe Dodge Lodge* (ⓣ603/466-2727), where you can rent a bunk ($35) or a private room ($70 double, $93 quad) and hang out with fellow hikers. The *Dolly Copp Campground* (ⓣ603/466-2713; $15) has 177 **campsites** and is open from mid-April through mid-October.

On the east side of Rte-16 across from the visitor center, local favorite **Wildcat Mountain** (ⓣ603/466-3326 or 1-800/255-6439, ⓦwww.skiwildcat.com) offers some of the best and most challenging **skiing** ($42 midweek, $52 weekends and holidays) in the state during the winter, as well as **mountain-biking** and **gondola rides** to the 4062-foot summit of Wildcat Mountain (daily: mid-June to mid-Oct 10am–5pm; late May to mid-June weekends only; $9).

Mount Washington

The 6288-foot **MOUNT WASHINGTON**, the highest peak in the northeastern US, was named for George Washington before he even became president. Over the years, other mountains in this "Presidential Range" have taken the names of Madison, Jefferson, and even Eisenhower – though it should be noted that Mount Nancy was called that long before the Reagans were in the White House, and Mount Deception just happens to be close by.

Driving and hiking to the summit

On a clear day, you can see all the way to the Atlantic and into Canada from the top of Mount Washington, once called the "second greatest show on earth" by P.T. Barnum, but the real interest in making the ascent lies in the extraordinary severity of the weather up here. The wind exceeds hurricane strength on over a hundred days of the year, and in 1934 it reached the highest speed ever recorded anywhere in the world – 231mph.

On the way to the top, you pass through four distinct climatic zones, with century-old fir and ash trees so stunted as to be below waist height, before emerging amid Arctic tundra. The drive up the **Mount Washington Auto Road**, ascending eight miles up the east side of the mountain from Rte-16 south of Gorham (early May to late Oct – weather permitting – 7.30am–6pm in peak season; call ⓣ603/466-2222 to check weather conditions), is not quite as hair-raising as you may expect, although the hairpin bends and lack of guard-rails certainly keep you alert. There's a $16 toll for private cars and driver (plus $6 for each additional adult and $4 for kids). Specially adapted minibuses, still known as "stages" in honor of the twelve-person horse-drawn carriages that first used the road, give narrated **tours** (daily 8.30am–5pm; $22, 90min round-trip; ⓣ603/466-3988, ⓦwww.mtwashingtonautoroad.com) as they carry groups of tourists up the mountain. Driving takes thirty or forty minutes under normal conditions. The record for the annual running race up the mountain, held each June, currently stands at an incredible 58 minutes 20 seconds.

Some fifteen **hiking trails** – in addition to the Appalachian Trail itself – lead to the summit of Mount Washington. Unequalled vistas, beautiful flora, and the satisfaction of reaching the top make this hike a particularly thrilling experience. The most direct route on the eastern side of the mountain is the **Tuckerman Ravine Trail**, which originates at the AMC Pinkham Notch Visitor Center (see p.513) and traverses the often snow-filled Tuckerman Ravine, a popular place for backcountry skiing. If you're in good condition, the 4.1-mile trail can be completed in about four and a half hours, and it is possible to hike up and back in one day, but don't forget that the weather at the top of the mountain is very unpredictable, and potentially very dangerous: even when it's seventy degrees and sunny at the base, the summit, some 4000 feet above, can be below freezing. The weather can change very quickly, and you should not hesitate to turn back should any signs of a storm become apparent; indeed, each year the conditions claim several lives – although the roll-call of the 124 victims to die on the mountain does include the duo that attempted to slide down on "improvised boards."

For hikes to the summit that originate on the west side of the mountain, see p.507. You can also ride to the top on the coal-fired steam train of the **Mount Washington Cog Railway**, originating in Bretton Woods – also detailed on p.507. Incidentally, unless otherwise posted, you can **camp** anywhere on Mount Washington below the tree line 200 feet from the trail and water sources, and a quarter-mile from any road or facility.

The summit

On the summit, you'll see the remarkable spectacle of buildings actually held down with great chains; many have been blown away over the years, including the old observatory, said to have been the strongest wooden building ever constructed. At the newer (and hopefully stronger) **weather observatory** (Ⓣ603/356-2137, Ⓦwww.mountwashington.org), scientists research the various effects of wind, ice, and fog; their various findings are displayed at a small museum downstairs (Fri–Tues 10am–5pm; $5). You can climb the few remaining feet to the actual summit point, sadly surrounded with cement structures – including a large viewing platform – and smothered by photo-snapping tourists. The **Tip Top House**, once a hotel for wealthy travelers, has been turned into an unremarkable historic museum (entry $2), providing "a link between the mountain's past and present" through antique furniture and a restored interior.

Gorham and beyond

Spread out along the northern reaches of the White Mountain National Forest, working-class **GORHAM** can be used as an inexpensive base from which to visit Mount Washington and other nearby peaks. Basic, affordable **accommodation** can be found at the *Hikers Paradise Hostel*, 370 Main St (Ⓣ603/466-2732 or 1-800/470-4224, Ⓦwww.hikersparadise.com), where you can get a bed, sheets, full kitchen, and full (shared) bath for $15. For **camping**, the *Moose Brook State Park*, Jimtown Road, off Rte-2 in Gorham (late May to mid-Oct;

First-in-the-nation presidential primary

The mountains of the "Presidential Range" might have made the state's name in tourist guides, but New Hampshire, and the tiny mountain village of **DIXVILLE NOTCH**, are really famous for a quite different presidential connection: the primary election. Since 1952, New Hampshire has been the first state in the US to hold its presidential primary, which more or less marks the start of the winnowing process to see who each party's presidential candidates will be, and Dixville Notch has had the privilege of being the first town in the state – and therefore the nation – to report its results. Every four years, the tiny electorate of Dixville Notch file into the ballroom at the *Balsams Hotel* just before midnight on election day, to cast votes at the stroke of midnight. Since 1968, Dixville Notch has never failed to successfully predict the Republican nominee, and the state as a whole has a good record for picking the candidates eventually nominated by both Democrats and Republicans to run for president (current leader George W. Bush notwithstanding). Due to the high media profile of the New Hampshire primary, as well as the state's compact size and relatively small electorate, campaigning is based very much on knocking on doors and actually meeting the people. The larger hotels in Manchester and Concord start to fill up with the entourages of the major candidates a year or so before the election; many of the fringe candidates, meanwhile, stay at churches, college dorms, or the homes of supporters. Indeed, the primary's popularity and easy access have encouraged a number of lesser-known candidates to participate. New Hampshire voters have been wooed by visionary candidates such as Russell Fomwalt, who recommended that the military occupy high schools to prevent violence; the "common sense candidate" Frank B. Legas, who ran a classified ad in the *Concord Monitor* describing himself as a "frugal presidential candidate"; the innovative Austin Burton (alias Chief Burning Wood), who once tried to pay his $1000 filing fee by mailing a snakeskin to the Secretary of State; and the environmentally-friendly Caroline Killeen, who argued that "America needs trees, not Bushes."

Ⓣ603/466-3860; $15 per site), has 62 secluded tent sites. Reasonably priced homemade Italian **food** can be had at *La Bottega Saladino* on Main Street (Ⓣ603/466-2520), while the *Golden Maple*, across the street at 245 Main St (closed Mon; Ⓣ603/466-2766), is good for cheap Cantonese and Polynesian specialties.

Up north on Rte-16, **DIXVILLE NOTCH** is a quiet hideaway centered on the sprawling turn-of-the-century *Balsams Grand Resort Hotel* (mid-Dec to late March & mid-May to mid-Oct; Ⓣ603/255-3400 or 1-800/255-0800 in NH or 1-800/255-0600 outside NH, Ⓦwww.thebalsams.com; ❾), another of the last grand White Mountains resort hotels. Built in the 1860s, the enormous red-roof-capped palace has 202 guestrooms, its own lake, 15,000 acres of land, a golf course, and a ski area. Rates include all meals and use of facilities. Dixville Notch is also the first town in New Hampshire to announce the results of its **primary elections** (see box, above).

Incidentally, if you've ventured this far north, don't miss the chance to **eat** a down-home meal at *Errol Restaurant*, at the intersection of Rte-16 and Rte-26 in **ERROL VILLAGE** (Ⓣ603/482-3852), where they serve cheap steaks, eggs, seafood, sandwiches, and "mooseburgers."

8

Maine

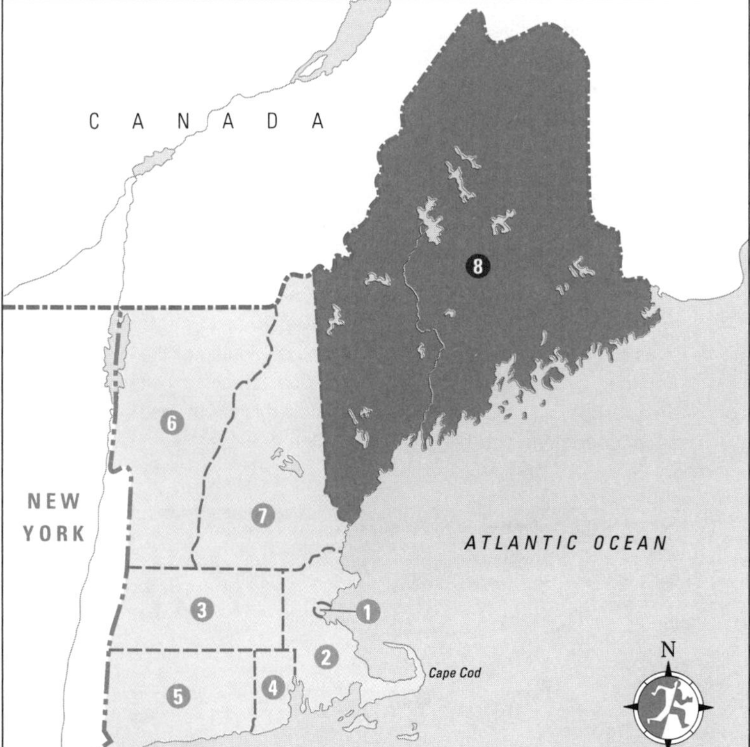

CHAPTER 8

Highlights

* **Southern coast beaches** Although the water can be chilly, Maine's popular southern beaches are uniformly picturesque. See p.523
* **Portland** As cosmopolitan as the state gets, coastal Portland has everything on offer, save big-city aggravation and high prices. See p.529
* **Camden** Among Maine's most beautiful, Camden's harbor is filled with windjammers and protected by verdant forest. See p.558
* **Castine** Nearly surrounded by the waters of Penobscot Bay, this tiny town of gardens and hilly streets is one of New England's most majestic. See p.566
* **Acadia National Park** Bike, boat, hike, climb, or simply commune with nature in the state's recreational mecca. See p.573
* **Bethel** Close to the White Mountains, remote Bethel is the quintessential New England small town and a hub for winter and summer outdoor adventures. See p.584
* **Mount Katahdin** In the deepest heart of Maine, the beginning of the Appalachian Trail sits atop this 5300ft peak. See p.594

8

Maine

As big as the other five New England states combined, **MAINE** has barely the population of Rhode Island. In principle, therefore, there's plenty of room for its massive summer influx of visitors; in practice, the majority of these make for the extravagantly corrugated **coast**. In the shoreline's southern reaches, the beach resort towns of **Ogunquit** and **Old Orchard Beach** quickly lead up to Maine's most cosmopolitan city, **Portland**. The **Mid-Coast**, between the quiet college town of Brunswick and blue-collar Bucksport, is characterized by a wildly irregular seashore, with plenty of dramatic, windswept peninsulas and sheltered inlets to explore, though in the well-touristed towns of **Boothbay Harbor** and **Camden**, you'll certainly have company on your wanderings. **Down East**, beyond the moneyed Blue Hill Peninsula, **Mount Desert Island** holds Maine's most popular outdoor escape, **Acadia National Park**, in addition to the bustling summer retreat of **Bar Harbor**. Farther still up the coastline, you'll find less cooperative weather and increasingly desolate scenery, capped by the candy-striped lighthouse at **Quoddy Head**, the easternmost part of the country.

You only really begin to appreciate the size and space of the state, however, farther north or **inland**, where vast tracts of mountainous forest are dotted with lakes and barely pierced by roads – more like the Alaskan interior than the RV-clustered roads of the Vermont and New Hampshire mountains. This region is ideal territory for hiking and canoeing (and spotting moose), particularly in **Baxter State Park**. In the northwestern part of the state, closer to the New Hampshire border, a cluster of ski resorts lie scattered about the mountains, highlighted by **Sugarloaf USA**, perhaps the finest place to ski in all New England.

Although Maine is in many ways inhospitable – the **Algonquin** called it the "Land of the Frozen Ground" – it has been in contact with Europe ever since the **Vikings** explored it, around 1000 AD. For the navigator Verrazano, in 1524, the "crudity and evil manners" of the Indians made this the "Land of Bad People," but before long European fishermen were setting up camps each summer to dry their catch. Francis Bacon in turn said that the English settlers were "worse than the very Savages, impudently lying with their Women, teaching their men to drink drunke, and . . . to fall together by the eares."

North America's first agricultural **colonies** were in Maine: de Champlain's **French** Protestants near Mount Desert Island in 1604, and an **English** group that survived one winter at the mouth of the Kennebec River three years later. In the face of the unwillingness of subsequent English settlers to let them farm in peace, local Indians formed long-term alliances with the French and, until as late as 1700, regularly drove out streams of impoverished English refugees.

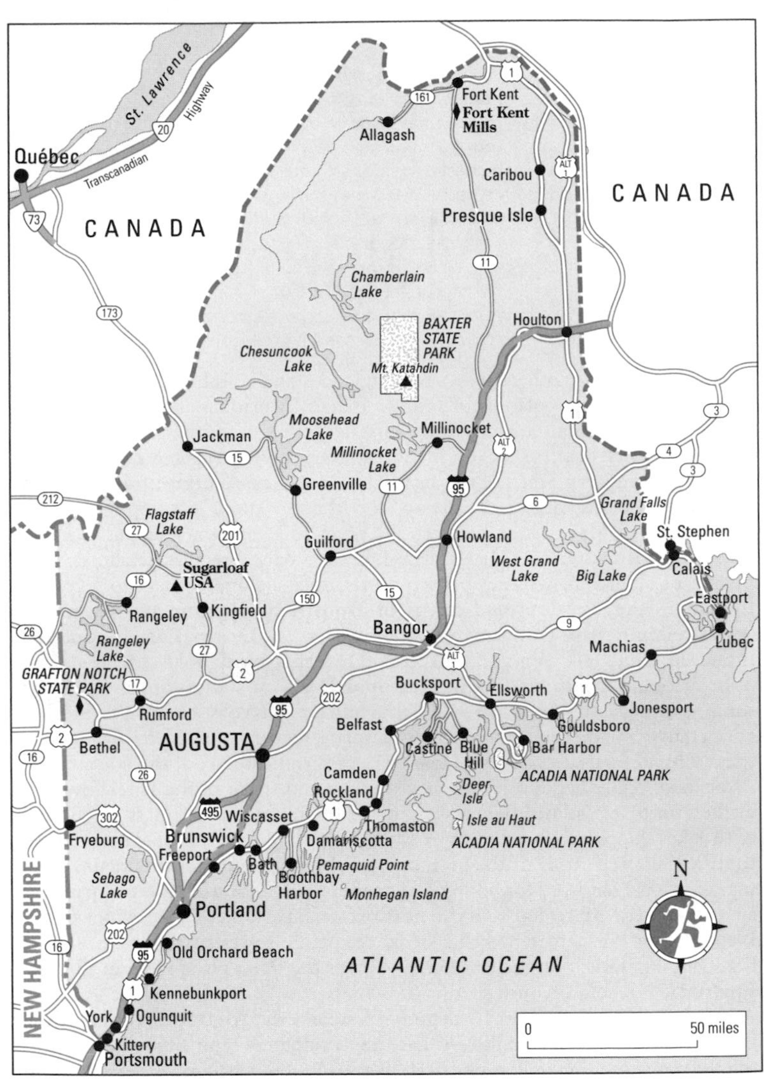

By 1764, however, the official census could claim that even Maine's black population was more numerous than its Native Americans.

At first considered part of Massachusetts, Maine became a separate entity only in 1820, when the Missouri Compromise made Maine a free, and Missouri a slave, state. In the nineteenth century, its people had a reputation for conservatism and resistance to immigration, manifested in anti-Irish riots. Today, the **economy** remains heavily based on the sea, although many of those who fish also farm, and long expeditions are rare. Recently they have been selling their catch direct to Russian factory ships anchored just offshore. Lobster fishing in

Finding your way in Maine

With public transport falling a long way short of meeting travelers' needs, the vast majority of visitors to Maine **drive**. Much the most enjoyable route to follow is US-1, which runs within a few miles of the coast all the way to Canada. Many hotels, restaurants, and attractions can be found along US-1 – but their addresses may or may not reflect that. In each coastal town, US-1 usually becomes a named street; sometimes several names are used. All this may make your destination deceptively difficult to locate, but the locals will inevitably provide cheerful assistance, so just relax and allow a few extra minutes. You should be prepared for backups at the height of the summer season, however. If you're in a hurry, I-95 offers speedy access to Portland and beyond. In the interior, the roads are quiet and the views spectacular; many routes belong to the lumber companies, who keep careful track of who you are and where you're going (and charge you for the privilege). At any time of year, bad weather can render these roads suddenly impassable; be sure to check before setting off.

particular has defied gloomy predictions and has boomed again, as evidenced by the many thriving **lobster pounds**.

Maine's climate is famously harsh. In winter, most of the state is under ice; in early 1998, a severe ice storm left many residents huddled in their homes without power or running water for several weeks. Summer is short and usually heralded in early June by an infestation of tiny black flies, though the tourist season doesn't come into full swing until July. **Fall colors** begin to spread from the north in late September – when, unlike elsewhere in New England, off-season prices apply – but temperatures drop sharply, becoming quite frosty by mid-October.

The southern coast

Running between the two shopping hubs of **Kittery** and **Freeport**, Maine's **southern coast** is its most settled part. Blessed with the state's best **beaches** – indeed, most of the state's beaches – the southern coastline was already a popular summer vacation spot by the mid-nineteenth century, when frequent trains brought city-dwellers up from Boston and New York or down from Canada. The eleven-mile strip of sand at **Old Orchard Beach** is still one of the finest in the country, attracting correspondingly huge crowds in July and August. The other popular beach resort town in the area, **Ogunquit**, only slightly less overrun in summer, is more attractive, with a long-established artist community and a collection of excellent restaurants to boot. Though commercial development has scarred some of the area's landscape with malls and fast food, you can still find attractive old towns with plenty of historical interest, such as **York**, the first chartered city in America, and beautiful **Kennebunkport**, best known as the site of ex-president George Bush's summer home. In the northern part of the region, the coastline becomes more varied and prone to peninsulas, harbors, inlets, and islands. At the mouth of the

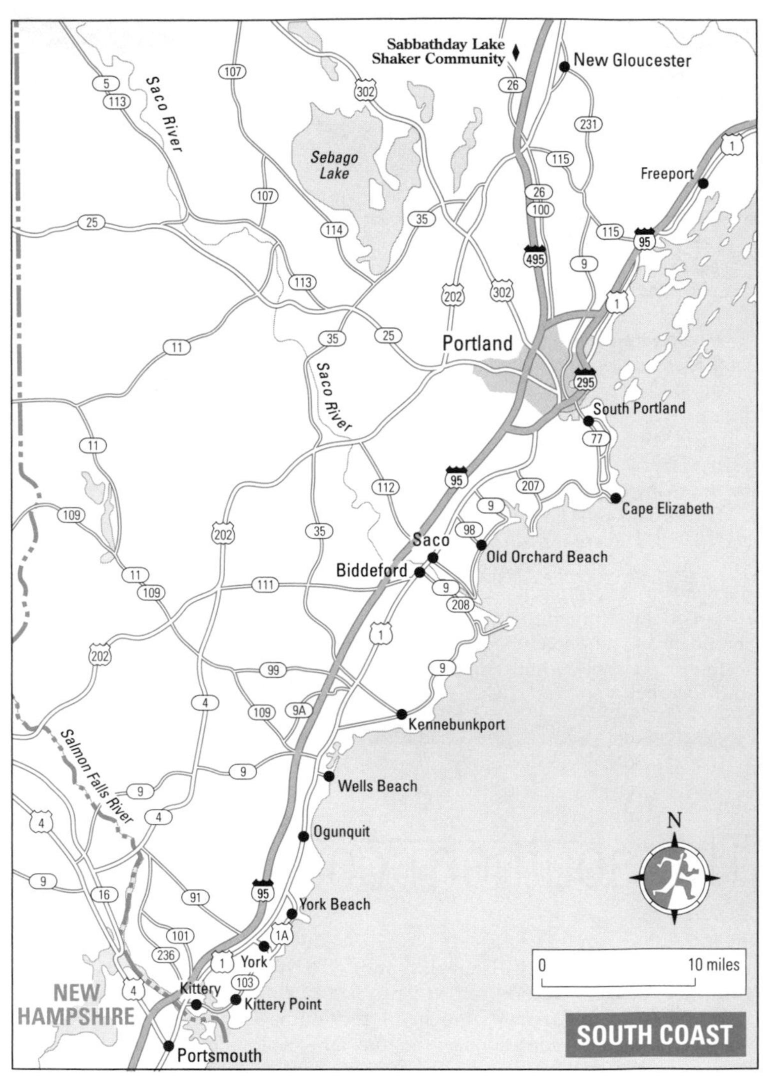

Fore River, Maine's largest city, **Portland**, has experienced a cultural resurgence over the past few years, with a young population, respected art museum, lively music scene, and creative restaurants.

If your aim is to blast north towards lesser populated (and visited), more physically dramatic stretches of the coast, stick to fast-moving **I-95**; otherwise, **US-1** is the major artery, with innumerable turnoffs every few miles that lead to the seaside villages.

Kittery and York

KITTERY is only just in Maine, right across the Piscataqua from Portsmouth, NH (see p.448), and it makes for an excellent place to get oriented, namely at its very complete **information center** at the intersection of I-95 and US-1 (daily: summer 8am–6pm; rest of year 9am–5.30pm; ⓣ207/439-1319), which has scads of brochures, weather information services, and volunteers who can give insiders' tips and help make reservations. If you follow US-1 through Kittery, you'll pass a nearly endless string of **outlet shops** (ⓣ1-888/KIT-TERY, ⓦwww.thekitteryoutlets.com), though these lag behind the quality of those in Freeport, about 75 minutes up the road. In the Maine Outlet mall, the Kittery Chamber of Commerce runs its own tourist information center (Mon–Fri 9am–5pm).

The small spit of land south along Rte-103 called **Kittery Point** makes for a pleasant drive, taking you a few miles and a thousand cultural light years from the outlet-shopping hordes. It also takes you past the **First Congregational Church**, Maine's oldest house of worship, to a rocky cliff overlooking the Portsmouth Naval Shipyard (also called the Kittery Naval Yard) on Seavey Island, where the treaty ending the Russo–Japanese War of 1905 was signed. Kittery was a major **shipbuilding** center by the mid-eighteenth century, when the *Ranger* sailed out of a Kittery shipyard under the command of Revolutionary War hero John Paul Jones. For an overly detailed look at the city's naval, shipbuilding, and cultural history, including a 12ft model of the *Ranger*, stop off at the **Kittery Historical and Naval Museum**, on Rogers Road near the intersection of US-1 and Rte-236 (June to mid-Oct Tues–Sat 10am–4pm; $3).

Close by is one of Kittery's best places to **eat**, *Cap'n Simeon's Galley*, 90 Pepperrell Rd (May to mid-Oct daily; mid-Oct through April closed Tues; ⓣ207/439-3655), with a well-priced menu specializing in seafood and an outdoor deck overlooking Kittery's picturesque Pepperrell Cove. Back on US-1 is longtime local favorite *Bob's Clam Hut* (ⓣ207/439-4233), a campy fish shack dating from the 1950s. Some of the best **places to stay** in town are the clean, adequate *Coachman Motor Inn*, 380 US-1 (ⓣ207/439-4434; ❺), right near the outlets, or try *Melfair Farm B&B*, 11 Wilson Rd (ⓣ207/439-0320; ❹), or *Enchanted Nights B&B*, 29 Wentworth St (ⓣ207/439-1489; ❹).

Surfing Maine's southern coast

A small number of hardy souls brave the cold tumult of the Northern Atlantic to pursue the unlikely pastime of **surfing** off Maine's coast; indeed, it's said that there are only a hundred or so Maine residents who surf regularly year-round (twenty of those in Portland), no matter the weather. While 50°F waters in Northern California are considered cold, the water here in January can dip below 40°F, daunting even with the newest developments in wet-suit technology. Though wave and tide conditions are usually best in fall and winter, on certain warm summer days, the waves come up and the crowds swell with the tides. The best spots are at **Higgins Beach**, south of Portland in Scarborough, **Fortune Rocks** in Biddeford, **Gooch's Beach** in Kennebunkport, **Old Orchard Beach**, **York Beach**, and **Wells Beach**. For equipment **rentals** and **information** on conditions, contact Moose County, 610 Congress St, Portland (ⓣ207/761-8084), or Wheels and Waves, on US-1 in Wells (ⓣ207/646-5774).

York

YORK, a few miles north of Kittery off US-1, bears the distinction of being America's first chartered city, incorporated as Georgeana in 1642 – though it was subsequently demoted to the status of "town" in 1670. Its past is very well preserved in the series of seven buildings that comprise Old York. **Jefferd's Tavern**, 5 Lindsay St, offers a starting place for the tour of the old buildings (mid-June to mid-Oct Mon–Sat 10am–5pm; ⓣ207/646-4974; $7, family rates available), with a visitors' center where tickets are sold. There are occasional hearth-cooking demonstrations in its working kitchen. Foremost among the structures is the **Old Jail**, 207 York St, the earliest British Colonial public structure still standing on its original site, dating from 1653. It was used as Maine's primary prison until the Revolution and continued to confine York County prisoners until the Civil War. Inside, a museum reconstructs the surprisingly plush jailer's quarters, traces York's tumultuous history of threats from Indian raids and pestilence, and has displays on some of the more colorful criminals to do time here. Other highlights in Old York include the **Old Schoolhouse**, which houses exhibits on education in the eighteenth century; the **John Hancock Warehouse and Wharf**, which has displays on early American maritime history and navigation; and the **Old Burying Yard**, where it's rumored that a grave covered with a stone slab was thus protected to prevent its occupant, reputedly a witch, from escaping. In fact, the slab was actually placed there by her husband to prevent cattle from grazing on her grave. If you'd like to talk to her (or one of her friends) yourself, you may want to attend one of Ghostly Tours' sometimes candle-lit strolls through the town (ⓣ207/363-0000).

As well as its historical attractions, York boasts several fine beaches and invigorating cliff walks. Head beyond Old York, for example, towards Nubble Light, at the end of Shore Road, off Rte-103, at York Beach, where you'll find one of Maine's most picturesque lighthouses, situated on an island of its own and observable from a rocky promontory.

Practicalities

York boasts some fine **accommodation**, of which the best is the 40-room *York Harbor Inn*, on Rte-1A in York Harbor (ⓣ207/363-5119 or 1-800/659-7863, ⓦwww.yorkharborinn.com; ⑥), a beautifully appointed inn on the shore with several very inviting common areas. It also has a restaurant, which serves inventive takes on seafood, as well as the less expensive *Cellar Pub*, for burger-and-beer cuisine. The *Apple Blossom*, 25 Brixham Rd (ⓣ207/351-1727; ⑥), is one of many B&Bs in the area, a 1727 farmhouse set on eleven acres. A number of cheaper motels and B&Bs can be found along Long Beach Avenue, including *The Willows*, at no. 3 (ⓣ207/363-9900; ⑥), a cozy Victorian home.

As for **food**, the *Lobster Barn*, on US-1 in York Village (ⓣ207/363-4721), has a relaxed atmosphere and well-priced lobster dinners that are served outdoors under a tent when weather permits. Or if you prefer your seafood in a more appropriate setting, *Fox's Lobster House* (ⓣ207/363-2643) is located within a stone's throw of Nubble Light. *Fazio's*, 38 Woodbridge Rd, York Village (ⓣ207/363-7019), has traditional Italian dining at great prices. In York Village's main square, *Village Café*, 226 York St (ⓣ207/363-7171), is good for a light snack or lunch. Out at York Beach, *The Goldenrod*, 2 Railroad Ave (ⓣ207/363-2621), has been churning out saltwater taffy for more than a hundred years; they also have an old-fashioned soda fountain, which serves simple sandwiches and breakfast foods. Just north in Cape Neddick, local institution *Flo's*, US-1 across from Mountain Road (closed Wed), cooks up nothing but juicy hot dogs, flavored with a special sauce, in its nondescript roadside shack.

Ogunquit

Approaching the small oceanside town just north of York, it's not difficult to imagine why Maine's Native Americans named the place **OGUNQUIT**, meaning "beautiful place by the sea" in their dialect. Though the area was much more attractive before it was developed into a summertime resort, its most prominent and stunning feature – the beach – still makes it a worthwhile spot for a visit. In the nineteenth and twentieth centuries, Ogunquit enjoyed fame as the vacation spot of choice for such rich and famous folks as Bette Davis and Tommy Dorsey, and its beachfront was lined with wooden luxury hotels, most of which are gone today. Also gone is the town's reputation as an artists' colony, though a few galleries remain to illustrate that chapter of its history. The town has a little bit of a privileged attitude, but streets named Whistling Oyster Lane and Ho Hum Hill point to the playful character underneath.

Information and getting around

The **Ogunquit Chamber of Commerce**, just south of Ogunquit Village on US-1 (daily 9am–5pm; ⓣ207/646-2939 or 1-800/639-2442, ⓦwww.ogunquit.org), has brochures year-round and operates as a fully staffed **information center** from May to October (daily 9am–5pm; ⓣ207/646-5533). The town is small and parking can be tricky, so it may be a good idea to use the **trolley** ($1), which connects Perkins Cove, Ogunquit Square, the beach, and the strip of motels along US-1 to the north. Wheels and Waves, a mile or two north of Ogunquit Square along US-1 (ⓣ207/646-5774), rents **mountain bikes** and has maps of local cycling trails.

If you're looking to get out on the water, a number of **sailing cruises** depart from Perkins Cove. Both Finestkind (ⓣ207/646-2214) and Silverlining (ⓣ207/361-9800) run several cruises daily from May to October; the *Bunny Clark* caters to deep-sea fishing enthusiasts (ⓣ207/646-2214; $40 half-day, $60 full day); and the *Deborah Ann* charters whale-watching expeditions from mid-June to August (ⓣ207/361-9501).

Accommodation

The pier at the beach has some decent **hotels** that tend to be high-priced due to their proximity to the ocean. Shore Road has a number of good-quality **B&Bs** within walking distance of the beach, town square, and Marginal Way. The stretch above Ogunquit Square along US-1 North has cheap **motels**, and once you get to the town of **Moody**, a mile out, prices drop precipitously. The best **camping** in the area is at *Pinederosa Campground*, 128 North Village Rd in Wells (ⓣ207/646-2492), or *Dixon's Coastal Maine Campground* (ⓣ207/363-3626), 1740 US-1 in Cape Neddick.

Beachmere Inn Shore Road ⓣ207/646-2021 or 1-800/336-3983, ⓦwww.beachmereinn.com. Beautiful rooms in quirky, turreted old wooden hotel that backs up on Marginal Way. The restored inn also operates a few more modern, motel-style buildings nearby. ❻

Hideaway 65 S Main St ⓣ207/646-3787. This funky, no-frills guesthouse has a sunny and casual atmosphere. May–Sept only. ❻

Juniper Hill Inn 196 US-1 N ⓣ207/646-5401 or 1-800/646-4544. Luxury beachside accommodation with pool, weight room, and spacious, if

somewhat plain, rooms. ❻
The Nellie Littlefield House 9 Shore Rd ☎207/646-1692. Individually designed, well-appointed B&B rooms just outside the square. ❼
Pine Hill Inn 13 Pine Hill Rd ☎207/361-1004. Quiet, secluded B&B in a Victorian cottage off of Shore Road closer to Perkins Cove. ❻
Seacoast Motel US-1 N ☎207/646-2187. Cheap, basic, and clean motel north of the square. ❹
Terrace by the Sea 11 Wharf Lane ☎207/646-3232. Plush motel located on the water's edge with spectacular views from many of its rooms. Closed Nov–March. ❹
Wells-Ogunquit Resort Motel 203 US-1 N ☎207/646-8588 or 1-800/556-4402. Impeccably kept modern motel rooms with cable and refrigerators. May–Oct only. ❸

The Town

Ogunquit Square, along Main Street (US-1), is the center of town, home to most of Ogunquit's best restaurants, coffeehouses, and quirky shops. East of the square, Beach Street leads over the Ogunquit River to the three-mile spit of white sand that is Maine's finest **beach**. The water is always freezing, but the tide is mellow and the sand great for sunbathing. Parking near the pier costs $5, but there's a better way to access the beach: take US-1 north of Ogunquit Square and go left on Ocean Road, which leads to a less populated area of the beach – with free parking.

Perkins Cove, a pleasant knot of restaurants and shops a few miles south of Ogunquit Square, is best reached by walking along **Marginal Way**, a windy path that traces the crescent shoreline from Ogunquit Beach. The two-mile trail offers unspoiled views of the Atlantic's rocky coast, particularly stunning in fall when the churning sea contrasts with the changing foliage. The folk art, pottery, and jewelry shops and galleries in and around the cove itself warrant maybe an hour's browse, and there are a few places to grab some ice cream or saltwater taffy for a sweet treat. A half-mile south of Perkins Cove at 543 Shore Road is the **Ogunquit Museum of American Art** (July to mid-Oct Mon–Sat 10.30am–5pm, Sun 2–5pm; ☎207/646-4909; $4), which has a decent collection of twentieth-century work, only a fraction of which is on display at any given time. Best are the Marsden Hartleys and the Rockwell Kent seascapes inspired by the surrounding area. The views of the Atlantic from the plate-glass windows provide a stunning complement to the art.

Eating, drinking, and entertainment

You'll find the standard profusion of **lobster shacks** and touristy seafood restaurants all over Ogunquit, but the best eateries are in the town square and around Perkins Cove. There are also a couple of decent pubs and **bars** in town, offering occasional live musical acts and friendly piano bar sing-alongs.

For more serious entertainment, the **Ogunquit Playhouse** along US-1 south of town (mid-June to Aug; tickets ☎207/646-5511, info 207/646-2402) has been called "America's foremost summer theater" for most of its seventy years, and usually attracts a few big-name performers each season.

Arrows Restaurant Berwick Road, just outside Ogunquit Square ☎207/646-9898. Excellent, New American cuisine in a Victorian house surrounded by gardens. Though it's very expensive, with mains at $40, you'll get excellent service and value for the price. Reservations recommended. Weekends only Oct–Nov, closed Dec–April.
Barnacle Billy's Perkins Cove ☎207/646-5575. A traditional restaurant, with a casual café next door. Lobster and fried fish favorites, as well as ice cream and other snacks.
Blue Star Grille US-1 ☎207/641-2200. Casual American family dining that won't break the bank – a rarity in this town – with most entreés under $15.
Hurricane Oarweed Lane, Perkins Cove ☎207/646-6348. Great views of the Atlantic from nearly every seat in this simple seaside eatery,

where fresh seafood is the specialty. Entreés go for $15–20, but cheaper appetizers such as lobster gazpacho can be a meal in themselves.

Jackie's Too 59 Perkins Cove ⓣ207/646-4444. The most popular of the cove area restaurants, with super-fresh seafood and outdoor dining when weather permits.

Jonathan's 2 Bourne Lane ⓣ207/646-4777. Live entertainment – musical and otherwise – nightly from April to Oct, with a decent restaurant serving seafood, pasta, and creatively prepared meats. Reservations recommended.

Native Grounds 139 Main St, Ogunquit Square ⓣ207/646-0955. Funky joint for light lunch fare. Create-your-own sandwiches and good soups of the day, to be enjoyed in pleasant outdoor seating area.

The Old Village Inn 30 Main St ⓣ207/646-7088. Upmarket seafood with a New American twist. Try the tequila lime shrimp or *osso buco*; the lobster bisque, too, is locally famous. There's also a cheaper pub menu if you're strapped for cash.

Poor Richard's Tavern 2 Pine Hill Rd ⓣ207/646-4722. Authentic old-time New England pub grub in a 1780 Colonial building that was once a coach stop on the road between Boston and Portland.

Two Guys Pizza 185 Main St ⓣ207/646-0888. Laid-back Italian in a homely little loft, with casual dinners, fresh sandwiches, and salads.

Vinny's East Coast Grill US-1 North ⓣ207/646-5115. Another lower-cost option, with casual diners, featuring sandwiches and salads.

Yum Mee 349 US-1 ⓣ207/641-8788. Twenty-two specialties, plus all the usual choices. For a lark, try the "Hawaii Four-O": lobster, beef, chicken, and pork in a flaming rum sauce.

North to Portland

The coast meanders on a bit from Ogunquit, with worthwhile stops slightly more spread out than at its most southern reaches. In this thirty or so mile stretch up to Portland, the main points of interest are in **Kennebunkport** and **Old Orchard Beach**.

Kennebunkport

The recent history of **KENNEBUNKPORT** illustrates the truth of Oscar Wilde's famous aphorism, "There is only one thing in the world worse than being talked about, and that is not being talked about." Kennebunkport was perfectly happy as a self-contained and exclusive residential district before its worldwide exposure as the home of (the senior) **George Bush**'s "summer White House." If anything, locals seemed to feel that George lowered the tone of the place by becoming president. There were complaints at having to bear the extra cost of policing (the far smaller and poorer Plains, Georgia, home of Jimmy Carter, paid up with pride), and talk of a "lower class" of gawking visitor clogging the streets and driving the old money away. However, interest subsided significantly after Bush lost the presidency to Bill Clinton in 1992, and now it's quite apparent that Kennebunkport isn't that different from any other

The Maine Diner

One of the best of Maine's many diners, the *Maine Diner* lies on US-1 North in the town of **Wells**, just above Ogunquit (ⓣ207/646-4441, ⓦwww.mainediner.com). An eatery with an old-school authenticity and a modern flair, this 1953 throwback serves your typical burger-and-fries but also ventures into more atypical gourmet food, often using fresh produce picked from the garden out back. Owned by the Henry Brothers since 1983, it's packed from 7am until 9pm (or "until closing" once the cold weather sets in) by devoted locals and tourists who fill the vinyl booths and long counter and feast on the blueberry pancakes, pulled BBQ pork sandwiches, crabmeat melts, and the grapenut custard dessert.

place along the coast – which bothers the locals even more. Bush's son, current president George W. Bush, has not been a regular visitor here.

The only sight worth stopping for in the area is the **Seashore Trolley Museum**, on Log Cabin Road off Rte-9 or US-1 (daily May to mid-Oct 10am–5pm; $7.50; Ⓦwww.trolleymuseum.org), which holds a surprisingly engaging display on the history of the trolley car (of all things) in northern New England. You can take a twenty-minute ride on a vintage trolley car through the Maine woods, along a stretch of track that used to be part of a line that allowed travelers to go from Bangor to Washington DC, entirely by trolley. Moose have occasionally been spotted along the way. Last, and best, is the collection of old trolleys from around the world, including the original New Orleans trolley that ran along Desire Street, inspiring the Tennessee Williams play *A Streetcar Named Desire*.

Although there's really nothing else to see or do here, there are some good **places to eat** if you're passing through. *Alisson's*, 8 Dock Square (Ⓣ207/967-4841), is a fun, relaxed place to hang out and chow on seafood. They have a late-night menu, for this area at least (food is served in the pub until 11pm Fri & Sat, until 10pm the rest of the week), as well as a lively bar. In the Lower Village section of town, *Grissini Trattoria and Panificio*, 27 Western Ave (Ⓣ207/967-2211), has reasonably priced Italian food that you can eat on an outdoor patio. *Federal Jack's*, off Rte-9, makes great appetizers – try the Goat Island mussels or Maine steamers – and features an on-site **microbrewery** that produces an excellent Shipyard Ale.

Old Orchard Beach

During the late nineteenth and early twentieth centuries, **OLD ORCHARD BEACH** (OOB, in local parlance) stood alongside Ogunquit as a classic New England resort town, drawing upper-crust citizens from all over the eastern seaboard to stay in its massive wooden seafront hotels. After World War II, its popularity and property values declined steadily, and in 1980 the town attempted to rectify the situation by refurbishing its decaying, carnivalesque pier. Almost overnight, OOB regained its status as a major hotspot, though it resembled the spring-break town of Fort Lauderdale more than the posh resort of old. Things have calmed down a bit, even if a slightly corny party atmosphere remains, especially along the waterfront.

The main draw here is the **beach**, a fantastic seven-mile strip of white sand that competes with any in New England. It can get intolerably crowded during summer and holiday weekends, in which case you'd do better to find another stretch of shore. It's free, but **parking** can be pricey; lots that charge $5–7 per day are reasonable. Just off the beach is the **pier** and Palace Playland (Ⓣ207/934-2001), with classic amusement-park attractions such as a Ferris wheel, bumper cars, and a vintage carousel dating from 1906. The entirety of **Old Orchard Street** (which leads down to the pier and beach) and **Grand Avenue** (which runs parallel to the ocean), are dotted with attractions, including instant-photo booths, cotton-candy vendors, and stores where you can design your own souvenir T-shirt. It's hopelessly tacky, but at least with its campy carnival vibe it's an alternative to its sedate neighbors.

Practicalities

The **Old Orchard Beach Chamber of Commerce**, on First Street (Ⓣ207/934-2500, Ⓦwww.oobme.com), operates an information center of sporadic availability and can help arrange accommodation. In any case, you

Exchange. In more recent years, downtown Portland, particularly along **Congress Street**, has also undergone a renaissance of sorts, spurred by a high concentration of artists, some wise city planning, and the opening of a new L.L. Bean outlet in the late 1990s. These successes, and a small but unexpected wave of immigration in the mid-1990s, have revitalized the city, keeping it at the heart of Maine life – but you shouldn't expect a constant hive of energy. Portland is simply a quite pleasant, sophisticated, and, in places, very attractive town, where one can experience the benefits of a large city at a lesser cost and without the hassle.

Arrival

Both I-95 and US-1 skirt the peninsula of Portland, within a very few miles of the city center, while I-295 goes through it; **Portland International Jetport** (Ⓣ207/774-7301) abuts I-95. Most major carriers serve the airport, which is connected with downtown by regular **city buses** (#5; no service Sun; Ⓣ207/774-0351; $1).

Amtrak's *Downeaster* pulls into Portland four times daily from Boston's North Station (one-way $21; Ⓣ1-800/USA-RAIL, Ⓦwww.thedowneaster.com), arriving at the Portland Transportation Center (Ⓣ207/828-3939). From the terminal, located three miles from the city center at 100 Thompson Point Rd just off Congress Street and adjacent to I-295, shuttles, city buses, and taxis can ferry you downtown.

Also arriving here, Concord Trailways (Ⓣ207/828-1151 or 1-800/639-3317) is the principal **bus** operator along the coast, with frequent service from Boston and Bangor. Vermont Transit Lines (Ⓣ207/772-6587 or 1-800/552-8737) has direct connection service with Greyhound and runs to Montréal, New Hampshire, and Vermont as well as to points throughout Maine from its station at 950 Congress St, on the eastern edge of downtown.

Car rentals are available from the local offices of Alamo (Ⓣ207/775-0855), Avis (Ⓣ207/874-7500), Budget (Ⓣ207/774-8663), Enterprise (Ⓣ207/772-0030), and National (Ⓣ207/773-0036); consult Basics (p.33) for toll-free phone numbers. **Parking** can be a real hassle in Portland. The parking meters charge 25¢ per half-hour, but finding a parking place can sometimes seem well-nigh impossible. The city makes up for this to some degree with a glut of parking garages, including the Fore Street Garage at 439 Fore St, and the Custom House Square Garage at 25 Pearl St.

Information

The **Convention and Visitors Bureau** is at 305 Commercial St (mid-May to mid-Oct Mon–Fri 8am–6pm, Sat & Sun 10am–6pm; rest of year Mon–Fri 8am–5pm, Sat & Sun 10am–3pm; Ⓣ207/772-5800, Ⓦwww.visitportland.com), but there's a more friendly – and less harried – information office at the Jetport (Ⓣ207/775-5809). Furthermore, all manner of details concerning transportation, whether bus, boat, or train, within the area can be found at Ⓦwww.transportme.org. The Portland Public Library at 5 Monument Square, at the corner of Congress and Elm streets (Ⓣ207/871-1700, Ⓦwww.portlandlibrary.com), has free **Internet access**.

City transit and local ferries

Downtown Portland and the Old Port are each compact enough to stroll around, though they're served by a comprehensive **bus and trolley** system

(Ⓣ207/774-0351; $1); stop by the Metro Pulse at the Elm Street Garage near Congress Street for a detailed route map. Cyclemania, 59 Federal St (Ⓣ207/774-2933), rents **bicycles** for $15 a day, which you can ride around the city's hundreds of acres of undeveloped land. Call Portland Trails (Ⓣ207/775-2411, Ⓦwww.trails.org) for more information on bike or walking trails all over the city. **Tour companies** abound; one of the best, and most entertaining, is Mainely Tours, which gives an overview of town history from a jaunty trolley, sometimes with assistance from Newman – the quite large Samoyed mix who belongs to the owners (3 Moulton St; May–Oct; $13; Ⓣ207/774-0808).

Between mid-May and mid-October, the Prince of Fundy Company's *Scotia Prince* **ferry** leaves Portland for Yarmouth in Nova Scotia at 9pm every evening, returning the next day. The standard high-season fare is about $160 per adult round-trip; you can take your car with you, but it's prohibitively expensive. There are always various discount and excursion fares available, however (details on Ⓣ207/775-5616 or 1-800/482-0955).

Accommodation

Finding a room in Portland is no great problem if you book in advance during the summer and fall, but you'll generally pay more for **accommodation** in town than for space in one of several **budget motels** that cluster around exit 8 off I-95. The extra cost can be worth it, however; Portland has some great old renovated hotels and you'll save in transportation costs by staying closer to downtown or the Old Port. The closest **campground** is *Wassamki Springs*, 56 Saco St, off Rte-114 in Scarborough, towards Westbrook (Ⓣ207/839-4276; May to mid-Oct only).

The Danforth 163 Danforth St Ⓣ207/879-8755 or 1-800/991-6557, Ⓦwww.danforthmaine.com. Portland's best accommodation has twelve spacious rooms, ten with private baths and working fireplaces, in an 1820s Federal-style home within walking distance of the Old Port. Elegant full breakfast served. ❻

Eastland Park Hotel 157 High St Ⓣ207/775-5411 or 1-888/671-8008, Ⓦwww.eastlandparkhotel.com. Luxury accommodation, centrally located. ❻

Embassy Suites 1050 Westbrook St Ⓣ207/775-2200 or 1-800/EMBASSY. Spacious suites for the price of a hotel room, overlooking Portland's tiny Jetport. Rates include full breakfast and afternoon cocktails. ❼

Holiday Inn by the Bay 88 Spring St Ⓣ207/775-2311 or 1-800/345-5050, Ⓦwww.innbythebay.com. Fairly standard link in the *Holiday Inn* chain, with 239 rooms, many of which overlook Casco Bay. ❼

Inn on Carleton 46 Carleton St Ⓣ207/775-1910 or 1-800/639-1779, Ⓦwww.innoncarleton.com. A nicely restored, clean Victorian brownstone on a quiet street in Portland's historic district. Breakfast included. ❽

Inn at St John 939 Congress St Ⓣ207/773-6481 or 1-800/636-9127, Ⓦwww.innatstjohn.com. Quaint, comfortable rooms in a renovated old hotel located a short drive from the museums and convenient for public transport to the Old Port. No elevator. Breakfast included. ❸

Portland Harbor Hotel 468 Fore St Ⓣ207/775-9090 or 1-888/798-9090, Ⓦwww.theportlandharborhotel.com. The city's newest hotel, in a great location near the waterfront; many rooms overlook the English garden. ❽

Portland Regency Hotel 20 Milk St Ⓣ207/774-4200 or 1-800/727-3436, Ⓦwww.theregency.com. Fancy rooms – some with bay views – in a beautifully renovated brick armory building not far away from the Old Port. ❼–❽

Super 8 208 Larrabee Rd Ⓣ207/854-1881 or 1-800/800-8000, Ⓦwww.super8.com. Budget suites with kitchenettes and free continental breakfast near I-95. ❸–❹

Travelodge 1200 Brighton Ave Ⓣ207/774-6106. Good-value chain offers affordable doubles on the western edge of the peninsula near the Maine Medical Center. ❺

West End Inn 146 Pine St Ⓣ207/772-1377 or 1-800/338-1377, Ⓦwww.westendbb.com. Charming 1871 townhouse in the historic district. Full breakfast included. ❺–❻

The City

Central Portland consists of two main districts. **Downtown** refers to the city's business district, bisected by Congress Street, where you'll also find several museums, the Civic Center, and a smattering of good restaurants. The **Old Port**, to the southeast, is lively and bustling with shops, bars, and eateries. Commercial Street runs along the water's edge, but Fore Street, just inland, has most of the area's attractions.

Downtown Portland

Portland's single best destination, the **Portland Museum of Art** (PoMA), in the heart of downtown at 7 Congress Square (Tues, Wed, Sat & Sun 10am–5pm, Thurs–Fri 10am–9pm; June to mid-Oct also Mon 10am–5pm; $8; Ⓣ207/775-6148, Ⓦwww.portlandmuseum.org), was designed in 1988 by the renowned I.M. Pei and Partners, and many parts of the museum afford superb views of the bay, including some through porthole windows. One of the museum's high points is the stunning collection of glassworks: encompassing the 1840s to the present, the European and American lamps and vases glow in a riot of color as if naturally fluorescent. Elsewhere, ships and images of the sea are prevalent, as reflected by Winslow Homer's sentimental seascapes, but there's also the pull of the forest. *Woodmen in the Woods of Maine* by Waldo Peirce, rich and dark, was a Public Works project commissioned by the Westbrook Post Office in 1937 and is displayed here with the clouded-glass mailroom door still intact. There's also a rotating collection of modernist works by the likes of Nevelson, Indiana, and Rauschenberg. Adjoining the main building are the impressive Federal-style **McLellan House**, built for a city shipping magnate in 1800, and the **L.D.M. Sweat Memorial Galleries**, both recently opened after twenty years in the dark and an $8 million restoration. The Sweat Galleries focus on American art (and especially landscapes) through 1900, incorporating both decorative and fine-art pieces. Scenes specific to Maine are well depicted here in works by naturalist Frederic Church (see the romantic *Mount Katahdin from Millinocket Camp*) and in the evocative Edward Hopper pieces.

Among several excellent smaller art galleries in the newly resurgent downtown area, one of the best is the **Institute of Contemporary Art** at Maine College of Art, 522 Congress St (Wed–Sun 11am–5pm; Ⓣ207/879-5742), which stages interesting modern art exhibits such as "Do It," with do-it-yourself artworks crafted in accordance to the written instructions of several well-known artists from around the world. Also worth a look, the fascinating **Museum of African Tribal Art**, 122 Spring St (Tues–Fri 10.30am–5pm, Sat 12.30–5pm; free; Ⓣ207/871-7188), was established in 1998 to showcase a rich collection of over 500 wood and bronze masks and artifacts; unfortunately, only a small portion of the collection is on view at any time due to limited space.

Not all that much of old Portland survives thanks to the fires over the years, though various grand mansions can be seen along Congress and Danforth streets in the downtown area. A few of the oldest houses are open to the public, most notably the **Wadsworth-Longfellow House** at 485 Congress St (June–Oct Tues–Sun 10am–4pm; Nov–May Wed–Sat noon–4pm; $6), Portland's first brick house, built in 1785 by Revolutionary War hero Peleg Wadsworth, grandfather of poet Henry Wadsworth Longfellow. Longfellow spent his boyhood here and wrote a number of pieces about the local harbor and lighthouses. The house is furnished with the Longfellow family's own housewares. Next door, at 489 Congress St, the **Maine History Gallery**

(June–Oct daily 10am–4pm; free with admission to Wadsworth-Longfellow House, otherwise $4; Ⓦwww.mainehistory.org) has rotating displays of art and Maine-related historical artifacts, as well as an extensive library. Another building that survived the fires, slightly west of downtown, the period-furnished **Tate House**, 1270 Westbrook St (mid-June to Sept Tues–Sat 10am–4pm, Sun 1–4pm; Oct Fri–Sun same times; $5; Ⓦwww.nentug.org/museums/tatehouse), was the home of Captain George Tate, mast agent for the British Royal Navy, from 1755 to 1794. The exterior of the building merits attention for its clerestory, an indented wall rising above the gambrel roof on the second story, while the furnishings and decorations inside reflect a style typical of a wealthy eighteenth-century official. Closer to the Old Port, the **Victoria Mansion**, at 109 Danforth St (May–Oct Tues–Sat 10am–4pm, Sun 1–5pm; $8; Ⓦwww.victoriamansion.org), an Italianate brownstone constructed in 1859 for a wealthy hotel magnate, is blessed with an exquisite interior. The walls and ceilings are ornamented with frescoes, and there's a freestanding staircase made of Santo Domingo mahogany. Stained glass and floor-to-ceiling gold-leaf mirrors are also prevalent. **Tours** of Portland's historic houses and architecture can be arranged through Greater Portland Landmarks, 165 State St (Ⓣ207/774-5561; $8 for tours).

Old Port district

For relaxed wandering, the restored **Old Port Exchange** near the quayside, between Exchange and Pearl streets, is quite entertaining, with all sorts of red-brick antiquarian shops, specialist book and music stores (especially on Exchange Street), and other esoterica. Several companies operate **boat trips** from the nearby wharves. The *Palawan*, a vintage 58-foot ocean racer, sails around the harbor and to the Casco Bay islands and lighthouses from DeMillo's Marina off Commercial Street (daily in summer; 2hr trip morning $20, 3hr afternoon $40; Ⓣ207/773-2163 or 1-800/284-PAL1), while Bay View Cruises, 184 Commercial St, offers seal-watching excursions all year (June–Sept daily; May weekends; $8; Ⓣ207/761-0496). Casco Bay Lines runs a twice-daily **mailboat** all year, and additional **cruises** in summer, to six of the seemingly innumerable Calendar Islands in Casco Bay, from its terminal at Commercial and Franklin streets ($10–16; Ⓣ207/774-7871, Ⓦwww.cascobaylines.com). Long, Peaks, and Cliff islands all have accommodation or camping facilities.

If you follow Portland's waterfront to the end of the peninsula, you'll come to the **Eastern Promenade**. Once the bastion of the town's wealthy families, (who've since moved on to the **Western Promenade**), it became almost exclusively residential after the last fire and is remarkably peaceful for so close to downtown. A big beach lies below the headland, while above, at the top of Munjoy Hill at 138 Congress St, is the shingled, eight-sided 1807 **Portland Observatory** (June to mid-Oct 10am–5pm; $3), the oldest remaining operational signal tower on the Atlantic; you can climb its 102 steps for an exhilarating view of the bay and the city.

South Portland

Across the harbor, in South Portland at Fort Williams State Park, lies the **Portland Head Lighthouse** (take Rte-77 south and follow the signs), the oldest in America, commissioned in 1790 by George Washington. Though it is no longer functional, it houses an excellent **museum** on the history of Maine's lighthouses (June–Oct daily 10am–4pm; April–May & Nov–Dec weekends only 10am–4pm; $2). The small but intelligent collection traces lighthouse his-

Portland's Festivals

As with many larger New England cities, Portland hosts its share of **festivals** outside of the typical holiday celebrations. Craft booths, plenty of food, and lots of people watching are standard. In some cases, you should call ahead to double-check dates.

Old Port Festival, first Sun in June. Old Port Exchange. Crafts and food booths, music, and other live entertainment (Ⓣ207/772-6828).

Greek Heritage Festival, last weekend in June. 133 Pleasant St. Greek food (especially good fresh-baked pastries), traditional music, and folk-dancing exhibitions (Ⓣ207/774-0281).

Portland Symphony Orchestra Independence Pops Concert, around Independence Day. Free outdoor concert by the PSO followed by fireworks (Ⓣ207/773-6128).

Italian Street Festival, weekend before Aug 15, Feast of Assumption. Federal Street. Ethnic celebration featuring band music, kids' games, Italian food (Ⓣ207/773-0748).

6Alive's Sidewalk Art Festival, late Aug. Congress Street. Downtown area blocked off for 350 booths featuring work from artists from all over the US and Canada (Ⓣ207/464-1213).

Key Maine Jazz Festival, last weekend in Sept. Party spotlighting hot local talent and national acts, to benefit youth music education (Ⓣ207/839-8880).

Portland Festival of World Cinema, mid-Oct. Independent new films and classics, international and Maine-made, at the Cannes of New England (Ⓣ207/772-9234).

Maine Brewer's Festival, first Sat in Nov. Maine's finest microbrewers serve up their best efforts with food, games, and tunes (Ⓣ207/771-7571, Ⓦwww.mainebrew.com).

Victorian Holiday, Nov 29–Dec 31. Downtown and the Old Port feature holiday- and winter-themed events in Old Victorian style.

New Year's Portland, Dec 31. Music, dancing, and arts-and-crafts city-wide. "Family"-oriented events mean no alcohol (Ⓣ207/772-9012).

tory back to 300BC when Ptolemy II built a lighthouse on the island of Pharos at Alexandria Harbor. Best are the displays combining lighthouse literature and art, such as Longfellow's paean *The Lighthouse* and Edward Hopper's forlorn watercolors, each of which were inspired by Portland Head. Five miles south of Portland, another lighthouse commissioned by George Washington, the **Cape Elizabeth Lighthouse**, is one of the more recognizable landmarks of the state, captured on countless postcards and posters. A short drive through the neighborhoods of Cape Elizabeth, with its stately homes and comfortable spaces, is also pleasant. Nearby, **Two Lights State Park** has easy shoreside trails and picnic areas (day-use fee $1). The lighthouse is still operational, as the occasional and unpredictable ear-splitting blasts from its horn alert anyone in the vicinity.

Eating

Portland's relatively low rents and young, hip population have given rise to a concentration of experimental, though still quite affordable, **restaurants**. Throw a rock in the Old Port district and you'll hit one; check around the downtown area near the Portland Museum of Art, too. Also in the downtown area, you'll find the **Portland Public Market**, along Cumberland Avenue between Elm and Preble streets (Mon–Sat 9am–7pm, Sun 10am–5pm; Ⓣ207/228-2000, Ⓦwww.portlandmarket.com), an indoor food bazaar where you can buy fresh breads, organically grown vegetables, a variety of local beers, specialty cheeses, and a whole host of other yuppyish eats.

Be wary of the larger, more touristed restaurants along the waterfront, where the ambience may be grand, but the food is probably bland. People eat out a lot here, so at least inquire about reservations Thursday through Sunday.

Inexpensive

Aurora Provisions 64 Pine St ☏207/871-9060. Upscale market/deli with mouth-watering sandwiches, a full selection of coffee, drinks, pastries, salads, desserts, and a small seating area. Closed Sun.

Becky's 390 Commercial St ☏207/773-7070. The best breakfast spot in Portland, serving hearty American portions, including homemade muffins, from 4am (for the fishermen) until 9pm. On weekends, the place is open all night.

Federal Spice 225 Federal St ☏207/774-6404. Eclectic international fare influenced by South American, Southeast Asian, and Caribbean cuisine, all very hot, spicy, and cheap.

Flatbread Company 72 Commercial St ☏207/772-8777. Tasty pizza, made with flatbread dough, their own sauce, and all-natural ingredients, in a hip waterfront location.

Granny's Burritos 420 Fore St ☏207/761-0751. Super-cheap burritos and quesadillas served on no-frills benches downstairs. There's table service, beer and wine upstairs. Open until midnight on Fri and Sat.

Bombay Club 675 Congress St ☏207/874-6631. Good tandoori dishes, with lunchtime and evening specials.

Silly's 40 Washington St ☏207/772-0360. Burgers, pies, and particularly fine milkshakes in a space adorned with wacky Americana.

Moderate to expensive

Aubergine Bistro 555 Congress St ☏207/874-0680. Classic French cooking with an American flair in a sophisticated setting. Try the swordfish loin with lemon and ginger or rump steak with red leek Béarnaise. Extensive wine bar. Closed Mon; brunch only Sun 11am–2pm.

Bakehouse Café 205 Commercial St ☏207/773-2215. Casual Caribbean-influenced food at candlelit tables in a small but sleek bakery/restaurant. The light pasta entreés cost $8–12, and many selections can be ordered in half portions.

Boone's 6 Custom House Wharf ☏207/774-5725. Traditional waterfront restaurant in old wharf buildings, overlooking the fishing docks since 1898. Good lobster and grilled seafood in general.

Café Uffa 190 State St ☏207/775-3380. Reasonably priced creative fare – the grilled salmon is particularly savory – in a funky neighborhood café.

J's Oyster 5 Portland Pier ☏207/772-4828. Classic old-school raw bar serving oysters and steamers right on the waterfront.

Lobster Shack 225 Two Lights Rd, five miles south of Portland, just below the Cape Elizabeth Lighthouse ☏207/799-1677. Great for fresh seafood – try the clamburger or lobster stew.

Natasha's 82 Exchange St ☏207/774-4004. New American cuisine, featuring wraps, pasta, salads, paella, eggplant casserole, and risotto, with a cool *trompe l'oeil* outdoor wall. Closed Mon.

Perfetto 28 Exchange St ☏207/828-0001. Modern Italian and New American cuisine in Ikea-dominated environs. Best are the North Beach *cioppino*, a light seafood stew, and pomegranate chicken.

Ribollita 41 Middle St ☏207/774-2972. Reasonably priced, fresh handmade pasta in a cozy, narrow dining room with brick walls. Closed Sun and Mon.

RiRa 72 Commercial St ☏207/774-4446. A more creative choice for dinner than one would expect from an authentic Irish bar (albeit, one with cupboards full of antique china in the dining room). Lunch, featuring some more traditional Irish favorites, can be had for under $10.

Sapporo at Union Wharf, 230 Commercial St ☏207/772-1233. Sushi bar on the water with fresh seafare, teriyaki, tempura, and Japanese beer.

Village Café 112 Newbury St ☏207/772-5320. No-nonsense, reasonably priced family dining; well-cooked steak and seafood plus a selection of Italian dishes.

Walter's Café 15 Exchange St ☏207/871-9258. New American cuisine in a hip, high-ceilinged dining room with an open kitchen. Most entreés go for $11–17.

Wine Bar 38 Wharf St ☏207/773-6667. Really more a restaurant than either a café or wine bar. They do serve good vino by the glass and bottle, and have inventive French/New American fusion fare, such as lobster and brie ravioli, and chicken and apple burritos. Very casual.

Entertainment and nightlife

The bar-restaurant distinction is blurry in Portland; most watering holes serve food, and many eateries have good selections of microbrews and wine. There are a good many **bars** scattered throughout the Old Port District, of which a number feature live rock music. ID policies are strict and bars aren't allowed to serve after 1am. **Cafés** are becoming increasingly popular with Portland's youthful population and frequently offer Internet access. They're generally as crowded and lively as bars on the weekends. The **club scene** is somewhat tamer, but there are a few intense dance and music venues.

There are several options for the **performing arts** in Portland. Chamber music, opera, dance, and touring theater productions are often featured as part of PCA Great Performances series held at City Hall's Merrill Auditorium (tickets ⓣ207/842-0800, ⓦwww.pcagreatperformances.org), while the Portland Stage Company puts on larger-scale productions at the Portland Performing Arts Center, 25A Forest Ave (ⓣ207/774-0465). Maine Arts, Inc (ⓣ207/772-9102, ⓦwww.mainearts.org) and Portland Parks and Recreation (ⓣ207/874-8793, ⓦwww.ci.portland.me.us) both sponsor free outdoor noontime and evening jazz and blues concerts at various locations throughout the city during the summer. You can find indie-type films at The Movies, 10 Exchange St (ⓣ207/772-9600). The free *Casco Bay Weekly* (ⓦwww.cascobay-weekly.com) and *Face Magazine* have listings of all local events; Maine's biggest gigs take place each summer at Old Orchard Beach, roughly ten miles south of Portland, but some mid-level shows come to town at the Merrill Auditorium, 20 Myrtle St. Call PorTix (ⓣ207/842-0800) for all area ticketing sales and information.

Sports fans should take a trip to Haddock Field, an intimate baseball stadium on Park Avenue where the minor-league **Portland Sea Dogs** (now affiliated with the Boson Red Sox) play from May to October. Tickets are wildly inexpensive (the prices top out at about $8). Call ⓣ207/879-9500 for ticket and schedule information. Other sporting choices: Portland Pirates hockey (ⓣ207/828-4665) and harness racing in nearby Scarborough Downs (ⓣ207/883-4331).

Cafés

Arabica Coffee House 16 Free St ⓣ207/879-0792. Mellow café with numerous types of imported java.

Habana Cigar Café 398 Fore St ⓣ207/874-4055. Wide selection of stogies and specialty coffees, including banana split latte and almond joy.

Breaking New Grounds 13 Exchange St ⓣ207/761-5637. Sleek but warm two-story interior, packed with young hipsters. Particularly strong caffeine beverages.

JavaNet Café 37 Exchange St ⓣ1-800/JAVA-NET. It's part of a burgeoning chain, but the coffee's good, the couches are comfy, and there's Internet access for $8 an hour.

Portland Roasting Co 111 Commercial St ⓣ207/761-9525. Euro-style coffeehouse with in-store roasted beans and the standard cappuccinos and lattes.

Bars and microbreweries

Brian Boru Public House 57 Center St ⓣ207/780-1506. Traditional Irish pub serving Guinness, with a big, if typical, menu and plenty of benches.

Bull Feeney's 375 Fore St ⓣ207/773-7201. Another Irish option, with live music on the weekends.

Great Lost Bear 540 Forest Ave ⓣ207/772-0300, ⓦwww.greatlostbear.com. According to *The Malt Advocate*, one of the Top 10 Beer Bars in the US. Try one from their 53 taps, including fifteen state microbrews. Food's decent here, too.

Gritty McDuff's 396 Fore St ⓣ207/772-2739, ⓦwww.grittys.com. Portland's first brewpub, making Portland Head Pale Ale and Black Fly Stout. Food, folk music, long wooden benches, and a friendly (if a little self-consciously British) atmosphere, which can get rowdy on Saturday nights.

Old Port Tavern 11 Moulton St ⓣ207/774-0444. Relaxed downstairs pub in the heart of the Old Port with great burgers and a good selection of brews. Live entertainment some nights.

The Shipyard Brewing Co 86 Newbury St ⓣ207/761-0807 or 1-800/BREW-ALE, ⓦwww.shipyard.com. Maker of one of Maine's finest microbrews. While there's no pub here, free tours are offered 3–5pm daily.

Three Dollar Dewey's 230 Commercial St ⓣ207/772-3310. Raucous beer hall, with a wide selection of micro- and macrobrews. They also have a typical burger menu.

Dance clubs and music venues

Asylum 121 Center St ⓣ207/772-8274. Loud, somewhat stylish dance club/bar popular with Portland's twentysomething singles set. DJ and dancing on weekends as well as occasional up-and-coming bands. Cover $5–12.

Big Easy Blues Club 55 Market St, ⓣ207/871-8817. Mellow blues joint with local acts, mostly blues with some jazz and rockabilly shows, rather tame on weekdays; more active on weekends.

Club Fore 32 432 Fore St ⓣ207/775-3510. Loud DJs on the weekends; free admission.

Geno's 13 Brown St ⓣ207/772-7891. Rock venue featuring mostly local indie acts.

Sisters 45 Danforth St ⓣ207/774-1505. Lively lesbian dance club.

Freeport

Sixteen miles north of Portland along the coast, **FREEPORT** is one long outlet shopping mall, though the town was once one of Maine's primary shipbuilding centers, where huge logs were shipped from the northern pine forests to make masts for schooners; this is still evident in the wide shape of the town square at Main and Bow streets, which was created to give the gigantic logs plenty of room to swing as they were turned on their way to the mast landing. Freeport's prominence was such that it was chosen as the place where the treaty to separate Maine from Massachusetts was signed in 1820, in the **Jameson Tavern**.

The shipping industry fell into disrepair following the Civil War, but Freeport managed a big comeback fifty years later when a fishing-boot maker by the name of **Leon L. Bean** planted the seeds of what has become an unbelievably successful outdoors-wear manufacturer. L.L. Bean's store stood alone along Freeport's Main Street for decades, until the 1980s, when it was joined by countless factory outlets and Freeport developed its current character.

Sabbathday Lake Shaker Community

North of Portland off of Rte-26, at 707 Shaker Rd in **NEW GLOUCESTER**, is the Sabbathday Lake Shaker Community, the last remaining active settlement of its kind. Founded in 1783, the village is made up of seventeen buildings, all constructed in the beautifully functional fashion typical of the Shakers. Though their numbers have dwindled to a mere seven, the remaining Shaker members remain true to their simple, celibate, and religious lives; they welcome visitors to their 10am Sunday worship service. Tours of the grounds (every hour on the half, starting at 10.30am, last tour at 3.15pm; $6.50 introductory tour, $8 extended tour) take in several of the buildings, including the meeting house, where the Shaker Museum has many of the religious community's innovative furniture, textile, and farm tool designs on display (end of May to mid-Oct Mon–Sat 10am–4.30pm; ⓣ207/926-4597). It's all well worth the detour, though the Canterbury Shaker Village in New Hampshire (see p.466) is more impressive.

Arrival and information

The best way to get to Freeport is by **car** – there's no public transport, and the closest a bus comes is in Portland, from where you'll need to take a **taxi** or van the rest of the way. Try Classy Taxi (ⓣ207/865-0663 or 1-800/499-0663) or Freeport Taxi (ⓣ207/865-9494). Mermaid Transportation (ⓣ1-800/696-2463, ⓦwww.gomermaid.com) also offers **van** service to Freeport from Portland for $15 round-trip. Drop by the incredibly complete Freeport Merchants' Association (ⓣ207/865-1212 or 1-800/865-1994) on Mill Street in a restored old tower, for reams of area **information** as well as public restrooms, an ATM, and a staff of senior citizens who will provide far more assistance than you'll ever need.

Accommodation

There's no shortage of quality **B&Bs** in town, but if you're low on cash, some cheap motels line US-1 south of Freeport. (Better still, stay in Portland and make a quick trip through Freeport.) The best nearby **camping** is at the oceanside *Recompense Shores*, 134 Burnett Rd (ⓣ207/865-9307), near Casco Bay, which has one hundred well-kept and spaced sites. You can also camp along the shores of the bay at the *Flying Point Campground*, 10 Lower Flying Point Rd (ⓣ207/865-4569), which is near nature trails and the town beach.

Brewster House 180 Main St ⓣ207/865-4121 or 1-800/865-0822. B&B set in a beautifully restored Queen Anne cottage with antique furnishings. ⑥

Freeport Inn & Café 31 US-1 S ⓣ207/865-3106 or 1-800/99-VALUE. Excellent-value rooms, clean and comfortable, and a café serving hearty breakfasts all day. ⑤

Harraseeket Inn 162 Main St ⓣ207/865-9377 or 1-800/342-6423. Wonderful clapboard B&B inn with some 80 rooms and an indoor pool. ⑦

Maine Idyll Motor Court 1411 US-1 N ⓣ207/865-4201. Basic cottage quarters in woodsy area a few miles north of town. ③

Village Inn 186 Main St ⓣ207/865-3236 or 1-800/998-3649. Motel-style units in the rear building, breakfast in the dining room of the proprietors' home. ⑤

White Cedar Inn 178 Main St ⓣ207/865-9099 or 1-800/853-1269. Seven rooms in a pleasant Victorian home. Breakfast served in bright sunroom. ⑥

The Town

Freeport owes virtually all of its current prosperity to the invention by Leon Leonwood Bean, in 1912, of a particularly ugly rubber-soled fishing boot. The boot is still available, and **L.L. Bean's** has grown into a multinational clothing conglomerate, housed in an enormous 90,000-square-foot factory outlet building on Main Street (ⓣ1-800/441-5713 or 207/552-6879, ⓦwww.llbean.com) that literally never closes. In theory, this is so pre-dawn hunting expeditions can stock up; all the relevant equipment is available for rent or sale, and the store runs regular workshops to teach backcountry lore. However, with the outdoor look in vogue, L.L. Bean's is now more of a fashion emporium. It's worth a spin just to gawk at the four stories packed with more camping supplies and dense plaid outerwear than the eye can see; there's also a full café, a trout pond with a waterfall, and a self-congratulatory chronicle of the chain's history located just inside the main entrance. There are plenty of other **outlet stores** nearby, with chic fashion stops like Donna Karan, Brooks Brothers, and Jones NY, alongside the ones geared toward rugged outdoorsmen (Patagonia, Timberland, and North Face). The **Frost Gully Gallery**, 1159 US-1 N (Mon–Fri noon–5pm; ⓣ207/773-2555), usually has a fine display of oil paintings by both local and nationally known artists, and will provide a respite from the blatant commercialism found elsewhere in town.

Now a lone reference to the city's life before Bean, the **Soldiers and Sailors Monument**, on Bow Street, was dedicated by Civil War general Joshua Chamberlain. The monument's cannons were used at the Battle of Bull Run and on Sherman's march to the sea. To get even farther away from the shops, however, head a mile south of Freeport to the sea, where the very green cape visible just across the water is **Wolfe's Neck State Park**. In summer, for just $1, you can follow hiking and nature trails along the unspoiled fringes of the headland. For another – and rather bizarre – change of pace, check out the **Desert of Maine**, on Desert Road off I-95 exit 19 (May to mid-Oct; ⓣ207/865-6962, ⓦwww.desertofmaine.com; $7), a vast expanse of privately owned sand deposited just inland from Freeport by a glacier that slid through eight thousand years ago. The result was a tiny, self-contained desert ecosystem that engulfed the surrounding homes and trees, which you can still see half-buried in sand. There's a kitschy gift shop for souvenirs, a display of little test tubes of sand from locations all over the world, and a small museum housed in a 1783 barn.

Eating and drinking

Restaurants in the area cater to the upscale crowd that seeks out the outlets. They're all done up to match the town's strict aesthetic zoning laws; even the *McDonald's* is disguised by a weathered-clapboard motif.

Broad Arrow Tavern 162 Main St, in the *Harraseeket Inn* ⓣ207/865-9377. Traditional Maine food prepared over wood-fired oven and grill in a faux hunting lodge.

China Rose 23 Main St ⓣ207/865-6886. Reputed to be some of Maine's best Szechuan and Hunan cuisine. Also has a surprisingly good sushi bar.

Gritty McDuff's Brewpub 187 Lower Main St ⓣ207/865-4321. Standard bar food with a fine selection of local microbrews, including many made on the premises. Seasonal outdoor dining.

Harraseeket Lunch & Lobster Co off Rte-1, South Freeport ⓣ207/865-4888. Extending on its wooden jetty into the peaceful bay, this makes a great outdoor lunch spot.

Isabella's Sticky Buns Bakery Café 2 School St ⓣ207/865-6635. Breakfast, coffee, and sandwiches; open from 6am.

Jameson Tavern 115 Main St ⓣ207/865-4196. Excellent traditional American fare in a historic setting – this is where the papers were signed that separated Maine from Massachusetts. Meat-oriented menu highlighted by steak au poivre. Wash it down with the house brew, Jameson's Black and Tan. The taproom menu has lighter, less expensive fare.

Lobster Cooker 39 Main St ⓣ207/865-4349. A particularly good roadside seafood shack specializing in lobster and crabmeat rolls.

The Mid-Coast

Stretching roughly from the quiet college town of **Brunswick** up to blue-collar **Bucksport**, Maine's central coast is a study in geographic, economic, and cultural contrasts. The shore here is physically different from the southern coast, prone to dangling peninsulas such as the **Harpswells** and **Pemaquid Point** where you can diverge from well-traveled US-1, which traverses the jagged coastline. Much of this region prospered in the late nineteenth century as a major shipbuilding and trading center, as evidenced by its wealth of attrac-

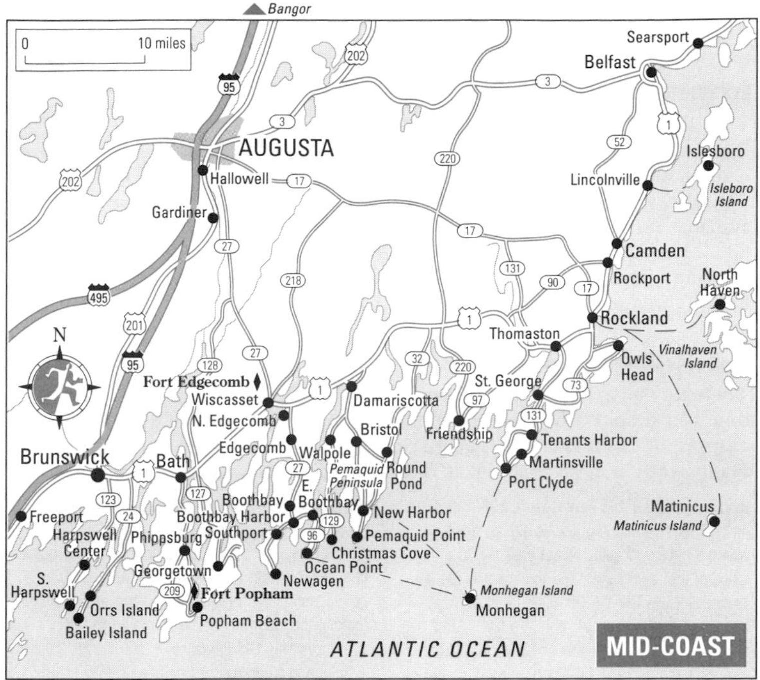

tive old captains' homes; today, only **Bath** remains as a ship manufacturer. Throughout, the focus is still unquestionably the sea, be it for livelihood, nourishment, or entertainment. Consequently, one of the best ways to see the area is by boat; from most coastal towns, you can catch a scenic boat tour. Indeed, remote **Monhegan Island**, somewhat of an artists' retreat eleven miles offshore near New Harbor, is only accessible by boat.

Lobsters are a way of life in Maine, and the state's largest producer of the ugly crustaceans is **Rockland**, which is also home to the Farnsworth Museum. Busy **Camden**, just beyond Rockland, is known for its fleet of recreational **windjammers** and as the New England headquarters of MBNA Bank. Picturesque fishing villages such as **Round Pond** and **Tenants Harbor** – tiny windows into the real Maine – can be found throughout, somehow managing to coexist with overrun summer tourist resorts like **Boothbay Harbor**, which is all but deserted in the winter. In the face of dwindling industry, it's hard to say what might happen to these smaller settlements, though sadly many have already reluctantly begun to promote tourism.

Brunswick and the Harpswells

Only a few miles farther on from Freeport is **BRUNSWICK**, home since 1794 of the private, well-respected Bowdoin College (Ⓦwww.bowdoin.edu). The town is attractive enough, with a concentration of old brick and clapboard homes and buildings, but apart from the small campus itself – at the south end of Maine Street – and a couple of unobtrusive cafés, there's little evidence of student life here.

Information and getting around

The Bath–Brunswick **Chamber of Commerce** at 59 Pleasant St in Brunswick (☎207/725-8797, Ⓦwww.midcoastmaine.com) is particularly helpful, with a typical array of brochures and a knowledgeable staff.

Public transport to and from Brunswick is infrequent but nevertheless available. Vermont Transit/Greyhound stops at the depot at 9 Pleasant St (☎1-800/231-2222), from where you can catch **buses** to most other parts of New England. Concord Trailways (☎1-800/639-3317) stops at 162 Pleasant St before continuing north to Searsport or south to Boston.

Accommodation

There isn't an abundance of **places to stay** in Brunswick, though most of the time you shouldn't have trouble finding a good-value room. The best place to **camp** is at the *Orrs Island Campground*, on the island of the same name in the **Harpswells** along Rte-24 (☎207/833-5595; end May to mid-Sept).

Brunswick B&B 165 Park Row ☎207/729-4914 or 1-800/299-7914. A gracious old inn decorated with antiques and quilts within easy walking distance of the town center and the college. 5–6

Tower Hill Inn Rte-24, Orr's Island ☎207/833-2311 or 1-888/833-2311. Set on a tiny island accessible via a bridge, this small inn has three attractive rooms, with American, European, and Oriental furnishings. 6–7

Harpswell Inn 108 Lookout Point, Harpswell ☎207/833-5509 or reserve at 1-800/843-5509. An exceedingly comfortable place, the white home with black shutters hosts nine rooms and three suites, and is centered on a pleasant green, overlooking the lobster boats in the cove. 5–6

Travelers Inn 130 Pleasant St ☎207/729-3364. A quiet and clean no-frills hotel half a mile from the town center. 4

The Town

Free tours of **Bowdoin College**, which counts among its alumni Henry Wadsworth Longfellow, Nathaniel Hawthorne, and Franklin Pierce (see p.471), begin at the Moulton Union (Mon–Fri at 9am, 11am, 2pm & 4pm; ☎207/725-3000) and take in the intriguing **Peary-MacMillan Arctic Museum** (Tues–Sat 10am–5pm, Sun 2–5pm; ☎207/725-3416; free). After decades of disagreement, experts now generally conclude that former student Admiral Robert Peary was the first man to reach the North Pole in 1909; whatever the truth, his assembled equipment and notebooks hold a powerful fascination.

Another distinguished alum of the college, Civil War hero General Joshua Chamberlain, graduated in 1852 and became a professor at the school in 1855. With no military training, he volunteered to serve in the Civil War at its onset, and would go on to fight in 24 battles, win the Congressional Medal of Honor, and, at the end of the war, be selected by Ulysses S. Grant to accept the formal surrender of the Confederate troops. He later went on to become governor of Maine and, in 1871, president of Bowdoin College. Chamberlain's varied career is documented at the **General Joshua L. Chamberlain Civil War Museum**, 226 Maine St (June–Sept Tues–Fri 10am–3pm; $5; ☎207/729-6606). Tours of his restored home begin twice each hour.

The **Bowdoin College Museum of Art**, in the Walker Art Building (Tues–Sat 10am–5pm, Sun 2–5pm; free; ☎207/725-3275), designed by noted

Harriet Beecher Stowe

Harriet Beecher Stowe (1811–1896), a native of Litchfield, Connecticut, moved to Brunswick with her family from Ohio in the summer of 1850 when her husband, Calvin, took a position as a professor of religion at Bowdoin College. While her family struggled financially, it was here that Stowe formulated and wrote *Uncle Tom's Cabin*, the emotional anti-slavery novel that would go on to sell millions of copies all over the world. The book is credited with bringing morality and respectability to the abolitionist cause, and when Abraham Lincoln met Stowe several years later he reportedly remarked, "So you're the little lady who wrote the book that started the war."

It is said that Stowe conceived of the death of Uncle Tom while sitting at worship in Brunswick's historic **First Parish Church**, 223 Maine St (☎207/729-7331), and then proceeded to write the entire story in a fiery passion in just a few weeks. The passage of the 1850 Fugitive Slave Act, which stipulated that it was illegal for any citizen to assist an escaped slave and demanded that escaped slaves be apprehended and deported back to the "rightful" owner, further outraged Stowe, who, encouraged by her husband, published her violent story serially in the *National Era*, an abolitionist weekly. The **Harriet Beecher Stowe House** at 63 Federal St is now privately owned.

architect Charles McKim, is also worth a look. There's a Winslow Homer Gallery filled with etchings, engravings, and other memorabilia from the one-time Maine resident, in addition to works by Gilbert Stuart, old Flemish masters, and more modern paintings and sculptures by the likes of Mary Cassatt, Andrew Wyeth, and Robert Rauschenberg. Other galleries house photography, ancient art, and special exhibits.

The ideal time to visit Brunswick is Labor Day weekend, in early September, when the town hosts a **Bluegrass Festival** (☎207/725-6009) out on Thomas Point Beach, reached by following Rte-24 from Cook's Corner.

The Harpswells

South of Brunswick, the narrow, forested peninsulas collectively known as the **Harpswells** make for a welcome escape from the bustle of US-1. The only problem is that once you get to the end of one of the thrusts of land, you have to turn right back around and retrace your tracks. Rte-123 weaves down the Harpswell Neck past Maine's **oldest meeting house** (1757) in Harpswell Center, and clear down to South Harpswell, where the Basin Cove Falls, created by the tidal flows, are popular with canoeists and kayakers. Rte-24 heads down another long, finger-like strip to **Bailey Island** (one of Casco Bay Cruise Line's stops), first crossing Orrs Island and then the **Cobwork Bridge**, which allows tides to flow right through it. Bailey Island's highlight is the **Giant Staircase**, off of Rte-24 on the eastern shore of the island, a massive waterfront stone stairway that's fun to explore and traverse. On Orrs Island, you can rent **kayaks** from H2Outfitters (☎207/833-5257 or 1-800/20-KAYAK); they also provide instruction and lead day and multi-day trips.

Eating and drinking

Bohemian Coffee Company 111 Maine St ☎207/725-9095. Brunswick's hip crowd hangs at this pleasant sidewalk café.

Bombay Mahal 99 Maine St ☎207/729-5260. Inexpensive Indian specialties, such as a good chicken curry for $8.45.

Cook's Lobster House Garrison Cove Road, Rte-24, Bailey Island ☎207/833-2818. They've been dishing out deliciously fresh lobster, shrimp, scallops, and shellfish on their outdoor decks since 1955 – be warned that it can get busy when the Casco Bay Lines cruiser dumps passengers off in summer.

Dolphin Marine 515 Basin Point Rd, South Harpswell ☎207/833-6000. A tiny, almost hidden, restaurant that serves up reasonably priced and simple yet robust seafood meals overlooking the ocean – don't miss the fish chowder.

Kitchen 4 Pleasant St ☎207/729-5526. Cheap calzones, sandwiches, soups, and other flavorful dinners in a cafeteria-type dining room.

Richard's 115 Maine St ☎207/729-9673. Tasty, good-value German and American cuisine. The German entreés are available in two sizes, the larger of which is huge; you can also get your favorite wursts by the pound.

Star Fish Grill 100B Pleasant St ☎207/725-7828. Relatively new restaurant – and easily Brunswick's best – with a catch of fresh local seafood, fresh produce, and vegetarian dishes served in an informal yet sophisticated atmosphere.

Bath

Approaching the small, community-minded town of **BATH** on US-1, it's hard to miss the rather enormous and industrial-looking supply cranes, tools of the massive **Bath Iron Works** shipyard, that hulk rigidly towards the sky along the Kennebeck River. In fact, the town of Bath has an exceptionally long history of **shipbuilding**; the first vessel to be constructed and launched here was the *Virginia* in 1607, by Sir George Popham's short-lived colony, just south of Bath in Phippsburg. Shipbuilding continued to be a major industry in the region throughout the eighteenth century, and between 1800 and 1830, some 288 ships set sail out of Bath's port. Bath Iron Works, founded in 1833, attracted job-seeking Irishmen in such numbers as to provoke a mob of anti-immigrant "Know Nothings" to burn down the local Catholic church in July 1854. Smaller trading vessels gave way to larger ships and in 1841, Clark & Sewall, one of the major builders at the time, launched the *Rappahannock*, then the largest ship in the world at 1133 tons. Despite changes in the shipbuilding market, Bath's military contracts were never in short supply, and during World War II, more destroyers were built here than in all Japan.

Accommodation

Bath is not short on good-value **accommodations**, mostly of the inexpensive bed and breakfast variety. There's **camping** south of town along the water in Perry Cove at the *Meadowbrook Camping Area*, Meadowbrook Road (May–Sept; ☎1-800/370-2267) and at Thomas Point Beach at 29 Meadow Rd (May–Sept; ☎1-877/872-4321) on the protected Thomas Bay. Two more campgrounds lurk farther south along the Phippsburg Peninsula: *Hermit Island* at the end of Rte-216 (late June to mid-Oct; ☎207/443-2101), where you can rent small boats and camp near a white-sand beach, and *Ocean View Park*, near Popham Beach (mid-May to Sept; ☎207/389-2564).

Benjamin F. Packard House 45 Pearl St ☎207/443-6069 or 1-800/516-4578. The period-furnished rooms in this 1790 Georgian house are a very good deal; full breakfast included. ❺

Fairhaven Inn on North Bath Road ☎207/433-4391 or 1-888/443-4391. You'll find a bit of rural flavor here – hiking and cross-country skiing trails are right nearby – plus a fine breakfast. ❺

Galen C Moses House 1009 Washington St ☎207/442-8771. A colorful restored mansion whose proprietors are almost as eccentric as the decorations; a delicious gourmet breakfast is included. ❻

Glad II 60 Pearl St ⓣ207/443-1191. Small B&B very close to the museum. ❹

Inn at Bath 969 Washington St ⓣ207/443-4294, ⓦwww.innatbath.com. An 1810 Greek Revival house, with friendly service and tastefully decorated rooms. ❼

Small Point B&B 312 Small Point Rd, Rte-216, Phippsburg ⓣ207/389-1716. A restored 1890s farmhouse in an isolated coastal location, this B&B offers good value and wonderful morning repasts.

The Town

With more than seven thousand employees, **Bath Iron Works**, two miles south of the town center, is the largest private employer in the state – and, thanks to a continuous stream of government contracts, the only shipbuilder remaining in Bath. As the place churns out massive destroyers and cruisers, shift workers keep the factory running around the clock; you should take care to avoid driving anywhere in Bath around 3.30pm, when shifts change and the town's roads come to a halt. The works are only open to visitors for special occasions such as ceremonial launchings – grand affairs that take place twice yearly and feature speeches by senators and the like. However, at the **Maine Maritime Museum**, 243 Washington St, next to the Iron Works (daily 9.30am–5pm; $9.25; ⓣ207/443-1316, ⓦwww.bathmaine.com), you can tour the old Percy & Small shipyard, check out the mildly intriguing lobstering exhibit, explore several visiting historic vessels, or browse the Maritime History Building, where galleries house an interesting range of ship-related paintings, models, photographs, and artifacts. The museum also runs **boat trips** along the Kennebeck River (for an extra $10; call for schedules). To fully enjoy the museum, take advantage of the detailed one-hour guided **tours** of the shipyard that are offered in the summer.

Walking tours of another sort, led by enthusiastic town historians, begin at the Winter Street Church, across from the 1847 **Chocolate Church**, 804 Washington St – named for its unfortunate dull grey-brown paint job, and now an arts center housing a theater and gallery – and lead up and down Bath's streets, highlighting examples of Georgian, Federal, Italianate, and Gothic Revival architecture. If you'd rather not cough up the dough for a live tour guide from Sagadahoc Preservation Incorporated ($10; ⓣ207/443-2174), you can pick up one of several exhaustive brochures at the church that annotate various routes.

A pretty fourteen-mile drive south along Rte-209 leads to the inviting crescent-shaped **Popham Beach** ($2; ⓣ207/389-1335), at the end of the

AMC huts on Georgetown Island

The **Appalachian Mountain Club** (general information ⓣ617/523-0636, reservations 207/547-4477, ⓦwww.outdoors.org) maintains a couple of excellent low-budget **accommodations** on Georgetown Island. At the *Knubble Bay Camp*, a friendly riverfront cottage with a nice porch and a kitchen (open all year; $90 per two-day weekend, $135 per three-day weekend, $45 per weekday, discount for members), there's bunk space for twelve as well as tent sites. The site is accessible by car and parking is available ($1 per day). You can also rent canoes for $15 per day. A much more primitive option is the secluded wilderness campground at Beal Island (closed in winter; $8 per night), which is only accessible by canoe or kayak from the cottage.

Phippsburg Peninsula, and part of a 529-acre state park. Outside of its scenic sands, there's **Fort Popham**, a nineteenth-century granite fort, with some nicely situated picnic benches that face the ocean and a marker that locates the **Popham Colony** site, where the first attempt at English settlement of the northeast coast was made in 1607. You can catch a **boat ride** at the Sebasco Harbor Resort, at the end of Rte-217 (☎207/389-1161), where the *Ruth* cruises the Casco Bay during the summer ($8).

The **Georgetown Peninsula**, just east from Bath and down Rte-127, contains another superior beach at **Reid State Park** (☎207/371-2303), where the dunes flatten out into 1.5 miles of beautiful sandy seashore.

Eating and drinking

The majority of Bath's **restaurants** are hearty no-nonsense grub-holes that cater to off-duty BIW employees.

Beale Street Barbeque and Grill 215 Water St ☎207/442-9514. Slightly more upscale than most in-town restaurants, with hickory-smoked Memphis barbecue plates in an airy, modern dining room. Takeout available.

The Cabin 552 Washington St ☎207/443-6224. Near the museum, the *Cabin* dishes out thick, cheesy pizzas ($6 or $8) in dark, wooden booths.

Five Islands Lobster Company Rte-127, on the wharf in Five Islands ☎207/371-2990. A good, casual lobster pound, where you're encouraged to get messy while eating.

Front Street Deli 128 Front St ☎207/443-9815. Beer on tap and sixteen different varieties of "Destroyers" (sandwiches), each named for a US battleship.

Kennebec Tavern 119 Commercial St ☎207/442-9636. A huge selection of seafood, at a tavern pretty much right on the water.

Kristina's 160 Centre St ☎207/442-8577. Inventive American dishes and great homemade breads and desserts.

Robinhood Free Meetinghouse Robinhood Road, Georgetown, south of Bath along Rte-127 ☎207/371-2188. This is one of Maine's premier restaurants, and well worth the detour. Housed in Georgetown's former town hall, the creative American bistro integrates interesting touches of Cajun, Italian, Szechuan, and German cuisine into its many entreés, all of which cost over $20.

Wiscasset

WISCASSET, ten miles on from Bath, is dominated by the bridge which carries US-1 over the Sheepscot River – and in the summer, the gently arching span is itself dominated by slow-moving cars usually headed to or from the coast farther north. Tourism, though, is catching on here, perhaps partially on account of Wiscasset's easily accessible town center, right where the bridge meets the river's west bank. In fact, the town lumberyard, grocery, and newsstand have all been replaced by antique shops and art galleries to welcome visitors (changes that have been very unwelcome to locals). Further removal of the town's character occurred in 1997, when two famous **shipwrecks**, the four-masted schooners *Luther Little* and the *Hesper*, which sat in the shallow waters of its narrow and picturesque bay for more than sixty years were carted away – rotted beyond recognition.

The Town

Like many of Maine's coastal towns, Wiscasset prospered in the late eighteenth century as a shipbuilding and lumbering center. The large homes and mansions of wealthy shipping merchants and lumber barons still stand in the town's

historic district, situated near US-1 and the waterfront, the best example of which is the towering white Federal-style **Nickels-Sortwell House** on US-1 (Main Street) at Federal Street in the center of town (June to mid-Oct Wed–Sun 11am–4pm; $4). Commissioned by shipmaster William Nickels in 1807 (he lost his fortune only a few years later due to the devastating effect of the Embargo Act of 1807 and the War of 1812), the house features fine woodwork throughout and a restored garden. Hourly historical tours lead through the period furnished rooms and up the handsomely curved, three-floor stairway.

The **Musical Wonder House**, 18 High St (June–Oct daily 10am–5pm; $1; Ⓦwww.musicalwonderhouse.com), is proof that if you amass enough of an obsolete technology, the collection will someday hold a mysterious fascination. This 1852 sea captain's mansion is stuffed with player pianos, phonographs, and antique music boxes, most still in working order, and the eccentric owner of the place takes particular delight in showing off his bizarre treasures. Daily listening tours are separated into two parts following a roughly chronological order ($8 for one half or $15 for both); one half is enough.

A couple of blocks off the main drag, the **Maine Art Gallery**, housed in an old schoolhouse building on Warren Street (mid-May to Oct Tues–Sat 10am–4pm, Sun 1–4pm; free; Ⓣ207/882-7511), exhibits – and sells – the works of up-and-coming Maine artists.

Practicalities

Accommodation possibilities in the area include the comfortable and modern *Wiscasset Motor Lodge* (April–Nov only; Ⓣ1-800/732-8168; ❸), around three miles south at 596 Bath Rd (US-1), and the *Sheepscot River Inn* (Ⓣ207/882-6343 or 1-800/437-5503; ❺), which offers rooms and cottages on Wiscasset Harbor. The *Cod Cove Inn* on Rte-1 (Ⓣ1-800/882-9586; ❻) is a bit more upmarket, with balconies, views of the sea, cable television, and phones. The good-value *Marston House*, on Main Street (Ⓣ207/882-6010; May–Oct; ❺), has homely rooms and a tasty light breakfast. The lakeside **campground** *Downeast Family Camping*, at Gardiner Pond, four miles north on Rte-27 (Ⓣ207/882-5431 or 1-877/213-5431; Memorial Day–Columbus Day), features an impressive cathedral stand of Norway pines.

For **food**, head to *Sarah's Café* on US-1 (Water Street) in the center of town (Ⓣ207/882-7504), where you can get pizzas, salads, sandwiches, pasta, and even some Mexican dishes at the right price. Just across the street, *Treats* (Ⓣ207/882-6192) has a great selection of gourmet baked and picnic goods, including sandwiches, fresh breads, imported cheeses, pastries, a huge wine selection, and good fresh coffee. For the best view in town, try *Le Garage*, on Water Street (Ⓣ207/882-5409), where seafood, steak, and vegetarian entrées ($8–18) are served in the glassed-in porch.

Boothbay Harbor

Due south from Wiscasset on Rte-27, the seaside town of **BOOTHBAY HARBOR** is for no obvious reason one of Maine's most crowded resorts. Much of the town's history as a prosperous fishing and shipbuilding center has been obscured by tourism, which has been an active pursuit here since the late nineteenth century, resulting in a wealth of predictable shops and restaurants. Nevertheless, the village is beautifully situated on a well-protected harbor, and has a lively town center, some good inns, and ample opportunities to explore the sea and surrounding coast. For a more genuine Maine experience, however, you might fare better in the less popular neighboring Pemaquid Peninsula (see p.550) or even the Blue Hill Peninsula (see p.563), closer to Bar Harbor.

Arrival, information, and getting around

Less than fifteen miles south of US-1 along Rte-27, several towns near the end of the Boothbay Peninsula share similar names, the most active of which, Boothbay Harbor, is crowded into a tiny strip of land on the western edge, along **Commercial Street** and Townsend Avenue. The rest of the settlement spreads out around a tiny cove, thinning into quaint residential neighborhoods southwest on Southport Island and southeast towards Ocean Point. Oak and Commercial streets are one-way headed west, while Townsend is one-way east, heading back to Rte-27.

The town is not easily reached via **public transport**; Concord Trailways stops in Wiscasset twice daily, from where you can catch a taxi; call Boothbay Stage Line at ⓣ207/633-7380 for information. The *Rocktide Inn* and *Cap'n Fish's* both run **courtesy trolleys** from the Boothbay Harbor Region Chamber of Commerce to various points in the town during summer days until 5pm. The chamber, just north of town on Rte-27 (ⓣ207/633-2353), is a very good source of **information**, with binders on local accommodations and a reservation service. The Boothbay Harbor Memorial Library, 4 Oak St (ⓣ207/633-3112), has free **Internet access**.

Though it's quite likely you'll have arrived by car, Boothbay Harbor is definitely not well designed for auto travel and is best explored **on foot**. The town's windy, narrow, and confusing streets are packed with cars all summer long and **parking** can be a nightmare. It's a good idea to park farther out – say along West, Howard, or Sea streets – or take the shuttle into town from the information center on Rte-27.

Accommodation

You can always find some sort of **place to stay** in Boothbay Harbor, but if you want a shorefront room in the summer, plan to call ahead at least a month in advance. In addition to several large, undistinguished resort-style motels, complete with all the modern conveniences, there are lots of smaller bed and breakfasts in the town center and on the eastern shore of the harbor. Prices are considerably lower at the beginning and end of the tourist season – early June and September – and many places close down completely by mid-October.

Anchor Watch B&B 9 Eames Rd ⓣ207/633-7565, ⓦwww.anchorwatch.com. Pamper yourself in this beautiful little B&B on a quiet peninsula just outside of the town center. ❼

Captain Sawyer's Place 55 Commercial St ⓣ207/633-2290. The rooms are not huge and the view is partially obscured, but the price is cheaper than most of the other places on the strip. Continental breakfast included. ❹

Linekin Bay B&B 531 Ocean Point Rd/Rte-96, East Boothbay ⓣ207/633-9900. Cozy and romantic 1870s-era home overlooking Linekin Bay, though only two of the rooms have ocean views. Open all year. ❺

Topside Inn 60 McKown St ⓣ207/633-5404. Pleasant rooms in an old sea captain's house on the top of a hill, giving you a great view of the harbor. Open May to mid-Oct. ❺

Sur la Mer Inn 18 Eames Rd ⓣ207/633-7400 or 1-800/791-2026. Upscale, spacious accommodations with the best ocean view in town (and a hot tub) at the end of a quiet, dead-end street. Enjoy the breakfast buffet (eggs, Danish, smoked salmon, fresh fruit) on the huge porch. ❹–❾

Welch House 56 McKown St ⓣ1-800/279-7313, ⓦwww.welchhouse.com. This gabled white-clapboard house perched on a hill affords excellent views from its rooftop deck. Light and airy guest rooms are tastefully furnished and a buffet breakfast is included. ❻

The Town

Aside from taking a quick stroll around the town's hilly, shop-lined streets, Boothbay Harbor's main attraction lies in the inordinate number of **boat trips** on offer from the harbor behind Commercial Street. Some depart for Monhegan Island (see p.552), while others circle along the rocky coast, taking in the dramatic scenery from the water. Balmy Days Cruises (Ⓣ207/633-2284 or 1-800/298-2284) is as good as any of the outfits on the waterfront, with all-day trips to Monhegan Island costing $30 and harbor tours for $9. A cruise aboard the traditional windjammer *Appledore V*, departing from the wharf four times daily (May–Oct; 2hr round-trip; Ⓣ207/633-6598), costs $22. In general, smaller boats depart from Ocean Point; try Captain Roger Marin's 40ft sailboat (Ⓣ207/882-1020). If you'd rather explore the coast under your own power, contact the Tidal Transit Company (Ⓣ207/633-7140), which offers **kayak** rentals ($12 per hour) and tours ($30) and also rents **bikes** ($20 per day).

On foot, the most immediate view of the harbor is from the 1000-foot-long wooden **footbridge** that connects downtown to the east side of town. If you venture all the way across, head south along Atlantic Avenue to the well-lighted and highly visible **Our Lady Queen of Peace** church, which has a lobster trap next to the altar and some fine architectural details. Unless you're on the move with small children, skip the rather unimpressive state-run **Marine Resources Aquarium** on McKown Point Road in West Boothbay Harbor (June–Sept daily 10am–5pm; $3; Ⓣ207/633-9542), which houses a touch tank in addition to a small number of other displays.

Ocean Point and Southport Island

There's plenty of less crowded land to explore in the area surrounding the busy town. At the end of the pretty fifteen-minute drive south along Rte-96 to desolate **Ocean Point**, you are rewarded with views of the horizon across the open ocean, interrupted only by Squirrel Island, a sparsely populated fishing village, Fisherman Island to the south, and Ram Island, with its prominent lighthouse. A few miles north on the same peninsula, the **Linekin Preserve** maintains a few miles of **hiking** trails on nearly a hundred acres of wilderness between Rte-96 and the coast.

On relatively deserted **Southport Island**, south on Rte-27, you can drive all the way down to Newagen, affording views of the Cuckolds Lighthouse, a half-mile out to sea. Along the western side of the island, the keepers of **Hendrick's Head Light** (now privately owned and visible only from the water) once adopted the only survivor of a terrible shipwreck – a tiny baby girl that they found floating in the debris, tucked away inside a feather-lined box.

Eating and drinking

For all the big tourist money that comes into Boothbay Harbor every summer, the culinary scene is surprisingly drab. While standard gourmet meals are available at several of the smaller inns, prices are often prohibitively high. Your best bet probably is to head to one of a handful of **lobster pounds** on the outskirts of town. Many restaurants close between October and May.

Blue Moon Café 54 Commercial St Ⓣ207/633-2349. Of the places right on the water, this is probably the least expensive; better still, it serves a variety of delicious hot and cold sandwiches, including veggie specials. There's indoor and outdoor seating, and it's open for breakfast and lunch.

Brud's 13 Atlantic St (no phone). As famous as a hot-dog stand can be in these parts, operated by the same man for more than fifty years.

Ebb Tide 43 Commercial St Ⓣ207/633-5692.

Cheap, greasy breakfasts are served all day at this plain blue-collar joint right in the center of town. Dinners are cheap and greasy, too.
Lobsterman's Co-op 97 Atlantic Ave ⓣ207/633-4900. Working lobster pound that dishes up ultra-fresh lobsters at minimal prices, as well as a range of sandwiches.
MacNab's Tea Room Back River Road ⓣ207/633-7222. A nice alternative in these parts: scones and scone sandwiches, salad, soup, and a wide assortment of teas (formal teas by reservation). Tues–Sat.
P&P Pastry Shop 10 McKown St ⓣ207/633-6511. Tempting sweets doled out from a little pink house.
Robinson's Wharf Rte-27, Southport Island ⓣ207/633-3830. Lots of indoor and outdoor seating at this lobster pound, where you can pick out your very own lobster. In addition to fresh seafood, they serve burgers, sandwiches, and blueberry pie.
Spruce Point Inn Atlantic Avenue ⓣ207/633-4152 or 1-800/553-0289. Boothbay's finest formal dinner spot, with New American fare such as chicken with tropical salsa, shrimp amaretto, and lobster spring rolls. There's a great view of the water, too, but it all comes with a price: entrées go for $15–25. Reservations recommended.

Damariscotta and the Pemaquid Peninsula

The compact town of **DAMARISCOTTA**, just off US-1 across the Damariscotta River from neighboring Newcastle, does not have any sights worth noting, although its Main Street is a good place to stop for lunch or a stroll.

From town, River Road leads south to **Dodge Point**, where you can **hike** along several miles of trails or hang out on the sandy **beach** along the Damariscotta River in summer. It's also a popular spot for **fishing**, where anglers fish for striped bass, bluefish, and mackerel. You can dig for clams in the offshore tidal flats – contact the Newcastle Town Office (ⓣ207/563-3441) for rules and regulations.

Damariscotta is a pleasant place to stay while exploring the rest of the Pemaquid Peninsula; the best **accommodation** can be found at the *Newcastle Inn* (ⓣ1-800/832-8669; ❽-❾), on River Road in Newcastle, a spot with lots of character and fifteen unique rooms named for lighthouses; similar quality but less expensive lodgings are yours at *Flying Cloud B&B*, also on River Road (ⓣ207/563-2484; ❺), an immaculately restored 1840s sea captain's home with five guest rooms and an elegant yet homely atmosphere. You might also try the *Brannon-Bunker Inn* on Rte-129 in Walpole (ⓣ207/563-5941 or 1-800/563-9225; ❹), where the owner is a bit obsessed with World War I.

The *Salt Bay Café*, on Main Street (ⓣ207/563-1666), is a local **restaurant** favorite, with simple but fresh seafood, soups, sandwiches, and steaks. On US-1 east of town in **Waldoboro**, *Moody's Diner* (ⓣ207/832-7785) is a long-standing haunt of police and truckers – open 24hrs and oozing nostalgia – that offers a typical selection of burgers and fries.

The Pemaquid Peninsula

Meaning "long finger" in the native language, the **Pemaquid Peninsula** points some fifteen miles south of US-1 along routes 129 and 130, culminating in the rocky **Pemaquid Point**. Controversial archeological studies have made as yet unsubstantiated claims that the first European settlers touched down here before they landed at Plymouth. A small state-run museum on the site of the would-be settlement, **Colonial Pemaquid**, just west of New

Harbor off of Rte-130 (late May to early Sept daily 9am–5pm; $2), houses ancient pottery, farming tools, and other household items. Over the years, ongoing excavation has also unearthed stone walls and foundations dating back to the seventeenth century. Within the eight-acre historical site stands a 1908 replica of **Fort William Henry**, the original built in 1677 by English settlers to ward off pirates, the French, and Indians, who are believed to have inhabited the peninsula as early as two thousand years ago. Though the robust fortress was thought to be rather impenetrable, it was defeated three times in the seventeenth century. There are good **ocean views** from the top of the massive stone citadel.

Nearby, the sands of **Pemaquid Beach**, just off Snowball Hill Road, are some of the most inviting in the state, and are correspondingly crowded on sunny summer weekends. Nevertheless, it's a great place to catch some rays, and even though the water can be cold, swimming is not impossible (parking $1). There's another, smaller **beach** all the way around the bend near the end of Rte-129 on Rutherford Island at **Christmas Cove**, so named by Captain John Smith after the day he discovered it.

Just north of Pemaquid Beach, from Shaw's Fish and Lobster Wharf in quaint **New Harbor**, Hardy Boat Cruises runs daily **boat trips** (9am) out to Monhegan Island for $27 round-trip, in addition to seal watches ($13), puffin watches ($18), and shorter scenic cruises ($10 and up).

South along Rte-130, at the tip of Pemaquid Point, the **Pemaquid Point Lighthouse** ($1) sits on a dramatic granite outcrop constantly battered by the violent Atlantic surf. You can wander around the small park for a good view of the salt-stained lighthouse, built in 1827 and still operational, but be careful not to get too close to the slippery rocks at the water's edge. The adjoining keeper's quarters have been transformed into the small **Fishermen's Museum** (May–Oct 10am–5pm; donation requested), containing uninspired exhibits related to the local fishing trade and, more interestingly, a map of Maine with a photo and description of each of the state's 68 lighthouses.

Another potential diversion on the Pemaquid Peninsula is the **Thompson Ice House**, Rte-129 north of South Bristol (July & Aug Mon, Wed & Fri 1–4pm). While modern refrigeration has eliminated the ice industry, this ice house was in operation for 150 years, harvesting ice from a nearby pond and

Maine lighthouses

There is probably no better place to observe **lighthouses** than on the Maine coast, where some 68 of the structures direct ships of all sizes through the varied rocky inlets and along the jutting peninsulas from Kittery up to Quoddy Head. For centuries much of Maine's economy has centered on the sea, and the lighthouses here have become symbols of this dependence (not to mention the saving grace of many a passing ship). Consequently a series of museums serves to illustrate their history and importance, none more prominent than the **Shore Village Lighthouse Museum** in Rockland (see p.555). There's even a quarterly publication, *Lighthouse Digest*, devoted to the curious structures. Some of Maine's most dramatic lighthouses include the lonely **West Quoddy Head Light** (p.577), a candy-striped beauty in Lubec; the scenic **Pemaquid Point Light** (see above), south of Damariscotta; and the **Cape Elizabeth Lighthouse** (p.535), near Portland, which was commissioned by none other than George Washington. The *Elms B&B* in Camden runs structured **lighthouse tours** of varying lengths in conjunction with one of the local boats – call ⓣ207/236-6250 or 1-800/755-3567 for more information.

shipping it to points as far as South America. Business mostly halted here in 1986, but the building, which sports ten-inch-thick sawdust-insulated walls, has been restored into a museum and working ice-harvesting facility. In the summer, you can check out a display of the tools of the defunct trade and gaze at photos depicting ice harvesters in action. In February, townspeople still gather to collect ice from a local pond using old-fashioned tools before burying the clear blocks in hay until summer, when they are sold to local fishermen.

Practicalities

Just back from the Pemaquid Lighthouse, you can enjoy reasonably priced American **food** with a fine view of the water at the small café that adjoins the Sea Gull Gift Shop (ⓣ207/677-2374). The *Anchor Inn* on Harbor Road in Round Pond (ⓣ207/529-5584) is another good bet, with crab cakes, lobster, pastas, and succulent steaks in a rustic dining room overlooking the harbor. There are also a number of traditional **lobster pounds** on the peninsula in New Harbor and Round Pond, all of which are good.

If you'd like to **stay** close to the lighthouse, the *Hotel Pemaquid*, only 100 yards away at 3098 Bristol Rd, Rte-130 (June–Oct; ⓣ207/677-2312; ④), offers Victorian furnishings in casual surroundings – some rooms share baths. Another option is the *Gosnold Arms* on Rte-32 in New Harbor (ⓣ207/677-3727; ⑤), with country furnishings and superb harbor views. Basic **campsites** are available up the road near Pemaquid Beach at the *Sherwood Forest Campsite*, on Pemaquid Trail in New Harbor (ⓣ207/677-3642 or 1-800/274-1593; $18), which has its own swimming pool.

Monhegan Island

Deliberately low-tech **MONHEGAN ISLAND**, eleven miles from the mainland, has long attracted a hardy mix of artists and fishermen. It also attracts its fair share of tourists, but for good reason: it's the most worthwhile jaunt away from the mainland along the entirety of the Maine coast. Sailor David Ingram recorded the first description of the place in 1569, calling it "a great island that was backed like a whale." Indeed, not much has changed since artist Robert Henri first came here in the early 1900s looking for tranquility and solitude – there are no banks, credit cards are not readily accepted, very few public phones are available, and there's only one public restroom ($1). Though there were already a few artists residing on the island at the time, Henri introduced the place to his students George Bellows and Rockwell Kent, which solidified the place as a genuine artist's colony. Edward Hopper also spent time painting here, and the youngest of the Wyeth family, Jamie, currently calls Monhegan his summertime home.

The small village – occupying only twenty percent of the island – huddles around the tiny harbor, protected by Manana and Smutty Nose islands. Other than a few old hotels and some good restaurants, there's not much here – even automobiles are seldom heard; just as well, because there are some seventeen miles of **hiking trails** that crisscross the eastern half of the island, leading through dense stands of fir and spruce to the headlands, 160ft above the island's eastern shore. Monhegan Associates publishes a reliable **trail map**, available at most island stores.

The **Monhegan Island Lighthouse**, on a hill overlooking the village (and a great place to watch the sunset), was erected in 1824 and automated in 1959. You can check out the **Monhegan Historical and Cultural Museum**

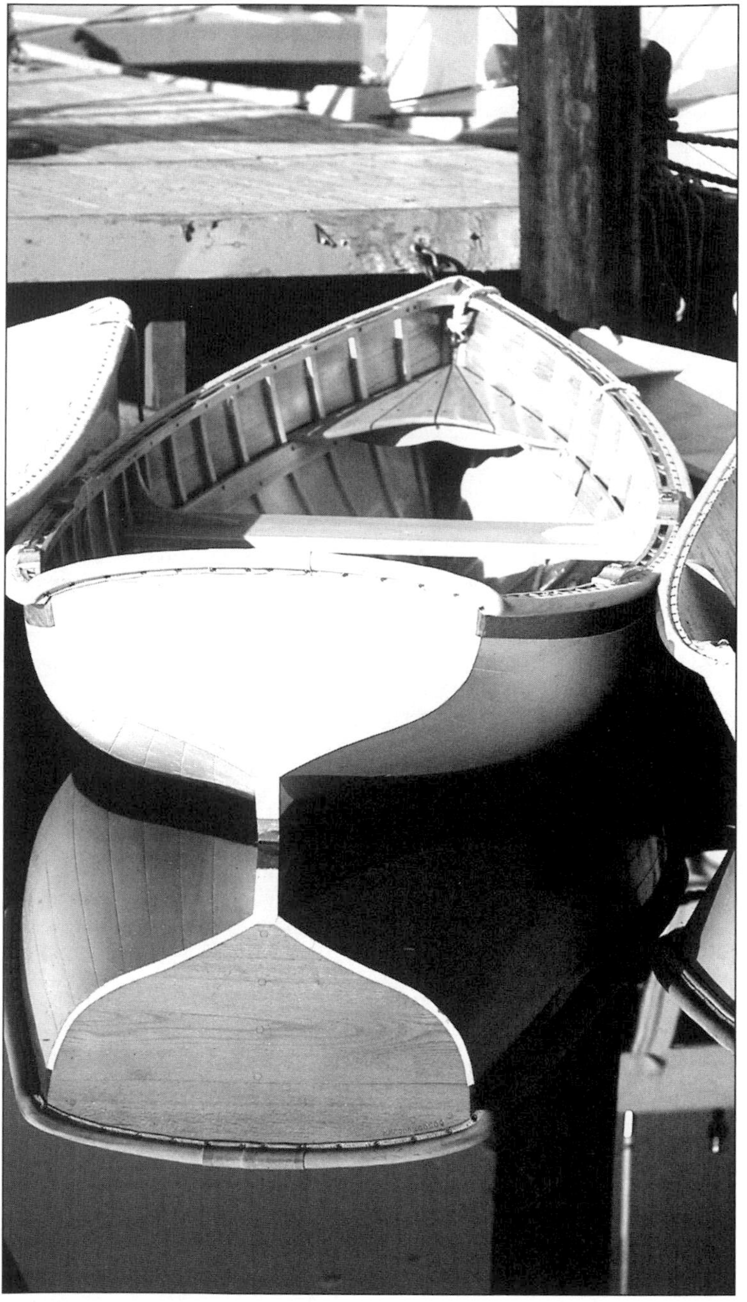

△ Rowboats, Mount Desert Island

Getting to Monhegan Island

To insure a spot with one of the three boats that connect the mainland with Monhegan Island, you should call in advance. The boats depart from Port Clyde for Monhegan three times daily during the summer and less often during the winter, arriving about an hour later, depending on which boat is in service ($16 one-way, $27 round-trip; ⓣ207/372-8848, ⓦwww.monheganboat.com). From Boothbay Harbor (see p.547) you can take the *Balmy Days III* (end of May to mid-Oct; $30 round-trip; ⓣ207/633-2284 or 1-800/298-2284, ⓦwww.balmydayscruises.com), which departs once daily at 9.30am and takes ninety minutes. The *Hardy Boat* takes 70min to get from Shaw's Wharf in New Harbor (see p.551) to Monhegan (late May & early Oct departs Wed, Sat & Sun at 9am; June–Sept daily at 9am; $27 round-trip; ⓣ207/677-2026 or 1-800/278-3346, ⓦwww.hardyboat.com).

inside the former keeper's house (July–Sept daily 11.30am–3.30pm; donation), which recently opened a new building to house the work of Monhegan artists, including a few paintings by Rockwell Kent and Jamie Wyeth. Other rooms display artifacts, photographs, and documents relating to the island's history and natural features.

In summer, some of the artists in residence on the island open their **studios** to visitors. For times and locations, check the bulletin boards around town. You can also see works by local artists at one of several **galleries** – the Lupine Gallery (ⓣ207/594-8131) at the end of Wharf Hill Road has a consistently good grouping of local works on display.

Practicalities

There's not a great deal of accommodation choice on the island, so you should plan on reserving your room well in advance of your visit. The largest place to stay is the Island Inn (May–Oct; ⓣ207/596-0371; ❼), a remodeled 1807 structure overlooking the harbor. Many of the rooms at the funky *Trailing Yew* (May–Oct; ⓣ207/596-0440; ❹), spread out among several buildings, do not have heat or electricity, while the guest accommodations at *Shining Sails B&B* (ⓣ207/596-0041, ⓦwww.shiningsails.com; ❺) are modern with private baths; some even have small decks with ocean views. The *Hitchcock House*, at the top of Horn's Hill (ⓣ207/594-8137; ❹), offers efficiencies, a cabin, and several rooms.

The island's several sit-down **restaurants** are all good, hearty, and surprisingly affordable affairs. At the *Trailing Yew* (see above), big family-style seafood dinners cost just $18 per person. The *Monhegan House Café* (ⓣ207/594-7983) is a little more formal, with a menu featuring simple meat, fish, and vegetarian dishes. You can get good pizza and sandwiches at *North End Pizza*, up the hill and to the right from the wharf (ⓣ207/594-5546). For light **snacks and coffee**, head to the *Barnacle* (late May to mid-Oct) overlooking the wharf; it houses the only espresso machine on the island and serves salads, sandwiches, and home-baked goodies. In the heart of the village, the Monhegan Store (ⓣ207/594-4126) sells groceries, alcohol, and sandwiches.

Rockland

Seaside **ROCKLAND** was once a solidly working-class factory town, not only Maine's largest distributor of lobster (which it still is), but also home to prosperous sardine canneries. However, the last of these closed down in the late 1990s, and residents have been forced to cultivate tourism to make ends meet. Clearly a city in transition, unpretentious locals have begun to accept their newfound dependence on outsiders – slowly replacing no-nonsense appliance stores with cute little gift shops.

The Town and around

The town's centerpiece is the outstanding **Farnsworth Museum**, 352 Main St (late May to mid-Oct daily 9am–5pm; rest of year Tues–Sat 10am–5pm, Sun 1–5pm; $9; ⓣ207/596-6457), established in 1935 at the bequest of reclusive spinster Lucy Farnsworth, who rather surprised the town when her will left $1.3 million to build a museum in her father's honor. Spreading over several buildings, including the **Wyeth Center**, a beautiful gallery space in a converted old church that holds two floors' worth of works by Jamie, Andrew, and N.C. Wyeth, the impressive collection spans two centuries of American art – much of it Maine-related. In fact, the highlight is the permanent "Made in Maine" exhibit, which features landscapes and seascapes by Fitz Hugh Lane, portraits by Frank Benson, familiar watercolors by Winslow Homer, and, of course, more big canvases from the Wyeths, like *Adrift* (1982) and *Airborne* (1996). The museum does not own *Christina's World*, Andrew Wyeth's most famous work (it's at the Museum of Modern Art in New York), but you can visit the field and home depicted in the painting at the **Olson House**, Hathorn Point Road, just outside of town in Cushing (late May to mid-Oct daily 11am–4pm; $3 or free with museum admission). Admission to the museum also gets you into the **Farnsworth Homestead**, tucked between museum buildings on Elm Street (late May to mid-Oct Mon–Sun 10am–5pm), a fine example of preserved Victorian opulence.

Another worthwhile museum in town, the **Shore Village Lighthouse Museum**, 104 Limerock St (June to mid-Oct daily 10am–4pm; rest of year by appointment; ⓣ207/594-0311; donation), lets you peruse one of the largest collections of lighthouse memorabilia and artifacts in the country. It's fun to press the buttons that trigger various foghorns and bells, but the real attraction is the curator, who probably knows more about lighthouses than anyone in existence. The **Owls Head Transportation Museum**, two miles south of Rockland on Rte-73 at Owls Head (April–Oct daily 10am–5pm; rest of year daily 10am–4pm; $6; ⓦwww.ohtm.org), is a similarly niche-oriented spot, with an interesting (mostly working) collection of cars, motorcycles, trains, and planes from a bygone era, including a full-scale replica of the Wright Brothers' 1903 *Flyer*.

The harbor

From Rockland's enormous **harbor**, a number of powerboats and **windjammers** compete for your business with offers of everything from leisurely morning breakfast cruises to week-long island-hopping charters. The majority set sail for three to six days at a time, costing a little more than $100 per night, including all meals. If you've got the time and money, do it. You really can't go wrong with any of the options, but a few boats to try include the 68-foot *Stephen Taber* (ⓣ207/236-3520 or 1-800/999-7352), the 92-foot *American*

Lobster

Though August is Maine's official Lobster Month, **lobsters** are everywhere in the state all year: on corny T-shirts, in countless restaurants, even on the state's license plates. Indeed, lobstering is a way of life around here and many residents in the smaller coastal towns depend on the crustaceans for their well-being. It's hard to believe, considering their status today, but lobsters were once so plentiful that they washed ashore, where they were easily collected – and even fed to servants in the seventeenth and eighteenth centuries.

Though financially and physically difficult, **lobstering** is a profession steeped in tradition and pride, with old hands staking their territory over many years. Lobsters are caught with basic traps, their ownership denoted by a series of colored bands on a floating marker, which you can see bobbing on the water's surface all up and down the Maine coast. Though some 56.7 million pounds were caught commercially in the state in 2000 (a record), there are strict laws governing the capture of lobsters – the minimum size is 3 and 3/16 inches from the eye to the end of the main body (the carapace) and the maximum length is 5 inches. It takes roughly seven years for a lobster to grow to this size, which usually translates to about 1.5 pounds. The largest lobster ever recorded, measuring 3.5ft and weighing in at an astounding 44 pounds, was caught off the coast of Nova Scotia in 1977.

When being prepared for consumption, lobsters are usually boiled, upon which their color changes from a greenish brown to the familiar bright red that you see gracing so many signs and brochures. Despite the myth, lobsters do not have vocal cords – the "screaming" noise sometimes heard while cooking is air escaping from the lobster's body cavity. Though lobsters have long been believed to contain high levels of cholesterol, the Lobster Promotion Council has been spreading word that newer studies reveal cholesterol levels on a par with chicken. Heaps of butter and mayonnaise are in fact the main culprits in a fattening lobster meal.

Unless you're enjoying it prepared in a gourmet restaurant, the task of **eating a lobster** is not a clean or easy one. The claws must be pulled off and cracked open (frequently done by hand, though there may be nutcrackers available for this purpose), the hard-shelled body and tail snapped apart, and the pale flesh dug out with fingers or tiny forks. It's acceptable – even encouraged – to suck the very last bit of the soft white meat from inside the legs and flippers. If you're having trouble getting to the meat, your waiter – or just about any other local – will be more than happy to assist you.

Festivals celebrating the crustacean are held yearly in several cities along the coast. The largest is the **Rockland Lobster Festival**, the first weekend in August, when some 50,000 people gather to eat, drink, and listen to music. Call the Chamber of Commerce (ⓣ207/596-0376) or visit ⓦwww.therealmaine.com for more information.

Eagle (ⓣ207/594-8007 or 1-800/648-4544), or the 95-foot *Heritage* (ⓣ1-800/648-4544). If you're having trouble finding what you want, stop by the Chamber of Commerce at Harbor Park, call the Maine Windjammer Association (ⓣ1-800/807-9463), or call the North End Shipyard (ⓣ1-800/648-4544). In late June, the Rockland breakwater serves as the finish line for the **Great Schooner Race**, predecessor to early July's **Schooner Days**, when the harbor fills up with a fleet of the sailing ships and the town occupies itself with live music, crafts, and lots of food.

Down the road at 517A Main St, the **Maine State Ferry Service** (ⓣ207/596-2202 or 1-800/491-4883) runs modern vessels at frequent intervals out to the summer retreats of Vinalhaven (75min; $10.50) and North Haven (1hr; $10.50), and less frequently to remote Matinicus Island, all of which make for relaxing day-trips from the mainland. For views of the harbor and the sea beyond without actually boarding a boat, head to the **Rockland Breakwater**, a manmade cement and rock structure jutting not quite a mile into the water and providing additional protection for the harbor. To get there, take Waldo Avenue south from US-1 (just past the Penobscot Bay Medical Center) to Samoset Road. Go right on Samoset and the road will dead-end into Marie Reed Park, at the base of the breakwater.

St George Peninsula

South of Rockland, the pretty **St George Peninsula**, in particular the village of Tenants Harbor, inspired writer Sarah Orne Jewett's classic Maine novel *Country of the Pointed Firs*, which gives descriptions of the landscape so deft that you can still pick out many of the sites depicted in the book. Jewett wrote much of the book in a tiny schoolhouse in Martinsville, though it's since been rebuilt. Boats sail from the hamlet of Port Clyde, at the tip of the peninsula, to **Monhegan Island** (see p.552). You may recognize Port Clyde's picturesque 1857 Marshall Point Lighthouse from the Tom Hanks movie *Forrest Gump*; there's a small historical museum in the old keeper's house.

Thomaston

The attractive little town of **THOMASTON**, straddling US-1 just west of Rockland, has the largest cement manufacturing plant in New England, but it's best known as the former home of the **State Prison**, on Main Street. The bleak facility – used for the filming of Stephen King's *The Shawshank Redemption* – was demolished in 2000, but the state maintains the store that sells various inmate-made handicrafts, mostly wood furniture (daily 9am–5pm; ⓣ207/354-2535). You might also want to check out **Montpelier**, at the junction of Rte-131 and US-1, a faithful 1926 reproduction of a huge white mansion built on the same site in 1794 by Henry Knox, Secretary of War under President George Washington (June to mid-Oct Tues–Sat 10am–4pm; $6; ⓦwww.generalknoxmuseum.org).

Practicalities

Thanks to Colgan Air you can **fly** to Rockland's Knox County Regional Airport direct from Boston for about $150 round-trip. The **bus station** is at the Maine State Ferry building, 517A Main St, just a short walk away from the **Chamber of Commerce**, at the public landing off of South Main Street (summer Mon–Fri 9am–5pm; rest of year 8am–4pm; ⓣ207/596-0376), which has comprehensive listings and information.

A good **place to stay** in the town center is the *Captain Lindsey House Inn*, 5 Lindsey St just off Main Street (ⓣ207/596-7950 or 1-800/523-2145; ❻-❼), snugly decorated with down comforters and puffy pillows, in an updated 1837 house. The *Old Granite Inn*, 546 Main St (ⓣ207/594-9036 or 1-800/386-9036, ⓦwww.midcoast.com/~ogi; ❹-❻), has clean, basic rooms right across from the ferry terminal. South of town, along the water in Tenants Harbor, the *East Wind Inn* (ⓣ207/372-6366, ⓦwww.eastwindinn.com; ❺) is a cozy old building with a huge porch and a formal dining area.

The best **food** in town can be had at funky and perennially crowded *Café Miranda*, tucked away at 15 Oak St just off Main Street (ⓣ207/594-2034); the appetizing array of international entrées ranges from saffron risotto with roasted mussels ($14.50) to Armenian lamb ($16.50). Situated at 1 Commercial St right on the harbor, *The Landings Restaurant* (ⓣ207/596-6563) has an ever-changing menu that centers on hearty portions of seafood. The atmospheric *Waterworks Pub and Restaurant*, 7 Lindsey St just off Main Street (☎207/596-2753), is half sit-down restaurant, half easygoing pub, that is deservedly popular. Another popular spot, the *Brown Bag*, 606 Main St (☎207/596-6372 or 1-800/287-6372), makes scrumptious breakfasts, freshly baked goods, and creative veggie options for lunch. *Second Read*, 328 Main St (☎207/594-4123), is a friendly place to drink **coffee**, with light lunch offerings, pastries, a broad selection of used books for sale, and occasional live music.

Camden

The adjacent communities of **Rockport** and **CAMDEN** split into two separate towns in 1891 over a dispute as to who should pay for a new bridge over the Goose River between them. Rockport was at that time a major producer of powdered limestone, manufacturing some two million casks of the stuff in the late nineteenth century, but a fire at the kilns in 1907 not only put an end to that business but also destroyed the ice houses that were the town's other main source of income. Now it's a quiet working port, among the prettiest on the Maine coast, home to numerous lobster boats, pleasure cruisers, and, other than an impressive grouping of rather wealthy-looking homes, little else. Camden, on the other hand, has clearly won the competition for tourists; indeed, it's one of the few towns in Maine that attracts visitors year-round. The place feels a bit more sophisticated than most coastal spots, thanks to the success of MBNA Bank, which set up their New England headquarters here in the late 1980s. The essential stop in town is **Camden Hills State Park**, which affords beautiful coastal views and has good camping. Camden's other highlight is its huge fleet of wind-powered schooners known as windjammers, many of which date back to the late nineteenth century, when the town was successful in the now-defunct shipbuilding trade.

Arrival and information

Camden's **information office**, down at the Public Landing (☎207/236-4404, Ⓦwww.camdenme.org), is usually a big help with finding a place to stay; they also stock a typically dizzying array of brochures. You can get free **Internet access** at the brand-new Camden Public Library, located partially underground across from Harbor Park. Published every Wednesday and available at many shops, *Steppin' Out* has comprehensive **listings** of all the goings-on in the area.

Concord Trailways' closest **bus** stop is in Rockport at the Clipper Mart on US-1. Once here, downtown is actually compact enough to be explored **on foot**. If you've got your car, know that **parking** can be a problem, but with patience you can usually find something on Chestnut Street or in the quiet residential areas just outside of town.

Accommodation

While **accommodations** in Camden are plentiful, they are not cheap; it's very difficult to find a room for less than $100. The budget spots congregate along US-1 farther north in Lincolnville. There are over a dozen B&Bs in the immediate area, but you'd still be well advised to call in advance if you plan on staying here, especially on summer weekends; Camden Accommodations runs a

reservation service (☎207/236-6090) for a fee of $15–20. Most of the hotels and B&Bs stay open all year here. Camden Hills State Park (see below) is one of the best places to **camp** along the coast (☎207/236-3109), though it's often filled.

The Belmont 6 Belmont Ave ☎207/236-8053 or 1-800/238-8053, Ⓦwww.thebelmontinn.com. Decorated with conservative elegance, this stately inn sits on a residential street just beyond the commercial district. The dining room is open to the public, serving gourmet meals in a formal atmosphere. 5–7

Camden Maine Stay Inn 22 High St ☎207/236-9636, Ⓦwww.camdenmainestay.com. Three-story white-clapboard 1813 inn, with eight inviting rooms, of which two share a bathroom. 6–7

Captain Swift Inn 72 Elm St ☎207/236-8113 or 1-800/251-0865, Ⓦwww.swiftinn.com. Four rooms in a restored 1810 house – ask for one in the rear if possible, as the traffic on US-1 (Elm Street) can be bothersome. 5–6

The Elms B&B 84 Elm St ☎207/236-6250 or 1-800/755-3567, Ⓦwww.elmsinn.net. A Colonial home on the southern end of a long strip of B&Bs along Elm Street. The rooms are cozy (you can choose and reserve your room directly from the user-friendly website), and the bubbly owners – lighthouse enthusiasts – offer a range of lighthouse tours. 5

Good Guest House 50 Elm St ☎207/236-2139. There are only two guest rooms in this pleasant home, which happens to be one of the best-value options in the center of town, with a couple of large, clean, beautifully decorated rooms. 4

Snow Hill Lodge US-1, Lincolnville ☎207/236-3452 or 1-800/476-4775. Basic, budget option north of town. 3

Swans House B&B 49 Mountain St ☎207/236-8275 or 1-800/207-8275. A beautiful little B&B that's nicely situated outside of town near the hiking trail to Mount Battie. 6

The Town and around

As in Rockland, Camden's specialty is organizing sailing expeditions of up to six days in the large schooners known as **windjammers**. Daysailers, which tour the seas just beyond the harbor for anywhere from two hours to all day, include the *Appledore* (☎207/236-8353), the *Surprise* (☎207/236-4687), and the *Olad* (☎207/236-2323). Sails on these boats cost anywhere from $25 to $80 and can often be booked on the same day – each vessel usually has an information table set up along the public landing. Longer **overnight trips**, including all meals, can cost from $350 to $900 (for six days) and should be booked in advance; the boats stop at various points of interest along the coast, such as Castine, Stonington, and Mount Desert Island. Contact the Maine Windjammer Association (☎1-800/807-9463), the Windjammer Wharf (☎1-800/999-7352), or the North End Shipyard (☎207/594-8007 or 1-800/648-4544) for information and schedules.

In the center of town, immaculately maintained **Harbor Park**, right where the whitewater of the Megunticook River spills into the sea, is a good spot to relax or have a picnic after wandering the town's small shopping district, which runs south from Main Street along the water. Farther down Bayview Street, which holds many of the shops, tiny **Laite Beach** looks out onto the Penobscot Bay.

Camden Hills State Park and Kelmscott Farm

Just north of town, US-1 leads towards **Camden Hills State Park** ($2.50 entrance fee), the best spot around for **hiking** and camping. Rather than drive, pick up the **Mount Battie Trail** (45min) that begins at the north end of Megunticook Street, a short walk from the town center. The panoramic views of the harbor and Maine coastline from the top of 790-foot Mount Battie are hard to beat; on the summit, you can climb to the top of the circular World

Edna St Vincent Millay

Edna St Vincent Millay came to Camden with her divorced mother, Cora, and two sisters in 1900, when she was eight years old. Her mother encouraged all the sisters in the arts, and Edna (she insisted on being called "Vincent") excelled in writing. As a young child, she had poems published in *St Nicholas*, a children's magazine, and by the age of twenty, she won international recognition with her poem, *Renascence*, which she first recited aloud at the *Whitehall Inn*, 52 High St (☎207/236-3391 or 1-800/789-6565). Today, the inn maintains a small collection of writings, photos, and scrapbooks that depict her playful childhood in Camden. Millay reputedly lived a rather carefree adulthood as well – an acknowledged bisexual, she had many affairs with women, and when she finally married a man, it was on quite open terms. A lifelong smoker, she died of heart failure in 1950. Her locally famous poem, *Afternoon on a Hill*, supposedly describing her wanderings in the Camden Hills, was published in 1917.

I will be the gladdest thing
Under the sun!
I will touch a hundred flowers
And not pick one,
I will look at cliffs and clouds
With quiet eyes,
Watch the wind bow down the grass
And the grass rise,
And when lights begin to show
Up from the town,
I will mark which must be mine
And then start down.

War I memorial for the best vantage point. It was here that poet Edna St Vincent Millay (see box, above) penned part of her most recognized poem, *Renascence*, which is commemorated with a small plaque. There's a variety of other trails in the area, including ones that head to the summits of **Ocean Lookout** and **Zeke's Lookout**; you can get a decent free hiking map at the ranger station in the parking lot at the park entrance just off of US-1. Farther out, on Rte-52 in Lincolnville, **Kelmscott Farm** (May–Oct Tues–Sun 10am–5pm, other months 10am–3pm; $5; ☎207/763-4088, Ⓦwww.kelmscott.org) best appeals to those with an animal sensitivity; the foundation, which houses twenty rare breeds of pigs, chickens, sheep, and the like, was established to promote animal biodiversity. There's no petting or feeding, however – the focus is more on quality education.

Eating and drinking

Camden has a satisfying array of **eating and drinking** spots – from gourmet restaurants to casual seafood joints to busy bars. One thing is for sure: on summer weekends, they're all going to be packed, so plan on waiting for a table. There's also a somewhat active **nightlife**, for Maine at least.

Camden Bagel Café 26 Mechanic St ☎207/236-2661. Popular morning spot with tables in a sunny dining area; lots of fresh bagels, coffee, sandwiches, and salads.

Camden Deli 37 Main St ☎207/236-8343. Great variety of bulging sandwiches and deli salads, right in the center of town, overlooking the harbor. They also serve beer and wine.

Cappy's Chowder House 1 Main St ☎207/236-2254. This cramped, child-friendly bar and restaurant is the place to go in town for a casual drink or meal.

Chez Michel US-1, Lincolnville Beach ☎207/789-5600. A few miles north of Camden, this unassuming seaside restaurant specializes in fine French cuisine.
Frogwater Café 31 Elm St ☎207/236-8998. A lively, informal joint with tasty renditions of steak, seafood, pasta, chicken standbys, and plenty of veggie options.
Gilbert's Publick House Bayview Street (under *Peter Ott's Steakhouse*) ☎207/236-4320. With lots of beer signs and a big-screen TV, the *Publick House* looks a little like a fraternity basement, but that doesn't stop people from filling up the dance floor to the tune of cheesy Top-40 hits and alternative rock, sometimes live (Thurs-Sat).
Lobster Pound Restaurant US-1, Lincolnville Beach ☎207/789-5550. Casual and wildly popular restaurant serving heaps of the bright-red crustaceans.
Peter Ott's Steakhouse Bayview Street ☎207/236-4032. Quality, traditional tavern fare at moderate prices with some seafood options for good measure. Fun atmosphere.
Sea Dog Brewing Co 43 Mechanic St ☎207/236-6863. The food portions are hearty, but the real treats are the handcrafted beers, brewed on-site. It gets loud on weekend nights.
Waterfront Restaurant Bay View Street ☎207/236-3747. The delicious clam chowder, fisherman's stew, and fresh seafood pastas are a bit expensive ($15–23), but you can't beat the dockside seating.
Zaddik's Pizza 20 Washington St ☎207/236-6540. Family-friendly joint that serves up the best pizza around, in addition to salads and a small selection of Mexican entrées.

Rockport

Just south of Camden, **ROCKPORT** preserves its past in the remnants of the old **lime kilns** by pleasant Marine Park, next to the harbor, which is also a good place for a picnic. The tiny town center holds a couple of decent galleries, such as the **Maine Coast Artists Gallery**, 162 Russell Ave (Tues–Sat 10am–5pm, in summer also Sun noon–5pm; $3; ☎207/236-2875), where local artists display their works, and the **Maine Photographic Workshops**, nearby at 2 Central St (☎207/236-8581), which is somewhat well known for its school of photography. Right across the street, the friendly *Corner Shop* (☎207/236-8361) serves up one of the best **breakfasts** in the area, with big and cheap omelets in a sunny dining room.

Belfast

Homely **BELFAST** feels like the most lived-in and liveable of the towns along the Maine coast. Here the shipbuilding boom is long since over (and the chicken-processing plant that regularly turned the bay blood-red has also gone), but the inhabitants have had the waterfront declared a historic district, sparing it from over-commercialization and condo development. As you stroll around, look out for the old-fashioned Western Union office (complete with jukebox) and any number of whitewashed Greek Revival houses, particularly prevalent along the wide avenues in the southern half of town between Church and Congress streets. Belfast was a lively center in the 1960s and its stores, community theater groups, festivals, and the WBYA (101.7 FM) radio station attest to its continued vibrance.

The convivial **information office** (☎207/338-2896), at the foot of Main Street by the bay, is next to the old railroad station, used by the **Belfast and Moosehead Lake Railroad** (☎207/948-5500 or 1-800/392-5500, Ⓦwww.belfastrailroad.com). Ninety-minute excursions ($15) in reconditioned Pullman cars run from here up the lush banks of the Passagassawakeag River, along tracks laid in 1870 to connect logging operations with the sea – though whatever impression you might get from their advertisements, the trains are pulled by diesel, not steam. En route to the villages of Brooks and Burnham Junction, you pass through thick forests, at their most colorful in the fall. The same company offers cruises on an old-style paddleboat in Penobscot Bay ($16); a combination ticket saves $3.

Practicalities

Up from the rail terminal, *90 Main* (ⓣ207/338-1106) is a good bet for **food**, with creative fare such as blueberry chicken with a bagel and cream cheese on the side, a full-service bakery downstairs, and live music on weekends. At 2 Fairview St, *Young's Lobster Pound* (ⓣ207/338-1160) serves up $11 fresh-boiled lobster dinners, among the best in the state, with sunset views. *Darby's*, at 105 High St (ⓣ207/338-2339), is a bit overpriced but nevertheless serves up delicious food such as pecan haddock, pad thai, and filet mignon; the adjoining **pub** specializes in Scotch whiskeys. *Rollie's Café*, back up the hill at 37 Main St (ⓣ207/338-5217), is a rough-and-ready bar open until 1am every day of the year. The *Gothic*, 4 Main St (ⓣ207/338-9901), is a nice little spot for **coffee**, ice cream, and pastries.

For **accommodation**, try the *Alden House*, 63 Church St (ⓣ207/338-2151, ⓦwww.thealdenhouse.com; ❺–❻), a beautiful 1840 Greek Revival house run as a B&B by two genial hostesses; the comfortable *Thomas Pitcher House*, 19 Franklin St (ⓣ207/338-6454 or 1-888/338-6454; ❺); or the *Jeweled Turret Inn*, 40 Pearl St (ⓣ207/338-2304 or 1-800/696-2304; ❺–❼). Along US-1 across the Passagassawakeag River in East Belfast are several inexpensive motels, including the *Gull* (ⓣ207/338-4030; ❹).

Bucksport

Named after founder Colonel Jonathan Buck, who's buried at the Bucksport Cemetery near the Verona Bridge, quiet **BUCKSPORT** was first settled as a trading post in 1762. Today, the Champion International Paper Company's enormous riverside factory dominates the town's skyline and employs a high percentage of its 4900 inhabitants. The town is trying hard to shed its workaday image to attract more visitors, but the problem is, there's not a whole lot to do here. One place worth checking out is **Northeast Historic Film**, in the restored 1916 Alamo Theater building at 379 Main St (Mon–Fri 9am–4pm; ⓣ207/469-0924, ⓦwww.oldfilm.org), which collects and screens film and video related to the heritage, culture, and history of northern New England. There's a tiny exhibit in the lobby, but the real treat is the chance to watch one of the regularly scheduled matinees.

Even if you hold no particular interest in the military, the hulking **Fort Knox**, just across the Penobscot River from Bucksport (May–Nov daily 9am–sunset; $2; ⓣ207/469-7719), still merits a wander round its castle-like structure. You can climb up and down circular stairways, stagger through countless tunnels that disappear into total darkness, investigate officers' quarters, and clamber to the top of thick granite walls, from which you can admire Bucksport's factory skyline. With all the cannon mounts – there are over 130 in all – it's hard to believe that this place never saw any action, though it was manned from 1863 to 1866 during the Civil War.

Down East Maine

So called because sailors heading east along the coast were also usually heading downwind, **Down East** Maine has engendered plenty of debate over its boundaries – some wishing to draw its western line at Ellsworth, or Belfast, or even include the entire state in their definition. It's all a matter of pride, of course; to be a downeaster means to be tough and fiercely independent – though it would be unfair to say unfriendly. For the purposes of this book at least, we've defined "Down East" as the Maine coast east of Bucksport, including the **Blue Hill Peninsula**, home to several wealthy summer towns, **Mount Desert Island**, the most visited place in the state, and the nearly deserted shoreline that stretches a hundred lonely miles between the strip mall town of Ellsworth and the point farthest east in the United States at **West Quoddy Head**.

As you make your way up the coast – particularly once you pass Mount Desert Island and **Acadia National Park** – the terrain and the population become more rugged and less prone to tourism. The weather here is also less forgiving, and the coast near the Canadian border is normally foggy for half the year.

The Blue Hill Peninsula

It used to be that the **Blue Hill Peninsula**, reaching south from Bucksport, was a sleepy expanse of land, too far off the primary roads to attract much attention. But word is slowly getting out about this beautiful area, blanketed with fields of wild blueberries and their pinkish-white flowers, and dotted with both dignified old-money towns like **Castine** and **Blue Hill** and hardcore fishing villages like **Stonington** and **Deer Isle**. Even farther off the established tourist trail, **Isle au Haut** is a remote outpost accessible only by mail boat. In the smaller towns between, you'll find close-knit communities of people who can trace their ties to the peninsula back for several generations. At once friendly and suspicious, year-round residents are understandably protective of the privacy they have come to cherish. As you might expect, the main draw down here is the quiet tranquility that comes with isolation, and while the area presents ample opportunities for exploration, you might find yourself content with a good book, an afternoon nap, a gourmet meal, and a night in a posh B&B.

Arrival, information, and getting around

The Blue Hill Peninsula is deceptively large, and, with somewhat indirect roads, it can take well over an hour to reach its southernmost point. It's a good idea to pick up a detailed DeLorme map before you set out to explore the area – even some of the locally produced plans can't seem to keep all the different numbered roads straight. **Cycling** is a good way to get around; your best bet for renting (about $65 a week) is probably at the Activity Center in Blue Hill on Rte-172 (℡207/374-3600), where you can rent a canoe or kayak by the week as well. Public transport is not available, though if you're really in a bind, you can grab a **taxi** by calling Airport & Harbor Taxi (℡207/667-5995) or Transportation Matters (℡207/348-2674).

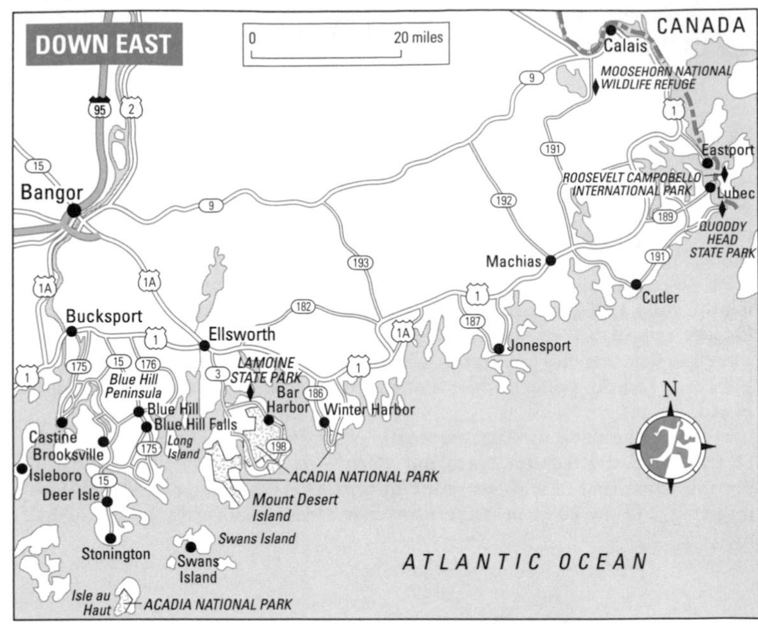

The only formal **information center** is way down on Little Deer Isle (Ⓣ207/348-6124), but most inns and shopkeepers can provide just about all the information you need, including regional maps. The local chambers of commerce maintain **websites** at Ⓦwww.bluehillme.com and Ⓦwww.deerislemaine.com.

Accommodation

Cheap **accommodations** on the Blue Hill Peninsula are non-existent, unless you make it clear down to Stonington. If you're not traveling in the offseason, plan to spend $100 or more per night; for a comparable amount, you may be able to rent a small house or cottage. There are only two official places to **camp** here, both on Deer Isle. *Sunshine Campground*, way out near the end of Sunshine Road (Ⓣ207/348-6681), has 22 sites from the end of May through mid-October, while *Greenlaws*, in Stonington (Ⓣ207/367-5049), is more RV-oriented.

Blue Hill and around

Blue Hill Inn Union Street Ⓣ207/374-2844 or 1-800/826-7415, Ⓦwww.bluehillinn.com. Romantic 1830 inn with inviting rooms and decor. Guests are treated to outstanding gourmet meals. (A small apartment, Cape House, is available in winter for $165 per night, two-night minimum.) May to November only. 6

Captain Isaac Merrill Inn One Union St Ⓣ207/374-2555. Ancient white-clapboard house in the center of town with fireplaces throughout and a decent restaurant downstairs. 6

Heritage Motor Inn Rte-172 Ⓣ207/374-5646. Pleasingly located and moderately priced motor inn with good-sized rooms, some with views. 5

Oakland House 435 Herrick Rd, Brooksville Ⓣ207/359-8521 or 1-800/359-7352, Ⓦwww.oaklandhouse.com. Stay in the immaculately refurbished old stone inn or one of the rustic cabins strewn about the property, which is situated in an impossibly remote area along the Eggemoggin Reach. Follow the signs down Rte-15 to get there. ⑦

Castine

Castine Inn Main Street ⓣ207/326-4365, ⓦwww.castineinn.com. One of the few old inns (1898) in the state that was actually built as an inn, this Castine fixture now offers updated amenities and has friendly, helpful hosts. Also see "Eating and drinking," p.567. Open May to Oct ⑤–⑧

Manor Inn Battle Avenue ⓣ207/326-4861, ⓦwww.manor-inn.com. Constructed as a summer home for a yachting commodore, the *Manor* looks a little incongruously like a New England castle of sorts. The inn offers fourteen rooms beautifully decorated in eclectic lodge style, plus immediate access to hiking and cross-country skiing trails. ⑥–⑧

Pentagoet Inn Main Street ⓣ207/326-8616 or 1-800/845-1701, ⓦwww.pentagoet.com. A welcoming old 1894 inn with sixteen rooms – restored to reflect an earlier era with the help of the antique-buff owners and period steamboat lithos – and a huge porch. The inn also has a lively pub, *Passports*. May to Oct only. ④–⑦

Stonington

Boyces Motel Main Street ⓣ207/367-2421 or 1-800/224-2421. It's not the nicest of places, but the somewhat run-down ambience still manages to appeal. Plus, it's cheap. They also have full apartments, with kitchens and living rooms for $60 per night (offseason). Open all year. ③

Inn on the Harbor Main Street ⓣ207/367-2420. Stonington's fanciest (and priciest) accommodations, though that's not saying a whole lot. It also has the best location, with a fine view of the harbor. Open all year; breakfast included. ⑥

Pres du Port B&B W Main Street at Highland Avenue ⓣ207/367-5007. This old house, filled with quirky furniture, overlooks the bay; call ahead for reservations. May to Oct only. ⑥

Blue Hill

Though wealthy **BLUE HILL**, at the intersection of routes 172, 176, and 15 adjacent to the Blue Hill Harbor, makes a fairly good portion of its living from tourism, you'd be hard pressed to find a Maine T-shirt or even a lighthouse figurine around town. It's not that there's much to see here, but plenty come for its quietude nevertheless.

Several well-known writers, among them E.B. White, have made their home in Blue Hill, whose population supports two excellent bookstores. North Light Books, on Main Street (ⓣ207/374-5422), is a great source for **travel books** and maps as well as fiction, specialty titles, and art supplies, while the larger Blue Hill Books, 2 Pleasant St (ⓣ207/374-5632), is a more comprehensive independent bookseller.

It's a relatively short walk (30–45min) up to the top of **Blue Hill Mountain**, from which you can see across the Blue Hill Bay to the dramatic ridges of Mount Desert Island. The trailhead is not difficult to find, halfway down Mountain Road between Rte-15 and Rte-172. South on Rte-175, **Blue Hill Falls** is a good spot to give kayaking a try: Rocky Coast Outfitters, on Grindleville Road (ⓣ207/374-8866), offers helpful instruction and the occasional tour, while at Maine Coast Experience, farther south in Brooklin on Reach Road (ⓣ207/359-5057 or 1-888/559-5057), you can rent a kayak ($50 per day) and set your own agenda. They also offer **whale-watching** trips and, for the romantically inclined, sunset cruises.

Community radio

In Bucksport and the surrounding area, tune your radio to community-run **WERU**, 89.9 FM, which broadcasts a wide range of lesser-known music, local news, and liberal commentary from its headquarters in East Orland.

Castine

CASTINE, nearly surrounded by water on the northern edge of the Penobscot Bay, is one of New England's most quietly majestic towns, with nicely kept gardens, enormous elm trees arching over many of the hilly streets, and a subdued sophistication found in only the wealthiest of communities. Named for Jean Vincent d'Abbadie de St Castin, a Frenchman who was deeded the land in 1667, the historically disputed peninsula has been occupied at various times by the French, British, Dutch, and, obviously, Americans. The British assumed control in 1779 when General Francis McLean stormed ashore with seven hundred men and built **Fort George**, now little more than a few mounds along Wadsworth Cove Road. The Americans responded by sending 32 vessels carrying some 1400 men, and what followed was arguably the worst American naval defeat in history. Unable to agree on a plan of attack on the weaker British forces on land, the Americans sat in the bay until a larger British fleet arrived, forcing them to retreat up the Penobscot, abandon their ships, and walk back to Boston. Among the officers court-martialed upon their return was Paul Revere, whose military career never really recovered. The military battles that occurred here are noted throughout town with various plaques and signs; a brochure and **map** entitled *Welcome to Castine* is available at any local shop for a full listing of all the historic sites.

Castine's small population is a mix of summer residents, a number of well-known poets and writers (Elizabeth Hardwick, founder of *The New York Review of Books* among them) and year-round people, many of whom are employed by the **Maine Maritime Academy**, with buildings both along the water and back on Pleasant Street. It's pretty tough to miss the *State of Maine*, the huge ship that's usually docked at the landing (except in the months of May and June) and used to train the academy's students, who give tours in the summer (call ⓣ207/326-4311 for schedules, or walk up the plank and ask). Take a stroll down **Perkins Street** to check out the string of enormous mansions looking out over the water. Between these ostentatious summer retreats are a number of old historic buildings, such as the 1665 **John Perkins House**, the town's earliest, which is occasionally open to the public. When you tire of wandering around the town, Castine Kayak Adventures (ⓣ207/326-9045) runs various **sea kayaking** tours ($55–105, includes equipment and instruction) from Dennett's Wharf next to the public boat landing.

Stonington and Isle au Haut

When you cross over the enormous suspension bridge onto Little Deer Isle and traverse the causeway onto **Deer Isle**, be prepared for a shock. It's said that many locals never even bother to leave the island, and by the time-warped feel of the place, that doesn't seem too far-fetched. Clear down at the end of Rte-15, it doesn't get much more remote than **STONINGTON**, a working-class town whose residents have long had a reputation for superior seamanship; many pirates and smugglers reputedly made port here in the late nineteenth century – no doubt due to its incredible isolation. Over the past hundred years, the place has found hard-earned prosperity in the sardine canning and granite quarrying businesses. The history of the granite quarries is brought to life at the newly opened **Deer Isle Granite Museum**, on Main Street (June–Aug Mon–Sat 10am–5pm, Sun 1–5pm; ⓣ207/367-6331; donation), which counts as its centerpiece a working model of the quarry as it stood in 1900.

Mailboats headed for **ISLE AU HAUT** ("I'll ah hoe") depart from the Stonington landing several times daily (no service Sunday; ⓣ207/367-5193; $25 round-trip). On this lonely island, you can explore the less-visited part of **Acadia National Park**, clambering over the rocky shoreline and feeling your way through the cool foggy breeze and dense stands of spruce trees. Alternatively, you can charter your own boat for a reasonable price from Captain Bill at Old Quarry Charters, in Stonington (ⓣ207/367-8977, ⓦwww.oldquarry.com), who, in addition to Isle au Haut, will take you anywhere on the Maine coast.

Eating and drinking

Most of the **eateries** on the peninsula cater to the expensive tastes (and fat wallets) of wealthy summer residents; **Castine** and **Blue Hill** have the best concentration of places, though even on the remote **Deer Isle** there are a couple of prix-fixe gourmet spots.

Blue Hill and around

Arborvine Main Street ⓣ207/374-2119. Mid-range priced dishes like mushroom and leek risotto and local Damariscotta River oysters, in an 1800s-style home. Try the plum napolean with whipped cream for dessert.

Firepond Main Street ⓣ207/374-9970. Enjoy a romantic candlelit gourmet feast in this intimate dining room near the town center. Entrées such as fresh local seared salmon with apricot couscous, veal with sundried tomatoes, and vegetarian risotto cost $15–19.

Hancock's of Blue Hill 118 Ellsworth Rd ⓣ207/374-3272. Fresh-baked goods, delectable salads, and some vegetarian offerings. Closed Tues.

Morning Moon Café Rte-175 and Naskeag Point Rd, Brooklin ⓣ207/359-2373. South of Blue Hill and known as simply "The Moon," this is a popular gathering spot for breakfast and lunch. Closes 2pm.

The Pantry Restaurant Water Street ⓣ207/374-2229. Cute little breakfast and lunch restaurant serving incredibly cheap and simple sandwiches, waffles, eggs, and the like.

Castine

Castine Inn Main Street ⓣ207/326-4365. Bold flavors from dishes such as orange muscat duck and beef tenderloin with a red-wine port sauce. There's also a friendly little pub.

Castine Variety Main Street ⓣ207/326-8625. The real draw here is not the food – although you can get a pretty good milkshake – but rather the opportunity to catch up on the town news while sitting at the tiny counter in the back of the store and chatting with the well-connected proprietor.

Dennett's Wharf 15 Sea St ⓣ207/326-9045. Dine on typical sea fare and then wash it down with one of several Maine microbrews on tap, all while enjoying a fine view.

Stonington

Fisherman's Friend School Street ⓣ207/367-2442. Packed with semi-friendly locals, this no-nonsense eatery serves up just what you'd expect to find in a remote fishing community: fresh, delicious, and sometimes greasy seafood.

Harbor Café Main Street ⓣ207/367-5099. A very casual spot for sandwiches, coffee, and muffins in the center of town.

East to Mount Desert Island

Aside from a short strip of quaint brick gift shops and a couple of cafés along the old part of Main Street (US-1), most of **ELLSWORTH** has been overdeveloped into a disastrous sprawl of parking lots and chain stores. There's predictably little to see, although on a cloudy day you might check out the **Woodlawn Museum**, on Rte-172 just south of US-1 (June–Sept Tues–Sat 10am–5pm, Sun 1–4pm; May and Oct Tues–Sun 1–4pm; $6), a huge and splendid nineteenth-century house with original furnishings amidst a pleasant park and two miles of trails. Otherwise, stop here only for provisions or a quick bite to eat before you head south to Mount Desert Island. The *Riverside Café*, at 52 Main St (☎207/667-7220), is a friendly local haunt for a quick **breakfast** or **lunch**.

If you're arriving in the Acadia region in high season (July and August) and the traffic is unbearable along busy Rte-3, head off down Rte-184 to **Lamoine State Park** ($2), just north of Mount Desert Island along the shores of Frenchman Bay. There are no hiking trails, but there are plenty of beautiful spots to have a picnic or wander the coast. The 61-site **campground** (mid-May to mid-Oct; park info ☎207/667-4778, reservations ☎207/287-3824; $20 per night) here is rarely full – maybe because it offers no hookups or hot showers – and has some well-situated tent sites that offer views of the island. Nearby, Lamoine Beach is the best **swimming** beach in the area.

Mount Desert Island

Considering that several million visitors come to **Mount Desert Island** each year, that it contains most of New England's only national park, and that it boasts not only a genuine fjord but also the highest headland on the entire Atlantic coast north of Rio de Janeiro, it is quite an astonishingly small place, measuring just sixteen by thirteen miles. It is, of course, simply one among innumerable rugged granite islands along the Maine coast; the reasons to select this one, however, are plentiful. Aside from its obvious charms, Mount Desert is the most accessible of the islands (it's been linked to the mainland by bridge since 1836), possesses the best facilities, and offers water- and land-based activities galore.

The island was named *Monts Deserts* (bare mountains) by Samuel de Champlain in 1604 and fought over by the French and English for the rest of the century. Although all existing settlements date from long after the final defeat of the French, the name remains, still pronounced in French (more like *dessert*, actually). After landscape painters Thomas Cole and Frederic Church depicted the island in mid-nineteenth-century works, word spread about its barren beauty, and by the end of the century, tourism was a fixture here. America's wealthiest families – among them the Rockefellers, Pulitzers, and Fords – erected palatial estates in **Bar Harbor**, and later (under the leadership of Harvard University president Charles Eliot) established the public land trust that would later become Acadia National Park, the first national park donated entirely by private citizens. In 1947, a fire destroyed many of the grand cottages, including Bar Harbor's "Millionaire's Row," putting an end to the island's grand resort era. The fire didn't entirely tarnish the island's luster, however, and the place now attracts vacationing middle-class families and outdoors enthusiasts in addition to the frighteningly rich.

Somes Sound roughly divides the island in half; the east side is more developed and ritzy, holding the island's social center and travel hub Bar Harbor as well as **Northeast Harbor**, the site of huge summer homes for many a CEO. The west side, known to some as the "quiet side," is rather sedate, with a few genuine fishing villages and year-round settlements like low-key **Southwest Harbor**, actually fast catching on as a popular destination in its own right. **Acadia National Park**, which covers much of the island, can offer less sedate travelers camping, cycling, canoeing, kayaking, hiking, and bird-watching, though you're hardly ever very far from civilization.

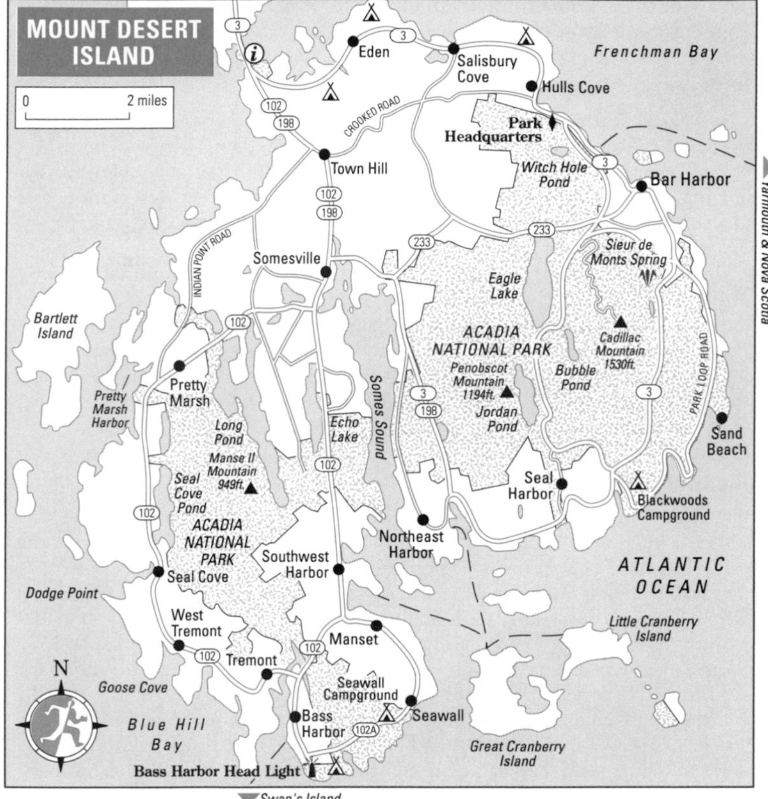

Arrival, information, and getting around

If you're **driving**, Mount Desert is easy enough to get to along Rte-3 off US-1, although in high summer roads on the island itself get congested (and the horse-drawn tours don't help). **Public transport**, however, is minimal. Vermont Transit Lines **buses** (☎1-800/552-8737) run to Bar Harbor from Boston, Bangor, and Portland for a couple of months in summer, starting in mid-June. West's Coastal Connections (☎207/546-2823 or 1-800/596-2823) travels between Bangor and the border town of Calais via Ellsworth.

Mount Desert is also accessible via airplane, though **flights** are relatively infrequent and expensive. Bar Harbor/Hancock County Airport (☎207/667-7432), on Rte-3 in Trenton, has a limited service run by Colgan Air; Bangor International Airport, 45 miles away, is served by Continental, Delta, and Northwest. If you're coming from (or have a desire to visit) Yarmouth, Nova Scotia, the speedy "Cat" **ferry** takes two and three quarter hours to reach Bar Harbor (one-way fares: mid-June to mid-Sept cars $95, people $55; mid-May to mid-June and mid-Sept to mid-Oct cars $85, people $45; ferries leave Bar Harbor daily at 8am; ☎1-888/249-7245).

Once here, take advantage of the free Island Explorer **shuttle buses**

(ⓦ www.exploreacadia.com), which travel through Acadia to Bar Harbor, and even out to the airport.

Information

The **Acadia Information Center**, on Rte-3 just before you cross the bridge to Mount Desert Island (daily: May–Aug 9am–8pm; Sept to mid-Oct 9am–5.30pm; ⓣ 207/667-8550 or 1-800/358-8550), is an advisable stop for lodging and camping information if you don't already have a reservation, and they have decent free maps of the island. There's also a tourist information office in Bar Harbor at the ferry terminal (ⓣ 207/288-5103).

There are three **information** outlets at Acadia during the summer, the best of which is the Hulls Cove Visitor Center, just off of Rte-3 at the entrance to the Park Loop Road (May–Oct daily 8am–6pm; ⓣ 207/288-4932). Here you can inquire about hiking routes and purchase maps. You can also obtain more information about the park by writing or calling the National Park Service at **Park Headquarters**, PO Box 177, Bar Harbor, ME 04609 (ⓣ 207/288-3338, ⓦ www.nps.gov/acad).

Accommodation

Rte-3 into and out of Bar Harbor (which becomes Main Street on the way south) is lined with budget motels, which do little to improve the look of the place but satisfy an enormous demand for accommodation. Rates increase drastically in July and August, and anywhere offering sea views will cost a whole lot more. In season, it's difficult to find a room for less than $100 in Bar Harbor; elsewhere, prices are a little less exorbitant. Despite the island's 4500 rooms, everywhere tends to be booked up early, so call ahead to check for availability. For help with **reservations**, call or stop in at the Acadia Information Center (see "Information" above). If you're really pressed for cash, it's cheaper to stay in **Ellsworth** and drive onto the island each day, though the drive to the far south end can be quite time-consuming, with all the auto congestion. **Camping** in Acadia itself is a better (and prettier) budget option but spaces are in short supply; here too you will need to call well in advance for July and August, although smaller private campgrounds scattered about the island are usually not full (see box, opposite).

Bar Harbor

Acadia Hotel 20 Mount Desert St ⓣ 207/288-5721 or 1-888/876-2463, ⓦ www.acadiahotel.com. One of the more affordable spots in town, the rooms in this old hotel are newly renovated but a bit overdone. You get a discount if you reserve through the website. ❻

Bar Harbor Inn Newport Drive ⓣ 207/288-3351 or 1-800/248-3351, ⓦ www.barharborinn.com. Perhaps the grandest hotel in town, the 153 rooms in the inn's three buildings have modern amenities, and are decorated attractively, yet unfussily. The eight-acre property is right on Frenchman Bay, and the views from many of the rooms can't be beat. ❺–❽

Bass Cottage in the Field 14 In the Field ⓣ 207/288-3705. Authentic down-at-the-heels Victorian relic from the golden age of Bar Harbor. Some rooms share baths, singles available. ❺

Hatfield B&B 20 Roberts Ave ⓣ 207/288-9655, ⓦ www.hatfieldinn.com. On a quiet side street a short walk from the center of town, this small, country-style B&B offers friendly service and a laid-back atmosphere. ❻

Maples Inn 16 Roberts Ave ⓣ 207/288-3443, ⓦ www.acadia.net/maples. Peaceful little B&B with antique four-poster and canopy beds. Open all year. Prices are thirty percent less in winter. ❻–❼

Mount Desert YWCA 36 Mount Desert St ⓣ 207/288-5008. Centrally located women-only accommodation. Open sporadically – call ahead. Beds in shared rooms start at $35. Beds also available from $75 per week (single) or $140 (double).

The Tides 119 West St ⓣ 207/288-4968. On a fairly residential street but still within a few

Camping On Mount Desert Island

There are three **campgrounds** in Acadia National Park, two public and one private. **Blackwoods**, near Seal Harbor (☎207/288-3274), is open all year, with reservations taken starting in February (through the National Park Service, ☎1-800/365-2267, or through Ⓦ reservations.nps.gov; $20). At **Seawall**, off Rte-102A near Bass Harbor (☎207/244-3600; $14 walk-in, $20 drive in), campsites are available on a first-come first-served basis (closed Oct to mid-May). The Appalachian Mountain Club maintains the private **Echo Lake Camp** (July & Aug; ☎207/244-3747; $380 per week), an extremely popular lakefront camp in Acadia National Park between Somesville and Southwest Harbor, with tent sites, beds, a dining room, kitchens, shared bathhouses with hot showers, canoes, and kayaks; rates here include three family-style meals a day. The following list of privately owned campgrounds on the island is not exhaustive but it should be sufficient; for a more complete guide, contact the information center. Most charge about $25 per night, or more for a waterfront location.

Barcadia Rte-3, Bar Harbor (mid-May to mid-Oct; ☎207/288-3520).
Bass Harbor Bass Harbor (mid-May to Sept; ☎207/244-5857).
Mount Desert Bar Harbor Rd/Rte-198, Somesville (mid-June to Sept; ☎207/244-3710).
Mount Desert Narrows, Rte-3, Bar Harbor (May–Oct; ☎207/288-4782).
Quietside West Tremont (mid-June to mid-Oct; ☎207/244-5992).
Spruce Valley Rte-102, Bar Harbor (mid-May to Oct; ☎207/288-5139).
White Birches, 195 Seal Cove Rd, Southwest Harbor (mid-May to mid-Oct; ☎207/244-3797).

minutes of the center of town, this elegant, somewhat formal white mansion affords ocean views from several of its luxurious rooms. 8

Ullikana B&B 16 The Field ☎207/288-9552. The place to go in town for a romantic splurge; nicely decorated rooms and unbelievably sumptuous breakfasts. 7

Southwest Harbor and the west side

The Claremont 25 Clark Point Rd, Southwest Harbor ☎207/244-5036 or 1-800/244-5036, Ⓦwww.claremonthotel.com. Classic old-fashioned wooden hotel with tennis and croquet, a few minutes from Acadia National Park on the quieter side of the island. Mid-May to mid-Oct. 8

Emery's Cottages on the Shore Sand Point Road ☎207/288-3432 or 1-888/240-3432. Well-equipped individual cottage units in green parkland overlooking Fisherman's Bay. From $38 off-season to $66–118 peak season.

Inn at Southwest Harbor Main Street, Southwest Harbor ☎207/244-3835, Ⓦwww.innatsouthwest.com. Brilliant old Victorian inn in the center of town with a cozy living room, cheery bedrooms, and an attentive innkeeper. Very inexpensive offseason rates. 6

Lindenwood Inn 118 Clark Point Rd, Southwest Harbor ☎207/244-5335 or 1-800/307-5335. This first-class inn offers tastefully redecorated rooms and African accents in a stylish turn-of-the-century captain's home. Breakfast included. 5–7

The Yellow Aster 53 Clark Point Rd, Southwest Harbor ☎207/244-4422 or 1-800/724-7228, Ⓦwww.acadia.net/yellowaster. Spotless and bright four-room B&B decorated with local artwork, with wholesome organic breakfasts and a bit of a new-agey feel. 6

Bar Harbor

The town of **BAR HARBOR** began life as an exclusive resort, summer home to the Vanderbilts and the Astors, but the great fire of October 1947 that destroyed their opulent "cottages" changed the direction of the town's growth. Many of the old-money families rebuilt their summer estates in hyper-rich **Northeast Harbor**, southwest along Rte-3, and Bar Harbor is now firmly geared towards tourists – though it's by no means downmarket. There's not all that much to do in town, even in high summer. However, the ambience is suf-

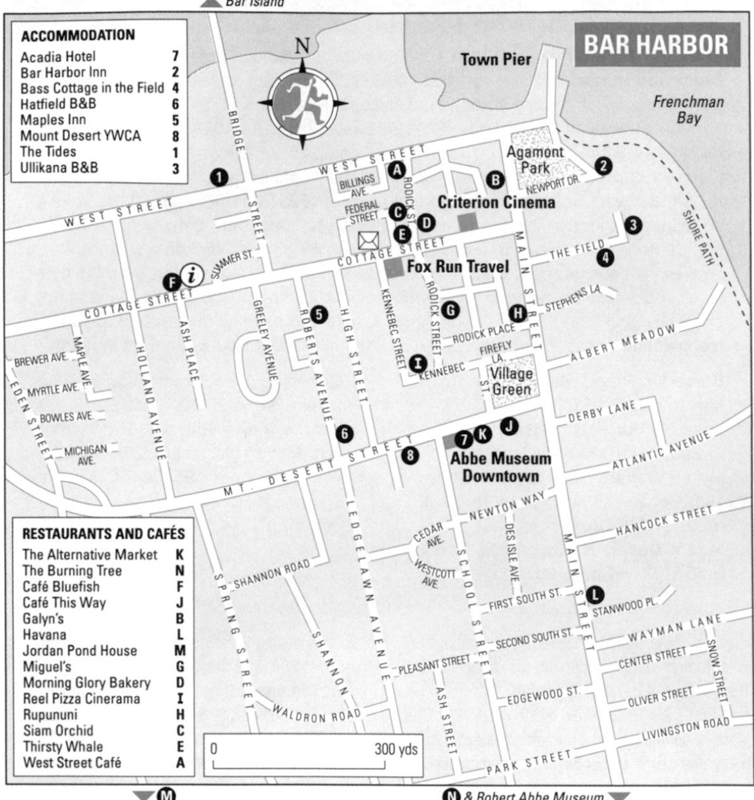

ficient for it to take a while to realize that once you've strolled around the village green, and walked along the **Shore Path** past the headland of the *Bar Harbor Inn* and along the coast for views of the ocean and Frenchman Bay, you've seen most of what Bar Harbor has to offer.

In high season up to 21 different **sea trips** set off each day, for purposes ranging from deep-sea fishing to cocktail cruises. Among the most popular are the **whale-watching** trips run by Bar Harbor Whale Watch Company, 1 West St (ⓣ207/288-2386 or 1-800/WHALES-4). Cruises, which depart adjacent to the Town Pier, take about three hours and cost around $39. With Downeast Windjammer Cruises, you can also enjoy a two-hour trip on the impressive **schooner** *Margaret Todd* or a deep-sea fishing experience on the *Janna Marie* (leaving from the *Bar Harbor Inn* pier daily June–Oct; ⓣ207/288-4585; $27.50–37.50). If you'd rather steer your own ship, rent a powerboat for the week from Harbor Boat Rentals, at the town pier (ⓣ207/244-0557).

One of the town sights in its heyday was the "Indian Village," a summer encampment where Native Americans came to sell pottery, necklaces, and trinkets to tourists; it was cleared away in the 1930s to make room for a new ballpark. Now the only signs of the island's first inhabitants are the artifacts at the **Robert Abbe Museum**, which were found at Fernald Point near Southwest Harbor and attributed to a nomadic people who made birch-bark canoes.

What became of them is encapsulated by a classic understatement on a map contrasting the tribal areas of 1600 with the modern reservations: "The native population did not view territorial boundaries as we do today." The museum has opened a location downtown at 26 Mount Desert St (June to mid-Oct daily 10am–5pm, Thurs–Sat until 9pm; rest of year Thurs–Sun 10am–5pm; $4.50, children $2; Ⓣ207/288-3519, Ⓦwww.abbemuseum.org), and maintains its original building, which shows Maine archeological findings and relates the history of the institution, a couple of miles south of Bar Harbor at Sieur de Monts Spring, just off the Park Loop Road (daily June to mid-Oct: July & Aug 9am–5pm, other months 10am–4pm; $2).

Acadia National Park

ACADIA NATIONAL PARK, sprawled out over most of Mount Desert Island, the Schoodic Peninsula to the east, and Isle au Haut, is the most visited place in Maine. It's visually stunning, with dramatic rolling hills carving smooth rocky silhouettes into the misty horizon. Dense stands of fir and birch trees hide over 120 miles of **hiking trails** (see box, overleaf) that pop into view on the island's several boulder-like summits. In fact, there's all you could want here in terms of mountains and lakes for secluded rambling, and such **wildlife** as seals, beavers, puffins, and bald eagles is not scarce. The two main geographical features are the narrow fjord of **Somes Sound**, which almost splits the island in two, and **Cadillac Mountain**, an unbelievable place to watch the sunrise, though the summit of the 1530-foot mound offers tremendous ocean views at any time of the day (assuming clear weather). It can be reached either by a moderately strenuous climb – more than you'd want to do before breakfast – or by a very leisurely drive, winding up a low-gradient road.

Much the most enjoyable way to explore is to ride a rented **bicycle** around the fifty miles of one-lane gravel-surfaced "**carriage roads**," built by John D. Rockefeller Jr as a protest against the 1913 vote that allowed "infernal combustion engines" onto the island. Keep your eye out for several ornate **granite bridges**, commissioned by Rockefeller and built by architects William Welles Bosworth and Charles Stonington. Three Bar Harbor companies rent mountain bikes for less than $20 per day: Bar Harbor Bicycle Shop, at 141 Cottage St on the edge of town (Ⓣ207/288-3886), Acadia Bike & Canoe, across from the post office at 48 Cottage St (Ⓣ207/288-9605), and Acadia Outfitters, at 106 Cottage St (Ⓣ207/288-8118). Southwest Cycle does the same on Main Street in Southwest Harbor (Ⓣ207/244-5856 or 1-800/649-5856). All provide excellent maps and are good at suggesting routes. Carry water, as there are very few refreshment stops inside the park.

If you'd prefer to get out on the water, you can take a 4-hour guided **kayak tour** ($45) from May to October with National Park Sea Kayak Tours, 39 Cottage St (Ⓣ207/288-0342 or 1-800/347-0940, Ⓦwww.acadiakayak.com), which also leads overnight sea kayaking trips. (They also offer downhill bike rides from the top of Cadillac Mountain.) Just up the street at 48 Cottage St, Coastal Kayaking Tours offers similar kayaking trips, including overnight island camping packages (Ⓣ207/288-9605 or 1-800/526-8615). With an abundance of rocky cliffs and overhangs, **rock climbing** is also popular here, and Acadia Mountain Guides (Ⓣ207/866-7562 or 1-888/232-9559) conducts half-day and full-day climbs, with prices scaled from $50–100 a head, depending on the number of people in your group.

The park is open all year, with a summer-only **visitors' center** in Hull's Cove

(May to mid-Oct) at the entrance to the Loop Road north of Bar Harbor (see "Information," p.570). The entrance fee is $10 per car for a seven-day pass, or $5 if you enter on bike or cycle. Many visitors do nothing more than drive the length of the Park Loop Road, which admittedly winds through some of the park's most arresting areas, but you should also make the effort to get onto the trails. The only fee collection station is on Park Loop Road near **Sand Beach**, five miles south of Bar Harbor, a gorgeous strand bounded by twin headlands, though the water is almost always arctic. Because there are so few parking spots near the beautifully sheltered cove, you should either bike over from Bar Harbor or plan to arrive early in the day.

Hiking on Mount Desert Island

It's no secret that Mount Desert Island offers some of the most exhilarating **hiking** in New England – most of its 100 miles of trails are only deserted in the dead of winter. Though by no means exhaustive, the following list highlights some of the best hikes. If you plan on exploring the island's trails extensively, get your hands on a copy of the detailed guidebook *A Walk in the Park*, published locally ($12) and available at the park visitors' center. The Southwest Harbor Chamber of Commerce (℡207/244-9264 or 1-800/423-9264) prints a decent map (free) of the west side of the park, detailing some two dozen hikes.

Easy:

Flying Mountain Trail, five minutes north of Southwest Harbor, just off of Rte-103 on Fernald Point Road. This short hike takes about an hour round-trip, affording beautiful views at the top of 284-foot Flying Mountain.

Jordan Pond Loop Trail, from the Jordan Pond parking area. A 3.3-mile loop that roughly follows the water's edge.

Ship Harbor Nature Trail, at the southern end of the park off of Rte-102A near the Bass Harbor Head Light. An easy 1.3-mile trail that loops out along the coast and back.

Moderate:

Bubble Rock Trail, starting at Bubble Rock parking area. Two 1-mile forest loop trails, with some vistas of Jordan Pond.

Great Head Loop, beginning at Sand Beach on the Park Loop Road. Scenic 1.5-mile trail leads along towering cliffs right above the sea.

South Ridge Trail, departing from Rte-3, near the Blackwoods Campground. This trail is the best way to get to the top of Cadillac Mountain, the highest point on the island at 1530ft. The 7.4-mile round-trip is not particularly strenuous but very rewarding.

Strenuous:

Acadia Mountain Trail, a few miles south of Somesville, on the east side of Rte-102. A relatively steep ascent to the top of the 700-foot mountain, with fine views of the Somes Sound. 2.5 miles round-trip.

Beehive Trail, just north of the Sand Beach parking area. A short one-mile trip up iron rungs on exposed ledges. There's a swimming pond near the top called the Bowl.

Mansell Mountain, at the south end of Long Pond, near Southwest Harbor. Trees impair the views from the 950-foot summit, but the two-mile hike along the Perpendicular Trail features stairways carved into the rock and unparalleled seclusion.

Penobscot Mountain, departing from near the Jordan Pond House. Panoramic views, second only perhaps to those from Cadillac Mountain.

The Schoodic Peninsula

A small section of Acadia National Park lies isolated at the end of the **Schoodic Peninsula**, some eight miles south of US-1 along Rte-186, where Schoodic Point overlooks a rocky shoreline that spills out into the crashing surf, creating many natural picnic benches. Watch out for the menacing gulls, who easily quell their fear of humans in search of sandwiches to grab.

The Point's the most scenic of stops on the peninsula, though there are plenty of places to pull off Rte-186 and explore a bit of the coast on foot. The pleasant little village of **WINTER HARBOR**, northwest of the park along Rte-186, is a worthwhile stop, if for no other reason than to grab a thick milkshake at local hangout *JM Garrish*, 352 Main St (Ⓣ207/963-5575), an old-fashioned soda fountain where you can also munch on huge homemade muffins and cheap sandwiches. If you prefer, you can take the ferry over from Bar Harbor – there are six round-trips a day ($24; Ⓣ207/288-2984).

If you are in the area, don't miss the yearly **lobster festival** in Winter Harbor, held the second Saturday in August, when lobster lovers converge on the tiny town to down heaps of the tender meat, shop for crafts, listen to live music, and watch a parade.

Southwest Harbor and Bass Harbor

The western half of Mount Desert Island was for many years unflatteringly called the "Backside" by well-heeled and snooty residents of Bar Harbor. But while its quiet hamlets still maintain a much slower pace than Bar Harbor proper, the area is not without appeal, especially if you're seeking solace from the crowds.

SOUTHWEST HARBOR, along Rte-102 across from Northeast Harbor, is the center of this side's action, so to speak. The small "downtown" is graced with a couple of top-notch restaurants and the surrounding area has a smattering of cozy, out-of-the-way accommodations. The streets here are quiet at 8pm on Saturday nights in high summer – though how long it will remain that way in the face of increased tourist traffic is up in the air. Regardless, Southwest Harbor makes for a good base from which to explore the western half of Acadia, and, if you plan on visiting the neighboring Swans Island or Long Island, the state ferry is only a couple of miles away in Bass Harbor.

South along Rte-102, **BASS HARBOR** is even further removed, the simple homes that line its streets reflecting the modest middle-class lifestyle of its residents. At the southernmost tip of the island, just off of Rte-102A, you'll find the much-photographed **Bass Harbor Head Light**, perched on the rocks and tucked behind the trees. Though the 1858 structure is not open to visitors, you can walk down a short seaside path for excellent views of the lighthouse and the ocean beyond. If you prefer to explore the water itself, take a three-hour lunch **cruise** from Island Cruises ($25, lunch not included), to the fishing village of Frenchboro on Long Island, or a two-hour nature cruise aboard the 40-foot *R.L. Gott* (mid-June to mid-Oct; $18; Ⓣ207/244-5785). The Maine State Ferry also runs **boats** between Bass Harbor, Swans Island, and Frenchboro several days per week (Ⓣ207/244-3254).

Eating and drinking

Mount Desert's most memorable **eating** experiences are to be found in the many **lobster pounds** all over the island, but for nightlife Bar Harbor is where the people are. Cottage Street is a much more promising area to look for food and evening atmosphere than the surprisingly subdued waterfront. As usual, **seafood** is everywhere, although, thankfully, there are some more creative options available.

As for other diversions, the Art Deco Criterion cinema at Cottage Street (Ⓣ207/288-3441) looks exactly as it did when it was built in 1932 and shows current favorites. But perhaps the most unusual of choices is the Great Maine Lumberjack Show (on Rte-3 in Trenton; mid-June to Aug every night at 7pm; Ⓣ207/667-0067, Ⓦwww.mainelumberjack.com). Hosted by Timber Tina, a logging sports champion who has competed around the world, it's campy family fun, with bits of history, humor, axes, and sawdust flying through the air.

Bar Harbor

The Alternative Market 16 Mount Desert St Ⓣ207/288-8225. Bag lunches, big sandwiches, soups, smoothies, and fresh squeezed juices.

The Burning Tree Rte-3, Otter Creek Ⓣ207/288-9331. A few miles south of Bar Harbor, this outwardly unimpressive seafood restaurant spices up its brilliant entrées ($15–20) with tasty Southwestern and Caribbean touches. Reservations a must in July and Aug; closed Mon and Tues starting in Sept. Closed mid-Oct to mid-June.

Café Bluefish 122 Cottage St Ⓣ207/288-3696. Cute, eclectically decorated little restaurant specializing in basic seafood and poultry dishes with a twist, such as pecan-crusted halibut ($17.95) and award-winning lobster strudel ($22.95).

Café This Way 14 Mount Desert St Ⓣ207/288-4483. Creative light California cuisine, the likes of maple salmon over sautéed greens or butternut squash ravioli (entrées $16–22). Breakfast daily, dinner Mon–Sat 6–9pm.

Galyn's 17 Main St Ⓣ207/288-9706. A good bet for relatively affordable ($11–30 per entrée) fresh gourmet seafood, with an attractively understated decor with candlelit tables.

Havana 318 Main St Ⓣ207/288-CUBA. American dining with a Latin sensibility, which translates into cilantro and sweet corn crabcakes and filet mignon with chimichurri.

Jordan Pond House Park Loop Rd, Acadia National Park Ⓣ207/276-3316. Worthy concession restaurant in the heart of Acadia National Park between Bar Harbor and Northeast Harbor. Serves light meals, ice cream, and popovers (light, puffy egg muffins, a longtime Acadia tradition). Tea is served in the beautiful lakeside garden 11.30am–6pm.

Miguel's 51 Rodick St Ⓣ207/288-5117. Hopping Mexican joint with a typically calorie-laden menu and a happy, margarita-swilling crowd.

Morning Glory Bakery 39 Rodick St Ⓣ207/288-3041. Fresh-baked breads, coffee, and pastries served at a purple-trimmed cottage.

Siam Orchid 30 Rodick St Ⓣ207/288-4060. Large selection of authentic Thai food with polite service; most entrées cost under $10.

Reel Pizza Cinerama Village Green Ⓣ207/288-3828 takeout, 207/288-3811 movie info. Eat pizza and watch intelligent films on the big screen. It's a simple concept, but it works. Movie tickets are $5.

Rupununi 119 Main St Ⓣ207/288-2886. Overpriced pub grub served until late – stick to the burgers. The bar stays open until 1am.

Thirsty Whale 40 Cottage St Ⓣ207/288-9335. As rowdy as Bar Harbor gets. Live music every night of the week in season.

West Street Café 76 West St Ⓣ207/288-5242. Family restaurant serving basic seafood at very reasonable prices.

Southwest Harbor and Bass Harbor

Beal's Lobster Pier Clark Point Road, Southwest Harbor Ⓣ207/244-7178. Fresh seafood for under $10, on a rickety wooden pier crammed full of lobsters. Closed Nov–April.

Chef Marc & Eat a Pita 326 Main St, Southwest Harbor Ⓣ207/244-4344. A great casual, cozy, and affordable spot with delicious, healthy gourmet food (pastas, salads, pita sandwiches, seafood), candlelit tables, and friendly service. Lunch and dinner served. Credit cards not accepted.

Deck House Restaurant & Cabaret Theater Great Harbor Marina Ⓣ207/244-5044. Full dinner plus more than a dozen songs performed in the round nightly, June–Sept.

Preble Grill 14 Clark Point Rd, Southwest Harbor Ⓣ207/244-3034, Ⓦwww.preblegrill.com. Classy and deservedly popular spot with flavorful grilled meats and Mediterranean favorites with regional ingredients.

Seafood Ketch McMullen Avenue, Bass Harbor Ⓣ207/244-7463. Great super-fresh seafood overlooking Bass Harbor. Reservations recommended.

Thurston's Lobster Pound Steamboat Wharf Road, Bernard Ⓣ207/244-3320 or 1-800/235-3320. Dine on your lobster of choice at the only true lobster pound on the island with a casual cafeteria-style layout overlooking Bass Harbor. Open end of May to Oct.

East to Canada

Looking at a typical map of the United States, you'd never dream that Canada stretches for five hundred miles beyond Maine to the east. In fact, few travelers venture far along the hundred miles of Maine coast beyond Acadia National Park, which is one reason the bulk of Down East Maine remains so little touched by change. Another reason is that this is bleak and windswept country, where high cliffs are battered by harsh seas. In summer, though, the weather is usually no worse than in the rest of Maine, and the coastal drive can be exhilarating. At those points where the road runs next to the sea, you get a real sense of the overwhelming power of the ocean, sweeping into the Bay of Fundy to create the highest tides in the nation. Tourism is not big business in these parts, but each village has one or two B&Bs and low-priced restaurants. Outside of just the rugged scenery, highlights include **West Quoddy Head**, the easternmost point in the United States, and the quiet seaside town of **Eastport**.

Machias

One of Maine's more picturesque locations, **MACHIAS**, on US-1, sports a little waterfall right in the middle of town, and was the unlikely location of the first naval battle of the Revolutionary War, in 1775, when the townsfolk, brandishing pitchforks, swords, and firearms, commandeered the British schooner *Margaretta* after refusing to provide it with provisions. The attack was planned in the still-standing gambrel-roofed **Burnham Tavern**, Rte-192 just off of US-1 (mid-June to mid-Sept Mon–Fri 9am–5pm; $2; ⓣ207/255-4432), which is set up as the tavern probably looked two hundred years ago, serving as a small museum to commemorate its place in history.

The best place to **eat** here is the *Artist's Café*, 3 Hill St (ⓣ207/255-8900), with its moderately priced and frequently changing menu; chicken parmesan and lobster linguini are typical offerings. Meals are also good value at *Helen's Restaurant*, 32 Main St (ⓣ207/255-8423), part of the *Machias Motor Inn* (ⓣ207/255-4861; ❹), which has sundecks and superb views. The restored *Riverside Inn and Restaurant*, on US-1 in East Machias (ⓣ207/255-4134; ❺), overlooks the Machias River and has a tasty prix-fixe menu six days a week. Cheaper and less romantic, but still comfortable, is the *Bluebird Motel*, a mile south of town on US-1 (ⓣ207/255-3332; ❹).

East of town, Rte-191 heads along a regal and desolate portion of shoreline known as the **Bold Coast**. From the parking lot along Rte-191, just a little ways east of **CUTLER**, two **hiking loops** head out to the windswept coast and back. There's a small beach at Long Point Cove and you can sometimes catch a glimpse of humpback whales from the cliffs. The Quoddy Regional Land Trust (ⓣ207/733-5509) has information on the trails and campsites along the way.

West Quoddy Head, Lubec, and Campobello Island

With a distinctive red-and-white striped lighthouse dramatically signaling its endpoint, **WEST QUODDY HEAD** is the easternmost part of the United States, jutting defiantly into the stormy Atlantic. You can see Canada just across the Bay of Fundy, though for a better view, take the east three-mile trail in **Quoddy Head State Park** that traces a winding line along precipitous cliffs.

Just beyond the turnoff for Quoddy Head, tiny **LUBEC** was once home to more than twenty sardine-packing plants. The number has dwindled to just one, but the remnants of **McCurdy's Fish Company**, on Water Street, are enough to evoke visions (and maybe even smells) of more prosperous times. Of several decent B&Bs in town, try the *Peacock House*, 27 Summer St (Ⓣ207/733-2403, Ⓦwww.peacockhouse.com; ❺), the largest and most elegant, or the *Home Port Inn*, 45 Main St (mid-June to mid-Oct; Ⓣ207/733-2077 or 1-800/457-2077; ❺), an old 1880 house with seven guestrooms. The *Sunset Point Trailer Park*, on the west end of town, has several cheap **campsites** overlooking the water (Ⓣ207/733-2150).

Campobello Island

Lubec is the gateway to **CAMPOBELLO ISLAND**, in New Brunswick, Canada, where President Franklin D. Roosevelt summered from 1909 to 1921, before he became president, and returned to sporadically during his time in office. The barnlike house is now open to the public, and it's furnished just as the Roosevelts left it. Perhaps the most interesting room, however, is the photo gallery on the south end, depicting FDR at various stages in his political career. The rest of **Roosevelt Campobello International Park** (mid-May to mid-Oct daily 9am–5pm; free; Ⓦwww.fdr.net), located on Canadian soil but held jointly with the United States, is good for a couple of hours of wandering. There are several coastal trails and picnic areas, and the drive out to **Liberty Point** is worth the effort.

Eastport

The seaside town of **EASTPORT**, afloat on Moose Island between Cobscook and Passamaquoddy bays at the end of Rte-190, is attractive and welcoming, though it's quite a ways off the beaten track. Canada is only several miles away, but the closest border crossing is thirty miles north in Calais; the bridge to Campobello Island in Lubec is forty miles from here by car – you have to drive all the way around Cobscook Bay. Despite its remote location, the town has capitalized on its deepwater commercial port near the downtown area since the late nineteenth century. A second shipping pier was recently constructed at Estes Head on the south edge of town, but it remains to be seen if the expansion will develop into a profitable venture. Cargo ships aside, the quiet town maintains the lonely air of a remote outpost, with spotty weather, hills that slope gently toward a collection of Canadian islands just across the bay, and lots of old brick and clapboard buildings. In fact, strewn about are structures from virtually every American architectural period from the Colonial (1775-1800) on through Gothic Revival and Queen Anne Victorian (1890-1910). The *Eastport Walk-About*, a pamphlet available in downtown stores, describes 82 such properties in detail, including the lives of the homeowners themselves.

A result of the somewhat active local arts community, the Eastport Gallery, on Water Street (Ⓣ207/853-4166), is worth a spin, usually housing an interesting collection of works by Maine artists in its two-story exhibit space.

Practicalities

There's not a whole lot to do in Eastport, but there are several decent **restaurants** grouped along Water Street, and some good-value **accommodation** is spread throughout the town's empty streets. *La Sardina Loca* at 28 Water St (Ⓣ207/853-2739) serves a host of Mexican entrées for less than $10 in a wonderfully eclectic interior. The *Second Chance Saloon*, 9 Arnold St (Ⓣ207/853-2735), dishes up steaks, seafood, and excellent chili in a casual setting. *Sunrise*

Café, at the tugboat pier, and the funky *Leisure's by the Sea* (66 Water St ☎207/853-4172) are great places to fill up on caffeine or snacks; both also have occasional live music. The *Weston House*, a boxy 1810 Federal-style home on 20 Boyton St (☎207/853-2907 or 1-800/853-2907; ❹–❺), has huge rooms that overlook the water, while the *Kilby House Inn*, 122 Water St (☎207/853-0989 or 1-800/435-4529; ❹), is a snug old Victorian. Halfway between Eastport and Lubec off of US-1, **Cobscook Bay State Park** has the best **camping** around (mid-May to mid-Oct; ☎207/726-4412), with over a hundred beautifully situated campsites and good facilities.

Calais

The border between the United States and Canada weaves through the center of **Passamaquoddy Bay**; the towns to either side get on so well that they refused to fight in the US–UK War of 1812, and promote themselves jointly to tourists as the **Quoddy Loop** (information ☎207/853-6036, Ⓔoldsow@quoddyloop.com). It's perfectly feasible to take a two-nation vacation, but each passage through customs and immigration between **CALAIS** (pronounced "callous") in the States and **St Stephen** in Canada does take a little while – and watch out for the confusion stemming from the fact that they're in different time zones. No trace now remains of Samuel de Champlain's 1604 attempt to found a colony on the diminutive St Croix Island, which you can see from an overlook on the main road. In town, the *Wickachee Dining Room*, on Main Street (☎207/454-3400), serves big plates of seafood and steak. West's Coastal Connections (☎207/546-2823 or 1-800/596-2823) runs a once-daily bus from Calais to Ellsworth and Bangor. The **visitors' center**, 7 Union St (☎207/454-2211), has loads of information on activities and accommodations and a helpful staff.

Nearby, the Baring division of the **Moosehorn National Wildlife Refuge**, between Rte-191 and Charlotte Road (☎207/454-7161), is a good place to catch a glimpse of a bald eagle or woodcock; they maintain some fifty miles of hiking trails – also good for cross-country skiing in winter.

Inland Maine

The vast expanses of the **Maine interior**, stretching up into the cold far north, consist mostly of evergreen forests of pine, spruce, and fir, interspersed by the white birches and maples responsible for the spectacular fall colors. Only in the remote north is much of it genuine wilderness, however; elsewhere what you see is more likely to be woodlands cultivated by the timber companies.

Distances are large. Once you get away from the two largest cities nearer the sea – **Augusta**, the capital, and **Bangor** – it's roughly two hundred miles by road to the northern border at **Fort Kent**, while to drive between the two most likely inland bases, **Greenville** and **Rangeley** (where exiled psychologist Wilhelm

Reich lived and is buried), takes three hours or more. Driving (there's no public transport) through this mountainous scenery can be a great pleasure, but you do need to know where you're going. There are few places to stay, even fewer gas stations, and beyond Bangor many roads are tolled access routes belonging to the lumber companies: gravel-surfaced, vulnerable to bad weather, and in any case often not heading anywhere in particular.

This landscape has evolved in a very unusual way. Many communities grew up without roads to serve them, back in the days when the timber harvest was floated downriver to the sea; other more recent settlements have only ever been accessible by seaplane. Now that mighty trucks carry the tree trunks instead, roads are finally being pushed through, amid complaints that they are ruining the whole feel of the place.

If you have the time, this is great territory in which to **hike** – the **Appalachian Trail** starts its 2000-mile course down to Georgia at the top of Mount Katahdin – or **raft** on the swift **Penobscot** or **Kennebec** rivers. **Skiing**, too, is a popular activity, particularly at **Sugarloaf** or in the area around **Bethel** near the New Hampshire border, where the White Mountain National Forest extends into Maine.

Especially around the beautiful **Baxter State Park** and enormous **Moosehead Lake**, the forests are home to deer, beaver, a few bears, some recently introduced caribou, and plenty of **moose**. These endearingly gawky creatures (they look like badly drawn horses and are virtually blind) tend to be seen at early morning or dusk; in spring they come to lick the winter's salt off the roads, while in summer you may spot them feeding in shallow water. They do, however, cause major havoc on the roads, particularly at night, and each year significant numbers of drivers are killed in collisions with these hefty creatures.

Augusta and Hallowell

The capital of Maine since 1827, **AUGUSTA**, thirty miles north of Brunswick, is much quieter and less visited now than it was a hundred years ago. The lumber industry here really took off after the technique of making paper from wood was rediscovered in 1844, and Augusta also had a lucrative sideline at the time: each winter hundreds of thousands of tons of **ice**, cut from the Kennebec river, were shipped out as far as the Caribbean, in a trade now all but forgotten by history. There are informative displays on that past in the **Maine State Museum** (Mon–Fri 9am–5pm, Sat 10am–4pm, Sun 1–4pm; free; ⓣ207/287-2301, ⓦwww.state.me.us/museum), housed inside the ugly governmental complex that's shared by the Maine State Library and Archives just south of the capitol on State Street. Walking through dimly lit hallways past the well-designed and intriguing (if slightly outdated) "Twelve Thousand Years in Maine" exhibit, you actually get quite a good sense of how the state has developed over the centuries. Also of note is "Made in Maine," centered on a functional three-story water-powered mill and including re-created shops, factories, and homes from the eighteenth and nineteenth centuries.

Next door, the 180-foot dome of the imposing **Maine State House** (Mon–Fri 8.30am–4.30pm), a Charles Bulfinch design, is visible from nearly anywhere in Augusta. The rather impressive granite structure, completed in 1832, has been subject to several renovations that have nearly doubled its size. You can take a self-guided **tour**, though unless you have a particular interest

△ Moose, Baxter State Park

in politics or architecture, this should kill no more than twenty minutes of your time. If you're so inclined, free guided tours can be arranged by calling ⓣ207/287-1408.

Hallowell

Just two short miles south of Augusta beside the gently sloping banks of the Kennebec River, the quaint haven of **HALLOWELL** is far more pleasant than its governmentally focused neighbor, especially along its main drag, **Water Street**, lined with some excellent **restaurants** and a couple of diverting bookstores and antique shops. Once a major port for lumber and granite, as well as a shipbuilding center, the place boasts a number of stately historic homes left over from those prosperous times, mostly perched in the picturesque hills above town. A small population of artists and craftsmen have arrived in recent years; for **information** on visiting one of the many studios in the area, contact the Kennebec Valley Chamber of Commerce (ⓣ207/623-4559).

Practicalities

If you plan to stay in the Augusta area, the best-value **accommodation** is the *Best Inn* at 65 Whitten Road at the Maine Turnpike's Augusta Winthrop exit (ⓣ207/622-3776; ④). The sole **B&B** is over in Hallowell, the *Maple Hill Farm*, set on 62 acres on Outlet Road, off of Shady Lane (ⓣ207/622-2708 or 1-800/622-2708, ⓦwww.maplebb.com; ④-⑤); you can feed the farm animals in the morning before enjoying a delicious breakfast. Decent family **camping** is available in Winthrop at the *Augusta West Lakeside Resort* (May 15–Oct 15; ⓣ207/377-9993).

For **food**, the lobster rolls at *Burnsie's Homestyle Sandwiches*, on Hitchhorn Street next to the capitol (ⓣ207/622-6425), are favorites with the politicians, while *Curly's*, 750 Main St (ⓣ207/933-2745), does tasty, moderately priced seafood. The *Thai Star*, 611 Civic Center Drive (ⓣ207/621-2808), is another good bet, with an authentic menu featuring spicy crispy duck, yellow curry, and jasmine rice. Along the short main drag of Hallowell, *Slates*, 167 Water St (Tues–Sat; ⓣ207/622-9575), is one of the best restaurants in the state, with a friendly atmosphere, fair prices, and original entrées like shrimp and scallops with coconut pie sauce over jasmine rice. Nearby, at *Higher Grounds Coffeehouse and Tavern*, 119 Water St (ⓣ207/621-1234), patrons sip their coffees and teas while surrounded by local art and (occasionally) live tunes.

Bangor

BANGOR, 120 miles northeast of Portland at the intersection of Rte-1A and I-95, is not a place to spend much time, although its plentiful motels and the big new Bangor Mall on Hogan Road north of town make it a good last stop before the interior. As Maine's third largest city (33,000 people), the place is noticeably more urban and rough around the edges (for Maine, at least) than the state's smaller towns, serving as a major source of goods and services for the stretch of coast twenty miles south. The town is also along the main transportation route between Portland and points farther east and north, so if you're using public transport, you may well find yourself here with an hour or two to kill.

In its prime, Bangor was the undisputed "Lumber Capital of the World." Every winter its raucous population of "River Tigers" went upstream to brand the felled logs, which they then maneuvered down the swiftly flowing Penobscot River as the thaw came in April, reaching Bangor in time to carouse the summer away in the grog shops of Peppermint Row. Bangor also exported ice to the West Indies – and got rum in return. The forests were thinning and the prosperous days were coming to an end, however, when in October 1882, Oscar Wilde addressed a large crowd at the new Opera House and spoke diplomatically of "such advancement . . . in so small a city." A devastating fire in 1911 leveled much of the city, although a fair number of the lumber barons' lavish mansions survived.

Arrival, information, and accommodation

Many of the major airlines service the newly renovated **Bangor International Airport** (Ⓣ207/947-0384) on the western edge of town. Frequent **bus service** is available from Bangor to most other parts of the state. Concord Trailways, which docks at the Transportation Center at 1039 Union St (Ⓣ207/942-0807), can take you to Bar Harbor, Ellsworth, Portland, Camden, and other smaller coastal cities. The CYR Bus Line (Ⓣ1-800/244-2335) heads north from the Trailways Center to Caribou, stopping in several small towns along the way. Vermont Transit Lines/Greyhound has a terminal at 158 Main St (Ⓣ207/945-3000), from which you can travel to Boston via Portland and Portsmouth or connect with Greyhound routes to other destinations. If you're spending any time at all in Bangor, you will find **BAT Community Connector** (Ⓣ207/947-0536; 75¢, carnet of five tickets $3) to be a handy means of getting around – look for the red bus with the black and gray bat outline on the side. Pick up a route map at the Bangor Depot on Main Street.

There's a helpful **information** center at the Bangor Region Chamber of Commerce, 519 Main St (Ⓣ207/947-0307, Ⓦwww.bangorregion.com), which has the typical collection of brochures and hotel information. Right in the center of town is Bangor's best **place to stay**, the *Phenix Inn*, 20 Broad St (Ⓣ207/947-0411; ❼), an old green-brick building with 33 comfortably furnished rooms. Cheaper are the *Motel 6*, 1100 Hammond St (Ⓣ207/947-6921 or 1-800/466-8356; ❷), and the *Main Street Inn*, opposite the Paul Bunyan statue at 480 Main St (Ⓣ207/942-5282; ❸). For a somewhat grander experience, the *Lucerne Inn* in nearby Holden combines accommodation, access to golf facilities, a lakeside setting, three-course dinner, and continental breakfast (Ⓣ1-800/325-5123; ❼).

The Town

One of the mansions that survives along West Broadway, complete with a spider web-shaped iron gate, is now the suitably Gothic residence of horror author **Stephen King**, a Maine native who relocated here in 1980. You can browse the full collection of King's works, including some limited editions and collectibles, at Bett's Bookstore, 26 Main St (Ⓣ207/947-7052).

Bangor's other claim to fame, the 31-foot **Paul Bunyan** statue along Main Street south of downtown, is perhaps the largest such statue in the world – excepting one or two in Minnesota – though it looks more like a brightly painted model airplane kit than a statue. Bunyan was allegedly born here in 1834, though several other prominent logging towns across the US would probably dispute that claim. From mid-May until the end of July there's

harness racing at Bass Park on Main Street (ⓣ207/947-6744), just behind the statue; admission is $1 but the potential to lose money is unlimited. The same venue hosts the **Bangor State Fair**, in the last week of July and the first in August (ⓣ207/990-4444).

Closer to downtown, a few short blocks off Main Street in a building designed by notable Boston architect Richard Upjohn (who also built the Isaac Farrar Mansion across the street), the **Bangor Historical Society Museum**, 159 Union St (April–Dec Tues–Fri 10am–4pm; $4; ⓣ207/942-5766), presents some of the state's better historical exhibits in its stately first-floor galleries and more modern upstairs space. The society also conducts special guided "Best of Bangor" bus tours every other Saturday of the month, July through September, departing from the Chamber of Commerce at 10.30am ($5).

If you've got the time, drive up to the **Thomas Hill Standpipe**, off of Union Street on Thomas Hill Road. The massive cylindrical water tank was constructed in 1897 and still provides 1.75 million gallons of water to the residents of Bangor. Though there's really not much to it, the strange shingled structure is set on a hilltop with a partial view of the landscape. A couple times a year, and usually in the first week of October, the standpipe's observatory is opened to the public, providing panoramic views of the surrounding countryside. Call the Chamber of Commerce (ⓣ207/947-0307) for details.

A few miles north of Bangor, the Maine Center for the Arts (ⓣ207/581-1755), at the University of Maine in **Orono**, runs a series of big-name concerts each summer. Orono is named after the eighteenth-century Chief Joseph Orono; a small island nearby is now a rather sad reservation running summer bingo sessions.

Eating and drinking

Bangor does not have any great wealth of good **places to eat**, though there's an incongruous amount of ethnic eats. For fresh bagels and a huge selection of other kosher foods, you can't beat *Bagel Central*, 33 Central St (ⓣ207/947-1654), while the *Oriental Jade & Sampan Grill*, 411 Main St (ⓣ207/947-6969), serves a wide selection of curries and noodles next to the Bangor Cinema.

The place to **drink** in town is the *Sea Dog Brewing Company*, 26 Front St near the marina along the Penobscot (ⓣ207/947-8009 or 1-888/4-SEADOG, ⓦwww.seadogbrewing.com), which has frequent live music and a good selection of handcrafted brews. The brewery also offers lunch, cocktail, and lobster-bake boat trips of varying lengths on the *River Dog* cruise boat (May to mid-Oct; ⓣ207/947-7194; $8–15). The *Whig and Courier*, 18 Broad St (ⓣ207/947-4095), is a straightahead pub, with burgers, cheesesteaks, and a wide variety of beers on tap. Across the street, the *New Moon Café*, 21 Main St (ⓣ207/990-2233), is a favorite hangout for Bangor's hip younger set, with snacks, coffee and espresso, and live music.

Bethel and around

The remote, quintessentially New England town of **BETHEL**, nestled in the Maine woods about seventy miles north of Portland, may appear rather sleepy, but it's an excellent year-round base from which to explore the outdoors, most notably in the **White Mountains** and **Grafton Notch State Park**. With a prestigious college preparatory school, the Gould Academy (ⓦwww

.gouldacademy.org), and a well-known managerial training center, the NTL Institute (Ⓦwww.ntl.org), Bethel has long attracted a rather academic and prosperous population; in fact, the town was once home to famous neurobiologist Dr John Gehring's clinic for people with neurological disorders.

Arrival and accommodation

Bethel is not accessible via public transit, though you can catch a ride from Portland on the Bethel Express (Ⓣ207/824-4646) or the Airport Car Service (Ⓣ1-800/649-5071) for about $90 (it works out considerably less the more passengers there are); call at least 24hrs in advance. A similar service is operated by Airport Limo & Taxi (Ⓣ207/773-3433 or 1-800/517-9442). Bethel does, however, have a good concentration of **places to stay** once you do get there. The local Chamber of Commerce, Cross Street (Mon–Fri 8am–5pm, Sat 10am–6pm, Sun noon–5pm; Ⓣ207/824-2282 or 1-800/442-5826, Ⓦwww.bethelmaine.com), can help you out if you need. For **camping**, *Crocker Pond Campground* off of Songo Pond Road (Rte-5) just south of town (Ⓣ207/824-2134; $12; mid-May to mid-Oct), has eight secluded and rather primitive campsites that are maintained by the US Forest Service, while the more family-oriented *Bethel Outdoor Adventures*, 121 Mayville Rd (Ⓣ207/824-4224 or 1-800/553-3607), has both RV and tent sites on the banks of the Androscoggin River.

Bethel Inn and Country Club on the Common Ⓣ207/824-2175 or 1-800/654-0125. A full-service four-star resort, with a golf course, tennis courts, a health club, and fine dining. 7–8

Briar Lea B&B 150 Mayville Rd Ⓣ207/824-4717 or 1-877/311-1299, Ⓦwww.briarleainnrestaurant.com. Renovated 150-year-old Georgian farmhouse with a full-service formal dining room, and quite affordable too. 4

Chapman Inn on the Common Ⓣ207/824-2657, Ⓦwww.bethelmaine.com/chapmaninn. Another fine option B&B-like option, also with dorm beds ($25 summer, $35 winter, including breakfast). 4–5

Holidae House Main Street Ⓣ207/824-3400. Another decent option, with double rooms starting at $69 in summer and $89 in winter. 3–4

The Town

The **Bethel Common**, at the south end of Main Street along Broad Street, is flanked by a number of stately white-clapboard nineteenth-century homes and dominated by the sprawling **Bethel Inn and Country Club** (see above), whose yellow Victorian buildings and first-rate golf course spread out over several acres of grassy terrain. The 1813 Federal-style Dr Moses Mason House, part of the **Bethel Historical Society's Regional History Center** is also on the common (July & Aug Tues–Sun 1–4pm; other months by appointment; $2; Ⓣ207/824-2908), holds an engaging and worthwhile museum that includes murals by painter Rufus Porter, period furnishings, and special exhibits relating to regional history. You might also get a quick look at the **John Hastings Homestead**, the former home of a founder of the Gould Academy across the street that was built in 1820 and has been preserved as it stood a century ago. For a more detailed look at the town's architectural highlights, pick up the **walking tour** brochure at the Historical Society or the Chamber of Commerce.

Skiing and other activities

Just a few miles north of Bethel off of Rte-2 on Sunday River Road, the **Sunday River Ski Resort** ($49 for a full-day lift ticket; Ⓣ207/824-3000 or

1-800/543-2754, Ⓦwww.sundayriver.com), is fast becoming one of the major alpine ski areas in New England. Their snowmaking system (copied by other resorts) guarantees "the most dependable snow in the Northeast" for skiing between November and May, with seventeen lifts servicing eight mountain peaks. In summer, Sunday River doubles as a popular **mountain-bike** park. The attraction here is the chance to ride the lifts up the hill with your bike so you can speed down at breakneck pace. The White Cap Base Lodge distributes maps, sells lift passes ($20 half-day, $24 full-day), rents bikes, and offers instruction; if you don't use the lift, however, this is a cost-free activity. Stop by Bethel Outdoor Adventures, 121 Mayville Rd (Ⓣ207/824-4224 or 1-800/533-3607), for route advice, maps, and **bike rentals** ($25 per day). They also rent **canoes** and **kayaks** and do guided trips.

Bethel is also known for its **cross-country skiing**, and there are several privately owned resorts in addition to the trails maintained in the White Mountain National Forest and Grafton Notch State Park. Some 25 miles of cross-country ski trails penetrate the wilderness at the beginner-oriented *Sunday River Inn* and Cross Country Ski Center, on Sunday River Road (Ⓣ207/824-2410). Don't miss the trail that leads to the 1872 Artist's Covered Bridge, off of Sunday River Road, which is a good spot for swimming during the summer. You can also cross-country ski at Carter's Cross Country Ski Center, with eighteen miles of trails at its location off of Rte-26 in Oxford, and forty miles of groomed trails in Bethel on Intervale Road (Ⓣ207/539-4848).

Eating, drinking, and entertainment

Breau's Pizza & Subs Rte-2 Ⓣ207/824-3192. Casual place for excellent pizza that also serves ice cream, clam chowder, lobster rolls, and hearty breakfasts.

Café Di Cocoa Lower Main Street Ⓣ207/824-5282. Bold vegetarian and ethnic specialties, sandwiches, soups, and espresso in a funky dining room. Winter, weekends only; rest of year, several nights a week.

Great Grizzly north along Rte-2 in Newry Ⓣ207/824-6271. Absolutely smokes all the time, filled with winter revelers or summer mountain-bikers.

Java House Lower Main St, near the railroad tracks Ⓣ207/824-0562. Where to get your caffeine fix, though note it's only open until 3.30pm.

Kowloon Village in the Mountain View Mall along Walker's Mill Road Ⓣ207/824-3707. Surprisingly flavorful Chinese food, including a $5.95 lunch buffet.

L'Auberge Country Inn and Bistro Mill Hill Road off the Common Ⓣ207/824-2774 or 1-800/760-2774. Perhaps the best restaurant in town, where gourmet meals (rack of New Zealand lamb, escargot with pernod) are unfussily served in a beautifully converted country barn (the seven guestrooms there start at $89).

Mother's 43 Main St Ⓣ207/824-2589. Another fine place with many loyalists, where you can dine on concoctions like grilled breast of duck with honey-ginger and soy glaze in a cozy book-lined dining room (entrées $12–19).

Suds Pub Lower Main Street Ⓣ207/824-6558. Hot spot for drinking in town, with live entertainment five nights per week and a good selection of microbrews until 1am.

Sunday River Brewing Co north of town along Rte-2 at Sunday River Road Ⓣ207/824-4253. Particularly popular with skiers, serving freshly brewed ales and hearty pub fare, with occasional live music.

Maine's White Mountains

Bethel sits just on the edge of the fifty thousand acres of the **White Mountain National Forest** that fall within Maine's borders, the center of which is **Evans Notch**, just as spectacular as any found in New Hampshire. Stop by their helpful **visitors' center**, 18 Mayville Rd, Bethel (Ⓣ207/824-2134), for maps, hiking suggestions, and information on campsite and shelter availability. The Evans Notch Ranger District maintains five **backcountry shelters** in the forest, some nothing more than a sleeping platform with a pit toilet, but providing a unique experience in the middle of nowhere. All are accessible only on foot (located at least a couple of miles away from the trailhead) and charge a small fee. Particularly good **hikes** through stands of birch and pine in the forest include the moderately difficult 6.3-mile (about 5hr) **Caribou Mountain Loop**, starting at the trailhead on Rte-113, following the Mud Brook Trail and ending at the summit of Caribou Mountain, and the easier 1.8-mile loop that begins on Rte-113, across the bridge just north of *Hastings Campground* and leads up to the **Roost**, a granite overlook providing views of the Wild River Valley and Evans Notch.

North from Bethel: Grafton Notch State Park

North of Bethel, Rte-26 bisects beautiful **Grafton Notch State Park** (mid-May to mid-Oct; $2; ⓣ207/824-2912), a patch of rugged mountains, gurgling streams, cascading waterfalls, and bizarre geological formations. Among these, the **Screw Auger Falls**, where the Bear River has carved out a twisting gorge through the solid granite, is good for wading. Just north, easy trails lead to **Moose Cave Gorge** and through the 45-foot-deep **Mother Walker Falls Gorge**, which features several natural stone bridges. More difficult trails head up **Old Speck Mountain**, Maine's third highest. Follow the 3.8-mile (one-way) **Old Speck Trail**, which traces the Appalachian Trail, from the Grafton Notch trailhead parking area up numerous switchbacks, past the Cascade Brook Falls to the Mahoosuc Trail, which eventually affords sweeping views at the summit. A somewhat shorter option is the **Table Rock Loop** (a two-hour jaunt with some very steep sections) that also departs from the main trailhead parking area up Baldplate Mountain to Table Rock, where you are treated for your efforts with mountain views. The State Park Office, or the Bethel Chamber of Commerce (see p.585) can provide you with maps and other necessary info. There is no camping in Grafton Notch State Park.

Rangeley

RANGELEY is only just in Maine, a little way east of New Hampshire and fewer than fifty miles from the Canadian border, at the intersection of routes 4 and 16. Furthermore, as the café/bar *Doc Grant's*, Main Street (ⓣ207/864-3449), makes a great show of telling you, it is equidistant from the North Pole and the equator (3107.5 miles), though that doesn't mean it's on the main road to anywhere. It has always been a resort, served in 1900 by two train lines and several steamships, with the real attraction then being the fishing in the spectacularly named Mooselookmeguntic Lake.

Today there's still one primary, albeit unorthodox, attraction, the remote **Wilhelm Reich Museum**, Dodge Pond Road, about halfway along the north side of Rangeley Lake, a mile up on a side track off Rte-16 (July & Aug Wed–Sun 1–5pm; Sept Sun 1–5pm; $4; ⓣ207/864-3443, ⓦwww.wilhelmreichmuseum.org), where Wilhelm Reich eventually made his American home after fleeing Germany in 1933. Although he was an associate of Freud in Vienna and wrote the acclaimed *Mass Psychology of Fascism*, Reich is best remembered for developing the orgone energy accumulator. He claimed it could create rain and dissipate nuclear radiation; skeptical authorities focused on the not very specific way in which it was said to collect and harness human sexual energy. In a tragic end to his career, Reich was imprisoned after a wayward student broke an injunction forbidding the transportation of his accumulators across state lines, and he died in the federal penitentiary in Lewisberg, PA, in November 1957. He is buried here, amid the neat lawns and darting hummingbirds, and his house remains a center for the study of his work.

South of town along Rte-17, it's worth seeking out **Angel Falls**, which, at ninety feet, are the highest in Maine. There's a good **swimming** spot at the base. Getting there is a bit complicated; take Rte-17 eighteen miles south of Oquossoc, go west onto the dirt road and across the bridge at highway mile marker 6102, turn right onto the railroad line, after 3.5 miles, turn left on the gravel road and follow the marked trail. Nearby, in the old mining town of Byron, you can also swim in the crystal clear waters of **Coos Canyon**, just off of Rte-17.

Practicalities

The *Rangeley Inn* on Main Street (ⓣ207/864-3341, ⓦwww.rangeleyinn.com; ⑤) stands between Rangeley Lake and the smaller bird sanctuary of Haley Pond, so you can stay right in town and have a room that backs onto a scene of utter tranquility; there's also a gorgeous old wooden dining room. *North Country Inn B&B* on Main Street (ⓣ207/864-2440, ⓦwww.northcountrybb.com; ⑤) is a good second choice. Otherwise, the Chamber of Commerce (see below) can provide lists of private home/condo rentals and "remote campsites" around the lake – which really are remote, several of them inaccessible by road. The *Red Onion*, 77 Main St (ⓣ207/864-5022), is good for an array of inexpensive **food** including pizza, steak, and pasta; the *People's Choice Café*, also on Main Street (ⓣ207/864-5220), is pricier, though the portions are huge and the desserts divine.

Twenty miles north of Rangeley, the peaceful *Grants Camps* beside Kennebago Lake (ⓣ1-800/633-4815) arranges fishing, canoeing, and windsurfing, with accommodation in comfortable cabins overlooking the lake, including all meals, costing around $100 per person per day; there are lower weekly rates. A more accessible **campground** is *Cathedral Pines* (ⓣ207/246-3491), just north of Stratton on Eustis Road. At its entrance stands a memorial to **Benedict Arnold**'s expedition to Québec in 1775, which passed this way, and to Colonel Timothy Bigelow, who climbed the mountain in a "vain endeavor to see the city of Québec."

Rangeley Lakes' **Chamber of Commerce**, down by Lakeside Park (ⓣ207/864-5364 or 1-800/MT-LAKES, ⓦwww.rangeleymaine.com), has details of various activities, including snowmobiling and moose-watching **canoeing** expeditions. One fun thing to do is take a **seaplane** trip with the Lake Region Air (ⓣ207/864-5307) – a fifteen-minute tour, flying low over vast forests and tiny lakes, costs $25 per person.

Sugarloaf USA and Kingfield

The road east of Rangeley cuts through prime moose-watching territory – in fact, locals call Rte-16 "Moose Alley." After about fifty miles, in the Carrabassett Valley, looms the huge mountain of **SUGARLOAF USA**, Maine's biggest ski resort (lift tickets $53; ⓣ207/237-2000 or 1-800/843-5623, ⓦwww.sugarloaf.com). A spectacular place for skiers of all abilities (with

AMC mountain huts in western Maine

The Appalachian Mountain Club, based in Boston (☎617/523-0636, ⓦwww.outdoors.org), maintains a host of remote **mountain huts** and **camps**, and there's a concentration in western Maine near the White Mountains. If you have your own tent and cookstove, these well-kept facilities offer endless outdoor options, especially if you're kayaking or canoeing. If you have questions or to make reservations, call or write the Pinkham Notch Visitor Center, PO Box 298, Gorham, NH 03581 (☎603/466-2727). Other AMC mountain huts in Maine are located on Mount Desert Island (see p.571) and near Georgetown Island, south of Bath (see p.545).

Cold River Camp, North Chatham, NH (June to mid-July $77, mid-July to Aug $88, Oct–April $30, discounts for summer weeks). Situated in the beautiful and undeveloped Evans Notch area of the White Mountain National Forest near the Maine border, this 100-plus-acre site offers a full range of facilities such as cabins, electricity, hot showers, linens, recreation hall, and a screened tea house. Rates include meals and firewood. Three nights minimum stay in summer, cash only.

Swan's Falls Campground, Fryeburg (mid–May to mid-Oct; ☎207/935-3395; $6 per night nonmembers, $5 members). Eighteen tent sites, several shelters, toilets, and hand-pumped water in a pine forest along the Saco River near the White Mountains. Some campsites are accessible by car and all are quiet during the week. Parking costs an additional $5 per day.

Walker's Falls Campground, East Brownfield (mid-June to early Sept; nonmembers $6 per night, members $5). This remote Saco River campground with five shelters, pump water, toilets, and several tent sites is primarily an overnight stop for canoeists. There is no auto access.

over 120 trails), this condo-studded center would be a more popular destination if it weren't for the fact that the nearest airport is a two-hour drive away in Portland. Summer activities include guided **mountain-bike tours** over the extensive trail system on the ski mountain; you can set one up, or just rent a bike courtesy of the Sugarloafer Shop (☎207/237-6718). There's also a full complement of hiking, canoe trips, and cookouts, plus a **golf** course designed by Robert Trent Jones Jr. Near the base of the Sugarloaf access road, just off of Rte-27, the amiable *Sugarloaf Brewing Company* (☎207/237-2211) brews up seven delicious original beers and also has a decent menu of filling pizzas and pub food.

Kingfield

The best base for Sugarloaf is fifteen miles south in the tiny town of **KINGFIELD**. The gorgeous *Inn on Winter's Hill*, 33 Winter Hill St (☎207/265-5421 or 1-800/233-9687; ❻-❼), is a lovingly restored Georgian Revival house with big rooms, an outdoor pool, hot tub, tennis court, and an option for sautéed veal with apple Chambord sauce at the excellent *Julia's* dining room (winter only). Down on the main street, the *Herbert Grand Hotel* (☎207/265-2000; ❺) has less attractive but functional rooms and a good restaurant. On Rte-142 in Weld, southwest of Kingfield, the *Lake Webb House* (☎207/585-2479; ❸) offers very affordable accommodations in an old farmhouse with a huge porch; breakfast is included. For **food**, *Longfellows Restaurant* on Main Street (☎207/265-4394) serves pastas, sandwiches, and chicken; entrées are two-for-one on Tuesdays, while *The Village Inn Restaurant*, Rte-27, Belgrade Lakes (Thurs–Sat 5–9 pm; ☎207/581-1154), is the place to get award-winning roast duckling.

Kingfield was the birthplace of twins Francis and Freelan Stanley, who invented, among other things, a steam-powered car and the dry-plate photographic process (which they sold to Kodak, amassing a considerable fortune). The **Stanley Museum** on School Street (June–Oct Tues–Sun 1–4pm; Nov–May Mon–Fri 9am–5pm; $2; ⓣ207/265-2729, ⓦwww.stanleymuseum.org) celebrates their story. Part of the main room is given over to their sister Chansonetta, a remarkable photographer whose studies of rural and urban workers have been widely published. Other exhibits include working steam cars from the early 1900s – ask nicely and you just may get a ride.

Moosehead Lake and around

Serene waters lap gently at the miles of deserted, thickly wooded shores around desolate **Moosehead Lake**, which at 117 square miles is the largest in Maine. As part of Maine's remote interior, the region was once relatively unknown, visited by Maine families, snowmobile fanatics, and serious hunters and fishermen; it's only now that more widespread discovery is taking place. **Greenville** is the sole settlement of any size on the lake, and it makes a good base from which to explore the area, especially if you're after moose sightings or if you intend to go whitewater rafting; though **The Forks**, a sporty settlement along the **Kennebec River** and US-201, has emerged as the center of the whitewater industry. West of the lake along Rte-15, gritty **Jackman**, big with the **snowmobile** crowd in winter, is the last stop before the Canadian border on the way to Québec.

Getting to Moosehead Lake

Moosehead Lake is roughly two and a half hours from Portland by car; the best way is via I-95 as far as Newport to Rte-11, Rte-23, and then Rte-6 N. While the majority of the **roads** in northern Maine are owned and maintained by huge logging and paper conglomerates, the public is often permitted access. On the **Golden Road**, for example, which connects Millinocket with the Quêbec border, travelers can pay a $4 fee at one of several gates for the privilege of driving its 96-mile length. Keep in mind, however, that the often unpaved roads are used primarily by logging trucks and that services are few and far between. Use caution and always yield to passing logging trucks. Distances are great and poor road conditions dictate slow travel speeds; be sure you have a good map and plenty of gas before you set out. In the towns especially, pay attention to the posted **speed limits** – local police are not shy about giving tickets if you're going only a few miles per hour too fast. For **information** on road availability and fees, call the Northern Paper Company at ⓣ207/723-2229.

Greenville and around

With a population of 1800, the rugged outpost of **GREENVILLE**, at the southern end of Moosehead Lake, is another nineteenth-century lumber town that now makes its living primarily from tourism. People come from all over to see wild **moose**, indigenous to the area, and which the town has been quick to exploit; there is nary a business around here that doesn't somehow incorporate the animal into its name. For several weeks in June, there's even an annual celebration, creatively named **Moosemainea** (call ⓣ207/695-2702 for more information). The Bullwinkle Guide Service (ⓣ207/695-3681) offers three-hour guided moose-watching tours daily during summer and early fall, while the *Birches Resort* (see below) offers, for $25, moose-spotting cruises, where you're also likely to see eagles, bears, and peregrine falcons.

The town isn't exceptionally pretty and it's certainly not very large, but it is well positioned for explorations throughout the Maine woods. With a bank, grocery store, post office, and a handful of shops and restaurants, it is also the area's commercial center. The main attraction is the restored **steamboat**, *Katahdin*, which tours the lake and serves as the floating Moosehead Marine Museum (cruises: June weekends only; July–Sept Tues, Fri, Sat & Sun 12.30pm, Wed 10am; 3-hour cruise $20, 5-hour cruise Wed $26; ⓣ207/695-2716). Near the dock, tiny **Thoreau Park** has a couple of picnic tables and a sign commemorating and describing the writer's 1857 visit to Moosehead Lake.

You'll soon want to get out of town, however, and a good way to explore is on a **mountain bike**; you can rent them ($25 per day), along with canoes, kayaks, and camping equipment at Northwoods Outfitters, on Main Street (ⓣ207/695-3288 or 1-800/530-8859, ⓦwww.northwoodsoutfitters.com). Greenville is also the largest **seaplane** base in New England; contact Currier's Flying Service (ⓣ207/695-2778) or Folsom's (ⓣ207/695-2821) for flight times and prices.

If you do choose to wander, one spot worth a visit is **Kineo**, an isolated nature preserve in the middle of the lake. Island trails lead to the top of dramatic **Mount Kineo**, whose flint-like cliff face rises some 800ft above the lake's surface. Shuttle boats to Kineo leave from Rockwood (daily 8am–5pm; $5).

Other good **hikes** in the area include the trip through **Gulf Hagas**, a 300-foot gorge fifteen miles east of town off of Greenville Road; the walk to an old B-52 crash site on nearby Elephant Mountain; and difficult climbs to the summits of 3196-foot **Big Moose Mountain** and 3230-foot **Big Spencer Mountain**. Contact the Chamber of Commerce for more information.

Practicalities

The **Chamber of Commerce**, just south of town on Rte-6/15 (9am–5pm: summer daily; Nov–Dec Thurs–Sat; rest of year Mon–Fri; ⓣ207/695-2702), has lots of information about area activities and accommodation. As an alternative, the **Maine Forest Service** (ⓣ207/695-3721) can provide information on their many free campsites in the area. There's not much in the way of interesting **food** options here; the local favorite is *Flatlander's*, on Main Street (ⓣ207/695-3373), which grills up cheap burgers and hot dogs along with a selection of basic seafood and meat dishes. Also in town, the relatively new *The Black Frog*, on Pritham Avenue (ⓣ207/695-1100), serves a variety of items (bacon-wrapped scallops, fettucini al Moosehead, fried chicken, BBQ pork) with a healthy dose of humor, and *Kelly's Landing* (ⓣ207/695-4438) is good for lunches and big weekend breakfasts.

Accommodations are generally upscale wilderness retreats that were built for rugged hunters, though there are exceptions. The *Birches Resort*, north of Greenville near the small village of Rockwood (ⓣ207/534-7305 or 1-800/825-9453, ⓦwww.birches.com; ❹–❽), for example, offers both rustic (tents, yurts) and first-class accommodations along with a host of outdoor activities. There's also a rather gourmet dining room overlooking the lake. More traditional choices back in Greenville include the Queen Anne *Pleasant Street Inn*, on Pleasant Street (ⓣ207/695-3400; ❻), and the comfortable *Lake View House*, on Lily Bay Road (ⓣ207/695-2229; ❻), which also has excellent lake views. The region's luxury hotel, also on Lily Bay Road, is the *Lodge at Moosehead Lake* (ⓣ207/695-4400; ❽),with a beautiful hillside location.

North of Greenville, the *Kineo House Inn*, an old cottage with six guest rooms (ⓣ207/534-8812; ⑤), is the only place to stay on Kineo; boat shuttle service and breakfast are included.

Jackman

Fifty miles west of Greenville, there's not much to **JACKMAN**, another old logging town that's somewhat reluctantly attempting to make the transition into a tourist destination. Situated next to deserted Wood Pond, less than twenty miles from the Canadian border (many of the radio stations here are in French), its main attraction is as a haven for **snowmobiles**, which take over the parking lots and surrounding lumber roads in winter. You can rent one of the noisy craft at *Dana's Rentals* on Main Street (ⓣ207/668-7828) or the *Sky Lodge* on Hwy-201 (ⓣ207/668-2171), from about $130–180, depending on the day of the week and how much power you want. **Ice fishing** is also popular in winter and several local businesses sell non-resident licenses, bait, and tackle. In summer, a forty-mile circuit known as the Moose River **Bow Trip** is one of the better flat-water **canoe trips** in the state, with good fishing and several **campsites** scattered along the way. The Jackman Moose River Chamber of Commerce, Main Street (ⓣ207/668-4171, ⓦwww.jackmanmaine.org), can help you locate a guide, if you so desire. The newly refurbished *Bishops Motel*, right in the center of town at 461 Main St (ⓣ1-888/991-7669, ⓦwww.bishopsmotel.com; ④), provides basic, clean **rooms** at reasonable rates. *Sally Mountain Cabins,* 9 Elm St (ⓣ207/668-5621 or 1-800/644-5621; $26 per person), has rustic cabins along the lake with full kitchens and private baths. The *Moose Point Tavern*, 16 Henderson Rd (ⓣ207/668-4012), is the best place to **eat** in town, not just for its views of the lake, but its hearty selection of meat dishes, including venison steak with blackberry sage sauce ($16.95); there's also a pleasant bar on the premises.

Baxter State Park and the far north

Driving through northern Maine can feel as though you're trespassing on the private fiefdoms of the logging companies; only **Baxter State Park** is public land. However, you're pretty much free to hike, camp, and explore anywhere you like, so long as you let people know what you're doing (only a sensible precaution, after all). The scenery is pretty much the same everywhere, although of course to get the best of it – to experience what Thoreau described in *Maine Woods* – you need to leave your car at some point and set off into the backwoods. You can read an excerpt from *Maine Woods* in the "New England in Literature," section on p.622.

Katahdin Iron Works and Millinocket

Five miles north of Brownsville Junction on Rte-11, an inconspicuous left turn leads to the **Katahdin Iron Works** at Silver Lake (summer daily 9am–5pm), built in 1843. It's quite remarkable how little remains of what one hundred years ago was a thriving industrial community: one solitary brick oven and the tower of the blast furnace, stark and forlorn at the end of a few miles of gravel track. In good summer weather, it's possible to continue along the track across the hills to Greenville.

Whitewater rafting

The **Penobscot** and the **Kennebec** are the two most popular rivers in Maine for the exhilarating sport of **whitewater rafting**, which has caught on in the past decade as a major recreational activity here. **The Forks** (population: 35), along Hwy-201 between Kingfield and Greenville, is the undisputed rafting center, and the majority of the outfitters are based there, along with the deluxe lodges and camps they've built to house the eager outdoors enthusiasts. Run from mid-May to mid-October, most trips depart in the early morning and return by mid-afternoon and require advance reservations. Levels of difficulty vary, but the rafting companies insist that people of all athletic abilities are welcome on most trips, which, as dictated by state law, are all led by certified "Maine guides." However, many companies do have age requirements, of which you must be aware if there are children with you. Raft Maine (ⓣ1-800/723-8633, ⓦwww.raftmaine.com) is an association comprised of several outfitters that can answer your questions. The following is but a partial list of potential - and reliable - options.

Magic Falls The Forks ⓣ207/663-2220 or 1-800/207-RAFT(7238), ⓦwww.magicfalls.com. One of the smaller, more personal rafting companies. Runs the Kennebec, Penobscot, and Dead rivers. One-day trips cost $70–99, with several special events planned. There's a new lodge with a bar and riverside cabins.

New England Outdoor Center Hwy-201, thirteen miles past Bingham in Caratunk ⓣ207/723-5438 or 1-800/766-7238, ⓦwww.neoc.com. A family-oriented outfit that puts on day-trips on the Kennebec, Penobscot, and Dead rivers, as well as two-day combination packages at a variety of accommodation types. They operate facilities both in Caratunk, south of The Forks, and at the Rice Farm, near Millinocket; there are also lakeside cabins on Millinocket Lake. Rafting trips cost $79–119 and include a guide, equipment, and a nourishing grilled lunch.

Northern Outdoors Hwy-201, The Forks ⓣ1-800/765-7238, ⓦwww.northernoutdoors.com. The oldest (since 1976) and largest of Maine's whitewater outfitters, running both the Kennebec and the Penobscot and offering longer overnight trips. One-day trips cost $85–122, including lunch. The outfit operates relatively upscale facilities at the *Forks Resort Center* and the Penobscot Outdoor Center, near Baxter State Park.

Professional River Runners Hwy-201, West Forks ⓣ207/663-2229 or 1-800/325-3911, ⓦwww.proriverrunners.com. Smaller outfit, family-owned and -operated, that runs both single-day and overnight trips; their guides are particularly good. No accommodations, but will help with referrals. Full-day trip on the Penobscot or Kennebec costs $55–100.

Wilderness Expeditions *The Birches Resort*, off of Rte-15, Rockwood ⓣ1-800/825-9453, ⓦwww.birches.com. Another of the large, full-scale resorts, with a base off of Rte-157 near Baxter State Park, along Hwy-201 just north of The Forks, and on Moosehead Lake near Rockwood. In addition to whitewater rafting, they offer many other activities, including kayaking, moose-cruises, eco-tours, and, in winter, cross-country skiing and snowmobiling. The facilities are top-notch. One-day rafting trips cost between $85 and $135, depending on the month, day, and river. Half-day trips are also available.

Farther north, **Millinocket** is a genuine company town, built on a wilderness site by the Great Northern Paper Company in 1899–1900 as the "magic city of the North." Public curiosity was so great that three hundred people came on a special train from Bangor to see what was happening. In 1990 the company was taken over by multinational Bowater Incorporated, and although the townspeople made a killing from cashing in their stock, their homes were almost unsaleable, and their jobs became tentative at best. The hundred-year-old manufacturing facilities still churn out nearly twenty percent of the newsprint produced in the United States. There's nothing to see or do here, but you might consider stopping off to pick up some supplies or grab a hot meal at the *Appalachian Trail Café*, 210 Penobscot Ave (Ⓣ207/723-6720).

It's also not a bad place to **stay** if the weather's bad; try the standard *Pamola Motel*, 973 Central St/Rte-11 (Ⓣ207/723-9746; ③), which provides a free continental breakfast. Next to Millinocket Lake, ten miles northwest, several whitewater rafting companies have set up lodgings and **campsites** as bases for their trips down the Penobscot River (see box on p.593 for details). There are dogsled races in February and March.

The park

By now you're approaching the southern end of sprawling and unspoiled **BAXTER STATE PARK** itself, with (on a clear day) the 5268-foot peak of imposing and beautiful **Mount Katahdin** visible from afar. Entrance to the park, collected at the Togue Pond Gate on Park Tote Road, costs $8 per car, and you should plan to arrive early in the day, as only a limited number of visitors are permitted access each day (though this limit rarely comes into effect outside of July and August). The enormous park – covering over 200,000 acres – was the single-handed creation of former Maine governor Percival P. Baxter, who, having failed to persuade the state to buy the imposing Katahdin and the land around it, bought it himself between the 1930s and 1960s and deeded it bit by bit to the state on condition that it remain "forever wild." A 2600-acre parcel was recently added and, amid some controversy, the State Park Authority refused to prohibit hunting and trapping on the newly acquired land. Nevertheless, the park's majestic green peaks (46 in all) and deserted ponds remain tremendously remote and pristine, and sightings of bears, bald eagles, and (of course) moose are not uncommon.

Hiking and camping

Hiking is the major pursuit here; indeed, the **Appalachian Trail** originates in the park at the top of Mount Katahdin. Among the park's 186 miles of trails, don't miss **Knife's Edge**, a thrilling walk across a narrow path that connects Katahdin's two peaks. The higher and typically more crowded of these, **Baxter Peak**, can also be reached via the **Hunt Trail** (5.2 miles, from Katahdin Stream), the **Cathedral Trail**, and the **Saddle Trail** (both around 2 miles, originating at Chimney Pond). For a less crowded but equally rewarding jaunt, head to the top of Hamlin Peak on the two-mile **Hamlin Ridge Trail**, which starts at Chimney Pond. Wherever you plan to hike, stop beforehand at either the headquarters in Millinocket, 64 Balsam Drive behind *McDonalds* (Ⓣ207/723-5140, Ⓦwww.baxterstateparkauthority.com), the visitors' center at Togue Pond (at the south entrance to the park – also a good place to **swim**), or at any of the park's campgrounds for a detailed **hiking map**. Water in the park is not treated and you should take care to carry as much as you'll need.

There are ten designated places to **camp** in Baxter, providing an array of options from basic tent sites to cabins equipped with beds, heating stoves, and gas lighting. Prices range from $8 to $22 per person per night and most sites are open from mid-May to mid-October. Reservations are accepted only via regular mail – again, try the Millinocket park headquarters.

North to Canada

The northernmost tip of Maine is taken up by **Aroostook County**, which covers an area larger than several individual states. Although its main activity is the large-scale cultivation of potatoes, it is also the location of the **Allagash Wilderness Waterway**, where several whitewater rafting companies put their boats in (see box, p.593).

Britain and the United States all but went to war over Aroostook in 1839; at **Fort Kent**, the northern terminus of US-1 (which runs all the way from Key West, Florida), the main sight is the solid cedar **Fort Kent Blockhouse**, built to defend American integrity and looking like a throwback to early pioneer days. *Doris' Café* (Ⓣ207/834-6262) at Fort Kent Mills on Rte-161, just off Rte-11 towards Eagle Lake, can provide big breakfasts.

Contexts

Contexts

A brief history of New England

It's generally accepted that people of mixed Mongolian descent, from northeast Asia, crossed the frozen Bering Straits and established settlements on the American continent sometime between 12,000 and 25,000 years ago, gradually spreading eastwards over the next several millennia, and arriving in New England between 9000 and 3000 BC. It's unclear whether or not they were the ancestors of the Algonquins, who greeted the Europeans when they arrived in the sixteenth and seventeenth centuries, or whether they became extinct.

Native peoples and early Europeans

The first documented **Europeans** to visit these shores were not English, but Norse. In about 1000 AD, King Olaf of Norway commissioned Leif Eriksson to bring Christianity to a new Viking settlement in Greenland. Like the pilgrims who were to follow six centuries later, Eriksson was blown off course, and came ashore somewhere between Newfoundland and Massachusetts. Discovering a new land where wild grapes grew in abundance, he dubbed it Vinland the Good.

Early European settlers applied the name **Algonquin** to the various groups of hunting peoples they encountered on the east coast of North America. Fiercely independent of each other, yet linked by the various dialects of the Algonquin tongue, and by common cultural ties and organizational structures, it's unlikely that they arrived in New England much before the fourteenth or fifteenth centuries – not long before the first European settlers. By 1600, there were only about 25,000 of them, broken into a dozen or so tribal nations, among them the **Narragansetts** of Rhode Island, the **Abnaki** of Maine, and smaller groups such as the **Niantics** and **Pequot** in Connecticut. They all took great advantage of the land, hunting, fishing, and growing crops such as beans, squash, tobacco, and corn.

European explorations

In the sixteenth century, Spanish conquistadors had focused almost exclusively on the southern regions of what is now North America, leaving the Dutch, English, Portuguese, and French to explore the inhospitable shores of New England – motivated not so much by the spirit of adventure, as by the determination to find an easy passage to the Orient and its treasures. Six years after Columbus's first voyage, in 1492, **John Cabot** nosed by the shores of New England, in search of the elusive Northwest Passage. Cabot, who came ashore somewhere in Labrador, claimed all America east of the Rockies and north of Florida for England, and was awarded a generous £30-a-year pension by King

Henry VII on his return. Meanwhile, **Giovanni de Verrazano**, for Francis I of France, traveled as far north as Rhode Island's Narragansett Bay, though the thought of establishing a settlement scarcely crossed his mind.

In 1583, **Sir Humphrey Gilbert** became the first Englishman to attempt the settlement of North America. Sailing from Plymouth, in the English county of Devon, he aspired to set up a trading post at the mouth of the Penobscot River, but he lost his life in a violent storm on the crossing over. More Englishmen followed him. Between 1602 and 1606, Bartholomew Gosnold, Martin Pring, and George Weymouth set out to tap New England's lucrative sassafras bark, used by the Indians to cure many ailments, and regarded in Europe as an effective panacea for all ills. Meanwhile, farther north, the French were making inroads: Samuel de Champlain had traversed the lake that today bears his name as early as 1609.

In 1606, King James I granted a charter to the **Virginia Company of Plymouth**, with permission to establish a colony between North Carolina and Nova Scotia. A year later, a hundred adventurous souls led by Pring, Raleigh, and Sir Fernando Gorges set out from Plymouth, their ships laden with trinkets to barter, food, and livestock. Arriving on Parker's Island off the coast of Maine, they made a short go of it, but were soon repelled by the hostile winter weather.

Despite their lack of success, they took home with them stories of a land of fast-flowing streams and rivers, of verdant forests, and friendly native peoples – so positive a picture, in fact, that the Plymouth Company commissioned distinguished surveyor **John Smith** to research the region's potential for development. Sailing along the Massachusetts coast in 1614, he named the region "**New England**." It was his book, *A Description of New England*, that persuaded the Pilgrims to migrate to these shores.

The Pilgrim Fathers

By the early seventeenth century, Europe was in religious turmoil: on mainland Europe, Luther, Calvin, and the other Protestant reformers had started a religious revolution against Roman Catholicism. The new **Church of England** that was created claimed to be both Catholic and reformed in an attempt to appease the varying factions within its ranks. The religious zealots who opposed all aspects of Catholicism, called **Puritans** on account of their apparent purity, enjoyed a degree of respectability during the reign of Elizabeth I, with growing numbers of followers in all walks of life. However, after the accession of the Catholic king, James I, in 1603, the Puritans found themselves increasingly harassed by the authorities.

Sixty-six of them negotiated a deal with the Plymouth Company to finance a permanent settlement in North America, where they would be free to practice their own religion. Chartered by Separatist leader John Carver, the *Mayflower*'s passenger list included the English Separatists, plus hired help, including Myles Standish, professional soldier, and John Alden, a cooper. In all, just over one hundred passengers set sail aboard the *Mayflower* from Southampton, England, on September 16, 1620.

After two months at sea, they reached the North American coast at **Provincetown, Cape Cod**, on November 19. The same day, 41 men signed the so-called **Mayflower Compact**, in which they agreed to establish a "Civic Body Politic" (temporary government) and to be bound by its laws:

IN THE NAME OF God, Amen. We, whose names are underwritten, the loyal subjects of our dread sovereigne Lord, King James, by the grace of God, of Great Britaine, France and Ireland king, defender of the faith etc., having undertaken, for the glory of God, and advancement of the Christian faith, and honour of our king and country, a voyage to plant the first colony in the Northerne parts of Virginia, doe, by these presents, solemnly and mutually in the presence of God, and one of another, covenannt and combine ourselves together into a civill body politick, for our better ordering and preservation and furtherance of the ends aforesaid; and by virtue hereof to enacte, constitute and frame such just and equall laws, ordinances, acts, constitutions and offices, from time to time, as shall be thought most meete and convenient for the generall good of the Colonie unto which we promise all due submission and obedience. In witness whereof we have hereunder subscribed our names at Cape-Codd the 11, of November, in the year of the raigne of our sovereigne lord, King James, of England, France, and Ireland, the eighteenth, and of Scotland the fiftie-fourth. Anno. Dom. 1620.

The Compact became the basis of government in the Plymouth Colony and **John Carver** was elected their first governor. The new arrivals had landed on a virtually barren stretch of the coast, and soon resettled across the bay, arriving at what is now Plymouth, Massachusetts, on December 26, 1620.

The early colonists

Only half of the colonists survived the first winter on American soil. Unaccustomed to the extreme cold, and living in shelters built of tree bark, many died from pneumonia; scurvy and other infections killed many more. It would have been even worse but for **Squanto**, a Native American who had spent time in England. He managed to enlist the support of Massassoit, the local Wampanoag sachem, who signed a Treaty of Friendship, and plied the visitors with food. Exactly a year after their arrival in Plymouth, the surviving Separatists could sit down with the Indians to enjoy a feast of roast game, eel, fruits, vegetables, and cornbread. Weeks later, they were joined by 35 more, laden with provisions, and by 1624 Plymouth had become a thriving village of thirty cottages. News of the community's success reached England, and in 1629 another group, led by London lawyer John Winthrop, obtained a royal charter as the "Company of the Massachusetts Bay in New England." That summer Winthrop and more than 300 settlers arrived at Salem; thousands more followed in the 1630s, as persecution of Puritans, led by Charles I's sidekick, Archbishop William Laud, intensified. Dozens of new communities were formed, many, such as Dorchester, Ipswich, and Taunton, named after the towns and villages the settlers had left behind. By 1640, the **Massachusetts Bay Company** had a population of about 10,000.

As the European population grew, so did the perceived need for clergy, preferably trained in New England. In 1636 **Harvard College** was established for that specific purpose, while a General Court was formed to administer the colony's affairs, including justice.

At this stage, new arrivals in the colonies were not limited to Massachusetts. In **Connecticut**, the Rev. Thomas Hooker established the community that became Hartford, while Theophilus Eaton and John Davenport founded New Haven. But frictions were already developing among the more zealous settlers, who were rapidly showing themselves to be even less tolerant than their oppressors back in England. The **Rev. Roger Williams**, hounded out of the Massachusetts Bay Colony in 1636 for his liberal views, established a new settlement of twenty families at Providence, in 1638, on land made available by two Indian sachems he'd befriended. The new **State of Rhode Island and Providence Plantations**, in its 1663 charter, guaranteed religious freedom for all: Jews, Huguenots, even the despised Quakers. Communities were also established in New Hampshire in 1638, and Maine in 1652.

Meanwhile, zealous Puritans worked at **converting** the Indians to their faith, translating the Bible into Algonquin, and setting up special communities for Christian Indians along the Connecticut River and on Cape Cod, which became known as "praying towns." Several Algonquins were sent to Harvard to train as Christian clergy – although only one completed the training successfully – and by the 1660s, the Christian faith accounted for one-fifth of all Indians. However, the settlers' arrogant attempt to persuade the Indians to give up their native culture and traditions, and mirror their own culture and beliefs, led to profound unhappiness, and eventually bloodshed.

At first, the new settlers and the Native Americans were able to co-exist peacefully, though **diseases** introduced by the colonists may have been directly responsible for a plague which killed more than a third of all the Algonquins. As the colonists ventured south, they began to meet growing resistance from the Indians, particularly the proud Pequot tribe, with whom war erupted in 1636, at Fort Mystic and Fairfield; many lives were lost on both sides. Then, in 1675, Narragansett leader Metacom, also known as Philip, persuaded feuding groups of Indians, principally the Nipmuck, Narragansetts, and Wampanoags, to bury their differences and join in a concerted campaign against the settlers. Known as **King Philip's War**, hostilities culminated in the **Great Swamp Fight** in Kingston, Rhode Island. More than 2000 Indians were slain, including Metacom himself. Even more significantly, it signaled the breaking of the Indian will.

The road to revolution

Up until the middle of the seventeenth century, the colonies had largely been left to take care of their own political structures. England, after all, was preoccupied with its own domestic concerns – a bloody civil war, the beheading of Charles I, and the establishment of Oliver Cromwell's parliamentary republic – and was scarcely interested in events happening three thousand miles away. The resulting vacuum was a breeding ground for the seeds of separatism, sentiment fueled by speculation that the Crown would soon seek to appoint its own governor to take charge of colonial affairs.

In 1686, King James II revoked the northern colonies' charters and attempted to create a **Dominion of New England** stretching from Maine to New Jersey. Spun as a security measure to protect the English communities from the French and the Indians, it was in reality an attempt to keep tabs on an increasingly defiant and potentially troublesome populace. The king's first gubernatorial appointee, Joseph Dudley, an Anglican, was succeeded by Edmund Andros, who imposed taxes as the disenfranchised populace grew increasingly frustrated.

A new respect between the Crown and colonies was temporarily forged in 1689, when the "Glorious Revolution" brought Protestants William and Mary to the British throne. The despised Andros was removed and put in jail, and the old powers of self-government restored. When King George III came to the throne in1760, he demanded obedience from America and soon demonstrated that he would go to any lengths to get it. In a move designed not so much to raise revenue as to remind the colonists who was boss, he was responsible for the **Revenue Act of 1764**, imposing taxes on sugar, silk, and wine, which resulted in a boycott of British goods and supplies.

The situation deteriorated further in 1765, with London's introduction of the **Stamp Act** and the imposition of taxes on commercial and legal documents, newspapers, and even playing cards. Throughout New England, protests erupted. Tax officials were the defendants in mock trials, and their effigies hanged. The bulk of the demonstrations were peaceful, but in Boston, the houses of stamp-man Andrew Oliver and Governor Thomas Hitchinson were plundered. The British prime minister, William Pitt, **repealed** the Act in March 1766.

Then, in the summer of 1767, new British prime minister Charles Townshend arrogantly taunted the colonies with his famous remark, "I dare tax America." The subsequent **Townshend Acts**, which introduced harsh levies on imports such as paper, glass, and, most provocatively, tea, prompted the dispatch to Boston of two regiments of redcoats. On March 5, 1770, a crowd of several hundred Bostonians gathered to ridicule a solitary "lobster-back" standing sentinel outside the customs house. Initially peaceful, the scene turned ugly as stones and rocks were thrown, and seven nervous reinforcements arrived, one firing on the crowd without orders. In the panic, more shots followed. Three colonists were pronounced dead and two were mortally wounded: the first martyrs in an event that was to become known as the **Boston Massacre**.

Things would have deteriorated more rapidly but for the **economic prosperity** that New England, and particularly Boston, was beginning to enjoy. Eventually, the Townshend Acts were repealed, though not the tax on East India tea, which was boycotted by the colonists. Dutch blends were smuggled in, and a special brew called Liberty Tea was concocted from sage, currant, or plantain leaves. Britain responded in September 1773 by flooding the market with its own, subsidized blend – half a million pounds of the stuff.

Resistance focused on Boston, where the **Massachusetts Committee of Correspondence**, an unofficial legislature, and the local chapter of the **Sons of Liberty**, a fast-growing pseudo-secret society, organized the barricading of the piers and wharves and demanded Governor Hutchinson send home the tea-filled clipper *Dartmouth*. When he refused, sixty men disguised as Mohawk Indians, Samuel Adams and John Hancock among them, surreptitiously climbed aboard and dumped 350 crates of the tea into Boston Harbor. The date was December 16, 1773, and the event captured the world's imagination as the **Boston Tea Party**.

This blatant act of defiance rattled Parliament, which introduced the so-called "**Coercive Acts**": the Boston Port Act sealed off the city with a massive naval blockade. Meanwhile, American patriots from Massachusetts, Rhode Island, and other states gathered in Philadelphia for the **First Continental Congress**, convened on September 5, 1774. Though British garrisons still controlled the major towns, such was the antagonism in rural areas that policing them was becoming virtually impossible for the British. All the while locals continued to stockpile arms and munitions.

In April 1775, London instructed its Boston commander General Thomas Gage to put down rebellion in rural Massachusetts, where the Provincial congress had assumed de facto political control. On the night of April 18, Gage dispatched 700 soldiers to destroy the arms depot in Concord, while at nearby Lexington seventy colonial soldiers, known as Minute Men, lay in wait, having been pre-warned of the plan by Paul Revere and William Dawes.

On Concord's Town Common, British musket fire resulted in the deaths of eight Americans. The British moved on to Concord, oblivious to the ambush which resulted in the deaths of 273 British soldiers, British retreat, and American jubilation. As news of the victory spread, rumors of plunder and pillage by British troops further fueled American resentment.

A couple of months later, the war intensified with the **Battle of Bunker Hill**, on Boston's Charlestown peninsula, which General Artemus Ward of the Continental Army had ordered to be fortified – though it was actually nearby Breed's Hill, not Bunker, where the American forces were stationed (see p.106). On June 17, the redcoats attacked twice, but were twice rebuffed. The third attempt succeeded, because the Americans ran out of ammunition. For this reason alone, the much-celebrated order "don't fire until you see the whites of their eyes" was given – some say by Colonel. William Prescott, others General Isaac Putnam – specifically to save on ammunition. Bunker Hill, with 1000 British casualties, was an **expensive triumph for the Crown**. Worn down by lack of manpower, low morale, and growing American resistance, less than a year later an embattled General Gage ordered a **British withdrawal** to Halifax, Nova Scotia.

The **Declaration of Independence** – with fifty-six signatories, fourteen of whom were from the New England states of **Massachusetts**, **Connecticut**, **New Hampshire**, and **Rhode Island** – was adopted by the Continental Congress on July 4, 1776.

Even after victory, all was not plain sailing. In a move designed to protect the states' newly independent status, the thirteen independent colonies hammered out an integrated union in 1781, though not without the concern that a centralized federal system would be just as bad as British rule. For that reason, heroes Sam Adams and John Hancock gave only grudging support to the Constitution, and representatives from Rhode Island consistently voted against it, relenting only after the Bill of Rights was added.

With the Declaration of Independence, the families who had settled **Vermont** pondered their future. In January 1777, the state proclaimed itself independent, and at Windsor in July, seventy delegates unanimously adopted a constitution that was almost an exact replica of Pennsylvania's. Vermont remained an independent state until 1791, when it was admitted to the Union as the **fourteenth state**.

Maine's statehood was not gained until 1820, after the eastern part of the state had been occupied by the British during the War of 1812. According to the Missouri Compromise of 1820, Maine was admitted to the Union as a free (anti-slavery) state, balanced by Missouri, a slave state.

Nineteenth-century development

New England had started out as a predominantly **agricultural region**, particularly the areas away from the coast, where maritime trading and commerce was found. Maine and New Hampshire developed important trades in timber, agriculture, and fishing, with some shipbuilding on the coast at Bath, Maine, and Portsmouth, New Hampshire. The opening of the **Champlain Canal**, connecting Lake Champlain to the Hudson River, made it possible for Vermont farmers to ship goods to New York City, stimulating agriculture and wool production, at least until the 1860s when dairy farming began to take hold. But, apart from some lush pockets of Vermont, the soil was generally poor; plowing was difficult, and the long, cold New England winters meant that for a large part of the year the ground was frozen solid. The land lent itself to little more than subsistence farming – with small farms, wheat, corn, pigs, and cattle – and New England could never compete with the vast wheat- and dairy-producing areas of the growing Midwest.

But New England's true prosperity came first as a result of its **connection with the sea**; fishing, especially for cod, was important, as was the production of whale derivatives, especially oil, used for heating and lighting. More adventurous sea captains, many of them based in Boston or Salem, Massachusetts, ventured farther afield, and brought back great treasures from India and China, including tea, spices, silk, and opium.

Several communities, such as Newport, Rhode Island, flourished on the back of the **Triangular trade**; ships unloaded West Indian molasses, reloaded with rum, then sailed to Africa, where the rum was exchanged for slaves, in turn shipped to the West Indies and traded for molasses. **Shipbuilding** industries flourished, particularly in places such as Essex, Massachusetts, which earned a reputation for manufacturing swift, easily maneuverable vessels. But the first two decades of the nineteenth century showed how volatile maritime trade was, especially with so many political uncertainties, notably the Napoleonic Wars, Thomas Jefferson's Embargo Acts (which prohibited all exports to Europe and restricted imports from Great Britain – a response to British and French interference with American ships), and the War of 1812. There was a clear need for New England to diversify its economy if its prosperity were to grow.

The Industrial Revolution

In 1789, **Samuel Slater**, a skilled mechanic from England, sailed from his native land to New York disguised as a laborer. The emigration of skilled mechanics was forbidden by the British government, and there were serious penalties for those found smuggling the specifications and drawings for the pioneering industrial machinery that had earned Britain her nickname as the "workshop of the world." Slater, though, had been able to memorize the specifications of his boss Richard Arkwright's factory-sized cotton spinning machine, which was set to revolutionize the highly inefficient existing system of individual looms. Financed by Moses Brown, a Providence Quaker, he set up the nation's first successful **cotton mill** at Pawtucket, Rhode Island. The working conditions here were hellish, and these, together with the poor rates of pay, inspired the nation's first industrial strike in 1800.

Another entrepreneur determined to duplicate British weaving feats was Bostonian **Francis Cabot Lowell**, a self-styled "industrial tourist." Determined to duplicate British ingenuity in America, he spent $10,000 of his own money plus $90,000 from his "Boston Associates" to set up a small mill with a power loom and 1700 spindles at Waltham, west of Boston. Lowell's **Merrimack Manufacturing Company** proved extremely profitable, with sales at $3000 in 1815 and reaching $345,000 in 1822. In 1826, having already uprooted to Chelmsford, the business moved again, to a purpose-built community named "Lowell" after its founder. Lowell's enlightened, anthropological approach was continued by his associates after his death: young female workers lived in dorms to protect their honor, received education, and were given sufficient time off to engage in a variety of leisure pursuits.

New England was fast becoming the **industrial center** of the US, home to some two-thirds of the nation's cotton mills, half of which were in Massachusetts. Tiny Rhode Island processed twenty percent of the nation's wool and in Connecticut **Sam Colt** and **Eli Whitney**, known for his invention of the cotton gin, manufactured the first firearms with interchangeable parts. Connecticut also became home to a thriving watch- and clock-making industry. In the fields of paper and shoe manufacture and metalworking New England, and particularly New Hampshire, was unsurpassed.

Culture and education

New England, particularly Boston, had always set a strong standard as far as **education** and **literature** were concerned. The nation's first secondary school, Boston Latin, opened in 1635, closely followed by Harvard in 1636. In Connecticut, Yale University was established in 1701, while Rhode Island's Brown University, originally Rhode Island College, came into being in 1764. Farther north, New Hampshire's Dartmouth College dates from 1769, and Bowdoin College in Maine from 1796.

In 1639, America's first printing press was set up in Cambridge, where the *Bay Psalm Book*, *New England Primer,* and freeman's oath of loyalty to Massachusetts were among the first published works. The colonies' first newspaper, *Publick Occurrences, Both Foreign & Domestick*, came into being in 1690, and was succeeded by the more popular *Boston News-Letter* in 1704. By the 1850s, more than 400 periodicals were in print. Libraries such as Hartford's famous Wadsworth Atheneum and the Providence Atheneum both came into existence in the mid-nineteenth century, while in 1854 the Boston Public Library, with 750,000 volumes, became the world's first free municipal library.

At the same time, the region became home to some of the nation's greatest thinkers, philosophers, essayists, artists, and architects. Among them were Henry David Thoreau, the **transcendentalist** philosopher and essayist; Louisa May Alcott, author of *Little Women*; Winslow Homer, noted for his marine watercolors; poet Emily Dickinson; and novelists such as Nathaniel Hawthorne, whose most famous book, *The House of the Seven Gables*, was set in Salem, Massachusetts. In Connecticut, Mark Twain had set up home at Nook Farm, near Hartford, as had Harriet Beecher Stowe – author of *Uncle Tom's Cabin.*

Not coincidentally, a strong cultural identity developed, focusing again on Boston, where the 1871 founding of the **Museum of Fine Arts** was followed a decade later by the Boston Symphony Orchestra and the Boston Pops. New Haven became an important focus for theater in Connecticut, with the establishment of the Long Wharf, Schubert, and Yale Repertory theaters.

The Civil War

The type of **anti-slavery** sentiment Stowe had advocated in *Uncle Tom's Cabin* was echoed by a number of northerners, though in general, when it came to **slavery** New Englanders held ambivalent views. Laws in all of the New England states had **outlawed** the practice. Still, it would prove to be the catalyst for the bloodiest conflict ever seen on American soil, the **Civil War**.

From the moment of its inception, the unity of the nation had been based on shaky foundations. Great care had gone into devising a Constitution that balanced the need for a strong federal government with the aspirations for autonomy of its component states. That was achieved by giving Congress two separated chambers – the House of Representatives, in which the number of representatives from each state depended on its population, and the Senate, where each state elected two members, regardless of size. Thus, although in theory the Constitution remained silent on the issue of slavery, it allayed the fears of the less populated southern states, that the voters of the north might destroy their economy by forcing them to abandon their "peculiar institution." However, it soon became apparent that the system only worked so long as there were roughly equal numbers of "free" and slave-owning states.

At first, it seemed possible that the balance could be maintained – in 1820, under the Missouri Compromise, Missouri was admitted to the Union as a slave-owning state at the same time as Maine was admitted as a "free" one. In 1854, the **Kansas–Nebraska Act** forced the issue to a head, allowing both prospective states self-determination on the issue. John Brown's raid on the Armory at Harpers Ferry, West Virginia, in which he intended to raid arms for a slave rebellion, was quashed, and Brown hanged. The Civil War began. Though **no battles** were fought in New England, the region sent thousands of men to bolster the Union cause, many of whom would never return. In the end, it was not so much the brilliance of the generals as sheer economic power that won the war for the Union. It was the north, with New England leading the way, that could maintain full trading with the rest of the world while diverting spare resources to the production of munitions.

Into the twentieth century

Civil War, the Industrial Revolution, a vast intellectual flowering, all these things and more combined to create the vast sea change for New England in the latter half of the nineteenth century. Perhaps most important, the frontiers of the US moved west, and other regions began to play their part in the development of the nation. Despite its **diminishing influence** on the national stage, New England continued the strong tradition of social reform exemplified by William Lloyd Garrison and others long before the Civil War started, paving the way in the fields of prison reform and health and mental health provision.

Meanwhile, the ethnic and religious make-up of New England was changing rapidly. No longer was it the preserve of white Anglo-Saxon Protestants; **Irish immigrants** began pouring over in the 1840s, following the potato famine. Soon more than a thousand Irish immigrants a month were arriving in Boston, while Catholics from Italy, French Canada, Portugal, and Eastern Europe accounted for two-thirds of the total population growth during the nineteenth century. Indeed, by 1907, seventy percent of Massachusetts' population could claim to be of non-Anglo-Saxon descent. Even in less developed New Hampshire, one out of every five had adopted, not inherited, the US flag.

Such waves of immigration provoked some backlash, with the openly racist **Know-Nothing** party gaining governorships in Massachusetts, Rhode Island, Connecticut, and New Hampshire; membership of the American Protective Association and Immigrant Restriction League increased dramatically; and signs such as "No Irish Need Apply" were found on the doorsteps of many a business.

Still, immigrants soon found ways of working the political system, especially the Irish, and in 1881, John Breen from Tipperary became the first Irishman to take up an establishment position – as mayor of Lawrence, Massachusetts. This had a profound motivating effect on his fellow countrymen, and three years later, Hugh O'Brien won the Boston mayorship, while Patrick Andrew Collin represented Suffolk County with a congressional seat in the nation's capital. By the turn of the twentieth century, immigrants were represented at all levels of government.

But political scandal and **corruption** were never far away. "Boss" Charlie Brayton and the *Providence Journal* ring bought their way to office in Rhode Island, with individual votes costing $2 to $5, and up to $30 in hotly contested elections. Others abused the privileges of the solid ethnic support they enjoyed: **James Michael Curley**, elected Boston mayor four times, and voted governor of Massachusetts 1934–1938, did much to improve the welfare of the poor, but also doled out jobs and money to community leaders who carefully manipulated the electorate and its votes.

With the huge influx of mainly poor immigrants, especially from Catholic countries, a "**New Puritanism**" began to take hold. Encouraged by Catholic leader William Cardinal O'Connell and the closely associated **Watch and Ward Society**, moralists lobbied for the prohibition of, among other things, Hemingway's *The Sun also Rises* and a variety of plays and books.

The southern exodus

As time passed, other regions began to challenge New England's claim to be the manufacturing capital of the US. Many companies **moved south**, where costs were much lower, and by 1923 more than half of the nation's cotton goods were being woven there. Industrial production in Massachusetts alone fell by more than $1 billion during the 1920s, while unemployment skyrocketed in some towns to 25 percent, and up to 40 percent after the Wall Street crash. The **Great Depression** hit New England particularly hard and, with few natural resources to draw upon and human resources moving to the South, industry in New England never really recovered. From the boom days of the late nineteenth century, when hundreds of thousands of New Englanders were engaged in textiles, the figure had dropped to fewer than 70,000 by the 1970s. By 1980, the region which had given birth to America's Industrial Revolution was headquarters to only fourteen of the nation's top five hundred companies.

Modern times

Political collaboration, instead of confrontation, between New England's "Brahmin" political set, and the second- and- third-generation sons and daughters of immigrants, began to pay off in a common quest to find an answer to New England's economic and social problems, and by the 1980s the region was beginning to experience something of an **industrial resurgence**. New industries, such as the production of biomedical machinery, electronics, computer hardware and software, and photographic materials sprang up throughout the region, but especially along Route 128 west of Boston, which has become New England's so-called Silicon Valley. During this period, Boston became the country's mutual fund capital, Hartford's insurance industry continued to flourish, and tourism became the region's second largest source of income. The region became known for its political stability and, at the same time, for leading the way with anti-pollution laws, consumer rights, handgun controls, and civil rights legislation.

The nationwide economic slump in the late 1980s and early 1990s continued to cause problems in those larger urban centers which had failed to address the social consequences of the demise of traditional manufacturing industries.

But the area rebounded again. Increasing, almost unparalleled prosperity accompanied by low unemployment – especially in the latter half of the 1990s – meant that more money was freed up for the benefit of long-neglected areas that needed attention – roads and infrastructure, crime prevention, schools, and social provision – although significant problems remain to be tackled. At the same time **urban regeneration**, sometimes on a spectacular scale (in Providence, Rhode Island, for example), and the continued development of new, mostly computer-related and service industries, has put the region more or less back on track.

The present and the future

Like most of the country, the region took another hit with the slowdown of the economy in the wake of the bursting of the dot-com bubble and September 11, 2001. On the whole, however, positive factors remain in place. Ethnic tensions are less of a problem here than they have ever been. Significant measures to protect the environment have been enacted in several states, and improvement in the frequency and duration of rail services along the northeast corridor – and in commuter services generally – will lead, planners hope, to fewer cars on the road. Time will tell how successful Amtrak's new *Downeaster* service between Boston and Portland, Maine, will be. As for the never-ending, multi-million dollar "Big Dig," which will take most of Boston's north–south traffic underground, current estimates are that the bulk of the work will be finished by 2004 – although no one is holding their breath.

Politically, liberalism and, to an extent, libertarian values, remain prominent. Vermonter Bernie Sanders has a claim as the lone **socialist/independent** congressman; the storied **Kennedy** family of Massachusetts continues to hold sway in the national consciousness, if with less political influence; and in January 2002 the Vermont Supreme Court rejected challenges to the state's **civil union laws**, reconfirming it as the most gay- and lesbian-friendly state in New England – if not the nation. Both tickets in the 2000 presidential campaign had strong ties to New England. Democratic vice-presidential candidate **Joe Lieberman** comes from New Haven, Connecticut; while the country's new president, **George W. Bush**, matriculated in the same city and has connections with Maine, where his family owns a home at Kennebunkport – though liberalism is certainly something he cannot be faulted for, and he was mostly rejected by New England voters in favor of Al Gore.

New England on film

As picturesque and as rich in narrative as New England is, the region has always seemed inhospitable to the young turks of Hollywood. For one thing it is as far from Los Angeles, both geographically and psychologically, as you can get in the continental United States; for another, the weather, though undeniably cinematic, is famously unpredictable. Nevertheless, there are plenty of films set in New England.

Films drawing their inspiration from the region often have a particularly local subject matter – academia, witchcraft – or sometimes literary adaptations. Indeed, Hollywood has gamely hacked away at whole schools of unfilmable New England novels, usually failing more spectacularly with each attempt.

The following films are all set in one of New England's six states (though Massachusetts, and especially Boston, predominates). They weren't, however, necessarily filmed in New England: many were shot in California, some in England, and quite a number conveniently across the border in Canada. The entries preceeded by ★ are highly recommended films.

The Actress George Cukor, 1953. A unique portrait of Boston in the early 1910s, *The Actress* is based on a play by Ruth Gordon about her early life in nearby Wollaston. Though the film, which stars Jean Simmons as Gordon and a deliciously cantankerous Spencer Tracy as her father, is largely studio-bound, it is full of historical tidbits.

★ **Affliction** Paul Schrader, 1998. One of the best New England movies of recent years, this brooding tale of violence shattering the placid surface of a snowbound New Hampshire town hardly does wonders for the tourist trade. Nick Nolte is superb as the divorced small-town cop stumbling through middle age, whose father's legacy of abuse is too heavy a load to bear.

Alice's Restaurant Arthur Penn, 1969. Built around Arlo Guthrie's hit song of the same name, this quizzical elegy for counterculture brought the hippie nation to the Berkshire town of Stockbridge in western Massachusetts.

★ **All That Heaven Allows** Douglas Sirk, 1955. Sirk's splendid technicolor masterpiece recounts the forbidden romance of a middle-aged widow (Jane Wyman) and her strapping, Thoreau-quoting gardener (Rock Hudson). This devastating portrait of small minds of the local country-club set served to show that the Puritanism of the seventeenth century was alive and well in post-war New England.

Between the Lines Joan Micklin Silver, 1977. Shot on location, this multi-character comedy-drama documents the dying throes of counterculture in late 1970s Boston by focusing on the ragtag staff of underground newspaper *The Back Bay Mainline* (based on the real-life *Real Paper*).

★ **The Bostonians** James Ivory, 1984. Merchant-Ivory's high-minded Henry James adaptation is set in 1875 Boston. New England women's libbers and a Southern male chauvinist battle for the soul of one very pliable young woman in the drawing rooms of Cambridge, on the lawns of Harvard, and on the beaches of Martha's Vineyard. Vanessa Redgrave and Christopher Reeve, as the opposing armies, are superb.

The Boston Strangler Richard Fleischer, 1968. Boston is set on edge by a series of brutal murders. Shot like a documentary, with a panoply of split-screen effects, this true-life crime story, starring a jittery Tony Curtis as the titular handyman, starts out well but soon gets bogged down in psychobabble.

Carousel Henry King, 1956. Loutish Maine carnival barker Billy Bigelow (Gordon MacRae), who resorts to crime to support his wife (Shirley Jones) and unborn child, is killed in a robbery attempt. Years later, heaven's Starkeeper allows him to return to earth to see his daughter graduate from high school. Though its non-sunny tone may have been responsible for its expensive failure on release, *Carousel* is nonetheless an excellent and fondly regarded musical. Includes the tunes "June Is Bustin' Out All Over" and "You'll Never Walk Alone."

Christmas in Connecticut Peter Godfrey, 1945. Barbara Stanwyck plays a Manhattan magazine writer who has faked her way to being the Martha Stewart of her day. When her publisher asks her to invite a war hero to her Connecticut farm for Christmas, Stanwyck has to conjure up the idyllic New England existence she'd only written about. Unfortunately the results are convoluted, and the studio-built Connecticut is – ironically – clearly a fake.

Cider House Rules Lasse Hallstrom, 1999. Surprisingly well-received adaptation of John Irving's novel (see "Books"), in which a shifting Maine backdrop sets the stage for a somewhat didactic, if winning, meditation on love, suffering, and the thorny issue of abortion.

A Civil Action Steve Zaillian, 1998. John Travolta struts his stuff as a cocky ambulance-chasing Boston lawyer who loses everything but regains his soul when he takes up the case of a group of families in a nearby town who believe their children developed leukemia after drinking contaminated local water. A rainy, wintry vision of New England enlivened by Robert Duvall as a devilish old pro who'd rather be at Fenway Park than in court.

The Crucible Nicholas Hytner, 1996. A riveting adaptation of Arthur Miller's classic allegory of McCarthyism, set during the Salem Witch Trials of 1692. Winona Ryder and her friends are spied dancing by firelight and accused of witchcraft; to save themselves they start naming names. Daniel Day-Lewis is suitably tortured as Ryder's Puritan lover caught between Plymouth Rock and a hard place.

Dead Poets Society Peter Weir, 1989. This inspirational film, pitting arch-conservative academe versus freethinking progress, seems like the classic New England movie. It was in fact shot in Delaware and the film itself makes no mention of specific locale. However, if any movie deserves mention as an honorary New England movie, this is it.

Dolores Claiborne Taylor Hackford, 1995. On a dreary island off the coast of Maine, a housekeeper (Kathy Bates) is suspected of murdering her wealthy employer, and even her neurotic journo daughter from New York (Jennifer Jason Leigh) thinks she's guilty. This lovingly crafted Gothic sleeper was adapted from a Stephen King novel, and, although it succeeds admirably in conveying the weather-beaten charms of the Maine coast, it was actually shot in Nova Scotia.

The Europeans James Ivory, 1979. Shot against the gorgeous fall foliage of New Hampshire and Massachusetts, Merchant-Ivory's genial adaptation of Henry James's novella pits New England sobriety ("There must be a thousand ways to be dreary and sometimes I think we make use of them all," pines Lisa Eichhorn) against the dizzy charms of a couple of European visitors to the suburban countryside of nineteenth-century Boston.

Far From Heaven Todd Haynes, 2002. Haynes's ode to Douglas Sirk (see *All That Heaven Allows*) stars Julianne Moore as a perfect 1950s Connecticut housewife, confronted first with sexual anxiety as a result of her husband's activities, then with racial pressures when she takes up with their gardener (Dennis Haysbert).

★ **Good Will Hunting** Gus Van Sant, 1997. When money-minded producers suggested shooting their script up in Canada, Beantown buddies Ben Affleck and Matt Damon insisted that the verisimilitude of Boston locations was essential to their script about a South Boston townie tough who is a closet math wizard. They got their way, and the rest is history.

The House of the Seven Gables Joe May, 1940. Fusty superstition battles liberal enlightenment in eighteenth-century Massachusetts in this histrionic adaptation of Nathaniel Hawthorne's Gothic family saga. George Sanders and Vincent Price play yin-yang siblings fighting for control of their accursed family mansion, against a background of abolitionism and the birth of photography.

★ **The Ice Storm** Ang Lee, 1997. Suburban living in 1970s Connecticut – bell-bottoms, key-parties, etc – is laid bare in all its formica-covered splendor in this rather dour adaptation of Rick Moody's novel, starring Kevin Kline, Sigourney Weaver, and Joan Allen. The production design, if nothing else, is priceless, and the titular squall that climaxes the film a magnificent specimen of New England weather.

In the Bedroom Todd Field, 2001. Against the backdrop of Maine's small harbor-town lobster docks (and filmed all over the coast), a college-age boy begins seeing a local divorcee with an angry ex-husband. After an unexpected tragedy, his parents (Sissy Spacek and Tom Wilkinson) dissect the affair and their pivotal roles in this emotionally draining drama. Wilkinson wins the best-Maine-accent-by-a-foreigner award.

★ **Jaws** Steven Spielberg, 1975. Spielberg's toothsome blockbuster took the well-worn New England trope of the destructive outsider disrupting the well-ordered life of the community and gave it its ultimate id-like expression in the form of a killer shark who wreaks havoc on the shores of Martha's Vineyard (known here as Amity Island).

★ **The Last Hurrah** John Ford, 1958. The great John Ford was born and raised in Maine, but this is one of his few depictions of the Northeast. Spencer Tracy plays the no-nonsense Irish-American mayor of a New England town (a thinly veiled Boston) whose career is on the wane. It's talky and sentimental, but pulls no punches in its depiction of the snobbery of the local bluebloods towards the Boston Irish.

★ **Leave Her to Heaven** John M. Stahl, 1945. A stunning, too-little-known gem, in which Gene Tierney plays a woman who loves too much. Half of this gorgeously colorful movie takes place in New Mexico, but the scenes in Maine – especially a devastating scene involving a rowboat, a lake, and a pair of sunglasses – are indelible.

Little Women George Cukor, 1933; Gillian Armstrong, 1994. Despite the reams of New England literature massacred by Hollywood, Louisa May Alcott's timeless classic, set in Concord, has fared remarkably well, with not one but two wonderful adaptations. The first, made by George Cukor in 1933, stars a rambunctious Katherine Hepburn as Jo; the second, made some sixty years later by Gillian Armstrong, has Winona Ryder in the lead role and Susan Sarandon as the ever-wise Marmee.

★ **Love Story** Arthur Hiller, 1970. The Harvard preppie (Ryan O'Neal) and the working-class Radcliffe wiseacre (Ali McGraw) fall head over heels against a backdrop of library stacks, falling leaves, tinkling pianos, and low-rent Cambridge digs. The tragedy in this four-hankie blockbuster only kicks in when the lovebirds relocate to New York.

★ **Malice** Harold Becker, 1993. In a small college town in Massachusetts (the film was shot at Smith College in Northampton) the blissful life of newlyweds Bill Pullman and Nicole Kidman is rocked by the arrival of diabolically charismatic Harvard doctor Alec Baldwin – a surgeon with a "God complex." A devilish little thriller.

Misery Rob Reiner, 1990. Adaptation of popular Stephen King novel, and certainly one of the more successful screen transformations, with a chilling Kathy Bates as novelist James Caan's biggest fan. The dreary and ominous New England backdrop is perfect – though most action takes place inside a house.

Moby Dick Lloyd Bacon, 1930; John Huston, 1956. Melville's classic, which begins in New Bedford, Massachusetts, has been given at least two very different treatments by Hollywood. Lloyd Bacon's early version, starring John Barrymore, runs a skimpy 75 minutes and turns Captain Ahab's monomaniacal quest into a love story with a happy ending. John Huston's reverential 1956 version, with Gregory Peck as Ahab, is visually striking, but still unequal to the task.

Mystic Pizza Donald Petrie, 1988. The film that put both Julia Roberts and Mystic, Connecticut, on the national map. Shot on location in Mystic and nearby Rhode Island, this mildly entertaining tale of the romantic travails of three young waitresses at the local pizza joint is set in the town's Portuguese lobster-fishing community.

Next Stop Wonderland Brad Anderson, 1998. The title of this thinking woman's indie romance actually refers to the greyhound racing stadium at the end of one of Boston's subway lines where luckless nurse Hope Davis finally crosses paths, after many a false start, with the man of her dreams. The Boston aquarium has a major supporting role.

On Golden Pond Mark Rydell, 1981. The pond of the title is really Squam Lake in New Hampshire's Lakes Region, where, one summer, a crabby Boston professor (Henry Fonda in his final film) and his wife (Katherine Hepburn) get in touch with their inner child. A breathtakingly picturesque but schmaltzy tear-jerker that probably did more for New England tourism than all the other films listed here combined.

The Perfect Storm Wolfgang Petersen, 2000. George Clooney, Diane Lane, and Mark Wahlberg star in this adaptation of Sebastian Junger's bestseller about a swordfishing boat's doomed journey into the heart of the "storm of the century." The film's best moments are on shore, in its rich portrait of the fishing community of Gloucester, Massachusetts; once at sea, it's an empty special-effects extravaganza.

The Raid Hugo Fregonese, 1954. A brutal Civil War tale of a band of escaped Confederate prisoners, who, in 1864, infiltrated the picturesque Vermont town of St Albans intending to raze it to the ground. Based on a true story, this little-known gem stars Van Heflin, Lee Marvin, and Anne Bancroft, who plays the beautiful Yankee widow whose hospitality puts a spanner in the Rebs' plan of action.

Reversal of Fortune Barbet Schroeder, 1990. Opening with a jaw-dropping aerial sequence of the mansions of Newport strung along the Rhode Island coastline, this devastatingly witty film dramatizes the case of Claus von Bülow, who was convicted of attempting to murder his heiress wife Sunny, and then acquitted in the Rhode Island Supreme Court with the help of Harvard lawyer Alan Dershowitz.

The Russians Are Coming! The Russians Are Coming! Norman Jewison, 1966. A comic vision of Cold War paranoia in which a Russian submarine runs aground off fictional "Gloucester Island" somewhere on the New England coast, causing panic in this archetypally dozy community. A precursor, of sorts, to *Jaws,* this blockbuster farce was actually shot on the coast of Northern California.

The Scarlet Letter Victor Seastrom, 1926; Wim Wenders, 1973; Roland Joffe, 1995. Hawthorne's masterpiece has been treated about as woefully by Hollywood as Hester Prynne was treated by the good people of Salem. The first, silent, adaptation of the book, starring Lillian Gish, is the best, though it reduces Hawthorne's symbol-laden complexities to a tragic pastoral romance. Wim Wenders' 1973 version – filmed in Spain with German actors – is about as much fun as Salem on the Sabbath, while the 1995 Demi Moore vehicle supplies the story with some racy sex scenes and a new happy ending.

Splendor in the Grass Eli Kazan, 1961. Though its handful of scenes set at Yale University are confined to studio sets, Kazan's Kansas melodrama bears mention for the pivotal role that New Haven's legendary pizza pie plays in the proceedings. To wit, Warren Beatty reneges on his promise to return to high school sweetheart Nathalie Wood when he is seduced by a pizza and marries the pizza-maker's daughter.

Starting Over Alan J. Pakula, 1979. Burt Reynolds leaves his unfaithful, song-writing wife in their swanky Manhattan pad and moves to a cold-water Boston flat to start over. A wonderful and little-known comedy romance, co-starring Jill Clayburgh, written by James L. Brooks, and shot by Bergman's cinematographer Sven Nykvist.

★ **State and Main** David Mamet, 2000. A slick Hollywood film crew lands in uptight small-town Vermont after having been run out of New Hampshire for unknown, but undoubtedly lurid, reasons. Mamet uses all his trademarks to take on sometimes obvious targets, but this screwball comedy, by virtue of its winning performances and often hilarious dialogue, still feels fresh.

The Swimmer Frank Perry, 1968. A splendid curio adapted from a John Cheever short story, in which upscale rural Connecticut is imagined as a lush Garden of Eden through which broad-chested, swim-suited Burt Lancaster makes his allegorical way home one summer afternoon, going from swimming pool to swimming pool.

There's Something About Mary Farrelly Brothers, 1998. If Rhode Island is to go down in the annals of cinema history it would have to be as the site of Ben Stiller's notorious pre-prom mishap with a zipper in this gross-out masterpiece. There are some nice views of the Providence waterfront before the film relocates to Miami in pursuit of the eponymous object of desire.

Tough Guys Don't Dance Norman Mailer, 1987. Set in Provincetown, on the beckoning fingertip of Cape Cod, Mailer's bizarre retelling of his own novel is a convoluted affair involving an overintoxicated writer (Ryan O'Neal), a gay-bashing sheriff, a Southern millionaire, a buxom Bible-bashing gold digger, drug-dealing lobster men, and a severed head.

The Trouble with Harry Alfred Hitchcock, 1955. A black comedy painted in the reds and golds of a perfect Vermont fall. The trouble with Harry is that he keeps turning up dead and everybody, including his young wife (Shirley MacLaine in her debut), thinks they may have killed him. The trouble, meanwhile, with fall in Vermont is the weather, and, though shooting began on location, Hitchcock's crew eventually had to retreat to Hollywood with truckloads of leaves to finish the film.

The Verdict Sidney Lumet, 1982. Gripping courtroom thriller, with Paul Newman as an alcoholic has-been lawyer given one last lease on life – trying a medical malpractice suit against a big Massachusetts hospital.

Vermont is for Lovers John O'Brien, 1993. A charming, semi-documentary, indie comedy about a New York couple who travel to Vermont to get married, come down with a bad case of cold feet, and turn to the locals – all real Vermonters and neighbors of O'Brien – for advice. Scene-stealing septuagenarian sheep farmer Fred Tuttle then had a spin-off in O'Brien's spoof of Vermont politics, *Man with a Plan* (1995).

Walk East on Beacon Alfred L. Werker, 1952. A very matter-of-fact thriller about FBI agents ferreting out communists in Cold War Boston. Shot documentary-style, the film tempers its pinko-bashing paean to Hoover's boys with the more engaging nuts and bolts of their activities and plenty of vivid location footage.

White Christmas Michael Curtiz, 1954. Singing and dancing army buddies Bing Crosby and Danny Kaye take a break from hoofing in Manhattan and take the train up to Vermont for a skiing holiday, only to find there hasn't been snow all year. One of the very few musicals to be set in New England, beloved for its Irving Berlin score, and that magical snowy finale.

The Witches of Eastwick George Miller, 1987. An arch, handsome, but ultimately hollow adaptation of John Updike's novel about three love-starved women who conjure up a rather unwelcome visitor to their sleepy Massachusetts town. The film was shot in Cohasset, just south of Boston – as picture-perfect a New England town as you, or the Warner Bros. production designers, could hope to find.

Books

Below are some of the best books to employ New England as a backdrop for storytelling and otherwise; publishers are listed after the title, US/UK if not published in both territories, and o/p denotes out of print.

Travel, impressions, poetry

James Chenoweth *Oddity Odyssey* (Henry Holt US). Fun little book that tries to point out some of the more intriguing and humorous episodes and myths surrounding the sights and major players in New England's history.

★ **Emily Dickinson** *The Complete Poems* (Little, Brown). The ultimate New England poet, who spent all her life in the same town – indeed the same house – and quietly recorded the seasons, local incidents, and her own thoughts on life in a series of insightful poems.

Robert Frost *The Collected Poems* (Henry Holt). Frost's poems skillfully evoke the New England landscape, especially "New Hampshire," and remain classics, despite their sometimes too-familiar feel.

★ **Robert Lowell** *Life Studies and For the Union Dead* (Noonday Press). Unbelievably affecting stuff from arguably New England's greatest twentieth-century poet, tackling family and social issues with striking precision.

Henry Wadsworth Longfellow *Poems and Other Writings* (Library of America). Longfellow celebrated both common and heroic New Englanders in his sometimes whimsical verse; perhaps a bit light for some, but very much central to New England society over the mid-nineteenth century.

Henry David Thoreau *Cape Cod; The Maine Woods; Walden* (Penguin US). Walden is basically a transcript of Thoreau's attempt to put his transcendentalist philosophy into practice, by constructing a cabin on the banks of Walden Pond, near Concord, Massachusetts, and living the simplest of lives based on self-reliance, individualism, spiritual enlightenment, and material frugality. Nature also plays a part in *Cape Cod* and *The Maine Woods*, accounts of the writer's walking trips published after his death. An extract from *The Maine Woods* is printed on pp.622–625.

History, culture, and society

Jack Beatty *The Rascal King: the Life and Times of James Michael Curley, 1874–1958* (Addison Wesley o/p). A thick and thoroughly researched biography of the charismatic Boston mayor and Bay State governor, valuable, too, for its depiction of big-city politics in America.

William Corbett *Literary New England: a History and Guide* (Faber). A guide to the literary haunts of New England – full of trivia, basically, but entertainingly so.

Malcolm Cowley *New England Writers and Writing* (University Press of New England). A compilation of previously published essays on nineteenth- and twentieth-century New England writers (some of whom Cowley knew personally), and including discussion of the work of Hawthorne, Whitman, and John Cheever, among others. Also included are writings by Cowley himself on aspects of New England life.

David Hackett Fischer *Paul Revere's Ride* (University of Massachusetts Press/Oxford University Press). An exhaustive account of the patriot's legendary ride to Lexington, related as a historical narrative.

Sean Flynn *3000 Degrees* (Warner). Gripping retelling of the 1999 four-alarm fire in Worcester, MA, that resulted in the death of six firefighters.

★ **Sebastian Junger** *The Perfect Storm* (Fourth Estate UK; HarperCollins US). A dramatized account of a storm off the New England coast in 1993, and a rip-roaring read of a book.

★ **Mark Kurlansky** *Cod* (Penguin). Does a fish merit this much obsessive attention? Only in New England. Kurlansky makes a good case for viewing the cod as one of the more integral parts of the region's fabric.

★ **J. Anthony Lukas** *Common Ground: a Turbulent Decade in the Lives of Three American Families* (Vintage US). A Pulitzer Prize–winning account of three Boston families – one Irish-American, one black, one white middle-class – against the backdrop of the 1974 race riots sparked by court-ordered busing to desegregate public schools.

Louis Menand *Metaphysical Club* (Farrar, Straus and Giroux USA). Arguably the most engaging study of Boston heavyweights Oliver Wendell Holmes, William James, Charles Sanders Pierce, and John Dewey ever written, this Pulitzer Prize–winning biography links the foursome through a short-lived 1872 Cambridge salon and extols the effect of their pragmatic idealism on American intellectual thought.

Nat Philbrick *In the Heart of the Sea: the Tragedy of the Whaleship Essex* (Penguin). Basically the story behind *Moby Dick*, and a true one at that, exploring the Nantucket whaling industry through the *Essex*'s saga. Gripping, if a bit too straightforward.

Douglass Shand-Tucci *The Art of Scandal: the Life and Times of Isabella Stewart Gardner* (HarperCollins US). Astute biography of this doyenne of Boston society, who served as the inspiration for Isabel Archer in Henry James's *Portrait of a Lady*. The book includes evocative photos of Fenway Courtyard in Gardner's Venetian-style palace – which is now the Gardner Museum.

Dan Shaughnessy *The Curse of the Bambino* (Penguin). Shaughnessy, a Boston sportswriter, strikes a chord with every long-suffering Red Sox fan by examining the team's "curse" – no championships since 1918 – that began just after they sold Babe Ruth to the Yankees.

Scott Turow *One L: the Turbulent True Story of a First Year at Law School* (Warner Books). Turow, author of the thriller *Presumed Innocent*, recounts his first year at Harvard Law, and all the trials, tribulations, and tension that it entailed. It's quite a well-written, evocative book, but mainly of interest to law students and lawyers.

Hiller B. Zobel *The Boston Massacre* (W.W. Norton). A painstaking account of the circumstances that precipitated one of the most highly propagandized pre-Revolution events – the slaying of five Bostonians outside the Old State House.

Architecture and design

Mona Domosh *Invented Cities: the Creation of Landscape in Nineteenth Century New York and Boston* (Yale University Press US). Fascinating historical account of how these very different cities were shaped according to the values, beliefs, and fears of their respective societies.

Elaine Louie and Solvi dos Santos *Living in New England* (Simon & Schuster). Well-illustrated coffee-table book about the interiors, rather than architectural styles, of New England homes.

Naomi Miller and Keith Morgan *Boston Architecture 1975–1990* (Prestel). Contextualizes Boston's transformation into a modern city, with emphasis on the building boom of the 1980s, but also detailing the early development and architectural trends of centuries before. Plenty of photographs, too.

★ **Susan and Michael Southworth** *AIA Guide to Boston* (Globe Pequot US). The definitive guide to Boston architecture, organized by neighborhood. City landmarks and dozens of notable buildings are given exhaustive but readable coverage.

Nature and specific guides

★ **Appalachian Mountain Club** *Maine Mountain Guide: The Hiking Trails of Maine* (Appalachian Mountain Club). Meticulous hiking guide, with detailed color maps, that should get you through both the popular and more backwoods sections of the state.

Marilyn Dwelley, Fay Hyland *Trees and Shrubs of New England* (Down East Books). Accessible field handbook to outdoor New England, useful if you'll be doing some hiking and camping through various parks and mountains.

Tom Wessels *Reading the Forested Landscape: Natural History of New England* (Countryman Press). Less an outdoors guide than a deconstruction of why the land and trees are like they are today. Uniquely informative.

Fiction

★ **Louisa May Alcott** *Little Women* (Puffin). A semi-autobiographical novel, drawing on family experiences, Alcott's novel remains a classic to this day.

Gerry Boyle *Lifeline* (Berkley). Hard-hitting suspense novel about an ex-big city reporter looking for solace in small-town Maine, only to find that crime exists there, too. Others in the series include *Bloodline* and *Deadline*.

James Casey *Spartina* (Vintage). Set in the fishing world of Narragansett Bay, Rhode Island, this memorable, spare work about a man struggling with pretty much every imaginable aspect of his life captured the National Book Award in 1989.

John Cheever *The Wapshot Chronicle* (Vintage). Better known for his short stories, this was Cheever's first novel, and documents the weird doings of the Wapshot family, of St Botolph's, Massachusetts. The sequel, *The Wapshot Scandal*, continues the family saga.

Michael Crichton *A Case of Need* (Signet USA). Winner of the 1969 Edgar Award for best mystery novel, this gripping medical thriller, which opens with a woman bleeding to death in a Boston hospital, was written long before Crichton conceived of the hit television drama *ER*, and under a pseudonym to boot.

Bret Easton Ellis *The Rules of Attraction* (Picador UK; Vintage US). Another of Ellis's sex, drug, and booze-driven narratives, this time charting the romantic progress of a few students through Vermont's fictional Camden College. Still, strangely compelling.

Mary Eleanor Freeman *A New England Nun and Other Stories* (Penguin Books). Relatively unknown these days, Freeman enjoyed quite a fashion about 100 years ago for her tales of rural New England life. Worth seeking out.

Elizabeth Graver *Unravelling* (Hyperion). In distinct and compelling fashion, Graver charts a young woman's progress on the bleaker edges of New England life: its farms and factory mills.

Nathaniel Hawthorne *The House of the Seven Gables*; *The Scarlet Letter*. Born in Salem, Massachusetts, in 1804, one of Hawthorne's ancestors was a judge at the famous witch trials, and this (and the curse that ensued) provides the story for *The House of the Seven Gables*. *The Scarlet Letter* is a moral tale of guilt, judgment, and redemption. Both Penguin and Bantam do low-priced paperback editions.

George V. Higgins *Penance for Jerry Higgins* (Abacus UK). Ace crime writer and former district attorney who portrays the seamier side of Boston life in this and most of his other novels.

★ **John Irving** *The Cider House Rules* (Black Swan UK; Vintage US). Irving writes huge, sprawling novels set all over New England. This one, suitably Dickensian in scope, is neither his most popular (*The World According to Garp*) or beloved (probably *A Prayer for Owen Meany*). But it is perhaps his best – a fascinating meditation on, of all things, abortion.

Henry James *The Bostonians* (Penguin). James's soporific satire traces the relationship of Olive Chancellor and Verena Tarrant, two fictional feminists, in the 1870s.

Sarah Orne Jewett *A Country Doctor* (Bantam US). One of the lesser-known late nineteenth-century New England novelists, but one of the most locally evocative. Packed full of period detail, this novel, about a Maine woman who refuses marriage so she can pursue her ambition to become a doctor, is a marvellous account of life in rural Maine.

Denis Johnson *The Resuscitation of a Hanged Man* (Penguin). Not Johnson's best work, but still a diverting, suspenseful read, in which a Provincetown disc jockey starts tracking the life of a lesbian with whom he becomes enamored.

★ **Jack Kerouac** *Maggie Cassidy* (Penguin). The protobeatnik grew up in New England; here, he traces the arc of a youthful romance, to fine effect, with an equally fine setting in a small Massachusetts mill town.

Stephen King *Different Seasons*; *Dolores Claiborne* (Penguin). Born in Maine, King is incredibly prolific, and doesn't always hit the mark; some of his writings do manage, though, quite well to evoke his home state and region; these are two of the better ones.

Wally Lamb *She's Come Undone* (Simon & Schuster). This debut novel is a harrowing and brutal story of a young girl in harsh circumstances, which is lightened by hopeful humor. Its first-person female narrative, despite being written by a man, is credible and moving.

Dennis Lehane *Darkness, Take My Hand* (Avon). Lehane sets his mysteries on the working-class streets of South Boston; they are all excellent and evocative, but this is probably the cream of the crop. His most recent, *Mystic River* (William Morrow), is highly recommended, too.

H.P. Lovecraft *The Best of H.P. Lovecraft: Bloodcurdling Tales of Horror and the Macabre* (Ballantine). The best stories from the author who Stephen King called "the twentieth century's greatest practitioner of the classic horror tale." An extract from his story, *The Dunwich Horror*, is printed on p.625.

★ **Herman Melville** *Moby Dick* (Penguin). The incomparable story of a man's obsession with a great white whale. Plenty of descriptive prose on the whaling industry and its effect on places like New Bedford and Nantucket.

Grace Metalious *Peyton Place* (Northeastern University Press US). A saucy and sexy, if not particularly well-written, romp through a small New England town's existence. The book that inspired the TV show and movie of the same name.

John Miller and Tim Smith (eds) *Cape Cod Stories* (Chronicle US). Well-selected stories, essays, and excerpts from a mostly predictable crop of writers – Thoreau, Updike, and so on.

★ **Arthur Miller** *The Crucible* (Penguin). This compelling play about the 1692 Salem witch trials is peppered with quotes from actual transcripts and loaded with appropriate levels of hysteria and fervor – a must for witch fanatics everywhere.

Susan Minot *Folly* (Washington Square Press US). This obvious nod to Edith Wharton's *Age of Innocence* is set in 1917 Boston instead of New York, and details the proclivities of the Brahmin era, in which women were expected to marry well, and the heartbreak that ensues from making the wrong choice (whence, folly).

Rick Moody *The Ice Storm* (Warner). Two neighboring families from Connecticut whose process of collapse is a tawdry Seventies tale of alcoholic excess, wife-swapping and adultery, and alienation – all brought to a shuddering and tragic climax by the storm of the book's title. Made into a stylish and affecting movie.

Sylvia Plath *The Bell Jar* (Harper Perennial US). Angst-ridden, dark, cynical – everything a teenaged girl wants out of a book. The second half of this brilliant (if disturbing) autobiographical novel about Esther Greenwood's mental breakdown after a summer spent working at a New York fashion magazine, is set in Boston suburbs, where she winds up institutionalized in a mental hospital.

★ **E. Annie Proulx** *Heartsongs* (Fourth Estate UK; Macmillan US). Gritty stories of life in rural and blue-collar New England – beautifully crafted tales that evoke elemental themes. Also worth your while, Proulx's novel *The Shipping News* won the National Book Award and the Pulitzer Prize for fiction.

George Santayana *The Last Puritan* (MIT Press). The philosopher's brilliant "memoir in the form of a novel," set around Boston, chronicles the short life and education of protagonist Oliver Alden coming to grips with Puritanism.

Wallace Stegner *Crossing to Safety* (Penguin). The saga of two couples who form a lifelong bond, set partly in Vermont. It might seem a bit slow and sentimental at a glance, but Stegner's strong writing should win you over.

John Steinbeck *The Winter of Our Discontent* (Penguin). A late work by Steinbeck, published in 1961, and examining the collapse of an old New England family under pressure from the modern world.

Eleanor Sullivan *Murder in New England* (Castle). A collection of pulpy murder mystery stories by Isaac Asimov, Ed Hoch, and Brendan DuBois, among others, fixating on the death of a Harvard man, eerie happenings off I-95, and Rhode Island lights.

Donna Tartt *The Secret History* (Penguin UK; Ballantine US). An "It" book from the early 1990s, and one that actually resonates, this centers on a small group of students at a fictional Vermont college, modeled after Bennington, and the murderous turns their elite cadre takes. Short on landscape, but a surprisingly diverting tale.

John Updike *The Witches of Eastwick* (Ballantine). Satirical witchy tale set in rural 1960s Rhode Island and chock-full of hypocrisy, adultery, and wickedness; in short, a fun read.

David Foster Wallace *Infinite Jest* (Little Brown and Co US). Not the kind of book you want to pack for your travels (it's a whopping 1088 pages), some of this sprawling and often hilarious opus's best passages take place at Enfield, a tennis academy outside Boston, while other nuggets involve a Cambridge store owner in a Canadian separatist terrorist plot.

★ **Edith Wharton** *Ethan Frome* (Penguin). A distilled portrait of stark, icy New England that belies the fiery emotions blazing underneath. The title character's perverse, tragic odyssey is riveting; the writing simple and superb, especially evocative of the Massachusetts farmscape in which the story is set.

New England in literature

New England is as literary a landscape as the United States has to offer; indeed the region's writers perhaps figure more prominently in the American literary canon than those of any other region. There are the early nineteenth-century nature writers, Thoreau and Emerson; the poets, Emily Dickinson, Henry Wadsworth Longfellow, Robert Frost, and Wallace Stevens; nineteenth-century novelists like Nathaniel Hawthorne, Henry James, and Edith Wharton; not to mention more recent authorial heavyweights like John Updike and Richard Ford. And, of course, Boston and Cambridge have long been centers of academic research and writing.

We've selected deliberately wide-ranging pieces of writing below, and printed them chronologically. First there is the opening passage of Thoreau's posthumously published account of trekking through Maine in the mid-nineteenth century; second, a flight of fantasy from H.P. Lovecraft, but one very deeply rooted in the landscapes and cultural traditions of New England; and, last, a contemporary piece of reportage about the sea and the fishing industry by adventure writer Sebastian Junger.

The Maine Woods

Henry David Thoreau was born in Concord, Massachusetts, in 1817 and spent all his life in New England before dying of tuberculosis at the age of 45. He was a nature writer above all, but only published two books during his lifetime, *A Week on the Concord and Merrimack Rivers*, published in 1849, and *Walden*, a searching and introspective story of the two years he spent living in a homemade hut not far from his home. He was unrecognized as a writer while he was alive, and in fact was regarded as something of an eccentric, both locally and by the literary establishment. "If I seem out of step with the world," he said, "it is because I hear another drummer." The following extract is taken from the opening pages of **The Maine Woods**, a story of several walks undertaken between 1846 and 1857, through what was in those days a relatively wild and undiscovered part of the region, still inhabited by native tribes and where the main activity was logging. It was published posthumously, having been edited by his sister Sophie and a friend, Ellery Channing, and is nowadays available as a Penguin paperback.

On the 31st of August, 1846, I left Concord in Massachusetts for Bangor and the backwoods of Maine, by way of the railroad and steamboat, intending to accompany a relative of mine, engaged in the lumber trade in Bangor, as far as a dam on the west branch of the Penobscot, in which property he was interested. From this place, which is about one hundred miles by the river above Bangor, thirty miles from the Houlton military road, and five miles beyond the last log-hut, I proposed to make excursions to Mount Ktaadn, the second highest mountain in New England, about thirty miles distant, and to some of the lakes of the Penobscot, either alone or with such company as I might pick up there. It is unusual to find a camp so far in the woods at that season, when lumbering operations have ceased, and I was glad to avail myself of the circumstance of a gang of men being employed there at that time in repairing the injuries caused by the great freshet in the spring. The mountain may be approached more easily and directly on horseback and on foot from the northeast side, by the Aroostook road, and the Wassataquoik River; but in that case you see much less of the wilderness, none of the glorious river and lake scenery, and have no experience of the batteau and the boatman's life. I was fortunate also in the season of the year, for in the summer myriads of black flies, mosquitoes, and midges, or, as the Indians call them, "no-see-ems," make traveling in the woods almost impossible; but now their reign was nearly over.

Ktaadn, whose name is an Indian word signifying highest land, was first ascended by white men in 1804. It was visited by Professor J. W. Bailey of West Point in 1836; by Dr. Charles T. Jackson, the State Geologist, in 1837; and by two young men from Boston in 1845. All these have given accounts of their expeditions. Since I was there, two or three other parties have made the excursion, and told their stories. Besides these, very few, even among backwoodsmen and hunters, have ever climbed it, and it will be a long time before the tide of fashionable travel sets that way. The mountainous region of the State of Maine stretches from near the White Mountains, northeasterly one hundred and sixty miles, to the head of the Aroostook River, and is about sixty miles wide. The wild or unsettled portion is far more extensive. So that some hours only of travel in this direction will carry the curious to the verge of a primitive forest, more interesting, perhaps, on all accounts, than they would reach by going a thousand miles westward.

The next forenoon, Tuesday, September 1, I started with my companion in a buggy from Bangor for "up river," expecting to be overtaken the next day night at Mattawamkeag Point, some sixty miles off, by two more Bangoreans, who had decided to join us in a trip to the mountain. We had each a knapsack or bag filled with such clothing and articles as were indispensable, and my companion carried his gun.

Within a dozen miles of Bangor we passed through the villages of Stillwater and Oldtown, built at the falls of the Penobscot, which furnish the principal power by which the Maine woods are converted into lumber. The mills are built directly over and across the river. Here is a close jam, a hard rub, at all seasons; and then the once green tree, long since white, I need not say as the driven snow, but as a driven log, becomes lumber merely. Here your inch, your two and your three inch stuff begin to be, and Mr. Sawyer marks off those spaces which decide the destiny of so many prostrate forests. Through this steel riddle, more or less coarse, is the arrowy Maine forest, from Ktaadn and Chesuncook, and the head-waters of the St. John, relentlessly sifted, till it comes out boards, clapboards, laths, and shingles such as the wind can take, still, perchance, to be slit and slit again, till men get a size that will suit. Think how stood the white-pine tree on the shore of Chesuncook, its branches soughing with the four winds, and every individual needle trembling in the sunlight,—think how it stands with it now,— sold, perchance, to the New England Friction Match Company! There were in 1837, as I read, two hundred and fifty saw-mills on the Penobscot and its tributaries above Bangor, the greater part of them in this immediate neighborhood, and they sawed two hundred millions of feet of boards annually. To this is to be added the lumber of the Kennebec, Androscoggin, Saco, Passamaquoddy, and other streams. No wonder that we hear so often of vessels which are becalmed off our coast, being surrounded a week at a time by floating lumber from the Maine woods. The mission of men there seems to be, like so many busy demons, to drive the forest all out of the country, from every solitary beaver-swamp and mountain-side, as soon as possible.

At Oldtown, we walked into a batteau manufactory. The making of batteaux is quite a business here for the supply of the Penobscot River. We examined some on the stocks. They are light and shapely vessels, calculated for rapid and rocky streams, and to be carried over long portages on men's shoulders, from twenty to thirty feet long, and only four or four and a half wide, sharp at both ends like a canoe, though broadest forward on the bottom, and reaching seven or eight feet over the water, in order that they may slip over rocks as gently as possible. They are made very slight, only two boards to a side, commonly secured to a few light maple or other hard-wood knees, but inward are of the clearest and widest white-pine stuff, of which there is a great waste on account of their form, for the bottom is left perfectly flat, not only from side to side, but from end to end. Sometimes they become "hogging" even, after long use, and the boatmen then turn them over and straighten them by a weight at each end. They told us that one wore out in two years, or often in a single trip, on the rocks, and sold for from fourteen to sixteen dollars. There was something refreshing and wildly musical to my ears in the very name of the white man's canoe, reminding me of Charlevoix and Canadian Voyageurs. The batteau is a sort of mongrel between the canoe and the boat, a furtrader's boat.

The ferry here took us past the Indian island. As we left the shore, I observed a short, shabby, washerwoman-looking Indian—they commonly have the woe-begone look of the girl that cried for spilt milk,—just from "up river,"—land on the Oldtown side near a grocery, and, drawing up his canoe, take out a bundle of skins in one hand, and an empty keg or half-barrel in the other, and scramble up the bank with them. This picture will do to put before the Indian's history, that is, the history of his extinction. In 1837 there were three hundred and sixty-two souls left of this tribe. The island seemed deserted to-day, yet I observed some new houses among the weather-stained ones, as if the tribe had still a design upon life; but generally they have a very shabby, forlorn, and cheerless look, being all back side and woodshed, not homesteads, even Indian homesteads, but instead of home or abroad-steads, for their life is domi aut militae, at home or at war, or now rather venatus, that is, a hunting, and most of the latter. The church is the only trim-looking building, but that is not Abenaki, that was Rome's doings. Good Canadian it may be, but it is poor Indian. These were once a powerful tribe. Politics are all the rage with them now. I even thought that a row of wigwams, with a dance of powwows, and a prisoner tortured at the stake, would be more respectable than this.

We landed in Milford, and rode along on the east side of the Penobscot, having a more or less constant view of the river, and the Indian islands in it, for they retain all the islands as far up as Nicketow, at the mouth of the East Branch. They are generally well-timbered, and are said to be better soil than the neighboring shores. The river seemed shallow and rocky, and interrupted by rapids, rippling and gleaming in the sun. We paused a moment to see a fish-hawk dive for a fish down straight as an arrow, from a great height, but he missed his prey this time. It was the Houlton road on which we were now traveling, over which some troops were marched once towards Mars' Hill, though not to Mars' field, as it proved. It is the main, almost the only, road in these parts, as straight and well made, and kept in as good repair as almost any you will find anywhere. Everywhere we saw signs of the great freshet,—this house standing awry, and that where it was not founded, but where it was found, at any rate, the next day; and that other with a waterlogged look, as if it were still airing and drying its basement, and logs with everybody's marks upon them, and sometimes the marks of their having served as bridges, strewn along the road. We crossed the Sunkhaze, a summery Indian name, the Olemmon, Passadumkeag, and other streams, which make a greater show on the map than they now did on the road. At Passadumkeag we found anything but what the name implies,—earnest politicians, to wit,— white ones, I mean,—on the alert to know how the election was likely to go; men who talked rapidly, with subdued voice, and a sort of factitious earnestness you could not help believing, hardly waiting for an introduction, one on each side of your buggy, endeavoring to say much in little, for they see you hold the whip impatiently, but always saying little in much. Caucuses they have had, it seems, and caucuses they are to have again,—victory and defeat. Somebody may be elected, somebody may not. One man, a total stranger, who stood by our carriage in the dusk, actually frightened the horse with his asseverations, growing more solemnly positive as there was less in him to be positive about. So Passadumkeag did not look on the map. At sundown, leaving the river road awhile for shortness, we went by way of Enfield, where we stopped for the night. This, like most of the localities bearing names on this road, was a place to name which, in the midst of the unnamed and unincorporated wilderness, was to make a distinction without a difference, it seemed to me. Here, however, I noticed quite an orchard of healthy and well grown apple-trees, in a bearing state, it being the oldest settler's house in this region, but all natural fruit and comparatively worthless for want of a grafter. And so it is generally, lower down the river. It would be a good speculation, as well as a favor conferred on the settlers, for a Massachusetts boy to go down there with a trunk full of choice scions, and his grafting apparatus, in the spring.

The Dunwich Horror

Much like Thoreau, **Howard Phillips Lovecraft** was a literary outsider. Born in Providence, Rhode Island, in 1890, he spent all his life in New England apart from a brief and unsuccessful marriage (when he lived in New York), until his death in 1937. He was something of a cult author while he was alive, read only by a handful of mystery and fantasy fiction fans, and he remains relatively unknown to this day. He's perhaps best known for his creation of the so-called **Cthulhu Mythos**, a pantheon of ancient gods that lurk beneath the surface of our everyday lives, influencing terrible events and destined one day to rise again. It's this combination of ancient horrors and everyday occurrences that makes Lovecraft's stories so distinctive – and still so resonant and frightening. They have all the classic motifs of horror fiction, but mix with this a local sensibility and evocations of ancient and sinister New England landscapes. Like many of his tales, the following extract, from the opening of **The Dunwich Horror**, is not describing real locations or events, but it is typical in the authority – and underlying fear – it brings to its subject.

When a traveller in north central Massachusetts takes the wrong fork at the junction of the Aylesbury pike just beyond Dean's Corners he comes upon a lonely and curious country. The ground gets higher, and the brier-bordered stone walls press closer and closer against the ruts of the dusty, curving road. The trees of the frequent forest belts seem too large, and the wild weeds, brambles, and grasses attain a luxuriance not often found in settled regions. At the same time the planted fields appear singularly few and barren; while the sparsely scattered houses wear a surprisingly uniform aspect of age, squalor, and dilapidation. Without knowing why, one hesitates to ask directions from the gnarled, solitary figures spied now and then on crumbling doorsteps or on the sloping, rock-strewn meadows. Those figures are so silent and furtive that one feels somehow confronted by forbidden things, with which it would be better to have nothing to do. When a rise in the road brings the mountains in view above the deep woods, the feeling of strange uneasiness is increased. The summits are too rounded and symmetrical to give a sense of comfort and naturalness, and sometimes the sky silhouettes with especial clearness the queer circles of tall stone pillars with which most of them are crowned.

Gorges and ravines of problematical depth intersect the way, and the crude wooden bridges always seem of dubious safety. When the road dips again there are stretches of marshland that one instinctively dislikes, and indeed almost fears at evening when unseen whippoorwills chatter and the fireflies come out in abnormal profusion to dance to the raucous, creepily insistent rhythms of stridently piping bull-frogs. The thin, shining line of the Miskatonic's upper reaches has an oddly serpent-like suggestion as it winds close to the feet of the domed hills among which it rises.

As the hills draw nearer, one heeds their wooded sides more than their stone-crowned tops. Those sides loom up so darkly and precipitously that one wishes they would keep their distance, but there is no road by which to escape them. Across a covered bridge one sees a small village huddled between the stream and the vertical slope of Round Mountain, and wonders at the cluster of rotting gambrel roofs bespeaking an earlier architectural period than that of the neighbouring region. It is not reassuring to see, on a closer glance, that most of the houses are deserted and falling to ruin, and that the broken-steepled church now harbours the one slovenly mercantile establishment of the hamlet. One dreads to trust the tenebrous tunnel of the bridge, yet there is no way to avoid it. Once across, it is hard to prevent the impression of a faint, malign odour about the village street, as of the massed mould and decay of centuries. It is always a relief to get clear of the place, and to follow the narrow road around the base of the hills and across the level country beyond till it rejoins the Aylesbury pike. Afterward one sometimes learns that one has been through Dunwich.

Outsiders visit Dunwich as seldom as possible, and since a certain season of horror all the signboards pointing toward it have been taken down. The scenery, judged by any ordinary esthetic canon, is more than commonly beautiful; yet there is no influx of artists or summer tourists. Two centuries ago, when talk of witch-blood, Satan-worship, and strange forest presences was not laughed at, it was the custom to give reasons for avoiding the locality. In our sensible age – since the Dunwich horror of 1928 was hushed up by those who had the town's and the world's welfare at heart – people shun it without knowing exactly why. Perhaps one reason – though it cannot apply to uninformed strangers – is that the natives are now repellently decadent, having gone far along that path of retrogression so common in many New-England backwaters. They have come to form a race by themselves, with the well defined mental and physical stigmata of degeneracy and inbreeding. The average of their intelligence is woefully low, whilst their annals reek of overt viciousness and of half-hidden murders, incests, and deeds of almost unnamable violence and perversity. The old gentry, representing the two or three armigerous families which came from Salem in 1692, have kept somewhat above the general level of decay; though many branches are sunk into the sordid populace so deeply that only their names remain as a key to the origin they disgrace. Some of the Whateleys and Bishops still send their eldest sons to Harvard and Miskatonic, though those sons seldom return to the mouldering gambrel roofs under which they and their ancestors were born.

No one, even those who have the facts concerning the recent horror, can say just what is the matter with Dunwich; though old legends speak of unhallowed rites and conclaves of the Indians, amidst which they called forbidden shapes of shadow out of the great rounded hills, and made wild orgiastic prayers that were answered by loud crackings and rumblings from the ground below. In 1747 the Reverend Abijah Hoadley, newly come to the Congregational Church at Dunwich Village, preached a memorable sermon on the close presence of Satan and his imps; in which he said:

> *It must be allow'd, that these Blasphemies of an infernall Train of Daemons are Matters of too common Knowledge to be deny'd; the cursed Voices of Azazel and Buzrael, of Beelzebub and Belial, being heard now from under Ground by above a Score of credible Witnesses now living. I my self did not more than a Fortnight ago catch a very plain Discourse of evill Powers in the Hill behind my House; wherein there were a Rattling and Rolling, Groaning, Screeching, and Hissing, such as no Things of this Earth cou'd raise up, and which must needs have come from those Caves that only black Magick can discover, and only the Divell unlock.*

Mr. Hoadley disappeared soon after delivering this sermon; but the text, printed in Springfield, is still extant. Noises in the hills continued to be reported from year to year, and still form a puzzle to geologists and physiographers.

Other traditions tell of foul odours near the hill-crowning circles of stone pillars, and of rushing airy presences to be heard faintly at certain hours from stated points at the bottom of the great ravines; while still others try to explain the Devil's Hop Yard – a bleak, blasted hillside where no tree, shrub, or grass-blade will grow. Then too, the natives are mortally afraid of the numerous whippoorwills which grow vocal on warm nights. It is vowed that the birds are psychopomps lying in wait for the souls of the dying, and that they time their eery cries in unison with the sufferer's struggling breath. If they can catch the fleeing soul when it leaves the body, they instantly flutter away chittering in daemoniac laughter; but if they fail, they subside gradually into a disappointed silence.

These tales, of course, are obsolete and ridiculous; because they come down from very old times. Dunwich is indeed ridiculously old – older by far than any of the communities within thirty miles of it. South of the village one may still spy the cellar walls and chimney of the ancient Bishop house, which was built before 1700; whilst the ruins of the mill at the falls, built in 1806, form the most modern piece of architecture to be seen. Industry did not flourish here, and the nineteenth century factory movement proved short-lived. Oldest of all are the great rings of roughhewn stone columns on the hilltops, but these are more generally attributed to the Indians than to the settlers. Deposits of skulls and bones, found within these circles and around the sizeable table-like rock on Sentinel Hill, sustain the popular belief that such spots were once the burial-places of the Pocumtucks; even though many enthnologists, disregarding the absurd improbability of such a theory, persist in believing the remains Caucasian.

The Perfect Storm

Sebastian Junger is a freelance journalist; he contributes to *Outside* magazine, the *American Heritage* and *Men's Journal*, among other publications. The extract below is taken from his bestselling book, **The Perfect Storm**, which describes the horrendous hurricanes of October 1991, that took place off the New England and northeast Canada coasts. As well depicting the frightening conditions experienced by deep-sea fishermen during a storm at sea, the book examines the nature and history of the Massachusetts fishing industry, and reconstructs, from interviews and a great deal of poetic license, the lives of those involved. It's a compelling read, and one which shows another, far grittier side to New England's twee fishing towns and clapboard cottages. The extract below is reprinted by kind permission of W.W. Norton and Fourth Estate.

Early fishing in Gloucester was the roughest sort of business, and one of the deadliest. As early as the 1650s, three-man crews were venturing up the coast for a week at a time in small open boats that had stones for ballast and unstayed masts. In a big wind the masts sometimes blew down. The men wore canvas hats coated with tar, leather aprons, and cowhide boots known as "redjacks." The eating was spare: for a week-long trip one Gloucester skipper recorded that he shipped four pounds of flour, five pounds of pork fat, seven pounds of sea biscuit, and "a little New England rum." The meals, such as they were, were eaten in the weather because there was no below-deck where the crews could take shelter. They had to take whatever God threw at them.

The first Gloucester fishing vessels worthy of the name were the thirty-foot chebaccos. They boasted two masts stepped well forward, a sharp stern, and cabins fore and aft. The bow rode the seas well, and the high stern kept out a following sea. Into the fo'c'sle were squeezed a couple of bunks and a brick fireplace where they smoked trashfish. That was for the crew to eat while at sea, cod being too valuable to waste on them. Each spring the chebaccos were scraped and caulked and tarred and sent out to the fishing grounds. Once there, the boats were anchored, and the men handlined over the side from the low midship rail. Each man had his spot, called a "berth," which was chosen by lottery and held throughout the trip. They fished two lines at twenty-five to sixty fathoms (150–360 feet) with a ten-pound lead weight, which they hauled up dozens of times a day. The shoulder muscles that resulted from a lifetime of such work made fishermen easily recognizable on the street. They were called "hand-liners" and people got out of their way.

The captain fished his own lines, like everyone else, and pay was reckoned by how much fish each man caught. The tongues were cut out of the fish and kept in separate buckets; at the end of the day the skipper entered the numbers in a log book and dumped the tongues overboard. It took a couple of months for the ships to fill their holds—the fish was either dried or, later, kept on ice—and then they'd head back to port. Some captains, on a run of fish, couldn't help themselves from loading their ship down until her decks were almost underwater. This was called deep-loading, and such a ship was in extreme peril if the weather turned ugly. The trip home took a couple of weeks, and the fish would compress under its own weight and squeeze all the excess fluid out of the flesh. The crew pumped the water over the sides, and deep-loaded Grand Bankers would gradually emerge from the sea as they sailed for port.

By the 1760s Gloucester had seventy-five fishing schooners in the water, about one-sixth of the New England fleet. Cod was so important to the economy that in 1784 a wooden effigy—the "Sacred Cod"—was hung in the Massachusetts State House by a wealthy statesman named John Rowe. Revenue from the New England codfishery alone was worth over a million dollars a year at the time of the Revolution, and John Adams refused to sign the Treaty of Paris until the British granted American fishing rights to the Grand Banks. The final agreement held that American schooners could fish in Canada's territorial waters unhindered and come ashore on deserted parts of Nova Scotia and Labrador to salt-dry their catch.

Cod was divided into three categories. The best, known as "dun fish," was caught in the spring and shipped to Portugal and Spain, where it fetched the highest prices. (Lisbon restaurants still offer bacalao, dried codfish.) The next grade of fish was sold domestically, and the worst grade "refuse fish"—was used to feed slaves in the West Indian canefields. Gloucester merchants left for the Caribbean with holds full of salt cod and returned with rum, molasses, and cane sugar; when this lucrative trade was impeded by the British during the War of 1812, local captains simply left port on moonless nights and sailed smaller boats. Georges Bank opened up in the 1830s, the first railway spur reached Gloucester in 1848, and the first ice companies were established that same year. By the 1880s—the heyday of the fishing schooner—Gloucester had a fleet of four or five hundred sail in her harbor. It was said you could walk clear across to Rocky Neck without getting your feet wet.

Cod was a blessing but could not, alone, have accounted for such riches. In 1816, a Cape Ann fisherman named Abraham Lurvey invented the mackerel jig by attaching a steel hook to a drop-shaped piece of cast lead. Not only did the lead act as a sinker, but, jiggled up and down, it became irresistible to mackerel. After two centuries of watching these elusive fish swim past in schools so dense they discolored the sea, New England fishermen suddenly had a way to catch them. Gloucester captains ignored a federal bounty on cod and sailed for Sable Island with men in the crosstrees looking for the telltale darkening of mackerel in the water. "School-O!" they would shout, the ship would come around into the wind, and ground-up baitfish—"chum"—would be thrown out into the water. The riper the chum was, the better it attracted the fish; rotting chum on the breeze meant a mackerel schooner was somewhere upwind.

Jigging for mackerel worked well, but it was inevitable that the Yankee mind would come up with something more efficient. In 1855 the purse seine was invented, a 1,300-foot net of tarred twine with lead weights at the bottom and cork floats at the top. It was stowed in a dory that was towed behind the schooner, and when the fish were sighted, the dory quickly encirled them and cinched the net up tight. It was hauled aboard and the fish were split, gutted, beheaded, and thrown into barrels with salt. Sometimes the school escaped before the net was tightened and the crew drew up what was called a "water haull"; other times the net was so full that they could hardly winch it aboard.

Purse seining passed for a glamorous occupation at the time, and it wasn't long before codfishermen came up with their own version of it. It was called tub trawling and if it was more efficient at killing fish, it was also more efficient at killing men. No longer did groundfishermen work from the relative safety of a schooner, now they were setting out from the mother ship in sixteen-foot wooden dories. Each dory carried half a dozen 300-foot trawl lines that were coiled in tubs and hung with baited hooks. The crews rowed out in the morning, paid out their trawls, and then hauled them back every few hours. There were 1,800 hooks to a dory, ten dories to a schooner, and several hundred ships in the fleet. Groundfish had several million chances a day to die.

Pulling a third of a mile's worth of trawl off the ocean floor was backbreaking work, though, and unspeakably dangerous in bad weather. In November of 1880, two fishermen named Lee and Devine rowed out from the schooner Deep Water in their dory. November was a hell of a time to be on the Grand Banks in any kind of vessel, and in a dory it was sheer insanity. They took a wave broadside while hauling their trawl and both men were thrown into the water. Devine managed to clamber back into the boat, but Lee, weighed down by boots and winter clothing, started to sink. He was several fathoms under when his hand touched the trawl line that led back up to the surface. He started to pull.

Almost immediately his right hand sunk into a hook. He jerked it away, leaving part of his finger on the barbed steel like a piece of herringbait, and kept pulling upwards towards the light. He finally broke the surface and heaved himself back into the dory. It was almost awash and Devine, who was bailing like mad, could do nothing to help him. Lee passed out from the pain and when he came to, he grabbed a bucket and started bailing as well. They had to empty the boat before they were hit by another freak wave. Twenty minutes later they were out of danger and Devine asked Lee if he needed to go back to the schooner. Lee shook his head and said that they should finish hauling the trawls. For the next hour he pulled gear out of the water with his mangled hand. That was dory fishing in its heyday.

There are worse deaths than the one Lee almost suffered, though. Warm Gulf Stream water meets the Labrador Current over the Grand Banks, and the result is a wall of fog that can sweep in with no warning at all. Dory crews hauling their gear have been caught by the fog and simply never seen again. In 1883, a fisherman named Howard Blackburn – still a hero in town, Gloucester's answer to Paul Bunyan – was separated from his ship and endured three days at sea during a January gale. His dorymate died of exposure, and Blackburn had to freeze his own hands around the oar handles to continue rowing for Newfoundland. In the end he lost all his fingers to frostbite. He made land on a deserted part of the coast and staggered around for several days before finally being rescued.

Every year brought a story of survival nearly as horrific as Blackburn's. A year earlier, two men had been picked up by a South American trader after eight days adrift. They wound up in Pernambuco, Brazil, and it took them two months to get back to Gloucester. From time to time dory crews were even blown across the Atlantic, drifting hopelessly with the trade winds and surviving on raw fish and dew. These men had no way to notify their families when they finally made shore; they simply shipped home and came walking back up Rogers Street several months later like men returning from the dead.

For the families back home, dory fishing gave rise to a new kind of hell. No longer was there just the grief of losing men at sea; now there was the agony of not knowing, as well. Missing dory crews could turn up at any time, and so there was never a point at which the families knew for sure they could grieve and get on with their lives. "We saw a father go morning and evening to the hilltop which overlooked the ocean," recorded the Provincetown Advocate after a terrible gale in 1841. "And there seating himself, would watch for hours, scanning the distant horizon . . . for some speck on which to build a hope."

And they prayed. They walked up Prospect Street to the top of a steep rise called Portagee Hill and stood beneath the twin bell towers of Our Lady of Good Voyage church. The bell towers are one of the highest points in Gloucester and can be seen for miles by incoming ships. Between the towers is a sculpture of the Virgin Mary, who gazes down with love and concern at a bundle in her arms. This is the Virgin who has been charged with the safety of the local fishermen. The bundle in her arms is not the infant Jesus; it's a Gloucester schooner.

Index

and small print

Index

map entries are in color

INDEX

INDEX

N

O

P

Q

R

S

INDEX

Twenty Years of Rough Guides

In the summer of 1981, Mark Ellingham, Rough Guides' founder, knocked out the first guide on a typewriter, with a group of friends. Mark had been traveling in Greece after university, and couldn't find a guidebook that really answered his needs.There were heavyweight cultural guides on the one hand – good on museums and classical sites but not on beaches and tavernas – and on the other hand student manuals that were so caught up with how to save money that they lost sight of the country's significance beyond its role as a place for a cool vacation. None of the guides began to address Greece as a country, with its natural and human environment, its politics, and its contemporary life.

Having no urgent reason to return home, Mark decided to write his own guide. It was a guide to Greece that tried to combine some erudition and insight with a thoroughly practical approach to travelers' needs. Scrupulously researched listings of places to stay, eat, and drink were matched by careful attention to detail on everything from Homer to Greek music, from classical sites to national parks, and from nude beaches to monasteries. Back in London, Mark and his friends got their Rough Guide accepted by a farsighted commissioning editor at the publisher Routledge and it came out in 1982.

The Rough Guide to Greece was a student scheme that became a publishing phenomenon. The immediate success of the book – shortlisted for the Thomas Cook Award – spawned a series that rapidly covered dozens of countries. The Rough Guides found a ready market among backpackers and budget travelers, but soon acquired a much broader readership that included older and less impecunious visitors. Readers relished the guides' wit and inquisitiveness as much as the enthusiastic, critical approach that acknowledges everyone wants value for money – but not at any price.

Rough Guides soon began supplementing the "rougher" information – the hostel and low-budget listings – with the kind of detail that independent-minded travelers on any budget might expect. These days, the guides – distributed worldwide by the Penguin Group – include recommendations spanning the range from shoestring to luxury, and cover more than 200 destinations around the globe. Our growing team of authors, many of whom come to Rough Guides initially as outstandingly good letter-writers telling us about their travels, are spread all over the world, particularly in Europe, the USA, and Australia. As well as the travel guides, Rough Guides publishes a series of dictionary phrasebooks covering two dozen major languages, an acclaimed series of music guides running the gamut from Classical to World Music, a series of music CDs in association with World Music Network, and a range of reference books on topics as diverse as the Internet, Pregnancy, and Unexplained Phenomena. Visit **www.roughguides.com** to see what's cooking.

Rough Guide Credits

Text editors: Jeff Cranmer and Julie Feiner
Series editor: Mark Ellingham
Editorial: Martin Dunford, Jonathan Buckley, Kate Berens, Ann-Marie Shaw, Helena Smith, Olivia Swift, Ruth Blackmore, Geoff Howard, Claire Saunders, Gavin Thomas, Alexander Mark Rogers, Polly Thomas, Joe Staines, Richard Lim, Duncan Clark, Peter Buckley, Lucy Ratcliffe, Clifton Wilkinson, Alison Murchie, Matthew Teller, Andrew Dickson, Fran Sandham, Sally Schafer, Matthew Milton, Karoline Densley (UK); Andrew Rosenberg, Yuki Takagaki, Richard Koss, Hunter Slaton, Chris Barsanti (US)
Production: Link Hall, Helen Prior, Julia Bovis, Katie Pringle, Rachel Holmes, Andy Turner, Dan May, Tanya Hall, John McKay, Sophie Hewat
Cartography: Maxine Repath, Melissa Baker, Ed Wright, Katie Lloyd-Jones
Cover art direction: Louise Boulton
Picture research: Sharon Martins, Mark Thomas
Online: Kelly Martinez, Anja Mutic-Blessing, Jennifer Gold, Audra Epstein, Suzanne Welles, Cree Lawson (US)
Finance: Gary Singh
Marketing & Publicity: Richard Trillo, Niki Smith, David Wearn, Chloë Roberts, Demelza Dallow, Claire Southern (UK); David Wechsler, Megan Kennedy (US)
Administration: Julie Sanderson

Publishing Information

This 3rd edition published June 2003 by
Rough Guides Ltd,
80 Strand, London WC2R 0RL
345 Hudson St, 4th Floor,
New York, NY 10014, USA
Distributed by the Penguin Group
Penguin Books Ltd,
80 Strand, London WC2R 0RL
Penguin Putnam, Inc.
375 Hudson St, NY 10014, USA
Penguin Books Australia Ltd,
487 Maroondah Highway, PO Box 257,
Ringwood, Victoria 3134, Australia
Penguin Books Canada Ltd,
10 Alcorn Ave, Toronto, ON,
M4V 1E4 Canada
Penguin Books (NZ) Ltd,
182–190 Wairau Road, Auckland 10,
New Zealand
Typeset in Bembo and Helvetica to an original design by Henry Iles.

Printed in Italy by LegoPrint S.p.A.

680pp includes index
A catalogue record for this book is available from the British Library.

ISBN 1-84353-065-1

Help us update

We've gone to a lot of effort to ensure that the 3rd edition of **The Rough Guide to New England** is accurate and up-to-date. However, things change – places get "discovered", opening hours are notoriously fickle, restaurants and rooms raise prices or lower standards. If you feel we've got it wrong or left something out, we'd like to know, and if you can remember the address, the price, the time, the phone number, so much the better.

We'll credit all contributions, and send a copy of the next edition (or any other Rough Guide if you prefer) for the best letters. Everyone who writes to us and isn't already a subscriber will receive a copy of our full-color thrice-yearly newsletter. Please mark letters: "**Rough Guide New England Update**" and send to: Rough Guides, 80 Strand, London WC2R 0RL, or Rough Guides, 4th Floor, 345 Hudson St, New York, NY 10014. Or send an email to **mail@roughguides.com**.

Have your questions answered and tell others about your trip at **www.roughguides.atinfopop.com**.

Acknowledgements

Arabella Bowen wishes to thank Aimee O'Brien, formerly of the Greater Boston Convention and Visitors' Bureau, for her list of regional contacts; Alison Stein for her Cape Cod notes; Karen Whiting for sanity Sundays; Josh Fullan for too many things to mention here; and Rough Guide editor Julie Feiner for keeping me on track (and in Wellfleet oysters).

Todd Obolsky thanks Ted & Jo Panayotoff for their warm hospitality and breakfast; Renny Loisel in New Haven and Sheila Pastor at Yale; Kat Pustay; Kathryn Farrington (Newport); the Cady House and the State House in Providence; Robin Zinchuk and Julia Reuter (at the CoC), Gary Brearley, Fred Nolte and Sandra Frye in Bethel; Portland CVB; Ms. Kovalsky (raincheck from the NYC guide) and Mr. Silva.

Ross Velton (rvelton@yahoo.com) would like to thank the following people for their help and support: Diane Konrady, Lynn Barrett, Ed Eagan, Susanne Schaefer, Lori Harnois, Laurie Campbell, Monique Devine, Tara Rendon, Ann Claffie, Louise Filkens, Andrew Rosenberg, Richard Koss, Julie Feiner, Jeff Cranmer and Ron and Juli Velton.

Also, thanks to Amy Sorensen for excellent photo research, Melissa Baker for cartography, Tanya Hall for typesetting, Diane Margolis for proofreading, Todd Obolsky for indexing, and Hunter Slaton for key last-minute assistance.

Readers' letters

Thanks to all the readers who took the trouble to write in with their comments and suggestions (and apologies to anyone whose name we've misspelt or omitted): Simon Bennett, Ed Bowman, Bridget Blomfield, John Connolly, Caroline Fullard, Deidre Howard-Williams, Graham Lazorchak, G.B. Nute, Jaylene Roths, Robert Shea, Mike Stanley, Peter Wenban.

Photo credits

Cover

Main front image Pemaquid © Getty
Small front top image Newstate House © Axiom
Small front lower image North Conway, New Hampshire © Robert Harding
Back top image Vermont lower farm © Robert Harding
Back lower image Camden harbour © Getty

Colour introduction

WaterFire, Providence © Barnaby Evans/WATERFIRE PROVIDENCE
Gazebo, Vermont village green © John Warden/Network Aspen
Houses in Edgartown, Martha's Vineyard © Dave G. Houser/Houserstock
Portland waterfront © Nicholas DeVore III/Network Aspen
Fall foliage, Vermont © Michael J. Pettypool/Houserstock
Block Island lighthouse © Dave G. Houser/Houserstock
Clam chowder © Eising/StockFood
Boston's Trinity Church reflected in John Hancock Building © Ralph Morang/ www.newenglandphoto.com
Robert Frost house © Ralph Morang/ www .newenglandphoto.com
Billings Farm Museum, Woodstock, VT © Jon Gilbert Fox/Billings Farm Museum
Vermont's Green Mountains © Sandy Macys

Things not to miss

View of Burlington from Lake Champlain © Paul O. Boisvert
Shaker craftsman, Canterbury Shaker Village © Dave G. Houser/Houserstock
Old State House, Boston © Dave G. Houser/ Houserstock
Lobster dinner © Ralph Morang/ www.newenglandphoto.com
Harvard Square © Dave G. Houser/ Houserstock
Boat in Mystic Seaport © Christie Parker/ Houserstock
Gas light, Beacon Hill © Maureen Hancock
Performance at Tanglewood © Nicholas DeVore III/Network Aspen
Provincetown beach bungalows © Dave G. Houser/Houserstock
Naumkeag mansion and gardens © The Trustees of Reservations/A. Merullo
Sterling Library, Yale University © Michael Marsland/Yale University
Beach cottage on Nantucket © Dave G. Houser/Houserstock

Mount Mansfield, Stowe © Phil Schermeister/Network Aspen
Sunset on Block Island © Dave G. Houser/Houserstock
Mansion interior in Newport © Nichold DeVore III/Network Aspen
Mass MoCA © Doug Bartow/Mass MoCa
Monhegan Island © Ralph Morang/www.newenglandphoto.com
College Hill, Providence © Nichold DeVore III/Network Aspen
Worcester Art Museum © Robert Arnold /Worcester Art Museum
Oar House restaurant, Portsmouth © Ralph Morang/www.newenglandphoto.com
Bluberry buckets © Ben R. Frakes/Houserstock
Whale-watching boat © Ralph Morang/www.newenglandphoto.com
Kitchen exhibit, Shelburne Museum © Courtesy of Shelburne Museum
Grasses and village, Cape Cod © Nicholas DeVore III/Network Aspen
State House, Montpelier © Paul O. Boisvert
Litchfield farm © Jim McElholm/Litchfield Hills Visitors Bureau
Mount Abraham, on the Long Trail © Sandy Macys
Battle re-enactment at Exeter © Ralph Morang/www.newenglandphoto.com
Acadia National Park © Ben R. Frakes /Houserstock
Aerial of Faneuil Hall and Quincy Market © Nicholas DeVore III/Network Aspen
Mount Washington Hotel © Phil Schermeister/Network Aspen
Ben and Jerry's factory tour © Courtesy of Ben and Jerry's

Black and white photos

Wheel of *USS Constitution* © Dave G. Houser/Houserstock
Aerial of Harvard Campus © Nicholas DeVore III/Network Aspen
Boston skyline © Ralph Morang/www.newenglandphoto.com
Cape Cod fishermen © Nicholas DeVore III/Network Aspen
Witch Trials memorial, Salem © Bill Bachmann/Network Aspen
Nantucket lighthouse © Dave G. Houser/Houserstock
Picnic on Tanglewood lawn © Stu Rosner/Boston Symphony Orchestra
Pontoosuc Lake, near Pittsfield, MA © A. Blake Gardner/Berkshires Visitors Bureau
Farm stand, Little Compton, RI © Peter Goldberg
Canoeing on the Blackstone River © Peter Goldberg
Mystic Seaport, CT © Christie Parker/Houserstock
American Clock and Watch Museum, Chester, CT © Donald Dziedzic/American Clock and Watch Museum
Covered bridge, Windsor/Cornish © Ralph Morang/www.newenglandphoto.com
Tractor, Vermont farm © Bob Handelman
Three churches, Marlow © NHDTTD/Arthur Boufford
Sap bucket © Ralph Morang/www.newenglandphoto.com
Gift shop, Boothbay Harbor © Ralph Morang/www.newenglandphoto.com
Row boats, Mount Desert Island © Ralph Morang/www.newenglandphoto.com
Moose, Baxter State Park © David Hiser/Network Aspen

roughnews
ROUGH GUIDES
Caribbean
San Francisco - p.7 | Dublin - p.10 | New Zealand - p.15 | Bond - p.19

Rough Guides travel

Europe
Algarve
Amsterdam
Andalucia
Austria
Barcelona
Belgium & Luxembourg
Berlin
Britain
Brittany & Normandy
Bruges & Ghent
Brussels
Budapest
Bulgaria
Copenhagen
Corsica
Costa Brava
Crete
Croatia
Cyprus
Czech & Slovak Republics
Devon & Cornwall
Dodecanese & East Aegean
Dordogne & the Lot
Dublin
Edinburgh
England
Europe
First-Time Europe
Florence
France
French Hotels & Restaurants
Germany
Greece
Greek Islands
Holland
Hungary
Ibiza & Formentera
Iceland
Ionian Islands
Ireland
Italy
Lake District
Languedoc & Roussillon
Lisbon
London
London Mini Guide
London Restaurants
Madeira
Madrid
Mallorca
Malta & Gozo
Menorca
Moscow
Norway
Paris
Paris Mini Guide
Poland
Portugal
Prague
Provence & the Côte d'Azur
Pyrenees
Romania
Rome
Sardinia
Scandinavia
Scotland
Scottish Highlands & Islands
Sicily
Spain
St Petersburg
Sweden
Switzerland
Tenerife & La Gomera
Turkey
Tuscany & Umbria
Venice & The Veneto
Vienna
Wales

Asia
Bali & Lombok
Bangkok
Beijing
Cambodia
China
First-Time Asia
Goa
Hong Kong & Macau
India
Indonesia
Japan
Laos
Malaysia, Singapore & Brunei
Nepal
Singapore
South India
Southeast Asia
Thailand
Thailand Beaches & Islands
Tokyo
Vietnam

Australasia
Australia
Gay & Lesbian Australia
Melbourne
New Zealand
Sydney

North America
Alaska
Big Island of Hawaii
Boston
California
Canada
Florida
Hawaii
Honolulu
Las Vegas
Los Angeles
Maui
Miami & the Florida Keys
Montréal
New England
New Orleans
New York City
New York City Mini Guide
New York Restaurants
Pacific Northwest
Rocky Mountains
San Francisco
San Francisco Restaurants
Seattle
Southwest USA
Toronto
USA
Vancouver
Washington DC
Yosemite

Caribbean & Latin America
Antigua & Barbuda
Argentina
Bahamas
Barbados
Belize
Bolivia
Brazil
Caribbean
Central America
Chile
Costa Rica
Cuba
Dominican Republic
Ecuador
Guatemala
Jamaica
Maya World
Mexico
Peru
St Lucia
Trinidad & Tobago

Africa & Middle East
Cape Town
Egypt
Israel & Palestinian Territories
Jerusalem
Jordan
Kenya
Morocco
South Africa, Lesotho & Swaziland
Syria
Tanzania
Tunisia
West Africa
Zanzibar
Zimbabwe

Dictionary Phrasebooks
Czech
Dutch
European Languages
French
German
Greek
Hungarian
Italian
Polish
Portuguese
Russian
Spanish
Turkish
Hindi & Urdu
Indonesian
Japanese
Mandarin Chinese
Thai
Vietnamese
Mexican Spanish
Egyptian Arabic
Swahili

Maps
Amsterdam
Dublin
London
Paris
San Francisco
Venice

Rough Guides publishes new books every month:

TRAVEL • MUSIC • REFERENCE • PHRASEBOOKS

Rough Guides music, reference & CDs

Music
Acoustic Guitar
Blues: 100 Essential CDs
Cello
Clarinet
Classical Music
Classical Music: 100 Essential CDs
Country Music
Country: 100 Essential CDs
Cuban Music
Drum'n'bass
Drums
Electric Guitar & Bass Guitar
Flute
Hip-Hop
House
Irish Music
Jazz
Jazz: 100 Essential CDs
Keyboards & Digital Piano
Latin: 100 Essential CDs
Music USA: a Coast-To-Coast Tour
Opera
Opera: 100 Essential CDs
Piano
Reading Music
Reggae
Reggae: 100 Essential CDs
Rock
Rock: 100 Essential CDs
Saxophone
Soul: 100 Essential CDs
Techno
Trumpet & Trombone
Violin & Viola
World Music: 100 Essential CDs
World Music Vol1
World Music Vol2

Reference
Children's Books, 0–5
Children's Books, 5–11
China Chronicle
Cult Movies
Cult TV
Elvis
England Chronicle
France Chronicle
India Chronicle
The Internet
Internet Radio
James Bond
Liverpool FC
Man Utd
Money Online
Personal Computers
Pregnancy & Birth
Shopping Online
Travel Health
Travel Online
Unexplained Phenomena
Videogaming
Weather
Website Directory
Women Travel

Music CDs
Africa
Afrocuba
Afro-Peru
Ali Hussan Kuban
The Alps
Americana
The Andes
The Appalachians
Arabesque
Asian Underground
Australian Aboriginal Music
Bellydance
Bhangra
Bluegrass
Bollywood
Boogaloo
Brazil
Cajun
Cajun and Zydeco
Calypso and Soca
Cape Verde
Central America
Classic Jazz
Congolese Soukous
Cuba
Cuban Music Story
Cuban Son
Cumbia
Delta Blues
Eastern Europe
English Roots Music
Flamenco
Franco
Gospel
Global Dance
Greece
The Gypsies
Haiti
Hawaii
The Himalayas
Hip Hop
Hungary
India
India and Pakistan
Indian Ocean
Indonesia
Irish Folk
Irish Music
Italy
Jamaica
Japan
Kenya and Tanzania
Klezmer
Louisiana
Lucky Dube
Mali and Guinea
Marrabenta Mozambique
Merengue & Bachata
Mexico
Native American Music
Nigeria and Ghana
North Africa
Nusrat Fateh Ali Khan
Okinawa
Paris Café Music
Portugal
Rai
Reggae
Salsa
Salsa Dance
Samba
Scandinavia
Scottish Folk
Scottish Music
Senegal & The Gambia
Ska
Soul Brothers
South Africa
South African Gospel
South African Jazz
Spain
Sufi Music
Tango
Thailand
Tex-Mex
Wales
West African Music
World Music Vol 1: Africa, Europe and the Middle East
World Music Vol 2: Latin & North America, Caribbean, India, Asia and Pacific
World Roots
Youssou N'Dour & Etoile de Dakar
Zimbabwe

check www.roughguides.com for the latest news

NOTES

NOTES

The ideas expressed in this code were developed by and for independent travellers.

Learn About The Country You're Visiting

Start enjoying your travels before you leave by tapping into as many sources of information as you can.

The Cost Of Your Holiday

Think about where your money goes - be fair and realistic about hov cheaply you travel. Try and put money into local peoples' hands; drink local beer or fruit juice rather than imported brands and stay in locally owned accommodation. Haggle with humour and not aggressively. Pay what something is worth to you and remember hov wealthy you are compared to local people.

Embrace The Local Culture

Open your mind to new cultures and traditions - it will transform you experience. Think carefully about what's appropriate in terms of you clothes and the way you behave. You'll earn respect and be more readily welcomed by local people. Respect local laws and attitudes towards drugs and alcohol that vary in different countries and communities. Think about the impact you could have on them.

Exploring The World – The Travellers' Code

Being sensitive to these ideas means getting more out of your travels - and giving more back to the people you meet and the places you visit.

Minimise Your Environmental Impact

Think about what happens to your rubbish - take biodegradable products and a water filter bottle. Be sensitive to limited resources like water, fuel and electricity. Help preserve local wildlife and habitats by respecting local rules and regulations, such as sticking t footpaths and not standing on coral.

Don't Rely On Guidebooks

Use your guidebook as a starting point, not the only source of information. Talk to local people, then discover your own adventure!

Be Discreet With Photography

Don't treat people as part of the landscape, they may not want their picture taken. Ask first and respect their wishes.

We work with people the world over to promote tourism that benefits their communities, but we can only carry on our work wit the support of people like you. For membership details or to find out how to make your travels work for local people and the environment, visit our website.

www.tourismconcern.org.uk

TourismConce

Campaigning for Ethical and Fairly Traded